For Reference

Not to be taken from this room

Encyclopedia of
Women and Religion
in North America

Editorial Board

Encyclopedia of
Women and Religion
in North America

❦

Edited by
Rosemary Skinner Keller
and
Rosemary Radford Ruether

Associate Editor
Marie Cantlon

VOLUME 2

Part V. Women in Orthodox and Oriental Orthodox Traditions

Part VI. Judaism

Part VII. Islam

Part VIII. Asian Religions

Part IX. Newer Religious Movements

Part X. Multidenominational Movements

INDIANA UNIVERSITY PRESS
Bloomington and Indianapolis

This book is a publication of

Indiana University Press
601 North Morton Street
Bloomington, Indiana 47404-3797 USA

http://iupress.indiana.edu

Telephone orders   800-842-6796
Fax orders   812-855-7931
Orders by e-mail   iuporder@indiana.edu

Library of Congress Cataloging-in-Publication Data

The encyclopedia of women and religion in North America / Rosemary Skinner Keller
and Rosemary Radford Ruether, editors ; Marie Cantlon, associate editor.
    p. cm.
  Includes bibliographical references and index.
  ISBN 0-253-34685-1 (cloth, set) — ISBN 0-253-34686-X (v. 1) — ISBN 0-253-34687-8
(v. 2) — ISBN 0-253-34688-6 (v. 3) 1. Women and religion—North America—
Encyclopedias. 2. Women—Religious life—North America—Encyclopedias. 3. Women—
Religious aspects—North America—Encyclopedias. I. Keller, Rosemary Skinner. II.
Ruether, Rosemary Radford. III. Cantlon, Marie.
  BL458.E52   2006
   200.82'0973—dc22   2005032429

1 2 3 4 5 11 10 09 08 07 06

Contents

Part V

෴

Women in Orthodox and Oriental Orthodox Traditions

WOMEN IN ORTHODOX
CHRISTIAN TRADITIONS
Demetra Velisarios Jaquet

THE MINISTRY OF women in Eastern Orthodox Christianity has historically taken different forms in different national churches, depending on their situation and cultural context. In view of the present times and current needs, Orthodox churches worldwide and more particularly women are in search of new forms of ministry that will respond to the problems of their societies. Since 1976 Orthodox women in America have concentrated primarily on the development of lay ministries and the renewal of the diaconate for both men and women. Currently the female diaconate has disappeared in almost all churches, and the male diaconate in many has been reduced to a liturgical function of assisting the priest with services and sacraments.

Care of home and offering philanthropy have typically been the major ministry outlets for Orthodox women. In America the charitable ministries of two national groups, the Greek Orthodox Philoptochos Society and the Antiochian Women, have been augmented since 1980 by a burgeoning number of parish-or diocese-sponsored social outreach ministries ranging from food banks to homes for the elderly, homeless, and disabled.

Traditional areas of women's service to the church have steadily grown, such as care of home and family, including the "little church in the home," the observance of family prayer and worship practices such as lighting votive candles and censing before the home icon corner. One factor limiting dialogue among women in American Orthodoxy is that while it is true that the Orthodox churches are one in faith and doctrine, in sacraments and moral teaching, they are divided in administrative terms, existing in separate "jurisdictions" that often look to different centers of ecclesiastical authority. The largest jurisdictions in America include the Antiochian Orthodox, the Greek Orthodox, and the Orthodox Church in America, primarily of Russian origin. This jurisdictional splintering effect makes it difficult for women in the same geographical area but different jurisdictions to meet each other, support each other, and work together.

The long-established and respected ministry of the Presbytera, Matushka, or Kourye, the wife of the priest, is supported in each American jurisdiction by its clergy wives' association. Religious education, also a well-established ministry for Orthodox women, is supported by diocesan and national training, conferences, and materials. In neither area are cross-jurisdictional gatherings within shared geographical areas yet the norm.

The establishment by the Standing Conference of Orthodox Bishops in America (SCOBA) of two major joint Orthodox projects in the 1990s, International Orthodox Christian Charities and the Orthodox Christian Mission Center, has created mission and outreach ministry opportunities for women never before available. Women are also active in the cross-jurisdictional efforts of the Orthodox Peace Fellowship, the Orthodox Christian Association of Medicine, Psychology and Religion, Orthodox Women in the Healing Professions, Orthodox People Together, and the Orthodox Christians for Life. Only a handful of Orthodox women are participating in Axios, a national Orthodox support group for gays and lesbians.

Orthodox seminaries opened their doors to women in the 1970s, and some have since employed a few women professors. Women earning degrees in theology from Orthodox and other seminaries have frequently turned to the ecumenical community to find opportunities for teaching and for active ministry in hospital and hospice chaplaincy, social work, pastoral counseling and spiritual direction, and homeless and prison ministries.

Ethnic-Immigrant and American-Born
Church Members

In the last thirty years the proportion of church members who were born in America or who came to Orthodoxy from other religious backgrounds has risen dramatically. This has led to positive growth but also new tensions among women in the American church.

For many members of Orthodox communities, and for the American public, "ethnic and immigrant" is still assumed to be a fully adequate description of the Orthodox churches in America. In fact, ethnic churches in America are gradually losing members, while the American mission effort is experiencing slow and steady growth. Since 1970 the Antiochian Archdiocese and the Orthodox Church in America (OCA) have led the effort to establish new, multiethnic or nonethnic Orthodox communities where none previously existed. For the first time since the 1900s, large numbers of adult converts are entering Orthodoxy—and not just by marriage.

Streams of immigrants in the early 1900s brought with them from their predominantly Orthodox home countries their cultural, national, and religious identities, forming communities that reflected both old and new in living interrelationship. The majority of American-born Orthodox women grew up in homes and immigrant parishes where past memories and "homeland" culture often perpetuated sociocultural practices of unself-consciously demeaning women. While sexual discrimination was gradually becoming more challenged in American society, the acceptance of such practices within the church by American-born cradle-Orthodox women was usually taken for granted as part of the gen-

Madame Elisabeth Behr-Sigel, Paris, France, (seated third from left) called "a mother of the Orthodox Christian Church," gave the keynote address at the "Discerning the Signs of the Times" Conference for Orthodox Christian Women in May 2003, at St. Vladimir's Orthodox Theological Seminary, Crestwood, New York. *Courtesy of Teva Regule.*

eral tension between one's ethnic and American identities. The emergence of the feminist movement provoked some clarity for naming the sins of sexism and hardness of heart and gave voice to many women's vague sense of discomfort with anti-woman rhetoric in the church fathers and theologians and negative, demeaning, or woman-denying practices in churches.

The 1988 mass conversions of two disparate groups—the Protestant "Evangelical Orthodox Church," an offshoot of the Campus Crusade for Christ with some 2,000 members in twelve communities, to the Antiochian Archdiocese; and the New Age "Holy Order of Mans," with some 3,000 members in twenty communities, to an Old Calendarist Greek Orthodox jurisdiction—testify to Orthodoxy's evangelical appeal (Stokoe, 109). This appeal for those who do not come from Orthodox ancestry is not limited to such movements as the evangelical Orthodox. In virtually every Orthodox community and institution, there are men and women who have become part of its life because they have consciously made a "faith decision," and this decision has brought them into the Orthodox Church.

At the same time, the Orthodox faith in America is also losing people, not just because of marriages outside the church and the lapse of the unchurched but also because women are taking their families to churches where women's gifts and talents in leadership and decision making are more readily welcomed.

In some quarters of Orthodoxy, the term *modernist* is always understood as synonymous with "a person who believes in and tries to promote dogmatic heresy in the Church." For some converts, the condemnation of "modernism" has been the appeal of Orthodoxy, particularly in response to the feminist movement. In the 1980s the unchanging rock of Orthodox dogma seemed

to offer safe haven for many in shock and pain at what they had seen and experienced in the rapidly liberalizing American churches. Many cradle-Orthodox priests and laity were startled into their first awareness of feminism by a handful of reactionary alarmists who condemned any discussion of women's concerns and interpreted interest in active parish ministry as having a hidden, radical feminist agenda.

Cradle and Convert

During this period cradle-Orthodox women, who had centuries of experience at carrying out the responsibilities of social ministry without any visibility or ecclesial authority, frequently became uncomfortable around women converts who were bringing their experience of active leadership with them into Orthodoxy and expecting to find programmatic ministries similar to those they had left behind.

Women converts from churches where women's leadership was the norm found its absence in conservative Orthodox parishes curious, giving rise to questions about why cradle-Orthodox women were refusing to accept leadership roles. To many cradle-Orthodox, it seemed inappropriate for converts to expect to find in Orthodoxy the same outward signs of ministry and piety they experienced in their former denominations. Eventually, the cradle-Orthodox response to this challenge was to suggest that the converts work on loosening their preconceived expectations of what "true faith" is supposed to look like.

An irony is that many spiritually committed cradle-Orthodox women, called to serve the church more fully but isolated in conservative parishes—those very dedicated Orthodox women leaders whom convert women were seeking but said they could not find—had gone underground in discouragement or had already left the church in frustration.

The Handmaiden magazine published by Conciliar Press expressed the experience, perspective, and enthusiasm of women among the evangelical converts to Orthodoxy during this time. In the summer and fall of 1997, letters of concern flooded the magazine in reaction to several articles promoting the traditional practice of females covering their heads in church. Recent convert Frederica Mathewes-Green of Baltimore, Maryland, wrote a letter to the editor that encapsulates the growing pains between cradle and convert women:

> Icons? Wow! Fasting? Terrific! Headcoverings? All right! For converts, Orthodoxy is a whole new rich, wonderful world. So many of the unfamiliar elements and practices of this faith strike us as fresh, challenging, and beautiful. We want to embrace it all.
>
> But in embracing headcoverings apparently we've sent some signals we didn't intend. The sharp reactions that sisters older in the faith have had against this practice have surprised us. We just didn't know....
>
> ...For convert women in majority-convert parishes, women's value is taken for granted.... In such an atmosphere of freedom and dignity, wearing a headcovering doesn't feel much different from wearing a prayer rope or kissing an icon. ...It doesn't feel like oppression or degradation, because nothing else in our experience is sending such a negative message.
>
> But sometimes I wonder if some of my Orthodox sisters have had a different experience. Perhaps some still retain painful memories of being disparaged and devalued; perhaps for some such a situation still exists. While wearing a headcovering feels to us like a lovely devotional practice, for others it apparently carries far different, and more painful, associations.
>
> This discussion isn't really about headcoverings; that's just the flashpoint. Maybe some of my Orthodox sisters don't feel they can expect to be treated with respect and valued for their gifts. If that's the case, we have a lot more to talk about than a scrap of fabric on our heads. (Mathewes-Green, 51–52)

Eventually, seeing pious customs within church tradition through the eyes of the new converts began to renew and restore their meaning for surprised cradle-Orthodox. At the same time, convert women gradually found appreciation for the hidden ministries of Orthodox women whose authentic spirit of humility and spontaneity caused them to persevere in charitable service to the church largely unconcerned about programmatic sustainability or public ministerial identity.

Orthodox Women, Western Feminism, and Asian Feminism

The conscience of the Orthodox Church in America has only gradually opened to some of the concerns of Western feminism. The question of the ordination of women to the priesthood had always been seen by Orthodox Christians as a barrier to the discussions of women's roles in the church. While the question of participation of women in the life of the church remains a vital concern, Orthodox women want to articulate their own terms of reference within the framework of their own sociopolitical context and within the spirit of their understanding of their own faith. Women's access to the sacramental priesthood is not a priority for many Orthodox women for two reasons. First, they are concerned with other urgent matters related to the question of ministry in the church, and second, they have a different understanding of the sacramental ministry.

A significant departure from Orthodox thought that sets Western feminism apart from Orthodox reality is the lack of distinction in feminist rhetoric between hierarchy and clericalism. In her article "The Fatherhood of God in Orthodox Theology," Sr. Nonna Verna Harrison clarifies:

> My conclusion regarding hierarchy is that it needs to be understood as an intrinsic aspect of the Church's life yet part of a larger whole, just as the ranking of Father, Son and Spirit based on the order of their relations of origin in no way exhausts their relationships with each other and does not compromise their equality or restrict their mutual self-giving.... Hierarchy's purpose is to include and unite, ultimately to spread and share divine life in Christ.... Oppression comes from its sinful misuse and distortion, not from the structure itself. (Harrison, 200–201)

Feminist theology as understood in the West is impossible for Orthodox to adopt, since the feminist theological critique as such is not operative within Orthodox theological systems. As a result, Orthodox women have by and large felt confused by the feminist agenda. Western feminism seems rooted in its reaction against extremes of hierarchical authoritarianism in the Western church, commonly called patriarchy. Women in Orthodoxy exist in a decentralized system whose theology values the harmonious balance of good patriarchy as hierarchical order with good spontaneity as peership. Yet while eschewing extreme authoritarianism in theory, in practice the church does not provide accountability structures against localized practices that cause abuse and invisibility for women. The struggles of Orthodox women as citizens end up being the same as the struggles of all other women within the ecumenical family. They are, together with their children, victims of war; victims of human rights abuses; they are refugees, asylum seekers; they suffer malnutrition; they are subject to sexual harassment, denigration, and exploitation. While experientially identifying with feminists in condemning the unjust, sexist social practices it addresses, at the same time Orthodox women are somehow aware that the theological rationale within Western feminist arguments and its implications for sacramental and spiritual life are alien to the Orthodox perspective. Unfortunately, the deep gap that separates Orthodox from non-Orthodox women on issues of participation in the church has been a stumbling block in building solidarity and community to face their common struggles.

Orthodox women's self-understanding as distinct from that of their Western Christian sisters is most similar to that of Asian Christian women. The two share in the struggle to differentiate themselves theologically from the dominant Western Christian feminist models, while sharing an anthropology of the harmonious distinctiveness and yet complementarity of male and female genders.

The Vision of Elisabeth Behr-Sigel

Madame Elisabeth Behr-Sigel, "the grandmother of Orthodox feminism," is a theologian and retired professor at St. Sergius Orthodox Theological Institute in Paris, France. She believes that most of the concerns that feminism addresses are in fact shared by Orthodox women but in differing cultural context, and her voice has since 1976 consistently provided hopeful witness for ecumenical dialogue around the ministries of women. Of her numerous publications in French, four important books have been translated into English. *The Ministry of Women in the Church* (1991), *The Ordination of Women in the Church* with Bishop Kallistos Ware (2000), and *Discerning the Signs of the Times* (2001) all express "her vision of the church as one of a community of men and women, clergy and laity, joined in the joy and peace of the Holy Trinity," and never shrink from challenging the Orthodox to articulate theology around ordaining women as priests. *The Place of the Heart* (1992) unpacks with grace and clarity the spiritual and theological underpinnings of lay and ordained ministry. Her deep involvement in the ecumenical dialogues on women in the church has given her a clarity and authority unique in Orthodoxy.

Madame Behr-Sigel outlines three next steps for Orthodox theology and practice to tackle regarding the re-examination of church teaching on women and, further, sees in Orthodox theology the opportunity to play a restorative role in translating the women's movement and feminist criticisms of tradition and society into creative growth and action. First, all canons referring to the ritual impurity of women (must) be once and for all abolished, following the lead of the Messiah who associated with prostitutes and permitted a woman with an issue of blood to touch him. Second, she expects that Orthodox anthropology, grounded in the fathers, can be explored and expounded to produce a human model for the ordering of society and, one might add, the current battles over the value of life in the unborn and elderly. Third, she would like to see a clarification of the meaning of the priesthood, especially as pertains to the function of the priest and the presence of Christ through the action of the Holy Spirit.

Behr-Sigel attributes many of the unfortunate and unfaithful extremes of corrupted Western women's movements to a fearful refusal by the church to assess the genuinely true and good impulse behind them. She discerns instead a very serious and Spirit-driven challenge to the Christian world. She explains:

> The contemporary women's movement (rather than the "feminist" movement) is, in spite of its weaknesses, a sign of that secret and irresistible force of the Spirit that is lifting humanity toward the Kingdom of the life-saving Trinity. This movement is certainly an ambiguous and sometimes irritating sign, written in clumsy letters and spoken of in consciously provocative terms. . . . Despite its excesses, the women's movement asks serious questions of the churches. In place of a Cartesian humanism of the male, master and possessor of the earth, we must substitute a new humanism pervaded with respect for the other, with tenderness and compassion for mankind and the whole of God's creation. (*Discerning the Signs of the Times*, 143–147)

The World Council of Churches Catalyst

The ecumenical movement has without doubt contributed positively to helping Orthodox women articulate and address their concerns. Over the last thirty years, the World Council of Churches (WCC) organized a number of unprecedented world conferences where Orthodox women from throughout the world became acquainted with each other and spoke out candidly for the first time. Their deliberations explored and revealed the many prejudices against women so often enacted in the name of Orthodoxy and challenged cultural misunderstandings about gender differences. Throughout this period WCC's continuing financial support was invaluable in light of the reluctance of the Orthodox churches to acknowledge, support, and provide resources for Orthodox women to attend ecumenical meetings and seminars.

The WCC Unit on Education and Renewal brought together Eastern and Oriental Orthodox women for a remarkable foundational meeting in Agapia, Romania, in September 1976. This first international consultation, on "Orthodox Women: Their Role and Participation in the Orthodox Church," held in the Agapia women's monastery, invited participants to share their experiences and to articulate the problems they face in their commitment to the church in its life and in society. Seven of the forty representatives were Romanian nuns, five were Orthodox clergy. Madame Behr-Sigel commented in her keynote presentation:

> It seems to me that in the Orthodox tradition, the problem of women's participation in the life of the Church is characterized by the tension between the affirmation of the equal dignity of men and women in Christ, and the recognition of their distinctiveness as something valuable and a gift of God. It is in the light of this tension today that the problem of the ministries or diaconal services to which women are called in our Orthodox communities arises in concrete terms. (*Orthodox Women, WCC Agapia Consultation Report*, 1976, 26)

Agapia was the first time that Orthodox women were called upon to articulate for themselves their concerns and propose solutions and ways in which they could contribute to their own church. Naturally, they sought answers consonant with the spirit of the doctrine of the church. Discussion centered on what role the Orthodox woman can play in the framework of the church and society and responded to the expressed needs of women to become more involved in theological education, church administration, and decision making in all levels of church life, social service, monasticism, and the strengthening of family life. Agapia recommended that the question of the ordination of women be studied in light of the Orthodox tradition for a more effective articulation of the Orthodox position in ecumenical dialogue. Also, special concern was noted for the human problems confronting women in societies involved in political conflicts, particularly for refugees, orphans, and other victims. A central focus was religious and spiritual education for women:

> Opportunities need to be provided by parishes and diocese for the higher theological training of Orthodox women. Such studies are important, not only for those who wish to be professionally engaged in the work of the Church, but for those who seek to be better informed lay persons, so that the life of the local parish may be enriched by the benefit of their educational experience.... Seminaries and Church councils at all levels are encouraged to examine the possibilities for new vocations, i.e. professional job opportunities or positions, for theologically trained women who can serve the emerging needs of the Church. Special courses ... in seminaries may be necessary [to examine] the role of women in the life of the Church, particularly in the vocational opportunities for service ... (and) to make the training of women for Church service meaningful and relevant. (*Orthodox Women*, 47–48)

The two American women participating in the historic Agapia consultation were Virginia Hampers, National Board member and Ecumenical Relations representative from the Greek Orthodox Philoptochos Society, and Dr. Constance Tarasar, executive secretary of the Orthodox Christian Education Commission and OCA delegate to WCC ecumenical consultations. Tarasar reflected on the spirit of the proceedings, hallmarked by the consultation's monastic presence, which set the tone for all subsequent consultations:

> Perhaps the greatest impression ... came to us in the vitality and joy of those abbesses and nuns who shared in our Consultation as participants. Their understanding of modern life, their concern for the mission of the Church, their desire to serve in any way possible—was a witness to all of us of St. Paul's words which call us "to lead a life worthy of the calling to which you have been called, with all lowliness and meekness, with patience, forbearing one another in love, eager to maintain the unity of the Spirit in the bond of peace" (Eph. 4:1–3). (*Orthodox Women*, 9–10)

The spirit of Agapia continued in 1987 when the WCC Programme on Justice, Peace and the Integrity of Creation sponsored a second consultation in Sofia, Bulgaria. The "Orthodox Perspectives on Creation" consultation focused on poverty and economic injustice, the environmental crisis, racism and discrimination, and injustice to women. It stated that

> it must be admitted that, due to certain socio-historical factors, the women have not always been provided with opportunities for active participation in the Church's life at parish and diocesan levels.... Such sinful divisiveness is not acceptable from an Orthodox Christian perspective (cf. I Cor., 11:11).... In particular Orthodox men must acknowledge that, as full members of the church,

women share in the intercessory vocation of the Church to stand in the presence of the Lord on behalf of all creation. In concrete terms . . . this means more opportunities for theological education for women and the opening of career opportunities in the Church for women. Serious consideration must be given to the re-introduction of the ancient order of Deaconess by the Hierarchies of the local churches. (*MaryMartha* Web site, "Consultations")

In 1988 the benchmark "Inter-Orthodox Theological Consultation," sponsored by the Ecumenical Patriarchate of Constantinople, met in Rhodes, Greece. The two previous consultations' call for fuller participation of women in the life of the church were reiterated, and the importance of the pastoral dimension to address issues raised by Orthodox women was highlighted. The revival of the apostolic order of deaconesses and minor orders of subdeacon, reader, cantor, and teacher was recommended. Careful evaluation of feminist theology was called for, stating that "not all issues raised by the feminist movement are theological issues, but some are social issues clothed in theological formulations" (*MaryMartha* Web site, "Consultations").

The 1988 Rhodes consultation encouraged serious consideration of the feminist initiatives regarding the use of inclusive language, the exegesis of specific biblical texts, especially in Pauline writings, and challenging the idea of the submission of women as it relates to bodily uncleanliness.

The significance of this conference is that from it emerged the most authoritative, unanimously advocated call, from a formal Inter-Orthodox Consultation that brought together official representatives and theologians from all the Orthodox churches, recommending to the regional churches the restoration of the order of women deacons. Affirming the ordination of women deacons and the importance of the ministry of all women in the life of the church, the conclusions state succinctly:

The revival of women deacons in the Orthodox Church would emphasize in a special way the dignity of woman and give recognition to her contribution to the work of the Church as a whole. . . . Furthermore, would it not be possible and desirable to allow women to enter in the "lower orders" through a blessing of the Church (cherothesia): sub-deacon, reader, cantor, teacher . . . without excluding new orders that the Church might consider to be necessary? This matter deserves further study since there is no definite tradition of this sort. (FitzGerald, *Women Deacons in the Orthodox Church*, 164)

Kyriaki FitzGerald, an Orthodox theologian, pastoral counselor, lecturer, and wife of a Greek Orthodox priest, offered an analysis of the two most significant results of the Rhodes Consultation. First, the consultation clearly affirmed that women deacons were ordained in the Byzantine period and recommended that this practice be restored. Second, and perhaps even more significant, the consultation clearly articulated an approach to ordained ministry and ecclesiology which "turned away from the Western Christian tradition [and] turned instead towards an approach to ordained ministry which reflects participation in the life of the Triune god . . . where no one person or ministry stands 'above' or 'apart' from the rest of the eucharistic community."

The diaconate, from this ecclesiological perspective, is not simply a liturgical ministry or a mere step on the way to higher "ranks" of clergy. . . . The diaconate is a full and parallel order of ordained ministry to which both men and women are called by God. (165)

Orthodox women met for the Second International Orthodox Women's Consultation titled "Church and Culture," sponsored by the WCC Sub-Unit on Women in Church and Society, in Crete in January 1990. Building on the work in Agapia in 1976 and in Rhodes in 1988, Madame Elisabeth Behr-Sigel addressed "Women and Ministry—Current Developments"; Fr. Thomas Hopko, New York, delivered a paper on "God and Gender"; and Professor Mary Thomas, India, presented "Visions for Participation and Decision Making by Women in the Orthodox Church." New recommendations for responsible family planning and participation and decision making were added to the previous list of concerns.

Between 1988 and 1998 the WCC Ecumenical Decade of Churches in Solidarity with Women sparked several more international consultations, involving more and more American Orthodox women delegates. The Decade Committee sponsored two conferences called "Discerning the Sign of the Times (Matt. 16:3): Women in the Life of the Orthodox Church," one in Damascus, Syria, in October 1996, and one in Istanbul, Turkey, in May 1997. In the introduction to *Orthodox Women Speak* (1999), the full text of the proceedings, editor Kyriaki FitzGerald emphasizes that both consultations again recommended evaluation of the role of the laity in the decision-making processes of the church:

We should underscore the seriousness with which these texts and the meetings which produced them were taken by church leadership. Four patriarchs . . . and a number of regional bishops were actively involved in the progress of the work. . . . Furthermore, there is an official quality to these statements, as they reflect the concerns of . . . representatives appointed by their presiding hierarchs, who themselves were acting on behalf of their regional synods. . . . We have now for the first time in history a consensus regarding some of the most important issues which concern Orthodox women . . . (a) global consensus discerned *from the perspective of Orthodox women*. (*Orthodox Women Speak*, 1–2)

Women's ordination to the priesthood was finally discussed openly during the Orthodox Fraternity conference in Vendee, France, in fall of 1996, at a study workshop on "Men and Women in the Church" led by Elisabeth Behr-Sigel, Veronique Lossky, and Nadine Arnoul. Much emphasis was placed on sexual inequality perpetuated at the parish level and the difficulties in countering it. Ordination to the priesthood was the central topic of Madame Behr-Sigel's presentation at the Orthodox Theological Society of America's Florovsky Lecture at St. Vladimir's OCA Seminary, Crestwood, New York, in May 2003 (Women's Orthodox Ministries and Education Network).

MaryMartha Journal

The first edition of *MaryMartha, International Orthodox Women's Network Journal* was published in time for the World Council of Churches Seventh Canberra Assembly in February 1991. In December 1998, after six volumes, the final edition of the journal was published in time for the WCC Eighth Assembly in Harare, Zimbabwe. Its editor Leonie Liveris, a Ph.D. historian of Orthodox women, from Perth, Australia, created the journal with WCC Ecumenical Decade funding and is considered by many to be the "mother of Orthodox feminism" for providing the average Orthodox woman a comprehensive, sustained information source about the WCC-sponsored women's consultations and the first international Orthodox forum for women.

Now online at http://members.iinet.au/~mmjournl/HOMEPAGE/html, *MaryMartha* is a Web site for Orthodox women who question the expected submissive and subservient roles in all aspects of their lives. The journal dedicates itself to

women who want to express and share their opinions, experiences, information and criticisms without the usual fear of enduring judgment, often prejudiced, whether from clergy or laity, women who need to express their opinions and not be silenced by the possibility of criticism if or when they are wrong. Its aim is to keep Orthodox women informed about the status of women in

our churches, at a time when the small gains a few women made during the Ecumenical Decade may well be lost due to a growing fundamentalism and nationalism in the Orthodox churches. . . .

In the words of Elisabeth Behr-Sigel, "It is time Orthodox women broke the silence that has been imposed on them, not by the genuine tradition of the Church, but by social customs and conventions. They should have the courage to speak out and express their view of things—the view, after all, of half the church—so that they can assume their responsibilities alongside the men as members of the people of God called by the Spirit to different forms of service." (*MaryMartha* Web site)

WOMEN and the *St. Nina Quarterly* Journal

As awareness of the international Orthodox women's consultations slowly grew in America, the Women's Orthodox Ministries and Education Network (WOMEN) was founded with funding from a WCC grant in 1994 by Demetra Velisarios Jaquet, an Orthodox pastoral counselor, chaplain, and educator at Regis University, Denver, to address the problems of jurisdictional splintering and isolation of women. The news of Orthodox women is often "buried" within their own jurisdiction, if publicized at all. It is very difficult to know or find out what articles and books are being written by Orthodox women, what addresses they are presenting, what conferences are taking place, without a communications network. The WOMEN Web site at http://www.orthodoxwomensnetwork.org/ electronically links Orthodox women across jurisdictions in America who are committed to more active parish, community, and ecumenical ministry within the context of the spiritual riches of Orthodoxy. While not promoting a feminist agenda, WOMEN works toward the development of ecclesiastically certified lay ministry training and restoration of the order of deaconess and offers a program for woman-to-woman mentoring.

In 1995 the WOMEN network supported the founding of the *St. Nina Quarterly* journal by its editor Teva Regule, an Orthodox musician and theologian in Brookline, Massachusetts. The *St. Nina Quarterly* is dedicated to exploring the ministry of women in the Orthodox Church and to cultivating a deeper understanding of ministry in the lives of all Orthodox Christian women and men. Online at http://www.stnina.org/, it features articles by leading Orthodox women theologians in keeping with its mission statement:

We profess firm faith in our Church's teaching that each of us is created in the image of God and called to grow into His likeness. We believe that all persons are endowed with gifts of the Holy Spirit in ways that uniquely express the fullness of their humanity and contribute to the fullness of the entire community of believers. Our mission is the discovery and cultivation of these gifts for the nurturance of the entire Body of Christ. (*St. Nina* Web site, "Mission Statement")

Growing American Awareness

At its All-American Church Council in Montreal in 1977, the Orthodox Church in America became the first jurisdiction to take up formal study of the issue of women and men in the church. The OCA's Ecumenical Task Force, Department of External Affairs, collaborated with its Department of Religious Education to produce a seventy-five-page, ten-chapter small group study book *Women & Men in the Church* (1980). Its introduction proclaimed, "The 'women's question' is one of the burning questions of the day. How people and churches respond to this question reveals how they respond to life itself, to God and the World, and to Christ and the Church." The OCA continued to encourage dialogue, publishing *Women and the Priesthood*, (1983), an anthology of Orthodox authors, reprinting a revised and expanded version in 1999.

The earliest feminist voice in America was that of Eva C. Topping, a Greek hymnographer and Greek and Latin scholar from McLean, Virginia, whose groundbreaking work identified itself as challenging the centuries-old patriarchal outlook of the church. Her two volumes of collected essays on Orthodox women saints unhesitatingly pointed out occasions of misogyny and antiwoman theology written and reinforced by successive Fathers of the Church. Her work also revealed feminist women of incredible spiritual strength and faith who defied emperors and patriarchs who they perceived as teaching wrong "truths" and were later proven to be so. Her essays in *Holy Mothers of Orthodoxy* (1987) and *Saints and Sisterhood* (1990) boldly challenged the American Church, clergy and laity, to question its actions and attitudes toward women.

By the 1990s conferences on women in Orthodoxy began to emerge in America as an outgrowth of the previous European consultations. The Summer Liturgical Institute at St. Vladimir's Orthodox Seminary in Crestwood, New York, sponsored "Women in the Church" in June 1991, analyzing the place and service of women in Orthodox worship and spiritual life.

Orthodox Christian Women of Montreal, founded by Mary Tkachuk, an Orthodox educator and wife of an OCA priest, from Montreal, Canada, has sponsored a one-day conference for women annually since 1992, launched in the first year by keynote speaker Julianna Schmemann, wife of the late theologian Fr. Alexander Schmemann.

In March 1994, Dr. Kyriaki FitzGerald and her husband, Fr. Thomas FitzGerald keynoted the Greek Orthodox Diocese of Denver Symposium on "Women in the Church—A Spiritual Foundation" in Dallas, Texas, followed by the Women's Orthodox Ministries and Education Network symposium with the same title in Denver, Colorado, in October 1995, keynoted by Dr. Valerie Karras, an Orthodox theologian and educator from St. Louis, Missouri.

In February 1997 "A Journey in Faith: A Conference for Orthodox Christian Women" met in Milwaukee, Wisconsin, organized by Cathie Callen of Milwaukee and keynoted by Frederica Mathewes-Green and Fr. John Matusiak. Two more conferences followed, the most recent "Serving in Faith" in 2003, sponsored by the Milwaukee Orthodox Christian Women's Association, the Society of the Myrrhbearing Women. In November 2000 the *St. Nina Quarterly Journal* and the Council of Eastern Orthodox Churches of Central Massachusetts offered "Gifts of the Spirit: A Conference for Orthodox Christian Women" in Dedham, Massachusetts, keynoted by Kyriaki FitzGerald. A second *St. Nina*–sponsored conference on "Authority in the Church" in May 2003 featured Elisabeth Behr-Sigel, by then in her midnineties, at St. Vladimir's Seminary, Crestwood, New York, in conjunction with the Orthodox Theological Society of America. These American conferences focused primarily on lay ministry and the restoration of the female diaconate, authority in church, and the responsibility of all members of the "royal priesthood" as a community in Christ.

Women Monastics

Orthodox monasticism, an integral part of any authentic Orthodox spirituality, has experienced a unique renewal in America over the last twenty-five years. Since 1970 an unprecedented twenty Orthodox monasteries, eight female and twelve male, were established throughout the United States and Canada. The Romanians have been the most active in supporting female monasticism in North America. Under the leadership of Mother Alexandra, the former Princess Ileana of Romania, a large English-speaking community in Ellwood City, Pennsylvania, and a smaller Romanian-speaking community in Rives Junction, Michigan, were established. With the exception of these two monasteries and the Orthodox Church in America's New Skete Monastery in Cambridge, New York, these new women's monasteries are generally small, typically numbering only one to three monastics, and financially insecure. Of special note are the publications emerging from monasteries, particularly compilations of the lives of women saints. Three volumes in a series produced by Holy Apostles Convent in Buena Vista, Colorado, provide a comprehensive compilation of scriptures, holy tradition, patristics, and other ancient writings with the liturgical and iconographic traditions of the church to provide a complete view of the numerous holy women in church history: *The Life of the Virgin Mary* (1989), *The Spiritual Mothers* (1991), and *The Holy Women Martyrs* (1991).

Holy Women of the Syrian Orient (1987) by Susan Ashbrook Harvey, *Holy Women of Russia* (1997) by Brenda Meehan, *The Lament of Eve* (1993) by Joanna Manley, and *A Cloud of Witnesses: Woman's Struggle for Sanctity,"* proceedings from the St. Mary Magdalene Conference (1992), all published by women, testify to the growing sources of women's scholarship emerging within the church. *The Female Diaconate* by Ellen Gvosdev (1991) and *Women Deacons in the Orthodox Church* by Kyriaki FitzGerald (1998) have provided clear historical evidence on the ordination, role, and function of the deaconess in Orthodoxy.

Present and Future

Almost thirty years after the Agapia, Romania, consultation, hundreds of pages of resolutions and recommendations have been gleaned from a thorough cross section of the women of the Orthodox Church. With soberness, clarity, and consistency, these resolutions call for action and education in the church around sexual double standards, human rights abuses toward women and children, and liturgical reform around sexist and misogynist references. They call for ecclesial guidelines and support for the restoration of the order of deaconess and a focused effort in spiritual and theological education on the unique gifts of women for the church. Of these comprehensive recommendations, a few are being addressed within the context of the general increase in lay ministry training and religious education resources in the American church, but no serious ongoing implementation resources or efforts have been placed into effect by any hierarch, diocese, or jurisdiction.

At the turn of the twenty-first century, American Orthodox women, linked electronically to Orthodox laity throughout the world, have just begun to be aware of the history of activity by their more outspoken European sisters and the obstacles resulting from jurisdictional splintering in America. Many discouraged women are attending church services but have given up on being allowed to contribute their leadership gifts in church affairs. Their energies are being given to the secular community, to organizations that not only confess but actually commit funds and resources for women's concerns and engage women in leadership and decision making.

Orthodox women seldom participate in or are cited in public debates concerning the complex social and ethical issues of the day. Orthodox women prominent in civic, professional, and business life, who routinely speak publicly of concerns for the community at large, continue to keep their voices silent in churches where reactionary, judgmental voices and established practices perpetuate the involuntarily submissive role and place for women in the Orthodox Church—often unnamed, usually passively tolerated, and seldom challenged.

The 2,000-year-old, decentralized Orthodox Church tends to progress by evolution, not revolution. Gradual attempts in American jurisdictions to establish departments of lay ministries, comprehensive religious education materials, and adult training programs for lay vocations are emerging at various paces. Although some concerns of Orthodox women are embedded within these areas, the resolutions and recommendations from the Orthodox women's consultations are not yet being specifically addressed.

Joint Orthodox theological consultations on ordination of women to the priesthood largely ended with the Ecumenical Decade (1988–1998); however, interest in ordination to deaconess is slowly growing, and lay ministries by women, especially in education and youth ministry, are becoming more common at diocesan levels. At the parish level, the practices regarding women's participation in lay leadership are widely divergent and inconsistent. What is permitted and encouraged in one parish is completely disallowed in the next, according to the guidance by the priest, a village tradition from long ago, or occasionally a directive from a bishop.

In her keynote address for the fifth annual meeting of the Armenian International Women's Association at Bentley College in May 1996, Orthodox theologian Dr. Valerie Karras offered encouragement for the future:

Education is vitally important so that our people can understand what the true theology of the Church is, and not make absolute the accretions and ideas of Old Testament ritual impurity that have crept in over time and become enshrined in the teachings of our grandmothers. . . .

Women theologians are still relatively few in number, but we are growing. . . . [W]omen also have pastoral roles to play today. Women serve as lay assistants in some Orthodox parishes, and . . . several are chaplains serving in prisons, hospitals, and hospices. . . . [they] are the modern-day equivalent of deacons and deaconesses.

The most important priority, therefore, is to encourage women to fulfill their spiritual calling in every way possible, which historically has included virtually every area of life the Church has to offer. . . . If women had such a diversity of active ministries in a time when women's societal roles were limited, what might we do in the Church of Christ in the twenty-first century? (*St. Nina Quarterly* 1.1 [1996]: 1, 4)

Raising questions about two millennia of church practice in which women have been excluded from participating equally with men is almost beyond the strength or spirit of most women. The job of winnowing out heretical sociocultural incursions from the truth of the faith requires a willingness on the part of both genders to acknowledge the sin of sexism when it occurs.

Orthodoxy has a history of courageous, outspoken, and challenging women, women who were often ignored, publicly criticized, or dismissed as misguided proponents of heresies in their time but who now wear holy crowns of martyrdom and sanctity. Their commitment was continually renewed and strengthened by their faith. Their stories and witness are a source of constant admiration and challenge, as they reveal historical evidence of the participatory role of women in the "royal priesthood of believers" (1 Peter 2:9). These are women to learn about and emulate in the twenty-first century.

It remains to be seen if the seeds of renewed commitment to truth and integrity, generated by the courageous Orthodox women of the European consultations in the late 1900s and planted by a handful of women in the New World, will be tended to fruition by the Holy Spirit's presence and action in the women and men clergy and monastics in the American Church.

SOURCES: Excerpts and summaries of international Orthodox women's conferences are archived at the *MaryMartha* Web site at http://members.iinet.net.au/~mmjournl/MaryMartha/CONSULTATIONS and at the Women's Orthodox Ministries and Education Network http://www.orthodoxwomensnetwork.org/. *Orthodox Women Speak* (1999), ed. Kyriaki Fitz-Gerald, documents the complete proceedings of the Orthodox women's conferences in Damascus, Syria, 1996, and Istanbul, Turkey, 1997. Echoing Eva Topping's perspective, Romanian theologian Anka Manalache addresses misogyny in Orthodox Church Fathers in her article "Orthodoxy and Women," in *Women, Religion and Sexuality,* ed. Jeanne Becher (1991). Sr. Nonna Verna Harrison provides an in-depth study of gender themes in the anthropology of the Greek Fathers in her article "Femininity and Masculinity in the Theology of the Cappadocian Fathers," *Journal of Theological Studies* (1990): 8. *Women Deacons in the Orthodox Church* (1998), by Kyriaki FitzGerald, offers the most comprehensive treatment challenging a common myth that the Orthodox Church had never ordained women as deacons. "Gender Issues and Sexuality," by Demetra Velisarios Jaquet, summarizes the concerns of the European consultations for an American audience in *Sickness or Sin?* ed. John Chirban (2001). Proceedings from the "Gifts of the Spirit Conference," Dedham, Massachusetts, in 2000 and "Discerning the Sign of the Times Conference" in Crestwood, New York, in 2003 are online at http://www.stnina.org/. Elis-abeth Behr-Sigel's landmark books in English are *The Ministry of Women in the Church* (1991), *Discerning the Signs of the Times* (2001), and *The Ordination of Women in the Church* (2000), with Bishop Kallistos Ware. See also Mark Stokoe, *Orthodox Christians in North America* (1995); Frederica Mathewes-Green, "Letter to the Editor," *The Handmaiden* 2.4 (Fall 1997): 51–52; Nonna Verna Harrison, "The Fatherhood of God in Orthodox Theology," *St. Vladimir Theological Quarterly* 37.2–3 (1993): 185–212; *Orthodox Women: Their Rule and Participation in the Orthodox Church* (1976).

ORIENTAL ORTHODOX TRADITIONS AND THE ARMENIAN APOSTOLIC CHURCH
Barbara J. Merguerian

THE ROLE OF women in teaching, preaching, pastoral work, and liturgical functions has been a subject of increasing interest (and in some cases controversy) in the Oriental Orthodox churches, all of whom trace their origins to the earliest years of Christianity. Men have dominated the clerical and administrative functions in these churches in modern times, and their attitudes toward women have been conservative. However, recent research has revealed many forms of active participation by women in the establishment and development of the Oriental Orthodox churches, raising questions about the retention of measures that were later additions and that restrict the role of women, particularly in liturgical practice. Today all these churches are faced with the problem of defining their basic underlying principles, which should remain intact, while identifying those peripheral areas in which modifications to meet new conditions are possible. Sentiment in America for modernization, including efforts to expand the role of women, must take into account the fact that these are hierarchical churches whose leaders are based abroad, making change a long and difficult process. Moreover, although these churches are each independent and self-governing, they have come together increasingly in dialogue in recent years, making it unlikely that any one will institute substantive alterations unless the sister churches are in agreement.

The Oriental Orthodox churches in America, including the Armenian Apostolic, Coptic, Ethiopian Orthodox, Syriac Orthodox, and Malankara Orthodox, are immigrant churches that face many issues in addition to religion, including preservation of language and culture, assimilation and acculturation, and intermarriage, among others. It is not unusual for members of the second and third generations, both men and women, to find established American Christian denominations more compatible with their religious needs; others find the tradition and ethnicity of their native churches a welcome haven from the secularism and rapid change that mark contemporary society.

Armenian Apostolic Church

The Armenian Apostolic Church is the oldest (established in Worcester, Massachusetts, in 1889) and the largest (with approximately 130 parishes) of the Oriental Orthodox churches in America. Women play an active role in the Armenian Apostolic Church, especially in the areas of education, music, community activities, and social service; in recent years they have entered increasingly into the lay administration of the church. In common with other Orthodox and Oriental Orthodox denominations, however, the church offers mixed (if not to say contradictory) images of women. As the mother of God, Mary is venerated, and a painting of mother and child appears prominently over the altar of most churches. Yet, as daughters of Eve, women have been barred by firm strictures from any participation in liturgical services and even from standing in the altar area. As one woman pointed out at an Armenian Church conference, "It is ironic, but true, that if today Mary, the mother of Christ, the most venerated woman in all of Christendom, were to appear in this church today, she wouldn't be permitted to go up to the altar" (Papazian, "Mary, Martha, and Men"). In recent decades the church has made determined efforts to appear more inclusive to women (by establishing and commemorating an annual "women saint's day," opening the doors of the theological seminary to female students, appointing women to upper administrative positions, and encouraging women's participation on local elected parish councils). The success of these efforts in maintaining the loyalty of increasingly well-educated and -assimilated parishioners remains to be seen.

Historical Summary

As an immigrant institution in America, the Armenian Apostolic Church has from its inception in this country endeavored to provide its members not only with religious support but with the means to ease adjustment to a new and unfamiliar society and at the same time to perpetuate their language, culture, and traditions. (One theologian has argued that the national focus of the church has hindered its spiritual development; see Guroian.) These auxiliary activities have provided a broad scope for the energies and talents of Armenian women. Innovations such as Sunday religious schools and Saturday Armenian language classes have become arenas for women's activism. Women's Guilds have planned and sponsored social events to foster com-

munity cohesiveness, as well as to raise funds to establish and operate the churches. In 1919 the church bylaws were amended to grant Armenian women twenty-one years of age or older the right to vote in the diocesan assembly and to be elected to the administration of the church (Zakian, 22). At the same time a proposal to ban mixed choirs as contrary to church tradition was not accepted, thus assuring that the voices of Armenian women would be heard in the celebration of the Divine Liturgy, which is such a central part of the observance of this faith.

The Armenian Church boasts a democratic basis historically, with its primates and other high ecclesiastical officers elected by mixed clerical/lay assemblies. This basis has been reinforced in America not only by the democratic nature of society at large but also by the fact that the local parishes have been almost exclusively responsible for the financing of the building and operation of the churches. If in the early decades most parish councils and diocesan assemblies were populated exclusively by males, that situation has now changed. To find women serving as members of parish councils and even as chairs of these councils is not uncommon today; women are also prominently represented at annual diocesan assemblies (for example, approximately 30 percent of parish council and diocesan assembly members were women in the Eastern Diocese of the Armenian Church of America in 2001–2002). On the other hand, it is rare to find women represented on the highest diocesan level (Louise Manoogian Simone, who was elected to the Eastern Diocesan Council in 1979 for a single term, remains the exception to the rule). Women are prominent in administrative positions; for many years a woman served as executive director of the Eastern Diocese, while today the codirectors of religious education and the director of its Armenian Language Lab are all women. Anxious to harness the talents and abilities of women, the church encourages this participation. One leading clergyman in America, the Very Rev. Aram Keshishian (subsequently elected Catholicos Aram I of the Great House of Cilicia in Lebanon), wrote an article in 1995 challenging women to assume a greater role in the church. He wrote:

In the Armenian Church, as in other churches, women have been excluded from the leadership. In all activities, at all levels, women have been delegated an auxiliary role to men. . . . Centuries-old, conservative mentality still persists, although occasionally—very small in number—women hold key positions. Times have changed; our needs have changed. . . . It is indispensable, therefore, that a renewed understanding and orientation be given to the role of women in the Armenian diaspora in

The movement in America to expand the role of women began modestly in 1969 when Rev. Arnak Kasparian called for the ordination of female acolytes and deacons. © 2004 Gale Zucker/www.gzucker.com.

general, and in the Armenian communities in the West in particular. (Keshishian)

Movement to Ordain Women

Given their active role in the educational, administrative, and social life of the church, it was inevitable that the question of the spiritual role of women in the church would arise, particularly with the emergence of the women's liberation movement and the decision in other Christian denominations to ordain women. The growing prosperity and sophistication of the community provided opportunities for a more careful study of church traditions in general and of the historic role of women in particular. It was apparent, for example, that the earliest saint and martyr of the Armenian Church was a women, Princess Sandukht, who lived in the first century and was murdered by her father, the king, because of her refusal to renounce her Christian faith; the much revered "enlightener" of the Armenian nation, St. Gregory, survived imprisonment in a pit for many years only through the clandestine assistance of another early saint, Princess Khosrovidukht; other female saints and martyrs followed in the ancient and medieval periods. Studies indicated that the Armenian Church formerly ordained deaconesses, although the practice had fallen

out of use; and convents have long existed in the Armenian Church, though much reduced in number in recent times. Personal pronouns in the Armenian language (in both classical and modern forms) do not differ by gender, so that the God of the Bible does not necessarily carry a masculine implication. And it is significant that, with the establishment in 1961 of a seminary in America for the education of the priesthood (St. Nersess, now located in New Rochelle, New York, and affiliated with St. Vladimir Orthodox Seminary), women have been admitted along with men.

The movement in America to expand the role of women began modestly, in 1969, when the Reverend Arnak Kasparian, a pastor in New Jersey, delivered a paper before the annual clergy conference of the Eastern Diocese titled "Ordination as an Acolyte and Deacon Must Not Be Denied to Qualified Females in the United States." Father Arnak cited in particular the shortage of males to perform liturgical functions as the rationale in favor of his argument and pointed out that women had been ordained to the lower ranks of the clergy during the early years of the church. Father Arnak raised some eyebrows later when, during the traditional ceremony just before Easter, he washed the feet of girls as well as boys. A decade later, in 1979, a respected Armenian American theologian, Dr. Hagop J. Nersoyan, published the paper "Women and Christian Priesthood" in the magazine of the Armenian Church Youth Organization of America, in which he examined, and then rejected, every possible argument against the ordination of women. "We seem to have found that, on balance, there are no rational or theological reasons against the ordination of women," Nersoyan concluded, and he suggested that the inclusion of women in the priesthood would result in a "better world" because *more* people who are willing, concerned, responsible, and competent can become what they want to be."

These early murmurings did not have any apparent effect on the hierarchy of the Armenian Church, but the movement continued. In 1982 Louise Kalemkerian, one of the first graduates from the St. Nersess Armenian Seminary, who had been appointed director of religious education at the Eastern Diocese, presented a paper titled "The Role of Women in the Armenian Church and Ordination to the Diaconate" at the Diocesan Assembly, held that year in New Britain, Connecticut (the paper was published subsequently by the Western Diocese of the Armenian Church of America, in 1986). Kalemkerian later recalled that, as she began her presentation, several of the clergy present "got up and walked out" (*Invisible No More?* 31). In her paper, Kalemkerian began by citing women's services to the church as teachers and leaders in the education ministry. "Indeed, it is the women of the church who are spearheading the movement for retreats, educational programs, spiritual growth seminars, Bible studies, and the like," she pointed out. Why not "provide new avenues of service" by opening the ministry of the diaconate to women, thereby allowing them to fill a real need in the church? Such women, she argued, could not only assist the priest in liturgical services, including baptisms, weddings, and funerals; they might also conduct services on college campuses or in nursing/old age homes, provide visitations and counseling to the sick and bereaved, assist immigrants to adjust to their new homes, and even be assigned to small parishes without priests. "God continues to call women into the ordained ministry," she pointed out. "The need of the present day for more workers in the harvest may lead us in the church to rethink our conventions of an all-male diaconate and return to the traditions of earlier times" (Kalemkerian, Role of Women).

A major milestone was passed in 1984 when a college student, Seta Simonian, became the first woman in America to receive ordination as an acolyte (*tbir*—the first four steps of the clergy) in the Armenian Church. The service took place in St. Andrew Church in Cupertino, California, with Archbishop Vatché Hovsepian, primate of the Western Diocese, presiding. Two years later, in 1986, the Armenian American faithful were astonished to find in their midst a visitor, Sister Hripsimé

Sassounian, who had been ordained a deaconess in Istanbul in 1982 by the Armenian Patriarch there and was visiting relatives in Los Angeles. The only deaconess in the Armenian Church as far as anyone could remember, Sister Hripsimé participated in several services in America, most notably during the Feast of the Assumption, when she assisted Archbishop Hovsepian during a celebration of the Divine Liturgy at St. Mary Armenian Church in Yettem, California. That same year a new publication, *Side by Side*, devoted to the interests of Armenian women in the church, was independently published in Boston. The Eastern Diocesan Assembly meeting in Racine, Wisconsin, in 1986 overwhelmingly (96–22) passed a resolution calling for the ordination of qualified women to the diaconate. The resolution stated, in part:

> The ordination of women to the diaconate is not a revolutionary idea. It is a practice and tradition which has fallen into disuse. We know of no part of Church Canon Law that prohibits women from providing the services associated with the diaconate, and the historical precedents speak rather eloquently that there is none. On the contrary, the evidence supports the belief that the exclusivity of males in the diaconate constituted a change from early church practice. (*Invisible No More?* 60)

With the exception of a handful of supportive clergy, the church hierarchy remained unmoved by the flurry of activity in the late 1980s on behalf of a more active women's ministry. The sole innovation was that, in the late 1980s and early 1990s, young girls were allowed to stand at the altar, as candle-holders, with the provision that such service would cease when they reached the age of twelve (and presumably became "impure"). When Louise Kalemkerian, who was serving at the time as the director of religious education at the Eastern Diocese, requested ordination as a deaconess, she was repeatedly and firmly rejected by the primate. Finally, in 1991, she "decided that God's call was stronger than I could withstand" and left the Armenian Church to be received into the Episcopal Church, where she was ordained subsequently into the ministry; she now serves as pastor of Emmanuel Church in Stamford, Connecticut. "For me it has been an incredulous journey, a very difficult one, but nonetheless very rewarding," she says. "I know I am doing what I have been called to do." Nonetheless, she recognizes that she "will always be part of the Armenian Church and it will always be part of me," because in that church she heard the gospel that "calls all human beings into full relationship with Jesus" (*Invisible No More?* 31–32). In leaving the Armenian Church to follow her call, Reverend Kalemkerian is not unique. An earlier example is the Reverend Flora A. Keshgegian, who was raised in the Armenian Church and, in the 1970s, became one of the first women to be ordained in the Episcopal Church. She is now an author (her latest book is *Redeeming Memories: A Theology of Healing and Transformation* [2000]) and a professor of systematic theology at the Episcopal Theological Seminary of the Southwest. Another route is being followed by Paula Jurigian, a graduate of St. Nersess Seminary who subsequently received two master's degrees, one in pastoral care and the other in higher education administration; she is now a novice in the Roman Catholic Order of the Sisters of Notre Dame de Nemur.

The door to women's ordination to the clergy was firmly closed in 1995 by the head of the church, Karekin I, Catholicos of All Armenians, whose seat is located in Echmiadzin, Armenia. In a letter issued on the occasion of the United Nations Fourth World Conference on Women in Beijing that year, the catholicos cited women's active role in the church as "preachers, educators, members of religious orders, benefactors, most active servants in social service, mothers *par excellence*, even martyrs in the defense of and the lively preservation of the Christian faith." Nonetheless, he stated flatly:

> The Armenian Church does not allow the priestly ordination for women. This attitude should never be considered as an attitude of discrimination. The church follows the Tradition (with a capital T) and has to respect that Tradition. The question of ordination of women has never emanated from the life of the Armenian Church. It has been considered as a foreign question that has not affected the life of the church. Women in the Armenian Church are fully satisfied with their active engagement in all aspects and areas of service of the church. (*Invisible No More?* 58)

This categorical statement by the head of the Armenian Church, while no surprise, was a deep disappointment to those in America who had been looking for a ray of hope that the situation of women might change. Some wondered on what basis the catholicos could presume to speak on behalf of "women in the Armenian Church." This issue was raised by several of the participants at the 1996 annual meeting of the Armenian International Women's Association, held in Boston, which took as its theme "Invisible No More? An Expanding Role for Armenian Women in the Church." A special guest at the meeting was Seta Simonian Atamian, the first (and to date only) woman ordained in America to the level of acolyte (*tbir*) in the Armenian Church, by then married and living in Boston. She described her experiences in the Western Diocese, where she had the opportunity to serve at the altar and to assist at weddings, funerals, and baptisms, with the support and encouragement of the pastor and congregation; she had been led to believe that she would be ordained as deacon "when the time was right." Nothing prepared her for the cold rejection she would experience after moving to Boston. "I knew that I would be a novelty to the Eastern Diocese," she recalled. "After all I hadn't heard of any other female acolyte anywhere else in the country." She hoped that she had "paved at least a small path" and wanted "to support and serve as an encouragement for other interested women to come forward." To her astonishment she was flatly rejected at the first Armenian Church she attended in the Boston area, on the grounds that the primate of the Eastern Diocese did not allow "those kinds of things." At the second church the pastor was welcoming and sympathetic but limited her participation to morning service litanies and special off-the-altar processions; even here she felt the disapproval of the congregation and longtime service servers. "I felt I couldn't fight the battle by myself," she concluded. "After all I had a new life and career to start. Slowly I stopped even attending church because it felt empty. Something had slipped away." Atamian summarized her dilemma, and that faced by many Armenian American women, as follows:

> Now as a mother I'd like my children to learn and participate in the rich tradition of our church, but I wrestle with the idea of exposing my daughter to a church that is patriarchal and inconsistent. I don't want her to feel alienated or inferior as a female. I also don't want my son to think that our family considers those values acceptable. (*Invisible No More?* 51–53)

The Armenian Church today faces many challenges. It has never fully recovered from the losses (especially in terms of experienced clergymen) sustained during the Armenian Genocide of World War I. In America it has long been divided into two competing administrations based on political divisions that no longer seem relevant or even comprehensible to most churchgoers. The head of the church, the catholicos in the Republic of Armenia, is preoccupied with the effort required to revive a church that barely survived seven decades of atheistic communist domination. The church in America faces a host of issues, ranging from language (the classical Armenian used in the liturgy is intelligible only to a small minority), administration (married clergy are ineligible for the higher positions), intermarriage (this has reached proportions considered alarming by many), and contemporary questions (the church's stance on divorce, abortion, and homosexuality is somewhat ambiguous, contradictory, or unclear). Those who raise women's concerns are often brushed aside as troublemakers or told to wait until the "more important" issues are resolved.

The strength and viability of the Armenian Church—which in 2001 proudly celebrated its 1,700-year anniversary—has been its ability to adjust to change while retaining its core principles. That flexibility in nonessential areas is being tested increasingly. The situation of Armenian American women has evolved in past decades. A recent study by the Eastern Diocese provided comparative statistics about women in the Armenian Church between the years 1978 and 2002; the study indicates that the number under the age of forty who work outside the home doubled in that period (from 40 percent in 1978 to 80 percent of the total in 2002); those enrolled in the Women's Guild fell from 50 to 20 percent of the total; and college graduates increased from 40 to 80 percent. "Thirty or forty years ago women came and cooked and held a bazaar," Father Untzag Nalbandian observed in presenting the statistics at a leadership workshop of the Women's Guild. "But now women are educated and raising children and don't have time to do these things." The clergyman's list of the ways today's women can serve the church, however, appears no more than a sanction of the status quo: In addition to education, he mentioned sponsoring Sunday coffee hour and making *mahs* (communion bread), helping at social events or joining the choir, conducting Bible study, serving on the parish council, or organizing ecumenical/interfaith activities (*Reporter,* March 9, 2002, 11–12).

The impetus in the late 1980s toward ordaining women appears to have abated, and many women have made the difficult decision to leave the Armenian Church. Most remain, however, and serve the church in various long-accepted capacities. Clearly women have the power to effect major change in the church, particularly affecting the role of women, if they determine to do so. It remains to be seen if they will accept the challenge placed before them:

> Marys and Marthas of the Armenian Church: Don't be timid. Don't be afraid. Take the bold initiatives that are necessary if we expect our church to survive. (Papazian)

SOURCES: General information can be found in Christopher Hagop Zakian, ed., *The Torch Was Passed: The Centennial History of the Armenian Church of America* (1998), and Vigen Guroian, *Faith, Church, Mission: Essays for Renewal in the Armenian Church* (1995). On women, see Abel Oghlukian, *The Deaconess in the Armenian Church* (1994); M. Christin Arat, "The Deaconess in the Armenian Church," in *Voices of Armenian Women,* ed. Barbara J. Merguerian and Joy Renjilian-Burgy (2000), 86–118; Louise Kalemkerian, "The Role of Women in the Armenian Church and Ordination to the Diaconate" (1986); and *Side by Side,* vol. 1 (1986–1987) and vol. 2 (1991). A useful collection of documents and statements is

in the Armenian International Women's Association publication *Invisible No More? An Expanding Role for Armenian Women in the Church* (1996). The evolution of the community is described by Anny Bakalian, *Armenian-Americans: From Being to Feeling Armenian* (1993). Relevant articles can be found in the periodicals *The Armenian Church* (Eastern Diocese of the Armenian Church of America, New York) and *Outreach* (Eastern Prelacy of the Armenian Church of America, New York), among them Iris Papazian, "Mary, Martha, and Men in the Armenian Church (*Outreach,* 1984), and Very Rev. Aram Keshishian, "The Role of Women in the Armenian Church and Society" (*Outreach,* 1995). The English-language Armenian press is also useful in this regard (especially the *Armenian Mirror-Spectator, Armenian Reporter,* and *Armenian Weekly*).

AN ORTHODOX PERSPECTIVE ON FEMINIST THEOLOGY
Valerie A. Karras

IN A RADIO address delivered on October 1, 1939, Winston Churchill described Russia as "a riddle wrapped in a mystery inside an enigma." For the average mystified Westerner, that famous phrase may equally well describe Russia's predominant religion, Eastern Orthodox Christianity. While Orthodoxy is the second-largest Christian communion in the world, with somewhere from 215 million to as many as 300 million faithful, it is a distinctly minority faith in western Europe and North America. In the United States, for example, only about 2 percent of the population is Orthodox. Moreover, despite increasing numbers of nonethnic converts in the West, Orthodoxy is usually associated with ethnic groups whose roots lie in eastern Europe and the Middle East. Most of the Orthodox churches are, in fact, the "original," continuously existing churches of the Christian East, rooted in the Greek-speaking half of the Roman Empire. They continue the early church's decentralized organizational structure, so each national or regional church (e.g., Church of Greece, Church of Russia, Patriarchate of Antioch) is self-governing. This decentralized, often ethnic-based structure, which historically has been one of Orthodoxy's strengths, has resulted in a fragmented, incoherent, and marginalized Orthodox presence in western Europe and North America. Each ethnic group has set up in these "diaspora" regions of the West a daughter church dependent on its own east European or Middle Eastern mother church, creating the untraditional and uncanonical situation of multiple Orthodox jurisdictions within a single geographic area.

The nature of the Orthodox Christian faith also baffles most Westerners. Two words that may best describe Orthodoxy are *traditional* and *mystical*. Neither of these words has been particularly important to North American culture. *Mystical* has only recently come into vogue, primarily through Far Eastern religions (i.e., Western Christians have simply leapfrogged over Eastern Christianity since they are usually unaware of its very existence), and *traditional* seems to have an almost pejorative ring, especially in the United States. Additionally, Orthodoxy does not engage in active proselytism (activities aimed at conversion) among non-Orthodox Christian peoples, including the majority of Americans. Thus, the religious insularity of many Orthodox has combined with the ignorance of most Westerners to create a common perception of Orthodoxy as impenetrable, ethnic, quaint, backward, and constitutionally opposed to, or at any rate unconcerned with, feminist theology.

Orthodoxy and Feminist Theology—Only a Passing Acquaintance?

To a certain extent this is true. The majority of Orthodox, even in North America, view feminism as irrelevant—or at least ill-suited, as a sociopolitical concept, to the Orthodox ethos. There is no popular, widespread movement for the ordination of women to the priesthood and episcopacy, and even the limited push for the ordination of women to the diaconate—which would revive a well-documented tradition of the early and Byzantine Church—eschews the more strident and assertive tones of women's ordination movements in Western Christian churches. Advocates of greater ecclesial participation for Orthodox women do not speak in terms of "rights," which is a political rather than theological concept. Rather, congruent with the spiritual and traditional foundations of Orthodox theology, advocates of a restored female diaconate offer arguments based on the church's tradition, history, and liturgical theology, applying the practices of the past to a modern situation.

The example of ordination reflects the broader state of Orthodox theology vis-à-vis feminist theology. As in Western Christian churches, Orthodox women theologians have become visible only in the last couple of decades, especially in the United States. However, there is no Orthodox feminist theologian akin to a Mary Daly or even to a Rosemary Radford Ruether. In other words, Orthodox theologians—whether male or female—have not challenged the basic tenets of the Orthodox Christian faith or criticized Orthodox theology as fundamentally patriarchal. In fact, compared with other major Christian confessions, Orthodox theology has had relatively little interaction with feminist theologies. Among North American Orthodox, there are only a few written Orthodox responses to Christian feminism: an article by Kyriaki Karidoyanes FitzGerald in a difficult-to-find edited volume (Limouris, ed., *The Place of the Woman* [1998]); a small booklet by Deborah Belonick (*Feminism in Christianity* [1983]) that is simply a revised version of her master's thesis from an Orthodox seminary; and a chapter by Valerie A. Karras (Saint Louis University) in the *Cambridge Companion to Feminist Theology* (2002). Since these works are brief, they tend to treat feminist theology as a generic whole; the first two, in particular, differentiate some strains of thought but do not respond to specific feminist theologians. FitzGerald, conscious of the dearth of literature in this area, notes in her article the painful lack of substantive Orthodox responses to the questions and issues raised by feminist theology (FitzGerald, 287).

Appearances can be deceiving, however. It is true that the debates and theologies sweeping through most of Western Christianity for the past two or three decades have scarcely created a ripple within Orthodoxy in terms of direct dialogue and reflection. On the other hand, feminist theology has not left Orthodox Christianity entirely unaffected. The theological "surface waters" may appear serene and static, but there is continuing movement below the surface, movement in several different directions. While some Orthodox resent what they perceive as ecumenism's imposition of Western concerns and agenda on the Orthodox Church, others have welcomed the opportunity to ponder practices and beliefs that have been uncritically accepted as traditional in Orthodox thought.

An important aspect of Orthodox ecclesiology in this regard is the absence of a "magisterium." That is, there is no official teaching authority distinct from the church as a whole; no one has the authority to speak unilaterally and authoritatively for the entire church, much less to bind the church to such a unilateral teaching. Bishops normally speak on behalf of the church, especially when they meet in synod and articulate a theological tenet collectively (conciliarity is the norm in Orthodoxy). Occasionally, however, the decisions of synods composed of hundreds of bishops have been negated by the collective will of the church. Therefore, it is meaningful to note that while the "official church"—that is, the clergy and laypersons chosen by presiding bishops to represent Orthodoxy in bilateral and ecumenical dialogues—has been almost uniform in its insistence on traditional ecclesiastical roles for Orthodox women, and has criticized much feminist theology as heretical, the attitudes of Orthodox as a whole have been nowhere near as monolithic.

When examining Orthodox perspectives on feminist theology, it is interesting to note that despite sometimes radically divergent views the framework of debate for nearly all Orthodox theologians is the same: a reliance predominantly on early church theology ("patristics") and on traditional practices, especially liturgical ones. These twin pillars—theology and worship—undergird

Historians such as Susan Ashbrook Harvey, professor of religion at Brown University, are engaged with feminist theology. Harvey, for example, has explored feminine imagery in Orthodox Trinitarian theology. *Courtesy of Teva Regule.*

virtually all discussions of feminist theology from an Orthodox perspective. What differs is how theologians have appropriated the patristic theology and liturgical life of the early church and applied them to a modern, Western context. Particularly noteworthy are the varying understandings of the relationships *between* theology and liturgical life. In other words, the relationship between theory and practice is often understood differently and therefore results in widely differing attitudes toward feminist theology and the ecclesial life of women.

Orthodoxy in the West

Orthodox resistance to feminist theology, and particularly to its implications in nontraditional ecclesial roles for women, is readily seen in a number of venues, but the real flashpoint is the ordination of women to the priesthood. Tensions have mounted within the World Council of Churches on both sides of this issue, with the Orthodox churches becoming increasingly vocal in their resistance. Typical of the majority Orthodox approach was the original title of an international Orthodox conference held in Rhodes, Greece, in 1988. The title of both the conference and the volume of its published papers was changed to *The Place of the Woman in the Orthodox Church and the Question of the Ordination of Women* (the title apparently was given by a nonnative English speaker). However, the original title—"The Impossibility of the Ordination of Women"—provoked the primate of the Russian Orthodox Church in Great Britain, Metropolitan Anthony Bloom, to write to French Orthodox theologian Elisabeth Behr-Sigel an unpublished but widely circulated letter condemning the foregone conclusions of the conference organizers.

Bloom's brief critique touched on several fundamentals of Orthodox theology. These areas, and some others, have been center stage over the past thirty years in most articles and discussions found in Orthodox circles regarding feminist theology and women's roles in the church. They are the understanding of the Three Persons of the Trinity (Trinitarian theology); who humans are as theological beings (theological anthropology); the understanding of salvation (soteriology); and how worship does—or does not—express the church's Trinitarian theology, theological anthropology, and soteriology (liturgical theology). As noted earlier, Orthodox theologians have approached these areas, and understood the relationships among them, differently. Those differences reflect personal spirituality and experience but also reflect the cultural context of the theologians. The organizers of the 1988 Rhodes conference, and most of the "official" representatives in ecumenical and bilateral discussions, are from eastern European and Middle Eastern countries such as Greece, Russia, and Syria. By contrast, Bloom is a native Russian who grew up largely outside of Russia, converted to Orthodoxy as a youth, and has lived most of his life in western Europe.

Like Bloom, most Orthodox theologians and historians who have questioned other Orthodox writers' theological arguments used to support traditional practices, and who have engaged more positively with feminist theology, have similarly come from a Western background and have often been adult converts to Orthodoxy: Bishop Kallistos (Ware) of Diokleia (Pembroke College, University of Oxford), Fr. Emmanuel Clapsis (Holy Cross Greek Orthodox School of Theology, Brookline, Massachusetts), Verna (Sister Nonna) Harrison (St. Paul School of Theology, Kansas City), Susan Ashbrook Harvey (Brown University), Leonie Liveris (a church historian in Perth, Australia), and the grande dame of Orthodox women theologians, Elisabeth Behr-Sigel (Paris, France). Several of these converts to Orthodoxy, similar to Jaroslav Pelikan (Yale) and Albert Raboteau (Princeton), have come to the Orthodox faith directly or indirectly through their academic and professional studies. Thus, they combine an understanding of Western Christianity—their roots—with a high degree of theological and historical knowledge of Eastern Christianity. At times they appear more aware of the Western basis of certain arguments used by some modern Orthodox theologians than do those raised in Orthodoxy. Ware observes that

> we are in danger . . . of taking over the criteria and arguments of non-Orthodox writers, without articulating an independent Orthodox standpoint, firmly based on Patristic principles. Orthodox opponents of the ordination of women priests have often relied, for example, on the Papal statement concerning women and the priesthood *Inter Insigniores* (October 15, 1976), without inquiring how far the conception of priesthood assumed in this document in fact corresponds to the Orthodox understanding. (Ware, 6)

Therefore, it is important to review relevant areas of Orthodox theology to see how they relate to feminist theology.

Trinitarian Theology as Foundation

Theology in its true sense—"teaching about God"—lies at the heart of all Orthodox thought. Orthodox theology is theocentric; that is, it is based primarily on divine revelation and spiritual experience, as opposed to an anthropocentric approach relying more on human intellect and social experience. For instance, Orthodox moral theology is grounded in Trinitarian theology, not on the natural law theory of Aristotle that underlies much of the ethical discourse of the Latin West. Therefore, Orthodox theologians of all stripes bristle at feminist theologians who facilely discard the traditional names and understandings of the persons of the Trinity as products of a premodern, patriarchal culture. The understanding of names as metaphors, brought out so well by feminist theologian Sallie McFague, is not the problem for most Orthodox; nor is the use of feminine imagery for God. In fact, in the Christian East, feminine imagery for the divine dates back not just to the medieval period, as in the West, but to the earliest centuries of Christianity. Susan Ashbrook Harvey has lifted up feminine imagery for all three Trinitarian figures from a second-century Christian Syriac work known as the *Odes of Solomon*, which depicts Jesus Christ in feminine terms in Ode 8: "I fashioned their limbs/ and my own breasts I prepared for them/ that they might drink my holy milk and live by it" (Harvey, 127). In Ode 19, it is God the Father and the Holy Spirit who are feminized:

A cup of milk was offered to me
And I drank it with the sweetness of the Lord's
    kindness.
The Son is the cup,
And He who was milked is the Father,
And She who milked Him is the Holy Spirit.

Because His breasts were full,
And it was not necessary for His milk to be
    poured out without cause.
The Holy Spirit opened her womb,
and mixed the milk of the two breasts of the
    Father. (125)

Verna Harrison quotes Clement of Alexandria (Egypt), who lived in the late second century and who, in his spiritual and ethical manual *The Teacher (Paedagogus),* used similar imagery for both the Father and Jesus, for example: "The food is the milk of the Father, by which alone the little ones are nursed. . . . We who have believed in God through him [the Logos = Jesus Christ] take refuge upon the 'care-banishing breast' of the Father, the Logos" ("The Care-Banishing Breast of the Father," 404). In another work, Harrison cites Gregory of Nyssa, who, like Clement, wrote in Greek. In his commentary on the Song of Songs (the book from the Hebrew Bible sometimes titled the Song of Solomon), written in the late fourth century in Cappadocia, a central region of Asia Minor (modern-day Turkey), Gregory averred: "No one can adequately grasp the terms pertaining to God. For example, 'mother' is mentioned in place of 'father.' Both terms mean the same, because the divine is neither male nor female" ("Male and Female in Cappadocian Theology," 441).

Nevertheless, as Emmanuel Clapsis has shown in "Naming God: An Orthodox View," Gregory and others both insisted on an asexual understanding of the name *Father and* argued for the irreplaceability of that name for the first person of the Trinity for two reasons: It is the revealed name, used by Jesus Christ himself, and it images a particular type of relationship among the persons of the Trinity. The Christian tradition, and especially Orthodox Christianity, understands God not as an impersonal force or monistic being with three modes or faces (an early heretical belief known as modalism) but as a being whose very manner of existence is irreducibly tripersonal and interrelational and whose activities are always united. Some feminist Christian theologians have substituted the traditional names of "Father, Son, and Holy Spirit" with "Creator, Redeemer, and Sanctifier" (or Sustainer), hoping by the use of nongendered names to avoid a patriarchal understanding of God. From an Orthodox perspective, the goal is an admirable one; the means are not. Harrison, in an article on the fatherhood of God, deconstructs the patriarchal, power-based understanding of fatherhood and constructs in its place a self-emptying (kenotic) one:

> In thinking of God the Father, one is struck by his awesome self-renunciation. From eternity to eternity, he gives his own essence, all that he is and has, all his attributes including his sovereign

authority and power, to the Son and the Holy Spirit. He does not withhold anything for himself alone but remains unique simply as the Source of the Godhead which he shares with the other two. His essence, his uncreated radiance and all his activities are theirs also. ("The Fatherhood of God," 190)

The feminist names describe, in a cosmocentric and even anthropocentric way, what God *does* (e.g., "create"), but the traditional names evoke who God *is*. In other words, they reveal to us the personal and relational nature of God in God's own Self: three distinct persons who exist without beginning as a "community" of love and mutual indwelling. Moreover, unlike the feminist names, the traditional names do not divide the unity of the Godhead by assigning activities to separate persons of the Trinity. For Orthodoxy, all three persons have the same divine capacities and properties, and every divine activity is Trinitarian, with each person acting in a personal way. For example, whereas the name *Creator* is applied to the first person of the Trinity (as though only the first person is Creator), Irenaeus of Lyons, a Greek-speaking bishop of the mid-third century, described the Son and Spirit as the "two hands of the Father" in the act of creation. Thus, the fourth-century Nicene-Constantinopolitan Creed—the only ecumenical creed of Christianity—refers to the creative activity of the second and third persons of the Trinity as well by describing the Son as the one "through whom all things were made" and the Holy Spirit as the "Life-Creator," thereby showing that the creation of life is a single activity of the three persons. Ironically, then, the traditional names may be seen as more "feminist" than the modern feminist names because while the feminist names for the persons of the Trinity view them primarily in terms of their activities or "work," the traditional names emphasize the fundamentally relational and personal nature of God.

The Implications of the *Imago Dei* in Theological Anthropology

Orthodox Trinitarian theology has striking implications in the area of theological anthropology. Since Orthodox anthropology retains the theocentric focus of Orthodox theology generally, the essence of human existence is derived, with some obvious differences, from the manner of divine existence. Humanity is a microcosm, composed of elements of both the physical and the spiritual worlds, and thus is a mediator, uniting them. Still, for the Orthodox, as Panayiotis Nellas has shown in *Deification in Christ* (21), the core of human existence is theological—it is based on the creation of humanity described in the first chapter of the book of Genesis, that is, human beings as the image of God (Genesis 1:26–27). Therefore, if God is neither male nor female, then humanity's sexual differentiation is not part of this *imago Dei*, this "image of God." Certain sex-linked traits may reflect aspects of God's nature (giving life, protecting, nurturing, etc.), but the patristic writers of the Christian East have almost unanimously interpreted Genesis 1:27 ("male and female God made them") in an inclusive sense, not a normative one. In other words, *both* man and woman are created in the image of God, but human sexual differentiation is not in itself a reflection of who and what God is intrinsically.

This means that, unlike much of Western Christian anthropology, the mainstream of Orthodox theology has for almost two millennia agreed with feminist theology in rejecting the idea that the man is the normative human person. The implications are even more significant when Orthodox anthropology is refined by distinguishing among various states of human existence: before the Fall from paradise (prelapsarian), after the Fall (postlapsarian), and in its resurrected, or ultimate (eschatological), state. These distinctions are evident, though usually not systematically, in early Christian writing and are further nuanced by distinguishing between (1) God's original plan for humanity (to be fulfilled in the resurrection) and humanity as it was actually created before the Fall and (2) postlapsarian humanity B.C. and A.D.

Orthodox anthropology can thus look very different at different stages of human existence. Since at least the third century, Eastern Christian theologians have distinguished between the *image* and the *likeness* of God (Genesis 1:27). The image of God is "hard-wired" into all human beings and includes such qualities as reason and free will; according to Orthodox theology, these traits continue to exist in all human beings even after the Fall. The likeness of God refers to the realization of our full human potential and involves a synergistic relationship between a human being and God that culminates in an ever-deepening union called *theosis*, or deification. This process begins in our current, fallen condition but is fulfilled only after death, in the resurrection. Because it posits a *substantive* difference between our current existence and our resurrected existence, Orthodoxy differs markedly from most feminist theologies, which project a future only incrementally different from the present. In fact, some feminist theologians do not believe in any continued personal existence beyond death.

While most Orthodox theologians agree on these basic ideas regarding different stages of human existence, they disagree on the nature of the *relationship* between our current existence, including our sexual differentiation, and our future existence in the resurrection. As numerous scholars, both Orthodox and non-Orthodox, have demonstrated, most of the early Greek Christian writers believed that sexual differentiation is not an essential property of human existence and therefore speculated that the distinction of sex will be utterly abolished in the resurrection. Interestingly, this line of thought is appealing to many feminist theologians since sexual distinction becomes irrelevant to ultimate human existence. However, since Orthodox theology distinguishes between our current, fallen existence and our future, resurrected state, some Orthodox theologians accept the idea of a sexually undifferentiated humanity in our resurrected future existence while—in contrast to feminist theology—affirming distinct roles for men and women in our current stage of existence, including the exclusion of women from the priesthood.

Moreover, not all modern Orthodox theologians believe that sexual distinctions *will* be abolished in the resurrection or that it is not essential to human nature. Similar to some French feminist theologians in the generation following him, Russian émigré to France Paul Evdokimov (*Woman and the Salvation of the World* [1994]) proposed a novel anthropology that included sex as a theologically constitutive element while avoiding a one-to-one correspondence to the persons of the Godhead (e.g., between men and the Father), by using the Virgin Mary and John the Baptist as models for female and male existence, respectively. Others, primarily in North America (e.g., Thomas Hopko and Kenneth Paul Wesche), have gone beyond Evdokimov. They are uncomfortable with what they perceive as an overreliance on Platonic thought in much patristic anthropology, criticizing it as too dualistic, that is, that it separates body from soul and spiritualizes human nature excessively (it should be noted, however, that many other scholars disagree with this characterization). These American Orthodox theologians have attempted to construct a theology that includes sexual differentiation as an essential element of human nature and associate a specific human sex with a specific person of the Trinity: men with the Father or the Son, and women with the Holy Spirit.

Women and the Priesthood: Liturgical and Salvific Implications

Although these efforts to associate a particular human sex with a particular person of the Trinity have been rejected by most Orthodox theologians, particularly those who specialize in early Christian thought, a similar line of reasoning can be seen in a typical argument used by many Orthodox against the ordination of women to the priesthood: The priest functions liturgically as an icon of Christ, so because Jesus was a man, priests must be men as well. This argument is borrowed from the 1976 Vatican encyclical *Inter Insigniores*, cited above, and demonstrates Kallistos Ware's concern that

Orthodoxy is responding to questions arising outside its tradition with answers derived outside its tradition. There are several reasons why the Orthodox Church has not been well equipped to deal with this issue. Most Orthodox still live in traditional societies, and even those Orthodox who live in Westernized societies often retain traditional values and beliefs with respect to the church. Furthermore, the priest—and even the bishop—is not seen as the epitome of holiness. Rather, the model is the "holy man" or "holy woman," that is, the ascetic monk or nun, who may be either male or female and is usually not ordained. Moreover, as mentioned previously, authority ultimately belongs to the church as a whole: The decision of no one bishop or group of bishops is authoritative unless the church as a whole recognizes its authority. This is why Elisabeth Behr-Sigel, noting the lack of organized Orthodox pressure groups for women's ordination, comments that "the Church is viewed by Orthodox not as a pyramid of authorities, but as a 'mystery of communion' " (Behr-Sigel, 31–32). Finally, the strong pull of tradition has meant that most Orthodox theologians believe that if the church has had a consistent practice for two millennia, then there must be a theological basis to that practice.

This has led to an attempt to work backward from practice to theory—to assume that the exclusion of women from the priesthood must be fundamentally theological—based on arguments foreign to Orthodox theology. The notion that the priest functions primarily in the place or role of Christ is one such example. As this idea began appearing in Orthodox theological circles in the late 1970s, it was rebutted by traditional Orthodox liturgical theology and practice. In the Orthodox liturgy, the priest primarily functions as the representative or icon of the *church*, in other words, on behalf of the whole people, the Church. The priest normally faces east when praying, as does the rest of the congregation, and all but one of his prayers are in the first-person plural. Furthermore, the central focus of the Eucharist in terms of the "change" of the bread and wine into the Body and Blood of Christ is not the words of institution, as in Roman liturgical theology, but the calling down by the people of the Holy Spirit upon the gifts (the *epiclesis*).

From an Orthodox perspective, there is an even more serious theological problem in making the argument that a man somehow is more an icon of Christ than a woman. This is because the Orthodox theology of salvation is not based on Western Christian atonement theory (that we are saved by Jesus' death, which literally "pays" God the price for our sins) but on the incarnation: Jesus Christ existentially shares our complete human nature and redeems and transfigures it by uniting it to the divine nature through his own person as the God-Man. Since at least the fourth century, a catch-phrase of Orthodox theology has been, "What is not assumed is not saved"—that is, if Jesus' human nature is in any way incomplete, then that element of human nature is not saved. In fact, early theologians did not see Jesus' maleness as significant, in part precisely for this reason. Even the dismissal hymn (the *apolytikion*) for the Orthodox Feast of the Circumcision of Christ emphasizes not Jesus' masculinity but his humanity: "Being God in essence, without change you took on human form, most merciful Lord, and, fulfilling the Law, willingly consented to bodily circumcision in order to put an end to ephemeral things and to strip away the covering of our passions."

So the theological importance placed on the maleness of Christ by some modern theologians appears to be not only untraditional but theologically problematic. This is evident in the writings of Harrison (Harrison, "Orthodox Arguments") and of Constantinos N. Giokarinis, a Greek theologian whose 1995 doctoral dissertation—"The Priesthood of Women"—at the University of Thessaloniki was on the ecumenical implications of the Orthodox Church's opposition to the ordination of women. Both scholars reject arguments against the ordination of women based on the idea of distinctly male and female "natures." Even some Orthodox theologians who initially embraced the *in persona Christi* argument for the exclusion of women from the priesthood, most notably Bishop Kallistos (Ware) of Diokleia ("Man, Woman, and the Priesthood of Christ"), have since reevaluated and repudiated this theology upon deeper reflection. Furthermore, theologians participating in the international Orthodox–Old Catholic theological dialogues of 1996 acknowledged that there are no solid theological arguments against the ordination of women (the Old Catholic Church broke with Rome in the nineteenth century over such issues as papal authority). A few voices have publicly and in print affirmed the theological validity of the ordination of women to the priesthood, if not its pastoral practicability in the near future. In an interview in the *St. Nina Quarterly*, Susan Ashbrook Harvey asserted:

It is, of course, my conviction that there will be no ordination of women to the Orthodox priesthood for the next few hundred years. But it is also my conviction that there someday will be. The reason is not because of women and their place in society but because the priesthood is something to which the Holy Spirit calls the individual, and the Holy Spirit calls whom the Holy Spirit will. We cannot tell the Holy Spirit whom to call. Women are called to the priesthood—we know this, we see this. Women leave churches that don't ordain women if they must have that call fulfilled. Women have always had to respond to the call of

the Spirit in ways that can be disturbing to society. The stories of women saints are full of such actions. (Harvey, in Regule, 7–8)

Conclusion

Two things may be said with respect to the "Orthodox perspective on feminist theology." First, there is relatively little direct interaction between Orthodox theology and non-Orthodox feminist theology; comparisons and contrasts must be done, for the most part, on one's own. Second, the Orthodox literature dealing with some of the issues of feminist theology, such as anthropology of gender and ordination, is not monolithic. There is no single Orthodox perspective. Orthodox approaches range from conservative views justifying traditional practices that limit roles for women to thoughtful questioning of such practices in a modern context, based predominantly, however, on traditional Orthodox theology in areas such as anthropology, the theology of salvation, and liturgy. Some Orthodox writers and speakers, such as Eva Topping, have been as outspoken as their Western Christian counterparts in denouncing traditional Orthodox practices and views that segregate or marginalize women:

Recently a notice, repeated four times in my parish bulletin, began with this sentence: "All young men between the ages 10–18 are invited to serve [as acolytes] in the Holy Altar." Four times it painfully reminded *all* young women between the ages 10–18 that they will never receive such an invitation. For no reason other than that they are females, they are denied the joy and privilege of serving God at the altar. For older women it is just one more reminder of the discrimination we, our mothers and foremothers have experienced for almost 2000 years. (Topping, 2–3)

This broad spectrum of Orthodox perspectives may be seen in several recent journals aimed at Orthodox women. *The Handmaiden* is published by a small, denominational (Antiochian Orthodox Christian Archdiocese), northern California house called Conciliar Press, which was founded by converts to Orthodoxy from evangelical Protestantism. Its mission statement distinguishes between equality before God and "sameness of earthly roles" and supports a male-only priesthood; the publication provides a mix of book reviews, Lenten recipes, saints' lives, spiritual reflections, and theological articles (often of a conservative nature). *MaryMartha*, which received funding from the World Council of Churches, originated in Australia as the brainchild of Leonie Liveris, who converted to her husband's Orthodox faith and went on to obtain a doctorate in church history from Edith Cowan University in Perth. *MaryMartha* was international in character—its writers and readers coming primarily from Australia, North America, and western Europe—and provided news and challenging theological reflections in both English and French (it has since ceased publication). The *St. Nina Quarterly* comes out of Boston (and is also available online at http://www.stnina.org/) under the auspices of the Women's Orthodox Ministries and Education Network (WOMEN); it boasts a pan-Orthodox editorial board with more extensive theological credentials than the other two journals but has been sporadic in publication. Its issues provide a mix somewhat similar to *The Hand-maiden* but with more theological emphasis, including articles by several of the world's best-known Orthodox theologians. Its editorial board has taken no formal position on women's ordination or other issues but is perceived by some as liberal and feminist; so far, no articles on the ordination of women to the priesthood have been published in the journal.

Unlike some early Orthodox conferences on women, all these journals, as well as the more recent international Orthodox conferences on women, have been organized and are run by women. In a church where men have traditionally held almost all formal positions of authority, perhaps this flourishing of Orthodox women theologians, speakers, writers, and activists is a small sign that feminism has breached the millennia-old ramparts of Orthodoxy.

SOURCES: Gennadios Limouris, ed., *The Place of the Woman in the Orthodox Church and the Question of the Ordination of Women* (1992); Deborah Belonick, *Feminism in Christianity: An Orthodox Christian Response* (1983); Susan Frank Parsons, ed., *Cambridge Companion to Feminist Theology* (2002); Kari-doyanes FitzGerald, "An Orthodox Assessment of Feminist Theology," in Limouris, ed., *The Place of the Woman* (1992); Kallistos Ware, "Man, Woman, and the Priesthood of Christ," in Peter Moore, ed., *Man, Woman, and Priesthood* (1978); Sallie McFague, *Metaphorical Theology: Models of God in Religious Language* (1982); Susan Ashbrook Harvey, "Feminine Imagery for the Divine the Holy Spirit, the Odes of Solomon, and Early Syriac Tradition," *St. Vladimir's Theological Quarterly* 37 (1993): 111–140; Verna Harrison, "The Care-Banishing Breast of the Father: Feminine Images of the Divine in Clement of Alexandria's Paedagogus I," *Studia Patristica* 31 (1997): 401–405; Verna F. Harrison, "Male and Female in Cappadocian Theology," *Journal of Theological Studies* 41 (1990): 441–471; Emmanuel Clapsis, "Naming God: An Orthodox View," *Ecumenical Review* 44 (1991): 100–112; Verna Harrison, "The Fatherhood of God in Orthodox Theology," *St. Vladimir's Theological Quarterly* 37 (1993): 185–212; Panayiotis Nellas, *Deification in Christ: Orthodox Perspectives on the Nature of the Human Person* (1987); Paul Evdokimov and Anthony P. Gythiel, *Women and the Salvation of the World: A Christian Anthropology on the Charisms of Women* (1994); Elisabeth Behr-Sigel and Kallistos Ware, *The Ordination of Women in the Orthodox Church* (2000); Nonna Verna Harrison, "Orthodox Arguments against the Ordination of Women as Priests," *Sobornost* 14 (1992): 6–23; Constantinos N. Giokarinis, "The Priesthood of Women" (Ph.D. diss., University of Thessaloniki, 1995); Teva Regule, "An Interview with Susan Ashbrook Harvey," *St. Nina Quarterly* (Fall 1997); Eva Topping, "Orthodox Eve and Her Church," Occasional Papers, No. 2, The Patriarch Athenagoras Orthodox Institute, Berkeley California, 1991.

Part VI

❧

Judaism

REFORM JUDAISM
Karla Goldman

LEADERS OF REFORM Judaism in the United States have often celebrated their movement's role in emancipating Jewish women from the many restrictions that Judaism has traditionally imposed upon women's ability to participate in and lead public worship. Historians generally see the American Reform movement as growing out of the German Reform Judaism that emerged in the early nineteenth century as an attempt to adapt traditional Jewish worship to the perceived demands for rational religious practice brought by the Enlightenment. Although it is true that the direction of the American movement was largely shaped by mid-nineteenth-century immigrant rabbis from German-speaking lands, American Reform Judaism found a distinct expression that was both more radical and broader than German Reform in terms of actual practice.

This distinctiveness emerges most clearly in the way that women's changing roles have continually and centrally shaped the emergence and evolution of Reform Judaism in the United States. Although mid-nineteenth-century German Reform leaders made the case for women's equality in Judaism and the abolition of anachronistic laws and customs that stifled the public expression of women's religiosity, it was only in the United States that practical innovations adopted by the Reform movement actively redefined the nature of women's participation in public worship. Chief among Reform Judaism's liberating innovations were the abolition of a separate women's gallery within the synagogue in the 1850s and the ordination of the first American woman rabbi in 1972. In addition to these important institutional changes, Reform congregations have also provided important sites for Jewish women to work out the tensions between evolving societal expectations for women and the roles identified with traditional Jewish practice.

Efforts to adjust the American synagogue to reflect American understandings of female religious identity long predated the emergence of an American Reform movement in the mid-nineteenth century. American synagogue builders in the eighteenth century had already begun to do away with the partition barriers that kept women out of sight in traditional women's galleries. American Jewish women quickly seemed to realize that American culture demanded women's presence at public worship. Moreover, American Jewish leaders came to understand that the segregation and seeming subjugation of women behind opaque barriers was hardly the way to achieve respectability as an American religion. By the 1850s, open American synagogue galleries offered tiered rows of seats, carefully affording a clear view to the many women who took their place at regular worship services.

A number of other innovations that helped to redefine women's place in Jewish worship, and that would become characteristic of American Reform practice, found a place in synagogues that congregants still expected to be sites for traditional worship. A desire for a more formal worship service led many congregations to introduce mixed male and female choirs, challenging the usual orthodox proscriptions against hearing women's voices during worship. In addition, the introduction by the 1850s of confirmation services in many American Jewish congregations signified, in part, an effort to celebrate the Jewish education and identity of girls together with those of boys.

The departure that most clearly heralded the arrival of a Reform style of worship and definitively separated that style from traditional Jewish practice was the introduction of the family pew. The earliest instance of the mixed seating of men and women in the synagogue may have arisen as a matter of convenience. In 1851, a break-away Albany congregation, Anshe Emeth, led by reformer Isaac Mayer Wise, adopted the mixed-gender use of family pews when the group moved into a former church building and adopted the existing design rather than build additional balconies to create a customary women's gallery. Similarly, three years later, Temple Emanu-El in New York City utilized the existing family pews of the church building that they had bought to serve as their new synagogue. Within the new Emanu-El building, family pews were one component of a wide range of revisions of traditional synagogue practice that included an abridged liturgy, elaborately orchestrated organ and choir music, emphasis on a service leader who intoned the worship service in distinguished and modulated tones, and a regular vernacular sermon. With the exception of mixed seating, all these reforms found parallels in German Reform efforts. Family pews, however, remained an exclusively American innovation until well into the twentieth century.

Women never could have been integrated into the main sanctuary at Emanu-El if the congregation itself had not been transformed. In traditional Jewish worship settings the male congregants played a vital part in the proceedings, participating in the Torah-reading service and other aspects of the ritual. Although a traditional service would have a leader, it was understood that he mainly marked time for the congregation as each individual chanted (quietly or with more volume) his own way through the liturgy. By contrast, services at Temple Emanu-El were guided and orchestrated by a leader—who having moved from the reader's traditional position in the midst of the congregation to an elevated position at the front of the sanctuary became the center of attention and of the service. One observer of the congregation in its 1854 building described a service in which "[t]he minister and reader do all the praying, the organ and choir perform the music." The congregants themselves had been transformed into spectators: "The visitors appear as mere dummies . . . the visitor acts no part, but that of *auditor*. . . . [E]xcept for an occasional rising from the seat, the congregation does not participate in the worship" (Goldman, 134). Women became emancipated just in time to become part of an assembly that was rapidly losing its identity as a traditional *kahal* (community); the congregation was now often referred to as an "audience" (134). Women did gain a kind of equality with men as worshippers in the sanctuary, but it was a role that had already been greatly devalued. Women had gained the right to join men in the shrinking role of congregant.

Introduced at a period when many American synagogues were just beginning to explore the implications of departing from strict adherence to traditional synagogue practice, it took some time for family pews to be widely adopted. Still, despite the limited spread of family pews in the 1850s and early 1860s, Temple Emanu-El's grand new sanctuary was occupied by some of the nation's most prominent and accomplished Jewish citizens and offered an influential model for an Americanized version of Jewish public worship.

An emerging Reform Judaism found expression in the many opulent synagogues that arose in urban centers from New York to San Francisco in the years after the Civil War, all proclaiming the prosperity, achievement, and refinement of the nation's Jews. These temples were home to a self-conscious and focused effort, driven by German-trained rabbis, to create a public Judaism that would satisfy the needs of an Americanized Jewish population. Acculturated rabbis and lay leaders hoped to thus associate themselves with the decorum and respectability of religious sanctuaries occupied by established members of America's social and religious elites.

Apart from a few determinedly orthodox settings, all the synagogues built to house this Americanized Judaism emphasized the repositioning and integration of women within Jewish religious space. Male Jewish leaders saw the introduction of this innovation as completely consistent with their drive for respectability. The 1863 annual address of the president of the Indianapolis Hebrew Congregation proudly reported that in the congregation's new building, "Ladies & Gentlemen are seated together which," as he pointed out, "is nothing more than civilization demands" (Goldman, 130).

Offered a place in the sanctuary, Jewish women occupied the family pews of these magnificent temples in force, continuing a trend that had marked early-nineteenth-century American synagogues. In a departure from the traditional pattern of synagogue worship, but in keeping with the attendance patterns of most American Christian denominations, women quickly came to dominate attendance at weekly Sabbath services as men increasingly attended to business concerns on the Jewish day of rest. The extent to which these synagogues were shaped by women's presence was again a distinctively American phenomenon. Neither family pews nor synagogues filled with women found any parallel in European Jewish experience. The success of the mid-nineteenth-century reformers in shaping a decorous and refined synagogue ceremonial that became the dominant expression of American Judaism had perhaps unforeseen consequences when it came to devising new public identities for women beyond that of synagogue-goer. The reorientation of worship space and gender roles within the synagogue, which Reformers would later describe as acts of emancipation for women, had decidedly mixed effects. Although Jewish women's attendance patterns may have emulated the pew dominance of American Christian women, mid-nineteenth-century Jewish women did not participate in the explosion of voluntary and organizational activity identified with women in Protestant churches of the same era. In Christian churches, women's numerical dominance of the pews was reinforced by their central role in general church-related activity. Historians have described the years after the Civil War as an era when the expansion of Christian women's work for benevolence and social reform was incorporated locally and nationally into organizations that gave life and vitality to churches and to church work.

This, however, was a time when the Reform synagogue's intense emphasis on refining synagogue ritual rendered many other communal activities suddenly irrelevant. The narrowing of the congregation to the limited sphere of public worship undermined the existence of the many groups, like female benevolent societies, which had earlier been active players within broadly defined synagogue communities. Although women's view of the proceedings within emerging Reform sanctuaries changed, they moved no closer to active participation or leadership in the religious life of their synagogues. Those active synagogue affiliations that remained, spiritual leadership and lay governance, remained exclusively in male hands. Even the question of who could be a "member" of a synagogue continued to be limited to those (men) who enjoyed the full rights and responsibilities associated with traditional synagogue worship. These limitations generally stretched only far enough to encompass widows of deceased members and, in some cases, unmarried women, so that they could be included among the dues-payers of the congregation.

Thus, although Reform leaders would often celebrate their introduction of the family pew in bringing gender equality to Jewish religious life, the second half of the nineteenth century brought mixed results in forwarding the public position of women in America's Reform congregations. Male synagogue leaders did often request aid from women within their communities to raise funds with which to build synagogues or to pay off debts. In many Southern and other small communities, in fact, women often took primary responsibility for raising funds and pushing for the building of synagogues. In most cases, however, these organized efforts were short-lived and did not translate into permanent organizations or sustained collective influence within their congregations and communities.

Formal organization of the Reform movement grew from the founding of the Union of American Hebrew Congregations (UAHC) in 1872 and Hebrew Union College (HUC) in 1875. Although women from seventy-nine (mainly southern and midwestern) communities responded to President Isaac M. Wise's call to commit one dollar a year to aid HUC's indigent students, women generally played little role in these institutional developments. Although Wise had often advocated the creation of a female theological seminary, nothing along these lines ever emerged. A few female students did enroll at the early Hebrew Union College, but none advanced very far in their studies.

Congregational religious schools constituted one important area where women associated with Reform congregations did expand their involvement in synagogue, serving as both teachers and supporters. Even in these settings, however, women were often explicitly excluded from leadership roles and could not serve on the congregational boards that governed the schools. Still, congregational religious schools offered girls a supplementary religious education that was equivalent to that of boys. Many nineteenth-century Reform congregations rejected the exclusively male bar mitzvah, adopting the confirmation ritual observed on the festival of Shavuot (in May or June) as the primary adolescent rite of passage, a practice that incorporated equality for girls in religious education. During confirmation services, girls, together with boys, offered prayers and speeches, demonstrating their learning and commitment.

Not until the late 1880s did new structures emerge to absorb the latent energies of the women within Reform congregations. The first Jewish Sisterhood of Personal Service organized by Rabbi Gustav Gottheil of New York's Reform Temple Emanu-El in 1888 provided a prototype that was quickly emulated in Jewish congregations throughout the country. These groups of Americanized Jewish women, especially in New York, at first focused their energies on the impoverished eastern European Jewish multitudes lately arrived in the United States. Women from many of New York's uptown synagogues, ranging from Reform to Orthodox, formed sisterhoods of personal service that cooperated in dividing responsibility for care of the city's immigrant districts. Sisterhood members engaged in a broad range of social welfare work directed toward aiding newly arrived immigrants. The most common activity was that of "friendly visiting," wherein sisterhood workers would visit the homes of immigrant families to assess their needs and, if necessary, dispense material aid. Interested in training immigrants to become both self-sufficient and sufficiently American, the sisterhoods of personal service in New York and San Francisco, and similar groups in other cities, also offered vocational schools, classes and clubs for working girls, child day care and kindergartens, and employment bureaus. Acculturated Jewish women throughout the country created religious schools that attempted to expose immigrant children to an Americanized form of Judaism. Many sisterhoods dispensed these services from settlement house–like buildings of their own. Although the work of these organizations was outwardly directed, it brought a measure of shared purpose and community to the women of these congregations.

Between 1880 and 1920, over 2 million immigrant Jews flowed into the United States, deterred only by World War I and then finally by the Immigration restriction acts of 1921 and 1924. In many locales, acculturated women remained a vital part of congregational and communal efforts to welcome and support the new arrivals throughout this period. Despite the dedicated work of these women, the numerous "professionalized" Jewish social service organizations that emerged around the turn of the century to address the needs of new immigrants ultimately marginalized the benevolent activities of the female "friendly visitors" who were often associated with congregations.

This did not, however, bring an end to the era of growing Jewish women's activism. Building on the model that their own organizations had helped to spark, sisterhood workers refused to simply retreat to their homes. The activation of women's energies that had arisen to meet the needs of new immigrants had inspired a general awakening of organized activism among more acculturated Jewish women at both the local and national level that began to match the intensity of Christian women's commitments to causes like temperance and missionary work. Much of this energy found its expression within synagogues.

Instead of gathering as ad hoc groups of women to advance particular and limited congregational projects, women in many Reform synagogues around the country during the 1890s started to approach their responsibilities on a permanent organized basis. Congregations, in turn, began to depend on synagogue women's groups to take responsibility for the physical, charitable, and social needs of the community. This activation of female energy for the benefit of the congregation intersected with efforts by graduates of Hebrew Union College to expand the institutional work of Reform congregations beyond the narrow scope of worship. Women's groups offered services in whatever ways congregations would allow them to participate. In some communities this meant that they became more involved in addressing the needs of religious schoolchildren or in furnishing and decorating their temple buildings. In other synagogues, women's participation became the key to sparking a general expansion of congregational cultural and charitable activities. The emergence of synagogue auxiliary associations offered women, for the first time, positions on various committees devoted to congregational work and opportunities to be officially recognized for their communal contributions. A wave of temple building in the 1890s and early twentieth century became necessary to encompass the expanding and variegated institutional life made possible by women's emerging activism.

The first national organization to emerge from the rising tide of Jewish women's activism was the National Council of Jewish Women (NCJW). This movement was spearheaded by women associated with Chicago's Reform Sinai Congregation. They took the lead in creating a Jewish Women's Congress that took place at the Columbian Exposition and World's Fair held in Chicago in 1893. Participants from around the country who came to the Congress embodied and articulated the ways in which Jewish women were finding their way into a public world of Jewish activism. The subsequent creation of the National Council of Jewish Women offered acculturated Jewish women in communities across the country a structure that could facilitate and validate their activism as Jewish women.

Adopting a range of issues and concerns that ranged from immigrant welfare, religious education for children, and the creation of study groups among NCJW members and classes with rabbis to the effort to ask synagogues to afford women access to membership, NCJW provided thousands of women with a channel into which they could invest their energies as Jewish women. NCJW's ability to offer itself as a organization that represented the religious interests of Jewish women was, however, undermined by conflicts between members of the leadership who were associated with a desire for radical Reform measures within Judaism and more traditionally inclined leaders and members. Conflict over issues like whether the Sabbath should be observed on the traditional Saturday or on Sunday, as was advocated by some radical Reformers in the United States, drew the Council into fruitless debate. The resulting inability to address women's issues that arose within Jewish religious settings helped give rise to a new generation of national Jewish women's groups.

Carrie Obendorfer Simon (1872–1961) was one of the leading figures in the creation of the Reform movement's National Federation of Temple Sisterhoods. She drew upon her experience of the expansion of Jewish women's public identities that had redefined American synagogues and Jewish communities in the 1890s and translated this into a form of women's organization that would do much to define twentieth-century American synagogues, whatever their denomination. Simon's mother had been a founder of the Cincinnati chapter of the National Council of Jewish Women. Thus, as a young woman, Carrie Obendorfer would have been intimately familiar with the new possibilities being opened to women within Jewish communities. After her marriage at age twenty-four to Hebrew Union College graduate Abram Simon, Carrie Simon found herself in many settings where she had the opportunity to push these possibilities in new directions.

As the National Council of Jewish Women stumbled over the differing religious approaches of its diverse membership, Simon, as a rabbi's wife first in Sacramento, then in Omaha, and finally in Washington, D.C., became engaged with the work of congregations at a local level. A sisterhood was founded at Temple Israel of Omaha in 1903, and Carrie Simon herself founded the Ladies Auxiliary Society of Washington Hebrew Congregation in 1905, for the purpose of "congregational work, pure and simple, and to endeavor to establish a more congenial and social congregational spirit" (Nadell and Simon, 65). Simon focused her efforts on synagogue women's groups that, although they had been established in some congregations as organizations intended to assist needy immigrants, had turned increasingly to attending to the needs of the synagogue community.

In 1913 the male leadership of the Union of American Hebrew Congregations issued a call "to all ladies' organizations connected with congregations belonging to the Union" to send delegates to a meeting to be convened in Cincinnati "for the purpose of organizing a Federation of Temple Sisterhoods" (Lefton, 17). The meeting, held in conjunction with the national UAHC convention, was attended by 156 delegates (mainly the wives of UAHC delegates) from fifty-two congregations. Carrie Simon was elected as the organization's founding president, and Rabbi George Zepin became its executive secretary.

The preamble adopted by the delegates, with its declaration that "the increased power which has come to the modern American Jewess ought to be exercised in congregational life" (Lefton, 27), reflected its framers' recognition that the new organization was built upon recent transformations in Jewish women's public lives. And just as the emergence of women's activism within acculturated Jewish communities helped bring about the formation of the National Federation of Temple Sister-

Carrie Obendorfer Simon was one of the leading figures in the creation of the Reform movement's National Federation of Temple Sisterhoods. She drew upon her experience of the expansion of Jewish women's public identities that had redefined American synagogues and Jewish communities in the 1890s and translated this into a form of women's organization that would do much to define twentieth-century American synagogues, whatever their denomination. *Used by permission of the Jewish American Archives.*

hoods (NFTS), the creation of a framework for the work of women in Reform congregations at the national level helped to transform the identity and work of Reform Jewish women at a local level. With the founding of NFTS, many local congregations that had not previously had women's membership organizations created sisterhoods, and the work of many existing women's organizations was transformed by the advent of a national organization. The energy engendered by the creation of NFTS encouraged tens of thousands of women to focus their energies on congregational life and on the broader efforts of American Reform Judaism.

The contributions of both new and reconfigured sisterhoods to the educational, material, and social life of American Reform congregations were transformative. Sisterhood groups moved boldly to take on a vast range of responsibilities within their communities. Within a year of the return of their delegates from the Cincinnati founding convention, Cleveland's Tifereth Israel's Temple Women's Association reported on the work of twenty-six different working committees. The renamed sisterhood of Rodeph Shalom in Philadelphia described a similar advance as it reported on the formation of fifteen new working groups. Often responding to sug-

gestions from the national leadership, sisterhoods across the country took on concerns that ranged from the sponsoring of religious schools for immigrant children to the selection of decor for the ladies' lounge.

Congregational religious schools reflected the sudden infusion of new energy that accompanied the founding of the National Federation of Temple Sisterhoods. From the provision of "paper roller towels and waste baskets" in Cincinnati (Goldman, 207) to the expansion of holiday celebrations to provision of appropriate gifts for male and female confirmands to the creation and oversight of temple libraries, religious schoolchildren benefited from the careful attention that sisterhoods directed toward their religious education. Sisterhood efforts to create social spaces for students within their synagogues led to the expansion of leisure activities provided by synagogues for young people. Individual women and women's groups had often taken responsibility for providing the synagogue sanctuary with appropriate religious objects, but sisterhoods radically expanded this traditional practice. Women's groups around the country provided their congregations with organs, carpeting, furniture, and wings of buildings. With the mandate of expanding synagogue attendance, many sisterhoods redefined the social experience associated with the synagogue by, for instance, providing food at the end of worship services and transforming sparsely attended annual meetings into elaborate congregational dinners.

The sisterhoods worked to reshape more than the social component of congregational life. They also helped redefine the ritual calendar and practices of their communities. Reform sisterhoods took responsibility for overseeing congregational Seders that were often held on the second night of Passover (even though many Reform congregations technically rejected recognition of the holiday's second day). They provided entertainments for religious schoolchildren and food for congregational events. They sought out new members among the parents of Sunday School students and encouraged existing members to attend worship services. They raised funds and selected furniture.

On a national level, production of an annual art calendar attempted both to expose Reform Jews to Jewish art and, as one of the first English calendars to incorporate the Jewish calendar, tried to infuse the lives of sisterhood members with Jewish time. Other early initiatives that continued to define the National Federation of Temple Sisterhoods throughout its existence included the support of rabbinic education and Hebrew Union College, through funds for student scholarships. A national campaign raised money for the school's Sisterhood Dormitory that opened in Cincinnati in 1925, as a residence for rabbinical students. Another central and continuing effort was introduced with the founding of the Jewish Braille Institute in 1931.

The validation of women's participation in synagogue life offered by the creation of national Jewish women's organizations and by their practical work helped to transform women's political status within their congregations. The presence, contributions, energy, and activities that women brought to the Reform movement, nationally and locally, contributed to growing expectations that women should be recognized as full participants in the work of Reform Judaism. One of the early campaigns of the National Council of Jewish Women in the 1890s had been to appeal to congregations throughout the country to invite women's participation in synagogue governance, through participation on synagogue governing committees and as voting members of the congregation. Although a few congregations responded positively to these requests, more responded like the Bene Israel congregation in Cincinnati when it informed the NJCW representatives that they did not deem the appointment of women to congregational subcommittees to be "advisable at this time" (Goldman, 192). Still, as women expanded their auxiliary work, congregations began to depend increasingly upon their contributions. One reflection of women's increasing integration into the community can be seen in the number of congregations that acted to redefine their membership categories so that women who were neither single nor widowed could become "associate" members of their congregations.

The founding of the National Federation of Temple Sisterhoods in 1913 and the impetus that it gave to women's local contributions engendered even higher expectations for the recognition of women as full participants in synagogue life. Already in 1916, National Council of Jewish Women leader Rebekah Kohut, who was active in the sisterhood of New York's Temple Emanu-El, felt free to question "who would dare to say that a woman, as the President of the congregation, or women on the Board of Trustees, could not guide the destinies of the synagogue as successfully as men!" (Lefton, 43). Unlike the previous expression of similar sentiments within the Reform movement, Kohut's words were more than rhetorical. By 1915 a number of Reform congregations around the country were not only inviting women to attend annual congregational meetings but had also asked local sisterhoods to send representatives to attend synagogue board meetings. The incorporation of women into previously all-male boards of trustees solidified the contributions and status of women leaders within the congregational world.

In NFTS rhetoric, "religious equality" became synonymous with recognition of women's political status as voting members and potential leaders within their congregations. The passage of the Women's Suffrage Amendment to the U.S. Constitution in 1920 pushed most Reform congregations across the country to assign formal and full membership to all women within their communities. In most communities, this also meant that women were offered regular representation, chiefly through sisterhood officers, on congregational boards of trustees. The founding of the NFTS and the consequent expansion of women's contributions to synagogue life brought about a profound reconceptualization of the possibilities for women's authority in Jewish public life. At the organization's founding convention, the only speakers to address the assembled delegates had been rabbis and prominent Jewish men, lending their seal of credibility to the women's gathering. Sisterhood women came to understand, however, that their work within their communities, their changing status within congregational governance structures, and their contributions to the national Reform movement carried an authority of its own. When Stella Freiberg, as president of an organization that now claimed 50,000 members, addressed the NFTS national convention in 1925, she was able to point to national accomplishments like the group's success in raising the funds to build the Sisterhood Dormitory at Hebrew Union College. Freiberg's comments emphasized the belief that sisterhood women no longer needed men to validate their efforts as she declared, "I don't know how the rabbis will feel about it, but we have not called upon them to invoke us with their blessing. Our own women are doing it" (Lefton, 45).

Inevitably, the growth of a cadre of local and national sisterhood leaders, together with the logic implicit in the Women's Suffrage Amendment, confronted Reform leaders not only with the challenge of accommodating new roles for women in lay governance but with the question of female religious leadership. In 1920, Martha Neumark, a female student at Hebrew Union College and the daughter of an HUC professor, requested that she be allowed, like her male classmates, to serve a high holyday pulpit as a student rabbi. Faced with the possibility that Neumark might continue her studies and become a candidate for ordination, the college's Board of Governors and faculty and the Reform movement's federation of rabbis, the Central Conference of American Rabbis (CCAR), all took up the question of whether to approve, in principle, the ordination of women rabbis.

Some traditionalist-leaning members of the faculty expressed misgivings as to whether the Reform movement, in ordaining women, would irreparably sunder itself from the other movements in Judaism. Nonetheless, the faculty unanimously agreed that this innovation was consistent with the inclusive and progressive tenets of the Reform movement and equivalent to other major breaks with tradition accepted by the movement. Consideration of the issue at the 1922 CCAR convention was especially noteworthy for the decision of the delegates to invite female members of the audience—wives of the rabbis in attendance—to take part in the discussion. Although the faculty and the CCAR both voted to support the proposed change, HUC's Board of Governors, which had to make the final decision, ultimately rejected the proposal.

A number of women did continue to pursue studies within the Reform rabbinical institutions. Three women engaged in substantive study at New York's Jewish Institute of Religion (JIR), founded in 1922 by Rabbi Stephen S. Wise, during the 1920s and 1930s. Although the faculty accepted them as students, it does not appear that they ever expected that these women would become rabbis. In fact, when Helen Levinthal actually completed the JIR curricular requirements for ordination in 1939, the faculty chose to award her a Bachelor of Hebrew Letters degree rather than rabbinical ordination.

But even as the question of whether women should serve as rabbis lay dormant, sisterhood women in Reform synagogues continued to push, in far from radical fashion, against traditional limitations on Jewish women's religious identity. The "Sisterhood Sabbath" emerged in the early 1920s as a way to honor congregational sisterhoods for their manifold contributions to their communities. Promoted as a suggestion from the

National Federation of Temple Sisterhood leadership in 1922, the idea seemed to be to create an occasion that would encourage greater synagogue attendance and prompt rabbis to acknowledge the work of women within their communities. Congregations that reported the celebration of such an occasion in the early 1920s included Boston, Dallas, Richmond, Philadelphia, Seattle, Galveston, Cincinnati, and Toledo. Some sisterhoods described the sermons that their rabbis prepared for these occasions, but, intriguingly, many more reported on sermons that were delivered by their own members. The Sisterhood Sabbath quickly developed into an unusual opportunity for women's public religious expression. In addition to delivering sermons, sisterhood women commonly came to lead all or part of the Sisterhood Sabbath services themselves, or at least to participate in guiding some of the readings. A 1923 NFTS report noted the widespread phenomenon of sisterhood women conducting these services, "sermon and all" (Lefton, 82). Sisterhood Sabbaths, which are still celebrated in many congregations, offered an annual outlet for public religious expression on the part of sisterhood women. Although the leadership expressed through the delivery of a sermon and the guidance of a service may have been limited to once a year, the annual practice helped to change expectations about the possibilities of women's participation within public worship. Many sisterhoods also took responsibility for leading worship services during the summer when rabbis went on vacation and the attendance was smaller.

Throughout the interwar years, the energy and creativity of women within the Reform movement provided their communities with a rich congregational life. At the national level, NFTS provided critical support to the central efforts of the movement, particularly to Hebrew Union College, and sponsored the creation of the National Federation of Temple Youth. The appointment of Jane Evans (1907–) in 1933 as the organization's first executive director secured the organization's seriousness of purpose and effectiveness in action. With tireless devotion, even after her retirement in 1976, Evans worked to sustain individual sisterhoods across the country and provided the national organization with a consistent and broad vision. Evans never let NFTS retreat from its commitment to supporting women's advancement within their congregations and within Judaism, to responding to the social and political challenges of the contemporary life, and to the firm conviction that NFTS could make a difference in the lives of its members and the world.

During World War II, as had been the case during World War I, many women looked to their sisterhoods to formalize their contribution to the war effort. They knitted, crocheted, baked cookies, organized blood banks, sold bonds, conducted first-aid classes, and resettled Jewish refugees, all under the auspices of their congregational sisterhoods. Continued postwar growth in synagogue activity reflected a nationwide return to religion that enlivened both churches and synagogues through the 1950s. As synagogue organizational life flourished, sisterhoods were critical in sustaining synagogue life in older congregations and in creating new frameworks for community as old and new congregations found their way to the suburbs. The child-centered focus of these congregations in building religious schools and creating congregational holiday events provided a meaningful and demanding focus for sisterhood efforts. Attention to young people within the movement before the war had extended to concern about Jewish college students suddenly out on their own without a familiar Jewish context. NFTS worked to create a national network that could assist women in Reform congregations in offering local college students a comfortable Jewish context that could help them sustain their Jewish identities. After the war, sisterhood leaders were instrumental in assisting the National Federation of Temple Youth as it became a central and dynamic force in the Reform movement. Another critical postwar innovation guided by local sisterhoods was the introduction of synagogue gift shops. Not only did the sale of Judaica within the temple foster Jewish ritual practice within the home, a recurrent concern for NFTS, but it also helped to provide a steady source of income for the local groups.

The confirmation service with its egalitarian commitment to Jewish education for both boys and girls had been an early aspect of the Reform movement's agenda. As the bar mitzvah ceremony regained popularity in Reform congregations after World War I, however, confirmation ceremonies became increasingly a province for girls alone. The feminization of the group confirmation service, together with the bar mitzvah ceremony's emphasis on individual Jewish ritual skills and obligations, highlighted the gender inequity within Jewish worship that confirmation was meant to neutralize. Mordecai Kaplan, founder of the Reconstructionist movement, introduced the first bat mitzvah ceremony as a female counterpart to the bar mitzvah, for his own daughter in 1922. The bat mitzvah ceremony gradually took root within the Conservative movement in the 1930s and 1940s. The Reform movement's commitment to the confirmation rite, however, slowed acceptance of the bat mitzvah in Reform temples. Bat mitzvah ceremonies began to appear in Reform congregations in the 1950s and made more general progress in the 1960s. Varying in format, a Reform bat mitzvah often involved having a girl read or chant the weekly reading from the prophetic books of the Bible and give some kind of talk. By contrast, the bar mitzvah ceremony for boys took place during the Saturday morning service, with the prophetic reading in its traditional place following the traditional weekly Torah reading drawn from the Pentateuch. With the rise of the feminist movement, the idea of sustaining distinctive rituals to mark the religious obligations and duties of boys and girls, or of men and women, within Judaism became increasingly untenable. By the early 1970s, a Saturday morning bat mitzvah service identical in its requirements with the ceremony held for boys was in place in most Reform congregations.

Progress toward incorporating increasing equality for women at the level of Reform lay and religious leadership moved in fits and starts through the 1950s and 1960s, as the rhetoric of gender egalitarianism and equality of opportunity became more familiar in the broader culture. Male Reform leaders did not actively support, but did not prevent, a decision by Meridian, Mississippi's Reform congregation, to appoint Paula Ackerman (1893–1989), the widow of their deceased rabbi, to serve as the community's spiritual leader from 1951 to 1953. Neither did the movement prevent Reform congregations like the one in Meridian or others in Trinidad, Colorado, and Akron, Ohio, from turning to qualified women when they needed someone to lead services and provide spiritual leadership. When Central Conference of American Rabbis president Rabbi Barnett Brickner asked the Conference to declare a commitment to the principle of female ordination in 1956, he may have been prompted by these cases, by changing societal expectations for women as professionals, and perhaps by the leadership already shown by rebbitzins (rabbi's wives) like his own highly able and educated wife Rebecca Brickner. In any case, although his proposal received general approval, the question was "laid on the table" until those with opposing views could present their case or, as it turned out, indefinitely.

At the same time that the movement's male leadership failed to move forward in affirming their approval of the concept of women's religious leadership, Reform Jewish women continued to build a case for recognition of their abilities through their ongoing and assiduous work on behalf of their congregations and the movement. NFTS had long proved a training ground in communal leadership, offering those involved in its work opportunities to guide their own organizations and participate in the deliberations of local congregations and the national Reform movement. In a few instances, female leaders were able to find recognition as leaders outside of the framework of women's organizations. Jeanette Weinberg began a sixteen-year term as president of her congregation in Frederick, Maryland, in 1943. Natalie Lansing Hodes served as the founding president of her Philadelphia congregation in 1952. Most significantly perhaps, Helen Dalsheimer (1900–1974), national president of NFTS, became the president of Baltimore Hebrew Congregation in 1956, thus becoming the first woman to lead one of the Reform movement's largest congregations.

The ability of women to serve in these roles helped to keep questions of women's leadership within the Reform movement alive. Jane Evans, NFTS executive director, was particularly committed to pushing the movement on this issue. She initiated a broad consideration of the question of women's ordination in the organization, culminating in a general discussion at the group's 1963 convention. Reflecting shifting cultural currents and renewed attention to questions of women's equality, the delegates determined to request a meeting of all Reform Judaism's governing bodies in order to take up the question of women's ordination.

No such conference ever took place. In fact, the issue was ultimately resolved without any grand pronouncements from the movement's organizing bodies. By the mid-1960s, HUC-JIR president Nelson Glueck was making it clear that he would ordain a female candidate for ordination when the opportunity arose, moving the question from abstract commitment to practical reality. Sally Priesand (b. 1946) had come to Cincinnati from Cleveland in 1964 with every intention of becoming a rabbi. Along with a few other women, she entered the school's joint undergraduate program with the University of Cincinnati. As she continued her studies past the college level, it soon became clear that Priesand would be the one to create the opportunity that Glueck had been seeking. After Glueck died in 1971, Alfred Gottschalk followed through on his predecessor's commitment, ordaining Priesand as the first American woman rabbi in 1972. The Reconstructionist Rabbinical College ordained its first woman rabbi in 1974. The Conservative movement's Jewish Theological Seminary followed in 1985. Barbara Ostfeld Horowitz was invested at HUC-JIR's New York campus as the first seminary-trained female cantor in 1975.

These pioneering steps in allowing women to take on the most prominent roles of Jewish religious leadership have had profound symbolic and practical implications both within the Reform movement and beyond. The presence of women clergy has reconfigured expectations of what women should be allowed and encouraged to do in a wide variety of Jewish settings. Many see the ordination of Priesand, and of the some 300 Reform women rabbis who have followed her, as the ultimate realization of women's religious equality by the Reform movement. Indeed, the embrace of equality for women at every level of leadership and life emerged as an unshakeable core tenet of Reform Judaism during the last quarter of the twentieth century. Yet, inevitably perhaps, institutional realities within the Reform movement during this period have often failed to match the movement's commitment to its ideal of gender equality.

Although women, individually and collectively, had been prime shapers of Reform Judaism since its first emergence, the movement's central institutional and leadership structures had always been exclusively male. Accordingly, as in many arenas of American society, the Reform movement during the last quarter of the twentieth century became a setting for both the tension and the energy that so often accompany challenges to long-established patterns of gender order. Many women who found themselves in positions of status and authority within the Reform movement that had previously been occupied exclusively by men struggled to obtain respect and job security. At the same time, many encountered a hunger for the new perspectives and new questions that women rabbis could bring to the Reform religious framework.

Not surprisingly, many early women rabbis encountered hostility as they took on this new role. Moreover, little thought had gone into preparing Reform communities to accept women rabbis or to anticipating unfamiliar practical issues, such as the question of building maternity leaves into rabbinic contracts. In response, in 1976, when there were only three women Reform rabbis, the CCAR created a Task Force on Women in the Rabbinate, chaired initially by Sally Priesand, intended to work toward the successful integration of women into the rabbinate. Another significant force in shaping the place of women rabbis in the Reform movement arose with the creation of the Women's Rabbinic Network (WRN) in 1980. The WRN displaced an earlier organization, the Women's Rabbinic Association, which had brought together women rabbis from both the Reform and Reconstructionist movements.

As a constituent organization of the Central Conference of American Rabbis, the Women's Rabbinic Network serves dual purposes. Through newsletters and biennial meetings, it has reduced the isolation of individual members and offered forums to address common issues. In addition, the WRN has been extremely effective as an advocate for the issues faced by women and (like the NFTS before it) in opening formerly all-male hierarchies to female participation. One significant contribution has been offering female rabbis a broader context in which to understand the struggles they face in their individual rabbinates. Entering a professional culture based on the premise that one's wife could take care of family and life responsibilities, many women rabbis have struggled to accommodate their desire to meld family and personal lives with their career. The network has been an important agent in contesting a professional model that has become increasingly problematic for both men and women. Despite this important contribution and although by the early 1980s the number of female HUC-JIR students began to approach parity with that of their male classmates, women rabbis continued to face distinctive challenges. A 1980 survey of congregations by the WRN reported diverse fears that women rabbis would be too soft-spoken, too weak, too emotional, unable to balance family and career, and too unfamiliar. A 1994 survey of 103 Reform women rabbis showed that half of the respondents had experienced some form of sexual harassment in their professional roles.

Even as women rabbis faced persistent challenges, they also began to reshape Reform congregations and American Judaism in profound ways. As women took on formal roles in Jewish worship and ritual, many began to view Jewish ceremonies, liturgies, texts, and traditions in a new light; they became more aware of the relevance and significance of their own experience. Rabbi Laura Geller, ordained in 1976, was among the first to point out that women rabbis, as they broke down the traditional exclusivity of Jewish leadership, could offer congregants a sense of greater access to the sacred and help them think more critically about their concept of God. She was also a pioneer in formulating Jewish traditions that address the many stages of women's lives that had been overlooked by a male-centered tradition. She and her many colleagues have created ceremonies to mark baby namings, gay unions, weaning, the beginning and end of menstruation, miscarriages, abortion, and divorce, among other significant life events. Reform women rabbis have also been important participants in the creation of feminist midrash, reexaminations of biblical texts often from the perspectives of female participants and in emerging critiques of traditional Jewish liturgy.

The most radical efforts to accommodate Jewish practice and liturgy to evolving gender concerns have occurred for the most part outside the Reform movement. Reform liturgical efforts geared toward introducing gender-inclusive language have been slowed by worries about preserving the familiarity of traditional texts familiar for congregants with weak Jewish educations and by differing perceptions of the extent to which the language of traditional Jewish prayer should be seen as a male expression of religiosity. In 1993 the movement published a "gender-sensitive" liturgy meant to supplement the 1975 Reform prayer book *Gates of Prayer*. The newer edition avoids male pronouns in referring to God in its English prayers and translations. Changes in the Hebrew text are limited to adding the names of the matriarchs to liturgical references to the patriarchs. Although more comprehensive reform seems to be on the horizon, some still see current attempts at liturgical revision as too awkward and/or too radical.

Other reflections of the impact of women's changing roles within Reform congregations include the elaboration of Jewish prayers and worship services directed toward physical and spiritual healing. The work of Debbie Friedman, a musician whose music has been embraced by the Reform youth movement and Reform congregations, has been critical to this trend, as has the work of rabbis like Nancy Flam, who has been active in creating and directing a number of Jewish healing centers in California. The popular emergence of bat and bar mitzvah ceremonies for adults represents a general trend toward greater access to textual knowledge and authority among Reform congregants. Women, many of whom felt that their earlier Jewish educations were limited because of their gender, have been the most active in taking advantage of this innovation and in moving generally toward greater participation in congregational ritual and life. Many within the movement, in fact, have begun to express concern about a growing absence of men engaged in congregational participation and leadership.

In this context, where women can claim full access to religious and lay leadership, and as women have taken on professional roles both within and outside of Judaism, some question the continued relevance of gender-segregated congregational organizations. Although many sisterhoods continue to attend to fundamental social, spiritual, and material needs of their communities, other congregations have seen a waning energy within their sisterhood organizations. With so many women taking on professional responsibilities outside of the home, congregational leaders can no longer draw freely upon the energy and time of a cadre of talented female volunteers. As a result, much of the responsibility for sustaining a more limited range of congregational activities is increasingly undertaken by paid (male and female) staff members.

Meanwhile, many women now become involved in synagogue life and governance without first rising through a congregational women's organization. As women take on lay leadership roles that were once monopolized by men, many have become wary of the subsidiary role often ascribed to sisterhood groups. This same concern was reflected in the National Federation of Temple Sisterhoods' 1993 decision to change its name to Women of Reform Judaism, the Federation of Temple Sisterhoods (WRJ). The change of name reflected a desire to be seen not merely as an auxiliary service group but as an organization that puts its members and their interests at the center of the Reform movement. The national WRJ remains a strong institutional entity, but it too has adapted to a changing social and religious context.

In many ways Women of Reform Judaism continues to fulfill NFTS's traditional role within the movement, including its long-standing support of Reform youth activities and rabbinical education both for American-born students and for rabbinical students from around the world. Likewise, the commitment to social justice issues pioneered by executive director Jane Evans has been carried on by her successor Ellen Rosenberg, finding expression in campaigns for breast cancer prevention and gun control. In addition, WRJ has attempted to incorporate changing expectations for the content of women's relationship to Judaism by creating major national projects that focus on Torah as the center of Jewish life. In 2001, WRJ celebrated the completion of a "Women's Torah," to be used at significant WRJ gatherings, written by a professional male scribe but, symbolically, by all the women of Reform Judaism. The other major Torah project embarked on by WRJ is an ambitious women's Torah commentary that will offer historical and textual annotation and essays that illuminate the biblical text from the perspective of women's experience and scholarship. Through these projects, WRJ seeks to demonstrate the commitment of Reform Jewish women to redefining the tradition and texts of Jewish life.

As the WRJ's Torah commentary project suggests, women's voices and religious authority have come to play central roles in the continuing effort to interpret an ancient tradition to a contemporary world. Female leadership, whether rabbinic or lay, has indeed become an unquestioned feature of American Reform Jewish life. Still, for all this, enduring differentials in male and female rabbinical salaries indicate that limits to equality remain. Even though women rabbis have now been in the field long enough to qualify for positions requiring seniority, a survey of rabbinical posts at large congregations, of faculty positions at HUC-JIR campuses, and of leadership roles within the movement reveals strikingly few women in the central roles that determine the future of the movement.

Evidence from the early years of the twenty-first century, however, points both to the entrenched male-centered institutional culture of Reform Judaism and to the authentic possibility of meaningful shifts in this pattern. Although most major Reform leadership positions are still held by men, the current general portrait of the influence of women in the American Reform movement is one of great promise. In the early 1990s, the different HUC-JIR campuses had appointed only a few isolated women to their faculties. A few more were hired over the course of that decade. Since 2000, new appointments especially on the New York and Los Angeles campuses have multiplied the number of women on the HUC-JIR faculty many times over. At the institutional level, Rabbi Julie Spitzer in 1992 became the first woman to serve as a director of one of the UAHC's fourteen regional offices that offer assistance and support to congregations within their geographical area. In 2003, five women held similar positions. In the late 1990s, a few women were hired for the first time as senior rabbis at some of the movement's largest congregations, positions that have traditionally been associated with the highest stature within the Reform rabbinate. In 2003, Rabbi Janet Marder became

president of the Central Conference of American Rabbis, a position that is generally held for two years. Marder's accession to the CCAR presidency represents the first time that a woman has held one of the posts generally considered to constitute the core leadership of the Reform movement. (The male-held posts of Hebrew Union College–Jewish Institute of Religion president and Union of American Hebrew Congregations president constitute open-ended appointments with no specific time limits.)

Most significantly perhaps, the CCAR's central liturgical endeavors have been assigned for the first time to women. A new Reform Haggadah for Passover, the first in twenty-six years, edited by Rabbi Sue Levi Elwell, appeared in 2002. Meanwhile, a new Reform prayer book, edited by Rabbis Elyse Frishman and Judith Abrams, is scheduled for publication in 2005. All these liturgists have been associated with feminist challenges to the patriarchal texts and traditions of Jewish culture. Elwell, for instance, has already edited a feminist Haggadah and is also coeditor of a book titled *Lesbian Rabbis* (2001). Abrams is the founder of a school for adult Talmud study. Future mainstream Reform congregations and households will thus encounter Jewish ritual shaped by women who have been a part of the feminist liturgical ferment that has energized liberal Judaism's recent relationship to its ancient patriarchal texts.

More evidence of the growing power of women rabbis to shape the course of Reform Judaism was evident in the role of the Women's Rabbinic Network in pushing the CCAR to take a strong public stand on the religious validation of same-gender marriages or commitment ceremonies. Although the CCAR had passed a resolution indicating its approval of gay civil marriage in 1997, the intention of considering the question of religious officiation at such unions during the 1998 CCAR conference was deflected at the last moment for fear of introducing a debate that would be too controversial and destructive of unity within the movement. All indications were that the organization would try to avoid this issue as long as possible. In 2000, however, pushed by the WRN to place a vote on the CCAR conference agenda approving rabbinic officiation, the Reform rabbis made headlines with their resolution declaring that "we support the decision of those who choose to officiate at rituals of union for same-gender couples, and we support the decision of those who do not" ("Resolution on Same Gender Officiation"). The final cautiously worded resolution represented a compromise that nonetheless signified the acceptance of religious sanction for gay unions by a mainstream religious organization.

Thus, as the first women to become Reform rabbis have begun celebrating the twenty-fifth anniversaries of their ordinations, the accession of women to the highly symbolic role of rabbi is being felt at the core of the

Reform movement. Female clergy have after all found acceptance in Reform congregations in a fashion that still eludes the Conservative movement. Given all this progress, there is, however, a danger of forgetting the difficulties that remain. There are frequent instances of women finding that their placement or renewal in clergy positions is complicated by concerns about their marital status, child-care responsibilities, sexual orientation, wardrobe, personal appearance, or inability to get along with male supervisors. Women's rabbinic salaries, moreover, continue to trail those of men. In addition, although the faculty on some campuses of the Hebrew Union College–Jewish Institute of Religion is for the first time beginning to show the presence of more than just one or two female professors, the only HUC-JIR faculty members to be denied tenure since 1963 have been two professors who were each the first woman to be hired to the faculty of their respective campuses. Ironically, women who become victim to gender-based employment issues may suddenly find themselves battling the Reform movement's loud rhetorical commitment to gender equality, facing almost reflexive denials that gender bias could have played any role in their experience. None of these difficulties negates the overall and symbolic progress that women have found within the Reform movement, but they should remind those both inside and outside the movement that the journey is not over.

In the effort to create a religion with which acculturating American Jews could feel comfortable, American Reform Judaism has always been at the forefront of challenging traditional limits on women's roles in Jewish life. From family pews to women rabbis and cantors, the particular adaptations necessary to realizing the principle of religious equality for men and women have evolved along with the broader society's often confusing mix of expectations for proper gender roles. In whatever era, gendered transformation within Reform Judaism has brought forth possibility, ambivalence, and the suggestion of future innovations. The achievement of true gender equality within American Jewish culture, as within American society, may always remain elusive. The recognition, however, that a vibrant and relevant Judaism must respond to the challenges raised by the position of women in contemporary life derives from the earliest days and concerns of American Judaism's Reform movement.

SOURCES: *Beyond the Synagogue Gallery: Finding a Place for Women in American Judaism* (2000), by Karla Goldman, offers much material on the ways in which women's changing roles fueled and defined the development of the Reform movement in the nineteenth century. New roles for women in the 1890s are also covered by Felicia Herman, "From Priestess to Host-ess: Sisterhoods of Personal Service in New York City, 1887–1936," in *Women and American Judaism: Historical Perspectives*, ed. Pamela S. Nadell and Jonathan D. Sarna (2001), and by Faith Rogow in *Gone to Another Meeting: The National Council of Jewish Women, 1893–1993* (1993). The National Federation of Temple Sisterhoods published a pamphlet on its organizational history, "The Days of Our Years, Service through Sisterhood, 1913–1963," in 1963. Papers of the National Federation of Temple Sisterhoods/Women of Reform Judaism are found at the American Jewish Archives in Cincinnati. The most valuable secondary sources focused on National Federation of Temple Sisterhoods/Women of Reform Judaism include the articles "Ladies of the Sisterhood: Women in the American Reform Synagogue, 1900–1930," by Pamela S. Nadell and Rita J. Simon, in *Active Voices, Women in Jewish Culture*, ed. Maurie Sacks (1995), and "National Federation of Temple Sisterhoods," by Pamela S. Nadell, in *Jewish Women in America: An Historical Encyclopedia*, ed. Paula Hyman and Deborah Dash Moore (1997). Deborah Levine Lefton wrote a useful rabbinical thesis on this subject at Hebrew Union College (Cincinnati), "Women's Equality in the Synagogue: The National Federation of Temple Sisterhood's Search for Autonomy, 1913–1930" (2001). On the story of women's ordination, see Pamela S. Nadell, *Women Who Would Be Rabbis: A History of Women's Ordination, 1889–1985* (1998), and two articles by Ellen M. Umansky, "Women in Judaism: From the Reform Movement to Contemporary Jewish Religious Feminism," in *Women of Spirit, Female Leadership in the Jewish and Christian Traditions*, ed. Rosemary Radford Ruether and Eleanor McLaughlin (1979), and "Women's Journey toward Rabbinic Ordination," in *Women Rabbis, Exploration & Celebration*, ed. Gary P. Zola (1996). The Women's Rabbinic Network sponsored the summer 1997 edition of the *CCAR Journal* as a special issue on the occasion of the twenty-fifth anniversary of Rabbi Sally Priesand's ordination titled, "Wisdom You Are My Sister: 25 Years of Women in the Rabbinate." See also Central Conference of American Rabbis, "Resolution on Same Gender Officiation" (2000), available online at http://ccarnet.org.

TRADITION AND CHANGE—FINDING THE RIGHT BALANCE: CONSERVATIVE AND RECONSTRUCTIONIST JUDAISM
Shuly Rubin Schwartz

THE MIGRATION OF over 2 million eastern European Jews to the United States between 1881 and 1924 dramatically altered the landscape of American Jewry. Conservative Judaism and its intellectual offshoot Reconstructionist Judaism offered a vision of an American Judaism that proved most popular among these Jews during the first two-thirds of the twentieth century. Though Reconstructionist Judaism has—since 1968—been an independent denomination with a distinctive institutional structure, leadership, and ideology, its origins were so intimately intertwined with that of Conservative Judaism that the two movements merit treatment together.

Conservative Judaism

The *Judaism of the Golden Mean*, a term coined by Alexander Kohut, one of the early spokespersons of the movement, aptly describes the character of Conservative Judaism in the United States. This movement, which has seen as its mission both the conserving of traditional Judaism and its adaptation when deemed necessary to the changed conditions of modernity, has long been ambivalent about the role of its women. On the one hand, the movement considers itself bound by halakha, Jewish law, and since traditional law prescribes discreet religious obligations for Jewish women, the movement for decades dedicated itself to upholding traditional homemaker roles for women. On the other hand, commited to change within a halakic framework, Conservative Judaism was the first movement to seriously attempt to adapt Jewish law to resolve pressing issues for Jewish women. Because of the tension between tradition and change that characterizes the movement, the role of women in Conservative Judaism is both the most complicated and the most all encompassing among the Jewish denominations.

The Conservative movement began to take shape in this country under Solomon Schechter, president of the reorganized Jewish Theological Seminary (JTS) in New York City from 1902 to 1915. Schechter was certain that the future of Jewish life in America depended on women as well as men, and he was an early supporter of women's learning. One of his first actions was to permit Henrietta Szold to attend classes at the seminary. Szold, probably the most learned American Jewish woman of her time, and secretary of the Jewish Publication Society, began to take courses with rabbinical students after assuring Schechter that she would not seek ordination. Szold studied with the famed Talmudic scholar Louis Ginzberg, professor of Talmud at the Jewish Theological Seminary from 1902 to 1953, and she soon began translating Ginzberg's lectures, letters, and articles from German into English; she eventually assumed the mammoth task of organizing and translating the material that would eventually be published as Ginzberg's popular, multivolume *Legends of the Jews* (1998). Much has been made of Szold's personal relationship with Ginzberg, with whom she fell in love and who was thirteen years her junior, and of the effect of its breakup on her pioneering role in founding Hadassah, the Women's Zionist Organization. Szold's own words reveal that her acute pain stemmed in part from her belief that within the Jewish Theological Seminary community she had as-

sumed the role of Ginzberg's "affianced wife." When Ginzberg married Adele Katzenstein, Szold, who remained single, lost her place in the JTS community. Her experiences proved cautionary for other educated, single women of her time. A few years later, Schechter founded the Teachers Institute of the Jewish Theological Seminary in 1909, which accepted both men and women from its inception and offered Jewish higher education to men and women on an equal basis. From 1915 on, it also offered a professional teacher-training curriculum that enabled women to prepare for careers in Jewish education. Schechter's attitude toward both Szold and Jewish education for women characterized the movement's position for many decades. Convinced of women's capabilities, the movement was committed to equal educational opportunities of women at all levels as long as women did not seek ordination and remained committed to marriage and family life.

Mathilde Roth Schechter, wife of Solomon Schechter, modeled just the kind of woman her husband had in mind. Born in 1857, Mathilde Schechter grew up in Breslau, Germany. Her father died when she was young, and she received her education in the Jewish orphan home. Quickly distinguishing herself intellectually, Schechter continued her education at the municipal high school for girls. She then entered a teacher's seminary, where she received a well-rounded secular education. Not content to assume the life of teacher in a provincial German town, she taught in Breslau and Hungary and then continued her travels to England in 1885. There, she met Solomon Schechter—fittingly, in the Jews College library. A learned woman with a warm, giving personality, Schechter—by marrying Solomon—secured her place as a homemaker who would not only be at the center of a rich Jewish home life but would also be at the hub of Jewish intellectual life. She was a gracious hostess and always conducted their home as an open one. In the United States, Mathilde felt that these Open Houses provided a fitting background for her husband's activities, and they reinforced her helpmate role. Jewish Theological Seminary students were especially attracted to the Schechter home, for Mathilde's nurturance became legendary. Offering solace, a sympathetic ear, and sometimes material relief, she nourished many individuals in her graciously appointed home. According to 1907 Jewish Theological Seminary graduate Jacob Kohn, Schechter "had a faculty for gathering about her people not usually at home in drawing-rooms." Szold went further, noting that in this gentle, warm milieu "so many, many of us basked and were transformed." Even after her husband's death, Schechter continued to preside in her home (Kohn, 6; and Henrietta Szold to Frank Schechter, August 31, 1924, reprinted in Scult, "Mrs. Mathilde Roth," 125–126).

Women's League

Schechter's greatest lasting achievement was the founding of Women's League (later Women's League for Conservative Judaism) in 1918, which she described as the natural extension of her husband's work. Five years earlier, Solomon Schechter had established the United Synagogue of America (later the United Synagogue of Conservative Judaism) as the congregational arm of the movement, and he believed it to be one of his prized achievements. In founding Women's League, Mathilde explained that she was merely organizing an auxiliary branch of United Synagogue for the women, though it is apparent that from the start she had in mind a strong women's organization with its own independent agenda. Both Schechters were convinced of the indispensability of Jewish homemakers to the preservation of Judaism in the United States, and Women's League was developed to teach its members how to make and keep a home traditionally Jewish and how to beautify it through observance. Mathilde hoped Women's League would impress upon women the beauty and depth of the Jewish religious and literary heritage, but she also implored women to study Jewish history, holidays, kashrut (dietary laws), and Bible, not only to be better mothers but also for the sake of study itself.

The mothering instincts that came to the fore in her experiences with students in her home surely influenced Mathilde's fervent desire to create a Students' House that would provide kosher food, rooms, and a feeling of comfort and belonging to students attending colleges far from their homes. An extension of women's homemaking role, this Students' House became one of Women's League's first projects. Open to all students in the New York area, the building was located near Columbia University and the Jewish Theological Seminary. Jewish college groups held meetings there, and the seminary student organization sponsored lectures. The Students' House became a model that was soon replicated in other cities. Schechter also worked through Women's League on several projects designed to revive home observances. She initiated the preparation and distribution of a convenient card imprinted with the Sabbath kiddush (blessing over the wine) and *Friday Night Stories*, a collection of inspirational legends. Echoing her husband's critique of Reform Judaism, Schechter explained that

we cannot have spirit without forms, forms tenderly kissed into life and warmth by the spirit. By natural law forms will spring up genetically. Then why not keep to the old beautiful forms, hallowed by the used of centuries. The Jewess of this twentieth century ought to be the finest type of American womanhood: bred in the best American traditions, she should also know and lovingly gather all the sweet blossoms of our poetical Jewish customs and traditions. (Schechter, "Aims and Ideals of the Women's League")

Although not known for her public speaking, Schechter could capture her audience not only with her inspiring persona but also with the passion and commitment of her words:

The House of Israel is on fire, the House of Israel is falling to pieces! Shall we let destruction take its course? Or shall we try to build up and save our home, our beautiful Jewish home for our children and grandchildren? . . . The Women's League will try to help us find our way back home. We have lost our way. The world's darkest hours close in around us, and we need the divine light as never before to guide us aright! (Schechter, "Aims and Ideals of the Women's League")

Schechter succeeded in achieving many of her goals. When she left office in 1919, she could report fifty-seven affiliated sisterhoods with a membership of over 6,000. Moreover, Schechter was an enormously powerful role model for younger women who saw her as the embodiment of fineness in Jewish womanhood. Remembered not only as its founder but as the architect of its program, Schechter was invoked for decades afterward as the inspiration for the blueprint of service that continued to guide Women's League throughout much of the twentieth century. Fittingly given her values, the first Jewish Theological Seminary residence hall built outside its 122nd Street campus bears her name. The Mathilde Schechter Residence Hall on West 120th Street was dedicated in 1974 after decades-long fund-raising efforts on the part of Women's League women.

Why was Schechter's impact singular? In part because, unlike her friend Szold, Schechter succeeded first as cooperative spouse. Similarly educated, capable, and concerned about Jewish life, Schechter framed her activist achievements as an expansion of the supportive homemaker role in which she took so much pride. In this way, she epitomized the Conservative movement's approach to tradition and change for its early-twentieth-century women.

Following Schechter's lead, Adele Ginzberg (1886–1980), wife of JTS professor Louis Ginzberg, or Mama G., as she was affectionately known, also ministered to the seminary community. She hosted open houses on Sabbath and holidays and invited each member of the seminary's senior rabbinical school class for Sabbath lunch. Even after her husband's death in 1953, Ginzberg continued to invite students to her Sabbath table until shortly before her own death in 1980. Mama G. was especially noted for her devotion to the seminary sukkah

A learned woman with a warm giving personality, Mathilde Roth Schechter—by marrying Solomon Schechter, founder of the Jewish Theological Seminary—secured her place as a homemaker. Mathilde was a gracious hostess; the Schechter home was an open one, and served as the center of Jewish intellectual life. JTS students were especially welcome. *Courtesy of the Jewish Theological Seminary, Ratner Center for the Study of Conservative Judaism.*

(the ritual booth where Jews dine during the Festival of Tabernacles), a project she inherited from Schechter, which was also an extension of the traditional home-maker role. For decades, she raised funds, shopped, and supervised the decoration of the sukkah with fresh fruits, vegetables, and greenery. In her day, the sukkah became known throughout the city for its grand beauty. In tribute to her role in heading the sukkah decorating project for so many years, Women's League named the sukkah in her memory. Ginzberg was also one of the early supporters of equal rights for women in Conservative Judaism. When JTS women were first granted permission to carry the Torah on Simhat Torah (festival marking the completion of the Torah Reading Cycle) in 1975, Ginzberg, then an elder statesperson, was honored with holding one. Young women danced around her in tribute to her pioneering role in advancing this cause.

Schechter's influence can also be seen in the career of Carrie Dreyfuss Davidson (1879–1953), wife of rabbi and Jewish Theological Seminary professor of medieval Hebrew literature Israel Davidson. Her most notable and lasting accomplishment was her role in 1930 in founding and then serving as editor for over twenty years of Women's League *Outlook*. At first, the monthly magazine was a one-woman operation; Davidson wrote most of the editorials and book reviews, published the children's stories of authors like Sadie Rose Weilerstein

(1894–1993), and over time shaped the publication into a highly regarded and widely read journal. She penned countless articles on a variety of topics including Zionism, Jewish holidays, and Jewish education. The magazine continues to be an important vehicle for disseminating information on a wide range of topics of concern to Conservative Jewish women; it has a current readership of about 100,000.

Schechter's handpicked successor as president of Women's League, Fanny Binswanger Hoffman (1862–1949), had been a strong Jewish leader in her own right even before taking on this role. Hoffman had helped found and served as the first president of the Philadelphia branch of the National Council of Jewish Women, but her passion was Jewish education for children. She served as the first principal of the Sunday School of Mikveh Israel Congregation in Philadelphia. In 1885, she established the Young Women's Union as a branch of the Hebrew Education Society, whose first goal was the creation of a free kindergarten for the poor. Hoffman became one of the first Jewish female kindergarten teachers in the United States. President from 1919 to 1928, she solidified and expanded the work of her predecessor. Gently persuasive, she complimented women on each step that they took toward increased Jewish learning.

Deborah M. Melamed (1892–1954) extended Schechter's commitment to Jewish ceremonials through her very popular book, *The Three Pillars: Life, Practice and Thought for the Jewish Woman* (1927), which she dedicated to Schechter's memory. Well educated, Melamed earned a B.A. from Hunter College and continued her studies in education, psychology, and English literature at Columbia University until she married. Her Jewish education was equally rich: She studied in the first class of the Teachers Institute, and after moving to Philadelphia upon her marriage in 1915, Melamed continued her education at Dropsie College, where she was a fellow in Semitic languages (1915–1917). When her husband, Raphael, took a position as rabbi of B'nai Israel Congregation in Elizabeth, New Jersey, in 1923, Melamed began her lifelong work with the public schools, eventually becoming the supervisor of foreign languages in the Elizabeth schools, a position she held until her death in 1954.

The mother of two children, Melamed helped found the Elizabeth chapter of Hadassah. She also played an active role in National Women's League, serving as vice president and chairman of the education committee for many years. A popular writer, lecturer, and speaker, she was especially effective in reaching modern women with her knowledgeable yet accessible presentations. Bright and capable herself, it is not surprising that she argued that the function of Jewish women must move beyond sewing "the tallith bag which the wandering Jew has carried through the ages" to become comanagers with men of the Jewish spirit ("The Modern Woman and Traditional Judaism," *United Synagogue Recorder,* January 1921, 9).

The Three Pillars, the first guidebook of its kind in English, was published in 1927 to provide "a brief exposition of those aspects of Jewish life which have a special significance for the woman" (preface). Melamed's hope was that by breathing the spirit of life into these ceremonies, she would inspire Jewish women to seek a more observant and richer Jewish life. Written in a simple, welcoming manner, *The Three Pillars* reviews the Jewish life and holiday cycle. Melamed includes small sections on dietary and family purity laws but also incorporates information about a wide range of other topics, from minor fast days to the ritual hand washing performed before reciting the Grace after Meals. While not advocating a feminist position, Melamed does favor confirmation ceremonies for girls, as "an intelligent Jewish woman bespeaks a certain amount of Jewish training and education" (35). She also expects Jewish women to involve themselves with their husbands in the full range of Jewish observance, from blessing their children on Friday nights to attending synagogue. In her view, "[N]othing ought be permitted to stand in the way of regular attendance at services on Sabbath morning" (74). About Hanukkah, she notes its proximity in the calendar to Christmas and states: "Christmas trees, gifts or parties have no place in a Jewish home. Jewish children ought not to participate in school plays or other celebrations of the season" (129). In the section on Bible, she avers that "it is a mark of gross ignorance to be unfamiliar with the Bible; for a Jew to be ignorant of his Bible is nothing short of a tragedy" (65). Instantly popular, the book was well reviewed. By 1967, Women's League reported that it had gone through nine editions. Women's League received many letters praising its utility, with many women wondering what they had done without it.

During the period of rapid growth of the Conservative movement in the interwar and post–World War II period, congregational sisterhoods formed the backbone of the educational mission of the Conservative synagogue. Sisterhood women successfully initiated many projects that greatly enhanced Conservative Jewish life in their synagogues, offering financial support as well as volunteer hours. They provided assistance in Sunday and religious schools and were instrumental in organizing classes for mothers in Jewish living and observance. Typically, women also maintained the synagogue kitchen, both in terms of dietary laws and by serving as cooks and hostesses for the collations, luncheons, and dinners that were essential to the success of synagogue activities. Many groups also took it upon themselves to issue sisterhood cookbooks; these popular fund-raising projects were a potent vehicle for demonstrating on a local level that it was possible to keep the highest standards of dietary laws while cooking a wide variety of both Jewish- and American-style dishes. Synagogue women also introduced and staffed synagogue gift shops, and in this way, women were largely responsible for introducing Jewish ceremonial objects as well as Jewish books and artwork into the homes of Conservative Jews. Finally, these women were often instrumental in campaigns to decorate or refurbish synagogue buildings. Choosing curtains, carpeting, and wall hangings, women often set the tone for their community's house of worship. Eventually, many women moved up the ranks of synagogue administration from sisterhood to Congregational leadership positions, where they have played active roles as officers of Conservative congregations throughout the United States and Canada. During the period from 1980 to 1995, 79 percent of congregations had a woman serve as president.

Women's League provided inspiration on a national level for each of these local efforts through its publications and its leadership. For example, Betty Greenberg and Althea Osber Silverman shared their views on the beauty and spirituality of the Jewish home in "The Jewish Home Beautiful," a pageant first presented in the Temple of Religion of the World's Fair in 1940 and then published as a popular book by Women's League (1941). This book included descriptions, traditional recipes, illustrations of table settings, and music, all of which illustrated the potential for creating a Jewish home filled with beauty, spirituality, and the latest style. Althea Osber Silverman with her *Habibi and Yow* and Sadie Rose Weilerstein with her *K'tonTon* series became noted children's authors who made it easier for mothers to enrich their children's Jewish upbringing by providing adventurous, age-appropriate stories on Jewish customs and festivals. The combined efforts of all these women reinforced the message that one could both embrace American culture and transmit a full Jewish life to one's family. Through their writings as well as through their lives, these women reassuringly illustrated that Conservative Jewish living was compatible with the aspirations of upwardly mobile American women.

After World War II, Women's League's educational activities expanded tremendously in response to the increased pace of the Conservative movement's growth. Adele Ginzberg initiated a Girl Scout project in 1946 that led to the establishment of the Menorah Award for Jewish Girl Scouts in order to stress the importance of Jewish education and encourage Jewish scouts to participate in synagogue activities (and to parallel the Ner Tamid Award for Jewish Boy Scouts). The Judaism-in-the-Home project introduced in the 1950s, and chaired by Rose Goldstein and Anna Bear Brevis, produced instructional materials to teach this generation of sisterhood women the meaning of Jewish holidays and rituals in order to promote family observance. A series of Oneg Shabbat (Sabbath celebration) programs based on the weekly Torah portions were published under the leadership of Education Department chairmen Dr. Evelyn Garfiel, Rose Goldstein, and Adina Katzoff. In 1952, the newly created Ceremonial Objects and Gift Shop Department made Jewish ritual objects and other ceremonial items, including New Year cards, accessible to all sisterhoods. In 1959, Hadassah Nadich initiated the first calendar diary. Issued annually until 1986, these calendar guides promoted Jewish activities in the home, synagogue, and community. They were distributed to all sisterhoods so that local leaders could incorporate educational elements into their projects.

Women's League women also played a crucial role in the national Conservative scene through their fund-raising capabilities. Among their most successful projects was the Mathilde Schechter Residence Hall and the refurbishing of what is now called the Women's League Seminary Synagogue. In this way, Women's League women have made and continue to make an important difference in the quality of life for Jewish Theological Seminary students in New York and University of Judaism students in Los Angeles. In 2000, its annual fund-raising efforts raised $2.4 million.

At part of its commitment to further traditional Judaism, Women's League has long been involved with issues of social justice, human rights, and care for the poor, hungry, and homeless. One of its earliest projects was helping the Jewish blind through the Jewish Braille Institute. Women were trained to serve as transcribers of Braille, and the first Hebrew-English prayer book in Braille was underwritten by the league in 1954. During World War II, the league was active in the Supplies for Overseas Survivors Drive and in collecting food and clothing for the Joint Distribution Committee. Members were also trained to assume needed tasks in many different areas, including serving as Red Cross instructors and air raid wardens.

After World War II, Women's League accelerated its involvement with issues of public concern. Over the decades, Women's League has supported a liberal political and social agenda, promoting the elimination of discrimination in public places, zealously guarding civil lib-

Women's League Presidents	
Mathilde Schechter	1918–1919
Fanny Hoffman	1919–1928
Dora Spiegel	1928–1946
Sarah Kopelman	1946–1950
Marion Siner	1950–1954
Helen Sussman	1954–1958
Syd Rossman	1958–1962
Helen Fried	1962–1966
Evelyn Henkind	1966–1970
Selma Rapoport	1970–1974
Ruth Perry	1974–1978
Goldie Kweller	1978–1982
Selma Weintraub	1982–1986
Evelyn Auerbach	1986–1990
Audrey Citak	1990–1994
Evelyn Seelig	1994–1998
Janet Tobin	1998–2002
Gloria Cohen	2002–present

erties in the McCarthy era, advocating the separation of church and state, and calling for government funding to ameliorate deteriorating social conditions of the poor and the aged, in the cities, and in the global environment. League women have been particularly concerned with women's issues, and they passed resolutions urging the adoption of the Equal Rights Amendment, protecting battered women, and favoring a woman's right to choose. Pro-Zionist in the interwar period, Women's League has been a staunch supporter of the State of Israel since its founding in 1948. It has passed resolutions supporting the need for foreign aid and security and criticizing the Arab boycott and propaganda and the United Nation's discriminatory policies. In recent years, attention has shifted to religious issues, with Women's League asserting the need for religious pluralism and for the recognition of the Conservative movement in Israel, known there as the Masorti movement. The organization has also long evidenced concern for world Jewry and human rights issues throughout the globe. Finally, Women's League has become an increasingly independent voice as one of the constituent arms of the Conservative movement.

Jewish Law

Several difficult Jewish legal issues have long perplexed rabbinic leaders concerned about the inequality of women in traditional Judaism. The most difficult of these is that of the *agunah* (literally "chained wife"; a woman who has not obtained a Jewish divorce and is thus not permitted to remarry). The Conservative movement's long-standing commitment to resolving the status of the *agunah* is an important symbol of its concern with redressing gender inequities. The Rabbinical Assembly Committee on Jewish Law (since 1948: "and Standards") tried for over twenty years to resolve the dilemma, and the first breakthrough came with the adoption of what came to be known as the "Lieberman clause" (1953), a clause inserted in the *ketubah* (marriage document), written by Professor Saul Lieberman, professor of Talmud at the Jewish Theological Seminary. This clause made the Jewish marriage contract into a civilly binding agreement in which both husband and wife agreed to abide by the recommendations of a Jewish court of law if their marriage ended. Although widely used throughout the movement, it did not fully resolve the *agunah* problem. First, many rabbinic authorities hesitated bringing Jewish legal matters to the civil courts. Second, civil courts are reluctant to decide religious questions. This is true even in states like New York that have laws prohibiting one spouse from impeding the remarriage of another. Therefore, the Joint Bet Din (Jewish Court) of the Conservative movement has in recent years become more aggressive in dealing with this problem, both by training and certifying Conservative rabbis to write *gittin* (bills of divorce) and by using *hafkaat kiddushin* (annulment of the marriage) to free women from recalcitrant husbands. Based on a Talmudic text, though not universally accepted, *hafkaat kiddushin* is reserved for those severe cases where a Jewish divorce cannot be obtained, either because of the husband's extreme resistance or his disappearance. The Joint Bet Din deals with each case individually and, where necessary, grants approval for a local Bet Din to annul the marriage. This approach has protected and aided women beyond what the Lieberman clause accomplished without abandoning the movement's commitment to Jewish law.

The path of women from the periphery to the center of synagogue life began with the introduction of mixed seating in prayer services. By 1955, this characterized the overwhelming majority of Conservative congregations and served as a yardstick to differentiate them from Orthodox counterparts. Bat mitzvah, a coming-of-age ceremony for girls parallel to the popular bar mitzvah for thirteen-year-old Jewish boys, was first introduced in 1922 by Mordecai M. Kaplan—rabbi of the newly founded Society for the Advancement of Judaism, dean of the Teacher's Institute at the Jewish Theological Seminary, and later the founder of Reconstructionist Judaism—for his own daughter Judith. At a Sabbath morning service, she recited the blessings and read from the Torah. Bat mitzvah gradually grew in popularity within the movement. By 1948, approximately one-third of all

Conservative synagogues had introduced such a ceremony. Today it is nearly universally observed. The bat mitzvah ceremony took different forms over the decades, from group rituals that resembled confirmation to individual ceremonies at a late Friday evening service, where the bat mitzvah girl generally chanted a haftarah (selection from the Prophets). By the 1980s most bat mitzvah ceremonies came to resemble bar mitzvah services, where girls receive an aliyah (Torah honor), read from the Torah, deliver a speech about the Torah portion, and chant a haftarah. The rapid growth of the bat mitzvah ceremony in the post–World War II period can also be attributed to a desire on the part of Jewish educators to attract Jewish girls to supplementary religious schools. If they received the same education as boys until age thirteen, they too would celebrate their coming of age with a meaningful rite of passage. Because of this, girls came to share the same educational experiences as boys and were given the opportunity to lead in children's religious services. This became the norm at the movement's summer camps, Ramah, as well.

The Committee on Jewish Law and Standards of the Conservative movement responded to the changing role of women in the synagogue by deciding to permit women to be called up for aliyot (Torah honors) in 1955. After reviewing the halakic literature on the topic and noting that the prohibition was based more on long-standing custom than on law, the author of the responsum, Aaron H. Blumenthal, concluded that "the time has come for someone to reverse the direction in which the halachah has been moving for centuries" (Siegel, 279). At that time, the option was implemented in only a few synagogues in the Minneapolis area, but the precedent was established. In 1973 the Committee on Jewish Law and Standards went one step further, passing a *takkanah* (enactment), allowing women to count equally with men in the minyan (quorum of ten) that is necessary for public prayer. In that responsum, the influence of second wave American feminism is evident. Author Philip Sigal noted that he was influenced in his thinking by changing realities:

> We live in a radically changing world, and foremost among those transformations taking place is that of the status of women. The equalization of women with men had been progressing at an accelerating pace in recent years in various phases of the socio-economic context of society, as well as in new attitudes toward women in the sexual-moral sphere. (Sigal, in Siegal, 282)

The committee also adopted resolutions that further equalized men and women in areas of ritual, including serving as prayer leaders. In 1973, the United Synagogue of America also resolved to allow women to participate in synagogue rituals and to promote equal opportunity for women in positions of leadership, authority, and responsibility in congregational life. From 1972 to 1976, the number of Conservative congregations giving aliyot to women increased from 7 percent to 50 percent. By 1986, 83 percent of congregations counted women in the minyan.

In part, these changes came about in response to grassroots pressure for equality in synagogue ritual life. In 1972, Ezrat Nashim, a group of young, well-educated women, most of whom were products of the camps and schools of the movement, presented to the Rabbinical Assembly a call for the public affirmation of women's equality in all aspects of Jewish life. They demanded that women be granted membership in synagogues, be counted in a minyan, be allowed full participation in religious observances, be recognized as witnesses in Jewish law, be allowed to initiate divorce, be permitted and encouraged to attend rabbinical and cantorial school and perform as rabbis and cantors in synagogues, be encouraged to assume positions of leadership in the community, and be considered bound to fulfill all the mitzvoth (commandments) equally with men. They stopped just short of demanding rabbinical ordination and investiture as *hazzanim* (cantors) for women.

Ordination

This call evoked a sympathetic response from many Conservative rabbis; as expected, Women's League also became an early and vocal advocate of their position. This precipitated widespread, often heated and divisive debate within the movement over the next decade. Some women who wanted to become Conservative rabbis came to study at the Jewish Theological Seminary, and due to an unrelated academic reorganization effective with the 1974–1975 year, they were able to study in any class at their appropriate level. Preparing for ordination without being officially enrolled in the rabbinical school, they hoped that someday they would be ordained on the basis of their studies. In September 1977, JTS chancellor Gerson D. Cohen appointed a Committee for the Study of the Ordination of Women as Rabbis, which held hearings in cities throughout the country to get the perspective of laypeople as well as the view of its rabbis and scholars. The committee's final report of January 30, 1979, recommended, 11 to 3, that women be ordained, but the Rabbinical Assembly voted 127 to 109 to take no action prior to the decision of the JTS faculty. Pressure increased when one month later seminary students organized GROW, Group for the Rabbinical Ordination of Women, in an attempt to educate and organize political action. Late that year, the issue was brought to the Seminary Senate for a vote but was tabled when its divisiveness became apparent.

In 1983, the Rabbinical Assembly decided to consider for membership Beverly Magidson, a graduate of Hebrew Union College. Though widely supported, her admission fell short of receiving the necessary three-quarters vote of rabbis present. However, the consensus was that such approval was only a matter of time. This spurred the seminary to reconsider the issue, and on October 24, 1983, the seminary faculty voted thirty-four to eight, with one abstention and over half a dozen absent in protest, to admit women to the seminary's Rabbinical School. The Jewish legal basis for their acceptance was the *Teshuvah* (responsum) of JTS Talmud professor Joel Roth, which held that individual women could become rabbis (and prayer leaders) if they chose to assume the same degree of religious obligation as men. Individuals opposed to the decision to admit women formed the Union for Traditional Conservative Judaism, which became a separate group in 1990, changing its name to the Union for Traditional Judaism.

The first class to include women entered in the fall of 1984; the following spring Amy Eilberg was the first woman ordained by the seminary. Born in Philadelphia in 1954, Eilberg grew up as a Conservative Jew. She came to JTS in 1976 after completing her undergraduate work at Brandeis University. She studied Talmud for several years and then spent time in Israel studying and teaching at the seminary's Jerusalem branch. When JTS voted to admit women, Eilberg returned for one final year of study and was ordained in the spring of 1985. She began her career in the hospital chaplaincy. After a year in the congregational rabbinate, she became chaplain of Stanford University Hospital, providing spiritual healing to the ill and their families. Eilberg has played an instrumental role in the burgeoning Jewish healing movement and became involved in the Bay Area Jewish Healing Center. At the spring 1985 convention, the Rabbinical Assembly voted to admit for membership Beverly Magidson and Jan Kaufman, also a graduate of Hebrew Union College. Their membership was made effective July 1, 1985, to enable Eilberg, the seminary graduate, to be the first woman admitted to the assembly. There are currently 127 women members of the Rabbinical Assembly out of a total membership of close to 1,500. This includes those in Israel and Latin America. Women currently make up 40 percent of the student body at the JTS Rabbinical School and over 50 percent at the Ziegler School at the University of Judaism in Los Angeles.

The struggle for acceptance of women as cantors took a different course, since women had been eligible to study in the Cantors Institute since its inception in 1952 as candidates for the degrees of Bachelor, Master, and Doctorate of Sacred Music. In 1987, seminary chancellor Ismar Schorsch announced that JTS would confer the diploma of *Hazzan* to two women, Marla Barugel and Erica Lippitz. The Cantors Assembly voiced its disapproval and established a Committee of Inquiry to look into the question of admitting women. A resolution to admit women to the Cantors Assembly was defeated in 1988 (95 for, 97 against) and again in 1989 (108 for, 82 against, 2 abstentions) and 1990 (110 for, 68 against), because although the majority of the assembly had turned in favor of admission, the resolution failed to receive the necessary two-thirds vote. Women were finally admitted in December 1990 as a result of a decision by the Executive Council of the assembly. Today 68 of the 540 current members of the Cantors Assembly are women. Women make up almost 70 percent of the student body in the H. L. Miller Cantorial School at JTS.

The Roth *Teshuvah* guided the seminary synagogue until 1995, when Chancellor Schorsch announced that in the Women's League Seminary Synagogue the principle of full egalitarianism would be decisive in granting women religious status equal to that of men. This latter principle governs over 75 percent of Conservative synagogues today in which women participate equally with men. Some students have agitated for liturgical change as well, challenging the movement to address issues of sexism and patriarchy in the liturgy. The Women's League Seminary Synagogue, for example, now permits the inclusion of the matriarchs along with the patriarchs in daily prayer at the discretion of the prayer leader, and the most recent movement prayer book (1998) includes this as an option. Since 1995, JTS has had a master's program in Jewish Women's Studies.

After fifteen years in the rabbinate, women have begun to have an impact on the movement. Women, like their male counterparts, have chosen many diverse career options within the rabbinate. According to Rabbi Joel Meyers, executive vice president of the Rabbinical Assembly, the nature and challenges of rabbinic leadership are essentially the same for all rabbis, but women are generally more concerned about quality-of-life issues in terms of their families and private lives and are more likely to make adjustments in their careers for the sake of those concerns. Today, women serve as rabbis in only 4 percent of Conservative synagogues in the United States. Given the seniority system in terms of placement, they have only recently become eligible for positions in large congregations. Debra Newman Kamin was the first woman to serve as senior rabbi of a major Conservative synagogue, Am Yisrael Congregation in Northfield, Illinois (1995). Today only three other women occupy similar positions. Thirty-four women serve as the sole rabbis in congregations. Amy Eilberg was the first woman appointed (1986) to serve on the Committee on Jewish Law and Standards. The inclusion of women rabbis on the committee has begun to influence its decisions on many issues, including appropriate mourning rituals for women suffering a miscarriage or stillbirth.

Since 1986, the vast majority of Conservative synagogues have accorded women partial or full equality in religious services, although the official position of the movement is to endorse both egalitarian and nonegalitarian services, and both options continue to be offered at the seminary, Camp Ramah, and United Synagogue events. Ceremonies for the naming of baby Jewish girls, performed in an ad hoc, experimental way by individuals for a generation, have entered the mainstream with the publication of Women's League's *Simhat-Bat: Ceremonies to Welcome a Baby Girl* (1994). It is no longer unusual to see women reading Torah or donning Jewish religious garb for prayer. During the last twenty-five years small numbers of Conservative women have begun to wear tallith (prayer shawl) and tefillin (phylacteries); some women prefer the traditional wool tallith, with its black and white stripes, while others opt for more feminine colors, fabrics, and shapes. Some women wear *kippot* (skullcaps), but creative head coverings that more readily conform to the shape of women's hair have also been developed in response to a growing demand. Many women have chosen to undertake the necessary studies to become bat mitzvah as adults. Women's League instituted Kolot Bik'dushah in 1993; today, it consists of over 400 women nationwide who have the ability to lead a religious service and/or read from the Torah. Though egalitarianism has not been universally embraced by the movement, it is now the dominant position.

Certain Jewish legal issues have not yet been resolved, the most notable being the inadmissability of women as witnesses in Jewish legal matters. There is also great lack of uniformity in many of the changes that have been introduced. Taken as a whole, however, the movement has made great strides during the twentieth century in positioning itself as committed both to Jewish law and to gender equality, to equality of both education and opportunity, and the movement has emerged strengthened and more sharply focused as a result of this challenge.

Reconstructionist Judaism

Reconstructionist Judaism originated in the philosophy of Mordecai M. Kaplan. Since Kaplan was for decades involved in the Conservative movement and since his philosophy was intended to transform all of American Judaism, Reconstructionist Judaism did not take shape as a distinct movement until the 1960s. Yet it was imbued from the start with its founder's essential commitment to the full equality of women. A staunch supporter of democratic principles, Kaplan believed in giving everyone a voice. He was an outspoken supporter of the women's suffrage movement and held similar views with regard to women's role in Judaism. In fact, Kaplan's decision to establish his own congregation, the Society for the Advancement of Judaism, stemmed in part from his commitment to mixed seating for men and women in worship services. Kaplan believed Judaism to be a continuously evolving civilization, and he understood Jewish law to be a nonbinding yet important and sacred dimension of Jewish tradition. At the same time, he held Jewish law accountable to contemporary ethical standards. Because of these views, Kaplan had no problem instituting changes in women's roles to eliminate gender inequities. In addition to introducing mixed seating into his congregation during its first year, 1922, Kaplan also celebrated his daughter's bat mitzvah that same year. Yet he understood that true change would come about only through women's own efforts and initiative.

When women, influenced by second wave feminism of the 1960s, began agitating for change, they found in Reconstructionism a movement conducive to their views. For one thing, the movement has always been decidedly nonhierarchical: Kaplan removed the chosen people doctrine from the liturgy and chose to see himself as the "leader" rather than the rabbi of his congregation. Second, the Reconstructionist view of God as the power in the world that brings about righteousness and salvation is also gender neutral and thus receptive to feminist theology. Kaplan also promoted creative ritual and had himself in the 1940s already rewritten major sections of the liturgy to reflect his theological stance. Finally, since halakha was not seen as binding, the movement could easily resolve the *agunah* issue that had proven so thorny for the Conservative and Orthodox movements: It did so by creating egalitarian marriage documents and by declaring in 1980 that either spouse could initiate divorce. Thus, women would no longer be dependent on their husbands to grant them a divorce.

When the movement formed its own rabbinical college in 1968, the school's founders chose not to incur added controversy by including women in its first class. By its second year, however, Sandy Eisenberg Sasso was accepted without controversy. Sasso received her B.A. and M.A. from Temple University, and in 1974, she became the first woman ordained from the Reconstructionist Rabbinical College. Sasso is also the first woman to serve a Conservative congregation in partnership with her husband. She and her husband, Dennis C. Sasso, have been rabbis of Congregation Beth-El Zedeck in Indianapolis since 1977. Sasso is the author of several acclaimed children's books on Jewish themes, including *God's Paintbrush* (1992), *In God's Name* (1994), and *A Prayer for the Earth* (1996). She also writes a monthly column on religious and spirituality issues in *The Indianapolis Star*. She has served as past president of the Indianapolis Board of Rabbis and the Reconstructionist Rabbinical Association.

Inspired by Kaplan's views and unencumbered by a binding commitment to Jewish law, Reconstructionist Judaism has been in the vanguard in developing creative rituals that give voice to Jewish women's experiences. Women rabbis in particular, including Sasso, Linda Holtzman, Nancy Fuchs-Kreimer, and Rebecca Alpert, were the authors of pioneering ceremonies that focus on women's life-cycle events that had been devoid of religious celebration such as first menstruation, childbirth, weaning, and menopause. The movement has also been in the vanguard to promoting gender-neutral God-language and in experimenting with new liturgical forms to describe the Divine. In 1993, Reconstructionist rabbis passed a resolution recognizing and supporting rabbis' participation in same-gender commitment ceremonies, and the movement was the first to publish a commitment ceremony for same-sex couples in its *Rabbis' Manual* (1997).

Because of the movement's focus on Judaism as a civilization in its broadest sense, music and the arts have always been an important component. Judith Kaplan Eisenstein (1909–1996), daughter of Mordecai Kaplan, became a noted Jewish musicologist who single-handedly helped to create the field of Jewish music in this country. She earned both bachelor's (1928) and master's degrees (1932) in music education at Columbia University's Teachers College. She also studied at the Jewish Theological Seminary's Teachers Institute, where she later taught music pedagogy and the history of Jewish music from 1929 to 1954. Concerned about the dearth of materials in the field, she created them. She published several books in the field including a Jewish songbook for children, *Gateway to Jewish Song* (1937), and *Heritage of Music: The Music of the Jewish People* (1972), as well as several cantatas on Jewish themes (some of which she coauthored with her husband Ira). She is the author of translations of Chanukah songs—including "Oh Chanukah, Oh Chanukah, come light the menorah" and "Who can retell the things that befell us?" that have become so universally accepted that they have become part of the folk culture of American Jewry. She received her Ph.D. from Hebrew Union College–Jewish Institute of Religion in 1966 and taught there from 1966 to 1979. She also taught at the Reconstructionist Rabbinical College from 1978 to 1981. Through her long career, Eisenstein played an important role in promoting the idea of a distinctive Jewish music and influenced several generations of students to advance the field.

Given the movement's early commitment to egalitarianism and the fact that it took form as a separate denomination in the midst of the feminist struggle, it is not surprising that women have held top leadership positions in the movement from the start. Joy Levitt was the first female president of the Reconstructionist Rabbinical Association, from 1987 to 1989, followed by Sandy Sasso, 1989 to 1991, and Barbara Penzer, 1997 to 1999. Joy Levitt also served as editor of the *Reconstructionist* magazine from 1989 to 1993. Of the 226 Reconstructionist rabbis today, 105 are women. Over half of the current rabbinical students are women. In 1996, Kolot: The Center for Jewish Women's and Gender Studies was established at the Reconstructionist Rabbinical College to educate and influence future Jewish leaders.

The history of women in Conservative and Reconstructionist Judaism in America is one of increasing inclusion and acceptance into the mainstream of American Jewish religious life—both public and private. By the last quarter of the twentieth century, women had moved to the forefront of leadership in many areas, strengthening both denominations with their talent, wisdom, and commitment.

SOURCES: The most comprehensive sourcebook on American Jewish women is *Jewish Women in America*, ed. Paula E. Hyman and Deborah Dash Moore (1997). See also Women's League Archives, New York, New York, especially Mathilde Schechter, "Aims and Ideals of the Women's League," May 1918, "Mathilde Schechter" file. Mel Scult, "The Baale Boste Reconsidered: The Life of Mathilde Roth Schechter (*MRS*)," *Modern Judaism* (February 1987): 1–2A; Mel Scult, "Mrs. Mathilde Roth Schechter: Her Life and Letters" (unpublished manuscript); Jacob Kohn, "The Beauty of Mrs. Schechter's Character," *United Synagogue Recorder* (October 1924); Pamela S. Nadell, *Conservative Judaism in America: A Biographical Dictionary and Sourcebook* (1988); Pamela S. Nadell, *Women Who Would Be Rabbis* (1998); *Seventy-five Years of Vision and Voluntarism* (1992); United Synagogue of America, *They Dared to Dream: A History of National Women's League, 1918–68* (1967); *Women's League Outlook* (1930–); Deborah M. Melamed, *The Three Pillars: Life, Practice and Thought for the Jewish Woman* (1927); *Conservative Judaism and Jewish Law*, ed. Seymour Siegel (1977); Sylvia Barack Fishman, *A Breath of Life: Feminism in the American Jewish Community* (1993); Simon Greenberg, ed., *The Ordination of Women as Rabbis* (1988); Paula E. Hyman, "The Introduction of Bat Mitzvah in Conservative Judaism in Postwar America," *YIVO Annual* 19 (1990): 133–146; Marshall Sklare, *Conservative Judaism* (1972); Beth S. Wenger, "The Politics of Women's Ordination," in *Tradition Renewed*, ed. Jack Wertheimer (1997); Jack Wertheimer, *Conservative Synagogues and Their Members* (1996); Rebecca T. Alpert, "A Feminist Takes Stock of Reconstructionism," *Reconstructionist* 54 (1989): 18–19; Rebecca Alpert and Goldie Milgram, "Women in the Reconstructionist Rabbinate," *Religious Institutions and Women's Leadership*, ed. Catherine Wessinger (1996); and http://www.rrc.edu/, the Web site of Reconstructionist Rabbinical College.

ORTHODOX JEWISH WOMEN IN AMERICA: DIVERSITY, CHALLENGES, AND COMING OF AGE
Blu Greenberg

ORTHODOX JEWISH WOMEN have lived more than three centuries of Jewish life on these shores. What they have shared in common across the centuries is their ability to remain faithful to Jewish tradition while acculturating to America's ways, a highly complex task given America's openness and its melting-pot nature. Still, three centuries is no small measure of time. Despite its relatively small size and shared mission, this group is marked by a high degree of diversity. The diversity reflects, in part, the many definitions of Orthodoxy, ranging from ultra right to left wing post-modern. But it also reflects the differences in time and in country of origin as the Orthodox emigrated to this country.

There have been four major waves of Jewish immigration, and Orthodox Jewish women were represented and played a vital role in each. Indeed, it was the arrival of women that marks the beginning of Jewish settlement in this land. As is widely recorded, Jews date their presence here to September 1654, when twenty-three Jewish persons arrived in New Amsterdam from Recife, Brazil. History also records that other Jews had arrived earlier, but unique to the Recife group were the six women among the twenty-three. The presence of women meant that families would grow, and communities could be built. The single Jewish male immigrants of earlier days did not constitute a viable Jewish presence.

In each immigration, women came as members of families, as wives and daughters. Quickly they set down family roots and added stability. But significant numbers also came as single women, pioneering spirits who braved the dual challenges of being uprooted from their homes in the old country and adapting to a new language and culture. The after-pull of these single women, whose siblings often followed them, added to their enormous influence on Jewish life in America.

The first Jewish immigrants from Recife were Sephardim, or Spanish Jews, descendants of Jews from Spain and Portugal who had sought refuge in South America as they fled the Spanish Inquisition of 1492. Although they did not call themselves "Orthodox" (the term "Orthodoxy" did not enter the lexicon until the mid-nineteenth century, in response to the rise of European Reform Judaism), their religious behavior and modes of worship were guided by the same dictates of Rabbinic Judaism (the interpretation of Jewish law according to the wisdom of the Rabbis) that later came to be called Orthodox Judaism. In the late 1900s, the Sephardic communities and the synagogues they had built two centuries earlier would also self-apply the term "Orthodox." Among these synagogues are the two oldest in America, Congregation Shearith Israel in New Amsterdam (New York), founded in 1654, and Congregation Yeshuat Israel (the Touro Synagogue) in Newport, Rhode Island, built in 1763.

In truth, this pioneering Sephardic immigration of the seventeenth and eighteenth centuries could hardly be called a wave. By 1820, there were still only 5,000

Jewish settlers in North America, dispersed in small communities throughout the country. They lived as patriotic citizens trying to integrate themselves into the life of America, yet, at the same time, hold on to their distinct Jewish identity. This was no small task, certainly so for the women who carried the major responsibility for maintaining the household, as Jewish women had done for centuries wherever they lived. From individual letters and records of these first two centuries in America, we know that Jewish women dedicated themselves to the task of transmitting the practice of their faith to the next generation and concerned themselves that their children marry within the faith. The second major immigration took place between 1820 and 1880, when approximately 300,000 Jews arrived, primarily from Germany and central Europe. Jews from these lands were known as Ashkenazim, and most of these second wave immigrants were non-Orthodox, having already embraced liberal Reform Judaism in Europe. These Reform Jews proceeded to build community institutions that reflected their religious beliefs: a Jewish identity that was wide open to acculturation and assimilation in the New World.

Immigrants of this second wave came less for relief

While this Orthodox mother and daughter engage in an ancient tradition of hand washing, new values are also influencing their lives. There has been tremendous change in women's lives everywhere, even in what we tend to think of as insulated religious communities faithfully carrying forward ancient beliefs and practices. © 2004 Gale Zucker/www.gzucker.com.

from persecution than to find opportunity. They succeeded, both culturally and economically, and they built grand synagogues in major cities throughout the United States, many of which still stand today. The immigration of 1820–1880 also included a smaller number of Orthodox immigrants, and they, as well as the Sephardim who preceded them, followed this model of building stately synagogues.

The Orthodox were influenced by this second immigration group in other ways: the liberal Jewish women of the mid-nineteenth century created institutions—the independent benevolent societies and social service organizations—that helped Jewish women at every point along the religious identity spectrum to integrate into this new society. Not only were generations of Orthodox immigrants given aid, but the institutional structures built by liberal Jews also served as powerful models for Orthodox women of future immigrations.

The major immigration wave of Orthodox Jews began in the latter part of the nineteenth century. From 1880 until 1924, when the United States' Open Door policy began to be reversed, more than 2.5 million Jews arrived. These Ashkenazim came mostly from small towns in Russia and Poland. A great part of this immigration was fueled by religious persecution and discrimination in Eastern Europe. After each new series of anti-Semitic pogroms, thousands of Jews fled to escape the violence. The Orthodox Jews were mostly poor and Yiddish speaking. Their gradual acculturation in America took a great toll on their traditional way of life. By the thousands, women and men alike quickly abandoned the religious strictures with which they had grown up. The costs and gains for a woman who made that journey out of tradition were significant. Yet, women who stayed Orthodox were deeply committed to their way of life, and this commitment reflected itself in their work of community building.

The fourth immigration, consisting of some 400,000 Jews, began in the 1930s prior to World War II and resumed again after 1945, intersected by the war. The prewar group was fleeing Hitler's net as it spread across Europe; the post-war immigrants were survivors, hoping to rebuild their lives in the aftermath. The Nazis made no distinction between liberal and Orthodox Jews in their extermination campaign. Orthodox Jews who had heretofore considered America an unholy land, a place where strict observance of the law would be threatened by the open society, now desired only to leave Europe as quickly as possible. Haredi (Ultra Orthodox) Jews who were part of the prewar yeshiva worlds of Poland and Hungary emigrated, as did Hasidic Jews, remnants of some of the great Hasidic dynasties of Eastern Europe. In addition to the relatively small number of Hasidim and Haredim able to escape or survive the war, this immigrant population also included modern Orthodox Jews. Each of the groups along the Orthodox spectrum made a large impact on the existent American Jewish community. And each helped to reverse the drain Orthodoxy had suffered in the Americanization of previous immigrations.

One more immigration with identifiable contours should be referenced: the Jews of the Soviet Union. They came largely after the fall of the Iron Curtain in the 1980s. However, having been cut off from the Jewish tradition since the days of Stalin, most of these immigrants were of secular intellectual backgrounds and left little impact on Orthodox life in America.

In addition to the relatively distinct immigration waves, two social forces of the postwar period, fundamentalism and feminism, were to shape the character and public face of American Orthodox women. Both movements were responses to modernity: the *baal teshuva* movement, somewhat akin to "born again" Christianity, wished to reject the universalizing, difference-leveling, melting-pot tendencies of modern America, and embraced Orthodox fundamentalism in its place. The *baalot teshuva* (returning Jewish women) came primarily from secular and liberal backgrounds; as adults, they voluntarily accepted a strictly religious way of life. This was a clear reversal of the prewar generations pattern of Orthodoxy. Orthodox feminism took a different route. Drawn primarily from the modern Orthodox community, these women welcomed the values of contemporary culture. They embraced the new idea of gender equality as a means of heightening their Jewish commitment; they utilized the principles and standards of feminism as a means by which to enter more fully into the religious life of the community.

These, then, are the general differentiations and sources of diversity among Orthodox Jewish women in America. But what are their commonalities? What defines them as Orthodox women?

Shared Values

All Orthodox women perceive themselves to be inheritors of Rabbinic Judaism. All share a belief in the divinity of the Torah (starting with the five books of Moses). All affirm the binding nature of halakha, Jewish law and teachings of the Rabbis. All are careful to keep the Sabbath and other holy days. All abide by *kashrut,* the kosher food laws which include the purchase and preparation of meat that has been ritually slaughtered and the separation of meat and milk in cooking and serving, which requires double sets of dishes and utensils.

Orthodox women accept the laws of family purity which forbid sex during menstruation and seven days thereafter. These days of abstinence are concluded by a woman's ritual immersion in the waters of the *mikveh* (the ritual bath house where Jews fully immerse in water in order to purify themselves). This purification rite for women is biblical in origin and distinguishes Orthodox women from non-Orthodox. Because of its intimate and very private nature, the degree to which early American Orthodox women were able to observe these laws is generally not known, and the construction of the mikveh, the ritual bath house, was not amply recorded in the annals of early Jewish communities here.

Orthodox women accept differentiated roles for male and female in community settings, liturgical responsibilities, and household ritual, though certain aspects of this differentiation are currently coming under reconsideration by some women. Yet, all Orthodox women abide by the norms of separate seating for men and women in the synagogue. And even as they uniformly hold the study of sacred texts to be the highest value in Judaism, the majority of Orthodox women until very recently accepted the reality of differentiated educational opportunities for male and female.

Overwhelmingly, Orthodox women through the generations assumed the major responsibility for creating the special Sabbath and holiday ambience in the home. This includes festive meals and guests. The house should sparkle and glow. Attire should be special, children's as well as adults; Mary Janes for little girls become "Shabbos shoes." All this entailed extensive advance preparation of household and food, since the tasks of cleaning, laundry, shopping, cooking, polishing, and so on were forbidden activities on the holy day itself. The Sabbath is not a day for dusting or baking or ironing. Instead, the day should be spent in synagogue worship, Torah study, home rituals, and leisurely family feasts. Preparation for Sabbath and holy days was no small accomplishment, and the division of labor worked quite well for most women throughout Jewish history.

Gender differentiation in halakhic Judaism extended not only to religious responsibilities but also to public versus private roles. In general, women were primarily defined by the Rabbis of ancient times as "inside" persons. The phrase, "All honor of the king's daughter is within" (Psalms 45:14), was applied in the Talmud as an interpretive tag line to laws that exempted or excluded women from certain public roles. The psalmist did not explain "within" what, but the rabbis of every generation understood it to mean within the home and family, within the interior private spaces, within the boundaries of female modesty. Thus, though women were equally obligated to observe all the negative precepts (Thou shalt not . . .) as well as almost all the positive commandments, the few exemptions for women had to do largely with public roles and communal space: women were exempt from daily communal prayer, daily study of sacred texts in the House of Study (which also served as access route to religious leadership), and presence in the religious courts of law. It is no accident that three laws that came to be synonymous with "women's laws", i.e., *niddah, challah,* and *nerot* (family purity laws, the consecration of the dough in baking bread, and the lighting of Sabbath and holiday candles), were laws observed in the home or, as in the case of *niddah,* associated with very private personal behavior.

Leadership Roles

Given the combination of general American sociological constraints and Jewish halakhic ones, it is not surprising that for the first century and a half of Orthodox life in America, women do not emerge as national or religious leaders. No individual Orthodox woman of record rises to special prominence, and no national women's enterprises of that time have been brought down through history, a situation not unlike that of European Jewry in preceding centuries. But the good works of American Orthodox women were not totally confined to the home, nor were they devoid of female collegiality. To begin with, they formed auxiliaries, sisterhoods, and benevolent societies of institutions that primarily serviced the males: the synagogue and, to a lesser extent, the religious schools for boys.

The women's groups had several models before them. One was the *chessed* (acts of loving-kindness) societies formed by Orthodox men in local American communities. These, in turn, were based on the model of men's *chessed* groups in their countries of origin, structures that were honed in the separatist, second-class status, self-contained, and often vulnerable communities of premodern Europe where Jews had lived for fifteen centuries. Underlying all such societies was the powerful Jewish concept of interdependency of the "family," as expressed in the ancient Talmudic dictum, "All Israelites are responsible for one another" (*Babylonian Talmud, Tractate Shevuot* 39a). Charitable societies of many different kinds were formed so as not to leave the care of others to chance or to random acts of kindness.

Another factor in Orthodox women's new associations was the powerful and very present model of Protestant women's societies. The conventional Protestant title, "female benevolent society," was commonly used for Orthodox women's sisterhoods. Although there were many parallels in the focus on good works and in the programs created to carry them out, such as sewing

clubs and bake sales, the Jewish societies were also driven by distinctive Jewish concerns. America was the land of hope and of opportunity for all. Still, Jews felt a profound sense of minority status in this new country. Laboring under deep memories of anti-Semitism in the places they had left, these new communities felt an added responsibility not to let members of their faith become a burden on society. As in all immigrant populations, there were many newcomers who quickly became indigent. The women of the synagogue saw it as their responsibility to help the downtrodden in their own communities. In many of the charters or mission statements of these organizations are the words, "care for the indigent," or "to help our needy country-people to become self-supporting."

While women shared with men a general responsibility for the community's quality of life, in many instances the ladies auxiliaries took special interest in helping women. The Benevolent Hebrew Female Society of Congregation She'arith Israel, the earliest synagogue founded in America, states in its charter the task of "succoring of the indigent female." Widows, orphans, and other women in need were the natural focus of women's groups. Help for pregnant, birthing, and nursing mothers was a popular agenda for many of these groups in an age when maternity brought with it major upheaval.

Religious orphans became the special concern of Orthodox women groups. The major thrust of the German and, later, Russian immigration was to Americanize the children. Orphanages were an opportunity to take up this task. Jewish orphanages took in not only children whose parent or parents had died, but also children whose parents were alive but in need of temporary help in raising them. Children from religious homes initially placed in "Americanizing" orphanages had the religious stuffing knocked out of them. Such children often testified to feeling uncomfortable after returning to their own homes. Therefore, Orthodox women formed their own orphanage societies. They supervised and monitored these places so that the staff would adhere to the laws of kosher food, the observance of Shabbat and holidays, daily prayer, Jewish instruction, recital of grace after meals and the *Shema Yisrael* prayer, the central Jewish creed at bedtime, "Hear Oh Israel, the Lord our God, the Lord is One" (Deuteronomy 6:4).

Among the unique tasks for women was the formation of a women's *hevra kadisha,* the holy burial society. An integral part of traditional Jewish death rituals is the purification of the dead body by washing and dressing it in shrouds before burial. Blessings are recited as clear waters are poured over the entire body. Because of modesty considerations, separate men's and women's Hebrew burial societies were formed. In a letter recommending to "the ladies of Jewish persuasion of congregation Shearith Israel" that they create a woman's *hevra kadisha*, they are reminded that, "separated by peculiar laws and customs from the rest of mankind, there are none who can appreciate our situation, ascertain our wants or gratify our sympathies so readily as those of our own race and persuasion."

"Taking the bride to the marriage canopy," i.e., helping the bride to make a wedding and furnish her home was a common task of women's societies, Orthodox and non-Orthodox alike. Beginning in the mid-1800s, marriage was a primary motive for immigration among Jewish women. In many European states, Jews suffered restrictions such as the Bavarian *matrikel* which allowed only one Jewish son to marry and remain at home as heir to his father's estate. The chances of a Jewish woman finding a husband were slim. Thus, though the idea of a single woman leaving home and traveling across the ocean to a new country was not common to most immigrant groups, among Jews single women of marriageable age emigrated at the first opportunity. The Jewish American community already in place understood its responsibility to help these single women and regarded such direct assistance to the bride as wholly in the spirit of ancient Jewish tradition.

Other tasks undertaken by Orthodox women's auxiliaries were visiting the sick, creating burial societies, giving comfort and creating support networks for family survivors in the death of a loved one, feeding and clothing the poor, supplying kosher food to the elderly and infirm, and raising money for synagogue improvement projects. As time went on, some of the Orthodox women's groups, modeled after the Reform ladies auxiliaries, expanded their care to include the general neighborhood, not only to members of their own faith or immediate community. The Sisterhood of the Congregation Orach Chaim in Manhattan, for example, states as its general purpose: "to help the poor of the surrounding neighborhood. Activities include providing religious instruction for 400 children of the poor as well as supplying clothing to the needy children and creating mothers sewing circles." Also, as time went on, Orthodox women reached into the civic establishments. Note the broad range of activities of an Orthodox sisterhood in New York: "Purpose: to do social, educational, religious and philanthropic work by personal service. Activities: maintain Neighborhood House at 133 Eldridge Street, daily religious services and Talmud Torah, clubs, classes, kindergarten, entertainment, dancing, lectures, reading room, relief and neighborhood visiting, sewing circles to provide garments for the poor. Probation work in the Night and Day Courts with delinquent girls. Cooperation with reformatories and rescue homes."

Over the course of time, when "their own" were not engaged in the mighty struggle of resettlement, these women's organizations would indulge themselves in purely social events such as fashion shows and card games, so often associated with sisterhoods and ladies auxiliaries. But for the better part of their history, and for the larger focus of their work, sisterhoods were bent on helping others. Many of their charters resonate with a verse taken from the Talmud that is recited by Jews every morning in their daily prayer. It reminds a Jew that the tasks to complete in this world are "honoring father and mother, practice of kindness, early attendance at the house of study morning and evening, hospitality to strangers, visiting the sick, dowering the bride, attending the dead to the grave, devotion in prayer, and making peace between fellow men; and the study of Torah excels above all" (*Mishnah Peah* 1:1).

In the process of doing good, Orthodox women gained much from these associations. Sisterhoods served as vehicles of the socialization process for women who suffered the loss of extended family relationships that nurtured them in Europe. These societies and auxiliaries created a proto family in which immigrant women learned to become Americanized, democratized, and acculturated. They learned to run for office, hold elections, vote democratically, pay dues, keep budgets, take minutes, write by-laws, and follow organizational procedures. Considering that this was an era in which wives were given weekly allowances by their husbands, never signed checks or held joint bank accounts, these were tremendous steps forward. In the camaraderie of their shared work, women also learned about fashion and child-rearing, which contributed further to their acculturation. These competencies served them in good stead a generation or two later, when they would begin to form the national women's organizations of the next century.

National Organizations

At the turn of the twentieth century, Jewish Orthodox men's groups increasingly began to federate and form national organizations. Women's auxiliaries, which had until then acted quite independently, were asked to join the consolidated charities. Joining posed a challenge to women's autonomy and independence of thought and action. In some instances, women came aboard and were absorbed into the new organizations. They continued to make important contributions but did not continue to hold the primary leadership roles. In other instances, women decided to maintain or to form separate organizations. It was these separate national women's organizations that left their greatest mark, both on the women and on the community at large. Typically, the women's organizations created girl groups or young women's divisions to carry forth their values into the next generation. Indeed most of these organizations reflected the powerful interconnectedness between Orthodox women of America and their spiritual home in the land of Israel. These women felt themselves to be faithful and proud citizens of this country, yet also affirmed their responsibility as Jews to protect the national Jewish homeland of Israel. They represent multiple loyalty at its finest.

While each national women's group is different, the stories are quite similar, like variations on a theme. The Mizrachi Women's Organization of America, (now AMIT) is the most prominent and largest (currently 40,000 members) of Orthodox women's organizations and its founding story is a prime example. Mizrachi Women was founded by Bessie Gotsfeld (1888–1962). Born Bailke Goldstein in Przemysl, Poland, the Hasidic heartland of Galicia, Bessie emigrated to the United States in 1905 with her father Leon, stepmother Adela, and five younger siblings whom she helped raise after her young mother died. Bessie remained close to her family all her life, and they were her most valuable cohorts in building Mizrachi Women.

In 1909 Bessie married Mendel Gotsfeld, her English tutor. They settled in Seattle, Washington, in 1911, where they remained until 1919. Prewar Seattle was flooded with immigrants who, escaping the pogroms, had fled to Siberia and from there crossed the Pacific Ocean. Many Jewish refugees arrived in Seattle, and Bessie and Mendel, who were childless, reached out to help settle them.

Their home was open to all. One important guest was Rabbi Meir Berlin, a leader in the Mizrachi (men's) movement. Mizrachi had been founded in Europe in the late nineteenth century by a minority group of Orthodox rabbis who supported Theodore Herzl's call for a Jewish homeland. But the group soon parted ways with the general Zionist movement over a resolution of the fifth Zionist Congress in 1901 that advocated only national and secular education goals. Mizrachi wanted a religious educational system that would meet the needs of the religious minority in the Jewish community of Palestine. Its motto became, "The land of Israel, for the people Israel, in accordance with the Torah of Israel."

Mizrachi was deeply involved in buying and building up the land, and supporting synagogues, schools, and student dormitories in Palestine. Mizrachi raised funds for its projects by sending representatives to Jewish communities in the United States to deliver an address and form local men's chapters of Mizrachi. They did this in every city they visited, which is what Rabbi Berlin was doing in the Gotsfeld home in Seattle. The meeting of Meir Berlin and Bessie Gotsfeld generated the idea that simultaneous to forming men's chapters, women's chapters should also be formed. The women's job was to collect money and turn it over to visiting speakers. All around the country, women ran functions to supplement the men's funds; in fact, they brought in greater totals albeit in smaller individual contributions.

By 1919, Bessie Gotsfeld returned to New York and was active in establishing local Mizrachi women's groups in Brooklyn. There was a desire among the women to take on their own projects. Rabbi Meir Berlin urged Bessie to federate the individual women's groups. In November of 1924, the Achios Mizrachi (sisters of Mizrachi) was formed by representatives of the various New York groups. Adela Goldstein, Bessie's stepmother, became its first president. The founding members paid dues of $74 apiece, no small sum in those days. The concept of a national religious women's movement was a bold idea for Orthodox women at the time. They understood it to mean that they would have complete autonomy over funds they raised and full jurisdiction over their projects.

But to those rabbis who were the fund-raisers, the new organization was simply a more effective fund-raising engine. At the next Achios meeting, Rabbi Y. L. Fishman, a leader of Mizrachi (the generic title remained with the men's organization for several decades longer), was the honored guest. After his speech, when he realized how much money the women had raised, he insisted that the funds be turned over to him. Bessie replied that the ladies would consider his request and inform him of their decision at some other time. He was stunned and angry. How could they not turn over monies for Palestine, he insisted! Bessie calmly thanked him for his remarks and expressed regret that he had misunderstood, because the women had every intention of sending the monies to Palestine. She promised that representatives would meet with him the following day. It was the turning point for the organization.

The monies were not turned over. When the story became known, many additional women joined the group, a response that has become almost predictable today but was quite feisty then. In 1925, at the men's national conference in Cleveland, a delegation of women participated and formally constituted the national Mizrachi Women's Organization of America. And so a national religious women's movement came into being.

Gotsfeld volunteered to go to Palestine and survey local conditions in search of a suitable project for the newly formed organization. Travel to Palestine in 1926 was not a simple affair, especially for an ailing diabetic woman. Her first visit, personally financed, would last for six months. She returned with a novel project, a vocational high school for girls. Bessie's recommendation was inspired by a convergence of three factors: the burgeoning but male-centered religious Zionist educational system, her personal childhood experience, and the activities of the men's Mizrachi groups.

The Zionist rabbis who had emigrated to Palestine from Europe were responsible for the religious segment of the dual educational system. Operating out of the yeshiva model, they established religious high schools for boys but did not trouble themselves with girls' education. Orthodox female teenagers were overlooked and had few opportunities to gain knowledge and skills. An energetic, creative religious female adolescent had the choice of staying at home helping her mother with housework and child care while waiting for marriage, or working at a low level job such as maid or textile worker. For Americanized Bessie, herself progressively educated in Poland and America, this was deplorable. She had before her the model of men's Mizrachi work in the United States pursuing a commitment to provide a Jewish education for boys and girls in every city of sizeable Jewish population.

The women understood they had to be politic in proceeding with their novel school. So as not to rile the Jewish establishment, they finessed the language in a way that would forestall objections. "Domestic science," which included the subjects of cooking, baking, housework, laundry, and sewing was part of the first curriculum. Soon, the agricultural curriculum was added, eventually followed by courses in crafts and secretarial skills, followed by the educational sciences and all the academic disciplines. It was a nonconfrontational approach, and it worked. The school opened in 1933 and was the first of scores of institutions to be built by Mizrachi Women (later renamed AMIT Women) during the next eight decades. Most of the AMIT institutions had as their mission the goal of taking disadvantaged children and turning their lives around, classic women's work. But the second goal, to make women productive, creative, equal members of society was equally central to its institutions. AMIT produced many leaders of Israeli society.

AMIT also recognized talent and availed itself of it. The most significant Jewish female educator of the twentieth century was Nechama Leibowitz (1905–1997). She first came to prominence through Mizrachi Women, which engaged her as a teacher in its institution in the early 1940s and 1950s, when women teachers of religious subjects were a rarity. Subsequently, she was invited to teach in seminaries and men's educational institutions. Though Nechama, as she was lovingly called by generations of students, never set foot outside Israel from the day she arrived from Germany, she managed to educate most contemporary modern Orthodox American rabbis and educators who studied with her as part of a year's course in Israel.

AMIT played a significant role prior to and following World War II in housing and educating victims of the Holocaust. In the 1930s and 1940s, the organization had grown sufficiently strong to take in thousands of orphans from Europe and settle them in religious homes. This was at a time when many new immigrants to Israel were being forcibly secularized under the theory that a modern state required modern citizens. Many leaders believed that one could not be both modern and religious. In those pre-multiculturalist days, secular Zionist leadership did not hesitate to place religious children into secular institutions. AMIT's alternative religious schools were a particularly important contribution.

The first children's village was built in Raanana, Israel, in 1947 and was appropriately named K'far Batya (Bessie's village). It was built with her eye for detail about the dignity and personal needs of every individual child. On the theory that a woman's encyclopedia has room for personal anecdote, I take the liberty of sharing one that I believe reflects her work: Bessie Gotsfeld was a friend of my parents in Seattle, and the relationship was maintained throughout her life. In 1956, as a student in Israel, I was given a private tour by her of K'far Batya. At that time the school had opened its doors to the first group of Ethiopian children who were brought to Israel. As we walked the grounds, I recall her pointing with pride to the curtains on the windows of the girls' dormitories, small, separate one-story buildings that housed three or four girls each. She commented that it was important that each girl have a sense of privacy. What struck me as so remarkable was that the Ethiopian girls had come from villages in which they lived in one room tents, housing families of ten or twelve members. In all likelihood, these girls had never had a moment of privacy or a bed of their own for all their growing years, yet here was this diminutive women concerned with their self-esteem and self dignity.

Today there are fifty-five AMIT schools, youth villages, and child havens across Israel. Several hundred thousand children have received care and education in the projects. In time, AMIT was recognized for its educational competence by being named as the official sponsor of religious technical education in Israel. Many graduates, including Holocaust survivors who were nurtured back to health, became teachers and leaders in both America and Israel. Although AMIT's activities are dedicated to building Israel and providing an educational and religious environment for students there, in recent years the chapters have understood their mandate to be more than fund-raising. Like many women's organizations that have moved away in recent times from the fashion shows and card luncheons of yesteryear, AMIT'S monthly meetings feature speakers, discussion groups, and study of texts.

Women's Branch of the Union of Orthodox Jewish Congregations of America (UOJCA), is the national organization of Orthodox synagogue sisterhoods. It was founded in 1923 at the initiative of seven women from various sisterhoods in New York City, among them, the most prominent *rebbetzins* (rabbis' wives) of the time. The name, Women's Branch, tells its story: it was the women's arm of a national organization that was founded in 1902 to unify the growing number of modern Orthodox synagogues around the country and to initiate joint or nationwide projects. Inasmuch as only men filled synagogue leadership roles, UOJCA was in fact a men's organization. Yet by the 1920s, all its constituent synagogues boasted individual sisterhoods. Two decades after the founding of the UOJCA, a similar organization linking the sisterhoods was established, a time lag appropriate to the prevailing view that synagogue leadership was a man's purview.

Once up and running, however, Women's Branch accomplished a number of outstanding and lasting achievements, many of them not known nor properly credited in the wider community. While each sisterhood remained independent—allowing for differences among individual congregations and rabbis—the national group undertook projects that were of larger scope. These projects were appropriate to the grand mission of Women's Branch: to unite and strengthen all Orthodox Jewish women and to spread the knowledge of traditional Judaism.

One of its earliest projects dealt with kosher food supervision. The women's goal was to make it easier and less complicated to observe the central Jewish laws of *kashrut*, particularly for the Jewish homemaker, a woman. Women's Branch convened a kashrut committee to answer questions about kosher food. Their work was the beginning of nationalizing the kosher food industry. Out of their own pockets, the women paid a rabbi to investigate products and factories, and they worked diligently to persuade companies to use kosher ingredients. From this project grew one of the main enterprises of the UOJCA today, the Kashruth Division. This Division is a principle source of funding for the UOJCA and has been a primary source of its influence. The Division's UO certification is found on thousands of kosher food products worldwide.

In the 1920s, Women's Branch raised funds to build a boy's dormitory for Yeshiva College, now Yeshiva University in New York City. Women's Branch helped establish a post–high school Hebrew Teachers Training Institute for Girls. This institution was later renamed Teachers Institute for Women (TIW), and was absorbed into Yeshiva University. This author attended TIW, without knowing until this very writing that the school grew out of these women's initiative. Women's Branch also published a series of children's books, sponsored Braille Torah and prayer books for blind bar mitzvah boys and large print works such as a Passover Haggadah for the elderly, and helped finance libraries and mikvehs in Israel. In the 1930s it formed a peace committee of representatives from many of the major Jewish organizations to work together on preventing World War II looming on the horizon.

In the eighty years since its inception, Women's Branch has responded to changing needs in the Ortho-

dox community. In 1948, with the establishment of the state of Israel and the outbreak of the War of Independence, Women's Branch organized shipments of food and clothing. Sisterhood women everywhere knit warm caps for Israeli soldiers. In recent years, as a response to the phenomenon of late marriage and the increasing number of singles in the Orthodox community, Women's Branch organized "Bashert" (your intended one), a dating and matchmaking service. For the past twenty years, the growing number of Orthodox women joining the work force has led to the decline of sisterhoods everywhere. Women's Branch also weakened somewhat, but like other women's organizations, it is now the process of redefining new areas of activism for itself.

Emunah Women, like AMIT, is a national religious women's Zionist organization, but while AMIT was founded in the United States, Emunah first took root in Israel and only later transplanted to these shores. In 1947, following the United Nations vote on partition, the women of the Religious Women's Workers Party of Israel (Irgun Hapoalot) recognized the need to form an alliance with diaspora Jewry. Toward that end, the chairperson, Tova Sanhedrai, traveled to the United States to seek partners. She approached several women's organizations but was rejected by all of them. She then organized a core group of individual American women who agreed to a partnership, and the Hapoel Hamizrachi Women's Organization was formed. Several years later, the American group renamed itself Emunah Women. Several years after that, the Israeli partner also adopted the name the American women had chosen, Emunah.

Emunah means faith, and its mission is to keep faith with the needy and downtrodden of Israel. Most of American Emunah's projects focus on social service, welfare, and education throughout Israel. Among them are: the Golden Age Centers (senior housing) as well as clubs and restaurants for the elderly, reflecting the organizational core value Emunah that older persons should not have to endure the loneliness of eating a meal without companionship. The organization also has created residential houses for children from troubled backgrounds, vocational junior and high schools for disadvantaged children, family counseling services, parenting classes and the like. One of its most recent projects has been the very successful Torah Arts School for Girls, a high school in Jerusalem where girls can study theater, dance, and the arts, subjects not often taught in religious schools where acting is perceived as conflicting with the concept of female modesty.

Branching out, Emunah also developed a Holocaust Resource Center in America. In Israel, the organization developed Emunah College which combines high tech and the arts in its curriculum. During the massive immigration from the Soviet Union to Israel, Emunah in

America helped to support the absorption process. Though the bulk of the United States chapters' activity focuses on Israel, Emunah sees as its American challenge countering assimilation and intermarriage. Thus, in this country it sponsors educational, cultural, and group-identity projects such as Hebrew language courses, after school clubs, seminars on Judaism, and a Bar/Bat Mitzvah program. A principle of "keeping faith" with Israel led to stress on visiting the Holy Land. To service this need, Emunah runs a strong travel department that sponsors tours throughout the year.

In 1979, a third national women's organization focused on Israel was founded; Women's Division of Shaare Zedek Medical Center. Shaare Zedek is an Orthodox hospital in Jerusalem that follows Jewish tradition in all aspects of running the hospital, such as kosher food, daily prayer services, Sabbath elevators (that operate without the passengers having to press floor buttons), and no elective medical procedures or unessential writing done on Sabbath or holidays. The hospital is open to all who seek its care, regardless of race of religion. Though its women's division has non-Orthodox members as well, the group is primarily Orthodox in its associations and activities. The main work of the Women's Division is to raise funds, but it also sponsors health seminars both in Israel and the United States.

Agudas N'Shei U'bnos Chabad (Organization of Women and Daughters of Chabad) was founded forty years ago. Unlike the other women's organizations, it was founded by a man, the Lubavitcher Rebbe. The Rebbe was and after his death still remains the charismatic leader of the Hasidic outreach movement, known as Lubavitch (its place of origin in Lithuania) or as Chabad, the Hebrew acronym for Wisdom, Understanding, and Knowledge which are three important categories of mystical teachings that guide the movement.

The work of Nshei (women of) Chabad is defined by the general mission of the Chabad movement: outreach to other Jews to help them assume responsibility for Torah and Mitzvos (commandments), greater knowledge of Judaism, and faithful practice of ritual and law that, according to the Rebbe, was a better way of comprehending God than through meditation. The mission statement adjures that "every Lubavitch woman and girl is an active participant" in these tasks of outreach, with special emphasis placed on those practices that are largely the prerogative of women. Thus, the role of women is to go to where the people are: "homes, universities and colleges, at street corners and shopping centers, hospitals, old-age homes and in prisons. The emphasis is on action; women must go out of their homes to do this sacred work. Indeed, that is what Lubavitch Women have done for several decades: going to remote places with their husbands to build Chabad communities, not isolating themselves but rather acting

as auxiliary outreach workers, teaching Judaism in their new communities." N'shei Chabad also boasts a women's speakers bureau, unusual for the ultra Orthodox community.

In its most recently published statement of purpose, N'Shei Chabad describes an additional task, one that reflects an internal division within the Lubavitch community about which N'Shei has taken a clear position: "In addition, in recent years, the Lubavitch women's organization has been intensely focused on virtually every aspect of the campaign to publicize and teach about the imminent redemption." Active in every sphere of the campaign (and in most cases on the forefront) from teaching classes, publishing materials, arranging global gatherings, advertising, to managing public relations and media, they received a remarkable number of blessings from the Rebbe MH"M (Hebrew acronym for Messiah the King) for these activities. Their well-known Reception for Moshiach (the Messiah), celebrated simultaneously by many thousands of women around the globe, was the prototype for all later activities which used media to publicize the Rebbe's message concerning Moshiach and the Rebbe's identity as Moshiach. The International Moshiach Congress for Women developed a campaign of "goodness and kindness to hasten the Redemption of humanity" and to offer financial support for Moshiach projects. The bottom line of the page reads, "Long Live our Master, Teacher and Rebbe, King Moshiach Forever." All of this activity has been undertaken since the Rebbe died several years ago. Clearly, the N'shei Chabad is centered in the messianic wing of the Chabad movement.

In addition to their emphasis on the Rebbe as Messiah, Lubavitch women's work includes: a project that facilitates observance of kashrut such as assisting families in koshering their kitchens or promoting displays of kosher products in supermarkets; promoting observance of family purity laws through classes for brides and grooms; encouraging girls over three to light Shabbat candles every Friday night (in contrast to most other Orthodox groups, where this ritual is assigned to grown women, not girls); increased education for women and girls; and organizing hospital visits to the sick. Even as they have embraced the new messianic impulse of Chabad, the women continue to reach out into the community. For example, it was N'Shei Chabad that began the process of healing the rift between blacks and Jews in Crown Heights, Brooklyn, following the riots there in 1994.

Women's Division of Young Israel, like Women's Branch of the Orthodox Union, was formed to augment the work of its parent body, the National Council of Young Israel. But unlike the other national Orthodox organizations, women were part of the parent body. Founded in 1912 by "15 visionary young men and women," the synagogue-based National Council of Young Israel was organized to counter that era's challenge of assimilation. In the early 1900s, a six-day work week was the norm and most job opportunities carried the obligation to work on the Sabbath. In addition to this outside threat to Sabbath attendance, the Orthodox synagogue itself was not inviting to modern youth. It was often Yiddish speaking and had an old-world feeling. Young people in the process of becoming Americanized drifted away from their parent's religious patterns of community worship. Young Israel was formed primarily to attract the youth by creating a "palatable synagogue experience that was user friendly to new immigrants and their subsequent generations."

A chain of synagogues sprang up around the country, each carrying the title of the national entity and the name of the locale, for example, "Young Israel of Riverdale." In addition to giving the service a more modern feeling, using English as the language for all but Hebrew prayer, other "Americanized" programs were created. Friday night lecture series in English, Saturday night dances, and a broad range of social, educational, and recreational programs all helped Young Israel to achieve its goals.

But the young get older. And the needs changed through the decades. Men and women's roles became more separate within the Young Israel community. As the number of constituent Young Israel synagogues grew, so did the number of sisterhoods, and the Women's Division was formed to serve the needs of branch sisterhoods throughout the country. Publications, training programs, and individual branch consultations were among the activities of the national women's group.

Today, Women's Division is comprised of over 150 Young Israel sisterhoods in synagogues countrywide. Its members run the gamut, young and old, singles, married women, widows, grandmothers, those choosing careers and those not. Currently, Women's Division is undergoing a major transformation in programming to meet the needs of such a diverse group. Like so many Orthodox women's organizations that have enjoyed a long life, Women's Division has reinvented itself numerous times over the years. For example, an early enterprise was the college kosher kitchen program designed to make a traditional way of life easier to negotiate on campus. But two decades ago, eating kosher at most major universities no longer presented a problem, so that program was dropped. Today, Women's Division spends its time and money on current issues, such as family education programs and how to eliminate the scourge of domestic violence in the Orthodox community.

Women's Division happens to be the first national Orthodox, and perhaps first altogether of the denominations women's group, to harness the energy of a special group, *rebbetzins*. Operating behind the scenes, without remuneration in their individual communities, not formally organized or tapped into as a group, rebbetzins have nevertheless played significant roles in their communities, at times simply as role models or public "stars," but more often going far beyond such in their hands on work in community. Interestingly, just at the moment that the broader society, particularly the Christian church, is moving away from the two-person-one-salary clergy couple model, the National Council and Women's Division have recognized and lifted up this unique female leadership population. *The Rebbetzin's Letter*, something unimaginable twenty years ago, is now published five times a year. This rotating guest column is printed alongside *The Rabbi's Letter* and reaches 25,000 households and beyond. Women's Division also provides seminars for rebbetzins at an annual NCYI conference and Rabbinic Conferences.

Women's Division is not feminist in orientation. Moreover, the entire Orthodox community, of which it is an integral part, has shifted to the right. Yet, Young Israel was the first national group to recognize women in greater leadership roles. Its charter allows women to hold office up to and including the vice presidency of a synagogue, a charter item that predates feminism and has everything to do with the origins of Young Israel.

N'shei Agudah, or Agudah Women, is the female counterpart of a men's organization that represents the ultra Orthodox wing of the community. Though Agudath Israel of America (the men's organization) was formed before World War II, it rose to prominence during the war years as it tried to respond to the state of emergency facing the Jewish people and as ultra Orthodox refugees and survivors came to the United States. Because there is greater emphasis on separation of the sexes in the ultra Orthodox community, the creation of the women's group followed fairly soon.

The initial work of Agudah Women was to help resettle refugees, primarily in Israel. The American women met to organize food and clothing packages to send to Israel; they raised money to subsidize religious preschools, meeting the needs of a constituency blessed with many young children and facing the onslaught of changing social mores. The women also created an orphan home in Israel, based on the practices of an ultra Orthodox community that had been all but wiped out by the war.

In the 1950s, the primary work of Agudah Women in America was Shabbos group. Many Orthodox children were being educated in public schools and these Sabbath afternoon groups in local communities were a way of keeping the youth identified with their religious roots. Girls and boys groups were kept separate, as they were in most of the institutions of ultra-Orthodoxy.

Forty years ago, Agudah Women also created its version of the Fresh Air Fund, a summer camp scholarship fund that allowed needy children to choose any Orthodox camp they wished. Most of its programs today are social service in nature: matchmaking, lunch-lecture-exercise programs for elderly women, support groups for care givers and for "mothers of multiples," and a matchmaking service for older singles, which, in this community of early marriage expectations, begins with individuals over age twenty-five.

Among its unique projects are the Doula programs begun at a Brooklyn hospital in a heavily Orthodox neighborhood. Because ultra Orthodox tenets do not allow a husband to touch his wife during labor or be present with her in the delivery room (based on laws of family purity and values of modesty), women volunteer to be with the birthing mother. The waiting list of volunteers to serve as doulas is quite long.

Agudah Women, like the other women's organizations, has reinvented itself periodically, seeing its strength as a start-up organization. Once an idea and activity is taken over by the community, Agudah Women let it fly free and they move on to another project. At every annual convention, the women's leadership gathers for a round table thinktank to determine where the next need lies.

The latest of Orthodox women's organization of national stature is the Jewish Orthodox Feminist Alliance, founded in April 1997. JOFA was formed in response to the overwhelming interest in gender issues within Orthodoxy expressed at an international conference on that subject held a few months earlier. An unprecedented 1,400 women and their male supporters from all over the United States and from seven countries around the world participated. Until then, it was thought that Orthodox feminism was a radical, fringe element of the Orthodox community. The conference, and the one that followed one year later with 2,000 participants, placed the issue of equality for traditional women at the center of the modern Orthodox community's agenda, with a ripple effect into the right wing community. JOFA's mission is to expand women's roles within halakha, and chart new paths for women in the spiritual, intellectual, and ritual spheres of Jewish life. It also seeks to create a climate of equality for women in Orthodox communal institutions and social relationships.

Halakha, as mentioned at the outset, is the body of Jewish law and tradition that governs an Orthodox way of life. Many of the role divisions in Orthodoxy, such as women traditionally carrying secondary roles in the synagogue, houses of sacred study, and religious courts of law, have been codified into halakah over the centuries. Although Orthodox women today play increasingly public leadership roles in society at large, there is great resistance to tinkering with the roles set for women

by the tradition. Thus, for example, it is not surprising to find an Orthodox woman serving as judge in a civil court yet not be counted as part of the minyan, the quorum of ten men that constitutes the traditional Jewish congregation, and be quite content with that dichotomy in her life.

The agenda of JOFA has been to integrate the values of equality into women's religious lives, yet remain within the Orthodox community in the process. Thus, it has proceeded at a different pace and with a different agenda than the feminist core of the liberal denominations of Judaism. Orthodox feminists have taken care to conform to the boundaries of halakha even as they press for reinterpretation of the law to achieve greater equality and dignity for women. For example, Jewish divorce law favors the husband in that he is the one empowered to write the *gett*, the writ of divorce. Some men exploit this position, refusing to grant their wives a *gett* for reasons of spite or blackmail or as leverage in a custody battle (also blackmail). A woman without a *gett* is an *agunah*, anchored to an absentee husband and not able to get on with her life.

JOFA's Agunah Task Force addresses this problem of inequity and abuse. It monitors the rabbinic courts, as matters of marriage and divorce come under their jurisdiction, to ensure that women are treated fairly by the court's judges; it promotes dissemination of alternate halakhic methodologies that eliminate the husband's legal advantage in divorce proceedings; it raises community consciousness regarding the problem; and recently it helped create a powerful and effective international link for all groups and individuals, spanning forty-seven countries, that deal with this thorny issue. Being halakhic, and being an Orthodox feminist means not going outside the Jewish law for a resolution to a problem. A person not committed to halakha might be satisfied with a civil divorce when encountering difficulty within the religious system. Yet Orthodox feminists are committed to working within halakhic parameters to resolve problems and prevent abuse.

Among JOFA'S initiatives are: biannual conferences on feminism and Orthodoxy that bring scholars and participants together to deal with a broad range of issues, from cutting edge ones such as egalitarian Orthodox prayer services to traditional ones such as women's modesty in dress and hair covering in the context of women's self expectations in public life today; *Shabbat T'lamdeini*, a designated Sabbath of the year when synagogues around the world recognize and celebrate the contributions of women's new Torah learning and leadership; a gender and Orthodoxy curriculum project that designs and implements curricular materials which integrate the ethical messages of feminism with traditional Jewish teachings; publication of books on Orthodox women and ritual, such as new rituals for naming baby girls, bat mitzvah ceremonies, marriage rites, and death and mourning rituals.

One example of the development of women's role in ritual is the recitation of kaddish, the mourner's prayer. This prayer is recited by the mourner for a full eleven months after the death of an immediate family member. Every day, three times a day at synagogue services, the mourner recites the kaddish and the congregation responds. In past centuries, women mourners were neither obligated nor included in this disciplined prayer ritual. But women are now beginning to take up the daily kaddish as a formal responsibility, and are finding it to be, as its ancient rabbinic creators intended, a most healing ritual in the presence of a nurturing community.

The Jewish Orthodox Feminist Alliance has not been without its critics in the community. There are those who argue that feminism is antithetical to Orthodox Judaism and that the new values of women's equality undermine both the Jewish family and halakhic authority. The organization, however, sees itself as working to reinforce the centrality of the Jewish family and the binding nature of halakha, even as it responds positively to the new social revolution of these times.

Education

Orthodox women's education has been in the process of unfolding for almost two centuries now. Several factors have affected this process positively and negatively, among them: the extraordinarily high value that Judaism places on Torah study and sacred learning; the universal phenomenon of all pre-feminist cultures preventing women access to religious and intellectual leadership roles and the codification into halakha of these limits on Jewish women; the model of American public schooling for boys and girls alike; and two innovative Jewish educational experiments of nineteenth- and twentieth-century Europe. With the advent of new values of equality for women today, these forces have come together in a remarkable way, creating change in Orthodox women's lives that is greater than change in any other area of Jewish life.

From time immemorial, Torah study—which encompasses not only the study of the Five Books of Moses but all subsequent Jewish religious literature—has been accorded the highest value. The reader will recall the verse cited above describing those acts that constitute the examined life. The final phrase of that verse is: "and the study of the Torah excels them all."

Some rabbinic commentators have stressed the study of Torah brings one to the performance of all other acts of loving kindness and ritual behavior; others suggest that the reward for the intellectual pursuit of Torah study is as great as the reward for ethical and ritual deeds. Whatever the differences in interpretation, no

one disputes that such study conveys to the Jewish soul the centrality of this enterprise: Learn Torah. Study sacred texts. Give time and heart to this pursuit.

Yet, all this did not apply to women. Men were formally obligated to the daily study of Torah, women were formally exempt. The tradition further codified the prevailing, transcultural social norm into binding law. These limits on women's learning were carried forward through millennia of Jewish life. Educational institutions for men and boys were created in many places, but none were created for women. All these centuries, Jews revered their scholars, undeterred by the reality that they were overwhelmingly male.

In America, however, new forces were at work that would change the climate of women's education. In the earliest settlement on these shores, Jewish education suffered greatly. Jewish schooling, of both genders, had to stand back for the all-consuming process of establishing viable communities and households. Formal Jewish education was elementary and rudimentary. Those who were schooled in Jewish texts beyond the weekly Torah portion were taught primarily by a *melamed,* a private tutor hired by the family. Boys were often trained for bar mitzvah this way. Given the community's meager resources and the history of women's exclusion from Jewish education, hiring a *melamed* for a girl would have seemed unnecessary and too expensive.

With the expansion of the population and the rise of Orthodox synagogues, congregational schools began to be organized. Some were independent community enterprises but most were affiliated with an individual synagogue. For many decades these schools were the bases of American Jewish education and were supplementary to the secular public school education that Jews were receiving.

In pioneering America, an interesting pattern emerged. An individual Jewish community could initiate a new practice without much ado in the larger Jewish community. Thus, while boys took primacy in the formation of congregational schools, many of the schools allowed girls in the classes. This was in sharp contrast to the medieval and early modern European model, where no formal educational institutions for girls existed and girls' presence was not welcome. Such a school, an independent conglomerate, was founded in 1838 by Rebecca Gratz (1781–1869), leader of the Philadelphia Female Hebrew Benevolent Society. The teachers were all women (as in its counterpart, the American public school), and the girls were taught alongside the boys.

With the large Eastern European immigration from 1880 to 1916, Orthodox religious instruction began to be upgraded, to serve both as a tool of acculturation and as a preventive measure against losing the next generation to secular America. As communities and congregations grew, Sunday school expanded to a Sunday-morning-weekday-afternoon "Talmud Torah" model. In many places, girls were included in the improved and expanded educational facilities, particularly in smaller communities outside New York City. Some of these Talmud Torahs began as synagogue schools, and many others around the country were initiated by the Mizrachi leaders who visited different cities raising money for Zionist causes.

On the other hand, as Jewish education further intensified, girls began to be left behind, both in institutional structures and in educational content. In 1886, on the Lower East Side of New York where a heavy concentration of Orthodox Jews existed, Yeshiva Etz Chaim was founded. Because it was modeled after the religious schools in Europe, girls were simply not a consideration. No alternate institution was created to serve an equal number of girls from the community, nor is there record of anyone clamoring for such schools. Etz Chaim served as the model for many other yeshiva day schools that were to follow in the next century. Etz Chaim later became Yeshiva University, and it was not until the 1940's that women finally became part of that institution. (The original Etz Chaim moved to Boro Park in Brooklyn as an elementary school, and remained exclusively a boy's yeshiva until it closed six decades later.)

Moreover, as the Talmud Torahs around the country began to expand to a Sunday-plus-weekdays model, co-opting every afternoon had the desired effects. It expanded Jewish education, to be sure, but also increased social separation of Orthodox children from the general assimilatory culture. In addition, the curriculum shifted slightly to incorporate the traditional limits on what a girl could learn. Introduction to Talmud study, which was newly being taught in some of the schools, was relegated to boys only, as, of course, was Bar Mitzvah instruction. This, plus the practice of separate seating that was a staple of synagogue life, prompted schools with larger populations to form separate classes for boys and girls.

Nevertheless, it must be said that a far greater number of girls were being formally educated in the Talmud Torahs of the United States than ever before in Jewish history. Moreover, the female counterparts of the boys in the fledgling yeshivas were given much better secular educations. This raised expectations for quality in women's learning and was to alter women's Jewish education in future decades. And, perhaps most important, the rise of the coed and girls-only yeshiva day schools of the Mizrachi movement began to give serious shape to Orthodox women's education in the twentieth century.

These American models were powerfully influenced by two exceptional schools systems created in Europe. One was the Hirschian schools of western Europe. Rabbi Samson Raphael Hirsch, leader of the Frankfurt and neighboring communities from 1851 to 1988, was considered by many to be the father of modern Orthodoxy, a movement later transposed to these shores. In response to a growing Reform movement in Germany, Hirsch taught that one can be modern yet not throw over the yoke of tradition. As one manifestation of this innovative philosophy, he introduced the idea of co-educational Jewish schools. This was rare indeed, and many of his Eastern European rabbinic colleagues fought him over this approach. But he prevailed on his own turf in western Germany.

Several decades later, the Hirsch schools became the model for the first two modern co-ed Orthodox day schools in the United States. These were the Yeshiva of Flatbush (Brooklyn) founded in 1928, and the Ramaz School (Manhattan) in 1936. These schools set the pattern for hundreds of day schools that would soon be created around the country and that educated most of the modern Orthodox women in the community today. They pioneered not only in structure but also in curriculum. Talmud was taught to the girls alongside the boys. This was a first in two millennia of rabbinic Jewish history. (Even today, many modern Orthodox and all ultra Orthodox day and high schools refrain from teaching girls Talmud.)

In the 1940s these two schools added high schools to extend and intensify their students' learning, and this pattern was followed by other day schools around the country. In 1946, there was no Jewish high school in Seattle, Washington, to continue the excellent Talmud Torah that existed there. Thirteen- and fourteen-year-old sons could be sent away to continue their education in a high school yeshiva on the East Coast, but one would not send a girl from home. The parents of this author moved to New York in order to secure Jewish high schooling for their three daughters. But today, Seattle and 50 other cities around the country boast Orthodox high schools for boys and girls. (In some modern Orthodox schools, classrooms are gender separate for Jewish studies but are joined for secular education.)

The first yeshiva day school created for girls only was the Shulamith School in Boro Park, Brooklyn, founded in 1929. It, too, was a pioneering school, the first of its kind in history. Although educationally its curriculum followed the spirit of the modern Orthodox Mizrachi movement, its model was actually derived from the ultra Orthodox Bais Yaakov movement in eastern Europe. In Cracow, Poland, seamstress Sarah Schenirer (1883–1935) felt that the Orthodox girls of her town were being swayed by the Polish feminist movement. Lacking a Jewish education, she argued, Jewish girls were vulnerable to leaving the fold. Even if they didn't leave, they would not be sufficiently knowledgeable to raise their own children Jewishly. With great political savvy and firm conviction in her mission, Schenirer persuaded the rabbis of her ultra Orthodox community to allow her to create a yeshiva for girls, though she did not use the name "yeshiva." Flouting the traditional yeshiva male association would have sabotaged her project. Prayers, Bible study, and Jewish law and tradition were taught in addition to the required secular studies of Poland. From 1917 to 1938, a vast network of Bais Yaakov schools for Orthodox girls was created all across eastern Europe. Sadly, by the time the war ended, only a small remnant of several hundred thousand young women educated by Bais Yaakov survived Hitler's onslaught. At the onset of World War II, the Bais Yaakov school system was transported to America, as was the Lubavitch Beis Rivkah school system. These schools would meet the growing needs of the postwar ultra-Orthodox community here.

Still, what was lacking were institutions of higher learning for women comparable to the dozens of men's yeshivot that existed. With the advent of the women's movement, one such institute, Drisha, was created by Rabbi David Silber in New York City. Unlike Sarah Schenirir, Silber asked no one for rabbinic permission. He simply opened a school that was parallel in teaching intensity to the all-male rabbinic schools. Though he was criticized for his bold move in teaching Talmud to adult women, he persisted. Today, his school has become the model for a score of women's institutions of higher learning around the world. And today, but one and a half generations since Talmud was first introduced to women, the Orthodox community boasts female teachers of Talmud and female scholars in rabbinic literature, phenomenon that would have been inconceivable forty years ago. It is fair to say that this is the most educated generation of Jewish women in all of Jewish history.

Conclusion

The new values for women that entered the life stream of human culture during the last third of the twentieth century have permeated every aspect of life. In consequence, there has been tremendous change in women's lives everywhere, even in what we tend to think of as insulated religious communities faithfully carrying forward ancient beliefs.

In Orthodox Judaism, women now hold positions that were undreamt-of 2,000 or 350 or even 20 years ago. This is the era of training Orthodox women in new skills, and bestowing upon them the formal credentials to match. Orthodox women now hold positions as master teachers of rabbinic literature, as congregational leaders and presidents of synagogues, as pleaders in religious courts, as heads of academies of learning, and as religious advisors able to make determinations on matters of Jewish law. While gender-distinct roles in the tradition have not become interchangeable, the general tenor of the change has been to honor women's public leadership; all this, in contrast to the traditional definition of a proper Jewish woman as an "inside person."

As a result of this shift in social order, there is the tendency to look back and perceive women of pre-feminist times to have been kept out of sight and under wraps, unable to use their abilities to the fullest, denied access, at best playing a role behind the scenes. Yet an examination of the totality of Orthodox Jewish women's lives in America offers us a different view. True, they were not heads of community, nor did they hold offices or purse strings. But they nevertheless built enduring communities, created unique institutions that helped future generations, took initiative where needed, and impacted powerfully on the quality of Jewish life in America. They did this as Orthodox women, despite the relentless and broad drive to assimilate them in the new country. They did this while holding fast to faith, community, and memory.

Recently, I had occasion to visit the old Jewish cemetery in Elmont, Long Island, where my maternal grandmother and parents-in-law are buried. Jewish cemeteries have within them community plots, as if to signify that the dead remain a part of the community. Though I had been there on numerous occasions, somehow I had never noticed how many of the communal plots were created by the ladies auxiliaries of this community or that one. The women purchased the land, commissioned the iron gates, created rules and regulations, took charge of the burial, kept the records. Similarly, in reading the labels on kosher foods, as every Orthodox Jew does, I now appreciate that it was a group of women who initiated the process of supervision that has made kosher food so much more accessible for my generation.

Women today are blessed to have been born in a time when society values women's dignity. Yet, we must also celebrate the lives and work of previous generations of women. For Jewish women are the products not only of the social revolution that wrought our new reality, but also of the women who went before us. They found ways to nurture and create where there was nothing. In doing so, they left a lasting mark on American Jewish life.

SOURCES: Joyce Antler, *The Journey Home: Jewish Women and the American Century* (1997); Charlotte Baum, Paula Hyman, and Sonya Michel, *The Jewish Woman in America* (1995); Hasia R. Diner and Beryl Lieff Benderly, *Her Works Praise Her* (2002); Idana Goldberg, *For the Honor of Her Sex and the Glory of Her Maker: Jewish Women's Religious Leadership and Political Action in Nineteenth-Century America* (2002); Blu Greenberg, *The Feminist Revolution in Orthodox Judaism in America* (1992); Paula E. Hyman and Deborah Dash Moore, eds., *Jewish Women in America: An Historical Encyclopedia* (1997); Jenna Weissman Joselit, *New York's Jewish Jews: The Orthodox*

Community in the Interwar Years (1990); Pamela S. Nadell, *American Jewish Women's History* (2003).

JEWISH WOMEN AND RITUAL
Hasia R. Diner

OVER THE COURSE of the 350 years that Jews have lived in North America, the nature of Jewish women's involvement with ritual has changed. By and large, it has been the history of expanding Jewish women's participation in the realm of public ritual. By the end of the twentieth century a majority of Jewish women, through the Reform, Conservative, and Reconstructionist movements, have not only stepped into public roles for the performance of rituals that had traditionally been the sole province of men, but they have also had a hand in creating new rituals for themselves.

At the same time, a set of religious rituals that had for centuries been the domain of Jewish women and were associated with the practice of "traditional Judaism" have fallen by the wayside. Orthodox Jewish women, their families, and their communities, who constituted approximately 10 percent of American Jewry in the 1990s, maintained these practices and continue to do so. Many of the observant have reinterpreted the meaning of those rituals in light of new conditions. However, the majority of American Jews found increasingly less meaning in the practice of women's ritual roles inherited from earlier times.

Women's rituals that continue to be practiced within the Orthodox communities work on an inner assumption that gender *is* an important divide and that men and women, by nature, have different roles to play in the performance of religious life. The differences between men and women expressed in different ritual roles represent, according to Orthodox Jews, divine decree, canonical texts, and Jewish law that can be reinterpreted, not changed. Those who maintain rituals consider that the fixed nature of laws renders them beyond the ability of "ordinary" Jews to change or abandon. Where modifications have crept in, Orthodox Jews, particularly women influenced by feminism, have claimed that the changes did not violate otherwise unchangable practices.

The evolution of Jewish women's ritual practice in North America requires some explanation of Judaism, its definition of ritual, and the role of women in these practices. To begin, the word *ritual* has no Hebrew equivalent. Within Judaism all practices that are defined as obligatory, as mitzvoth—commandments—might be considered rituals, since their enactment often involves appropriately staged ceremonies and liturgically mandated language.

Much of Jewish ritual grows out of basic Judaic legal practice and is governed by halakah, literally, "the way," the corpus of Jewish law. Normative Judaism, canonized in the Torah and the Talmud, and adumbrated by later codes, has for most of Jewish history been considered fixed. Most Jewish rituals involve the performance of those behaviors, the mitzvoth, that require particular acts accompanied by particular words.

That system specified three different kinds of mitzvoth, in terms of gender and gender role. Some mitzvoth apply to men and others only to women. Still, a vast complex of obligations governed both sexes. Keeping the Sabbath, observing the dietary laws, giving *tzedaka*, assistance to the needy, welcoming strangers, fell upon women and men alike. But the vast range of obligations that govern the public performance of Judaism falls into the category of male mitzvoth.

One of the most potent barriers to women's active participation in traditionally constituted Judaic public ritual, men's domain, involved the ban on the hearing of women's voices during prayer. Perhaps because considered as a source of sexual temptation, the woman's voice, *kol ishah*, had to be eliminated from communal prayer so as not to divert men's attention from the obligatory and lofty task at hand. Historically Jewish women received relatively little education in Jewish matters outside those associated with the home, further keeping them unable to serve as the voices of their communities.

But the synagogue was not necessarily the place most intensely related to the observance of Judaism, Jewish communal life, or the fulfillment of Jewish obligations. The home functioned, for much of Jewish history, as an equal, possibly more significant place in which Jewish ritual took place. All the practices associated with food, sex, family, Sabbath, and the like, began in the home. Here women joined men in ritual peformance. They had different but symbiotic roles to play in the enacting of basic Jewish practices. As one example, one can cite the centrality of kashruth, the dietary laws, to the functioning of the Judaic system. Both women and men in their homes guarded the sanctity of the home from its possible pollution by *treife*, impure, food. Women, as the family members most associated with the purchasing, storing, and cooking of food, served as the sentinels to insure the purity of the food and the performance of all rituals associated with this central aspect of the Judaic repertoire.

The ritual lives of Jewish women need to be further understood in the context of the reality that Judaism and its complex of behaviors mandated by law do not distinguish between the realm of the lofty and spiritual and the mundance and quotidian. After all, Jewish law governs nearly all matters considered in the Western sense to be mundane, seeing great meaning in clothing, food, and other seemingly prosaic aspects of everyday life. What a Jew eats and wears, for example, throbs with sanctity and as such can be consecrated by ritual behavior.

So, too, the rituals associated with the lofty and those associated with the ordinary carry equal weight. The act of washing one's hands before eating, consuming a piece of bread, or slaughtering a chicken under the standards of *kashruth* are accompanied by specified rituals that are of no less significance than the public reading of the Torah or the marching in procession in the synagogue with the *lulav* and *ethrog*, a bundle of branches and a citron, on the fall holiday of Sukkot.

Likewise, these mitzvoth and the rituals that accompany their performance do not distinguish in any substantive way between the realm of the "public" and the "private." Although some rituals have generally taken place in the home—lighting Sabbath candles, for example—in some communities, they have also been performed in public. Ceremonies associated with the holy time as mandated by the weekly, monthly, and yearly calendar and those linked to life cycle events—birth, coming of age, marriage, divorce, death, and burial— derive either from biblical law or from the elaboration of commandments in the Talmud and the responsa literature. In the long diasporic history of the Jewish people, these biblically and Talmudically prescribed practices have been shaped by local circumstance and practice, and wide variations have crept in. Over time local variations, often thought of as *minhag* or tradition, have taken on the force of law.

It was through the fulfillment of these obligations by women and men in living Jewish communities that the basic rituals associated with Judaism developed. The Bible, for example, enjoins Jews to "remember the Sabbath day and keep it holy." From this commandment, Jews developed a vast array of rituals—lighting candles and blessing them, reciting the kiddush over a glass of wine, listening to the public reading of the biblical portion of the week in the synagogue—and a set of iconic practices that have all the markings of sacred ritual—eating a rich and tasty meal, singing table songs, inviting strangers to share the good food, enjoying marital relations, and many more—as a way to act upon the biblical words. The lines between the two sets of rituals blurred and became indistinguishable.

In the realm of the mitzvoth, obligations whose fulfillment gave birth to Jewish ritual behavior, much has, according to halakah and by custom, been expressly limited to men. These rituals tended to be those that were time-bound, that required that they be performed at a fixed hour. According to Jewish law, Jewish women were exempt from these requirements because of their great responsibilities in the realm of the household and child care. Because of this, men traditionally thanked God in their morning prayers for not having made them women and therefore uncommanded to fulfill the many public acts of Jewish ritual.

Yet a good deal of Jewish women's ritual practice was in fact fixed in time, including those mandated by the observance of the Sabbath. Indeed of the three mitzvoth directed specifically at women, two made the Sabbath possible. First, women were required to fulfill the ritual of challah. In preparing the dough for the Sabbath bread, they were required to pinch off a bit of the batter, referred to as the challah, and throw it in the fire as a way to remember olden practices associated with the Temple and the Levites who served in it. The Sabbath bread took its name from this act and not from the shape of the loaf. By performing this ritual act, Jewish women transformed flour, egg, and water into consecrated challah.

In the twentieth century, most women no longer perform this mitzvah, as most purchase bread in commercial bakeries. Yet the commodification of challah does not in and of itself mean the end of the ritual. Among the most observant, women make sure that the bread that they serve on the Sabbath is ritually pure, that the baker fulfilled the challah obligation. Thus, by patronizing those bakeries that observe this practice, the act of shopping becomes a vehicle for performing the ritual.

Women were also obligated to light the candles to usher in the Sabbath and holidays. This act, accompanied as it was by the blessing "Blessed are you Lord, our God, King of Universe, who has sanctified us with God's Commandments and Commanded us to light the Sabbath candle," brought the Sabbath into the Jewish home. For centuries women added their own personal prayers as they lit the candles. It *had* to be done before the sunset, or at the very moment when the sun went down. Since Jewish law forbade the making of fire on the Sabbath, time was of the essence, and women, those who lit the candles, made the Sabbath with their act and words.

Additionally all food for the Sabbath had to be prepared in advance, and the house was, by custom, meticulously cleaned in anticipation of sacred time. In most times, in most places, it was Jewish women who did this crucial work that transformed mundane time into sacred time. With their baking, frying, roasting, and broiling, as well as with their scrubbing, sweeping, and polishing, the calm of Sabbath was made possible. The chores of housekeeping were as such sacred rituals tied to a particular time.

Those acts—lighting the candles, preparing a rich meal, and fostering a peaceful atmosphere—made the Sabbath, much more than the public prayers to which men alone went. Additionally, the recitation of the blessing over the wine, traditionally a male ritual, is not pegged to a particular moment, and the celebrant has much greater leeway in terms of when he performs his responsibility.

Neither of the normative Jewish women's obligations, candles and challah, continue to inform the lives of a majority of Jewish women. Of the two, lighting Sabbath candles has a wider appeal, although according to various communal polls, somewhat more than a quarter of American Jewish women do so on a regular basis. Since most American Jews do not observe the Sabbath as a day of rest and as a moment for family ritual, it is not surprising that women's sanctified role within the Sabbath culture has eroded. Given the decline in the observance of kashruth in general, there is no reason to assume that American Jewish women or men think of challah as anything other than a braided loaf of bread.

The third ritual obligation directed specifically at women involved family purity, a complex of laws that regulate sexuality within marriage. Halakah forbids couples from having sexual relations during the time of the wife's menstrual period or for seven days after. Women then are required to immerse themselves in a ritual bath, a *mikvah*. Only then may they resume sexual contact.

Women had the chief responsibility for the supervision of these laws of *niddah*. Here, too, marking time, counting days, and making sure that the visit to the *mikvah* takes place at the correct moment have tremendous import. The sexual fate of the couple, as such, lays in the hands of women and in their knowledge as to how and when to perform the ritual.

Additionally the rituals surrounding the *mikvah* make it clear that the binary of public and private do not fit well the structure of Judaism. Judaism itself makes no distinction between these two spheres. What goes on within the home is as much part of the sacred universe of religious ritual as what is conducted in the synagogue, and women did, even in traditional, premodern communities, have public spaces for the performance of their religious obligations. The *mikvah* was a highly public space. The community maintained it through communal funding, and a female attendant was typically employed to make sure that the women performed the rituals properly. While the purpose of going to the *mikvah* was to be able to fulfill a private and indeed intimate act, it required public space and public funding.

While no scholar has heretofore studied the history of *mikvah* use in the United States or the changing rates of observance of the laws of *niddah* (sometimes referred to as *taharat ha-mishpacha*, or family purity), most agree that this practice has for decades—if not longer—had little hold on the vast majority of American Jews. Bits and pieces of autobiographical and memoir material from the nineteenth century and early parts of the twentieth make scattered reference to *mikvah* observance. Rachel Calof, for example, a Russian Jewish homesteader on the Dakota prairie in the early twentieth century, left a memoir in which she described how she and the few other Jewish women in the vicinity found a way to build for themselves, without any kind of rabbinic oversight, a *mikvah* so that they might engage in the ritual of immersion into its waters. Jewish newspapers at times advertised in their "help wanted" section for a "bath house" attendant, a woman who oversaw the *mikvah*.

Survey data and other historical material indicate that most American Jews do not consider that their marriages must be regulated by this practice. As such, both its home-based and *mikvah*-based rituals have largely been abandoned by non-Orthodox Jews. Rabbis of the liberal denominations do not require women to attend to the *mikvah* even before marriage, a ritual once universally observed by Jewish women.

In addition to these three specified women's rituals, other commonly practiced behaviors, rooted in Jewish law, gave women a locus for ritual practice. In the traditional functioning of Jewish communities, other kinds of ritual roles and ritual behaviors also fell upon women. While not one of the three specified women's mitzvoth, a variety of practices associated with women's charitable works, including support for widows, caring for the sick and orphans, and helping poor girls put together their doweries, brought women into a range of community tasks, each of which had its own attendant rituals.

None demonstrates this better than women's roles in matters surrounding sickness, death, and burial. Jewish law regarding death and burial, for example, operates upon the principle of *kibbud ha-met*, or respect for the deceased. The body must be treated with reverence as it is prepared for burial, which includes the process of *tahara*, or ritual washing. Just as the normative laws of modesty make it anathema for a woman to appear undressed in front of a man, so too in death, she must be attended by other women. So *hevrot nashim*, or women's burial societies, were a regular feature of Jewish community life. Women got together, washed the bodies of the recently departed females of their community, sewed shrouds, recited Psalms, sat with the bodies until burial, and accompanied them as a group to the cemetery for the *levayah*, or funeral.

In Jewish communities across America, from the early nineteenth century onward, such societies existed. They often called themselves Hebrew Ladies' Benevolent Societies. They performed the traditional functions of the *hevrot nashim*. In order to support their activities, they used currently popular methods of fund-raising—theater parties, card parties, "strawberry festivals"—as well as charging membership dues. They understood themselves to be fulfilling a basic Jewish need through the performance of a basic Jewish women's ritual.

Much of the history of Jewish women's ritual lives in America derives from the basic nature of Judaism. But that history also developed in relationship to the specifics of American life. American culture lent a great deal of autonomy to individuals in shaping the institutions that they wanted. The separation of church and state derived from the First Amendment to the Constitution stripped all clergy and all religious bodies of the power of the enforcement of orthodoxy, in practice or thought. Institutions had to conform to the "consent of the governed" since membership was utterly voluntary, and the history of all American denominations, Judaism included, was one in which members dissatisfied with the liturgy, practices, beliefs, or styles of the clergy "walked with their feet," left the congregation and created new ones. Laypeople basically hired the clergy, paid their salaries, and whatever authority the clergy had derived from the will of the members and not from the state. If congregants did follow the dictates of the clergy, it was because they chose to and not because of any kind of duress, buttressed by the power of the government.

Furthermore, most Jewish rituals do not necessarily require an ordained rabbi to perform them. Rituals associated with the home or with everyday life are performed by all Jews. Some rituals do need a person with training, but not necessarily a rabbi. A ritual circumciser, a *mohel*, performs a ritual act, as does a *shochet*, who slaughters animals to render the meat kosher. So the woman who attends the *mikvah* functions as a ritual professional. Many of the ritual functions performed in America by rabbis, like conducting prayer services, officiating at funerals, and even performing marriage ceremonies, were as much products of the American social and political environment as they are manifestations of Judaism. Indeed, one of the most important changes in Judaism in America has been the elevation of the rabbi in public ritual. While rabbis lost, over time, much of their legal authority in America, they gained a highly public realm of ritual leadership.

Likewise, individual clergy were free to experiment with new modes of worship, create new texts, and innovate with new rituals. National bodies and hierarchies had less authority than elsewhere. This had a direct impact on the ritual options of Jewish women in the United States to a degree not matched by their coreligionists in other countries. It also emboldened American rabbis to tamper with tradition.

As such, in the creation of new rituals and roles for Jewish women in America, the American context played a crucial role. The new rituals created for and by women like the bat mitzvah, which began in the 1920s, and the inclusion of women in other publically performed Jewish rituals, long limited to men, did not have a counterpart in Europe, even western Europe. American Jewish women, unlike their sisters in Europe, moved into the synagogue at an early date and by their mere presence transformed the space. Scholars like Paula Hyman and Marion Kaplan have pointed out that under the impact of modernization of the early nineteenth century, European Jewish women did not begin to flock to the synagogues. They became much more the guardians of home-based rituals, associated with family meals, visiting on the Sabbath, and the celebration of holidays in the domestic sphere. Unlike Jewish women in America, their Germany counterparts did not move out into the public sector of the synagogue.

But in America the opposite happened. Starting in the early nineteenth century, Jewish women began to attend synagogues on Sabbath morning. Their presence in the synagogues, which until the middle of the century were physically designed with a separate women's gallery, caused a great deal of discussion in the Jewish press and among rabbis since this represented a historic change. Traditionally the synagogue, the site for the performance of one crucial Jewish ritual, the weekly reading of the Torah on the Sabbath and holidays, was a male space, although women attended. No matter the number of women who attended synagogue outside of America, their presence made little impact on the conduct of the worship service. Women might sit in a separate room, built on to the back or the side of the synagogue, or they might sit in a balcony, but they were not to be seen or heard. This was the locus of male ritual.

Scholars who have studied the impact of modernization upon American Jewish women's public religious lives have stressed the significance of women's entry into the synagogue in the early nineteenth century. By the middle decades of the century, women begin to outnumber men as synagogue-goers on Sabbath mornings. Jewish men, most historians have asserted, who made a living in commerce, used Saturdays to operate their stores. Their wives, sisters, and mothers in essence began to replace them in the American synagogues. Rabbis, editors of Jewish publications, and others concerned with the state of Judaism in America fretted over the increasing number of women who filled the houses of worship on any given Sabbath. Although it was not until the 1890s that women were first allowed to become actual members in synagogues—a practice initiated by Philadelphia's Mikve Israel—rabbis understood that in some ways they had to cater to women and be concerned about their sensibilities.

Not only did American rabbis of the liberal denominations see women as active participant members of their congregations, but they increasingly observed the anomaly between the expansion of public roles for women in America and the unchanging and limited roles for women within Judaism. In the latter part of the nineteenth century individual rabbis expressed concern that this gap needed to somehow be narrowed. One important ritual arena where this played itself out was that of weddings.

This was a particularly notable ritual with great symbolic meaning. In America, a culture that venerated marriage as the goal of all women and that celebrated the place of the married woman in her home, the Jewish wedding ceremony seemed anachronistic. Weddings in American culture were understood to be for and about women, yet Jewish weddings placed the groom at the center stage. How weddings were performed was shaped by the dictates of halakah in which men took or acquired wives.

Jewish women stood passive and silent at their weddings, and traditionally they had little ritual role to play, other than to be there. Men initiated marriages (and divorces as well). Men recited the appropriate formulas, and women stood by silently. While women could not be married off against their will and they received a *ketubah*, or contract, specifying their rights within the marriage, when it came to standing under the marriage canopy, the mute woman stood by as her husband-to-be intoned the words that she was "consecrated to him according to the laws of Moses and the Jewish people."

With the development of the Reform movement in the nineteenth century in Germany and in the United States, the binding and legal nature of Jewish law was scrutinized and found to be inappropriate for the modern world. Reform rabbis like Kaufman Kohler in America in the latter part of the century specifically cited the passive role of women in the wedding ritual to be shameful to women and deviating from the liberal spirit of his age, which he saw as one that valorized women and gave them greater autonomy. He considered one of Reform Judaism's greatest achievements to be the reformulation of the wedding ceremony in which the woman could speak, articulate her will, and have a role in the public ritual. "Reform Judaism," wrote Kohler, "has pulled down the screen from the gallery behind which alone the Jewish Woman of old was allowed to take part in the divine service" (Goldman, 152). In the expansion of women's ritual roles within Judaism, in the liberal movements, brides were increasingly able to give rings to their grooms, and they too were able to intone words in either English or Hebrew to indicate that they were active participants in this pivotal ritual.

The American tradition of religious innovation, the freedom of clergy to tinker with liturgy and traditional practice, and the high levels of congregational autonomy all fostered an environment in which rabbis took note of women's presence and sought ways to enhance their participation. Nothing demonstrates this ritual freedom and its implications for women greater than the creation of the bat mitzvah ceremony by Rabbi Mordecai Kaplan in 1922. In that year Kaplan, himself the product of a traditional upbringing and education and a graduate of the Jewish Theological Seminary, called his daughter Judith up to the *bimah*, altar, on the occasion of her twelfth birthday to read from the Torah and mark her coming of age.

Jewish law considered a young woman upon becoming twelve years of age responsible for performing all the commandments appropriate for her sex, age, and station in life. She was obligated to assume responsibility for her actions. But this ascendancy to the age of obligation took place—historically—devoid of any public ritual or any festivities. This obviously stood in stark contrast to the events marking a boy's attainment of manhood, long associated with age thirteen. Boys were called to the Torah to recite the blessings over the reading from the scroll. They might give a learned discourse, and their families hosted friends and kin with food, drink, and merriment.

Kaplan was not the first modern Jew to feel the need to redress this imbalance. Jacob Ettlinger, a neo-Orthodox rabbi in Germany in the mid-nineteenth century, called for a ceremony for girls, but as a staunch traditionalist he envisioned it to be outside of the synagogue and disconnected from the public performance of Jewish ritual and worship. Likewise, in some Jewish communities in Muslim lands, families celebrated their daughters' attainment of their majority with home ritual.

But Kaplan's boldness was not in his interest in celebration but in his assertion, with his daughter as a model, that a girl should mark, Jewishly, her maturation in the synagogue in the context of public worship. He was acutely aware that just two years earlier women in the United States had been given the right to vote. He saw the expansion of professional and educational opportunities for women around him, and as the founder of Reconstructionism, a movement that sought to harmonize the Jewish and the American civilizations, he worried about the lack of equality for women within Judaism.

He was concerned that as increasing numbers of Jewish women experienced equality in their American lives, be it at school, on the job, and in the political sector, they would find their Jewish lives limiting, narrow, and offering little to enlist their loyalties as women. In the bat mitzvah that he created for his daughter and that he advocated for other Jewish girls, he saw a way in which new ritual could enhance the meaning of Judaism in America.

The bat mitzvah as envisioned by Kaplan took decades to catch on. At the time Kaplan called his daughter to the Torah, the Reform movement had largely abandoned the bar mitzvah and had substituted for it the confirmation ceremony. This ceremony had its roots in Europe in the early nineteenth century. It was intended by reforming rabbis to be a solemn moment when young Jews, sixteen years old, would swear, publicly, their loyalty to Judaism. From nearly the start, girls were included in the rite that was to replace, for boys, the bar mitzvah, which reformers saw as taking place at too young an age and having become formulaic and outmoded. The confirmation spread rapidly in America, and in Reform and Conservative congregations girls and boys marched to the *bimah* on Shevuoth, the holiday celebrating the giving of the Torah. Since, therefore, many Reform congregations were not celebrating bar mitzvah at the time Judith Kaplan was called to the Torah in 1922, they had no need to create an analogous ritual for girls.

Most American Jews at the time Kaplan created the bat mitzvah were either immigrants from eastern Europe or their American-born children. When they participated in religious rituals and when they attended services, they tended to go to Orthodox congregations, whether they were personally observant of the mitzvoth or not. They had little interest in or exposure to the kind of ritual innovation coming out of Kaplan's Society for the Advancement of Judaism.

It was, however, in the 1950s as American Jews participated in the massive movement to the suburbs and in the largest congregational building boom in American Jewish history that the bat mitzvah began to take off. In this period Reform congregations returned to the bar mitzvah, which had been abandoned, and in doing so, they also included girls with a ceremony of their own. In the post–World War II embrace of bat mitzvah Conservative congregations initially allowed girls to participate only in the Friday night service, while the more central service, that of Saturday morning, was reserved for boys. Likewise, it took several decades for a majority of Conservative congregations and their rabbis to allow girls to read from the Torah.

The rise of the women's movement made it impossible for Conservative congregations and their rabbis to continue a practice that privileged the experiences of boys over girls, and over the course of the next generation, bar and bat mitzvah became virtually indistinguishable in most congregations. By the 1980s, as the Conservative movement ordained women as rabbis and then as cantors, there was no longer any justification for separate and unequal coming-of-age ceremonies for boys and girls.

In the last two decades of the twentieth century, Orthodox Jews in America, the women in particular, have begun to find ways to allow for some kind of bat mitzvah for their daughters within the context of halakah. Sometimes a group of women meet in the home of the girl, and she recites a set of prayers, gives a talk about the Torah portion of the week, and a festive meal is served. In other congregations, women have been allowed to mark the bat mitzvah of their daughters in a separate room in which no men are present, or where fewer than ten men (less than a quorum for prayer) sit in the back, apart from the women. The fact that late-twentieth-early-twenty-first-century Orthodox Jews have found ways to incorporate this ritual into their religious lives indicates the profound impact of changing gender roles in the society as a whole and within Judaism.

Some of the earliest changes in women's ritual lives in the American synagogues came from rabbis and not the laity, from men and not from women. Rabbis increasingly saw the preponderance of women in the sanctuaries most Sabbath mornings. They also witnessed, particularly in the suburban congregations of the post–World War II era, the high level of women's activism in the functioning of the synagogues: organizing the religious school, creating parents' associations, staffing the social activities, launching ambitious fund-raising projects, decorating the new facilities, publishing the bulletin, and making possible the vast array of tasks necessary for any well-functioning voluntary association. The steps that individual rabbis took to bring their female congregants into the ritual life of their congregations might be seen as a form of thanks for, or at least a recognition of, the centrality of women to the synagogues.

In the Reform movement women had always been allowed up on the *bimah*, and as a movement that rejected the idea of halakah as binding, it had no inherent problem with women performing any particular ritual role in public worship. Reform congregations put great store on congregational singing, and as such, women, whose voices predominated, were involved with a basic ritual act. Women ascended to the *bimah* to speak, read, or just be present. During confirmation ceremonies, girls and boys together appeared in front of the congregation.

Given the involvement of women with public ritual in Reform congregations, it may not be surprising that the first women who began to ask, as early as the 1890s, why and when women might become rabbis came from the ranks of this liberal movement. Their comfort with women in Jewish ritual caused some of them to start thinking about a final step in putting women and men on an equal plane in all matters Judaic, including taking on the most visible and public ritual role, that of rabbi.

That would not happen until 1972 when Sally Priesand received rabbinical ordination at the Hebrew Union College. Until then, women in Reform congregations were involved in an ancillary fashion in the ritual of public worship on a regular basis. Since the end of the nineteenth century, for example, women in Reform congregations had organized themselves into sisterhoods, and throughout the country they staged the annual Sisterhood Shabbat. The women ran the service. They led the services, gave the sermon, and in the process took on, one day a year, the whole panoply of roles associated with public Jewish ritual life, as articulated by American Reform.

For the Conservative movement, the movement of women into public ritual proved to be a more difficult project. The movement, which took shape in the second decade of the twentieth century, considered itself as bound by halakah. It saw itself as operating within a historic system of interpreting the law, cautiously. Initially in recognition of the service women performed and under the influence of Mordecai Kaplan, who had written widely about women's rights—and wrongs within Judaism—Conservative rabbis began informally in the 1950s to allow women up to the *bimah*, to open the ark or read from the English translations of the prayers. They took it upon themselves, assuming rightly that they would not be censured by their movement's rabbinical body—the Rabbinical Assembly—to start counting women in the minyan and allowing women to recite the blessings before and after the Torah reading.

Not all rabbis did this. Some thought this wrong and held out well into the late 1970s in limiting the role of women in public ritual. Some rabbis, fearing traditionally oriented members, offered women greater ritual roles during the summer months, for example, when many congregants were away on vacation and when in fact the rabbi was often not present. The small steps within the Conservative movement took place, then, on an individual basis and without an ideological committment of the movement to the idea of women functioning fully in public ritual roles.

For most of American Jewish history the changes in women's placement and place in public ritual came about from the top down, and women themselves made few demands for greater equality. But this all changed with the social and cultural ferment of the late 1960s. Starting in this period, Jewish women began to make specific demands on Judaism and the institutions of the Jewish community. They spoke up, as women, for equality and for the right to participate in ritual life as Jews and not specifically as women. They were no longer content with individual rabbis making individual and piecemeal accommodations. They set the agenda, and the rabbis of the liberal denominations followed suit.

That the period of greatest creativity in the universe of Jewish women's ritual life, the era from the 1960s onward, coincided with a period of great cultural innovation in America in general reflected the high level of consonance between Jewish women and American culture. American Jews partook of the cultural trends of the larger society and experimented with grafting upon Judaism and Jewish ritual practice those elements of American culture that they found most appealing.

The new rituals for women that they created—the invigoration of the bat mitzvah ceremony, the creation of a public ritual for naming baby girls, or the *simhat bat*, the emergence of the adult bat mitzvah, which made it possible for older women who had never been exposed to Jewish learning and who had never had a public coming-of-age ceremony to do so, to name just three—born of this era, reflected the fervor of both the feminist movement of the late 1960s and the efflorescent counterculture of that same historic period. Jewish women, and men, participated actively and probably out of proportion to their number in the population in both movements.

The first of these held up to scrutiny all social and cultural practices that privileged men and placed women in marginal and subservient positions. Why, Jewish feminists asked, did Judaism mandate a set of public rituals to richly celebrate the birth of sons—the *brit milah*, or circumcision, as well as the *shalom zachar*, a festive meal served by the parents of the baby boy on the Sabbath before the circumcision—whereas the birth of daughters was marked merely by the father of the newborn coming to the synagogue and pronouncing the girl's name? Why should Jewish ritual valorize men and not women from the moment of birth onward?

Rather than just lament the inequity, starting in the late 1960s, American Jewish women and their husbands began to experiment with new rituals to make the birth of daughters as joyous and as publically notable as the birth of sons. They believed they had the right to create such new forms of ritual practice because of the critique of Judaism launched by Jewish feminism. They also did so because the mood of American society in the closing decades of the twentieth century was one that promoted autonomy and popular expression in the religious realm. One of the important Jewish by-products of this counterculture was the *havurah* movement, independent clusters of young Jews who met, worshipped, and celebrated Jewish life cycle events without rabbinical supervision or involvement.

It was in these *havurot* that such rituals as the *simhat bat* had its first stirrings. Those who created this practice had no particular models to follow, since they were doing it themselves, and they freely borrowed from the traditional liturgy but changed the words to make it either gender neutral or specifically female. They added other kinds of readings, drawn from Hebrew poetry, from Yiddish literature, or from other, even non-Jewish sources. They wrote their own prayers as well.

Notably, within a decade or two of the innovations of the counterculture and the autonomous creation of new Jewish rituals for women, like the *simhat ha-bat*, the rabbis of the Conservative, Reform, and Reconstructionist movements began to adopt this practice themselves. They began to participate in these home-based rituals, and their prayerbooks and rabbis' manuals included material on what had been a marginal practice, inspired by feminism.

The thrust of the feminist critique against limitations on women's participation in Jewish ritual was aimed at the Conservative movement. Since Reform and Reconstructionism were unworried about the hand of halakah in structuring public worship, they were free to respond quickly and without an intense, anguished battle. Orthodoxy, on the other hand, was out of the question, in terms of allowing women equality in public ritual. But the Conservative movement that sees itself as walking a line between tradition and change has been the locus of much of the rancor over just how far women could enter into the world of ritual.

Feminists objected fervently to the idea that women did not count, literally. Jewish public prayer required a quorum of ten men, and this was still observed in the Conservative movement in the early 1970s when the Jewish feminist movement took off. In 1973 the Rabbinical Assembly passed a resolution permitting rabbis to count women, although it still left open the possibility that some rabbis might not feel comfortable doing so.

Ritual lay at the heart of the feminist demands on Judaism. Jewish women took upon themselves, without asking permission, the right to wear the tallith, the fringed ritual prayer shawl worn by men, and tefillin,

phylacteries. They demanded to be called to the Torah to chant the weekly portion and recite the blessings.

While much of the feminist argument was framed in terms of demands, Jewish feminists considered themselves empowered to create new rituals and to take upon themselves the symbols of traditional rituals. So in addition to the *simhat bat* ceremony, Jewish feminists since the 1970s have organized *rosh hodesh* groups. *Rosh hodesh* is the beginning of the new month, and there had long been an association in traditional Judaism between women and this monthly event. In modern America, Jewish women have formed groups to meet on *rosh hodesh*, recite poetry, discuss texts, recite prayers—new and old—and mark the time as their special moment. Likewise, women Jewish artists, working in fabrics having created new *kippot*—head coverings—for women, using colors and designs not conventionally worn by men.

In many communities, thousands of women gather annually for a feminist Seder, the ritual marking the beginning of Passover. They use an expressly feminist Haggadah, the book of readings for the Seder, and experiment with new songs and rituals. Over time the forms developed for feminist Sedarim have migrated into the mainstream. For example, feminists fixed upon the image of Miriam, the sister of Moses and Aaron, as a woman who they wanted to celebrate at Passover. Miriam had, in midrash, been associated with water and its life-giving properties. So they created a Seder ritual, using a cup, now called a "Miriam's Cup," to be placed on the holiday table. Haggadoth published by the end of the twentieth century have begun to include the filling of Miriam's Cup as a ritual moment and have provided the words, developed a feminist Sedarim, to be sung by families in their homes.

In a curious twist of historic irony, some Jewish feminists in Conservative congregations in particular are beginning to talk about reclaiming the *mikvah* as a woman's space. They have begun to write in publications like *Lilith* about the spiritual value of the ritual of immersion. This was made possible by the fact that in the 1980s in a number of cities Conservative synagogues built their own *mikvaot*, primarily in order to fulfill the rituals associated with conversion to Judaism. Given the increasing tension between the Orthodox and the liberal movements, Conservative-sponsored *mikvaot* offer their own rabbis as well as their colleagues from the Reform

In many communities thousands of women gather annually for a feminist Seder, the ritual marking the beginning of Passover. They use an expressly feminist Haggadah, the book of readings for the Seder, and experiment with new songs and rituals. Over time the forms developed for feminist Sedarim have migrated into the mainstream. © 2004 Gale Zucker/www.gzucker.com.

and Reconstructionist movements, a friendlier environment in which to function. This in turn provided a venue for Jewish women influenced by feminism to experience the *mikvah* and the public rituals of *niddah*.

At the beginning of the twenty-first century, Jewish women in America have more ritual roles than they ever had before, although, for most, they do not involve the practice of rituals that had for centuries been synonymous with Judaism and women's roles within it. Yet the newly created ritual life of Jewish women appears to be one of the areas of greatest growth, creativity, and vibrance on the American Jewish ritual scene.

SOURCES: Karla Goldman, *Beyond the Synagogue Gallery: Finding a Place for Women in American Judaism* (2000). Paula Hyman, *Gender and Assimilation in Modern Jewish History: The Roles and Representations of Women* (1995). Pamela S. Nadell, *Women Who Would Be Rabbi: A History of Women's Ordination, 1889–1985* (1998). Riv Ellen Prell, *Prayer and Community: The Havurah in American Judaism* (1989). Ellen Umansky and Diane Ashton, eds., *Four Centuries of Jewish Women's Spirituality: A Sourcebook* (1992).

JEWISH LAW AND GENDER
Norma Baumel Joseph

THE CENTRALITY OF Jewish law (halakah) in traditional Jewish life raises many questions for contemporary Jewish communities. In America, the divergent denominations have responded with a variety of distinct positions and interpretations of that law and of its place in determining Jewish practice and identity. One of the most serious and contentious issues is the place of women within that halakic system and its influential determination of gender roles. The practice, study, and promulgation of Jewish law traditionally have been a male occupation. Although women were always obligated to observe the legal rules, many women, especially in the modern period, felt excluded or invisible.

In the early 1970s many feminists wrote of their disenchantment with androcentric interpretations of legal premises and processes. Rachel Adler's 1971 essay "The Jew Who Wasn't There" complained that "[women] are viewed in Jewish law and practice as peripheral Jews" (Heschel, 13–14). Since traditionally women were legally exempt from many ritual acts, she argued that Jewish women were denied positive religious associations, and all that was left to them were the negative commandments. Although factually inaccurate, she expressed the perception and sentiment of many Jewish women. Some, like Paula Hyman, argued that the problem was not halakah per se. In calling for the full participation of women in religious observance, Hyman noted, "The

most formidable barrier to change and to the acceptance of women as authority figures and as the equals of men lies in the psychological rather than halachic realm" (Koltun, *Response* 7.2 [Summer 1973]: 72). Jews in general were not ready for the full inclusion of women in communal enterprises. On the other hand, Cynthia Ozick, commenting on these laws of ritual exemptions, framed the issue poignantly and precisely: "To exempt is to exclude, to exclude is to debar, to debar is to demote, to demote is to demean" (Heschel, 126). Rachel Biale, in her classic *Women and Jewish Law*, aptly compared the process of legal development in Judaism to a birth. "Women have participated in the evolution of the Halakhah only in the 'prenatal' and 'postpartum' stages of the process" (3). They may ask some of the questions and are bound by the decisions, but they do not have any active role in the decision-making process: They are not the birthing agents of the law. To a certain degree, by not creating the texts themselves their voices are halakically—and in some communities literally—silent.

Inasmuch as women do not produce the texts, Jewish law would appear to be a poor source for information and research on women. Their silence and invisibility in itself sustains a critique of Judaism. As Judith Hauptman noted: "Jewish law is and was sexist: it does not extend to women the same opportunities for spiritual expression and public leadership as it does to men" (396).

Yet these legal documents and codes describe the issues that affected women's experience and expose the assumptions, explicit and implicit, that governed their lives. The terms of discourse used reveal gender codes that reflect cultural patterns and structure legal perceptions. Moreover, the link between women and modernity in a traditional context is of particular significance in the study of religion, and it is exposed in the legal systems explored. Irrevocably, women's increasing critique of and active role in the legal system of the various denominations—Reform, Orthodox, Conservative, Reconstructionist—have changed the face of Judaism.

The history of Jewish law is as long and complex as the history of Judaism itself. The many sources and resources available often yield a confusing maze requiring years of training and practice. In questionable matters, individuals are expected to seek direction and decision from a rabbinic scholar rather than decide matters for themselves. Historically, few men and most women were rarely ever given the tools to explore or study this heritage. Few were in a position to wield the instruments of legal determination: to make authoritative and binding legal decisions.

Jewish law begins with biblical pronouncements that are then interpreted, applied, and generated in the Mishnah (finalized end of second century) and Talmud (sixth century). These two texts, containing the commentaries, decisions, and discussions of the early rabbis, are the classical texts of Jewish law. In order to engage any legal question today, it is expected that one can respond to these formidable ancient texts. Subsequent generations of rabbis (male) attended to the process of elaboration and accommodation that produced a wide variety of legal structures and strategies, including commentaries, codes, and responsa (authoritative legal decisions made in response to questions of law). In the sixteenth century the quintessential code of Jewish law, the *Shulhan Arukh*, was written by Rabbi Joseph Caro (Spanish/Sephardic) and revised for European (Ashkenazic) Jews by Rabbi Moses Isserles. In the following centuries, other compilations and codes were produced, but the most prolific form has been the responsa format of question and answer. The process of creating these legal documents and texts is ongoing in all Jewish communities today as many Jews attempt to live by the codes of conduct initiated in the Bible and adhered to through thousands of years.

The law itself is not limited to matters of ritual or religious ceremony. It covers matters of civil and criminal regulation as well. In each arena—ritual, civil, and criminal—there are gender distinctions that have become increasingly problematized in the modern period. Yet legal rulings do not easily fall into comprehensive gender categories. There are cases of similar and dissimilar treatment, some of equal treatment, protectionism, and/or restriction. The object of the full range of legal pronouncements is to determine whether one is obligated, exempted, permitted, or prohibited regarding the performance of different acts. In Jewish criminal law, women and men were generally treated the same, whether they were the victims or the culprits. The associated monetary fines that were frequently based on capacity to earn do differentiate between male and female. Significantly, women were not allowed to be witnesses in most criminal and civil cases. Moreover, despite the biblical precedent of Deborah, the Talmudic sages deemed women unable to sit as judges in rabbinic courts of law.

In Jewish civil law, there were elements of equal opportunity and those of clear disenfranchisement for women. As Judith Romney Wegner discovered: "[T]he sages chose to perceive woman sometimes as *person* and sometimes as *chattel*" (175). A woman could own property and present claims before a rabbinic court. She could write a will and make contracts. Significantly, marriage required the woman's consent if she was no longer a minor under her father's control. A woman over twelve and a half could not be married against her will, and any sexual act that was forced on her by any man was deemed rape and prosecuted. Despite these examples of enfranchisement, the rabbis understood the man to be the central player both ritually and civilly. Consequently and problematically, the male is deemed

the initiator of marriage proceedings, and only the husband can divorce the wife. This latter form of discrimination—to be further discussed—is one of the most vexing legal problems in contemporary Jewish society.

It is in the arena of ritual law that we find the conspicuous gender distinctions that have produced such a far-reaching reaction in the modern period. In the vast array of traditional Jewish ritual law, women are exempt from fourteen rites (Biale, 10–43). The Talmud exempts women from Shema (a fundamental prayer) and tefillin (phylacteries) but obligates them in standard prayer, mezuzah (an amulet on the doorpost), and grace after meals. It further specifies that women are exempt from sitting in the sukkah (for festival of booths), waiving the *lulav* (palm fronds), hearing the shofar (ram's horn), wearing *tsitsit* (fringes), and tefillin. These are the rituals from which women are released. They are classified as positive acts that are limited as to time, but there is no clear explanation given for these exemptions, which have been rabbinically defined and refined over the years.

Throughout history, there have been shifts in women's performance of some of these rituals. Many have entered the repertoire of pious women so much so that memory of the exemption status is fading. Thus, for centuries women have gone to considerable lengths to hear the shofar on Rosh Hashanah. Some have argued that because of the behavior of these women, the legal category has shifted to one of obligation. Rabbinic authorities have in fact required women to perform certain previously exempted rituals. For example, Rabbi Joseph Caro, author of the *Shulhan Arukh*, refers to the necessity for women to say the Shema prayer, even though the Talmud exempts them. Strikingly, educating females, initially listed as an exemption, was once considered a prohibition by many. Today it is considered an obligation and a right by many Jews, particularly in the Orthodox community.

There has been a great deal of confusion and misinformation in this area of exemptions. The current interest in women's participation in religious life, especially public ceremonial, has compounded the importance of these deliberations. Some people argue that women were exempted from the fourteen rituals discussed above because of their competing responsibilities on the domestic scene. Since the Talmud presents some of the exemptions under the category of positive time-bound commandments, rabbinic theorists posit the domestic role as the competition for a woman's time. Hence, she is exempted from specific ritual performance. But reliance on this principle as a generating decree is rejected by the Talmud itself. In fact, many of the exemptions do not correlate with the Talmudic principle of positive acts that are time bound. Thus, women are equally obligated to fulfill the commandment of kiddush (blessing over

It is in the arena of ritual law that the conspicuous gender distinctions are found that have produced such a far-reaching reaction in the modern period. But throughout history, there have been shifts in women's performance of some of these rituals. © 2004 Gale Zucker/www.gzucker.com.

the wine) for the Sabbath and holidays as well as of matzo on Passover, both of which are very specific as to time elements. Moreover, women are exempt from Torah study, which has no time qualification. However, some of the exemptions do correlate with a domestic/public divide. Women were exempt from those rituals that are the central focus of public prayer, especially tallith, tefillin, and *aliya l'torah* (called up during services to read from the Torah). In the Orthodox world, they do not constitute the quorum of ten for prayer, thus keeping women away from the public performance of these rites and preventing them from standing as representatives of the communal group. Combined with their exemption from the world of Torah study, these rules left the prized public sector of Judaism open to men only.

One of the most ironic elements in these regulations is that according to the Talmud women are considered exempt from the procreative commandment. Clearly, this exemption has never been equated with a prohibition. Indeed, many contemporary portrayals of women's religious responsibilities often emphasize their procreative/domestic role to the exclusion of other roles. This form of reasoning flies in the face of strict legal decrees while clearly complying with the design of Judaic family patterns. Undoubtedly, this exemption undercuts any attempt to equate exemptions in general with prohibitions, as well as repudiating any simplistic public/domestic explanation of the exemptions themselves.

Attempts to find one overarching explanation for these exemptions have usually failed. Moreover, the complete history of women's ritual practice is veiled and hence not available as a decisive explanation or blueprint. Nonetheless, the contemporary climate of increased women's presence, participation, and representation has transformed the gendered map of ritual performance. The current practice among American Jewish women varies by denomination and by individual preference. The story of these developments is the making of modern Judaism.

In the past 200 years, Jewish life has been confronted with a whole new set of norms, attitudes, and values. The Jewish community has accommodated to life in the Western world in a variety of ways. Hundreds of rabbis—predominantly male—have written thousands of legal decisions (responsa) in an effort to solve the pressing problems and map out a guide for proper Jewish behavior. Responsa are literally answers that trained, recognized rabbinic authorities dispense in response to specific questions. Through these texts, rabbis shape and control their community as they respond to the pressing needs of their coreligionists. They are the outcome of a legal process that is reactive rather than legislative, particular rather than general, individual rather than communal. The specific decisions deal with unusual, anomalous, and questionable events. The questions arise because the issues are new, legally unprecedented, and the questioner, as a member of a community, is unsure of the correct or required action. Despite this reactive element, the result is a series of legal decisions that are used as precedents in subsequent cases and are clues to the transformation of a community.

Since law variously reflects, molds, and rejects social transformation, it can be used as an excellent source to examine religious convention and gender shifts. It is remarkable that contemporary Jewish historians and sociologists continue to focus on the law's tendency to perpetuate traditional patterns of living. Yet it can be argued that it is precisely through adherence to halakah and to halakic patterns that the Jewish community has developed some of its most innovative approaches to American life. Contemporary responsa are a direct source for an understanding of the method by which traditionalists survive in the modern world, what principles and norms govern their approach, and how these are enunciated and activated. In the process of meeting modernity, these traditionalists, even those who denounce modernity, have brought their communities into the twentieth century. Saliently, the dynamic tension between tradition and modernity is played out in the decisions concerning women's religious lives.

Two hundred years ago, the Jewish community considered itself bound to rabbinic Judaism. With the advent of modernity, the nature of the community and its relationship to that tradition changed. Alternative ways of being Jewish emerged. Reform, Orthodox, Conservative, and Reconstruction sectors of Judaism flourished in America. Conspicuously, these denominations have approached legal issues and decision making quite distinctly, contributing to a shift in perspective from a position of self-evidence to one of self-consciousness. All these groups draw upon the classical rabbinic legal tradition, affirm the message of law, and claim their continuity with premodern Judaism and commitment to Jewish heritage. Yet their diverse adherence to law's absolute authority sets the stage for a range of positions on women's practice of Judaism.

The Reform movement, which came to North America from Germany in the nineteenth century, inaugurated the debate with its initial opposition to the absolute authority of the law and suggestion of gender equality. Even so, Reform Judaism generated an appreciation of law's significance while balancing it with the commitment to the autonomy of the individual. In this community, halakah is a reference point, a part of a cherished heritage, but it does not have dominion. The rabbis are not considered bound by the law, but they do see themselves as legitimate interpreters of Jewish tradition. Thus, Jewish law continues to influence and guide both Reform community standards and rabbinic responses while individual practice varies from synagogue to synagogue and from person to person.

An opposing position is found in the Orthodox sector, where there is a complete acceptance of and commitment to the absolute supremacy of halakah. This position was articulated in Europe and established institutionally in America by the end of the nineteenth century. Notably, the standards and procedures of the Judaic legal system are considered timeless. Since the law derives from an eternal God, it is deemed immutable and binding on all Jews. The rabbis, as scholars of the law, are charged with the responsibility of interpreting and applying the law to specific situations. The process of legal unfolding is sacrosanct and can only be engaged in by those committed to and learned in it. Thus, all issues related to gender must be adjudicated within the system, item by item, individual by individual, rabbi by rabbi, rather than based on some notion of progress, public opinion, or gender equality. Moreover, these decisions are to develop internally based only on legal precedents and not necessarily conforming or suited to contemporary standards.

The Orthodox denial of change particularly distinguishes this group from the Conservative position. Conservative Judaism, formed in the United States at the beginning of the twentieth century, is in theory also committed to the binding authority of Jewish law. But within this orientation, halakah can and does change, evolving historically as rabbinic leaders innovate in response to the altered circumstances of life. As in the Reform movement, there is a law committee that frequently decrees specific decisions that individual congregations can accept or reject. This legislativelike role has enabled the movement to make certain comprehensive decisions concerning women.

The Reconstructionist movement is similar to the Reform in its stance on law. Law is part of the heritage of the past emanating out of the life of the community. As such, it is worthy of study and consideration but not unquestioned or unconditional obedience. People can choose what path to follow, how to practice, and whom to accept. Within this view, the parameters of the community's lifestyle dictate practice. Thus, modern egalitarianism is a value pursued. The denominations have developed gender-inclusive platforms in distinctive ways, but none yet offers comprehensive equality. Though access to greater ritual participation and public leadership is increasing across the board, it by no means addresses or solves all the major issues.

The noted distinctions between the movements are both obvious and subtle. Increasing women's ritual presence and leadership introduces the question of change and continuity. All the groups claim some form of continuity, with the Orthodox being the most adamant and persuasive on this point. Change is rejected by the Orthodox officially. Nonetheless, any examination of the vast collections of responsa literature attests to the fact that Jewish law has changed over time. Rather, the controversy rests on the question of whether the law embraces change as a halakic value. In this and in locating the details of legal positions, there is great debate, ambiguity, and even confusion.

One caveat: This discussion focusing on law skews the communal portrayal. Regardless of affiliation, the vast majority of Jews are not concerned with Jewish law, and their ritual practice of Judaism is quite indistinguishable, no matter what their synagogue affiliation. Nonetheless, there are important differences from sector to sector in the roles and rituals applied to women. And in these stances, Jewish legal deliberations often play a decisive role.

Plainly, changes in the role, ritual, and public participation of women in the modern period have generated heated debate and great tension in the Jewish world. The formal legal reactions to women can be seen as the vehicle for a community's reaction to modernity in general. Although most accounts focus on the restrictive and conventional nature of such legislation, it is also necessary to seek the creative and dynamic tendency hidden in the legal system. One might argue that the struggle toward modernity has been problematized through the prevailing attitudes about women. Women's issues can thus be seen as a test case that discloses an apprehension about and an embrace of modern living.

There are many divergent and intriguing arenas that expose these complex tendencies and intersections of gender, law, and modernity. In these domains, the question of women's place, initiative, and responsibility contested existing legal practices. Historically, women were recipients of legal pronouncements, accepting of male decisions and actions. Modernity raised questions about individual action, choice, responsibilities, and rights. Western legal systems understand issues in terms of rights and entitlements. Jewish law operates on the basis of obligations rather than rights. Women's rights as persons challenged traditional Judaic legal norms and yielded new blueprints, new problems. These challenges required new interpretations and applications while exposing the law to be dynamic and unexpectedly resilient.

One of the most radical changes in the role of women took place in the twentieth century. Traditionally, women were not educated in Torah texts; they were neither teachers nor students. Aside from sporadic exceptions, women's knowledge was based on practice, experience, and observation rather than formal study. By the beginning of the twentieth century, this was deemed by some to be insufficient for Jewish survival.

Could Judaism survive if education was to remain the preserve of the elite, primarily a male elite? Until the modern period, most Jews picked up all they needed to know by living within the confines of the community. Life was the classroom; parents, the educators. Certainly there were educated women in Jewish history, but they were exceptions to the rule that legally excluded women. When in the beginning of the eighteenth century, education was democratized in the Western world, Jews eagerly grasped the full benefit of schooling. Education was called upon to solve social ills and to provide economic security. In Europe and especially in North America, public education for the masses became the norm. Jews recognized that secular education was the ticket of admission to advancement in an open society. Factors such as the spread of the Enlightenment, free government schools, and increased compulsory education also had an impact on formal religious education for girls. The Judaic and text content of these classes varied from place to place but was generally limited. In the nineteenth century, there were several schools or classes for women in countries such as Italy, England, Iraq, Morocco, Germany, Poland, and Russia.

In such an environment, Jewish women, no less than Jewish men, desired to be educated and to educate. In the United States of America, the first schools were mainly congregational based. The great east European immigration at the end of the nineteenth century increased the need for schools. As in the past, the main educational effort was directed at boys. But many women, like Rebecca Gratz, Rebekah Kohut, and Henrietta Szold, embraced Jewish education in addition to secular study. Synagogues and Jewish women's organizations added classes for the general Jewish education of their members in order to strengthen Jewish life.

These distinguished examples anticipated and participated in a paradigm shift, but they did not assume an authoritative standing, nor did they present a reasoned legal legitimation for this break with the past. The conclusive breakthrough originated in Europe with variations in the East and West. In eastern Europe, at the beginning of the twentieth century, one woman, Sarah Schenirer (1883–1938), sought to establish a school to teach women about Judaism. She was a pioneer in advocating a combined program of secular and religious education for girls. Schnirer wanted to develop fully integrated religious graduates who would be knowledgeable about the world while also able to maintain a faithful respect for tradition and traditional authorities. Her model was so successful that by 1937 there were approximately 250 schools with over 35,000 students in Beth Jacob schools spread all over Europe.

Significantly, Schnirer understood that rabbinical authorization and support were essential. After receiving approval from the rabbis of the Gerer and Belzer Hasidic groups, she went to Rabbi Yisrael Meir HaKohen of Lithuania who endorsed her plans with a legal edict. He claimed that the law prohibiting a father from teaching his daughter no longer applied because of extenuating circumstances. Girls were no longer learning about the tradition by emulating their mothers. It was necessary to break with convention and teach daughters formally. In fact, he ruled, teaching women was now not an issue of permission but of duty, of mitzvah. His reasoning was based on a fear that without the basic rudiments women would leave the faith and not instruct their children properly. According to this cult of domesticity, women were seen as the prime educators because of their maternal role. He was not legislating a new standard because it was better for women; rather, he was protecting the traditional role division.

In western Europe, Rabbi Samson Raphael Hirsch of Frankfurt/Main also extended Torah studies to women. There had been schools for girls in Germany with very limited Jewish content in the nineteenth century. Hirsch claimed that women always had at least limited access to study. He redirected the effort by proclaiming that it was necessary now to educate all girls. According to him, women were obligated to study. His ideal, however, also reified a map of divided gender roles. Given these European legal precedents, Jewish education for women established deep roots in America. Many rabbinic leaders and institutions assumed girls' education to be normative. One of the great American Orthodox decisors (authoritative legal decision makers), Rabbi Moses Feinstein shifted the parameters by making it obligatory for a father to pay for his daughter's education, a radical transposition from Talmudic antecedents. It was self-evident to him that girls must get a good Jewish education. Unlike many of his predecessors, he did not bemoan the contemporary trend of educating females. Curiously, he claimed that educating females was an unremarkable change; that the legal issues were simple. Of course, given the historical process and the heightened social acceptance, it does seem simple today.

Two points stand out. This new standard was legitimated in the Orthodox world first by those who maintained that the law does not change. Surprisingly, by proclaiming continuity while denying change, the practice of universal education for female Jews became normative. These legal approaches established as a given for all segments of the Jewish world that girls must be formally educated. Significantly, the new was proclaimed in such a way that it was immediately accepted as part of a traditional Judaism and not perceived as a threat even by the traditionalists.

Across North America, Jewish schools proliferated. Initially, most educational efforts took place in synagogue contexts. After World War II, boys and girls entered Orthodox day schools in almost equal numbers. Some maintained separate classes or schools for boys and girls; other were coeducational. Some taught the same subjects to both; others maintained a separate curriculum. By the 1950s girls as well as boys could get an excellent Jewish education especially in centrist Orthodox schools. The gender gap in education was most pronounced in right-wing Orthodox schools and non-Orthodox supplementary education. In the 1970s the study of Jewish texts post high school accelerated. Jewish studies programs in universities further enabled the illiterate as well as well-educated women to broaden and deepen their studies. The rabbinical seminaries of the Reform (Hebrew Union College–Jewish Institute of Religion), Conservative (Jewish Theological Seminary), and Reconstructionist (Reconstructionist Rabbinical College) movements opened their doors and increased advanced text study to women. The Yeshiva University of the Orthodox community did not allow women into their seminary but established Stern College for women's continued education. Notably and controversially, Rabbi Joseph B. Soloveitchik inaugurated the first Talmud lecture for women there. In fact, aside from the Reconstructionist Rabbinical College, which opened its doors to men and women at its inception in 1968, early controversy was part of the process in all the movements. Henrietta Szold (1860–1945) was an educator, essayist, editor, social and communal worker, Zionist organizer, and politician; she had to agree that she would not request a degree upon completion of her studies before she was accepted into the Jewish Theological Seminary. The Reform Hebrew Union College was theoretically open to equal education but also took time to graduate learned women. These conflicts occurred in the first half of the twentieth century. The second half explodes with opportunities for women to advance as Jewish students and scholars. Some seek professional degrees and jobs; others propose only to learn, to sit and study for the love of Torah. There are proliferating institutes such as the Drisha Institute for Jewish Education in New York, where any woman can study without any formal program or degree expected. In all sectors and in all topics women have gained in knowl-edge and influence. Jewish women today are far more likely than their grandmothers to have received some formal Jewish education. The consequences of this rev-olution are varied and profound, contributing to, rather than detracting from, Jewish survival.

The legal analysis that brokered this transformation is still developing. In all likelihood none of the original players anticipated the far-reaching and long-term af-fects of such legislative innovation: independent knowl-edgeable women, leaders, women who could be rabbis. For although none of the rabbinic proponents of women's education envisioned female rabbinic leaders, their early decisions unequivocally opened the path for that eventuality.

The Reform seminary was the first to formally ordain a female rabbi in 1972. The path to that level was long and convoluted. Although committed to the ideal of male/female equality since at least 1845, the implemen-tation of the abstract commitment took time and soci-etal approval. The process was simpler and speedier in the Reconstructionist Rabbinical College. Their doors were unconditionally open to women since 1968, and they ordained their first female rabbi in 1973. Con-versely, the Conservative movement followed a more difficult process. The issue was debated for almost ten years. Those who opposed did so on halakic grounds, claiming specific prohibitions as well as the weight of previous halakic standards. The role of teacher, pastor, or preacher was not the problem. The two outstanding legal obstacles involved women in the prohibited roles of witness and prayer leader. Both these tasks were seen as legally prohibited to women in all traditional sources. The initial discussion in the Conservative movement of-fered that female rabbis would desist from those two auxiliary actions in the same way that a rabbi who is a *cohen* (descended from the priestly class) does not of-ficiate at a funeral. But there were those who contended that an argument could be made for women performing all the roles of a rabbi by accepting complete ritual ob-ligations. Thus, Rabbi Joel Roth wrote a responsum as-serting that if women accepted the obligation to pray daily at fixed times—as part of a voluntary acceptance of all mitzvoth—they would be counted as part of the minyan (prayer quorum) and therefore able to represent the community as prayer leaders. In the matter of wit-nesses, Roth recommends setting aside the biblical pro-hibition because the expectation today is that women are reliable. Other submissions offered that the prayer leader no longer represents the congregation since they all have books and can read from them. Thus the leader is merely a musician who enhances the service. Some claim that the witness prohibition is not biblical and is therefore easier to change. The debate expanded with numerous suggestions, opinions, and papers. The ordi-nation of women was finally accepted in 1983. Women were not accepted into the cantorial program until 1987.

The legal impediments were perceived differently among Orthodox and right-wing Conservative Jews. While most agreed that the major obstacle of the pro-hibition to female education was no longer problematic, the issue of women as scholars and teachers of Jewish law still lingered for some. However, the question of women as witnesses involved a more serious impedi-ment. The Talmud links the ability to be a judge to the ability to testify. If the law maintains that a woman can-not testify in a court of law, then as a direct consequence she cannot sit in judgment. This legal disability is indeed significant since the ability to function as a *dayan* (judge) encompasses the rabbi's competence to prom-ulgate legal decisions. Other halakic barriers include is-sues of modesty, of women standing before a male con-gregation, or coming into close proximity to a male for private advising. Although many of these considerations disappear in the context of modern society and its stan-dards of interaction, for some they remain troublesome. A more substantive problem is raised in the legal rulings of Maimonides (Rabbi Moses ben Maimon, 1135–1204). Citing the biblical statement concerning the appoint-ment of a king "from amongst your brothers" (Deuter-onomy 17:15), Maimonides defines that the king must be male and applies this to all positions of authority. This decision coupled with the legal questions about a woman standing as representative of the congregation, especially if she is not equally obligated, has remained of primary concern in the Orthodox world. Even though there are examples of Jewish women in history acting as teachers, preachers, and halakic decision makers, those chronicles are not treated as legal precedent for ordi-nation. Hence, aside from two exceptional Israeli Or-thodox rabbis who have decided to ordain two women, so far the Orthodox rabbinate is closed to women.

Be that as it may, there are significant developments in the Orthodox world, especially in Israel. The first ma-jor step was the training of women as rabbinical court advocates in Israel. These female advocates appear in rabbinic courts to plead divorce cases and advise women in the complicated area of Jewish divorce. Their training is intense, and after two or three years they receive a certificate from the Chief Rabbinate of Israel. This pro-gram began in Israel in 1990 but as yet has not found a home in America, which does not have a Directorate of rabbinical courts. A second step is the Orthodox ha-lakic accreditation of women as halakic advisers for is-sues relating to menstrual laws and rites. By locating their expertise in divorce and menstruation, these two programs for women concentrate on female issues and claim that women are better able to advise and represent women. There is now a Halakic Hotline staffed by these specialists that receives calls from Orthodox women all over the world. Ironically, these novel programs are predicated on claims for traditional standards of modesty and are consistent with traditional forms of gender separation. Yet the revolution behind these formats is based on women's intellectual achievements and ushers in an era of female guidance and authority. In the United States, two synagogues in New York attempted to include women professionally by hiring women as rabbinic interns. Instead of offering halakic expertise, these women were given pastoral duties. Regrettably, instead of expanding, that endeavor has evaporated. Nevertheless, given the increased level of scholarship and commitment among women and the communities' growing need for resources, Orthodox women will soon take their place as leaders with authority and influence. Blu Greenberg, renowned Orthodox feminist, predicted Orthodox female rabbis within this decade.

Considering the increased importance of synagogues in the practice of American Judaism, it is to be expected that numerous legal developments are synagogue based. The Reform movement was the first to introduce mixed pews in America (Albany, New York). In like manner, when the Conservative movement followed, there was no uniformly accepted legal decision. In 1941 Boaz Cohen argued that there was no legal basis other than justifying this move by abrogating the law and citing the radical statement of "it is time to work for God and break the law of God" found in Psalms 119:126. Others presented the notion that there were always variations in synagogue seating. The Orthodox movement vehemently refused to accept any form of mixed seating, and in the 1950s it became the symbol of the division between the movements. Numerous legal issues were raised, with some prominent Orthodox authorities claiming that separation during prayers was biblically mandated.

One of the big issues in the 1940s was the presence of women on synagogue boards. Once debated both in Conservative and Orthodox rabbinic writings, today most synagogues in both camps allow and even expect women to take their place as lay leaders. The legal issue remains focused on the interpretation and extension of Maimonides's ruling on placing women in positions of power. In 1959 the United Synagogue (Conservative) voted that all women are eligible to be members and hold office.

In 1955 the Conservative movement undertook a discussion about aliyot (sing. aliyah: being called up to read from the Torah scroll during synagogue services) for women. Linked to the growing bat mitzvah phenomenon, two positions emerged: for and against. Again individual synagogues were left to decide policy independently, and many were very slow to accept this practice. Although Jewish law theoretically includes women among the seven people who are called to read from the Torah during services, the Talmud notes that it was not the custom to do so because of the community's honor. Without any permissive decree or precedent in this, Conservative rabbis such as Aaron Blumenthal based their approval on a reinterpretation of community honor and a need to extend equal status to women, given American standards. Some rabbis allowed this aliyah as an additional one after the prescribed seven, or only on special occasions. By 1973, the Conservative movement was prepared to include women in the quorum for worship services (minyan). Some rabbis, such as Philip Sigal, argued that since minors and slaves were able to be counted for the minyan and women were frequently listed alongside those two categories, then by analogous extension, women could be counted for the quorum. Prominent rabbis such as David Feldman were opposed because they could find no legal justification. Instead of accepting any one of the various position papers, the Committee on Jewish Law and Standards passed a statute (takkanah) allowing women to be part of the minyan. In the Reform community, the issue had long been resolved with women counting equally. On the other hand, since they did not necessarily require a minyan (decided in 1936 and affirmed in 1989), this eligibility did not have the same valence.

In the Orthodox world women are not counted in the minyan or given aliyot. But there are other changes in practice that are noteworthy. Women dancing with the Torah scrolls on the holiday of Simhat Torah, which literally means "rejoicing in the Torah," commemorating the end and beginning of the annual cycle of weekly Torah readings, became symptomatic of an increase in ritual activity. Although according to the sixteenth-century Code of Jewish Law women are allowed to see, touch, and read from the Torah scrolls, some authorities forbade women to touch the Torah when menstruating. Women's public performance of ritual depended on the application of these rulings and opinions. Similarly, the recitation of the mourner's prayer (kaddish) was at first restricted. The question was first raised in Amsterdam in the seventeenth century. As then, some rabbis today authorize women to say this prayer and others ban it. While both the Conservative and Reform law committees consented to women's kaddish, neither made it mandatory. Actually, although some women recite this prayer occasionally, not many women have carried on for the complete eleven-month mourning period for parents. It is not necessarily easy to find a daily minyan that is female friendly for this purpose. But as more women practice these rituals publicly and write about them, they set a new norm for individuals and for the community.

Women's tefillah (prayer) groups were established in several communities as women tried to maximize their personal public prayer experience. The initial focal point was Rosh Hodesh, the new moon, traditionally known as a woman's holiday. Products of modern Jewish educational institutions, some women knew how to pray but were not satisfied with their normal routine. They understood the importance of ritual participation and sought to increase their roles as practicing Jews. Influenced by the prevailing women's movement as well as by traditional patterns of gender separation, they resolved to pray together once a month. Although women from across the Jewish spectrum attended the services, this arrangement was particular to the Orthodox community. Unlike Conservative and Reform Jews, the women accepted the model of gender separation. They did not elect to bypass the *mehitsa*—the partition separating men and women during prayer. Acting according to Orthodox norms, they asked for rabbinic approval. Submission to halakic authority—customarily male authority—marked this endeavor as significantly different from other feminist activities. Yet the prayer service challenged notions of participation, public ritual, and gender separation. One outgrowth is the still-active court case in Israel. Initiated in 1988 by North American women, the Women of the Wall have been trying to pray at the Western Wall in Jerusalem with Torah reading as the women's tefillah (prayer) groups do in America. The Israeli government and courts have not yet settled the case.

Although the women maintain that they are acting according to halakah, the backlash has been vigorous and unexpected. The debate surrounding the legal status of such expressions differs in Israel and America. In Israel the case revolves around security and custom, not particular to Jewish law. In America it focused on the question of the quorum and whether women are abandoning the main communal service. It is ironic that the women themselves do not claim minyan status. Although there is legal precedent for challenging the gender restriction of the minyan concept, the women's groups consciously opted to avoid halakic controversy by choosing not to claim the status of a prayer quorum. Hence, they do not say certain prayers and avoid the minyan format. It is further curious that women are being told not to separate from communal prayer but that their presence at that prayer service is not necessary. They have been accused of undermining the legal categories of prayer, of gender, and of communal commitment. Despite the disapproval, some women continue to gather in small groups to participate in a legitimately recognized form of public, personal, and communal prayer. Curiously, both sides have relied on the same responsum of Rabbi Moses Feinstein. The women contend that they can touch, read from, and dance with a Torah and that Jewish law in general and Rabbi Feinstein's letter specifically support such activity.

More important, the women maintain that they act out of a sincere commitment, requesting that the permissible be permitted them. This type of argument is repeated in many situations of ritual exemptions and voluntary obligation such as women wearing prayer shawls (*tsitsit, talit*) and phylacteries (tefillin). There is a debate in classical rabbinic law on women using these items. The Reform position was expressed by Rabbi Solomon Freehof, who wrote that women could wear the prayer shawl. The Conservative position was not uniform, but in 1990 Rabbi David Golinkin wrote a responsum permitting women to don phylacteries. These decisions left the choice up to the individual congregation and woman. Even though most women from all the denominations have chosen not to put on these ritual artifacts, the legal debate about their usage extends the range of the possible, the permitted, and the ideal.

Life cycle rituals, some celebrated at home and others in the synagogue, were initiated from within the general population and more readily accepted. Since there were no legal ramifications to expanding baby-naming ceremonies for girls, these celebrations were creative, informal, and popular. Bat mitzvah ceremonials, on the other hand, caused debate in all sectors. Bat mitzvah ceremonies, paralleling bar mitzvah services for boys, increased in popularity in the latter half of the twentieth century, allowing some women to take a central role in public synagogue rituals.

The terms *bar* and *bat mitzvah* refer to one who is subject to the law and connotes membership in the community. The legal standard of twelve years for girls and thirteen for boys dates back to the Talmud. The Talmud advances the concept of a male and female age of maturity as a juridical status, referring to a person who is no longer a child and must legally act as an adult. Thus, after their respective twelfth and thirteenth birthdays, girls and boys must fast on Yom Kippur. For a woman, this involves acting on her own behalf, no longer dependent on her father, mother, or brother for marital arrangements, for example.

Bat mitzvah ceremonies, apparently inaugurated in Italy and Iraq in the nineteenth century (with France and Germany a bit later), have developed in twentieth-century America along denominational lines. Beginning slowly, most notably, though not the first, in 1922 with the bat mitzvah of the daughter of Rabbi Mordecai Kaplan, founder of the Reconstructionist movement, there were many different locations and patterns. The Reform rabbinate was initially opposed since they preferred the later confirmation rite. Many saw bat mitzvah as a step backward to gender discrimination. The first Reform ceremony was held in Chicago in 1931, but American Reform responsa of 1913 and 1954 both banned the bat mitzvah as being counter to tradition. By 1979 the American Reform Responsa #33 claimed that bar/bat mitzvah are virtually universally observed and that there was no conflict with the Reform ceremony of confirmation.

The 1950s and 1960s witnessed a ceremonial evolution in the Conservative movement. At first, this practice was also controversial but quickly moved into mainstream Conservative practice. Friday nights were originally reserved for the bat mitzvah and Shabbat mornings for the boys' ceremony. Given the various formats, these early ceremonies remained synagogue-based modest affairs, symbolic of adulthood. In the early 1950s, the Rabbinical Assembly began to discuss the legal and ritual issues related to this growing phenomenon. The decision on granting aliyot to women was a direct result of this deliberation. Thus, the ritual celebration of bat mitzvah became ensconced within Reform, Conservative, and Reconstructionist congregations in the 1970s and 1980s. Through the 1970s many in the Orthodox movement sought ways to fit a bat mitzvah into their established order of observances.

Contemporary Orthodox responsa on bat mitzvah remains divided. Some rule against any celebration; others limit the context; and still others are more accepting of the exercise. For the traditional halakists, there are major questions to be settled before innovative practices such as celebrating a bat mitzvah may take place in synagogues. The central issues include what a woman may do or say on this occasion, where it may take place, who can participate, and what are the legal and liturgical responsibilities that ensue. Equally important is the legal question of where this idea originated and who introduced it. For some, the entire project is tainted because its source is in the non-Orthodox sector.

The variety of styles and formats both invigorates and confuses. In the Conservative, Reconstructionist, and Reform movements, most girls have a bat mitzvah celebration in which their performance is identical with a bar mitzvah. Even though in some communities this marks the only time a girl reads from the Torah or Haftorah (weekly readings from the non-Torah biblical texts), nonetheless, the members feel it appropriate to acknowledge her coming of age with a Torah ritual. For some the ceremony is held Friday night; for many others, it takes place during Sabbath morning services. In the Orthodox communities, there is great resistance to a public performance in the synagogue. Some prefer home- or school-based rites. Others permit the use of synagogue when there are no prayer services. Many prefer a ceremony that is based on an educational format rather than as a form of worship. Noteworthy are the increasing numbers who celebrate their bat mitzvah at the separate women's prayer services for Rosh Hodesh. In this array, one fact stands out: In almost every Orthodox community today, there exists some format for the recognition and celebration of a girl's initiation as an adult Jew on her twelfth birthday.

Marriage ceremonies traditionally relied on male action and female consent. Without a woman's consent the marriage is not valid, but the man is the one who "takes a wife": He gives the gift, usually a ring, to her and pronounces the formula of marriage. In the contemporary context of increasing her ritual performance, some rabbis have permitted the bride to give the groom a ring and to say some fitting words. In many Reform and Conservative marriages the bride says the same words as the groom. Legalists have argued about the nature of the second ring as well as the implications of her speech act. Double ring ceremonies are increasingly adopted in all the movements. At issue is the nature of the legal contract of marriage. Is it the man who establishes the contract and whatever the bride does is window dressing, or is the nature of the legal relationship equitable? Changes have also been made to the *ketubah*, the marriage contract, in the non-Orthodox denominations. Additionally, there is an increase in the role of female friends in the wedding ceremony, with some women saying the blessings (*Sheva brachot*) under the canopy or later at the meal. The main problem within marriage law has always been the implication for divorce procedures, one of the most vexing problems in Jewish law today. Jewish divorce, like any other, can be simple or complicated, a release or a tragedy, straightforward or a swindle. It can set people free to resume or reinvent their lives, or it can embroil individuals and families in a never-ending cycle of abuse. The intent of rabbinic Judaism was to ensure a tolerable disengagement. Regrettably, the current implementation in the Jewish legal system does not meet that minimal standard. Many individuals, women and men, rabbis and volunteers, in all the denominations have labored to maintain a fair practice. And in some cases it works.

However, the biblical account of divorce found in Deuteronomy, while accepting marital breakups, establishes a procedure that is at the heart of the problem. "When a man has taken a wife, and married her, and it come [*sic*] to pass that she find [*sic*] no favour in his eyes, because he has found some unseemliness in her: then let him write her a bill of divorce, and give it in her hand, and send her out of his house. And when she is departed out of his house, she may go and be another man's wife" (Deuteronomy 24:1,2). According to the literal message, the man is the initiator, the actor. And while rabbinic law established that there need be no grounds for divorce other than mutual consent, it enforced the structured order of the verse: The male is the active legal principle. He must initiate, author, and give the document to her. She receives it and only then is free to resume control of her life.

While in most cases Judaism's tolerant acceptance of divorce enables a decent split, in too many situations this male prerogative becomes the means for extortion, vengeance, and affliction. Certainly not a biblical ideal. Thus, although her consent to the divorce is necessary, the wife is still at the mercy of the husband. In the course of the centuries-long development of Jewish law, many improvements have been incorporated into the system in an attempt to limit the man's unilateral power and prevent misery. The rabbis were aware of and sensitive to women's vulnerability, but they preserved the pattern whereby the get (the divorce document) is given freely by the man to his wife, which she must voluntarily accept. Without this document, neither partner may remarry according to classic Jewish law.

Today, this affects many Jews. There have been various attempts to solve or ameliorate the condition, but throughout Israel and in the Orthodox community outside of Israel, the pattern of insisting on the biblical directive has left too many women *agunot* (pl.). An *agunah* (sing.) is a woman who cannot remarry because her husband is unable or unwilling to give her a get (Jewish divorce). The term actually means anchored or tied down and is first found in verb form in the biblical story of Ruth (1:13). The original Talmudic use of the word was limited to cases in which the man had disappeared and literally could not act as a legal instrument in the Jewish divorce proceedings. In America, popular usage has expanded the term to apply to all cases of women who are unable to remarry because their husbands will not acquiesce and give the divorce document. Since the rabbinic court cannot authorize the writing of the get, and only a man can initiate the proceedings, problems arise most frequently for women, although the term can be applied to men (*agun*).

The problems for women within this system are obvious. Procedurally dependent on her husband and on a rabbinic court, her future children also become pawns in this tug of war. If a woman without a get gives birth, her newborn children will be considered the product of an adulterous union and hence be categorized as *mamzerim*, Jews who are not allowed to marry other Jews. A *mamzer* can be a rabbi but can only marry a non-Jew or another *mamzer*. There is no remedy. To be sure, both a man and a woman can be found guilty of adultery, but the category depends on the marital status of the woman only. The applicable result is that the woman suffers the most from an incomplete divorce. The irony is that if the Jewish process of divorce was established to set one free, even to encourage remarriage, the current reality is one in which the process itself has created a group of people who are not free. And the numbers and problems are increasing.

Exact numbers are actually hard to come by, but the numerical dimensions of this issue should not be the primary consideration. For Jewish society today, divorce constitutes a major moral problem: not because of the increase in numbers, nor because of the guilt of either party—but because of the inequities of the process, the failure of Jewish law, and the indifference of the larger community. People no longer married, no longer living together, are still tied to each other. Bound together and abandoned. The implication for the credibility, viability, and continuity of Jewish law is crucial.

The Reform movement often relies on local civil divorce courts, accepting a civil decree as terminating a marriage. Citing the injustice of Jewish divorce, Reform rabbis might additionally issue a Jewish divorce after the civil one, but they will perform a wedding for those without a get. Some rabbis today have noted that it is proper to write a get rather than rely on the secular state, while others feel that it is inappropriate to use halakah when they do not accept its binding authority. Regardless of the attention to the details and desirability of a get, the bottom line is that since 1869 the Reform movement has recognized civil divorce as sufficient.

Not so the Conservative rabbinate, which consistently has required a separate rabbinic Jewish divorce. In 1953 the Conservative movement accepted the Lieberman clause inserted in the *ketubah* that stated that if a Jewish divorce had not been effected after the civil divorce, then both parties agreed to appear before the movement's rabbinic court and obey its decision. There was great debate over this clause as well as over the recommendation of a conditional marriage so that neither proposal solved the problem. They then decided to apply the ancient rabbinic prerogative to dissolve marriages with annulments. The Conservative movement empowered its central court to intervene and act unilaterally to effect a divorce or annulment when there are insurmountable problems. In 1980 the Reconstructionist *Beth Din* (court of law), issued a get written on behalf of a woman to her husband. This is known as the first egalitarian get, but Reconstructionist rabbis still recommend convincing the husband to issue a traditional divorce.

In the Orthodox community, the rabbis have been most active on individual cases rather than on comprehensive solutions. Many are now requiring a prenuptial agreement wherein both parties agree that if they intend to divorce, they will go through with a complete Jewish divorce. Some of these contracts then obligate the man to give the woman a daily maintenance fee until such time as he actually gives her the get. There are also some who are using annulments with increasing frequency, but this has engendered great debate. Without a recognized get, the possibility increases that many Jews will be considered *mamzerim* and not be able to marry other Jews. Since the Orthodox community strictly adheres to the law and its procedure, it is the scene of the greatest inequities and most vigorous activism. There are numerous books, articles, and legal decisions on the laws of Jewish divorce, contemporary problems, and proposed solutions. As Rivka Haut, an Orthodox activist, wrote: "The tragedy of the *agunah* is causing many in the Orthodox world to reevaluate Rabbinic constructs of marriage and divorce" (*Lifecycles*, in Orenstein, ed., 189).

The proliferation of unsettled cases has convinced many individuals and organizations to come forward. There are solutions within Jewish law and vehicles for action. Social awareness and education are the first steps. There are numerous groups and resources available. Some organizations have taken on the task of working with individual cases; others have promoted educational formats. Working within both the secular and Jewish systems, activists have initiated both civil and halakic remedies. New York is the center of numerous organizations such as G.e.t., Inc., Agunah, Inc., Lema'an Bnos Yisrael International, and Beth Din of America (RCA). Canadian activities are mobilized through the Coalition of Jewish Women for the Get and in 1990 succeeded in getting federal legislation passed. In Israel, aside from the work of the special directorate of the Chief Rabbinate, women work through a confusing array of organizations such as Israel Women's Network and Icar, International Human Rights Watch, Ohr Torah Legal Aid Program, Organization for Women Denied a Divorce, and Mevo Satum: The Dead End. Many of these organizations were founded and staffed by women volunteers. Aside from the major denominational courts (*batei din*), there are numerous rabbinic courts that follow their own standards and processes. Confusion reigns.

Likewise, there is a plethora of legal issues and options when it comes to conditions of fertilization, birthing, and abortion. Although there is a great bias in favor of fertility in Judaism, in all the legal discussions the central concern is always the life of the mother. Thus, birth control will be permitted when the mother's life is threatened in some way. The legal discussions focus on why and who but also on how. The method used cannot violate certain canons of law. In the first part of the twentieth century, with the availability of rubber, rabbinic experts such as Rabbi Joshua Baumol determined that a diaphragm was usable in all situations wherein the talmudically approved sponge or tampon (*mokh*) was permitted. Then in the 1960s with the appearance of the pill, which conformed to halakic standards, many authorities implemented lenient positions across the denominational divide. Abortion presented other thorny problems. All the discussions use the same biblical and Talmudic precedents. All understand and agree that saving the mother's life requires, not permits, abortion even in the ninth month. The fetus is not a complete human being yet; the mother's life is sacrosanct. Yet all are uncomfortable, if not forbidding, of abortion on demand:

Convenience is not accepted as a justification. Maternal pain, suffering, and anguish form the only valid basis for abortion in all the responsa. The classic tension between reverence for all forms of life and the need to save an existing life render judgments of compassion, caution, and human concern. Given these agreed-upon standards, there is still a great deal of disagreement and debate. Nonetheless, most Jewish organizations support civil legislation that maintains the legality and accessibility of abortion so that religious authorities, in cooperation with medical specialists, may determine when an abortion is mandated halakically. Today, cases of surrogacy, in vitro fertilization, artificial insemination, and cloning, to name just a few, present Jewish legalists with a wide range of demanding and complicated problems. But they also present the law with the potential for effective application and development. Every decision attests to the dynamism inherent in a legal tradition of thousands of years.

Yet some feminists such as Judith Plaskow found the legal system to be contrary to feminist designs. The problem with legal texts is multifaceted. Most significantly, women's voices are not heard. They may ask the questions and live with the decision, but they do not create—and have no part in the creation of—the legal text. It is of course ironic to search for a woman's voice in a tradition that bans the (singing) voice of a woman for fear of its effect on men.

Plaskow lists three objections to law as a medium for the feminist scholar and activist alike. First, the content of the legal material is problematic, especially since women are often objects within this system, treated as an undifferentiated group. The male experience is the legal norm. The lists of exemptions and obligations privilege men and create a community of practitioners in which only men are the ritual experts and women do not participate fully in the life of the community. She further questions whether law typifies a woman's style of management. Many feminists agree with Plaskow's suggestion that law may not be women's mode of operation and, therefore, is not an arena for feminist praxis, attention, or transformation. The final objection is to the structure of the legal process itself. Women have not historically been either the creators or agents of legal formation. Issues of access and agency challenge contemporary legal positions. In *Standing Again at Sinai*, Plaskow opined:

The place of halakhah in the feminist transformation of Torah stands, then, on the boundary of past and future. The history of what halakhah has done to women and of women's relationship to halakhah is part of the broader reconstruction of Jewish memory. Women's halakhah, however, and women's self-defined relation to halakhah await the present and the future. (74)

But Jewish law is the link with generations of the past, with a cherished history and a vibrant heritage. Is it not redeemable? Perhaps the very confusing diversity signals a flexibility and openness that are the foundation for continued involvement and application. Since the legal system was established as a responsive one, much of its content can be addressed in today's language and terms, using women's experience to pry it open. All social systems are based on legal systems. Women work and live in societies based on rules. Moreover, the women who ask these questions of their rabbis accept rabbinic authority within the hierarchy of a legal process. It is fitting to attend to that legal heritage. As Judith Hauptman noted, Jewish law can be equated with principled change. Blu Greenberg challenged many with her probing image of the halakic path that is responsive to rabbinic discretion. She has persistently claimed, "A central theme seems to emerge: where there was a rabbinic will, there was a rabbinic way" (44). On the other hand, Tikva Frymer-Kensky observed that attention to the human element in the decision-making process permeates feminist analysis as well as rabbinic decisions. Additional scholars such as Judith Romney Wegner, Miriam Peskowitz, and Rachel Adler have approached Jewish law with both a feminist critical perspective as well as with transformative propositions for understanding and applying that system. In *Engendering Judaism*, Rachel Adler presented her personal approach to Jewish law.

By renewing halakhah we bridge the gap between the impoverished world of meaning we currently inhabit and the richer and more vital worlds that might be. Our mission . . . is to make connections where there has been a rift, to make conversation where there has been silence, to engender a new world. (58)

The study of Jewish law, as well as its promulgation, traditionally has been androcentric, both as a subject and as a vocation. The recent inclusion of women in the equation, in the capacity of learned teacher, scholar, decisor, and/or rabbi, has changed that landscape conceptually and practically. We now await those legal engagements and determinations as women expand the map of Judaic tradition, gaining access, invoking their own agency, and redeeming their place within the covenant.

SOURCES: The best general introduction to the topic of women in Jewish law is found in Rachel Biale's *Women and Jewish Law: An Exploration of Women's Issues in Halakhic Sources* (1984). Many of the direct Hebrew legal sources affecting women's lives were collected by Getsel Ellenson in his classic *HaIshah Ve-HaMitsvot*, 3 vols. (1977). These have been translated into English: *Serving the Creator* (1992), *The Modest Way* (1992), and *Partners in Life* (1998). Early examples of the Jewish feminist critique can be found in Susannah Heschel's edited volume *On Being a Jewish Feminist* (1983). Some earlier legal arguments can be found in Elizabeth Koltun's edited volume *The Jewish Woman* (1976). Judith Plaskow presents one of the clearest feminist critiques and appreciation of Jewish legal processes in her influential book *Standing Again at Sinai* (1990). For a clear contextualized presentation of the issues as they developed in American Jewish life, see Sylvia Barack Fishman, *A Breath of Life: Feminism in the American Jewish Community* (1993). Placing women in synagogue life from both a historical and ritual perspective, Susan Grossman and Rivka Haut edited *Daughters of the King: Women and the Synagogue* (1992). Paralleling that historical approach, the legality and evidence of women's Judaica education can be found in the excellent volume by Shoshana Pantel Zolty, *"And All Your Children Shall Be Learned": Women and the Study of Torah in Jewish Law and History* (1993). Interestingly, as Jewish women scholars entered the field, their voices and research on Jewish law were collected into a volume edited by Micah Halpern and Hannah Safrai, *Jewish Legal Writings by Women* (1998). Scholars such as Judith Romney Wegner, Judith Hauptman, Miriam Peskowitz, Daniel Boyarin, and Charlotee Fonrobert have written books on gender in Talmudic law from a variety of perspectives. For an example of the intersection of law and policy today as it affects women's lives, see Norma Baumel Joseph, "Ritual Law and Praxis: Bat Mitsva Celebrations," *Modern Judaism* 22.3 (Fall 2002): 234–260. Finally, some of the contemporary issues are illuminated in the documentary film *Untying the Bonds . . . Women and Jewish Divorce* (1997) and in the volume edited by Rivka Haut and Phyllis Chesler, *Women of the Wall* (2002). See also Judith Hauptman, "Women and Prayer: An Attempt to Dispel Some Fallacies," *Judaism* 42 (Fall 1993); Judith Romney Wegner, *Chattel or Person? The Status of Women in the Mishnah* (1988); Debra Orenstein, ed., *Lifecycles: Jewish Women on Life Passages & Personal Milestones* (1994); Blu Greenberg, *On Women & Judaism: A View from Tradition* (1981); and Rachel Adler, *Engendering Judaism: An Inclusive Theology and Ethics* (1998).

ANTI-SEMITISM
Riv-Ellen Prell

ANTI-SEMITISM, THE hatred of Jews, in the United States has taken various forms in different periods and regions. Its roots clearly lie within Europe, most likely beginning with state support of Christianity in the fourth century by the Emperor Constantine. Ironically, the nineteenth-century term *anti-Semitism* was invented by those who adhered to its tenets. These ideologues drew on the principles of a false racial science that asserted the existence of a Jewish or Semitic race in order to oppose extending citizenship to Germany's Jews.

With each wave of settlement from the seventeenth

to the twentieth centuries the European immigrants brought anti-Semitism with them to the New World. Persistent and virulent, it has nevertheless led to the same magnitude of discrimination as those faced by American Catholics or people of color. In contrast to Europe, anti-Semitism in the United States has, practically speaking, never been state sponsored, nor has the state sanctioned violence against Jews. Until the mid-nineteenth century, anti-Semitism was largely directed against the Jews for the practice of Judaism. By the late nineteenth century, and well into the twentieth, this prejudice came to focus instead on Jews as a stigmatized people, and its religious component became secondary.

The most persistent form of anti-Semitism has been a series of widely circulating stereotypes that constructed Jews as socially, religiously, and economically unacceptable to American life. They were made to feel marginal and menacing. Jews have suffered the very real consequences that those attitudes created. Particularly in the twentieth century, Jews in the United States were deprived of open access to all educational opportunities, the right to many types of employment, housing, and social acceptance.

Most anti-Semitic stereotypes expressing anxiety about Jews were directed primarily at men, although Jewish women were also objects of hate. Jews consistently have organized to defend themselves against these accusations, and since the nineteenth century, Jewish women's organizations have been a major force to combat prejudice. Conversely, both men and women organized around hatred of Jews in the United States in the twentieth century, creating a variety of organizations that attacked Jews, including women's organizations.

Anti-Semitism is further complicated by "self-hatred," or internalized anti-Semitism. For example, in 1918 a New York Jewish journalist, Marion Golde, asked Mrs. Sholem Asch, wife of a distinguished Yiddish writer, what she thought of young Jewish women living on New York's lower East Side. She commented upon "their awful coiffures, the clumsy and ungraceful costumes, the indiscriminate and tasteless use of cosmetics, their extravagance in dress and atrocious taste." Mrs. Asch then explained that she had asked her gentile friends, "What do you think is wrong with our girls?" They told her, "They do not want to learn; they have no taste" (*American Weekly Jewish News*, March 24, 1918). These offensive images of young Jewish women drew on classical anti-Semitic ideas about Jews of the period. Their appearance and demeanor were vulgar; Jewish women were excessively interested in possessions. Asch's view echoes many, but by no means all, of the traits ascribed to Jews by American anti-Semites.

That Jews and non-Jews alike shared many of the same negative stereotypes reveals one of the most insidious qualities of anti-Semitism—its internalization by the very people against whom it is directed. Stereotypes based on hate create a double victimization, one external and one internal to the group. Gender, rarely included in any discussion of anti-Semitism, is one of the channels through which anti-Semitism is translated from the dominant culture to the stigmatized one. As non-Jews slur Jews, so Jewish men often paint Jewish women with slightly altered versions of the same stereotypes. Far less frequently, Jewish women have used cultural venues to belittle Jewish men.

The stereotypical image of "the Jew" is part of a dynamic process that reveals how Americans understood their relationship to immigrants, the economy, and social class differences. In projecting their fears about a changing nation and the incorporations of non-Protestants and people of color, Americans expressed some of their deepest held beliefs about their nation. Americans' anxieties about "others" had different implications for Jewish women and men.

The Eighteenth Century: Relative Tolerance and Expanding Rights

The first significant enclave of Jews in America did not develop until 1740. This period was characterized by expanding rights for Jews. Indeed, England gave Jews the rights of citizenship in the American colonies before granting it to them in England. British tolerance of Jews was closely linked to the need for whites with business experience to populate the New World. The more fluid boundaries between groups allowed significant interaction between Jews and Christians.

Before the American Revolution, Jews nevertheless suffered from a number of onerous laws that included church taxes, the denial of political liberties, and Sunday closing-laws forcing Jews to refrain from work on the Christian Sabbath, a burden since they did not work on Saturday when they observed the Sabbath. Although the Founding Fathers never considered denying Jewish males the right to citizenship in the Constitution, state laws continued to limit Jewish involvement in civil society. Citing their loyalty and participation in the Revolutionary War, Jews pressed the right to vote and hold office within states. They gained greater freedom and increasingly became acculturated to the Protestant-dominated nation.

A more aggressive anti-Semitism developed in the first half of the nineteenth century. From 1795 to 1835, a Protestant religious revival, the Second Great Awakening, led activists and ordinary citizens to seek to transform the United States into a Christian nation. Conversion of non-Christians became an important strategy. Christian congregations grew from 2,500 in 1780 to 11,000 in 1820, then to 52,000 by 1860. This period was one of considerable population growth. However, scholars argue that the growth of congregations reflected active efforts at conversion rather than a demographic change.

Women evangelists played a central role in this work of spreading Christianity. Cultural norms of propriety often barred them from males. Therefore, they approached women and children, particularly Jews. Their efforts mobilized Jewish women to write and organize in response to this threat to Jews' ability to practice their religion. Both Jewish and Christian women began to shape public lives in the context of religious antagonism and defense.

Christianizing efforts affected Jews in various ways. During this period, many communities persisted in forcing businesses to close on Sunday. Jewish children were required not only to learn about Christianity in public schools but to see themselves described in their textbooks as recalcitrant sinners for their refusal to convert.

The theater and other cultural venues disparaged Jews, often portraying them adorned with heavy jewels as a sign of their greed. Journalists routinely blamed them for a variety of social ills; Jews often responded with letters to the press defending themselves.

A number of Jewish women writers and activists came to prominence in response to the period's religiously inspired anti-Semitism. Rebecca Gratz (1781–1869), the most influential Jewish woman in the nineteenth century, was born in Philadelphia to a large, philanthropic, merchant family. Well educated for a woman of her day and an active writer, her status and abilities brought her into contact with many Christians. As her own commitment to Judaism grew, intense evangelism by Christian women catalyzed her to defend her religion and people. In 1819 Gratz gathered the women in Philadelphia's Mikveh Israel Congregation to found the country's first Jewish charity, to operate outside the structure of a synagogue. The Female Hebrew Benevolent Society provided food, fuel, shelter, and later a traveler's aid service and employment bureau for needy Jews. These services protected poor Jews from Christian proselytizing as food, clothing, medicine, and education were offered to bring Jews to the church. Similarly, the Jewish Foster Home she founded in 1855 countered Christian foster homes where Jewish children faced pressure to convert to Christianity. Gratz's commitment to Jewish education, training women teachers, and creating philanthropic institutions outside the confines of the male-dominated synagogue allowed her simultaneously to develop a vibrant American Judaism and to create a critical role for Jewish women in it.

During the late nineteenth century educated Jewish women wrote about both the anti-Semitism endangering Jews in Russia, as well as their own experiences in the United States. These women were the descendants of both German Jews and those from Spain and Portugal (Sephardim). They drew on the Jewish woman's tradition of acting as "a mother in Israel," who protected the Jewish "nation" by protecting her family. For example, Alice Hyneman Rhine (1840–?) wrote an article titled "Race Prejudice in Summer Resorts" to challenge anti-Semitic attitudes that excluded Jews from vacation spots they had previously patronized. "In all civilizations, it has been said, The Jew must be of gold to pass for silver, but when he is of thrice refined gold he is still only a Jew. . . . For the obliteration of a prejudice so unjust the Israelite can only look forward with hope to a time when broader culture shall prevail among his Christian fellow men" (*The Forum* 1887). In this passage, Rhine evokes the double edge that characterized elite Jewish women writers' response to anti-Semitism. On the one hand, these authors tried to demonstrate the injustice and inaccuracy of anti-Semitic portrayals. On the other, they express the fervent wish and longing to realize America's promise of equality between Jews and Christians.

Emma Lazarus (1849–1887), the most widely read Jewish writer in the nineteenth century, turned to Jewish subjects and anti-Semitism in the last decade of her life. In 1882 and 1883, she published three essays in *The Century*. In "The Jewish Problem," she was so pessimistic about the persistence of anti-Semitism that she advocated a Jewish homeland as the answer to European discrimination against Jews. These writers had greater access to circles of influence, which emphasized their sense of marginality and what they certainly experienced as a "taint" of Jewishness.

By the second half of the century, the immigration from Germany and central Europe swelled the number of Jews in America. In 1820, roughly 3,000 Jews lived in the United States. By 1840, there were 15,000. While the United States' population doubled between 1789 and 1839, the Jewish population increased fourfold. After 1865, when there were more than 160,000 Jews in the United Sates, the rise of the Jewish population, in conjunction with economic and social changes in the United States, ushered in a more virulent era of anti-Semitism. It was less concerned with the religious heresy of Judaism than with fear of Jews and money. German Jews became part of the nation's system of finance and banking, leading to their relationships with northeastern industrialists who needed finance capital. This alliance became the focus of political hostility from unlikely partners—Populists and the descendants of America's oldest elites.

Nativism, the term most commonly associated with hostility to immigrants, was not uniform. Regions of the country might be virulently anti-Chinese but perfectly comfortable with Jews. Other regions might be accepting of Catholics but hostile to Jews. The nation was characterized by intergroup "tensions" so diverse there was no attempt to categorize them within a single term. And anti-Semitism was found among not only the native born but new immigrants such as the Irish. Hence, in the nineteenth century, hostility against many groups of immigrants was intractable.

Certainly, following the Civil War, Protestant evangelizers persisted in efforts to make America Christian. Attempts to convert Jews and to demand Sunday business closings continued. In response to the nation's depression of 1890, a new form of hatred of Jews emerged. John Higham, the first American historian to have written on anti-Semitism, described this new form as "ideological," noting that it developed alongside "social" anti-Semitism. Ideological anti-Semitism quite simply blamed the ills of the nation on Jews, treating them as pariahs who must be contained and separated from "true" Americans.

Ideological anti-Semites constructed "the" Jew as Shylock, Shakespeare's character in his play *The Merchant of Venice*. He was sly and conniving and preyed on virtuous Christians. Early-twentieth-century Populist ideology rejected banking, commerce, and credit as a denial of meaningful labor. The "dishonest" work of urban American entrepreneurs was juxtaposed with the honest work of agrarian citizens. In this antiurban and antiinternationalist ideology, Jews were cast as the chief architects of the changing economy, the embodiment of a commercial, bourgeois society.

If Shylock was male, much of the social liability that came from an unnatural love for money was also associated with women. Their jewelry, manners, and upward striving were under constant scrutiny. These same qualities were associated with Jewish men, of course, but women, whose adornment so often reflected the economic wealth of their husbands, became a special target for criticism. A common image of the late-nineteenth-century Jew was a male or a female draped in heavy chains of gold. For example, Harriette N. Baker, a popular novelist of the time, wrote *Rebecca the Jewess* in 1879. Rebecca's attraction and ultimate conversion to Christianity is in part expressed in the novel by her loss of taste for rich jewelry and elaborate and showy clothes as she begins to learn about Christianity. Only as a Christian woman does she do good deeds.

Anti-Semitic literature of the period portrayed unscrupulous Jews as observant of minute religious laws and indifferent to ethics, or guided in their cunning by sacred literature, such as the Talmud. In either case, Judaism was cast as entirely inauthentic and best supplanted by Christianity, the true faith of love and charity.

Nevertheless, many scholars have commented upon American's ambivalence about Jews for most of the eighteenth and nineteenth centuries. *The* Jew was to be cas-

tigated and contained. However, particularly in the nineteenth century, the Jew of one's own acquaintance was often admired. The very qualities for which Jews were lauded—hard work and economic success—became the cudgel with which they were attacked and ultimately excluded from elite institutions. By the 1880s, social discrimination became the nation's norm.

As the nineteenth century drew to a close, the images of Jews became more menacing, particularly around issues of gender and sex. For example, writer Ignatius Donnelly (1831–1901), an important figure in the national Populist movement, provided key ideological components in his vision of Jews as a destructive force in the modern world. In his 1891 novel *Caesar's Column*, the villain, Prince Cabano, is not merely a Shylock with economic designs. He also lusts after gentile women. He corrupts not only the economy but Christian womanhood as well. These charges would become prominent in the early twentieth century, as anti-Semitism became a racial strategy to purify the nation.

In the last decades of the nineteenth century a new alliance emerged between old-stock patricians and the captains of industry. Private schools, social clubs, resorts, and universities were created and expanded, all of which excluded Jews from, in some cases, institutions that had previously accepted them. A more aggressive era of anti-Semitism began in the 1920s and reached alarming proportions during the 1930s and into the war years.

The Racialization of Anti-Semitism, 1900–1930s

After the peak of Jewish immigration in the first years of the twentieth century, when more than 2 million eastern European Jews arrived, nativists finally succeeded in influencing Congress to virtually halt immigration from eastern Europe in 1924. This virulently anti-Semitic and anti-Catholic movement focused on the "racial" qualities of these "outsiders." A growing preoccupation with the science of race cast differences between groups as "inherited" and unequal. The United States needed to be preserved as a nation of Americans—white Protestants—who stood at the apex of that hierarchy. For example, the editors of *Life* magazine responded to letter-writers who protested the appearance of anti-Semitism of cartoon images of men with exaggerated noses personifying commercial interests preying on naked and vulnerable women in their pages. They wrote defensively, "[*Life*] never criticized the Jews for their religion, but for their racial characteristics" (*Life* 1901). A new era of anti-Semitism had begun.

Jewish women continued to combat anti-Semitism, but now for the first time through their own national organization. The National Council of Jewish Women, founded in 1893, was one of the first Jewish organizations to engage in antidiscrimination work, establishing the Committee for Purity of the Press in 1905. Members reviewed newspaper accounts about Jews and publicly objected to anti-Semitic articles and stories.

One of the most menacing accusations of Jewish male criminal behavior was that they controlled prostitution, which was called "white slavery." Greedy, degenerate, and corrupting Jewish men were accused of preying upon innocent young women, Christian and Jewish, and enslaving them for profit. These accusations drew on the economic and cultural fears of the era. Jews were part of an international conspiracy; they profited from the labor of others who they victimized in urban centers where young women were particularly vulnerable. The Jew then embodied greed, cosmopolitanism, urbanism, and perversity.

Scholars attribute the increasing popularity and acceptability of anti-Semitism in the 1920s and 1930s to the large number of immigrants and their children in the United States resulting from eighty years of immigration and transformations in American life and economy. Increasing anxiety about communism and radicals further expressed Protestants' fears of America under siege.

Sympathy for hatred of Jews came from many different sectors of society, whose interests were often in conflict with one another. What united them was the defensiveness created by groups who attacked enemies of the nation as dangerous because they were different. For example, feminists in the suffrage movement began to distance themselves from their Jewish Socialist allies as criticisms of the feminist movement of the period mounted. They were often the same accusations directed at Jews—disloyalty, radicalism, and conspiracy. As common cause became a liability, some suffragists drew a sharp line between themselves and Jews.

The Women's Ku Klux Klan was a striking example of right-wing women's activism and investment in anti-Semitism and racism. In the resurgent Klan of the 1920s, newly enfranchised white, Protestant women were eager to keep America pure by limiting the rights of Catholics, Jews, and African Americans. Klan women labeled Jewish men sexually perverse because of their connection to the film industry whose films broadcast "immoral sex" and their "procurement" of white Protestant girls for dance halls. They blamed the Jewish fashion industry for forcing sexually alluring clothing on young women.

Indiana, a stronghold of the Women's Klan, counted 32 percent of its native-born female population as members during the 1920s. Their economic and political clout was considerable as they refused to vote for any non-Protestant candidate. Their leaders reiterated that Jews had no place in public office. Economic boycotts were even more successful. Through women's networks

and word of mouth, consumption became a weapon in the war fought by the Klan for racial supremacy. One woman proclaimed, "There will be no Jewish businesses left in Indianapolis" (Blee, 147). Innumerable Jewish and Catholic merchants lost businesses and left the community because women patronized Protestant stores exclusively.

In the 1930s, for the first time in several decades, a significant sector of mainstream Protestants and Catholics engaged in anti-Semitism as well, castigating Jews for their refusal to relinquish their "difference" and defining that difference as dangerous. For example, *The Christian Century*, a popular Protestant journal, published a series of articles condemning Jews during this decade. One writer noted, "If this racial group . . . insists upon living apart in biological and cultural, as well as religious, aloofness, let it take the consequences" (*Christian Century*, May 13, 1936).

The Christian Front Organization, formed in big cities of the eastern United States, was made up of Catholics who espoused anti-Semitism, labeling Jews as a menace to the country. Father Charles Coughlin of Detroit, who used radio and his own newspaper to widely circulate a message of hatred of Jews, was one of their well-known spokespeople.

The racism of this era's anti-Semitism affected the more affluent German Jews and their descendants, as well as the working-class east European immigrants and their children. The upper reaches of society closed doors once open to affluent Jews by excluding them from private clubs and resorts, where they previously had been accepted. Channels for mobility, particularly education and employment, were severely restricted.

In this period the leadership of American higher education introduced quota systems. Harvard dramatically limited the numbers of Jewish students accepted in 1922, and hundreds of liberal arts and professional schools followed suit. They asserted that failure to contain Jewish enrollment would lead to Jews soon becoming the majority of the student body, keeping out better classes of Americans and introducing values of unbridled competition and aggression.

Ivy "sister" schools, such as Barnard and Radcliffe, and all-female institutions within other colleges implemented similar policies. Both state and private colleges created offices of admission and alumnae committees to screen candidates on the basis of character and personality. Using the language of "social anti-Semitism," they rejected Jewish students because they lacked refinement. Their policies succeeded. Between 1928 and 1932, for example, the number of Jews in northern New Jersey increased dramatically, but Jewish female enrollment at Douglas, the women's counterpart of Rutgers College, declined from 17 percent to 11 percent. The admissions committee accepted 61 percent of Christian applicants but only 31 percent of Jewish women, despite high qualifications. Radcliffe College, with one of the highest percentages of Jewish students, reduced the number of Jews admitted by almost half between 1936 and 1938, despite an increase in applications for admission from Jewish women.

By the 1940s the Seven Sisters colleges collectively had a reputation for "flagrant discrimination," although the percentage of Jewish women admitted varied among them. M. Carey Thomas (1894–1922), president of Bryn Mawr college, blocked both the admission of black students and the promotion of Jewish instructors. Her institution had one of the lowest admission rates of Jewish women.

Like higher education, employers in the workplace openly discriminated against Jews by the late 1920s in their help-wanted ads. Working-class Jewish women were particularly targeted for exclusion. Such female oc-cupations as stenographer, bookkeeper, and secretary most frequently excluded Jews. Jewish women began to wear crosses, because in order to find work they were forced to hide their identities by changing their names and lying about their religion. Jews understood that businesses would not hire them because they feared alienating non-Jewish clients.

Quotas, discrimination, and an ongoing debate over Jewish inferiority created an environment in which Jewish women and men constantly confronted not only discrimination but a sea of anti-Semitic images and stereotypes they often turned against one another. These stereotypes particularly drew on differences between classes and genders, native and nonnative born.

The diary of a young Jewish woman living in Massachusetts in the early 1920s illustrates this dynamic. Helen Labrovitz (b. 1907) often drew distinctions between "good" and "bad" Jews in her entries. She ex-

ILL·GOTTEN RICHES.

Though you try to put on a "Four Hundred" air,
And dress in such style that we all have to stare;
Your last bottom dollar you safely may bet,
That you'll ne'er into decent society get:
For there's none that don't know that your Daddy's big pile
Was gathered by methods despicably vile.

Offensive images of young Jewish women drew on classic anti-Semitic ideas: Their appearance and demeanor were vulgar; Jewish women were excessively interested in possessions. *Used by permission of the American Jewish Archives.*

pressed repulsion at other Jewish girls and reiterated her satisfaction that she "did not look Jewish." In high school she yearned for acceptance from non-Jewish classmates and often expressed despair about rejection of her because she was a Jew. In her adolescent years, Helen internalized American anti-Semitism, blaming her Jewishness for causing pain.

How not to "look," "sound," "act," or "appear" Jewish was the basis of advice and even threats advanced by affluent Jews to one another, as well as to working-class Jews whom they attempted to control. Anxiety about display led Jewish men to urge Jewish women not to wear jewelry at resorts and Jewish women to condemn one another's taste. In newspapers Jewish women advised their affluent sisters to soften their voices and alter their nasalized tones, to simplify their dress because of their "Oriental" (curvaceous and large) bodies, and to monitor their behavior. Affluent women and men charged young Jewish working-class girls of gaudy attire, outlandish hairstyles, and excessive desire for beautiful things. Like young Helen Labrovitz, Jews intent on entry to the middle class internalized the negative and punishing images of social anti-Semitism and worked to contain their differences in hopes of an acceptance that was not forthcoming.

Jewish agencies worked hard to combat these forms of discrimination and joined forces with other minority organizations, such as the National Association for the Advancement of Colored People, to open opportunities. But as the United States entered World War II, anti-Semitism reached new heights.

The War Years—Growing Anxiety and Hate

Anti-Semitism, like all other forms of racism in the United States, reached a high point during the years of World War II. American Jewish organizations began to systematically measure attitudes toward Jews as the war against the Jews in Europe alerted them to the possible vulnerabilities of Jews and other minorities in the United States. For example, the American Jewish Committee surveyed a sample of voters, better educated and hence presumed to be less anti-Semitic. When asked, "Do you think Jews have too much power in the United States?" 43 percent agreed in 1940, 48 percent in 1941, and 51 percent in 1942. In 1944 and 1950 Jews were consistently listed as a greater menace than German Americans, Japanese Americans, radicals, Negroes, and foreigners. In 1944 and 1945 those surveyed were asked if they would support a campaign against Jews and "other hypothetical groups" who might be considered a threat to the nation. Over 40 percent said they would, and more Americans supported such a campaign against Jews than, for example, against Negroes or Catholics. Much of the antagonism directed to Jews in this period

was tied to the war. Isolationists blamed Jews for America's entry and associated Franklin Roosevelt's support for the war with his supposed Jewish ancestry and the presence of Jews in his administration.

One of the most popular isolationist groups was a loose confederation of organizations known as the Mothers' Movement that had between 5 and 6 million members. It began in California in 1939 after Hitler invaded Poland. Its members did not succeed in keeping the United States out of the war but did slow Roosevelt's ability to support the Allies in Europe until the bombing of Pearl Harbor. One of its leaders, Elizabeth Dilling, campaigned against communism, Judaism, and Roosevelt in an effort to keep America Christian. She proclaimed communism "the political vehicle and tool of Judaism." She aligned her anticommunism to the work of the Mothers' organizations in order to support German fascism as the best way to fight communism and Jews.

The Mothers' Movement often masked its anti-Semitism by members appealing to motherhood as the basis for opposing the war. The conventions of the years preceding the war dictated that women committed to influencing public opinion were most successful when they focused on issues pertinent to child welfare. In fact, anti-Semitism was at the core of this group's ideology. One of its founders argued that "Jews started World War II as part of a plot to destroy Christianity" ("Catherine Curtis and Conservative Isolationist Women, 1939–1941," 83).

The war years were a frightening time for American Jewish men and women who faced Jewish genocide in Europe and widespread anti-Semitism in the United States. From the depression to the war's end, the many anxieties that beset Americans were often expressed in their attitudes about and prejudices toward Jews.

The Postwar Period—
Optimism and Disappointment

In September 1945 America's new relationship with Jews was symbolized by Bess Myerson's crowning as Miss America. If a young Jewish woman from the Bronx embodied American beauty and values, surely the end of the war ushered in a new era. In the two following years Laura Z. Hobson's *Gentleman's Agreement* was a bestselling novel and film, marking a seismic shift in attitudes toward Jews that developed after the American victory in World War II. The story's protagonist, a Christian journalist, assigned to write about anti-Semitism, assumed a Jewish identity and found anti-Semitism among his friends and indignity in everyday life for himself and his child. The book's message was that hating Jews had no place in a democratic United States.

The growing unacceptability of anti-Semitism was reflected in a number of postwar opinion surveys of American attitudes that revealed declining fears of Jews and far fewer negative associations between Jews and money. Throughout the 1950s, job discrimination, restrictive policies at resorts, and housing discrimination began rapidly to fall away. Social discrimination certainly persisted among the wealthiest Americans. Only court decisions finally forced the integration of exclusive neighborhoods and elite social clubs. The decade following the end of World War II, therefore, was a particularly optimistic one for American Jews. Judaism was counted as one of America's three great faiths along with Protestantism and Catholicism. Economic opportunities were great, and Jews began a mass exodus to suburbs in disproportionate numbers to assure good educational opportunities for their children. Many young families were particularly optimistic about living the American dream, which included socializing with neighbors.

Research concerned with Jewish-Christian relationships of the period demonstrates that for all of the opportunities realized by Jews, anti-Semitism persisted. Sociological studies of suburbs of Chicago, Boston, New York, Cleveland, and other cities revealed the disappointments of young Jewish families, particularly the young mothers who spent practically all of their time in their new neighborhoods. Phrases like "the golden ghetto" and "five o'clock shadow" reflected the fact that Protestants rarely invited Jews to their homes or shared real friendships. More disturbing was the fact that Christian residents began to leave the suburbs when Jews arrived or that Jews who bought new homes were directed to neighborhoods almost entirely shared with other Jewish families. Some Jewish suburban women reported that when they joined women's community organizations, they quickly became "Jewish" rather than civic clubs. Among more affluent Jewish suburbanites, country club membership and other signs of status were unattainable. Businessmen often explained their policies as the choice of their wives who did not want to be around Jewish women.

During this period the negative stereotype of the Jewish mother—suffocating, overly emotional, and impossible to satisfy—entered the popular culture in the writing and comedy routines of Jewish men. The image resonated with anxiety about women and the loss of male autonomy in the society at large. A novelty book, *How to Be a Jewish Mother*, by Dan Greenburg became the bestselling nonfiction book of 1964. Jews' own anxiety about acceptability in the larger society continued to be expressed by projecting onto mothers what was deemed unattractive about being a Jew, meaning their difference from the larger society.

By the 1980s, when a substantial number of Jews moved into the upper middle class economically, many of these barriers fell. Decreased tolerance for discrimination and Jews' economic success were responsible for this transformation in American society. Anti-Semitism certainly persisted at the end of the twentieth century. However, it became increasingly associated with the extremist political fringe of the United States.

Feminism and Anti-Semitism

Women's political activism became the site of accusations and denials of anti-Semitism in the 1970s and 1980s. Many of the movements on the Political Left in this period were grounded in issues of identity, long suppressed in postwar America's building of a consensus culture. Race, gender, sexuality, and ethnicity became rallying points. Activists vied with one another to name the true cause of oppression—class versus race, race versus gender, for example—and to link their own identities to that cause. Politically active Jewish women participated not only in these groups but in the struggle to locate themselves as Jews in a politics based in identity. In the women's movement, there were two arenas in which the charges of anti-Semitism were raised and denied by some women.

Jewish women in great numbers embraced second wave feminism and were disproportionately involved in its membership and leadership. A much smaller number of women became active in what would be called Jewish feminism. Women who participated in the wider feminist movement sometimes found that their Judaism marginalized them from a hoped-for universal sisterhood. Their concerns with anti-Semitism were often rebuffed, in a way no other minority group's concerns were, some believed.

Feminist religious activism was one important arena of those conflicts. Jewish feminist scholars of religion in the 1970s introduced the problem of anti-Semitism when they raised the alarm that some Christian feminist writing blamed Judaism for patriarchy. "The ultimate solution" to the feminist problem was Christianity because "Jesus was a feminist." The feminism of Jesus was consistently drawn in contrast to first-century Judaism and thus implied that Christianity was a feminist corrective to Judaism. Jewish feminist scholars such as Judith Plaskow argued that these assertions often were based on sloppy and ahistorical scholarship, reducing the complex textual tradition in Judaism to a monolithic assertion of patriarchy. Like Susannah Heschel, Plaskow understood those accusations' long-standing assertions of the superiority of Christianity as the only true religion to be the very antithesis of a feminist ethic.

Many Christian feminists have made the apostle Paul the chief target of their critiques of the inherent sexism of Christianity, but others have argued that he was constrained by the limitations of the Jewish milieu in which he lived. However, this made Paul, like Jesus, all the more remarkable for transcending these limitations. While few Christian feminists, particularly in the United States, claimed that it was solely the Jewish roots of Christianity that were the root of the problem, Jewish feminists have found the language of blame in the writings of European and some American Christian feminist thinkers.

Some feminists evoked the Goddess as the source of a just, egalitarian society that had existed in ancient times. According to this version of history, in the work of Goddess feminist Merlin Stone, the Goddess was destroyed by Israelites who replaced her with the "Father God of the Hebrew Bible." Patriarchy was therefore ushered in by Judaism. The perennial accusation of Jews as slayers of God/Jesus was translated anew into Jews as slayers of the Goddess. While Stone's position was clearly a minority one among Goddess feminists, it had real currency in the 1970s and early 1980s. Jewish feminist scholars continued to express their concern that Judaism was regularly portrayed as the problematic religious system between the ideal periods of Goddess worship and early Christianity.

Feminism faced an even greater challenge for Jewish women when Letty Pogrebin, a founder of *Ms. Magazine* and longtime activist, published a 1982 article identifying the problem she called "Anti-Semitism in the Women's Movement." The anti-Semitism she documented was complex. She linked it to anti-Israel stands taken by radical activists who were also feminists. Jewish women, Pogrebin learned, felt marginalized from the women's movement by some feminists' refusal to acknowledge Jews' right to a homeland as a legacy of the Holocaust.

Jewish feminists complained that they found themselves and other American Jews repeatedly portrayed as rich, bourgeois, privileged, intellectual racists and oppressors not entitled to their own experiences and fears of discrimination. Jewish lesbians made similar charges against lesbian activist groups. Other minority groups' experience of oppression were readily accepted and acknowledged, but Jewish women felt theirs was not.

These concerns were heightened and complicated by three highly visible international events held from 1975 to 1985 under the auspices of the United Nation's Decade of Women. At these events Jewish women experienced well-organized and aggressive anti-Zionism and anti-Semitism from women from several nations. What Western women, among them both Israeli and diaspora Jewish women, believed was key was the economic and social equality of women with men. Third World women understood equality to mean the redistribution of world wealth and the end of Western domination, which would alter world economic systems. Personal liberation became synonymous with national liberation, and anti-Zionism dominated the proceedings of the 1975 meeting in Mexico City. By the 1980 and 1985 conferences Israel's right to exist was no longer challenged, and the Palestinian issue was confronted more precisely with demands for statehood and economic support for women. Nevertheless, the centrality of anti-Zionism to the women's agenda remained an issue that united African and Asian women.

In addition to the formal proceedings with resolutions condemning Zionism, Israeli and Jewish women from the diaspora were verbally attacked in public as well as in private with delegates leaving meetings where Israeli feminists spoke. The United Nations' Decade of Women presented a devastating challenge to American Jewish feminists who believed that gender was sufficient to forge alliances.

Many related issues were addressed seriously at the 1983 National Women's Studies Association Conference attended by 1,500 people, which held a plenary session on racism and anti-Semitism in the women's movement. The panel members addressed the sources of oppression of several minorities and offered a feminist analysis to address the problem of "competing oppressions" and to acknowledge the forms of racism that separated women from one another.

In this same time period in the 1970s and 1980s a new stereotype of Jewish women emerged that was particularly offensive to Jewish feminists, the Jewish American Princess (JAP). The JAP is the young, dependent woman whose affluence, expressed by her insatiable desire for consumption, is underwritten by her father or husband. In novels, films, greeting cards, novelty items, and above all jokes, JAPs were ubiquitous.

Like other forms of internalized anti-Semitism, the JAP synthesized all the classic social and ideological anti-Semitic images of the nineteenth and twentieth centuries, projecting them on a young Jewish woman. She was greedy, cunning, unwilling to labor honestly, excessive, loud, and parasitic. The stereotype circulated among Jews and served as a critique of Jewish women by Jewish men and even other Jewish women. If Jewish women "really" were JAPs, then criticizing them distanced other Jews from this unattractive person. Just as in another era there were "white" and "black" Jews, and "good" and "bad" Jews, in these decades of rising consumerism, growing American Jewish affluence, and changing ideas about families and women, the Jewish woman was accused of embodying everything that was unattractive and a source of anxiety in this period.

The offensiveness of the JAP image was taken seriously within the Jewish community as the result of the fall 1988 issue of the Jewish feminist magazine *Lilith*. An article reported on the work of Syracuse University sociologist Gary Spencer, who documented how widespread graffiti and personal attacks focused on JAPs were on college campuses. He documented the fact that the graffiti was anything but harmless. It frequently praised Nazism and threatened Jewish women with rape and death. Jewish defense organizations called on members of the Jewish community to boycott JAP novelty items and to stop telling these jokes with their anti-Semitic overtones. The campaign was successful in reducing the commercial market for such items, but the humor persists with new innovations for several generations.

In the 1990s Jewish women became far more self-conscious about their portrayal in the media. The Morning Star Commission, thirty leading Los Angeles film and television professionals, was organized by Hadassah of Southern California, a Jewish women's organization, to respond to the negative stereotyping of Jewish women. They concluded, based on research with focus groups, that there are persistently negative images of Jewish women in the media, and they urged executives to address the problem of negative stereotypes. At the same time, this decade, and the first of the new century, has seen an increase in independent Jewish women filmmakers and artists whose work offers far more complex and interesting portrayals of Jews in general and Jewish women in particular.

Jewish women have encountered anti-Semitism as both women and Jews, from those who hated their religion as well as those who defined Jewishness as the embodiment of America's enemies or a worldwide Zionist conspiracy. Jewish women, like other victims of racism, have also been the target of those who internalize self-hatred. They have also organized to combat anti-Semitism directed at all Jews, and Jewish women in particular, in their own communities as well as on global stages. Their fight against anti-Semitism has often been joined to the struggle against other forms of oppression, just as it has often served to solidify Jewish women who have been separated by other forms of social difference. The persistence of anti-Semitism is as significant as its increasing banishment, for the most part, to the fringes of American society. Nevertheless, the persistence of anti-Semitism in the twenty-first century in the form of accusations of American Jewish power controlling foreign policy on the floor of Congress, as well as in right-wing publications, makes clear that it is a form of racism that will not soon disappear.

SOURCES: The most important books on anti-Semitism in America that touch on issues of women are Leonard Dinnerstein, *Anti-Semitism in America* (1994); Michael N. Dobkowsi, *The Tarnished Dream: The Basis of American Anti-Semitism* (1979); John Higham, *Send These to Me: Jews and Other Immigrants in Urban America*, rev. ed. (1984); David Gerber, ed., *Anti-Semitism in American History* (1986); and Charles Stember, ed., *Jews in the Mind of Americans* (1966). Works on Jewish women that touch on anti-Semitism in the eighteenth and nineteenth centuries are Diane Lichtenstein, *Writing Their Nations: The Tradition of Nineteenth-Century American Jewish Women Writers* (1992), and Dianne Ashton, *Rebecca Gratz: Women and Judaism in Antebellum America* (1997). Important works on Jewish self-hatred include Sander Gilman, *Jewish Self-Hatred: Anti-Semitism and the Secret Language of the Jews* (1982), and Riv-Ellen Prell, *Fighting to Become Americans: Jews, Gender, and the Anxiety of Assimilation* (1999). Works on women and anti-Semitism include Glen Jeansonne, *Women of the Far Right: The Mothers' Movement and World War II* (1996), and Kathleen Blee's *Women and the Klan: Racism and Gender in the 1920s* (1991). Works on anti-Judaism in Christian feminism include Susannah Heschel, "Anti-Judaism in Christian Feminist Theology," *Tikkun* 5.3 (May–June 1990): 25–28, 95–97, and Judith Plaskow, "Blaming the Jews for the Birth of Patriarchy," in *Nice Jewish Girls*, ed. Evelyn Torton Beck (1984). The archive of the American Jewish Committee, New York City, New York, has files on women and anti-Semitism.

Part VII

❦

Islam

ISLAM, WOMEN, AND THE STRUGGLE FOR IDENTITY IN NORTH AMERICA
Yvonne Yazbeck Haddad

THE EARLY HISTORY of Muslims in the United States, both immigrant and African American, reveals a great deal of women's participation in building the foundational institutions of Islam and creating a space and a place for Islam in the American religious mosaic. The understanding of Islam for a growing number of believers is different both from the image of the religion that has been part of the Western heritage and from that which has historically shaped the experiences of their sisters overseas. Muslim women therefore are not only participating in the public square in growing numbers, but they are actively helping to determine the nature and appropriateness of that participation in conversation with each other, with the men of the American Muslim community, with the opinion makers of contemporary America, and also with women across the world through networking and direct communication. The identity of Muslim women in America is increasingly defined by the women themselves as they assume individual and corporate responsibility for determining who they are, what they will do, and how they will be in conversation with other women around the world.

The history of Muslim women in America is not a long one, compared with that of most Islamic societies. But it is now sufficiently established that one can point to its roots, its development, and its great heterogeneity. It is primarily a history of immigration to a new land, a new implant into a society that had a small group of indigenous Muslim women—almost exclusively African American—who chose Islam for their religion. The first Muslims to arrive on the continent of America were Africans brought through the slave trade. Because of forced conversion to Christianity, however, only traces of their original Muslim identity have been written into the American historical record. It is through the waves of immigration over the last 130 years, beginning with the earliest arrivals from the Middle East and now representing virtually every part of the world, as well as through the conversion of black, Latino, and white Americans, that the history of Islam in America is being played out.

Studies on early immigrants show that the women assumed a pioneering role in creating a space for Muslims in North America. In both Canada and the United States, the women were active in establishing mosques and Islamic centers, in helping to raise funds for such projects, in providing instruction about Islam to their children, and in supervising the activities of the group. Women were also active in the forming of the Federa-tion of Islamic Associations in the 1950s, which was created in the hope of providing a space where young Muslims could meet, discuss issues of mutual concern, and hopefully find appropriate spouses.

A significant change in the constituency of the Muslim community in the United States occurred in the 1970s. The immigration of Muslims to North America after the revocation of the Asia Exclusion Act includes a large number of highly educated, already Westernized professional Muslims. The majority of these new Muslim immigrants did not qualify for entry as "your tired, your poor" of Lady Liberty fame. They did not engage in digging ditches and installing railroad tracks or peddling their goods on street corners, as was true of the early Muslim immigrants for many decades. Today a significant number are the energetic, the wealthy, and the technologically productive who have landed some of the best jobs in America and are helping to maintain America's leadership in the scientific, medical, and technological fields. A growing number of these professionals are women, working as bureaucrats, psychologists, physicians, technicians, lawyers, professors, and businesspeople.

The globalization of the world and the technological revolution have made it possible for the most recent immigrants to be more able to maintain communication with the families and cultures they left behind. While earlier generations of Muslims in America quickly found themselves distanced from and out of touch with "home," today the situation is dramatically different. New modes of communication, from cell phones to the Internet to cable allowing them to access television broadcasts from all over the world, ensure that being Muslim in America no longer means losing contact with one's family, country, and culture of origin. Muslims know instantly what is happening around the world, and in turn the ideas they generate dealing with Islam and gender and the decisions they make about roles and opportunities for Muslim women in the West reverberate back and help shape the discourse in their home countries.

More recently, in addition to the new wave of professionals coming to further their education and tap into the financial resources of America are also substantial numbers of refugees from countries wrenched by civil wars and often suffering the results of Western exploitation. Some have called these people the "collateral damage" of American ventures overseas in such countries as Afghanistan, Iran, Iraq, Lebanon, Somalia, Palestine, and elsewhere. Along with the refugee populations, including numbers of women who regardless of their former social and economic positions find themselves severely disadvantaged in America, are those who have come seeking asylum for either political or religious reasons. Also part of the American scene are Islamists wanting refuge from secular leftist governments, as well as transnationals who go back and forth freely from the United States to their home countries.

Muslim Women as Battleground

American Muslims, women and men, immigrant and indigenous, secular and religious, inevitably have as part of their own histories experiences of encounters between Islam and the West that play an important part in the current processes of self-identification. The intimate encounter between Islam and the West during the period of Western colonialism, highlighting both political-economic and social-cultural differences, irreparably shaped relationships between Muslims and citizens of what has now become their home. Western colonization of Islamic territories was justified, among other reasons, on the basis of helping to improve what was depicted to be an inferior and backward Islamic culture. One of the significant factors in that assessment was what the West believed to be the "miserable status" of women as segregated, uneducated, swathed, and generally mistreated. European colonialists claimed that the conquest of Muslim nations, and the process of plundering their resources, was part of their "civilizing mission," culturally and politically defined as a mandate to modernize backward peoples. Muslim women, they reasoned, were calling for assistance in liberation from their condition of oppression, which the West was only too ready to provide.

Parallel to the colonialist enterprise was the Christian missionary campaign that perceived colonialism as a God-given opportunity to convert the Muslims to Christianity. The missionary movement grew in strength during the nineteenth century as part of mainline denominational activity. It thrived between the 1920s and late 1940s of the twentieth century under the protection and encouragement of European colonialism. Currently it continues with vigor, especially as part of the efforts of American evangelical churches. Western missionary strategists reasoned that "oppressed" women would be the most obvious place from which to begin the penetration and conversion of Islamic societies. Thus they identified as one of their primary goals the release of Muslim women from the yoke of male domination. Consequently, the missionaries are perceived as having served as agents for the subjugation of Islamic society precisely by undermining the role of women in the process of trying to present to them a better, that is, Christian, way of life. Both male and female missionaries shared in producing for Western consumption the stereotypes of "the repressed and downtrodden females." Muslims coming to, and making their home in, the West in the latter part of the twentieth century, and

now in the twenty-first century, not only immediately encounter the residue of these long-propagated stereotypes, but they carry with them the defensive polemic and ideological responses to them generated in Muslim nation–states for over a century.

Part of the baggage carried by Muslim immigrants, then, is colonial history, a history that reflects not only the impact of the Western incursion itself but also its concomitant stereotyping. For many Muslim women from areas that struggled to achieve independence from Western colonialism, the twentieth century was one in which women fought for and won their place in society as part of the professional workforce, the military, and in other public spheres. Often their expectations were raised as to the roles that were possible, and necessary, for them to play in the process of nation-building. That these expectations were frustrated after independence was won, especially in Algeria, where they were expected to return to the private sphere, has been a source of anger and deep discontent on the part of many Muslim women. In the wake of such movements as the Islamic revolution in Iran under Khomeini and the Taliban in Afghanistan, their apprehension that the achievements in liberating women in various Muslim countries were now going to be reversed has increased. For some, the new environment of America is a challenge as well as an opportunity, a context in which to achieve what they believe to be their legitimate Islamic rights of involvement and public participation in the life of the community and in shaping Islamic norms worldwide.

Other Muslim women arriving from abroad have brought with them a variety of cultural expectations, shaped and influenced by the many different societies from which they have come. Those cultural assumptions often have supported the notion that women should be subservient to men and that their sphere of activity should be confined as much as possible to the home. Such an orientation characterizes many of the movements that may be placed under the umbrella designation of "Islamist," movements that have changed and influenced many Muslim women's lives whether or not they have chosen the Islamist ideology as their own mode of religious and political response.

In addition to carrying this complicated baggage, immigrant Muslim women have also needed to adjust to the realities of the American environment itself. Despite the rhetoric about America as the great "immigrant-welcoming" land, expectations have been frustrated as Muslims have often found that it is not easy to be accepted into Western society. While they share with many other immigrant groups the difficulties of assimilation and even integration, Muslim women have had to bear the additional burdens of representing a religion that has never been appreciated by Western Christians, one that by their colonial and missionary efforts they have even tried to eliminate. It has been the particular responsibility of American Muslims, therefore, to sort out in one complex process their struggles to claim their rightful roles and responsibilities (1) as citizens of America, (2) as inheritors of particular cultural interpretations, and (3) as defenders or critics of faith and culture in the face of strong tendencies on the part of Americans to foster ungenerous and often hurtful stereotypes about Arabs and Muslims in general and Muslim women in particular.

Other realities contribute to the struggles Muslim women must engage in the American context. As representatives of different cultural contexts vie for leadership of American Islam, the question of women's rights and roles often becomes a kind of political football. While some Muslim women continue to cherish and hold on to the particularities of the cultures from which their parents and grandparents came, others of the second, third, and fourth generations both want to challenge traditional worldviews and to distance themselves from the claims of a particular cultural heritage. The task facing American Muslim women also has not grown easier as a result of escalating political tensions around the world. The violence associated with some Islamic movements has served to

hone American fears of Islam and to foster yet more stereotypical responses to what is depicted as the oppression of Muslim women in Afghanistan, Iran, Saudi Arabia, Pakistan, and elsewhere. As a result of Israel's operation "Defensive Shield" and the new modes of resistance appropriated by Palestinians, Muslim women have been portrayed in the American press as fanatic and proud supporters of the suicide attacks of their young sons. American Muslim women are being called to respond to all of these issues.

Islamic feminist discourse, whatever its form, is formulated as a response both to Islamic traditionalism and to the West, its norms, its different kinds of feminism, and its social problems. It represents a century of encounter with colonialism, Christian exceptionalism, and the projection into the international context of what are perceived in the West to be universal models of womanhood as developed by the feminist movement in the United States. Several Arab and Muslim women who were members of the National Organization for Women (NOW) were alienated when the organization refused to condemn the 1982 Israeli invasion of Lebanon and its relentless bombing of Beirut, which resulted in the death of 20,000 Lebanese and Palestinian civilians. Azizah al-Hibri, executive director of Karama, an organization of Muslim women lawyers, breaks out in tears every time she recalls this bitter experience. It is at such moments that Muslim women realize that the solidarity they seek with American feminists will not be realized. The kinds of discourses projected by many Muslim women in the West are clearly the result of immersion in a new context influenced by liberationist discourse and by postmodernist analyses. Muslim women feel and exercise the freedom to analyze and critique texts and traditions in ways not possible in most Muslim societies. Whatever kind of Islamic feminism is adopted, the tendency is to posit it as clearly different from "Western feminism," often with little apparent interest in seeing that Western feminism itself has evolved and transmuted into a variety of forms of expression and interpretation. In some models, Western feminism is used as a kind of foil or antithesis of both Islamism and Orientalism, allowing for the creation of "new" space for Muslim women not identified with any of those. This approach characterizes the work, for example, of Shahnaz Khan in Canada.

Women scholars such as law professor Azizah al-Hibri are following the models of the early socialist-nationalist trained academics of the middle to late decades of the twentieth century, who identify themselves as Muslim and are engaged in scholarly research on women's issues in Islam unbiased by doctrinal affirmations articulated by medieval jurists. *Copyright © Doug Berelin.*

The Discourse on Muslim Women in North America

Before World War II few efforts were made by Muslims, still small in number and geographically spread across the huge American continent, to think about what it means to be Muslim in a Western context. Most Muslims were concerned about economic survival and generally tried to maintain the social structures of Islam as they had been interpreted in their home countries. Very few texts were available at all on the religion of Islam, and virtually none written by and for Muslims. The earliest written materials available to Muslims interpreting the role of women were either those produced overseas and exported to the United States or the contributions of Muslim men in the American context telling women what they should do and what their appropriate roles are in traditional Islamic culture.

Some of the earliest texts on Islam written by Muslims in America dealt with the issue of women. These texts were prepared by men who generally affirmed traditional roles. Muhammad Abdul Rauf, at one time imam of the Islamic Center of Washington, D.C., the "showcase" mosque of America built in the 1950s, was among the first to try to define women's roles and responsibilities. Male assumption of the exclusive right to make such assessments was illustrated in a public encounter at the American Academy of Religion between Abdul Rauf and Riffat Hassan, one of the early prominent Muslim female academics in the United States. Hassan, whose scholarly project was the exegesis of the Qur'an as a document affirming equality between men and women, was chastised publicly by Abdul Rauf as not having the authority to make such statements. Abdul Rauf's conservative understanding of women's rights and roles has been echoed by a number of male interpreters whose writings continue to be highly influential. In addition to such scholars who were writing specifically for an American audience, the Muslim community in America has continued to be influenced by fatwas issued in Egypt, Iran, Iraq, and other centers of Islamic authority. Here again, of course, men are writing their opinions about what is appropriate for women within the Islamic context.

Since the 1970s a large number of books on Islam have been published under the aegis of such organizations as the Islamic Society of North America and the International Institute for Islamic Thought, affirming the superiority of the Islamic worldview. These texts have received worldwide distribution as they are available by mail order, in mosque bookstores, and at annual conventions of regional and umbrella organizations. They are discussed in women's study circles, and their worldview is propagated from the pulpits. This material

tends to reiterate Islamist views developed overseas as a response to what is experienced as the cultural onslaught of the West.

The most prominent feature of Islamic literature on the role of women is its apologetic tone, regardless of the gender or ideological orientation of the author. Such literature demonstrates the overwhelming impact of Western ideas on Muslim society and the role of women over a century of engagement. It tends to provide a comparative perspective declaring the superiority of Islam and the Islamic model. Islam, it declares, has liberated women, a liberation decreed by God and not a gift from men. It granted women rights to life, to education, to conduct business, to maintain their property, and to keep their names, rights they had to struggle to achieve in the West. This literature demonstrates the progress that has been made as the paradigm of Muslim woman has evolved. Whereas at the beginning of the twentieth century the debates focused on whether women should be educated, today this right is affirmed as explicit in the Qur'an. Now the discussion is about what subjects it is appropriate for women to study and what contributions they can make to society. The fact that there are instances where Muslims impede the education of their daughters is due to residue of tribal and social customs of patriarchy that have no room in Islam.

This does not mean that some of the traditional views have not survived. They are preached by conservative imams who maintain that women's work must be confined to the home, to the raising of her children and the pleasing of her husband. She is the mother and wife providing comfort and love and maintaining Islamic culture in the home. While it is true that the Qur'an affirms that men and women are created from the same cell, that both were tempted in the Garden, both were expelled for their disobedience and both will be equally held accountable on the Day of Judgment, traditionalists maintain that still there are differences. These biological and emotional differences determine social and political distinctions between the two genders; the witness of one man being equal to that of two women is said to be due to the fact that women are emotional, while men are rational. Each gender has been assigned a different role. Males are superior because they are the protectors of women. Together, male and female, in their divinely dictated separate but complementary roles, they have been charged with creating a cohesive virtuous society.

Also available for over a decade now is the corpus of information, debates, and polemics expanding the battle over the role of Muslim women into cyberspace. In the process, vast Web sites have been colonized by various Muslim advocates as well as by anti-Muslim protagonists. These sites are maintained by apologists, radical and conservative Muslims, fundamentalists, pro-Western feminists, Western anti-Islamists, and a few who appear to be perpetually confused. It is clear that they are cognizant of each other's postings and indulge in providing point and counterpoint answers and refutations. The information includes such topics as the Qur'anic and prophetic teachings on gender issues, narratives about the wives of the Prophet ("The Mothers of the Believers") and the early Muslims, and information about relevant legislation of various Muslim nation–states. It also provides several fatwa sites that provide access to Q&A sections that address the most commonly asked questions about male-female relations, dating, sex, and how to live an Islamic life according to the dictates of the tradition. The sites also offer virtual access to authoritative opinion on these issues for those who are seeking guidance from scholars throughout the world on personal issues relating to gender, marital relations, and the daily concerns of life.

From within the Muslim community itself comes pressure from the traditional leadership to conform to traditional Islamic values that see woman as a protected ornament not available for interaction with males or even, in some cases, for public view. Emphasis on the maintenance of such values becomes enhanced as the community (in its great variety of forms) expresses concerns about disintegration, absorption into American culture, and abandonment of the faith. Parents are worried about the effects of socialization on their children, these concerns covering everything from fear of the degenerate culture of the West with its temptations of drugs, pornography, and other social ills to the possibility of intermarriage and children being raised outside of the faith. Many Muslims who come from countries where Islam is the dominant religion struggle with how to organize an Islamic community in the secular West where Islam has to reconceive itself as a minority religion. Often this means reinforcing conservative interpretations of the rights and role of women. Muslim women in America thus find themselves caught between these external and internal pressures.

The very diversity of the population of Muslim women in America, as well as the relative freedoms available to them in the Western cultural context, has opened up a wide range of possible avenues in which to affirm one's affiliation with Islam, to define the parameters of the community, and to combat the many forms of American prejudice. Ethnic affiliations, class and educational levels, professional involvements, tolerance for diversity, and many other factors reflect differences in the kinds of Islamic discourse being fostered by American women. They are also subject to two strong pressures: One is external and the other is internal. From the outside is the American pressure to homogenize, indigenize, and assimilate all immigrants. This pro-

cess involves creating a consensus on values that promote capitalism, a culture of consumption, private morality, standards of dress, beauty, and social interaction. This is balanced by pressure coming from within the tradition of Islam itself.

In many cases, Muslim women, probably including a majority of those who have chosen to convert to Islam in America, opt to support the opinions and analyses as articulated by the medieval authorities, seeing them as reflecting the eternally binding and valid nature of the Qur'an and the Sunna (the precedent of the life of the Prophet and his teachings). They affirm that as God's divine word the Qur'an is clear in meaning and thus is not in need of reinterpretation beyond what the early exegetes provided. For these women, Islam is divinely dictated and ultimately a closed system, valid and binding in all of its minute details, including prescriptions for and about women, for all time. Those who choose to express their opinions publicly in written or oral discourse support an Islam that does not need to adjust to changing circumstances, times, or environments any more than absolutely necessary. The basic teachings of Islam, supported by conservative propagators of the faith in America and by the fatwas, regulations, and interpretations of many Muslims on the international scene, are seen as injunctions to be followed by all believers. This interpretation of Islam seems to create an Islamic culture wherever Muslims live, with as little accommodation as possible to local customs or circumstances. No one has the right to challenge what God and his prophet have determined. This kind of conservative interpretation entails the personal commitment to wear Islamic dress, covering everything but the face and hands, and in some more extreme interpretations means wearing the full-face veil and gloves. Women who opt for this Islamic alternative are often disinclined to interact with women (or men) who are not Muslim or to participate fully in the public sphere, although some take the opportunity to speak out for conservative Islam whenever they feel it will provide a chance for either interpretation or propagation of the faith.

On the opposite end of the spectrum are women scholars, following the models of the early socialist-nationalist trained academics of the middle to late decades of the twentieth century, who identify themselves as Muslim and are engaged in scholarly research on women's issues in Islam that is unbiased by doctrinal affirmations articulated by medieval jurists. Sometimes they identify themselves as modernists or progressives, even feminists (though generally distinguishable from what they define as "Western" feminists), identifying and challenging the roles of patriarchy in Islam and working for reform both within Islam and within the secular structures. They tend to see the Qur'an as open to reinterpretation by each generation as it engages with the context of its environment, responding to the challenges of the time. They view the Qur'an as a revelation that is "a mercy to humanity," rather than a fixed text that constrains human development.

One of the Qur'an verses that has engendered the most discussion among Western scholars of Islam, for example, as well as among Muslims themselves, particularly in light of Islamic feminist critique, is chapter 4, verse 34, which says that men have authority over women and that if a woman is disobedient to her husband, he has the right to beat her. Traditional and literalist interpreters have insisted that this is a divine injunction specifically regulating relations between men and women. However, a number of Muslims who are writing from the perspective of an "Islamically committed feminism," living both in Muslim countries and in diaspora, have argued that such a verse can only be understood when it is viewed in the larger context. When one understands and affirms the egalitarian message of the Qur'an, an interpretation that calls for dominance and brutality can be nothing but incorrect. Scholars such as Riffat Hassan, Amina Wadud, Amira Sonbol, and Asma Barlas argue a variety of alternative interpretations unencumbered by patriarchal assumptions.

Carving up a New Space for Muslim Women in the United States

The first Muslim women to achieve public acknowledgment in the American context were those who gained prominence as scholars and academics in the 1970s. For the most part they were educated overseas, and most received graduate degrees in the United States. Generally they represented the modernized, educated Arab women who were products of the nationalist-socialist discourses of their respective home countries. Among them were women like Afaf Lutfi al-Sayyid Marsot, the first Muslim woman to become president of the Middle East Studies Association of North America, elected to that position by the association's Muslim and non-Muslim membership. Marsot was one of the first, in the American context, to put forward the argument that it is social practice rather than Islam itself that has determined the position of women in society and that, for example, despite Qur'anic injunctions that she sees as supporting women's financial rights, family and social practices have often hindered the realization of these rights.

A few, such as Leila Ahmed, have even gone so far as to claim that women were better off before Islamic laws that served to subjugate them were introduced. Often the primary concern of these Muslim feminists is political. As Muslim women now living in the United States they apply tools of political and social analysis to

political situations elsewhere in the world. Among them, for example, are Iranian women such as Mahnaz Afkhami, who played prominent roles in prerevolutionary Iran, then immmigrated to the United States when threatened under the Islamic regime. Other Iranian scholars whose work is being read and integrated into Muslim consciousness include Shahla Haeri, Haleh Afshar, Afsaneh Najmabadi, and Guity Nashat, among others. Their academic pursuits are often focused on Iran, considering the implications for women of events and interpretations taking place in that country for Muslim women in general. One can find similar examples of Pakistani, Arab, and other Muslim women in America analyzing current realities for women in their countries of origin.

Secular feminists are increasingly being viewed with suspicion by the growing number of practicing Muslims. This criticism is based not so much on the fact that they may not be wearing Islamic dress or participating in Qur'an circles as on a conviction that their criticism of what obtains in Muslim society has become instrumental in reinforcing Western prejudice. By appropriating Western discourse, they are accused of participating in undermining their faith and denigrating the role of their sisters. They are perceived as tapping into the Western paradigm of essentializing Islam and perpetuating an image of the faith as ossified in the past. Critics charge that their efforts serve neocolonial justifications for the continued dominance of Muslim societies by the West and that by breaking rank they are undermining the solidarity necessary for the true liberation of Muslims from bondage to Western power and dictates.

Other feminist Muslim women, both in the United States and overseas, seek to reconcile Islam and feminism. They have increasingly abandoned the efforts of the earliest Muslim secular feminists, who emulated colonial bureaucrats and missionaries, to compare the condition of Muslim women with Western norms; rather, they have opted to address the issues from within the faith. Their gender paradigms of equality and liberation are grounded in the Qur'an and in Islamic jurisprudence. They are working on examining traditional narratives of Islamic history, law, and other Islamic sciences. Amira Sonbol, for example, argues that historically Islamic law was flexible and in many cases served to work in favor of women. Modern legal reforms based on Western secular models, she insists, have in fact fostered the subjugation of women. This kind of argumentation provides another challenge to the Western presupposition that modernization and Westernization are necessarily good for women, while Islamic law, considered archaic and repressive, is not. The work of Sonbol and others in this area is not only serving to challenge prevailing paradigms of historical interpretation but has implications for bringing about changes in contemporary laws in Egypt, Jordan, and other Muslim countries based on new understandings of what was historically true and verifiable.

Many of these women, though certainly not all, will also choose to define themselves as Islamic feminists but within carefully articulated dimensions. For these women Islam is an eternally valid system for all times and places, but it is one that must be seen in the light of constantly changing times and circumstances. Eternality of the Qur'an is understood to be less in the specific style and articulation than in the spirit of truth. While the principles of the Qur'an are eternal, and reflect the unchanging nature of God, local interpretations can vary. The term *gender jihad* has come into popular use as a way of categorizing the efforts of these women who are contesting the prescriptions of the traditionalists, the reactionaries, and the fundamentalists but who are clearly working with a mandate to affirm the divine message of the Qur'an and the ultimate viability of the Islamic system. Those who practice the so-called gender jihad are struggling to create new and viable interpretations of Islam based on the Qur'an and the Sunnah, opening the discourse to new possibilities of individual interpretation and collective consensus. They are trying to provide corrective definitions that break out of the confines of scripted and prescribed molds, looking for ways in which to make an Islamically valid contribution to twenty-first-century thought and life. They want to create an attractive alternative to both dogmatic traditionalism with its constraining patriarchal overtones and to liberal feminism that they feel has forfeited Islam and its teachings to the changing whims and values of a West that can never appreciate Islam. Affirming God's guidance for all humanity in all times, they are grounding their discourse in an Islamically validated modern lifestyle.

These modern Muslim feminists see Islam not as fixed and unchanging but as dynamic and constantly open to interpretation. Rather than the essentialized perception of a static Islam, their efforts are geared to prove that the Qur'an pioneered human, civil, economic, and civil rights for women. They acknowledge that patriarchy has played a dominant role in the classical interpretations of the Qur'an but deny that the text itself fosters patriarchy or in any way advantages men over women. They see the Qur'an as a whole unit, based on the concept of the oneness of God. Thus they do not extract verses about women to analyze alone or out of context but see them as part of an inseparable whole. Basic to their starting point is the understanding that the Qur'an is God's divine word and that God as essentially just could never author anything that promotes injustice. Thus verses that might be seen in any way to be privileging men over women must be reinterpreted in light of the overall Qur'anic presentation of God's justice.

Similar ideas have been propagated among the African American Muslim women. Some of the earliest works on Islam available to American audiences were those written by the leadership of the Ahmadiyya movement in Islam that pioneered Muslim missionary activity in the West. Their missionaries were especially active throughout the first half of the twentieth century in the African American community. Their interpretations of women's roles have been classically traditional and appear to have impacted the indigenous Islamic movements that arose in the African American community. The Nation of Islam (NOI), thriving throughout the decades from the 1940s to the 1970s, was a male-dominated organization. A recent effort to address the situation was made by Louis Farrakhan when he appointed the first woman imam of a mosque in Atlanta. Even in the last several decades, which have seen the transition of most NOI members under the leadership of Warith Deen Mohammed to a form of Sunni Islam, some African American women have expressed their disappointment that becoming Muslim has not allowed them any more gender equality than they experienced either as members of the Nation or as Christians. Warith Deen Mohammed, noted for naming a chain of Islamic schools after his mother, Sister Clara Muhammad, preached sermons on several occasions asking women to empower African American men by accepting a lesser status. Some African American Muslim women feel that they are the victims of triple oppression in American society—as Muslims, as African Americans, and as women—and that the last two forms of oppression are not absent in the Muslim community itself. Two prominent African American Muslim women scholars with an international following, Amina Wadud and Aminah McCloud, have made their voices heard through writing and other forms of public expression, calling for the gender equality that they feel is legitimately theirs as Muslims as well as identifying the relationships between gender and racial prejudices.

Other American Muslim women have opted for an expression of Islam that provides an alternative to textual or historical-critical analysis, to conservative affirmations of the perfection of Islam as a way of life, and to modernist-secularist discourse. These women are advocates of one of the many expressions of Sufism or personal engagement with the divine. They find that this path liberates them from concern with doing daily battle with a society that rejects Islam on so many levels and allows them to maintain their Islamic identity in a more quietist and personalized way. In its transcendence over the mundane, Sufism allows women to engage with the divine on a level where all creatures are equal, where one is free from the effects of stereotypical treatment, and where issues of gender equality are not given prominence of place.

Muslim Women and the American Public Square

Today in the American context a great range of female Muslim voices is being heard. It is not only academics who are contributing to the discourse, although they can increasingly be found in major American campuses teaching history, sociology, anthropology, religious studies, international relations, literary criticism, and women's studies as well as scientific disciplines. There are increasing numbers of women activists, journalists, officers of local and national organizations, health professionals, and many others who are eager to have a part in explaining and interpreting the role of women in Islam and in the West.

Since the 1970s, and very much continuing today, Muslim women in America have found it necessary to assume active leadership roles in the United States and to become political activists as well as scholars. One of the pioneer activists for Arab American rights and a leader in the struggle against prejudice and distortion of Arab and Muslim women, for example, was the late Hala Salam Maksoud. Maksoud was one of the highest-profile Muslim women activists, one of the founders of the American Association of University Graduates and of the American Council for Jerusalem and a powerful and charismatic president of the American-Arab Anti-Discrimination Committee. The contributions of such women, combining their experiences of achievement both in their home cultures and in American academia, have made them significant agents in helping shape the discourses of generations of Muslims both in the United states and overseas.

A younger generation of American-born Muslim women, of both immigrant backgrounds and converts, is coming into its own. They are more actively engaged in the public square and in holding America accountable to its constitutional guarantees and promise of freedom of religion and choice. Some are working on the staff of congressmen providing input on Islamic causes. Others have organized charity and human rights groups seeking to ameliorate the condition of less fortunate people both in the United States and overseas. Still others are working to correct the information on Islam and Muslim women in school textbooks, in the media, and in the movie industry. An African American woman has been elected judge in Maryland. California activist Laila al-Marayati has served with distinction on the Committee on Religious Freedom to which she was appointed by President Bill Clinton. While such women are disturbed by the continuing diatribe against Islam and Muslim women such as that used to justify the war against the Taliban, they are certain of their identity as American and Muslim and working to change America from within, to create a more just society.

The discourse about women that now takes place on a number of different levels in America is thus deeply influenced and shaped by what Muslims bring with them, by the circumstances that affect them when they arrive, by their continuing contact with the countries and cultures from which they came, and by the dominant Western paradigm of diatribe and denigration of their roles. Women now living in America from a great range of backgrounds, including African Americans who must respond to both American and foreign cultural expectations and pressures, are in the process of trying to respond to dominant stereotypes of women, both Western and Islamic. Their writings and their public presentations as well as their modes of participation in American culture are all reflective of a response to an image of the Muslim women, whether that image is one propagated by the Western media or fostered by the traditional conservative interpreters of Islam. Women in the American context of course do not always agree, and the differences and distinctions in their understandings reflect the ways in which their respective formative influences determine how they see the world and themselves in it.

SOURCES: Mahnaz Afkhami, *Women in Exile* (1994). Haleh. Afshar, *Women and Empowerment: Illustrations from the Third World* (1998). Leila Ahmed, *Women and Gender in Islam: Historical Roots of a Modern Debate* (1992). Yvonne Yazbeck Haddad and John L. Esposito, eds., *Daughters of Abraham: Feminist Thought in Judaism, Christianity and Islam* (2002). Yvonne Yazbeck Haddad and John L. Esposito, eds., *Islam, Gender and Social Change* (1998). Shahlaa Haeri, *Law of Desire: Temporary Marriage in Shi'i Islam* (1989). Riffat Hassan et al., eds., *Women's and Men's Liberation: Testimonies of Spirit* (1991). Azizah Al-Hibri, *Women and Islam* (1902). Shahnaz Khan, *Muslim Women Crafting North American Identity* (2000). Afaf Lutfi a-Sayyid Marsot, *Women and Men in Late Eighteenth-Century Egypt* (1999). Aminah McCoud, *African-American Islam* (1999). Afsaneh Najmabadi, *The Story of the Daughters of Quchan: Gender and National Memory in Iranian History* (1998). Guity Nashat, *Women and Revolution in Iran* (1983). Abdul Rauf, *The Islamic View of Women and the Family* (1979). Amira Sonbol, *Women, the Family and Divorce Laws in Islamic History* (1996). Amina Wadud, *Qur'an and Women: Rereading the Sacred Text from a Woman's Perspective* (1991).

AFRICAN AMERICAN MUSLIM WOMEN
Aminah Beverly McCloud

ISLAM, THE WORLDVIEW of over 1 billion people, is over fourteen centuries old, but as an American religion, it is relatively new to the consciousness of U.S. citizens. Nevertheless, Muslims have been in the United States since before it was a nation. It is critical to understand what Islam is before exploring what has attracted millions of African American women to its beliefs and practices during the twentieth century. Most African American women who came to Islam found a totally different worldview, coming as they did from either no particular religious affiliation or from Christianity, both Protestantism and Catholicism. While there has been a great deal of speculation about why these women moved away from the familiar to something totally new, there is no quick answer. In numerous interviews and community publications, these women often expressed serious disillusionment with Christianity and even more dismay about life without a religion that honored them as women.

Women abandoned Christianity for a variety of reasons: It asked them to accept the degradation heaped upon them by white Americans and turn the other cheek; and/or because God was white, they felt "Christianity did not really serve our community and families" (Interview, 1999, in Chicago). Others searched for a religion connected to their roots in Africa. In the early years of the twentieth century, the connection with Africa was directly associated with a heightened awareness of the fight of the Ethiopians against their Italian colonizers. Still others came to Islam because it was different, and the Muslim communities put an emphasis on the femininity of black women, their beauty, and their need to be respected and affirmed. In an interview with a reporter from Newark, New Jersey's *Star Ledger*, Safiyya Sharif asserted, "For many women, one of the core attractions was the restoration of the black family, plagued by social ills like poverty, a history of oppression, etc." (March 14, 1999). Others insist that it was the Qur'anic assertion of the equality of men and women along with the affirmation of modesty that attracted them to Islam. Most African American Muslim women, in various interviews over the last thirty years, vigorously state that they are not "blind to the inequities that exist" either in African America or the Muslim world but say that in Islam at least the origin of inequities is not the religion (Interview with Ameena Bey, 1989).

All African American Muslim women, even those who are now third and fourth generation, say that Islam is the truth for them, that they can only be Muslim. There are many estimates of the actual numbers of Muslims in the United States. The only numbers that researchers agree on are that close to half of all Muslims are African American and almost half of them women. Using the prevailing figures, it is estimated that there are approximately 4 to 5 million African American Muslims today, and since there are slightly more males than females, a little less than 2.5 million are women, and all these numbers are growing.

In Islam the house of worship is called the *masjid* (mosque). However, there are no pictures, statues, or benches, no choir pit, no pulpit, no musical instru-ments, collection plates, or ushers. Prayers are held five times daily, and on Fridays there is a congregational prayer. In the worship there is gender separation. Every Muslim strives to memorize the Qur'an because it must be recited during prayers. So Muslims begin by memorizing the short suras near the end first. Muslims from every ethnic group participate in any *masjid*, usually one that is close to their place of business or school or home during the day. Anyone who moves into the worldview of Islam is definitely experiencing something different. The Qur'anic view of womanhood is different than that of men, though male scholars have spent a great deal of time offering translations that subordinate women to men. Fortunately, there are and have been women scholars of Islam who also provide close readings of the text who write constantly, recovering what the text actually says about the equality of women regarding knowledge. Additionally, the Prophet Muhammad's wives are sources of law and etiquette.

According to the only African American Islamic woman theologian, Amina Wadud, "the Qur'an asserts the distinctions between women and men but does not propose that this is a part of their natures. It also does not propose a set of roles for the genders." She continues, pointing out that "the Qur'an encourages all believers, female and male, to follow their beliefs with actions and for this it promises them a great reward" (15). Perhaps because there is no belief in a plague on the human soul from birth, nor a concept that women are made from men, some African American women are attracted to Islam. The emphasis on individual responsibility is an important element as well.

Muslim women are everywhere. One distinguishing mark is their veils, but not all women wear them. Most women however, are modest in dress. They wear African head wraps, scarves, and conservative hairstyles. African American Muslim women are housewives, teachers, university professors, engineers, physicians, dentists, and attorneys as well as involved in a whole host of other careers. They are probably the most traveled of all African American women. This is directly due to their participation in a worldview that assumes a community of believers who interact across ethnic, national, and racial lines because of the Qur'anic injunction to seek knowledge.

At the center of Islam sits the Qur'an, the last revelation of God revealed through the Prophet Muhammad ibn Abdullah in seventh-century Arabia. Muslims believe that since the beginning of time, God has revealed Himself to humankind through prophets and messengers. The Qur'an asserts that the primordial message has always been to worship God, the one God. All the prophets and messengers are mentioned in the Qur'an (not by name but by category), and portions of the stories about a few are mentioned, such as Moses, David,

African American Muslim women are housewives, teachers, university professors, engineers, physicians, dentists, and attorneys as well as involved in a host of other careers. They are probably the most traveled of all African American women due to their participation in a worldview that assumes a community of believers who interact across ethnic, national, and racial lines because of the Qur'anic injunction to seek knowledge. *Used by permission of Aminah McCloud.*

Joseph, Jesus, and of course, Muhammad. The Qur'an also asserts that God has infused each human being with a connection to God, and it is the challenge of this life is to remember that connection. There is a way to live justly. Humans are vicegerents, not masters of the world; the best person is the most pious one. There is no inherent superiority or inferiority of races or classes. People are created as different "tribes" and are commanded to come to know each other. There is an emphasis on the Day of Judgment, when each person, regardless of when they died or religion, will be judged on their beliefs and their actions.

Islam does not have an ordained clergy. Each individual is expected to become knowledgeable and responsible for their actions to God. Wealth is not scorned but is seen as putting a greater responsibility on an individual in the arenas of charity and justice. Practice is essential to the realization of God-consciousness and justice. Besides praying five times daily, Muslims fast from food, drink, and carnal pleasures from sunrise to sunset for thirty days during the ninth lunar month (Ramadan), pay an annual tax on wealth above a certain amount to purify it, and at least once in a lifetime, if able, make a pilgrimage to Mecca in Saudi Arabia to reenact primary events of Islamic history.

Beginning in Arabia in the seventh century, Islam spread rapidly to the West, moving first through eastern Africa, Egypt, and the Sudan to the western outpost of the African continent—the Maghrib (Morocco). Simultaneously, it moved north into what is now called the Middle East and east through the Indian subcontinent, into China and through the Federation of Soviet States. By the ninth century, Islam had begun to implant itself in West Africa. By the time of the burgeoning slave trade in the fifteenth century, West African Muslims had established centuries-old Islamic traditions vying for power with traditional religion. Many of the African slaves in the New World were Muslim and educated.

Most historians of the Atlantic slave trade, writing in the late twentieth century, held that African slaves had no monotheistic religion, disregarding the Islamic tradition. They relegated African traditional religion to shouts and stories of which slaves had some memory. Only recently has concrete evidence been found about the lives of African Muslim slaves. Thanks to Allen Austin (*Muslim Slaves in Antebellum America*) and Sylvaine Diouf (*Servants of Allah*), we now have some information on African Muslims in the New World and thus a possible context for female African Muslim slaves to begin a conversation.

Diouf asserts:

The most dynamic segments of the Muslim population were made up of well read, well-traveled, cosmopolitan, multilingual, resourceful, adaptable men [and women] who were prompt to see and seize opportunities, even in familiar surroundings, and who were unafraid of the unknown. (39)

Since we know that in African Muslim history girls and boys were educated in Islamic schools and that some women were teachers who knew the Qur'an by heart, we can deduce that these women were among those kidnapped and transported to the New World. However, most of the information on female Muslim slaves comes from the narratives of their descendants.

Ed Thorpe, an eighty-three year-old former slave, recalled his grandmother Patience Spalding, who came from Africa, in these terms: "When muh gran pray, whe knell down on duh flo. She bow uh head down tree time an she say "Ameen, Ameen, Ameen." (61)

Rachel Anderson, seventy-three years-old, remembered her great-grandmother: "Muh great gran— she name Peggy—I membuh she pray ebry day, at sunrise, at noon, an at sunset. She kneel down wen she pray an at duh en she bow tree times, facin duh sun. (61)

In addition to prayer, female African Muslim slaves probably participated in many of the rituals of Islam such as fasting and giving to charity even though there were constraints on both their bodies and actions. In spite of their attempts to keep coherent Islamic knowledge and practice, time took its toll, and by the time of the Emancipation Proclamation, only fragments remained. Islam in twentieth-century America began anew.

The Moorish Science Temple

The Moorish Science Temple of America, founded as the Canaanite Temple by Noble Drew Ali in 1913 in Newark, New Jersey, is the first known instance of an African American community asserting ties to Islam in the twentieth century. By 1928, the Moorish Science Temple of America had temples in fourteen cities including Chicago, Philadelphia, and Detroit.

Islamic belief in the Moorish community focused on central Qur'anic concepts such as justice, a purposeful creation of mankind, freedom of

will, and humankind as the generator of personal action (both good and bad). At the core of Moorish teachings was the assertion that the primary need of African Americans in the first few decades of the twentieth century was a historically accurate nationality—i.e., a national identity that gave them some connection with a homeland. (McCloud, 11)

Pearl Ali, who married Noble Drew Ali when she was a teenager in the 1920s, is the best known of the Moorish women because of her establishing the Young People's Moorish League and other social work activities. In addition to directing activities inside and outside the community, Women in the Moorish Science Temple of America worked to establish stable religious homes with a focus on morality. Moorish women were careful about their appearance, fastidious about the upkeep of their homes, and loving, protective mothers. They also were activists in the black community, contributing as volunteers in women's shelters, nursing homes, and soup kitchens. *The Holy Koran of the Moorish Science Temple* by Noble Drew Ali provided some instruction for women in the community in a segment titled "Marriage Instructions for Man and Wife":

Remember thou art made man's reasonable companion, not the slave of his passion; the end of thy being is not merely to gratify his loose desire, but to assist him in the toils of life, to soothe his heart with thy tenderness and recompense his care with soft endearments. (23)

With the uniqueness of their names, Bey or El, with their heads wrapped in seven yards of cloth, usually red, these women were conspicuous when they worked as maids in the late 1920s and 1930s. They quickly gained a reputation for being prompt, efficient, and honest. Because they did not drink, smoke, or gamble, their integrity was above reproach and even earned them respect (Interview with Jamila Abdur Rahman, 1995). In the year 2000, there are Moorish Science women. Their surnames and head wraps still identify them. Some Moorish women moved on into mainstream Islam in the middle decades of the twentieth century after hearing immigrant Muslims lecture about Islam in urban communities. One group of immigrants in particular, the Ahmadiyyah Movement, in Islam was especially influential.

The Ahmadiyyah Movement in Islam

Members of this movement came to the United States as early as 1920. The Ahmadiyyah Movement in Islam originated in 1880 as an Islamic reform movement in the Punjab region of India in response to missionary activities of Christians, the increasing hostility of Hindus, and the inability of Muslims to act against either one. The founder, Gulam Ahmed (d. 1908), asserted that Muslim scholars had misunderstood basic fundamentals of the Qur'an such as Jesus' death on the cross and the end of prophethood with Prophet Muhammad. These differences led to Ahmed's followers' separation from the main body of Muslims. By the latter part of the twentieth century the community was labeled heretical by most Muslim courts. Nevertheless, members of this community were largely responsible for the majority of the Islamic literature in the United States and the African American communities' first general exposure to Islam in 1921.

African American women who learned about Islam through this community were introduced to the Qur'an and to a multiracial international community. White Christianity and racism in America became the issues of injustice attacked by this community. Islam's focus on racial injustice and its connection to mainstream religion attracted many African Americans. During the early decades of the twentieth century the Ahmadis had several newspapers that served as organs of protest and contributed to the growth of Islam in the United States. African American women who joined this community were taught Arabic and the practices of Islam and, in general, were acclimated to a cultural Indian Islam. There is a particular intracommunity organization around age and gender. Nasirats (girls, ages seven to sixteen) and Young Lajna (young women, ages sixteen to twenty-one) have their own social activities separated from males. Each group has its own constitution and a nationally standardized program. Each group's activities are organized around worship, education, and service to humanity.

This community's African American women are especially well traveled. Since the community is both distinct and international, members travel for study and visiting other Ahmadi in India a great deal. Women are national and international officeholders and do a significant portion of the community's public relations work. Because their initiation to Islam was to "orthodoxy," that is, the Qur'an, Islamic history, and the Arabic language, these Muslim women frequently mixed with other immigrant communities. They also participated in local groups serving the general black community from soup kitchens to literacy programs. Ahmadi African American women are indistinguishable from other Muslim women and remain active in the general black as well as Muslim worlds.

Women in the Nation of Islam

Newspapers have periodically run pictures of women in the Nation of Islam—all in white veils, praying in long rows with palms up. Muslim women in the NOI greet each other and every visitor to a warm smile and sonorous, "As salaam alaykum" (peace unto you). Politeness, courtesy, complementary jewelry, correct posture, a look of peace and good health—these are the terms used to describe these women by those outside of the Nation of Islam.

The Nation of Islam came into being during the Great Depression of the late 1920s and early 1930s. African Americans, in general, and black women in particular were severely constrained in the labor market. Situated at the bottom of the economic ladder, with extraordinary family and community obligations, life was a living hell. The pragmatic message that Elijah Muhammad (1897–1975) brought to the black community was both a relief and a promise. His message gave black people a place in the history of the world, a rationale for their current situation as ex-slaves in the United States, and a program for present and future well-being.

Though every strata of society suffered during the Great Depression, blacks and poor whites suffered the most. The Nation of Islam offered few material incentives but did provide assistance for its hardworking members when unemployment, illness, death, and other calamities struck. It also refocused the minds and efforts of members. Rather than pursuing wealth for personal gain, wealth was pursued for the common good. Prosperity was not in what others could see; it was in economic programs that helped all black people. Social mobility was reframed and aimed to deriving personal gratification from within the Nation. Women and men who exemplified the best moral qualities were seen as role models. The Nation engaged itself, at all levels, in aspects of nation building. Activities for socializing and opportunities for work were cornerstones of identity formation, promoting membership and solidarity. Men were schooled in the ideas on moral living, abstaining from drugs or gambling.

One attraction this community had for black women was the shift of responsibility for the home from women to men. Men were undeniably the heads of NOI households and took pride in being maintainers and supporters. These men were encouraged to bring the earned money home to the family and to take an active role in the lives of their children. Since there have always been more men than women in the Nation, women joined to find those "ideal" husbands.

Clara Muhammad (1898–1972), wife of Elijah Muhammad, was an indispensable agent in the Nation of Islam. She introduced her husband to Fard Muhammad, the Supreme Teacher of the Nation Islam. Additionally, she was the leader of the Nation while her husband was jailed and began the first University of Islam in the 1930s. As the "first lady" of the Nation, Clara Muhammad was the primary responsible person in teaching and training women in the Muslim Girls Training classes. This remarkable woman died in 1972 (Interview with Zakiyyah Muhammad, biographer of Clara Muhammad).

Female members of the Nation of Islam are required to attend Muslim Girls Training classes. These classes are now more than fifty years old. Here young women use *The Holy Qur'an, The Message to the Blackman, Our Savior Has Arrived,* and *How to Eat to Live* to learn about Islam, black history, managing households, and diet. This community is really an enclave inside the larger black community. Women are taught to value themselves as women, wives, and mothers along with demanding respect from black men for their modesty. In the Muslim Girls Training classes, women are constantly asked to reflect on their behavior in private as well as in public. They are at all times to act as models of womanhood. They are also taught to be efficient in homemaking—household cleaning, cooking, care and education of children, and care of their husbands.

In the text *How to Eat to Live,* Elijah Muhammad laid out this diet: Eat one meal per day, between four and six in the evening. He excluded or modified the amount of many foods that are now known to cause problems such as pork, candies, white sugar, and white bread and recommended drinking water instead of soda. All alcohol was prohibited, as was smoking. This program, which includes fasting, has kept members of the Nation of Islam fit and trim and thus able to combat many of the diseases that plague the black community such as high blood pressure and heart disease.

Women in the Nation are distinguishable by their uniform dress and accompanying veils. As symbols of unity, modesty, and financial responsibility, this dress is worn on occasions of public meetings, affirming their participation in and adherence to a set of specific guidelines. They have assisted in the reform of thousands of women from lives of crime and drug addiction. Likewise, black communities have benefited by the membership of hundreds of NOI physicians, dentists, teachers, and lawyers. The women have developed multifaceted talents while holding to the same women's programs for over sixty years. This consistency of purpose has attracted many black women to the Nation of Islam.

The fundamental center of the Nation of Islam's philosophy is a belief in one God, Allah, his messenger, and the presentation of Islam to "Negroes" in North America through the teachings of Fard Muhammad and his student the Honorable Elijah Muhammad in the third decade of the twentieth century. What has been idiosyncratic is this community's dedication to the uplift of African Americans by asserting that while their continuing role as the scapegoats of society is primarily their fault, the origin of their condition lies in the story of the creation of "whiteness." The leaderships' teachings

on why the degradation of African Americans is necessary for the existence of whiteness has "hit a chord" in the hearts of most African Americans.

Nevertheless, African American women in this community have persisted in their war against poverty, drugs, poor health care, and other ills plaguing the black community. Tynetta Muhammad, widow of the Honorable Elijah Muhammad (d. 1975), runs a clothing business while engaging the larger Muslim and African American community across the nation on issues of culture and, additionally, writes for the community newspaper *The Final Call.* Mrs. Khadijah Farrakhan, the wife of Minister Louis Farrakhan, does public relations for the community regarding international affairs. Minister Ava Muhammad (graduate of Ministers Class) has made sure there is a woman's voice at the ministerial level in the Nation of Islam.

In the early 1990s as the Nation of Islam changed its theology and moved into mainstream Islam, NOI women kept to the Nation's principles of behavior. They still are dressed uniformly on public occasions, while their everyday dress has taken on a syncretic style designed by women in the community. This style includes modifications on the Pakistani *shalwar khameez* (long tunic blouse over pants with matching veil) and long shirt matching skirt sets. Very little, if any, makeup is worn, although earrings and necklaces are used as accessories.

The confidence in their religious history as well as ethnic position continues to make this community of women unique. At least three generations of Muslims share in this community.

Darul Islam (The House of Islam)

As stated previously, African American Muslim women have participated in the larger Muslim community since the 1920s. The State Street Mosque in Brooklyn, New York, was founded in 1924 or 1925 under the leadership of Shakyh Daoud Faisal. This community was directly associated with the Muslim world but also fought the accepted American designation of black Americans as Negroes. Faisal, like Noble Drew Ali and Elijah Muhammad, felt that African Americans should reclaim their Islamic heritage and also lay claim to an American allegiance. Darul Islam forged ties with the Muslim world mostly through its hospitality to immigrants and visiting seamen in ports in New York and New Jersey. Along with the Moorish Science Temple of America and the Nation of Islam, this community used the Ahmadi translation of the Qur'an until other translations became available. Weekly teachings consisted of learning the beliefs and practices of Islam along with reading the Qur'an and studying Arabic.

In keeping with an adherence to a more conservative

Islam, Darul Islam's practices included some cultural practices such as prohibition of photographing people, of wearing shoes in the home, and of mixing women and men. Islamic law concerning what to eat as well as private sexual etiquette was strictly observed. The maintainers and transmitters of information on Islamic culture were women. African American women in this community rarely associated with non-Muslim African American women in the early decades. Like their sisters in the Ahmadiyyah Movement, the Nation of Islam, and the Muslim world, they developed their own supportive and active community. In the late 1930s and early 1940s, women organized schools for both children and adults in East Coast neighborhoods to teach the basics of reading and writing. They also ran soup kitchens and clothing distribution centers. These activities continued into the twenty-first century.

Although Darul Islam did not have a concrete program like the Nation of Islam for either efficient living or thrift, Islamic patterns assisted them in areas of financial responsibility. Muslims do not eat pork, gamble, drink alcohol, or indulge in drugs. Monies spent in the larger black community on narcotics or gambling were rerouted to the maintenance of the community. Women, most often, sewed their families' clothing, and food was purchased in cooperation with other families.

Since most African American women who become Muslim find themselves engaged in a different worldview and sometimes estranged from their nuclear families, they also make new friends and sometimes even create new families within the Muslim communities. These surrogates become the only families for some, while others make continuous successful attempts to stay in touch with their "natural" families. Many African American non-Muslims still see Islam and its believers as a kind of "failed Christianity," thus keeping them from sharing in its solutions for urban problems. This is most evident in larger African American women's organizations that Muslim women are not invited to join, nor are their accomplishments in the black community usually recognized. One of the oldest black newspapers in the United States is *The Muslim Journal*, which for over twenty years has been managed by an African American woman, Ayesha Mustapha, who has received neither awards nor any recognition by black journalists' organizations for this feat.

The practical demands of Islamic beliefs and practices led to a distinctive organization of domestic space. Because empty space is needed for prayer, many African American Muslim homes tend have minimal furniture, especially furniture that is difficult to move. Muslims pray in every room of the house except the kitchen and bathroom. Many women try to replicate some part of the Muslim world. There are rugs, incense holders, and small wooden boxes from India or Pakistan, wall hangings from Afghanistan or Bangladesh, calligraphy from the Middle East, and drums and artifacts from West Africa. Most African American Muslim homes mark a separation and difference from the outside world. As Muslims pray on the floor, shoes are removed upon entering to prevent bringing dirt into the home.

There are African American Muslim women who belong to the Shi'a Muslim community. This is the smaller branch of Islam found mainly in Iran. Beginning in 1979 with the overthrow of the shah of Iran and the American hostage crisis, the Ayatollah Khomeini, through emissaries, sent hundreds of tickets to the African American Muslim community for members to study and learn about Shi'a Islam in Iran. As a direct result, some stayed, studied, and married there, while others returned to the United States and contributed to the larger community of Sunni Muslims. They travel to Iran often for study purposes.

Many women left the Nation of Islam after 1975 when Elijah Muhammad's son attempted to move the entire community into "mainstream" Islam. They followed Warithudeen Muhammad, in the American Muslim society. Dr. Constance Shabazz, a medical internist, spends a significant portion of her time working with AIDS patients. Dr. Bambade Shakoor, a clinical psychologist, travels across the nation to counsel young black women and hold "rites of passage" programs. Dr. Zakiyyah Muhammad works to keep a national Muslim educators group together. She also promotes spiritual wellness programs for black women in all religious communities. The list of women and activities that women in the American Muslim society support or initiate is long and continuously growing.

African American Muslim women also participate in Sufi communities. Long understood as mystical Islam, Sufism in America at first attracted European Americans who later became Muslim. In the late 1970s, however, Sufism in America directed its focus toward fulfilling the diversity that is intrinsic to Muslim general culture. Shakyhs from Senegal and Gambia brought the Tijaniyyah Order to the eastern coast of the United States, while shakyhs from Lebanon brought the Naqshabandiyya Order to all regions. While only a few African American Muslim women have joined these orders, the numbers are increasing.

The many cultures of the Muslim world all center on a core set of values and practices found in the Qur'an. Each culture also has its particular ethnic expression of Islam. African American Muslim communities are new to Islamic history and are in the process of concretizing their experience. That African American Muslims are different on many levels is obvious. They come from a strong work ethic like all their Muslim sisters but generally are not subservient or submissive. Raised to be independent they have committed themselves to a worldview that thrives on communalism. Women in the Muslim world, just like men, have been taught that at the bottom of any ladder the African American sits. Only since 1990 have immigrant Muslim women discovered the knowledge and resources that African American Muslims can bring to the Islamic world.

SOURCES: Texts and articles on African American Muslim women are few. Thus, this essay used a variety of source materials on African Islam such as Allen Austin's *Muslim Slaves in Antebellum America* (1997), and Sylvaine Diouf's *Servants of Allah* (1998). Amina Wadud's *Qur'an and Woman* (1992) provides an examination of the Qur'an's view of women, while Aminah McCloud in *African American Islam* (1995) explores African American Muslim women culturally. African American Muslim women are often directly addressed in Muslim community literature such as the texts of the Nation of Islam—*How to Eat to Live* (1972), *The Message to the Blackman* (1965), *Our Savior Has Arrived* (1974), and the texts of the Moorish Science Temple, *The Holy Koran of the Moorish Science Temple* (1968). Additional information was obtained through interviews with women from some of the communities.

WOMEN, ISLAM, AND MOSQUES
Ingrid Mattson

ONE DAY, AFTER a particularly frenzied day of driving her children between home, school, and the mosque, I heard an American Muslim mother exclaim, "Sometimes I wish women were forbidden to drive in *this* country." With this tongue-in-cheek reference to the prohibition on women driving in Saudi Arabia (an uncommon edict in the Muslim world), this woman was clearly implying that such a restriction would be impossible in America. Indeed, urban planning and the exegencies of modern life not only force most American women into their cars many times a day, but they also require women to be involved in the public sphere to a greater extent than was true in the premodern West or is still true in many traditional Muslim societies. Significantly, the complexity of contemporary American life has also forced, and permitted, Muslim women to enter the public spaces of the Islamic community in numbers perhaps unprecedented in history.

The mosque has always been the center of Islamic communal life and religious practice. The first mosque established by the Prophet Muhammad in Medina (Saudi Arabia) in 610 C.E., was alive with the presence of women. The Prophet's wives and unmarried daughters lived on one side of the mosque. Another side was home to a number of poor and needy men and women, including a slave woman who had escaped an abusive master. Between these two sides of the mosque was the prayer space, where women could be found joining congregational prayers, performing individual acts of worship, or engaged in group discussion and learning. At the same time, there is evidence in the Qur'an and from reports about the Prophet Muhammad that women were discouraged from being too visible in the public sphere. The streets of Medina were not always safe, and young women in particular could attract unwanted attention. Consequently, women, especially young women and those who did not live near the Prophet's mosque, were encouraged to pray at home. In any case, women were not required to attend Friday congregational prayer, nor was it considered better for them, as it was for men, to pray the obligatory five daily prayers in the mosque. Over time, as Islam spread throughout Asia, Africa, and Europe, Muslim authorities increasingly stressed the threat posed to chastity by the interaction of men and women outside the home, including the mosque. By the premodern period, it became unusual for any woman, other than very elderly women, to frequent the mosque.

This situation began to change after the European colonization of the Muslim world. In the twentieth century, as secular, Western ideologies began to spread in the Muslim world, men and women who were interested in Islam "as a complete way of life" began to consciously organize for worship and to discuss strategy for changing society. With the spread of modern media, it also became increasingly unlikely that women who remained in their homes were better protected from temptation than those who went to the mosque. Perhaps most important, given that more and more women were seeking secular education and employment, some argued that discouraging them from coming to the mosque made them more vulnerable to secular trends. By the late 1960s, increasing numbers of women were worshipping in mosques in the larger urban centers of the Middle East and South Asia, although in most areas women still generally stayed out of the mosques.

This change also affected Muslims in the United States and Canada, where immigrant Muslims had established mosques as early as the 1920s and 1930s (earlier African American Muslim slaves joined together in prayer when possible, but the secretive nature of these meetings did not normally permit the public performance of prayer and the transmission of religious practices to the young). In these mosques, activities rarely exceeded Friday congregational prayer; consequently, there was minimal involvement of women. The fact that these communities often did not pass a strong faith commitment to their children was a lesson to later generations. Muslims who came to America in the 1960s therefore had learned about the threat to religious commitment posed by the general secularizing trends of modernity "back home," as well as the threat to a distinct Muslim identity from assimilation pressures in their new homeland. The increased participation of women in public, organized religious activities, including those held within the mosque, have been seen by some as a solution to these problems.

In the last few decades, one of the most important functions mosques have undertaken has been the religious education of children. Most Muslims, like most Americans of other faiths, need or want to enroll their children in the public school system. This leaves weekday evenings and weekends for religious education. As a result, although the Islamic holy day of congregational prayer is Friday, "Sunday School" has become as much a part of the average American Muslim child's education as it has for American children of other faiths. Again, as is true in other faith communities, it is normally the mothers of these children who organize and teach in weekend schools. Although some Muslim communities now have separate facilities for teaching children, and a growing number have opened full-time religious day schools, most religious education is conducted within the mosque. This necessitates the regular presence of women, a necessity that has been somewhat problematic because, according to many Islamic traditions, men or women in a state of major ritual impurity (because of sexual intercourse or menstruation) should not enter the prayer hall. For this reason, many communities have renamed their main building an "Islamic Center" and have designated a specific place within that center that is the *masjid* or *musallah*, that is, the "place for prayer." Within the other areas of the center, ritual purity is not a requirement for entrance.

This need to have women provide religious education to children opened the door to women's presence in the mosque more than anything else. Even women who were not accustomed to praying in the mosque found themselves in the building at prayer time and so joined the congregation. Sometimes limited space made this difficult, since men and women form separate lines for prayer. Although a woman can be the prayer leader (the "imam") in a group of women, a man always leads the prayer of a mixed-gender group; consequently only a man can be the official prayer leader for the entire community. In a mixed-gender group, the usual arrangement for prayer is that men form parallel rows behind the imam, and women form parallel rows behind the men. Muslim scholars trace this division to the normative practice of the Prophet Muhammad (the sunna), and many say that the wisdom behind it is to preserve the dignity and modesty of the women, since ritual prayer involves prostration. Unfortunately, because many mosques are converted houses, or quickly become too small for the growing Muslim community, women often find themselves squeezed into less-than-desirable spaces for prayer. This tendency has been vigorously resisted by many Muslim women and has even motivated some who were previously "apolitical" to question male domination of mosque leadership. When men have expressed surprise or claimed ignorance about the problems women have with the spaces assigned to them in the mosques, women have pointed out that it is precisely this inability of men to be aware of all their needs that necessitates their representation among the leadership of the mosque. This is particularly true in American Muslim communities where many women, unlike women in traditional Muslim societies, do not have male relatives to represent their concerns.

Increasingly, Muslim women are insisting on having more space designated for them in the mosques. How this space is delineated is another concern. Although there was no physical barrier between men and women in the Prophet's mosque, over the centuries, many Muslim societies used walls or curtains to separate the two genders. In contemporary America, many Muslims seem to prefer a separate balcony where women can see but not be seen. Whatever the form, assigning permanent separate spaces for men's and women's prayer is a source of great controversy among Muslims, with an equal number of men and women, it seems, favoring or disfavoring such a partition. Some women like the private space where they can rest, recline, and even nurse children away from the gaze of men. Other women resent the barrier presented to their participation in lectures and discussions that frequently occur in the prayer space. To accommodate both demands of gender segregation in prayer and communication within the community, some centers, such as the Islamic Foundation of Greater St. Louis in Ballwin, Missouri, have built separate prayer spaces for men and women but also have an auditorium in which men and women can attend lectures and meetings together.

Although more opportunities have opened for women to participate with men in religious instruction in the American mosque, it is still more common for men and women to be instructed separately. Some imams offer weekly lessons just for women, following the example of the Prophet Muhammad who set aside one day a week to meet privately with the women of his community. Even more commonly, women have their own study circles in the mosque or in their homes. Although formal religious schools and seminaries were important in the traditional Muslim world, they never replaced the "study circle" (*halaqah*) as the most common means of transmitting religious knowledge. Study circles form when a group of people gather around an individual whom they recognize as having some beneficial religious knowledge. Throughout Islamic history, distinguished female scholars have transmitted the sacred sciences to male and female students in study circles held in their homes.

In Muslim communities across America, study circles

In many American communities, it is not uncommon for women to form study circles even when no one among them has more religious education or knowledge of Arabic than any other. In such cases women meet to pray, socialize, and discuss their problems. They may form a kind of Islamic "book club" or pledge to support each other in learning and memorizing passages of the Qur'an. *Used by permission of Rabia Bajwa.*

are normally held weekly but can spring up spontaneously anytime a learned person visits a community. There is no ordination in Islam; only the community's recognition of a person's religious learning and piety provides justification for authoritative interpretation. However, it is the duty of every Muslim, even those with little knowledge, to share what they know with those who know less. While the leader of one study circle might be a scholar, another might be an otherwise ordinary person who happens to recite the Qur'an better than anyone else in the group. In America an immigrant woman with no advanced religious education, but who speaks Arabic, the language of the Qur'an, might find herself in a position of leadership over a group of American or non-Arabic-speaking immigrant women. Similarly, in America, the wives of imams often assume the role of teacher, counselor, and adviser to the women of the community. Often this motivates the imam's wife to increase her own study of religious texts, in order to answer the women's questions more knowledgeably. On the other hand, in many American communities, it is not uncommon for women to form study circles even when no one among them has more religious education or knowledge of Arabic than any other. In such cases women meet to pray, socialize, and discuss their problems. They may form a kind of Islamic "book club" or pledge to support each other in learning and memoriz-

ing passages of the Qur'an (a highly recommended act of worship) from audio tapes and CDs.

Although there are women's study circles in many mosques, women often prefer to meet in their homes for a number of reasons. As mentioned previously, some mosques do not have comfortable areas for women to meet, and sometimes this is an indication that their presence in the mosque is not encouraged. Most women indicate, however, that meeting in their homes is more convenient, especially if they have small children. Further, in the privacy of a home, with no men around, women can remove their veils and relax. This reflects an aspect of tradititional Islamic gender segregation, whereby no man is permitted access to the space in which women are meeting. One important consequence is that if only women are present when it is time to perform one of the five daily prayers, one of the women will lead the others as the imam of the congregation.

Most commonly, the home is also the location for celebrating female rites of passage. In Islamic law legal maturity commences with puberty, usually determined by the onset of menstruation in females. Traditionally, this is the age when a girl begins to wear the *hijab* (veil) and is required to perform all the ritual duties of Islam, such as prayer and fasting. Many Muslims in America do not adhere to the practice of veiling, which means that family and community support for a girl who veils needs to be strong. This is especially true for Muslim teenagers in America who are a small minority in an adolescent culture that revolves, to a great extent, around what is "fashionable." This explains the origin of the "*hijab* party" among religious Muslim American teenagers, particularly Arab immigrants. At a *hijab* party, a newly veiled girl and her friends will style their hair, put on makeup, wear fancy dresses, and dance with each other. The *hijab* party allows girls to dress as beautiful as prom queens, enjoy music and dancing, yet maintain their public modest dress and adhere to the restriction on social mixing with males.

Among more learned families, girls might be feted not for having reached the age of puberty but for having attained a certain level of knowledge. Among South Asian Muslims parties are commonly held in honor of children who have completed the recitation of the Qur'an with a scholar. At these parties the child recites in front of guests, who invoke blessings on the child and partake in food distributed by the family. Religious occasions, like the two annual Eid festivals, are further opportunities for religious and social gatherings among women. Beautification, particularly in the form of applying henna designs on the hands and feet, is a common shared activity among women on such occasions.

Although in traditional Muslim countries such parties are normally held in the home, they are frequently held in Islamic centers in America. There are a number of reasons for this. One reason is that the homes of many Muslims in America are not spacious enough to accommodate entertaining men and women separately. For Muslims who observe gender separation on social occasions, the local Islamic center is often a more suitable location for such gatherings. In other cases, the Islamic center is considered the natural location for any social gathering that has religious significance, because in America that is where one finds one's Muslim "family." Universally, Muslims consider themselves "brothers" and "sisters"; in America, in the absence of extended family for most Muslims, brotherhood and sisterhood in faith acquires even greater significance.

Sisterhood forms the explicit or implicit ideological basis for many Muslim women's organizations in America. Most immigrant Muslims leave their extended families behind in their home countries, and most American Muslim converts separate emotionally and spiritually from their non-Muslim families to some extent. To compensate for these lost or loosened bonds, there is a need for close relationships to be formed with other Muslims. One occasion when sisterhood becomes especially evident is when a woman is suffering from an illness or recovering from childbirth. At such times, Muslim women in a community often coordinate efforts so that a different woman brings a prepared meal to their "sister" every day. Visiting the sick is not only a

highly meritorious act in Islam; from an Islamic legal perspective, an ill person has a "right" to assistance and visits from other Muslims. A Muslim also has a right after death to have his or her body prepared in a proper manner for burial. In Islamic law, this entails bathing the body of the deceased and then wrapping the body in plain white strips of fabric. Even in death Islamic modesty prevails, so that except in some cases where a man or woman prepares the body of his or her spouse, women prepare women and men prepare men. Larger mosques often have groups of volunteers on call for this purpose; in smaller communities, three or four family members and close friends prepare the body.

The sisterhood that binds Muslim women as they support each other in times of trouble can form the basis for more formal associations among women. On the local level, Muslim women have joined to establish assistance programs for refugees from Muslim countries, food pantries for the poor, and other kinds of social services. Another sphere of society that has attracted the attention of many Muslim women is the public school system. On an individual level, women often become involved with their children's schools when they become aware of discrimination there because of their religious or ethnic identity. In many cases, the mother's involvement with the school is limited to giving presentations about Islam on religious occasions. In other cases, more ambitious efforts have been made. For example, in the early 1990s, two young Muslim women, Ameena Jandali and Maha Elgenaidi, founded the Islamic Networks Group (ING) in the San Francisco Bay area. Initially focusing on public schools, the women gave formal presentations on Islam to teachers and students and addressed issues of bias and stereotyping in the curriculum. Later ING expanded their efforts to other public institutions, including police, corporations, and media. After less than ten years in existence, ING was sponsoring approximately 700 presentations a year about Islam.

All Muslims are vulnerable to stereotyping and prejudice in America, but Muslim women have a particularly difficult time. On the one hand, like Muslim men, they suffer from stereotypes of Muslims as violent, backward terrorists. On the other hand, Muslim women are often assumed (by "well-meaning" persons) to be oppressed by their religion. If they wear a veil, often the assumption is that they have been forced to do so by their male relatives. As a result, Muslim women who observe religious practices in general, and religious dress in particular, are constantly trying to find ways to express their own authentic experiences. The Internet is an especially rich resource for Muslim women's support groups, study circles, and creative expression.

American Muslim women have actively addressed international situations in which Muslims have been victims of violence and oppression. Muslim women have rallied and lobbied, along with men, for the rights of Palestinians under Israel rule, Bosnians during the Serb assault, and Iraqis suffering from economic sanctions. The victimization of women in such situations has been an area of particular concern for many American Muslim women's organizations. For example, in 1992, after learning about the enslavement of Bosnian Muslim women in Serbian rape camps, a group of Muslim women established an organization called Women in Islam (WII). Women in Islam was based in New York City in order to establish a presence close to the United Nations. WII director Aisha al-Adawiya was present at the 1995 Beijing Women's Summit, and the group has won official nongovernmental organization (NGO) status at the United Nations.

Another Muslim women's organization established to address national and international issues of human rights is *Karamah*: Muslim Women Lawyers for Human Rights. Founded by lawyers and academics Azizah al-Hibri and Asifa Quraishi, *Karamah* is particularly focused on abuses of women's rights perpetrated in the name of Islam. Al-Hibri and Quraishi have written critiques, for example, of Taliban rule in Afghanistan and Pakistani rape laws. The organization's priority, however, is to help solve Islamic legal issues that are particularly problematic for American Muslim women. For example, the group has written about the problems impeding a just interpretation of Islamic marriage contracts in American courts. Describing their agenda they write,

When we talk of human rights abuse, we often direct our attention to governments and institutions. We must not forget, however, that the most basic of our rights emerge within our private and our domestic spheres. KARAMAH is founded upon the idea that education, dialogue, and action can counter the dangerous and destructive effects of ignorance, silence, and prejudice.

The Muslim women lawyers and legal scholars of *Karamah* generally try to draw upon the methodology of traditional Islamic jurisprudence to argue for Muslim women's rights. A number of other Muslim women's organizations have a more secular orientation or draw upon controversial modern revisionist interpretations of Islamic law. Perhaps the most prominent of these organizations is the Muslim Women's League (MWL) of southern California, under the leadership of physician Laila al-Marayati. The MWL's publications convey a sense of urgency regarding the circumstances in which many Muslim women live. They decry the fact that religion is often used to justify a limitation on Muslim women's opportunities for education, economic independence, and simple self-preservation. They write,

To all those who are committed to the Islamic principles of justice and truth, we call upon you to join us in our efforts by organizing similar groups in your community, participating in Muslim as well as non-Muslim organizations that are part of this struggle, educating yourselves and others about Islam, and by working together without divisiveness and ill-will.

Dr. al-Mariati and the MWL have received a significant amount of support and attention from non-Muslim activist and political organizations. Whether they will be able to affect the Muslim community as deeply as they desire remains to be seen, given that their ideological approach to Islamic law and normative discourse is often considered unorthodox. There is no doubt, however, that American Muslim women in general are determined to join together and to join with sympathetic Muslim men and non-Muslims to realize their full humanity within the broad context of Islamic tradition.

SOURCES: See the following Web sites: Islamic Networks Group, at http://www.ing.org/; Women in Islam, at http://womeninislam.org/; *Karamah*, at http://www.karamah.org/; and Muslim Women's League, at http://www.mwlusa.org/. For the early history of Muslims in America, see Sylviane Diouf, *Servants of Allah: African Muslims Enslaved in the Americas* (1998).

WOMEN'S ISSUES IN AMERICAN ISLAM
Jane I. Smith

AMERICAN MUSLIMS IN the United States and Canada comprise a rich, complex, and extremely diverse population of somewhere around 6 million. They are immigrants from a variety of countries as well as indigenous Americans, representing many races and ethnic/cultural groups, speaking a range of languages, and often choosing to present themselves in very different ways. The first Muslims to immigrate to America came from Syria and Lebanon in the late 1800s. By the early 1900s their numbers had increased, and they began to form small struggling communities across the country. Immigrant Muslims now represent over sixty nations in Asia, Africa, the Middle East, and Europe. Some are fleeing political oppression and come as asylum seekers, others are looking for economic or educational training, and still others are already skilled professionals who want to join the American workforce.

Many Muslims are not new to this continent but are African Americans, Latinos, Native Americans, or Caucasian citizens who have chosen to adopt the faith of

Islam. Most American Muslims are Sunni, and about a fifth of the population is Shi'ite. Some who call themselves Muslim identify with heterodox, sectarian groups. American-born and immigrant Muslim women make up the most heterogeneous female Muslim population in the world. Some wear their Islam, both literally and figuratively, with pride and with overt zealousness. Others choose to practice the religion privately and in family settings rather than as part of the public arena. A significant number of Muslims, men and women, remain publicly and privately unobservant and do not participate in either Islamic practices or ritual occasions.

American Muslim women are notably freer than their sisters anywhere in the world. Because public education is mandatory, they are guaranteed opportunities for schooling. If they choose, and their families support it, women generally are able to find jobs, possible prejudice against the headscarf notwithstanding. Most women drive or use public transportation, have access to some kind of health care and other social services, and enjoy a degree of autonomy in determining how they will live both publicly and privately. On the other hand, many Muslim women need to learn what their rights and opportunities are and how to take advantage of them. In terms of religious practices, women have the chance to participate in the public observance of Islam in ways never available to them in a number of other countries. It is also the case, however, that many American imams and other religious leaders, including African Americans, are conservative in their views about women, sometimes making open and active participation difficult to achieve.

Identity Formation

The rhetoric of American Muslim leaders, and of many of its youth, celebrates the diversity of American Islam at the same time that it seeks to emphasize commonalities over distinctions. Spokespersons stress the interpretation of Islam as a social and religious system that does not distinguish on the basis of race, gender, ethnicity, or national origin, a doctrine that has added to the appeal of Islam to many otherwise disadvantaged American citizens. Yet for practical purposes, the diversity of American Islam, and of its women, offers a range of challenges to the community at the same time that it represents a variety of individual and familial choices. Muslim women are learning that the transition from a mainly ethnic affiliation in which Islam is one component to finding primary identity as a member of a minority religion in which ethnicities are often divisive can be very difficult.

Given the range of identities and of potential choices, what are the kinds of issues with which Muslim women struggle to figure out who they want to be as members of the equally diverse American public? For both immigrants and Americans who have chosen Islam, the task of discovering, or formulating, their sense of identity is crucial. Immigrant women must seek a balance among such factors as their sense of commitment to Islam as a common bond, the particularities of the cultures from which they have come, and the reality of now being resident in (or citizens of) the United States or Canada. To which of these affiliations do they feel the greatest affinity? Some decide to adopt hyphenated identities in which these several associations are acknowledged, but even then the order suggests choices. Is one a Pakistani-American-Sunni Muslim? An American who happens to be Muslim and happens to come from Nigeria? Different kinds of occasions tend to bring out unconscious allegiances that may affirm the sense of community of American Muslims or may serve to emphasize the differences and distinctions.

Here again the very fact of being able to choose how to think about who one "really is" provides an opportunity rarely found in other countries and cultures. In most Muslim societies definitions are confined by the general homogeneity of the culture as well as by the ideologies generated by the state. In America options are at least theoretically open, although the extent to which Muslim women are able to, or should, exercise those options varies greatly according to the expectations of family, subcommunity, and particular religious leadership. These choices are the subject of a great deal of private and public conversation and attention, both in local arenas and on the programs of national Muslim association meetings.

A large number of American Muslims find their primary identity not so much through membership in the Islamic community as by being Americans who happen to be part of an Islamic heritage. They have accepted the fact that they live in and operate out of the American context and do not worry about possible compromises. Women of this orientation often find themselves struggling to determine where to look for the appropriate guidelines as to their own identity and place in their families, their communities, and American society as a whole.

All Muslims, regardless of their origin or degree of religious observance, are aware of the dominant American attitude toward Islam and Islamic values. They know that the American public is generally unappreciative of what it believes to be the sexist and repressive attitudes of Muslims vis-à-vis women. A variety of influences have shaped American perceptions of women in Islam, including a long history of Western prejudice and misunderstanding, reports of current practices in regard to women in some countries of Asia and the Middle East, the often distorted images of oppressed Muslim women that are perpetuated by the media, mov-

Many Muslim women, and men, in America today are assuming the responsibility of publicly challenging negative stereotypical images. One such effort is *Azizah*, a magazine that describes itself as "The Voice for Muslim Women" and dispels many of the myths surrounding Muslim women's lives. *Copyright © Azizah magazine.*

ies, and pulp fiction, and even the choice of many Muslim women in America to dress in ways that seem to Americans inevitably to be the result of male attempts at subjugation. Many Muslim women, and men, in America today are assuming the responsibility of publicly challenging such negative stereotypical images.

Identity issues for Muslim women include the extent to which they choose, or are allowed to choose, whether and how to participate publicly in the practice of Islam. A great number of often competing ideologies, both imported and homegrown, come into play as Muslims deal with the challenge of living in a non-Muslim country in which the religion of Islam is often misunderstood and underappreciated. Some spokespersons for Islam from more conservative parts of the Islamic world, as well as some African Americans, want to keep the Islamic community as separate as possible from the rest of American culture. They fear that overly associating with the Western way of life will lead to the degeneration of the faith. In this interpretation women are discouraged from participating in activities outside the home.

Growing numbers of Muslims in America, however, are now persuaded that if Muslims are to gain a voice in helping shape American attitudes and policies, it is necessary for everyone to be more publicly active, including women. National Muslim associations such as the Islamic Society of North America (ISNA) and the Islamic Circle of North America (ICNA) have moved from an original conviction that American society ought to be avoided to advocating participation for both women and men, although on strictly Islamic terms and by Islamic definitions.

To live in Western society without being influenced by it is difficult; thus the discourse about women's public participation inevitably is influenced, positively or negatively, by the claims of Western feminism. Some Muslim women choose to define themselves as feminists—but within an Islamic understanding. They may adopt certain of the feminist assumptions about freedom of access and opportunity for men and women. They reject, however, the common assumption that feminist formulations of equality are necessarily appropriate in the Islamic context and struggle to determine which ideas are most effective and consonant with Muslim values as they work to define their identity within their own family and communal settings.

Conversion to Islam in America

AFRICAN AMERICANS

The choice of many African Americans to adopt Islam as a religion and way of life has taken different forms over the last century, and numbers of converts continue to grow. Originally attracted to Elijah Muhammad's Nation of Islam, many blacks since the death of the Elijah have followed the leadership of his son Warith Deen Mohammed in identifying with mainstream Sunni Islam. Imam Mohammed's followers now call themselves the Muslim American Community. The Nation of Islam, now a small movement, continues under the primary leadership of Louis Farrakhan. Other Sunni movements are also part of the complex of African American Islam, as are a variety of heterodox movements, many only tangentially identified with the religion. For many blacks the choice to convert has centered on their hope that the egalitarian and nonracist doctrines of Islam will guarantee that they can be free of the forms of racist oppression they have experienced in America. African American women are important contributors to public efforts to formulate Islamic identity in the Western context, and they are increasingly vocal when they experience what they see as familiar forms of racial or gender oppression by their husbands or men of their community or by some Muslim immigrants, especially male leaders.

For many black women Islam truly has provided a vehicle for self-affirmation, participation in a welcoming community, and the practice of faith within a reasonable and manageable structure. They find the Islamic emphasis on the direct responsibility of the individual to God straightforward and refreshing. Some African American Muslim women are from very poor social and economic circumstances, are accustomed to being on welfare, and hope that Islam will offer them a better life. Others come to Islam from the context of black power groups, seeing in the religion a way of political participation as well as philosophical and spiritual satisfaction. Most Muslim women who are black choose to adopt Islamic dress and Islamic names and to participate as much as possible in Friday prayers and other mosque activities. Many are active in women's associations.

Life for African American women is not always as good as they may have expected. Certain Islamic restrictions, such as a general ban on most kinds of music, can be difficult to accept. In many ways African American Muslim women face a triple prejudice evident in the society and culture: against women, against blacks, and against Islam. Often they have had a hard time explaining their choice of conversion to parents and family. The loneliness they experience with the breaking of those bonds may be exacerbated if they are not made to feel welcome by their immigrant Muslim sisters. The ethnocentricity of some immigrant communities may mean there is little tolerance for African Americans who are newly come to the faith. Many blacks experience difficulties in keeping their jobs when they appear in Islamic dress. Those who continue on the welfare system find that the already humiliating experience of being "on the dole" is made even more difficult if social workers respond in prejudicial ways to their being Muslim.

Still, almost all black women who adopt Islam believe that, despite the difficulties, it is far preferable to the racism and sexism of general American culture. As numbers grow and communities solidify, women are finding in their sisters a positive sense of support and solidarity. The strong affirmation of the family generated by Elijah Muhammad in the old Nation of Islam has been continued by Imam Warith Deen Mohammed and provides a welcome change from the broken families and fatherless homes that many have experienced.

OTHER AMERICAN CONVERTS

Women from other racial-ethnic groups in the American context may also decide to adopt Islam, although their numbers are considerably smaller than those of African Americans. Many have been attracted by the movements of *da'wa* (educating about Islam and/or inviting others to accept to Islam) that are active in the United States and Canada. The reasons for their choice are many, including marriage to Muslim men, rejection of Christianity as ineffective in changing social structures, and attraction to what they see as the clear and straightforward structure of Islamic faith and practice. While conversion of non-Muslim wives to Islam is not mandated, a large number of women who enter into such marriages report obvious pressure to convert. Many indicate that they do so out of respect for their husbands and new families or because they do not want to raise their children in a household in which two religions are observed.

Some American women encounter Islam in the academic context and are attracted by the long history of Islamic culture and its holistic view of art, literature, science, and philosophy. Hispanic and Native American women are coming to adopt Islam, though as yet only in very small numbers, because they see in it elements that resonate with cultural characteristics common to their own ethnic associations such as respect for family and elders, appreciation of the rhythms of nature, and the integration of religious and spiritual beliefs with the whole of life. Increasing public efforts at *da'wa* are bringing the faith to the attention of more women as well as men.

The spiritual practices of Islamic Sufism (mysticism) are attractive to many American women. Also appealing are what they see as the Islamic emphasis on community over the individuality of Western culture and the conviction that the family with its specific responsibilities for women and men is a significant alternative to what seem to be crumbling Western family structures. They feel welcomed and supported in the American Muslim community and form an active part in forming its definition. The Islamic ideals of family, dedication to God, and a disciplined life are appealing options to much of current Western society.

These converts, too, often experience struggle and pain as consequences of their choice of a new religion and identity. Some are shocked to discover that they are more marginalized in the Islamic community than they had expected. Less surprising, but nonetheless difficult to deal with, is the misunderstanding and sometimes rejection they experience from their own families and groups. Family tensions grow as new converts adhere to Islamic customs not understood or appreciated by those unfamiliar with the faith. The adoption of Islamic dress may cause stress and embarrassment to family members, and the disinclination to continue to observe Christian or Jewish holidays may make family gatherings difficult or impossible. The choice of Islam on the part of young Muslim women often appears to parents as a rejection of themselves and of the religious or cultural values that they had struggled to inculcate in their children.

Male-Female Relationships

Relationships between the sexes have always been of paramount importance in Islam, and they remain so in the American context. Notions of propriety are very important to most Muslims, often most obviously in the ways they determine what is and is not appropriate in terms of women's interaction with men, girls with boys. Some women prefer not to be in the company of men outside of their families at all, others feel that this is acceptable if they are appropriately dressed, and still others interact freely with members of the opposite sex within certain clearly understood boundaries. Some conservative Muslims feel that men and women shaking hands with each other is not proper.

Throughout most of the history of Islam male-female relationships have been characterized by the institution of patriarchy. Although it may take different forms in the American context patriarchy persists as a dominant theme. New opportunities for education and employment have gone a long way to change both the structure and the discourse about relative roles and opportunities for women, as have the pressures of Western secularism

and "equal opportunities" for both genders, much as that discourse has been resisted by many in the Muslim community. Within families major decisions generally are made by males. Few women choose to engage in activities or assume roles that are not generally approved by their husbands or fathers. Whether or not this will change in the near future is unclear, although Muslim organizations and councils are increasingly featuring conversation about the roles and functions of women in society at large as well as within the family.

An integral element in public discourse about Islam is the insistence that it is the first of the major world religions to truly liberate women and that the Qur'an guarantees parity with men in terms of both rights and responsibilities unparalleled in other scriptures. A few verses in the Qur'an, such as chapter 4, verse 34, that suggest men have authority over women are the focus of continuing discussion between male leaders of Islam and Muslim women who find traditional interpretations to be unreasonable and oppressive. If God is just, they argue, and the Qur'an is God's word, then what seems inequitable and thus apparently unjust in the Qur'an must simply be reinterpreted in a more evenhanded light. Some American women academics are arguing publicly that new interpretations must be suggested to challenge what they identify as the male bias of Qur'an interpretation and that women are the ones who must undertake this exegetical task.

Finding a Marriage Partner

In traditional Muslim cultures marriage is negotiated by families, though this is undergoing significant change and rethinking in many Islamic societies today. Some immigrant groups in both the United States and Canada still adhere to arranged marriages, although with subtle differences from traditional expectations. Such customs vary with the length of time that immigrants have been in the West. Many younger women refuse to accept such arrangements, insisting that they are capable of making their own choices or that God will lead them to appropriate unions. Popular Muslim journals are sometimes used by individual men and women, or their families, to "advertise" for a mate, with very specific descriptions of the characteristics desired in a mate—such as piety, age range, or special interests—and the qualifications of the available partner.

These journals also publish articles on the elements of a good Islamic marriage, what potential partners should be looking for, and the importance for both parties of a well-thought-out and reasonable marriage contract. Female advocates and others are prompting young women to be wise in their insistence on such a contract as an essential component of a truly Islamic marriage, urging them to see that a carefully crafted contract can be an effective deterrent to future problems in the marriage. The importance of *mahr*, or dowry, as essential to a valid Islamic marriage contract is also stressed. Challenging the traditional understanding of *mahr* as a kind of bride-price, they insist rather that it is the element of the contract that makes clear the conditions by which a woman is willing to engage in marriage. Many young Muslim women, while accepting the importance of this contractual element, are using it as a way not only of providing security for themselves but of ensuring a fair and equitable basis for marriage by insisting that the amount not be more than the male can easily afford.

Socialization of young women and men is a very important issue for American Muslims. Some families do not allow either boys or girls to date or socialize with each other, within or outside the community. Others apply a double standard and allow boys freedoms not available to girls, often engendering feelings of frustration and anger on the part of the daughters. Some acknowledge that life in America involves a degree of capitulation to American culture and leave it up to their children to make wise and Islamically informed choices. When young people find the allure of American teen culture too appealing to resist, parents experience great consternation. Alternative means of socialization are being developed both locally and nationally, opportunities for youth to meet and get acquainted that do not involve the dating process per se. Mosques and Islamic centers feature activities for mixed groups of chaperoned youth, bringing them together through service opportunities or social encounter. Organizations such as Muslim Youth of North America (MYNA) and the Council of Muslim Communities of Canada (CMCC) invite youth to conferences, summer camps, and other activities in which they interact with members of the opposite gender but not in all activities and with carefully selected adult chaperones.

Muslim Marriages

According to Islamic law, Muslim men may marry Christians and Jews (the so-called People of the Book or those who have also been the recipients of God's revelation), but Muslim women may only marry Muslim men. Men naturally take advantage of this alternative more often in the United States and Canada than in societies where Islam is the dominant culture, putting an additional burden on young Muslim women who may find that the pool of available partners is very small. Marriage has been considered a sacred institution in Islam, despite the fact that it is not a sacrament in the Islamic understanding but a legal contract guaranteeing rights to both partners. Remaining single has not been an option for women in most Islamic societies but is

being entertained by a few Muslim women in America for whom finding a suitable partner is difficult, who resist the traditional practice of arranged marriages, or whose pursuit of vocation or career makes marriage a choice rather than an expectation.

Some Muslim women are even opting to contravene Islamic law and marry outside the faith. To the alarm of many families, the incidence of interfaith marriage is clearly on the rise, with Muslim women marrying Christians, Jews, Buddhists, Hindus, and others. For more traditional Muslims in America, particularly immigrants from conservative cultures, not only are interfaith marriages totally unacceptable (often for men as well as for women), but even interethnic, international, and interracial Muslim marriages are to be avoided. Some young American converts are expressing their frustration that potential marriage partners are inaccessible to them because of the insistence of families that their children, especially their daughters, marry "one of their own."

The custom of marrying one's cousin is still followed in certain immigrant communities, although this practice fades with length of residence in the West. Other families view marriages between two Muslims as such a preferable alternative to an interfaith marriage, or no marriage at all, that they are supportive of almost any such union. Certainly Muslims who are born in the United States or Canada are more open to marriage outside the narrow restrictions of family or racial-ethnic identities. Some unions have taken place between Sunni and Shi'i partners, although neither community looks officially with much favor on them. In American culture where many Muslims do not consider themselves observant, and may even identify as secular, intermarriage between those who are practicing Muslims and those who are not is also increasingly common. There are very few instances of marriages between immigrant and African American Muslims.

The Qur'an allows men to take up to four wives on condition that they relate equitably to all. Throughout the history of Islam this permission has been interpreted as a sanction for polygyny on the part of those males who could afford it. Current exegesis of this Qur'anic permission, however, stresses both the particular conditions under which such a practice is supposed to be observed (e.g., a lack of males in the community and the concern that a single women be outside a conjugal structure) and the acknowledgment also in the Qur'an that it is extremely difficult to relate with complete fairness to more than one marriage partner. American law also clearly stipulates that polygynous marriages are illegal. While it is not legally possible for an immigrant to bring more than one wife into the country, some have managed to get around this stipulation. In both Canada and the United States there are some instances of Muslims in polygynous (usually bigamous) unions, but not more than is true for other American groups such as the Mormons.

In the early days of African American Islam, particularly in the Nation of Islam, polygyny was sometimes seen as appealing. Imam Warith Deen Mohammed, since taking over leadership of most of the former Nation members, has spoken out forcefully against the practice as not consonant with the expectations and requirements of American society. A few African American groups still participate in polygynous marriages, sometimes with the justification that it counters the "absent father" trend in African American culture and helps create solid family units in which all females are provided for. Certain immigrant communities, particularly African, continue to engage in such marriages, although the practice is certainly not supported by the leadership of American Islam. While an imam might sanction polygyny if the partners are not U.S. citizens, and if foreign embassies approve, none will perform or honor such marriages if they are not contracted before entry into the country. Virtually all Muslim women in America as elsewhere oppose polygyny.

Family Disruption

Of greater concern to many Muslim women than the possibility of a cowife is the fact that traditionally divorce has been easier for men to effect than for women. The Qur'an stipulates that the *talaq*, or divorce decree, must be a three-month affair, assuring both that the wife is not pregnant and that the husband is serious in his intent. Islamic law does provide for the barely permissible possibility that the triple statement of intent to divorce can be said at one time. This has been an all-too-common practice in many Islamic societies. While many governments are acting to make it illegal, the threat still lingers in the minds of many women. Spokespersons for Islam in America are clear in their counsel to men that they should not resort to such an option. Divorce is also possible for women to initiate according to Islamic law, although generally the acceptable grounds for such divorce are much more specific than is the case for men. Muslim women, particularly those well versed in Islamic law, are active in helping Americans understand their rights according to Islamic as well as civil law.

The Prophet Muhammad is reported to have said that there was nothing more hateful to him than divorce, and certainly the sanctity of marriage is a strong theme in Islamic culture and in American Muslim communities. Nonetheless, the traditionally low incidence of divorce in Muslim families is rising in both the United States and Canada. Although U.S. family law recognizes Islamic marriage without a civil ceremony as a form of common-law marriage, it does not recognize Islamic divorce, which may lead to legal difficulties. Muslim leaders are active in calling for careful counseling for couples before they enter into marriage, as well as for those who are experiencing difficulties within their marriages or after divorce has been effected. While it is traditional for a Muslim father to take custody of both boys and girls at a relatively young age, divorced mothers in America are much more often allowed to keep their children. There is great concern that children of divorced parents are more likely than others to lose any active affiliation with Islam and to cease participation in Islamic activities, including holidays and festivals.

Violence and sexual abuse within the Muslim family, while formally condemned and certainly abhorred by women, is being recognized as an evil in the Islamic community that must be faced and addressed. The Qur'an verse that has been understood to grant men authority over women concludes with the injunction that men also have the right to beat them (however lightly) if they are disobedient (i.e., if wives refuse to acknowledge the conjugal rights of their husbands). Contemporary Islamic discourse in the West as elsewhere strongly condemns any such activity as wife-beating and favors a range of alternative interpretations of the real meaning of the verse. Whether done out of belief that it is sanctioned by scripture or simply part of a pervasive American phenomenon to which attention is increasingly being called, sexual abuse is being identified and addressed with candor in the Muslim community. Abuse of wives by husbands tends to be tolerated more by first- than second- or third-generation immigrant families and less by those who are educated in the principles of Islam and are aware of the campaign against spousal abuse in American society at large. Muslim leaders and agencies are working to eliminate this injustice that they argue has no place in Islam.

Women's Changing Roles in Family and Society

Many Muslim women in America are giving increasing attention to appropriate ways to relate to the wider contexts in which they find themselves. What does it mean to be Muslim in American society? The roles that women play in Islamic culture(s) are generally related to factors such as age, family relationships and responsibilities, and status in the community. In traditional societies it is very clear that expectations for females are specifically related to their movement from childhood through puberty, marriage, and aging. American Muslims are actively engaged in the effort to identify which elements of Islam are essential, mandated by Qur'an and Sunna (the way of life exemplified by the Prophet Muhammad), and which are cultural rather than religious.

Definitions of women's roles are clearly subject to cultural and ethnic variations that come to play as Muslims try to determine how closely they want to or are able to stick with traditional ways and what kinds of adaptations or changes are desirable or necessary in a new context.

Immigrants from more traditional cultures often find that opportunities available to them in American society are unacceptable or undesirable in terms of family and community expectations. Part of the struggle for women is to determine what they want in the new culture, what price they are willing to pay for it in terms of parental or conjugal disapproval, and what the implications of different choices may be not only for themselves but for their children. Often these choices are related to matters of education and employment.

While educational opportunities are often unavailable for women in home cultures, and education for women is sometimes frowned on or disallowed, the situation is markedly different in the United States and Canada. Muslim leaders are vocal in their insistence that education for all Muslims was part of the platform of the Prophet Muhammad and that the Muslim community cannot function if all of its members are not as well educated as possible. Nonetheless, some families prefer not to have daughters or wives continue with higher education, fearing that it will discourage them from fulfilling responsibilities at home or expose them to currents and trends opposed to traditional Muslim structures. In general, however, support for women's education in the American Muslim community is high.

The matter of employment is more complex. While traditionally many Muslim men have not wanted, or allowed, their wives to work, circumstances are changing in many places of the world and clearly are different in the American context. Some families look favorably on women's outside employment because it allows women to use their educational training, brings in extra income, and gives women an opportunity for professional fulfillment. Women who choose to work in the public arena are faced with a range of choices. Are certain professions more appropriate for women than others? If there is disagreement about employment, should a woman contravene the desires of her husband and family? Will a woman be compromised in any way if her work situation puts her into direct and constant contact with men?

The mobility of individuals and families characteristic of American society presents problems for women who want to work. Uprooted not only from their home culture but also from the aid and support of extended families, many women who worked full-time in their countries of origin cannot do so in America because they do not have other family members nearby to help take care of the children. In some instances women who have ad-vanced professional training choose to take time away from their work to raise their families, often resulting in their inability ever to rejoin the workforce. When elderly parents are in the home, often experiencing loneliness and isolation, added pressures are put on younger women to remain at home rather than go out to work.

Islamic Dress

Many American Muslim women are convinced that public participation in employment, whether it is blue-collar or professional, is directly related to the way in which they dress. The issue of "Islamic dress," which in its most common form means covering the hair, arms, and legs, has many dimensions. Women often believe that if they are dressed modestly, they are free to enter any profession because there is no danger that the men with whom they work will make unwanted advances. Unfortunately the very garb that in her own understanding, or that of her family, allows a woman to work may mitigate against her professional advancement or even getting a job in the first place. Many employers look askance at a woman wearing a *hijab* or headcover, fearing that customers or other employees will think it strange or that it may indicate some kind of religious fanaticism on the part of the wearer. The headscarf is sometimes prohibited in the workplace as part of general regulations against clothing that attracts too much attention. Ironically, regulations that may have originated in response to clothing considered too skimpy, such as miniskirts, now may prohibit clothing that serves the opposite purpose.

In recent years organizations such as the Council for American Islamic Relations (CAIR) are working hard to expose cases of prejudicial treatment in the workplace. Instances where women are not hired because of the scarf, or where it can be proved that they are not allowed professional advancement because of their dress, are immediately reported and publicized in the Islamic press and over the Internet. Companies who practice such discrimination may be forced to apologize, to reinstate or promote a female worker, or even to undergo special kinds of antidiscrimination training.

In Canada some Muslim students have been sent home from school for wearing *hijab* on the grounds that it does not conform to school dress code. The issue is of particular relevance in Quebec, where the headscarf is often interpreted as a political statement. Francophone Québécois may accuse those who wear the scarf of being anti-French in light of the strong French response against Islamic dress since the early 1990s. Even though such dress fits with Canadian policies of multiculturalism, many citizens of Quebec interpret it as one more critique of the French identity of many citizens of Quebec. Both Canadian and U.S. feminists have been articulate in describing the *hijab* as a symbol of subordination and oppression of women. Such arguments affect Muslim women in several ways. While some adopt certain elements of the critique and are themselves articulate in opposing Islamic dress, albeit in their own terms, others deeply resent such "interference" on the part of those who are not Muslim. Oppression comes in many forms, they argue, not least from those feminists who want to save Muslims from what many believe to be a commandment from God.

Most convert women, though far from all, do decide to wear a form of Islamic dress. Some immigrants are content to continue wearing a version of the dress characteristic of their home cultures, and others adopt Western dress completely. Still others decide to dress more conservatively than they would have done in the societies from which they came. Most Muslim women do cover themselves in one way or another when they attend the mosque. Within the Islamic community itself the issue can be divisive. Those who choose to wear the *hijab* are sometimes sharply critical of other Muslims who are not comfortable with it or do not feel that it is appropriate for them. Those who leave their heads uncovered may consider some of their sisters a bit foolish in the degree of their zealousness. On the whole, however, Muslims try to respect the right of a woman to make her own decision about dress, as about other things, and wish that the rest of the American public would do the same.

Practice of the Faith

While many American Muslim women choose not to participate actively in the mosque or Islamic center, others attend prayer services regularly and support the public practice of Islam. Some immigrant women find that they have the opportunity, and thus the desire for, greater public participation in religious activities than was true in their home cultures. More are attending Friday prayers, lectures, or functions. In some of the larger Islamic centers, classes are held for women in the study of Qur'an and the Arabic language, even providing special instruction for the elderly. Muslim women's home study groups are a growing phenomenon in America. Young Muslim women have begun to engage in exegesis of the Qur'an and to participate in discussions of religious texts that used to be strictly an arena for men. A few lone voices are now being heard on the American scene calling for the institution of women as imams or prayer leaders; but thus far they are not influential, and the function of imam remains the province of males.

Following to an extent the model of women in churches and synagogues in America, many Muslim women serve their mosque communities not only by organizing bake sales and teaching classes but in some cases serving as fund-raisers, moderators of congregations, and primary spokespersons in the public profession of the faith. Women who formerly would have attended the mosque only for special occasions are now participating in Friday (or Sunday morning) prayers and other special services. Without the support of an extended family, many women find that the mosque or Islamic center itself provides community and a context for socializing. Such participation has become especially important for those Muslims who feel that social interaction with non-Muslim Americans is to be avoided or for whatever reason choose not to have women involved in the workplace. Mosque attendance, formerly primarily for males, has become a family event.

Non-Muslims find it easy to question why Muslim women participate in prayer in a different area from men. Women pray either at the back of the hall behind the men, on one side with the men on the other (often separated by a partition), on a second-floor balcony where they can see the men and the imam below, or occasionally in very conservative mosques in a separate room with the service broadcast over a speaker or through closed-circuit television. Not all women agree on the most appropriate form of separation, and some feel that "separate but equal" is not served by extreme segregation. Virtually all Muslim women, however, say that not mixing with men during the prayer service is helpful for them, as well as for the men, in concentrating on the ritual rather than on each other.

Following one of the Sufi or mystical religious paths has a particular appeal for some women. While Sufism in America often has been more a New Age movement than a truly Islamic one, more recently there has been a growth in adherence to more traditional Sufi orders, with leaders trained in the classical disciplines. Some women are particularly attracted to practices of dancing or chanting. Even women who do not choose to participate in Sufi practices are increasingly emphasizing the spiritual dimension of Islam in their teaching and writing, trying to help their sisters understand that the religion is more than rules and regulations about dress and behavior. Women are increasingly articulate about the importance of Islam as a religion of reason, moderation and spiritual achievement.

Growing numbers of Muslim women in America recognize that their work within the community must extend beyond the traditional context of family and neighborhood and even beyond the often newly discovered context of mosque and Islamic center. They are engaging in different forms of community cooperation and in public efforts to help educate the American public about Islam. Mothers are working with public schools to share elements of faith and practice with teachers and non-Muslim children. They are cooperating with other interested citizens to see that school curricula are free of demeaning stereotypes and inaccurate information about Islam. During the month of Ramadan when observant Muslims fast from dawn to dusk, some high school girls are making it their special responsibility to visit hospitals and nursing homes for the elderly, helping non-Muslims understand what the "fast" means for them.

Networking and Organization

Networking with other Muslim women, while it carries different connotations in America than in traditional cultures, is a natural move for many immigrants who have always had strong bonds with other women in the community. The informal nature of this activity is now being replaced by more formal structures, such as women's groups and networks that often function as extended families. They are new in a number of ways, however, not least in the heterogeneous nature of their composition, sometimes including both immigrant and indigenous women. Gatherings differ widely in purpose, from religion to support groups to agencies for political action. Muslim women's centers can be found in most major cities of the United States and Canada. Women work with each other in nongovernmental organizations (NGOs) and civic organizations, health and educational agencies. Many have grown up participating in Muslim youth organizations and are extending their experience and training by taking their place in the leadership of the American Muslim community.

The list of formal organizations for Muslim women, both national and international, grows daily, many dedicated to bringing abut better understanding of rights, responsibilities, and opportunities for women. Among the most prominent are *Karamah*: Muslim Women Lawyers for Human Rights; Rahima Foundation, which pursues charitable activities for Muslim families; the North American Council for Muslim Women (NACMW), which initiates programs and provides services to women; the Sisterhood Is Global Institute, which works to improve women's rights; Sisters in Islam, which reinterprets Islamic principles and practices in light of the Qur'an; and many more. Some differences naturally exist between organizations that favor *da'wa* as a primary activity and those more interested in women's rights per se; women who choose to be involved have a great range from which to select.

Few groups have been more active than Muslims in making use of the Internet to stay in communication with each other both at home and abroad and in using electronic means to work for equity for Islam in the Western context as well as for propogating the faith. The proliferation of women's Islamic organizations in Canada and the United States reflects to a great extent the opportunity for access to instant information and communication. Most Islamic journals have sections or articles about or for women, with clear instructions as to how to connect with other women or to find assistance with particular problems, and the number of journals specifically for women is growing. Many are available online.

A Range of Choices

As broad as the spectrum of American Muslim women themselves is the range of possibilities open to them for involvement, or lack of it, in the many structures of American society. As women differ in terms of place of origin, racial-ethnic affiliation, education and professional involvement, and observance of Islamic practice, they also differ in the degree to which they choose to identify with American life and culture. Some decide to relegate their Islamic identity to the private realm or simply ignore it in the effort to "belong" and to succeed professionally and socially. This decision is applauded by some Muslims and criticized by others. At the opposite extreme are those Muslim sisters who try to reject the norms of Western culture and to dress, speak, and live in as close adherence as possible with what they understand to be the dictates of Qur'an and tradition. Still others find themselves between these alternatives, clear about their Muslim identity and willing to publicly claim it, perhaps participating in mosque activities or at least Islamic holidays, but not setting themselves apart from other Americans by practice or dress. Subject to pressures from within and without the Muslim community, women struggle to determine what is possible, acceptable, and workable. Some might wish that they could be more open about their criticisms of certain elements of Islamic tradition but do not wish to be seen as participating in American prejudice against Islam. Others regret that they are not able to be more public about their affiliation with Islam, or to wear Islamic dress, but know that such a choice would have serious professional and social ramifications that they are not able or willing to assume.

However they may choose to frame their responses, Muslim women who are working for a contemporary reinterpretation of Islam in the West are struggling to determine a viable alternative to traditional structures that have served to repress women, on the one hand, and to the influences of Western secularism (and sometimes feminism), on the other. Many call for women to exercise their right of individual interpretation of Qur'an and tradition. They see Islam as a dynamic and flexible system, rather than a static and rigid set of rules and regulations, and want to open up avenues of participation in which women as well as men are the public faces of Islam. In the process they will be very important contributors to the definition of an American Islam that flows directly out of its many contributing streams but that will have its own structures, definitions, and contributions to make to the complex picture of religious society in the United States and Canada.

SOURCES: Carole L. Anway, *Daughters of Another Path: Experiences of American Women Choosing Islam* (1996). Laleh Bakhtiar, *Sufi Women of America: Angels in the Making* (1996). Yvonne Y. Haddad and John Esposito, eds., *Muslims on the Americanization Path?* (1998). Yvonne Y. Haddad and Adair T. Lummis, *Islamic Values in the United States: A Comparative Study* (1987). Azizah al-Hibri, "Islamic Law and Muslim Women in America," in *One Nation under God? Religion and American Culture*, ed. Marjorie Garber and Rebecca Walkowitz (1999), 128–144. Aminah Beverly McCloud, *African American Islam* (1995). Evelyn Shakir, *Bint Arab. Arab and Arab American Women in the United States* (1997). Jane I. Smith, *Islam in America* (1999). Earle H. Waugh, Baba Abu-Laban, and Regula B. Qureshi, eds., *The Muslim Community in North America* (1983).

Part VIII

~

Asian Religions

BUDDHISM

ORIGINS OF BUDDHISM IN NORTH AMERICA
Lori Pierce

BUDDHISM IN NORTH America emerged from two distinct but not unrelated streams. Buddhism was first brought to the United States beginning in the mid-nineteenth century as the natal faith of immigrants from China and Japan. Asian workers also were recruited as laborers to build railroads, dig mines, and plant and harvest crops. They often lived and worked in filthy, dangerous, and dehumanizing conditions. Like many immigrants from Europe, they anticipated earning enough money to help support their families and return home. And like many immigrants from Europe, many found that after many years away they could not afford, or no long desired, to return home. But unlike European immigrants, Asian immigrants were barred from citizenship. It was for their own comfort and for their American-born sons and daughters that they built and established permanent Buddhist institutions in order to retain a sense of their ethnic and cultural identity in a foreign land.

Even as Asian Buddhists were migrating to the West, Westerners—Europeans and North Americans—were gradually becoming aware of Asian religions, especially the religions of India, Sri Lanka (Ceylon), China, and Japan. It would take several generations of scholars to fully and clearly understand the many forms of Buddhist worship and belief that developed in Asian countries and cultures. Driven by intellectual curiosity, European and American scholars began to translate Buddhist texts into Western languages. The first Buddhist text printed in the United States appeared in the Transcendentalist periodical *The Dial* in 1844. By the time Asian Buddhists spoke at the World's Parliament of Religions, which took place at the Chicago World's Fair in 1893, many upper-middle-class Americans were well aware of and curious about Buddhism. A very few converted, but many more read books and magazines, joined study groups, and developed a sympathy of Buddhism as a philosophy, if not as a style of devotional worship and practice.

Women made significant and long-lasting contributions to the effort to establish Buddhism in North America in the years before World War II. As scholars, seekers, and women of faith, they were instrumental in establishing institutions and forging the network of relationships that facilitated the transmission of Buddhism as a faith and as religious institutions from Asia to North America.

Asian Buddhist Communities from China and Japan

Chinese immigrants were the first to bring Buddhism to North America. Driven from home by the effects of poverty, famine, and war, Chinese migrants were lured to North America during the gold rush. Once the rush for wealth abated, Chinese workers were recruited to work on railroad building projects across the continent. They also settled into small towns and established businesses and farms. Attracted by the promise of high wages on sugar plantations, Chinese workers migrated to Hawaii, beginning in the 1850s. They, too, quickly established a beachhead in Honolulu, Lahaina, and Hilo and became small businessmen, rice and taro farmers, and merchants.

Between 1860 and 1880 the Chinese community in the United States grew from 35,000 to nearly 110,000. This rate of growth frightened many Euro-American workers and politicians. Chinese workers in the United States and Canada were illegally taxed, barred from specific professions, and excluded from public places. This bigotry culminated in the passage of the Chinese Exclusion Act of 1882, which, for the first time, placed a racial barrier to immigration on a specific ethnic group.

Chinese communities in rural and urban areas built small temples and shrines dedicated to a wide variety of gods and goddesses, including Buddhist deities such as Guan Yin, the Bodhisattva of Compassion. These temples were the site of community celebration and individual devotion. Our knowledge of women's roles in these temples is limited by two factors: Women were a minority in Chinese communities during the earliest decades of Chinese immigration (less than 10 percent of Chinese migrants), and the roles of those women who did migrate to North America were circumscribed by the patriarchal social structure of Chinese society. Women migrants were wives of wealthy merchants, family servants, or prostitutes. Prostitutes who were lured or sold into service were virtual slaves having little to no freedom of movement. Without status, they had few opportunities to contribute to or participate in community worship. Family servants would have had greater access to temples and opportunities for home and family religious observance. The wives of merchants and other middle-class Chinese men would have had the greatest access to and ability to comment on worship and religious life, but again, the patriarchal nature of Chinese communities kept them in the home. Except for the rare oral history, we have little knowledge of their participation in the religious life of the Chinese community.

What we do know of the temples suggests that women were frequent and important worshippers and participants. Temples dedicated to female deities to whom women felt a special affinity suggests that women's spiritual needs were an important consideration to the community.

Japanese immigrants began migrating to North America and Hawaii in large numbers beginning in the 1880s. During the Meiji era (1868–1912), the Japanese government relaxed its restrictions on travel and allowed its citizens, largely poor farmers, to sign labor contracts abroad. As Chinese workers moved from plantations to towns, they were replaced by thousands of impoverished Japanese workers. Many women also migrated to Hawaii as workers and as wives. Although the Issei (first generation) were focused on making enough money to support their families in Japan and then return home, many eventually settled and began to raise families in Hawaii and North America. By the time Hawaii was annexed as a territory of the United States in 1898, there were over 80,000 Japanese migrants living there.

The vast majority of Japanese immigrants were Buddhists, and a large number of that group belonged to one of the two largest sects of Jodo Shinshu, or Pure Land Buddhism. Other Japanese Buddhist sects established temples in North America including the Soto Zen, Nichiren, and Tendai traditions.

Women were instrumental in the founding and perpetuation of Jodo Shinshu Buddhism in North America and Hawaii. The wives of missionary priests who were sent to the United States and Hawaii by the Nishi Hongwanji (later known as the Buddhist Churches of America, or the BCA) acted as more than just helpmates for their husbands. These *bonmori*, or missionary wives, acted as liaisons between the immigrant community and other bureaucracies. Often the conditions were harsh and austere; Shinobu Matsuura (1896–1984) described the dreadful living conditions of workers in Guadalupe, California, conditions so poor that she took it upon herself to open a children's home to shield the youngest from the miserable conditions. Shigeo Kikuchi, (n.d.), the wife of a missionary on the island of Hawaii, described her life as remarkably busy from morning to night. Living in an isolated rural community, she might be called on to host visitors at any time; in addition to her own domestic chores, she also taught Japanese-language school and acted as a mediator between members of the Japanese and Euro-American communities. She wrote and translated letters and other official documents and often kept money and papers for safekeeping. She helped to facilitate weddings and engagements and also helped to educate young girls for their roles as wives, teaching them cooking and sewing and other tasks their own mothers might have been too busy to teach them. Jane Imamura, the daughter of Shinobu Matsuura and wife of Ryo Imamura of the Berkeley Buddhist Church, remembers taking care of her own family as well as a large number of Nisei (second-generation) students from the University of California

Women were instrumental in the founding and perpetuation of Jodo Shinshu Buddhism in North America and Hawaii. The wives of missionary priests who were sent to the United States and Hawaii by the Nishi Hongwanji (later known as the Buddhist Churches of America) acted as more than just helpmates for their husbands. *Hawaii Federation of Honpa Hongwanji Hawaii, Buddhist Women's Association.*

who adopted the Buddhist temple as a home away from home. She ran a dormitory and hosted student activities such as debates and discussion groups. A community lucky enough to have a Buddhist priest and his wife took full advantage of them as figures of authority and guidance.

Japanese women, under the leadership of a missionary priest and wife, also formed social organizations that served to further the mission of the Buddhist temple. Most temples had a fully functioning *fujinkai*, or women's league. The *fujinkai* carried out a variety of tasks, keeping the temple and community center clean, supplying it with flowers for services and special occasions, organizing holiday celebrations and fund-raisers, and helping with the management and operation of Sunday dharma school and Japanese-language schools. This was, of course, in addition to their domestic work and whatever wage labor they might engage in. Temples did not rely on funding from any central authority, and so fund-raising events such as bazaars and carnivals were important sources of revenue. The *fujinkai* often took the lead in these fund-raising ventures, using community celebrations such as the *obon* festival (which commemorates the spirits of the dead) as an opportunity to raise funds for the community as well.

Although Japanese Buddhism is seen as primarily an "ethnic" institution, it does have a history of promoting and facilitating interethnic cooperation and dialogue. Many Euro-American Christians taught English to Japanese immigrants, worked with social institutions such as the Young Women's Christian Association (YWCA), and gave professional and personal support to Buddhist immigrants.

Jodo Shinshu temples, especially those in urban areas, hosted a small but influential number of Euro-Americans who, having learned about Buddhism on their own, sought a *sangha* to which they could belong. Many priests and bishops, especially in the early years of the twentieth century, took advantage of the presence of Euro-Americans who wished to convert to Buddhism, inviting them to study groups and to participate in the education of the first generation of American Buddhists, the children of Japanese immigrant parents. In Hawaii, for example, Ernest and Dorothy Hunt work closely with the influential Bishop Yemyo Imamura in creating an "English Department." The English Department literally and symbolically translated Buddhism into English; Dorothy Hunt wrote poetry and hymns that became an official part of the worship service in Buddhist temples around the county. Her poems appeared in Buddhist periodicals like *Light of Dharma*. She and her husband were also favored speakers among the young

Buddhists of the Nisei generation. As native English speakers and as Americans, they often felt an affinity to Euro-Americans like the Hunts who spoke about Buddhism from a Western point of view they shared.

In Tacoma, Washington, Sunya Pratt actively participated in the life of the Tacoma Buddhist Church for more than sixty years. Born in 1898 in England, she moved to the United States in 1919 with her husband James. She was head of the Tacoma Buddhist Society in 1934 and was ordained in 1936. The May 11, 1936, issue of *Time* magazine took note of this unusual event, the ordination of a Euro-American woman into the Japanese Buddhist sect. Pratt wrote for Buddhist periodicals, especially those aimed at young Buddhists, urging them to remain committed to their Buddhist faith in spite of obstacles. She was officially appointed a minister in the Buddhist Churches of America in 1953, and in 1985 she was awarded a certificate from the Japanese government in recognition of her years of service to the Japanese American community.

Women like Pratt and Hunt were unusual for their time; they risked being ostracized from the larger Euro-American community because of their involvement with Japanese Buddhists, especially in the years leading up to the internment of the entire mainland Japanese American community during World War II. They were instrumental in helping to bridge the gap between the Japanese and Euro-American communities and served as role models for the Nisei generation who often felt pressured to convert to Christianity in order to fully assimilate. Euro-Americans who converted to Buddhism "proved" that one could be fully Buddhist and fully American.

After World War II, the Berkeley Buddhist church sponsored lectures and language classes that taught Nisei and Euro-Americans about Buddhism and Japanese-language skills. Gary Snyder and other "beat" poets and philosophers took part in these events, continuing the tradition of the Buddhist church reaching out to Euro-Americans.

Euro-American Buddhists

Missionaries in Asian countries were among the first Euro-Americans exposed to Buddhist beliefs and practices. They wrote detailed descriptions of Buddhist ritual and belief as far as they could comprehend it. Although their intention was to describe the strengths and weaknesses of Buddhism in order to give other missionaries an understanding of what they were up against, these descriptions also stoked the curiosity of Euro-Americans who sought to understand the totality of the world's faiths in order to understand the human condition.

In addition to missionaries, European intellectuals were also instrumental in conveying an understanding of Buddhism to Western audiences. Many were trained as linguists, and while they were in service to the British colonial authority in India and Sri Lanka, they began to recover and translate Buddhist texts from Pali. The study of religion as an academic discipline emerged from the work of early Orientalists such as Brian Hodgson, Eugene Burnouf, T. W. and Caroline Rhys Davids, and Friedrich Max Müller.

Drawing on the work of both missionaries and Orientalists, Hannah Adams (1755–1831), a distant relation of John Adams, published *An Alphabetical Compendium of the Various Sects* (1794), an early comparative study of the world's religions. Several years later, Lydia Maria Child (1800–1880) published *The Progress of Religious Ideas through Successive Ages*. Both of these women wrote during an age of religious progressivism. "Asiatic" societies in Britain and the United States produced scholarly journals and forums at which linguists, archeologists, and philosophers lectured on these newly discovered faiths, especially Hinduism and Buddhism. Child and Adams were able to compile their books based on the research of these Orientalist scholars, and although not immensely popular, these books opened the door to the understanding of non–Judeo Christian faiths in the United States.

Buddhism became the adopted faith of a small but influential group of Euro-Americans in the early twentieth century. Initially many who had become disenchanted with traditional Christianity began to explore other religious faiths and new religious movements such as Transcendentalism and Spiritualism. Transcendentalists like Ralph Waldo Emerson, Henry David Thoreau, and Bronson Alcott introduced Americans to a romantic vision of religious faith that eschewed creeds and theology and promoted individual self-expression, a love of nature, and appreciation for religions outside of the monotheistic traditions. In 1844, the Transcendentalist periodical *The Dial* published the first English translation of a Buddhist sutra (scripture) in the United States. Although long thought to be Thoreau who produced the translation, it was in fact the editor, Elizabeth Palmer Peabody (1804–1894), who translated a section of the Lotus Sutra from French into English.

Spiritualism gained popularity during the same era and capitalized on the spiritual malaise that occupied many women and men upon the death of loved ones. Anxious to restore a connection to their loved ones, the bereaved called on a medium, one who was believed to be able to communicate with the dead. At a time when women's leadership roles were restricted in traditional Christian churches, many women were active and prominent in the spiritualist movement. One of the women most responsible for the transmission of Buddhism to North America capitalized on this interest in Spiritualism, Madame Helena Petrovna Blavatsky (1831–1891).

Blavatsky gained notoriety based on her claim to be able to communicate not with the ordinary dead but with a realm of advanced masters whose wisdom surpassed our own. Blavatsky was a Russian émigrée ostensibly of noble birth. Extremely charismatic, she attracted a large following. In 1875, along with Henry Steel Olcott, she founded the Theosophical Society. Although the original stated mission was the investigation of fraud in the spiritualist movement, Olcott and Blavatsky quickly became interested in Asian religions, especially their more esoteric expressions. Theosophy gradually became less associated with Spiritualism and more associated with the investigation and exploration of Asian religions. Olcott and Blavatsky founded Theosophical Lodges in India and Sri Lanka, where they came in contact and formed associations with Asian Buddhists. In 1880 Olcott and Blavatsky traveled to Sri Lanka and became the first Euro-Americans officially to convert to Buddhism. Blavatsky never became an active member of the Buddhist faith, but Olcott went on to promote Buddhism in Japan, South Asia, Europe, and North America.

The signal event in the transmission of Buddhism to a North American audience was the World's Parliament of Religions. Staged at the World's Columbian Exposition in Chicago in 1893, it was the first international, interreligious conference. Although some of the organizers of the Parliament intended to demonstrate the superiority of Christianity by comparing it to other religions, the effect was the opposite. For the first time Westerners heard about non-Christian religions from the actual practitioners of those faiths; Japanese, Chinese, and South Asians spoke about Buddhism with such conviction that many were convinced of its viability if not its superiority.

The Parliament touched off something of a Buddhist fad across the continent. Anagarika Dharmapala, a young Sri Lanka Buddhist who had come under the influence of Olcott and Blavatsky, traveled to the United States, speaking about Buddhism at sold-out Theosophical lodges. Soyen Shaku, a Buddhist priest who had spoken at the Parliament, returned to the United States in 1906 and, traveling with his translator D. T. Suzuki, embarked on a well-publicized speaking tour. For North American audiences, the difference between Theosophy and Buddhism was vague, and the presence of Buddhist personalities like Dharmapala and Soyen Shaku in Theosophical halls further blurred the distinction between the two groups.

Most who attended these lectures never converted to Buddhism. Although it became somewhat fashionable to call oneself a Buddhist, most Euro-Americans did not become serious about Buddhism as a faith. For some Buddhism was a weigh station on the way to other religious expressions. For example, Marie deSouza Canavarro (1849–1933), the first woman to formally convert

to Buddhism in the United States, had begun life as a Catholic, became interested in Theosophy, converted to Buddhism, and finally became a Bahai. For a period of years in the first decade of the twentieth century, however, Canavarro was one of the most popular lecturers on Buddhism in the country. Canavarro may first have been exposed to Buddhism while she was married to the Portuguese ambassador to Hawaii. There she met Anagarika Dharmapala on his return trip to Sri Lanka after the Parliament. Under Dharmapala's instruction, she converted to Buddhism. In 1897 she moved to Sri Lanka, where she opened a school for Sinahlese girls. As Sister Sanghamitta, Canavarro was a regular correspondent to Paul Carus in Illinois, editor of *Open Court*. She lectured widely around the country and became a well-known speaker.

On his stopover in Hawaii, Dharmapala also met Mary Elizabeth Mikahala Foster (1844–1930). Foster, a part-Hawaiian woman, had married into a wealthy land-owning family. Both Euro-American and Hawaiian members of the upper class were Christian, so members of Foster's family did not take kindly to her growing interest in Theosophy and Buddhism. Foster donated large amounts of money to various charitable causes directed by Dharmapala. Dharmapala sent Foster a cutting from the tree under which the Buddha attained enlightenment; the tree still grows in Foster Garden, now a famous botanical garden in Honolulu. In addition to her charitable work with Buddhists in Sri Lanka, Foster was also a friend to Jodo Shinshu Buddhists in Hawaii, helping them secure land to build the head temple in Honolulu. Although she had requested a Buddhist funeral, upon her death her family demonstrated their disregard for her religious commitment by giving her a proper Christian burial.

Most Euro-American women who became interested in Buddhism in America did not enjoy the economic privilege that allowed them to follow up on their newfound faith by traveling to Asia. The historical record, however, retains the stories of women who were able to travel widely in the Buddhist world. These women expanded American Buddhists' range of contact with Asian Buddhists and European scholars who were central to the project of translating Buddhist texts, philosophy, and history into Western languages. For example, the British scholars I. B. Horner (1896–1981) and Caroline Rhys-Davids (1857–1942) were both experienced researchers, translators, and scholars of South Asian Buddhism. Both had extensive experience living in Asia and later taught Buddhist studies in England, Horner at Cambridge and Rhys-Davids at Manchester University. Both served as presidents of the Pali Text Society, an organization dedicated to the preservation and translation of Buddhist texts.

Beatrice Erskine Hahn Lane Suzuki (1870–1939) was

a fellow scholar, translator, and student of Buddhism. Although she is often only remembered as the wife of D. T. Suzuki, she was also a scholar in her own right. Beatrice probably gained an interest in Buddhism through her mother, Emma Erskine Hahn Lane, a medical doctor and Theosophist. Beatrice was educated at Radcliffe and also earned a master's degree from Columbia. She met D. T. Suzuki at a lecture by Soyen Shaku on his tour of the United States in 1906. They were married in December 1911 and moved to Japan. There they founded and coedited *Eastern Buddhist*. Suzuki wrote poetry, essays, and stories that were published in Buddhist periodicals and in the Japanese English-language newspaper *Osaka Mainichi*. She also wrote two scholarly books, *Japanese No Plays* (1932) and *Mahayana Buddhism* (1938).

Because D. T. Suzuki was an "alien ineligible for citizenship," Beatrice risked losing her citizenship when she married and moved to Japan with him. Ruth Fuller Everett Sasaki (1892–1967) took a similar risk—alienation from family and friends for befriending and later marrying a Japanese citizen. Sasaki had become interested in Buddhism long before she met her second husband. Her first husband Edward Everett was a prominent Chicago banker, so Ruth Fuller could afford to indulge her interests. She became interested in Buddhism through her experiences with an eccentric, self-styled religious teacher, Pierre Bernard, also known as "Oom the Omnipotent." Later she traveled to Japan, where she met D. T. and Beatrice Suzuki. On a return trip, she became one of the first Western women to train in a Zen monastery, Nanzenji. During her travels she met members of the Buddhist Lodge, a British group of Buddhist converts and sympathizers. One of the members of the lodge, Alan Watts, would later marry Fuller's daughter Eleanor.

Fuller met Shigetsu Sasaki (also known as Sokei-an) in 1938 in New York City. Sasaki had established the First Zen Institute in America. Here, those who had been reading about Buddhism came to receive instruction in sitting meditation and koan study. Ruth and Sasakai shared the teaching duties; Sokei-an focused on *teisho* (sermons or teachings) and *sanzen* (individual interviews with the teacher in which koans are discussed). Ruth, because of her experience in a Japanese monastery, taught students the rigors of sitting in and maintaining the correct meditation postures. The two enjoyed a close relationship but did not marry until 1944. (Because Sasaki was a Japanese citizen, he was interned during the war.) Sasaki died in 1945. Ruth returned to Japan after the war, looking for a teacher to replace Sasaki at the First Zen Institute. She took up the study of Japanese and Chinese and eventually established a branch of the First Zen Institute at Daitokuji monastery. She enlisted interested Europeans and Americans inter-

ested in the study and translation of Buddhist texts. Gary Snyder, Burton Watson, and Philip Yampolsky were among her collaborators in this work.

The work of the Sasakis at the First Zen Institute would not have been possible, had it not been for the efforts of Mary Farkas (1910–1992). In addition to carrying out the day-to-day administrative work of keeping the institute running, Farkas was the longtime editor of the institute's journal, *Zen Notes*. This handmade publication faithfully recorded and transmitted Sokei-an's teaching, and after his death, when the First Zen Institute had no teacher, his words served as a substitute for a teacher.

There were countless other women whose tireless efforts helped to establish Buddhism in North America on a firm foundation. Chinese women perpetuated their faith in the privacy of their families, passing along to their children a devotion to Buddhist saints. Nameless hundreds of Japanese women—immigrants and their daughters—established Buddhist women's associations in order to support the mission and work of the Buddhist Churches of America. The wives of missionary priests like Jane Imamura made Euro-American and Japanese American students welcomed in their homes. Mrs. Alexander Russell hosted Soyen Shaku, who taught her entire family Zen meditation. Elsie Mitchell traveled extensively throughout Japan and was a founding member of the Cambridge Buddhist Association. Buddhism flourished in North America because of a strong network of connections that crossed gender and ethnic boundaries. Immigrant Japanese workers shared their space and their faiths with upper-class Euro-Americans who found their way to Buddhism.

SOURCES: There are a limited number of secondary sources that address the histories of Buddhist communities in the United States and none that successfully describe the intersection of Euro-American and Asian American traditions. There are several unpublished theses and dissertations on Japanese American Buddhism but only a few published histories: Louise Hunter's *Buddhism in Hawaii: Its Impact on a Yankee Community* (1971); Tetsuden Kashima's *Buddhism in America: The Social Organization of an Ethnic Institution* (1977); and Donald Tuck's *Buddhist Churches of America: Jodo Shinhsu* (1987). On Mary Foster, see Patricia Lee Masters and Karma Lekshe Tsomo, "Mary Foster: The First Hawaiian Buddhist," in *Innovative Buddhist Women: Swimming Against the Stream*, ed. Karma Lekshe Tsomo (2000). There are only a few published memoirs by Japanese American Buddhist women, and they include Shinobu Matsuura, *Higan Compassionate Vow* (1986); Shigeo Kikuchi, *Memoirs of a Buddhist Woman Missionary in Hawaii* (1991); and Jane Michiko Imamura, *Kaikyo: Opening the Dharma. Memoirs of a Buddhist Priest's Wife in America* (1998). The most comprehensive overviews of Buddhism in the Euro-American community are Rick Fields, *How the Swans Came to the Lake: A Narrative History of Buddhism in America* (1992); Stephen Prothero, *The White Buddhist: The Asian Od-*

yssey of Henry Steel Olcott (1996); and Thomas Tweed, *The American Encounter with Buddhism 1844–1912: Victorian Culture and the Limits of Dissent* (1992). For a description of the World's Parliament of Religions, see Richard Hughes Seager, *The World's Parliament of Religions: The East-West Encounter, Chicago 1893* (1995).

WOMEN AND ZEN BUDDHISMS: JAPANESE, CHINESE, KOREAN, AND VIETNAMESE

Miriam Levering and Grace Jill Schireson

ZEN, AN ASIAN Buddhist tradition that first came to the West from Japan, emphasizes meditation and intensive self-examination as a way to wisdom, compassion, self-knowledge, and freedom from self-concern. In North America groups of Zen practitioners embody and reshape Japanese (Zen), Chinese (Ch'an), Vietnamese (Thien), and Korean (Son) Zen traditions. In the nearly 100 years since its introduction, Zen in North America has become truly North American, as this Asian contemplative and monastic tradition has established itself as a lay-centered movement. North American Zen is more active, individualistic, egalitarian and engaged, media friendly, synthetic, and universalistic than its Asian counterparts (McKinney, 1). Recently the sexual revolution, increases in higher education for women, the women's liberation movement, and middle-class women's growing economic independence gradually have created a culture in the United States and Canada in which middle- and upper-class women lead publicly and expect their concerns to be addressed. In Asian cultures, women have always supported Zen, but only exceptional women have received the most rigorous monastic training. One major change that has occurred as Zen adapts to North American conditions is that wherever whites are in the majority, women have come to play a greater role. Largely white Zen communities are the only ones that have been studied, so the role of women in those communities is the focus of this essay. In those communities, wherever new leadership has developed following the death of the Asian founder, women teachers have taken on public roles.

Typically, Japanese- and Korean-derived Zen groups in North America have "Zen centers" in large cities, training monasteries or retreat centers in the countryside, and smaller affiliated "sitting groups" in smaller communities. In 2000 there were approximately 2,000 centers. Zen centers are headed by a teacher certified to give dharma transmission or teaching authority to students. The community of a Zen center is those who carry out daily liturgies of worship, periodic special ceremonies honoring Buddhas (fully awakened ones) and bodhisattvas (powerful saints who are close to becoming Buddhas), and twice-daily practice of seated meditation. Members also participate in periodic longer practice sessions (*sesshins*), commonly lasting seven days, and follow the basic moral and behavioral precepts of Mahayana Buddhism, the form of Buddhism dominant in East Asia. In some Zen traditions, students try to embody the meaning of koans, stories about the enigmatic sayings and doings of earlier masters. An example is the famous dialogue in which a monk asked the teacher Joshu, "Does a dog have the Buddha-nature?" Mahayana Buddhism teaches that all sentient beings have the Buddha-nature, a fact the questioning monk surely knew. Joshu replied, "No!" Students today are asked to understand what Joshu meant by that "No!" and to demonstrate that meaning, often nonverbally. Most members of Zen centers in North America are married; many are supported by jobs in the larger society and some by center-created cottage industries. Spiritual authority rests in the teacher or teachers, and institutional authority in a board of directors. Holders of monastic offices assist the teacher in training students. Advanced students take ordinations as priests. Priests can perform ceremonies such as daily offices, weddings, and funerals. Often they can teach students under the supervision of a fully certified teacher but cannot grant teaching authority to students of their own without dharma transmission. Obtaining dharma transmission often takes many years. On attaining dharma transmission, former students often start their own sitting groups and aspire to build or inherit the leadership of Zen centers. As one can see from this description, authority is acquired not from an institution but from a single senior person who chooses one to "inherit his (or her) dharma." As in Asia, father-to-son transmission as part of a long genealogical lineage going back to the Buddha as the original ancestor remains the central metaphor for the foundational structure of authority. At Zen centers teachers are supported by dues and donations but also by producing books and workshops for persons beyond the center. Teachers of small sitting groups depend on outside income. Chinese and Vietnamese Zen groups in North America, heirs to a tradition of gender-segregated monasticism, follow this pattern to some extent but strongly encourage future teachers to become celibate monks and nuns.

At all these levels women have "arrived" in large sections of North American Zen, particularly in the Japanese-derived Zen groups in which leadership has already passed from the Asian or Asian-trained founder to a second generation of leaders, usually of European descent. By the 1980s women constituted more than half of many centers' members, were on the boards of nearly every Zen center, had attained dharma transmissions in several schools of Zen, and were head teachers at several

Zenkei Blanche Hartman began sitting in 1969 at the Berkeley Zen Center, was ordained a priest in 1977, and became abbess of the San Francisco Zen Center in February 1996. *Used by permission of Renshin Judy Bunce, San Francisco Zen Center.*

Zen centers. By 2000 many more women had obtained dharma transmission, there were more Zen centers, and women were in more prominent leadership roles. Some teach at smaller sitting groups. Some head branches of large organizations that remain under the direction of the founding Asian teacher or assist at larger centers. Recently a number of women have been installed as abbesses (a combination of chief executive officer and chief spiritual teacher) of Zen centers, including all the largest and longest established centers. The San Francisco Zen Center installed Zenkei Blanche Hartman as abbess in 1996, and Ji Ko Linda Ruth Cutts as abbess in 2000. The Los Angeles Zen Center installed Wendy Egyoku Nakao as abbot in 1999. Karen Sunna became abbess of Minnesota Zen Center in 1998. The Chapel Hill (North Carolina) Zen Center installed Taitaku Pat Phelan as abbess in 2000. Other abbesses and abbots include Mitra Bishop at Mountain Gate, a monastic community in New Mexico; Dai-en Bennage at Mt. Equity Zendo near Williamsport, Pennsylvania; Diane Eishin Rizzetto at Bay Zen School in Oakland, California; and Roko Ni-Osho Sherry Chayat at the Zen Center of Syracuse, New York. Karuna Dharma directs the International Buddhist Meditation Center in Los Angeles, a Vietnamese Zen group. Since 1984 Linda Haju Murray has directed the Ann Arbor, Michigan, temple of the Zen Lotus Society founded by the Korean teacher Samu Sunim. Linda Sujata Klevnick directs the Society's Toronto temple. Toni

Packer, dharma heir of Philip Kapleau-roshi, and Charlotte Joko Beck, dharma heir of Maezumi-roshi (see below), established important centers in San Diego and Rochester, New York.

Early History of Zen in America

The development of Western Zen began in 1893 when a Japanese Zen priest, Shaku Soyen (1860–1919), came to the World Parliament of Religions in Chicago. Shaku Soyen and members of his lineage inspired and led the first, tiny Western Rinzai Zen sitting groups. This might not have happened without a woman who offered financial support and hospitality, Mrs. Alexander Russell. She was also the first person of European descent to study a Zen koan on North American soil.

In 1929–1930 Miriam Salanave of Oakland, California, studied for five months in Zen monasteries in Kyoto, Japan. In North America Soyen Shaku was followed by others in his lineage, including Sokei-an Sasaki, who began the Buddhist Society of America in New York in 1931, later called the First Zen Institute of America. In 1938 he ordained Ruth Fuller Everett (?–1967), who played a major role in bringing Japanese Zen to North America. In 1944 the pair married. Following her husband's dying wishes, Ruth Fuller Sasaki spent many years in Japan practicing Zen at the historic temple Daitokuji in Kyoto. She also organized and participated in translating Zen texts and founded a subtemple for Westerners at Daitokuji. Back in New York, though not a teacher, Mary Farkas (1910–1992) held leadership for the First Zen Institute of America; she became its general secretary in 1949.

In the 1950s Zen began to attract the attention of mainstream North American culture. Daisetsu (D. T.) Suzuki (1870–1966), Alan Watts, and Jack Kerouac introduced in books and lectures an attractive but romanticized account of Zen spirituality and art. The interest in Zen at this time coincided with and contributed to a radical questioning of Western values. However, the early stirrings of public interest in Zen in North America did little to challenge the Western construction of gender with its subordination of women.

Zen's Growth and a New Role for Women Zen Practitioners

In the 1960s one strong woman leader was Elsie Mitchell (b. 1926), who with her husband John founded and led the Cambridge Buddhist Society in the late 1950s. Elsie Mitchell went to Japan to study the practice of meditation with a Soto Zen priest, Rindo Fujimoto. In 1960 she published, with her own introduction, Fujimoto's lecture *The Way of Zazen*, the earliest English-language guide to Soto-style "just sitting."

In the 1960s Zen grew in North America, and a number of Asian teachers arrived. While men were the acknowledged leaders, women flocked to the practice in large numbers. On the East Coast Yasutani (1885–1973) began his teachings, as did Nakagawa Soen and Eido Shimano. A woman who became a great American Zen teacher, Maurine Stuart-roshi (1922–1990), studied with these teachers. She later taught Zen at the Cambridge Buddhist Society and was a pillar of support for women practicing Zen.

On the West Coast in the early 1960s two Japanese Zen priests who had originally come to minister to immigrant communities began to work with Western students: Shunryu Suzuki (1904–1971) and Hakuyu Taizan Maezumi-roshi (1931–1995). Joshu Sasaki (1907–) arrived in Los Angeles late in the decade. Hsuan Hua (1918–1995), a teacher of Chinese Ch'an, attracted in California a number of North American women Ph.D.s, many of whom sought full ordination as nuns. In 1969 Dharma Master Hung Ch'ih became the first American woman from this group to be ordained in Taiwan as a nun, vowing to keep the 348 precepts defining appropriate world-renouncing behavior for nuns, an act that has constituted full ordination for women in Buddhism for 2,500 years.

Among Shunryu Suzuki's first hippie Zen students were three "proper" ladies. Of the three women, Jean Ross (1916–1996), had a rare gift for Zen. She was born in Detroit, Michigan, on August 16, 1916. The granddaughter of a Methodist minister, she was a nurse by profession. Suzuki encouraged her to practice in Japan, where in 1962 she was one of the first Westerners and the first woman of any nationality to study at Eiheiji, the oldest and largest monastery of the Japanese Soto Zen sect. Ross's seven-month training period at Eiheiji was longer than that of any foreigner in the 700-year history of the temple. Ross later taught in California but became discouraged by the events and atmosphere at the San Francisco Zen Center during the 1980s under Suzuki's successor Zentatsu Richard Baker and left the Zen community.

By the late 1960s Westerners who had studied in Japan returned to North America to teach. In 1965 Philip Kapleau founded his own Zen Center in Rochester, New York, and published a highly influential book, *The Three Pillars of Zen* (1965). And an American, Robert Aitken led the Diamond Sangha in Hawaii. Peggy Jiyu Kennett (1924–1996), a British subject who trained in Japan, also moved to California from Japan to found Shasta Abbey Zen Monastery in 1970. Kennett was the first female Zen teacher in North America to have been officially recognized as a teacher by the Soto Zen sect in Japan.

Kennett began her training in Malaysia, where she was ordained as a nun in the Chinese Buddhist *sangha* (monastic order). However, her true intent was to train in Japan under the Abbott of Soji-ji, Keido Chisan Koho, who gave her dharma transmission in 1963. Soji-ji is one of the two official training monasteries of the Soto Zen sect; Kennett was the first Western woman to complete training in this authentic Japanese tradition and to establish a Soto Zen school in America. With Koho's support, Kennett-roshi became abbess of her own temple in Japan and held other positions within the Japanese Soto hierarchy. Her adaptation of Zen for Westerners has been likened to Japanese Soto Zen with a flavor of the Church of England, for she believed that Zen in North America should adopt Western monastic dress and liturgical forms. For example, she set the traditional Buddhist liturgy to music based on Gregorian chants. Kennett's organization became the Order of Buddhist Contemplatives in 1978. The order has founded temples and meditation groups in Britain, Canada, Germany, and the Netherlands as well as the United States and has ordained and certified a relatively large number of women teachers.

The 1970s brought the Korean teacher Seung Sahn (also known as Soen Sa Nim) and Samu Sunim to the West. Political exile also brought the Vietnamese teacher Thich Nhat Hanh who, though centered primarily in France, teaches frequently in North America. Another Vietnamese teacher, Thich Thien-an came as a scholar to North America but, like the others, began to devote his attention to a Western congregation. The most influential Chinese teacher on the East Coast at present, the Ven. Sheng-yen, founded a center in Elmhurst, New York. He found an eager audience for his teaching among Chinese immigrants in New York but also attracted many non-Chinese-speaking students.

In the late 1970s and early 1980s the broader women's movement began to affect Zen communities in North America. Deborah Hopkinson and Susan Murcott, members of the Diamond Sangha led by Robert Aitken-roshi in Hawaii, began in 1979 with the encouragement of their teacher to publish the *Kahawai Journal of Women and Zen*. This important periodical brought women's voices to the fore in North American Zen communities. It offered resources to practitioners seeking to understand women's history in Zen and provided a forum in which to explore women's perspectives on practice.

In 1982 the Providence Zen Center, led by the Korean Master Seung Sahn (Soen Sa Nim), started an informal women's discussion group. A year later and in 1983 the center offered a workshop called "Feminist Principles in Zen," with Maurine Stuart, Susan Murcott, Barbara Rhodes of the Providence Zen Center, and Jacqueline Schwartz, later Jacqueline Schwartz Mandrell, of the Vipassana Buddhist community. In 1984 and 1985 the Providence Zen Center held two more conferences on "Women in American Buddhism." From then on women's retreats and conferences became common. Sandy Boucher's book *Turning the Wheel: American Women Creating New Buddhism* (1993) and Lenore Friedman's *Meetings with Remarkable Women: Buddhist Teachers in America*, first published in 1987, introduced readers to the startling fact that Zen in North America had women teachers. Boucher summed up the women's goals:

> the altering of the language of chants and sutras to eliminate male bias, the insistence that women in numbers equal to men be allowed to give lectures and perform religious offices, the creation of support structures to give mothers the opportunity to do their spiritual practice, the incorporation of body movement into practice situations, the allowing of psychological content as a useful point of focus in practice, the integration of group therapy into the schedule of activities of a center, the very *acknowledgement* of therapy individual or otherwise as useful, the recognition of autonomous women teachers and establishment of women-led centers and retreats. (385–386)

These goals resonate with those of the more general feminist and women's spirituality movements in North America.

However, beginning in 1983 and continuing through-

out the 1980s many Zen centers were rocked by the discovery that men Zen teachers had been having sexual relations with women students. Zen centers lost members, and feelings of abuse and betrayal drove a number of women from practice. Maurine Stuart led all-women retreats in California as a special effort to help women heal from the hurt that resulted from sexual intimacy with their male Zen teachers. Stuart was not particularly drawn to the women's movement in Zen, but she felt this "separatist" approach was needed to heal the wounds women had experienced, and she found that women-only retreats had a special quality. She tried to dispel the myth of the enlightened teacher who can do no wrong, which she felt had led students and male teachers astray. "Don't put anyone's head above your own," she told her students (in Chayat, ed., xxxii).

Women Change the Character of North American Zen

The 1990s saw significant accomplishment of many goals outlined by Sandy Boucher. More women certified teachers and dharma heirs emerged into public teaching and leadership roles in many lineages. Many teachers and leaders have thought about the roles that their own gender and their awareness of gender differences have played in the development of their practice and teaching styles. Their chosen activities reflect in part the success of the women's movement in Zen. The lives and teaching styles of Sherry Chayat, Blanche Hartman, Linda Ruth Cutts, and Wendy Nakao are representative of this new generation of women teachers.

Roko Ni-Osho Sherry Chayat was born in Brooklyn in 1943. She began studying Buddhism on her own in the early 1960s while pursuing a degree in creative writing at Vassar College. She began formal Zen training in 1967 at the Zen Studies Society with Eido Shimano-roshi, Yasutani-roshi, and Soen-roshi. She received lay ordination (an initial set of vows for laypeople and a Buddhist name) from Maurine Stuart-roshi and priest's ordination from Eido-roshi. Chayat was acknowledged by Eido-roshi as a dharma teacher in the Rinzai tradition in 1992. Two years later he gave her an *inka*, or a certificate of enlightenment, in the Hakuin/Torei lineage of the Rinzai sect. She became the first American woman to receive official Rinzai dharma transmission.

Chayat teaches at Hoen-ji, the Zen center of Syracuse. At Hoen-ji both Zen and Tibetan Buddhism are taught and practiced. Chayat also supports the integration of meditation as supportive treatment in a variety of medical conditions, and her center runs a program called "Well/Being Contemplative Practices in Healing" to help health-care professionals, their clients, and the wider community benefit from the healing power of mindfulness. The Syracuse Zen Center also leads meditation at Syracuse University, Syracuse area schools, recovery and justice system institutions, hospitals, and corporations.

Zenkei (Inconceivable Joy) Blanche Hartman was born in 1926 in Birmingham, Alabama; she fell in love with Zen in the early 1970s while a graduate student at the University of California at Berkeley and an active wife and mother of four children. She studied with Suzuki Shunryu-roshi and was ordained as a priest by Richard Baker-roshi (Suzuki-roshi's dharma heir) in 1977. While her family questioned her ordination in the Buddhist faith, they came to appreciate the benefits of her increased attentiveness and compassion. An important part of her understanding came from her contact with the Japanese nun Joshin-san, who came to San Francisco to teach the traditional Japanese Buddhist sewing of the priest's robe. Sojun Mel Weitsman of the Berkeley Zen Center gave her dharma transmission in 1988.

Blanche Hartman served two terms as abbess of the San Francisco Zen Center. One reason for accepting this position in 1996 was that she knew how much women needed to see a woman step into this role. Her honesty, humility, and particularly her relentless self-examination inspired her students. Recently she gave dharma transmission to her first dharma heir, Barbara Kohn. She found this experience to be one of almost overpowering intimacy and gratitude.

Blanche Hartman has offered various special teachings for women. In 1992 she led an all-female practice period at Rinso-in, Suzuki-roshi's home temple. This is the first time in the 500-year history of the temple that women have conducted a training period there. She has also led women's all-day retreats at the Green Gulch Zen Center in Mill Valley, California. Additionally, she has honored lost and aborted children by performing a ceremony attended by grieving women centering on Jizo Bosatsu, the bodhisattva whom Japanese Buddhists revere as a savior of souls from the hells and a protector of children.

Jiko Linda Ruth Cutts, born in 1947 in Minneapolis, Minnesota, was ordained as a priest by Zentatsu Richard Baker at the San Francisco Zen Center in 1975 and has lived at the San Francisco Zen Center's three practice places, Tassajara Zen Mountain Center, the City Center, and Green Gulch Farm. Cutts has three children and now lives with her husband and their two children at Green Gulch. Linda received dharma transmission, certification to teach independently, from Tenshin Reb Anderson in 1996 and became co-abbess of the San Francisco Zen Center in 2000.

Cutts adopts a horizontal style of organizational interaction similar to that used by other women teachers; she calls it working as an "ensemble." In thinking about her new role as abbess, she notes that in a patriarchal society the expected model of leadership is based on a conventional male-centered consciousness. Members of the organization expect this style of leadership, and she knows that she herself also carries the same internalized expectations. Cutts knows that being true to herself, not imitating others, is the way to meet the job as abbess fully and with joy.

Cutts has been able to find already present in Zen practice a resonance with women's experience. She believes that her own self-exploration in both therapy and Zen have opened her to facets of Zen ritual and practice that express women's insights and meet women's needs. For example, Zen emphasizes practicing with the body as well as the mind and accepting one's own body as a vehicle for practice. In Zen the term *blood vein*, a central term referring to the passing down of ordination from teacher to student, can be seen as a powerful feminine image of life-giving force. The daily liturgy performed by Zen students every morning, a collection of set prayers and scripture readings, invokes the feminine Maha Prajna Paramita, who is Transcendental Wisdom and the figurative Mother of the Buddhas, as well as the feminine Kuan Yin, the Bodhisattva of Infinite Compassion. These images already embedded within the existing rituals and ceremonies give women material to work with. But in the first year of her abbacy Cutts also helped develop a new ceremony to honor female teachers and ancestors.

Sensei Wendy Egyoku Nakao was born in Hawaii in 1948 of Japanese Portuguese descent. In 1978 she moved to the Zen Center of Los Angeles (ZCLA) to study with Maezumi-roshi. Ordained as a priest in 1983, she was given dharma transmission by Bernard Tetsugen Glassman-roshi in 1996. Nakao became the third abbot of ZCLA in 1999 and is a founding member of the Zen Peacemaker Order, an international order of social activists engaged in peacemaking based on three tenets: penetrating the unknown, bearing witness to joy and suffering, and healing oneself and others. She believes Zen practice needs to be rooted in one's flesh and bones and in social service as well.

Nakao has emphasized traditional Zen meditation practice but also has encouraged more horizontal relationships and communication at the Zen Center. At her suggestions, the Los Angeles Zen Center holds councils on relationships and addictions where everyone is encouraged to speak from the heart. She has also taken part in a project to recover and chant in the liturgy the names of women teachers from the Buddha's time to the present. Nakao has felt supported and encouraged by the male teachers of her lineage, but she believes that her own gender has encouraged her to give more support to the members.

Gender and the Direction of North American Zen

Both women and men are creating in North America forms of Zen that are more active, individualistic, egalitarian, and engaged, as well as media friendly, synthetic, and universalistic, than their Asian counterparts. But in addition, women teachers are affecting Zen practice in America in ways that may be connected with how they experience and construct their gender in this culture. Characteristics particularly associated with women teachers are integration of practice with everyday life and less formalism and hierarchy. Another trend worth noting is that Zen communities welcome persons in same-sex relationships.

First, women teachers connect practice in everyday life. The foremost proponents of this in writing and speaking have been Charlotte Joko Beck, founder of the Ordinary Mind Zen School based in San Diego, and Toni Packer of the Springwater Center. Their books *Everyday Zen* (1989) and *Nothing Special* (1993) (Beck) and *The Work of This Moment* (1990) (Packer) have inspired many. Many of the female Zen teachers are married and have children. They write about the integration of practice into every aspect of their daily life (Dresser). Female Zen teachers have been very active in the pioneering efforts of "socially engaged Buddhism," a term derived from the writings of Vietnamese teacher Thich Nhat Hanh. Catronia Reed and Michele Benzamin-Masuda, teachers in Thich Nhat Hanh's Order of Interbeing, work with at-risk children at juvenile hall and prison camp and visit local correctional facilities to lead classes in mindfulness, meditation, and martial arts. Japanese Zen teacher Maylie Scott (?–2001) of Arcata, California, worked in prisons and homeless shelters as well as demonstrations against armaments. Karuna Dharma, abbess of the International Buddhist Mediation Center in Los Angeles, ordained by Thich Thien-an in the Lieu Quang school of Zen (Thien) from Vietnam, took on the work of assisting the Vietnamese refugees as part of the function of her center.

Many of the women Zen teachers hold or have held jobs that have made use of the wisdom and compassion that are said to be the fruit of Zen practice. In this way their professional lives and their lives of Zen practice have been mutually enriching. For example, Korean Zen Master Seong Hyang (Barbara Rhodes) of the Kwan Um School of Zen (Korean Son tradition) has been a nurse working in hospice care. She is able to use the Zen understanding of impermanence, the mindfulness built through meditation, and the compassion for all sentient beings that is taught through Zen practice with her suffering patients. At the same time working with aging and dying patients personally and concretely enriches and informs her Zen understanding of what is called "The

Great Matter," or the problem of life and death. The same is true for Maylie Scott as a social worker, Karuna Dharma as a teacher, or Karen Sunna as a psychologist. The Zen priest Madeline Ko-i Bastis, founder and director of the Peaceful Dwelling Project in East Hampton, New York, is the first Buddhist to be board-certified as a hospital chaplain.

Some women teachers have dropped or changed the status symbols associated with the authority of the teaching position. In Asian countries, Zen teachers were surrounded with symbols of elevation: wearing distinctive, elaborate teachers' robes, ascending a seat elevated high above the assembly to teach, and so forth. Both Toni Packer and Joko Beck have stopped wearing their priest's robes. Wendy Nakao, Maylie Scott, and Angie Boissevain of the Floating Zendo speak of stressing horizontal or circular forms of communication as opposed to the formerly strictly observed vertical hierarchical model. Nakao's regularly scheduled "council"-style meetings mentioned above are held in a circle. She has been particularly active in building relationships within the *sangha*. To her colleagues, Maylie Scott described her primary teaching objective as empowering the *sangha* by making sure she is the facilitator, not the "star."

Ancient Indian Buddhist rules excluded those whose sexuality was not "normal" from taking monastic vows. But gay men and lesbian women, as well as bisexual and transgendered persons, excluded from many Jewish, Islamic, and Christian congregations, are welcomed in North America's semimonastic, semilay Zen communities. Some women abbesses are in same-sex relationships. Leaders who have given particular emphasis to feminist issues and the needs of lesbians, bisexuals, gays, and transgendered persons include Kuya Minogue, who codirects Amazenji, a women's retreat center in British Columbia, Canada, which includes traditional Zen meditation and earth-based women's spirituality; Catronia Reed, who is herself a transsexual; and the late Sarika Dharma, a teacher at the International Buddhist Meditation Center (Vietnamese) who founded a Lesbian Zen Group in Los Angeles.

Issues Arising as Women Enter the Leadership of Zen Practice

The issues most on the minds of women leading Zen communities include the need to attend to and augment feminine dimensions of the tradition and the need to clarify boundary issues to foster equality and protect women. Specifically, women teachers are concerned about their lack of Asian female role models and the lack of female images in Zen's iconography, liturgy, and literature.

North American Zen women are painfully aware that the Asian Zen traditions do not provide enough female role models. Many female American Zen teachers have virtually no historical figures to emulate, and they have never personally known female counterparts in Asia. This may result in "making it up as we go along." Understanding how women in Asia have worked with lower-status and conflicting roles may be an enormous help to women Zen teachers. Contact with their Asian counterparts, learning to appreciate both the difficulties they have endured for the sake of the practice and the creative ways they have found to persevere, could be helpful to North American female Zen teachers. Korean Zen Master Barbara Rhodes of Providence, Rhode Island, described how while traveling as a nun in Korea she was surprised by the lack of respect she consistently encountered. Further, understanding the depth of the Asian Zen female tradition might help to counteract the possible dilution of Zen practice resulting from the less formal American style. Dai-en Bennage, an American abbess who studied in Japan with and received dharma transmission from Soto Zen abbess Shundo Aoyama, describes the mostly lay American practice this way: "Wonderful but scary. Who's reading the whole encyclopedia? We need a few who will go the whole nine yards" (Friedman, 343–344). A number of senior Zen practitioners in North America believe that studying with female Asian counterparts, while demanding, may take North American women Zen practitioners to new levels of understanding.

Another concern is that there are few liturgical elements that have come from Asia that refer to women or female images of awakening and advanced spiritual attainment and practice (bodhisattvahood). The same is true of the classic Zen literature. There are few references to women practitioners in the stories used to illustrate and encourage the development of the Zen insight. Currently scholars are translating the stories that are told of female teachers in the history of Asian Zen. Sallie Jiko Tisdale, a lay dharma heir of Kyogen and Gyokuko Carlson in Portland, Oregon, and Vicki Austin, a dharma heir of Mel Weitsman, have collected the names of female teachers from India, China, Japan, and America and worked their names into chants for the Zen liturgy, as have Linda Cutts, Wendy Nakao and others. Many feel that the full empowerment of North American female Zen teachers will not be complete until these historical female teachers are known and honored.

Women are also concerned about the status of female images in the meditation halls. Many North American women Zen teachers do have a statue of Kuan Yin, the bodhisattva of compassion, who since 900 years ago has often been portrayed in female form in East Asia. But the myth of Kuan Yin as usually presented may only serve to support the stereotype of the nurturing, docile, or kind woman as opposed to the wise or warriorlike qualities associated with male figures. Wendy Nakao ad-dresses this somewhat by using the image of Prajna Paramita, "Great Transcendent Wisdom," who is sometimes referred to in scriptures as the Mother of all the Buddhas, as a complement to Kuan Yin.

Ambivalence about Power

Women in North American Zen also face challenges in maintaining their status and power in the face of a postfeminist and antifeminist culture. The new, less hierarchical Zen teaching roles adopted by many women Zen teachers display the relative comfort with which women can step out of the spotlight. However, there is a danger that this trend may go too far, and women may lose the authority and leadership they have gained over the last twenty years.

The prevalence of marriage among North American Zen teachers presents special challenges. There are also now in North America many examples of women dharma heirs sharing teaching responsibilities with their husbands. Where the man is the acknowledged spiritual senior in the couple, the way the co-abbacy is expressed usually implies a gender hierarchy with which North Americans are perhaps too comfortable. Where the woman is the senior member of the team, it is hard to predict how marital dynamics will affect teaching roles. While married coteachers may divide responsibilities equally, there is always the danger that status and power struggles may bubble below the surface of the marital relationship and spill over into the partners' coteaching situation. Where the male coteacher is also the dharma heir of his wife, the situation may be even more complicated.

Boundary Issues

The new custom of men and women practicing and teaching together that obtains in North American Zen has brought up many issues concerning maintenance of boundaries in student-teacher and student-student relationships that will need clarification. Male Zen teachers have reportedly had sex with their female disciples, some of whom later became their dharma heirs. Some women have felt victimized by the teacher's advances. It is important for women Zen practitioners to understand the unconscious impulses that might pull them into this type of relationship and the difficulties involved. North American male Zen teachers also need to be trained to understand the kinds of situations and impulses that lead to this kind of intimacy. Spiritual practice should offer the opportunity to experience a relationship of intimacy and trust between teacher and student without crossing over into sexual behavior that may damage both the student and the community.

Zen communities in North America are now instituting "ethics statements" to educate about limits to appropriate behavior and to establish community processes for correcting misconduct. In North America, female Zen practitioners have a historic opportunity to participate equally in a deep spiritual awakening. They feel that protecting this opportunity for other men and women is an important responsibility.

SOURCES: Rick Fields's *How the Swans Came to the Lake: A Narrative History of Buddhism in America* (1981; 3rd rev. ed., 1992) is the basic source for the history of American Zen and includes references to women in North American Zen's early history. Helen Tworkov, *Zen in America* (1994), adds important case studies. James Ishmael Ford, "Holding the Lotus to the Rock: Reflections on the Future of the Zen Sangha in the West," http://www2.gol.com/users/acmuller/articles/ZENINAM.htm, and Laurence O. McKinney, "Buddhist Modernism and the American Buddhist Lineage," *CyberSangha*, 1995, http://www.newciv.org/CyberSangha/mckinsu95.htm, provide interesting reflections on the Americanness of North American Zen. *Women & Buddhism*, a special issue of *Spring Wind-Buddhist Cultural Forum* 6.1–3 (1986), is an invaluable source on the history of women in North American Zen. Lenore Friedman, *Meetings with Remarkable Women: Buddhist Teachers in America* (1987, 2000), gives portraits of important women teachers that provide in-depth coverage of their perspectives on gender and feminism. *Buddhist Women on the Edge: Contemporary Perspectives from the Western Frontier*, ed. Marianne Dresser (1996), and *Being Bodies: Buddhist Women on the Paradox of Embodiment*, ed. Lenore Friedman and Susan Moon (1997), give Zen women's feminist thinking and reflection on Buddhism and daily experience. See also Roko Sherry Chayat, ed., *Subtle Sound: The Zen Teachings of Maurine Stuart* (1996).

THE WAY OF THE ELDERS: THERAVADA BUDDHISM, INCLUDING THE VIPASSANA MOVEMENT
Sandy Boucher

THERAVADA MEANS THE "Way of the Elders." The orthodox original form of Buddhism followed in Sri Lanka, Burma, Thailand, Laos, and Cambodia has taken two distinct forms in the United States. The Asian immigrant communities have established religious centers run by monks who perpetuate the traditional forms of practice, teaching, and devotion. These ethnic temples operate not only as spiritual but also as cultural and social centers, serving the needs of the immigrant population, particularly those most recently arrived. Due to the rise of immigration from Asia in the 1970s and 1980s, a conservative estimate is that by 1990 there were between one-half and three-fourths of a million immigrant Theravada Buddhists in the United States who attended 142 immigrant Theravada temples. Women's

participation in these temples followed the Asian Theravada model of devotion and support for the monks, with a few immigrant women wearing the robes of monastics. A fascinating development is the participation of some native-born North American women in these *sanghas* (communities) as nuns, where they encountered many obstacles.

A second phenomenon that engages vastly larger numbers of Westerners, the "Vipassana movement," has proven to be a major player in the development of American Buddhism. *Vipassana* denotes the type of meditation done by those who follow the Theravada path. Called "insight meditation," this practice trains the student to observe phenomena such as thoughts, emotions, and physical sensations in a nonjudgmental manner, thus developing insight into the impermanence of all existence, the nature of suffering, and the insubstantiality of the self—aspects of life known as the "Three Marks." Another important element in most Vipassana centers is cultivation of the *Brahma viharas*, or "Divine Abodes" of loving kindness, compassion, empathetic joy, and equanimity.

These Vipassana centers were established not by immigrant monks but by young Americans who had learned to meditate in Asia and returned to the United States to offer courses. Chief among these pioneers were the four founders of the Insight Meditation Society in Barre, Massachusetts, and a somewhat older married woman, Ruth Denison.

The receptivity of young Americans to Eastern religions grew in part from the hippie drug culture of the 1960s and early 1970s. Young people turned away from society's expectations of them and went searching for a spiritual explanation for the visions and insights they had experienced under the influence of hallucinogenic drugs. Spokesmen like Aldous Huxley, Alan Watts, Timothy Leary, and Richard Alpert (Ram Dass) led the way. In a context of Vietnam War and nuclear threat, young people sought to step into an alternative reality, to cultivate values of wisdom and compassion rather than consumerism and aggression. Buddhism offered a practice to develop those qualities.

First Women Teachers

Ruth Denison, whose training had taken place in Burma, began offering courses in meditation in the United States in 1975. Later she established Dhamma Dena Desert Vipassana Center in the Mojave Desert near Palm Springs, California. She augmented traditional Vipassana meditation practice with innovative dance and movement meditations and was the first teacher to conduct an all-woman retreat. A colorful and innovative guide, she trained a number of women and men teachers who now lead their own *sanghas*. Denison is best known for her emphasis on the body, the First Foundation of Mindfulness, as the object of intensive and meticulous investigation, and for her creative, imaginative teaching style. Now in her early eighties she continues to offer both mixed and women's retreats at Dhamma Dena and travels to other states to teach.

The founders of the Insight Meditation Society (IMS) were in their twenties when they returned from Asia in the mid-1970s. Among them were two women, Sharon Salzberg and Jacqueline Schwartz (the men being Jack Kornfield and Joseph Goldstein). These four determined that in order to bring the benefits of Buddhist practice to their fellow Americans, as Salzberg recounts, they would leave aside the "heavy cultural overlay" of devotional practices and traditional teachings on rebirth, stages of enlightenment, and monastic renunciation: Principally they would teach the "wisdom-practice" of Vipassana or insight meditation and would also emphasize the "life-practices" of loving kindness (*metta*), generosity (*dana*), and morality (*sila*). *Metta* is a traditional practice designed to evoke an attitude of deep kindness for all beings, starting with oneself and expanding out to encompass the entire universe; *dana* practice teaches the interdependence of all phenomena and the benefit of letting go of attachment; *sila* is based upon the five precepts—to refrain from killing, stealing, sexual misconduct, harmful speech, and misuse of intoxicants. The young founders of IMS chose to emphasize these practices in their search for a Western idiom that would allow the *Dhamma* (teachings) to be accessible and meaningful to American seekers like themselves.

They established the Insight Meditation Society in a former Catholic novitiate in Barre, Massachusetts, in 1976 and began to offer retreats. Soon IMS became the major venue for teaching Vipassana meditation to Westerners, with students regularly attending retreats in Barre and inviting the four teachers to give courses in other settings.

After some years of teaching at Insight Meditation Society, cofounder Jacqueline Schwartz encountered difficulties. In 1983 she had become aware of discrimination against women and began to look critically at the male-supremacist Theravada tradition in which she was teaching. Ultimately the contradictions between her growing feminist consciousness and the reality of her situation became extremely uncomfortable, particularly as she received little support from her fellow teachers to pursue her examination of sexist bias at IMS. Finally, in October 1983, she made the decision to leave the Theravada tradition and her role as an IMS teacher, while retaining her loyalty to Buddhism. She met with her fellow teachers and friends and told them, "As a woman, I could no longer represent a tradition which taught and believed women to be a lesser birth and life, and whose texts contained very clear passages of discrimination against women" (Boucher, *Turning the Wheel*, 38). Schwartz's resignation brought her to the attention of many women practicing Buddhist meditation and contributed to the exploration of the nature of Western women's participation in Buddhism that was taking place in academic and other quarters.

Sharon Salzberg, on the other hand, has maintained her allegiance to Insight Meditation Society and Theravada Buddhism. She teaches within the tradition of her Asian teachers Goenka, Munindra, Mahasi Sayadaw, U Pandita Sayadaw, and the Indian female teacher Dipa Ma. In Asia, she asserts, she had discovered that enlightenment is possible, and her effort to convey this truth and to teach the path leading to it includes a commitment to offer this opportunity to everyone. In her teaching Salzberg emphasizes the practice of loving kindness, showing how it arises naturally from our awareness of the impermanence and interpenetration of all phenomena. She explains:

> Lovingkindness is a capacity we all have. . . . We only have to see things as they actually are. . . . Upon close examination we come to understand that each aspect of our present reality arises . . . from a vast ocean of conditions that come together and come apart at every moment. Seeing this is the root of compassion and lovingkindness. . . . Lovingkindness is a view rather than a feeling. It is a view that arises from a radical perception of nonseparateness. (*Voices of Insight*, 265–272)

Salzberg has continued her teaching and organizational work, writing several books—*A Heart as Wide as the World* and *Lovingkindness: The Revolutionary Art of Happiness*—and editing *Voices of Insight: Teachers of Buddhism in the West Share Their Wisdom, Stories, and Experiences of Insight Meditation*, and in the process has become an important teacher and force in American Buddhism, an inspiration for women and men alike. Of her continuing endeavor, she writes that "the work of transplanting a teaching from one culture to another continues to be our deepest creative effort, offering many challenges in integrity, compassion, discriminating wisdom, and the ability to let go and start anew when we've made a mistake" (*Voices of Insight*, 2).

Illustrious Forebears

While the sexism of the Theravada tradition and the misogyny of some texts point to obstacles for women, alternatively there is a historical precedent that offers great inspiration for Theravada female meditators. In the India of 2,500 years ago, the Buddha himself established a female monastic order, and many of its adherents (*Bhikkhunis*) achieved enlightenment and functioned as celebrated exponents of the teachings and leaders of large groups of women renunciants (what we would now call "nuns"). Enlightened women were called *Theris* (female elders); their verses (*gathas*) composed on the occasion of their enlightenment were gathered into a volume called the *Therigatha,* which forms part of the official Pali canon. (Pali is the sacred/literary language in which the Buddhist canon was transcribed from its original oral form.) Individual *Theris* are sometimes named in the *suttas* (discourses of the Buddha) in association with the Buddha and his many monastic and lay followers. Eminent laywomen also are chronicled in the Buddhist scriptures, for their support of the community of monks and nuns and for their own spiritual attainment. This documented history of women's achievement in original Buddhism offers validation and encouragement to contemporary women, giving proof as it does of women's capacity for full enlightenment within the tradition, as well as their early assumption of leadership. The verses of the *Theris* also often describe difficulties unique to female roles and conditioning, with which contemporary women can identify (Rhys Davids).

Other Women Teachers

The so-called Vipassana movement has grown steadily since the early 1970s, with at least 300 weekly meditation groups currently meeting throughout the United States and approximately 100 retreats offered each year. Conservatively, 50,000 people attended Vipassana retreats between 1970 and 1995. The majority of these students are women. In 1995 there were seventy lay Vipassana teachers in the United States. While accurate figures are difficult to gather, it appeared that half of the teachers of the American groups and retreats are women.

The Vipassana movement has from the beginning welcomed female teachers. In 1981 Jack Kornfield moved from Massachusetts to Marin County, California, where he established Spirit Rock Meditation Center, which quickly grew to rival Insight Meditation Society in Barre in influence. IMS adhered to the more traditional forms of practice while adjusting and expanding to meet the needs of its students; Spirit Rock's teachers, many of them therapists, brought a more psychological perspective to their teaching, and the center hosted conferences and seminars bringing together teachers from the major Buddhist traditions. In both these centers, women regularly teach and determine policy. Carol Wilson, Christina Feldman, Michele McDonald-Smith, and Narayan Liebenson Grady provide a strong women's perspective at IMS. Sylvia Boorstein, a therapist by profession, has written several popular guides to Vipassana meditation, among them *It's Easier Than You Think* and

Don't Just Do Something, Sit There, and teaches at Spirit Rock. Julie Wester, a student of Ruth Denison, leads family practice retreats at Spirit Rock, and Anna Douglas is a regular teacher there. Across the country are scattered Vipassana centers, many of them headed by women teachers such as Kamala Masters in Hawaii, Marcia Rose in Taos, New Mexico, and Sama Cowan in Fayetteville, Arkansas. Numerous other female Vipassana teachers travel throughout the United States, making regular teaching rounds to small regional centers and groups. Among them are Mary Orr, Sharda Rogell, Taraniya, Debra Chamberlain-Taylor, Sara Doering, and Myoshin Kelley.

One teacher has taken it upon herself to address the spiritual needs of lesbians. Arinna Weisman, a student of Ruth Denison, leads retreats in various parts of the country for lesbians, and, with Eric Kolvig, for lesbians and gay men. She has also opened a center in Northampton, Massachusetts, named Dhamma Dena Meditation Center (like Ruth Denison's center), which welcomes a diverse range of people. In Berkeley, California, another Denison student, Carol Newhouse, leads the Lesbian Buddhist Sangha, a meditation group whose biweekly sittings are typically attended by thirty to forty women.

Monasticism for Women

Among the Buddhist centers established by immigrant communities from Burma, Thailand, Sri Lanka, Kampuchea, and Laos offering teachings and service to their various communities, the Sinhalese Washington, D.C., Buddhist Vihara, established in 1966, and Wat Thai of Los Angeles, established 1971, are the oldest. Despite language barriers and cultural differences, a number of American women have become "nuns" in one or another of these centers, hoping to benefit from the intensive training and sheltered lifestyle that monasticism typically offers. A major impediment to this goal is that in contemporary Theravada Buddhism women cannot be fully ordained. The nuns' order established by the Buddha 2,500 years ago in India flourished for a thousand years and then died out. While in other parts of Asia (Hong Kong, Taiwan, Korea) it is believed that the order persisted unbroken, and full ordination of women is offered, the Theravada establishment in Southeast Asian countries almost universally rejects that ordination as illegitimate. The effect of this is that while Theravada women may wear robes, shave their heads, and observe strict monastic practice, they are viewed by monks and laypeople as religious nonentities who do not deserve instruction or material support. (Note: In 1996, Sakyadhita, an international organization of Buddhist women, convinced the male clergy in Sri Lanka to allow nuns from Korea and Taiwan to plant the seed of ordination again. In the next seven years 200 Sri Lankan Bhikkhunis received full ordination. This movement meets resistance from conservative clergy and laypeople, but it is a beginning.)

The American women who were moved to leave home and take the robes have found themselves in precarious positions. They cannot live at the immigrant Buddhist centers, as monks are not allowed to sleep under the same roof as a woman; they are not supported financially and thus must work at jobs, while being hampered by monastic vows such as not handling money and not eating after noon; and they are given only haphazard instruction. A woman who wishes to be called Sister Nanda (her anonymity reflects the delicacy of the relationship with immigrant groups) took the robes and struggled for thirty years to accommodate herself to the strictures of several immigrant Asian centers. During that time she found that the majority of the monastic rules for nuns were unworkable in the West, concluding, "Of the over three hundred *Bhikkhuni* precepts [rules for fully ordained nuns], perhaps one hundred or less can be followed in a Western environment." It also be-

came clear that the Asian monastic establishment had little interest in providing systematic instruction for Western female renunciants. A Western nun had to pursue her training on her own, with perhaps some help from an individual teacher. In some centers the novice nun was expected to devote all her effort to maintaining the institution and caring for the laypeople of the *sangha*, leaving no time for her own spiritual cultivation. These conditions, combined with the precarious material situation of nuns, led Sister Nanda to dream of establishing a Women's Dharma Monastery in the United States; she sought to organize her sisters in robes to this end. She worked with various organizations attempting to develop a more accessible and practical form of monasticism for Westerners. But finally, as she saw little substantive change occurring, and as she was getting older, she made the decision to take off the robes and return to lay life. Sister Nanda says,

> I decided to leave the Order to avoid perpetuating more difficulties. Concentrating on personal practice became the primary focus. I was nearing retirement age and could live independently on an earned Social Security allowance. To some degree, I miss the companionship of sister nuns. I try to keep the non-monastic Ten Precepts [moral guidelines for devout postulants or laypeople] and many of the workable *Vinaya* [monastic] rules. For me, it has been a fulfilling and wise choice to lead an independent committed celibate Dhamma lifestyle.

Her experience perhaps exemplifies the situation of an ordinary Western nun in these Asian immigrant settings. Other Western women in Theravada robes have gone to Asia to experience the monastic life at its source; some have continued to live in Asian monasteries, adapting themselves to the prevailing cultural expectations for women. A few others have found a home in European monasteries run by Western Theravada monks. These women are given instruction and are working to create a fully empowered nuns' *sangha*, yet they remain subject to the traditional discriminatory rules that restrict behavior and prevent women's full ordination.

The Venerable Ayya Khema was an extraordinary Theravada nun who became an international spokeswoman for equal rights within the *sangha* monastic community. She took ordination at the Chinese Hsi Lai Temple near Los Angeles in 1988, becoming a *Bhikkhuni* (fully ordained nun). *Used by permission from Bhiuuhu Nyanabodhi.*

Activism within the Monastic *Sangha*

A most extraordinary Theravada nun who became an international spokeswoman for equal rights within the *sangha* was the Venerable Ayya Khema. Ayya Khema took ordination at the Chinese Hsi Lai Temple near Los Angeles in 1988, becoming a *Bhikkhuni* (fully ordained nun). She was a well-respected teacher who frequently led retreats and gave lectures in the United States. Many women students journeyed to Sri Lanka to live with her as eight-precept (postulant) nuns in the nunnery she established at the invitation of the Sri Lankan government. Raised in a German Jewish family in wartime Germany, Ayya Khema was incarcerated in a concentration camp; as a teenager she was liberated by the U.S. military and brought to this country where she became a U.S. citizen and lived for many years. Later, she lived in Australia as a married woman, mother, and farmer. There she found Buddhism and first took the robes. Until her death on November 2, 1997, however, she was grateful to her first adopted country and proud of her U.S. citizenship.

Ayya Khema was gifted with a quick mind, great resolve, and tremendous clarity in expounding the dharma (teachings). She also knew how to build institutions, founding the forest monastery Wat Buddha Dhamma in New South Wales, Parappuduwa Nuns Island in Sri Lanka, a Buddhist center called Buddha Haus, and a Theravada monastery named Metta Vihara in Germany. She wrote a shelf of dharma books in both English and German, among them *Be An Island Unto Yourself; All of Us: Beset by Birth, Decay and Death; Being Nobody, Going Nowhere; When the Iron Eagle Flies;* and *Who Is My Self?* She was one of the founders of Sakyadhita, the international association of Buddhist women, and often gave talks at their conventions.

Over the years Ayya Khema spoke up for ordination of Theravada nuns on several continents and in countless gatherings, great and small. As so visible a spokeswoman, she drew much critical fire, yet she never sacrificed her convictions in order to be accepted by the Southeast Asian Buddhist establishment. Her name and her efforts became known throughout the Buddhist world, wherever there were women in robes. Indeed, the changes in attitude and behavior toward nuns that have come about, still partial and gradual in many areas but happening nevertheless, grow out of the activism and strong inspiration of Ayya Khema and a few other valiant, determined female renunciants. Nothing could be more essentially Buddhist than spiritual equality, regardless of gender; Ayya Khema knew that in her challenge to the establishment she expressed the deeper truth of Buddhist teachings.

Scholar Activists

Joanna Macy, a scholar of religion who has strong ties to the Tibetan tradition as well as Theravada training, maintains that the misogynist texts were later additions to the Buddhist canon and that the teachings and intentions of the Buddha were profoundly egalitarian. She writes, "As American women opening to the Dharma, we are participating in something beyond our own little scenarios. We find ourselves reclaiming the equality of the sexes in the Buddha-Dharma. We are participating in a balancing of Buddhism that has great historic significance" ("The Balancing of American Buddhism," 6).

Macy is best known for her spiritual/political work in the fields of environmentalism and the antinuclear movement. For years she led Despair and Empowerment workshops, encouraging participants to go past their psychic numbing and experience their fear and sorrow at the threat of nuclear holocaust. She delineated the guiding principles of this work in *Despair and Personal Power in the Nuclear Age.* A passionately committed and articulate spokeswoman, Macy asserts that the threat of the destruction of humanity through nuclear war or accident can be viewed as an unprecedented opportunity for spiritual growth.

Macy developed, with others, a workshop called the Council of All Beings in which participants take on the identities of other species and engage in a dialogue with the representatives of the human species on ecological issues. And she has spearheaded the Nuclear Guardianship Project that proposes the deactivated sites of nuclear production facilities become sacred pilgrimage places attended by guardians who watch over the spent fuel, making sure it is contained. All her work is based on the Buddhist perception of the interrelationship and interdependence of phenomena. And she urges Buddhists to engage more actively with the problems and issues of our contemporary condition, stating: "Instead of emphasizing that in our enlightenment we move into a sense of *sunyata*, emptiness, there is stress now on moving into fullness, or moving into interrelationship, interdependence. That's what we wake up to—our relationship with all that is" (Boucher, *Turning the Wheel,* 276).

Another Buddhist academic is Rina Sircar, who may be said to bridge the monastic and lay forms. Dr. Sircar, originally from Burma, established the Department of Buddhist Studies at the California Institute of Integral Studies in San Francisco, where she holds the World Peace Chair in the Philosophy and Religion Department, teaching courses in Theravada Buddhism and the Pali language. Dr. Sircar maintains a strong relationship with the Burmese monastic tradition, living a ten-precept renunciant's life. She helped establish the Theravada monastery and retreat center Taungpulu Kaba Aye in Boulder Creek in 1978 and runs the Taungpulu Kaba Aye Meditation Center in San Francisco, where she leads retreats and gives discourses, works with the sick and dying, and performs weddings and funerals.

The Cake as Well as the Icing

"The western teachers went to Asia and saw the great cake of Theravada Buddhism, but they brought back the icing and left the cake!" The icing, according to Dr. Thynn Thynn, a Theravada lay Buddhist teacher in northern California, is Vipassana meditation. Dr. Thynn Thynn, who was born in Burma and lived many years in Thailand before coming to the United States, is a medical doctor who worked in public health in both countries, a wife, and mother to two children. Author of the book *Living Meditation, Living Insight*, she teaches how to apply meditation within the full responsibilities of job and family. She has established a residential lay center called Sae Taw Win II (the original exists in Burma), to "establish the Theravada tradition in the United States." A woman of great warmth and friendliness, Dr. Thynn Thynn works to create a Dhamma community that welcomes families and children and old people. This community is based on the "cake," that is, the Buddhist scriptures—*suttas* (discourses of the Buddha) and *Abidhamma* (the codified teachings)—the precepts, and devotional practices "to open the heart." Fundamental to this body of teachings is the doctrine of karma and rebirth. The spiritual and psychological foundation provided by the teachings, Dr. Thynn Thynn points out, supports the community, providing safety and proper motivation. "Vipassana meditation is the icing" on top of that. On September 9, 1999, Dr. Thynn Thynn, in a monk-led ceremony at Sae Taw Win II, took eight precepts (vows) and donned the brown robe of a "yogi." She went through this formal ordination to bring awareness to her friends, family, and students that she was "starting the tradition here." The practice she teaches, however, remains lay oriented. She calls it "daily life practice" and emphasizes its derivation from the Vipassana tradition.

It is the same discipline as the sitting practice of Vipassana—paying attention to the mind-states—but you're doing it in daily life instead of sitting on the cushion. You're doing it with your eyes open, while working at your job or at home relating to your family. You observe the mind-states, without judgment, and as you observe them you notice that they dissipate and fall away. This gives balance in one's life, and develops equanimity."

Directions for the Future

At the beginning of the millennium, Theravada Buddhism was finding its way in the United States. Many teachers, some of them doctors and therapists, were teaching the mind training of pure Vipassana practice in medical and other secular therapeutic settings. Here the word *Buddhism* might never be mentioned, and the practices were offered as stress-reduction or relaxation techniques. In general the Vipassana movement was strongly lay oriented. Yet some voices urged that to turn away from the monastic roots of the Buddha's teachings was to lose the source and continuity of Buddhism and risk a gradual dilution in the American setting. Other commentators saw many practitioners combining traditions, incorporating practices from Zen or Tibetan or other forms of Buddhism into Theravada practice, which might lead to a future hybrid form that could be called American Buddhism.

Meanwhile, the monks in the immigrant centers continued to offer traditional teachings to their communities. They were guardians of the strict Theravada tradition and as such provided cultural and social as well as spiritual support to Asian immigrants and to some Westerners. (Abhayagiri monastery, a recently established Western male–led institution in northern California, offers traditional monastic practice for men only.) Communication and cooperation between the Asian immigrant *sanghas* and the teachers and students involved in the Vipassana movement continued to be sparse, but there *were* Western Vipassana teachers who cleaved to their Theravada roots while seeking to address the needs of Western students.

At the other end of the spectrum from those who taught only the mindfulness practice, Sharon Salzberg, with her Insight Meditation Society coteacher Joseph Goldstein, addressed the need for cultivation of a more intensive relationship with the traditional teachings by establishing a Forest Refuge in Barre, Massachusetts. Here people come to pursue a longer-term practice than they find in the usual Vipassana center. A more personal relationship between teacher and student is developed in order, in Salzberg's words, "to plant deep roots, to access the depth, the awe, of what the Dharma can be."

SOURCES: Some quotes were drawn from private interviews with Sharon Salzberg, Dr. Thynn Thynn, and Sister Nanda. Two major books on American Buddhist women provide material on Theravada practitioners. Sandy Boucher's *Turning the Wheel* (1988, 1993) offers an overview of American women's participation in Buddhist practice, with a delineation of the issues, and portraits and photographs of eighty Buddhist women. Lenore Friedman's *Meetings with Remarkable Women* (1987, 2000) profiles leading female Buddhist teachers. Boucher's *Opening the Lotus* (1997) contains a contact list of women Buddhist teachers and women-led centers. Sharon Salzberg includes numerous articles by contemporary Theravada women teachers in her *Voices of Insight* (1999). The *Therigatha* verses by enlightened women elders can be found in *Psalms of the Early Buddhists. I. Psalms of the Sisters* (1909) by Mrs. Rhys Davids, M.A., and in the more recent *The First Buddhist Women* (1991) by Susan Murcott. Books by Ayya Khema (*Be an Island Unto Yourself*, 1986; *All of Us: Beset by Birth, Decay and Death*, 1987; *Being Nobody, Going Nowhere*, 1987; *When the Iron Eagle Flies*, 1991; and *Who Is My Self?* 1997), Sharon Salzberg (*A Heart as Wide as the World*, 1997, and *Lovingkindness*, 1995), Dr. Thynn Thynn (*Living Meditation: Living Insight*, 1998), Sylvia Boorstein (*It's Easier Than You Think*, 1995, and *Don't Just Do Something, Sit There*, 1996), and Arinna Weisman (*The Beginner's Guide to Insight Meditation*, 2001) offer the Theravada teachings from a woman's perspective. Joanna Macy expresses an "engaged Buddhist" sensibility in her *Despair and Personal Power in the Nuclear Age* (1983), *World as Lover, World as Self* (1991), and "The Balancing of American Buddhism," *Primary Point* 3.1 (February 1986). The history, nature, and scope of Theravada Buddhism in the United States are explored in Charles Prebish's *Luminous Passage* (1999), and Prebish's and Kenneth Tanaka's *The Faces of Buddhism* (1998), as well as in Don Morreale, ed., *The Complete Guide to Buddhist America* (1998).

TIBETAN BUDDHISM
Amy Lavine

THE ADVENT OF Tibetan Buddhism in North America started in the 1960s with the arrival of several important Tibetan meditation teachers representing the largest schools of Tibetan Buddhism. These schools are the Nyingma, the oldest school of Tibetan Buddhism dating back to the first entry of Buddhism in Tibet, circa the ninth century C.E.; the Sakya tradition, dating from the eleventh century C.E.; the Kagyu school, which traces its lineage to the adept Tilopa in the tenth century C.E.; and the Gelug school, which is the school of the Dalai Lamas and traces its heritage to Tsongkhapa in the fifteenth century C.E. The primary differences emerged among these schools in the emphasis each placed on scholastic learning and meditation practice as well as political power and influence. For example, the Kagyu school is known as the tradition most concerned with meditation practice, particularly sitting practice, and the Gelug school secured the longest-lasting political influence over the whole of Tibet, beginning in the fifteenth century. Today, the Gelug school may be considered to be the best known of the four schools because of the prominence of the Dalai Lama around the world.

The Chinese communist invasion and subsequent occupation of Tibet starting in the 1950s compelled hundreds of thousands of Tibetans, including a large number of religious specialists such as monks, nuns, and lamas (religious authority figures senior to monks or nuns), to flee their homeland in search of refuge in more welcoming countries. The majority of Tibetans settled in India and Nepal, recreating many of the Buddhist institutions that had been decimated by the Chinese. A smaller but influential segment of the Tibetan population eventually moved to North America where they have established exile communities in several large cities as well as enclaves in rural and suburban areas. Tibetan lamas traditionally as well as in contemporary times have a multitude of roles: They may be monks or nuns (although the majority are men), unmarried lay adepts, or married householders; they may be the head of monasteries or solitary hermits; they may be scholars or unlettered practitioners. In time, the Tibetan lamas attracted significant numbers of Western practitioners, many of whom converted, through a Tibetan Buddhist refuge ceremony, to the religion. This group of new Buddhists plays a critical role in the cultivation of Tibetan Buddhism in North America, and women are emerging as a particularly powerful and authoritative voice within this community as lay believers and ordained nuns.

This essay explores the role women have played in the cultivation of Tibetan Buddhism in North America, both by Tibetan believers and non-Tibetan (predominantly Western-born) practitioners. Although Western converts make up the largest number of practicing Tibetan Buddhists in North America, it is important to consider the ways in which lay Tibetans are contributing to the development of their native religious and cultural traditions in diaspora. The differences represented by these two groups are briefly assessed below in terms of cultural priorities and ritual practices. Following this consideration, the essay investigates the modes of authority available to women in Tibetan Buddhist communities (primarily Western convert in nature) in North America, which contribute to the expansion of the religion in its latest incarnation far beyond the gender boundaries placed on it in Tibet. Lastly, several issues of particular relevance to women practitioners are addressed, including the role of the feminine principle in Tibetan Buddhism, the place of the family in the lives of practitioners, and the dialectic of lay and monastic practice that constitutes Tibetan Buddhism in the West in general.

Traditionally in Tibet, the status of women within the religious hierarchy of Tibetan Buddhism, which was also the system that governed the country, was relatively insignificant. Women did not hold positions of religious authority beyond the role afforded to them as nuns in the large monastic system that constituted as much as 20 percent of the male population in premodern Tibet. The number of nuns made up considerably less of the overall female Tibetan population. In North American diaspora communities the traditional religious hierarchy continues to be relevant to Tibetans in terms of their general values and orientations. This is manifest most intensely in the widespread devotion displayed toward the Dalai Lama, the Tibetan people's spiritual and temporal leader. However, the status of women as the transmitters of religious and cultural customs has improved. Tibetan Buddhism in North America can be thought of as constituting two separate realms: that populated by several generations of ethnic Tibetans who have formed relatively close-knit communities in a few dozen cities in the United States and Canada, and the convert community that has fused together the traditional roles of lay and monastic practice in their approach to the scholastic and ritual aspects of the religion.

Assuming much of the responsibility for passing down the customs and ritual practices that defined lay religious practice, as well as social life, in Tibet, Tibetan women in North America have accepted the considerable challenge of making their native traditions attractive to younger generations of refugees, most of whom have never been to their homeland. Increasing numbers of immigrants are being raised in Western countries and have not even had the opportunity to experience the reconstitution of Tibetan culture that has occupied thousands of Tibetans living in India. Therefore, these Tibetan women attempt to pass on the basic religious practices that define lay Tibetan Buddhist practice as well as the traditional food, dress, folk music, and dance within the diaspora community.

The rituals that constitute diaspora Tibetan religion are quite different than the practices that engage the convert communities. It is rare to find nonmonastic Tibetans who practice meditation or who engage in the sustained study of Buddhist teachings beyond the recitation of prayers. Tibetans focus their ritual activities on familial practices, such as the daily maintenance of a home altar (containing water bowls, incense and candles lit daily, and photographs of the Dalai Lama and possibly another important Tibetan teacher) and the recitation of prayers, and communal events, such as the Tibetan New Year (called Losar) and the Dalai Lama's birthday. These two events celebrated by the Tibetan community in exile are among the few times during the year that Tibetans wear traditional dress (and usually more women participate in this show of ethnic pride than men), chant as a large group the prayers of refuge, compassion, and long life for the Dalai Lama, and participate in the devotional exercise of presenting the ceremonial white silk scarf, called a *khata*, to a large photograph of the Dalai Lama. In addition, more and more young Tibetans are learning traditional folk music and dance that they perform at these occasions.

Many ethnic Tibetans feel a strong obligation to preserve and recreate traditional Tibetan rituals and customs in exile that faithfully represent the contours of lay Tibetan Buddhist life as it was once lived in their homeland. There has also been a fusing of the religious with the political for many Tibetans living in diaspora in North America, seen, for example, in the communal recitation of prayers that always initiates political events, such as demonstrations for a free Tibet or the commemoration of the Tibetan uprising of 1959. This latter event remembers the large-scale protest movement that precipitated the eventual exodus of the Dalai Lama from Tibet in the face of increasing pressure from the Chinese communist forces for his submission to their rule. One important event commemorated occurred on March 10, 1959, and involved thousands of women marching in Tibet's capital Lhasa in protest against the invasion of their homeland by the Chinese. Large numbers of refugees turn out each year in New York City to recall this important moment of Tibetan protest that also marks the emergence of Tibetan women into the political sphere for the first time in their history. The fervor among Tibetan women living in diaspora toward their own cultural and religious traditions revolves around their understanding that it is essentially up to those living outside Tibet, and who are thus free to engage in religious practice, to keep their traditions alive. There is little expressed desire among this population of women to embrace the traditionally monastic rituals of meditation practice or the intensive study of Tibetan Buddhist teachings that is so popular among Western converts. They see their own obligations as involving the reconstitution of their cultural and lay religious traditions outside of Tibet in the expressed hope that someday their country will become free of the tyrannical rule of the Chinese, and then Tibetans will feel moved to relocate back to their homeland.

Although there are no specific statistics confirming the numbers of convert practitioners of Tibetan Buddhism today, it is clear from the personal observations of those involved in writing about this population that the numbers are increasing yearly. Beginning in the 1970s as Tibetan teachers started arriving on North American soil, Western converts were attracted to the teachings and practices offered by these Tibetan meditation masters. Up until recently, the Tibetans who came to teach such converts were all men. However, the students they attracted were fairly evenly dispersed between men and women. As these communities formed into primarily practice and study groups, the traditional Tibetan distribution of religious labor was transformed so that lay practitioners became increasingly interested in, and capable of, performing what had always been the ritual practices of ordained monks and nuns. The foundation of this practice is sitting meditation in the form called *shamatha-vipassyana*, translated as calm repose and extending insight. Some Western practitioners have received various empowerments (called *abhisheka*) from Tibetan teachers that prepare them to perform the more mentally and physically challenging practices of Vajrayana Buddhism (another name for the kind of Buddhism practiced in Tibet), which are grouped under the category of tantric practices. These rituals include extensive sessions of sitting meditation, elaborate visualizations, the recitation of various mantras in Sanskrit and Tibetan, the ceremonial offering of symbolic cosmic diagrams called mandalas, and for more advanced practitioners, the complicated reading of Vajrayana texts known as *sadhanas*. The level of commitment, time, and effort required for these practices is traditionally reserved for those who reside in a monastery, as most Tibetan teachers believe it to be extremely difficult to integrate such practices with ordinary lay life. This is why many Western practitioners reserve a period of time, often once a year, to spend in a secluded retreat environment where their primary obligation is to practice without the distractions of everyday life.

Within the new territory being cultivated by Western converts to Tibetan Buddhism, women have discovered many positions of authority that had previously been denied to them in other religious organizations, including the earlier Buddhist communities. Due in large part to their intense devotion, focus, and discipline, women excelled at meditation practice as well as at both the intellectual and experiential knowledge essential to the accurate and authentic teaching of Tibetan Buddhism. In many communities across North America, Tibetan teachers gave women the authority to lead meditation practice sessions, retreats, and seminar-type workshops where they taught the principles of Tibetan Buddhism to large groups of converts. Over several decades, women who started out practicing alongside men were recognized by their Tibetan lamas as exceptional practitioners and worthy of increasingly significant responsibilities and authority within the growing number of practice and study centers across the country. Many of these women traveled to India or other parts of Asia to receive empowerments (instructions and transmissions to practice more advanced rituals) and teachings from other Tibetan teachers. Some chose to become ordained as Tibetan Buddhist nuns, while others chose to remain lay practitioners in order to balance the demands of Buddhist practice with those of ordinary American life.

A remarkable and controversial ascension of a Western-born convert to Tibetan Buddhism was that of Catherine Burroughs who became Jetsunma Ahkön Lhamo, one of the few Western *tulkus* recognized by a Tibetan lama to be the reincarnation of a siddha or Buddhist saint. Burroughs had led an informal New Age group prior to her exposure to Tibetan Buddhism. During an auspicious meeting with Burroughs while visiting her center in Poolesville, Maryland, Penor Rinpoche, the head of the Palyul lineage of the Nyingma school of Tibetan Buddhism, recognized her as a bodhisattva, or great Tibetan teacher reincarnated as this American woman. Eventually, during a visit to his monastery in India, Burroughs was informed by Penor Rinpoche that she was the reincarnation of Ahkön Lhamo, an obscure but important seventeenth-century Tibetan female meditation adept who had not been recognized since her death. The figure of the *tulku* is a vital character on the landscape of Tibetan Buddhism. Transmitting authority from generation to generation, the *tulku* is the officially recognized reincarnation of an important teacher or meditation specialist who traditionally had a great deal of power over a particular monastery and the region surrounding it. A *tulku* is not necessarily someone who has taken monastic vows; especially in the Nyingma school, many *tulkus* marry and have families.

In time, Jetsunma (a title she chose for herself) attracted a group of practitioners to study and practice at her center in Maryland. They built a number of impressive Buddhist structures including a *stupa*, or reliquary, for remains of the Buddha or an important Buddhist teacher. Even more remarkable for a North American *sangha*, or Buddhist community, is the number of converts who, in a show of intense devotion for Jetsunma as their teacher and guru, made the life-altering decision to become monks or nuns. Such a decision involves wearing traditional Tibetan monastic robes; living in community with others (separated by gender); and taking a series of vows, including not killing, stealing, using abusive speech (such as lying or gossip), refraining from sexual relationships, drinking, and listening to music for pleasure or dancing. In a shift from the more disciplined and ascetic lifestyle of Buddhist monastics in most of Asia, American monks and nuns are permitted (and in some cases strongly encouraged) to work for a living, contributing a portion of their earnings to their monastic community. Controversy surrounded Jetsunma as she attempted to integrate her newly sanctioned role as *tulku* with the demands placed on her by the devotion of her followers. As there was no blueprint for how an American might "become" a *tulku*, and as her own guru, Penor Rinpoche, offered little advice in this area, she stumbled with several self-serving expectations, such as the request for a large salary to be paid her by the center. Jetsunma herself had not taken any monastic vows and seems to have used her position of authority to attract several lovers (both male and female) and spouses from among her students. Furthermore, her allegedly spiritual accomplishments seem to have included some rather dubious practices for a Tibetan Buddhist teacher (such as the channeling of a voice known as Jeremiah), which were remnants of her previous role as a New Age teacher. She also claimed that recognition as a Tibetan *tulku* meant that she herself was a "living Buddha," a claim strongly refuted by Penor Rinpoche. A number of her students have since left her center and publicly questioned her abilities and her effectiveness as a Buddhist teacher. It should, however, be noted that the behavior attributed to Jetsunma is similar in certain ways to behavior attributed to several Tibetan teachers who adhere to what has been called the "crazy wisdom" (*yeshe cholwa* in Tibetan) lineage in the Kagyu and Nyingma schools.

The story of Jetsunma Lhamo is the most extreme example of a Western woman's experience with Tibetan Buddhism. There are numerous other cases where a woman has slowly ascended in the hierarchy of convert Tibetan Buddhist communities through the hard work of practice and study and eventually been rewarded with positions of great esteem. One fascinating example is that of Lama Margaret Ludwig whose Tibetan name is Ani Dechen Drolma. Lama Margaret took nun's vows in 1977 with Dezhung Rinpoche, a lama in the Sakya tradition of Tibetan Buddhism. In 1998, Hidgal Dagchen Sakya, an important Sakya lama, conferred on her the title of lama, an indication of her accomplishments as a Buddhist teacher and practitioner. Lama Margaret is a resident teacher of Sakya Thubten Kunga Chöling, better known as the Victoria (British Columbia) Buddhist Dharma Society, where she has aided and assisted Geshe Tashi Namgyal, the other resident lama. Lama Margaret's work focuses on her position as Buddhist prison chaplain at Wilkinson and William Head Correctional Institutions. In 1992, she established a Buddhist meditation group at William Head, which regularly meets twice a week. In her work with prisoners, she stresses the need for healing instead of punishment and careful training of the mind as a way to eliminate negative thoughts and anger.

A number of women Buddhist teachers have achieved positions of influence in other Canadian *sanghas*. The Venerable Cecilie Kwiat has studied and practiced within Theravada and Vajrayana traditions since 1965. Kwiat was appointed by the Sixteenth Karmapa, the leader of the Kagyu school of Tibetan Buddhism who died in 1981 (and whose reincarnation has since been recognized as a Tibetan boy who grew up in Tibet, escaping into India in 2000), to be the first resident teacher at the Karma Kagyu Centre of Toronto (North America's largest Kagyu center at the time). She now lives, teaches, and leads retreats in Calgary, Canada. The Venerable Bhiksuni (Anila) Ann McNeil is a sixty-five-year-old Canadian who has been a Tibetan Buddhist nun for twenty-five years. She was one of the first Westerners to be ordained and spent years with her first teacher Lama Yeshe. Before becoming a nun, Anila Ann was a ski in-

Tsultrim Allione is an important Tibetan Buddhist teacher who has worked with a number of Tibetan lamas and is the author of the classic *Women of Wisdom. Courtesy of the Tara Mandala Retreat, Pagosa Springs, Colorado.*

structor in Canada and a travel agent in Greece. She now serves as the Buddhist chaplain for federal prisons in lower mainland British Columbia and currently teaches in Vancouver at Zuru Ling Centre.

Tsultrim Allione is another important Tibetan Buddhist teacher who has worked with a number of Tibetan lamas and is now an internationally recognized teacher in her own right. Tsultrim was ordained as a Buddhist nun in 1969 by the Sixteenth Karmapa in Bodhgaya, India. After three and a half years she decided to return to lay life. Tsultrim then wrote the classic *Women of Wisdom* and has been empowered by Chögyal Namkhai Norbu Rinpoche to teach the practice of Chöd, an intensive meditation practice that is body centered and requires the practitioner to imagine various parts of her body, such as her limbs, being severed from the whole body. The purpose of this practice is to foster detachment from one's own body and the essential understanding of impermanence as an experiential reality. She is now one of the principal teachers at Tara Mandala, a retreat center in Pagosa Springs, Colorado. Tsultrim, who has raised two children on her own, focuses her teachings on how women practitioners can integrate the demands of their lives as American women with the rewards of Tibetan Buddhist meditation.

One valuable development in the Shambhala lineage of the Kagyu school of Tibetan Buddhism is the group of women converts who are known as *acharyas*, or senior teachers. Students of the late Chögyam Trungpa Rinpoche, these women have practiced and studied Tibetan Buddhism for many decades and recently were given this honor by Trungpa Rinpoche's son, Sakyong Mipham Rinpoche, the head of the Shambhala community. Among the duties *acharyas* perform for the Shambhala community are to act as meditation advisers to students, teach seminars and workshops in Tibetan Buddhism as well as in the meditation program of Shambhala Training, offer refuge and bodhisattva vows, impart transmissions and instructions for other Vajrayana practices, and lead portions of the seminary in which all students who wish to become official Shambhala practitioners must participate. Graduates of this seminary take lay vows to become Vajrayana practitioners with the Sakyong as their root guru. There are eighteen *acharyas* in total, and six of these are women. One of the most famous is the Venerable Bhiksuni Pema Chodron, a student of Chögyam Trungpa. Bhisuni Pema is the resident teacher and abbess of Gampo Abbey on Cape Breton in Nova Scotia, a Karma Kagyu monastery affiliated with Shambhala International. Alongside ordained monks and nuns, several lay students participate at Gampo Abbey in the traditional three-year retreat, which has been modified for Westerners to six years with alternating periods of time on and off retreat so that participants may work to raise funds for their time in retreat and take care of any family or personal demands during that time. Bhiksuni Pema has published several successful books on Tibetan Buddhist practice and has achieved international renown as one of the most influential and important Tibetan Buddhist teachers practicing today.

Another influential Buddhist teacher is Karma Lekshe Tsomo, an American-born woman who studied for five years at the Library of Tibetan Works and Archives and several years at the Institute of Buddhist Dialectics, both in Dharmsala. Today, she teaches Buddhism and World Religions at the University of San Diego. A fully ordained American nun practicing in the Tibetan tradition, Karma Lekshe established Jamyang Choling Nunnery in Dharamsala. She is president of Sakyadhita: International Association of Buddhist Women, an organization whose mission is to promote world peace through the Buddha's teachings and to create a communication network for Buddhist women. Karma Lekshe has helped organize nine national and international Sakyadhita conferences since 1987 and has helped found eight education programs for women in the India Himalayas.

Considering issues that face women practitioners of Tibetan Buddhism, it is important not to make an essentialist argument about supposed differences in approach, interest, or competence between the genders. That certain themes emerge when one focuses on women practitioners and teachers of Tibetan Buddhism is not meant to signal that men do not find these same themes equally compelling or decisive in their relationship to Buddhist practice and study. However, as women gain strength and influence through their own efforts and understandings, their experiences will necessarily shed valuable light on particular aspects of Tibetan Buddhism that may not have occurred to, or taken on the same importance for, their male counterparts. One of the most essential concepts in Tibetan Buddhism is that of the feminine principle, which is associated with the wisdom aspect of the teachings. As Judith Simmer-Brown, an *acharya*, puts it:

> In the Tibetan tradition, the wisdom aspect of the teachings is associated with the feminine, which is depicted in the form of the *dakini*, while the skillful means aspect of compassion is more masculine. Without joining the masculine and feminine aspects we can't become fully enlightened, and I've reflected a great deal about how this relates to my gender being female. . . . In my life, I'm trying to identify the ways in which my gender might be helpful to wake things up for myself and others, and at the same time, trying to step over the ways

in which my gender might be an obstacle—getting stuck in particular aspects of hesitation or emotionality or whatever. (30–31)

The figure of the *dakini* that Simmer-Brown mentions is an important character in Tibetan Buddhism. Similar to a trickster in effect, the *dakini* is a feminine figure who traditionally acted as a kind of spiritual guide for Indian or Tibetan seekers on the path to enlightenment. *Dakinis* often humiliate male practitioners by showing the transparent nature of their intellectual knowledge, which is deemed insufficient to realize true awakening. In other Tibetan stories, *dakinis* often encourage female practitioners to celebrate their feminine nature. These female characters, often acting as consorts to a deity or adept, illuminate the importance of experiential, nonconceptual awareness on the Tibetan Buddhist path. *Dakinis* can act both as an outer visionary guide appearing to the practitioner when she is in a deep state of meditative awareness or as an inner principle reflecting the wisdom and compassion that are central to Tibetan Buddhism. One of the most famous *dakinis* was Yeshe Tsogyal, the consort of Padmasambhava, otherwise known as Guru Rinpoche, the legendary founder of the Nyingma school and the Indian master who helped secure a place for Buddhism in Tibet in the seventh century. Many North American female Tibetan Buddhist teachers use the figure of the *dakini* to interest women practitioners, offering them an image of a powerful, authoritative, sexual woman to encourage their participation and empowerment within the often male-dominated world of Tibetan Buddhism.

A common theme echoed by most women Tibetan Buddhist teachers concerns the high level of consciousness practitioners need to cultivate to integrate their family and Buddhist lives. With the basic contours of their ritual and meditation practice conforming more to monastic rigors than to the relative leniency of lay life, women converts must work hard to balance their time and energy between domestic responsibilities and meditation, between work and Buddhist study, and between familial relationships and commitment to their Buddhist *sangha*. Some communities arrange for child care during certain meditation or study sessions. Other groups have developed simple teachings suited to school-age children designed to expose them to basic Buddhism while their mothers devote their efforts to more advanced practice. Growing up as they have in an environment where their parents (one or both) meditate regularly in a shrine room in the home, it is quite normal for children to make time for their parents' religious life whether they participate or not. Many women wait until they have finished with the more intense demands of raising children before devoting their lives to Buddhist practice and

study; still others decide not to have children, placing their maternal instincts on the formation and nurturing of Buddhist communities.

One difference between the ethnic Tibetan diaspora community and the convert community is in the realm of culture and politics. At this stage in Tibetan Buddhism's entrance into the religious landscape of North American religion, few Western-born converts are involved with the political struggles of Tibetans in their quest for a free Tibet, nor do many seem interested in integrating Tibetan cultural artifacts into their primarily meditation-focused ritual universe. Conversely, exile Tibetans are not engaged in the practice of meditation that consumes the convert community. Although Tibetan women have contributed significantly to the preservation and reconstitution of the cultural traditions of Tibetan Buddhism in North America, women in the convert communities are more involved in transforming the structure of Tibetan Buddhism on a systemic level. These women have profoundly influenced the creation of an American Vajrayana through their meditative expertise, their interest in exploring the meaning and significance of the feminine principle as represented in the embodiment of wisdom in the figure of the *dakini*, among others, their methods of teaching, and the ways in which they empower other women to assert themselves in the operation and leadership of convert communities. The recognition of Jetsunma Lhamo as a bona fide *tulku* was one important way for convert women to begin to influence the general composition of Tibetan Buddhism as it entered a new cultural, social, political, and religious context. The emergence of women practitioners, teachers, nuns, and scholars within Tibetan Buddhist communities ensures that women will continue to influence and direct the development of the ritual and communal arrangement of Buddhism in North America.

SOURCES: In *Women of Wisdom* (1987, 2000), Tsultrim Allione gathers together vivid biographies of six Tibetan female mystics and describes her own experiences as a Tibetan Buddhist nun, thus providing an inspirational account of women who have attained enlightenment and liberation in a variety of difficult situations. *Buddhist Women on the Edge: Contemporary Perspectives from the Western Frontier* (1996), edited by Marianne Dresser, presents the voices of American women on their experiences of Buddhist practice. In thirty thoughtful and provocative essays, a diverse range of contributors—dharma teachers, scholars, monastics, practitioners, and sympathizers—explore the challenges and rewards of integrating Buddhist practice in the West. Leonore Friedman's *Meetings with Remarkable Women: Buddhist Teachers in America* (1987, 2000) celebrates the flowering of women in American Buddhism, exploring this phenomenon by interviewing some of the women who teach Buddhism in the United States. The seventeen women written about vary in background, personality, and form of teaching. Together they represent the growing presence and influence of women teachers in America. Richard Hughes Seager, in *Buddhism in America* (1999), begins with a brief introduction to Buddhist beliefs and history in both Asia and the United States. Seager then presents six profiles of Buddhist traditions exported to the United States from Japan, Tibet, Southeast Asia, and elsewhere. The last section considers Americanization and recent developments in gender equity and progressive social change. *Buddhist Women across Cultures* (1999), edited by Karma Lekshe Tsomo, documents both women's struggle for religious equality in Asian Buddhist cultures and the process of creating Buddhist feminist identity across national and ethnic boundaries as Buddhism gains attention in the West. The book contributes significantly to an understanding of women and religion in both Western and non-Western cultures, and *Buddhism through American Women's Eyes* (1995), edited by Karma Lekshe Tsomo, portrays Buddhism in a fresh, personal, and dynamic way, suggesting its richness, variety, and pragmatism, providing a vision of Buddhism's future in North America. See also Judith Simmer-Brown, "Women's Liberation," *Shambhala Sun* (July 2000): 30–31.

HINDUISM

HINDUISM IN NORTH AMERICA INCLUDING EMERGING ISSUES

Vasudha Narayanan

HINDUISM, WHICH IS the dominant religion of India, going back to sources that are more than 4,000 years old, is also the religion of more than 1.5 million people in the United States. While a substantial number are immigrants, primarily from India, Sri Lanka, Malaysia, and the Caribbean, there are also local people who either have converted to Hinduism or have adopted a significantly identifiable Hindu way of life. There is considerable diversity among the North American Hindu population: Some have come directly from South Asia; some are in a double diaspora—that is, descended from a Hindu immigrant community outside of South Asia and then moved to North America; and some have ancestors who came from Europe or Africa and initially had Judaeo-Christian backgrounds. The Hindus from India are further divided into communities based on the language (there are about eighteen official ones in India), caste, sectarian affiliation, professional groups, interest groups focusing on classical music or dance, and so on. The differences between the communities in the first few years after the migration are directly related to the caste, class, educational qualifications, place of origin of the community members, and their relationship to the host country. Through processes of assimilation, accretion, and adaption, some traditions are renewed and revitalized, while others are marginalized and discarded.

Hindu women in America tend to conflate their religious traditions with their culture. Like other Hindu women who have migrated to other countries, they largely use performing arts to retain and preserve their culture. Retention of their Hindu names without Anglicizing them, Indian food habits, and pride in wearing ethnic clothes on festive occasions largely serve as markers of their Indian/Hindu identities.

History

Many American sailors encountered Hindu traditions and culture when they traveled to India in the eighteenth century and kept detailed logs of what they witnessed. While early translations of Hindu sacred texts influenced the New England Transcendentalists such as Ralph Waldo Emerson and Henry David Thoreau, it was through the visit of Swami Vivekananda (1863–1902), a delegate to the World Parliament of Religions in Chicago in 1893, that Americans came to know about at least one branch of Hindu teachings—the Vedanta philosophy—in a direct manner. The Vedanta philosophy looks primarily to sacred texts known as the Upanishads (c.

sixth century B.C.E.), the Bhagavad-gita (c. second century B.C.E.), and the Brahma Sutras as sources for its worldview. At Vivekananda's behest, the first Hindu temple known as the "Vedanta" temple was built in San Francisco in 1905 and functioned primarily as a meditation center, and the Indian swamis in the Ramakrishna monastic order organized by Vivekananda came to North America and founded Vedanta Societies in major cities. A branch of women renunciants, following the tradition in India and a parallel order of women, have now established an interfaith *ashram* (retreat center) near the Vivekananda monastery in Ganges, Michigan. There are also monastic communities of women connected with the Vedanta Societies in California.

Although Vivekananda is one of the better known religious figures who visited the United States, other holy men including Paramahansa Yogananda (1893–1952) and Baba Premananda Bharati (1868–1914) also visited the country. In the early twentieth century, a few thousand Indian men, including Sikhs and Hindus, came to work on the West Coast of the United States and Canada. Since Hindu women did not migrate at that time, the men married Mexican American women. For several decades in the early part of the twentieth century, the United States closed its doors to Asian immigration.

After the changes in the immigrant laws in 1965, the arrival of Indian professionals and their families led to the building of the first large South Asian Hindu temples. The first two temples that claimed to be "authentic" were built in Flushing, New York, and in Penn Hills, Pennsylvania. They grew out of the many classes in performing arts that were being conducted for the new immigrants and young second-generation Indo-Americans. Many women who came in the mid-1960s were those whose husbands had migrated to Canada and the United States. After the mid-1970s, there has also been a steady flow of students and professional women from South Asia. The Hindu population now has large numbers of first- and second-generation immigrants from India. Although until the 1980s many of the Hindu women who came here arrived as wives of men who had chosen to migrate, in the last twenty years there have been increasing numbers of students and professionally trained women who came here to study or work and decided to stay on. It is important to note that many women came and continue to come to join their husbands in North America; many of them are well educated, and a fair number have professional degrees.

There are many ways in which one may classify Hindu institutions in North America. One is by the devotees' place of origin: Thus, there are temples that largely serve North Indians, South Indians, people from the Indian state of Gujarat, immigrants from Guyana, and so on. There are also institutions whose members are of European descent. Ethnicity is largely conflated with religion in the Hindu traditions, and there is great diversity in the language and the culture of worship. One may also classify institutions as those primarily devotional in texture and others that emphasize more self-effort—meditation, yoga, and so on. While most Hindu institutions in the United States and Canada are not exclusively devotion or meditation oriented, in general most temples are devotional in spirit with trained male priests of the Brahmin caste doing the formal worship and rituals.

The many social divisions known as "caste" in the Hindu traditions are present, though in a much more diluted way, in America. There are further divisions along community lines; that is, members of the same caste may choose different philosophical traditions or deities to worship. Thus there are Vaishnava (followers of Vishnu), Shaiva (Shiva), and other communities that worship the Goddess. Many marriages are still arranged within caste groups in India, but the boundaries of the caste and community groups have widened considerably in the diaspora.

A Taxonomy of Hindu Communities

Hindu communities in the post-1965 immigration era can be classified in many ways. One easy division is by *area of origin:* North India, South India, Sri Lanka, Trinidad and Tobago, South Africa, and so on. Hindus from various geographic areas tend to worship together. A further subdivision for the Indian communities is by *language groups;* such groups include the Tamil Sangam ("society of Tamil"), Kannada Koota (The Kannada [people's] group), and the Gujarati Samaj (The Gujarati Society). Two large language-based groups with strong organization are the TANA (Telugu Association of North America) and ATA (American Telugu Association), and they hold very large annual meetings. These groups cut across religious boundaries and castes and are found in all major metropolitan areas. There are also Hindu communities based on *caste.* Some people prefer to use the term *community* interchangeably with *caste;* thus there are pan-American groups that have members of the Bhant caste, the Patel/Patedhar community, and so on. These groups are specific communities/castes from particular regions in India, and there are dozens of similar groups. There are also other communities based on sectarian affiliation; thus the Swaminarayan community (which has built one of the largest Hindu temples at Neasden, just outside London) has temple communities in hundreds of cities and towns all over North America. A sectarian community that relies exclusively on the salvific power of Sri Vishnu-Narayana and the teachings of the nineteenth-century preceptor Swaminarayan, its members feel comfortable in a temple where their monotheistic faith is not compromised with shrines dedicated to other Hindu deities. Thus, this movement has seen it as a priority to have its own temples where the community can regularly gather. It is also a community that is in the forefront of volunteer work and gathering food for the homeless in the Americas. There also large social organizations for some sectarian communities. The Vira Saiva or Lingayat community, whose members are exclusive followers of Shiva in Kanataka, India, has pancontinental gatherings every other year. Specific communities that focus on *veneration of a particular teacher or guru* are also to be seen in most parts of the Americas. There are Sai Bhajan groups—that is, communities that meet weekly or fortnightly to sing hymns in praise of the teacher-saint Sathya Sai Baba (b. 1926). Many other gurus like Ma (Mother) Amritanandamayi have loyal followers who also meet regularly.

There are also many cyber communities based on sectarian affiliation; email listservs are dedicated to particular traditions where men and women want just to discuss the sacred texts—Sanskrit and vernacular—of their tradition or matters relevant to living a religious life on the American continent.

A general rule of thumb in North America is that the smaller the geographic area under consideration, the more inclusive the group. A large city may have very specific groups based on caste, community, and language lines; smaller towns like Allentown, Pennsylvania, may have one large shared worship facility for Hindus, Sikhs, and Jains. Cyber communities now bring together people from all over the world in virtual forums to discuss matters of mutual interest.

Rituals

LIFE CYCLE RITUALS

Women from almost every Hindu tradition and community celebrate various life cycle and regular calendrical rituals at home, in public spaces, and in temples. Life cycle rituals begin during the prenatal months; the pregnant mother and the father of the child may observe several rituals like *simantam* ("parting of the hair") for the safe delivery of the child. This ritual is conducted during the eighth month of pregnancy. There are also other rituals that are region specific. A popular woman's rite in many communities in South India is called *vala kappu* ("bracelets and amulets"), and this rite is accompanied by a ritual called *poochutal* ("adorning with flowers"). The pregnant woman is dressed in heavy silk saris, and women of all ages slip bangles and bracelets on her arm. These bracelets are supposed to be protective, like amulets, and safeguard the woman from the effects of the evil eye and evil spirits. This ritual of celebration and protection is observed by many South Indian

women in the United States and Canada and frequently doubles as a baby shower.

Childhood sacraments include the naming of the child, first feeding of solid food, tonsure, or cutting of the child's hair, and piercing of its ears. The beginning of education for a child is called *vidya arambha*, or "the beginning of learning." Some of these are celebrated with a large Indian community in attendance. Puberty rites for girls associated with the first menstruation are still practiced in India in many communities but almost never in the Americas except in the company of a few close women friends.

Marriages are seldom arranged by consulting horoscopes—as they are frequently done in India—in America; most young men and women get to meet and know the person they wed. Nevertheless, families regularly introduce young women to men who are of the same linguistic group, caste, and community. While it is hard to come by hard numbers, ordinarily marriages are not arranged among second-generation immigrants in America, at least not in a traditional sense as in India. When they are, the bride and groom frequently have considerable time to get to know each other's families. The major exception is seen in the case of Indian Hindu students who are potential immigrants and young first-generation immigrants. Many of them, especially young male students and technological workers who are on temporary visas from India, go back to the home country and marry according to the wishes of their parents and then bring their spouses to the United States or Canada. Alongside these marriages, many younger generation Indo-Americans and Indo-Canadians also marry outside their religious traditions and raise children with dual religious heritage. Wedding rituals may take a whole day with much dancing, singing, and merriment. Young brides add "Western" rituals to a traditional Indian wedding by including bridesmaids in traditional Indian clothing at their weddings. The wedding ritual in the diaspora is usually a traditional Hindu ceremony officiated by a male brahmin pries, but the reception is a completely Western occasion with both Indian folk and Western dancing.

FESTIVALS

While Deepavali, or the festival of lights, is celebrated by almost all Hindus around the new moon that comes between mid-October and mid-November, Navaratri (nine nights) is largely celebrated by women. It lasts for nine nights and ten days. It is celebrated all over India by Hindus but in different ways and for different reasons. The festival begins on the new moon that occurs between September 15 and October 14. The nine nights and ten days are dedicated to the goddesses Sarasvati, Lakshmi, and Durga. Sarasvati is worshiped as the goddess of learning and performing arts; Lakshmi is the

A Hindu Gujarati bride in her wedding splendor displays the henna patterns on her hands. *Courtesy of Vashudha Narayanan.*

Lakshmi and Sarasvati, draped with garlands of fresh flowers, are placed in front of the display of dolls and worshiped. Many South Indian women continue to celebrate this festival lavishly, and on any given Navaratri weekend in Chicago or the Bay Area, invitees may visit fifteen or twenty homes where the festival is celebrated with an open house.

Some Hindus believe that during these nine/ten days the goddess Durga killed the buffalo-demon Mahisha. Hindus in the state of West Bengal call this festival "Durga Puja." While in India, Bengali Hindus make enormous statues of Durga and worship her, in America smaller images are made. After nine nights, these images are immersed in a river in India and disposed of in other ways in America. For these ten days the spirit of the goddess is believed to be in the image. In the state of Gujarat, during Navaratri, women do circular dances called *garbha* (womb) all through the night. A sacred lamp, considered to be a manifestation of the goddess, is placed in the center, and women dance around it. While traditionally done only by Gujarati Hindu women, in the Americas Hindus from all areas tend to join the festivities. The largest *garbha* dances are held in New Jersey, where over 10,000 Hindus participate. *Dandiya*, a dance with sticks, reminiscent of Krishna's dance with the cowherd girls, is also performed during Navaratri. The traditional dances are now done to contemporary music, and "disco dandiya" is very popular, as is "pop-bhangra," a dance from the state of Punjab. In many campuses across the United States and Canada, second-generation Hindu women participate in these dances with considerable enthusiasm.

VRATAS OR VOTIVE RITUALS

Annual or occasional votive rituals done by women are common all over India and are continued by immigrant Hindus. Women of a family and friends gather together on particular days of the year and celebrate the goddess by fasting and feasting and then perform rites (*vratas*) for the happiness of the entire family. The *Varalakshmi Vrata* (the votive ritual for Lakshmi who grants all boons) is conducted in late July or early August by many women from South India. While it is a domestic ritual in India, here there are large celebratory gatherings at homes and in temples. Many women in the Americas congregate at temples and perform the ritual worship together.

The *karva chauth*, performed the fourth day after full moon, is a ritual observed by women of the Punjab area

goddess of fortune who gives wealth in this life and liberation in the afterlife; Durga is a goddess of strength and power. In the region of Tamilnadu, it is largely considered to be a festival for women; it is the time when a room is set apart and filled with exquisite dolls for the play of the goddesses. Elaborate tableaus are set up depicting mythological scenes (similar to the nativity scenes that one sees around Christmas), and usually in the center are large images or clay dolls of the goddesses. Every evening during this fall festival, women and children dressed in bright silks visit each other, admire the *kolu* or display of dolls, play musical instruments, and sing songs (usually in praise of one or the other of the goddesses) from the repertoire of classical music. Songs composed by Tyagaraja and Diksitar (musicians who lived in the state of Tamilnadu around the late eighteenth century) are particularly favored. It is a joyous time of festivity, music, elegance, and beauty; it is a glorious celebration of womanhood. The last two days are dedicated to the goddesses Sarasvati and Lakshmi; these are special countrywide holidays. Large pictures of in the month that falls roughly between mid-October and mid-November. Women eat while there is still starlight and begin their fast soon by dawn. They fast the whole day and are exempt from doing their regular household chores. During the day, a special story giving the "origin myth" of the ritual is read by one of the older women in the gathering. The ritual is for the well being and longevity of the husband and makes the point that the woman, through the proper observance of the ritual, has enough power and good merit to create happiness for the husband. Varieties and forms of this ritual, or similar ones to obtain a husband, are found all over India in different Hindu castes and communities. While this ritual is usually undertaken by a woman with other women in the family in India, in the United States and Canada women dressed in bridal finery usually gather in someone's home and undertake the fast together to keep each other company. The observance creates a sense of community among the women who participate and a feeling of keeping the values they grew up with in India. Even women who think they ordinarily do not participate in patriarchal power structures observe this or other fasts if it is something they grew up with in India in an effort to hold on to tradition in a new land. In eastern Uttar Pradesh, Madhya Pradesh, and Bihar in India—and by extension, women from these states who have migrated to North America—women fast in a ritual called Teej (third day after new moon) for the welfare of their families, and women from these areas continue the ritual in America. Teej in other parts of northern India is celebrated with women returning to their natal homes and spending the day by participating in fun activities including feasting.

Drama, dance, and music are perceived to be vehicles of religious expression and conveyors of yearning in the Hindu tradition. Classical music and dance were considered to have been given by gods and goddesses to human beings. Even now, the Goddess Sarasvati is worshipped as the patron goddess of music and learning. The *Bharata Natya Sastra*, the treatise on classical dance, is considered to have the essence of the four Sanskrit Vedas (the oldest sacred texts in India, frequently thought of as being revealed in some fashion) and claims to be the fifth Veda. The performing arts therefore provide an alternative avenue to salvation, paralleling other ways to liberation seen in post-Vedic literature. While pure music and dance (as distinguished from music and dance with devotional content) is itself said to be of divine origin and understood to lead one to the divine, usually singing and dancing are connected with the bhakti, or devotion, contained in the lyrics being sung. Devotion to the deity is expressed through a number of *bhavas*, or attitudes; these include the loving attitudes connected with service, ma-

ternal love, romantic love, and so on. The combination of the emotional lyrics sung with the abandon of devotion is said to be a path through which one can reach the divine goal of one's choice. In the United States and Canada, dance, especially the style called Bharata Natyam, has become one of the *primary* ways in which young girls learn about their religion and culture. In almost every town and city, women who have learned this dance form in India—or elsewhere—teach the art to young girls. This form of dance is taught in temple halls and private studios and performed in almost all major Indian cultural forums in America. The songs speak about the various deities and their manifestations; to learn dance is to know the stories, the emotions, and where relevant, the allegorical meaning associated with the narratives. While sacred texts are not memorized, the stories are heard and danced. The Chicago area alone has about a dozen major Bharata Natyam dance teachers, whose studios have hundreds of young students as well as several smaller schools. While the students in the United States tend to be largely young Hindu girls of South Asian heritage, in Canada, there is a larger proportion of women of European ancestry. Unlike the United States, in Canada, due in large part to differences in public policy and multicultural awareness, Indian classical dances are better known among the larger population and, like ballet, have become part of a secularized dance training.

South Indian Hindu women in the Americas are also largely involved with regular meetings—teaching and learning classical and semiclassical (*bhajan*) music. Groups of women meet regularly in many towns, some weekly, some less frequently, to learn and sing religious songs. Some women's groups gather on an ad hoc basis to learn or recite prayers like the Vishnu Sahasranama (the thousand names of the God Vishnu) or the Lalita Sahasranama (the thousand names of the Goddess Lalita/Parvati). In towns where there are no temples this becomes the primary way of expressing communal religiosity. An annual event showcasing South Indian classical music is one that was instituted in India by Bangalore Nagaratnammal (1878–1952). This is the Tyagaraja Utsava (Festival of Tyagaraja), named after an eighteenth-century composer. Bangalore Nagaratnammal was a very talented woman from a traditional courtesan family and was apparently greatly devoted to music and to the Hindu tradition. The celebration she started in the birthplace of the musician Tyagaraja has grown to be one of the best known music festivals in India and for Hindus in the diaspora. Tyagaraja Utsavas are celebrated with great eclat not just in Tiruvaiyaru, the place where Tyagaraja lived, but in every major city in the United States and Canada. The most prominent festival is in Cleveland, Ohio. Men and women sing in the festival that lasts one day in smaller towns, a long weekend in larger cities, and a week long in Cleveland. Women musicians are now the lead singers in many of these festivals in India and abroad.

Apart from the religious content of the songs, it is through the identification with the composer's emotions that the singer or dancer participates in the spiritual community. When a singer or dancer recites the woman poet Andal's (eighth century) verses, or dances her songs, she is participating in her devotion to the god Vishnu. Dances, music, and rituals at home and in the temple are based on participation of the devotee in the myths of the many saints and the many acts of redemption attributed to the gods Vishnu, Shiva, or the Goddess. The devotees participate in the passion and surrender of the saints whose verses they utter, and through this identification, they link themselves to the devotional community extending through time. Thus the devotion of the saints and the composers of the prayers are appropriated by the devotee who recites or sings or dances the words. While dancers have their own studios in some of the larger metropolitan areas, in many smaller towns they tend to teach in temples. In fact, the impetus for building some of the earlier temples in Pittsburgh and other places came from a need to have a community center where children could be taught to dance and pray with their parents.

DOMESTIC WORSHIP

Worship at home is generally called *puja*. Worship of the deity or a spiritual teacher, especially at a home shrine, is one of the most significant ways in which Hindus express their devotion. Many Hindu households set aside some space (a cabinet shelf or entire room) at home where pictures or small images of the gods and goddesses (Rama, Krishna, Lakshmi, Durga) are enshrined. A woman's *puja* may involve simple acts of devotion done daily, like the lighting of oil lamps and incense sticks, recitation of prayers, or the offering of food to the deity enshrined in the altar. Usually all members of the family can participate in daily *puja* for personal devotions, but more elaborate or specialized rituals of worship, like the one done to Satyanarayana (a manifestation of Vishnu) on full moon days, may involve the participation of a male brahmin priest or special personnel. Regular singing of devotional songs, either alone or in groups, frequently takes place in front of family *puja* shrines. While the time devoted to *puja* varies widely in each household both in India and in America, on the whole, the longer and more elaborate worship with food offerings to the deity done fairly regularly in India is less frequent in America because of time constraints.

Leadership Roles

Priests who officiate in temples are usually male brahmins. It is thus not just a gender but a caste issue. Hindu priests are generally not trained in seminaries or expected to have detailed knowledge of scriptures, though a few in this country have some knowledge of the sacred texts. Nor are they expected to fulfill pastoral obligation or to be a minister to the congregation. Many of them are ritual specialists who have detailed knowledge of how to conduct either hourlong or weeklong rituals. It is not an occupation or role that many people in India or in the diaspora aspire to, and thus women's ordination or priesthood is not much of an issue in the Hindu traditions.

Many women take active roles in the initiation, planning, and building of temples in the United States and Canada. Unlike women in India, they are also presidents and members of various temple committees. They also appropriate and initiate new rituals in temples; for instance, in the Hindu Temple of Atlanta, women now ritually carry a palanquin with the icon of the goddess, a task done by men in India.

A major twentieth-century phenomenon has been the rising popularity of women gurus. Many of them are Hindu by birth but espouse generic "interfaith" theologies. The rituals they conduct are grounded in the Hindu tradition. Well-known Hindu women gurus, who have large followings and who visit the American continent regularly, are Ma Amritanandamayi (more popularly known as Ammachi) and Ma Karunamayi. Ma Jaya, a Brooklyn native of Jewish origin, is also largely "Hindu" and "interfaith" in her worship and meditational rituals. She lives in the Kashi Ashram in Sebastian, Florida.

Hindu women considered to be ethnic Westerners are seen in many communities in America. The Mother's Place, or Sri Saradeswari Ashram, is a small monastery and retreat center in Ganges, Michigan. A few women renunciants, primarily of European ancestry, follow the way of life set by the parent order in Calcutta and have many Hindu and interfaith activities at their center. The largest number of Western Hindu women are probably with the International Society of Krishna Consciousness. There are approximately 80,000 members of this society in the United States alone, and about 50 percent of them are women. Many of these women have been working hard for representation on their governing boards and in organizing conferences and seminars.

Emerging Issues

With more than a half million Hindus in the United States and several hundred thousands more in Canada, all with diverse ancestry, backgrounds, language, and educational skills, there are many areas of concern and celebration. While many Hindus come here from India for professional opportunities, they also enjoy the freedom to be selective about the traditions they choose to follow, a freedom that is harder to come by in India with older relatives and an instilled sense of respect for custom and practice. In India, women's rituals are frequently done under the watchful eye of an elder relative or friend; in the diaspora, some rituals are retained, some adapted, some innovated, and some discarded. In larger American cities, where there are large Hindu temples, there are now Sunday School classes for young children on how to ritually worship (do *puja*) and conduct home worship. While these rituals have great diversity in India and are tailored according to caste and community, in the United States they are made uniform and homogenous.

The family structure is still considered as central in the diaspora as it is in India. With the exception of people from Gujarat, whose families in America tend to include older-generation immigrants, most Hindu families in America are nuclear in structure. Many of them, however, tend to have parents and relatives who come and visit their immigrant children for several months at a time. This is particularly true at times when the young couples become parents themselves. Parents and grandparents are then invited to come and be with the family to help with the baby, especially in the first few months when the mother has to go back to work outside the home.

Embedded as they are in a "majority" culture in India, the identity of first-generation immigrant women and their sense of belonging to a place are problematized when they make a new home in the Americas. From their names to appearance to celebration of festivals, there are issues with which women wrestle. Many women have Sanskrit or vernacular names that are connected with some manifestation of the sacred. Should they be anglicized like the Chinese women? Should they wear the Indian clothes they are so fond of, the dot on the forehead that articulates the identity of an Indian and sometimes a distinctively Hindu womanhood? Is the family to celebrate religious holidays after a full day's work and Little League or postpone them until the weekend, well past the sacred auspicious time? Most women see all this as part of their larger Hindu identity, just as their music and dance are part of their culture. Hindu women ordinarily end up keeping traditional names or abbreviating them; they usually wear Indian clothes for most social and religious events. Many of them make compromises with festivals whether observing Hindu rituals or celebrating Christmas. Hindu families say they celebrate Christmas "for the children" as a nonreligious event. They usually have some form of tree and give presents to the children. Dual traditions are particularly seen in households where one of the parents is Hindu and the other of European ancestry. With the increase of what is popularly called "mixed" marriages, Hindu traditions are adapted and selectively followed to fit into a religious environment of compromises in the family.

Despite being raised Hindu, second-generation women frequently see themselves as culturally different from the new immigrants. Nevertheless, there is a pervasive notion in many academic and social sectors that Hindu women who have been raised in the Americas share more with their Indian sisters than with American women. This notion manifests itself in issues like the "cultural defense" in legal cases. In the isolated cases where the Hindu women are accused of harming or killing their husbands, the defense may argue that they allegedly did so because of emotional or physical abuse. A further argument is that it is an act of desperation brought about by a certain worldview and cultural conditioning that encourages years of quiet submissive behavior on the part of the woman even under abusive circumstances. This defense is built on many stereotypes and, like other stereotypes, has some elements of truth but also limitations.

There are areas where there seems to be little interface between religion and some social issues. Like women from every race and economic class, some Hindu women are subjected to abuse. There are various shelters that focus on helping such women in the large metropolitan areas. Reaching out to a larger South Asian population of many religions, these institutions bear Indian names: *manavi* (woman), *sakhi* (friend), and *raksha* (protection). These institutions seldom have any direct connections with any one religious tradition. While open to any woman, they are particularly concerned with counseling those from South Asia. These institutions thus have a loosely held perception that patterns of cultural responses are shared by women from the subcontinent.

There is also not much interface between the religious institutions and gay and lesbian people from India. While there are complex reactions to such phenomena in India, only recently have Hindu women gone public with their lifestyle in America. The religious institutions do seem to either condemn or openly make spaces for gays and lesbians and, at least in the last century, seem not to concern themselves with any kind of sexual issue and do not recognize such matters as coming within their provenance. The situation is similar for issues such as contraception and abortion where individual choice and privacy have been the key issues. Thus, while the word *religion* covers several areas (like dance and astrology) in the Hindu tradition that are not part of the general Western understanding of the word, there are also topics like abortion, contraception, and gay rights discussed by religious institutions in the West that are ignored in practice in Hinduism. While these topics are discussed in dharma (righteousness, duty) texts written in the first millennium c.e., Hindus, in general, have balanced text with custom and practice. They have had a far more ambiguous relationship with the sacred texts than the Judaeo-Christian-Islamic traditions.

Hard evidence on the issue of "dowry" in the Americas is hard to get. While dowry is not sanctioned by the scriptures, the giving of monies or goods by the bride's parents to the son-in-law and his family had become a custom in many parts of India. The practice in India today, when it does occur, is not connected with religion or Hinduism exclusively; it is a custom extensively in vogue among Muslims and Christians in India. To a large extent, the intention behind the original custom among Hindu families was laudable—to help the bride financially. Women in most communities in India, according to Hindu law, did not inherit immovable property, and the gift of jewels and goods was to balance the situation. The custom spiraled out of control. It is hard to get information on this issue because most Hindu parents give their daughter many gifts including jewelry at the time of wedding and do not call this dowry. If the term is to be used simply for goods demanded from the bride's family and not those given voluntarily, we can say that the custom is not popular in America.

To understand Hindu communities and women in the Americas, therefore, we have to take into account their diverse ethnic backgrounds, their nebulous connection with religious institutions and scriptures, and the differences between first- and second-generation immigrants. We further have to note that issues important in the Judaeo-Christian traditions are ignored by Hindu institutions. In transmitting their traditions, Hindu women have relied largely on ritual and the performing arts. Almost a million strong, large numbers of Hindu women work outside their homes, and the second generation of Indo-American and Indo-Canadians, while quite integrated in the only homeland they have known, also continue to maintain Hindu and ethnic traditions.

NEW HINDU MOVEMENTS
Kathleen M. Erndl

THE TERMS *HINDU* and *Hinduism*, problematic in India, are even more so in North America. Originally, the term *Hindu* was applied by Turkic- and Persian-speaking invaders as a geographic and ethnic designation for the peoples living east of the great river Sindhu, known as the Hindu in Persian (and Indus in English; hence India). Eventually, and especially under British colonialism, Hindu came to be a religious designation opposed to Muslim. One problem in defining Hinduism stems from the wide diversity of beliefs, practices, and cultural groups included under its umbrella. It is highly decentralized, with no historical founder, no equivalent of a pope or council with final authority in religious matters, and no agreement on which sacred scriptures or articles of belief are essential for all Hindus. Today, *Hinduism* refers to the religion of the majority in India and is generally understood to include all of the religious traditions indigenous to India, except for those that have established a distinct religious identity of their own (Buddhism, Jainism, and Sikhism, but even they are sometimes included within the rubric of Hinduism). However, some modern Hindu-inspired religious movements, both in India and abroad, including most of those surveyed in this essay, either avoid or explicitly reject the term *Hinduism*, preferring to be known by the name of their particular organization or spiritual lineage and emphasizing their universality. Although the term *Hinduism* has been and is today highly contested, it may be used as a convenient designation for a diverse but continuous tradition, including common elements of belief and practice.

The worldview of Hinduism includes a belief in samsara, the realm of birth and death in which human and other sentient beings undergo a series of rebirths determined by karma or intentional actions. Liberation from samsara (*moksha*) is attained through the practice of various disciplines or paths, yogas, such as ritual and ethical action (karma yoga), devotion to a personal deity (bhakti yoga), or meditation and transformative wisdom (jñana yoga). In all of these paths, the goal is to eradicate ignorance, desire, and ego, thus severing the bondage of karma and ending the cycle of rebirth. Brahman is the name of the ultimate spirit or reality, while the atman is the individual soul. Some Hindu philosophical schools assert the ultimate identity of brahman and atman (nondualism), others their unity (qualified nondualism), and still others their distinctness (dualism), with numerous intermediate positions. These matters are the purview of the ancient Vedic texts known as the Upanishads, and the various philosophical schools devoted to them are known collectively as Vedanta ("end of the Veda," i.e., Upanishadic philosophy).

Hindu-inspired movements in North America have generally emphasized some form of yoga practice combined with some form of Vedanta philosophy in the context of individual spiritual development under the guidance of a guru or spiritual preceptor. More culturally specific aspects of Hinduism in India such as the caste system, purity and pollution, family-oriented rituals, and folk practices involving the worship of village deities, spirit possession, and animal sacrifice have not generally taken hold in the newer Hindu movements popular in North America.

New Hindu movements are a selective transmission to North America of modern Hindu movements in India that, beginning in the late eighteenth and early nineteenth centuries, tended to emphasize the universality of the Divine under many names, the irrelevance of gender in the spiritual path, and the social and educational uplift of women (Falk). They are also compatible with the experimental and eclectic nature of American religion, particularly its more radical wing, which values individuality, reason, and personal experience over and above social norms, traditional authority, and religious dogma. New Hindu movements draw their membership from the same pool of spiritual explorers, as do such movements as Spiritualism, New Thought, Theosophy, New Age, and Neo-Shamanism. In all of these movements, the presence of women, both in leadership and support roles, is noteworthy.

North American interaction with Hindu ideas and practices can be divided into three periods (Trout, 4–6). The first began in the early nineteenth century. Hindu philosophical texts were increasingly available in English translation and attracted the attention of American intellectuals such as the Transcendentalists Ralph Waldo Emerson, who was deeply affected by Upanishadic thought, and Henry David Thoreau, who took a copy of the Bhagavad-gita with him to Walden Pond. This period was characterized by intellectual interest in such ideas as reincarnation, karma, and monism, often taken out of their original contexts, rather than in wholesale conversion to Hinduism as a religion and by contact through sacred texts in translation rather than with Hindu religious leaders. The second period (1893–1965) was ushered in by Swami Vivekananda, disciple of the charismatic Bengali mystic Sri Ramakrishna. Vivekananda's dramatic appearance at the World Parliament of Religions in Chicago in 1893 put a face on Hinduism and led to the establishment of the first and most influential Hindu groups in North America, the Ramakrishna Mission and Vedanta Society. Other Hindu leaders such as Paramahansa Yogananda followed Vivekananda, establishing their own centers and organizations, and multiple varieties of Hindu movements grew slowly but steadily. The third period, 1965 to the present, saw a proliferation of religious and spiritual movements originating in India, due in part to the lifting of racist immigration policies, dating from the 1920s and earlier, which had made it difficult for many Asians to immigrate to the United States. These movements are based on the teachings of an ever-growing number of charismatic Indian and even some American gurus, many of whom are women.

Brief sketches of five New Hindu movements, with particular emphasis on women's roles and contributions, are presented here. The first two, Ramakrishna Mission/Vedanta Society and Self-Realization Fellowship, were founded during the second time period referred to above. The other three, International Society for Krishna Consciousness, Siddha Yoga, and Kashi Ashram, were founded during the third period. They are in no way representative but have been chosen out of dozens of likely candidates to give some sense of the variety of gender ideologies and religious beliefs and practices, as well as the importance of women in the New Hindu movements.

Ramakrishna Mission and Vedanta Society

The oldest and most influential Hindu movement in America, the Vedanta Society was founded by Swami Vivekananda (1863–1902), who also subsequently established the Ramakrishna Mission of the Ramakrishna Order, headquartered at Belur Math, outside of Calcutta, India. The spiritual ancestor of this movement was Sri Ramakrishna (1836–1886), the famous Bengali saint. Ramakrishna was an ecstatic mystic who combined an intense devotion to the Mother Goddess Kali, for whom he served as a temple priest for many years, with both esoteric tantric practice and a universalist Vedanta philosophy. He experimented with the devotion toward the cowherd deity Krishna, in which he took on the feminine persona of the milkmaid devotees, as well as with other religions such as Islam and Christianity. One of his major gurus was a woman known as the Bhairavi, a wandering tantric holy woman who initiated Ramakrishna into esoteric meditative practices involving visualization and trance. Remaining celibate throughout his life, he regarded his child-bride as an incarnation of Kali and often worshipped her. His wife, later known as Sri Sarada Devi, became a guru in the movement after Ramakrishna's death. However, Ramakrishna himself had an ambivalent attitude toward women and sexuality, often warning his disciples against the temptations of the twin evils, "women and gold."

Late in his life, Ramakrishna took on a disciple who under the name Vivekananda was to deliver his message to the world. After completing a Western-style education and spending time as a member of the rationalist reform movement Brahmo Samaj, Vivekananda sought out Ramakrishna to guide him to a personal experience of the divine.

In 1893 Vivekananda heard about a World Parliament of Religions to be held in Chicago in connection with the Columbian Exhibition. While dominated by Protestant Christians, the Parliament was the earliest attempt to provide a forum for the exchange of ideas among adherents of faiths from all over the world, including Hinduism, Buddhism, and Islam. Vivekananda arrived in the United States months before the Parliament, ran out of money, and had to beg for sustenance and, having no formal invitation, made it onto the program only after the interventions of well-wishers. His speech at the Parliament made him a celebrity. His powerful personality, oratorical skills, and exotic turban and saffron robes made him a sought-after lecturer throughout the United States in the years following the Parliament. His organizational skills and ability to synthesize the many-faceted tradition of Hinduism led to the founding of the New York Vedanta Society in 1896, followed by others in cities across the continent. A dynamic synthesis of social service and Vedantic philosophy, his message was appealing to European Americans looking for religious alternatives. Today, the message appeals equally to Hindu Indian immigrants, who increasingly comprise the membership of the Vedanta Societies.

Many of Vivekananda's most active disciples, supporters, and financers were women. One example was Miss S. E. Waldo who transcribed his 1895 lectures on raja yoga, dealing with meditative methods of "psychic control," into a book of the same name. Another was Mrs. Sara Bull, a wealthy widow who ran a fashionable salon in Boston, attracting such intellectuals as William James and the young Gertrude Stein. After dabbling in Theosophy and New Thought, she embraced Vedanta in the mid-1890s. During her life, she financed much of Vivekananda's work both in America and in India. When she died, she willed most of her substantial fortune to the Ramakrishna Mission in India. Her bequest set off a scandal in which her daughter contested the will, citing "undue influences." Lurid newspaper coverage of the story perpetuated racist stereotypes of swarthy foreign charlatans masquerading as holy men and seducing pure naive white women. Though the guru-disciple relationship is emotionally and spiritually intimate, there is no evidence of such seduction, and in fact the women attracted to Vedanta were generally well educated, capable, and independent minded.

Swami Vivekananda taught that the real nature of men and women is divine. He was radically egalitarian for his time, offering women opportunities for entering the monastic life on the basis of their spiritual qualifications, not their gender. However, Vivekananda's idealism did not always translate into practice in the various Vedanta centers; it often gave way to a more conservative status quo. The organizational structure of the movement is such that there is no overall American Vedanta Society. Instead, each Vedanta Society is governed by a local board of trustees and is under the jurisdiction of the Ramakrishna Mission in India, which posts a monk of the Order to be the spiritual guide of each society. The monks sent from India varied from progressive to reactionary along a continuum of attitudes toward traditional gender roles, both American and Indian. Disagreements over women's leadership sometimes led to schisms in the organization.

The most prominent example of such disagreement concerns Swami Paramananda (1884–1940), a close disciple of Vivekananda's, who went even farther in his commitment to gender equality than his master, giving the three highest leadership roles in his Vedanta centers to women. Two were American women who served as his next in command. They were Sister Devamata (Laura Franklin Glenn, 1867–1942), a former Episcopal lay sister who instituted a hybrid Indian-Western style of monastic discipline at the Boston Vedanta Centre.

Srimata Gayatri Devi (1906–1995) followed her uncle, Swami Paramananda, to the United States to work in his Vedanta centers. She developed a reputation as a gifted teacher, administrator, and spiritual leader. Upon her uncle's death, she assumed the leadership of the centers over the objection of the Ramakrishna Mission in India. Gayatri was the first female head of a Hindu community in the United States and led the community until her death in 1995. *Used by permission of the Vedanta Centre, Cohasset, Massachusetts.*

Sister Devamata was Paramananda's first disciple and the first Western woman ordained to teach Vedanta (1910). Her successor was Sister Daya (Georgina Jones Walton, 1882–1955), a former Los Angeles socialite and Theosophist. The third was Paramananda's Indian niece, a young widow later known as Srimata (Reverend Mother) Gayatri Devi (1906–1995), who joined the order and accompanied her uncle to Boston with the reluctant assent of her in-laws. While in India, she had been close to the Nobel laureate poet Rabindranath Tagore and had been a follower of Mahatma Gandhi. In her uncle's Vedanta centers, she developed a reputation as a gifted teacher, administrator, and spiritual leader. On one occasion when Paramananda and some of the sisters visited the Providence Vedanta Society led by his brother-monk Swami Nikhilananda, Gayatri was prevented from addressing the congregation on the grounds that she was a woman. Paramananda objected strongly, saying that surely Vivekananda would have understood. Before his death in 1940, Paramananda chose Gayatri Devi to lead his three centers (in Boston, Cohasset, Massachusetts, and La Crescenta, California), but the Ramakrishna Order headquarters in India refused to recognize her and insisted that the congregation accept a male swami posted from India. This disagreement over succession led to the withdrawal of the community from the Ramakrishna order and the establishment of a new order of Ramakrishna Brahma-Vabin, which continues to follow the tradition. Reverend Mother Gayatri Devi, the first female head of a Hindu community in the United States and the first Indian woman ordained to teach Vedanta (1927), led the community until her death in 1995. She chose as her successor an American woman, Reverend Mother Sudha Puri Devi (Dr. Susan Schrager, 1942–), the first American woman to head a Vedanta center in the Ramakrishna tradition.

Self-Realization Fellowship

Paramahansa Yogananda (1893–1952) was born Mukunda Lal Ghosh into a well-to-do Bengali family the same year Swami Vivekananda spoke in Chicago. His family's guru, Lahiri Mahasaya, was a yogi who propagated kriya yoga, a system of physical yoga postures, breathing exercises, and bodily and mental purification techniques efficiently and scientifically designed to bring about "ecstatic union with the Divine" in a very short period of time. At the age of seventeen, after experimenting with several paths, Yogananda was initiated by one of Mahasaya's disciples, Sri Yukteshwar. Both Mahasaya and Yukteshwar were disciples of the mysterious Swami Babaji, an adept who had lived in his physical body for many centuries in the Himalayas and who would appear from time to time to his devotees.

Yogananda chronicled these and many other saints whom he met on his spiritual pilgrimage throughout India in *Autobiography of a Yogi* (1946), arguably the most widely read work coming out of the new Hindu movements.

Yogananda came to America in 1920 to attend the International Congress of Religious Liberals, held under the auspices of the Unitarian Church. Soon afterward, he moved to Los Angeles, which was to become the headquarters for over 150 Self-Realization Fellowship (SRF) Centers worldwide. He remained in the United States for over thirty years until his death, the first Hindu guru to teach in the West for such an extended period of time. Yogananda was a yogi rather than a philosopher, renowned for performing miracles and "mind over matter" exercises, which he himself considered commonplace. Like his own gurus, Yogananda taught kriya yoga, which is based on the classical Indian yoga system of Patanjali. However, he packaged it a way that was palatable to Westerners, stressing its compatibility with both science and Christianity and making extensive use of marketing strategies borrowed from New Thought such as mail-order yoga courses. He taught that God was a universal spirit who could be worshipped as He or as the Divine Mother.

Yogananda's two most important female disciples were Sri Gyanamata (1889–1952) and Sri Daya Mata (1914–), the current head of SRF since 1955. Gyanamata, then known as Mrs. Edith D'Evelyn Bissett, had met Yogananda in 1924 in Seattle, where she was impressed with his magical and healing abilities. She came to live at his monastery in Mt. Washington, California, shortly before her husband's death in 1932 and shifted to Encinitas a few years later, remaining in the community until her death in 1952. Though her health was poor, she served as spiritual adviser to the nuns and sometimes took charge of the whole community during Yogananda's absences.

Daya Mata, born Faye Wright in Salt Lake City, at the age of seventeen, attended a lecture by Yogananda. She instantly recognized him as one who knew God and accepted him as her guru. She took a series of classes from Yogananda, during which time her face was swollen and bandaged due to a chronic blood disorder. Within seven days, in keeping with Yogananda's prediction, the disease had disappeared. Shortly afterward, she moved to Mount Washington and dedicated her life to Yogananda's cause. Low-key and self-effacing by nature, her own preference was to practice mediation and stay in the background, but Yogananda kept pulling her into administrative organizational work, telling her that she must also learn to serve God through right activity. Gradually, Daya Mata assumed more and more responsibility over the leadership aspects of the organization. While her family had initially opposed her decision, eventually her mother and sister became nuns at Mount Washington, and her brother became Yogananda's secretary. Little has been published about her personal life. In her own writing and in official SRF publications, she is always presented as keeping the emphasis on Yogananda and his teachings rather than on self-promotion.

International Society for Krishna Consciousness

His Divine Grace A. C. Bhaktivedanta Swami Prabhupada (1896–1977) founded the International Society for Krishna Consciousness (ISKCON). Born Abhay Charan De, he came from a wealthy Bengali family and received a Western-style education before embarking on a spiritual path, but the face of Hinduism he presented to the West was very different from that of his predecessors. Unlike them, he rejected the monistic view of the divine that sees personal deities as mere manifestations of the impersonal Divine. Instead, he embraced a form of Vaishnava devotionalism, originating with the Bengali saint Chaitanya Mahapraphu (1485–1533), who is considered to be the incarnation of Krishna, the supreme and personal Lord, and Radha, his divine consort and ideal devotee.

After spending thirty years in business, Prabhupada took renunciation and at the age of seventy came to New York where he began to preach among the drug addicts, hippies, and derelicts of the Bowery. He taught them the path of ecstatic devotion to Lord Krishna embodied in the famous mantra that begins "Hare Krishna" and encouraged them to sing and dance in the streets wearing saffron or white robes. The "Hare Krishnas," as they are popularly known, formed an exclusive cohesive community based on strict discipline (no meat, eggs, or fish; no illicit sex; no intoxicants, including caffeine; no gambling). One unique feature of this movement is that all devotees are initiated as *brahmanas,* traditionally the highest Hindu caste subject to numerous ritual responsibilities and purity restrictions. All details of life were regulated, including daily routine, arranged marriages, and education for the children in ISKCON's own schools, known as *gurukula.* Many of the devotees spent their time as missionaries, where they became a familiar sight distributing literature and soliciting donations in public places such as parks and airports. Gender roles were extremely rigid. Women were told they could only be wives and mothers; yet, ironically, many were forced to place their children in the movement's boarding schools so that they could be free to travel as missionaries or otherwise serve the temples. Formal renunciation (*sannyasa*) was closed to women, and they were excluded from becoming gurus, temple presidents, or members of the Governing Body Commission (GBC) that Prabhupada set up shortly before his death.

After the death of Prabhupada in 1977, ISKCON became embroiled in a number of controversies and criminal cases; allegations of wife abuse, child abuse, and even murder were brought forward; several major schisms and purges in the organization ensued. For the last decade or so, ISKCON has been taking stock of mistakes made in the past and has resolved to return to Prabhupada's original teachings. In response to a court case brought against ISKCON by children raised in the *gurukula* boarding schools, the organization established in 1997 a Child Protection Task Force led by senior members, social workers, and attorneys. Women devotees have begun speaking out as well. They argue that Prabhupada himself made no distinction between male and female devotees and that discrimination based on gender has no place in the movement. An example of the "new woman" is Radha devi dasi (Rebecca Corina), author of a declaration of fundamental human rights for ISKCON members (1998). A Harvard Law School graduate and practicing attorney, Radha is on the board of directors of the ISKCON North American Women's Ministry.

Although there is some evidence of women gurus in the early Chaitanya movement in Bengal, all of the initiating gurus in ISKCON are men, and whether or not women can be gurus is a hotly contested issue in the movement. It was only in the late 1990s that a few women were appointed to the Governing Body Commission. However, women's voices are being raised and heard. In response to a presentation of the ISKCON Women's Ministry, a resolution issued in 2000 by the GBC expressed regret for past mistreatment of women in the movement and affirmed "the need to provide equal and full opportunity for devotional service for all devotees in ISKCON, regardless of gender" ("Minutes").

Siddha Yoga

Swami Chidvilasananda (1954–), known more familiarly as Gurumayi (One Who Is Immersed in the Guru), is probably the most well known female Hindu guru today. She inherited her mantle from Swami Muktananda (1908–1982), who, following the command of his own guru Swami Nityananda, first came to the United States in 1970 and established the Siddha Yoga Dham of America (SYDA) Foundation in 1974. His original organization, Shree Gurudev Siddha Peeth, and ashram (spiritual community) are headquartered in Ganeshpuri, India. Before his death in 1982, he appointed both Chidvilasananda and her brother, who became known as Swami Nityananda (b. 1962), as his successors. They served as co-gurus in the movement until 1985, when Nityananda was forced to step down under circumstances that have never been fully understood.

Muktananda was a charismatic guru who taught an

eclectic blend of devotionalism and the esoteric teachings of Kashmir Shaivism, a monistic form of tantra in which the male deity Shiva is the supreme brahman but which emphasizes the dynamic activity of *shakti*, the female aspect of the Divine. Muktananda is best known for imparting to his devotees an experience called *shaktipat*, "the descent of power," a type of initiation done through glance or touch in which the devotee feels the grace of the guru, undergoes spiritual transformation, and becomes prepared to undergo further realization. Gurumayi continues this tradition and has also continued to formalize and refine the doctrinal aspects of the teaching through the recruitment of Indological scholars as devotees and the sponsoring of research on various forms of Hindu philosophy.

The two main centers of Siddha yoga in North America are in South Fallsburg, New York, and Oakland, California. When she is not on tour visiting the hundreds of Siddha yoga centers worldwide, Gurumayi divides her time between these centers and the Ganeshpuri ashram. The organization has become so large that it has lost the face-to-face intimacy between guru and disciple that characterized it in the beginning. Now the message is spread mainly through "intensives" (weekend workshops) and retreats led by senior students and through video and satellite broadcasts of Gurumayi giving teachings. The main draw, however, remains the charismatic presence of the guru, who is said to be spiritually present, even when physically absent. The goal, according to Siddha yogis, is to realize the guru as one's own higher self.

The movement attracts large numbers of women, many of whom are well-educated professionals. It also attracts a sizable number of lesbian and gay followers, drawn perhaps to the gender-neutral conception of the deity, the charismatic female guru, and the fact that a superstar of the lesbian music industry, Meg Christian, gave up her music career to become a Siddha yoga devotee some years ago. In spite of these factors, Siddha yoga, at least in its official stance, is socially quite conservative. Gurumayi has no feminist agenda, rarely speaks on women's issues, and although she has initiated a few male and female *sannyasis*, encourages her followers to form heterosexual marriages. Married heterosexual couples who visit her ashrams are allowed to share living quarters, while same-sex couples, even those with children, are not.

Kashi Ashram

The Ma Jaya Neem Karoli Baba Kashi Ashram was founded in Sebastian, Florida, in 1976 by Ma Jaya Sati Bhagavati, an American-born spiritual teacher. Though rooted in Hinduism and emphasizing the worship of the Mother Goddess Kali and tantric meditative practices, Kashi Ashram is an interfaith community sponsoring visits by religious leaders and housing shrines to all the major world religions on its lush subtropical campus. Ma Jaya is a trustee in the Governing Council of the Parliament of the World's Religion and participated in the World Parliament of Religions centennial in Chicago in 1993 and a subsequent Parliament in Cape Town, South Africa, in 1999. Ma Jaya and Kashi Ashram also have a strong social service mission with hospices for the dying, AIDS awareness and advocacy programs, antipoverty initiatives, and educational programs for children and adults. In keeping with her commitment to social justice and religious pluralism, Ma Jaya founded World Tibet Day in 1998 with Tenzin Choegyal, brother and adviser to the Dalai Lama.

Ma Jaya, born Joyce Green, grew up in poverty in a Brooklyn Orthodox Jewish family. As a young married woman on Coney Island, she began to have visions while practicing yogic breathing exercises in order to lose weight. Her first visions were of Jesus Christ carrying a cross, who told her to "teach all paths" in spite of her protestations that she was Jewish. These were followed by a series of posthumous visitations by Indian male gurus, including the sixteenth-century Sufi saint Shirdi Sai Baba; Swami Nityananda, who was the guru of Swami Muktananda, founder of the Siddha Yoga Dham discussed above; Ramana Maharshi (1879–1950), one of the most famous Vedantic saints of modern India; and finally, Neem Karoli Baba (1900?–1973), whom Ma Jaya refers to as her true Guru. She has also seen visions of the goddess Kali and other deities such as Hanuman, the monkey god. Upon establishing her ashram in Florida, she and her devotees continued their religious practice, which includes devotional chanting in Hindi and Sanskrit and intense meditative practice, drawn from the Hindu tantric tradition, which involves activating the chakras (energy centers) along the spine and guiding the *shakti* or *kundalini* (the female energy) until it unites with Shiva, the supreme reality, at the top of the head. At the same time, they initiated their social service programs. It is fitting that many of these would focus on death and dying, as the goddess Kali is mistress of the cremation grounds. Her outspokenness (which she describes as *khutzpah)* and unconventional behavior have evoked both admiration and controversy.

Of the New Hindu groups surveyed here, Ma Jaya's is the most explicitly feminist. Ma Jaya describes herself as a feminist, not of the type who excludes men but of the type who recognizes and encourages the power of women. She has run workshops for women only and for men only, as well as mixed. She has initiated both male and female *sannyasis* (renunciants), and most of the administrative officers, as well as *pujaris* (ritual temple officiants), are women. In terms of the latter, Ma Jaya has broken with traditional Hindu practice and allows the women *pujaris* to worship the images even during their menstrual periods. The rejection of this specific purity regulation is unheard of, even among the most socially progressive and egalitarian Indian Hindu religious leaders. One might attribute this to Ma's American cultural background, but the Orthodox Judaism of her childhood has similar restrictions. Also, Ma Jaya is the only New Hindu religious leader who has publicly advocated for lesbian and gay rights. She performs same-sex marriages, and although she encourages celibacy, she allows both same-sex and opposite-sex married couples to live at the ashram.

With Ma Jaya, an American-born Hindu guru, we come full circle, as she incorporates the ecstatic Kali worshipping of Ramakrishna with the social service and even the World Parliament of Religions leadership of Vivekananda.

SOURCES: Douglas Renfrew Brooks et al., *Meditation Revolution: A History and Theology of the Siddha Yoga Lineage* (1997). Diana Eck, *On Common Ground: World Religions in America* (1997), CD-ROM. Robert S. Ellwood and Harry B. Partin, "The Ganges Flows West: Indian Movements in America," in *Religious and Spiritual Groups in Modern America*, 2nd ed. (1988). Nancy E. Falk, "*Shakti* Ascending: Hindu Women, Politics, and Religious Leadership during the Nineteenth and Twentieth Centuries," in *Religion in Modern India*, ed. Robert D. Baird (1995), 298–335. Carl T. Jackson, *Vedanta for the West: The Ramakrishna Movement in the United States* (1994). Sri Daya Mata, *Only Love* (1975). "Minutes of the Annual General Meeting of the ISKCON GBC Body Society," Sri Dham Mayapur, March 2, 2000, Section 500, available at http://www.iskcon.com/Download/GBC/Resolutions/gbc_2000.txt. Karen Pechilis Prentiss, *When the Goddess Comes to Life: Encountering Female Hindu Gurus in India and the West* (2002). Radha Devi Dasi, "Fundamental Human Rights in ISKCON," *ISKCON Communications Journal* 6.2 (December 1998): 7–14. Rhada Devi Dasi, ISKCON Women's Conferences, Radhadesh, Belgium, June 28–29, 1998, New Ramana Reti, Alachua, USA, September 25–30, 1998," *ISKCON Communications Journal* 6, no. 2 (December 1998): 73–85. Richard Hughes Saeger, *The World's Parliament of Religions: The East/West Encounter, Chicago, 1893* (1995). Polly Trout, *Eastern Seeds, Western Soil: Three Gurus in America* (2001). Thomas A. Tweed and Stephen Prothero, *Asian Religions in America: A Documentary History* (1999). Paramahansa Yogananda, *Autobiography of a Yogi* (1946, 1988). Catherine Wessinger, "Woman Guru, Woman Roshi: The Legitimation of Female Religious Leadership in Hindu and Buddhist Groups in America," in *Women's Leadership in Marginal Religions: Explorations outside the Mainstream*, ed. Catherine Wessinger (1993). Also see these selected Internet sources: International Society for Krishna Consciousness, http://www.iskcon.com/, and http://www.vaisnava.net/women.htm (Women's Ministry); Ma Jaya Neem Karoli Baba Ashram, http://www.kashi.org/; Ramakrishna Order of the Vedanta Society, http://religiousmovements.lib.virginia.edu/nrms/ramakrishna.html; Self-Realization Fellowship, http://www.yogananda-srf.org/; and Siddha Yoga Meditation, http://www.siddhayoga.org/.

CHINESE RELIGIONS

RELIGIONS OF CHINESE IMMIGRANT COMMUNITIES AND CHINESE RELIGIONS PRACTICED IN NORTH AMERICA BY NON-CHINESE PEOPLE
Vivian-Lee Nyitray

RECORDS DOCUMENT CHINESE immigration to the United States as early as the 1780s, but the first great wave of Chinese immigration occurred during the California gold rush of the 1840s. Mining companies required a steady supply of reliable, cheap labor, resulting in the mass transport of contract laborers—"coolies" (*ku li,* or "bitter labor")—from China. By 1851, there were 25,000 Chinese in California, most of them having come from the southeast coastal provinces of China. By the end of that decade, demand for cheap labor had shifted to the transcontinental railroad companies, for whom the Chinese constructed the most difficult and dangerous portions of track. Chinese labor subsequently turned to agricultural development in California's Central Valley, to salmon canning in the Pacific Northwest, and to textile mills and the garment industry across the country. By 1875, there were more than 100,000 Chinese workers in the West, accounting for almost 25 percent of the workforce in California.

Under pressure from white laborers who had traveled west in search of jobs during the recession of the 1870s—and who found themselves undercut by cheaper Chinese labor—Congress passed the Chinese Exclusion Act in 1882, barring all immigration of Chinese laborers. One significant effect of the act was the perpetuation of the already large sex ratio imbalance in Chinese communities in America. During the first period of immigration, few Chinese women accompanied their husbands to the States. In the aftermath of the Exclusion Act, the court system classified all Chinese women as laborers, thus automatically denying their entry—an exclusion that extended even to the wives of resident Chinese Americans. By 1890 the male-to-female ratio of Chinese in America was twenty-seven to one.

The earliest Chinese temples in America were founded in California in the 1850s; by 1880, there were dozens of temples throughout the western states. Enshrined deities almost always included Tianhou (also known as Mazu), the Empress of Heaven. As the patron goddess of seafarers and inhabitants of coastal and riverain communities, Tianhou figures prominently in the religious history of Chinese migrants worldwide. Other significant dieties were Guangong (also known as Guandi), the god of both warfare and literature; the Jade Emperor, highest ranking of the gods; Chenghuang and Tudi, the gods of cities and of the earth, respectively;

and the Buddhist bodhisattva Guanyin (Kuan Yin), the Goddess of Mercy pledged to the support and salvation of all beings. Of economic necessity, a local temple would house multiple deities of both Buddhist and Taoist origin, their combined presence on the altar illustrating the diverse religious interests of the heterogenous immigrant community.

A prime example is the Bok Kai Temple in Marysville, California, originally constructed in 1854 at the entrance to this historic placer gold mining town located about thirty-five miles north of Sacramento. The principal god is Bok Kai, associated with water and the cardinal direction north; he is here flanked by six other deities including Tianhou and Guanyin, both of whom are focal devotional figures for Chinese women. The temple also holds a religious tablet dedicated to Jinfa, or Gold Flower Lady, a midwife-goddess whose presence demonstrates attention to the needs of the women of Marysville's early Chinatown.

The initial Chinese Exclusion Act was augmented by the 1892 Act, which added Chinese doctors and priests to the excluded category; later acts and amendments continued to tighten immigration rules until the 1924 Immigration Act essentially closed the doors to Chinese immigration. The 1892 professional exclusionary provisions adversely affected the flow of immigrant Buddhist priests to replace ill or aging priests in America. In contrast, Taoist priests, who could hold other jobs and marry, were able to train others (often family members) to carry on temple operations with relative ease. For this reason, primarily family-run Taoist institutions such as the Bok Kai Temple survived to provide religious services throughout the period of exclusion. Traditionally, temple caretakers were older men, but necessity sometimes propelled women into this capacity. They cleaned the temple grounds, maintained the incense burners, instructed worshippers and provided offering goods for them, organized feasts, and generally kept an eye on the premises. Today, female caretakers, generally elderly new immigrants who might otherwise not find employment, continue to perform these tasks in temples such as the Tien Hau (Tianhou) Temple in San Francisco.

Having embraced the Chinese as allies in the prelude to World War II, Congress repealed the Exclusion Act in 1943 and authorized the resumption of limited Chinese immigration. The American government also moved to reunite families by permitting the immigration of Chinese American citizens' wives and by passing the War Brides Act, which allowed the immigration of Chinese women who had wed American military men serving on the Pacific front. Between 1945 and 1947, 80 percent of all Chinese immigrants were women; by 1950, the male-to-female sex ratio was 1.89 to 1. Amendments to the 1952 Immigration Act in 1965 eliminated pref-

erential treatment for European immigrants. Subsequent amendments mandated a flat quota of 20,000 immigrants from any country outside the Western Hemisphere and ultimately recognized China, Taiwan, Hong Kong, and Singapore as discrete countries of origin. As a result, the U.S. resident Chinese population, which had been approximately 250,000 prior to 1965, rose dramatically—increasing tenfold to nearly 2.5 million people by the year 2000. The Chinese are the second largest immigrant group in America today, surpassed only by those coming from Mexico. It must be noted, however, that "Chinese" is not a monolithic term. Ethnic Chinese immigrants have come not only from greater China, that is, mainland China, Taiwan, Singapore, and Hong Kong, but also from Southeast Asian nations impacted by centuries of Chinese economic migration. Since 1975, a significant number of ethnic Chinese have been admitted to the United States as refugees from Vietnam, Laos, and Cambodia.

Although many of the earliest Chinatowns have disappeared, those in large urban areas have been revitalized in the wake of post-1965 reforms. Today the majority of recent Chinese immigrants, regardless of their socioeconomic status, tend to live and work in ethnically and linguistically isolated communities that continue to reflect social practices and preferences from their countries of origin. Not surprisingly, then, elements of belief and practice drawn from the entire traditional Chinese religious complex—Confucianism, Taoism, Mahayana Buddhism, and diffuse practices such as geomancy and techniques for fostering qi (vital energy)—continue to exert significant influence on the lives of Chinese women in North America.

Although few members of the Chinese immigrant community would identify Confucianism as their primary religious practice, it is clear that the tradition suffuses the culture. In the Confucian view, any individual is understood as positioned within a network of relationships that originate in the extended family and radiate outward through society. The resultant image of personal integrity as rooted in interpersonal responsibility forms the basis of the Confucian understanding of humanity. Although the philosophical core of the traditions was not fundamentally inimical to women, the historical incorporation of yin-yang theories during the Han dynasty (c. 200 B.C.E.–200 C.E.) had profound consequences for women. Yin-yang theory posits that all things are the product of the interaction of the complementary forces of yin, which is weak, passive, inauspicious, and destructive, and yang, which is strong, active, auspicious, and constructive. When this schema was incorporated into existing Confucian notions of relationships, the result was a hierarchy in which women were essentialized and identified negatively with yin qualities. Furthermore, Confucian tradition defined spousal roles and duties in the dichotomous terms of private (wife) versus public (husband), and thus a woman's role came to be understood as one of dependency and inferiority, albeit potentially tempered by her domestic value as wife and mother.

In traditional China, a woman once married was not expected to maintain close ties to her natal family. In modern Chinese immigrant families, however, especially among those more recently arrived, there is a pressing need for all children to assume responsibility for their parents and grandparents, particularly those who might have neither English-language proficiency nor a reliable source of income. Thus the core Confucian virtue of filiality ("son-ness," often translated as "filial piety") has come to encompass daughters to an ever greater extent, demanding of them lifelong emotional, material, and financial support that historically would have been directed primarily to their husband's family. In order to meet these multiple demands, familial expectation for a woman's educational achievement and professional development is strong, placing a double burden on girls and women to fulfill not only private responsibilities but, within the context of school and the workplace, public ones as well.

Beyond the deep-seated but generalized respect for Confucian virtues and familial values, there are formal institutions that specifically self-identify as Confucian, for example, the Confucius Center in Chicago or the Confucius Church in Stockton, California. Such institutions are usually administered by one or more senior men from the Chinese community and function as umbrella organizations and cultural centers. These Confucian centers typically offer language and calligraphy classes and fine arts and martial arts instruction, and they host traditional celebrations at holidays such as Confucius's birthday (Teachers' Day) and Lunar New Year. They may assist families with the maintenance of traditions relating to ancestral veneration by operating a traditional cemetery or by holding memorial ceremonies at appropriate times on the lunar calendar.

Finally, some Western and Western-trained scholars in recent years have begun to discuss Confucianism as a world religious tradition holding great promise as spiritual resource for people whose heritage is not traceable to China or to other Confucianized Asian cultures. Starting with the "Boston Confucians" surrounding intellectual historian Tu Wei-ming, North American scholars of the tradition are acknowledging in highly personal ways the impact of what is for them a vital and profoundly important religiophilosophical tradition.

Historically, the counterpart to Confucianism was Taoism, a tradition that valued yin qualities yet manifested androcentric structures of authority in its sectarian movements. It is often difficult to isolate Taoism as a distinct religious practice, and it is impossible to ac-

curately count its adherents. The more philosophical aspects of Taoism, such as reverence for the natural world and investigation of its processes, have been broadly influential and have always complemented Confucian emphases on social practice. Practical Taoist ideals, such as the cultivation of longevity and the maximizing of benefit and happiness in everyday life, are manifest not only in sectarian Taoist traditions with centuries-long lineages but in diffuse "folk" traditions ranging from martial arts to traditional medicine and *feng shui*. Devotional impulses have yielded a syncretic Buddho-Taoist pantheon wherein Taoist deities, Buddhas, and bodhisattvas are worshipped side by side, each having jurisdiction over different realms of human concern. In North American temples, it is also not uncommon to see statues and images of Confucius enshrined or displayed.

Among sectarian Taoist traditions in North America, the temples of the Fung Loy Kok Institute of Taoism are notable. Founded in 1987 by Master Moy Lin-shan of China and Hong Kong, Fung Loy Kok operates more than 200 centers worldwide. In Denver and Tallahassee, Toronto and Vancouver, Fung Loy Kok's mission is to further the teaching and practice of self-cultivation through chanting, meditation, *qigong* (techniques for fostering and conserving *qi*, or vital energy), scripture study, and visualization exercises. Devotional attention is paid to the Jade Emperor and to the bodhisattva Guanyin and also to the Taoist Immortal Lu Dong Bin. Community service is stressed as a way to promote charity for others.

Other Taoist temple communities focus their worship on Tianhou, the Empress of Heaven, and/or Guangong, the god of war and literature. As noted above, many of these temples are more accurately described as Buddho-Taoist, given their simultaneous devotion to Buddhist and Taoist sacred figures. These temples are generally small and cater to the preferences and traditions of the local immigrant community. In much the same manner as the nineteenth-century temples reflected the varied needs of immigrant Chinese hailing from different provinces, post-1965 temples reflect the new immigrant communities—pooling their resources to serve a diverse yet economically constrained population. The Tien Hou (Tianhou) Taoist Temple of Houston, for example, was established in 1986 by a group of ten Chinese and Vietnamese Taoists and Buddhists; it now counts over 500 members from the surrounding Chinese, Vietnamese, and Laotian immigrant communities. Observation suggests that most temple activities are undertaken by middle-aged or older women, but that is perhaps as much a function of available time and lack of outside employment as of relative piety.

Further complementing the historical dyad of Chinese Confucianism and Taoism were devotional and meditative forms of Buddhism. In addition to Chan

Buddhism, discussed elsewhere in this volume, of special significance to North American Chinese immigrant groups are two forms of what is called Engaged Buddhism. Engaged Buddhism is the name given to an increasing number of Buddhist groups whose focus is on the lay community's sociopolitical concerns as well as their spiritual needs. Buddhist doctrines and institutions are updated to consider contemporary issues of differential resource allocation, environmental degradation, and the status of women, children, and oppressed groups. The overall aim is to relieve the suffering of all beings worldwide. Within the Euro-American Buddhist community, prominent proponents of Engaged Buddhism include the Vietnamese Zen master Thich Nhat Hanh, Roshi Bernard Tetsugen Glassman, and Dr. Joanna Macy, but their teachings have had little impact on Chinese American Buddhists. Rather, two schools that originated in Taiwan—Fo Guang Shan Buddhism and the Tzu Chi Buddhist Compassion Foundation— count tens of thousands of North American Chinese followers.

Fo Guang Shan (Buddha's Light Mountain) was established in 1967 by Venerable Master Hsing Yun. Although Master Hsing Yun traces his lineage through the Lin-chi sect of Chan Buddhism, Fo Guang Shan is a hybrid creation blending Chan-influenced meditation with Pure Land devotionalism in order to promulgate a humanistic Buddhism. The hope is to create a Pure Land (paradise) here on earth. In just thirty years, Fo Guang Shan has grown to become Taiwan's largest Buddhist monastic order. In 1988, a daughter institution, Hsi Lai Temple ("Coming to the West" Temple), opened in Hacienda Heights, California, a Los Angeles suburb ringed by communities with significant Chinese immigrant populations. Hsi Lai is arguably the largest Buddhist temple complex in North America and has been active in expanding Fo Guang Shan's reach. A sister temple has been established in San Diego, and Hsi Lai is the American anchor for the International Buddhist Progress Society, a network of Fo Guang Shan–affiliated temples and chapters. In 1991, to complement and assist the monastic order, Master Hsing Yun also founded the Buddha's Light International Association (BLIA), a lay organization that stresses community service. BLIA is organized in more than two dozen countries and claims more than 2 million members worldwide.

With regard to women, Fo Guang Shan has the largest female monastic population of any contemporary Buddhist order. The chief administrator of Hsi Lai Temple is Venerable Abbess Tzu Jung, and Hsi Lai's resident nuns, most of them ethnic Chinese from Taiwan and Southeast Asia, clearly outnumber the monks. Master Hsing Yun maintains a strong interest in advancing female ordination across the three traditions of Theravada, Mahayana, and Vajrayana Buddhism; to this end,

in February 1988 he organized the first International Full Ordination Ceremony for monks and nuns in Bodhgaya, India, during which women were ordained in Theravadin *bhikshuni* (nuns') traditions that had been defunct for centuries. That same year, another 200 women were ordained at Hsi Lai Temple. In Taiwan, in a deliberate effort to blur the boundaries between monastic and lay populations, and to increase spiritual opportunities for women, Master Hsing Yun established an order of laywomen celibates who reside on temple grounds. At Hsi Lai, in recognition of the needs of dual-career couples and the double duty that devolves upon working wives, the temple offers child-care and elder-care programs.

Through the Buddha's Light International Association, ordinary laywomen are active in every aspect of temple affairs, although they are most visible in service rather than management capacities, for example, providing early childhood education or staffing the welcome center, the stalls selling incense and offering items, the tea room and dining hall, the museum, and the gift shop. There is a Women's Association and a predominantly female choir, and there are special short-term retreats for mothers and housewives. Although most members of BLIA are ethnic Chinese, non-Chinese members—referred to as Western Buddhists—are increasingly common and are often featured in the association's publications. Moreover, scholars have observed something of a dividing line being drawn in the congregation: Cultural activities and sutra recitations attract a predominantly Chinese population, while dharma lectures (talks on doctrine, ethics, and practice) and meditation courses have greater appeal for non-Chinese.

The second significant Engaged Buddhist group is the Tzu Chi Buddhist Compassion Foundation, founded in 1966 by Venerable Master Cheng Yen. Although less widely known than Fo Guang Shan outside the Chinese community, Tzu Chi claims a larger membership and has garnered an international reputation for its humanitarian efforts. In a phrase similar to that of Fo Guang Shan Buddhism, Tzu Chi's goal is to "expect the Pure Land in this world," a hope they nurture through their fourfold mission of charity, medicine, education, and culture. There are several dozen ordained nuns, but Tzu Chi is primarily a lay—and overwhelmingly female—organization.

In the early 1960s, as a young woman in rural Taiwan, the future Master Cheng Yen shaved her own head, ignoring centuries of novitiate training tradition in favor of getting her life's plan under way at once; she later received formal ordination from Master Yin Shun, a highly respected senior monk. Beginning with a half dozen housewives who sold handmade goods and donated a share of their daily profits, Tzu Chi has grown to be the largest charitable organization in Taiwan and claims over 5 million followers (almost all of whom are ethnic Chinese) in more than thirty countries. The vast majority of Tzu Chi members are women; the men's auxiliary, the Faith Corps, was not established until 1989. Tzu Chi's mission focuses on international relief efforts and on the provision of local medical services for the indigent. In Taiwan, the foundation has established its own hospital, medical school, nursing school, and one of the country's first hospices. Contradicting deep-seated Chinese belief about the necessity of keeping one's body intact (whether out of Confucian respect for one's ancestors or out of the folk belief that it will be needed in the afterlife), Tzu Chi also developed the first bone marrow registry in Asia along with a remarkable body donation program to provide cadavers for its medical school. In the same spirit, Tzu Chi has begun to promote global awareness of organ donation programs.

Tzu Chi lay volunteers mobilize quickly to assist in disaster relief worldwide, often cooperating with other international charitable and relief organizations. In honor of Tzu Chi's work, Master Cheng Yen was awarded the Republic of the Philippines' 1991 Ramon Magsaysay Award, the so-called Asian Nobel Prize. She remains a perennial nominee for the Stockholm-based Nobel Peace Prize. There are more than 50,000 Tzu Chi members in the United States, with dozens of branches spread across virtually every state; there are thousands more active members in Canada, notably in Vancouver.

The first American branch was founded in 1989 in southern California. It offers nursing scholarships to inner-city students in Los Angeles, conducts mobile immunization clinics for migrant workers in the farms of California's Central Valley, and crosses the U.S.-Mexico border to organize short-term medical and dental clinics in rural Mexican towns. A free clinic, opened in 1993 to serve the greater Los Angeles area, has seen more than 1,800 volunteers over the past ten years—the great majority of them women—donate their time, money, and energy to provide medical and dental care for the needy. Other American and Canadian branch offices mirror these efforts.

Despite these phenomenal successes, Tzu Chi's future is unpredictable. It seems likely that the foundation can survive the eventual passing of its charismatic founder, but the question of whether it can overcome its essentially Taiwanese character and cultivate a global character remains open. The organization maintains an extremely close affinity with Taiwan; its members worldwide are typically recent immigrants or expatriate Taiwanese corporate families. Most business and social affairs are conducted in Mandarin and/or Taiwanese, making Tzu Chi a comfortable place for those with limited English-language skills but a more daunting environment for second- or third-generation members who may have only rudimentary fluency in a Chinese language. In North America, non-Chinese volunteers are few and are typically people who have been previously helped by Tzu Chi or who have had prior exposure to the organization in Taiwan (and thus have Chinese-language skills). There are, however, a few individuals with expertise in traditional art forms, such as martial arts or Chinese chess, now teaching at Tzu Chi Humanities schools, such as those established since the mid-1990s in Los Angeles and Houston. At these schools, young children and adolescents are tutored in Chinese language and traditional customs as well as in Tzu Chi ethics and practice.

Aspects of Tzu Chi practice demonstrate the tenacity of traditional Confucian views of women. In her dharma talks, Master Cheng Yen consistently urges women to be filial to their parents-in-law, to attend to their husbands' needs, to educate and nurture their children, and to be capable housewives. The Tzu Chi Foundation retains a strongly essentialist view of women, who are understood to be naturally gentle and to have been born with compassion; thus "a mother's heart" remains the starting point for one's interactions with others. Yet at the same time, women are urged to "work like men" in their efforts to fulfill Tzu Chi's mission, and despite Master Cheng Yen's Confucian emphasis on home and family as the center of women's lives, the women who join Tzu Chi are engaged in activism that extends far beyond the traditional confines of "inner" and "private." Participation in medical outreach efforts, environmental clean-up projects, and international relief work offers women new avenues for social participation, enabling them to utilize and expand upon their existing skills as well as to learn new ones. Finally, it should be noted that even within the family, preliminary research indicates that men who participate in Tzu Chi activities adopt more egalitarian views toward household chores and child-rearing; that is, Tzu Chi membership diminishes the differentiation of household labor along traditional sex-role lines. Simultaneously conservative yet subversive, Tzu Chi is a significant spiritual resource and forum for action for Chinese women in North America.

Other, non-Buddhist, sectarian traditions are evident within the Chinese immigrant community, among them Yiguandao (I-kuan tao), sometimes discussed in scholarly literature as "the Unity Sect." Founded in 1930 in China and outlawed in both China and Taiwan for many years, the tradition draws its inspiration from a syncretic mix of Confucianism, Taoism, Buddhism, and other practices. The focal deity is the Golden Mother (known by various names, including the Golden Mother of the Jasper Pond, the Queen Mother, and the Eternal Mother), with secondary attention to the bodhisattva Guanyin and celestial Buddhas and to various gods of the traditional popular pantheon. Primary practices include meditation, the recitation of scripture, and most controversially, ecstatic communal rituals of salvation. Yiguandao's American headquarters are in Santa Monica, California. The number of adherents is difficult to ascertain. Claims of 2 million practitioners are made for Taiwan, but no reliable estimates are available for U.S. membership. As with many East Asian New religions, female authority is more readily accepted, and the spiritual status of laywomen can equal that of male devotees.

A final sectarian organization deserving of mention is Falun Gong, or Falun Dafa. Branded in China as "an evil cult," Falun Gong believers in North America have gained media attention for their protests against Chinese repression. Founder Li Hongzhi lives in exile in New York. His followers practice breathing and movement exercises, and they study his writings, a combination of Buddhist, Hindu, and apocalyptic ideas. Because there is no official membership and people often practice in their homes or in small groups, it is impossible to estimate the number of followers in North America. The Web site for the Falun Dafa Information Center in New York has links to groups in forty-five states.

Falun Gong's popularity among nonethnic Chinese is at least partially attributable to a general interest in practices known as *qigong*. *Qigong*, or "the working of *qi*," seeks to enhance the free circulation of vital energy within the body. Since 1965, nonethnic appropriation of *qi*-related practices such as *tai chi*—a series of rhythmic movements or "forms" designed to circulate one's *qi* and to develop physical and spiritual balance—has risen steadily and prepared the way for a broader acceptance of other Chinese traditions. Introduced through books such as *The Tao of Physics* and *The Tao of Pooh*, Chinese traditions perceived as conferring practical benefits have attracted increasing numbers of students from various ethnic backgrounds, along with the teachers to train them. These various martial, meditative, and medical traditions are thought to harmonize the individual with the workings of cosmic forces, collectively known as the Tao, and to thereby enhance personal happiness, success, and longevity. Many local temples, such as the Fung Loy Kok temple in Denver, house *tai chi* centers where instructors and students of all backgrounds and religious orientations practice *tai chi*. Other successful organizations, such as the network of International Healing Tao Centers, established during the 1980s by the husband-wife team of Mantak and Maneewan Chia,

Branded in China as an "evil cult," Falun Gong believers in North America have gained media attention for their protests, such as this one in Pasadena, California, against the Chinese government's repression. Founder Li Hongzhi lives in exile in New York. His followers practice breathing and movement exercises, and they study his writings, a combination of Buddhist, Hindu, and apocalyptic ideas. Because there is no official membership and people often practice in their homes or in small groups, it is impossible to estimate the number of followers in North America. *Used by permission of the San Gabriel Valley Newspaper Group.*

promulgate traditional principles but are not associated with devotional temples. In hundreds of North American communities, private martial arts academies, acupuncture clinics, and traditional Chinese medicine schools have proliferated since the 1970s. Female students are plentiful, particularly in gentler forms of practice such as *tai chi*. Nonetheless, the ranks of instructors remain overwhelmingly male, even among the nonethnic Chinese population.

Certain traditions, such as *feng shui*, have only recently but very visibly moved beyond the confines of the immigrant community. *Feng shui*, or geomancy, is the ancient art of mapping the flow and concentration of *qi* in a plot of land so as to situate graves, homes, and businesses in the most auspicious way. With large-scale Chinese immigration to certain areas such as California, New York, Vancouver, Seattle, Houston, and Toronto, mainstream builders and realtors have responded to their clients' concerns for good *feng shui*. Many firms retain *feng shui* experts of their own. The mortuary business has been similarly affected. At a 1996 University of California conference on Chinese religions in diaspora, a Chinese Protestant pastor reported that his congregation was unimpressed by the prestige and reputation of Los Angeles' Forest Lawn Cemetery, the "Cemetery to the Stars," instead strongly preferring burial in other cemeteries perceived as having more favorable *feng shui*.

Beyond the ethnic Chinese community, *feng shui* has gained an especially wide following as its application has spread from the traditional siting of graves and buildings to landscaping and interior design. Historically, Chinese *feng shui* masters were men, but in the new North American nonethnic appropriation—particularly in interior design—women figure prominently. There are now several thousand *feng shui* consultants in North America. Advice is offered on every aspect of the layout of home or business: The orientation of doors and windows, the function of particular rooms, and even the balance of colors, furniture, and accessories within the structure are all correlated with traditional yin-yang and five elements theories. The alternation of yin and yang and the rotation of the five elements (metal, wood, fire, water, and earth) are understood to influence the natural flow of *qi* in a building and, by extension, the health, wealth, and spiritual harmony of all within its walls.

As Asian Christianity is discussed in a separate essay, it can simply be noted that, owing to successful nineteenth-century missions to China and the work of home missions among early immigrant Chinese workers, Protestant Christianity has long had a significant historical presence in the Chinese American community. Today, many first- and second-generation college students, having experienced the casually Christian civil religion of American public school education, are embracing nonsectarian Protestant Christianity through the fellowship of college Bible-study groups. One exception to the dominance of Protestantism among ethnic Chinese is found among immigrants from Vietnam, where the legacy of French colonialism has kept Roman Catholicism on a nearly equal footing with devotional Buddhism. However, Chinese American Christian feminists are finding that, whatever their sectarian affiliation, Christian patriarchal ties are reinforced by the persistence of patriarchal Confucianism, thus creating a double bind for them to undo.

The history of Chinese religions in North America—from the necessarily syncretic practices of early immigrants to the contemporary diffusion of traditional practices among the broader Euro-American population—is significant but understudied. In seeking to understand that history, there is much patient, microhistorical work yet to be done, particularly if we hope to more clearly discern Chinese American women's participation in shaping the transmission and transformation of their collective tradition.

SOURCES: Information about the history of Buddho-Taoist temples in America, as well as aspects of Engaged Buddhism in North America, appears in the following collections: Pyong Gap Min and Jung Ha Kim, eds., *Religions in Asian America: Building Faith Communities* (2002); Charles S. Prebish and Kenneth K. Tanaka, eds., *The Faces of Buddhism in America* (1998); Thomas A. Tweed and Stephen Prothero, eds., *Asian Religions in America: A Documentary History* (1999); Duncan Ryuken Williams and Christopher S. Queen, eds., *American Buddhism: Methods and Findings in Recent Scholarship* (1999); David K. Yoo, ed., *New Spiritual Homes: Religion and Asian Americans* (1999); and Diana Eck, *On Common Ground: World Religions in America* (1997), CD-ROM. For the history of the earliest Taoist temples in California, see Jonathan X. H. Lee, "Journey to the West: Tianhou in San Francisco" (master's thesis, Graduate Theological Union, 2002). An illustrated history of Master Cheng Yen and the Tzu Chi Buddhist Compassion Foundation is available in English: *Lotus Flower of the Heart: Thirty Years of Tzu Chi Photographs* (1997); for more on shifting sex-role stereotypes in Tzu Chi families, see Lu Hwei-syin, "Fei guan nan nu" [Disregarding "man" and "woman"], *Tzu Chi Monthly* (March 1997): 35. Robert Cummings Neville offers an intriguing discussion of the liveliness of Confucian debate in North American academic circles in *Boston Confucianism: Portable Tradition in the Late-Modern World* (2000). Other relevant works include Richard Hughes Seager, *Buddhism in America* (1999); and although a nonacademic work, an intriguing look at the appropriation of Chinese tradition is offered by Elizabeth Moran et al., *The Complete Idiot's Guide to Feng Shui*, 2nd ed. (2002).

JAPANESE RELIGIONS

RELIGIONS OF JAPANESE IMMIGRANTS AND JAPANESE AMERICAN COMMUNITIES
Ruth M. Tabrah

WOMEN HAVE PLAYED an important but underappreciated and rarely acknowledged role in Japanese religion and culture. The traditional religions of Japan are Shinto, the indigenous polytheistic "Way of the Gods," and Buddhism. The two are closely intertwined and formed the basis of the Japanese culture brought by immigrants to Hawaii and North America more than a century ago. A controversial element of that culture was its ideal of subservience in women.

In the introduction to a book she is writing about Japanese American women, Grace Miyamoto, a Californian who has spent her married life in Hawaii, says,

> Like my mother and my grandmother before me, I was raised to be submissive, docile, conservative and obedient, "the ideal Japanese woman." Fortunately for me I grew up American and being a fairly typical teenager, I began to rebel during those difficult years. My mother and I had many arguments about hair styles, makeup, clothing, curfews, teen activities like dances, something she was not remotely familiar with.

This cultural model, which most Japanese American women refused to follow, certainly did not fit the 6 women in the first group of 141 immigrants to leave Japan. Like the men in their group the 6 women were city people, independent, and daring enough to set out from Yokohama on May 17, 1868, to work in the sugar cane fields of Maui, a destination that was a mystery to all of them. When they left Yokohama, the men cut off their topknots as a sign of farewell to the old gods. All of them, including the 6 women, made vows not to quarrel and to help each other in the new land. Because they left Yokohama one day before Emperor Meiji ascended the throne, in the usual patriarchal view of history, they were named the "First Year Meiji Men."

Not until a hiatus due to a shift in imperial power (from Tokugawa to Meiji) did immigration to the independent Kingdom of Hawaii resume. The majority who came from 1885 on were bachelors, most of them members of Japan's largest sect, Jodo Shinshu (Shin Buddhism). They were not particularly interested when the first Buddhist service was held in Honolulu in 1889 by a Jodo Shinshu minister. Ten years later, two Jodo Shinshu ministers arrived in California to serve the Japanese immigrants there. Since Americans considered

Buddhism suspect, a heathen religion of idol worshipers, Japan's consul-general in Honolulu advised Japanese arrivals to become Christians. "When in Rome do as the Romans do" was advice that most immigrants ignored. In 1898, the year that Hawaii became an American Territory, Satomi Honi and Yemyo Imamura were sent from Jodo Shinshu headquarters in Kyoto to establish the Honpa Hongwanji Mission of Hawaii. Funerals, memorial services, and occasional talks on Buddhism and its rituals had been the venue of Buddhism in Japan. Shinto shrines were where one got married and later introduced one's young children to the ancient gods. Quite differently in Hawaii and mainland America, Buddhist temples became places of spiritual support and social centers for immigrants and their "picture brides," an innovative long-distance version of an arranged marriage—one in which a young woman must be adventurous enough to risk spending the rest of her life with a stranger she knew only from his photograph.

A typical picture bride was seventeen-year-old Kiyono Doi. In childhood she had suffered a disease that left her with badly bent legs. She despaired of anyone wanting to marry her until distant relatives brought her a photo of a young man and asked if she would be willing to go to Hawaii and become his wife. Without hesitation she agreed. A photo of her was sent to the prospective groom. He sent her passage money, and Kiyono set out to cross the ocean on a slow steamer, leaving behind family and everything familiar to her. Some of the picture brides on her ship brought with them a jar of earth from the homeland. Others brought the Buddhist prayer beads common to the Japanese Buddhist tradition.

What Kiyono brought with her was the inner strength of her Buddhist faith and a capacity for hard work and endurance. She needed both in the remote Big Island district of Ka'u where her husband leased five acres in Wood Valley to become an independent cane planter. Kiyono's youngest daughter Connie remembers her mother telling her what a shock it was to have a primitive lean-to shack as her first home. Both Kiyono and Saroku Doi had been Jodo Shinshu in Japan, but in Wood Valley the only temple nearby was another denomination—Nichiren-shu. Never mind, Kiyono thought. It was Buddhist.

None of the network of temples that had been built by Yemyo Imamura, the dynamic bishop of Honpa Hongwanji Mission, was close to Kiyono Doi's new home. Had there been, she would have noticed a big difference from the temple she had attended in Japan. Bishop Imamura was Americanizing Buddhism, installing pews instead of the traditional tatami matting, introducing gatha (hymn) singing and responsive readings as part of a regular weekly Sunday service. Ministers from Japan were kaikyoshi (overseas missionaries) who spoke only Japanese. Imamura's ambition was to have services in English, so during the 1920s he sent a number of young English-speaking Nisei (second generation) to Japan to study for the ministry. In a radical departure from tradition, several young women were included. Conservatives upset by this evidently had never read Nihon Shoki, the chronicles of ancient Japanese history that state Japan's first Buddhist priest was Nun Zen-shin, a young Japanese woman ordained in 584 c.e. after a year of study in the Korean Kingdom of Silla.

Assuming that Buddhism made workers more docile, plantation bosses often donated land for temples, whatever their sect. In Japan, Jodo Shinshu temples were the property of priestly families, passed on from one generation to the next. Ownership of Jodo Shinshu's overseas temples was of necessity either the congregation, the Honpa Hongwanji Mission of Hawaii, or on the mainland, the Buddhist Churches of America (which then included Canada). As the monastic traditions of Nichiren-shu, Soto Zen, Rinzai Zen and Shingon-shu took root in Hawaii and North America, temple ownership continued with local headquarters. When the immigrant population skyrocketed, animosity of Americans increased. In California Japanese immigrants lived under the threat of the Chinese Exclusion Laws. In Hawaii a "Gentleman's Agreement Act" made in 1907 between Japan and the United States raised worries among the Issei (first generation) that their island-born children would be denied the citizenship that was their birthright, a status guaranteed every child born in the Territory of Hawaii. The agreement restricted emigration from Japan to Hawaii for a sixteen-year period ending in 1924. Only picture brides and immigrants related to those already living in Hawaii were to be allowed entry.

During the 1920 strike by Japanese plantation laborers, anti-Japanese sentiment peaked. The Hawaii Sugar Planters Association demanded elimination of the Japanese-language press and closure of the language schools immigrant children attended for an hour and a half every day after public school. Hawaii's Haole (Caucasian) leadership, once so supportive of Bishop Yemyo Imamura, reviled him for sympathizing with the strikers. They filed a lawsuit aimed at closing the language schools, but on February 21, 1927, when the case reached the U.S. Supreme Court, the justices decided in favor of the Buddhists, saying loyalty to America and the religious values of Buddhism were being taught, not loyalty to Japan. America's Freedom of Religion Act had been put to the test. Language schools remained open. All of Kiyono Doi's ten children attended the one taught by the Nichiren priest and his wife.

The Court's favorable decision intensified anti-Japanese prejudice. Strangely enough the Japanese themselves were prejudiced against Okinawan immigrants who to outsiders looked Japanese. Yasuko Matsunaga, an Okinawan (Ryukyu Islander) Nisei who grew up in the plantation community of Kekaha, Kauai, reminisced in an interview how this prejudice affected her and her family. Social support for her parents came from Okinawan neighbors and "from *tokoro mono*, people who came from the same village or area of Okinawa." As to spiritual support, Yasuko's parents were sustained by the belief systems they had grown up with in Okinawa, principally the belief in a life after death and continuation of family relations after death. "I'm not sure if it was Shinto or Buddhist," she says, "but my parents had a *kamisama dai* [gods' shelf] where they offered rice and either tea or water."

I converted to Christianity when I was in the sixth or seventh grade. The fact that my parents were not strong committed members of the Buddhist church made it easier for them to accept my conversion. My mother, particularly, was aware of and open to change but she once mentioned to me that my grandmother, whom I had never met, came to her in a dream and spoke of her unhappiness and concern about my becoming so different from them, that is, a Christian. I could understand my mother's concerns as expressed in her story of this dream so there was no anger in my response to her that there were certain areas in a person's life where not even a parent, much less a grandparent, had a right to interfere. I told her that this was such a case. The matter was purely between God and me. She heard me out and then said, "That's probably true." I don't remember opposition from either of my parents after that.

As a child I thought of Haoles as a race apart, richer, superior, our bosses. The Second World War with its influx of hundreds of GI's helped to change my perception. I was only a sixth grade kid but I realized there were all kinds of Haoles, many of them without money or education. As an Okinawan child the prejudice I felt from *Naichi* [those from the islands of Japan] touched me

In Hawaii and on the mainland, Buddhist temples became places of spiritual support and social centers for immigrants and their "picture brides," an innovative long-distance version of an arranged marriage. These young "picture brides," who are being processed at Angel Island immigration station in San Francisco, California, will meet and marry men who are strangers and who they will only know by their photographs. *Courtesy of State Museum Resource Center, California State Parks.*

more personally and deeply. We were teased for eating pork, for being hairy, etc. Generally these prejudices were kept on a sub-surface level. We had many friends among the *Naichi* girls but the feelings and attitudes were there and we all knew it. When, after I graduated from the University of Hawaii, Richard (a *Naichi*) and I announced we were getting married, my worried parents insisted on a meeting with his grandmother and uncle before anything was finalized. They wanted assurance from his family elders that I would be accepted and welcomed into the Matsunaga family. Fortunately, all worked out well.

During the war Hawaii's 139,000 Japanese were such a substantial proportion of the population that even in the anti-Japanese hysteria following the attack on Pearl Harbor, there were simply too many Americans of Japanese ancestry to be incarcerated. They were, in addition, too valuable as members of the workforce. In their panic to prove they were Americans, many became Christians. A few Buddhist lay leaders and almost all Buddhist and Shinto priests were arrested and sent to internment camps on the mainland. All Shinto shrines and all but one or two Buddhist temples were closed. A number were used by the military as barracks and offices. Otherwise, except for the ugly intolerance and discrimination against them, Hawaii's Americans of Japanese ancestry were not uprooted, their property and bank accounts were not confiscated, and they were spared the humiliating devastation of the camp experience. On the mainland only those in interior communities like Arizona, where immigrants had been farming since 1909, and those who moved inland, like Grace Miyamoto's large group of family and friends, were among the very few who were spared. Early in 1942 in northern California, on learning that all Japanese Americans on the West Coast faced incarceration, Grace's father leased farmland in Keetley, Utah, forty miles from Salt Lake City, where for the duration of the war he relocated his family, relatives, and many friends. Most of their Mormon neighbors were friendly, but even so the group was threatened with bombs thrown on the property.

Those who remained on the West Coast were taken to remote desert camps encircled with barbed wire, guarded by soldiers with sharp bayonets. The four years of internment were difficult beyond imagining for both Buddhists and Christians. Bitter memories of their wartime experience led many returnees to retreat after 1945 into the protective social cocoon of understandably ethnocentric temples and churches. One important exception was a surge of revitalized Jodo Shinshu in the Berkeley, California, Buddhist Temple where Reverend Kanmo Imamura, son of Hawaii's pioneer bishop, at-

tracted young, enthusiastic Japanese Americans and non-Japanese like Jack Kerouac, Gary Snyder, and Philip Whalen to his Buddhist Study Center. A vigorous partner in his outreach to new people was his wife, Jane Matsuura Imamura. In 1949 Kanmo Imamura opened the Institute of Buddhist Studies, a Jodo Shinshu seminary that today is a degree-granting member of the Graduate Theological Union.

Regrettably, the end of the war did not end anti-Japanese prejudice. Buddhist author Mary Wada Roath remembers, "When I was a child my mother and I were walking in downtown Los Angeles when a woman came up and spat in my mother's face. The same thing happened in the 1980's when I was crossing a street. A man walking towards me spat at me." Such instances were rare in Hawaii. There the worst aftereffect of the war years was a sharp decline in membership of all Japanese Buddhist sects. Those who had become Christian to prove they were American tended to remain so. The population drain of families leaving for better jobs and living conditions in Honolulu closed many small temples in plantation communities on the neighbor islands. However, for individuals like Kiyono Doi's youngest daughter, new opportunities for education opened in these same communities, changing their future. To solve a teacher shortage, the University of Hawaii had sent idealistic student teachers who drilled students in English until they had no trace of a pidgin accent and moved them from learning by rote to innovative approaches. When Connie Doi graduated from high school and told her parents she wanted to go to college, her father's reaction was, "Girls don't go to college," but her mother Kiyono encouraged her daughter: "If you want to go, find a way."

The way for her and countless others was summer employment at Honolulu's Dole Pineapple Cannery. Free boat transportation for neighbor islanders, free room and board, and good wages enabled a student to earn enough to attend the University of Hawaii, where many from Buddhist families were exposed to and became Christian. In the postwar years the GI Bill armed veterans of Japanese ancestry with degrees in medicine, dentistry, law, business, and political science so that by Hawaii's statehood in 1959 island veterans became a major force in professions and careers from which they had formerly been restricted. This broad social change, affecting the lives of Japanese American women as well, was not mirrored in temple organization. Even the once progressive Jodo Shinshu had, since the death of Yemyo Imamura in 1932, retreated into conservative ritual that gave little insight into the rich doctrinal treasures of Shin Buddhism. Yet in the 1950s the sect had a cadre of young members who ardently supported the Young Buddhist Association, pioneered in encouraging a Jodo Shinshu fellowship in Berlin, Germany, and petitioned

Jodo Shinshu's headquarters in Kyoto to provide an English translation of the Seiten, the writings of their founder Shinran whose "True Pure Land" version of Mahayana Buddhism opened the gate of enlightenment to all beings, both monk and laity. Translation of Shinran's writings was the prelude to new activity inspired by Kanmo Imamura when, in the 1960s, like his father before him, he became Hawaii's bishop. Under him, more young Americans of Japanese ancestry returned to Buddhism. His wife Jane was equally inspiring. "Imagine! A minister's wife who reads *Time* Magazine!" marveled one young Buddhist who was also thrilled when, in 1975, a Buddhist Study Center opened in an old house adjacent to the University of Hawaii campus. The center quickly became a gathering place for students and a magnet drawing all ages to its two-week summer sessions featuring speakers like Dr. Rita Gross, who in 1985 gave a two-week seminar on "Buddhism and Feminism." In 1989, in celebration of its centennial, Honpa Hongwanji Mission of Hawaii built a handsome new center on the same site and plans one day to have a pan-Buddhist seminary.

Hawaii's liberal difference impressed native Californian Reverend Joan Ishibashi during her fourteen years as a Christian minister there. In June 2000 she was promoted to executive associate with Wider Church Ministries, a Covenanted Ministry of the United Church of Christ in Cleveland, Ohio. A Sansei (third-generation) Japanese American, Buddhism was not her family background. Both her parents were kibei Nisei, Americans of Japanese ancestry who had been sent to Japan to be educated. Her father returned from Japan in 1941 with severe tuberculosis. During the war he was interned in a sanitarium where the only visitor he had was a Quaker missionary. "Through her," says Reverend Ishibashi, "he was exposed to Christianity. Through him, my Mom was converted. They never fully understood the tenets of Christianity so we still celebrated Obon [the Buddhist midsummer festival of joyous respect for the ancestors]." Her parents joined a Japanese Christian church close to their home in suburban Los Angeles

so we could interact with other Japanese Americans. I think the cultural stuff was more important to my parents than the faith stuff. My sister and I attended Japanese language school at the church and we even prepared for the Little Tokyo Los Angeles Obon by learning the dances at church. Included in the teachings and sermons of our Christian church was our struggle to understand what it means to be a minority in a majority culture. My family was baptized together so I was brought into the Christian faith by my parents.

The only place I saw other AJA's was at church, which is one of the reasons we joined. I did not feel different in terms of religion. All my friends were Christian. But I did feel different being Japanese and was constantly teased about that.

Far beyond "teasing" was the ugly anti-Japanese prejudice she and her family experienced.

Back in the 1940's, because he was Japanese, my father was refused medical care in a hospital in Bakersfield, California. In 1959, a petition signed by people living in the neighborhood where my family wanted to move was given to the person who wanted to sell us his house, telling him they did not approve of him selling his house to us. They did not want us moving into their neighborhood because we are Japanese. In the late '70's, when I was in seminary in Washington, DC, a man came driving toward me like he was going to run me over and screamed at me, "You fucking gook!"

Less devastating but still personally disturbing was the refusal of her mother-in-law in Nebraska to display Joan's picture in her house even though she had pictures of everyone else.

Things were different when Joan became the minister of a Christian church in Hawaii in 1986. "It was the first time I had lived in a place where there was a large Japanese population. It was quite liberating for me after having lived in California, Nebraska, Maryland, and New Jersey. Although I was once refused service in a restaurant in Waikiki, I think it was because I was with an African-American man." She is an outspoken feminist who challenges the old model of an ideal Japanese woman and points out that this still affects how others see her. "While my Caucasian and African American colleagues here in Ohio and back East see me as quiet and 'sweet,' my AJA friends think I tend to be loud and outspoken. Both my sister and I are independent and my parents have preferred having daughters like that." Neither her ethnicity nor her gender hindered steady advancement in her denomination. Joan Ishibashi became one of the leading Japanese American Christian women in America.

Both ethnicity and gender continued to be a hurdle for women who wished to become ministers in Buddhist Churches of America. They were expected to avoid "making waves" as did Rev. Carol Himaka, one of Buddhist Churches of America's three women clergy. In 1993 she knew she was risking her career by filing a sexual harassment suit against a fellow minister whose obscene overtures were abhorrent to her. A lawsuit was the only channel open to her in the church's tight, male-dominated hierarchy. In filing a suit she knew she would be reviled and condemned by her male colleagues, but that was the least of it. She had been director of the Office of Buddhist Education. The powerful weapon used against her by Buddhist Churches of America's National Council was their closure of that office, a move that left her without a job. She tried to amend her lawsuit, charging unfair retaliation. To the dismay of her many lay supporters, the court dismissed her entire suit. She was left in limbo until the bishop made the unprecedented announcement in a 1996 issue of Buddhist Churches of America's newsletter, *Wheel of Dharma*, that the power to hire or fire ministers was in the hands of each individual temple. This was a chance seized by Enmanji, a liberal Jodo Shinshu temple in Sebastopol, California. They immediately fired the minister whom they had long petitioned the bishop to remove and hired Reverend Carol Himaka. She was still there as Buddhist Churches of America, still a male-dominated hierarchy, began a second century in America.

The liberalism that impressed Joan Ishibashi in Hawaii is exemplified in the ministry of Jodo Shinshu's Reverend Jan Youth, a Kauai native and former educator who switched careers in midlife. She is a trailblazer working in socially engaged Buddhism as hospital, hospice, and prison chaplain and in ecumenical networking with other Buddhist sects, with all kinds of Christians, with local rabbis, and representatives of Hawaii's diverse religious communities. One of five fully ordained women ministers in Honpa Hongwanji Mission of Hawaii, Jan tells her story with characteristic humor, sincerity, and enthusiasm. Her decision to become a minister was a spontaneous one made in 1989 when she signed up for a course at Honolulu's Buddhist Study Center. Participants were told that if they so wished, the course might lead to qualifying for training to receive *tokudo*, the ritual by which one is ordained as a Shin Buddhist priest In the interview given those registering for the course, Jan was asked "Would you consider becoming a minister?" She impulsively answered, "Yes," resigned from her position in Hawaii's Department of Education and went off to the Institute of Buddhist Studies in Berkeley for two years.

For her, ministry has been an exhilarating career change and yet in many ways not a distinct one. She sees little difference between her former career as educator and her present one as minister:

The only real change is that I now wear a different uniform (black priest's robe and colorful surplice). What I see as the whole purpose of both education and Buddhist ministry is to help people gain insight into their lives and the meaning of life itself.

That's the *bodhisattva* role, to enable them to awaken to their own enlightenment.

While she was studying for the ministry in Berkeley, her high school graduation class was about to hold a reunion in Las Vegas. "You better go," a friend advised, "because when you get to be a minister you can't be seen in a casino." Needless to say, Jan rejected that advice. Her two years on the mainland convinced her that "those in Buddhist Churches of America as well as Japanese Americans in general retain more of Japanese culture than I do. Even the temples on the Mainland seem to be archives of Japanese culture. By contrast," she muses, "Hawaii is a breakaway place, exploring new universal dimensions in Shin Buddhism."

Despite a continuing decline in membership Shin Buddhism is still the largest Buddhist sect in Hawaii and one of the most progressive, welcoming the flood tide of Buddhist immigrants from Southeast Asia that followed the Immigration Act of 1965. The impact on Hawaii was minimal compared to the huge numbers of new Southeast Asian, Korean, and Chinese immigrants swelling mainland America's Buddhist population. About the same time Soto Zen and Rinzai Zen, neither of which had made much of an impact on Japanese immigrants, began to attract large numbers of Caucasians and some African Americans. Zen centers sprang up in such unlikely places as Wichita, Kansas, Atlanta, Georgia, and St. Paul, Minnesota. In the summer 2000 issue of *Tricycle*, Anne Simpkinson in her article "Riding Two Horses" says of this phenomenon, "In America Japanese Buddhism has a new face and a new feel. Meditation halls are arranged in an egalitarian circle, a nod to Native American Council Meetings." It is a circle that, unlike traditional Zen, includes men and women but few Japanese Americans like Wendy Egyoku Nakao, abbot of the Zen Center of Los Angeles, one of America's leading Buddhist teachers.

In a 1998 talk given at the North American Conference of Buddhist Women in Claremont, California, and reprinted in the spring 1999 issue of *Turning Wheel*, the abbott said, "When we sit in a circle, there's a flattening of the hierarchy. Everyone gets heard and everyone realizes the tremendous wisdom and compassion that is inherent in every single person, not just the teacher. We have learned that our diversity is not a problem. It's our strength." Nakao grew up on the Big Island of Hawaii, "in a Japanese-Portuguese family, and my koan was: how can I be both? My Portuguese friends talked a lot and laughed a lot. My Japanese friends were much quieter. Where did I belong? I agonized over this true-life koan of mine. I was still agonizing when I was in my twenties and one day a friend said to me, 'You're so lucky to be both.' Then I realized the obvious. I am all of it. The diversity is me."

Diversity is now the hallmark of the Buddhism brought to America by Japanese immigrants, but Shinto, Japan's indigenous, polytheistic "Way of the Gods," is no longer flourishing in America. Only a handful of Shinto shrines still exist in Hawaii and on the mainland. Another profound change is in traditionally monastic Buddhist sects such as Tendai, Shingon, and Nichiren-shu. They have followed the practice initiated by Jodo Shinshu's founder, the thirteenth-century Japanese monk Shinran who took a wife and raised a family of six children, forging a new identity as both monk and layperson. Although membership in Buddhist Churches of America and Honpa Hongwanji Mission is still declining, Buddhism is now said to be the fastest growing religion in America. Like Zen, Tibetan Buddhism is extremely popular among Euro-Americans. The Nichiren temple in Wood Valley, near Kiyono Doi's old home in the Big Island's remote southern district of Ka'u, has become a Tibetan Buddhist center often visited by the Dalai Lama. An increasing number of Americans, male and female, are shaving their heads, donning saffron-colored robs, and taking vows as monks and nuns in the monastic Buddhist traditions of Southeast Asia.

Numbers of those in the United States whose forebears condemned Buddhism are now Buddhists themselves, while most of the grandchildren of Japanese immigrants are no longer so. Until recently, many Americans of Japanese ancestry who remained Buddhist relegated their religious commitment to attendance at funerals and memorial services. Many of those who are Christian, Protestants and Catholics, tend to regard their church membership as more social than spiritual, although many embrace charismatic preachers, fundamentalist services, and sects like Jehovah's Witnesses. Others, like Rosemary Goto, a Jodo Shinshu minister's daughter, have chosen Hinduism's Siddha Yoga as their spiritual path. Mary Beth Nakade of Kona is a wife and mother who is training at her home temple, Daifukuji, for the traditional Soto Zen ministry.

No one is sure how many Japanese Americans are without religious affiliation. There are no reliable statistics on the diverse "new" religions of Japan such as Risso Koseikai, an offshoot of Buddhism that is followed by contemporary Americans of Japanese ancestry. In Hilo, Hawaii, committed Christian Yasuko Matsunaga estimates Hilo Hongwanji has more members than any Christian church in the Big Island city of Hilo. In Honolulu, the Hawaii Association of International Buddhists is an active group to which all leaders and some members of the twenty-nine diverse Buddhist groups in Hawaii belong. The current president is Japanese American abbot Irene Matsumoto of Palolo Kuan Yin Temple. Two past presidents have been Jodo Shinshu. In Hon-

olulu's Hawaii Betsuin, the magnificent temple built by Yemyo Imamura in 1916, among the 2,000 predominantly Japanese American members are most of Kiyono Doi's children and grandchildren. Three of her great-grandchildren attended Hongwanji Mission School, which since 1949 has been the only Buddhist elementary school in the United States.

Like every immigrant group in America, today's Americans of Japanese ancestry are proud of their cultural heritage and at the same time totally American in lifestyle, allegiance, and family values. As to the old ideal of a Japanese female, Hawaii's late Congresswoman Patsy Takemoto Mink, a Sansei (third-generation) Christian, said in an interview with the author of this essay, " 'Oriental' women like myself are not naturally submissive or subservient. I grew up believing I could do anything!" She spoke for the vast majority of Japanese American women who, like Japanese American men, tend to choose non-Japanese spouses, excel in a wide range of careers, live in pluralistic communities like Washington, D.C., New York City, Los Angeles, San Francisco, Chicago, and Honolulu, and enjoy the aesthetics of Japanese culture. Few of them understand or speak the Japanese language.

What has been ongoing and remarkable among these descendants of Japanese immigrants has been their respect for the diverse religions transmitted through the personal example and leadership of women like Wendy Egyoku Nakao, Patsy Takemoto Mink, Mary Wada Roath, Jane Imamura, Grace Miyamoto, Yasuko Matsunaga, Joan Ishibashi, Jan Youth, Carol Himaka, Rosemary Goto, and Mary Beth Nakade and, in their own caring way, by picture brides like Kiyono Doi.

SOURCES: Connie Doi Fukumoto and Rosemary Tamekuni Gogo, who are quoted and whose stories are told in this essay, were interviewed in person. Those who are quoted and told their stories via email interviews were Yasuko Matsuura, Grace Miyamoto, Joan Ishibashi, Carol Himaka, Jan Youth, Mary Wada, and Mary Beth Nakade. Quotes and information about Abbot Wendy Egyoku Nakao were taken with her permission from her article "Trust Yourself" sent the interviewer by Mary Beth Nakade. The quote from late Congresswoman Patsy Takemoto Mink was given in a telephone interview in 2000. References to Jane Matsuura Imamura were based on the knowledge and memory of the author's personal friendship. Specific reference to a woman being the first Japanese Buddhist priest was from *Nihongi: Chronicles of Japan from the Earliest Times to A.D. 697*, translated from the original Chinese and Japanese by W. G. Aston, 2 vols. in one (1972). For general background the author of this essay relied on Marianne Dresser, ed., *Buddhist Women on the Edge: Contemporary Perspectives from the Western Frontier* (1996); Ellison Banks Findly, ed., *Women's Buddhism/Buddhism's Women, Tradition, Revision, Renewal* (2000); and Karma Lekshe Tsomo, ed., *Buddhist Women across Cultures: Realizations* (1999). For the history of

Japanese Americans in Hawaii, the resource was The States and the Nation Series Bicentennial library volume *Hawaii, a History*, by Ruth M. Tabrah (1980). Personal observation and participation are also the basis for the reference to Dr. Rita Gross's 1985 seminar on "Buddhism and Feminism" at Honolulu's Buddhist Study Center. She made a lasting impact on those who attended, 90 percent of whom were Japanese Americans, female and male.

OTHER RELIGIONS

WOMEN AND JAINISM IN NORTH AMERICA
Anne Vallely

JAINISM IS AN ancient and enduring tradition whose origins scholars trace to the sixth century B.C.E. Jains contend that their tradition, which has no creator God but claims that all living beings have godlike souls, is beginningless and eternal. Jainism is not widely known outside India, yet its maxim "Ahimsa Paramo Dharma" (nonviolence is the supreme path) has had a major influence on many religions, including Christianity. Women tend to dominate religious practices, and they enjoy a status that is unparalleled among other religious traditions in the Indian subcontinent.

Why the Jain tradition is not better known in the West is difficult to say. Perhaps it is because the Jain community is numerically small, or because its followers never sought to convert others. Jain religious practices are also arduous and forbidding. The possessionless and egoless itinerant ascetic, wandering from region to region with no attachments to person, place, or thing, is an unlikely North American hero. Yet, for the Jain community, the ascetic represents the highest spiritual ideal. Each year, the Jain diaspora community invites ascetics from India to spend time with them, in the hope that their presence will inspire and reinforce the community's commitment to its ancient values.

Jainism in North America is being transformed into a transnational religious entity, drawing upon the symbolic and cultural capital of India and at the same time adapting to its new sociocultural environment. Out of this interplay between traditional ascetic values and the unequivocally nonascetic culture of North America, a new form of Jainism is emerging. One of the most significant outcomes of this cultural negotiation may be its effect on women, since ideals of femininity and women's roles have traditionally been defined through the parameters of ascetic practice.

The cultural heroes of the Jain tradition have always been those courageous women and men who renounce worldly life to pursue a spiritual path of nonviolence. And—as has been the case throughout history—three times as many women adopt this path as do men. Although the overall number of ascetics is small, representing just a tiny fraction of the total community, the ideal that they embody defines the community's distinctive character.

Newcomers to North America, the composition and character of these roughly 60,000 Jains are still very much in flux. Even though Jains have been immigrating to North America since the late nineteenth century, no self-perpetuating community existed until the 1970s when the laws of the United States and Canada (formerly restrictive to non-Europeans) opened up to Asians. In the early years, home shrines served the community's needs, but by the 1980s temples were being erected throughout North America to accommodate the community's growing numbers. In 1981 an umbrella association called "JAINA" (Jain Associations In North America) was established as a nonsectarian organization to foster and support these communities. The association now comprises fifty-seven Jain societies that support youth activities, schools for religious learning (*pathshalas*), annual pilgrimages to India (*yatra*), interfaith activities, and matrimonial information services. Its most important function is a biennial socioreligious convention that attracts thousands of Jains from all over North America.

The geographical and cultural distance from India has been an impetus to adapt beliefs, practices, and organizations. For example, sectarianism has become a contentious issue in North America: The Jain tradition is composed of two major sects, called the Svetambara and the Digambara, each with their own ascetic traditions. The historic differences between the two are doctrinal in nature, stemming from different interpretations of ascetic practice, but they also tend to overlap linguistic and geographic divisions. Discord now exists between those who want to retain a sectarian heritage and those who are working to create a nonsectarian Jainism in North America.

There are no fully fledged ascetic orders outside of India, and their absence in North America is associated with the advent of a more fluid and less doctrinal form of Jainism. Ascetics act as powerful symbols of the tradition, and their presence ensures the continuation of orthodox practices. Without them, a wider variety of religious beliefs and practices is possible, allowing formerly established ideas of what constitutes an ideal Jain life to be debated and broadened.

In India, being a pious Jain woman (whether lay or ascetic) is demonstrated through behavioral purity—restrained bodily demeanor, self-control, religious devotion, and fasting. From a young age, a girl is instructed in the fundamentals of Jainism by a female family member. She begins to fast periodically, learns in minute detail food limitations, performs rituals, and is expected to visit the female ascetics (*sadhvis*). Religion becomes the primary means through which female integrity is demonstrated, and the religious life of laywomen is essentially ascetic in its ethos. For many Jain girls in India, especially those in conservative areas of the country (e.g., in Rajasthan and Gujarat), marriage or becoming a *sadhvi* are the only viable options. In North America, by contrast, renunciation is not a realistic, or desired, choice. And, for most, marriage is but one of many opportunities and not an end in itself.

The Pious, the Traditionalist, and the Unorthodox: Three Women in North America

Samaniji Mangalpregya, Paulomi, and Inaya all identify with the Jain tradition, and each considers her life to be guided by its teachings. Samaniji Mangalpregya is an ascetic from India, currently living in New York. Her purpose in coming to the United States was to inspire the Jain community here to greater piety. She has no possessions—neither home, money, nor belongings. Her daily life is a series of carefully considered acts—meditating, preaching, "begging" for alms—each performed mindfully, so as not to cause violence and to accrue karma. She seeks the highest and most ancient goal of Jainism, namely, transcendence of worldly existence. This otherworldly ethos has come to occupy a backseat as Jainism takes root in North America. The ascetic teachings of egolessness and nonattachment have locked horns with the rather antagonistic values of a culture where identity is often defined by what is "possessed" and where ego aggrandizement is a cultural norm. For Paulomi and Inaya—two young Jain women who have been reared in North America—renunciation is inconceivable and, perhaps more important, not greatly esteemed. Yet both define themselves as "Jain" and consider the development of North American Jainism to be as authentic and legitimate as that found in India.

THE PIOUS

Samaniji Mangalpregya ("Samaniji" for short) sits cross-legged in a simple white sari. Each morning, she wakes before dawn in New York City, just as she does in the village of Ladnun, Rajasthan, her hermitage in India. As in India, her day will be a discipline of mindfulness: Every word she speaks and every move she makes will be done with great care. Her message is always the same: A life of nonviolence and nonattachment is the only way to rise above the petty worries and selfishness that characterize human existence. A full social life with husband, children, friends, and wealth never tempted her. Ever since she was a little girl, Samaniji wished only for a life of spirituality and tranquility. At the age of sixteen she entered into a "training school" that prepares young girls for ascetic life. There she gradually learned to give up her attachments to things, to places, to ideas, even to family members.

Ascetic discipline came easier to Samaniji than to many. She gained inner peace through relinquishing attachments and discovered that her aptitude made her a natural mentor to the other girls. In 1985 she took initiation into the ascetic order as a *samani*, a title that means equanimity and restraint. *Samani* is a category of ascetic with less rigorous demands than that of a *sadhvi* and was created to allow ascetics to travel outside of India. In fact, strict vows of nonviolence prohibit *sadhvis*

For many Jain girls in India, marriage or becoming a *sadhvi* are the only viable options. In North America, by contrast, renunciation is not a realistic, or desired, choice. And, for most, marriage is but one of many opportunities, not an end in itself. Like many young Jain women, Paulomi is charting new ground and does not see herself as neatly fitting into either of Jainism's two traditional female vocations: that of an ascetic or homemaker. *Courtesy of Anne Vallely.*

from traveling by any means other than by foot, so preclude the possibility of these ascetics visiting the diaspora communities. The creation of the *samani* category enables these semiascetics to travel abroad freely and reach Jain communities wherever they may be. It also allows them more time to pursue scholarly interests. Samaniji, who received her M.A. in Jainology and comparative philosophy at the age of twenty-five, is an associate professor of Jainology at the Jain Vishva Bharati Institute in Rajasthan. Because of her proficiency in English, oratory skills, and scholarly knowledge, she travels the globe as a representative of Jainism. She spends long sojourns among Jain congregations in North America in the hope of kindling the spirit of nonviolence and nonattachment in the harried and spiritually besieged communities.

In spite of being away from India, and away from her guru, Samaniji maintains her daily routine and vigilance. Waking well before dawn each morning, "the most tranquil time of the day," Samaniji moves slowly as she settles into a lotus position and begins her meditation. As spontaneous, unmonitored activity leads to the death of countless living beings that surround us at all times, she wears a mouth-shield to prevent harming subtle beings in the air and as a reminder to refrain from speaking violent words. Her preoccupation with not harming any life form—however small—is rooted in the Jain cosmology and rigorous ethical system.

Jainism posits a fundamental division of all existing things into two categories: that which has a soul, called *jiv*, and that which is devoid of soul, called *ajiv*. All living beings have souls, whether they be in the form of a blade of grass, an insect, an animal, or a human being. And all are in karmic bondage. *Ajiv* represents physical matter, also called karma, that attaches to the soul and shackles it. The soul, hindered from realizing its true and eternal nature, will go through a continuous cycle of death and rebirth until it attains *moksha*, or spiritual liberation. The only way out of this cycle is to free the soul from bondage; this can be achieved only through an ascetic life of total nonviolence.

Once the sun has risen, Samaniji can move about freely. As in darkness, even cautious movements may inadvertently cause harm to unseen beings. Before changing from her night to day sari, she performs *pratilekhna*—the meticulous inspection of her clothes and objects around her for tiny life forms. Once dressed, she will continue her meditation. Later the host of the home where she is a guest will offer her something to eat. Jain ascetics cannot prepare their own food. Plants, water, fire, electricity—all the things necessary for cooking—are considered alive. So to cook any food involves violence. This is unacceptable. Since all aspects of physical reality are imbued with life, the harm done to any one of these lives results in karmic inflow. In India ascetics are even forbidden from accepting food if it has been prepared expressly for them, because this would implicate them in the violence involved in food preparation. Instead they wander through villages, begging for alms, and only accept leftover food from strictly vegetarian families.

But for Samaniji, the exigencies of living in North America require her to accept food that has been prepared for her. Nevertheless, she carries out the rite as faithfully as possible: She will enter the kitchen with her begging bowl, just as she would in India, and accepts only a small portion of properly prepared vegetarian food.

For the remainder of her day Samaniji will teach meditation and relaxation techniques, give lectures at colleges and religious centers, visit families, and counsel individuals. Her presence is in great demand; the diaspora community has so few opportunities to meet with ascetics that all try to benefit from her presence.

From the ascetic perspective, America is a land of materialism, violence, and sexual impropriety—a land where the Jain community is besieged with temptations to sin. Samaniji sees her mission as providing inspiration for (and occasionally chastening) the community through the example of her own piety. In India, she receives considerable reverence and respect, possessing a degree of prestige and authority that is rare for women in society. Indeed, the prominent status of female ascetics within Jainism is remarkable and highly atypical of other religious traditions in India. In North America, Samaniji's popularity stems less from her prestige as an ascetic than it does from her ties to tradition. Many within the community, especially first-generation immigrants, are concerned about the dilution of traditional values and eagerly support visits by ascetics. Most of the younger generation do not have the appetite for sermons on the minutiae of *ahimsa* or the karmic repercussions of living a materialistic life. Samaniji tailors her discussion to the needs of the community as she sees it and focuses on the teaching of Jain meditation and techniques of stress management. Actually, the significance of her presence in North America is her power to symbolize the traditional path: She is part of a deliberate effort by the diaspora communities to recreate a transnational identity for Jainism, drawing upon the "homeland" to reconstitute itself.

The Traditionalist

Paulomi is a bright, charming "doer" about as far removed from ascetic quiescence as one can get. A jet-setting, high-tech computer wizard in her mid-twenties, she juggles a challenging career and family demands and is actively involved in local and international Jain organizations. Like many young Jain women in North America, she is charting new ground: Participation in the public domain has not been available to women until recently. Outside the ascetic path, marriage had long been regarded as the noblest vocation for Jain women, and the cultural ideal of the benevolent mother and faithful wife remains influential.

The important role played by laywomen in Jainism has long been valued. A Jain proverb states: "Rearing a boy brings forth a good man, rearing a girl, brings forth

a good family." Women are widely perceived to embody religious power and to be inherently more pious than men. Their religiosity is believed to be an important factor in the well-being of the family. Women are almost single-handedly responsible for the socialization of their children, providing religious instruction, teaching the intricacies of Jain dietary rules, and instilling in them tolerance and reverence for all life.

Paulomi has learned this well. She strives to lead an observant life. She refrains from eating meat and eggs, consumes no alcohol, and has deliberately chosen a career in computers because of its nonviolent nature. "What violence does the movement of electrons from one circuit to another ever cause a living being?" she asks rhetorically. She regularly attends temple and fasts during Paryushan, Jainism's most significant religious observance (a festival of atonement celebrated over an eight-day period in September) during which repentance and forgiveness are stressed. Her ethical decisions are reinforced by her beliefs in karma and reincarnation and grounded in tradition.

But, like many women her age, Paulomi does not see herself as neatly fitting into either of Jainism's two traditional female vocations: that of an ascetic or homemaker. Most of the women of her mother's generation forfeited personal careers for the sake of their families. Lata Champsee, the current president of the Jain Society of Toronto (and the second woman to hold the position in the society's short history), contends that the Jain organizational structures remain largely male dominated and that being a woman president has not been without its obstacles. Nevertheless, she maintains that things are quickly changing and that the past ten years has seen the restructuring of Jain organizations in North America. Through constitutional amendments, Women's Chairs have been established to promote women's participation. As a result, many older women, now that their children are grown, are becoming active in Jain societies.

Paulomi does not want to wait. Like many young women in North America, she plans to have it all: a happy family life and a successful career. Reared in cosmopolitan Toronto, she contends that she feels more Canadian than Indian. But she is not willing to abandon the traditional Jain social life from which she and her brother have benefited so much.

Her mother, in addition to being her closest friend, is her inspiration and role model. She instilled in her children the importance of close family ties and tradition. Paulomi lives with her family, speaks Gujarati at home, is active in Jain society and in temple life, and will likely have an arranged marriage (which she is quick to point out is little more than a family-approved introduction). And, unlike many young Jains, she is not critical of the role that sectarian differences continue to play in the North American environment. Paulomi's acceptance of established practices and ritual dimensions of Jainism makes her more traditional than many in her age group.

In India, Jains of different sects tend to live in separate social worlds. Since the fourth century B.C.E., the Jain community has been divided into two major branches, named after their ascetic orders: the Svetambaras ("white clad") and the Digambaras ("sky clad"). The names denote the ascetics' comportment: The Svetambara ascetics wear white robes, whereas the Digambara are unclad. The Svetambara maintain that their white robes are simply a symbol of purity. But to the Digambara, clothes reveal a degree of attachment to one's body that should be abandoned in ascetic life. The divisions are ancient, and the sects have developed independently of each other, with their own texts and practices. Linguistic and geographic differences overlap with sectarianism, entrenching the differences even further.

Many hoped that with the birth of a new community in North America sectarian differences would disappear, and, indeed, several organizations with nonsectarian mandates have been established. But this ideal is far from being achieved. The vast majority of Jain immigrants to North America are from the Svetambara sect and are Gujarati speaking. Those outside this dominant group were too few in number to establish their own temple or societies, so they allied themselves with the dominant group. But the non-Svetambara and non-Gujarati-speaking Jains have often felt alienated and excluded from the dominant group, and as the community has grown, it has become an increasingly contentious issue. Recently, for instance, after a twenty-five-year history, the Toronto Jain community decided to separate along sectarian lines and establish a Digambara temple.

Paulomi maintains that sectarian (and caste) differences are merely social markers that facilitate understanding. She provides an example: When her parents were newly arrived in Canada, they did not know anyone at all. Starting out in a foreign land with unfamiliar customs was difficult. They had no idea even where to live and chose their first apartment after seeing a sign written in the Gujarati language posted in the lobby of a building. Whether or not their neighbors were Jain, they could not tell, but their common language represented a link with home and made them feel at ease. The comfort of linguistic and cultural familiarity underscores the motive for retaining sectarian ties. Paulomi believes that as long as sectarian differences are socially meaningful, there is little point in denying their existence. But she acknowledges that they are of little importance to most second-generation Jains. "Within a

generation," she says, "these divisions will probably be meaningless."

THE UNORTHODOX

Inaya describes herself as "100% American." Most comfortable in a pair of worn jeans and a sweatshirt, she is outspoken as well as strikingly pretty. Her parents moved to England from India when she was a baby and then to the United States when she was six years old. She has never been to India, though professing a keen interest in the country of her cultural heritage. And like most young Jains who grew up in North America, she considers asceticism to be an alien and unlikely path.

At twenty-two she is a busy university student pursuing a degree in economics. She characterizes herself as a feminist, a human rights and animal rights crusader, earnestly working toward a more equitable world. Ultimately, she hopes to work in the field of economic development, where her social and political interests will have an outlet. Jainism provides the philosophical basis for her belief, grounding her concerns in a coherent ethic that has worked for thousands of years for millions of people. For Inaya, Jainism is about doing good in the world, not about ascetic withdrawal from it. But the ideas she embraces are rooted in ascetic values. "Jainism teaches us to rise above our desires for things and to not harm or interfere with others," she says. "These simple ideas encourage us to live with respect and restraint. What could be more important?"

Her own values and goals have been shaped by Jain ideals of nonviolence and nonattachment and, above all else, by the ideal of tolerance. The Jain principle of *anekantvada*, which means "multiple perspectives," encourages tolerance for dissenting views. It asserts that all truth is partial and that all views share in truth. For Inaya, it is an exquisite expression of open-mindedness and one she strives to adopt in her own life. "In my apartment, I have icons of Mahavir, the Dalai Lama, Guru Nanak, Jesus and the Buddha. They are all inspired teachers," she explains.

For Inaya, however, Jain ethical principles are separate from philosophical theories of karma, reincarnation, and nirvana. "I don't know what I believe in," she said, "but I certainly don't feel attached to these ideas." She explains that Jain teachings on tolerance and nonviolence are ends in themselves, that they transcend religious dogma. In this way, Inaya is expressing a view that is increasingly common among young Jains who grow up in North America.

Though reared as a Jain, she maintains that the label is something she could dispense with. "Sometimes, I will say I am Hindu, for simplicity's sake," she says. The fact that Jainism is a little-known tradition does not concern her, so long as the ethical teachings remain alive. In fact, her commitment to Jainism is provisional: "Where it's progressive, I embrace it; where it isn't, I drop it." And when it comes to the question of gender, she finds that as a Jain she has occasion both to celebrate and to denounce it.

She complains that although Jainism espouses a radically egalitarian philosophy, it remains a patriarchal tradition. "It deserves praise for having recognized the legitimacy and importance of lay and ascetic women's roles in the community, from the very beginning. But women have always been considered subordinate to men." For instance, although women are far more involved in religious life than men, until very recently they had been excluded from the structure of authority, prestige, and power. Even within the ascetic orders, where they outnumber men and have had illustrious careers, women are subordinate to the monks. Over 2,000 years ago, a debate over the question of female spirituality began that still divides the community. According to Inaya, it reveals deeply held biases against women. The debate centered on the question of the possibility of attaining nirvana immediately following a life in a female body. Those of the Digambara sect argue that nirvana can never be achieved from a female body—that a woman must be reborn as a man before spiritual liberation can occur. The Svetambara sect claim that a woman can attain liberation directly, albeit with greater difficulty than a man. This issue continues to be a central question over which the two sects remain divided. Women are not initiated as full ascetics among the Digambara. Whereas, among the Svetambara, female asceticism is well institutionalized, with females outnumbering males and, as a consequence, wielding a considerable degree of influence in the community. Though the two sects disagree on questions of female religiosity, both hold the same negative understanding of female nature as flawed, associating sexuality with sin. And although theoretically *sadhvis* and *munis* are considered as equals in the Svetambara sect, in practice the *sadhvis* are subordinate.

Inaya, like most North American Jains, is from the Svetambara sect. But she does not derive much comfort from that: "The ideas that they [the Svetambara and Digambara] share in common are greater than their differences," she maintains. However, she is sanguine about the future, arguing that in religiously and culturally pluralistic North America, new ideas are constantly being inserted into religious debate, and old, antiquated ones discarded. "This is the force of *anekantvada*," she beamed.

Samaniji, Paulomi, and Inaya represent three distinct views of Jainism among myriad visions. The differences and diversity within the community are vast, and an accurate portrait would need to include a discussion of many others—for instance, of the women whose faith is expressed through ritual and temple-based practices and of the grandmothers who followed their families to Canada (often without knowing English) and who have sought to preserve the ascetic basis of the tradition here. Yet, in large part, the young women's views are representative of the majority. Their lives illustrate some of the changes occurring in women's roles, and in Jainism itself, as the community takes root in North American soil. Each embodies modern aspirations and traditional values in a way that challenges conceptual frameworks that would set them apart. And in spite of their divergent views, each woman emphasized the centrality of *ahimsa* in their own lives, illustrating how traditional Jain teachings continue to have striking contemporary relevance. Jainism's egalitarian philosophy has withstood the caprice of history and remains the core of the tradition today as in its ancient past. As Paulomi puts it, "No matter what epoch one lives in, the ideal of nonviolence is unchanging and everlasting."

SIKH WOMEN IN NORTH AMERICA
Nikky-Guninder Kaur Singh

SIKH WOMEN CAN be recognized by the circular steel bracelet worn around their right wrist. Although the short-styled hair is becoming more popular with the young generation, Sikh women usually have their hair long, either neatly braided or put up in a bun. They can also be distinguished by the *salwar* (loose pants), *-kameez* (shirt to the knees), and *dupattas* (long sheer scarves) that they wear. Westerners tend to confuse this north Indian form of dress with the sari, which is approximately six yards of material draped by most women in India. In recent years, the *salwar-kameez* has become very popular with women from different religious backgrounds, and fashion designers are even incorporating contemporary Western styles into this traditional Punjabi dress. Sikh women can just as easily be recognized from their surname "Kaur," meaning princess, which remains the same whether they are married or unmarried. Then there is the greeting exalting the all-encompassing Timeless One ("Sat Sri Akal") with folded hands. This is uniquely Sikh. There are also some North Americans who are deeply devoted to Sikhism through the 3HO (Healthy, Happy, Holy Organization) founded by Harbhajan Singh Yogi, but unlike Punjabi Sikhs, they wear predominantly white clothing.

Immigration

The first Sikh immigrants to North America appear exclusively to be males who came to the West Coast of this continent between 1901 and 1923. They were agricultural laborers who left their wives and families in search of economic opportunities. The British annexation of the Punjab in 1849 offered Sikhs opportunities to become a part of the imperial workforce and migrate to distant lands. A substantial number served in the British army in a variety of countries, and many were employed as soldiers and clerks in British colonies on the Malay Peninsula and in East Africa. Advertisements by steamship companies and recruitment to work on the Canadian Pacific Railroad attracted these first "passenger" migrants to the North American continent. These so-called bachelors (even though some were married back in India) were severely isolated from their families as an expected temporary absence from the Punjab often became a lifetime spent abroad. There were barely any Sikh women in this early group of immigrants, and the Sikh men often married Spanish-speaking women on the western rim, creating a biethnic community erroneously termed "Mexican-Hindus" (also "Mexidus"). A few did return to India. Growing up in the Punjab in the late 1960s, this author remembers attending a gala "remarriage" of her cousin's grandmother; the groom who had left his newly-wed wife fifty years ago to work in America was returning to her and to his son and grandchildren he had never seen! Women were rare partners in the first wave of Sikh migrations. The pervasive anti-Asian feelings, and a series of exclusionary acts and immigration restrictions, made their entry into the New World almost impossible.

Since the relaxation of immigration laws after World War II, and especially after the elimination of national quotas in 1965, there has been a dramatic surge in the Sikh population, both male and female, all across North America. The New Family Reunification policy opened doors to a second wave of Asian immigration through which Sikh men and women from all stratas of society arrived in increasing numbers. Political crises in India have also impelled the increase in migrations over the last few decades. In the 1980s, the Sikh quest for an independent Khalistan led to a tragic political situation, driving many young Sikhs to North America whose families are now finding a home here. Another set is the case of the "twice migrants" who were initially settled in Uganda, Kenya, and Iran, but due to political turmoil in their adopted countries, families were forced to migrate. Many settled on this continent.

There are about 234,000 Sikhs in the United States, and the numbers are even higher for Canada. In British Vancouver they constitute 2.3 percent of the population. Although the Punjab-like terrain of California still attracts the Sikhs (Yuba and Sutter counties form the largest and most prosperous Sikh farming communities outside India), recent Sikh migrants are highly urban based. Sikh women arrive in the United States of America not only on visas for wives, mothers, daughters, and sisters but also independently to pursue education or enter a variety of careers. They are successful in various dimensions of American life including business, medicine, academics, law, engineering, computers, public health, and

The Sikh holy scriptures feature music and poetry along with musical instructions compiled by the Sikh gurus in celebration of the Supreme Being and life. One of the main activities in Gurdwaras (Sikh places of worship) is the singing of this poetry. This religious singing is called kirtan. *Photo © 2005 Sandeep Singh Brar.*

politics. Like their male counterparts, they are energetic and enterprising, but sadly, even in the New World, the talents and potential of many Sikh women continue to be stifled by age-old societal norms.

Sikhs are transnational and remain closely tied with their families and communities in India. How to preserve Sikh identity in the modern West is a vital concern for diasporic Sikhs. To begin with, Sikh society never quite freed itself from ancient Indian patriarchal structures. Threatened by the modern West, these patriarchal formulations are carried over the oceans and upheld with even greater urgency by the immigrants. Since women are literally the reproducers of the community, the preservation of "Sikhness" in the New World falls primarily on them. As a result, Sikh women become subject to strict control. Control over their reproductive rights leads to the reproduction of the family's identity and that of the Sikh community at large. The situation of Sikh women on the North American landscape ends up being paradoxical: Their Sikh faith provides them with a window of opportunity, and they come to the land of opportunity; they should be doubly free, but many only find themselves doubly oppressed.

Heritage

Guru Nanak and the Origins of Sikhism

At its foundation, Sikhism is very egalitarian. The religion can be traced to the person and ideology of Guru Nanak. He was born in the Punjab in 1469 in Talwandi, a village in northern India that is now in Pakistan. Lying on the border of India and Pakistan, the Punjab continues to be the homeland for the Sikhs from which they have migrated to all parts of the globe. The Punjab of Guru Nanak's time was torn by social and religious divisions, and women's status was very low. Practices of sati (widow immolation) and purdah (veiling and seclusion of women), and strong attitudes toward menstrual pollution, were widely prevalent. Guru Nanak's close association with his mother (Tripta), wife (Sulakhani), and sister (Nanaki) must have raised his awareness about the tragic plight of women in his milieu. His older sister Nanaki (after whom Nanak was named) must have been especially significant because he spent many of his formative years with her and even went to live with her in her new home after she got married. Nanak rejected all austere and ascetic practices that were exclusive to caste, class, and gender. Early in life he refused to go through the upanyana ceremony of wearing the sacred thread reserved for upper-caste Hindu boys. Nanak mixed freely with people of different religious backgrounds and traveled extensively, spreading his message of the singularity of the Ultimate Reality

and the consequent unity of humanity. Poetry became his medium of expression. At the end of his travels, he settled in Kartarpur, a Punjabi village he founded on the bank of the river Ravi. A community of disciples grew around him here. It was not a monastic order of any kind but a fellowship of men and women engaged in the ordinary occupations of life. Men and women shared equally in the Sikh institutions of seva (voluntary labor), langar (community meal), and sangat (congregation). Together they listened and recited sacred hymns; together they cooked and ate langar; together they formed a democratic congregation without priests or ordained ministers.

The pattern of inclusivity set up by Guru Nanak in Kartarpur continued, and women were not excluded by any of the successor gurus from any aspect of religious life. There are ten gurus in Sikhism (Guru Nanak, Guru Angad, Guru Amar Das, Guru Ram Das, Guru Arjan, Guru Hargobind, Guru Har Rai, Guru Har Krishan, Guru Tegh Bahadur, and Guru Gobind Singh). For the Sikhs the same light is reflected in Ten different bodies, and the same voice speaks through all Ten. The Guru Period, beginning with the birth of Guru Nanak in 1469 to the death of the Tenth in 1708, offers many examples of women leading Sikh institutions of sangat and langar, reciting sacred poetry, fighting boldly against oppression and injustice, and generating liberating new rituals. Their vital participation in varied dimensions is deeply etched in Sikh memory. Mata Khivi, wife of Guru Angad (Nanak II), is fondly remembered for her liberal direction of community meals. With Mata Khivi's generous supervision and her plentiful supply of kheer (delicious rice pudding), langar became a real feast rather than a symbolic meal. Guru Amar Das (Nanak III) even assigned leadership roles to women. In order to consolidate the growing Sikh faith, he created a well-knit ecclesiastical system and set up twenty-two manjis (dioceses or preaching districts), covering different parts of India. Along with men, women served as supervisors of these communities. Guru Amar Das's daughter Bibi Bhani married her father's successor, Guru Ram Das, and became the mother of Guru Arjan. Sikhs remember Bibi Bhani as a strong woman with immense moral fervor. In her various roles of daughter, wife, and mother of gurus, she had tremendous impact on the development of Sikh values. Her son, Guru Arjan, who became the fifth guru, compiled the Guru Granth, the Sikh holy book, and created the Sikh sacred space, the Harimandir, the Golden Temple of modern times. Guru Arjan's poetry contains a wealth of feminine images as if to underscore the importance of his mother's voice in his life, and the holy volume he compiled remains the universal matrix containing the verses of the Sikh gurus, Hindu religious poets, and Muslim saints.

Guru Gobind Singh and the Cultivation of Sikh Identity

The Sikh ideal of Oneness became effective as a vital social reality with Guru Gobind Singh's creation of the Khalsa (Community of the Pure) in 1699. His father, Guru Tegh Bahadur, gave up his life for human values when Gobind was barely nine. His mother, Mata Gujari, brought up her son courageously. While visiting India, Sikhs pay homage at the two shrines dedicated to her near the town of Sirhind: Gurdwara Mata Gujari, where she spent the last few days of her life, and, just a mile away, Gurdwara Joti Sarup, where she was cremated.

Guru Gobind Singh's Khalsa came into being when the first five initiates sipped *amrita*, the alchemical nectar, from the same bowl—discarding all divisions of caste and class. As Guru Gobind Singh stirred the water in a steel bowl with his double-edged sword to the accompaniment of scriptural recitations, his wife, Mata Jitoji, added sugarpuffs into the bowl, therewith combining the alchemy of steel with the sweetness of sugar. Through the drink the initiates were physically and psychologically nourished to fight against oppression and injustice and uphold freedom and equality.

The *amrita* (drink) initiation is open to both Sikh men and women, and both are equally enjoined to wear the emblems of the Khalsa, popularly known as the five Ks:

1. *kesha*, or uncut hair—denoting the natural order of the human condition

2. *kangha*, a comb tucked into the *kesha* to keep it tidy

3. *kara*, a steel bracelet worn on the right arm

4. *kaccha*, short breeches

5. *kirpan*, a sword symbolizing self-defense and the fight against injustice

Guru Gobind Singh marked the internal transformation of Sikh men and women with a new identity. The five Ks are basic to the construction of the individual subject: They serve as a means of refining the physical and the psychological self; simultaneously, they constitute a social practice and are a means of intensifying social relations amongst the Sikhs. The *amrita* is sipped from the same bowl, sealing the pledge of equality and faithfulness. Sikhs celebrate Mata Jitoji as an active copartner in the creation of the Khalsa. When they drink *amrita* they enter the family of the Khalsa and declare themselves to be the direct descendants of Guru Gobind Singh and Mata Jitoji, their two equally important spiritual parents. Men are given the surname of *Singh*, meaning "lion," and the women, *Kaur*, meaning "princess." Their rebirth into the Order represents an anni-

hilation of their family (caste) lineage, of their confinement to a heredity occupation, of all their stifling beliefs and rituals. Women are liberated from tracing their lineage to their father or adopting a husband's name after marriage. As Singh and Kaur, Sikh men and women are enjoined to help the weak and fight the oppressor.

In his battle against injustice, Guru Gobind Singh was assisted by Mai Bhago. She was a courageous woman from the Amritsar district who rallied men to fight for the guru against the imperial forces. She herself fought in the battle at Muktsar in December 1705 for the guru and was injured. Thereafter, she accompanied Guru Gobind Singh as one of his personal bodyguards. Sikhs have built shrines in her memory.

The Tenth Guru ended the line of personal gurus by passing the succession not to another person but to the Guru Granth, the holy book of the Sikhs. The First Sikh Guru had bequeathed his inspired poetry to his disciple, Guru Angad, and appointed him as his successor. The Second Guru carried on the tradition of sacred poetry, which he felt was important for the aesthetic pleasure it imparted to human life as well as for the knowledge it transmitted. The transference of guruship from Nanak to Angad was repeated successively through the installation of the Tenth Guru, Gobind Singh, in 1675. Just before he passed away in 1708, Guru Gobind Singh declared the sacred book his successor. The body of the Ten Gurus, their flesh and blood conceived in the mother's body and fed on her placenta, was identified with the Guru Granth and made the Guru Eternal.

Worship

Guru Granth

Across centuries and continents, the Guru Granth remains the focal point of Sikh worship, whether private or public. The sacred book is the center of all Sikh rites and ceremonies; it is the sole visual and aural icon. When Sikhs immigrate to foreign lands, they carry with them their most revered possession. To have a room enshrining the Guru Granth is the aspiration of most Sikhs. Both at home and in public places of worship, the Guru Granth is treated with the highest respect and veneration. It is draped in cloth, called *rumala*, placed on quilted mats, and supported by cushions. A canopy hangs over it for protection, and a whisk is waved over it as a sign of respect. Sikhs everywhere bow before the Guru Granth and seat themselves on the floor. Shoes are removed and heads covered in the presence of their holy book by men and women alike. The Guru Granth is opened at dawn. This act of opening the holy book is called *prakash*, "making the light manifest." *Vak*, or "the divine command"—the message for the day—is obtained by opening the book at random and reading the passage on the top of the left-hand page. After dusk, the Guru Granth is closed. The closing ritual is called *sukhasan*, which means "to place at rest."

The Guru Granth is read for all rites of passage, for any family celebration—a new house, a new job, an engagement, and for all times of uncertainty and difficulty—sickness, death. The reading may be a *saptah*, a seven-day reading, or it may be an *akhand*, a forty-eight hour, nonstop reading of its 1,430 portfolio pages, during which several readers take turns. Anyone, male or female Sikh, who can read Gurmukhi script may read the Guru Granth. Some mothers complete the reading annually to correspond with the birthday of their child.

Kirtan is the singing of the scriptural verses. Harmonium and tabla (a set of drums) are the most common musical accompaniments. *Ragis* (professional singers) are invited by Sikhs to perform at homes and in shrines in North America. Daily Sikh homes and cars resound with *kirtan* tapes and CDs.

Special social functions and rites of passage are marked by the *bhog* ceremony. The word *bhog* literally means "pleasure." In this context it signifies the gratification attained by having concluded a reading of the scriptures. It is similar to the Greek word *eucharist*, which means "thanksgiving" and, in the spiritual sense, refers to the Christian sacrament of Holy Communion. *Bhog* involves reading the concluding pages of the Guru Granth, saying *ardas* (the Sikh counterpart of the Lord's Prayer in Christianity), and partaking of the Sikh sacrament of *karahprashad*, which concludes every religious ceremony.

Karahprashad is the sweet sacrament consisting of equal portions of butter, flour, sugar, and water. During its preparation, Sikh men and women keep their heads covered, their feet bare, and recite hymns from the Guru Granth. When the *karahprashad* is ready, it is put in a large, flat dish and placed on the right side of the Guru Granth. After readings from the Guru Granth, the aromatic sacrament is distributed to the entire congregation.

For the Sikhs their Holy Book represents the Infinite One. There is no priesthood in Sikhism, so both men and women can directly approach their sacred text. Both are free to read and recite the sacred verse at home or in public, and any Sikh from within the congregation can be chosen to lead worship. However, unwritten laws are the ones that govern Sikh life, for public worship is a privelege granted to men. Women play a very active role in devotional practices at home, but when it comes to conducting worship in Gurdwaras—whether they are located in the homeland or in the New World—it is invariably the male lips that recite the sacred verses, the male hands that touch them, and the male lens that interpret them.

The sacred verses in fact are empowering for women.

The gurus who uttered them are men, but they adopted a female tone and imagery in their quest for the Divine. Woman was envisioned as being physically, psychologically, and spiritually more refined. Throughout the Guru Granth (GG) her body, her activities, her dressing up, her tenacity, her longing are prized. *She* is the model in forging a sensual and palpable union with the Transcendent.

The absolute transcendence of the Ultimate Reality is affirmed abundantly in Sikh scripture, yet in order to grasp That One, a variety of images are used. For example, the One is expressed as both Father and Mother: "you are my Father and you are my Mother" (GG:103). Similarly, "you are my Father and Mother, and your Name is like milk in my mouth" (GG:713). Although traditional exegetes and translators have underscored the masculine dimension, the feminine is powerfully present in the Guru Granth. The Mother in her female gender, and in her feminine qualities, is exalted. Her natural processes are celebrated. Again and again, we are reminded that we are created from the mother's blood, we are lodged in her womb, and we our first nurtured by her milk. Guru Nanak reprimands those who stigmatize menstrual blood. He poignantly questions: "Why call her inferior from whom all great ones are born?" (GG: 473). The imagery of conception, gestation, giving birth, and lactation is vigorously present in the Sikh sacred text. Its metaphysical and aesthetic poetry is inspiring for both male and female devotees.

Gurdwara

In public, Sikh worship is conducted in a Gurdwara—literally, door (*dwara*) to enlightenment (*guru*). The shrines serve as a central point for the local Sikh community: They are the source of information, assistance, food, shelter, and fellowship. For the newly arrived Sikhs, locating the Gurdwara is an important initial step. The Sikh community creates and maintains its social, cultural, intellectual, and political links through the Gurdwara. The first Gurdwara in North America was built in 1909 in Vancouver, followed by another in Victoria. The first Gurdwara in the United States was built in Stockton, California, in 1912. While being a religious hub, Stockton was also a storm center for political activity: the Ghadr (revolution) Party with its goal to overthrow the Britsh Raj in India had its genesis here. For decades Stockton was the only Sikh center, but today there are more than 150 Gurdwaras in America. Many start out on a rotational basis in homes, in a basement of a church, or in a community hall. Where there are large Sikh populations, Gurdwaras are being designed to accommodate huge gatherings. A spacious Gurdwara like the Ontario Khalsa Darbar, with thirty-eight acres and over 35,000 square feet of building (located close to the airport in Toronto), allows Sikhs to celebrate their special festivals in the thousands. Simultaneously, it enables persons living in the neighborhood to pay daily homage before starting off for their jobs—just as many Sikhs do back in India. Even for an occasional visitor, the Gurdwara offers a wonderful opportunity to pay homage, listen to *kirtan*, partake of the delicious *langar*, visit the library, and meet with fellow Sikhs. With exactly the same sights, sounds, accents, smell, and spirit as the Gurdwaras in the Punjab, the North American Gurdwaras take immigrants back home, back into the recesses of their deepest self.

The Gurdwaras are designed on the architectural pattern of the Harimandir in Amritsar. Built by the Fifth Guru, its four doors are an architectural symbol for welcoming people from the traditional four castes of Indian society. The Gurdwaras are open spaces where the devotees can freely enter or leave any time. There is no central chamber from which any male or female is excluded, for the Guru Granth is the focal point to which everyone has equal access. The principle of *seva* of the first Sikh community established by Guru Nanak in Kartarpur pervades all Sikh shrines as men and women together clean the precincts, cook *langar*, recite poetry, and give Punjabi instruction. The exception is that there are no women *granthis* (official readers) affiliated with any of the Sikh Gurdwaras, and so the men lead worship by taking *vak* (reading out the divine command for the congregation), reciting *ardas* (prayer that begins and concludes every ceremony), and distributing *karahprashad* (the Sikh sacrament). Daily ceremonies like *prakash* (opening of the Guru Granth) and *sukhasan* (putting to rest in the evening) in Gurdwaras, the annual celebrations of Baiskahi and Gurpurabs (birthday or death anniversaries of the gurus), and all rites of passage for Sikh men and women are conducted and administered almost exclusively by men. The sexism and subjugation they directly experience in public places resonate deeply in the inner psyches of Sikh men and women, legitimizing women's deference and subordination to their fathers, brothers, uncles, and husbands.

Celebrations

True living for Sikhs involves remembering the One Reality as often and as intimately as possible. There is the urge to link daily rhythms of life with historic memories, seasonal moods, and human transitions. Interestingly, wherever Sikhs migrate, they not only celebrate their own rituals on the new soil but also participate wholeheartedly in the customs and traditions prevalent in their adopted country.

The daily spiritual routine (*nit nem*) consists of recitations of hymns from the various gurus, including Guru Nanak's Japji, which is read or recited or heard on tape in the morning. For the English-speaking generation, the Gurmukhi verses are transliterated into Ro-

man script. The Japji expresses the quintessence of Sikh philosophy, leading the worshipper through the five stages of spiritual development from earthly duty to spiritual bliss.

Annually, Sikhs celebrate Gurpurabs (literally "the day of the Guru"), which include birth anniversaries of their gurus, important historical events, and the martyrdom of their heroes. During Gurpurabs, uninterrupted readings of scripture take place, intellectual symposiums are held, and musical performances are organized. All over the world Sikhs joyously celebrate the birth of Guru Nanak, the installation of the Guru Granth in the Golden Temple, and the birth of the Khalsa. Baisakhi, which is also the first day of the Sikh calendar, commemorates the momentous initiation of the Khalsa by the Tenth Guru. On the day that Guru Gobind Singh transformed Guru Nanak's personal and mystical experience into a public, social, and institutional ritual, Sikhs initiate new members into the Khalsa family. New yellow Sikh flags replace the old ones in Gurdwaras. Huge Sikh processions with colorful floats carrying the Guru Granth and, depicting different aspects of Sikh life, are becoming a familiar sight in North American cities. Because of the large population of Sikhs in and around metropolitan areas, a recent phenomenon has been to pool together the resources of the various communities for the celebration of major events. For instance, during the 300th anniversary of the Khalsa in 1999, Sikhs from the Washington, D.C., area got together and held religious, cultural, and intellectual activities at the National Convention Center in the U.S. capital.

The Punjabi folk dances *Bhangra* and *Gidda* are popular performances during sociocultural Sikh celebrations. *Bhangra* is traditionally performed by a group of men. It dates back to the fourteenth century, originating in a region in west Punjab (now a part of Pakistan). But in modern times, *Bhangra* has become extremely popular with both Sikh men and women. Dressed in bright colors, the group dances in an elemental rhythm to the beat of a large drum and sing songs celebrating Punjabi village life. The vigorous steps and sounds create a primal connection with the earth. The audience encircles the dancers, clapping and joining in with the dancing and singing. With the migration of Sikh communities to the West, this Punjabi folk dance has become the latest rage with young music lovers in Britain, Europe, and Canada. The modern form of *Bhangra* combines North Indian folk music with a kaleidoscope of contemporary styles including reggae and western pop.

Gidda, choreographed in gentle and lithesome movement, is the typical folk dance for Sikh women and is very popular during engagement and wedding celebrations. Like *Bhangra*, *Gidda* celebrates nature and her bountiful gifts through the seasons of spring, summer, monsoon, autumn, and winter. Amidst sparkling agrarian scenes, *Gidda* captures simple activities that form a rich reservoir of Sikh memory. In vibrant and playful colors and sounds, the women recreate scenes left behind in the Punjab: how the mothers and grandmothers milked cows, cooked mustard seeds, did needlework, fanned their children in the summer heat, bought glass bangles, churned milk in the morning, carried water in earthen-ware pitchers sturdily balanced on heads, helped with ploughing and harvesting. While evoking nostalgic memories, *Gidda* also affords women a mode of dancing out their oppressive life. The patriarchal structure of Punjabi society, combined with the rigidity of the joint family system, becomes restrictive for women even in Western countries. *Gidda* opens the way to articulate *her* oppression, *her* hopes and dreams. The individual anguish is rendered in a collective idiom. Women sing freely and vent their frustration. In a popular folksong, a woman asks her father for "a cow, a buffalo, two bulls with bells, and a female camel with anklets" so that she can break away from her in-laws and start out life independently with her husband. Such rustic songs are sung over sophisticated sound systems in elegant Hilton ballrooms reserved by Sikh wedding parties across North America. Sikhs are known for their heartiness and zest; and *khera*, or cheerfulness, their prized virtue, manifests itself in song and dance.

While maintaining the foundations of their own faith and culture, Sikhs participate in traditions such as Easter, Thanksgiving, and Christmas. Thus they promote pluralism in an essential way. For Thanksgiving, Sikh men and women prepare vegetarian meals in Gurdwaras and serve them to the needy and the homeless in their communities. They incorporate Hanukkah and Christmas into Divali, the Indian festival of lights; Hanukkah candles and Christmas trees are making their entry into Sikh homes. Sikhs joyously interact with their American neighbors and friends—exchanging gifts, sharing sweets. They also want to share their culture, so women and men relay *kirtan* and Sikh discourse on local televisions. For Sikhs, sacred space and sacred time merge into the singular experience of the sacred that is beyond all space and time.

Rites of Passage

In Sikhism there are four rites of passage: name-giving, *amrita* initiation, marriage, and death. Though they are the same for both sexes, they end up being different for men and women. Guru Nanak, the founder, rejected elaborate and exclusionary rituals and ushered in a way of life that would be the same for men and women from all castes and classes. Nanak's refusal to go through the cardinal *upanayana* ceremony (the rite of passage reserved for all uppercaste boys in his culture)

and his criticism of the officiating priest are boldly imprinted in Sikh memory. The Sikh gurus followed his example and repudiated all the oppressive and exclusionary rites, as well as those who conducted them. They envisioned an egalitarian community for both men and women. But in practice families have different expectations of and different obligations to their daughters and sisters than those for their sons and brothers. And again, though in theory both men and women can conduct any of the rites, they end up being primarily officiated by men.

NAME-GIVING

In Sikh thought, both boys and girls are equally the embodiment of the divine spark. Yet Sikh families pray for the birth of a son, and the common Indian blessing "May you be the mother of a hundred sons" resonates in the pyches of most Sikh families even in North America. The child is named in consultation with the holy book. While the spine of the book rests on the cushions, a reader (either of the parents at home or an official reader in the Gurdwara) holds the Guru Granth closed with both hands and then gently lets it open at random. The child is named beginning with the first letter appearing at the top of the left-hand page of the Guru Granth. Sikhs do not have different names for boys and girls. The addition of the name *Kaur* or *Singh* indicates the gender of the child. The child also receives its first *kara*, or steel bracelet. The recitation of *kirtan*, readings from the Guru Granth, recitation of *ardas*, and the partaking of *langar* are the central activities, just as they are for all Sikh rites of passage. But the ceremonies for a son are a much more celebratory affair—the gatherings often surpassing that for a wedding.

AMRITA INITIATION

No particular age is prescribed for initiation. It may be as soon as a boy or a girl is old enough to be able to read the scripture and comprehend the articles of the Sikh faith. Or it may be later in life—some people even wait until their own children are grown up. The initiation is open to all. According to the Sikh Ethical Code (The Rahitmaryada), "Any man or woman of whatever nationality, race, or social standing, who is prepared to accept the rules governing the Sikh community, has the right to receive amrit initiation." Zealous proselytization is alien to Sikhs.

Amrita is prepared by putting the elemental drink of water and sugarpuffs in a steel bowl and stirring it with a small sword while the ambrosial word is recited. Any Sikhs who are already members of the Khalsa can be one of the Five Beloved (*panj pyare*) who administer the ceremony. In everyday life, however, women do not administer this significant Sikh rite. The whole point of Guru Gobind Singh's *amrita* ritual was to shatter exclusivist rites and rituals and include people from all castes and classes into the new family of the Khalsa. His call on that historic Basiakhi day in 1699 was to the entire gathering—to both men and women. The first five volunteers happened to be men—but this was not the guru's request. He even erased the hegemony between himself and his disciples by kneeling in front of those Five and sipping the *amrita* they prepared and administered. Sikhs vividly and proudly remember how their revered guru was initiated by his initiates just the way he had initiated them, but what they forget is to apply his moral vision of absolute equality. How can Sikhs go against the model of their own guru? He had requested volunteers from a congregation of men and women, so how can modern Sikhs tacitly exclude women from initiating new members into the Khalsa, and likewise, from officiating all other Sikh rites and ceremonies? The male dominance in public worship is unconsciously taken into the home, and male domination is reproduced in the home, the extended family, and Sikh society at large.

WEDDING

Anand Karaj (*anand* = bliss, *karaj* = event), the Sikh rite of wedding, began as a very simple ceremony. No words or gestures are directly exchanged between the bride and groom, nor any legal formalities performed between their families. The marriage takes place either in a Sikh Gurdwara or in the home of the bride with everyone seated on the floor in front of the Guru Granth. Anand Karaj begins with the father of the bride handing one end of a scarf (about two and a quarter yards in length) to the groom and the other to his daughter. Through the auspiciously colored scarf (pink, saffron, or red) the couple is bonded together. Holding each end of the scarf, the groom and the bride then walk around the holy book four times. The four circumambulations by the couple correspond to the four *lavan* passages read in solo by the official reader of the Guru Granth. After each circling of the book, the bride and the groom touch their foreheads to the ground and rejoin the congregation by seating themselves on the floor in front. Bowing together to the Guru Granth marks their acceptance of each other. They are solely—and equally—bound to the sacred word rather than to any legal or social authority. The rite concludes with Guru Amar Das's rapturous hymn, *anand* (bliss)—the name of the wedding ceremony itself. With its focus on the bliss that results from the union of the individual with the Divine, this popular scriptural hymn by the Third Guru is liturgically recited at the conclusion of all Sikh congregational services and joyful ceremonies. It is sung by a plurality of voices to the accompaniment of various musical instruments. The celebratory singing of *anand* is followed by *ardas* recited by the officiating member of the congregation, with everybody standing up. After *ardas*, the congregation bows in unison to the Guru Granth and sits down. At this point, the Guru Granth is opened at random, and the first passage on the left-hand page is read out loud. It is regarded as the *vak* (the divine command) for the entire congregation but is especially significant for the newlywed couple. Anand Karaj ends with the distribution of the warm and sweet sacrament (*karahprashad*) to everyone.

Marriage between children, once a common practice in India, is forbidden. Divorce is legal in Sikhism, and both men and women can remarry. However, divorces are few, and it is rare that a widow would remarry.

In contemporary times, the simple marriage ceremonies have become extremely opulent, dowries extravagant, and gifts to the daughter and her in-laws for every rite, ritual, and festival, exorbitant. In both North America and India, marriages are transformed into elaborate affairs, and the quantity and quality of what is hosted for or given to the daughter reinforces the power and prestige of her father. Daughters are regarded as "beautiful" commodities whose marriages are arranged and conducted with a view to build up their status and honor. The not-so-wealthy feel extreme pressure to squeeze out their hard-earned money to keep up with the cultural norms. The son is wanted more and more for the accretion to his father's assets, the daughter less and less for the depletion she extorts. Frightened by Western ideals of individuality and independence, some Sikh parents even send their teenage daughters to live with their extended families and be educated back in India. Marriages are arranged through relatives, matrimonial ads in newpapers, and friends, and often daughters brought up in the West are married to bright doctors and engineers in India whom they are required to help settle in the New World. And young women in India are married to men settled in distant lands as a means of sponsoring entire families' emigration. The process has been interpreted by sociologists as the "sacrifice of the daughter for the sake of son" (Bal, 107). The most popular English-language newspaper in the Punjab poignantly captured this modern tragedy: "Young bright promising girls are literally bartered away by their parents looking for an opportunity to send other members of the family to the land of lucre" (*The Tribune*, June 15, 1996). Economic and social demands of contemporary Sikh culture are so strong and pervasive that Sikh teachings against elaborate rituals and "object"-ionable treatment of women by the gurus go unheeded.

DEATH

Life and death are regarded as natural processes, and just as each day that dawns must set, so must all people depart. Sikh life is intergenerational, and even in the nuclear family systems of North America, couples often continue to live with their children and parents, thus bringing together three generations under the same roof. An expectant mother is sure to receive help from her mother or mother-in-law, who will fly across continents. And much to the amazement of Western friends, their visits do not last a week but months and sometimes years—until the time the child is ready to attend school. The elderly are not consigned to homes for the aged. Among all diasporic communities, there is always the wish to go "home" to India to die.

In India the dead body is carried on a stretcher by the closest male relatives and friends of the family to the funeral grounds where it is cremated. As customary from ancient times, the pyre is lighted by the oldest son. The body returns to the elements it is made up of: Fire merges with the fire that is lighted, air to air, earth to earth, and the ashes and bones (called *phul*, literally, flowers) are immersed in flowing waters of rivers and streams. Even in North America when a Sikh dies, the body is taken to the mortuary and cremated. The family members later take the ashes back to India and immerse them in the Sutlej, one of the five rivers of the Punjab. In the interim the ashes are not brought into the home but left in the local Gurdwara. Death in the family is marked by the initiation of a reading of the Guru Granth. The *bhog* ceremony takes place on the tenth day with the final prayers recited for peace to the deceased. In order to fit schedules in North America, *bhog*, which can be at home or at the Gurdwara, is arranged over weekends. Family members try to keep the memory of their loved ones alive by making gifts to the needy, to schools, to libraries, to hospitals, and to their Gurdwara back home and/or local. At the death anniversary, the family will supply *langar* to the community. Sikh families may even send money to Gurdwaras back in the Punjab to have continuous reading of the Guru Granth (*akhand path*) at shrines such as the Golden Temple. Incidentally, two of the chairs for the study of Sikhism in North America (University of Santa Barbara and Hofstra University) were created by the donors in memory of their mothers. The final rite of passage is significant in Sikhism insofar as it represents the return to the Divine that we all come from. Birth and death are accepted as a part of the natural rhythm of life. Sikh philosophy and ethics stress living in tune with the Transcendent in this world.

Status of Women in the Community and Challenges of Modernity

The ideological equality of women is not replicated in the practical sphere. In an attempt to formalize the message of the gurus in the twentieth century, the Sikh Code of Conduct was published in 1950 by the highest Sikh executive committee. The Code developed several rules that would combat female oppression:

> Twice it makes the point that Sikh women should not veil their faces.
>
> It prohibits infanticide and even association with people who would practice it.
>
> It allows for widow remarriage and underscores that the ceremony be the same as that of the first marriage—a marked difference from the custom where the widow was shamefully wrapped in a sheet and carried away to a brother of the dead husband.
>
> Sikhs should be free of all superstitions and not refuse to eat at the home of their married daughter. The assumption underlying this injunction most likely is that daughters should not be treated like an object or piece of property passed on at marriage to the husband and his family.
>
> Dowry is prohibited. Neither a girl nor a boy should be married for money. Child marriages are not permitted. A girl should marry only when she has attained physical and mental maturity.
>
> There is no prohibition against abortion.

In spite of the ethical code and Sikh scriptural message, gender equality has to be constantly reaffirmed against ancient patriarchal values that have dominated India for centuries. The egalitarian message enshrined in their words is far from being translated into a social reality. The restrictive customs of feudal Punjabi society make their way across the globe. But as traditional Sikh life intersects with modernity, Sikh women face an even greater set of problems.

The primary challenge for a Sikh woman in the West is the upkeep of the five Ks. In modern society where magazines constantly flash chic hairstyles, how are women to keep their hair untouched by scissors? Some even worry about shaving their legs or plucking their eyebrows. In reaction to modernity, in order to define themselves, Sikh women sometimes take up wearing turbans, which is also a way of seeking equality with Sikh men.

And how do Sikh mothers maintain the *kesha* of their sons and daughters? In a culture where all boys have short hair, how does a mother send her little son off to school in braids? There is a real psychological struggle between pride in preserving Sikh formats and the taunts made at her son by his peers who have only seen girls with long hair and braids.

Should women date like their Western peers? Although not a religious issue, there is a strong social prejudice against dating. Whereas it is all right for sons to develop casual relationships even with Westerners—though of course not to marry them!—Sikh parents are extremely protective and controlling when it comes to their daughters. Young women often feel tension and resentment against their families for upholding double standards between themselves and their brothers as expressed in (Tweed and Protheros, 312–314).

Sikh women are also caught in a double bind. Their traditional values force them to retain their primary obligations of childbearing and child rearing. They are responsible for cooking, cleaning, and taking care of their households. And yet their new society expects and encourages them to work full-time outside the home. Living up to these two demanding standards simultaneously is no easy task.

Although legal, divorce is still a stigma in Sikh society. Without friends and family, new brides from India upon joining their husbands may end up suffering in silence. Often those who arrive as dependents on the visas of their husbands discover independence that creates its own set of pressures. Studies show that wife beating, abuse, and battering are increasing alarmingly in the Sikh community, but for the most part, these matters are hushed up.

The obsession of having sons is so great that many Sikh mothers have their female foetuses aborted. Ultrasound, amniocentesis, and other modern technologies are misused to preserve the legacy, business, property, and status of the fathers, as Christine Fair explores in her study "Female Foeticide among Vancouver Sikhs."

Loneliness and isolation prevail in the cases of mothers and grandmothers who come as babysitters to help out their working daughters or daughters-in-law. They find their life in North America as a golden cage and miss the rhythms of Punjabi life with the washerwoman, the newspaperman, vegetable seller, and friends and relatives dropping by during the course of the day. Many Sikh professionals subscribe to the American dream. Their life in the suburbs makes family isolation more acute.

Sikh mothers are very concerned about passing on Sikh heritage to their children. Many diligently offer Punjabi classes and teach Sikh history to youngsters in Gurdwaras. Many drive for hours to make sure their children learn about Sikh scripture and perform *kirtan*. Camps are held during the summer as a way of bringing children together and giving them a sense of tradition. North American Sikhs actually are much more conscious about maintaining their identity and the spirit of their religion on the new soil than their counterparts back in India who take Sikhism for granted. Young Sikh mothers, who probably attended English-medium schools in postcolonial India and did not learn the script for their sacred text (Gurmukhi), are making sure their children are learning it in their new society.

On the other hand, arriving in the "First World" many Sikh women feel insecure and tend to bond with their own. Language barriers often deter them from establishing friendships not only with Western and Middle Eastern women but even with other South Asians who do not speak Punjabi.

And while rights of Sikh women are great on paper, they have to find ways to enforce them. When several prominent Sikh men were asked if women are allowed to serve as the Panj Pyare (the Five Beloved chosen by the community to officiate Sikh rites), the answer was always in the positive. But when asked whether women actually do so, the answer was no and the absence blamed on the women themselves: "They don't want to." Yet in 1989 when a group of women asked to be the Panj Pyare who lead the Baisakhi procession in New York, the women were rejected. Sikh women have to retrieve and demand what belongs to them by right. It is imperative they learn the words of the Guru Granth and the ethical code, so that they can ensure their practice. Otherwise, male lips and patriarchal lenses will continue to veil the feminist openings of Sikhism. Sikh women have to be strong and resilient and keep demanding the space granted to them by their tradition both in the symbolic interpretations and in the ritual practices.

The first generation of Sikhs were concerned about social and economic success; the second generation is aware of their rights in the land of liberty and equal opportunity. A recent phenomenon has been the organization of forums at universities by undergraduate and graduate men and women. During such forums there are lectures on issues vital to Sikhism, workshops on Punjabi culture, and an opportunity for young people to meet socially. Racial and gender issues are also discussed. Instead of building Gurdwaras, these youngsters urge their parents to build shelters for women. They express concern about the lack of academic studies in Sikhism on North American campuses. Caught between tradition and modernity, between East and West, between the older generation and the new, students try to grapple with the philosophical and ethical issues of their religion. Issues taken up in such seminars are often continued on the Internet. Web sites promoting the role of women in Sikhism (Sikhsisterhood) and organizations linking Sikh women (Nanaki) are becoming more and more accessible.

Over all Sikh women in North America are at an exciting threshold. The values enshrined in the Guru Granth have immense import for a pluralistic society. The quintessential experience of the One Reality in Sikhism shatters the Western dualistic framework that subordinates the body to the mind and generates all kinds of *ism*s, sexism, racism, classism, and casteism. The election of Bibi Jagir Kaur in 1999 as the president of the

Shromani Gurdwara Prabhandak Committee (SGPC) was a landmark event. Established in 1920 to manage all Sikh shrines, the SGPC is the highest Sikh executive committee that sets rules and regulations for Sikhs to follow throughout the world. The lifting of the ban on women from reciting *kirtan* in the Golden Temple under her tenure paves the way for further emancipation.

Many Sikh women have already made their mark on this continent. Their initiative and energy have brought success in many business ventures, professions, and arts. Shauna Singh Baldwin's novel *What the Body Remembers* was nominated for the Booker Prize in 2000. Here from a Sikh woman's perspective we have a poignant recollection of the partition of India and Pakistan in 1947. The famous Sikh painter Amrita Sher-Gill (1913–1941) continues to inspire young Sikh artists in the West. A view painted by Sher-Gill from her ancestral home in the Punjab, *Landscape*, received great acclaim at Sotheby's in New York (September 2000). Sikh anchorwomen like Gurvir Dhindsa in the United States, Monica Deol in Canada, and British-born Daljit Dhaliwal on CNN are popular personalities in the television industry. Gurinder Chadha, also British, has established herself as a well-known film director. Sikh organizations in North America are beginning to recognize the contributions of Sikh women, and the Sikh Centennial Foundation in Toronto honored them in April 1998.

But the full benefit for women can be reaped only through exchange and engagement. With a few exceptions, North American female scholars have not seriously entered the world of Sikh women. The multivalent and complex feminine imagery of the Sikh sacred text remains closed to most feminist scholars in religion. We need to redress the current imbalance and Eurocentricism of feminist perspectives on religion. In turn, Sikh women need to tap into the resources offered by Western feminists. Elizabeth Schüssler Fiorenza, Rosemary

Ruether, Mary Daly, Judith Plaskow, and Rita Gross are scholars whose work can be studied to develop methods and techniques to gain insight into the female experience within Sikhism. The "divide-and-rule" policies of the Masters have kept us splintered far too long, and their dualisms of monotheism versus polytheism, East versus West, modern versus traditional, Sikh versus Catholic, have blocked our access to our singular Creator. How can we make use of the windows of opportunity offered by Sikh gurus, Hebrew prophets, or Vedic seers if we do not even communicate with one another? A dialogical relation is much needed. Thus we will recover the richness and empowerment of our particular religious landscapes—which we can celebrate together in the vibrant New World and pass on to our daughters.

SOURCES: Gurpreet Bal, "Migration of Sikh Women to Canada: A Social Construction of Gender," *Guru Nanak Journal of Sociology* (April 1997): 97–112. N. G. Barrier and V. A. Dusenbery, eds., *The Sikh Diaspora* (1989). P. Bhachu, *Twice Migrants: East African Sikh Settlers in Britain* (1985). Harold Coward, John R. Hinnells, and Raymond Brady Williams, *The South Asian Religious Diaspora in Britain, Canada, and the United States* (2000). C. Christine Fair, "Female Foeticide among Vancouver Sikhs: Recontexualizing Sex Selection in the North American Diaspora," *International Journal of Punjab Studies* 3.1 (1996): 1–44. Jasbir Kaur Puar, "Resituating Discourses of 'Whiteness' and 'Asianness' in Northern England: Second-Generation Sikh Women and Construction of Identity," *Socialist Review* 24.1–2 (1995): 21–53. Nikky-Guninder Kaur Singh, *The Feminine Principle in the Sikh Vision of the Transcendent* (1993). Nikky-Guninder Kaur Singh, "Why Did I Not Light Up the Pyre: The Refeminization of Ritual in Sikhism," *Journal of Feminist Studies in Religion* 16.1 (Spring 2000): 63–85. Pashaura Singh and N. G. Barrier, eds., *The Transmission of Sikh Heritage in the Diaspora* (1996). "Things That Make You Ask *Kion*?" in *Asian Religions in America: A Documentary History*, ed. Thomas A. Tweed and Stephen Prothero (1999), 312–314.

Part IX

∾

Newer Religious Movements

WOMEN IN COMMUNITARIAN SOCIETIES

Rosemary Radford Ruether

COMMUNITARIAN SOCIETIES IN America have a long history, going back to pre–Revolutionary War settlements. In the 1840s and again in the 1960s communitarian movements arose that claimed to emancipate women. Women's marginalization was seen as stemming from the separation of work from home, productive labor from unpaid domestic work, segregating women in the domestic sphere and cutting them off from the larger world of work and politics. Communal societies saw themselves as overcoming this split. Home and work, domestic and productive work, daily life and political leadership would be integrated into one community, overcoming the separation of male and female spheres and roles. Communal child raising would overcome the women's exclusive responsibility for children and make this the work of the whole community, men as much as women.

However, the actual record of communal societies in America has been ambiguous in regard to gender equality. Most have been male founded and male dominated. Even those founded by women, including some woman-only groups, have been hierarchical in their concept of leadership. Still communalism continues to proclaim the possibility of utopia in American society and, with it, the hope of more just relations among all humans, overcoming both class and gender hierarchy.

The communitarian impulse in the Christian tradition is an ancient one, having roots in Jewish religious communitarians, such as the Essenes, in the first century C.E. The New Testament book of Acts describes the first Christians in Jerusalem as "having all things in common" and laying their possessions at the feet of the apostles for distribution to those in need (4:32–34). This text became an inspiration to future generations of Christians who saw the communal life as a renewal of the original apostolic community. Western Christian monasticism, following the Rule of St. Benedict in the fifth century, brought together communal living, prayer, and work, inspiring continual renewals through the Middle Ages. Monastic life for both men and women came to the Americas with the Spanish in the sixteenth century. Nineteenth-century immigration planted new seeds of Catholic monastic life in the United States. Today, active orders of social service and cloistered contemplative orders, such as the Benedictines and the Cistercians, dot the American landscape from coast to coast.

The mainstream of the Reformation, while rejecting both celibacy and monastic life, saw a renewal of communitarianism by Anabaptist Protestants. Some, such as the Hutterites, followers of Jakob Hutter, adopted communal life in the Tyrol in 1528, consciously imitating the apostolic example by laying their worldly goods on a cloak before their leaders. In 1530 the Hutterites fled persecution into Moravia and in the eighteenth century migrated to Russia. Beginning in 1874, renewed persecution drove thousands to immigrate to the United States and Canada. Here they have faced hostility because of their pacifist refusal of military service. Today Hutterites are both the longest-lasting and most successful group of religious communitarians, numbering some 400 communities, averaging 100 per community, mostly spread across the northern plains of Alberta, Manitoba, Saskatchewan, South Dakota, and Montana.

Communitarian movements in North America often have been seen as short-lived failures, but this ignores the long history of both Catholic monasticism and communal Anabaptists. Many experimental communities were only one stage in a longer life of a religious community. After the communal phase ended, organizations founded by the movement, such as joint stock companies, schools, cooperatives, and credit unions, remained.

Many Christian communitarians have been pacifist and have seen their movement as the beginning of the realization of the millennium, the thousand-year reign of Christ on earth. Open lands, religious freedom, the vision of America as a "new world" where millenarian hopes could be realized, attracted many such movements. Already in the colonial period a number of communitarian experiments were planted on these shores. Jean Labadie, a mystical French Calvinist, founded the celibate double (male and female) monastery of Bohemia Manor in Maryland in 1683. German pietists, inspired by the mystic Jacob Boehme, founded the community of the Woman in the Wilderness (the name inspired by Revelation 12:6) near Philadelphia in 1694. They saw themselves as imitating the first Christians who fled into the wilderness to await the return of Christ. Each of these colonies lasted about a decade and a half.

A longer-lasting colony, Ephrata Cloister, was founded by German Baptist Conrad Beissel, in 1732, in the Germantown, Pennsylvania, area. It took the form of celibate orders of both men and women, together with a third order of married people who farmed the surrounding lands. The celibate orders lasted until 1844, while the married group continued into the twentieth century. The Moravian Brethren, a renewal of the Hussite church, a Czech reform movement of the fifteenth century, planted a number of colonies in North America in the mid-eighteenth century, beginning in Bethlehem, Pennsylvania. The Moravians lived communally for several decades before dissolving the "General Economy" into private property in 1762.

In the eighteenth century the German pietist movement, critical of the formalism of German Lutheranism, renewed the communitarian impulse. Experiencing persecution from the Lutheran state church, several of these pietist communities emigrated, adopting celibacy and community of goods in the process of transplanting and refounding their communities in the United States. Among these German groups was the Harmony Society, founded by George Rapp, who built their first American colony in Harmony, Pennsylvania, in 1804. In 1814 he moved the community to Indiana, where they built the village of New Harmony. In 1825 they sold their buildings and land to the Owenites and built a third village of Economy near Pittsburgh. The society was dissolved in 1905.

Other German communitarians that migrated to the United States were the Zoarite Separatists, who settled in Ohio, and the Inspirationists, who developed seven villages in Amana, Iowa, in 1854. They converted their property and industries into a joint stock company in 1932, while continuing as a worship community. Although these groups migrated as individual families from neighboring villages in Germany, they adopted communal property and sought to live celibate lives. A group of Swedish Separatists, led by Eric Jansson, migrated to western Illinois in 1846, building the communal village of Bishop Hill. Jansson was assassinated by a dissident member in 1850. More dissension was caused when some leaders sought to impose celibacy on the community. The communal system was dissolved in 1861, but some colonists continued to live as farmers on their shares of land.

The best known of the religious communal societies are the Shakers who migrated from England, under the leadership of Mother Ann Lee, in 1774. By the first half of the nineteenth century, eighteen Shaker communities had spread from Maine to Kentucky. Celibacy and community of goods were key elements in their vision of themselves as the messianic church of Christ's Second Appearing. A period of withdrawal into spiritualist experiences, called "Mother's work" (the appearances being seen the work of Mother Ann Lee), and rejection of active evangelizing caused the Shakers to gradually decline in the latter half of the nineteenth century. In 1965 the new wave of interest in communal living brought potential converts to the Shaker way of life, but the ministry decided not to admit them, believing that they did not understand the original inspiration of the church. At the end of the twentieth century a few elderly Shakers continued to live in the last remaining community at Sabbath Lake, Maine.

The industrial revolution in England and France in the early nineteenth century spawned utopian socialist movements that sought in communal living alternatives to the exploitative conditions of early industrialism. Although militantly critical of the established churches in their countries, the utopian socialists often held quasi-religious millenarian views of their experiments. English textile factory owner and reformer Robert Owen bought the Rappite village of New Harmony in Indiana in 1825 and assembled a community to live there. Owen's lectures on communalism aroused great public interest. He recruited scientists and educators to live in New Harmony but failed to take leadership himself. New Harmony collapsed as a communal society in 1827. Several daughter Owenite communities, such as Nashoba, founded by British feminist Frances Wright, had similarly short lives. New Harmony lived on as a center of social reform, scientific investigation, innovative pedagogy, and the historical study of communal societies in America.

American interest in communalism was also sparked by two French utopian socialist thinkers, Charles Fourier (1772–1837) and Etienne Cabet (1788–1856). Fourier envisioned large communities of 1,620 men, women, and children (seen as the ideal number), living in phalanxes, grand palacelike structures, surrounded by factories and farmlands, all working in harmony as each took up the work to which they were "naturally" attracted. A number of Americans, including the Transcendentalist Brook Farm, tried to adopt Fourier's plans in the 1840s and 1850s but were never able to generate his ideal numbers or architectural plan. The last attempt to create an American phalanx died out in 1892, although the vision often continued in small-scale producer and consumer cooperatives.

Cabet's followers did not try to recruit North American followers but remained determinedly French in language and culture. They first tried to create a colony in Texas, then moved on in successive efforts to Illinois, Missouri, Iowa, and finally California. The California colony dissolved in 1898, but remnants of the colonists continue to make fine cheese and wine in the areas where they settled, such as Nauvoo, Illinois.

Two American-founded religious movements were the Oneida Perfectionists and the Church of Jesus Christ of Latter-day Saints (LSD) (Mormons). The Perfectionists were founded by John Humphrey Noyes, who sought a way of life of perfect holiness. He and his followers developed a society in Oneida, New York, in 1844 where they sought to purge themselves of all selfishness by adopting communal property, shared sex, and child raising. The experiment flourished for the first generation and then was dissolved into a joint stock company in 1881.

The LDS Church arose from the visionary experiences of Joseph Smith in western New York. The Saints sought to found the new Zion successively in several locations in Ohio, Missouri, and Nauvoo, Illinois. They developed a system of communal ownership of property by the church, which then leased it back to church members. Smith also initiated the system of polygamous marriage in Nauvoo. In 1844, a mob, fearful of growing Mormon power, killed Smith and his brother Hyrum in a jail in Carthage, Illinois.

Brigham Young took over the leadership of the movement and led the Mormons to their new Zion in the Salt Lake area of Utah. Although the last colony practicing communal property ended in 1885, it remains an ideal vision for Mormons. Communal practices continue in large church property holdings used for education, worship, social welfare, and help for poorer members. Mormons today are a major denomination with over 5 million members worldwide.

Other smaller communal movements growing out of perfectionist Protestantism also arose on American soil after the Civil War. One particularly interesting movement was the Sanctificationists of Belton, Texas, which began as a Methodist prayer meeting in 1866. Martha McWhirter led the group's separation from the local church and founded a cooperative society in 1876. The group flourished through their cooperative industries. Renaming themselves the Woman's Commonwealth, they moved to Washington, D.C., in 1898, where their numbers dwindled as the elderly members died.

New waves of communitarianism arose in the late

nineteenth and early twentieth centuries, sparked by Theosophical visions and by socialist labor movements. The Koreshan Unity movement was founded by Cyrus Reed Teed. Teed experienced a transcendental vision of a divine Mother in 1869 and proclaimed himself her messianic son. In the 1870s he gathered a communal group around him that moved from Syracuse, New York, to New York City, then to Chicago, and finally sought to build their New Jerusalem in Estero, Florida. They too adopted celibacy as the ideal spiritual way of life by which to harmonize male and female "energies." The community dwindled after Teed died in 1908, and its property became a Florida state park in 1961.

The American branch of the Theosophical movement, founded by Helena Blavatsky, Henry Steel Olcott, and William Q. Judge in 1875, went through various splits. One group, led by Katherine Tingley, founded a school and community on 330 acres on Point Loma, California, in 1897. This became headquarters for spreading the Theosophical vision of spiritual renovation through cultural and educational projects. Tingley was accidentally killed while on a European tour in 1929. The Point Loma properties were sold, and the colony dispersed in 1942.

Leaders of the radical wing of the American labor movement attempted several communal socialist colonies in California between 1885 and 1937, many inspired by Edward Bellamy's socialist vision in *Looking Backward* (1888). Among these were the Keweah Cooperative Commonwealth (1885–1892), the Altrurian colony in Napa Valley (1894–1895), and the Rio de Lllano colony in the Antelope Valley in 1914, which ended its days in Louisiana in 1937. During the Great Depression in the 1930s, New Deal federal government's efforts to create work for the unemployed resulted in a number of cooperative homesteads.

Jews fleeing pogroms in Russia established a series of agricultural colonies that spread from New Jersey to Colorado and the Dakotas from 1882 to 1940. These colonies were inspired by the same vision of Jewish renewal through communitarian socialism that created the kibbutzim in Palestine. Jewish philanthropists, such as Baron de Hirsch, who sponsored migrants to Palestine, also helped fund the American colonies. American Jewish charitable organizations, fearing the concentration of poor Russian Jews in American urban slums, also funded the colonies. While short-lived, these commu-

The American branch of the Theosophical movement, founded by Helena Blavatsky, Henry Steel Olcott, and William Q. Judge in 1875, went through various splits. One group, led by Katherine Tingley (left), founded a school and community on 330 acres in Point Loma, California, in 1897. *Used with permission of the Point Loma Theosophical Community.*

nities served to disperse Jews into rural areas across the United States and contributed to founding agricultural colleges and credit unions for farmers hard hit by economic crisis.

American blacks, hardest hit by the depression, also developed a variety of efforts to create cooperative businesses in poor urban areas. Some also purchased land for efforts at collective farming. One of the most ambitious of these efforts was the Father Divine Peace Mission. At its height in the late 1930s the mission had some 150 centers with as many as 10,000 core followers. Many members lived communally and ran low-cost restaurants, stores, and industries to provide both employment and services for the poor, mostly black, communities. Although paternalistic in his style (proclaiming himself to be God), Father Divine strongly supported both racial integration and gender equality. Much of the rank and file of his following came from divorced or widowed poor black women who looked to the Peace Mission for survival.

The New Left of the mid-1960s inspired a new wave of American communal living. Many of the urban communes were chaotic and short-lived, but some of the groups that migrated into rural areas formed more lasting colonies. Among these is The Farm, which began as a New Age movement in the Haight-Asbury section of San Francisco in the late 1960s. Its leader, Stephen Gaskin, and 250 followers moved to rural Tennessee, where they have sought to live their vision of "natural" life, including mutual sexual pleasure. The commune developed a special role for women as midwives to guide women through childbirth as a peak spiritual experience.

Another New Age community, Twin Oaks, was founded in rural Virginia in 1967. They have sought to overcome gendered division of labor through a system of labor credits. Some lesbians, who grew out of the gay New Left, sought to create separatist communities by moving to rural areas in Oregon, Wisconsin, Minnesota, and New Mexico, buying land together and creating partially self-sufficient movements of "country lesbians."

At the beginning of the twenty-first century, communitarianism continues to inspire utopian experiments. An important new impetus for such societies comes from American Buddhism, which brings together renewed monasticism and ecological living. Christian apocalyptic fundamentalism also has its communal side. Some experimental groups have ended in disaster, such as the Jonestown mass suicide in November 1978 and the fiery end of the Branch Davidians at Waco, Texas, in April 1993. Despite great diversity of inspiration, utopian communities generally share a vision of separation from a debased society around them and hope for perfectibility of humanity through personal transformation and reorganized social relations.

How has this vision been related to gender relations and female roles? There are four shared aspects of the transformed self and society in these utopian communities related to women, gender symbolism, and gender relations: (1) androgynous God-language and visions of a new humanity where gender division is overcome; (2) alternative forms of family and sexual relations; (3) female founders and leadership; and (4) claims of gender equality and changes in gender-based division of labor.

Androgynous Divinity and a New Humanity

Utopian groups with a mystical inspiration have often believed in androgynous divinity. God and the spiritual powers of the universe were seen as composed of complementary principles, male and female. Often this was connected with an idea of a new humanity that will overcome the split between masculinity and femininity in the human person. This ideal was related to a theory of original human nature, its fall, and redemption. In this theory the original humanity was androgynous and spiritual. Maleness and femaleness were united in a blessed spiritual union. The fall into sin brought a division of male and female and a capitulation to the "lower" animal self, often identified with the "female" side. Redemptive spiritual transformation will overcome this split and its resultant fall into "carnality" (in the double sense of sin and fleshly mortality).

These ideas have their roots in ancient Jewish and Christian gnosticism of the first centuries C.E. Sometimes influenced by its Jewish development in Kabbalism, such ideas were revived among Christians in the sixteenth to eighteenth centuries and figured in the theories of mystics, such as Jacob Boehme (1575–1624) and Emanuel Swedenborg (1688–1772). Many communal groups that arose in Europe in this period were influenced by the thinking of these mystical philosophers.

The Shakers developed a distinctive and systematic theory of androgynous deity and a restored spiritual humanity. They taught that God who created humanity in "our" image must be both male and female, in order for humans, as male and female, to image God. They revived the ancient biblical symbolism of God as feminine Wisdom, claiming that God as male and female unites power and wisdom. As this was put in the *Testimony of Christ's Second Appearing*, the Shaker Bible:

> Thus we may see the true order and origin of our existence, descending through proper mediations, not only in the state of innocent nature, but in the state of grace: proceeding from an Eternal *Parentage*; the Eternal Two, as distinctly Two, as *Power* and *Wisdom* are Two; and as *Father* and *Mother* are two; yet immutably, unchangeably, *One Spirit*; One in *Essence* and in *Substance*. (516)

Shakers believed that humanity as male and female mirrors divine maleness and femaleness, but the original harmony of the human pair was broken by sin, resulting in a fall into animal lust, manifest in sexual intercourse. From lust arise all forms of human disorder and sin: avarice, gluttony, violence, and war. Redemption comes through successive revelations of God, culminating in the revelation of the male side of God through the male (Jesus Christ) and then of the female or Wisdom side of God through Christ's bride, Ann Lee. Humanity is called to arise from its present animal state to become a regenerated humanity through adopting celibacy and restoring harmonious parity of male and female in the Millennial Church. All people are to be gradually gathered up into this millennial humanity that will overcome all forms of lust and violence and eventually shed the mortal for the immortal state of life.

An important testimonial to the importance of the Shaker vision of the divine female is found in Rebecca Jackson, a black woman evangelist who became a Shaker elderess. Jackson records in her journal the empowering effect of this view of the divine as she looked out over the assembled worshippers.

One night we went to meeting and while they were worshipping God, I saw the head and wings of their Blessed Mother at the center of the ceiling over their heads. She appeared in glorious color. Her face was round like a full moon, with the glory of the sun reflecting from her head, formed itself into a round circle with a glorious crown. . . . And what a Mother's look she gave me! And at that look, my soul was filled with love and a motion was in my body, like one moving on the waves of the sea. I was happy. (Humez, 154)

Jackson goes on to link this vision of God the Mother with her own call to evangelize, "to make known the Mother of the New Creation of God." After Jackson became a Shaker, she was appointed the elderess of a black Shaker community in Philadelphia.

Shaker theology closely links celibacy and spiritually regenerated humanity where maleness and femaleness, spirit and body, are harmonized. Several German communitarians, also influenced by Boehme and later by Swedenborg, held similar views of divinity and redeemed humanity. These views were a major impetus for their adoption of celibacy. The Harmony Society, under George Rapp, cultivated ardent devotion to Sophia, the virginal feminine "side" of God. They saw such devotion as lifting the devotee above the carnal to spiritual union with the divine.

One prayer invokes Sophia as the "Harmonists' goddess": "O Sophia . . . play now your golden strings: Bind with loving golden chains those who follow you to the designated goal. . . . Sophia, from your glances rapture flows into my heart. . . . This flame feed the blessed heavenly love." True spiritual love for Sophia is contrasted to base animal lust: "Let no Delilah sneak into my heart and rob me of my strength! . . . O heal what is wounded, cut what is unclean! Give me, noble Virgin, a virgin-heart; give me a hero's spirit for my sufferings . . . until my spirit rests with you; nothing but you I want to love. My heart is refreshed with increasing fiery-zest. Call me yours, then I am free" (King, 113–120).

Some spiritualists, Christian Scientists, and Koreshans also believed in an androgynous deity. Ex-Universalist minister Thomas Lake Harris, founder in 1875 of the Brotherhood of the New Life in Santa Rosa, California, wrote that "we further conclude that the creative Logos, 'God manifested in the flesh,' is not male merely, nor female merely, but the two-in-one, in whose individual and social likeness, in whose spiritual and physical likeness, we seek to be reborn, is the pivot of our faith and the directive force of our life" (Harris, 143–147). Mary Baker Eddy, founder of Christian Science, wrote, "The ideal man corresponds to Intelligence and Truth. The ideal woman corresponds to Life and Love. We have not as much authority, in Divine Science, for considering God masculine, as we have for considering Him feminine, for Love imparts the highest idea of Deity" (552–554).

In spite of the male pronoun for God, we see in Eddy a common tendency in Victorian American spirituality to reverse the traditional Christian dualism in which femaleness represented the flesh and maleness the spirit. Instead, femininity was seen as representing superior spiritual virtue. The revelation of the feminine "side" of God was regarded as necessary to complete the revelation of God and fulfill human transformation. This was also the Shaker view. Cyrus Teed, founder of the Koreshan Unity, had similar ideas. Teed had a personal revelation of God the Mother through whom he saw himself as receiving the power of transformation into a biune spiritual humanity.

Mormons also believed that there is a "Mother in heaven," alongside God the Father. They conceived of both God the Father and God the Mother as literally physical, gendered supernatural persons. For the Mormons, the existence of a divine Mother alongside a divine Father was pictured as the divine prototype of Mormon patriarchal marriage, which requires two parents. But the Mother is the silent partner beside her divine husband. According to current Mormon teaching, while the divine Mother exists, she is not to be prayed to.

These nineteenth-century ideas of divine androgyny and the revelation of the female aspect of God were all but forgotten after 1920. Thus the revival of quests for the "goddess" or female divinity was seen as a radical departure from monotheist tradition when religious feminists began to claim this concept in the 1970s. Post-Christian feminists, some identifying themselves as Wiccans, see themselves as renewing ancient Goddess traditions before the rise of patriarchy. They have developed forms of spirituality and worship that focus on female deity. Such Goddess-centered spirituality is seen as necessary, not only for restoring the well-being of women but also for the redemption of a world torn by violence, perpetrated by a split-off masculinity.

One song from Goddess spirituality cries: "Goddess of life, please speak through me, though your world is bloodied and torn. There'll be a full moon rising on the ruins of our dreams if your life force is not soon reborn." The song goes on to speak of the bloody destruction of the old Goddess-centered spirituality, concluding with the words:

> [A]nd now in this time we gather again and our open hearts fill the world with truth, with a vision of power that makes each other whole, circling and spiraling the Earth. Goddess of life, you speak through me, though our world is bloodied and torn. There is a full moon rising on the birthing of our dreams as your life force is this night reborn. (*Pilgrim Warrior Songbook*, 2–3)

Sexuality and Family

Communal life, work, and property challenged the basic institutions of the nuclear family, private property, and the split between home and work. Even those communitarian societies that have separate houses for heterosexual couples and their children, and manifest traditionally gendered division of labor and male rule, such as the Hutterites, still challenge the dominant nuclear family in several ways. There is no private property to be passed down through the paternal line. Every individual must subordinate themselves to the collective good of the community. Both men and women do productive work that is essential to the economic maintenance of the whole community. Children, although they sleep at home with their parents, are socialized from the age of three to fifteen in collective schools and eat with their age group in the community dining room. At fifteen they become adults, join an adult male or female workforce, and are expected to marry soon after.

A number of American communal societies have adopted celibacy, either as an ideal to which to aspire or as a rule for the whole group. The relation of celibacy to the status of women is complex. This seems to depend on whether celibacy is defined primarily from the perspective of men or from that of women. Early Christian celibacy often suggested that women's subordinate status was dissolved by renouncing sex and marriage. Celibate women were no longer defined by sex and pro-

creation but became spiritually equal to men. However, as Christian celibacy became a requirement for a priesthood reserved for men alone, even celibate women were seen as threatening sexual temptresses. Celibate men must strictly separate themselves from all contact with women, less they be tempted and capitulate to their lower animal "side." Thus male clerical celibacy has reinforced a patriarchal view of femaleness as linked to inferiorized body and sexuality.

But Catholic celibate women have often covertly assumed a different view. Through celibacy women can free themselves from subordination to men and from the burdens of childbearing. They are freed to pursue intellectual and spiritual paths of life in independent and self-governing women's communities. There has been a continual tension in Catholicism between the male clerical view of celibate women and celibate women's own view of themselves, a conflict that has been renewed in American Catholicism since 1965, as some Catholic nuns have become consciously feminist.

Protestant celibate communal societies reveal variations of such male and female perspectives on celibacy. The German sects Rappites, Zoarites, and Inspirationists reflected a primarily male view of celibacy. Women were linked to sexual temptation representing a capitulation to the male "lower" self. Celibacy meant subordination of women and strict separation of the sexes. Men become spiritually transformed by rejecting sexual relations with women. For the Rappites, love for the divine feminine Sophia sublimates love into spiritual union with God and prevents capitulation to some "Delilah" who might "rob me of my strength" (King).

The Shakers held a mixed view of celibacy. Early Shaker documents talk of the female as representing the "animal half" of "man." Celibacy overcomes the fall of the higher self into sinful lust. But Shaker writings in the later part of the nineteenth century become increasingly feminist in their view of celibacy. Like Catholic nuns, celibacy is defined as freeing women from subjugation to men and the burdens of childbearing and allowing them an equal spiritual life. Sex is seen as the tool by which men have ruled over women. Shaker Elderess Anna White wrote in 1891:

> Woman appears in her rightful place, at once the equal of man in creation and office at the hand of God. . . . To Ann Lee may woman look for the first touch that struck off her chains and gave her absolute right to her own person. . . . Daughters of Ann Lee, alone among women, rejoice in true freedom, not alone from bondage to man's domination, but freedom also from the curse of that desire for her husband by which, through the ages, he has ruled over her. (White and Taylor, 256)

The Koreshans also had a mixed view of celibacy. Cyrus Teed strongly affirmed the equality of women in political and economic life. He saw the spiritual transformation of each person as proceeding through a process of liberation from lust, culminating in celibacy, through which male and female energies were united and every person became spiritually biune. But he often formulated this as the incorporation of female energies into a biune male, who then reigns as the perfect human. He saw himself as the exemplary expression of this perfected androgynous and even immortalized human.

The Sanctificationists of Belton, Texas, a female celibate community, saw celibacy primarily as practical. By celibacy women free themselves from male economic domination and are able to collectivize their work to become self-sufficient. This allows women in community together to pursue leisure time as they wish and to lead more satisfying lives than is possible under the regime of childbearing, unpaid housework, and legal and economic dependency on husbands.

Communal societies have also developed other alternatives to monogamous marriage. Male leaders of two nineteenth-century movements formulated forms of marriage and sexuality that became notorious. One of these was Mormon polygamy, and the other was "complex marriage" in the Oneida community. Mormon founder Joseph Smith, during his presidency of the Latter-day Saints in Nauvoo, Illinois, declared that he had received a revelation from God to restore polygamy as practiced by the biblical patriarchs. God also commanded Smith's wife, Emma, to accept this revelation. She refused to do so and eventually became the leader, with her son Joseph Smith II, of a group of Latter-day Saints that did not follow Brigham Young to Utah. The group that rejected polygamy became the Reorganized Church of Latter-day Saints.

Mormon polygamy was seen as a privilege of male leaders who were allowed the largest number of wives. Mormons have been adverse to birth control. Women are exhorted to have as many children as possible to clothe with bodies souls created by God in heaven. Yet not all Mormon women have seen polygamy as oppressive. Some experienced it as creating a community of women who could work together, sharing household and child-raising tasks.

John Humphrey Noyes interpreted the Christian ideal of having "all things in common" as sharing both goods and sexuality. He taught that any man could have sexual access to any woman in the community, but only through a complex system of application through a supervising community. Older men and women, seen as spiritually more advanced, were given preference in sexual relations, being the initiators of younger men and women into sexuality. Communal sexual access was combined with a strict ethic of nonattachment of any person to another person. Everyone should purge themselves of "stickiness" to a sexual partner. The community intervened to separate partners who were becoming too exclusively attached to each other.

Complex marriage was combined in the Oneida community with the practice of "male continence" by which men were trained to have sex without ejaculation. This avoided the "waste" of male seed and also prevented conception. In this way Noyes believed the procreative function of sexuality could be separated from the "amative." Women could enjoy sexual pleasure without fear of pregnancy. After a period of time when few children were produced in the community, Noyes embarked on a project of "sterpiculture." The most spiritually advanced members would be encouraged to procreate in order to produce superior offspring, Noyes himself having a priority in this process. Parents were to avoid "stickiness" to their children. The children were to be raised communally, belonging to the whole community as collective parents, not to one particular set of parents.

A few groups, notably the Fourierite phalanx Modern Times and the Owenite community of Nashoba, founded by Frances Wright, advocated "free love." Free love did not mean having many sexual partners at the same time but as ending woman's economic dependency and easing divorce laws. A woman and man would be allowed to separate amicably from unsatisfactory relations and form another, more satisfying partnership.

The communal movement of the late 1960s and 1970s, by contrast, saw free love as dissolving all restrictions and allowing any desired type of partnership, such as several partners at the same time or even group sex. The Tennessee New Age community The Farm originally sought to stabilize plural relations by creating committed marriages of four or more persons. But this proved unworkable for long-term relations. The community returned to monogamous, even if serial, partnerships.

Some authoritarian "cults" have become notorious for what outsiders have seen as sexual exploitation of women. This typically has taken the form of a male leader claiming total power over all other members, men and women, based on privileged access to God or even as being himself a Messiah or incarnation of God. This occurred in Cyrus Spragg's New Jerusalem, Illinois, in the mid-nineteenth century. Spragg was expelled from the Mormon Church and went on to attempt various communal alternatives. After moving his group to New Jerusalem, Spragg had a temple constructed into which he withdrew to meditate and direct the community from within. He ordered a virgin to serve him every night, claiming that one of them would become the mother of the Messiah. A rival suitor for one of the women broke into the temple and shot Spragg, who thereafter disappeared. Whether he had been killed or "ascended" spiritually remained in doubt. In any case, the community dissolved shortly thereafter (Muncy, 222–223).

Some cultlike communities in recent decades have manifest a pattern of a male authority figure claiming privileged sexual access to the women of the community. This occurred in the Children of God, founded by Pentecostal missionary David Berg, also in Jim Jones's People's Temple and David Koresh's Branch Davidians. Sexual exploitation by male leaders also developed in 1960s New Left communes. Repelled by such experiences, some women withdrew into lesbian colonies, such as the "country lesbians," and began to explore the possibilities of more egalitarian bonding between women.

Women Founders and Leaders

Few communal societies have been founded by women, although there have been notable exceptions. Many more communal societies, both in the nineteenth century and today, have claimed that their new arrangements for male and female relations would liberate women from male domination. But the actual practices of such societies have been ambivalent. Women have sometimes been allowed to participate in the political process or cultural leadership in communities but seldom given primary leadership. Leadership in communal societies has typically been charismatic and authoritarian, with one leader, usually the founder, holding superior power as an inspired figure.

Christian tradition did not accept the possibility of women in ordained priesthood, but it did recognize that God might choose a woman to be a prophet. Prophecy did not violate women's subordination, since God used the woman prophet as a vehicle of God's word, rather than the woman speaking on her own authority. Radical Protestant church traditions from which communal societies have sprung continued this view. They often saw prophecy renewed in their own societies, claiming that in their own ranks "your sons and your daughters shall prophesy," as they had in apostolic times.

The Amana Inspirationists particularly relied on what they saw as privileged prophets or *Werkzeuge* (inspired instruments) to lead them. One of these prophets was Barbara Heinemann, who in 1818 received the gift of inspiration at the age of twenty-two after a struggle of faith. Heinemann was regarded as having lost her prophetic gift and status when she married a schoolteacher in the community, George Landmann, in 1823. Twenty-six years later, after the community's immigration to America, Heinemann (now named Landmann) was seen to have regained her prophetic powers. She retained this role until her death in 1883. However, her special gift did not elevate other women to leadership. Patriarchal government in church and community affairs remained intact.

Claims of prophetic inspiration allowed several other women to found and lead communal societies in the eighteenth and nineteenth centuries. One of these was Jemima Wilkinson (1752–1819). Wilkinson grew up in a Quaker family in Pennsylvania and was converted in a New Light Baptist revival in 1774. When she fell ill and then revived, she interpreted this as having died and been resurrected. No longer her former self, her body was occupied by the Holy Spirit. God's Spirit had descended into the world to use her body to proclaim the last chance of repentance to a perishing world. Calling herself the "Universal Public Friend," Wilkinson embarked on an evangelizing mission in 1776.

Wilkinson, a striking beauty with long glossy curls and a deep voice, adopted the garb of a white cravat, flowing robes, and a man's gray beaver hat. She traveled seated on a blue velvet saddle on a spirited horse, attended by twelve disciples. Her preaching style was charismatic and compelling, although her message was essentially that of revival preachers of the time. She herself adopted celibacy, although she did not demand this of her followers. Wilkinson preached for fourteen years in the New England area, during which time she gathered several hundred converts, some of them wealthy and influential.

In 1790 Wilkinson immigrated with some 300 followers to the Seneca Indian territory of Genesee County, New York. They settled on a large tract of land where most were expected to farm individual parcels. Wilkinson and her immediate followers, many of them celibate women, occupied a central community house. Conflict and lawsuits, which continued after Wilkinson's death in 1819, marred the last days of this communal experiment.

The most notable woman founder of a communal society is Mother Ann Lee. Only the Shaker tradition developed a theory of women's elevation to equal status that mandated a pattern of equal male and female women leaders. Lee, as a young married woman in England, was in prison for "disturbing the peace" when she had a series of visions in prison that showed her that the fall of Adam and Eve into sin was caused by the sexual act. Only through renouncing sex is salvation possible. She became convinced that she was Christ's chosen instrument to proclaim this saving truth to a fallen, lust-filled world.

After several attacks on her community by English church and civil authorities, Lee had another revelation that the community was to immigrate to North America. She led this migration in 1774. After securing land near Albany, Lee conducted several preaching tours in the area. Here again she excited antagonism, both as a woman claiming spiritual authority and as the leader of a celibate community. She died in 1784, after a violent beating by a mob.

Lee justified her own special authority by claiming to be the bride of Christ, a traditional Christian term for the Church and for the Virgin Mary that Lee applied to herself. Drawing on the existing legal custom that a widow could represent an absent husband, Lee claimed that since Christ had died and was absent, she as his bride was his representative. Her followers accepted her in this special role, linking her with the revelation of divine Wisdom, or the female side of God.

After her death, the Shakers went through several stages of reorganization under James Whittaker and Joseph Meacham. Meacham shaped the organizational structure and much of Shaker theology about Lee. He chose Lucy Wright to be coleader with him. Meacham died in 1796, and Wright continued as sole leader until 1821. But Wright lacked the same theological claim as Lee. Although she maintained her position as leader for twenty-five years, some male Shakers objected to sole female rule. Thereafter the Shakers institutionalized a system of comale and cofemale rule.

Separating spiritual from economic leadership, there was to be a coelder and -elderess in every community and over the whole movement. Codeacons and -deaconesses administered the temporal business of the community. This coleadership of a male and a female was seen as reflecting the duality of God as male and female and the parallel revelation of Christ in Jesus and Mother Ann Lee. However, in the declining years of the Shakers, there ceased to be enough male members to hold parallel office. Shaker women became sole leaders in many communities.

Another significant female community founder was Frances Wright (1795–1852), herself a leading feminist abolitionist lecturer when she affiliated herself with the Owenite movement. Wright founded Nashoba in Tennessee in 1825 as an abolitionist community to free Negro slaves. Believing that Negroes debased by slavery needed to gain self-sufficiency, she bought slaves and planned to have them earn their freedom through their labor. She also sought to model equal leadership of men and women, as well as "free love." This combination of race, gender, and sexuality became explosive in the antebellum South.

Like Owen, Wright was more interested in lecturing about her ideas than settling down to the tasks of management. The community fell apart in economic disarray. In 1830 Wright arranged for the remaining emancipated slaves to immigrate to Haiti, the one Caribbean nation ruled by blacks who had overthrown slavery and colonial rule. Wright's leadership role depended on her exceptional class status as a white educated woman of means, not on a real ability to institutionalize gender and race equality in her community. In that period women had no right to own property or represent themselves at law, so Wright's freedom to operate as an independent agent in the larger society was limited and dependent on friendly men, particularly Robert Owen's son, Robert Dale Owen.

Another significant woman leader was Martha McWhirter, founder of the Sanctificationists of Belton, Texas, later called the Woman's Commonwealth. In 1876 McWhirter led a group of mostly women followers out of the Belton Methodist church into a process of self-emancipation from economic dependency on husbands. The women professionalized their own domestic skills by selling butter, eggs, rugs, and other home products. They then created a communal laundry. This represented a decline in class status for women who had been middle-class wives. But the women saw this as preferable to being at the mercy of their husbands. Several of the women had suffered physical abuse at their husbands' hands, particularly when they sought to separate themselves from them.

The women then bought a hotel and ran it themselves, cooking the meals, doing the laundry and cleaning, as well as managing the enterprise. They became prosperous and in 1898 were able to purchase a large house and move to Washington, D.C. Their collective profits were lucrative enough to enable each of them to work only four hours a day and spend the rest of their time in recreation and educational pursuits.

Although McWhirter was the leader of this process, she seems to have had a particular skill in bringing out the capacities of all the women, enabling the community to operate as a shared project. For a while these women held their own religious services, but these were replaced by mutual interpretation of dreams and "a delicate sense which belongs to the whole community, rather than to any individual member, which enables them to detect any mistake they have made or false step they have taken, by causing an unpleasant reaction to be felt in the whole body" (Garrison).

Several women in the spiritualist and Theosophical movement became important community founders but, in contrast to McWhirter, did not see their leadership as one to be shared with other women or to emancipate women generally. Mary Baker Eddy saw herself as a uniquely inspired font of revelation. She preferred to surround herself with docile males, in whose hands she lodged the governance of the Christian Science Church, rather than to empower a woman with rival charisma. In Christian Science women have predominated in the role of healing practitioners. Katherine Tingley followed a similar path, as the unique spiritual leader surrounded by docile male followers, in her Theosophical community in Point Loma, California. Other women played more traditional roles, such as teachers, in her school.

Some women have led major communal movements in the last period of their existence. Gertrude Rapp, the carefully educated granddaughter of George Rapp, was a leader of the Rappite Harmonists after her grandfather died in 1847. Edna Rose Ritching, a white Canadian women whom Father Divine married in 1946 when she was twenty-one years old and he was sixty-seven, inherited the leadership of the Peace Mission when he died in 1965. She was given the title Mother Divine. But this type of female leadership follows a traditional patriarchal pattern in which women are allowed a substitute leadership for a dead male relative who they are seen as representing.

Gender Equality and Women's Work Roles

This history does not suggest an impressive record of communal societies as vehicles of women's emancipation, despite the claims that some communal movements have made in this regard. In some cases communalism has actually increased women's sexual and economic exploitation. Women have fared best in those few communities where a woman is the founder and women predominate in the membership, where there has been a conscious theory that a goal of the community is gender equality, and where this theory has been translated into democratization of decision making and women's control of the economic profits of their own work.

The Woman's Commonwealth accomplished these goals by separating from economic dependence on their husbands, professionalizing their domestic skills so that they earned profits from this work, rather than serving as unpaid labor for their husbands. They achieved a unique rapport with each other in shared guidance of the group. The group was mostly all female (one or two men occasionally lived with the women, and the son of Martha McWhirter lived in the community for much of his life). They were relatively small, peaking at fifty members. They only lasted through the lifetime of the first generation and so did not face the problem of institutionalizing a system of passing on the leadership. Their experience shows that women need not do what has been defined as male work in order to be emancipated. They only have to gain economic control over their work, whatever it may be, and to make this work sufficiently lucrative.

The Shakers followed the traditional gendered division of labor, with women doing the "indoor" work, such as cooking, sewing, basket making, and broom making, and men the carpentry and farmwork. But by returning to preindustrial household economy where men's and women's work are equally productive and necessary for the maintenance of the community, they prevented one type of work from being seen as inferior to the other. Women were not unpaid workers dependent on men as paid workers. Most of both men's and women's work went into an unpaid consumer economy,

while the work of both was marketed. At first male Shakers did most of the marketing of the community's goods, but as male members declined in numbers, women ran the Shaker stores, kept the accounts, and maintained the community economically by their handiwork.

The Owenites and Fourierites made the most sweeping claims that women would be emancipated through their version of communal living. They believed that the communalization of property and work would overcome the split between unpaid domestic labor of women and the paid labor of men upon which women were economically dependent. In addition, they saw communal child raising as freeing women from isolation in child care. But the reality of life in these groups was more ambivalent. In some cases, women were allowed to share in male roles, as educators or writers, or did outdoor physical labor untypical of middle-class white women at that time. Women could participate in community discussion and sometimes vote. But the men did not take on any of the traditional work of women.

The result of this one-sided "emancipation" of women into some aspects of the "male sphere," without a corresponding sharing of men in women's work, was a double shift for women. In New Harmony and Brook Farm, women could be intellectual leaders and do "outdoor" work. But they were also expected to do the cooking, cleaning, and sewing for the whole community, including a number of single males. Although there was communal child raising, women did this work as well. Thus communalism increased rather than decreased women's work.

The result was that many women, generally of middle-class background, found themselves having to do an extended double workday, without the servants they were accustomed to in the private family of the time. Owenite and other utopian socialist communities were plagued with unhappy wives who had not chosen to join such communities but were brought into them by enthusiastic husbands attracted to socialist theories. They were treated as appendages of their husbands, without decision-making power or authority over their own children, while being burdened with far longer hours of arduous labor than in the private household. The few intellectual women, such as Frances Wright, who participated in such communities did not help ordinary wives, since they acted as "honorary" men who could write and lecture but expected other women to do the domestic work for them.

The Oneida Perfectionists also were hardly emancipatory in women's work roles. Here men dominated the income-producing work and made the financial decisions. Women did the housework, laundry, and sewing for both men and women. They also proudly took on skilled jobs hitherto untypical of middle-class white women's work at the time, such as printing and running machines in the silk factory. Sometimes they were allowed to drive the team of horses or work in the machine shop. But boys were educated for college, being then sent to the finest universities, while girls left the community's school at twelve to be incorporated into women's work and sex roles.

Oneida women did wear the bloomer outfit that allowed them freedom of movement, in contrast to the confining long skirts and stays of middle-class female dress. Mothers had their children taken from them at the age of one to be raised in a separate nursery and school by male and female teachers. While this freed them from isolated child rearing, many women experienced as agonizing the demand that they stifle their love for their own children. Noyes himself was a paternalistic autocrat, who subordinated both male and female members to his will, so in a sense the genders were equalized in their dependency on him. A system of spiritual hierarchy allowed some women to rule over younger women and men, but within the framework of ultimate rule by the great Father.

The new wave of communes from 1965 have yet to be studied systematically, but general impressions do not suggest that their record is freed from the ambivalence of their nineteenth-century ancestors. New Left communes, as well as cult movements, have a questionable record of sexual and economic exploitation of women. The primary exceptions may be lesbian communes where women bond together to do the economic work jointly, while owning and managing their means of subsistence.

The New Age community The Farm represents a mixture of reversion to traditional male and female division of labor and gender complementarity, while seeking to modify male aggression and idealize female mothering. Promiscuity is forbidden and abortion is discouraged. By making midwifery a specialty of a leadership group of women, this traditional role is elevated to the highest status of spiritual mediation, as well as a source of income.

The most ambitious effort to equalize gender work roles in a communal society of both men and women is Twin Oaks, begun as a Skinnerite experiment in rural Virginia in 1967, which used behaviorist incentives for work. It has worked out a system of labor credits in which each member must do forty-seven hours of work a week but receive labor credit for all types of work, from car repair to child care to backrubs. There is an organized effort to train women to do traditionally male work (carpentry, machinery) and to train men to do women's work. Thus Twin Oaks has an organized if somewhat mechanistic system for overcoming gendered division of labor and giving equal status to all kinds of work. They are guided overall by a preference for the values traditionally associated with women, rather than those associated with men. Nurturing rather than aggression is the norm for relationships. It is perhaps symptomatic that female members outnumber men. This system has proved to have a reasonably successful longevity.

Utopian movements have been a Janus-faced phenomenon since the nineteenth century. They have claimed to represent the dawning of a new world of freedom, equality, and justice, overcoming gender, class, and sometimes race hierarchies. They have also sought to restore preindustrial agrarian and handicraft economies. By producing much of their own subsistence needs and marketing the produce of their joint labor, they have altered the dependency of the privatized household on the capitalist economy. Only a few have sustained themselves beyond the founding generation. The most long lasting are the most traditional, celibate religious orders and the Hutterite communal patriarchy.

Yet communal living continues to attract men and women deeply alienated from the dominant capitalist society, with its gender, class, and race hierarchies and its increasing gap between rich and poor. At the beginning of the twenty-first century, looming ecological disaster is added to the other ills created by existing social and economic arrangements. Communalized farming and handicrafts take on a new attraction as a way of restoring sustainable relations of human production, consumption, and the ecosystem.

Significantly one of the groups presently pioneering new forms of community life that address the ecological crisis are Catholic nuns. Drawing on their traditional structures as women's religious communities who own their own land, the primarily Catholic ecofeminist movement, Sisters of Earth, seeks to join spirituality and sustainable living in new forms of community for the future. The most important center for this movement is Genesis Farm, New Jersey, founded by Sister Marie Teresa McGinnis. Genesis Farm offers hands-on earth literacy programs for those who want to start their own ecojustice centers. The oldest form of Christian communalism may yet be a significant harbinger of an alternative future, as these religious women seek to reenvision their relation to each other and to the earth on which we live.

SOURCES: Wendy E. Chmielewski, Louis J. Kern, and Marlyn Klee-Hartzell, *Women in Spiritual and Communitarian Societies in the United States* (1993). Mary Baker Eddy, *Science and Health, With Key to the Scriptures*, 68th ed. (1895). George Garrison, "The Sanctificationists of Belton," *The Charities Review* (November 1893): 29–46. "Goddess of Life," from *Pilgrim Warrior Songbook* (n.d.), 2–3. Thomas Lake Harris, writing to W. A. Hinds, August 22, 1877, reprinted in *American Communities* (1878), 143–147. Jean Mahon Humez, ed., *Gifts of Power: The Writings of Rebecca Jackson* (1981). Hilda Adam

King, *The Harmonists* (1973), 113–120. Raymond Lee Muncy, *Sex and Marriage in Utopian Communities* (1973). Donald E. Pitzer, ed., *America's Communal Societies* (1997). *Testimony of Christ's Second Appearing* (1856). Anna White and Leila S. Taylor, *Shakerism* (1904).

MORMON WOMEN
Claudia L. Bushman

MORMONISM, OR FORMALLY the Church of Jesus Christ of Latter-day Saints, is often considered an uncongenial religion for women. The church is directed by an entirely male priesthood and once practiced polygamy, not a female-friendly marital practice. The Latter-day Saint Church has appeared on the national scene to oppose abortion, gay marriage, and the Equal Rights Amendment. Within the church, women's voices are absent at the highest levels of the bureaucracy.

Yet women have always played an important part in Mormon history, and many are deeply devoted to the faith. Active Mormon women outnumber active Mormon men. Latter-day Saint beliefs encourage women to develop their abilities as potentially God-like individuals even as they assert that family relationships are all important. Mormon women have independently supported themselves in many fields and enjoyed suffrage in Utah as early as 1870. An increasing number of young Mormon women serve full-time church missions, along with the men. In everyday church affairs, women pray, preach, organize, and teach.

The Latter-day Saint Church was begun by Joseph Smith, an uneducated farm boy who saw visions and who translated and published the Book of Mormon, a history of ancient Israelites in the Americas. Smith's mother Lucy Mack Smith was the more religious of his parents, and her efforts to take her family to church precipitated her son's religious crisis. When Joseph's father refused to attend, the son was confused. Praying to know which of the local competing churches was the right one, he received his first vision in 1820 at the age of fourteen. Lucy believed that God was involved. In Smith's second vision, three years later, the Angel Moroni identified himself as one of the writers of an ancient book written on gold plates that gave an account of the former inhabitants of the continent and how they had come from Jerusalem. Smith was allowed an annual visit to the place where the plates were buried and later "translated" and published the history as the Book of Mormon.

Smith's wife Emma Hale also believed in him. Joseph and his father had hunted for treasure near Harmony, Pennsylvania, while they boarded at the farm of Isaac Hale, Emma's father. Joseph was immediately drawn to Emma, who eloped with him against her family's wishes. In 1827, when Smith went to the Hill Cumorah to retrieve the gold plates, his wife went with him. She was involved in the founding work of the church, serving as his first scribe as he translated the plates. Her testimony to the translation is one of the more convincing. Eleven men testified to seeing and handling the golden plates, described as thin golden sheets, about eight inches square, bound with three large gold rings, but Emma noted that Joseph picked up the dictation each day without having the previous passage read back. Her husband's translation from the ancient text was inspired, she said, because on his own he could not even write a decent letter. She never saw the plates, which were kept on a table covered by a silk handkerchief, but said that she touched them while dusting.

Smith's translation was published as the Book of Mormon in March 1830, the work of three months of dictated translation. People intrigued by the book began to believe, and on April 6, 1830, Smith organized a church with about fifty people. He was then just twenty-five. The church defined itself as a restoration of a pure Christianity by means of heavenly visitations, revelations, and the direct passing on of authority to the young prophet and his followers. Mormons consider themselves Christian without being Catholic or Protestant. They profess a deep belief in Jesus Christ, the need for baptism, repentance, and living a Christian life. Mormons believe in the Bible and in the Book of Mormon, subtitled "Another Testament of Jesus Christ."

The Book of Mormon says little about women, less than the Bible. The long narrative historical record of early peoples of the Americas from about 2200 B.C.E. until 421 C.E. charts political, religious, and military changes. Only six women are mentioned by name, none a major figure. The book shows women participating in household and religious activities, in family terms. Mothers of 2,000 young warriors, for example, are credited with teaching their boys faith. The book promotes gender equality: "All are alike unto God," both "black and white, bond and free, male and female" (2 Nephi 26:33).

Within a decade, the church numbered more than 20,000, growing despite persecution wherever they settled. Because of cultural and religious differences, their gathering in large disciplined groups threatened other residents with the loss of local political control. Their outspoken claims to divine authority and later their marital practices added to the antipathy. Dogged by their enemies, Mormons moved to Ohio, to Missouri, to Illinois, and finally to Utah, where the church established a powerful theocracy in the valley of the Great Salt Lake. At the turn of the twenty-first century, Mormonism counted more than 11 million adherents settled in most of the countries of the world, more than half outside the United States.

From New York to Nebraska, 1830–1847

Under Joseph Smith's direct leadership, this was a time of settlement and exodus, of revelation and organization. After the organization of the church in 1830, Smith continued to receive divine revelations. Few mentioned women. In one of these, Emma Smith was told to devote herself to learning and to writing. She was instructed to compile the first book of Latter-day Saint hymns and did so with the assistance of W. W. Phelps, a converted newspaper editor.

Another revelation bestowed priesthood authority on Smith, who conferred it on all men but to no women. Priesthood holders were forbidden to exercise unrighteous dominion. The Doctrine and Covenants, a collection of Smith's revelations, noted that the power of the priesthood should only be exercised by persuasion, long suffering, gentleness, meekness, and love. Based on the account in Genesis, Mormons believe that the genders are equal, both created in the image of God, but that they have different roles. Men and women are to marry and have children, to create families. Men are to support the family, the women to nurture children and to supervise a happy home. Motherhood and priesthood are often considered parallel roles. The establishment of the Kingdom of God is inextricably linked to the establishment of family groups. Kinship is a central organizing principle within Mormonism, where members call each other brother and sister. Women joined the church in numbers equal to men. The new gospel promised generous spiritual gifts, and Mormon women enjoyed these along with the men, speaking in tongues and interpreting the speech of others. Women put their hands on the heads of other women and children and blessed them, healing them from illness. The New Testament predicted that these signs would follow faith. Women were considered particularly gifted in receiving these powers.

Belonging to this new church required sacrifice from women. Because Mormons were instructed to gather to Zion, most left their homes to move to new settlements. Once there, the men were sent on long missions, leaving women behind to tend and support households. Frequently at odds with their neighbors because of their strange faith and their growing numerical strength, Mormons were driven from their homes, and the women bore the brunt of this displacement. During stable periods, women helped build up the church.

In 1833, in the Mormon settlement of Kirtland, Ohio, work began on an ambitious two-story Mormon temple, 80 by 59 feet, with a 100-foot tower that dwarfed the settlement and nearly bankrupted the people. As men labored on the building, women sewed curtains to divide up the large rooms. The temple was dedicated in March 1836, and according to witnesses, the event was accompanied by spiritual manifestations. Visitors sighted angels and pillars of light. Church meetings, a school, and a weekly day of fasting and prayer took place there. When local opposition against the Mormons increased the next year, they left behind their homes and the temple and headed west.

In Missouri, again unwelcome, the Mormons were attacked by local people who burned their cabins and haystacks. Missouri governor Lilburn Boggs issued an order to drive the Mormons from the state or to exterminate them. At the small Mormon settlement Haun's Mill, 240 armed men killed about 20 Mormons. Smith was captured, charged with treason, and sentenced to death by firing squad, a sentence the officer refused to carry out. With Smith in jail, the Saints crossed the Mississippi River to Illinois. Smith escaped from jail and planned the city of Nauvoo, Illinois, his last and most ambitious settlement. The Mormons lived there for six years.

Joseph Smith's attention to women enlarged in the last years of his life. In 1842, the organization of the women's Relief Society gave them an official role. Seeing the need for a charitable association, the women proposed a constitution. Recognizing the potential, Smith redirected the organization's purpose, saying that he had desired to organize the sisters in the order of the Priesthood and that the church organization was not perfect until the women were organized. The "Female Relief Society of the City of Nauvoo," he said, helped the sisters to "provoke the brethren to good works in looking to the wants of the poor—searching after objects of charity, and in administering to their wants to assist; by correcting the morals and strengthening the virtues of the female community, and save the Elders the trouble of rebuking; that they may give their time to other duties &c. in their public teaching" (Derr, Cannon, and Beecher, 30). Emma Smith, the society's first president, said, "We are going to do something *extraordinary* . . . we expect extraordinary occasions and pressing calls" (31). The women contributed what they had, solicited donations from the rich, and helped the poor and suffering as they could. The women sewed shirts and mittens for temple workers and distributed food to the hungry. Joseph Smith told the women that they would have the privileges, blessings, and gifts of the Priesthood. These gifts would follow their virtuous lives and conversation. Smith told the sisters to be united with their brethren in meekness, love, and purity. When the Saints moved west in 1847, the Relief Society disbanded but was reestablished in 1867 in Utah.

More important in the expansion of women's role were newly revealed temple ceremonies that included women in the ordinances. In 1843 at the temple built in Nauvoo, women received the temple endowment along with men and officiated in the temple in the name of the Priesthood. Salvation was conceived as a family matter, coming to men and women in family groups. In special rituals husbands and wives were married for eternity and their children linked to them. This process extended to baptism by proxy for relatives already dead, again uniting the family over time.

Also in the revelation explaining eternal marriage was the command to practice plural marriage, called by the Mormons *celestial marriage* and technically termed *polygyny*. Additional women could be sealed in marriage in the temple to men already married. Smith may have received this revelation as early as 1831, but he was slow to teach it, partly because his wife Emma resisted and opposed the practice. He secretly married as many as thirty-three other women. He told followers of the teaching in 1843, and slowly and reluctantly, after prayers and tears, many complied with his instruction, feeling that salvation was to be found in Mormonism, despite the trials of plural marriage. This practice of plural marriage was the most drastic and dramatic, most noteworthy and notorious aspect of women's lives in the early church. Although the practice was officially discontinued in 1890, the legacy remains.

In 1844, Joseph Smith, who had been evading arrest by moving from place to place for years, shut down a dissident press in the Mormon city of Nauvoo. The countryside was outraged and called for his arrest and execution. He fled west, but Emma, who thought he was deserting his people and family, urged his return. He surrendered to authorities for trial, and Governor Ford of Illinois guaranteed his safety. But Ford left town, and a mob of a hundred disguised men stormed the jail where Smith and his friends were detained, killing Joseph and his brother Hyrum. Succession to church leadership turned on the family. Some thought Joseph Smith had named his son to succeed him as president, but other claims were advanced. Brigham Young, the president of the Twelve Apostles, asserted his quorum's leadership and eventually prevailed but not without creating a major schism. When the majority of the Saints left Nauvoo in 1846 to go west, many, including Joseph Smith's wife Emma and his mother Lucy, remained behind. Emma Smith's devotion to her husband had been

Many women lived in households as second or third wives, sharing husbands and limited incomes. The teaching of plural marriage, quietly disclosed to the faithful in 1843 by Joseph Smith, was made public in 1852. Fewer than 20 percent of church members were ever active in this practice, but accurate figures are elusive because many marriages were secretly performed and divorce easily granted. *Used by permission of Southern Utah University Special Collections.*

tried by plural marriage, and the Mormons going west were ever more openly polygamous. Some years later in 1860, the remaining Illinois group formed the Reorganized Church of Jesus Christ of Latter-day Saints (RLDS) with Joseph Smith III as the leader and prophet. Emma Smith joined her son's church that continued to be led by lineal descendants until 1996. The RLDS church long denied that Smith had ever taught plural marriage. More Protestant in style than the Utah group, the church opened the priesthood to women in 1984 and became known as the Community of Christ in 1999. These two Mormon groups have coexisted for many years, gradually drifting farther apart.

Pressure to leave Illinois continued, and on February 5, 1846, the first group of Mormons crossed the Mississippi. Nine women are said to have given birth to babies on that first freezing night in Montrose, Iowa, American refugees from their own people. Two years later the Nauvoo Temple was burned.

The Mormon Israel headed west and built a temporary community called Winter Quarters near Council Bluffs, Iowa. After settling in, the group was drained of manpower by the creation of the "Mormon battalion," a group enlisted to help the United States in the war against Mexico. As 500 men marched west to provide income for the Saints, a largely female group remained, enduring the cold, malnutrition, and disease. Given power and wisdom to teach and bless each other, the women transcended daily suffering. Journals of the period include accounts of miraculous healings, a practice later discouraged. Spiritual experiences united the women in a close sisterhood distinct from the home and congregation.

The first wagon train consisting of 150 men under Brigham Young's direction set out to the Utah valley in the spring of 1847, arriving in July. The second, much larger wagon train, with 1,553 women and men, 2,212 oxen, 124 horses, 587 cows, 358 sheep, 716 chickens, and some pigs, a moving agricultural village with everything but land, set off around July. Mary Isabella Horne, one pioneer, owned three wagons that carried a small cooking stove, a rocking chair, and food for eight people for eighteen months, meant to last until the next year's harvest. Women kept house along the trail. When they passed Young's party returning from Utah to Winter Quarters, they roasted a fat steer for a feast, improvising a table for a thousand diners, no small achievement in heavily falling snow.

A Period of Pioneering, Patriarchy, Polygamy, and Persecution, 1847–1896

Under the direction of Brigham Young in the Salt Lake Valley, women pioneered new territory under primitive conditions. Mary Isabella Horne first lived in a tent in a fort and then in a two-room log house without doors or floors. She improvised a corner bed by inserting poles into holes in two log walls. The poles met where the one bed leg sat on the floor, and strips of rawhide were interlaced for the spring. A rag in grease made a lamp. She had brought two windows, as well as the stove and rocking chair. Packing boxes became cupboards, tables, and stools. Constrained from bringing much, these women contrived to create familiar homes.

Many women lived in polygamous households as second or third wives, sharing husbands and limited incomes. Polygamy, quietly disclosed to the faithful in 1843, was made public in 1852. Fewer than 20 percent of church members were ever active in this practice, but accurate figures are elusive because many marriages were secretly performed and divorce was easily granted. Men in positions of leadership, with sufficient incomes, were encouraged to marry another wife. Very few had more than two or three wives. The common plural family was a middle-aged pair with a second, and maybe a third, younger wife. Polygamy created a strong female society, with bonds between sisters, mothers, daughters, and sister wives, occasionally visited by men.

Many wives admitted that the life was difficult. They faced the loss of their husband's loyalty and affections even as they consented and defended the principle to others. Mary Jane Done Jones considered polygamy to be a trial to a woman, but just as hard on the man. Much adjustment was required. Augusta Joyce Crocheron thought that any woman could be a one and only wife but that Christian philosophy, fortitude, and self-discipline were required for polygamists who had to cast out selfishness and rise above petty slights.

Smith's revelation gave no justification for the practice but the Old Testament pattern. However, polygamy provided homes for single immigrant women without family connections. The greatest number of such unions was contracted in the 1850s, a time of near starvation. Extra hands helped make a living and provided Mormon husbands for women who might have married out of the faith. The principle encouraged female independence and cooperation with sister wives who divided up the labor. Frontier shortages of goods and cash and absent men imposed unusual responsibility on women, while plural marriage enforced the boundaries against other Americans, strengthening the community's internal bonds. In the greater world, this practice was considered a threat to the American home and widely denounced, isolating Mormons morally just as they were isolated geographically.

To organize women in the Mormon settlements, the Relief Society was revived under the direction of Eliza R. Snow in 1862. Snow, a writer and a poet who joined the church in Ohio in 1835, had been one of Joseph Smith's plural wives and a leading practitioner of spiritual gifts. She later married Brigham Young. Mormon women concentrated their energies on family life and toward building up the kingdom through the Relief Society, which granted them both economic and ecclesiastical identities. Relief Society activities helped women sustain themselves and benefited the community. They built Relief Society Halls furnished with cooking and sewing equipment and encouraged cooperative activities, producing brooms, baskets, straw hats, and other items, sometimes sold in their cooperative general stores. The Relief Society helped staunch the flow of dollars eastward for imported goods. The society and the later Retrenchment Society helped women stifle frivolous desires for fashionable clothes and redirect demand toward neat, homemade articles.

In response to the policy of self-sufficiency, the women obediently practiced sericulture to produce their own silk dresses. They planted mulberry trees and fed smelly silkworms. The worms sometimes took over whole houses, unless killed by ants, rats, or disease. The women produced silk handkerchiefs, collars, dresses, and stockings. They built a silk factory before sericulture was abandoned as impractical.

The Relief Society stored wheat against possible famine. They gleaned the harvested fields for overlooked kernels and sold the eggs laid on Sundays to purchase grain. In time the women amassed huge stores of wheat in society granaries. From these supplies the women gave out wheat for bread during droughts or sold the grain to help build chapels. In 1880, the sisters loaned out 35,000 bushels of wheat for seed.

The Relief Society encouraged women to study and practice midwifery. Particularly in childbirth, Mormons felt that women should be treated by other women, as a matter of modesty. Midwife Patty Sessions, who lived to be ninety-nine, attended 3,977 births and had only two difficult cases. Hannah Sorenson claimed to have delivered 4,000 babies safely.

When medical training improved, Mormon women, who had relied on the natural and folk remedies of their time, traveled east to earn degrees. Although Mormons still believed in divine healing, Brigham Young asserted that women should have the "privilege of studying." He noted that women were not only useful to "sweep houses, wash dishes, and raise babies, but that they should study law . . . or physic." The time had come, he said, that women should "come forth as doctors in these valleys of the mountains" (Bushman, 58). Toward the end of the century, a higher percentage of women from Utah studied medicine than from any other state or territory.

Ellis Shipp left her four small children with another of her husband's wives while she studied at the Women's Medical College in Philadelphia in the 1870s. Pregnant after a summer visit home, she returned to Philadelphia

and delivered her fifth child the day after her last exam. Back in Salt Lake City, she was part of a steady stream of eastern-trained female doctors who taught nursing and obstetrics to Relief Society delegates from far-flung congregations. When these students returned home, they taught what they had learned to their communities. In the 1880s, the women created a hospital in Salt Lake for medical treatment, maternity care, and training.

While attempting self-sufficiency in the desert west, the Mormon women could not escape the scrutiny and disapproval of eastern observers who considered them slaves and concubines, prisoners in their own homes. Protestant churches raised funds for missions to Utah to save the mistreated women and opened schools to save the children. Polygamy was considered an ill equal to slavery. The national government denied six petitions for statehood because of polygamy, hostility to outside capitalism, and the power of the Mormon theocracy. In 1862 Congress passed the Morrill Anti-Bigamy Act, which levied heavy financial penalties against the church.

This move to halt polygamy encouraged feminist action in Mormon women who surprised the nation by getting the vote soon after women in Wyoming and by exercising it first. Observers hoped that with this suffrage, Mormon women would vote out polygamy, but they made no effort to do so. These Utah voters forged a bond with eastern suffragists Elizabeth Cady Stanton and Susan B. Anthony, who visited them in the West. The Utah women produced a length of their homemade black silk for a dress for Anthony.

Easterners hoped that the Transcontinental Railroad in 1869 would help the women escape their oppression. John Coyner, a Presbyterian educator in the West, wrote in 1879 that he had once believed that Utah's women were held captive by their men, unable to escape from the degradation of their position. He was sure that they would welcome the chance to escape this thralldom. But he was surprised to find that he was mistaken.

The women eloquently defended their chosen lives in public mass meetings, protesting the passage of the Cullom Act by the U.S. House of Representatives, which required all polygamist prosecutions to be heard by federal, rather than local, judges and juries. When this news reached Utah, 3,000 Mormon women gathered in the Salt Lake Tabernacle to demonstrate, asserting that Mormon practices were the "only reliable safeguard of female virtue and innocence" against prostitution. Suffrage leader Sarah M. Kimball said on this occasion, "We have been driven from place to place, and wherefore? Simply for believing and practicing the counsel of God, as contained in the gospel of heaven." Eliza R. Snow noted that if Mormon women were the "stupid, degraded, heartbroken beings that we have been represented, silence might better become us." But "as women of God, women fulfilling high and responsible positions, performing sacred duties—women who stand not as dictators, but as counselors to their husbands, and who, in the purest, noblest sense of refined womanhood, are truly helpmates—we not only speak because we have the right, but justice and humanity demand that we should" (Tullidge, 384, 392). This political activism and female support for polygamy surprised the country. Mormon women entered the political sphere, and the bill failed to pass the Senate.

Church leaders encouraged the women to speak out, and their voice became the independent newspaper the *Woman's Exponent*, subtitled "The Rights of Women of Zion and the Rights of Women of all Nations," published from 1872 to 1914. The first issue of this feminist public face proclaimed that the journal would discuss "every subject interesting and valuable to women." Included were reports and articles on women around the world, on Latter-day Saint women's organizations, editorials, articles, and poetry. Correspondents from widespread church settlements spoke for themselves and encouraged others to speak. The paper supported gender equality, equal pay, exercise, sensible clothing, and educational and professional advancement. With circulation of about a thousand, the paper was influential beyond the numbers and the boundaries of the church, widely read and quoted.

Female activity did not stay governmental action, which took over the territorial government and punished polygamy with fines or imprisonment. In 1882, all believers in polygamy, practicing or not, were disenfranchised, after twelve years of female suffrage. An appeal to the U.S. Supreme Court was denied. Over 1,000 men went to prison for "unlawful cohabitation." Others disappeared to the safe houses and hiding places of the "underground." The Edmunds-Tucker Act of 1887 enforced the 1862 law that dissolved the corporation of the church, confiscated church property, disinherited children of polygamous marriages, and forbade Mormon governmental participation, disenfranchising all women. The Supreme Court upheld this law. National woman suffrage leader Belva Lockwood stated that no despot could have more fully denied the rights of these Mormon women than did the government of the United States.

At this low point, the church's president Wilford Woodruff foreswore the practice of polygamy, declaring his intention to submit to the laws forbidding plural marriage and urging others to do likewise. His document, the Manifesto, read at the church's General Conference in 1890, stunned the congregation, who nonetheless unanimously approved it. For fifty years the church had preached, practiced, and protected this form of marriage. Suddenly it was stopped. One plural wife wrote, "I was there in the tabernacle the day of the Manifesto, and I tell you it was an awful feeling. There Pres. Woodruff read the Manifesto that made me no longer a wife and might make me homeless. . . . But I voted for it because it was the only thing to do" (Young, 411).

The Utah Territory Woman Suffrage Association had been organized in 1889 and soon numbered fourteen chapters, most under LDS sponsorship. Whether female suffrage should be included in the new state constitution was hotly debated, and universal suffrage prevailed. In 1896, Utah became a state, the third in the Union with a female vote. Democrat Martha Hughes Cannon won a state senate seat contested by her Republican husband Angus. Plural marriage and hostilities with the greater world ended as statehood began.

A Time of Outmigration from Utah to the West and East Coasts, 1896–1950

Mormon women, as mothers and managers, held to the conservative domestic style of rural agrarianism as the church rebuilt its organization to achieve respectability and financial stability. Around the turn of the century, however, leaders began to reverse the pattern of gathering to Zion, encouraging new converts not to immigrate to Utah but to remain in their own areas, building up the church there. This changed policy was coupled with outmigration, mostly to the West Coast, as Mormons left the Valley for educational and business opportunities. Women, transplanted to new climes, recreated the cultural richness of life in Zion in new places. As Mormons migrated away from the Utah center, the women adapted church culture to new conditions.

The public voice of Mormon women remained the Relief Society, numbering 22,000 members in more that 400 units in 1888. Their properties were valued in excess of $95,000. They owned 32,000 bushels of stored grain. Charitable work continued, and in 1898 the Relief Society trained nurses, giving free education to those willing to aid charity cases. All local groups cared for the sick and prepared the dead for burial. The Mormon women also directed the organizations that taught the children and young women and taught in the Sunday School.

Much changed in the church at the turn of the century besides a new state government and the end of polygamy. Joseph F. Smith, son of Joseph Smith's brother Hyrum, the first church-born president, moved toward consolidation and systematization. Presiding over 168,331 men, women, and children, Smith recognized a changed political and economic situation. The Mormon settlements that had focused inwardly on themselves for fifty years now saw themselves as part of the national population. Formerly they had emphasized the differences between Mormons and others. They now looked for similarities.

As the first major schism had been caused by disagreement over polygamy, so its cessation caused another schism. Many felt that plural marriage had been abandoned for practical rather than religious reasons. Zealots secretly contracted new plural marriages, and a stronger prohibitory statement was issued in 1904. Polygamists gathered in clandestine groups to continue plural marriage. At the beginning of the twenty-first century, Utah and nearby states still had about 30,000 of these fundamentalist polygamists, most of them excommunicated from the larger church.

Prejudice against the Mormons still remained. In 1898, many objected to seating the elected Democratic congressman from Utah, B. H. Roberts. As a church leader and a known polygamist, he seemed unqualified for national office. Women's groups, religious congregations, and newspaper writers sent a barrage of anti-Roberts petitions to Congress, and he was denied office. In 1903, when Reed Smoot, another devout, but monogamous, Mormon was elected to the Senate, the petition movement was repeated. Smoot, however, was seated.

The Relief Society, still led by early converts, continued its spiritual emphasis. The group seemed old-fashioned to younger women, and leaders moved toward more progressive courses of study and training for mothers. Women's clubs came to Utah, and several lineage societies were organized in the 1890s. Descendants of the pre-1869 Mormon settlers organized the Daughters of Utah Pioneers to celebrate their ancestors' secular accomplishments.

Grain saving continued, and the women sent sixteen carloads of wheat to San Francisco after the 1906 earthquake. The next year they sent more to counter a famine in China. In 1918 all the Relief Society wheat was released for war use. About 200,000 bushels were sold to the U.S. government for $1.20 a bushel. The decision to sell the Relief Society's wheat was made by priesthood leaders without consulting the Relief Society. Dismayed by this disregard, the Relief Society leaders asked for a clarification of their role and were defined into subordinate status. Their own "Circular of Instructions" in 1915 said that "while acting independently in their own sphere of activity, [they were] under the controlling power of the priesthood, vested in the Presidency of the Church, the Presidency of the Stake, and the Bishopric of the Ward" (Derr, Cannon, and Beecher, 213). Formerly independent groups became subordinate levels of a hierarchy.

Emmeline B. Wells, secretary of the Relief Society for two decades and the longtime editor of *Woman's Exponent*, became general Relief Society president at age eighty-two. In 1914, Wells replaced the privately owned *Woman's Exponent* with the official *Relief Society Magazine* (1914–1970), which included articles and lesson materials for classes on literature, theology, genealogy, mother training, and handwork. Record keeping improved. These developments modernized the old Relief Society. The new motto "Charity Never Faileth" combined biblical language, an emphasis on good works, and an optimistic tone.

All the women's activities of the Salt Lake groups were repeated in hundreds of other administrative units and congregations known as branches, districts, wards, and stakes far from the headquarters of the church in the United States and increasingly in other countries. Women built halls, stored grain, taught lessons, visited the sick, raised funds, and forwarded the society's charities. In 1917 the Relief Society reported 45,339 members who spent 36,581 days with the sick, made 78,066 visits to sick persons, helped 5,868 families, and prepared 2,311 bodies for burial. They paid out $53,883 for charitable purposes that year. This work was also forwarded by pairs of missionary sisters who joined the previously male missionary force.

Charismatic gifts, the staples of Mormon women's lives in the past, were practiced less often and less publicly. The church leadership announced in 1914 that any good sister with faith and a belief in the efficacy of prayer could bless children and adults, but it would be better if the women called in the male elders of the church rather than giving the blessings themselves. The general movement was for religious manifestations to come within recognized lines of priesthood authority, within doctrinally defensible limits.

In another important change in tradition within this period, Emmeline B. Wells, in ill health, was released from her office as Relief Society president. Prior to her tenure, all presidents had served until death, as had all male presidents of the church. The male presidents of the church continue to serve until death, but Relief Society presidents now have shorter tenure.

Relief Society members moved deeper into welfare during the Great Depression in the 1930s. The church, which had always taken care of its own, felt a tension with government programs. Should they relinquish their responsibility for the poor? They shared the burden. Then in 1935, the Relief Society Social Service Department, already working on employment, adoption, and foster care services, moved with the larger church to develop a more extensive Church Security Plan that helped people help themselves, earning what they needed. Eventually farms, warehouses, and stores serviced church members in need.

Continued social service characterized the Relief Society during World War II. President Amy Brown Lyman noted that religion and true social service were just about the same thing, both aiming toward salvation. Saving and rescuing human beings was a religious ideal. Efforts to strengthen family life, a common thread of the organization, became urgent in wartime. Despite and because of the need for wartime female labor and the hasty courting and marriage of many young people, the church continued to stress the value of full-time homemakers. When mothers with young children went to work, the church asserted, the very foundation of the family, all the things the husband was fighting for, were endangered. The church had always strictly proscribed any extramarital sexual relations, and the relaxed moral standards of the period alarmed leaders. The church's Correlation Committee, a group named to rethink all programs, began in 1940 to simplify and consolidate all organizations and activities to relieve the burdens on members.

In 1947, church members, more than a million strong, celebrated the centennial of the pioneers' entrance into the Salt Lake Valley. At that time, mothers were encouraged to hold a weekly family hour and many complied, believing that the greatest good that parents could do was in their own homes. Although they also fulfilled societal roles, most felt that family concerns had precedence over other involvements. This family priority influenced role expectations for women who were taught good household management and thrift. The emphasis on producing children and devoting effort to raise them, along with natural childbirth, breast feeding, and homemaking, brought Mormons into mainstream style in postwar America.

Mormon women had effectively managed many programs, but generally as the outgrowth of their own mothering efforts. That they were skillful homemakers, good managers, expert cooks, and good parents was assumed. They also nurtured and helped the young through teaching and taking them into their homes as they did in the case of the "Indian Placement Program," where they provided homes and expenses for young Native Americans so they could attend better schools. At its height in 1970, this program placed 5,000 young people a year.

The somewhat contradictory ideas of developing personal abilities while centering lives in the family come from the early days of the church and have been sustained to the present. Mormon women are encouraged to gain education so they can support themselves, but they are also encouraged to devote primary effort to their families that statistically have one more child than the non-Mormon Americans next door. Their fertility rates follow national peaks and valleys. At the same time, Mormon women are effective managers of the church programs that support children, young people, and women. Many have managed large operations and have had demanding and successful careers in the church. What Mormon women were and have always been is conscientious, gifted, and enthusiastic amateurs, learning new skills whenever necessary.

A Time of Rapprochement to National Norms and International Growth, 1950–2000

Following World War II, when American women returned to their homes from wartime employment, Mormon women, always domestic and nurturing, achieved their highest level of national approval. They had been domestic all along. During this period of pride in woman's traditional accomplishments, Mormon women also managed ever larger church cultural and social activities.

In the 1960s, a new feminism emerged nationally along with civil disruption. The National Organization for Women (NOW) was founded in 1966, and in 1972 the U.S. Congress passed a proposed Equal Rights Amendment (ERA) to the Constitution. Legal abortions became available. The church responded conservatively, fearing that social change would disrupt stable family life. Good homes seemed the only corrective to the nation's ills, and that wholesome environment reflected a home-based wife and mother.

The tension of a woman doing justice to her responsibilities at home and achieving her potential in the world was articulated by Relief Society President Belle Spafford as she became president of the National Council of Women in 1968. "Although I believe that a woman's primary place is in the home, I think that her world is expanding and changing. Today it is becoming more and more essential for her to be a contributing citizen in her community" (Derr, Cannon, and Beecher, 337). Even though church policies are conservative, the attainment of an individual's personal goals as well as dedication to the family and church are inextricably intertwined in LDS belief.

Women's role in the church has been simplified in recent decades. In the continued effort to streamline the administrative structure of the growing church, changes were made that reduced women's responsibilities. Women's administrative work has been cut back as traditional values are newly emphasized. A single committee now plans curricula for all church groups, rather than each organization devising its own lessons. The Relief Society gave up its financial autonomy, turning over more than $2 million to the general church. All fundraising activities—bake sales, bazaars, and so on—were curtailed to allow more energy for women's important work in the home. The *Relief Society Magazine*, along with other auxiliary organs, was discontinued, and the church published three new consolidated magazines, one each for adults, teens, and children.

The women adjusted to the new program, but at the same time, a few stirrings of Mormon feminism were heard. Some of the sisters in Boston, trained in the cooperative amateurism of church service, met to discuss their lives as Mormon women against the background of current feminist movements and their own conservative church upbringing. They discovered the feminism of early Mormon women and tried to emulate it. Their independent newspaper *Exponent II* has been published for more than twenty-five years.

In 1978 the church came under fire from pro-ERA forces who charged discrimination against women. In 1972, the Equal Rights Amendment had passed Congress, and the proposed amendment was submitted to the states for ratification. The first thirty of the required thirty-eight states ratified the proposed amendment within a year. But momentum slowed, and objections surfaced. Relief Society President Barbara Smith objected to the blanket approach of the Equal Rights Amendment for dealing with discrimination against women. Although she supported equal pay and women's rights to careers, she felt that enforcement of this amendment would demand a single approach that would create new problems for a society already troubled. Other opposing voices were raised, and the church, usually averse to involvement in political matters, stood against the ERA as a moral issue. Leaders feared the amendment would threaten the future.

Mormon women were drawn into political activity on both sides of the ERA. Media writers criticized Mormon opposition, as the church quietly gathered money to oppose ratification. Feelings ran high as state meetings of the International Women's Year (IWY) in 1975 approached. The basic recommendations, including endorsement of the ERA, abortion on demand, and lesbian rights, had been developed at an earlier conference, but Utah women wanted to frame their own recommendations. Fearing that attendance would be scant, ten women from each Relief Society were invited to attend. The invitation, however, went out from the priesthood rather than the Relief Society. The manner of invitation led to charges that the Mormon male hierarchy had packed the Utah IWY conference. Some advocates of particular stands lobbied the groups in advance, as others urged them to vote their consciences. The stage was set for conflict.

Attendance at the Utah IWY meetings by the dutiful Mormon women numbered more than 12,000, five times the expectation. Materials ran short, and tempers flared. The conference elected fourteen delegates to the national meeting, all of whom rejected the proposed agenda. The original plan of action, however, passed at the national meeting, even as the ERA itself went down to defeat, three states short of ratification. The explosive IWY gave domestic Mormon women some experience in practical politics, although most were on the conservative side, rather than the radical side they had espoused in the previous century. Many were polarized and politicized as much media attention came their way.

In 1987 President Ezra Taft Benson sounded the familiar note for women. "No career approaches in importance that of wife, homemaker, mother." He told mothers to teach their children the gospel in their own homes, at their own firesides. "Your children will remember your teachings forever, and when they are old, they will not depart from them" (Derr, Cannon, and Beecher, 427). The long-term aim is to reestablish the earth family in heaven, but that seemingly conservative idea had radical implications. A Mother in Heaven as well as a Father in Heaven is a belief first articulated by Eliza R. Snow in the hymn-text "O My Father": "Truth is reason, truth eternal, tells me I've a mother there [in heaven]." This belief has long been accepted by church members. In recent years, feminists seeking role models and direction have made much of the Mother in Heaven, a figure so shadowy as to make individual interpretation necessary. Perhaps fearing a cult of the Mother, church leaders came out against these feminists. Gordon Hinckley, then a counselor to the president of the church, said in a speech in 1991 that he considered it inappropriate for anyone in the church to pray to a Mother in Heaven.

While Mormons have a long history of thinking for themselves in private, those who publicly oppose the church may well be excommunicated by church courts. In recent years women have been disciplined for speaking for the ERA, for advocating prayer to Mother in Heaven, for supporting open abortion laws, for urging the extension of the priesthood to women, for publicizing cases of "ecclesiastical abuse," for revealing LDS temple rites, for questioning the infallibility of church leaders, and for publishing books or articles deemed critical of the church or church policies, as well as for sexual improprieties. These actions have led many women to keep criticisms quiet.

While discouraging feminist activity, the church provides a wide variety of activities for people of all ages. Besides regular church callings in teaching, service and administrative posts, significant and satisfying responsibilities in a church with no paid clergy, many young women choose to serve full-time, short-term missions for the church. Female missionaries, who early served with husbands, were first sent out on their own, to be paired with other women, in 1850. Their contribution was enthusiastically noted over the years, and now about 20 percent of the missionary force, numbering about 60,000 in 2000, are women. Girls may choose to go on missions at age twenty-one, while boys are expected to go on missions at nineteen. As a group these young women are mature, motivated, and effective. The pool of female returned missionaries continues to grow, containing the best and brightest of young Mormon women. A significant number of older couples choose to serve missions of many kinds, teaching prospective members, managing church public relations, helping people work on their genealogy in Family History Libraries. The church commitment to temple rituals, where families over many generations are "sealed" together "through eternity" by special ordinances, fuels a huge genealogical operation. Workers microfilm records from around the world, which can be accessed for genealogical research. Many women are occupied with genealogy, doing the individual research necessary for temple sealings or digitizing records for the research of others.

In recent years the church has issued "The Family: A Proclamation to the World," underscoring the importance of the nuclear unit for the well-being of individuals and society. The proclamation states that fathers are to preside over their families in love and righteousness and are responsible to provide the necessities of life and protection for their families. Mothers are primarily responsible for the nurture of their children. The fathers and mothers "are obligated to help one another in these tasks as equal partners."

This emphasis on the family as the important church unit, however, has marginalized many single women, the proportion of whom may be as high as a third. Little heed is paid to the large group of intelligent, well-trained young women who realize that they may never find husbands in this family church. The problems of widows and single mothers who work to support their families in a church that preaches staying at home are also downplayed.

The family emphasis involves the church in contradictions. The church's financial resources are not available to support women at home if they can work or get help from their families. Church teaching also disapproves of working mothers with preschool children, while Utah has a larger proportion of such cases than any other state. Three large groups—single women, widows, and working mothers, many of whom are devout believers—sometimes find themselves in tension with the church.

To alleviate the problem, the church has muted its message that women must be stay-at-home mothers somewhat in recent years, aware of economic difficulties and the situations of many single women and converts. Leaders stress sisterhood, acceptance, mutual support. The church still teaches that no career is as important as child care, but the message is now more conditional, arguing against work to buy luxuries. This is an example of the way the church has responded to social change in women's roles: A short-term resistance to accelerated social change is accompanied by a pattern of long-term accommodation.

Women in the Church of Jesus Christ of Latter-day Saints are a significant presence, but the reordering of the church structure has steadily brought them under the control of the priesthood leadership, stripping away the autonomy and authority the LDS women had exercised in the early days. Doctrinally, the church maintains a middle ground by asserting that while women "share" the priesthood with their husbands, they are often told that their role is to "support the priesthood." Still the women have recently become more visible as more speak at General Conference, as special women's satellite meetings are held, and as temple ceremonies are modified.

Current church President Gordon B. Hinckley told an interviewer,

I think you'll find our women are very happy now. We have a dissident now and again, somebody who speaks out very sharply, very strongly. But that's very unusual. . . . They feel strongly about it. That's their prerogative. . . . We've heard it again and again. We feel they're not right. . . . If they speak out against the church in a strong, vigorous way, then possibly some action will be taken. (Ostling and Ostling, 364)

Some challenge the claim that Mormon women are content with their lot in the church, but the statement is likely true; most do support priesthood leadership. If they have complaints, they are far outweighed by the satisfactions of church membership. They find in the church a place for satisfying service and an opportunity for female companionship. They do not harbor a secret wish for complete autonomy. Mormon women want partnership with their husbands and a suitable environment for rearing their children. Most feel Mormonism helps them attain these goals.

SOURCES: Information on Mormon women can be found in general studies such as Leonard J. Arrington and Davis Bitton, *The Mormon Experience: A History of the Latter-day Saints* (1979); Richard N. Ostling and Joan K. Ostling, *Mormon America: The Power and the Promise* (1999); or specialized histories such as Claudia L. Bushman, ed., *Mormon Sisters: Women in Early Utah* (1976). Lucy Mack Smith's *Biographical Sketches of Joseph Smith the Prophet* (1969) is the best account of the young Joseph Smith. Accounts of early charismatic gifts can be found in Edward W. Tullidge, *The Women of Mormondom* (1877). The most recent history of the women's organization is Jill Mulvay Derr, Janath Russell Cannon, and Maureen Ursenbach Beecher, *Women of Covenant: The Story of Relief Society* (1992). Kathryn M. Daynes's *More Wives Than One: Transformation of the Mormon Marriage System, 1840–1910* (2001) is an excellent study of polygamy. See also Kimball Young, *Isn't One Wife Enough?* (1954) and "The Family: A Proclamation to the World," available online at http://owen.sj.ca.us.rkowen/LDS/family.html.

WOMEN IN THE REORGANIZED CHURCH OF JESUS CHRIST OF LATTER-DAY SAINTS
Rita M. Lester

CALLED A SAINT, a devil, and a Mormon enigma, Emma Hale Smith (1804–1879), the wife of Joseph Smith II and the mother of Joseph Smith III, is the "First Lady" of both the Church of Jesus Christ of Latter-day Saints (LDS) and the Reorganized Church of Jesus Christ of Latter-day Saints (RLDS). Her husband was the founder, and she, as the prophet's wife, was an "Elect Lady." Because Emma seems to have resisted the practice of plural wives and the leadership, especially of Brigham Young, immediately following her husband's death, and because her son Joseph Smith III would lead the reorganized branches of the church, Emma Smith plays an unparalleled role in the history of the Reorganized Church of Jesus Christ of Latter-day Saints, today known as the Community of Christ.

In 1830 Joseph Smith II believed that he received visions from God to restore the gospel before the second coming of Christ. Because of hostility toward this fledging religious community, Smith, his family, and his growing church membership moved from western New York state to Ohio, Ohio to Missouri, and Missouri to Illinois. After the murder of Joseph Smith on June 27, 1844, most church members moved from Nauvoo, Illinois, to what would become Salt Lake City under the leadership of Brigham Young. The group that moved to Utah are Latter-day Saints, also known as Mormons. But a significant number of church members did not go west but, instead, settled in places like Wisconsin, Iowa, Missouri, and Texas. These groups would gather together in 1860 under the leadership of Joseph Smith III and take the name the Reorganized Church of Jesus Christ of Latter Day Saints. Relations between the LDS and the RLDS church, the largest organizations to come out of Smith's movement, would be marked by contention and rivalry over recognition as the legitimate successor to the original church.

The RLDS church has been the subject of less academic research than their Utah-based sibling. This lack of attention may be due to their relatively small membership globally (less than 250,000) as compared to 10 to 12 million LDS around the world. Or perhaps it is due to the relative lack of tension between RLDS and other Protestant Christians in the United States. Or this lack of attention may be because many of the Mormon community's distinctive cosmological beliefs and ritual practices that establish the LDS community as distinctive, such as marriages sealed for eternity, baptism by proxy for deceased family members, and strongly encouraged missionary duty, are not practiced in the reorganized church. The RLDS church has tended to focus less on the historic persecution or their differences from other Christian denominations. This cultural accommodation allowed it members to live in low tension with the surrounding culture.

The most intense contemporary struggles in the RLDS church appear to be constructing an identity that is both consistent with its past while highlighting a more global, peace-oriented future and defining itself to outsiders as "not Mormon." In the twentieth century, the church has been committed to an intensified focus on a global peace initiative, the ordination of women, the institution of annual theology and peace colloquies, an increase in the number of nondenominational students and faculty at church-related colleges, and an intensified emphasis on theological education. Though LDS and RLDS share several significant elements such as history and priesthood structures, there are significant theological and sociological differences between the two traditions, differences that may have contributed to the RLDS church decision to change its name in an effort to distance itself from its similarly named Mormon sibling. In light of these identity struggles, the 2000 RLDS World Conference voted to change its name to Communities of Christ in June 2001.

The Relief Society and Plural Marriage

While in Nauvoo in the early 1840s, Joseph Smith II organized the women of the church into the women's Relief Society and nominated his wife Emma for president. By doing so, he instituted an ecclesiastical identity for women that seemed to parallel male priesthood (Newell and Avery, 117). The nineteen women present supported Emma's presidency (1842–1844) of the society. She was recognized as an "Elect Lady," that is, chosen for leadership, based on a revelation her husband experienced. According to L. Madelon Brunson, after the first Relief Society meeting, Joseph Smith wrote in his journal:

> The revelation was then fulfilled by Sister Emma's election to the Presidency of the Society, she having previously been ordained to expound the Scriptures. Emma was blessed, and her counselors (Elizabeth Ann Whitney and Sarah Cleveland) were ordained by Elder John Taylor. (*Bonds of Sisterhood*, 16)

About the society, Emma is said to have proclaimed, "We are going to do something extraordinary!" (Newell and Avery, 107).

Joseph Smith saw the Relief Society as one aspect of organizing the church more perfectly, as he and the

Called a saint, a devil, and a Mormon enigma, Emma Hale Smith, the wife of Joseph Smith II and the mother of Joseph Smith III, is the "First Lady" of both the Church of Jesus Christ of Latter-day Saints and the Reorganized Church of Jesus Christ of Latter-day Saints. In the early 1840s, Joseph Smith II organized the women of the church into the Relief Society and nominated his wife Emma for president. By doing so, he instituted an ecclesiastical identity for women that seemed to parallel male priesthood. *Used by permission of the RLDS/ Community of Christ Archives.*

all his persecutions . . . she was always ready to encourage and comfort him. . . . She was a queen in her home . . . and beloved by the people, who were many of them indebted to her for favors and kindnesses. (Newell and Avery, 118)

Though the organization patterns and objectives would change over time, the Relief Society afforded women personal, social, and spiritual involvement in the church.

In Nauvoo in the early 1840s, Joseph Smith II introduced plural marriage, that is, one man having more than one wife, to a small circle of church members. Emma Smith used the Relief Society as a counterbalance to oppose plural marriage. She required women of the society to sign statements certifying that each individual member had "not seen or heard anything improper or unvirtuous [*sic*] in conduct or conversation," most likely referring to the practice of plural marriage (118). In 1860, Joseph Smith III, first president of the Reorganized church, denied that his father instituted or practiced plural marriage, but polygyny did become a feature of the nineteenth-century Utah-based Latter-day Saint tradition. The RLDS has taken two approaches to plural marriage in the Nauvoo period. One was to deny that plural marriage was ever practiced. Since the 1970s, the church has been more open to the historical evidence of plural marriage but has focused on the women and men who never accepted the practice. Either way, plural marriage was rejected by the church.

The Relief Society continues in the Mormon but not the Reorganized tradition. Instead, there were numerous incarnations of women's organizations in the RLDS church whose functions were similar to the Relief Society, such as the Society of Gleaners, Zion's Aid Society, Mite Society, Sewing Circle, Prayer Union and Prayer League, United Daughters of Zion, and the Department of Women. Each provided opportunities for women to meet, share, lead, and contribute to church goals such as building a temple, earning money for church projects, easing the burdens of the poor, and educating children and adults.

Women also had access to the publishing arm of the church to communicate with each other. In 1886 Mar-

women members clearly embraced the early-nineteenth-century cult of true womanhood, a philosophy that women were naturally more nurturing and pious than men. A Mrs. Durfee, who was healed by Emma Smith and two counselors by a laying on of hands, said afterwards that "the sisters had more faith than the brethren" (114). The Relief Society, with its own ordained female officers, gave women leadership and administrative experiences in developing church publishing and education programs.

Though Joseph and Emma Smith would show signs of disagreement over plural marriage, the women of the Relief Society respected Emma Hale Smith's leadership. They were impressed by her fairness, her refusal to engage in gossip, and her compassion. As one member of the society, Emmeline B. Wells, wrote about Emma:

[She] was benevolent and hospitable; she drew around her a large circle of friends. . . . She was motherly in her nature to young people, always had a houseful to entertain. . . . She was very high-spirited and the brethren and sisters paid her great respect. Emma was great solace to her husband in ietta Walker began contributing a women's column to the *Herald*, a monthly church magazine, called the "Mothers' Home Column" under the name of "Sister Frances" in which she discussed the rights of women, the criteria for participation in church conferences, and the vital role of women in the church. The appearance of the subject of women in the priesthood in the *Herald* in the early 1960s was due at least in part to the effort of such publications and women's groups.

Women's Roles, Organizations, and Ordination

As the Reorganized church shifted from centralization to decentralization, women's organizations also shifted in structure, sometimes being autonomous, sometime being absorbed in other departments. During the presidency of Joseph Smith III until his death in December 1914, the church enjoyed stability, and the women's organization functioned as "integral [to] the church, but the organization method excluded [women] from administrative decision making" (Brunson, *Bonds of Sisterhood*, 54). In 1924 the Young Women's Bureau was absorbed by the Religion Department with the warning from Pearl Gardner that the history of the church would not be complete until it included the history of the women. Like Gardner, some women feared that the Religion Department would not make women's history a priority.

After World War I, President Frederick M. Smith placed renewed emphasis on stewardship, including women as stewards and religious educators. When in 1930 a new Department of Religious Education was announced, Blanche Edwards Mesley attempted to allay fears regarding the dissolution of the Department of Women by claiming that the creation of the Religious Education Department "need not mean the sacrificing of all the good work the Department of Women has done and is still doing" (65). At the 1934 RLDS World Conference, women facilitated meetings on Friendly Visiting, Home Beautification, Family Worship, Literature in the Home, as well as other topics, and the General Council of Women was created.

By 1940 the Women's Department had a budget and an office in the RLDS Auditorium in Independence, Missouri. In 1942 Director Pauline Arnson noted that RLDS congregations, or branches, were 61 percent female and that women should accept more congregational responsibilities. The Council of Women brought in more money than they spent (and published a Handbook to suggest moneymaking methods). In 1954 Alice Burgess, Arnson's replacement, focused on Zionic community (building a socially just and moral world), spreading the gospel message, community improvement, ethics and morality, education, literature and the arts,

and social services. With the death of President Israel Smith in 1958 and the resignation of Alice Burgess, the delayed October Conference appointed Kathryn Westwood as the women's leader. Westwood's publication efforts focused on the church youth in magazines such as *Stride*, instead of the more traditional "Home Column" in the *Herald*, which was discontinued in 1958, perhaps in response to the changing roles of women in society.

The 1963 World Conference attracted 2,000 women and promoted the Women's Department. The *Women's Newsletter*, later called *The Distaff*, was sent without charge to local RLDS women leaders. But in 1968, the Women's Department was moved out of direct contact with the presidency, and it was not until 1970, with Geoffrey Spencer as administrator of Education-Pastoral Services, that church administrators responded favorably to women's concerns about the lack of female involvement in decision making in the church. Marjorie Troeh was appointed as Westwood's successor, and the name changed to Women's Ministry Consultant. Though *The Distaff* was discontinued, new meetings were held to discuss images of the female as projected by society and the church. The Committee on the Roles of Women in the Church, which functioned from 1971 to 1973, submitted a report on the need to recognize, reconceptualize, and revitalize the role of women in the church and society. The report was endorsed by the RLDS presidency and used in regional institutes by women and administrators. The Women's Ministry Commission met for the first time on April 19, 1974, to advocate for more paid staff church employment for women, the appointment of more women to advisory committees, and for full equality.

Under the executive leadership of Imogene Goodyear, the RLDS church produced new worship resources and in 1978 adopted an Inclusive Language policy for church publications. The New Zealand National Church and Adelaide District of Australia proclaimed their readiness to ordain women in the early 1980s, but this progress was not without a backlash. There were resolutions offered at the general church level to endorse the idea that women should never hold RLDS priesthood offices. The Women's Ministries Commission, started in 1981, attempted to address the goal of equality through task forces such as Women as Witnesses, Policies on the Participation of Women, Pastoral Unit Participation, and Women's Literacy. In 1982 the topic of whether or not scriptures excluded the ordination of women was hotly debated at the church's World Conference in Independence, Missouri. The church resolved that there should be no "barriers to ordination based on race, ethnic or national origin, or gender" (1982 World Conference Minutes, 268–331).

After motions of referral, studies, and reports to the

presidency, women were accepted into ordained positions in the RLDS church in 1986. The priesthood, like the LDS church, is largely voluntary but has two categories of priesthood: Melchizedec (high priests and elders) and Aaronic (priests, teachers, and deacons). Bishops, evangelists, apostles, and presidents are specialized offices of the high priesthood, and elders are helpers to the high priests and conduct Aaronic ordinations. The First Presidency of the church is the President-Prophet and two counselors. The Second Presidency is the Council of twelve, the Apostles. The Apostles are drawn from the missionary quorum, the Seventies (seven quorums of seventy), who, in turn, draws their members from the lower priesthood levels. The RLDS priesthood structure is hierarchical in that persons are most often called to higher positions of authority after service in lower positions. Until the most recent presidency of W. Grant McMurray, the role of President-Prophet was filled by male descendants of the founder of the church. McMurray is the first President-Prophet who is not related to Joseph Smith II and Emma Smith. There as yet has not been a women President-Prophet in the RLDS church.

The President-Prophet of the church presents revelatory material to the general church body and delegates at the biennial RLDS World Conference, who then discuss and vote on accepting the revelation and canonizing it into the book the Doctrine and Covenants. Revelation is understood to come from God to the president, but it is discussed and a vote is conducted as to whether or not to accept the revelation into church policy. Revelation was offered by then President Wallace B. Smith to the assembly of delegates at the 1984 World Conference in 1984. When approved, this statement was accepted into the RLDS record of continuing revelation, the Doctrine and Covenants (156:8–10), as inspired counsel and direction to the church.

A number of church members left the church because of this revelation. More traditional or conservative (called Restorationism) RLDS who had looked to church authorities for infallible leadership found themselves in the unusual position of rejecting the revelation of the President-Prophet. Paradoxically, liberal church members who had tended to question the authority of the hierarchy on issues of revelation found themselves in the position of championing this revelation from "on high."

Since 1986 women have been more fully integrated into church leadership structures and are members of the highest and most prestigious ministerial and administrative bodies such as Linda Booth and Gail Mengel in the Council of Twelve (Apostles), and Mary Jacks Dynes, president of the 5th Quorum of Seventies (missionaries). But ambivalence persists. In the July 2000 issue of the *Saint's Herald*, Apostle Linda Booth discussed her personal experience of ordaining a man to the office of high priest who did not recognize her authority and would not receive communion from her because she is a woman (*Saint's Herald*).

Biographies of Women and Theology

Most Reorganized Church of Jesus Christ of Latter-day Saints' writings on women are published collections of individual faith journeys. In Roy Cheville's *They Made a Difference* (1970), out of twenty-nine short biographies, there are two, Emma Smith and Marietta Walker, who wrote the *Herald* "Home Column" and were significant in the creation of RLDS-affiliated Graceland College (now University) started in 1885. According to *Living Saints Witness at Work* (Barlow), Graceland College was also instrumental in the lives of two women who served as English faculty and later as presidents of the college, Velma Ruch and Barbara Higdon. This style of writing about women by collecting short biographies, testimonies, or "faith journeys" can also be seen in *33 Women of the Restoration* by E. M. Phillips (1960), its sequel *Dedicated to Serve* by Phillips (1970), *First Ladies of the Restoration* by Frances Hartman Mulliken (1985), and *Extending the Call: Testimonies of Ordained Women*, edited by Carol Anderson Anway (1989). All were published through an RLDS publishing company, and all exemplify the tendency to favor individual faith biographies over an analysis of the roles of women churchwide.

The church has traditionally focused more on history than theology, but the last quarter of the twentieth century witnessed a wave of theological inquiry in church publications like the *Herald*, as well as the more scholarly series *Restoration Studies* and the Graceland/Park Press series *Theology*. Women often contribute essays and serve on the boards as editorial advisers of these publications. Though restoration churches were historically anticlerical in the sense that they did not require and were even suspicious of a religiously educated clergy, increasingly church conferences and publications include topics such as gender in religious imagery and language, revisioning the meaning of priesthood, and issues in feminist theology. This focus is most likely because RLDS women and men increasingly attend Protestant seminaries and earn theological degrees. Annual theological and peace colloquies held in the 1980s and 1990s exemplify an openness of the RLDS church to general theological and social issues, and many of the papers presented are published by Herald House or the Graceland/Park Press. The church was also granted a six-year renewable affiliate status membership with the Association of Theological Schools (ATS) in June 2000, so church representatives are now eligible for appointment to ATS committees or task forces.

The most recent mission statement reads: "We proclaim Jesus Christ and promote communities of joy, hope, love and peace." And because the church strives to meet the needs of the new millennium, the RLDS church, in its program Transformation 2000, testifies, in the words of current President W. Grant McMurray, "[W]e are called to a journey of transformation . . . dedicated to the pursuit of peace and reconciliation and healing of the spirit."

Though small in number and theologically inconspicuous, the Reorganized Church of Jesus Christ of Latter-Day Saints, recently renamed the Community of Christ, embarked in the twenty-first century on a global mission and identity marked by the promotion of peace and reconciliation that includes the ordination of women and the commitment to involve women and issues of gender equity at all levels of church life.

SOURCES: Carol Anderson Anway, ed., *Extending the Call: Testimonies of Ordained Women* (1989). T. Barlow, ed., *Living Saints Witness at Work* (1976). Alma Blair, "RLDS Views of Polygamy," *The John Whitmer Historical Association Journal* 5 (1985): 16–28. Lois Taylor Braby, "Beyond Equality . . . to Justice," in *Restoration Studies III*, ed. Maurice L. Draper (1986), 61–65. Richard Brown, ed., *Theology: From Tradition to Task* (1993). L. Madelon Brunson, *Bonds of Sisterhood: A History of the RLDS Women's Organization, 1842–1983* (1985). L. Madelon Brunson, "Stranger in a Strange Land: A Personal Response to the 1984 Document," in *Restoration Studies III*, ed. Maurice L. Draper (1986), 108–115. Roy Cheville, *They Made a Difference* (1970). Don Compier, "The Faith of Emma Smith," *The John Whitmer Historical Association Journal* 6 (1986): 64–72. Margaret Wilson Gibson, *Emma Smith: The Elect Lady* (1976). Imogene Goodyear, "The Legacy of Early Latter-day Saint Women: A Feminist Critique," *The John Whitmer Historical Association Journal* 10 (1990): 21–23. Richard Howard, "The Changing RLDS Response to Mormon Polygamy," *The John Whitmer Historical Association Journal* 3 (1983): 14–28. Richard Howard, "What Sort of Priesthood for Women at Nauvoo?" *The John Whitmer Historical Association Journal* 13 (1993): 18–30. Frances Hartman Mulliken, *First Ladies of the Restoration* (1985). Linda King Newell, "Emma Hale Smith and the Polygamy Question," *The John Whitmer Historical Association Journal* 4 (1984): 3–15. Linda King Newell and Valeen Tippetts Avery, *Mormon Enigma: Emma Hale Smith, Prophet's Wife, "Elect Lady," Polygamy's Foe, 1804–1879* (1984). Emma Phillips, *Dedicated to Serve: Biographies of 31 Women of the Restoration* (1970). Emma Phillips, *33 Women of the Restoration* (1960). Velma Ruch, "To Magnify Our Calling: A Response to Section 156," in *Restoration Studies III*, ed. Maurice L. Draper (1986), 97–107. *Saints Herald* 147. 7 (July 2000), foreword. Steven Shields, *Divergent Paths of the Restoration* (1990). Patricia Struble, "Mite to the Bishop: RLDS Women's Financial Relationship to the Church," *The John Whitmer Historical Association Journal* 6 (1986): 23–32. Alan Tyree, ed., *Exploring the Faith: A Series of Studies in the Faith of the Church Prepared by a Committee on Basic Beliefs* (1987). Emmeline B. Wells, "LDS Women of the Past: Personal Impression," *Women's Exponent* 36.7 (February 1908): 1.

VODOU, SPIRITISM, AND SANTERÍA: HYBRIDITY AND IDENTITY IN CARIBBEAN RELIGIONS
Carlos F. Cardoza-Orlandi

VODOU, SPIRITISM, AND Santería are religions of the diaspora *and* religions of the New World. Vodou and Santería belong to the large spectrum of African diaspora religions that find new grounding and vitality in the New World, particularly in the Caribbean and most recently in North America. Spiritism is a French diaspora religion that finds a new effervescence as it cross-fertilizes with Roman Catholicism and other African diaspora religions in the New World, particularly in Brazil, in the Caribbean, and most recently, in North America. These religions can be characterized as "religions-in-a-journey." They have accompanied their followers, whether uprooted from their homelands or as immigrants in search of adventure, prosperity, and freedom, for many years and under difficult circumstances. These religious traditions have traveled, not as missionary religions seeking new converts and new territory but as partners in solidarity with people whose life is characterized either by uncertainty, oppression, struggle, and liberation or by great curiosity and search for the unknown. These religions are intertwined with the threads that make the tapestry of people at the margins—social and religious—and yet struggling for their own survival.

In their new context, Vodou, Spiritism, and Santería have experienced deep changes in their structures—rituals, mythology, moral and religious thought, and ethical agency—making them different, yet connected, to their "mother" religions in their places of origins. For instance, these traditions experienced a change in their iconography and religious calendar, given that they were practiced in secrecy within the structures of Roman Catholic evangelization and catechism. Furthermore, they also changed their ritual configuration and elements as they found themselves in a different social structure—being slaves, free slaves, or marginalized immigrants—and social context—from rural or semirural contexts to slavery in plantations and urban life.

Yet they have preserved certain elements of their ethos and worldview that allow observers to recognize their roots in the African and European soils. Among those elements, we find in Vodou and Santería the preservation of the Fon peoples of Dahomey and Yoruban languages, the role of drums and drum playing in their rituals, and the *reciprocity* that shapes the relationship or "serving of the spirits" in these Afro-Caribbean religions. Moreover, in the last two decades of the twentieth century, international conferences of Yoruba and Dahomey religions were held in Africa, in the Caribbean, and in North America recognizing the differences of these traditions in their different contexts and, at the same time, fostering a sense of continuity and connection despite their separate developments as religions in particular contexts.

In Spiritism, followers continue to use the Christian scriptures, particularly the gospel of John, and Allan Kardec's—French spiritist who created the system of doctrines and practices known as Spiritism—commentaries as sources for metaphysical reflection (*El Evangelio Según el Espiritismo* [The Gospel According to Spiritism], *El Libro de los Espíritus* [The Spirits' Book], and *El Cielo y el Infierno* [Heaven and Hell]). The domain of the spirits is deeply connected with daily life: It is a source for discerning the meaning and direction of physical life and the continuity for optimum progress in this world and in the world of the spirits. Originally based on experimentation and research, Spiritism seeks to explain physical life as a multidimensional, multitemporal, reality that is connected with the world of the spirits, one that is also submitted to scientific laws and experimentation, albeit eternal laws. Even in the most remote communities where Spiritism is practiced, the observer will discover a "positivist dimension" in the approach and resolution of problems and conflicts with the spirit world.

These vibrant and tenacious religions have, however, a level of *hybridity*, a level of *syncretism* in their own contexts, particularly in the New World, that may be considered their bloodlife, their main source of identity (Stevens-Arroyo and Pérez y Mena). Though grounded in old traditions from Africa or more recent metaphysical explorations from Europe and the United States, Vodou, Spiritism, and Santería are religions that project and portray the history and relationship of the conqueror with the conquered, the colonizer and the colonized, the slave owner and the slave. They have served many who belonged to different social classes and had different levels of political participation and influence. However, they also project and portray the resilient and resisting character of marginalized and oppressed people. These religions mix, adopt, adapt, and reconfigure their structures in order to provide force and direction to many people who live at the margins of mainstream religious practices and beliefs, particularly women in the Caribbean and North American societies.

The Religions

VODOU

Vodou means "spirit." Vodou, or the religion of the spirits, is practiced by more than 90 percent of the Haitian population. It is frequently mentioned that 95 percent of the Haitian population is Roman Catholic and that all Haitians practice Vodou! As Karen McCarthy Brown has mentioned in her work on Vodou, many Haitians prefer to speak of their religion as "serving the spirits," rather than calling it "Voodoo"—which is a pejorative term for the religious practice (3–12).

Media and cinema have given these religions, but particularly Vodou and Santería, a negative and distorted picture. Unfortunately, terms such as *zombi*—a disembodied spirit of a person used for magical purposes or a spiritless body raised from the grave to do labor—and the racist and ethnic biases that characterize the West have dismissed the richness, tenacity, and creativity of Vodou in Haitian history and beyond. For example, a number of historians attribute the beginning of the Haitian revolution and slave revolt of the early nineteenth century to Vodou rituals that made warriors indestructible against the forces of the colonizer. An early victory and the establishment of the first Caribbean and black republic did not well suit the growing colonial economy of the Caribbean. Its religious force could not be appreciated, much less recognized, over and against the European Christian empires and missionary endeavors in the region.

Vodou is a religion with a strong African influence. Though we have very limited information on the early years of Vodou in Haiti, we know that there were three African groups that have shaped the tradition in its new context: the Yoruba, the Dahomey, and the Kongo. Affinities between names of African spirits and Haitian spirits are very common, though the new context has given these spirits a different connotation (Brown, 100–103).

Vodou is a religion with a complex set of rituals and ceremonies that relate the practitioners with the spirit world. The spirits, or *Iwas*, grouped in families called *nanchons* (nations), have familial and territorial connections. In rural Haiti, a person inherits a particular *nanchon* through paternal or maternal relationship. Spirit nations also inhabit a particular territorial perimeter that would render responsible for these spirits those living in that territory.

With immigration to urban centers, two *nanchons* have emerged as predominant groups absorbing the others; they are the *Rada* and the *Petro*. These groups of spirit nations not only provide information about the history of the *Iwas*; more important, they provide the "ethos of the *Iwas* as well as the characteristic attitudes

Vodou is a religion with a complex set of rituals and ceremonies that relate the practitioners with the spirit world. The spirits or *Iwas*, grouped in families called *nanchons* (nations), have familial and territorial connections. In rural Haiti, a person inherits a particular *nanchon* through paternal or maternal relationship. Spirit nations also inhabit a particular territorial perimeter that renders those living in that territory responsible for these spirits. *Copyright © Bettmann/ CORBIS. Used by permission.*

with which the devotees approach them" (Desmangles, 97). The character and personality of a spirit nation will illustrate the character and personality of those who serve the *Iwas* of that particular *nanchon*.

Not all the *Iwas* are equal. Vodou has a range of spirits that move from the spirits of the dead (*lemò*) to the ancestral spirits who are patrons of protection, health, and guidance to the community (*gèdè*). This spirit world is configured and related to the devotee through a repertoire of rituals. In the rural setting these rituals are flexible, simple, and less rigorous. In the urban context, the rituals have become structured and organized, projecting the complexity of daily life in the urban context. Vodou provides both a priest (*oungan*) and a priestess (*manbo*) with ritual practices that go from simple candle lighting for the dead to a grandiose feast with animal sacrifice that can last for a week. Drumming, dancing, eating, and drinking are part of these celebrations held in an open area rural area or in the temple (*ounfò*) in

the urban context. Similar to Santería, drum beating is used to invoke the spirits in order to "ride" the devotee—possess the follower—creating a direct link between the human and the spirit worlds.

This repertoire of *Iwas*, the ritual practices, and the worldview of Vodou have been shaped and organized in a significant way by the influence of Haitian Roman Catholicism. Some scholars of the religion characterize the relationship between Vodou and Roman Catholicism as symbiotic (Desmangles, 103–108, 174–181). Whether symbiotic or of another nature, it is evident that Vodou devotees call themselves Catholics. Because many of the rituals of the Roman Catholic tradition are part of more elaborate Vodou rituals, devotees attend mass, are baptized, have their first communion, and expect the Roman Catholic priest to reject and disapprove their religion. In addition, many Catholic prayers, images, and saints' names are used in Vodou rituals.

Moreover and similar to Santería, the history of the

Vodou tradition includes the development of a dual system between the *Iwas* and the Roman Catholic saints. For instance, la Virgen de los Dolores is Ezili in the Vodou pantheon, Saint Patrick is Dambala, and Saint James is the warrior Ogou.

Vodou rituals and worldview seek the healing and well-being of a person and the community. Bound by territory in the rural area or by new religious and familial relationships in the urban context, Vodou, in its search for the well-being of the person and community, is a continuous interaction between the world of the spirits and the human condition. Hence, unless the problem comes directly from God, in which situation the Vodou priest or priestess cannot do anything (Murray, 14–22), healing comes from the reconfiguration of human relationships, including the dead and the *Iwas*, through ritual, adivination, charms, and herbal potions.

Finally, with the immigration of Haitians to North American cities, Vodou also makes its way to a new context. One of the most important resources to understand the new changes and challenges for Vodou in the North American context continues to be Karen McCarthy Brown's *Mama Lola: A Vodou Priestess in Brooklyn*. Describing the issues of immigration and mobility, the role of women in the inner-urban context, and the religious and social problems of an emerging new religion in a North American city, Brown provides the reader with insight into and sympathy with this rich and ongoing religion from the Caribbean.

SPIRITISM

Spiritism as it is known and practiced in the Caribbean and in many North American cities is a syncretistic religion. The system of beliefs and rituals is a combination of Allan Kardec's doctrines and Afro-Caribbean religiosity (Pérez y Mena, 146–152). Kardec's work is grounded in the following doctrines: (1) There are spirits of dead persons who are capable of communication and interaction with the living and visible world; (2) these spirits belong to an invisible but yet natural world that can be investigated, though it is eternal and preexistent; (3) this world of the spirits has a hierarchy where those closer or closely identified with the material world are evil; (4) spirits in this world are free and progress toward perfection via reincarnations as they fulfill their missions; (5) Christian charity is the supreme expression of virtue and makes spiritual evolution possible (Christ is considered the most elevated spirit); and (6) the communication and interaction between the world of the living and the world of the spirits is through a *medium* or *medium-unidad*.

Though Kardec understood Spiritism as a philosophy with spiritual connotations, Spiritism developed as a religion in the New World. Spiritism flourished as it sought to be a tradition of Christian charity with an awareness of the spirit world and its moral and progressive agency in both the material and spiritual worlds. The presence and grounding of the Roman Catholic tradition in Latin America and in the Latin Caribbean (particularly the emphasis on the saints), the already present Afro- and indigenous beliefs in the world of the spirits and the communication with the dead, and the predisposition of the elite for spiritual things, on the one hand, and their prejudice toward anything Afro-indigenous spiritual, on the other, were religious and social factors that grounded and proved to be a catalyst for the tradition. It is no surprise that many of the Roman Catholic saints are the spirits to whom requests and needs are addressed in the tradition.

Spiritism, hence, practices *reciprocity*. The relationship between the world of the spirits and the material world is based on a mutual need: The spirits' mission, in order to move into perfection, is to be performed in both the world of the spirits and the material world, whereas the material world needs the spirit world in order to find well-being and guidance in difficult times. The human element that mediates this reciprocity, which embodies the in-betweenness of these two worlds, is the *medium*, a person of unique gifts, deep Christian love, and clairvoyance. The *medium* exercises *el pase* (the "pass"), which unlocks the pathways making the spirits available for the community gathered around the table or, in more recent locations, a church-type configuration.

As the religion continued to ground itself in the Latin American and Latin Caribbean soil, the *medium* not only provided the source of connection between the material and the spirit worlds but also began to execute similar practices of adivination, herbal remedies, healing rituals, and problem solving as those performed by the priest and priestess in Vodou and in Santería. These new functions of the *medium* show the level of syncretism that Spiritism experiences with other Afro-Caribbean traditions.

Mediums are both men and women. In the Caribbean, there are a significant number of women who carry this important responsibility, though most of them remain anonymous. More recently, the role of the *mediums* has also expanded to the treatment of maladies, trying to eliminate the consequences of evil, the *causas* of evil, becoming, therefore, a socioreligious space of contested spiritual warfare with psychophysical healing implications.

Finally, just as with Vodou and Santería, Spiritism makes its way to North America in the hearts and minds of the immigrant community. It is also in this new space where Spiritism develops and appropriates elements of the Afro-Caribbean religions (Pérez y Mena, 149–152) and continues to be nourished by other Hispanic/Latino religious influences—other expressions of Roman Catholicism, Pentecostalism, New Age, and so forth.

SANTERÍA

Santería, the religion of the *Orishas,* is the name used to identify this Afro-Caribbean religion by many who study and some who practice the religion. Most practitioners, however, call it the religion of the *Orishas.* Beautiful, mystic, historical, and communal, Santería shares a similar history with Vodou and Spiritism. It is a religious tradition with its roots in Africa, particularly from the Yoruba, a strong continuity with Yoruban mythology and rituals, and yet with a unique grounding and vitality in the Caribbean soil and in many cities in North America.

Santería emerged in the nineteenth century as thousands of African slaves were brought to Cuba from West Africa, particularly Nigeria and Benin. African slaves were introduced as a commodity in order to provide the brutal labor needed for the booming sugar economy of the region. The Roman Catholic Church continued to uphold its responsibility of evangelizing the African soul in order to keep the body of the slave in chains. The irony was, as Joseph Murphy says, "[T]he slaves were brought into a world of hatred and greed; yet they survived and built within it a spiritual world of beauty and order" (23).

One of the most important social spaces for the preservation and transformation of the Yoruban religion in the Caribbean was the *cabildo.* The *cabildo,* or social club, kept the cultural and religious vitality of different African ethnic groups. The Roman Catholic Church established and organized the *cabildos* in order to provide Christian instruction and social aid to the different ethnic groups in the culturally diverse Cuban society of the nineteenth century. Far was the Roman Catholic Church from discovering that the same sacred/social space created for evangelization and social support would become the sacred/social space for the recovery and rediscovery of the *Orishas* in a new context and with a unique flavor. The *lucumi,* or "friends," found a place to preserve and develop their religious tradition.

Today, Santería, the religion of the *Orishas,* has a more public face. Homes of the priests, or *babalawo,* have become places of worship and consultation. Frequently, a follower of the faith will have an altar for her/his *Orisha,* and the *santeros* will have a room or a space at home to celebrate ceremonies and gather the community. Another social space where people will find artifacts, herbs, saints, and other items for the practice of the faith is the *botánica.* *Botánicas* can be found in almost any major city of the United States, the Caribbean, and some in Canada. Most recently, Santería has public worship spaces where devotees and sympathizers of the religion come together for celebrations, particularly the ceremonial events called *bembés* or *tambores.*

Santería continues to have a syncretistic and symbiotic relationship with Roman Catholicism. Given the nature of the religion and the persecution of the Roman Catholic Church, the leaders of Santería used the iconography of the Catholic saints to preserve the identity and devotion of the spirits, of the *Orishas.* Consequently, Saint Anthony is Elleguá, Saint Barbara is Changó, Our Lady of Mercy is Obatalá, Our Lady of Regla is Yemayá, and so on. The reader should not be confused; the religion of the *Orishas* is a wonderful example of religious syncretism but continues to be predominantly an Afro-Caribbean religion in continuous interaction and exchange with the cultural and religious vitality of its context.

Santería is a religion of *lo cotidiano* (of daily life). In its metaphysics, the religion of the *Orishas* believes that every human being has been given a destiny, a path to follow, by Olodumare, or God. It is the purpose of the human being to live this path rather than ignore, resist, or evade it. The *Orishas,* or spirits, have the power to guide the devotee in this path. As a result, the metaphysics of the tradition are ultimately grounded in a close and reciprocal relationship between the devotee, the *Orisha,* and the community that practices Santería.

Santería takes four devotional expressions. The first and probably the most distorted by media is sacrifice. The religion of the *Orishas* is a religion of reciprocity. Devotee and *Orisha* have a mutual enriching relationship that is nurtured by sacrifices and food for the spirit(s) and the devotees. *Oblations* and sacrifices of food continue to preserve and deepen the reciprocal dependency of spirit and follower. Feasts and celebrations are communal in character; community and spirits share food as one.

The second expression—one that is also frequently misrepresented in media—is spirit possession. The *batáa,* or drums, are played in a *bembé o toque de tambores* to invoke and feast with the *Orishas.* The possession of the *Orishas* of their priest and followers becomes an epiphany of interaction and celebration between the spirits and the community. On these occasions, the *Orishas* dwell, embodied in their followers, in the earthly life to provide divine advice and wisdom for daily life problems and challenges.

The third expression is divination, or *la voz de los caracoles* (the voice of the shells). Migene González-Wippler and Joseph Murphy provide interesting and accessible interpretations to the difficult and complex divination practice in Santería (González-Wippler, 110–132; Murphy, 49–69). For the practitioner of the faith, divination becomes the means by which to receive clarity and direction in daily life decision making. For the *padrino* or *madrina* (priest or priestess), the ritual of divination is a complex reading of symbols interwoven with the stories of the *Orishas*, which become metaphors or archetypes to help the practitioner make decisions congruent and coherent with the path of the *Orisha.*

This author will never forget the first time he saw this beautiful young woman walking down Himrod Street on the West Side of Manhattan. She was exotically and beautifully dressed in white, moving as though "walking in the clouds." She had recently been initiated—or she recently had her *asiento* in the Santería religion. Initiation is the most secret of all rituals in Santería. Experts in the traditions have been unable to describe the details of the rituals, though the ceremony has the exuberance and effervescence of the possession of the *Orishas*. Initiations are similar to Christian baptisms in that they represent a *discontinuity* with a way of living and understanding life and a *discovery* of a new path, the way of the *Orisha.* As the practitioner continues to grow in her/his reciprocal and mutual relationship with the *Orisha*, the faithful discovers her/his humanity in the character and path of the *Orisha.* Both the human and the divine are interwoven and interlocked in the path of the *Orisha:* It is both the humanization of the divine and the divinization of the human experience.

The Religions and Christianity: A Personal Appraisal

This author has been interested in the encounter between these religions and the Christian religion for almost ten years. These religious traditions, given their history and developments in primarily Christian environments, and their interaction with the Christian religion, provide a window for critical, religious, and theological reflection regarding the postmodern proposal of hybrid cultural identities.

As mentioned above, these religions have appropriated Christian elements and worldview in order to continue their life in the New World. Early in their history, the imposition of Roman Catholic Christian expressions provided an opportunity for transformation that made the traditions become Caribbean, rooted in their new context. Moreover, the encounter with Roman Catholic Christianity made them recreate and reimagine themselves in a context of adversity; they rediscovered the creative force of the spirits rather than reifying the spirits of the never-returning past in the present. In this process, inadvertently, the Christian faith proved to be critical in the preservation and development of the traditions.

Today, many expressions of these religious traditions live in a symbiotic and syncretistic relationship with Roman Catholicism and some expressions of Protestantism—though very few. In fact, they continue to evolve,

by incorporating and transforming their ethos and worldview as they find themselves facing new religious adaptations and confrontations with the Christian religion. Most of the confrontations, however, are with Pentecostal and neocharismatic expressions. Some of these confrontations are both creating (1) a complex exchange of religious beliefs and practices between the Christian religion and the traditions and (2) a developing practice of publicly claiming the particularity of the religious traditions (without looking back to Africa) over Christian traditions and expressions in the New World. These encounters and interactions between Vodou, Spiritism, and Santería and the Christian religion need to be further explored and studied as part of the hybrid nature of Caribbean cultures and the future effect of religions in the North American context.

Finally, as a Christian historian and theologian involved in interreligious dialogue with people who practice Vodou, Spiritism, and Santería, this author continues to find among many of them a perplexing hunger for understanding their faith and the Christian faith in a different mode than just syncretism, confrontation, or alienation. After eight years of dialogue, a female follower of the religions of the *Orishas* told this author that her *Orishas* followed Jesus. In a course this author taught in the Caribbean, he met a woman—a distinguished leader of a Protestant denomination—with whom he has kept a close relationship for the past seven years, who continues to struggle with her spiritist background and gifts. She finds that rather than accepting the polarized relationship between her Protestant faith and her spiritist background and ethos, she thrives in living the tensions between the traditions; she has discovered both the seeds of the Christian faith in her spiritist faith and the seeds of Spiritism in her Christian religion. This author believes, however, that the most eloquent statement that characterizes the perplexity and hunger of understanding the history and development of the encounter between these faith traditions and the Christian religion in this hybrid postmodern world is by a friend who follows the paths of the *Orishas*. In a recent email to this author regarding our hybrid religious identity, she stated:

> I feel like I can finally express myself about the two most important Spiritual journeys [Santería and Christianity] that I have ever undertaken without being looked at as if I was crazy or something. For the last few years I have not had much contact with my Santería family because of this feeling. To them Santería or Orisha is the only way and they neither have the time nor the inclination to try to understand both of our traditions. Even when I try to explain that Orisha was preserved

and kept alive by our ancestors via Christianity, to them I sound like one of the slave masters; it's been very painful, so I have kept my distance, but never letting go of my belief in Orisha. . . .

Yes I agree it's important to preserve both of our identities, not just one or the other. My father was an Orisha priest and yet always managed to balance his two faith communities. I wish to do the same.

These traditions are alive and well in our North American context. They represent the new religious landscape of faiths that continue to belong to immigrant communities but that are also growing and grounding a new religious experience for the Americas. They also provide a different starting point for religious and theological studies, a challenge to find in our scholarly work a new vision for the way we imagine our disciplines, and an opportunity to contribute to a new religious project that promotes an awareness of life beyond the unidimensional Western history and the typical religions-against-each-other model.

SOURCES: The following are invaluable sources: Allan Kardec's *El Evangelio Según el Espiritismo* (1983), *El Libro de los Espíritus* (1982), and *El Cielo y el Infierno* (1984); Anthony M. Stevens-Arroyo and Andrés Pérez y Mena, eds., *Enigmatic Powers: Syncretism with African and Indigenous Peoples' Religions among Latinos* (1995); Karen McCarthy Brown, *Mama Lola: A Vodou Priestess in Brooklyn* (1991); Leslie G. Desmangles, *The Faces of the Gods* (1992); Gerald F. Murray, "The Phantom Child in Haitian Voodoo: Folk-Religious Model of Uterine Life," in *African Creative Expressions of the Divine*, ed. K. Davis and E. Farajaje-Jones (1991); Andrés I. Pérez y Mena, "Puerto Rican Spiritism as a Transfeature of Afro-Latin Religion," in *Enigmatic Powers: Syncretism with African and Indigenous Peoples' Religions among Latinos*, ed. Anthony M. Stevens-Arroyo and Andrés Pérez y Mena (1995); Migene González-Wippler, *Santería: The Religion* (1989); Julio Sánchez, *La religion de los Orishas* (1991); Angela Jorge, "Cuban Santería: A New World African Religion," in *African Creative Expressions of the Divine*, ed. K. Davis and E. Farajaje-Jones (1991); and Joseph M. Murphy, *Santería: An African Religion in America* (1988).

CHRISTIAN SCIENCE
Sarah Gardner Cunningham

LIKE MORMONISM, SEVENTH-DAY Adventism, Jehovah's Witnesses, and Pentecostalism, Christian Science was founded in North America. Unlike most other indigenous American religious movements of the nineteenth century, Christian Science was founded by and is still closely identified with the experience and writings of a single woman. Mary Baker Eddy wrote the textbook of Christian Science, *Science and Health with Key to the Scriptures*, she incorporated the Church of Christ, Scientist, as an institutional organization, and she exercised personal leadership over the church until her death. Christian Science historiography still centers on Mrs. Eddy's biography. And Christian Science exercised a particular appeal to women, both as an alternative to male-dominated orthopathic medicine (conventional medical treatment with medications or surgery) and as an opportunity for remunerative employment as a Christian Science practitioner.

On a theological level, Christian Science is among the metaphysical religions, with New Thought and Theosophy, that stress the immanence of God—that God is not mysterious and disconnected from reality but accessible and knowable by human understanding. Historian Sydney Ahlstrom located Christian Science in the family of "harmonial" religious movements that originated in the nineteenth century. Harmonial religions commonly have charismatic founders, complex organizations, and highly developed belief structures. Adherents believe that spiritual wholeness, physical health, and even material prosperity derive from being connected to and in harmony with the unseen forces in the universe.

Though the church is now well over 100 years old and remains a sizable movement, Mary Baker Eddy received only a one-line mention in Mark A. Noll's recent *A History of Christianity in the United States and Canada* (1992) among women who were "other religious founders" (185). Despite its long history, Christian Science is usually grouped among "new religious movements" or even "cults" by sociologists studying its origins and growth. To find treatments of Christian Science that are neither worshipful paeans to Mrs. Eddy nor debunkers of her teaching is difficult. One of the best sources is the three-volume biography of Mrs. Eddy by Robert Peel, which is both sympathetic and thoroughly researched.

Mary Baker Morse was born in 1821 in rural Bow, New Hampshire. She was raised in a religious atmosphere permeated by Puritan tradition. From an early age she was plagued by poor health, including spinal pain and nervous complaints, and was educated at home. Twin interests in health and religion dominated her life. She wrote later, in her autobiography *Retrospection and Introspection*, that she faced a stark choice between the strict Calvinism of her father, with its emphasis on predestination to damnation or salvation, and a gentler trust in prayer and God's love offered by her mother. Though she found comfort in her mother's views, she did not find in conventional faith more than temporary relief from her suffering.

When Morse was fifteen the family moved to the larger town of Sanbornton, and in 1843 she married George Washington Glover. She became pregnant immediately but, when George died only a year after their marriage, found herself a twenty-two-year-old widowed mother. She returned to the Morse household and spent a miserable nine years of illness and depression there. Her family, judging her incapable of caring for her son, gave him to family friends to raise. (They later migrated to the Midwest; Mrs. Glover never regained custody of her only child, George Washington Glover, Jr.) During this period she cast about for remedies to her situation, including morphine as well as homeopathic treatment (using a minute amount of a substance that in a healthy person would produce a similar symptom) and hydropathic medicine (internal or external treatment with water). In 1853 she married a second time, to an itinerant dentist, Dr. Daniel Patterson, partially in an attempt to recover her son. This marriage was a disaster, as Mary Baker Morse Patterson was spectacularly unsuited to a life of constant travel. These were the lowest years of her life, when she began to move away from the orthodox Puritan faith that seemed unable to answer her suffering. Mr. and Mrs. Patterson finally separated in 1862 (though they were not divorced until 1873). Almost completely debilitated, Mrs. Patterson soon moved to Portland, Maine, where she made the acquaintance of a mesmeric healer, Dr. Phineas Quimby, who used non-material methods, including positive suggestion and an early form of hypnotism.

This acquaintance changed her life. She was treated by Quimby and found immediate and dramatic improvement in her mental and physical health. She then studied with him over a period of many months. A former clockmaker, Quimby had absorbed a rich amalgam of the teachings of the mystic Emanuel Swedenborg, the Transcendentalist Ralph Waldo Emerson, and the famous hypnotist Anton Mesmer, among others. He had seen the well-known showman Charles Poyen's demonstrations of mesmerism in 1838, moved into "magneting rubbing" of his patients in the 1840s, then began to emphasize suggestion and the corrections of "mental error" in curing disease. Quimby's practice was not religious; he believed he was practicing a science. Admitting he could not articulate all the theories behind his technique, he was confident the mental origins of disease could be rationally shown.

Quimby, who had become Mrs. Patterson's close friend and mentor, died in early 1866. Only three weeks later, on Thursday, February 1, 1866, in Lynn, Massachusetts, where she now lived, she was injured in a fall on winter ice. Though the severity of her injuries is in dispute, clearly this incident was the genesis of Christian Science. With Quimby's mesmeric treatment unavailable, Mrs. Patterson turned back to the Bible and discovered there "the great fact that I have since tried to make plain to others, namely, Life in and of Spirit; this Life being the sole reality of existence" (Gottschalk, 907).

On Sunday, February 4, 1866, after three days of prayer and study of Jesus' healing miracles, she was physically healed of her injuries. She believed she had discovered a principle lost since the time of Jesus: that Spirit, not matter, is ultimately real and that correct understanding of this principle could heal disease.

From her Calvinist upbringing, she preserved human dependence on the absolute majesty and sovereignty of God and on the necessity of reliance on the Bible to learn God's will. One could only repent of the sinful error of belief in matter by turning to God, not to the human mind. But she innovated the doctrine that healing was a practical "demonstration" of correct understanding of God's will for the world, almost a by-product of this understanding rather than a goal in itself.

Christian Science healing was effected by a trained practitioner, either in the presence of the patient or at a distance ("absent treatment"), using her understanding of divine Mind to "argue" the patient out of the false belief that rendered him susceptible to disease. Once the patient had received the truth of Science, the practitioner could explain in words the method of the treatment. The practitioner's mind did not effect the healing but the practitioner's ability to open the mind of the patient to God, either silently through thought or verbally through speech.

Though Mrs. Patterson denied strenuously that human mental power could heal, she did teach early in her career that human mental power could be used for ill. This was the notorious MAM, or malicious animal magnetism. While human mind was not real, any human being might be susceptible to aggressive evil thoughts wielded by another. Therefore, she later had circles of followers and students on perpetual guard, giving constant absent treatment to protect her from the MAM of her spiritual enemies.

For the next nine years Mrs. Patterson struggled to articulate her discovery in writing, teaching, lecturing, moving around New England in the mental healing subculture and always on the edge of bare subsistence. Finally, she was ready to formalize her movement and organize her students and followers. In 1875 she purchased a modest house in Lynn, which she called the "Christian Scientists' Home," and conducted the first public Christian Science service there on June 6. In the fall she published the first edition of *Science and Health with Key to the Scriptures*.

A small number of her followers were men. In 1877, at the age of fifty-six, she married a devoted student, a former sewing machine salesman named Asa Gilbert Eddy. Mr. Eddy continued as his wife's loyal supporter and partner, but there was no doubt she was the leader of the movement. Mrs. Eddy organized the Christian Science Association in 1876 and in 1879 officially incorporated the Church of Christ (Scientist). In 1881 she obtained a charter for the Massachusetts Metaphysical College to grant degrees in Christian Science practice, with herself as the college's president and sole faculty member.

The small church was riven by doctrinal and personal disputes and controversies in 1882, involving conflict over precedence and interpretation of the complexities of Christian Science practice. A substantial portion of the membership defected, and there were acrimonious lawsuits charging defamation and misappropriation of the church's name. The loyal few who remained gave Mrs. Eddy their vote of confidence and ordained her their pastor. Mrs. Eddy decided to give the church an opportunity to begin again in a fresh field and moved the headquarters to Boston. She did so in an atmosphere of personal tragedy: In 1882 Asa Eddy died. Mrs. Eddy blamed his death on "mental arsenic poisoning," malicious animal magnetism wielded by a jealous professional rival.

Mrs. Eddy found success in Boston. She sent students out across the country to spread the movement and in 1886 founded the National Christian Scientist Association to gather and bind her followers into a cohesive unit. Many of Mrs. Eddy's early students were "leaners rather than leaders" (Peel, *Years of Trial*, 10). In the mid-1880s she began to recruit actively more dynamic women who could themselves become exponents of the cause. One of these was Mrs. Augusta Stetson, married to a disabled Civil War veteran, who was seeking a means to support herself and her family.

Mrs. Stetson had found a modest success as an elocutionist, giving humorous and dramatic recitations at social gatherings and small theaters. She was taken with Christian Science after hearing Mrs. Eddy give a parlor lecture, enrolled in the Primary Class at the Metaphysical College (Mrs. Eddy waived the $300 tuition for this promising student), and was soon embarked on a career as a practitioner and teacher. Still, it was clear Mrs. Eddy meant to promote men to the upper reaches of church hierarchy; in 1886 the managers of the church's new Publishing Society she appointed were all male.

In 1888 the limitations of Mrs. Eddy's personal leadership became painfully clear. She had traveled to Chicago, a hotbed of New Thought activity, to bolster the work of Christian Scientists there and sharpen the distinctions between the two movements. New Thought encompassed a number of new movements that taught a "scientific" approach to metaphysical problems, that positive thought patterns could yield spiritual and material benefits. Mrs. Eddy insisted that Christian Science, which was strictly Christian and nonmaterial, must not be confused with New Thought. On June 14 Mrs. Eddy spoke before an audience of 4,000 women and was an enormous success. But in her absence a meeting of Scientists in Boston on June 17 ended with the defection of one-third of the church's membership (Satter, 1ff). One of the crises that had gripped Boston was the indictment for murder of Christian Science practitioner Mrs. Abby H. Corner of Medford in the deaths of her daughter and the daughter's baby in childbirth. Mrs. Eddy responded by hiring a close male aide, Ebenezer J. Foster, to teach the obstetrical course at the college and doubling the course's tuition to $100 (this when Harvard Medical School charged $200 for an entire year). She also legally adopted Mr. Foster as her son. The college would no longer accept students for the Normal (Christian Science teaching) course who had not already received Primary (the first level of Christian Science practice) degrees.

In an attempt to reach out to women outside the middle and upper classes, in March 1889 Mrs. Eddy opened a free Christian Science dispensary at 3 Boylston Place in Boston. Soon dispensaries opened in other cities, staffed and managed by women. However, the experiment in social service was a disaster; it demanded enormous commitments of time and resources and yielded few cures and fewer converts. The dispensaries gave way to Christian Science Reading Rooms, where the message of Christian Science would be available to the public free of charge, minus the social welfare overtones.

Then Mrs. Eddy began her reorganization of the church. Through 1889 she resigned from her offices: editor of Christian Science publications, pastor, teacher, and president of the National and Boston associations. In December she dissolved the Boston church, directing that it should continue "on a spiritual plane." This led to a flurry of defections, notably a group led by the later notorious Josephine C. Woodbury (who bore a child out of wedlock the next year, baptized it in a seaside tidal pool as "Prince of Peace," and claimed it was a virgin birth). Mrs. Eddy moved her home from Boston to Concord, New Hampshire, in order to distance herself physically from the church's headquarters. She was ready to complete the task of pioneering a new church in the wilderness: As one early observer wrote, the land had been initially cleared, and it was time to go back and root out the stumps and boulders.

In 1891 the church began to raise a building fund to construct a Mother Church edifice in Boston. Thereafter, every local church would be called First, or Second, Church of its city and would be a branch of the Boston church. Only the church in Boston would be the First Church of Christ, Scientist. Mrs. Eddy signed a deed of trust granting control of church property and funds to the board of directors. Hereafter Christian Scientists would have to be elected to membership in the Mother Church by a group of twelve First Members appointed by Mrs. Eddy.

This reorganization mirrored the corporate reorganizations going on in the American business community.

Mary Baker Eddy, the founder of the Church of Christ, Scientist, did not experience a revelation or a revival of faith but claimed to have discovered underlying principles of the universe. In this way Christian Science differs from other new religious movements that have appealed to women. Christian Science has at its base an intellectual, metaphysical knowledge. *Used by permission of The Mary Baker Eddy Library.*

The deed of trust ordered that the board of directors would constitute a "perpetual body or corporation," made up of men whose "business methods" Mrs. Eddy approved. In 1892 Mrs. Eddy directed that there would no longer be pastors or preachers in Christian Science churches. Hereafter the services would be led by First and Second Readers elected by each congregation, who would read preselected portions of *Science and Health* and the King James Bible, then read a sermon written for the day by a committee in Boston. In 1894 the first edition of the *Manual of the Mother Church* was published, a handbook of rules authorized by Mrs. Eddy herself, requiring only the rubber-stamp vote of the board of directors. There was a constant flow of new rules, some general, some specific, many of them clearly intended to curb the ambition of Mrs. Stetson in New York. In 1909, as Mrs. Eddy, in her late eighties, was clearly in failing health, the board of directors moved to excommunicate Mrs. Stetson and her followers. The charges were that Mrs. Stetson had engaged in malpractice using malicious animal magnetism, seeking to aggrandize herself and angling to succeed Mrs. Eddy. With Mrs. Stetson removed, after Mrs. Eddy's death in 1910 the stage was set for the future of the church under

"impersonal" leadership, its canon closed and its hierarchy secure.

The conflict within the Christian Science movement between Mrs. Eddy and Mrs. Stetson exemplifies the transformation directed by Mrs. Eddy. While there is copious evidence of Mrs. Eddy's absolute control over the church during her lifetime, she carefully institutionalized that control in the pages of the *Manual of the Mother Church* and appointed a board of directors to carry out the administration. As summarized by John K. Simmons, the charisma of Mary Baker Eddy was transformed into the covenantal code of the *Manual*. Mrs. Stetson's error was in taking Mrs. Eddy at no more than her original word and failing to "keep up" with the developments the Beloved Leader herself put in place. Many of the changes made in the *Manual*'s eighty-nine editions between 1895 and Mrs. Eddy's passing in 1910 were in direct response to challenges made by Mrs. Stetson.

Mrs. Eddy conscientiously facilitated the process of pouring her own charismatic authority into that document over the last fifteen years of her life, with such Weberian accuracy that the transformation could be a sociological model for routinization of charisma. . . . She once declared to a student that "This Church Manual is God's law, as much as the Ten Commandments and the Sermon on the Mount." (Simmons, 109)

Yet within the *Manual* are numerous articles that function as estoppel clauses; that is, they require the approval of the Pastor Emeritus (Mrs. Eddy) in order to be enacted. These include the appointment of key church officers (Article I) and any revisions to the *Manual* itself (Article XXXV). Therefore, while it appears to have been Mrs. Eddy's intent to institutionalize the leadership of the church under a male board of directors, the mechanism of that institution's bylaws seems to indicate her intent that the institution "wither away" within a matter of years after her death. When the first board member died in 1912, a substantial number of Scientists expected the remnant of the board to resign and return the branch churches to autonomous status. This did not happen, and the resulting lawsuits of the "Great Litigation" were not settled until 1921. The controversy became a battle between the officers of the Christian Science Publishing Society (the church's primary income producer) and the board of directors, both overwhelmingly male, over control of the church. In the end, the board was the victor and continues to direct the Mother Church in Boston and the church publishing activities and to supervise the branch churches. The leading dissenters from this model were women, Mrs. Stetson in the United States and Mrs. Annie C. Bill in the United Kingdom. Mrs. Bill had split from Third Church, London, over doctrinal matters, and upon Mrs. Eddy's death, she declared that the *Manual* itself was an eternal covenant not between Mrs. Eddy and her church but between all humanity and its divine creator. Seeking to reify the charismatic covenant by raising up the *Manual* as a divine document, Mrs. Bill founded the "Universal Design of Life" and invited world religious leaders, including the pope, to recognize her "Parent Church" as the genuine successor to Mrs. Eddy's. Renewed legal action by the board prevented Mrs. Bill from making a public claim to Christian Science authority, but her organization lasted until her death in 1937. A male follower, Francis J. Mott, attempted to reorganize the group as the Church of Integration, but he was unable to sustain it, and the church faded into obscurity.

The Church of Christ, Scientist, however, continued to thrive. Mrs. Eddy's first congregation of 26 members grew to 86,000 by 1906, 202,000 by 1926, and 269,000 by 1936 (Satter, 5). While the church has eschewed publication of formal membership data, sociologist Rodney Stark and historian Mary Farrell Bednarowski have estimated the membership of the church in the 1980s as somewhere between 200,000 and 250,000 (Bednarowski, *New Religions*, 12). In 1996, the *Christian Science Journal* listed 1,802 practitioners and teachers and 1,284 branch churches.

Bednarowski has provided helpful insight into Christian Science theology. Mary Baker Eddy did not experience a revelation or a revival of faith but claimed to have discovered underlying principles of the universe. In this way Christian Science differs from other new religious movements that have appealed to women, such as Wicca; Christian Science has at its base an intellectual, metaphysical knowledge rather than an emotionally driven, experiential basis. Mrs. Eddy wrote that "a corporeal God as defined by lexicographers and scholastic theologians is only an infinite fine being, an unlimited man,—a theory to me inconceivable" (Bednarowski, *New Religions*, 28) and "God is incorporeal, divine, infinite Mind, Spirit, Soul, Principle, Life, Truth, Love" (29). In this way Mary Baker Eddy broke profoundly with her Puritan roots and moved toward a nongendered God, away from the bearded father of traditional Christianity. In her later work *The Religious Imagination of American Women*, Bednarowski notes the now widely accepted view of American women as religious dissenters and places Mrs. Eddy squarely in that category. Still, Bednarowski also wishes to highlight ways in which women such as Mrs. Eddy are also powerful conservators of their religious traditions. This ambivalence is a potent dynamic as we have seen, in the origins of Christian Science, between the paramount role of the individual's understanding of ultimate reality and the necessity of fidelity to the church as defined by the board of directors. " 'Healing' provides one good opening into the expression of ideas that women find most creative in the allocation of their energies toward resistance and acceptance, struggle and hope" (Bednarowski, *Religious Imagination*, 155).

Author Beryl Satter sees the key to evolution of Christian Science, particularly Mrs. Eddy's bureaucratization of the movement after 1890, as an answer to the nineteenth-century question of what the force of the future was to be: male (middle-class white) desire, with his rational, competitive, materialist focus? Or the virtue of (white, middle-class) woman, with her spiritual, desireless, altruistic model? American Social Darwinism, rooted in the gendered nature of selfhood and the cultural dominance of Anglo-Saxon culture, adapted the thought of Herbert Spencer that vigorous, free competition between men would yield leadership of the "fittest" and lead therefore to economic prosperity and the progress of civilization. In this view women represent "refinement" but only as an ornament, a home-based support for men, and caretaker of children. Men's strength is intellectual, women's emotional. Opposed to this view were reform Darwinists such as Lester Ward and women's rights leaders such as Elizabeth Cady Stanton. They saw a necessary balance between the lust of men and the moderating influence of women, a requirement for partnership, albeit in different roles. The goal of the "new woman" would be to reform society so that both men and women would aspire to "pure, desireless, and rational character" (Satter, 12). This position eventually led to women winning the right to vote in 1920, following the horrors of World War I. It is important to see this as background to Mrs. Eddy's insistence that women, better suited to understand God as spirit, are best allied with men, better suited to manage the organized church.

> Woman has the finer spiritual nature. She more readily takes the impress of Christian Science. If as you say (I leave all statistics to the publication department) there are 13,000 women, against 5,000 men, out of a book total of 18,000, it shows that their minds are more receptive; their enthusiasm greater at the beginning of the struggle, but in the strength of man lies the power of carrying it on. (Mary Baker Eddy, *New York Herald*, May 5, 1901)

Christian Science was from its start primarily a movement of and for women. In 1890 some 75 percent of Christian Science practitioners were women, rising to 89 percent in 1910. According to religious census data in 1926, 75.5 percent of all Christian Scientists were female, 94 percent of them urban, in 1,914 congregations totaling 202,098 members, concentrated particularly in the Pacific Coast states. The church was criticized on this score by other Christian healing movements equally hostile to conventional material medicine. Charles Francis Parham, the Pentecostal leader, cited Christian Science as an example of how women could easily fall into spiritual error. To Parham Christian Science practice was a counterfeit of genuine Christianity, a perverted mirror of true Holy Spirit mediumship not far removed from the spiritualism of seances and parlor spectacles.

Mrs. Eddy's own theological language was richly gendered and valorized the female at the expense of the male. She identified the origin of human error with the "Adam-dream" of material consciousness and urged her followers, in the most violent and vivid imagery, to "rise in rebellion" and "mighty struggle" to "choke these errors" of false belief (Satter, 66). In a similar vein, Eve, made last in the ascending order of God's creation and the first human to confess her sin, is the model of Woman, leading to Mary the mother of Jesus and the women who were the first to witness the risen Christ. Woman's spiritual leadership culminates in Mrs. Eddy's (re)discovery of the truth of Christian health. Mrs. Eddy's *Key to the Scriptures* focused on Genesis and the twelfth chapter of Revelation, where archetypes of gen-

der play a central role. She saw the apocalyptic battle of Revelation as prefigured in the present age, in which " 'Material hypotheses challenge metaphysics to meet in final combat. In this revolutionary period . . . woman goes forth to battle Goliath' " (*Science and Health*, 570). Mrs. Eddy was in no doubt that Woman would win the battle. "This immaculate idea [Science], represented first by man [Jesus] and, according to the Revelator, last by woman, will baptize with fire; and the fiery baptism will burn up the chaff of error with the fervent heat of Truth and Love, melting and purifying even the gold of human character" (*Science and Health*, 565).

Mrs. Eddy, however, rejected the strictly bifurcated identification of woman with matter and man with spirit and intellect that was the common currency of the late nineteenth century. To her, matter was partially linked with man because men were more fully under its grasp. To the extent that matter was masculine, it was active and powerful and must be opposed by the loving strength of Spirit. But Mrs. Eddy's primary identification of matter was with the human body, especially as it was susceptible to the error of illness. It is important to understand the development of Mrs. Eddy's thought in the context of nineteenth-century medical practice. In the last decades of the nineteenth century there were significant advancements being made in anesthesia, surgical techniques, and physiological understanding. However, all too often, particularly in the case of "female complaints" (sexual health) the only treatments available were a combination of sedation with opiates, such as laudanum or morphine, and crude, even barbaric (by today's standards) surgery. Medicine was a profession almost exclusively reserved for men and was practiced by an increasingly elite fraternity unsympathetic to the social and psychological pressures that lay beneath many women's sufferings. To submit to conventional medical treatment was indeed to submit one's body to the control of an individual who would likely have little comprehension of the spiritual and emotional dimensions of illness and who would treat a patient as just so much matter.

Was Mary Baker Eddy a feminist? To what extent is Christian Science a feminist religion? Women who embraced Christian Science were deliberately and publicly turning their backs on the male medical establishment. In many cases they were defying their husbands and disturbing the religious unity of their households. However, the vast majority of converts remained married and living with their families. They did not become involved in women's issues such as temperance or suffrage, as both of those causes were rooted in the material world. Their sphere of activity centered in the church and in church affairs. Still, Mrs. Eddy supported some economic rights for women. In *Science and Health* she wrote:

Our [American] laws are not impartial, to say the least, in their discrimination as to the person, property, and parental claims of the two sexes. . . . If a dissolute husband deserts his wife, certainly the wronged, and perchance impoverished, woman should be allowed to collect her own wages, enter into business agreements, hold real estate, deposit funds, and own her children free from interference. (Tucker, 82)

The activist feminist leader Susan B. Anthony took a class in Christian Science in the 1880s in Washington, D.C. Anthony was nothing if not a thoroughgoing materialist. She found Christian Science entirely unsatisfactory as a method of improving the lot of woman. Mrs. Eddy had written in a letter to a colleague, "If the elective franchise for women will remedy the evil without encouraging difficulties of a greater magnitude, let us hope it will be granted" (Peel, *Years of Trial*, 109). This lukewarm endorsement, waffling on unspecified "difficulties," was far from the committed stance Anthony expected from her allies. She wrote that the spiritual abstractions of Christian Science were of little use to the suffrage struggle and that she would "have to go on knocking away to remove the obstructions in the road of us mortals while in these bodies and on this planet" and would leave to others who had "entered into the higher spheres, to revel in things unknown" (Tucker, 83).

Christian Science appealed to women on many levels: woman founded, offering relief from illness, and for many a lucrative profession. However, it offered no leadership roles for women above the local level. Mrs. Eddy brooked no competition from students and colleagues and instituted the board of directors to ensure no individual, man or woman, would succeed her. Therefore, when examining the experiences of women in Christian Science, it must be noted that the other prominent figures early in the movement all became dissenters, many founding their own movements: Augusta Stetson, Ursula Gestefeld, and Emma Curtis Hopkins, among them. Critics of Christian Science, including Mark Twain, also noticed the overwhelmingly female membership. They scoffed and made fun of Science on that score, attributing its appeal to women's "naturally" more emotional nature, their understandable if futile wishes to escape the demands of their bodies and their "normal" social and familial duties, as well as their ambition to make an easy living charging fees to "heal" their coreligionists.

Traditional historical explanations of the success of Christian Science view the movement through their own particular lenses (see McDonald). Sociologists of the late nineteenth century pointed to it as a response to the increasingly crowded, urbanized, mechanized stresses of the Industrial Age. Psychiatrists examined the facets of Mrs. Eddy's personality and her interactions with those around her. Rhetoricians pointed to her adept combinations of religious and scientific vocabulary. As women's studies grew as an academic discipline, feminist scholars offered their own explanations, focused on gender. To scholars such as Margaret Fox, Christian Science was a "nineteenth century women's protest movement" led by "a classic female hysteric who resolved her personal conflicts by developing Christian Science and assuming an extraordinary power role" over a body of followers who "wanted to enact dominance roles that society denied them access to" (McDonald, 89). Jean A. McDonald, however, raises the caution that "public women" such as Mrs. Eddy should not be evaluated by the same criteria traditionally applied to them by male historians: that a woman seeking power must somehow be "explained" by appeal to pathology or protest.

McDonald suggests that Mrs. Eddy's movement was particularly threatening to Victorian "manliness" because it offered direct competition to two male groups already insecure in their social prestige: clergymen and physicians. The heat of their rhetoric opposing Mrs. Eddy is an indication of the danger she posed. The clergy attacked Mrs. Eddy on moral grounds, that as a woman she was constitutionally unable to lead a Christian movement. Likening Mrs. Eddy to the serpent who corrupted Eden, a Baptist minister wrote that she had "coiled herself around the Christian system, breaking all the doctrinal bones of Christianity," then "slimed it over . . . [so it would] go down easy." She was also called "the modern witch of Concord," a "very Delilah who summons man to go to sleep in her lap" (McDonald, 96). Physicians used biological grounds to attack Eddyism, disqualifying women as perpetual children intellectually, endowed with smaller heads and wider hips than men to suit them for their duties as mothers. A woman who overworked her brain risked taxing her weak system and atrophying her uterus. One physician wrote, "Occasionally female physicians, if properly managed and controlled, may be useful (e.g. in a Mohammedan population) on the other hand . . . medicine . . . will not derive much benefit from their efforts" (97). There was even a particular diagnosis made of Mrs. Eddy, as a clear case of hysteria, "religious exaltation—with special crises at adolescence [puberty] and between 40 and 50 [menopause]—and self-importance exaggerated to a disease," "a simple melancholia characteristic of this age, a quiet dementia, a hallucinatory psychosis of paranoid type" (98).

By these accounts Mary Baker Eddy was indeed ill, and her system of Christian Science a symptom of that illness. That the practice of Christian Science offered women an opportunity for a lucrative profession was also used as a charge against it. Painting Mrs. Eddy and other Christian Scientists as no more than ambitious and money hungry was intended to undercut any theological or health claims of the church. The important point is that this ambition in a man was proof of his masculinity, his drive and desire to compete, to get ahead, to succeed. The same drive in a woman was monstrous, or at least corrupting of her nature, at the very least requiring "explanation."

Far from a mercenary motive, McDonald's examination of testimonial letters from converts in the *Christian Science Journal*, two-thirds of them from women, one-third from men, showed that a satisfying intellectual understanding of God was most often reported as the primary reason for conversion. Healing experiences figure very little in these letters, ambition not at all. McDonald raises the important point that it is responsible scholarship, even responsible feminist scholarship, to believe what these witnesses attest are their motives. Some clergymen were willing to concede that Christian Science might offer a more genuine spiritual life than what was commonly practiced in other churches. McDonald hopes that contemporary scholarship as well will take women's motives and choices seriously, without expecting women to conform to categories developed for the experience of men.

Mary Farrell Bednarowski has observed connections between the theology of marginal religious movements and women's leadership. She points to four common features: "1) a perception of the divine that deemphasizes the masculine, 2) a tempering or denial of the doctrine of the Fall, 3) a denial of the need for a traditional ordained clergy, and 4) a view of the marriage which does not hold that marriage and motherhoood are the only acceptable roles for women" (Bednarowski, "Outside the Mainstream," 209). In the case of Christian Science, Mrs. Eddy described God as "Father-Mother," not judging for sin but offering infinite love. Because the body is not real, then gender and any weaknesses attributed to women are also not real. Therefore, the human person, male and female, is already spiritually perfect. Mrs. Eddy went even further, to predict that sexuality and marriage would become unnecessary as error was overcome—"the unbroken levels of eternal harmonious living will be spiritually discerned, and men, not of the earth, earthly, but co-existent with God will appear" (*Science and Health*, 68–69). There is no marriage service included in the *Manual*. Mrs. Eddy herself was a role model of religious leadership, one that many of her followers chose to imitate. But in her church, Mrs. Eddy left few opportunities for women to advance into the top ranks and expected the highest offices to be held by men.

Recent Christian Science

Since 1980, the Church of Christ, Scientist, has weathered a long series of struggles, both legal and financial. Christian Science parents have been prosecuted repeatedly, most notably in Massachusetts, home of the Mother Church, for withholding conventional medical treatment from children who later died. A number were convicted, though most of the cases were reversed on appeal on First Amendment grounds of religious liberty. The church has lobbied intensively and effectively for legal changes to prevent further prosecutions. The board of directors decided to follow Mrs. Eddy's conviction that the church could best present its case in the mass media (which led in 1908 to the founding of the church's newspaper, the respected *Christian Science Monitor*). There was a scandal in 1992 when it was discovered that the board had secretly borrowed against church pension funds reserves to purchase and run a cable television network and a monthly magazine, both of which had lost hundreds of millions of dollars. However, sales of *Science and Health* continued strong, with more than 500,000 copies sold between 1993 and 1998. The church has also reached out to young people through college conferences designed to attract those who are "just interested" in the church's teachings. Christian Science has also benefited from a recent rise in interest in the spiritual aspects of healing on the part of mainstream medicine, said Virginia Harris, the chair of the board of directors. Not to be left behind, the church also has an official Web site (http://www.tfccs.org/).

The Destiny of the Mother Church, written by a former president of the Mother Church, Bliss Knapp, was published in 1993 and promoted by the church's board allegedly in exchange for a Knapp family bequest of $98 million. Knapp, who was a church leader and close friend of Mrs. Eddy, wrote that Mrs. Eddy was the fulfillment of the coming of the Holy Spirit foretold in John 16, the literal manifestation of God and the prophesied second coming of Christ. Though put forward by the official publishing arm of the church, this teaching is considered heresy by many in the church. Over 20 percent of the individual Reading Rooms refused to carry it.

Of course, church dissidents, too, have taken advantage of technology to spread their message. Mrs. Eddy and the board long attempted to restrict the distribution of unauthorized literature, but the Internet has allowed numerous dissident groups to promote their points of view using URLs such as http://www.christianscience.org/. The Mother Church has relaxed some of its restrictions in recent years, such as allowing members to seek conventional medical treatment without losing their church membership. A new initiative of the Mother Church is the Mary Baker Eddy Library for the Betterment of Humanity. Located in Boston with a satellite location in Seneca Falls, New York, the library is dedicated to "celebrating the transforming power of ideas . . . [with] the largest single collection by and about an American woman. The Library will be a forum for discussions of spirituality and health, women in religious leadership, journalism, and other topics related to the ideas, life, and achievements of Mary Baker Eddy" (http://www.marybakereddylibrary.org/).

Virginia Harris, who became chairman of the Mother Church board of directors in 1992, has taken bold steps to address some of the issues that troubled the church. Though she does not use conventional medical care, she has announced that the decision to use material medicine is an individual one. Harris has also encouraged cooperation with medical researchers studying the effects of state of mind on physical health and has spoken at medical conferences. She has promoted a vigorous advertising campaign to promote Christian Science as consonant with New Age spirituality.

Harris attended the 1998 conference marking the 150th anniversary of the Women's Rights Convention in Seneca Falls, New York. She has made it a priority to open the archives of the Mother Church to scholars and was instrumental in allowing Eddy biographer Gillian Gill unrestricted use of church archives. The Mary Baker Eddy Library is a testament to Harris's concerted efforts to modernize the church and broaden feminist awareness of Mrs. Eddy and Christian Science. "With the last decade of such a change in women and such a tremendous interest in spirituality, we really felt we didn't have a choice but to make [Christian Science] available and accessible to the public" (Blanton).

SOURCES: Mrs. Eddy's papers are collected at the Mother Church archives and The Mary Baker Eddy Library in Boston. Extensive collections of Mrs. Stetson's papers are at the Burke Library, Union Theological Seminary, New York, and the Huntington Library, San Marino, California. For more information, consult Sydney E. Ahlstrom's *A Religious History of the American People*, 2 vols. (1972), and his entry on "Mary Baker Eddy" in *Notable American Women*, ed. Edward T. James, Janet Wilson James, and Paul Boyer, vol. 1 (1975). Stephen Gottschalk is a premier historian of the church; see his "Christian Science and Harmonialism," in *Encyclopedia of the American Religious Experience: Studies of Traditions and Movements*, ed. Charles H. Libby and Peter W. Williams, 3 vols. (1988). Also recommended is *Mary Baker Eddy* (1998), by Gillian Gill, and the magisterial three-volume biography of Mrs. Eddy by Robert Peel: *Mary Baker Eddy: The Years of Discovery* (1966), *The Years of Trial* (1971), and *The Years of Authority* (1977). For women's experiences in Christian Science and feminist interpretations of the movement, consult Mary Farrell Bednarowski's *The Religious Imagination of American Women* (1999), as well as her earlier *New Religions and the Theological Imag-*

ination in America (1989) and her foundational article "Outside the Mainstream: Women's Religion and Women Religious Leaders in Nineteenth-Century America," *Journal of the American Academy of Religion* 48.2 (June 1980): 207–231; Jean A. McDonald, "Mary Baker Eddy and the Nineteenth-Century 'Public' Woman: A Feminist Reappraisal," *Journal of Feminist Studies in Religion* 2.1 (Spring 1986): 89–111; and Sarah Gardner Cunningham, "A New Order: Augusta Emma Simmons Stetson and the Origins of Christian Science in New York City, 1886–1910" (Ph.D. diss., Union Theological Seminary, 1994). In addition, see the following sources: Kimberly Blanton, "The Gospel According to Virginia Harris," *Boston Globe*, June 9, 2002; Mary Baker Eddy, *Science and Health with Key to the Scriptures* (1875, 1971); Caroline Fraser, "Suffering Children and the Christian Science Church," *The Atlantic Monthly* 264.4 (April 1995): 105–120; Beryl Satter, *Each Mind a Kingdom: American Women, Sexual Purity, and the New Thought Movement, 1875–1920* (1999); John K. Simmons, "Charisma and Covenant: The Christian Science Movement in Its Initial Post-charismatic Phase," in *When Prophets Die: The Postcharismatic Fate of New Religious Movements*, ed. Timothy Miller (1991); Rodney Stark, William Sims Bainbridge, and Lori Kent, "Cult Membership in the Roaring Twenties: Assessing Local Receptivity," *Sociological Analysis* 42.2 (Summer 1981): 137–161; Cynthia Grant Tucker, *Healer in Harm's Way: Mary Colson, a Clergywoman in Christian Science*, 2nd ed. (1994); and Barbara Wilson, *Blue Windows: A Christian Science Childhood* (1997). See also Mary Baker Eddy, *Retrospection and Introspection* (1891); Mary Baker Eddy, *Science and Health* (1875). Page numbers for quotes from *Science and Health* are to a 1975 reprint edition.

CLARA EVANS MUHAMMAD: PIONEERING SOCIAL ACTIVISM IN THE ORIGINAL NATION OF ISLAM
Debra Mubashir Majeed

IT IS NOT possible to fully understand the social activism of African American Muslim women without addressing the role and contributions of Clara Evans Muhammad (1899–1972), who served the *original* Nation of Islam (NOI) for four decades until her death in 1972. The use of the term *original* distinguishes the black proto-Islamic organization of Wallace D. Fard and Elijah Muhammad from as many as five other movements that include "Nation of Islam" in all or part of their names, including the movement led by Minister Louis Farrakhan since 1977.

Like so many unsung heroines of the African experience in North America, Clara lived her life communally, intertwining her day-to-day activities with those of other NOI members struggling to survive at a time and in a cultural milieu where African American women were the "oppressed of the oppressed." Thus, Clara embodied the sentiments of scholar Renita J. Weems:

If the truth be told, we today are who we are—if we are anybody—because some woman, somewhere, stooped down long enough that we might climb on her back and ride piggyback into the future. (Weems, 108)

Contrary to popular views of the Black Nationalist movement, which gained nationwide attention under the leadership of her husband Elijah, at least one woman was situated at the center of power during the late 1930s and early 1940s—a critical period in NOI history. Clara's leadership as the pioneer of the Islamic educational system, from which emerged both the Black Nationalist independent and Afrocentric education movements, and as supreme secretary of the Nation of Islam is a well-kept secret acknowledged by few observers of African American Muslims. Buried beneath most explorations of the original Nation of Islam as well are works that draw attention to Clara as the one who introduced her husband to the Islamic teachings of W. D. Fard, who organized the movement in 1930. While unfortunate, the lack of attention afforded her as a model of black womanhood or as an example of female activism is consistent with the prevailing image of Muslim women, the vast majority of the estimated 6 to 7 million American followers of Islam.

Many people view female Muslims as oppressed, powerless victims whose agency and visibility are dictated by the men around them. Characterizations of the original Nation of Islam that do not portray the organization as a stumbling block to women who desired to participate in the political and social affairs of their community are rare. Unsurprisingly perceptions of African American and other Muslim women are clouded by images of them as individuals whose activities are primarily restricted to the care and nurture of husbands and children. Ironically, support for these narrow characterizations often emerged from within the cultural atmosphere of the Muslim world, where the dehumanizing gender relations of some societies have been portrayed as the normative injunctions of Islamic law. Despite the emphasis on these reports, Muslim women and others have waged a campaign to depict the role and function of Muslim women more broadly. Among others Aminah

Clara Evans Muhammad served the original Nation of Islam for four decades until her death in 1972. Like so many unsung heroines of African experience in North America, Clara lived her life communally, intertwining her day-to-day activities with those of other NOI members struggling to survive at a time and in a cultural milieu where African American women were the "oppressed of the oppressed." *Courtesy of Mosque Care.*

McCloud, herself a Muslim, Cynthia S'Thembile West, Rosetta Ross, and Sonsyrea Tate, raised in the NOI, have developed research on the original Nation of Islam that gives depth to the lived experience of female members. Like Christianity and Judaism, Islam is not a monolithic global faith. What is more, the varieties of Islam in America preclude simple generalizations. Consequently, when media reporters, scholars, and others project the rigid customs and behavior of some Muslims as the beliefs and rituals of all Muslims, they not only perpetuate stereotypes, but in the case of the NOI, they miss more subtle stories of female Muslim leaders who wield considerable control over their lives and influence the direction of their religious communities.

Though her race, gender, and formal education may suggest otherwise, Clara Muhammad was far from powerless. A product of the post–Reconstruction South, Clara has not appeared in any published encyclopedias on black women, nor are any biographies or manuscripts dedicated to her life. Only in recent years have books on the NOI and/or Elijah Muhammad featured the name of "Mother Clara" in their indexes. In fact, this is one of the few published accounts to feature Clara Muhammad as the primary subject of public conversation since Elijah's alleged extramarital relationships were publicized in the early 1960s and her death in 1972. Nevertheless, Clara Muhammad's belief in education as a key to the liberation of black people and her devotion to the organization that today identifies with the worldwide Islamic movement led residents in Fulton Count, Georgia, in the summer of 2000, to celebrate her as one who pioneered the restoration of the female in the stable family life.

Clara was born in an era that necessitated the formation of the National Association of Colored Women's Clubs to combat the mythology of black womanhood. Her arrival on November 2, 1899, on a plot outside of Unadilla, Georgia, signaled the presence of the first baby girl born to Mary Lue Thomas and Quartus Evans. Apparently, like brother Carlton, later sister Rosalie, and most black people at that time, Clara was born at home with the assistance of a midwife. By 1900 Georgia was a prominent region within black America. The Peachtree State was home to almost 12 percent of all African Americans, including at least one Sea Island Muslim community. More than half of the African American residents of this former slaveholding state cultivated land in the agricultural center, the "black belt" that stretched across the middle and southwestern portions of the state. Some, like Clara's father, earned enough by sharecropping to rent the land on which their homes stood. Years later, the Evans family settled in the Cordele area and became a fixture of the rural black community. A devout Christian, Clara worshiped with her parents at Bethel Christian Methodist Episcopal Church, where,

according to relatives, her father was a church leader. Both in the choir and the congregation, Clara sang versus to songs like "I Never Can Forget," whose lyrics she later would adapt to fit her Muslim identity. It was in the "church house" around Thanksgiving 1917 that she first met her future husband, who attended nearby Zion Hope Baptist Church. The former Elijah Poole discovered early on that Clara's faith in her Creator was real and deep. After Sunday services, Poole would walk along Rock House Road to Clara's home for his 6 P.M. visit with her and her family. Against the wishes of her father, Clara eloped with Elijah on March 7, 1919, climbing out of a window during the night. For the first month, Clara's family was unaware that the newlyweds were sharing the home of Elijah's brother, Sam, a short distance away off of Highway 41. Clara and Elijah would later reunite with her family; according to some sources, Clara's first child was born in her parents' home in 1921.

In September 1923 Clara and her toddlers, Emmanuel and Ethel, migrated from Georgia and settled in Detroit, Michigan, joining Elijah who had left their southern home five months earlier. On paper, the Motor City appeared to be a likely choice of migration for two reasons. First, it was up North, and at the time almost any place in the Promised Land seemed light years away from lynching and other forms of oppression and discrimination that black people were subjected to in the South. Second, Elijah's father had moved to Detroit the year before, and in a letter to his son the elder Poole described the booming automobile factories. Still, life for these southern migrants was not easy. Urban industrial existence did not fulfill the dreams of Clara's family nor for the thousands of other African Americans who fled the social conflict of the South. Intimidation was pervasive, housing was in short supply, and good jobs scarce, especially for African Americans, whom Claude Andrew Clegg III described as being "on the fringes of industry" (15). Further, like many other southern-born immigrants, Clara and Elijah had little formal education. Clara did not proceed beyond elementary school; Elijah's formal education ended much earlier.

Theirs was a financially—and emotionally—challenged family as well. By 1926, Clara had moved from being a stay-at-home mom to accepting work as a maid. Employment for Elijah was unstable. The family could not always support the purchase of shoes or clothes. Sometimes the children were forced to wear shoes whose soles were reinforced with cardboard. Soon Elijah's financial support was limited to the income from the occasional odd job. Following the Great Depression's arrival in already poverty-stricken Detroit, Elijah began to drink steadily and heavily. The family was forced to accept public assistance. There were toddlers to feed and marital stress to relieve. By June of that year, the Poole household had grown to five children, three boys and two girls. Elijah and Clara could afford to put meat on the dinner table only twice a month. Recalling the days when her family was at its "lowest ebb," Clara says,

> I would go out and try to help him [Elijah], but with five small children, I could not work steadily. However, I was successful when I went door to door, asking for work. The people would question me, and I would tell them the truth. Some of them did not have any work, but they would give me a little money and some gave me food. This was Allah's work, but I did not know it then. ("An Invitation to 22 Million Black Americans," 19)

During this time, Elijah frequently stayed away from home, according to his son and successor, Warith Deen Mohammed, "ashamed because he couldn't bring her [Clara] anything." At times, Clara searched the streets for her husband, sometimes with at least one child in tow. When she would find him, among his drinking friends, she would "bring him on her shoulder," according to Mohammed, dragging him into the house and letting him fall on the bed. "My mother was a very strong lady." (Mohammed interview).

Clara's faith was severely challenged in her new northern environment. Without the closeness of her immediate or church families, Clara found herself searching for a tangible anchor in an environment where many disillusioned blacks hunger for a religion that spoke to their "material reality" and satisfied their psychological need for affirmation of their basic humanity and destiny (Clegg, 19). Understandably, then, she was intrigued when in September 1931 a girlfriend introduced Clara to the teachings of W. D. Fard, a silk salesman and former leader of the Moorish Science Temple of America (MSTA). Organizing former MSTA members under a separate organization he initially called Allah's Temple of Islam, Fard carried his message about the divine goodness of black people door to door throughout Paradise Valley, a predominantly black section of Detroit. According to Mohammed, the friend told his mother that "there's a man . . . he sells silks, and he says that black folk used to wear silk before they were brought to America, and that they were Muslims" (Mohammed interview). Clara accompanied her neighbor to one of Fard's meetings, during which Fard lectured on the history and future of black Americans. His messages represented a blending of Christianity, orthodox Islam, and Black Nationalist ideology with other belief systems. Fard was able to describe the origins of God and creation as well as what Muslims should eat and how they should dress. For Clara this new religion "dealt with all of the major questions people have posed about their place in the universe" (Clegg, 41). Soon after first meeting Fard, Clara wrote a letter to her mother declaring that "we have found the savior" (Historical Documentary). Such a declaration would have caught the ear of her Christian mother, whom herself awaited the return of "the savior." Followers of Protestant Christianity, still dominant religious expression among black people, and the original Nation of Islam, viewed their Creator and their God as one and the same. It was their understanding of the human manifestation of "the savior" that separated mother and daughter. Mary Lue Evans prepared for the return of Jesus Christ. As a Christian she believed Jesus to be the Son of Man who suffered and died on a cross and would ultimately win the battle between good and evil. Conversely, Clara celebrated the arrival of one whose teachings would *save* black people from their mental deaths, enabling them to survive the imminent destruction of white America. Elijah taught followers that Fard was the "Son of Man" about whom Jesus prophesied. Thus the NOI addressed Fard in terms Christians often used to refer to Jesus: as God in the flesh.

Clara's level of consciousness mirrored that of other African Americans who searched for an identity consistent with a reality that thirty years later Aretha Franklin would sing about—R-E-S-P-E-C-T—and the Rev. Jesse Jackson would preach about—"I Am Somebody." It was in the *nation*, not the *church*, that Clara found lasting solace, for the messages of Fard focused on God's concern for the earthly liberation of black people rather than heavenly rewards. Thus she, and a number of former Christian women, became the female support system of a charismatic leader who made them feel good about themselves, helped them empower their men and alter their way of life.

Following Fard's lecture, Clara characterized his teachings as something that "may help my husband" regain his dignity and self-respect. She was right. Within months of their meeting, Clara invited the mysterious teacher to dinner. Fard accepted and shared the meager table of Clara and Elijah. He and Elijah relieved Clara of kitchen clean-up duties so that she could put the children to bed. There was no question her husband asked that this charismatic teacher could not answer. After Elijah accompanied Clara to one of Fard's meetings, he informed his wife, "We're going home, we've got to take all of the pork out of the ice box, throw it away" (W. D. Mohammed interview). Elijah's response reflected the developing moral code of the NOI, which focused on cleanliness of the mind, spirit, and body. For the latter, strict dietary regulations challenged NOI members to forego the "slave diet" of cornbread, black-eyed peas, and chitlins, which was considered hard on the digestive system. Like traditional Muslims, NOI members also were instructed to abstain from eating pork, viewed as a meat from the animal that most resembled the white man. Not only was Clara instrumental in her husband meeting Fard and becoming a Muslim; she also served as the conduit through which his calling to teach his newly accepted faith was confirmed. Within months of Elijah's conversion, Clara went to hear Fard speak, while Elijah remained in their home near Detroit with the children. Before the meeting ended, Fard sought out Clara and asked her to deliver a message that would have profound implications for her husband and the growing Nation: "You tell him that he can go ahead . . . and start teaching [Islam], and I will back him up" (*History of the Nation of Islam*, 2). At the same time, Clara moved into position to become "the glue" that would hold together the community that Elijah would build for decades to come.

The year 1932 unveiled a series of events that illustrated why women were attracted to the patriarchal structure of the NOI, also finding an environment that afforded them a tangible sense of their own agency and capacity to promote change. No curriculum within the public educational system placed black people at the center of civilization, provided positive images of the black family or communal life, or pointed to the significant contributions made by Americans of African ancestry. The few textbooks or teaching lessons that intentionally featured black people served to extend negative stereotypes and foster black self-hate.

This was the atmosphere in which Fard began to encourage his followers to withdraw their children from the public school system of the "white devils" and instruct them in a home school environment. Elijah and Clara, also distrustful of the public school curriculum that promoted the culture of whites and reflected "lies" about blacks, complied. They envisioned an educational institution that would represent a counterdiscourse on black inferiority and black religion. Consequently, their six children became the first students in the newly formed University of Islam, operating from the home of its first instructor, Clara Muhammad, who, along with her husband, assumed the new surname given to them by their leader. In actuality, the "university" was an elementary and secondary school with curriculum similar to that taught in the public school system and content considered advanced. Initially it also was not a gender-segregated environment because all the students were members of the same primary or extended family. As other families enrolled, girls would sit on one side of the room, boys on the other. The goal was to form a school site inside each Temple location. By investing her talents, energy, and faith in this endeavor, Clara's work mirrored the slogan of the National Association of Colored Women—"Lifting as we climb." It was within the original Nation of Islam that she and others would respond to their marginalization in the larger society and carve out space in which they could direct their activist consciousness.

Two years later, a court order to close the home schooling project and the arrest of Elijah (along with thirteen teachers and administrators) led to a march on police headquarters in Detroit. The presence of independent educational systems developed to address the cultural heritage of students was not unusual, nor was the bias to which the schools could be subjected. Catholic schools in America began as a nineteenth-century phenomenon when church leaders in response to Protestant domination in the public schools developed a plan to build a school in every parish. While the NOI endeavor did not attract harassment from such racist groups as the Ku Klux Klan as the Catholic Church did in 1920, government pressure against the assembly of NOI members was mounting, seemingly as a result of a murder during religious rituals associated with Fard's early followers, building code violations of meeting locations, negative media reports, and accusations of the movement's cultlike status. What is more, home schooling was still illegal in Detroit in 1934. Such realities complicated the efforts of an organization that could not always rely on landlords to renew leases on property in which classes were conducted.

Many of the 700 participants in the 1934 march were women, who protested the arrest of their leaders as well as the state of Michigan's refusal to accept their decision to self-educate their children. The presence of this unarmed group was met by armed local police officers who attacked the black marchers—a scene that would become an all-too-familiar image during the civil rights movement two decades later. Before Elijah was released with six months' probation, officials also threatened Clara with arrest. She responded, "I will die as dead this door knob, before I allow my children to attend public school" (Muhammad and Shakoor-Abdullah).

The budget was low and supplies were scarce at Clara's school, compelling the mother of the Nation to call upon her creativity to enhance the learning of her students. Daily, Clara's youngsters gathered around the dining room table, pencils in hand, awaiting instructions from their teacher—a woman who never advanced beyond the seventh or eighth grade herself—who would write out their spelling and reading assignments on pieces of lined paper. Clara's own ideas, thoughts, and family history as well as Fard's teachings became sentences to be copied, word groups to be memorized, paragraphs that helped develop penmanship. While textbooks were not available initially, subjects still included basics—readings, writing, arithmetic—as well as Temple history or the founding of the original Nation of Islam and the myths about the origins of black people. Within their own educational system, wrote two Muslim scholars, a history was taught that "placed black people at the center of civilization and made them feel good about themselves" (Rashid and Muhammad, 179). "It was a curriculum that made a point of ignoring world history as we know it and United States history as we know it," added Mohammed, Clara's fifth son. "And we learned to think," he said, "to have our own thoughts. She'd ask questions and sought our opinions" (Mohammed interview).

When governmental attempts to arrest him compelled Fard to go into hiding in 1933, Elijah assumed control of the Detroit-based movement. Controversy surrounding his appointment led Elijah to move the headquarters of the organization to Chicago in 1934 and there open a second University of Islam. Education continued to be central to "building a nation." As the original Nation of Islam, marked by Elijah's philosophical blueprint, began to attract attention with its methods of black liberation, Clara's visible role extended beyond the school system. At the same time, other NOI women were attracting attention because of their presence in public protests. When Rosetta Hassan, a member of Temple #2 in Chicago, went to court over a dispute with a Greek immigrant on a streetcar, an estimated sixty Muslims joined her at the March 5, 1935, hearing. No charges were filed against Hassan, but as the jubilant group attempted to leave the courtroom, conflicting directives issued by bailiffs led to a scuffle between the Muslims and another black group. In the end, an estimated forty-four Muslims were arrested, including as many as twenty-eight women. External social concerns as well as the responsibilities of the NOI as a burgeoning network led Elijah to increase his dependence on his wife's administrative and leadership skills. He also relied on her ear and voice more often, as well as her ability to be, as some early members observe, "the glue that kept the movement together" and the model of black womanhood. As one new Muslim recalled, "[S]he had the courage to be different with great dignity. . . . I felt comfortable with her, which made it easier for me to get out of my expensive, low-necked dresses and put on one longer than all of my friends and associates" (Muhammad, "Month of November," 11).

During the next seven years, pressure from law enforcement authorities intent on detaining the NOI leader on any number of complaints, coupled with actual periods of incarcerations, allowed Elijah little time to focus on the day-to-day operations of his movement. Clara stepped in, consoling frightened members, solving disputes, and working with officials—some whose disapproval of her display of agency was apparent—to steer the course of the NOI. By 1942 female activism in the NOI was supported by leaders and members on some levels but still frowned upon by others. Educational activism was more easily accepted due to Elijah's recognition of women as "tone-setters" for the education of children (West, 44). Most leaders of the NOI, however, were not accustomed to dealing with female members other than in subservient roles. To be sure, the core teachings of the NOI implied that women's work was confined to the domestic sphere and that strong and stable family units were to a large extent the responsibility of female members. In fact, in Muslim Girls Training (MGT) classes, often taught by the daughter of Clara and Elijah, female members where informed that they were the key to the success of the black man. Yet for many women, the movement itself—as well as activities engineered to foster its success—was an extension of the home. That is why some NOI women unashamedly participated in public protests, held jobs outside the home— mostly as entrepreneurs in community businesses—and shared the messages of their leader, confident that their activism would further individual development as well as the progress of the NOI.

In this spirit Clara naturally took charge in 1942 when Elijah and other male leaders were arrested and convicted in Washington, D.C., on draft evasion charges. In addition to seeing to the needs of her children, Clara solicited members for financial support for her husband's bond and carried funds collected to Elijah in jail—at least once in a trunk full of $1 bills. As the NOI's designated supreme secretary, Clara intervened during Temple disputes and represented her husband at public engagements within the movement and in the larger society. When she addressed an audience, her messages were often characterized as spiritual or inspiring speeches for which she received a tremendous ovation. Ultimately, she gained the respect of NOI leaders, including some who would later develop splinter organizations. Outside the original Nation of Islam, her contributions and her husband's mission were sometimes viewed as one, even by other Muslims who did not accept Elijah's philosophy. According to her son Emmanuel Muhammad, "[S]he had held the family together all the while he was on the run, and while he was in prison. She gathered and sent or brought to my father and me whatever literature the prison permitted. She also typed verses of the Holy Qur'an, (which she and Elijah taught their children to read) and sent them to us" (Clegg, 154).

Through occasional personal visits, Clara maintained intimate connections with "her" school (now with locations across the nation) at least through about 1970, when she was photographed with an NOI leader who served as a principal then, Marva Salimah Salaam at the University of Islam in Chicago. No matter the location of the dozens of schools that operated by the 1970s, each time Clara arrived at a site she would announce, "I just came to see how the school was doing." Then she'd inquire, " 'Do you have everything you need here? If you don't, I'm going to tell my husband!' " Often Clara employed her own resources, rather than wait to inform the NOI leader. "Many times, she wouldn't tell him [my father] anything," acknowledged their son Mohammed. "She had savings, and she would say, 'take this [money] and get the typewriter or whatever they needed' " (Mohammed interview). She'd also remain in touch by attending annual graduation ceremonies, where she met each graduate with a gift.

For more than thirty years the University of Islam almost single handedly provided African American children with a worldview that promoted self-knowledge, self-reliance, and self-discipline. After Warith Deen Mohammed succeeded his father as leader of the original Nation of Islam in 1975, he renamed the educational enterprise the Clara Muhammad Schools in honor of his mother. In a series of reorganizations, Mohammed guided the NOI onto a path of traditional Islam, and its estimated 2.5 million supporters exist under the name American Society of Muslims. With about seventy-five units nationwide in 2000, Clara Muhammad Schools serve a broader group of Muslims and non-Muslim youngsters who consistently receive academic achievements awards. Accolades earned by the Clara Muhammad School in Milwaukee, Wisconsin, recipient of six first-place trophies in the 1999 Academic Olympics sponsored by Marquette University, is but one example. These institutions are among at least 200 around the country that comprise a national network of Islamic Schools. Clara Evans Muhammad, the Nation of Islam's "bonding apparatus," died on August 12, 1972, following a quiet battle with stomach cancer (Muhammad and Shakoorn-Abdullah). Before and after accusations emerged about her husband's relationships with other women, some inside the NOI wondered why she never left him. Karl Evanzz, author of *The Messenger: The Rise and Fall of Elijah Muhammad* (1999), theorizes that she—like many married women of her day—was too financially dependent. Halimah Muhammad of Atlanta offers a different perspective. "[My grandmother] recognized his mission; it was a great work, and [she chose to look] beyond his human frailties," she explains. "Wherever she saw she could do something . . . an opportunity to do work as a Muslim woman [she would]. She had the wisdom to know how to be graceful, to stand by a man whose mission was bigger than he was" (Halimah Muhammad interview).

The social activism of Clara Evans Muhammad and other female members of the original Nation of Islam is most evident in contemporary endeavors of women affiliated with the American Society of Muslims as well as the contemporary Nation of Islam orchestrated by Minister Louis Farrakhan. For instance, Laila Muhammad, a granddaughter of Clara, single mother and businesswoman, served as cochair of the Muslim American Society's 2000 international convention, which attracted an estimated 5,000 people. Her leadership role marked the second consecutive year that a woman organized

the annual gathering. (Her sister, N'Gina Muhammad-Ali, currently holds the same position.) Amazingly, soon after receiving a kidney transplant, Amatullah Rashad of Wilmington, Delaware, coordinated the 1999 convention. In 1999, Rashad and Amatullah Sharif were named Muslim Women of the Year. Sharif, a former secretary to both Elijah Muhammad and W. Deen Mohammed, his son and successor, delivered a presentation as the American Muslim representative at the Eleventh General Conference of the Supreme Council for Islamic Affairs, held in July 1999 in Cairo, Egypt. The weekly newspaper of the American Society of Muslims has been edited in the past ten years by Ayesha K. Mustapha, an award-winning journalist. Baseemah Abdullah is principal of the first Islamic school established in the city of Milwaukee in 1972. Indeed, in both associations, which trace their roots to the ministry of Elijah and Clara Muhammad, women employ self-defining strategies as educators, principals, photographers, entrepreneurs, real estate agents, therapists, attorneys, counselors, social workers, writers, publishers, administrators, fashion designers, and liaisons between their Muslim group, other religious institutions, and the larger society. They edit periodicals, establish international organizations, and create forums and support systems for new Muslim women as well as for immigrant women in whose traditional cultures women are not permitted to visibly exert influence or employ agency outside the home. A number of Muslim women hold advanced degrees, including the highest degree in their fields.

Perhaps the most visible contemporary example of female activism is the work of Minister Ava Muhammad, appointed in August 2000 as the national spokesperson for Minister Farrakhan. Muhammad, an Atlanta attorney, is the first woman in Farrakhan's organizations to serve in this capacity. Without a doubt, her gender will attract attention in the position once held under Elijah Muhammad by both Farrakhan and Malik El Shabazz, formerly Malcolm X. But it is her unprecedented role as Southern Regional Minister and Minister of Muhammad Mosque No. 15 in Atlanta that continues to be debated within some Muslim communities. In fact, she was installed on July 28, 1998, as part of a rare interfaith installation service at Hillside Chapel Truth Center, the Atlanta church pastored by Martin Luther King Jr.'s daughter, Rev. Dr. Barbara K. King. Noting the significance of her appointment and the religious environment in which it was celebrated, Minister Ava remarked, "[I]t is my fervent prayer that I succeed in my assignment, in order to help the Minister in his effort to destroy the myth that women are inferior beings who cannot preach the word or shepherd the flock. Through my appointment, Minister Farrakhan is manifesting the liberating force and power contained in the Teachings of the Honorable Elijah Muhammad." ("A Nation Can Rise No Higher Than Its Women").

As an activist educator in the classroom, in the home, and at the helm of a movement, Clara Evans Muhammad made the transition from being a woman whose identity was shaped by Western culture and the values of her husband and community "to one who shaped and defined what it really meant to be a Black Muslim woman" (Rahman, 71). Because she dared to speak and to act in a patriarchal world, Mother Clara challenged and inspired women and men for whom religiously motivated activism and social responsibility were integral to their daily lives. Her witness is connected to earlier traditions of black religious activism and continues to enable new generations to ride into the future and stake a claim to their divinely appointed destiny.

SOURCES: See Claude Andrew Clegg III, *An Original Man: The Life and Times of Elijah Muhammad* (1977); Mrs. Clara Muhammad, "An Invitation to 22 Million Black Americans," *Muhammad Speaks* 6.17 (January 13, 1967); W. Deen Mohammed, interview by author, tape recording, Chicago, Ill., November 5, 1997; *Historical Documentary*, prod. The Nation of Islam in America, 90 min, CORE (Coalition for Remembrance of the Honorable Elijah Muhammad), n.d., videocassette; Messenger Elijah Muhammad, *History of the Nation of Islam* (1955); S. Maryum Muhammad and B. Shakoor-Abdullah, "A Profile—Our First Pioneer Mrs. Clara Muhammad," *Muslim Journal*, October 1966; Queen Ester Muhammad, "Month of November—Tribute to Sister Clara Muhammad," *Muslim Journal*, November 26, 1999; Cynthia S'Thembile West, "Revisiting Female Activism in the 1960s: The Newark Branch of the Nation of Islam," *Black Scholar* 26.3–4 (Fall 1999): 41–48; Halimah Muhammad, conversation with author, Cordele, Ga., March 9, 2000; Hakim M. Rashid and Zakiyyah Muhammad, "The Sister Clara Muhammad Schools: Pioneer in the Development of Islamic Education in America," *Journal of Negro Education* 61.2 (1999): 178–185; Ajile Rahman, "She Stood by His Side and at Times in His Stead: The Life and Legacy of Sister Clara Muhammad, First Lady of the Nation of Islam" (Ph.D. diss., Clarke Atlanta University, 2000); and Renita J. Weems, *Just a Sister Away: A Womanist Vision of Women's Relationships in the Bible* (1988). See also "A Nation Can Rise No Higher Than Its Women," available online at http://www.finalcall.com/national/savioursday2k/min_ava.htm.

THEOSOPHY, NEW THOUGHT, AND NEW AGE MOVEMENTS
Catherine Wessinger, Dell deChant, and William Michael Ashcraft

THEOSOPHY, NEW THOUGHT, and the New Age movements are related in the interweaving of their his-

tories and the cross-fertilization of their ideas. Women have played significant roles in founding and leading groups in these three movements and in shaping their worldviews. Although understandings of gender roles vary, these movements have fostered women's religious leadership and nonpatriarchal understandings of ultimate reality.

Theosophy, New Thought, and the New Age movements are parts of a broader stream of religious thought that has been termed the "metaphysical movement" by historian J. Stillson Judah. The metaphysical worldview is monistic, meaning that there is one ultimate reality and everything is part of it; God is an immanent universal principle. The metaphysical movement has an optimistic view of human nature that rejects the Christian doctrine of original sin. The fallenness of the human condition is due to ignorance, not sin, and salvation comes through knowledge. The individual is always progressing, either in the afterlife or through reincarnation, or both. Jesus is a spiritual exemplar, not a human sacrifice who died to appease a vengeful God. The Christ principle, a higher state of consciousness that is attuned with God, is available to all. One's thoughts are believed to have the power to shape material events in one's life. Well-being is attained by utilizing the natural laws that govern the unseen reality that is consciousness/spirit.

Theosophy, New Thought, and the New Age movements represent a reaction against scientific materialism. All three assert that reality involves unseen, spiritual planes of existence that influence earthly well-being. A special emphasis is the power of thought/consciousness/spirit to change matter.

Women's roles in these movements illustrate typical social dynamics that legitimate women's religious leadership. These include a reliance on charisma—the believed claim that a person receives revelation from an unseen source of authority—to break through the restrictions of patriarchy. The earliest women leaders often relied on a male partner to institutionalize their movements. Subsequent women leaders combined in themselves charisma and administrative talent. Contemporary women in these movements continue to rely on charisma while going beyond it to rely on educational credentials to legitimate their religious leadership. A theological emphasis on charisma is continued in the view that God or the divine is immanent in nature and humanity.

Theosophy

In a culture that requires women be restricted to the domestic sphere, charisma—when the claim to revelation is believed by others—has the power to cut through patriarchy and propel the exceptional woman to religious authority. Often such a woman relies on a man to organize the religious institution that she inspires. This pattern was followed by the two founders of the Theosophical Society, Helena P. Blavatsky and Henry Steel Olcott. Blavatsky articulated a worldview that, when combined with the slowly increasing social expectation of equality for women, fostered the subsequent religious leadership of women such as Annie Besant and Katherine Tingley. Each of these women combined charisma, intelligence, oratorical skills, and administrative abilities. The Theosophical movement, of which the Theosophical Society is the parent, provides diverse opportunities for women to find spiritual sustenance and utilize their talents.

As first articulated by Helena P. Blavatsky, Theosophy is a synthesis of Eastern and Western religions with an emphasis on mysticism. Theosophy is a response to increasing interactions of diverse world religious traditions. Reality is seen as consisting of seven levels of spirit-matter, with the highest level being the most refined and the lowest level the most gross. The universe emanated from one impersonal source but is filled with beings who operate on various spirit-matter planes. These beings include *devas* (a Hindu term meaning gods), angels, evil spirits, fairies, and spirits of the dead who are in various stages of transition to their next lives. Blavatsky taught that there is an "Occult Hierarchy" of "Masters of the Wisdom," who are living men of ad-

vanced consciousness who know how to function consciously on all seven planes of existence. These men have seemingly miraculous powers due to their knowledge of how to manipulate the laws of nature. Blavatsky taught that these men guide evolution on Earth. The parent Theosophical Society popularized such Hindu and Buddhist ideas in the West as reincarnation and karma, chakras (centers of consciousness roughly aligned along points on the spine), and *kundalini* (a serpentlike feminine energy that lies dormant at the base of the spine), as well as the practices of meditation and yoga. (Yoga and meditation are believed to cause the *kundalini* to rise, activating the chakras along the way, to the top of the head, thus awakening enlightenment.) Several organizations are now part of the broad Theosophical movement that grew out of the Theosophical Society.

HELENA P. BLAVATSKY

Helena P. Blavatsky (1831–1891) was an unconventional Russian noblewoman who married at seventeen, then promptly left her husband to embark on a career as world traveler and spiritual seeker. She was the daughter of a military officer and a feminist novelist. Since her mother died when she was twelve, Helena spent much of her childhood in the home of her maternal grandparents. Her grandfather was a provincial

Helena P. Blavatsky was an unconventional Russian noblewoman who married at seventeen, then promptly left her husband to embark on a career as world traveler and spiritual seeker. Blavatsky was the first to articulate Theosophy, a synthesis of Eastern and Western religions with an emphasis on mysticism. *Courtesy of the Theosophical Society in America.*

governor, who had a library on occult subjects. During her childhood, Helena was noted for mysterious personages, voices, and strange happenings in her proximity. As an adult, Blavatsky attracted attention by manifesting Spiritualist phenomena such as the sound of unseen bells, raps, and causing tables to become alternately immovable or light as a feather. She also demonstrated psychic skills. Although she participated for a while in the Spiritualist movement, Blavatsky soon asserted that her powers were manifested by the exercise of her will and not by spirit possession. Blavatsky taught that Spiritualist mediums were possessed by low-order spirits masquerading as ghosts. Blavatsky's bias against such possession has been passed down to subsequent prophets in the Theosophical movement, who emphasize that they are not unconscious "channels" but instead are inspired or receive dictations from Masters while being fully conscious. Blavatsky gained authority for these ideas expressed in her two philosophical works, *Isis Unveiled* (1877) and *The Secret Doctrine* (1888), by asserting that these teachings were given to her by psychic communications from Masters of the Wisdom.

Blavatsky came to the United States in 1873. In 1874 she met Henry Steel Olcott (1832–1907), a Civil War colonel, New York City attorney, and Spiritualist journalist, at a Vermont farmhouse where Spiritualist manifestations were occurring. They quickly became collaborators and shared an apartment in New York City, dubbed the "lamasery." This became a salon for bohemian intellectuals and professionals attracted to Blavatsky's expertise in esoteric lore. A group of these seekers founded the Theosophical Society in 1875 with Olcott as the president and Blavatsky as the recording secretary. The society evolved the following three objectives:

> To provide a nucleus of the Universal Brotherhood of Humanity, without distinction of race, creed, sex, caste, or color.
>
> To encourage the study of Comparative Religion, Philosophy, and Science.
>
> To investigate unexplained laws of Nature and the powers latent in man.

The purpose of the Theosophical Society was to promote unity and equality among humanity and to present the "Ancient Wisdom" as revealed in Eastern religions and the Western occult traditions (as opposed to conventional Judaism and Christianity). Blavatsky became an American citizen in 1878. Olcott agreed to accompany Blavatsky to India in 1879, where in 1882 they established the international headquarters of the Theosophical Society in Adyar outside Madras.

Olcott and Blavatsky were a sensation in Sri Lanka and India. The Sinhalese and Indians were gratified to find two Westerners who expressed appreciation for Buddhism (in Sri Lanka) and Hinduism (in India) in opposition to the criticisms of Christian missionaries. Blavatsky and Olcott formally took the Buddhist five precepts for ethical living in 1880 in Sri Lanka. Olcott and other Theosophists worked to found schools to provide Sinhalese children with an education appreciative of Buddhism as an alternative to Christian mission schools. In India Olcott gave public lectures and established the Theosophical Society. Blavatsky became the focus of salons attracting Indian and British intellectuals. Masters appeared to Indians and British, and letters from the Masters mysteriously appeared ("precipitated") in various locations when Blavatsky was not present.

Blavatsky had in her quarters at Adyar, a special shrine in which she placed letters to the Masters to be picked up by occult means, and the Masters left their replies. Following allegations by employees that Blavatsky fabricated letters from the Masters and staged appearances of the Masters, a representative of the Society for Psychical Research concluded that Blavatsky was guilty of fraud. Blavatsky returned to Europe in 1885 in some disgrace, but there she wrote her magnum opus, *The Secret Doctrine*. She moved to London in 1887, attracted her most talented convert, Annie Besant, and taught disciples there until her death in 1891.

Annie Besant

Annie Besant (1847–1933), a British atheist freethinker, feminist, journalist, and social reformer, converted to Theosophy in 1889 after reading *The Secret Doctrine*. Besant was a noted speaker in an era in which women were discouraged from public roles. She had become a freethinker after separating from her husband, an Anglican clergyman, over her loss of faith in Christianity. Besant and her colleague Charles Bradlaugh, president of the National Secular Society, advocated for the right to publish information on contraception in 1877, and they took up numerous causes for social reform. Besant joined the Fabian Society of socialists, which advocated a gradual, nonrevolutionary transition to socialism, in 1885.

Like Blavatsky, Besant regarded herself as a student of the Masters. The development of psychic senses was important to satisfy Besant's rationalism; she believed that her spiritual experiences provided proof of a divine reality. Besant conducted her psychic research in partnership with Charles W. Leadbeater, a Theosophist who was formerly an Anglican priest, and in 1901 they published a small but influential book titled *Thought-Forms*, which contains paintings of the forms and colors that they said thoughts take in subtle spirit-matter. They asserted that the quality of one's thoughts have an effect on one's life experiences and can affect others. The belief in thought-forms remains influential today in the Theosophy, New Thought, New Age, and also neopagan movements.

Besant was elected president of the international Theosophical Society after Olcott's death in 1907. Besant spread the message worldwide through lectures and books. The society's membership grew to its peak of about 45,000 in the late 1920s. She toured the United States several times, and in 1893 Besant was one of the speakers at the Theosophical Congress at the World's Parliament of Religions, held in conjunction with the Columbian Exposition in Chicago.

Later in her Theosophical career, Besant promoted a young Indian, J. Krishnamurti (1895–1986), as the vehicle of the World-Teacher or Christ. Besant said that the Master who held the office of the World Teacher, or Christ, was the Lord Maitreya, who in Buddhism is the future Buddha. She believed that the Lord Maitreya would take Krishnamurti's body as a vehicle by which to deliver a new spiritual teaching to the world. Besant taught that the World-Teacher would found a new world religion that would raise the awareness of human beings to the level of *buddhi*, an awakened consciousness in which the divine oneness is perceived. Thus, a "New Civilization" would be built that actualized the "Universal Brotherhood" of the first object of the Theosophical Society. Annie Besant's concept of the New Civilization is an important forerunner of the contemporary New Age movement, which expresses the hope that human society will be perfected when a critical mass of people attain a high level of consciousness.

Besant taught that a "new race" consisting of people of diverse races who had developed the *buddhic* awareness would develop in southern California, New Zealand, and Australia. Besant identified the beautiful Ojai valley in California as the birthplace of the new race and the New Civilization. She purchased a home there for Krishnamurti, who continued to live and lecture in Ojai long after he had broken ties (in 1929) with the Theosophical Society and the messianic movement that Besant had built up around him called the Order of the Star (30,000 members). The population of Ojai is currently very New Age in orientation, although most are not directly affiliated with the Theosophical Society.

Besant did much important work in India. Whereas Olcott had focused much of his work on uplifting Buddhism, Besant regarded Hinduism as the most perfect expression of the Ancient Wisdom. She founded numerous Hindu schools to offer an alternative education to Christian mission schools. She also founded the Central Hindu College that became the Benares Hindu University. Besant, Margaret Cousins, and other women Theosophists founded the Women's Indian Association in 1917, which helped secure Indian women's right to vote, and also the All India Women's Conference in 1927 to promote Indian feminism. She worked for Indian Home Rule and was elected president of the Indian National Congress in 1917, but her Indian political career was eclipsed by Mohandas Gandhi, who is noted as the leader of the movement for Indian independence from Great Britain.

Katherine Tingley

Katherine Tingley (1847–1929) was a social reformer from Massachusetts who heard about Theosophy while living in New York City in the 1880s and 1890s. Under the inspirational leadership of William Q. Judge (1851–1896), president of the American Section of the international Theosophical Society, Theosophy became a household word in the United States in the closing decades of the nineteenth century. In 1895, after disputes with Olcott, Besant, and other leaders, Judge led the majority of the members of the American Section (about 6,000) in declaring independence from the Theosophical Society headquartered in Adyar, India. Tingley succeeded Judge as head of this growing American movement after his death in 1896.

Tingley directed the society's efforts toward social reforms of interest to women, especially education of urban poor children, rehabilitation of prostitutes, and feeding those in cities with little to eat. During the Spanish-American War Tingley and Theosophists provided medical and other aid to returning American soldiers and, upon President William McKinley's invitation, journeyed to Cuba to provide war relief to Cubans.

Tingley's most notable achievement was the establishment of a community in California. Beginning in 1900, she persuaded several hundred Theosophists to move to Point Loma, near San Diego, where their children and Cuban children were educated in the standard curriculum of the day, with an emphasis on the humanities and fine arts. Tingley called this educational effort Raja Yoga, borrowing an ancient Indian term to signify a holistic educational approach that developed a child mentally, emotionally, physically, and spiritually. She enlisted the aid of numerous women Theosophists, some with educational credentials, to provide the bulk of the teaching staff. The children lived in age- and gender-segregated groups supervised by surrogate parents. Although this separation of children from their natural parents (except for brief visits every two to four weeks) was criticized then and later, Tingley justified this measure as necessary for the child's proper development. Implicit in this arrangement was a critique of conventional mother/child relationships, which Tingley claimed could lead to the distortion of the child's ego and maim his or her spiritual and moral development.

Tingley believed that the mature souls reincarnating at that time in children were especially attuned to such education. Point Loma was founded to be a center in which such spiritually and morally advanced individuals could grow, then go out into the world to do good. But the opportunity to live in such a place carried costs to individual members of the community. Tingley demanded compliance from the adults and intervened in numerous marriages and other relationships when she thought it necessary to correct behaviors that did not conform to her standards. These were a combination of Victorian expectations and Theosophical doctrines.

Tingley was a public figure of some renown. She took positions against vivesection and capital punishment, opposed the United States' entry into World War I, and addressed audiences worldwide on Theosophical ideals during a long career. After her death in 1929, Theosophists carried on the Point Loma community through the middle decades of the twentieth century. The current president of the Theosophical Society (based in Pasadena) is the inheritor of this tradition. Grace F. Knoche was herself a Raja Yoga student trained in Point Loma's schools.

New Thought

New Thought is a decidedly American religious movement that emerged in the late nineteenth century, first taking hold in the developing urban centers of the mid- and far western United States. The roots of New Thought can be traced to the Church of Christ, Scientist, founded in 1875, and the broader mental healing (or "Mind Cure") movement. Like its precursors, New Thought is an expression of popular religious idealism, affirming that the fundamental basis of reality is mental and that mental states determine material conditions. New Thought resembles Christian Science in this regard, although it differs from the earlier movement in its positive evaluation of the physical world. Not only is the material world good and real; it is fundamentally spiritual.

Dubbed the "religion of healthy mindedness" by philosopher William James, the early success of the New Thought movement can be traced to several factors, including its empowerment of women in professional healing and ministerial roles. New Thought has been truly gender-blind, and in its formative period, this proved to be a tremendous boon to the movement's evangelistic efforts.

It is notable that the origins of New Thought can be traced most directly to the charismatic teacher Emma Curtis Hopkins (1849–1925), an independent Christian Scientist and former student of the founder of the Church of Christ, Scientist, Mary Baker Eddy (1821–1910). Although Hopkins is recognized as the founder of New Thought, preinstitutional influences also include the mental healing practice of Phineas Parkhurst Quimby (1802–1866), who taught Eddy.

EMMA CURTIS HOPKINS

Emma Curtis Hopkins (1849–1925) was born in Connecticut, the oldest of nine children in a prosperous family. She attended Woodstock Academy and later taught at the school. In 1874, she married George Irving Hopkins, a professor at Andover College in Connecticut, and had one son. Her husband divorced her in 1900 for abandonment. Hopkins's correspondence indicates that her husband physically abused her.

In December 1883 Hopkins, in what was a turning point in her life, attended a class in Christian Science offered by Eddy. By February of the following year she was listed as a "practitioner" in the *Christian Science Journal*. In September 1884 Hopkins became the editor of the *Journal*, a position she held until being fired in October 1885. Hopkins was not the only Eddy student to leave Christian Science in its early years. Others included Ursula Gestefeld, Mary Plunkett, and Augusta Stetson. Possible factors for the egress of talented women were Eddy's dogmatism, her radical idealism, and her authoritarianism. Reasons for Hopkins's dismissal are unclear, although it appears likely that her independence was not compatible with Eddy's desire to preserve doctrinal purity. There was also a disagreement over Hopkins's financial compensation.

In 1886 Hopkins and another Christian Science dissident, Mary Plunkett, began an independent Christian Science ministry and school in Chicago. During her first years there, Hopkins cooperated closely with other Christian Science dissidents, including George B. Charles (student of Eddy adversary A. J. Arens) and Ursula Gestefeld (1845–1921). In the late 1880s Gestefeld broke with Eddy due to differences over organizational structure and possibly the independence of practitioners. Her pamphlet "Jesuitism in Christian Science" offered a defiant stance against Eddy's attacks on her. After working briefly with Hopkins, Gestefeld developed her own system, called "Science of Being," and founded the Church of New Thought in Chicago. Gestefeld published a periodical, the *Exodus*; traveled widely spreading the gospel of healthy mindedness; and acquired a large national following.

As important as these other figures were to the early New Thought movement, Hopkins soon eclipsed them all. She opened the Emma Hopkins College of Christian Science in 1886. Over thirty students were in the first class, among them Kate Bingham, who would be instrumental in the healing of Nona Brooks, cofounder of Divine Science.

Hopkins found herself inundated with students, many of whom traveled great distances to study with her. The Hopkins Metaphysical Association was formed, and Hopkins traveled to San Francisco, Milwaukee, and New York to teach classes. By the end of 1887, the Association spanned the continent, claiming seventeen member groups in locations such as San Francisco, Denver, Chicago, New York, and Boston.

Hopkins's role in the developing association was that of spiritual leader. Her primary activities were preaching and teaching, with institutional concerns left to others. The delegation of organizational duties to competent lieutenants was a characteristic not only of Hopkins but also her students, the future leaders of the various New Thought groups. This approach is quite evident in the movements led by Charles and Myrtle Fillmore (Unity), the Brooks sisters (Divine Science), and Ernest Holmes (Religious Science). All the successful New Thought groups employed this Hopkinsian strategy. It can be reduced to this principle: Spirit is in charge. The spiritual teacher leads, has final authority, and delegates authority to competent lieutenants.

Hopkins and her association were involved in the labor and women's movements during her Chicago years. In 1888 the association supported the Ladies' Federal Labor Union in its efforts to improve the condition of Chicago's working women. In order to disseminate information at the World's Columbian Exposition of 1893, the association worked with the Queen Isabella Association, a women's social action organization. The association was also involved with the Women's Alliance and the Labor League.

In 1888 the college was reorganized to become the Christian Science Theological Seminary to prepare students for ministry. In 1889 Hopkins ordained the first graduates of the seminary: twenty women and two men. Hopkins's ordination of women marked the first time in American history (and possibly Western Christian history) that a woman ordained women. By 1893 Hopkins had ordained 111 persons, and the seminary had an enrollment of 350 students.

With the formation of the seminary and ordination of ministers, Hopkins laid the foundation for what became the New Thought movement. Until this time Christian Science and the Mind Cure groups had been lay movements. Eddy did not ordain ministers. With Hopkins's move, emergent New Thought ceased to be a lay movement of quasi-professional teachers and practitioners. Now it was a religious organization; its leaders were ordained ministers who began to establish churches, hold Sunday services, and preach. Thus the New Thought movement provided its leaders with cultural legitimacy.

Prior to Hopkins, popular religious idealism was essentially a healing movement known as Mind Cure. In Hopkins's work, healing became part of a more extensive enterprise. Her primary mission was the transformation of human consciousness and society.

Hopkins became known as the "teacher of teachers," and virtually all early New Thought leaders were Hopkins's students. These include Charles and Myrtle Fillmore (cofounders of Unity); Kate Bingham, the teacher of Nona Brooks (a founder of Divine Science); Melinda Cramer (a founder of Divine Science); Fannie Brooks James (a founder of Divine Science); Annie Rix Militz (founder of Homes of Truth); Frances Lord (who established New Thought in England); H. Emilie Cady (author of *Lessons in Truth*); Ella Wheeler Wilcox (New Thought poet with wide cultural acceptance); and Elizabeth Towne (publisher of the influential periodical *Nautilus* [1898–1954]). Near the end of her life, Hopkins tutored Ernest S. Holmes, founder of the Church of Religious Science.

When Hopkins closed the seminary in 1895, she moved to New York City where she lectured, met privately with students and clients, and wrote. Her two most notable books are *High Mysticism* (1920) and *Scientific Mental Practice* (n.d.).

Hopkins's students, the vast majority being women, founded and/or taught in New Thought denominations. Among these, three are of special note: Nona Brooks, Myrtle Page Fillmore, and Annie Rix Militz. Today, the majority of New Thought ministers are women, accounting for slightly over 60 percent of the nearly 1,600 ministers in the three largest New Thought groups—Unity, United Church of Religious Science, and Religious Science International.

NONA BROOKS AND DIVINE SCIENCE

Divine Science was one of the first distinct New Thought sects and is the oldest one still in existence. From among a number of persons who could be cited as founders of the movement, two are of special significance: Nona Brooks (1861–1945) and Melinda Cramer (1844–1906). Three others played decisive roles in Divine Science's formative period: Alethea Brooks Small (1848–1906), Fannie Brooks James (1854–1914), and Kate Bingham. Among these, Nona Brooks was the dominant force in the establishment and growth of Divine Science.

Nona Lovell Brooks was born in Louisville, Kentucky, the youngest daughter in a large and prosperous family. A reversal of her father's business and his death caused a significant decline in the family's standard of living. Her mother and other family members relocated to Pueblo, Colorado, and upon her graduation from the Charleston Female College, Nona joined them. The financial challenges of the family, her failure to secure a satisfactory proposal of marriage, and especially her own health condition led Nona and her sister, Alethea Brooks Small, to attend a class on mental healing in 1887. The class was led by Kate Bingham, a student of Hopkins. In a short time, Nona Brooks experienced a healing. The sisters' enthusiasm for the new teachings resulted in their dismissal as Sunday School teachers at the local Presbyterian church. Thereafter, the sisters became active in the mental healing movement. Before devoting her full attention to religious work, Brooks returned to college, attending Wellesley for one year in 1890.

Nona Brooks then relocated to Denver, where she found her sister, Fannie James, leading a group of women in the study of mental healing. Because Fannie's husband would not allow her to leave the house to visit persons requesting healings, their sister Alethea was asked in 1893 to come to Denver to facilitate this part of the ministry. The three sisters laid the groundwork for the institutional establishment of Divine Science. The organizational impetus came from yet another woman, Melinda E. Cramer, also a Hopkins student, who had begun a mental healing group in San Francisco in 1888. Fannie James was inspired to link her work in Denver with Cramer's group in San Francisco. The Denver ministry adopted the name of Cramer's group, Divine Science.

In 1898 the Brooks ministry was incorporated as the Divine Science College, and Nona was selected to be the minister. She was ordained by Cramer and conducted the first Sunday morning service in Divine Science history on January 1, 1899. Brooks served as the minister of the Denver church and leader of the Divine Science movement for thirty years. Although the Denver church grew and prospered during her tenure, and numerous students studied at the Divine Science College, Brooks was not strongly committed to institutional development, and the movement remained small.

After resigning her leadership of the Denver church in 1929, Brooks spent time in Australia, accepted speaking invitations from numerous churches and the International New Thought Alliance, and finally settled in Chicago where she ministered to a small Divine Science church. In 1938 she returned to Denver to serve as president of the Divine Science College. She continued writing and teaching classes at the college until a few days before her death in 1945.

Brooks's impact on the early New Thought movement was considerable. In addition to cofounding Divine Science, she contributed to the development of the International New Thought Alliance, helped popularize New Thought in the American West, and directly influenced Ernest Holmes, Emmet Fox, and other leaders of the movement. She wrote five books, of which the most popular are *The Prayer That Never Fails* (1935) and *Short Lessons in Divine Science* (1928).

Myrtle Fillmore and Unity

Perhaps the best known of Hopkins's students is Myrtle Page Fillmore (1845–1931), cofounder with her husband Charles (1854–1948) of Unity, the largest New Thought denomination. Myrtle Page was born in Pagetown, Ohio, into a Methodist family. As a youth, she was described as frail. She studied at Oberlin College and was licensed as a teacher in 1868. Upon graduation, she taught school in Clinton, Missouri. In 1874 she moved to Denison, Texas, hoping its warmer climate would ameliorate her various health challenges, which by this time included tuberculosis and malaria. In Denison she operated a small private school and also met Charles Fillmore, whom she married in 1891. They would have three sons. The couple settled in Pueblo, Colorado, where Charles became a real estate partner with Charles Small (husband of Alethea Brooks Small). During their Pueblo years, the couple was exposed to Spiritualism and possibly Theosophy. Myrtle was active in the Episcopal Church. Previously, the couple had attended Methodist churches. The Fillmore family relocated to Omaha, Nebraska, and then Kansas City, Missouri. By 1886 the Kansas City real estate boom ended, and the Fillmores faced financial difficulties. At the same time, Myrtle's tubercular condition reappeared.

In the spring of 1886, Charles and Myrtle attended a New Thought lecture by E. B. Weeks. Myrtle was inspired by a phrase Weeks used in the lecture: "I am a child of God and therefore I do not inherit sickness." As Myrtle's commitment to the new teachings grew and her health improved, Charles's interest increased. They traveled to Chicago to study with Emma Curtis Hopkins in 1886.

Myrtle pronounced herself healed in 1888. In 1889 the Fillmores gave up their secular pursuits and devoted themselves solely to the study and propagation of "Truth" teachings. The Unity movement was born that year with the inauguration of its first periodical, *Modern Thought*. The first issues included articles on and advertisements for Christian Science, Theosophy, Spiritualism, Rosicrucianism, the occult, "magnetic healing," Buddhism, and Vedanta, but the Fillmores quickly began to distance Unity from Spiritualism and other religious practices that did not accord with their conception of Christian Science.

In 1890 Unity's first prayer ministry was formed, largely as an outgrowth of Myrtle's healing work. Today it is known as Silent Unity and is the largest prayer ministry in the New Thought movement. Myrtle remained its director until 1916.

The Fillmores attended classes taught by Hopkins in

1890 in Kansas City and later attended her seminary in Chicago. In 1891 they were ordained by Hopkins, and the first issue of *Unity* magazine was published. In 1893 Myrtle founded the famous children's magazine *Wee Wisdom*.

In 1894, H. Emilie Cady, another student of Hopkins, began a series of articles for *Unity*. These articles were soon republished as the book *Lessons in Truth* (1920). Often cited as Unity's primary textbook ("next to the Bible"), *Lessons* went on to become the most widely printed book in the history of New Thought.

A major figure in Unity's early expansion was another student of Hopkins, Annie Rix Militz. Ordained at the same time as the Fillmores, Militz worked closely with them for nearly two decades.

A significant turning point occurred in 1903 when the movement became incorporated as the Unity Society of Practical Christianity. The new corporation unified the educational/congregational ministry in Kansas City and national outreach activities of Silent Unity with the critical link supplied by various periodicals. Myrtle's role in Unity began to diminish after 1903. Although she was among the first group of persons ordained into the Unity ministry in 1906 and she remained active in her position as the director of Silent Unity, by the end of the first decade of the twentieth century, Myrtle's presence as a Unity leader was eclipsed by Charles and her sons.

In 1907 Myrtle stepped down as editor of *Wee Wisdom*, and in 1916 she turned over the leadership of Silent Unity to Clara May Rowland. Myrtle died in the same year that she and Charles celebrated their fiftieth wedding anniversary. Two anthologies of her writings are published by Unity: *Myrtle Fillmore's Healing Letters* (1936) and *How to Let God Help You* (1956).

Annie Rix Militz and the Homes of Truth

Relatively little is known about the early life of Annie Rix Militz (1856–1924). Her major achievements were the founding of one of the first Hopkins-inspired groups, the Homes of Truth, publication of the influential New Thought periodical *Master Mind*, development of New Thought's "metaphysical" (allegorical) method of biblical exegesis, participation as an author and teacher in Unity during its formative period, and leadership in the International New Thought Alliance.

Like so many others, Annie Rix was introduced to New Thought through the teachings of Hopkins, who conducted classes in San Francisco in 1887. Rix, a schoolteacher in San Francisco at the time, attended with her sister, Harriet Hale Rix. In the course of the classes, Annie experienced two miraculous healings; one was of her lifelong affliction with debilitating headaches and the other was of total deafness in one ear. She ex-

claimed to her sister after the third class, "I have found my life work."

Later the same year, the sisters began their vocation as "metaphysicians," establishing the first Home of Truth (then called a "Christian Science Home") in San Francisco. In the 1890s Harriet started a second Home of Truth in Alameda, and by the first decade of the twentieth century, Homes of Truth had been set up throughout America.

After getting the Homes of Truth organization off the ground, in 1889 Annie Rix accepted an invitation to join the faculty of Hopkins's newly opened Christian Science Theological Seminary in Chicago, leaving Harriet and others in charge of the ministry in San Francisco. Annie Rix's career blossomed in Chicago. Her official position at the seminary was professor of Scripture Revelation, and in this post she refined the "metaphysical" method of biblical exegesis, an approach first used by Emmanuel Swedenborg in the eighteenth century and popularized in America by Eddy and later Hopkins. Annie Rix took the method further and, through her involvement with the Unity movement, helped establish it as one of New Thought's primary theological features. The Fillmores, Rix, and a number of other Hopkins students were ordained on June 1, 1891. Another ordinand was Paul Militz, himself a member of the seminary faculty. Annie Rix and Paul Militz married shortly after the ordination. By 1895 they had separated. All that appears to have remained of the relationship was the Militz name, which Annie retained.

Militz's relationship with Unity lasted much longer. In 1893 the first of her numerous articles appeared in *Unity* magazine. Soon Militz was established as the Bible scholar of the Unity movement. Militz's work served as the transition from Hopkins's rather loose and unfocused style of "metaphysical" interpretation to Unity's more systematic method.

Militz's last Bible lesson appeared in *Unity* in 1898, but she continued to write for the magazine, authoring two widely popular article series, "Primary Lessons in Christian Living and Healing" and "Spiritual Housekeeping." Militz was affiliated with Unity for eighteen years. Curiously, she has been entirely ignored in Unity authorized histories, although the movement continued to publish her most popular book, *Both Riches and Honor*, until the 1980s.

After her relationship with Unity ended, Militz devoted her energies to her own magazine, *Master Mind* (1911–1931). One notable feature of the magazine was the inclusion of articles offering instructions on how to establish "Truth Centers" (New Thought churches). Militz had been actively involved in setting up such centers since 1894 when she established a Home of Truth in Los Angeles. In 1899 she started another Home of Truth in

Chicago. Chicago was her base of operations until 1903, when she again returned to Los Angeles and made that city the headquarters for the rapidly expanding Homes of Truth movement. Militz traveled widely, teaching classes, inspiring persons (chiefly women) to become religious leaders, and setting up churches. By the end of the first decade of the twentieth century, the Homes of Truth was a national movement, with affiliated groups on both coasts and major inland cities such as Denver, St. Louis, and Minneapolis.

Militz was a firm believer in a widely held tenet of the early New Thought movement—physical immortality. Called "regeneration," this belief held that through spiritual discipline (including elimination of sexual desire) and harmonization of consciousness with Truth (Divine Mind), one could so perfect the body that death would not occur. Convinced that Militz had achieved this state, after her death on June 22, 1924, her followers refused to allow local morticians to prepare her body for burial. Expecting her to return to life, they stood by her corpse for three days, finally ending their vigil only when they felt assured she had truly left the world for a better place *and* after public health officials intervened. Today only one Home of Truth in Alameda, California, remains of Militiz's movement.

New Age Movement

The New Age movement became noticeable in the 1960s and grew increasingly prominent during the last decades of the twentieth century. The New Age movement and its various groups are centered chiefly in North America and western Europe, although it is influential throughout the world. The New Age movement readily appropriates beliefs from different religious traditions. The movement represents a melding of two types of spirituality: basic religion, which emphasizes that spiritual forces and beings affect material existence, and millennialism, which involves belief in an imminent transition to a collective salvation. Millennial New Age groups anticipate a radical transformation of humanity that will eliminate suffering.

The movement can be seen as a resurgence in the West of what historian of world religions Lewis Hopfe has termed "basic religion," the original pattern of human spirituality that is found in numerous indigenous religions. Possessing an animistic cosmology, basic religion includes belief in both impersonal forces and personal gods and spirits within the natural world. To attain well-being, one must be in harmony with these forces and spirits. Methods to achieve well-being include sacrifice, magic, rites of passage, ancestor veneration, and divination. The shaman is an individual who knows how to contact the spiritual world and reports what needs to

be done to achieve harmony with the invisible forces and spirits. The New Age movement borrows elements of basic religion from various traditions, and conversely, the New Age movement blends easily with animistic faiths such Japanese Shinto, Native American religions, African and African-based religions, and European pagan survivals.

The New Age movement draws on Theosophy, New Thought, Asian religions, indigenous religions, Western occultism, and mystical religious traditions. It includes belief in impersonal forces and personal spirits and gods, spirits of those who are deceased (ancestors), and the practice of magic, along with meditation and yogas. The ubiquitous sacred objects in the New Age movement are crystals and stones believed to possess special powers. There are numerous women shamans, healers, speakers, and writers in the New Age movement. Much of New Age activity is noninstitutionalized, with people reading books, listening to audiotapes, and watching videotapes. They attend New Age lectures and workshops and consult psychics who function as shamans and diviners to foretell the future and contact spirit guides. They go to healers who use crystals, aura cleansing techniques, and massage therapy. They participate in local circles devoted to alternative methods of healing such as Therapeutic Touch, promoted by Theosophists Dora Kunz and Delores Krieger. Women in the movement also found religious institutions and serve as ministers in churches.

A primary stimulus of the New Age movement was the richly diverse religious ecology that developed in America's postwar counterculture. Explicit forebears include Theosophy, Liberal Catholicism (associated with the Theosophical Society), Spiritualism, New Thought, the environmental movement, Asian religions, the "Beats" of the 1950s, and the hippie movement of the 1960s. In the late twentieth century, the New Age movement provided a context in which women could explore goddesses of the world religions and seek out spiritual foremothers as models of empowerment. Numerous New Age ideas and practices influence the neopagan and Wiccan movements.

The term *New Age* refers to the millennial aspiration for a new global civilization of peace and justice that is the First Object of the Theosophical Society, to be a nucleus of a "Universal Brotherhood." Annie Besant, the second president of the Theosophical Society, envisioned a "New Civilization." The terms *New Age* and *Age of Aquarius* were probably first used by Alice Bailey (1880–1949), who broke away from the Theosophical Society and said that her writings were dictated to her by Masters. Bailey's role during the formative period of the New Age movement is analogous to Hopkins's role in the formative period of New Thought. While both movements can claim other precursors, in the work of these women the respective movements were given both their first theological foundations and institutional models.

ALICE BAILEY

Alice Bailey (1880–1949) was born Alice La Trobe Bateman in Manchester, England. Raised in the Church of England, she evinced a keen interest in religion from an early age, becoming a Sunday School teacher in her teens. When she was fifteen, she was visited by a tall man, dressed in European clothes and wearing a turban, who entered the room and sat down next to her. The stranger reported that she had a great work to do, but in order to be successful she would have to become more responsible. She thought the stranger was Jesus. Much later, in 1915, she learned the visitor was Koot Hoomi—one of the Masters with whom Blavatsky had communicated.

When Alice was twenty-two, she was given an auxiliary position with the British Army through the Young Women's Christian Association (YWCA). Her work took her to India, but that journey apparently did not inspire any particular interest in South Asian religions. In 1907, upon her return to England, she married Walter Evans. The couple moved to America, where Walter entered Cincinnati's Lane Theological Seminary to prepare for the Episcopal priesthood. After the completion of his studies, the couple relocated to California. In 1915, they separated, then divorced in 1919.

In California, Bailey was introduced to the Theosophical Society, where she saw a painting of Koot Hoomi, the mysterious visitor she had first met twenty years earlier. She became active in the society and soon became the manager of the vegetarian cafeteria of the Theosophical school at Krotona in Hollywood.

While working at the American Headquarters of the Theosophical Society, Alice met her future husband, Foster Bailey, who soon became the society's national secretary. Prior to their marriage in 1921, several important developments occurred in Alice's life. She became editor of a Theosophical periodical, the *Messenger*, and a teacher in the movement. More important, in 1919 she had her first contact with the Master with whom she would work closely for the remainder of her career, Djwhal Khul (also Djual Khool), "the Tibetan," who had also communicated with Blavatsky. Djwhal Khul asked Alice to be his secretary for books he desired to dictate. After consulting with Koot Hoomi, she agreed to do so. Bailey's professional relationship with the Tibetan spanned thirty years. The first writing was partially serialized in the *Theosophist* magazine, beginning in 1920, then published as a book titled *Initiation, Human and Solar* (1922).

The major turning point in Bailey's development grew out of her involvement with the Esoteric Section (ES) of the Theosophical Society. Shortly after joining this inner group, Alice became critical of its dogmatic structures: the need to sever ties with other organizations, pledge loyalty to the leader (Annie Besant), and be appointed by Besant to became a disciple of a Master. During the annual convention of 1920 in Chicago, there was a power struggle between forces loyal to Besant and the Esoteric Section and others who believed that the ES had become too powerful. Below the surface was a hidden controversy regarding Alice's work with the Tibetan. Alice and Foster Bailey were terminated from their positions.

The couple moved to New York, where they married and in 1923 founded the Arcane School. Prior to establishing the school, the Baileys established Lucis Trust, which would become the school's publishing arm, and began a periodical, the *Beacon*. The challenges created for mainstream Theosophy by Krishnamurti's distancing himself from the role of the World-Teacher enhanced the profile of Bailey and the new school. By the time of Besant's death in 1933, Bailey's work was clearly a successful competitor with the parent Theosophical Society in the larger metaphysical movement.

Bailey was good at organizing and generating income for her religious groups. In addition to the Arcane School and the Lucis Trust, she founded the New Group of World Servers in 1932 and the Triangles in 1937. These groups functioned to empower persons through meditation and visualization as spiritual agents (light workers) and to form networks of such persons to accelerate the spiritual evolution of humanity and hasten the dawning of the New Age. In the mission of these two groups, the prototype for numerous New Age groups of today can be found.

In Besant's World-Teacher project, Theosophists had sought to produce a messiah who would inaugurate a new age; the Master known as the Lord Maitreya was to utilize the body of Krishnamurti as a vehicle to present a new religious teaching. Although Krishnamurti became an important spiritual teacher, in 1929 he distanced himself from the Theosophical Society and the role of World-Teacher, although he never denied being the World-Teacher. What Bailey did, on the other hand, was specify a millennial moment (clearly related to the advent of the nuclear age), rather than an identified messiah, and advanced a religious system that could support a millennial movement over time without an explicit institutional hierarchy aside from a supernatural one. The decisive text was *The Reappearance of the Christ* (1948), the unifying liturgy was the "Great Invocation" (1937), and the primary rituals were the "Three Festivals." The Three Festivals were celebrated during full moons in the spring: Easter (full moon in April), Wesak (full moon in May), and the Festival of Goodwill (full moon in June). These three celebrations represent the syncretistic dimension of the New Age movement. The full moon has affinities with the animism of basic religion, while Easter and Wesak (commemorating the Buddha's birth and enlightenment) are meaningful in Christianity and Buddhism, respectively. In Bailey's corpus there is a greater emphasis on the Christ than in parent Theosophy. For her the Christ is closely identified with Jesus of Nazareth even more so than the Lord Maitreya, the future Buddha (as Annie Besant asserted). Bailey's work also has a decidedly Christian, even evangelical, flavor. *Reappearance of the Christ* has frequent scriptural references and seems to function as a text designed to convert Christians to Bailey's version of Theosophy.

Bailey produced twenty-four books, of which eighteen were direct transmissions from the Tibetan Master. As many as 1 million persons may have had some degree of direct exposure to Bailey's writings. Many millions of others have heard or read the "Great Invocation," which calls on the Christ to return to Earth. After Alice Bailey's death, Foster Bailey directed the Arcane School until his death in 1977, at which time Foster's second wife, Mary Bailey, became president.

The principal contributions of Alice Bailey and the Arcane School to the New Age movement can be summarized as follows:

1. Articulation of the need to prepare spiritually for the return of the Christ (either as an individual or as a generalized elevation of consciousness) through the establishment of spiritual conduits by which the Christ and/or the spiritual powers of the Masters can be brought to Earth.

2. Development of collective rituals for the salvation of the planet. This gave the Bailey project an evangelical and salvific flavor and a global/universalist perspective characteristic of New Age groups today. To further this dimension of the mission, Bailey groups purchased or were given airtime on radio and television to broadcast the "Great Invocation."

3. Specification of rituals of meditation, prayer, visualization, and recitation of the "Great Invocation" to be conducted in groups that function as "points of light" and "light groups" to attract and focus spiritual energies to benefit the planet. Such rituals and spiritual networking projects are primary components in many New Age groups today.

As the formative visionary behind the New Age movement, Bailey is notable for the following contributions:

1. Simplification of Theosophy for widespread consumption;

2. A Buddhist-Christian syncretism that popularizes the concept of Masters;

3. Strong stress on the millennial dimension of Theosophy without specificity to date or discernible messiah;

4. Collective rituals that merge an animistic worldview with a millennial expectation;

5. Establishment of the first significant New Age network (consisting of meditation groups and the New Group of World Servers); and

6. Establishment of a loosely structured organization (like Hopkins's) that generated a number of subgroups and served as the model for New Age groups.

The emergence of Alice Bailey as a religious leader and the establishment of the Arcane School have similarities with the rise of Emma Curtis Hopkins and the development of her seminary and students' association. As Hopkins's work emerged from dissatisfaction with Eddy's form of Christian Science, so Bailey's began due to dissatisfaction with the parent Theosophical Society's control by Annie Besant. Although Bailey's organization has survived, while Hopkins's organization disintegrated less than fifteen years after its founding, both supplied theological foundations and institutional models for such movements as the New Age and New Thought.

Four major New Age leaders continued to develop the spiritual terrain first charted by Alice Bailey: Elizabeth Clare Prophet, Helen Schucman, Jean Houston, and J. Z. Knight.

Elizabeth Clare Prophet and the Church Universal and Triumphant

The Church Universal and Triumphant, whose messenger is Elizabeth Clare Prophet (1940–   ), is a New Age church within the wider Theosophical movement. In this church the Masters are considered to be "ascended" and spiritually influencing humanity from spiritual planes.

Elizabeth Clare Wulf married Mark L. Prophet (1918–1973) in 1961. Mark Prophet led the Summit Lighthouse, a movement based on Theosophical principles and descended from the I AM Movement of Guy and Edna Ballard. The I AM claimed that Ascended Master St. Germain appeared to Guy Ballard on the slopes of Mt. Shasta in California in 1929 and imparted ancient wisdom for the modern day to him. These teachings combined Theosophical doctrine with New Thought emphasis on mental healing. Mark Prophet's "dictations," or doctrinal speeches, purportedly came from the same Master who guided Blavatsky, El Morya. Elizabeth Clare Prophet became coleader of the Summit Lighthouse.

In 1962 the Prophets began the Keepers of the Flame, an inner circle of followers said to have been together millions of years ago in previous incarnations as workers for the betterment of humanity. Other organizational changes included a move in 1966 from their Washington, D.C., headquarters to Colorado Springs, the establishment of a Montessori preschool for children of Keepers of the Flame in 1970, and the beginning in 1971 of a series of workshops called Summit University.

Mark Prophet died in 1973, and Elizabeth Clare Prophet assumed sole leadership of Summit Lighthouse, which was renamed the Church Universal and Triumphant in 1974. Mark was elevated to the status of an Ascended Master and given the name Lanello. Elizabeth became the messenger of countless dictations from him and other Ascended Masters that she delivered to followers in meetings and later via satellite to centers nationwide and around the world.

By 1980 the movement had 25,000 members. Headquarters were moved to Santa Barbara, California, then Pasadena, and finally Malibu, before relocation to Royal Teton Ranch, adjacent to Yellowstone Park, near Corwin Springs, Montana.

During the 1980s the group experienced an episode dubbed the "shelter cycle." Mark and Elizabeth Clare Prophet taught that evil entities worked against the Ascended Masters by corrupting people on Earth, and the fruit of their labor could be found, among other places, in communist governments. In her dictations, Prophet warned of impending nuclear war between the United States and the Soviet Union. Many followers decided to build bomb shelters. Two thousand members sold their homes and moved to live close to shelters built on and near the Royal Teton Ranch. Two high-ranking officials were arrested for illegally purchasing arms to protect the faithful during the postwar chaos. One of these was Prophet's husband, Ed Francis (they divorced in 1996). In the aftermath of the shelter cycle, many members left the church. A reorganization followed. Prophet retired from active administrative oversight but retained her role of conveying messages from the Ascended Masters.

In November 1998 it was announced that Prophet has Alzheimer's disease, but she remains the church's messenger. The organizational changes have led to the church leadership becoming more accountable to members and the public. The stated purpose shifted emphasis from millennial concerns to individual spiritual liberation.

In contrast to the parent Theosophical Society, the church's worldview possesses several female Masters. One of the seven Chohans, or Ascended Masters most responsible for working divine power in the universe, is Lady Master Nada, Lord of the Sixth Ray. In a previous incarnation she was a priestess and lawyer in ancient Atlantis. Her special ministry is to serve and enable others to serve. She is also the Master who supervises the gift of tongues and their interpretation, meaning that she directs the divine vibrations of the seven rays of divine light that infuse the universe and thus also supervises all human and angelic speech and the very process of dictation itself. Among the other Masters are two feminine entities, Mother Mary and Kuan Yin, both of whom represent compassion and mercy. Among the lesser entities are the seven elohim, the builders of material form who carry the highest concentration of divine light that humans can perceive in our present state of evolution. They are androgynous beings, composed of masculine and feminine halves.

The earthly church organization also reflects the presence of the feminine. Elizabeth Clare Prophet is the messenger and Vicar of Christ for the church, and in 2001 the three-person presidency was composed of two women and one man. The seven-member Board of Directors had three women, and the twenty-two-member Council of Elders had twelve women. Many of these women were ordained ministers in the church, and women ministers also served as local leaders among the 237 congregations worldwide. As Prophet has withdrawn from active leadership, the ordained ministers increasingly have taken over various duties, and ordained women are on the Minsterial Council that oversees the church's ministries. Unordained women serve as staff members at the national level and in many capacities in local congregations.

HELEN SCHUCMAN AND *A COURSE IN MIRACLES*

If the Church Universal and Triumphant is an example of a highly institutionalized group, the *Course in Miracles* exemplifies an equally significant feature of the New Age movement: the loosely organized study group network. The network that has developed around *A Course in Miracles* is loosely structured, yet the text is one of the most popular spiritual study guides in the New Age movement.

The *Course* is a channeled document whose teachings resemble Christian Science. Great stress is put on the illusory nature of the material world and negative experiences such as pain, sickness, and death. Such experiences are the result of humanity's separation from God, maintained through fear and guilt that are generated by the human ego. They can be eliminated by overcoming the ego and rediscovering one's true spiritual nature as a child of God. The practical dimension of this realignment process is forgiveness and love. Although traditional Christian terminology is used throughout, the text is understood to be a correction of errors that have entered Christian theology.

The decisive figure among the many persons who

played roles in the origination and popularization of the *Course* was Helen Schucman (1909–1981), the reluctant channeler of the text. Born Helen Cohn, she was exposed to a variety of religious traditions in her youth, although at an early age she became skeptical of all religions. Despite her skepticism, she had several mystical experiences during her life, the most notable of which was the transmission of the *Course* from an unidentified disembodied being, whom she soon recognized to be Jesus.

She married Louis Schucman in 1933 and received her Ph.D. in psychology from New York University in 1957. Schucman's professional career began in 1958 when she accepted a position as a research assistant to William M. Thetford, a professor of psychology at Columbia University. In 1965, while working with Thetford and serving as an assistant professor of medical psychology, Schucman began having vivid mystical visions and dreams.

Fearing that she was becoming delusional, she confided in Thetford, who suggested that she keep written records of her experiences. Schucman followed this advice and on October 21, 1965, a powerful presence forced itself into her consciousness. More an audible energy than a being, the presence spoke to Schucman, saying: "This is a course in miracles. Please take notes." Thetford advised her to follow this direction. Schucman did so, and the message she received that night became the first page of the primary text of *A Course in Miracles*. The communications lasted from 1965 to 1972, resulting in three documents totaling 500,000 words: a 622-page text, a 478-page workbook, and an 88-page manual for teachers. The process of transmission occurred in two steps: The voice spoke to Schucman, who recorded the communication in shorthand; Schucman then dictated to Thetford, who typed the messages.

The manuscript lay dormant from 1973 until 1975. During this time, Schucman and Thetford apparently shared the material with only one other person, Kenneth Wapnick, who would later play an instrumental role in popularizing the *Course*. In 1975 a chance encounter with one of the leaders of the New York metaphysical community, Judith Skutch, set in motion the process that led to the publication of the *Course*. Skutch clairvoyantly sensed that Schucman had been having paranormal experiences, and she was given a copy of the manuscript. Skutch made it her personal mission to have it published. Skutch and her husband Robert established the Foundation for Inner Peace and published the first edition in a run of 5,000 copies in June 1976.

Since that time, over 1.5 million copies of the *Course* have been distributed. Although the primary vehicles for dissemination of the *Course*'s teachings have been over 2,200 small independent study groups, several organizations dedicated to promoting the *Course* have been founded. Among the largest of these is Wapnick's Foundation for *A Course in Miracles* (established 1984), which focuses on training teachers and today holds the copyright to the text. In 2001 the foundation moved from upstate New York, where it operated a residential education program, to Temecula, California, and shifted its emphasis to electronic education. Two other notable organizations are the networking groups, the Miracle Distribution Center, formed in 1978 by Beverly Hutchinson, and the Community Miracles Center, established in 1987. Interest in the *Course* has been furthered by celebrity authors such as Gerald G. Jampolsky, whose bestselling self-help book *Love Is Letting Go of Fear* (1979) was inspired by the *Course*, and New Age magus Marianne Williamson, whose *Return to Love* (1992) was subtitled *Reflections on the Principles of* A Course in Miracles.

Unlike many other New Age channelers, Schucman sought to remain anonymous. She played no role in the promotion of the text after its publication and admitted that she was not able to apply the teachings she received in her own life. In fact, she often expressed resentment about having to serve as the amanuensis of the disembodied presence whose message was communicated through her.

JEAN HOUSTON AND THE FOUNDATION FOR MIND RESEARCH

Jean Houston (1941–   ) is among the most popular of contemporary New Age teachers. Closely associated with the human potential movement, Houston has devoted her life to hastening the advent of planetary transformation through the expansion of human creativity and self-realization.

Born into a show-business family, her father (Jack) was a writer for such comedians as Bob Hope and Henny Youngman. Her mother (Mary) was a classical actor. Mary Houston was also a Christian Scientist. At the age of six, Jean had her first mystical experience. She later characterized the experience as a deeply felt realization that all things are part of a unitive and interrelated whole and that the entire cosmos is evolving. This early mystical insight led Houston to commit herself to assisting others in discovering their own inner potential.

Houston attended New York's High School for the Performing Arts and later Barnard College. She was active in the New York theater, receiving acclaim as both an actor and director. However, a severe head injury caused her to become temporarily blind and affected her academic work. The injury precipitated another mystical experience, one in which she was visited by a mysterious woman, who assured her that things would work out and she would have a wonderful and exciting life. The mysterious woman was none other than Jean Houston herself, visiting from twenty years in the future. Houston recovered her sight and mental abilities, whereupon she returned to her college studies with a heightened commitment.

While still in her teens, Houston traveled to Greece, where she studied ancient religions and archaeology. Sensing that the world was entering a period of accelerated change and recognizing that she could make positive contributions, Houston turned down several acting opportunities, choosing to pursue an advanced degree. She earned a doctorate in psychology from Union Graduate School in Cincinnati, studied and worked with Margaret Mead, and led seminars with mythologist Joseph Campbell.

Houston married Robert Masters in the early 1960s, and together they explored the mystical dimensions of altered states of consciousness produced by hallucinogenic drugs. Their inquiries resulted in the bestselling book *The Varieties of Psychedelic Experience* (1966) and the formation of the Foundation for Mind Research, which the couple still directs. In the late 1960s and early 1970s, Houston and Masters turned their attention to methods of achieving higher states of being without the use of drugs, producing another widely read text, *Mind Games* (1972).

Houston is the sole author of over a dozen books, including an autobiography, *A Mythic Life* (1997), and a New Age christology, *Godseed: The Journey of Christ* (1992). Perhaps her most notable book is *The Possible Human* (1982), which is also the title of the popular workshop she has presented to countless New Age audiences. The text and the highly interactive workshop provide participants with a wide range of techniques designed to enrich consciousness and creativity. Houston is a dynamic speaker, and her popularity on the New Age "consciousness circuit" is well earned. By the early 1990s, Houston was traveling over 250,000 miles a year giving "The Possible Human Workshop."

In addition to her work in the New Age community, Houston also has been keenly alert to the greater cultural ramifications of the human potential movement. A frequent lecturer at colleges and universities, she has visited over forty countries and served as a consultant to politicians, heads of state, business leaders, and government agencies. She also has served as president of the Association for Humanistic Psychology, an adviser to UNICEF (United Nations Children's Fund), and chair of the United Nations' conference of World Religious Leaders (1975). During the Clinton administration, she gained notoriety for her close association with Hillary Rodham Clinton, with whom she worked on Clinton's bestselling book *It Takes a Village*. The "notoriety" refers to reports that Houston was facilitating séancelike psychic encounters between Clinton and Eleanor Roosevelt.

Both Clinton and Houston readily admitted that Houston suggested that Clinton have "imaginary conversations" with Roosevelt. Both deny that anything resembling a séance occurred.

J. Z. Knight and Ramtha

A type of shamanism termed *channeling* has been a characteristic feature of the New Age movement. One of the best known channelers is J. Z. Knight (1946–   ), who is the medium for Ramtha, a 35,000-year-old warrior who had lived on the lost continents of Lemuria and Atlantis. (Lemuria and Atlantis figure in the Theosophical writings of Helena P. Blavatsky.) Unlike Helen Schucman, who was a reluctant channel for Jesus, Knight served as an enthusiastic medium for the ancient warrior and established Ramtha's School of Enlightenment to promulgate his teachings.

The teachings of Knight/Ramtha are found in various texts, the best summary being *The White Book* (1986). Ramtha's School offers teachings and techniques to assist individuals in becoming aware of their essential divinity and using it for positive purposes. Ramtha's teachings are vaguely Neoplatonic and resemble New Thought in their emphasis on the role of consciousness in the creation and modification of the material world.

Knight was born Judith Darlene Hampton in New Mexico. The family was poor and her father an abusive alcoholic. Her mother had psychic abilities that were revealed to Judith on several occasions. Knight's paranormal experiences began when she was quite young and included a close encounter with a UFO (unidentified flying object) or some higher life force, revelations by psychics that she had tremendous spiritual power and was destined for greatness, and various manifestations of her own psychic abilities.

In 1977 Knight and her second husband were living in Tacoma, Washington, when Ramtha first appeared. Knight was in her kitchen where she and her husband had been making pyramids to focus psychic energy in an effort to better preserve food. An imposing figure with the full splendor of a spiritual master, Ramtha introduced himself, saying: "I am Ramtha, the Enlightened One, and I have come to help you over the ditch." Then, in words familiar to many New Thought followers, he explained: "The ditch is limited thought." Fearing that Ramtha might be Satan, Knight sought assistance from a local Spiritualist church. There she met Lorraine Graham, who would help guide her into a deep and lasting relationship with Ramtha and her own role as a professional channeler.

In 1978 Knight channeled Ramtha publicly for the first time. When she channels Ramtha, Knight pulls back her hair, dresses in nonfeminine clothing, and takes on the mannerisms of a warrior-teacher. The initial event was successful, and Knight/Ramtha became a local sensation. Ramtha gave Judith the idea to begin charging people to attend gatherings when he would speak through her. By the early 1980s, Knight was traveling around the country presenting programs called "Ramtha Dialogues" and developed a national following. In 1984 she married Jeffrey Knight, her fifth husband; they divorced in 1989.

By the end of the 1980s, Knight was arguably the most well known channeler in the world and Ramtha a New Age celebrity. Knight institutionalized the movement, first as Sovereignty, Inc., then the Church I Am, and finally, its contemporary manifestation, Ramtha's School of Enlightenment, located in Yelm, Washington. The school offers a residential education program in spiritual self-development, with auxiliary organizations producing and marketing Knight/Ramtha books, audio- and videotapes, and other educational materials. Like other New Age learning centers, it is conceived as being a contemporary mystery school patterned on mystery schools of the ancient world, which were established to promote spiritual development.

In the early and mid-1990s, Knight briefly retired from public view, most likely due to several scandals and a spate of negative publicity—including an investigative report on the ABC television program *20/20*. She resumed her public career in the late 1990s, and by the turn of the century, Knight, Ramtha, and the School of Enlightment were again attracting significant numbers of followers.

Conclusion

Theosophy, New Thought, and the New Age movements continue to be important for contemporary women's religious lives. These movements have promoted worldviews that teach that spiritual realities and entities affect the well-being of humans' earthly lives. The New Age movement, in particular, represents a contemporary international resurgence of basic religion, the animistic religious pattern found in many indigenous traditions. There has been a concern with millennialism in these three but interrelated movements, in the expectation of an imminent transition to a collective salvation, either by catastrophic destruction of the old world (such as the shelter cycle of the Church Universal and Triumphant) or by noncatastrophic progress into a new age that may be aided by a messiah in the form of an individual (such as Annie Besant's World-Teacher) or accomplished by a general receptivity to the Christ principle (as articulated in the Alice Bailey writings). Women and men in all three movements have worked to improve society.

Women have been active in these three movements as shamans in touch with entities in the spiritual realm, theologians, philosophers, founders, teachers, writers, ordained ministers, and administrators. Charisma—believed claims of access to an unseen source of authority—remains important in legitimating women's religious leadership in these movements. Increasingly, women are relying on educational and institutional credentials, including ordination to ministry, to legitimate their religious leadership, but these more routinized forms of leadership have not displaced the importance of charisma in giving women a creative voice in articulating religious worldviews. In the twentieth century there were numerous women theologians and religious leaders who claimed that they were not speaking/writing their own words but those of exalted, often male, beings, the most noteworthy being Alice Bailey, Elizabeth Clare Prophet, Helen Schucman, and J. Z. Knight.

Theosophy and New Thought continue in their various institutional expressions, but their themes have also strongly influenced the diffuse New Age movement, which exists in both institutionalized and noninstitutionalized forms. The New Age movement influences the lives and outlooks of numerous women and men who read literature, attend workshops, visit psychics, healers, and shamans, and participate in alternative healing therapies. The ideas and practices of Theosophy, New Thought, and the New Age movements are influential in the neopagan/Wiccan movements, particularly in the concept of magic as focusing thought to change physical reality. Additionally, many neopagans and Wiccans believe in reincarnation and karma. Syncretism is the norm here, and many people who belong to mainstream religious institutions are touched by these movements. Theosophy, New Thought, and the New Age movements show every sign of continuing to be significant in the lives of women in the twenty-first century. They will continue to influence the spirituality of many women and provide contexts within which exceptional women will express their religious leadership.

SOURCES: J. Stillson Judah identified and described "the metaphysical movement" in *The History and Philosophy of the Metaphysical Movements in America* (1967). Robert Ellwood and Harry B. Partin provide excellent general treatments of many of these groups in *Religious and Spiritual Groups in Modern America*, 2nd ed. (1988). The book edited by Catherine Wessinger, *Women's Leadership in Marginal Religions: Explorations Outside the Mainstream* (1993), contains articles by Ann Braude on Christian Science, Robert Ellwood and Wessinger on the Theosophical movement, J. Gordon Melton on Emma Curtis Hopkins, and Dell deChant on Unity; the introduction by Wessinger discusses the importance of charisma to women's religious leadership. James Santucci provides a treatment of "Women in the Theosophical Movement," *Explorations: Journal for Adventurous Thought* 9 (Fall 1990): 71–94. The book edited by Daniel Caldwell, *The Esoteric World of Madame Blavatsky: Insights into the Life of a Modern Sphinx* (2000), presents recollections of Helena P. Blavatsky by her contemporaries.

Catherine Lowman Wessinger studies the life and thought of Annie Besant in *Annie Besant and Progressive Messianism* (1988). W. Michael Ashcraft's *"The Dawn of the New Cycle": Point Loma Theosophists and American Culture* (2002) is a sensitive and detailed study of gender roles and child-rearing practices in Katherine Tingley's Point Loma community of Theosophists. Evelyn A. Kirkley discusses women in the Point Loma community in " 'Equality of the Sexes, But . . . ': Women in Point Loma Theosophy, 1899–1942," *Nova Religio: The Journal of Alternative and Emergent Religions* 1.2 (April 1998): 272–288. Earlier treatments of the Point Loma community are Emmett A. Greenwalt, *California Utopia: Point Loma: 1897–1942* (1978), and Iverson L. Harris, Jr., "Reminiscences of Lomaland: Madame Tingley and the Theosophical Institute in San Diego," *Journal of San Diego History* 20.3 (Summer 1974): 1–32. Charles S. Braden's *Spirits in Rebellion: The Rise and Development of New Thought* (1963) is a pioneering study of the New Thought movement. J. Gordon Melton has provided additional pioneering work on individuals and groups in the New Thought movement. See Melton's "New Thought's Hidden History: Emma Curtis Hopkins, Forgotten Founder," *Journal of the Society for the Study of Metaphysical Religion* 1.1 (1995): 5–40, and "How Divine Science Got to Denver," *Journal of the Society for the Study of Metaphysical Religion* 7.2 (2001): 103–122. An important and extensive scholarly study of women in the New Thought movement is Beryl Satter's *Each Mind a Kingdom: American Women, Sexual Purity, and the New Thought Movement 1875–1920* (1999). The only book-length study of Emma Curtis Hopkins is Gail Harley, *Emma Curtis Hopkins: Forgotten Founder of New Thought* (2002). John K. Simmons reveals "The Forgotten Contributions of Annie Rix Militz to the Unity School of Christianity," *Nova Religio: The Journal of Alternative and Emergent Religions* 2.1 (October 1998): 76–92. A history of the Church Universal and Triumphant is found in J. Gordon Melton, "The Church Universal and Triumphant: Its Heritage and Thoughtworld," in *Church Universal and Triumphant in Scholarly Perspective*, ed. James R. Lewis and J. Gordon Melton (1994). Bradley C. Whitsel in *The Church Universal and Triumphant: Elizabeth Clare Prophet's Apocalyptic Movement* (2003) studies the church's shelter cycle. J. Gordon Melton's *Finding Enlightenment: Ramtha's School of Ancient Wisdom* (1998) is the first scholarly study of Ramtha's School of Enlightenment. J. Gordon Melton, ed., *New Age Encyclopedia* (1990), provides informative articles on many of the figures discussed here. Lewis Hopfe in *Religions of the World*, 5th ed. (1991), delineates the characteristics of basic religion.

SPIRITUALISM
Cathy Gutierrez

IN 1848, MEMBERS of the Fox family of Hydesville, New York, complained of a haunting. The Fox's adolescent daughters, Margaret and Katherine, devised a system of communication with the spirit called "alphabet raps," in which they would ask a question, and the spirit would respond by rapping out a response, one for A, two for B, and so forth. This incident would prove to be the spark for a new religious movement that would claim half of the U.S. population as believers during the nineteenth century and spread over the border to Canada and across the Atlantic to England and continental Europe. The effects of active communication with the dead were especially significant for women, who benefited not only by talking to their deceased loved ones but also by gaining entry to a burgeoning industry that allowed them financial gain as mediums and access to the traditionally masculine sphere of science.

Spiritualism was the late-blooming child of the Second Great Awakening, a period of fervent religious revivals that took place along the Erie Canal between the years 1820 and 1850. This period witnessed several momentous changes to American Protestantism as well as the birth of several new religious movements such as the Mormons and the Oneida Community. The Second Great Awakening began in the heady days of the new democracy and may be seen as a religious articulation of the values of populism and individualism. At the same time, urbanization and rapid industrialization disrupted modes of community, economics, and religiosity, as a mobile and literate youth moved westward along the Canal, uprooted from family and tradition. The era was both exciting and unsettling and called for new answers to old questions. Spiritualism was among the new religious systems that swept in to fill a vacuum of meaning in times of social flux.

In varying degrees, all the new religions coming out of the Second Great Awakening were characterized by espousing continued revelation. The traditional tenets of Christianity needed an infusion of new life in order to adequately respond to the changing times: Joseph Smith of the Mormons and John Humphrey Noyes of the Oneida Community claimed the power of prophecy, as Mother Ann Lee of the Shakers had decades earlier. The Christian canon, which had been perceived as closed, had to be reopened, and Spiritualism, no less than the others, offered a view of the good life and the afterlife that differed radically from prior forms of Christian thinking. Unlike other new movements, however, Spiritualism was not centered around a single charismatic leader who claimed direct experience of God but rather was diffused among the population with mediums, mostly women, who received religious—and secular— knowledge from the dead.

Women's full participation in religious life was already burgeoning in antebellum America. The Second Great Awakening saw a shift in ideas of salvation away from the Calvinist claim that the "elect," or saved, were predetermined. Instead, individuals became responsible for experiencing conversion and thereby being saved. During this period, itinerant preachers would go from town to town, spreading the word and encouraging conversion experiences; there is evidence that a few women numbered among the wandering preachers. Moreover, industrialization changed how much time women had for leisure and how they spent it. Whereas before the advent of factories women had been involved in the economic production on farms or in artisan shops, some women now had newfound leisure as members of the middle class who stayed at home while their husbands worked in industry. This newly created time was overwhelmingly devoted to religious pursuits and the creation of myriad benevolent societies that would have a serious impact on progressive reforms ranging from abolition to the call for women's rights.

Spiritualism's most notable commentator, historian Ann Braude, has argued that the movement's appeal to women initially lay in its exceptional capacity to allay grieving. Calvinist belief had previously held that children who died before the benefit of baptism were condemned to hell. Spiritualism sprang to life during the century's highest infant mortality rates and spoke directly to mothers' concerns about the state of their children's souls. As Braude has shown, communication with the dead was understood by believers to be utterly empirical and scientifically verifiable. During the era of the telegraph, telephone, and later photography, invisible communication across space was the very essence of current technology. Spiritualism posited that it was possible to communicate across the threshold of death and in so doing assured the grief-stricken that their loved ones were flourishing in the afterlife, surrounded by kind relatives and wise angels. The Calvinist policy of infant damnation was thus understood to have been empirically overturned—children were not only in heaven, but they grew up, went to school, even married in the afterlife (Braude, 32–55). In short, the dead completed the life cycles that had been denied to them on earth.

This theology of continued growth in heaven, both spiritually and physically, reflected the progressive ethos of the age and is frequently called a "postmillennial" religious attitude. Postmillennialism denotes a religious belief in the gradual march of humanity toward perfection, and one that was usually understood to be the precondition of the Second Coming. The world would be perfected slowly by human hands, and when this process was complete, Jesus would return to reign for a period of 1,000 years. On the one hand, Spiritualism exemplified this belief in progress perhaps better than any other movement of the century. Spiritualists projected the march of progress into the daily happenings of heaven, where the dead grew in both body and knowledge. Heavenly progress was mirrored on earth, and Spiritualists were at the forefront of the religious and political reform movements of the day. On the other hand, however, the ability to talk to the dead radically eclipsed many standard Christian beliefs, such as the centrality of church teachings and the existence of a final

judgment and even hell. Adherence to normative forms of Christianity differed widely, depending on geography, class, and circumstance, and it was frequently the case that one would both belong to a regular congregation, mostly Protestant, and practice Spiritualism in addition to churchgoing Christianity.

Before turning to specific characteristics of Spiritualism and their benefits for women, two influences on Spiritualism need to be addressed. Mesmerism and the writings of Emanuel Swedenborg shaped both the form and the content of Spiritualism and contributed to its roles for and effects on women. The first derives its name from the colorful figure of Franz Anton Mesmer, an eighteenth-century German thinker whose students stumbled across what we now call *hypnosis*. Mesmer was a medical doctor who developed a theory he called "animal magnetism," an unconventional but highly popular method for curing illness. Mesmer believed that the human body contained "magnetic fluid" and that sickness was the result of this fluid being out of balance. Since healthy humans were also magnetic, Mesmer believed that he could cure by readjusting this fluid in the patient by touching him or her with his hands or other magnetized objects. Despite the enormous popularity of animal magnetism and numerous recorded cures attributed to it, Mesmer failed to gain the official recognition he thought was his due, and the method remained on the margins of the medical establishment.

In the course of administering a magnetic cure, one of Mesmer's pupils, the Marquis de Puysegur, discovered what he termed "magnetic sleep," which would be the predecessor to trance states in Spiritualist mediumship. In the course of treatment, one of the marquis's patients lapsed into a trance state that resembled sleepwalking. In this state, the patient had a full consciousness but a different consciousness from his waking state. Under the conditions of magnetic sleep, the patient was able to diagnose his own medical condition and to perform acts that appeared to be paranormal. Puysegur called this ability the "sixth sense," and the combination of the ability to induce trance states and the ability of the entranced to supercede the limits of normal consciousness set the stage for Spiritualist mediumship (Crabtree, chapters 1–4).

The discovery of magnetic sleep quickly caught fire within the esoteric circles of Europe, including a large group of intellectuals who promulgated the works of Emanuel Swedenborg. Swedenborg was a seventeenth-century philosopher and mystic who, during numerous mystical visions, was able to view heaven. He described a three-tiered heaven with a complex society of angels and the dead. These societies mirrored those of earth but were free of any taint of wrongdoing or carnality. Two central tenets of Swedenborgian mysticism would inform Spiritualist theology: First, his visions implied that humans could have easy and repeated access to the afterlife. Second, what was found there was not a static heaven of sheer perfection but was rather a fluid and dynamic state marked by change and improvement.

America was already awash in esoteric belief handed down through secret societies like the Freemasons. This included Neoplatonic traditions that posited that individuals could ascend through levels of knowledge that culminated in apprehending ultimate reality. The popularity of Swedenborg's works can hardly be overestimated, and when Mesmerism was introduced to this side of the Atlantic in the 1830s, it found a fertile ground already in place. One man in particular, Andrew Jackson Davis, would finalize the marriage of these disparate cultural strains. Davis, known as "The Poughkeepsie Seer," had published tracts heavily influenced by Swedenborgian thought coupled with an American Transcendentalist view that the divine was manifest in the natural world. He called this amalgam "Harmonial Philosophy," and his works were popular before the incidents in Hydesville in 1848. When the Fox sisters demonstrated an apparent ability to communicate with the dead, Davis supported the nascent movement as the empirical demonstration of many of his Swedenborgian claims about the afterlife. While Davis would later denounce much of Spiritualism's excess in its more dramatic table-tipping phase, his initial advocacy and numerous publications brought vital publicity to the movement and provided it with the necessary theological backbone. Without Davis's support, Spiritualism might have remained too scattered and idiosyncratic to become a full-fledged religious phenomenon.

Mediumship

The central claim and ritual activity of Spiritualism was contact with the dead. From the outset there were two primary settings for communicating with those in the afterlife: On a small scale, seances were held in people's homes with a group of family and friends in attendance, and on a large scale, Spiritualists held exhibitions for the general public that resembled the tent revivals prevalent at the time. Both types required a medium, a person with talent and experience in entering trance states that allowed her to contact spirits and to relay their messages to the living. Mediumship took many forms and mutated greatly over the span of the sixty-odd years that Spiritualism flourished. These forms included the straightforward trance wherein the medium would allow the dead to speak through her, and her own consciousness was understood to be temporarily absent. As time went on, different methods were developed, ranging from the use of planchettes (like modern-day Ouija boards use) to automatic writing to the "materi-

alization" of the spirits in cabinets specially designed for séances. Even as styles in communication changed, one thing that remained constant was that the majority of mediums were women.

Spiritualism was largely predicated on the new discovery of electricity and the possibilities it held for human society. Spiritualists posited that people themselves were "charged" positively or negatively, and this dichotomy conformed to contemporary ideas about gender as opposite but complementary. Men, seen as more active, were positively charged, and women, both nervous and passive by nature, were negatively charged. Women's "natural" disposition thus made them better receptors for the spirit world, since the spirit world was positively charged and attracted to its opposite.

Braude has pointed out that this apparent boon to women, in terms of both respect and economic gain, took the form of a social paradox. Particularly in the large, public settings, the spirits who were contacted were often the famous and powerful dead, and they were called upon to give advice about the present historical situation. This roster includes Francis Bacon, Benjamin Franklin, Swedenborg, and even Shakespeare. The trance states that the female mediums entered paradoxically allowed them to expound on matters of politics and philosophy, but at the expense of being utterly passive—indeed, not even really "present" at all—while doing so. In fact, the younger and less educated the women were, the more their messages were understood to be authentic, since the vast run of people would not believe that a young woman could have come up with these thoughts on her own.

One of the best examples of this paradox of authenticity is the story of Cora Hatch. (Mrs. Hatch went through several husbands and thus several last names, but scholars generally agree to refer to her by the name she had when she first became a celebrated medium.) Cora Hatch began her career as a medium at age fourteen and by all accounts was one of the top three mediums of her generation. Cora was young and very beautiful, with long, blonde curls that were much commented on in the press. On stage, for thousands to observe her as the passive vehicle for the other world to inhabit, Cora Hatch exemplified the voyeuristic appeal of Spiritualism and the mixed blessing of women's public speaking.

Cora's renown made her the perfect test case for Spiritualism, and she complied with more than one request to be the object of scientific inquiry. Committees composed of well-respected members of the military, government, and scientific community tested her while in a trance state. The questions put to her were specifically designed so that her conscious self would be unable to answer them, or that was the assumption. In the late 1850s, one such committee asked her to respond, on behalf of the spirit world, to the following queries: (1) What are the natural principles governing the gyroscope? (2) What causes seeds of plants to germinate? (3) Did the races of man all spring from one mundane parent? and (4) Was Jesus of Nazareth divine or human? Her answers to these questions, given from the spirits, met with the surprised adulation of Captain Isaiah Rynders, the chair of the committee, who said that he "expected to be humbugged, and [was] agreeably disappointed" (cited in Fornell, 81).

While it is unfortunately true that the majority of books published by Spiritualists had male authors, women were represented in the book marketplace, particularly in the form of mediums relating or transcribing their communications with spirits while in a trance state. In 1858, Cora Hatch published *Discourses on Religion, Morals, Philosophy, and Metaphysics*, and in the introduction her husband made a point of reminding the reader that the topics discussed were mostly given to her by committees. Each discourse is a transcription of communications from the spirit world, and the breadth of knowledge about music, other cultures, history, and literature is impressive. On the eve of the Civil War, many of the discourses are devoted to the place of America on the world stage and the moral necessity of equality. The principles of democracy as the highest form of government are marshalled against those who uphold slavery, and the central role of women in shaping the moral realm is reinforced:

> [T]here is the worm, the serpent, gnawing daily and hourly; and you point to African slavery, saying, "It is a shame and blasphemy upon the American government!" Ask those who complain if the moral education of the people is not neglected. Ask if the mother, with the education she gives her child, does not administer the very elements of aristocracy, of pride, of ignorance, and of depravity. It is only those great men like Washington, who have had noble, moral mothers, and who have been instructed in their moral as well as religious nature, that shine forth in the firmament of your political constellations. (*Discourses*, 251)

In the condition of a trance state, Cora was able to critique not only the contemporary political situation but also religion itself as a vehicle of oppression and fear. Catholicism wrought "ignorance and superstition" on the believers, and Protestantism held the people in terror of a wrathful God. In the *Discourses* she lambastes Jonathan Edwards and John Calvin for the highest crime of perpetuating fear of the deity. Such criticisms provoked outrage among the general public, and in 1857 a riot broke out at one of her lectures. Cora Hatch's position on religion is exemplary of the more general Spiritualist relationship to normative Christianity: While usually upholding the tenets of Christian morals and the divinity of Jesus, Spiritualists either sought to reform aspects of their religion or parted ways with it on several counts. By instilling judgmentalism and fear in its adherents, Christianity was actually delaying the perfection of humankind.

One of the primary departures from Christian doctrine was the notion of humanity as fundamentally given to evil and to sin. Human nature, for Cora Hatch and other Spiritualists, was essentially good, and any evidence to the contrary could be accounted for by ignorance and the lack of social and economic equality. She writes, "Evil is a word that should be cast out of every vocabulary; for it does not follow that because the finite can not equal the infinite, it is evil. In our opinion, *the finite comprehension of good is all the evil that exists*, and as men's understanding enlarges, so will their ideas of goodness increase" (Hatch, 315). This understanding of human nature had the radical effect of dispensing with the concept of hell in its entirety; souls may repent, learn, and improve in the afterlife and thereby move forward to moral perfection after their deaths.

If Spiritualism gave women a platform for expressing their views on a variety of topics generally reserved for the masculine sphere, it also gave women an economic freedom and social mobility that was frequently denied to their more housebound sisters. Fame, money, and mobility all marked the upper echelons of mediumship, and like the paradox of passivity, these advances too had their price. The private life of Margaret Fox, one of the founding sisters of Spiritualism, reveals the benefits and costs of being a woman in the public eye. Margaret was thirteen when the Hydesville rappings occurred, and her sister Katherine just twelve. Daughters of a Methodist farmer, the Fox sisters became the object of almost instant celebrity in their small New York town when word spread of their ability to communicate with the spirit in their house. Hundreds of the curious came to their home to hear the conversations with the ghost the children had named "Mr. Split-foot," in an ongoing drama that revealed that the spirit had been murdered in the house and was seeking justice. The crowds and the publicity quickly became too much for their mother, a devout Christian and quiet woman, and the girls were moved to live with their sister Leah Fish in Rochester.

The spirits seemed to follow Margaret, with knockings and furniture movings happening only in her presence, even after her sister had been sent to live in yet another locale. While most Rochester residents were resentful of having this new and possibly demonic commotion brought into their lives, a handful formed a "spirit circle" and began to hold regular meetings at Leah's home. From this modest beginning, Spiritualism would shape the rest of Margaret's days. Initially, she

The private life of Margaret Fox, one of the founding sisters of Spiritualism, reveals the benefits and costs of being a woman in the public eye. Margaret was thirteen when the Hydesville rappings occurred, her sister Katherine just twelve. Daughters of a Methodist farmer, the Fox sisters became the object of almost instant celebrity in their small New York town when word spread of their ability to communicate with the spirit in their house. Margaret Fox is on the left, Katherine Fox is in the center, and Leah Fox Fish is on the right. *Courtesy of the Rush Rhees Library, University of Rochester.*

was subjected to ridicule, excruciating tests of authenticity, and even danger to her person on one occasion when the small hall where she was giving a demonstration erupted into violence and several men rushed the podium, apparently with the intent to harm her.

The publicity that these events generated brought Margaret to the attention of important men who were to champion her and give credence to the new movement she and Katherine had started. The first of these was John Edmonds, New York State Supreme Court judge, who became convinced of the presence of the dead by Margaret's innocent demeanor. Judge Edmonds would continue to be one of Spiritualism's most ardent proponents and the author of some of the most important Spiritualist tracts in the years preceding the Civil War. Edmonds's influence brought a roster of influential friends into contact with the Fox sisters, including Dr. Robert Hare of the University of Pennsylvania and Horace Greeley, the editor of the New York *Tribune*. Soon others started claiming the ability to contact the dead,

and within two years, Spiritualism spread across the country and into Europe.

Before she turned twenty, Margaret would come into the orbit of many of the most powerful and famous minds of her day, including P. T. Barnum–for whom the sisters gave demonstrations in his museum—James Fenimore Cooper, Jenny Lind, Michael Faraday, and Henry James. It was during this period of celebrity that the tone of the communications shifted from the consultation of deceased relatives for the grieving to the consultation of the famous dead for their advice on contemporary matters.

While living in Philadelphia with her mother in 1852, Margaret met Dr. Elisha Kent Kane, the internationally renowned Arctic explorer. The love affair that ensued was brief and tragic and illustrates the public distrust of women overstepping their social and class boundaries. Their correspondence reveals that Kane, gradually and almost in spite of himself, became smitten with the young medium and that the affection was mutual. However, Kane had an aristocratic background and a reputation to uphold, and associating with the founding member of a suspect and frequently radical upstart movement was socially problematic. He repeatedly scolded Margaret and urged her to quit the business of Spiritualism and to get a proper education befitting a young lady.

If Kane's tone was tempered by love, his family and friends' was certainly not; they disapproved of the association vehemently. During his many travels and even a two-year rescue mission to the Arctic, Kane remained trapped between his love for Margaret and the social taint of Spiritualism; his family forbade their marriage in the direst terms. Against their wishes, the two were married in 1856 in what appears to have been an unofficial Quaker ceremony, and he wrote Margaret into his will. The day after he announced their betrothal, he left for London, and Margaret would never see him again. He died in Cuba on the return trip a year later, and his family succeeded in making the draconian arrangement that Margaret could only receive her inheritance on the condition that she never publicly claimed to be his wife or use his last name.

The depression from this heartache lasted for years; in the meantime, Margaret's mother had taken her and her sister Katherine to live in Washington, D.C., in 1853, where the sisters would experience American political life firsthand. The effects of Spiritualism were starting to be felt on Congress, and politicians no less than scientists wanted the truth or quackery of Spiritualism determined. In 1861, Abraham Lincoln was introduced to Spiritualism by Nathanial Tallmadge, a former senator of Wisconsin. While Lincoln appeared unimpressed with communications from the spirit world, his wife believed in their veracity, and in 1872, disguised and using a false name, Mary Todd Lincoln consulted Margaret Fox to get in touch with her husband who had been assassinated almost a decade before. She was convinced of Margaret's success in this matter.

The following decade was a difficult time for Margaret, who tried to leave her life as a medium only to be forced to return for financial reasons. She fell into a dark depression and began drinking heavily. In the late 1880s, apparently under the influence of alcohol, she told a reporter from the *New York Herald* that her participation in mediumship was then and had always been a fraud. She sold her story to the papers and held a series of "exposé séances" to demonstrate the tricks of the trade. Public interest in Margaret's turnabout flared briefly but was quickly extinguished, and Margaret was forced to recant her own confession and return to mediumship, again for financial reasons. World weary and sad, she died in 1893, after an extraordinary life had taken its toll on her.

Being in the public eye brought many benefits to women but also held severe consequences for them. The rewards were rich, garnering them material gains and extraordinary respect within certain circles; mediums had the ear of the most powerful and famous people of their day, many of whom legitimized Spiritualism's claims and the role of women as religious leaders. But the costs were frequently high. Detractors denounced Spiritualism as hysteria, witchcraft, or just plain foolishness. Despite individual tragedies, mediums brought public recognition to women's authoritative role as intermediaries with the spiritual realm, offering consolation to the grieving and advice to the needy. For believers, mediums provided a glimpse of the afterlife and the values espoused in heaven itself. As such, they played a pivotal role in shaping the ethos of the day since the perfection of heaven could and should be imitated on earth. Those values conjoined the religious and the political, and Spiritualists were at the vanguard of social progress.

Progress and Politics

The creation of a middle class had given women ample leisure time to devote to religious pursuits, and during the Second Great Awakening these took the form of benevolent societies. These were charitable groups around the country that were devoted to a wide range of reform platforms. Foremost these reforms centered on abolition, women's rights, and temperance; some, however, were devoted to more esoteric causes such as the call for phonetic spelling and even underwear reform. Whatever the platform for improvement was, the benevolent societies embodied a postmillennial philosophy—it was humanity's central task to perfect the world, and this overwhelming responsibility could be accomplished one cause at a time, each aimed at eliminating injustice, inequality, and economic hardship.

Spiritualists embraced the progressive hopes of the day and carried them further than their predecessors had. While other Christian groups relied on a sense of basic human dignity and biblical morals to buttress their social agendas, Spiritualists had the additional theological support of having the workings of heaven itself as their guide in earthly matters. The spirits routinely and tenaciously told the living that in heaven all beings were equal, or at least had equal access to progress toward perfection. The famous dead and the common run of humanity alike advised the living to promote the causes of abolition and gender equality, and while members of "primitive" cultures were often consigned to the lower rungs of heaven, they were certainly not banished to hell. The progressive ethos of earth merely mirrored that of heaven, where every creature had an equal opportunity to advance to the upper tiers of heaven.

Spiritualist newspapers kept careful track of the Civil

War, monitoring not only the current events but their effects on the spiritual plane as well. One of the most widely circulated papers was *The Herald of Progress*, Andrew Jackson Davis's weekly based in New York City. While decidedly pro-abolition in tone, the *Herald* gave equal time to Southern correspondents and rebuttals (as was the policy for all matters, including Spiritualism itself). The editorials written on behalf of the paper decry the institution of slavery while at the same time asserting the harm done to all humanity by war. A typical example comes from an 1862 issue:

> The voice of justice—which is the voice of God— and which, as well as mercy, pleads for the weak and defenseless, has been crying "Let my people go." But in vain the cry! One half of this nation has been steadily lapsing toward barbarism, by reason of the exercise of irresponsible power, habits of indolence, and ungovernable passion. Meanwhile the other half have blinded their eyes and steeled their hearts against the claims of humanity—refused to recognize the brotherhood of man, and persisted in decreeing injustice, oppression, cruelty, and wrong as the portion of the defenseless few. (*The Herald of Progress*, June 21, 1862)

Prominent Spiritualists like Amy Post were involved in the Underground Railroad, and many Spiritualists recognized a family resemblance between their ritual practices and those of traditional African religions that also maintained contact with deceased relatives and often involved trance states. African Americans on occasion became mediums, and no less a figure than Sojourner Truth was counted among the believers. One of the more spectacular examples of African American believers was Paschal Beverly Randolph, a man of mixed race who worked as a medium for eight years before entering even deeper into the hermetic circles of Rosicrucians and magic. Randolph wrote nearly fifty books and pamphlets on Spiritualism and related matters and traveled to Europe and the Middle East where he observed a variety of clairvoyant and magical practices that he incorporated into his long career as a seeker of esoterica and a political radical, particularly in the arena of sexual love (Deveney).

Perhaps even more than abolition, Spiritualists focused on causes that affected women. The newspapers joyfully recounted the opening of women's colleges and constantly called for the equality of the sexes. Foremost among their concerns was the institution of marriage, which many denounced as "legalized prostitution." With men controlling the finances of the household, women were seen as forced to submit to their husbands' wishes in exchange for economic security. Rather than abolish marriage, Spiritualists called for reform so that marriage might reflect a true and spiritual state of love rather than a debased form of ownership of women.

As historian Mary Ryan has shown, new economic modes changed marital relations that were formerly cemented by shared labor to a more intangible relationship based on intimacy. These more ephemeral bonds brought romantic love into the spotlight mid-century, and Spiritualist thought reflected and expanded the prevailing mores. With their emphasis on the afterlife, Spiritualists posited that coupled souls remained so for eternity. By increasing the stakes of marriage and projecting its continuation into the hereafter, Spiritualists argued that easy and acceptable divorce was necessary to avert the possibility that one would remain eternally with the wrong person.

As part and parcel of marriage reform, Spiritualists propounded what they called "spiritual affinities," or natural attractions between two souls. Some reports of the afterlife claimed that there were schools of spiritual learning that lone individuals were denied access to; only the (heterosexually) coupled could enter. Since the spirits in heaven had bodies, it was also one of the favorite questions of the living to ask whether sex continued in the afterlife. The answer was generally a qualified "yes," in that spirit bodies did meld together but with the caveat that this process was not carnal: The meshing of bodies and souls was for the purposes of spiritual wholeness rather than the fulfillment of desire.

Spiritualism was associated, both in fact and in the popular mind, with the Free Love movement. Generally not as licentious as it might sound, the Free Love platform ranged from standard marriage reform to a sexual utopianism on the fringes of the movement. While it is nearly impossible to determine to what extent Spiritualism and Free Love were coextensive, it does appear to be the case that while not all Spiritualists were Free Love advocates, all Free Love advocates were Spiritualists. Against the backdrop of experimentation with sex and gender, Spiritualist Free Love was generally tamer than many of its cultural kin. The Oneida Community practiced "group marriage," wherein all members of the sect were expected to love all others equally. This Christian model of communal love was extended to include the physical expression of love, sex. The Mormons had implemented "plural marriage," commonly called polygamy, at the same time, and the Shakers found the highest religious expression of communal love to lie in absolute celibacy.

The farthest reaches of Spiritualist Free Love shared many of the utopian characteristics of these other movements. One example from mid-century used nothing short of Plato's *Republic* to argue for multiple sex partners, citing the love of a particular quality as the greatest good rather than its presence in a particular person: "I am, in the sense in which I am speaking, comparatively a fixed fact in always loving or having an affinity for certain attributes of other human beings. I love mentality. Some minds more than others, because their mentality is more in harmony with the particular development of mine—but I can love no one mind exclusively. If I love mind, to love one mind exclusively from another is impossible" (Kent, 25). Victoria Woodhull, president of the American Association of Spiritualists and the only woman of the century to run for president of the United States, was an ardent Free Love advocate. Her public lectures on the matter were broadly attended and generated enormous publicity for the movement, much of it negative. The utopian cast of these lectures is also evident, and in one she even went so far as to claim that better sex was the necessary path to inaugurating the millennium! These extremes were the exception rather than the rule of Spiritualist marriage reform.

Overall, progress both in earth and in heaven was the hallmark of Spiritualist thinking, and adherents' dedication to the cause of progress had very real repercussions for the political atmosphere of the nineteenth century. With the example provided by heaven, Spiritualists sought to bring earth into proper reflection of the divine, in which all creatures had equal capacity and equal rights, and individuals had only themselves to answer to if they failed to improve. With access to the world's great thinkers of past and present, humanity had no excuse for floundering in injustice and oppression, and change was called for on nearly every front.

Developments and New Directions

Almost from the outset, Spiritualism invited chicanery into its domain by the public demand for increasingly spectacular displays from the spirit world. Table tipping, gifts from the spirit world (flowers, gloves, and the like), the playing of musical instruments, and materializations of the dead themselves all became common occurrences in many séances. The element of theatricality contributed both to Spiritualism's popularity and to its eventual decline when these displays became too outrageous for even the most willing to believe. Two developments stand out as most important—spirit photography and the appearance of ectoplasm.

Spiritualism was grounded in the new technologies of communication; mediums were understood to serve as living telegraphs, transmitting messages from the space of earth to that of heaven. The advent of photography brought a new infusion of excitement over possible proof of the continued existence of the dead, and the technology was co-opted by Spiritualists almost as soon as it became available on a large scale. Spirit photographs flooded the market in an era when the cost of a "spirit-sitting" was three times the cost of a regular photograph. The public's appetite for the latest form of "proof" of the afterlife was insatiable. The appeal of spirit photography rested largely on the assumption that the camera is a more perfect eye than the human one. Photography was credited with absolute objectivity: Since it reproduced reality in ways that were recognizable, it could be trusted to do the same when what it reproduced was less familiar.

The implications of spirit photography for women were complex. On the one hand, photography literally served as an alternate "medium," one that was controlled by men. By creating static portraits of the dead, women were silenced both in life and in death: The male-dominated commercial field of photography served a similar function to that of the female-dominated field of mediumship, and photographs of both genders did not allow the dead the voice that they had in trance speaking. However, photographs of both corpses and spirits were immensely popular forms of enshrining memory, and the preservation of memory fell firmly within the domestic sphere during the Victorian period. Amid wreaths made from the hair of the dead and bronzed baby booties, women now had a new and more holistic memorial device to add to the relics of the dead that were commonly kept at the home.

Moreover, the majority of spirits photographed were women. Wives and daughters reappeared with their usually male relatives who had gone for a photographic sitting, thus reassuring the living of the continued bonds of the family past the time of death (Cox, 98–99). Spirit photography thus served to reinscribe the importance of the domestic sphere and women's continued fidelity to family. Women occasionally communicated about their own spirit photographs from beyond the grave, explaining the scientific process to their relatives. In one example, a wife explains the process to her husband: "Our thoughts produce our garments, the cut and coloring of the same, and the chemists, using their own magnetic power over the etherealised matter mould it so, and give to it an appearance such as we were in earth life" (Coates, 200). Women were thus in the peculiar situation of explaining scientific principles to men.

In a similar vein, the appearance of ectoplasm also gave women a voice in the scientific or pseudoscientific discourse of the day. Margery Crandon was the medium who first produced ectoplasm in America at a séance for the members of the *Scientific American Journal*. Margery also had the singular honor of being the cause of the lifelong and venomous dispute between Harry Houdini and Sir Arthur Conan Doyle, who disagreed about the authenticity of her mediumship (predictably, Houdini was the nonbeliever). *Ectoplasm* was the name given to a pliable, often gooey substance that was understood to be a residue from the spirit world. In Margery's case, this manifestation took the form of pseudopods, or strands of ectoplasm, produced from her navel, and one observer specifically referred to ectoplasm as an "umbilical cord," thereby linking mediumship with giving birth to the material of the beyond. Since Spiritualism was understood by believers to be truly empirical and a thoroughly scientific endeavor, it would not be overstating the case to say that these women were in fact giving birth to the discourse of science itself.

These new modes of spirit manifestations led to excesses that the public eventually proved unwilling to forgive. In addition to the loss of trust engendered by suspected charlatans, the spirit of optimism proved to be increasingly difficult to maintain in the years following the Civil War. As social problems seemed more intractable than ever and science and religion appeared to have parted ways, the ethos of progress took a fatal blow, and much of Spiritualism's hopefulness went down with it. Spiritualism would continue in myriad forms throughout the twentieth century, but its force as a religious movement proper would be lost by the first decades. Mediums continued to work and Spiritualist books continued to be published, but the true vitality of the movement would transmute into different expressions of religiosity.

Spiritualism's successors take a wide range of articulations from the religious to the secular. Perhaps foremost, many Spiritualists also subscribed to Theosophy, a movement begun by H. P. Blavatsky, herself a former medium, that posited that the truest knowledge of the world was secreted away in the writings of all cultures including that of the ancients. Blavatsky repudiated unconscious mediumship as unhealthy contact with low-level spirits, but she and other Theosophists continued to evince interest in mysterious powers and abilities latent within human nature, which they explored through meditation, yoga, and psychic phenomena. Psychoanalysis is also the unwitting heir to Spiritualism, which briefly provided an alternative interpretation of multiple personality disorders and hysteria, offering similar phenomena a more positive and religiously fecund understanding of women's experiences. The life force of Spiritualism continues today in televised mediumship and the numerous psychic services available to the general public. It is highly questionable, however, whether the modern manifestations of Spiritualism have the same regard and rewards for women as the radical and hopeful new movement had when it was young.

SOURCES: For the classic work on the Second Great Awakening, including a discussion of women as itinerant preachers, see Whitney Cross, *The Burned-Over District: The Social and Intellectual History of Enthusiastic Religion in Western New York,* 1800–1850 (1965). For the best discussion of the rise of the middle class and its effects on women, see Mary Ryan, *Cradle of the Middle Class: The Family in Oneida County, New York, 1790–1865* (1981). For the most extensive work on women and Spiritualism, see Ann Braude, *Radical Spirits: Spiritualism and Women's Rights in Nineteenth-Century America* (1989). For the background on Mesmerism, see Adam Crabtree, *From Mesmer to Freud: Magnetic Sleep and the Roots of Psychological Healing* (1993). For the definitive biography of Margaret Fox, and the one on which the author relies here, see Earl Wesley Fornell, *The Unhappy Medium: Spiritualism and the Life of Margaret Fox* (1964). See also Margaret Fox, *Memoir* (1866), and Cora L. V. Hatch, *Discourses on Religion, Morals, Philosophy, and Metaphysics* (1858). For extensive coverage of African Americans and Spiritualism, see John Patrick Deveney, *Paschal Beverly Randolph: A Nineteenth-Century Black American Spiritualist, Rosicrucian, and Sex Magician* (1997). For a typical example of Free Love writings, see Austin Kent, *Free Love: Or, a Philosophical Demonstration of the Non-Exclusive Nature of Connubial Love* (1857). For the gendered implications of spirit photography, see Robert S. Cox, "The Transportation of American Spirits: Gender, Spirit Photography, and American Culture, 1861–1880," *The Ephemera Journal* 7 (1994): 94–107. For a nineteenth-century account of spirit photography, see James Coates, *Photographing the Invisible: Practical Studies in Supernormal Photography, Script, and Allied Phenomena* (1921).

WOMEN IN THE NORTH AMERICAN BAHA'I COMMUNITY
Sandra Hutchinson and Richard Hollinger

THE BAHA'I FAITH was founded in the 1860s by Mirza Husayn Ali, a Persian nobleman known as Baha'u'llah (the Glory of God), who claimed to fulfill prophecies contained in all the world's major religious traditions of a divine messenger destined to inaugurate an era of world peace. Baha'u'llah began his religious leadership as a champion of the Babi Movement, a millenarian movement rooted in Shi'i Islam, that swept across Iran in the 1840s. His own teachings, which at once validated and transcended those of the Babi Movement, were characterized by their clear applications to modernity and by their global perspective. Not only did Baha'u'llah assert the validity of all the major world religions, but he also introduced new social teachings aimed at promoting world unity and social harmony: for example, the equality of the sexes; parliamentary governance and full civil rights for all people; education for all; a universal auxiliary language; a world monetary system and a global system of weights and measurements; and the elimination of prejudice based on race, religion, gender, nationality, ethnicity, or other social categories.

Baha'u'llah's teachings were elaborated upon by his son, 'Abdu'l-Baha and great-grandson Shoghi Effendi, both of whom inherited the leadership of the Baha'i world community and were the authorized interpreters of Baha'i scriptures. Their ministries spanned the years 1892 to 1921 and 1921 to 1957, respectively. Two aspects of Baha'u'llah's teachings in particular would exert a strong influence in shaping the role of women in the North American Baha'i community: first, Baha'u'llah's direct and repeated assertion that men and women had equal capacities; and second, his prohibition of a priesthood in the religion he had established. The absence of a priesthood militated against male domination of the administrative and pastoral functions in the community, while the teachings on gender equality ensured that all arenas of activity within the religion were open to women's participation. Because of these factors, and because they have traditionally composed the majority of the faith's adherents in the West, women have played not only a significant but often a dominant role in the development and maintenance of Baha'i communities.

In the late nineteenth century, the Baha'i Faith spread from Iran, its primary stronghold, to other parts of the Middle East as well as to East Asia, Russia, and North Africa. Confined mainly to Islamic enclaves in societies that were not predominantly Muslim, by the 1890s the Baha'i teachings had reached North America and, for the first time, claimed a significant number of converts from a Christian background. Like other small, non-Christian groups in North America, the Baha'is were, at first, few in number, transient in membership, and centered in major urban areas.

The Baha'i Faith was introduced in North America by Ibrahim Kheiralla, a Syrian Baha'i who immigrated to the United States in 1892 and began Baha'i classes. Kheiralla's presentation of the Baha'i teachings appealed to Western, Protestant students because it linked the history of the Baha'i Movement and the events of Baha'u'llah's life to biblical prophecies and because it portrayed ʿAbdu'l-Bahá, his son and successor, who was then living in Palestine, as Christ returned. Between 1895 and 1900, about 1,500 people in Chicago, New York, and several smaller cities became converts to the faith.

A number of women contributed to this process through the development, teaching, and promotion of the classes. Behind the scenes, Marian Miller, a veteran of various American metaphysical movements who married Ibrahim Kheiralla in 1895, played a significant role in the organization and presentation of the lessons. Maude Lamson, the secretary of the Chicago Baha'i group, maintained a national mailing list in order to notify potential students of upcoming classes in their area, carried on correspondence with people interested in the teachings, and helped organize new classes where there was sufficient demand for them. Eliza Talbot pub-

licized the classes in New York City through the New Thought networks of which she was a part, thereby contributing greatly to their success. Several Baha'i women taught the classes in various cities: Sarah Herron, in Philadelphia; Pearl Doty, in Baltimore; Mrs. W. G. Taylor in Cincinnati; and Lua Getsinger (née Moore, 1871–1916), in Ithaca, New York, as well as San Francisco and Washington, D.C.

One class taught by Lua Getsinger in 1898 had a significant impact on the nascent Baha'i community, as it led to the conversion of Phoebe Hearst, the widow of Senator George Hearst, who was well known for her philanthropy. Hearst played a key role in the establishment of the Baha'i Faith in North America by introducing the religion into elite social networks, by funding a number of Baha'i teachers and projects, and by bringing her philanthropic and business experience to bear on the shaping of what was then a loosely organized movement. One initiative she sponsored had a powerful and enduring impact not only on the handful of new American converts it directly touched but also on the evolution of the American Baha'i community as a whole: namely, a pilgrimage to Palestine that brought a number of new believers face to face with the leader of the Baha'i Faith, ʿAbdu'l-Bahá. Contact with ʿAbdu'l-Bahá proved transforming to these new believers and, through them, to the growing community in America. Not only did it give the new believers access to a more authoritative source of Baha'i doctrine than they had hitherto had, but this contact strengthened their commitment to their new faith and galvanized them to contribute to its expansion.

The pilgrimage also marked a signal point in the waning of Kheiralla's influence as he increasingly came into conflict with ʿAbdu'l-Bahá's interpretations of Baha'i doctrine. His growing defiance of ʿAbdu'l-Bahá's authority culminated, in 1901, in his break with the Baha'i community. However, Phoebe Hearst's financial support for other Baha'i teachers sent to North America by ʿAbdu'l-Bahá in 1900–1901 helped preserve the unity of the nascent Baha'i community during these events. Hearst was the first of a number of wealthy women who would leave their mark on the evolving Baha'i community. Women such as Laura Dreyfus-Barney (1879–1974), Agnes Parsons (1861–1937), Ella Cooper (1879–1951), and Amelia Collins (1873–1962) shaped the Baha'i community by financially supporting and guiding a wide range of undertakings, often without taking on a visible leadership role in them.

In the 1890s, organization in the Baha'i community was informal: The newly established local Baha'i groups elected or otherwise selected local officers when they felt they were needed. In the five locations for which records have survived, the community presidents were all men, while women served as secretaries in every community and held the positions of treasurer (New Jersey) and vice president (Kenosha, Wisconsin). In 1900, after Baha'u'llah's writings about community organization were translated, more formal consultative bodies were formed to oversee community affairs and to serve as the nucleus for community life. Some uncertainty among North American Baha'is as to whether or not women should serve on these bodies is reflected in their membership rolls: The first Chicago and Kenosha councils included women, but they were subsequently replaced by all-male bodies, which were soon in place in most other communities. A number of Baha'i women did, however, argue for a more public role for women in the community. As Corinne True, one of the leading Baha'is of Chicago, wrote: "Women in America stand so conspicuously for all that is highest & best in every department and for that reason it is contended the affairs should be in the hands of both sexes" (quoted in Stockman, 23).

True went on to spearhead the formation of an all-female council in Chicago that became known as the "Assembly of Teaching." Female Baha'i organizations were also formed in New York City and in other communities between 1901 and 1905. The rhetoric and activities of such bodies suggest that they were viewed as a "separate sphere for women." For example, Ida Brush, a member of the Assembly of Teaching, argued that the male and female councils had different functions and that if women interfered in the affairs of the male councils, "pure spirituality would cease." She continued:

We can liken this to the household—it is not home without the combined qualities of the husband and wife. The husband by his efforts provides the way and means for the home, the wife makes the home a haven of comfort and rest. (Quoted in Stockman, 18)

As is reflected in these remarks, the activities of such all-women bodies tended to follow a "social housekeeping" model, including the organization of meetings for the spread of the Baha'i teachings, the care of the sick in the community, the establishment of a school, and the pursuit of various philanthropic endeavors.

The practice of gender-specific councils began to be phased out in 1912 when 'Abdu'l-Bahá, then on a speaking tour of North America, asked that the male council in Chicago be disbanded and a new one elected. The new council was composed of both male and female members. Subsequently, all such bodies, which became known as "Local Spiritual Assemblies," were open to women. As of 1995, membership on these assemblies in the United States was 56 percent female, with 79 percent

of the secretaries and 40 percent of the chairpersons being women.

On the next tier of Baha'i community administration stands the National Spiritual Assembly (NSA). The first such body in North America had jurisdiction over both the United States and Canada. It evolved from the Executive Board of the Baha'i Temple Unity, which was formed in 1907 to oversee the construction of the Baha'i House of Worship in Wilmette, but it gradually assumed broader responsibilities, and in 1926 it was renamed the National Spiritual Assembly of the United States and Canada. As a result of the growth of the Baha'i population, in 1948 separate assemblies were formed in Canada and in the United States.

A sampling of the membership on the NSA of the United States since 1948 indicates that 36 percent of its members were women. The average female membership on the Canadian NSA between 1948 and 1994 was 24 percent, although in 1994 women were in the majority. It is difficult to accurately gauge the influence of individual women within these bodies, since their deliberations are not public and members have no individual authority. However, because their responsibilities gave them extensive contact with Baha'is in many localities, some National Assembly officers have clearly had a significant influence in shaping the community. For example, Charlotte Linfoot, the assistant secretary of the NSA in the late 1950s and early 1960s, carried on much of the correspondence of the National Spiritual Assembly and was probably the most prominent American Baha'i during this period. And Dorothy Nelson, who recently served as chair and vice chair of the National Assembly of the United States and who was its treasurer for many years, is undoubtedly one of the more influential Baha'i women in the country.

Another arm of Baha'i administration, referred to by Shoghi Effendi as the "learned branch," was inaugurated in North America in the 1950s. In 1951, Shoghi Effendi appointed a number of "Hands of the Cause of God" to take special responsibility for promulgating the religion and for educating its adherents about the Baha'i teachings, functions that were later carried on by the "Continental Boards of Counselors," first appointed in 1968. In 1952, the Hands of the Cause introduced another tier to the "learned branch" by appointing Auxiliary Board Members to assist them in their work, and in 1973, the members of these Auxiliary Boards began to appoint their own assistants.

The persons appointed to these positions have generally played prominent roles in the Baha'i community through public speaking and teaching classes at Baha'i schools, as well as through writing and publishing. Of the thirty-two Hands of the Cause appointed by Shoghi Effendi throughout the world in the 1950s, five were

North American women: his wife Amatu'l-Baha Ruhi-yyih Khanum (née Mary Maxwell), Amelia Collins, Corinne True, Agnes Alexander, and Dorothy Baker. Since its inception, the average female composition of the Auxiliary Board in North America has been 43 percent. There are no parallel statistics available for the numbers of women who have served as assistant Auxilary Board Members, but the trend in all three tiers of the learned branch is toward the greater participation by women. A 1995 survey of all those in the learned branch worldwide indicated that women made up almost half (47 percent) of the membership, a percentage that is likely to be higher in North America, where the participation of women in the Baha'i Faith has always been higher.

Recruitment of new members, referred to as "teaching the Faith" or "spreading the Message," has been the central focus of Baha'i activities since the religion was established in North America. Between 1900 and 1930, the number of Baha'is in the United States and Canada remained fairly static, at somewhere between 1,500 and 2,000. As of the 1930s, the Baha'i population began to grow as a result of the launching of a series of multiyear plans for the expansion of the faith, which were overseen by the National Spiritual Assembly. Updated usually every few years, these plans continue to serve as the focus of activity in the Baha'i community and have generated significant growth, leaving North America with 150,000 Baha'is and thousands of local communities by the end of the twentieth century. In 1946, the plans began incorporating goals relating to the establishment of the religion in other parts of the world. Largely as a result of these concerted and ongoing efforts, the Baha'i Faith has now spread to virtually every country in the world and claims about 6 million adherents.

In the early decades of the twentieth century, the main method of recruitment was through public speaking: formal lectures; classes; and informal meetings in homes, called "firesides." In the absence of a paid clergy, these efforts were undertaken by lay teachers and, as one history of the period recounts, "as soon as it was known that a Baha'i could speak in groups, that Baha'i was invited to nearby cities, and many a fireside group was confirmed this way" (*The Baha'i Centenary*). A survey of North American Baha'i communities conducted in 1938 identified 149 such teachers, 85 (65 percent) of whom were women. While the majority of these people were associated with teaching in one or two localities, a few played a significant role on the regional and national scene. For example, in the early years of the twentieth century, two very different Baha'i women came to the fore: Lua Getsinger, a forceful speaker trained in the theater, who traveled extensively on the West and East Coasts of the United States as well as in Europe and India; and Isabella Brittingham, the wife of a railroad employee from New Jersey, who visited almost every Baha'i community in North America. Several other women played important roles on the regional level in the formation of new Baha'i communities: Fanny Knobloch (1859–1949), a Baha'i from Washington, D.C., was active on the East Coast and Midwest of the United States in the 1920s and 1930s; Elizabeth Greenleaf (1863–1941), a widow from Chicago, traveled in the midwestern and southwestern states in the 1910s to 1930s; and Mary Hanford Ford (1856–1937), an author and literary critic, lectured in numerous cities and towns in North America and Europe in the 1930s.

Several women are especially noteworthy for single-handedly establishing new Baha'i communities: Ruth Moffett (1880–1978) and Orcella Rexford (d. 1946), both professional lecturers, as well as Mabel Ives (1878–1943), the wife of a Unitarian minister. These women usually gave public lectures on then-popular topics, such as diet, the pyramids, and theories of color, and then they invited their audiences to attend a series of classes on the Baha'i Faith. Sometimes hundreds of students attended these classes. Staying in a town for weeks, or even months at a time, to complete the classes, they recruited groups of new adherents and, in this way, established Baha'i communities in a number of localities.

Several other women deserve mention for their extensive international lecture tours. Martha Root (1872–1939), a Baha'i from Pittsburgh who supported herself as a freelance journalist, traveled the world almost continuously from 1919 until her death in 1939. Described by Shoghi Effendi as the "archetype of Baha'i itinerant teachers" (Effendi, 386), Root traveled through Asia, Europe, and North America several times. She also toured Australia and South America, giving lectures and speaking with people from all walks of life about the Baha'i teachings. One of the more dramatic results of her efforts was the conversion of Queen Marie of Romania, the first monarch to become a Baha'i. Mrs. Keith Ransom Kehler (d. 1933) began travel-teaching in the United States and Canada in the late 1920s and then undertook an extensive international trip in the 1930s that took her through Asia, Australia, New Zealand, South America, and Africa, ending only with her death in Iran in 1933. Lorol Schopflocher (1886–1970), a Baha'i from Montreal, began her international travels to spread the Baha'i Faith in the late 1920s, eventually traveling around the world nine times and visiting eighty-six countries. Finally, Amatu'l-Baha, in 1957, after the death of her husband Shoghi Effendi, the hereditary head of the faith, traveled extensively for several decades, visiting virtually every country of the world. Her travels are unique in that at an advanced age she undertook extended trips into the rural areas of the developing world, including a boat trip through the Amazon jungle, a two-year safari across Africa, and visits to rural villages on every continent. Her journeys inspired other Baha'is to travel and to settle in these areas, and they drew attention, within the Baha'i community, to the conditions of Baha'is residing in rural areas of the developing world.

Teaching took another form in the work of lay missionaries, known as "pioneers," who settled in a new location either permanently or for an extended period of time, in order to establish new Baha'i communities. Probably the first North American to do this was May Maxwell (née Bolles, 1873–1941), an American who became a Baha'i in Paris in 1898. At the request of ʿAbdu'l-Bahá, she remained in Paris until 1902, by which time she had formed a Baha'i group there. She then moved to Montreal, where she established another Baha'i community. Near the end of her life, she moved again, this time to Argentina for the same purpose. Alma Knobloch (1864–1943), a German American Baha'i from Washington, D.C., moved to Stuttgart in 1907 and remained there until 1920, establishing Baha'i communities in several German cities during that period. Fanny Knobloch, the sister of Alma, moved to Capetown, South Africa, living there from 1923 to 1926, with the purpose of establishing the religion. Agnes Alexander (1875–1971), a Baha'i from Honolulu, moved to Japan in 1914 and resided there intermittently until 1967, by which time she had established the Baha'i Faith in that country.

By the late 1930s, "pioneering"—that is, the practice of settling in locations where there were no other Baha'is—was the dominant method of spreading the Baha'i religion. Between the years 1937 and 1948, scores of Canadian Baha'is settled in new localities in Canada, 66 percent of them being women. Many of these women remained unmarried because there were few Baha'is for them to marry, if they chose to marry within their religion. In 1948, 134 Americans volunteered to pioneer within the United States. Of these volunteers, 69 were women and at least 19 were single women.

In the 1940s and in subsequent decades, many women also pioneered internationally, a service that was greatly lauded in the Baha'i scriptures and romanticized within the Baha'i community. Dorothy Baker (1898–1954), a prominent American Baha'i, summarized the experience of those who moved overseas to spread the Baha'i Faith as follows:

> Pioneering is ecstasy and tears; bad food, cold rooms, dark pensions, and periods of fruitless waiting; yearning souls, sudden illumination . . . and new conviction of the "power that is far beyond the ken of men and angels." (Baker, 9)

Between 1953 and 1963 about 250 Baha'is, mostly from Iran and North America, moved to new countries to establish the Baha'i Faith in "virgin territories." About half of these pioneers were women, but almost all the seventy-seven single women and most of the married couples had Western names, suggesting that North American women formed a significant percentage of this group. Furthermore, when couples pioneered, most of the actual work of spreading the religion was done by the women, since the men were usually occupied with earning a living.

It would be impossible here even to name those women who made significant contributions in this area, but two women who have been recognized as models within the Baha'i community should be mentioned: Ella Bailey (1865–1953) and Marion Jack (1866–1954). A retired schoolteacher who, at the age of eighty-eight, while she was in ill health and against the advice of friends, made the decision to settle in Tripoli, Ella Bailey explained her motivation, saying, "I do not find it such a sacrifice to give up living in a rest home" (*Baha'i World* 12, 686). Bailey died shortly after her arrival in Tripoli and was hailed as a martyr by Shoghi Effendi. A Canadian artist, who settled in Sofia, Bulgaria, Marion Jack remained at her "pioneering post" throughout most of World War II, despite the danger from the war and the threat of imprisonment because she held a British passport. After a brief evacuation, she returned to Sofia, residing there until her death. In a letter to a relative written following the war, she wrote: "Thank God I am able to help some people spiritually. . . . This is my compensation, and if I can only help people to renew their faith in God, I shall be more than grateful" (*Marion Jack: Immortal Heroine*, 11). These women and others inspired later generations of North American Baha'i pioneers.

Baha'i women have also played a dominant role in developing Baha'i communities. There is little doubt that, at the local level, women, more than men, have organized and hosted meetings, produced newsletters, maintained communications within the community, and engaged in other community-building activities. One clear indication of this is the extremely high percentage of women who have held the position of secretary of the Local Spiritual Assembly, a position that involves taking primary responsibility for internal and external communications. At a regional level, Baha'i women have been active in a number of endeavors that have fostered Baha'i identity and group cohesion, such as schools; the writing, production, and distribution of literature; the creation and performance of art; and the construction of a Baha'i House of Worship.

In the early decades of the twentieth century, summer schools where Baha'is and others could go to study the Baha'i teachings during vacations evolved into a popular institution in North America. One woman, Sarah Jane Farmer, had a singularly important role in their devel-

In 1939 the National Spiritual Assembly appointed a Race Unity Committee. One woman who made a major contribution to such efforts was Dorothy Baker, who traveled through the South from 1941 to 1942 to visit and speak at some thirty and, in the following year, fifty colleges. *Used by permission of the National Spiritual Assembly of the Bahais of the United States.*

opment, as she conceived of and established what was to become the first Baha'i summer school. In the 1890s, Farmer began using a resort hotel in Eliot, Maine, known as Green Acre, as a venue for conferences on progressive religious and social ideas, inviting leading thinkers to speak there, among them W. E. B. DuBois, Swami Vivekananda, John Greenleaf Whittier, Rabbi Silverman, Edward Everett Hale, Paul Carus, and Booker T. Washington. Eventually, Green Acre became known for its tolerant atmosphere and evolved into a center for the exploration of unconventional religious ideas.

Farmer learned of the Baha'i Faith in 1899, probably from Phoebe Hearst, who was an early supporter of Green Acre. When Farmer became a Baha'i in 1900, her vision for Green Acre began to change, as is reflected in the following excerpt from one of her letters:

My joy in the "Persian Revelation" [the Baha'i Faith] is not that it reveals *one* of the streams flowing to the Great Ocean of light, life and love, but that it is the perfect mirror of that Ocean. What, in Green Acre, was a vision and a hope becomes, through it a *blessed reality* now. It has illuminated for me every other expression of truth." (*Green Acre on the Piscataqua*, 34)

Reflecting her new allegiance to the religion, the programs at the school featured, with increasing prominence, Baha'i lecturers and teachers, until some of the early supporters of Green Acre began to oppose Farmer, feeling she had betrayed the original mission of the school. A rift between the Baha'is and the other supporters of Green Acre finally ensued, and the school became unapologetically Baha'i.

Eventually, Green Acre came to be viewed as paradigmatic of a Baha'i institution, inspiring the development of other schools. In 1927, another school was begun in Geyserville, California. John and Louise Bosch donated the property for this school, while Amelia Collins provided funding for improvements, such as an auditorium. In 1931, a Baha'i school was also established in Davison, Michigan, on property donated by Helen and L. W. Eggleston. Women have played a prominent role in all these schools, both as administrators and as teachers.

Another endeavor in which a woman, Corinne True, played the critical role was in the construction of a Baha'i House of Worship outside of Chicago. The idea of building a House of Worship for the Chicago community was not hers, but her zealous advocacy for and involvement in the project shaped the outcome to such an extent that she became known as the "Mother of the Temple." Originally conceived as a modest structure to serve as a center for the Chicago Baha'i community, a group no larger than a small church congregation, it evolved into a magnificent and innovative specimen of architecture that continues to be an important Baha'i symbol throughout North America.

True realized that the relatively small Baha'i community of Chicago could not undertake the project on its own and helped to organize a gathering for North American Baha'is to discuss and mobilize support for the project. The first convocation of Baha'is in North America, the convention became an annual event and led to the formation of the first regional Baha'i association: the Baha'i Temple Unity. True was elected to the Executive Board and served as its financial secretary for more than a decade. In this capacity she worked for decades to fund-raise and promote an expansive vision for the House of Worship. Of the House of Worship, she wrote:

> Will it not become a visiting point for all nations and people throughout centuries and cycles? The inflow thus produced will return an outflow of vitalizing spiritual influence and its accessories will shed the light of the highest sciences, arts and crafts and the most magnanimous works of charity and hospitality. (Rutstein, 93)

Women made one of their earliest and most substantial contributions to the Baha'i community through the production and distribution of literature. For several decades, much Baha'i literature, including some Baha'i scriptures, was available only in typescript. Mary Lesch (d. 1945), one of a number of women who typed and circulated these materials, recalled that copies of scrip-

tures "were made in large numbers and passed around among the friends [Baha'is]" (Lesch, 2).

Financing for some of the first Baha'i publications was provided by Phoebe Hearst, who backed the first Baha'i publishing organization, founded in 1900 and now known as the Baha'i Publishing Trust. For the first twenty-four years of its life, sales and book distribution for the publisher were handled by two women volunteers, Mary Agnew and Mary Lesch. Remembering the pioneering nature of that early venture, Lesch wrote:

> Oh! that some of the present day friends could know of the faith and assurance that came with it, of those days. . . . I knew nothing of the work before attempting it, but only with the help of God and possibly some little business sense and experience, tided me over those happy but trying days. (Lesch, 2)

Between 1924 and 1928, several other women volunteers assisted with this work, under the aegis of the Publishing Committee of the National Spiritual Assembly. In 1928, Marion Little (1891–1973) was named secretary of that same body and, as such, began overseeing the publishing operation, while, until 1943, the day-to-day operations were managed by Clara R. Wood. The efforts of these women appear to have increased the production and distribution of publications. The press distributed more than 100,000 titles per year in the 1930s and early 1940s, a remarkable accomplishment considering that no more than 5,000 Baha'is in North America constituted most of the market for English-language Baha'i books during this period. Eunice Braun was managing director of the Baha'i Publishing Trust from 1955 to 1971. Probably the most influential editor of the press in the twentieth century, Dr. Betty Fisher (b. 1935) served as general editor between 1971 and the late 1990s. Demanding a high standard of English, consistency in the transliteration of Arabic and Persian (the original languages of Baha'i scriptures), and the careful documentation of quotations and facts, Fisher's meticulous editing set the standard for English-language Baha'i publishing and helped shape the Baha'i discourse of the period.

In addition to book publishing, women also made an important contribution to the publication of Baha'i newsletters and journals. The most successful of the early Baha'i periodicals, *Star of the West*, evolved from the efforts of Gertrude Buikema to convey community news by means of circular letters and extensive personal correspondence. Initially, Buikema served as the managing editor and then coeditor of the magazine, which was published from 1910 to 1921. From 1919 to 1924, Ella Robarts published and distributed the *Magazine of the Children of the Kingdom,* the first Baha'i serial for children. In more recent decades, beginning in 1968, Betty Fisher has served as editor of *World Order*, a Baha'i scholarly journal; Renee Knight-Weiller has been the main editor of *The Spiritual Mothering Journal*, which began publication in 1985 and focuses on the spiritual aspects of child rearing.

Women also made significant contributions to Baha'i literature as authors, translators, and transcribers. For example, during 'Abdu'l-Bahá's 1911–1912 visit to America, several women stenographically recorded the English translations of his talks in different localities: Esther Foster and Emma C. Melick in the New York area; Marzieh Moss and Gertrude Buikema in Chicago; Edna McKinney (d. 1930) in Philadelphia, Boston, and Eliot, Maine; and Bijou Straun in the San Francisco Bay Area. These transcriptions were compiled into a book, *The Promulgation of Universal Peace* (1921), a widely used publication that touches upon many areas of Baha'i doctrine.

Another important book, *Some Answered Questions*, grew out of interviews with 'Abdu'l-Bahá conducted by Laura Dreyfus-Barney in Haifa between 1904 and 1906 and recorded in Persian by his secretaries. The Persian transcripts were translated into English by Barney and first published in 1908. The publication is one of the most important English-language Baha'i texts, which contains detailed answers to a wide variety of metaphysical questions and includes extensive explications of biblical passages.

Among the translators of Baha'i writings, one woman, Marzieh Gail (1908–1993), stands out as the foremost figure of the twentieth century. Her translations of Baha'i scriptures include *The Seven Valleys and the Four Valleys* (1945), *The Secret of Divine Civilization* (1957), and the *Kitab-i-Aqdas* (Book of Laws), which was not published but was widely circulated in typescript during her lifetime. She also translated *My Memories of Baha'u'llah* (1982), the memoirs of Baha'u'llah's barber, and assisted with the translation of other writings of 'Abdu'l-Bahá, such as *Memorials of the Faithful* (1971) and *Selections from the Writings of 'Abdu'l-Bahá* (1976). Also known for her work as an essayist and memoirist, Gail was one of the most prominent Baha'i woman writers of her generation. Her publications include *Dawn over Mount Hira* (1976), a collection of literary essays, as well as several books of personal recollections: *Khanum: The Greatest Holy Leaf* (1981), *Other People, Other Places* (1982), *Summon Up Remembrance* (1987), and *Arches of the Years* (1991). All these publications explore the central preoccupation of her literary as well as her personal life: the union of East and West.

One of the earliest and most widely read forms of literature generated by Baha'i women in North America is a unique and compelling form of memoir known as "pilgrim's notes." Based on informal diary jottings, the notes recount interviews and meetings with the then-head of the faith, 'Abdu'l-Bahá. Often framed by gripping accounts of personal transformation as a result of contact with 'Abdu'l-Bahá, many such pilgrim's accounts attempt to set down 'Abdu'l-Bahá's explanations of the teachings and writings of the Baha'i Faith. Though pilgrim's diaries do not represent an authoritative source of Baha'i doctrine, such accounts are significant as historical documents and hold value as inspirational literature.

Lua Getsinger, a member of the first Western pilgrim party to visit 'Abdu'l-Bahá in Palestine, is thought to have authored the first pilgrim's account in the form of a letter that was circulated among the Baha'is in 1899. May Maxwell, another member of that party, wrote a better-known account published under the title *An Early Pilgrimage*. In the following excerpt, she describes her first encounter with 'Abdu'l-Bahá in 1899:

Of that first meeting I can remember neither joy nor pain nor anything that I can name. I had been carried suddenly to too great a height; my soul had come into contact with the Divine Spirit; and this force so pure, so holy, so mighty, had overwhelmed me. (Maxwell, 12)

The form found more sophisticated expression in the 1911–1913 diary of Greenwich Village artist Juliet Thompson, one of the most colorful figures to come into contact with 'Abdu'l-Bahá during the prewar period. A book-length account of her various meetings with 'Abdu'l-Bahá in Europe, Palestine, and America, "The Diary of Juliet Thompson" contains a deeply personal record of her own spiritual awakening and transformation. The literary character of the diary can be seen in passages such as this one recounting her first meeting with 'Abdu'l-Bahá:

Suddenly my heart burst open to the outpouring from His Heart, like a rose beneath strong sunbeams. A beam seemed to pierce my heart. At that instant He flashed a lightning glance at me. When He left the room, as he did almost at once, my breast dilated as if a bird were spreading wings in it. (Thompson, 18–19)

Thompson's passionate discipleship of 'Abdu'l-Bahá is mirrored in *I, Mary Magdalene* (1940), a novel in which she imagines the relationship between Jesus and Mary Magdalene. The text of the novel is illustrated by her own sketches, which depict 'Abdu'l-Bahá as Jesus and herself as Mary. In addition to writing most of the pilgrim's accounts, Baha'i women of this early period also authored some introductory books on the Baha'i Faith:

Isabella Brittingham wrote *The Revelation of Baha-Ullah in a Sequence of Four Lessons* (1903), and Mary Hanford Ford, *The Oriental Rose or the Teachings of Abdul Baha* (1910).

Only a few other book-length publications were written by North American Baha'i women in the first half of the twentieth century. Penned by world traveler and journalist Martha Root, one of these works was a biography of the renowned Persian poet and Babi martyr Tahirih. Titled *Tahirih the Pure: Iran's Greatest Woman* (1938), Root's book is the first biography to be written by a Western Baha'i woman about one of her Eastern sisters. As such, the book stands not only as a pioneering effort to comprehend Root's life but also as a fascinating intercultural document. "My soul thrilled to understand her!" Root is quoted as saying (26). What follows is not only the story of Tahirih's life but also the tale of Root's own journey to the very roots of the Baha'i Faith in Iran and of her discovery of the rich culture, literary and religious, out of whose matrix it was born.

In the 1930s, Ruhiyyih Khanum, named Amatu'l-Baha by her husband Shoghi Effendi, emerged as a writer with the publication of a literary commentary on a history of a Babi movement, *Nabil's Narrative* (1932), titled "The Reflorescence of Historical Romance in Nabil." Over the decades, Amatu'l-Baha continued to write and publish across the genres, always in response to "a need perceived at the time" (Interview with Amatu'l-Baha, 1995). Her works include essays, poetry, plays, circular letters, history, and a full-length biography of her husband.

Amatu'l-Baha will perhaps best be remembered for her meticulously researched and movingly rendered biography of Shoghi Effendi, *The Priceless Pearl* (1969), as well as for her heartrending volume of lyric poems about Shoghi Effendi's death, *Poems of the Passing* (1996). Drawn from eyewitness accounts, personal diary entries, and historical documents; and given life by a rich dialogue of voices, both private and public, the portrait of Shoghi Effendi that emerges in *The Priceless Pearl* will undoubtedly remain unique in its ability to evoke the multifaceted personality of the late guardian of the Baha'i Faith. Similarly, her volume of intensely personal poems, documenting her own response to her husband's sudden and unexpected death, powerfully evoke an historical event so tragic that her transmutation of that loss emerges in the poems as an act of singular courage and sustained heroism.

In the 1980s, a number of Baha'is began to apply academic methodologies to the study of Baha'i writings and history, an approach that has generated a new form of Baha'i discourse. In addition to the contributions made by a steadily growing contingent of Baha'i women scholars to the academic study of the Baha'i Faith in a wide range of disciplines, from Women's studies to Middle Eastern history, the work of Christine Zerbinis, for many years the general secretary of the Association of Baha'i Studies, must be mentioned. By overseeing a wide variety of scholarly endeavors and publications, including the annual conference of the association, she was instrumental in creating a network of scholars interested in Baha'i studies and in fostering a milieu congenial to the growth of studies about the Baha'i Faith.

Women have also played an important role in the production of children's literature, both magazines and books. Not only have Baha'i women served as editors of children's magazines and authored a wide variety of children's books, both educational and imaginative; they have also played a key role as administrators of various bodies, such as the Educational Task Force, which continue to be devoted to ensuring that an ever-growing corpus of literature based on Baha'i themes and celebrating Baha'i history and experience is available to foster religious identity and a sense of community among Baha'i children. Aimed at producing a wide range of stories about the central figures of the Baha'i Faith, the Storybook Project, currently under way, is only one example of such undertakings.

During the first half of the twentieth century it was primarily in the field of literature that Baha'i women distinguished themselves. Only a few women visual artists emerged during these years, among them Greenwich Village artist Juliet Thompson and the little-known Canadian painter Marion Jack (1866–1954). The rich artistic legacy of portrait painter Juliet Thompson continues to be appreciated by Baha'is the world over in the form of a portrait of ʿAbdu'l-Bahá, in pastels, which took three half-hour sittings to complete.

Musicians, too, were few in the early part of the century. Louise Waite, a woman with no formal music training, was a composer and a leader of the "Vahid Chorale Society," the first North American Baha'i choir. Composing songs with a piano and voice, she hired others to transcribe her compositions. Waite revised Christian hymns, giving them Baha'i themes, and also wrote original compositions. Although others wrote Baha'i hymns, hers were by far the most popular, being widely used in the North American Baha'i community and beyond. One composition in particular, known as the "Baha'i Benediction," enjoyed such popularity that one contemporary Baha'is described the work as *pure and soul refreshing* music," while other listeners expressed these sentiments: "It brings such a wonderful peace into my heart"; "It carried me out into the great spaces nearer to God"; and "It penetrated the whole assembly . . . and bound us into one strong brotherhood" (Armstrong-Ingram, *Music, Devotions, and Mashriqu'l-Adhkar*, 77–80). The piece was used to open and close Baha'i meetings throughout North America until the use of Baha'i hymns fell out of fashion in the 1940s.

In the 1970s, new forms of Baha'i music began to take shape through the compositions and performances of Joan Lincoln, Mary Davis, and other artists who were influenced by the folk music that was then popular. Another woman, Mimi McClellan, pioneered musical comedy in a series of productions about Baha'i community life, such as "Every Friday Night" and "The Education of Henry Halifax." She has also composed children's songs, an opera on Tahirih, and settings for Baha'i scriptures.

Since the 1980s, Baha'i women have produced a large and diverse body of artistic work. Works in every genre—settings of Baha'i scriptures, classical music, jazz, youth dance workshops based on contemporary rap music, poetry, and quilting, to name only some—reflect a flowering of the arts in the Baha'i community in the last years of the twentieth century. One signal event, the Baha'i World Congress, convened in 1992 in New York City, served as an important catalyst to the production of dramatic and musical arts, bringing these arts to a new level of professionalism and raising the consciousness of the Baha'i community as to their importance in the presentation of the Baha'i Faith and its teachings.

In conclusion, in the fields of music, dance, visual art, theater, folk art, literature, architecture, and scholarship, Baha'i women have sought to integrate the teachings of Baha'u'llah into an artistic expression that with its celebratory tone and life-affirming themes stands apart from the searching, often iconoclastic expressions of modernism and postmodernism. The results are difficult at such close range to tally, but it can be said that the Baha'i belief that artistic work undertaken in the spirit of service constitutes an act of worship is clearly reflected in the wide range of media being explored by contemporary Baha'i women artists.

From the beginning, Baha'is in North America, both men and women, have put their social teachings into practice in the wider society by sponsoring social and economic development projects, by contributing to existing organizations and like-minded movements, and by creating new institutions to stimulate social change. North American Baha'is have consistently sought to facilitate the advancement of women, viewing it as one of the most important prerequisites for the achievement of world peace.

Another Baha'i social principle women within the community have actively promoted throughout the twentieth century is the elimination of racism. 'Abdu'l-Bahá was uncompromising in his opposition to racial segregation and, during the early years of the twentieth century, strongly encouraged Baha'is to integrate their own meetings wherever possible. During his visit to North America in 1912, he set an unforgettable example by bringing an uninvited black man to a dinner with white socialites, by refusing to stay in hotels that blacks could not visit, and by holding large public integrated meetings. In 1920, he instructed Agnes Parsons (1861–1934), a wealthy white socialite from Washington, D.C., then a very segregated city, to organize a convention for "the amity of the colored and the white." She wrote: "I thought I would like to go through the floor, because I did not feel I could do it" (Morrison, 136). But Parsons overcame the conventions set down by race and class and used her social position to organize and promote a Racial Amity Convention that was held in Washington, D.C., in 1921. Later, Parsons, along with other women such as Mariam Haney (1872–1965) and Pauline Hannen, helped to organize similar conventions and related activities that were held periodically in a variety of cities until the 1930s.

In 1939, the National Spiritual Assembly appointed a Race Unity Committee, which carried on similar activities in the 1940s. One woman who made a major contribution to such efforts was Dorothy Baker (1898–1954) by traveling through the South in 1941–1942 to visit and speak at some thirty colleges and, in the following year, fifty colleges. In the 1950s, Baha'i race unity activities became institutionalized by the establishment of Race Amity Day (later changed to Race Unity Day), a day on which Baha'is throughout the United States hold events in conjunction with other like-minded groups to encourage racial unity and draw attention to the issue of racial prejudice.

With such a deep commitment to racial unity, Baha'is were inevitably drawn into the civil rights movement. Although Baha'is rarely participated in activities as an organized group, individual Baha'is protested segregation in the 1950s and 1960s, and a few played significant roles in mobilizing support for the movement. Dr. Sarah Pereira, a professor at Tennessee State University and a prominent black Baha'i woman, encouraged her students to participate in sit-ins and organized their participation in one of the marches. Several Baha'i women were friends of the Martin Luther King family and are reported to have supported the civil rights protests in a number of ways behind the scenes. Baha'is have also been active participants in the National Association for the Advancement of Colored People (NAACP), the Urban League, and similar organizations, where they continue their work for race unity.

Efforts by Baha'i women to advance the social position of women have extended beyond North America. One of the earliest endeavors of this sort was undertaken by a handful of professional Baha'i women from the United States who settled in Iran to offer medical and educational services to women there. Two doctors, Susan Moody (1851–1934) and Sarah Clock (d. 1922), as well as a nurse, Elizabeth Stewart, settled in Tehran in the early part of the twentieth century to provide services to women in a Baha'i hospital. Moody also established a private clinic. Providing modern medical services that were not commonly available to women in Iran at that time, the Baha'i medical professionals were in great demand, and their presence had a significant impact on the capital, Tehran, by increasing the availability of modern medical care to women there. Stewart left Iran in 1924, but both Clock and Moody remained in Iran until their deaths in 1922 and 1934, respectively.

Lillian Kappes, another American Baha'i, was recruited to direct a Baha'i school for girls in Tehran. Kappes died in Iran in 1920, and her position was filled briefly, from 1922 to 1924, by Genevieve Coy (b. 1886). In 1929, Adelaide Sharpe took over the directorship of the school and held that position until 1934, when the school was closed by the government. Sharpe remained in Iran until her death in 1976, serving the Baha'i community there in various administrative capacities.

Throughout this past century, North American Baha'is have given high priority to the achievement of gender equality within their own community, primarily through educational activities and publications. In the United States, these efforts have received institutional support in the form of a national Office of Women's Affairs, a National Committee for Equality, and a 1997 position statement on gender equality issued by the National Spiritual Assembly of the United States. Baha'i institutions have also consistently supported the advancement of women outside the Baha'i community, through their offices at the United Nations and through the External Affairs Office of the National Spiritual Assembly of the United States. As would be expected, women have played a leading role in these endeavors.

Responding to Baha'u'llah's teaching that an international auxiliary language was essential to a unified world, a number of Baha'is, many of them women, have promoted the use of Esperanto, as well as the less popular Interlingua. One of the most influential advocates for Esperanto was Martha Root, who promulgated its use and met with Esperantists in many countries during her extensive world travels in the 1920s and 1930s. Other Baha'i women pioneers, such as Agnes Alexander in Japan, also encouraged its use in the countries in which they had settled.

Another way in which women within the community have supported the Baha'i vision of a unified world is through their ongoing support for institutions that foster international cooperation. In 1926, an International Baha'i Bureau was opened in Geneva to act as a liaison with the League of Nations and other international organizations. Its operations were managed by three American women in succession: Emogene Hoagg (1869–1945), Julia Culver (1861–1950), and Helen Bishop. Laura Dreyfus-Barney, a prominent American Baha'i residing in Paris, was a leading member active in the In-

ternational Council of Women from the 1920s to the 1960s. She served as the council's representative to the League of Nations and president of its Peace and Arbitration Commission; after World War II, Dreyfus-Barney helped to develop relations between the United Nations Children's Fund (UNICEF) and various nongovernmental organizations (NGOs) represented at the United Nations.

When the United Nations was established in New York, the Baha'is, in turn, opened a liaison office in New York known as the Baha'i International Community. Mildred Mottahedeh (1908–2000) served as first community representative to the United Nations, a position she occupied from 1948 to 1967, acting as a spokesperson for the Baha'i community on a variety of issues. From 1972 to 1977, Mary Powers worked at the Baha'i International Community, holding the positions of executive assistant, representative, and director of the Office for the Advancement of Women. Wilma Ellis, an African American Baha'i, served as administrator general of the Baha'i International Community from 1986 to 1996.

Finally, Baha'i women have founded several organizations devoted to social and economic development and to the advancement of women. For example, in 1958, Mildred Mottahedeh and her husband established a foundation, now known as Mottahedeh Development Services, which funded some of the earliest economic development projects initiated by Baha'is and contributed to their continued growth. Since the 1980s, social and economic development has become the focus of considerable Baha'i activity, with thousands of projects now under way worldwide. Founded by Juana Conrad in 1985, the Women's International League for Peace and Arbitration aims to encourage the arbitration of international disputes and to encourage women to be involved in international peace efforts. The Women's International League for Peace and Arbitration has initiated a number of programs, such as the "Spring Bud Program," a program that provides education to girls in China who because of their poverty would otherwise drop out of school. The Tahirih Justice Center, which provides legal assistance to women facing gender-based discrimination, was founded by Layli Miller Bashir, a Baha'i lawyer, in the wake of her success in obtaining a grant of asylum for Fauziyah Kassindja, a seventeen-year-old African girl who fled to the United States to avoid female genital mutilation.

In conclusion, Baha'i women have played a significant role in all areas of Baha'i activity in North America. In some endeavors, such as Baha'i publishing and the recruitment of new members, women have predominated, and in certain arenas, such as the development of Baha'i schools, individual women have made singularly important contributions. Without the contributions of North American women, it is doubtful the Baha'i Faith would have become what it is today: one of the most global of the world's religions. And in those arenas in which women are less well represented, the trend is toward ever greater female participation, as Baha'is struggle to manifest, in all aspects of their lives, Baha'u'llah's teachings on gender equality.

SOURCES: There are several academic articles discussing Baha'i women in North America: Gwen Etter-Lewis, "African-American Women in the American Bahá'í Faith, 1899–1919," *World Order*, 25.2 (1993–1994): 41–57; Robert H. Stockman, "Women in the American Baha'i Community, 1900–1912," *World Order* 25.2 (1993–1994): 17–34; Susan Maneck, "Women in the Baha'i Faith," in *Religion and Women*, ed. Arvind Sharma (1994); and Jackson Armstrong-Ingram, "A Question of Gender," in *Equal Circles: Women and Men in the Baha'i Community*, ed. Peggy Caton (1987). A good deal of information about the role and contributions of women can also be gleaned from more general histories, including *The Baha'i Centenary 1844–1944* (1944); Shoghi Effendi, *God Passes By* (1944); *Green Acre on the Piscataqua* (1991); R. Jackson Armstrong-Ingram, *Music, Devotions, and Mashriqu'l-Adhkar: Studies in Babi and Baha'i History*, vol. 4 (1987); Gayle Morrison, *To Move the World: Louis G. Gregory and the Advancement of Racial Unity in America* (1982); Robert Stockman, *The Baha'i Faith in America* (vol. 1, 1984; vol. 2, 1995); Will C. van den Hoonard, *The Origins of the Baha'i Community of Canada, 1898–1948* (1996); and in a number of historical articles published in the journal *World Order*. A number of biographies of individual women have been published, including Velda Metelmann, *Lua Getsinger: Herald of the Covenant* (1997); Dorothy Freeman, *From Copper to Gold: The Life of Dorothy Baker* (1984); Jan Jasion, *Never Be Afraid to Dare: The Story of "General Jack," Marion Elizabeth Jack, 1866–1954* (2000); Abu'l-Qasim Faizi, *Milly: A Tribute to the Hand of the Cause of God: Amelia Collins* (1977); Nathan Rutstein, *Corinne True: Faithful Handmaid of 'Abdu'l-Bahá* (1988); and Violette Nakhjavani, *Hommage a Amatu'l-Baha Ruhiyyih Khanum* (2001). Biographical information can also be found in several books by O. Z. Whitehead—*Some Baha'is to Remember* (1983), *Some Early Baha'is of the West* (1976), and *Portraits of Some Baha'i Women* (1996)—and in the obituaries in the serial publication *Baha'i World*. Published memoirs and diaries by women, in which women speak in their own voices, include Romana Brown, *Memories of 'Abdu'l-Bahá: Recollections of the Early Days of the Baha'i Faith in California* (1980); May Maxwell, *An Early Pilgrimage* (1969); Juliet Thompson, *The Diary of Juliet Thompson* (1983); Louilie Mathews, *Not Every Sea Hath Pearls* (1986); Marzieh Gail, *Other People Other Places* (1982); Marzieh Gail, *Summon Up Remembrance* (1987); Marzieh Gail, *Arches of the Years* (1991); Doris McKay, *Fire in Many Hearts* (1993); Florence Mayberry, *The Great Adventure* (1994); Agnes Parsons, *'Abdu'l-Bahá in America: Agnes Parsons Diary* (1996); Marion Yazdi, *Youth in the Vanguard: Memoirs and Letters Collected by the First Baha'i Students at Berkeley and at Stanford University* (1982). Archival records of Baha'i ad-

ministrative institutions are not generally available for research, but the U.S. Baha'i National Archives holds the personal papers of a number of women, including the Agnes Parsons Papers, 1902–1933; Sarah J. Farmer Papers, 1873–1948; Ella Cooper Papers, 1899–1950; and Martha Root Papers, 1899–1939. Some of the papers of Laura Dreyfus-Barney can be found in the Alice Barney Papers held by the Smithsonian Institution. In addition to the sources listed above, the following materials have been used in preparing this article: Dorothy Baker, "A View of Pioneering," *Baha'i News*, no. 207 (May 1948): 9; interview with Amatu'l-Baha conducted by Sandra Hutchison, February 17, 1995; Mary Lesch, "A Few Facts Regarding the Bahai Publishing Society," box 3, folder 1, Mary Lesch Papers, U.S. Baha'i National Archives; and *Marion Jack: Immortal Heroine* (1985).

WOMEN IN NEW RELIGIOUS MOVEMENTS SINCE THE 1960s
Susan J. Palmer

THE STATUS OF women in today's unconventional religions, popularly known as "cults," is often portrayed in anticult literature as a backlash against contemporary feminism, resulting in domestic enslavement in patriarchal enclaves or in degrading sexual experiments at the hands of charismatic prophets. There are plenty of testimonials of women ex-members who indeed regret their investments in demanding spiritual movements. Moreover, there have been a series of new religions that have perpetrated violent crimes, from the 1978 Jonestown mass suicide to the mass homicides in Uganda in 2000. Sensationalized news reports convey the message that all cults are potentially destructive and expoitative. A broad knowledge of contemporary marginal religions, however, suggests that women's participation in them is by no means a pathological nor tragic phenomenon. The argument can be made that the remarkable variety of women's roles in new religious movements (NRMs)—the sheer complexity and richness of their experiences—cannot be reduced to an anticult, journalistic stereotype. To be truly just, one must assess each group, if not each female member, as a unique case.

Since this is not practically possible, it is necessary to venture a few sweeping statements. First, women appear to make a conscious choice as to which new religion or gender role they find appealing. Second, radical religiously based gender roles, although extreme, may have their healing and restorative side. Third, it is important to note that new religious communal experiments do not occur in a vacuum, and as strange as many of these patterns of sexuality may appear, the motives that shape them do not necessarily originate exclusively from the "charismatic cult leader's" dark psyche. Rather, these alternative patterns of gender might be influenced by the countercultural experimentation and reshaping of gender roles that is an ongoing process in the larger society.

In order to analyze these larger social changes and to observe new religious responses to them, we need to step back and review recent history.

Social Background

The 1960s witnessed a dramatic rise in new religious movements in North America, mainly the result of a liberalization of the immigration laws, so that ethnic communities from the Orient and Middle East brought their religious experts with them. Some of these gurus, roshis, and imams proceeded to adapt their spiritual messages to America's "lost generation." "Hippies" were receptive to instruction in meditation techniques and exotic eschatological models, primed by their explorations of altered states of consciousness through the use of psychedelic drugs.

Profound changes in social and sexual mores were taking place. Rock-and-roll bands, birth control, the drive to legalize abortion, and the feminist movement opened the door not merely to casual sex but also to idealistic and utopian approaches to "free love." A new morality was being forged, influenced by political and antiwar protest, a burgeoning ecological consciousness, and the emphasis on natural foods and the body as Nature. This led to a casting off of artificial constraints and distinctions between the sexes. Men let their hair grow, and women discarded brassieres, high heels, and girdles.

Women were profoundly affected by the erosion of norms regulating gender roles in North America. In order to better understand the impact on women, it is useful to look at Mary Ann Glendon's comparative study of family law and social change since the 1960s. Glendon, in *The New Family and the New Property*, focuses on the threats to women's traditional roles and argues that the declining nuclear family is in transition, transforming into a new type. This "new family" is not a single model but represents a variety of coexisting types: single-parent households, reconstituted families, childless couples, gay couples, all nonnuclear patterns. The three characteristics of the new family that have the strongest impact on women are the fragility of the marriage bond, the relaxing of the parent-child bond, and the increase of women in the workplace.

Some women undergoing these social transitions presumably felt a sense of anomie or angst in their intimate relationships and sought spiritual guidance or comfort. Angela Aidala proposes that there is an "elective affinity" between the clear-cut roles found in religious communes and the need in contemporary youth to resolve gender-related ambiguities.

This essay approaches new religious movements as *social experiments*. The notion that NRMs serve a special function in society as laboratories of social and sexual experimentation has been explored by historians of American communes, Lawrence Foster, Jon Wagner, J. Gordon Melton, and others. Warren Lewis, the historian, writes in "Coming Again: How Society Functions Through Its New Religions": "[N]ew religions in the history of the American people have served at least one particular function: they have allowed the nation to explore, work out, and relieve deep cultural needs . . . to solve within [their] laboratories . . . some more general cultural problem" (191).

The groups in this study are organized under a typology of sex identity, originally borrowed from the philosopher Sister Prudence Allen and adapted to apply to new religious movements. It is interesting that these three types bear a close affinity to Rosemary Ruether's typology of eschatological, liberal, and romantic feminism, which Reuther interprets as reactions to patriarchal anthropologies in Christian history that speak of woman's original equality "in the image of God, restored in Christ" (199). This tripart typology is based on two variables: equality and difference.

A Typology of Sex Identity Applied to New Religious Movements

Sex complementarity regards men and women as endowed with different spiritual qualities and emphasizes the need for marriage as a union between to incomplete halves of the same soul, in order to form one androgynous, balanced, and harmonious being. Gender and marriage may continue on into the afterlife; ritual marriage between the living and the dead may be practiced. Marriage and procreation is understood as a path to personal salvation and a way to usher in the New Age or millennium. A dual or androgynous godhead is a feature of many of these groups.

Sex polarity groups agree that the sexes are spiritually distinct and separate, insisting that men and women should not unite and are irrelevant, even detrimental, to the other's salvation. Inequality is the order, since one sex is perceived as purer, or closer to God, at the expense of the other. Predictably, it is men who are usually held to be the superior sex, but some groups besides the Rajneesh—the Raelians, Dianic Wiccans, and the Brahmakumaris—view women as superior. Fears of spiritual pollution justify sexual segregation. In some movements the sexes are permitted to engage in limited, tightly controlled relationships as a necessary phase in the individual's spiritual development or to contribute children to the group.

Sex unity sees the body and its gender as a superficial layer of false identity obscuring the immortal, sexless spirit. Groups espousing sex unity might dress unisex and foster androgynous social personae; or they might play-act traditional sex roles while maintaining an inner detachment from the role. In neoshamanic or neognostic groups, there is often the notion that letting go of one's attachment to the body and gender is a necessary prelude to realizing one's godhood or infinite power. Sex unity groups often view gender as something that can be chosen or changed—through elective surgery for Raelians, through conscious rebirth, or through metamorphosis into a higher androgynous being for Heaven's Gate.

It is important to note that these types may not be found in their pure form, for mixtures of two types are common. Moreover, longitudinal studies of a group's history can show a transition from one type to another. Both the Hare Krishna and the Rajneesh (Osho) movements have shown a recent trend toward discarding their sex polarity views in favor of sex complementarity values that tend to foster more conventional, stable relationships between the sexes.

One finds in communal or millenarian groups that woman's role is clearly defined. This remarkable simplicity and clarity are achieved by emphasizing one role (or sometimes two) while deemphasizing or rejecting other roles. For example, the disciples of Rajneesh (now called "Osho") and of Raël define themselves as "lovers," reject monogamy and marriage, and tend to devalue, postpone, or even proscribe motherhood. Women in Reverend Moon's church are celibate "sisters" for many years before taking on the roles of wife and mother. The Children of God, now known as The Family, have evolved a more complex pattern of gender in which the normally incompatible roles of lover and mother are reconciled.

The Unification Movement

The Unification Movement (UM) started in Korea in 1954 when evangelist Reverend Sun Myung Moon (b. 1920) founded the Holy Spirit Association for the Unification of World Christianity. At the age of sixteen he received a vision of Jesus informing him that he was to be the Second Coming and must fulfill God's plan for the physical salvation of humanity. The Unification Movement expanded into North America in the mid-1960s to become a highly visible and controversial new religion after Reverend Moon spoke at rallies across the country in his Day of Hope tour (1972–1974).

This eclectic millenarian movement, founded by the Korean messiah, a former Presbyterian minister, has developed radical, alternative gender roles, based on the notion of correcting the Fall, when Eve was seduced by Satan and polluted by his blood that is still carried in the veins of humanity today.

Unification women are considered to be the spiritual "daughters" of Reverend Moon and Mrs. Moon and "sisters" to their other sisters and brothers in the church. Members call themselves the "The Family" and look across sex lines at siblings, not at potential lovers or spouses. In Moon's theology, woman is equal to man spiritually and indispensable for his salvation. Her equality derives from the Unificationist belief in an androgynous God, the "One True Parent of Mankind." Her importance as a wife and mother derives from the key role marriage and parenthood play in Reverend Moon's vision of humanity's salvation.

On joining, the new member moves into a communal residence and lives a celibate life devoted to missionary work and fund-raising until she or he is considered eligible for the Marriage Blessing, a ritual fulfilling the triple function of an arranged marriage, an initiation, and a purification from sin (equivalent to baptism in the Catholic Church).

The theological significance of his central ritual is found in *The Divine Principle* (the UM's sacred text, a compilation of Moon's revelations). This narrates the creation myth of an androgynous God who created Adam and Eve through physical parthenogenesis. In Moon's unorthodox version of the Fall of Man, the Archangel Lucifer, a mere spirit being who is jealous of God's love for His/Her fleshly children, seduces the pubescent Eve during her period of engagement to Adam. As a result of this primal abuse of love, humanity fell from grace and became the progeny of Lucifer, bearing the tainted blood of the fallen Angel for many generations. Then, in 1960, Reverend Moon, the "Third Adam," wed the "Perfect Woman" Hak Ja Han and overthrew Satan's dominion over the world. This messianic couple gave birth to thirteen "Perfect Children" (two are now deceased) and through the ritual of the Marriage Blessing are the True Father and Mother to tens of thousands of Unificationists.

In an interesting ritual innovation, Unification couples are matched by Reverend Moon and pledge their troth in the Holy Wine Ceremony. In this ritual, Reverend Moon stands in the position of Adam who drinks from the cup of wine and offers it to the bride-to-be, who stands in the place of the Fallen Eve. After drinking, she becomes the Restored Eve and offers the cup to her fiancé, who represents the seducer Lucifer. He drains the cup, thereby earning forgiveness, but does not assume the position of Adam until the consummation of the union during the wedding night (which is often postponed for three years or more). The wine contains the semen of Reverend Moon and the menstrual blood of Mrs. Moon, believed to have magical properties.

Unification mass marriages, involving thousands of interracial and intercultural couples, are performed every few years and have a millenarian significance. When Unificationists marry, they are ushering in the

The Reverend Sun Nyung Moon sprinkles water on bridal couples as he officiates at a wedding ceremony for 2,200 couples in a Unification Church ceremony at Madison Square Garden in New York City, July 1982. *Copyright © Bettmann/CORBIS. Used by permission.*

Restoration, the convergence of the spirit world and the physical realm.

The lives of male and female Unificationists are virtually identical during the phase of "coed monasticism," when they perform the same missssionary and domestic work, sharing ritual observances and priestly roles. After marriage, however, women tend to assume the traditional domestic role of wife and mother, while the husband is the breadwinner and church leader.

According to early reports, during the first phase of the movement in Korea, women greatly outnumbered men (although no precise statistics are available). Once the Unification Movement moved to the West, studies of sex ratios among Unificationists in Britain and North America indicate that the movement attracted more men than women. Eileen Barker, author of *The Making of a Moonie: Choice or Brainwashing?* found a ratio of 2:1 in favor of men, and James Grace (*Sex and Marriage in the Unification Church*, 104) found a similar ratio of 64 percent men to 34 percent women and notes that "the opening up of leadership positions for men might explain why there are considerably more male than female members in the movement."

The average age of Unificationists, according to Barker, "has remained fairly consistently around 23" (210). Finding the converts tend to come from conservative, religious families from the upper lower to middle classes, Barker suggests, "Moonies do not appear to be rejecting [their parents'] values . . . they [in joining the Unification Church] are responding to the opportunity to live *according to* those very standards."

Women's leadership and success in missionary work were outstanding during the initial stages of the movement when Moon's devotees in Korea and Japan were overwhelmingly women. It appears the Holy Spirit Association for the Unification of World Christianity functioned as a sort of liberation movement for women who wished to opt out of arranged marriage and the control of their husbands and parents—not unlike the early Christians. The church offered them opportunities for travel, ritual expression, and leadership. Moon instructed them to "live like virgins" until their marriage had been blessed by him. As a consequence, Reverend Moon was denounced as a heretic who disrupted family life.

Perhaps the most outstanding women in the leadership was Oon Young Kim, who compiled the *Divine Principle* and pioneered the first Unificationist "family" in the United States in 1960. She spent her last years teaching theology at the Unification Theological Seminary in Barrytown, New York. Another outstanding woman was Yun Soo Lim, who spearheaded the Japanese mission, then moved to California and married Mosé Durst in 1974. Together they directed the Oakland Family, an active recruiting center, whose coercive and deceptive methods were criticized by journalist Josh Freed in *Moonwebs* (1980), where the extraordinary evangelical success of their center was later explained as due to techniques of "brainwashing." Women founded the first branches of the church in several countries.

By the mid-1980s the Unification Church was burdened by a negative public image largely due to the propaganda of the anticult movement. It disbanded as a "church" and reorganized under different headings and projects, notably Women for World Peace, founded in 1991 by Mrs. Moon. Reverend Moon retired from active leadership, and his wife still tours the international Unification community and reads out prewritten speeches. Gender roles are less extreme, since Reverend Moon now blesses secular marrriages and does not require newlyweds to live separately.

The Rajneesh Movement/Osho Commune

This spiritual movement in the West was founded by a philosophy professor from Kuchwada, India, born into a Jain family. His name was Mohan Chandra Rajneesh (1931–1990). Teaching an eclectic, sophisticated blend of Eastern mysticism and Western philosophy, Rajneesh (or Bhagwan, as he was called by his disciples) established an ashram in Poona in India in the 1970s, then moved to Oregon in 1981 to build with the voluntary labor of his disciples a communal holy city, Rajneeshpuram, which was based on utopian principles of communal sharing, work as worship, nonviolence, meditation, free love, ecological harmony, and woman's rule. Rajneeshpuram collapsed in 1986 amid allegations of attempted murder, wiretapping, and financial abuse directed at the core group. The CIA and FBI moved in, and Rajneesh was forced to leave the country. After touring Europe and finding himself rejected at many borders, he assumed the title Osho and resettled in the Poona ashram, where he died in 1990. During the Rajneeshpuram (communal) phase of this movement, gender roles were clear-cut, extreme, and based on spiritual principles.

Rajneesh women have always tended to reject the role of wife and mother in favor of the role of "lover." To be a devoted disciple or "lover of Bhagwan" in the 1980s required living in the commune, where women and men were encouraged to engage in short-term, pluralistic heterosexual love affairs. This expressed an ideal of communal sharing and equality in love. The commune was called the "Buddhafield," where touching and erotic emotions were conduits for Bhagwan's "energy" that flowed through the charismatic community, propelling the individual towards enlightenment.

Disciples of Bhagwan referred to themselves as "lovers of Bhagwan." The spiritual quest and feelings of charisma evoked by the master's presence are linked to sexual desire and romantic love. Rajneesh, as the "enlightened one," is "beyond sex" and is perceived as male in relation to the disciple who surrenders to him and receives his energy in the initiation ritual. This explains Rajneesh's statement, "All my disciples are women." Upon initiation, men adopt the title of "Swami" and women, "Ma."

The message conveyed in the initiation *darshan* might be summed up as follows: "You are already enlightened. Don't strive for enlightenment, don't give up anything. Just relax and accept yourself and celebrate your beauty and spirituality as it is now."

In Rajneesh's system, women are regarded as spiritual superior to men: Modern research says they are sexually more powerful . . . as a corollary they are spiritually more powerful because it is sex energy that becomes transformed into spiritual energy. (Rajneesh, 1984; see "Woman")

In the early movement, at the Poona ashram, a core group referred to as the "power ladies" held the executive offices. At the height of the communal experiment in Rajneeshpuram, women held over 80 percent of leadership positions. These leaders were called "moms" or "supermoms," and the authority structure has been dubbed the "ma-archy" by the press. An interesting experiment in role reversal was tried out in the commune. Men were described as "soft" or "beautiful" and encouraged to develop feminine qualities, whereas women were referred to approvingly as "strong" and "dynamic." During the building of Rajneeshpuram, women drove earth-moving equipment, while the men took charge of the children of single parents and supervised the kitchen. Unisex fashions, perfume, and earrings were shared by both sexes, as were bathrooms and bedrooms.

Sexual and dietary taboos developed in the mid-1980s out of Rajneesh's prophecies concerning AIDS (acquired immunodeficiency syndrome) as a "spiritual disease" foretold by Nostradamus, the French medieval prophet. After settling down in Oregon in 1984, Rajneesh emerged dramatically from a three and a half-year vow of silence to announce that AIDS would decimate two-thirds of humanity by the year 2000. His red-garbed disciples would be among the survivors who would build a new society ruled by women. This New Age of Woman would be characterized by ecological harmony, technological advancement, strict birth control, and meditative consciousness. At that point, the group instituted precautionary measures against the HIV (human immunodeficiency virus) infection. Lovers were told to refrain from exchanging saliva by kissing and to wear latex gloves and condoms. Cooks and dishwashers wore plastic gloves and dipped tableware in bleach.

The Rajneesh movement has always strongly discouraged procreation. Rajneesh recommended "twenty years absolute birth control" due to the overpopulation of the planet. In order to achieve enlightenment, it was advisable to stay unattached and childless in order to "give birth to oneself." During its four-year existence, Rajneeshpuram did not witness the birth of a single baby among its 4,000-odd sexually active residents. In the Poona ashram, sterilization operations were a common practice among the leaders, particularly for men, since the operation was less intrusive for them, according to former member Kate Strelley.

In contrast to many of the best-known communal new religions that emerged out of the counterculture, the Children of God and the Hare Krishna, Rajneesh's disciples tend to be considerably older and to attract a higher ratio of female members. Studies of membership suggest that the average age of the "Rajeeshee" (prior to 1986) was in the upper thirties (Braun, 71). Rajneesh recruits tended to come from the middle and upper middle class. The "typical Rajneesh disciple was thirty-five, single or divorced, and childless, highly educated and professionally successful. Among the Rajneeshpuram residents, 83% had attended college, two-thirds had bachelor degrees, and twelve percent had doctorates" (Fitzgerald, 58). Surveys on sex ratios have consistently found that women outnumber men, although the ratio fluctuates between 3:1 and 6:4 (Palmer, 61).

Rajneesh in his book *A New Vision of Women's Liberation* presents a utopian vision of a society based on women's sexual, social, and spiritual liberation. His vision takes the recent changes resulting from the sexual revolution and the feminist movement (particularly the emphasis on nonprocreative sex and individual self-realization) to their ultimate conclusion. These are changes that have taken their emotional toll on some people and have created considerable confusion concerning the basic rules governing interpersonal relationships, particularly in the volatile area of short-term sexual relationships. Individuals who have chosen to remain single and childless were presumably sensitive to these cultural trends and affected by the "new narcissism" explored by Christopher Lasch. Thus, Rajneesh's charismatic portrait of a "Female Buddha" who will rule the New Age might have an inspirational appeal for middle-aged, ambitious, and childless women.

Rajneesh women fit the sex polarity model since they exhibit distinct spiritual and moral qualities superior to men. After the fall of Rajneeshpuram and the disbanding of the international communes, the *Rajneesh Times* reported a new policy to award men leadership positions and began to profile happy couples and the value of long-term relationships. This suggests a trend toward sex complementarity or perhaps a new kind of "sex mutuality."

The Children of God/The Family

The Family, best known in their early phase as the Children of God (COG), might be described as an ongoing self-correcting social experiment, and the task of redefining woman's role has been important in the development of this new religion. Anticult literature portrays COG women as sexually exploited "Happy Hookers for Jesus" or as baby-making machines enlisted to swell the group's ranks. The Family's own press releases and videocassettes paradoxically convey the contradictory impression of wholesome and conventional family-oriented Christian missionaries. A deeper investigation reveals something quite different. The Family is a Christian fundamentalist subculture, Bible-based, communal, and millenarian movement whose patterns of sexuality and parenting are quite as radical as those of the nineteenth-century Oneida Perfectionists, yet whose doctrines and ethics almost succeed in remaining within the boundaries of Protestant Christian orthodoxy.

If, as historian Warren Lewis has argued, "deep cultural needs" are being "worked out" within the laboratory of new religions, in the case of The Family it is interesting to observe how their experiments with gender echo, and indeed put into practice, certain feminist critiques of American motherhood. It could be argued that The Family has, if quite unintentionally, resolved many of the conflicts in woman's roles that the poet Adrienne Rich speaks of so eloquently. "Moses David" Berg was hardly a "feminist," nor would women's role in The Family impress feminist theologians. A cursory glance at the cartoons in The Family's newsletters would probably appall most feminists for reasons summed up in Ruth Wangerin's apt description: "In COG, 'Playboy' married the 'Total Woman'" (134).

Feminist poet Adrienne Rich (1929–) challenges the unexamined assumption that a "natural" mother is a person without further identity and that the isolation of mothers and children in the home must be taken for granted. She describes a situation journalists have dubbed role overload: "[W]e . . . were expected to fill both the part of the Victorian Lady of Leisure, the Angel of the House, and also of the Victorian cook, scullery maid, laundress, governess and nurse" (27). She astutely identifies the mother/lover dichotomy in American culture:

> Throughout patriarchal mythology . . . two ideas flow side by side: one, that the female body is impure, corrupt . . . a source of moral and physical contamination "the devil's gateway." On the other hand, as mother the woman is beneficent, sacred, pure, asexual, nourishing
>
> The asexual Victorian angel-wife and the Victorian prostitute were institutions created by this double thinking. . . . The body has been so problematic for women, it is easier to shrug it off, travel as disembodied spirit. (40)

The Family appear to have undergone a process of developing communal patterns in which these larger cultural conflicts have found a resolution. In order to understand this process, it is necessary to examine David Berg's background and the dynamics of his family relationships.

David Berg was born into a family of Christian fundamentalists in the southern states. His mother Virginia Brandt Berg was a famous traveling preacher, "the Amy Semple Macpherson of the East Coast." Berg, on growing up, emulated her missionary zeal and evangelical creativity, but he rebelled against her sexually repressive moral stance by taking plural wives after her death and writing the sexually explicit, even exhibitionistic *Mo Letters*. These letters convey paradoxical messages about traditional Christian marriage and women's priestly authority:

> If the Lord & we place a woman in authority over men she's not usurping that place, but coming by it rightly, by divine appointment & His ordination. . . . So, if you can't accept the God-given authority of a woman, Brother, you are not only defying the Lord Himself, but also the authority of your leaders! (*Mo Letters* 148:1:1139)

Berg married Jane (who later formed a schism to start her own mission as "Mother Eve") and worked as an assistant to a radio evangelist. In 1969 he moved with his family—who had become a singing missionary team featuring his four children as "Teens for Christ"—to Huntington Beach, California, a popular hippie hangout. The teens operated a successful coffee house where music was followed by Berg's fiery sermons denouncing the "system" and prophesying the endtime. The group formed into a caravan of traveling missionaries and Bible students, settling down for a while at a ranch in Texas, called the Texas Soul Clinic, where intensive Bible classes were held and the formation of the commune began.

Jane Berg, the mother of the prophet's four children, was a maternal figure for young converts during the first few years of the Children of God, but David Berg in his midforties received a revelation that compelled her to make way for the "New Church," his twenty-two-year-old secretary, whom he dubbed "Maria" after the Second Eve. His wife Jane, denounced as the corrupt "Old Church," was henceforth known as "Mother Eve." In *Old Love, New Love*: "A Prophecy of God on the Old Church, New Church" (August 26, 1969), Berg defends himself against possible charges of adultery and accuses his wife, the "Old Church," of "spiritual whoredoms." Maria became Berg's lifelong consort, "Mama Maria." Since 1969 she has assumed the role of "Faithful Scribe" (depicted in the *Mo Letters* in backless dresses and owl-like glasses) who follows the Prophet around, taking shorthand notes of his prophetic utterances, awaking at night beside him to tape record his dreams and revelations.

Berg consistently encouraged women to occupy the highest positions of leadership within The Family. He initially crowned "Queen Rachel," one of his early lovers, to be his successor. Within his own family, his two daughters Faith and Deborah have had a much stronger impact on the history of the movement than his two sons: Faith is hailed as the charismatic pioneer, and indefatigible missionary, and "inspirationalist," whereas Deborah is now one of her father's arch "detractors."

Berg's elder daughter, Deborah, became COG's first role model for mothers and wrote the early child-care materials, still in use. In 1978 she and her husband Jethro were denounced as dictators and were fired from the "Chain." She defected with her apostate lover and wrote a countercult diatribe against her father, accusing him of heresy and incestuous advances.

In 1977 Queen Rachel, who joined COG at the age of fifteen and became one of Berg's "wives," was viewed by many as the Prophet's successor (Wangerin, 136). She married an Italian count who donated his sixteenth-century villa to the movement, which became the center of a jet-setting "flirty fishing" operation near Florence. Rachel was fired from the Chain for withholding and reinterpreting information coming in from field reports and for levying unauthorized 25 to 50 percent taxes that enabled her to live an opulent lifestyle.

As Berg was forging a practical ethical system based on his Law of Love, he was influenced by the social changes occurring in the surrounding society and its pressures upon his small, separate society. The need to reconcile the "straight world" of evangelical Christianity represented by David Berg, his mother, wife, and daughters with the "hip" world of his youthful disciples recruited from the counterculture can, to some extent, explain the unusual patterns of sexuality in the early years. The sexual revolution ongoing in the 1970s was taken to an extreme inside the Family of Love.

In the letter "Maria Shall Shine" (DO 2192 3/86), Father David, by now old and sick, anointed Maria as his successor, the inspired prophetess who will guide his people through the coming Tribulation. Today, she is Mama Maria, the prophetess who leads the movement with "King Peter" since David Berg passed away in 1994.

WOMAN'S ROLE IN THE FAMILY

Family women are as "feminine" as any Christian fundamentalists. They groom their long hair and tie it up in elaborate knots with flowers and bows. They wear discreet makeup and frocks with puffed sleeves. But they are also comfortable with seminudity. Indoors they often wear revealing clothing such as low-necked or halter tops, shorts, and backless dresses. In David Berg's household, it was the custom for women to appear at the dinner table topless. Their apocalyptic literature and comic books from the 1970s feature topless women warriors flying around and participating in cosmic battles. Mothers breastfeed during meetings and morning devotions, and woman's physicality is not perceived as incompatible with positions of authority.

In COG marriages, the husband and wife are "betrothed" to each other but married to Jesus. Thus, there is a complex and paradoxical relationship between woman's role as wife in her private marriage and her public role, where she is often a leader or administrator in the community, fulfilling her "marriage to Jesus."

FLIRTY FISHING

The driving force behind this movement is and has always been the imperative to seek out new and fertile missionary fields. Patterns of gender have been altered to accommodate this central concern, notably flirty fishing.

Flirty fishing is based on the antinomian doctrine of David Berg's Law of Love. Berg argues that Jesus' prime commandment was to love and to share the self, which demanded personal sacrifice compassion in action. Love was compassion in action, so as long as the action was done in love and the spirit of sacrifice, there was no sin in breaking the Bible's laws against fornication or adultery. The inspiration for flirty fishing came from Berg's erotic dream of Atlanta, a fish-tailed goddess from lost Atlantis.

Flirty fishing became a highly controversial form of evangelistic outreach originated in London, England, in 1973, when Berg encouraged his consort Maria to make love to a lonely man they met at an Arthur Murray's dance studio as a successful ruse to get him to accept Jesus into his heart. In 1974 Berg and Maria moved to Tenerife in the Canary Islands and launched an aggressive flirty fishing mission field in a local nightclub. Flirty fishing was a highly successful recruitment strategy, for many of the men (called "fish") who responded to these "flirty" female missionaries joined the commune or donated their financial support. Many illegitimate children were born in the commune from "fish" fathers, and they were called "Jesus babies," since all members of COG considered themselves married to Jesus. Many communes in the international movement were investigated by the police, and David Berg was accused of operating a prostitution ring. The practice of flirty fishing was discontinued in the late 1980s, due to the concern over AIDS.

BIRTH AND PROSCRIBING CONTRACEPTION

The rejection of birth control and the inclusion of children in evangelical activity have had a strong impact on women's role in The Family. A high birthrate and a deemphasis on the "flesh father's" biological ownership of the child, combined with decisions by the executive to integrate children into missionary activity, have resulted in enhancing women's power.

Motherhood in The Family is prestigious. Childbearing takes precedence over all other tasks. Even a woman who holds key positions of authority in the international movement will not practice contraception. If pregnant, she delegates responsibility to her assistants and contin-

ues to work until labor begins. Upon giving birth, she will enjoy a rest period of six weeks and then assume the full load of her position with her baby and a full-time nanny, usually a teenage girl, at her side. Berg as a child had a full-time nanny who traveled with his famous evangelist mother. Berg's consort Maria also delegated the care of her children to nannies so she could continue in her role as "Faithful Scribe" to the "Lord's Endtime Prophet."

Woman are rewarded for giving birth, and home birth in the commune is a big event. The girls of the second generation receive training in midwifery and are keen to try out their new skills. Some husbands participate in the birth. One father said, "It's the purest expression of God's love. Whenever I hear there's going to be a birth I try to get in on it if I can!" (personal communication).

Motherhood is not perceived as incompatible with "sexiness," for sex and procreation have always been closely linked in Berg's theology:

What was God's *first* command to Adam and Eve? . . . to have sex! be fruitful and multiply. . . . God *told* them to have sex and he meant for them to *enjoy* it. . . . The Devil *hates* sex, but since he can't wipe it out he tries to *control* it & get the *credit* for it! So he has craftily deceived the World into thinking . . . that people have to break the law of God & the Bible & be the Devil's *sinners*! And the sad thing is . . . they believe his anti-sex lies . . . but . . . the Truth shall make you free! ("Thrilling Pictures of the Future," 51)

Thus, The Family's philosophical view of gender appears to be a mixture of "sex complementarity" and "sex unity" patterns, for women's roles are varied and complex. Woman is wife, mother, lover, sacred prostitute, priestess, missionary, and teacher. The traditional roles of mother and wife are emphasized, but women also enjoy equal opportunity in leadership roles, missionary work, and administration. Men and women are perceived as different but equal. Unlike other models of complementarity, husbands and wives are not treated as one unit, nor are single or divorced people seen as spiritually and socially incomplete (as they are, for example, among Mormons and Unificationists). David Berg's writings on women are a strange blend of the most patriarchal stances of a Christian fundamentalist with some of the most avant-garde ideals of feminine "empowerment" expressed by radical feminists. Berg expresses nothing but contempt for "women's lib":

God's law is that woman's desire shall be unto her husband . . . and the Devil's been trying to overthrow that ever since, of which woman's lib is a classic example. They don't want to *please* their husbands, they want to rule over them! . . . It's rebellion against the plan and order of God. ("Trust the Lord!: On Husband and Wife Relationships," DO 2135, 29/11/83)

The International Raelian Movement

The Raelians are the largest UFO (unidentified flying object) religion in the world, currently boasting over 60,000 people who have undergone the "baptism"—a ceremony in which the initiate acknowledges the extraterrestrials as his/her "creators" and is given the hope of immortality through cloning. The founder of this international movement, which has achieved status as a bona fide religion in Quebec and the United States, is Claude Vorilhon, a Frenchman known as "Raël" who became a famous contactee after the publication of his book Le Livré qui dit la verité ([*The Book Which Tells the Truth*], 1974). In this he describes his 1973 encounter of the Third Kind. He blossomed into a messianic prophet after his second encounter in 1975, when he claimed he was taken aboard the Elohim's spacecraft to visit their planet and was introduced to his biological father, an extraterrestrial named Yahwehn (Raël, *Let's Welcome Our Fathers from Outer Space*, 105).

The twofold mission of Raelians is to spread the message (that the aliens created us and will return to bequeath their scientific knowledge to us) and to build an embassy in order to welcome the aliens when they return.

Raël preaches the "sex unity" view of gender. Men and women possess identical abilities and are "biological robots" programmed to give the other pleasure. Not only gender but human life is an artificial construct, since extraterrestrial scientists created us in their laboratories from their own DNA when the planet was colonized. Since cloning will soon be possible, reproduction through sexual intercourse is considered outmoded, and the purpose of sex is for pleasure. Sex is a panacea for man's violent impulses (Raël urges his male followers to be more like women, for the "Age of Apocalypse is the age of women!"). Sexual pleasure is believed to stimulate the growth of new brain cells and links between neurons and can be used as a meditation technique to establish telepathic contact with the Elohim. Homosexuals are welcome and are prominent in the community, and Raelians make a point of participating annually in the international gay marches. Raël has encouraged the campers at the summer seminar to experiment with their own sex, in order to overcome social conditioning and to be able to make an informed choice based on direct experience regarding their sexual orientation.

Thus for Raelian women, their charismatic, meaningful role is that of lover or playmate. Women tend to dress seductively, and the optimum lifestyle for a Raelian is to engage in short-term, pluralistic sexual relationships with both sexes. Raël, however, makes it clear that everyone is free to live and love according to his/her own choice, and many leaders in the Structure appear to live in long-term heterosexual relationships, some of them (interestingly enough) with non-Raelians. Motherhood and parenthood are not exactly prohibited, but they are deemphasized and devalued, since the planet is overpopulated.

Women are eligible for all leadership positions in the movement's hierarchy, which is modeled on the Roman Catholic Church. Raël is the equivalent of the pope, supported by a five-tiered "Structure" of Bishops, Priests, Animators, Assistant Animators, and Probationers. The rank and file of the movement are just plain "Raelians" who have been baptized but who do not necessarily pay their tithing nor observe the rules (no recreational drugs, alcohol, or caffeine) and whose attendance at the monthly meetings may be sporadic. Since men outnumber women in the movement, women are still a minority in the Structure but have gained a stronger presence over the last ten years. In 1998 a new development had a profound impact on women's leadership role and sexual identity, the creation of the Order of Raël's Angels.

In July 1998 Raël announced that he had received a revelation from the Elohim to found a special women's caucus called the Order of Raël's Angels. The purpose was to "gather young women who consciously wish to put their inner and outer beauty at the service of their Creators and of their Prophets, when we [the extraterrestrials] arrive at the Embassy" (Raël, "The Order of Raël's Angels," 1). Within this Order, there are two levels: the Pink Angels and the White Angels. They can be identified by the pink or white feathers appended to their necklaces, and the number of feathers denotes their rank. Raël's Angels have two aims in which they play a nurturing role and a missionary role: to "make Raël comfortable" as well as the other thirty-nine prophets upon their advent (attending to their physical needs) and to spread the message to women outside the movement. The Pink Angels have a more specialized role, to prepare themselves for the aliens' advent, when they will become the companions and lovers for the Elohim and prophets. To prepare for the aliens' advent, the Pink Angels take vows of celibacy and follow a strict diet to protect the purity of their genetic code. Meanwhile, they may have sexual relations with the other Pink Angels and with Raël, since he is (to date) the only prophet and (half-bred) extraterrestrial on earth.

The Angels meet periodically in training seminars with Raël. Raelian women who feel a vocation for this mission fill out an application form and attach a photograph, and Raël makes the selection. They must be beautiful to qualify, since the Elohim stated, "We prefer to be surrounded by individuals of great beauty corresponding to the absolutely perfect original models of the different races that we once created on earth . . . [P]hysical flaws are all due to the errors of generations past, which have damaged our genetic code" (Raël, "The Order of Raël's Angels"). In March 1999 (the last time the Raelians permitted this author to conduct research in this area) there were 171 Angels, and only 6 were pink. A visit to a Raelian seminar in July 2000, however, indicated that the numbers have expanded considerably.

Raelian women the author interviewed commented on their initial fear that being an Angel implied a reversion to woman's traditional role in Christianity—that of a nurturer and domestic. But then they also argued they now felt superior to the men in the movement, for when the Elohim arrived, only women would be admitted to the Embassy to communicate with them, and the rest of the world would be dependent on these women who would act as advisers, courtiers, and public relations personnel for the aliens.

In September 2000 the Raelians held a press conference presenting eight Angels (out of fifty Raelian women) who had volunteered to be the surrogate mothers for Raël's cloning company, Clonaid. This captured the attention of the media, who began to treat Clonaid's claims seriously. Raël created this company in 1997 after the birth of Dolly the sheep. He appointed as Clonaid's director Dr. Brigitte Boisselier, a Frenchwoman and Raelian bishop with two Ph.D.s.

On Boxing Day 2003, Boisselier announced the successful birth of the world's first human clone. "We call her Eve," she said, evoking the Raelian's creation myth of how life began on our planet with the arrival of a team of extraterrestrial scientists who set up a laboratory and created the first humans from their own DNA. The Raelians soon became the focus of a worldwide media blitz, and a team of international scientists were gathered to test the clone. Boisselier triumphantly announced the birth of four more clones, but none of these babies were produced, and the media dismissed the whole event as a hoax. At the January 19, 2003, Raelian gathering in Montreal, Raël expressed his gratitude toward Boisselier for harnessing the media to help Raël inform the entire planet of the message, which increased his following from 50,000 to 60,000. Raël then rewarded her by appointing her as his successor.

These recent developments augure a feminization of the millennium for Raelians. "It is so important that the first cloned baby is a girl!" a Raelian informed this author. That Raël has named a woman to be his successor (although the overwhelming majority of Raelian bishops are male) suggests a strong trend toward women's leadership. In 2003 he appointed, for the first time, a woman (bishop Nicole Bertrand) to the highest office of Continental Guide for the Americas. One Angel interviewed by the author commented on the changes she perceived in woman's power in the movement:

> At first I was afraid that being an Angel I would be more like my mother and grandmother who are Catholics, that my job would be to wait on the men all the time, to cook dinner, arrange parties. . . . But then I realized that when the Elohim come, it is only *women* allowed to go into the Embassy to speak with them, and the whole world will depend on Raël's Angels for information. We will be like ambassadors or PR people. We will learn so much! It is an honor to be so close to the Elohim!

Until 1998 Raelian women fit the "sex unity" model, since autonomy was valued, and leadership unconditioned by gender bias. Women and men, whether homo or hetero, explored their sexuality as part of their work toward self-realization and physical salvation (worthy to be cloned by the Elohim). The institution of Raël's Angels, however, suggests a transition to the sex complementarity model, for we see women withdrawing into a separate enclave and cultivating "feminine" qualities so as to be ready to complement the godlike extraterrestrials. This might be compared to Unificationists marrying spirits (believed to originate in Korean shamanism) and to the Mormon's proxy wedding services for their dead ancestors.

Conclusion

This essay attempts to do three things. First, the alternative roles for women that have developed in some of the more successful new religions are described. Second, some of the social changes are identified that make these "sexual experiments" possible, even desirable, for the women who participate in them. Finally, the question of larger social significance of these radical patterns of sexuality and their evident appeal for contemporary women is addressed.

The "cult experience" appears *less* significant (or at least less threatening to mainstream religions) when one considers the well-documented high dropout rate. Sociologists have consistently found that between 80 and 90 percent of members participate in these movements for one, two, or three years—and then leave. The theory that new religions provide experiences analogous to those found in traditional rites of passage has been convincingly argued by a number of scholars, such as Melton and Moore (*The Cult Experience*) and Saul Levine (*Radical Departures: Desperate Detours to Growing Up*).

The "cult experience" may appear *more* significant within the context of our culture if one considers the possibility that these radical religions are fulfilling a function similar to tribal or traditional rites of passage. Contemporary women who choose to be ushered through these spiritual-sexual initiations seem to be healing past wounds and undergoing a psychological metamorphosis toward maturation. Far from being victims of "brainwashing," they are using the spiritual and therapeutic exercises of the group for their own ends. Temporarily encased in the enclosure of a masklike cocoon identity, they undergo a process of intensive social deconditioning. Uncomfortable with the limitations imposed by the commune, they reach a point where they are ready to expand beyond the boundaries of the sect. When they emerge, they are in some cases perhaps better equipped to cope with the complex problems that confront women living in North American society today.

Whether the group espouses sex unity, complementarity, or polarity, a common thread runs through their rhetoric, the dual notion of the androgyne. Women and men, whether they practice celibacy, free love, or monogamy, set aside their individuality and strive to build collective identity, to experience what sociologist Rosabeth Moss Kanter termed "communion." Through communion with the opposite sex, these new adepts strive to merge into an undifferentiated whole. Rejecting hierarchical relationships and social status, initiates embrace symbols of totality: the presexual simplicity of childhood or the harmony of androgyny. New religious movements may function as sheltered havens where women can recapture a sense of innocence and wonder and slowly recapitulate the stages of their own sexual and social development.

The strange phenomenon of a modern woman who chooses to adopt the stylized role defined by a living prophet, whether it is Rajneesh's sexually expressive "supermom" or Reverend Moon's celibate "wife," might best be understood as a contemporary version of the ancient and familiar search for the powerful religious and social epiphanies that can be experienced within the ritual passage.

SOURCES: Angela Aidala, "Social Change, Gender Roles and New Religious Movements," *Sociological Analysis* 46.3 (1985): 287–314. Christine Allen, "Two Medieval Views on Woman's Identity: Hildegarde of Bingen and Thomas Aquinas," *Studies in Religion/Sciences religeuses* 16.1 (1987): 21–36. Eileen Barker, *The Making of a Moonie: Choice or Brainwashing?* (1984). David Berg, *No Letters* (brochures of comics handed out by missionaries). Kirk Braun, *Rajneeshpuram, the Unwelcome Society* (1984). Lewis Carter, "The New Renunciates of Bhagwan Shree Rajneesh," *Journal for the Scientific Study of Religion*. 26.2 (1987): 148–172. Frances Fitzgerald, "A Reporter at Large: Rajneeshpuram," *The New Yorker*, September 22, 1986. Lawrence Foster, *Religion and Sexuality: Three American Communal Experiments of the Nineteenth Century* (1981). Mary Ann Glendon, *The New Family and the New Property* (1985). James Grace, *Sexual and Marriage in the Unification Church* (1985).

Rosabeth Moss Kanter, *Commitment and Community: Communes and Utopias in Sociological Perspective* (1972). Saul Levine, *Radical Departures: Desperate Detours to Growing Up* (1984). Warren Lewis, "Coming Again: How Society Functions Through Its New Religions," in *New Religious Movements: A Perspective for Understanding Society*, ed. Eileen Barker (1982), 191–215. J. Gordon Melton and Roger Moore, *The Cult Experience: Responding to the New Religious Pluralism* (1982). Hugh Milne, *Bhagwan, the God That Failed* (1986). Susan J. Palmer, *Moon Sisters, Kishna Mothers, Rajneesh Lovers: Women's Roles in New Religious Movements* (1994). Raël, "The Order of Rael's Angels," in Susan J. Palmer, *Aliens Adored: Raël's UFO Religion* (2004) and *Let's Welcome Our Fathers from Outer Space* (1987). Bhagwan Shree Rajneesh, *The Book: An Introduction to the Teachings of Bhagwan Shree Rajneesh* (1984). Adrienne Rich, *Of Woman Born: Motherhood as Experience and Institution* (1976). Rosemary Ruether, *Sexism and God Talk* (1983). Kate Strelley with Robert D. San Souci, *The Ultimate Game: The Rise and Fall of Bhagwan Shree Rajneesh* (1987). "Thrilling Pictures of the Future," poster series, Worlds Services, Switzerland (1984). Ruth Wangerin, "Women in the Children of God: Revolutionary Women or Mountain Maids?" in *Women in Search of Utopia: Mavericks and Mythmakers*, ed. Ruby Rohrlich and Elaine Hoffman Baruch (1984), 130–139.

WOMEN IN JEWISH RENEWAL
Reena Sigman Friedman

"IN THE RENEWAL community, the Shekhinah [feminine presence of God] is ascendant. Women's skills are valued, celebrated and nourished." Thus Rabbi Marcia Prager, a leading spokesperson for Jewish Renewal, described the experience of women in this contemporary movement in Jewish life.

Rabbi Prager, who serves as director of Professional Development of ALEPH (Alliance for Jewish Renewal) and as rabbi of P'nai Or Religious Fellowship in Philadelphia, honors her grandmother for inspiring her to pursue a life of religious leadership and providing her with many of the tools she would need in the rabbinate. "I came to congregational work with an array of interpersonal skills, such as conflict resolution, compassionate listening and pastoral care, which the women of my family taught me," she said, "and which now undergird my rabbinate. Everything I learned in rabbinical school I use, but the 'how' and 'to what end' are informed by my family and woman's experience" (Interview, December 19, 2000).

There is no doubt that as women have gained greater access to religious leadership over the past thirty years, they have brought a new dimension to these roles. The active involvement of women as both congregational professionals and laypeople has prompted a thorough reexamination of ancient religious traditions, including Judaism, in light of the insights gained from the feminist movement. While the impact of feminism has been felt across the Jewish spectrum, it has been most evident in liberal religious movements, including Jewish Renewal. As Dr. Arthur Waskow, director of the Shalom Center affiliated with ALEPH and editor of its *New Menorah* journal, put it, "I can't imagine Jewish Renewal in the last thirty years without the full involvement of women in Jewish life. . . . Jewish Renewal and feminist Judaism are very deeply intertwined" (Interview, March 7, 2001).

Jewish Renewal is a pluralistic, nondenominational movement striving to "empower individuals to respond to the call of Torah, nurture communities seeking to express themselves spiritually and provide the resources which assist individuals and communities in their searches for a meaningful spiritual practice" (ALEPH Web site). ALEPH serves as the umbrella organization for a network of Jewish Renewal communities, some fifty throughout the United States and other countries, including Brazil, Argentina, England, Switzerland, Israel, and Canada. (It is believed that there are more Renewal-type communities not affiliated with ALEPH.) The Shalom Center promotes activism, informed by Jewish values, on behalf of world peace and environmentalism. ALEPH also sponsors: a Rabbinic Program (open to students from all branches of Judaism either as a supplement to their studies in another rabbinical seminary or as a primary course of preparation for the rabbinate); an Association of Rabbis for Jewish Renewal (known as OHaLaH, an acronym for the Hebrew title, which also means "her tent" in Hebrew); a biennial, weeklong *Kallah* (international gathering of Jewish Renewal activists); and a quarterly, online journal, *New Menorah*. Among ALEPH's other affiliated projects are Elat Chayyim (a retreat center near Woodstock, New York, used for seminars during the summer and throughout the year), the Raysheet Chochmah Bet Midrash in the Boston area (an adult education program focusing on spiritual practice in Judaism), the Jewish Renewal Life Center in Philadelphia (a yearlong program of work, study, celebration, and community building), and the Spiritual Eldering Institute (which supports older people in their spiritual pursuits).

ALEPH was formed in 1993, with the merger of P'nai Or (Faces of Light) Religious Fellowship, founded (as B'nai Or/Children of Light) by Rabbi Zalman Schachter-Shalomi in 1962, and the Shalom Center, established by Arthur Waskow in 1982. P'nai Or, based in Philadelphia since 1975, as well as a number of similar communities in Boston, Vancouver (British Columbia), Berkeley (California), and other cities, had begun experimenting with innovative techniques for enhancing the experience of prayer, such as movement, chants, and meditation. While many of these practices were "borrowed" from other religions, Rabbi Schachter-Shalomi, known to many as Reb Zalman, points out that they have long

been part of the Jewish mystical tradition. In fact, it is these Jewish mystical movements, especially Kabbalah and Chasidut, that serve as the underpinnings of Jewish Renewal.

The new approaches to Jewish religious practice were part of a larger quest for spiritual meaning in the post-Holocaust era. As Reb Zalman has written of his own spiritual journey,

> I am a survivor of the eastern European Judaism from before the *Shoah* (Holocaust). . . . There was a time when after the Holocaust I believed that all we can do is create a Noah's Ark into which to gather the last bits of evaporating tradition and knowledge of the spiritual and liturgical know-how. . . . I have moved from this position, the one we call "restoration," one seeking to restore Judaism to its pre-Holocaust status. I am no longer interested in the Noah's Ark. Instead, I have embraced and propagated a vision of Jewish Renewal, one in which we metamorphose in the paradigm shift to be transformed again now as we have been transformed in the past. (Quoted in Singer, xix)

In Reb Zalman's view, the Holocaust, the bombing of Hiroshima and Nagasaki, the cold war, technological revolution, and corporate globalization have created a profound "paradigm shift" in the world. Such momentous events require a creative spiritual response. He believes that Jewish Renewal, emerging out of the "highest value traditions" found in Kabbalah and Chasidut, meets that challenge.

The early Jewish Renewal groups emerged during the 1960s and 1970s, a time of significant religious experimentation in the Jewish world and beyond. Some young people, influenced by the counterculture of those years, began to reevaluate their Judaism, spawning a variety of *havurot* (religious fellowships) and minyanim (prayer groups) that emphasized intimate, creative, and participatory styles of worship and Jewish practice. Involvement in the women's movement inspired many to examine Jewish tradition from a feminist perspective. Other young Jews, who could not find a place for themselves within mainstream Jewish institutions, began to look beyond the Jewish community to satisfy their religious yearnings.

Tirzah Firestone was one such young woman who, in the early 1980s, was searching for spiritual nourishment. Raised in a strictly observant family in the Midwest, she rebelled against the male-centeredness of the Jewish tradition as it was presented in her Orthodox day school. She movingly describes the painful alienation from her family that she suffered as she embarked on an exploration of various spiritual disciplines and eventually married a Protestant minister. It was Reb Zalman's visit to Boulder, Colorado, where Tirzah was living at the time, that opened the door for her return to Judaism. After attending Reb Zalman's lecture, Tirzah, a Jungian psychotherapist, became aware that there were others like her interested in "the feminine principle in Judaism, embodied spirituality, the use of dance and music in prayer and the immanence of God in daily life" (Interview, December 8, 2000). She eventually studied for the rabbinate, was privately ordained by Reb Zalman, and founded the Jewish Renewal Congregation of Boulder. She currently serves as the congregation's spiritual leader and is also a member of ALEPH's Spiritual Advisory Board.

Rabbi Firestone's story is similar to those of other individuals who were drawn to Renewal. Many, whether or not they had strong Jewish backgrounds, were attracted to Eastern and other religions. Through the influence of Reb Zalman and other Renewal leaders, these people eventually found their way back to Jewish life, discovering that there was a way to incorporate many of the spiritual practices they had mastered into Jewish prayer and observance.

Quite a few knowledgeable women from Orthodox backgrounds could not accept the relegation of women to second-class citizenship in traditional circles, yet hungered for the intense spirituality they had experienced in childhood. Several of these women ultimately found a home in Jewish Renewal. As Rabbi Shoni Labowitz, of Temple Adath Or in Fort Lauderdale, Florida, put it,

"When I began puberty, I was no longer able to sit in the men's section [of her Orthodox synagogue]. I felt that the God I was so close to had put me in *cherem* [excommunication]. I began journeying away [from my Jewish background] because I didn't feel that I had an equal place in it. In college, I returned to Judaism because I missed the melodies, tastes, smells, all the things I had loved in Jewish tradition. I loved everything about the way I was raised except being treated unequally. (Interview, February 26, 2001)

Rabbi Labowitz, who had also explored other religious traditions in India, Nepal, and Thailand, was powerfully drawn to the teachings of Reb Zalman and was privately ordained by him as well. "Rabbi Schachter talked about sensitive souls in Judaism that had been overlooked," she said, "and I felt I was one of those souls." (Interview, February 26, 2001).

Rabbi Leah Novick, also raised in an Orthodox home and well educated Jewishly, asserted, "Renewal gave me a place where I could get past my anger [at women's unequal status in traditional Judaism]. The movement has a lot of space for female leadership" (Interview, January 17, 2001).

Rabbi Leah, as she prefers to be called, is representative of a number of women who came to Renewal with extensive political experience and sought to integrate political activism with spiritual concerns. She was active in Democratic politics in New York State, served as Bella Abzug's chief Washington aide, and was coordinator of the International Women's Commission under President Jimmy Carter. Having been involved in the Zionist, civil rights, women's, and peace movements, she eventually made her way to the West Coast, where she joined the pathbreaking Aquarian Minyan in Berkeley, California. This encounter with a profoundly spiritual Jewish group, as well as other personal experiences, led her to seek rabbinic ordination from her mentor Reb Zalman in 1987 and to found Beit Shekhinah, a large *chavurah* in the Bay Area, which "grew out of my work and that of other women teachers who focused on bringing the Divine feminine into everything we did" (Interview, January 17, 2001). Rabbi Leah was also founder and former president of another group, Ruach HaAretz, and currently describes herself as a spiritual teacher.

As a student at the State University of New York at Stonybrook, Long Island (sometimes called "the Berkeley of the East") during the "sixties," Marcia Prager was deeply involved in political causes as well, primarily the antiwar movement. Although she herself had warm childhood memories of her Jewish home, many of her fellow (and sister!) activists were alienated from their Jewish roots. As Prager's Jewish ties were strengthened through several trips to Israel, she began to introduce Jewish holiday observance (of Passover, Succot, and the Sabbath) to her peers, seeking to demonstrate the link between their political ideals and traditional Jewish values. While many of her associates continued to resist any involvement with Jewish life, Prager went on to serve as Jewish Association of College Youth director (JACY) at Stonybrook and later to study at the Reconstructionist Rabbinical College (RRC), where she was ordained in 1989. After studying privately with Reb Zalman, she subsequently received *smicha* (ordination) from him as well.

Not all the women who became active in Renewal did so because they felt disenfranchised in traditional Judaism. Many, like Marcia Prager, had strong Jewish identities and were involved in the Jewish community. Yet they were searching for greater knowledge and spiritual depth, along with an enhanced role for women. As a child, Phyllis Berman enjoyed celebrating Jewish holidays at her grandparents' home and loved the Brooklyn Jewish Center, the vibrant Conservative congregation in which she was raised (and which enabled girls as well as boys to lead youth services). Berman's positive connections with Judaism were maintained at the University of Wisconsin, where Rabbi Max Ticktin was the inspirational Hillel director. During her junior year, Reb

Rabbi Leah Novick is representative of a number of women who came to Jewish Renewal with extensive political experience and sought to integrate political activism with spiritual concerns. *Courtesy of Rabbi Leah Novick.*

Zalman came to the university to lead a *Shabbaton* (a weekend of prayer and study), and Berman's initial impression of him as a powerful spiritual teacher was confirmed years later when she heard him again, at the Second National Havurah Institute. She continued to be involved in synagogue activities but was increasingly offended by women's exclusion from full participation and by the male God language of the traditional service. She began attending services and retreats sponsored by Reb Zalman's group B'nai Or. Berman now serves as codirector of Elat Chayyim Center for Healing & Renewal and was ordained as a rabbi in 2004.

Most of the women who have become leaders in Renewal were powerfully influenced by Reb Zalman who, they felt, spoke to their souls, enabling them to find new meaning in their Judaism. Many went on to study with him and to receive rabbinic ordination. Born in Poland and raised in Vienna, Reb Zalman attended both a traditional yeshivah (Talmudic academy) and a Zionist high school. He and his family fled the Nazis in 1938 for Belgium, spending time in an internment camp in France during the war. After arriving in New York in

1941, Reb Zalman studied at the Central Yeshivah Tomchei Tmimim in Brooklyn, New York (an institution of the Lubavitch movement, a branch of Chasidism), where he was ordained in 1947. He did outreach for the Lubavitch movement and received a degree in psychology from Boston University and a doctorate in Hebrew literature from Hebrew Union College in Cincinnati. Later, he worked in various educational and academic settings, mentored men and women through the ordination process, and influenced large numbers of people through his teaching and writing. Reb Zalman is currently professor in the Religious Studies Department of Naropa University in Boulder, Colorado.

While Reb Zalman is no longer officially connected with the Lubavitch movement, he maintains cordial relationships with certain segments of that community. In Boulder, he occasionally attends Shabbat services at the local Chabad (Lubavitch) congregation, as well as those of other denominations. Leaders of the Lubavitch movement do not share Reb Zalman's commitments to ensuring full equality for women in religious life, bringing halakah (Jewish law) up to date, applying an ecological awareness to observance of the Jewish dietary laws (known as "eco-Kashrut"), and integrating other spiritual practices into Judaism. Despite these differences, he believes that Chasidism and the Lubavitch movement, in particular, have significantly influenced the development of Jewish Renewal. As he concluded, "Lubavitch is into restoration and we are into renewal, and there is a difference. . . . [Nevertheless], what we are doing is very much built on my training with Chabad" (Interview, July 21, 2003).

(In fact, participants in a recent transdenominational conference in New York, sponsored by the Spirituality Institute, New York UJA-Federation, and other groups, discussed the impact of Chasidism on liberal Judaism in the United States. Reb Zalman and Rabbis Abraham Joshua Heschel and Shlomo Carlebach were identified as the "Neo-Chasidic rebbes" who have translated the rich Chasidic tradition into terms that could be understood and appreciated by contemporary Jews.)

Though raised in a traditional environment, Reb Zalman has come to recognize the transformative role that women play in Jewish life. Expanding on an insight of Rabbi Levi Yitzchak of Berdichev, the great Chasidic master, Reb Zalman says that "women represent the white letters of the Torah. In the past, women's contribution was not visible. Now it is, and it is becoming more manifest" (Interview, March 28, 2001).

In addition to Reb Zalman's influence, a number of women Renewal leaders acknowledged the impact that female role models, such as Lynn Gottlieb, a pioneer of Jewish Renewal, had upon them. After studying at both the Conservative movement's Jewish Theological Seminary and the Reform movement's Hebrew Union College, Gottlieb was the first woman ordained by Reb Zalman, along with Rabbi Everett Gendler, in 1980 before Renewal was designated as a movement. She became a symbol of women's quest for the rabbinate and maintained that feminism would introduce far-reaching changes in traditional Judaism. In 1973, even before she was ordained, she became spiritual leader of Temple Beth Or of the Deaf in Queens and was nationally known for her work with the deaf. In addition, she founded Bat Kol, a pathbreaking Jewish feminist theater troupe, and was instrumental in popularizing women's Rosh Chodesh groups (groups of women that meet to celebrate the start of the new Jewish month, traditionally a women's holiday).

Marcia Prager described a Kabbalat Shabbat (Friday evening) service led by Lynn Gottlieb that she attended during her student days: "She was a blend of Young Israel [a modern Orthodox movement] and Woodstock. . . . Different parts of my being were integrating and crystallizing. . . . I felt that I had permission to bring art, music and theater into the *davvenen* (prayer service). I had discovered an idiom that was completely authentic

for me" (Interview, December 19, 2000). Others credit Gottlieb with helping them to view traditional Jewish texts through a feminist lens. Hanna Tiferet Siegel remembered seeing an early performance by Bat Kol and being "transformed by the experience. I felt women really had a voice in the Torah. . . . I [realized] how powerful women are and how important it was to liberate that piece of Judaism that had been hidden for so long" (Interview, January 16, 2001).

Gottlieb's activities made headlines at a time when Jewish feminists were aspiring to positions of religious leadership, searching for female role models in Jewish history, and creating a variety of new rituals for women. Over time, these women began to take more active roles in mixed-gender groups as well, particularly in the hospitable world of Jewish Renewal. As Rabbi Geela Rayzel Raphael, a Reconstructionist rabbi with Renewal tendencies and a talented musician, noted, "Many feminists now felt they had a broader context in which to express themselves. Women brought all that creative juice to a larger community" (Interview, February 26, 2001).

The receptivity of Jewish Renewal communities to feminist innovation is in keeping with their general willingness to experiment with ritual, liturgy, and style of worship. This is of the utmost importance, in Rabbi Ayla Grafstein's view, because "really good ritual is never repeated, though the essential formats are there. No two [Renewal] services are quite the same" (Interview, February 26, 2001). Marcia Prager likens Renewal leaders to the Disney Corporation's "Imagineers," a group of creative employees known for their originality and inventiveness. "I often think of pioneering Renewal leaders as the Imagineers of the Jewish future," she said (Interview, December 19, 2000). Barbara Breitman, codirector of Lev Shomea, the Jewish Spiritual Direction program at Elat Chayyim, sees the movement as "the R&D [research and development] wing of American Judaism." In particular, she observed, "Renewal created the freedom and openness for women to explore. Women were able to develop within Renewal ritually, liturgically, artistically, creatively, in ways that they were not able to develop elsewhere" (Interview, March 20, 2001).

In the past thirty years, a variety of new rituals have emerged to celebrate turning points in women's lives. While this endeavor has by no means been limited to Renewal groups, their members have been very active in this area, creating rituals to mark such transitions as Rosh Chodesh (the beginning of the new Jewish month), the onset of menstruation or menopause, special birthdays, retirement, and so on. Phyllis Berman, who has done a good deal of writing and speaking on this topic, explains that acknowledging these private moments in women's lives "is just as powerful and important as the usual public rituals. It shapes the public consciousness as well" (Interview, December 27, 2000).

A number of Renewal groups, like others in the Jewish community, have tackled the often thornier problem of the language of prayer. While one can address the Divine in neutral terms in English, this is not possible in Hebrew, which has only masculine and feminine forms. Some have experimented with such descriptive phrases as *M'kor Chayim* (Source of Life) and *Ruach Ha'olam* (Spirit of the World) rather than the more traditional formulations, while others reinterpret the standard liturgy in new ways. Many women in Renewal have focused attention on the Shekhinah (literally "indwelling"), a term connoting the feminine presence of God, long part of Kabbalistic (Jewish mystical) tradition. Some feminist critics, on the other hand, take issue with this emphasis on Shekhinah because they feel that the term was originated by male thinkers and therefore does not accurately reflect the religious sensibilities of women.

In recent years, many of the liturgical innovations developed in Renewal communities have been compiled in siddurim (prayerbooks) such as *Or Chadash* (now called *Kol Koreh*) published by ALEPH as a resource to assist communities in their explorations. Individuals within the movement have produced their own creative siddurim, such as Shoni Labowitz's and Judith Gulko's *An Invitation to Prayer*, a beautifully illustrated volume that juxtaposes masculine and feminine renditions of the prayers on each page (in blue and gold letters, respectively), enabling the reader to make his/her own liturgical choices.

Another liturgical work that has had a powerful impact on Renewal communities, as well as the larger Jewish world, is Marcia Falk's *The Book of Blessings: New Jewish Prayers for Daily Life, the Sabbath, and the New Moon Festival* (1999). Although the author, a renowned scholar and poet, is not affiliated with the Renewal movement, her book of new blessings and prayers (in both English and Hebrew), poetry, meditations, and commentary has generated widespread interest.

The most striking features of Jewish Renewal services are their egalitarianism, high level of participation, spiritual intensity, and incorporation of a variety of creative techniques to enhance the experience. Most groups arrange their prayer spaces in a circular formation so that congregants can face each other, in order to maximize interaction and involvement. Efforts are made to relate the prayers, weekly Torah portions, and holiday themes to individuals' personal lives. It is common for chanting, meditation, music, dance or movement, drumming, or dramatic exercises to accompany the traditional prayers. As Barbara Breitman noted, "From the beginning Renewal brought the whole person into the religious experience and not just the mind" (Interview, March 20, 2001).

This emphasis on "praying with the heart and not only the head," as well as the tremendous support for the arts in Renewal circles, has provided women, especially those with artistic bents, with opportunities for self-expression. As Shoni Labowitz explained, "Renewal has given women an equal place in Judaism that can speak to their hearts, bodies and minds" (Interview, February 26, 2001).

The input of artistic women has done much to enhance collective worship. Rabbi Daniel Siegel, ALEPH's rabbinic director, recalled an outdoor Friday evening service at the first *kallah* when several of the female participants greeted the Sabbath with expansive movements using huge, flowing pieces of cloth. "It was a whole different way of placing people and using the space," he said. "This was an inspiring, ecstatic experience" (Interview, February 26, 2001).

Quite a few talented women have successfully integrated their passions for music and dance with their spiritual work in Renewal congregations. Rabbi Shoni Labowitz incorporates yoga, meditation, music, and dance into services for her congregation of over 300 families. Rabbi Shefa Gold, a well-known teacher, retreat leader, composer, and performer, developed and popularized a chanting service based on the repetition of key phrases from the traditional prayers, which makes use of breathing techniques and silence to allow the individual to "pray from one's depths." She emphasizes the *kavanot* (intentions, inner meanings) of the prayers rather than "saying all the words," noting that "moving energy [within a group of people] is what expands consciousness and makes prayer transformative" (Interview, November 24, 2000). Rabbi Hanna Tiferet Siegel, co-spiritual leader, along with her husband, Daniel Siegel, of Congregation B'nai Or of Boston, recently published a songbook, *Va'ani T'filati*, that features original musical compositions, translations, transliteration, and interpretation. In addition, she has produced five albums of Jewish "soul music," and her specially choreographed movements to accompany prayer have been widely adopted by many congregations. "I feel like I'm a sacred artist," she says, "with my music, dance and weaving. I like to have my hands in my Judaism" (Interview, January 16, 2001).

Other women have made their contributions to Renewal communities primarily in the area of the visual arts. Rabbi Ayla Grafstein, who has a strong background in media and the arts, has been gathering photographs and videotaping Renewal groups for many years with the goal of producing a documentary titled "Up With Joy: Experiencing Jewish Renewal." Shonna Husbands-Hankin brings her unique talents to the ancient art of *tallith* (prayer shawl) weaving, creating extraordinary, inspirational designs. Geela Rayzel Raphael described her own Husbands-Hankin original: "It's a Renewal *tallith*, part of the feminine tapestry of new traditions, which has given me the wings to do my work as a rabbi" (Interview, February 26, 2001).

Lynn Gottlieb's remarkable congregation Nahalat Shalom in Albuquerque, New Mexico, brings artistic expression and spirituality together in novel ways. Her congregants, many of whom are professional artists, share their interests through such activities as a Klezmer band, theater ensemble, art exhibits, community garden, poetry nights, and coffee houses. "My approach is as a craftswoman," says Rabbi Gottlieb. "I have given them a context to bring their art into Jewish life. . . . Renewal ties in the best of traditional Jewish culture with the creativity and egalitarianism of American Jewish life. But creativity, like the arts, has to be rooted in something. We need people with knowledge" (Interview, March 5, 2001).

Along with its emphasis on the creative and performing arts, Nahalat Shalom sponsors adult education classes, many of which focus on the study of traditional texts. While some have observed that the Renewal movement pays greater attention to artistic than intellectual pursuits, Renewal groups do engage in the text study that is historically central to Jewish life. Such study is an important component of congregational life, Elat Chayyim retreats, and the curricula of the ALEPH rabbinical program, Jewish Renewal Life Center, and Raysheet Chochmah Bet Midrash.

Women in Renewal have made valuable literary contributions as well. Spiritual autobiographies, such as Tirzah Firestone's *With Roots in Heaven* (1998), and theoretical works including Lynn Gottlieb's *She Who Dwells Within* (1995) and Marcia Prager's *The Path of Blessing* (1998) have guided many readers on their own religious journeys. Shoni Labowitz's work *God, Sex, and Women of the Bible* (1998) reinterprets traditional Jewish sources in the context of women's lives, and Tirzah Firestone's book *The Receiving: Reclaiming Jewish Women's Wisdom* (2003) chronicles the lives and teachings of seven Jewish women mystics, relating these to Jewish women today. Leah Novick has done extensive research on the many "lost women" of Jewish history, such as Dulcie of Worms, Malka of Belz, and Penina Moise, bringing their achievements to the attention of contemporary American Jews through her writings and a play about nine women's lives.

In addition to their many artistic and literary accomplishments, women have introduced new leadership styles to Renewal groups, stressing both cooperative decision making and conflict resolution. According to Daniel Siegel, "Women have joined the creative spiritual process and have also modeled other ways of doing things organizationally and structurally. I used to think of myself as the captain of the team and now I see myself more as a coach" (Interview, February 26, 2001).

In fact, Reb Zalman encourages women rabbis in the Renewal movement to cultivate their distinctive leadership styles rather than imitating traditional male models. "When women began to be ordained," he says, "they were asked to become female eunuchs. They had to do it like the men, and if they didn't, it was considered to be wrong. What was necessary was to let the feminine soul shine. I am impressed with what many of the women [Renewal] rabbis have done. They have made their contribution as women" (Interview, March 28, 2001).

Some women in Jewish Renewal have introduced a new category of religious leadership known as Eshet Hazon (Woman of Vision). The first woman to receive the title was Hanna Tiferet Siegel, during a special ceremony performed by a group of her women friends (with some men present) at a 1982 conference in Olympia, Washington. Since then, some forty women have been so honored by their peers or community members, initiating them into a kind of "spiritual sisterhood." The ritual, described by Daniel Siegel as "ordination from below," offers recognition to a woman who has distinguished herself as a religious leader in her community.

The many charismatic Renewal leaders are reaching out to significant numbers of American Jews in search of greater spiritual fulfillment in their lives. Renewal is a nondenominational movement, drawing leaders and participants from all sectors of the Jewish world. Quite a few of the rabbis currently serving Renewal communities were trained in denominational rabbinical schools; for example, Rabbis Daniel Siegel, Marcia Prager, Shefa Gold, and Geela Rayzel Raphael are all graduates of the Reconstructionist Rabbinical College. The Renewal approach appeals to individuals on various points of the Jewish religious spectrum. As Ayla Grafstein explained,

> Renewal Jews . . . view themselves as a bridge between all of the Jewish communities, and a connection point for the culturally assimilated and unaffiliated, because they believe their spiritual approach . . . has the power to reach beyond the labels and denominations which have all too frequently separated and fragmented the Jewish community as a whole. (*Up With Joy: Experiencing Jewish Renewal*)

Moreover, Renewal is clearly having an impact on the broader Jewish community. Practices once thought to be radical, such as healing services, meditation, physical movements accompanying prayer, "gender sensitive liturgy," and even handmade *tallitot* (especially those with "rainbow" designs), have gradually made their way into the mainstream. For example, the Jewish Federation of Greater Philadelphia recently cosponsored, along with ALEPH and other groups, a Jewish meditation conference in that city. As Reb Zalman commented, "We broke the ice for them [others in the Jewish community] to deal more with Jewish spirituality.... I think we can take a certain amount of credit and responsibility here" (Interview, July 21, 2003).

Women, in particular, are attracted to Renewal ideas and groups. According to Rabbi Daniel Siegel, women constitute more than half of the participants in Renewal *kallot*, retreats, and other functions, though slightly less than half of the movement's leadership (Interview, February 26, 2001). Marcia Prager, director of ALEPH's rabbinical program, reported that a little over half of the forty students in the program are women (Interview, December 19, 2000).

Women generally feel empowered in Renewal settings and are convinced that their ideas, feelings, and contributions are fully honored, appreciated, and welcomed by men within the movement. In Phyllis Berman's view, "Renewal went beyond [gender] equality, moving in a completely new direction. It was not women doing men's things as men did them, but rather men and women together doing something different" (Interview, December 27, 2000). And as Ayla Grafstein concluded, "Renewal is a very good place for women to develop their talents and to be respected, supported and well received. We are living in an extraordinary time, when Jewish Renewal's impact is being felt by the rest of the Jewish world" (Interview, February 26, 2001).

SOURCES: Much of the material in this article is based on a series of interviews conducted by the author with key figures in the Jewish Renewal movement. Citations indicating interview dates appear in the text. Among the sources consulted were the ALEPH Web site, http://www.aleph.org/; Tirzah Firestone, *With Roots in Heaven: One Woman's Passionate Journey into the Heart of Her Faith* (1999); Tirzah Firestone, "The Movement for Jewish Renewal," *Humanistic Judaism* (Winter–Spring 2000): 28–30; Lynn Gottlieb, *She Who Dwells Within: A Feminist Version of a Renewed Judaism* (1995); Judy Petsonk, *Taking Judaism Personally* (1996); Marcia Prager, *The Path of Blessing: Experiencing the Energy and Abundance of the Divine* (1998); Rami M. Shapiro, "The Three-Fold Torah," *Tikkun Magazine* 18.4 (July–August 2003): 53–55; *Sh'ma: A Journal of Jewish Responsibility* 27 (January 10, 1997): 525; and Ellen Singer, ed., *Paradigm Shift: From the Renewal Teachings of Reb Zalman Schachter-Shalomi* (1993). See also *Up With Joy: Experiencing Jewish Renewal*, UP WITH JOY: Productions (2001).

ANCIENT MATRIARCHIES IN NINETEENTH- AND TWENTIETH-CENTURY FEMINIST THOUGHT
Cynthia Eller

THE IDEA THAT ancient human societies were matriarchal is as old as the beginnings of literacy in the West.

Myths of past or distant societies where women formed the core of society and held significant power were told in classical Greece and have likewise been found in myths in a range of indigenous societies. These stories are full of local details and specific plots. Yet, at least to scholars and other interested observers, they do seem to indicate an enduring human fascination with the possibility of societies where gender and power interweave in atypical ways, ways distinctly at odds with the reigning (usually male-dominant) status quo.

Well into the Middle Ages and Renaissance, stories of Amazons and other fictive female societies flourished in the European imagination. As European imperialism extended its reach, so too did efforts to locate these fabled women somewhere on the globe. No Amazons were found, but European missionaries, military leaders, colonists, and ethnographers did report on customs that seemed unusual to those back home, telling of women who held important—sometimes leading—roles in their families, tribes, and economies. In line with nineteenth-century anthropological thinking, these "primitive" peoples (along with peasants and the urban lower classes in Europe itself) were regarded as living fossils of earlier phases of European civilization. As such, they exerted a special attraction for Europeans and other Westerners intent on reconstructing their own prehistoric roots. Between these emerging ethnographies and classical myths of women's former power, a theory began to be constructed in which human prehistory was somehow matricentric or matriarchal, eventually giving way—in the historical era and among "advanced" peoples—to patriarchal social organization.

Father Joseph François Lafitau, a French Jesuit missionary working with the Mohawks of Sault St. Louis outside of Montreal in the early eighteenth century, was one of the first to draw a connection between classical myth and "living fossils." His *Moeurs des sauvages amériquains* (*Customs of the American Indians*, 1724) described Iroquois society as a gynocracy, or "government of women," similar to that recorded for ancient Lycia by Heraclides of Pontus. Lafitau could not believe that such a strange custom could be independently invented on two sides of the world, and so he posited a huge migratory scheme according to which the Iroquois were in fact the Lycians, who were in turn the sons of Japhet expelled from the Promised Land by the Hebrews before they were gradually driven into Greece in one direction and across Asia in the other, from whence they finally came to the New World, settling in eastern North America.

However, Lafitau regarded these matriarchies as oddities. They did not reflect European society in its infancy but were simply peoples who had gone astray, degenerating from the perfection of Eden. It was left to Johann Jakob Bachofen, a Swiss jurist and independent scholar of the classics, to claim that ancient peoples like the Lycians were part of a larger pattern of female dominance that characterized all human prehistory prior to a decisive patriarchal revolution occurring in historic (or nearly historic) times. Bachofen described a "gynecocratic" society in which women ruled, largely through their role as mothers, until such time as men rebelled and seized the upper hand. In Bachofen's telling, ancient matriarchies were the cradle of human civilization, possessing of a glory and beauty all their own. But they had to be superseded in the interests of progress, as Bachofen deemed the emergence of patriarchy to be an advance for the human race.

Bachofen was quickly followed by an entire school of British and American anthropologists who proferred similar theories. These evolutionary anthropologists were less interested in the classics than Bachofen and more focused on a still growing body of ethnographic data. Thinkers such as John Ferguson McLennan in Britain and Lewis Henry Morgan in the United States developed a chronological scheme extending from an archaic time of "primitive promiscuity" and communal marriage through to evolution's apogee, Victorian England. They postulated earlier societies that accorded women a more central place, tracing kinship through the mother's line (of necessity, since, owing to "promiscuous" sexual relations, the father of any individual child could be one of many men). With the institution of female monogamy and/or the discovery of men's role in procreation (heretofore unknown in these societies), patriarchal social relations came into effect. Like Bachofen, these nineteenth-century anthropologists regarded male dominance as a necessary evolutionary advance. But also, like Bachofen, at least some of them seemed wistful for the lost matriarchy and hoped to reincorporate aspects of it into future societies.

From the beginning, myths of ancient matriarchy were obviously bound up with contemporary controversies around gender roles and sexual relations. Fantasies of communal marriage, for example, were closely tied to debates about appropriate sexual norms in Victorian England. A postulated female-centeredness in ancient societies echoed and answered themes regarding women's public role that were very much in the air as a result of early feminism. It would be only a matter of time, then, until someone decided to switch the moral valences in the theory of ancient matriarchy to tell its defeat as a story of regress rather than as one of progress. The first person to do this explicitly was Friedrich Engels. Shortly after Karl Marx's death (and working to some extent from Marx's notes), Engels produced *The Origin of the Family, Private Property, and the State.* It restated the theories of Bachofen and Morgan but construed the era of ancient matriarchy as a golden age of sorts and described the patriarchal revolution as simul-

taneous with the evils (and benefits) of private property and the state. Far from being a necessary or morally advantageous step, the turn to patriarchy was, in Engel's thought, a fall from grace, the "world historical defeat of the female sex" (120–121).

Soon after the publication of Engels's *Origin,* and sometimes independently of it, a number of feminists saw the revolutionary potential of the theory of ancient matriarchy and began to draw moral lessons from it. Like Engels, they portrayed "the Matriarchate" or "Mother-Age" as a golden era not only for women but for all humankind. As American feminist Matilda Joslyn Gage wrote in 1900, "[N]ever was justice more perfect, never civilization higher than under the Matriarchate" (15). Establishing the existence of this era was deemed crucial for feminist politics since it would defeat the argument that patriarchy was "natural," having existed in all times and all places. Indeed, the existence of ancient matriarchies could be said to furnish proof that women could manage social power wisely and well. As another feminist writer, Catherine Gasquoine Hartley, wrote in *The Age of Mother-Power* in 1914, "Whoever reflects soberly on the past history of women will not be surprised at their present movement towards emancipation. Women are reclaiming a position that is theirs by natural right—a position which once they held" (3–4).

In establishing this version of the theory of ancient matriarchy, late-nineteenth- and early-twentieth-century feminists in continental Europe relied on Bachofen's *Mutterrecht* (1897). British and North American feminists, on the other hand, were mainly indebted to the work of British and American anthropologists. Like these anthropologists, early feminists in England and North America emphasized the doctrine of survivals—that ancient customs were visible among living "primitive" cultures and the lower economic classes in Europe—in making their case for ancient matriarchy. For example, Matilda Joslyn Gage claimed that "every part of the world to-day gives evidence of the system; reminiscences of the Matriarchate everywhere abound" (14), while Carrie Chapman Catt, writing in 1914, described a living society occupying the center of Sumatra whose "fundamental institutions belong to the Matriarchate, or Age of the Mother's Rights" (738–739). Also like early anthropologists—particularly the American Otis T. Mason, author of *Woman's Share in Primitive Culture* (1894)—early feminists were eager to attribute specific technologies (such as pottery, agriculture, and weaving) to one sex or the other, generally to women.

The emerging doctrine of Darwinian evolution also had an impact on feminist thought regarding ancient matriarchies. Most Victorian-era anthropologists incorporated Darwinian thought by painting the shift from matriarchal to patriarchal societies as an evolutionary advance, a cultural "survival of the fittest" (as did Darwin himself, who argued that human evolution was leading to ever greater physical and intellectual superiority for men). Their feminist counterparts took quite a different tack: Drawing attention to Darwin's account of sexual selection, they claimed that it was women's choice of specific mates—in effect, women's breeding program—that allowed the human race to evolve. In fact, some feminists argued that it was women's breeding program that ultimately, if unintentionally, led to women's downfall. Breeding larger, stronger, smarter men—out of a pragmatic desire for their services and/or a benevolent desire to make their sons more nearly their own equals—women eventually created the conditions that made patriarchy possible. Maleness was a biological experiment that got out of hand. Though this argument suggested some female complicity in patriarchy, it also insisted, significantly, on the biological primacy of the female. Not only did women select their mates, but reaching farther back, they were the original life form from which maleness originated as "an excrescence, a superfluity, a waste product of Nature, discarded or expelled by the female or mother organism" (Swiney, *Awakening of Women,* 19).

This theory of female biological primacy was developed by American sociologist Lester F. Ward, who declared forthrightly that "the female not only typifies the race, but metaphor aside, she *is* the race" (Zilboorg, 278). Ward's work was taken up by feminists such as the British Frances Swiney and the American Charlotte Perkins Gilman, who, in dedicating her 1911 book *The Man-Made World or Our Androcentric Culture* to Ward, declared him to be "one of the world's greatest men . . . to whom all women are especially bound in honour and gratitude for his gynaecocentric theory of life, than which nothing more important to humanity has been advanced since the theory of evolution, and nothing more important to women has ever been given to the world."

Although early feminist versions of matriarchal theory were largely indebted to the work of male anthropologists and other male thinkers, there were also important feminist innovations to the dominant anthropological view. Foremost among these were conceptions of prehistoric sex and motherhood. As noted earlier, most anthropologists were enamored of the idea that prehistoric societies practiced "primitive promiscuity." Against the backdrop of Victorian sexual norms, anthropologists delighted in describing ancient mother-right societies as hotbeds of consensual, communal, often orgiastic sex, while simultaneously heralding the comparative chastity of their own society as an advance due to patriarchy. As a rule, feminists who spoke of ancient matriarchies rejected this interpretation, insisting, with Matilda Joslyn Gage, that "under the Matriarchate, monogamy was the rule; neither polyandry or promis-

cuity existed" (Gage, 16). With the interesting exception of Elizabeth Cady Stanton, who seems to have accepted the anthropological dogma of primitive promiscuity, these feminists, if they chose to discuss ancient matriarchies, described them as havens of chastity. It was, they said, the "Patriarchate" that engineered "the sacrifice of woman to man's baser passions" (Gage, 43–44). Women were occasionally held to account for their cooperation with men's sexual vices; for example, Frances Swiney notes that "women, to their lasting shame, have pandered to men's passions, instead of controlling them; have of their own free-will satisfied the lusts of the flesh and the pride of life; have to their everlasting ignominy trailed the white flower of womanhood in the dust" (*Awakening of Women,* 85). But clearly, for most early feminists, what was natural to women was chastity, and so a time of women's rule or centrality could only have been a time of sexual restraint.

The other innovation to matriarchal theory made by these feminists was a pronounced emphasis on motherhood. The traits presumably possessed by mothers were thought to give ancient matriarchies their characteristic benevolence. For example, feminist writer Eliza Burt Gamble described "maternal love" as "divine, uncreated, eternal" (78–79); for Frances Swiney it was "the purest and least selfish of emotions" (*Awakening of Women,* 109). More prosaically, Elizabeth Cady Stanton attributed the origins of human society and technology to "the instincts of motherhood," which led primitive woman "to make a home for herself and children" (3). This emphasis on motherhood was part and parcel of their understanding of women's role in their own societies. As described by Catherine Gasquoine Hartley, it was to be mothers:

> A woman's natural right is her right to be a mother, and it is the most inglorious page in the history of woman that too often she has allowed herself to be deprived of that right. . . . Let us, then, reacquire our proud instinctive consciousness, which we are fully justified in having, of being the mothers of humanity; and having that consciousness, once more we shall be invincible. (345)

Late-nineteenth- and early-twentieth-century feminists—especially when compared to later feminists—were relatively uninterested in the role of religion in ancient matriarchies. Many asserted the existence of Goddess worship as a direct consequence of women's leading role in society. But the impact of this worship was little discussed; it was typically taken to be an effect of women's centrality in society rather than a cause of it. An important exception here is Frances Swiney, a feminist and Theosophist who wrote of "the eternal creative Feminine Principle by which all exists" and "the

Divine Feminine Consciousness, the supernal Unity" (*Cosmic Procession*, vii, xi). Unlike her peers, Swiney seemed to believe that the Goddess existed, now as in ancient times, was moving society in a more feminist direction, and deserved to be worshipped. To that end, Swiney formed her own branch of Theosophy called "The League of Isis." She redeemed Jesus—and to some extent, Christianity—for feminist purposes by describing him as "a male organism" who was nevertheless "the outcome of the pure Feminine spirit and of the pure Feminine substance." Indeed, it was *because* he was male that Jesus proved "the mighty supremacy of the Feminine principle," since through "the elimination of the male element" in this male organism Jesus was rendered "free from taint, and able to develop the highest spiritual faculties" (*Cosmic Procession*, 129).

In sum, these feminists found a rhetorical use for the theory of ancient matriarchies, in no sense did this theory take a leading role in late-nineteenth- and early-twentieth-century feminism, nor did it take on religious form or function. Some feminists seemed to see the theory's usefulness for the women's movement and employed it judiciously, but they rarely rested their case on it. They refuted the antifeminist implications of both theories of universal patriarchy and theories of ancient matriarchy that saw it as an early stage of human culture that needed to be superseded in the name of progress, but ancient matriarchies rarely became the centerpiece of their political or religious work.

The theory of ancient matriarchy fell into disrepute among cultural anthropologists in the first decades of the twentieth century, owing mainly to shifting methodologies in the discipline. The matriarchal theory continued to find adherents (in popular culture and in other disciplines in the academy), but comparatively few of them were women, and fewer still were feminists. Beginning in the 1950s and 1960s, there was a renewed interest in the feminist potential of claiming a matriar-

Marija Gimbutas, an archaeologist specializing in Neolithic and Bronze Age cultures in eastern Europe and the Balkans, became a major scholar on ancient matriarchies. Beginning with the publication of her *Gods and Goddesses of Old Europe* in 1974, Gimbutas advanced the theory that Goddess worship, and a corresponding centrality for women, was a key characteristic of neolithic societies in Europe. *Courtesy of the Marija Gimbutas Collection, The Joseph Campbell & Marija Gimbutas Library, Santa Barbara, California.*

chal past. The first forms this interest took were socialist and psychological. On the socialist side, activists like Evelyn Reed and anthropologists like Eleanor Leacock and Karen Sacks returned to the work of Engels on ancient matriarchies to undergird a socialist feminist agenda, finding that patriarchy could not be regarded to be universal if it only entered human culture with the rise of the state or the development of private property. On the psychological side, latter-day Jungians began to develop theories of psychology (especially female psychology) based on the notion that there is a matriarchal stage in human history and world religion but, just as important, in each individual human psyche. Through the recovery of Goddess archetypes, light could be shed on personal and cultural struggles with issues of femininity.

Not until the 1970s, however, did the feminist use of the theory of ancient matriarchies truly blossom. Then it was through a much tighter association with Goddess worship: in the present, as an aspect of feminist identity and practice, and also in the past, as an outstanding feature of matriarchal societies. The neopagan revival had begun a few decades earlier in England, claiming roots in antiquity and a primary worship of "the Goddess." This new religion, which quickly spread to the United States, was perfectly poised to appeal to second wave feminists hoping to find alternatives to the masculine god of Western traditions. Zsuzsanna Budapest and Starhawk emerged as important leaders, adapting neopagan traditions they had earlier acquired to feminist use. Between their efforts and an even greater amount of grassroots spiritual creativity, neopagan feminist spirituality became a viable religious movement. A central part of its belief system and ritual practice revolved around the story of Goddess-worshipping ancient matriarchies, their overthrow, and their hoped-for reemergence at the end of the twentieth century.

This spiritual interest in ancient matriarchies produced a huge outpouring of ritual, poetry, song, and theater. Socialist and anthropological interest in ancient matriarchies was almost completely eclipsed by its spiritual counterpart, which in its turn adopted much of the psychological matriarchal theory pioneered by Jungians having to do with feminine and masculine archetypes in both an individual's life and the history of the world. Still, there was a great felt need to document the existence of ancient matriarchies historically and archaeologically, and many women rose to the challenge. Marija Gimbutas, an archaeologist specializing in Neolithic and Bronze Age cultures in eastern Europe and the Balkans, became the greatest authority. Beginning with the publication of her *Gods and Goddesses of Old Europe* in 1974, Gimbutas advanced the theory that Goddess worship, and a corresponding centrality for women, was a key characteristic of Neolithic societies in Europe. Gimbutas

did not initially conceive of her work as having a feminist agenda, but as it began to be embraced by feminists, Gimbutas gradually moved toward a more explicitly feminist interpretation of her own findings. By the time she wrote *The Language of the Goddess* (1989) and *The Civilization of the Goddess* (1991) in the late 1980s and early 1990s, Gimbutas had developed a grander, more unified theory of prehistoric Goddess worship and clearly saw and claimed its feminist implications.

Merlin Stone, in contrast, undertook her study of prehistoric Goddess worship (*When God Was a Woman* [1976]) in a self-consciously feminist way. She was, she wrote, trying to answer the question, "How did it actually happen? How did men initially gain the control that now allows them to regulate the world in matters as vastly diverse as deciding which wars will be fought when to what time dinner should be served?" (xi). Her hope was to unseat the continuing, insidious, intrapsychic power of the Adam and Eve myth over Jews and Christians (particularly Jewish and Christian women) by finally telling the truth about prehistoric Goddess worship and the patriarchal revolution that supplanted it.

This was the motive power behind most feminist uses of matriarchal theory in the 1970s—and indeed over the next thirty years. For many, including Stone and Gimbutas, practice of feminist spirituality followed on their discovery of the theory of ancient matriarchy. Others, such as theologian Carol Christ, approached the matriarchal theory by way of their desire for a feminist religion. Many who were so motivated have been able to negotiate a feminist religious option in the present without any absolute need for a past era of Goddess worship or matriarchy. As Christ states in *Laughter of Aphrodite*, "Though nourished by ancient symbols of Goddesses from around the world, women's imagination is by no means subject to the authority of the past. Instead, modern women joyfully discover what is useful to us in the past and reject what is not" (154). Still others—such as Gloria Steinem and Marilyn French—found an important political resource in matriarchal theory but did not initially see a need to combine it with any actual practice of Goddess worship or neopaganism.

The story contemporary feminists tell of ancient matriarchies is not identical with that told by their earlier counterparts. While they seem to draw similar lessons—that patriarchy is not universal, that change is possible, that what is "natural" for human beings is some form of sex egalitarianism under the aegis of female symbols, deities, or persons—they interpret the key themes of sexuality and motherhood differently. Far from emphasizing the chastity of matriarchal societies, contemporary feminists are inclined to celebrate their purported sexual freedom. The phrase "primitive promiscuity" is certainly not in vogue, but it is generally believed that prehistoric societies offered women (and men) numerous sexual opportunities without guilt or reproach. And motherhood, while still important in matriarchal thought, is less often pictured as the work of raising children and making a home and more often seen in the miracle of biological reproduction itself. Both these changes correspond to broader differences between first and second wave feminism.

There continues to be significant debate about whether or not ancient matriarchies actually existed. But there can be no question that the possibility of their existence has inspired feminist thought and action for over a hundred years, providing a new and potentially revolutionary angle on human history.

SOURCES: Johann Jakob Bachofen, *Myth, Religion, and Mother Right,* trans. Ralph Manheim (1967). Carrie Chapman Catt, "A Survival of Matriarchy," *Harper's Magazine* 128 (1914): 738–743. Carol P. Christ, *Laughter of Aphrodite* (1987). Cynthia Eller, *The Myth of Matriarchal Prehistory: Why an Invented Past Won't Give Women a Future* (2000). Friedrich Engels, *The Origin of the Family, Private Property, and the State* (1884, 1972). Matilda Joslyn Gage, *Woman, Church and State* (2nd ed., 1900; rept. 1972). Eliza Burt Gamble, *The Evolution of Woman* (1894). Charlotte Perkins Gilman, *The Man-Made World or Our Androcentric Culture* (1911). Marija Gimbutas, *The Civilization of the Goddess* (1991). Marija Gimbutas, *The Language of the Goddess* (1989). Catherine Gasquoine Hartley, *The Age of Mother-Power* (1914). Elizabeth Cady Stanton, "The Matriarchate or Mother-Age," *The National Bulletin (of The Woman's Tribune)* 1–5 (February 1891): 1–7. Merlin Stone, *When God Was a Woman* (1976). Frances Swiney, *The Awakening of Women or Woman's Part in Evolution* (1899, 1908). Frances Swiney, *The Cosmic Procession or the Feminine Principle in Evolution* (1906). Gregory Zilboorg, "Masculine and Feminine," *Psychiatry* 7 (1944): 266–290.

WOMEN IN THE WICCAN RELIGION AND CONTEMPORARY PAGANISM
Selena Fox

WOMEN HAVE PLAYED a prominent part in the development of the Wiccan religion and related forms of contemporary Paganism. Many of the women who have helped shaped the religion have lived in the United States. Among the best known and longest serving of these are three priestess-author-feminists: Starhawk, Margot Adler, and Z Budapest. More information about them and several others appears at the end of this essay, following a discussion of history, forms, beliefs, and practices.

Overview

The Wiccan religion is a worldwide Nature religion rooted in Pagan antiquity. It has developed into its present form in contemporary times. Also known as Wicca, Wicce, the Craft, the Old Religion, and witchcraft, its practitioners are typically known as Wiccans or witches. The Wiccan religion and related forms of Nature spirituality known as contemporary Paganism incorporate revivals, continuations, and adaptations of customs, mythology, symbology, folkways, worldviews, and spiritual practices from old Pagan Europe and the ancient civilizations of Mesopotamia, Egypt, Greece, and Rome. These include the celebrations of the cycles of sun, moon, and seasons; bonfires in rituals and festivals; ecstatic dancing, drumming, and music making; feasting and celebrations; trance and meditation; divination; intuition; magic as projected imaginal intention; and spiritual relationships with deities, ancestors, sacred places, animals, plants, Nature spirits, and other Divine forms.

History

In the twentieth century, several major influences converged to shape the Wiccan religion and Paganism into their twenty-first century forms. These include the writings and teachings of Gerald Gardner (1884–1964) and Doreen Valiente (1922–1999), the cofounders of Gardnerian Wicca in 1950s England; the back-to-Nature counterculture and human potential movements of 1960s America; the rise of feminism and environmentalism in the United States and worldwide in the 1970s; the development of the Pagan festival movement in the United States in the 1980s; and the growth of Pagan networking on the Internet in the 1990s. Three books by priestesses, first published in 1979, gave impetus to the growth of Paganism: (1) *Drawing Down the Moon,* by Margot Adler, which was the first comprehensive history; (2) *The Spiral Dance,* by Starhawk, which was a practical guide to rituals and other forms of spiritual practice; and (3) *Circle Guide to Pagan Groups,* by Selena Fox, which was a networking tool that facilitated contact among different traditions, making possible multitradition festivals and cultural growth. In the late twentieth and early twenty-first centuries, Wiccan and Pagan religious freedom victories and witchcraft imagery and themes in popular culture reflected and contributed to the growth of Paganism in numbers and visibility in society.

The history of the Wiccan religion, witchcraft, and Paganism is complex. There continues to be considerable debate among scholars and practitioners alike regarding its forms in Europe and North America prior to the 1950s, when Gardnerian Wicca began emerging in England. Over the years, within the larger Pagan community, there have been a variety of practitioners who have reported having contact with teachers and traditions that were different from and predated Gardnerian witchcraft. Most, although not all, of these teachers have been women, and most of these reports have been shared privately with other Pagans, rather than directly with scholars. Such reports have been difficult, if not impossible, to verify, due to a variety of factors, such as the lack of written records resulting from teachings being transmitted orally, privacy needs of practitioners, secrecy protocols of traditions, and practitioner concerns about possible anti-Pagan prejudice that might result from gaining greater visibility by participating in research. Further complicating research into this area have been instances in which some attention-seeking practitioners have made such claims that, upon investigation, proved to be spurious. Resulting exposés of false and distorted claims have caused some to discount all such claims as invalid and caused others not to pursue research at all. However, more, not less, research needs to occur in order to bring about a more complete understanding of the development of contemporary Paganism.

Forms

Some use the terms *Wicca* and *Wiccan* as synonymous with the Gardnerian tradition of witchcraft and forms directly derived from it. However, increasingly, Wicca is more typically used to include the wider range of paths that presently exist. Some practitioners prefer to use the word *witch* for themselves and *witchcraft* for their religion, but others do not because of these words' history of diverse and contradictory connotations. The term *witch* applies to both female and male practitioners; *warlock*, meaning "oath breaker," is not used to refer to male practitioners.

Due to decentralization, the rapid spread of information via the Internet, the emphasis on direct personal encounters with divinities, and other factors, there are now many Wiccan and witchcraft traditions. Some paths are named for a founding teacher, such as Gardnerian, Alexandrian, Cabot, and Georgian. Others, such as Seax (Saxon), Celtic, Egyptian, Italian, Scottish, and Welsh Traditional, are named for the cultural roots of the tradition's pantheon and customs. Multicultural animistic traditions include Circle Craft, Shamanic, and Faery. Feminist activist paths include Dianic, Wicce, and Reclaiming. Many practitioners blend teachings and practices from two or more paths and usually are known as Eclectic.

The term *Pagan* is used by practitioners and many scholars to describe both ancient and contemporary forms of polytheistic Nature religions. There is much diversity within contemporary Paganism. The major branches of Paganism include the Wiccan religion, Unitarian Universalism Paganism, Druidism, Teutonic Paganism (which includes Asatru, Odinism, and Heathenism), and Eclectic Paganism. Other branches include those rooted in a particular ethnic folk religion, such as that of Latvia, Lithuania, Estonia, and Iceland, and contemporary revivals of religions of ancient Pagan cultures. Many consider Goddess Spirituality, Green Spirituality, and Multicultural Shamanism as branches of contemporary Paganism, but not all practitioners of these paths would self-identify as Pagan, even though their spiritual practices and worldviews are similar. Each of the major branches of Paganism can be further subdivided into denominations commonly referred to as traditions, and within each tradition, there is considerable variation among groups and individual practitioners.

Pagan groups vary according to several factors, including size, structure, focus, and composition. Groups often are called *covens* in the Wiccan religion, *groves* in Druidism, and *kindred* in Asatru. Many groups consist of women and men and others are women-only or men-only. Most groups have at least one female leader, usually a priestess who has been trained in group leadership. Traditionally in Gardnerian groups, a priestess must be present in order for a ritual to happen. Many Wiccan and Pagan groups have both a priestess and a priest, sometimes a partnered couple. Some mixed groups and all men's groups are led by men. All women's groups typically have two or more women leading.

Some groups are initiatory and have several levels of initiation, each of which requires a process of training and study, usually lasting a year or more. Other groups are noninitiatory. Group structure varies from informal to formal, and leadership may be fixed, rotated, by appointment, or by election. Most, but not all, Pagan groups meet face-to-face. Many are small, with less than a dozen members. Others, such as churches, multitradition associations, festival communities, and online networks, are much larger, with hundreds or thousands of members. Although many Pagans are affiliated with some type of group, others practice on their own. No one knows how many Pagans there are in North America, and Pagan decentralization and diversity make estimates difficult. Some published reports have included estimates that have ranged from 100,000 to more than 5 million.

Values

Wiccans and Pagans celebrate and attune to Nature and Nature's rhythms and consider this central to spiritual practice. Humans are viewed as part of Nature, not as dominators or owners of Nature. Wiccans and Pagans endeavor to live life with consideration of others as well as oneself, endeavoring to be of service and to do no harm. The Wiccan Rede (Law), "And it harm none, do what you will," is considered by many to be the golden rule for Wiccans and Pagans on related paths. Most

Wiccans and Pagans believe in an afterlife and some form of reincarnation. The realm of the dead is sometimes called the Summerland or the Spirit world. Across traditions, a commonly held belief is that contact and communication with the dead are possible, especially at certain sacred times, such as Samhain.

Equality for women and men is valued by Wiccans and Pagans. Sexuality among consenting adults is considered sacred. Sexual harrassment, rape, and child abuse are anathema. Views on abortion vary among individuals and groups, but most consider this a spiritual decision that should be free of government interference. Diversity in sexual orientation within Pagan communities and paths is commonly accepted, and leadership roles in most traditions are open equally to heterosexual, gay, lesbian, bisexual, and transgendered Pagans. Marriage rites are performed for homosexual couples as well as for heterosexual couples. Although Pagans are from across the political spectrum, they join together in Pagan religious freedom efforts.

Wiccans and Pagans of many paths cherish and cultivate virtues such as integrity, honesty, reliability, responsibility, balance, perseverance, empathy, kindness, compassion, knowledge, service, courage, and freedom. In Asatru, there are Nine Noble Virtues: courage, truth, honor, fidelity, discipline, hospitality, industriousness, self-reliance, and steadfastness. Living in balance is important to many Wiccans and Pagans, and most endeavor to balance intellectual and intuitive perception; work and rest in daily living; social time with solitude. Furthermore, Wiccans and Pagans seek to cultivate and sustain good communication and healthy relationships with family, friends, community, Divine forms, and the greater Circle of Life.

Although some are born into Pagan families, most practitioners have adopted a Pagan path. Many women have found a spiritual home in the Wiccan religion and related paths because they include the honoring of the Goddess, the Divine feminine, in one or more of Her forms. Some women have become Pagan because personal empowerment and direct contact with the sacred are encouraged as part of spiritual development. The lack of rigid dogma is appealing to many women as well as the prevalence of women leaders. Wicca and many forms of Paganism are equal opportunity religions. Women called to pursue the path of ministry are able to do this without the discrimination against women clergy still found in some other religions.

Divine Forms

Wiccans and other Pagans honor what some term "The Divine" in one or more sacred forms. *The Divine* is a gender-neutral term for what is known in other religions as *God* (Christianity and Judaism), *Allah* (Is-

lam), *Tao* (Taoism), and *Great Spirit* (Native American). The Divine is viewed by most Wiccans and Pagans as immanent, or indwelling, and therefore personally accessible and experienced in ritual, meditation, and other types of spiritual practice. Many Wiccans and Pagans have a pantheistic philosophy that includes viewing The Divine not only as immanent but also as transcendent, being beyond the limits of total human comprehension. In that The Divine is viewed as a Great Unity and oneness, Wiccan and Pagan spiritual philosophy has a monotheistic dimension. However, most forms of the Wiccan religion and Paganism are usually termed *polytheistic* because The Divine is also viewed as multifaceted and taking many forms.

In most denominations, or traditions, of the Wiccan religion and Paganism, The Divine is honored in both female and male deity forms. Many worship The Divine as the Goddess and the God, as well as honor Their Unity as "The Great Mystery." Often the Goddess is honored as the Divine Mother and the God as the Divine Father, but these deities also take other forms, depending on tradition. Most Wiccans and many Pagans honor the Triple Goddess in the forms of Maiden (associated with the new and waxing moon), Mother (full moon), and Crone (waning and dark moon). Many honor the Dual God, symbolically represented by the sacred Oak of the waxing solar year and by the sacred Holly of the waning sun. Other forms of deity widely honored by Wiccans and Pagans include the Great Goddess of All, or Mother Nature; Gaia, or Mother Earth; the Green God, such as Dionysus; and the Horned God of the Forest and Fields, such as Cernunnos and Pan. Some practitioners center their worship on a particular deity form, but most honor several. Traditions that are inspired by or revivals of a Pagan religion associated with a particular culture usually work with the associated pantheon of deities, such as Celtic, Nordic, Greek, or Egyptian. Other Wiccans and Pagans, often whose own ancestry is mixed, may work with a multicultural pantheon. Some Pagans conceptualize and relate to The Divine in the form of Nature Spirits or as an interconnecting Divine force, rather than through anthropomorphic deity forms. The Wiccan religion and related forms of Paganism do not worship the devil and do not engage in malevolent or satanic practices.

In addition to honoring The Divine as oneness and through deity forms, Wiccans and most Pagans attune to The Divine through other sacred forms, including the spirits of animals, plants, places, ancestors, and the elements. In the Wiccan religion and many related forms of Paganism, the elements of Nature are invoked at the start of rituals and thanked at the end. Each of the elements is associated with a direction in the circle and has specific correspondences. One system commonly used is Earth in the North, air in the East, fire in the

South, water in the West, and spirit in the Center. Wiccan practitioners usually begin their sacred journey around the circle in a ritual with either the North or East, depending on tradition, and move clockwise. Elemental correspondences usually include a dimension of the human self as well as an associated force in Nature. Ritual implements are used to invoke and relate to each element. The element Earth, as soil and rock, usually represents the physical realm, the body, and material things. A pentacle platter of salt, a rock, and a dish of soil are some examples of ceremonial tools of Earth. The element air, as winds and breath, represents the mental realm, the intellect, and the thinking self. An incense burner, lit incenses, a feather, and an athame or blade are among the tools of air. The element fire, as flames and electricity, can represent the behavioral realm, willpower, lifestyle, and the doing self. A wand, sword, staff, and candle are some tools of fire. The element water, in its many forms such as springs, rivers, dew, rain, lakes, and seas, represents the emotional and social realm as well as the feeling self. A chalice, cup, and bowl with water are tools of water. Spirit as the fifth element represents the spiritual self, soul, and Divine Unity and usually is viewed both as the indwelling Divine as well as the interconnecting Divine force that permeates all of Nature. A cauldron, crystal, totem symbol, drum, and pentacle jewelry are examples of tools used to symbolize Spirit in some traditions. Many traditions work with these five elements, but others work with four elements, combining fire and Spirit. Some traditions do ritual invocations at seven directions rather than five and work with a sacred sphere that includes an axis at the center with Above as Cosmos and Below as Planet as well as Spirit as Unity at the midpoint.

Spiritual Practices

Wiccans and Pagans of many paths do rituals, meditations, and other forms of spiritual practice at their homes. Many have an altar, which is used as a focus for personal and household rituals. Some also have indoor and outdoor shrines and circles at home that are used for spiritual activities. In addition to rituals at home, many Wiccans and Pagans take part in group rituals held elsewhere. Most Wiccans and Pagans gather for group rituals in private homes, in public parks, in rented halls, at campgrounds, or other locations. Some individual practitioners and groups make pilgrimages and do meditations and rituals at ancient Pagan holy places, such as Stonehenge and Avebury (England), Newgrange (Ireland), and Delphi (Greece). Others journey to sacred land owned and cared for by some contemporary Wiccan and Pagan groups, such as Circle Sanctuary Nature Preserve in Wisconsin.

Sacred Symbols

The predominant symbol and form of ritual and social space for Wiccans and many Pagans is the circle. As in antiquity, the circle is considered sacred. The circle represents a variety of concepts, including wholeness, balance, continuity, cooperation, interconnectedness, the cycles of Nature, and community. The circle is used by individuals in personal rituals as well as by small and large groups for ceremonies and festivals. In group settings, a circle form can facilitate group cohesion, participation, and shared experiences. The *Circle of Life* is a term used to represent the greater community of all of Nature of which humans are part. In addition to the circle, other sacred Wiccan and Pagan symbols include, but are not limited to, the spiral, pentagram or five-pointed star, equal-armed cross, tree, and the eight-spoked wheel representing the Wheel of the Year. Most Wiccans wear a pentacle, or encircled pentagram, as the symbol of their religion. Teutonic Pagans usually wear a Thor's hammer and Egyptian Pagans an ankh. Many Pagans wear some kind of image representing the Goddess and/or God with which they are aligned.

Ceremonial Tools

In both individual and group practice, Wiccans and Pagans use ceremonial tools, also known as ritual implements. An altar with altar cloth is usually positioned in the center of the ritual circle, but sometimes it is located along the perimeter, such as at the North or East. On the altar are tools required by the ritual. The most commonly used tools include candles, chalice with water, wand, sacred herbs and oils, incense and incense burner, pentacle platter and salt, crystal, book of shadows (spiritual journal and collection of rituals), musical instruments (or audio recording player), seasonal symbols and decorations (usually vegetation prominent at the time of year), deity symbols, and Divine guidance tools, such as Tarot cards or Runes. If a feast is part of a ritual, food and beverages are also included. In addition, there may be particular tools required for specific rituals, such as photographs of deceased loved ones for a Samhain ritual or rings for a handfasting. Most traditions use some form of a table as an altar, but others, such as some Shamanic and Teutonic paths, use a designated area on the ground instead. Most practitioners have their own ritual implements that they use in their personal spiritual practice. Some groups have tools owned by the group and used only for group practice.

Life Passage Rites

Transition points in the cycle of human life also are celebrated with rituals across various forms of the Wiccan religion and contemporary Paganism. Birth rituals include rites to promote conception, bless pregnancy, and guide birth, as well as naming and welcoming rites for the newborn. The passage from childhood is marked with a coming-of-age rite, and the passage into the senior years is marked with a croning, saging, or elderhood rite. Marriage rituals, called *handfastings* in the Wiccan religion, usually include the exchange of rings or other tokens of love; the joining of hands of the couple with a ribbon, cord, or cloth (hence the name, handfasting); and the jumping of the broom by the couple at the end of the ceremony to signify the beginning of wedded life. When marriages end, a handparting, or divorce, rite may be held. End-of-life ceremonies include crossing-over rites during the final stages of the dying process, and after death, wakes, funerals, memorial services, and the release of bodily remains through burials or the scattering of cremains.

Sacred Year

The spiritual calendar commonly used by Wiccans and most contemporary Pagans is called the Wheel of the Year. It consists of eight holy times, or sabbats, that mark the beginning and midpoints of each of the four seasons. Some of the customs associated with celebrating the solstices and equinoxes, which begin each season, are from old Teutonic forms of Paganism. The seasonal midpoints, or cross quarters, are old Celtic fire festivals. Wiccan and other Pagans celebrate each of the eight sabbats with rituals and feasting on one or more days and nights at or near the festival times: Samhain on October 31–November 1; Winter Solstice or Yule on December 21; Imbolc on February 1–2; Spring Equinox on March 21; Beltane on April 30–May 1; Summer Solstice on June 21; Lughnassad on August 1–2; and Fall Equinox on September 21. Many Wiccans, some Druids, and other Celtic Pagans begin their spiritual new year at Samhain. Others begin the year at other points, usually either Winter Solstice, as is done by many Norse Pagans, or Spring Equinox, by Greek Pagans.

Samhain, or Summer's End to the Celts, celebrates the end of the harvest and the warmer half of the year. It is a time for remembering and honoring the dead, including ancestors, friends, and family members. For those who celebrate it as the spiritual new year, it also is a time of purification and release from outmoded patterns and a time for divining the future and making resolutions. Some customs connected with the secular folk holiday of Halloween, including trick or treating, costumes, bobbing for apples, and bonfires, have their origins in Samhain celebrations.

Winter Solstice is a festival celebrating the rebirth of the solar year, the beginning of winter, and the return of lengthening daylight. Since ancient times, it has been a time of peace and renewal. Many of the customs associated with Christmas have their roots in Pagan celebrations of Winter Solstice in ancient Rome (Saturnalia) and Scandinavia (Yule). Wiccans and other Pagans today include these old customs as part of their own celebrations, including exchanging gifts, decorating homes with wreaths and evergreens, feasting with family and friends, the kindling of lights, and the burning of the Yule log, traditionally of oak.

Imbolc is also known as Imbolg, Oilmec, Candlemas, and Brighid's Day. It includes the lighting of candles and the honoring of Brighid, Celtic Triple Goddess of inspiration, smithcraft, and healing. In the past, milk became associated with this holiday because it coincided with the time of lactation of ewes. Imbolc is a time for looking for the first signs of spring, including the reappearance of creatures after winter rest or hibernation. In America the spring prognostication roots of this Pagan holiday survive in the secular folk holiday of Groundhog's Day.

Spring Equinox, the time of equal day and equal night, is a welcome of springtime. It sometimes is known by the name of its associated Teutonic Goddess, Ostara or Eostre, whose name and symbols of baskets, eggs, and hare have become part of American and Canadian Easter celebrations. Some contemporary Pagan Ostara customs include egg decorating, egg hunts, and other egg games; the wearing of new clothes; and dressing in green to represent the greening land in climate zones covered by snow in the winter months.

Beltane is a spring fertility festival celebrated with Maypole dancing, bonfires, and the wearing of colorful garb and garland crowns of flowers and greenery. Some Pagan celebrations feature traditional English Morris dancing, with the use of ritualized movements to symbolize the awakening of fertility in the land.

Summer Solstice is also known as Litha or Midsummer in some traditions and is a celebration of the beginning of summer. Associated customs include candlelight processions and the kindling of large bonfires, dancing, singing, and revelry throughout the shortest night of the year, and greeting the rising sun on solstice morning. Some Swedish American Pagans continue the old custom of erecting and dancing around the Maypole at this holiday. Some Latvian and Lithuanian Pagans in North America continue the old tradition of kindling a fiery wheel to represent the sun.

Lughnassad, also known as Lammas, is the celebration of the first fruits of the harvest. Across many traditions, this is a grain festival and includes the baking and sharing of bread. In many places in North America at this time of year, the country fairs that feature food, arts and crafts bazaars, and games reflect some of the traditions associated with this Celtic Pagan holiday in the past.

Fall Equinox, a time of equal day and equal night, is the main harvest festival of the year. It is sometimes called Mabon, Harvest Home, and the Pagan Thanksgiving. One of its traditional symbols, which comes from ancient Greece, is a cornucopia overflowing with fruits, nuts, and vegetables. The ancient Pagan traditions of harvest thanksgiving and using the cornucopia as an abundance symbol continue on in secular Thanksgiving celebrations in Canada in October and the United States in November.

Lunar Cycle

In addition to celebrating the cycle of the sun and seasons, most Wiccans and other Pagans also observe the cycle of the moon. Most groups and individual practitioners celebrate the full moon, and some celebrate the new moon in addition, or instead. Some groups meet weekly and also observe the waxing and waning quarter moons. Lunar celebrations are known as Esbats in the Wiccan religion. Moon celebrations may take a variety of forms, depending on tradition. Most include invocations of the Moon Goddess, meditation, chanting, dancing, prayers/magic for healing and other purposes, sharing of food and beverages, and socializing. Drawing Down the Moon is an important part of coven full moon rituals in many traditions. In Gardnerian-based Wiccan groups, this typically takes the form of the Moon Goddess being invoked into the high priestess of the group by the high priest, then the entranced high priestess, serving as the living embodiment of Goddess, speaking guidance to individuals and to the group as a whole. In some feminist and Shamanic Wiccan traditions, Drawing Down the Moon may take a different form, with all practitioners evoking and attuning to the Moon Goddess within themselves.

Contributions of Individual Women

Women have played and continue to play an important part in the development of the Wiccan religion and contemporary Paganism in North America and around the world. Many individual women have made contributions, including those who have founded organizations, developed traditions, and written books. Here is a sampling of thirteen women elders and some of their contributions.

Sybil Leek (1923–1983) was an elder of Traditional Witchcraft and one of the first witches in the twentieth century to talk about witchcraft publicly through the media and in her writings. Born Angela Carta in Staffordshire, England, into a well-to-do family, Leek said she came from a long line of hereditary witches that traced its Pagan roots to 1134 in southern Ireland on her mother's side. Leek said she was initiated into the

Craft in southern France. She later moved to New Forest in England. She lived among gypsies and joined and became high priestess of their group, known as the Horsa Coven, which claimed a heritage that went back for many generations. During the 1950s, while walking alone in the New Forest, she had a mystical vision that guided her to educate the public about witchcraft. Media attention soon followed as she set about to do this work. After experiencing discrimination in her antique business because she spoke publicly about her religion, Leek left the New Forest. In the early 1960s, she moved to the United States. In 1968, her first book, *Diary of a Witch*, was published. She wrote more than sixty books during her life and was an internationally syndicated columnist. She helped dispel misconceptions about witchcraft as a religion. Leek was a teacher and mentor to many, including some who became witchcraft elders, such as Lady Sintana, founder and queen elder of Ravenwood Church and Seminary in Atlanta, Georgia, and Lady Athena (Christine Jones), a Celtic high priestess and author in Florida.

Yvonne Frost (1931–) is cofounder of the Church of Wicca tradition and the oldest witchcraft church and school in America. She was born Yvonne Wilson in Los Angeles. Raised fundamentalist Baptist, she searched for something that better matched her interest and explored comparative religions, which led her to discover Spiritualism. In the 1960s at work, she met her boss's boss, Gavin Frost, an English witch who worked in the aerospace industry. Wilson and Frost began studying psychic development and became romantically involved. Later they moved to St. Louis, Missouri, where they studied witchcraft and were initiated into a Celtic tradition. In 1965, they founded the Church and School of Wicca, which in 1972 became the first Wiccan church to receive federal tax-exempt status in the United States. In 1970, the Frosts married, and in 1972 they began working full-time for the church they founded, with Yvonne as bishop and Gavin as archbishop. After several moves, the Frosts relocated the church, school, and their home to New Bern, North Carolina, where they developed a survival community. She and her husband have continued teaching through the church and, from time to time, also make guest appearances at Pagan festivals.

Elizabeth Pepper (n.d.) is the cofounder of the *Witches Almanac*, one of the first witchcraft periodicals in the United States and the first to be publicly available on newsstands and bookshops nationwide. Pepper is a hereditary witch and an elder in Traditional Witchcraft. Pepper grew up in Providence, Rhode Island. Her parents and other members of her family practiced witchcraft, and all contributed to teaching Pepper. Pepper and longtime friend John Wilcock produced the first *Witches Almanac* in 1969 and published it for ten years. The *Almanac* later reemerged under a different publisher.

Pepper also has written and coauthored other works; her primary form of teaching is through her writing.

Z Budapest (1940–   ), one of the founders and elders of Feminist Witchcraft and women's spirituality, was born Zsuzsanna Mokcsay in Budapest, Hungary, on Imbolc and is part Transylvanian. She describes her family lineage as including a long line of women herbalists and healers. Two women were important influences in her life—her grandmother Ilona, who was an herbalist, healer, and suffragette who worked for the liberation of Transylvania, and Z's mother Masika, a psychic and artist whose work included Goddess ceramics. Z reports that her own psychic experiences began when she was three years old when her grandmother Ilona appeared to her as she died, and since that time, Ilona has served as her guardian spirit. The Hungarian revolt in 1956 disrupted Z's family life and schooling. Z escaped to Austria where she resumed studies. In 1958, she immigrated with her fiancé to the United States and shortly after they arrived married and in the next three years had two sons. Z continued her studies, including acting in Chicago and New York City. In 1970, after a near-death experience and the breakup of her marriage, she went to California and attended her first feminist rally. This was a pivotal experience. She became a feminist activist and worked at a local women's center. She realized the importance of developing a feminist theology and began doing so. At Winter Solstice in 1971, Buda-pest and six friends founded the Susan B. Anthony coven that helped begin the all-women's feminist Dianic Witchcraft tradition. Budapest taught, led rituals, initiated priestesses, opened a shop called The Feminist Wicca, and self-published the *Feminist Book of Lights and Shadows*, later known as the *Holy Book of Women's Mysteries*. Budapest also has written other books and has done media work, including hosting a radio program, working on a cable television show, and granting media interviews. Budapest has helped organize conferences, retreats, and lectures as director of the Women's Spirituality Forum in Oakland, California. Budapest also speaks at Pagan festivals and women's events.

Starhawk (1951–   ) is a feminist witch, author, activist, and cofounder of Reclaiming Collective. Her first book, *The Spiral Dance*, was published in 1979 and helped spark the rapid growth of the Wiccan religion and contemporary Paganism in the years that followed. This book continues to be one of the most widely read Wiccan books among Pagans. Starhawk was born Miriam Simos and had a Jewish upbringing that emphasized intellectual freedom. She earned a master's degree in psychology from Antioch West University and worked for a time as a psychotherapist. During her college years, she began studying and teaching about witchcraft. She practiced solitarily for several years and then, with some of her students, formed her first coven, Compost. In 1975, she met poet and Pagan priest Victor Anderson and later was initiated into his Faery Tradition, which provided some of the inspiration for *The Spiral Dance*. In the years that followed, Starhawk wrote a variety of other nonfiction and fiction books. She also has worked as a consultant on Goddess Spirituality films, including *Goddess Remembered*, *Burning Times*, and *Full Circle*. Starhawk is a longtime activist who continues to campaign for peace, a better environment, and social justice. She lives in California and travels internationally to present workshops, rituals, and lectures.

Margot Adler (1946–   ) is a Pagan priestess, author, and journalist. Her first book, *Drawing Down the Moon*, published in 1979, was the first in-depth and extensive history of the developing contemporary Pagan movement in America. It has been widely read by Pagan practitioners and scholars and over the years has served as a textbook on Paganism in religious studies courses at a variety of colleges and universities. Born in Little Rock, Arkansas, Adler grew up in New York City in an atheist-

Z Budapest, one of the founders and elders of Feminist Witchcraft and women's spirituality, was born Zsuzsanna Mokcsay in Budapest, Hungary. She describes her family lineage as including a long line of women herbalists and healers. *Courtesy of Marcella Paolocci.*

agnostic Jewish household. Her mother was a radical educator, her father and aunt were psychiatrists, and her grandfather was renowned psychiatrist Alfred Adler. Margot attended the University of California at Berkeley, receiving her bachelor's degree in political science in 1968. During her undergraduate and graduate years, she was politically active in the free speech, civil rights, and peace movements. In 1970, she received a master's degree in journalism from the Graduate School of Journalism at Columbia University in New York. Adler's broadcast journalism career has included working with Pacifica radio network, WBAI radio of New York, and National Public Radio. She also has been a Neiman fellow at Harvard University. Adler had an affinity for Pagan Greek myths since childhood, and in the 1970s, she began studying witchcraft. In 1973, she became a Gardnerian priestess and from 1976 to 1981 was priestess of a Gardnerian coven. In 1988, she married her longtime partner John Gliedman in a handfasting ceremony, which was the first to be written up in the society pages of the *New York Times.* Her son, Alexander Gliedman-Adler, was born in 1990. Her autobiography *Heretic's Heart* was published in 1997. Adler continues to travel widely, presenting rituals, workshops, and lectures at Pagan festivals and women's spirituality retreats.

Selena Fox (1949–) is a Pagan civil rights activist, founder of the Circle Craft tradition, and the high priestess of Circle Sanctuary, headquartered in Wisconsin. She has successfully worked on numerous Pagan religious freedom cases and helped lead campaigns that defeated federal antiwitchcraft legislation in 1985 and 1999. Fox has served as a consultant on Wiccan religious accommodation issues to the Pentagon and U.S. Department of Justice and is the first Wiccan to serve on the Religious Practices Advisory Board of the Wisconsin Department of Corrections. Fox is the executive director of the Lady Liberty League, an international Pagan religious freedom organization she founded in 1985. Fox was born Suzanne Marie Bisset in Arlington, Virginia, and was raised fundamentalist Southern Baptist. At seventeen, Fox began defining herself as a Pantheist. When she was twenty-one, as president of the classics honor society at the College of William and Mary, she led her first Pagan ritual. Shortly thereafter she began practicing the Craft with a family tradition witch. In 1974 Fox and others founded Circle, now known as Circle Sanctuary, which is one of America's oldest Wiccan churches and first international Pagan service institutions. In 1977, Fox founded Circle Network and in 1979 began publishing the *Circle Guide to Pagan Groups,* which along with *CIRCLE Magazine,* which she founded in 1978, provide contacts and information for Pagans of many paths worldwide. During the late 1970s and 1980s, Fox began organizing national multitradition campout festivals and became one of the founders of the Pagan fes-

tival movement. Fox has been active in interfaith work since the 1970s, and in 1999, she was the first head of a Wiccan church to serve on the Assembly of Religious and Spiritual Leaders associated with the Parliament of the World's Religions. In 1994, she and her husband, Dr. Dennis Carpenter, founded the Nature Religions Scholars Network associated with the American Academy of Religion. Fox also is a clinical psychotherapist and has a bachelor's in psychology from the College of William and Mary and a master's in counseling from the University of Wisconsin at Madison. She travels internationally, speaking at colleges and universities, Pagan festivals, and women's conferences. Her rituals, chants, writings, and photographs have been published in periodicals, books, and online.

Diana Paxson (1943–) is an elder in Asatru and is cofounder of Hrafnar, a heathen kindred. She has served as Steerswoman of the Troth, an international Asatru organization. Part of her work has been in researching and reclaiming the oracular tradition of ancient Scandinavia. With writer Marion Zimmer Bradley, Paxson cofounded an all-women's Goddess coven, Dark Moon Circle, in 1978 in Berkeley, California. Together, they also founded the Center for Non-Traditional Religion, which later evolved into the Fellowship of the Spiral Path. She also is one of the founders of the Society for Creative Anachronism, one of the oldest and largest medieval recreation societies in North America. Paxson has a master's in comparative literature and is a storyteller, teacher, and science fiction and fantasy writer. Paxson lives with her extended family in Berkeley, California, in a large home known as Grayhaven.

Laurie Cabot (1933–) is an author and founder of the Cabot tradition of witchcraft. Cabot was born in Wewoka, Oklahoma, and grew up in Anaheim, California. She began having psychic experiences when she was six. As a teenager, she met three female witches who trained and initiated her into the Craft. Cabot was married twice and had two daughters. In the late 1960s, Cabot moved to Salem, Massachusetts, and became visible as a practicing witch. She opened Crow Haven Corner, a witchcraft shop, which has been run by her daughter Jody since the late 1970s. In 1973, Cabot started the annual Witches Ball in Salem, and in 1977, then-governor Michael Dukakis granted her wish and gave her a citation naming her "the Official Witch of Salem" in recognition for her work with dyslexic children. In 1986, Cabot founded the Witches League for Public Awareness, a media watchdog group, and in 1988, she founded the Temple of Isis, a chapter in the National Alliance of Pantheists. Cabot has written several books on witchcraft.

Morning Glory Ravenheart (1948–) is a Pagan priestess, Goddess historian, and elder in the Church of All Worlds. Born Diana Moore in Long Beach, California, she was raised Pentecostal Christian by her parents, but at the age of sixteen, she began to study other paths, including Buddhism and then Paganism. She changed her name to Morning Glory in 1967. She teamed up with Church of All Worlds founder Oberon (then, Tim) Zell in 1974 and collaborated with him on a variety of projects, including the publication of the church's magazine, *The Green Egg*, breeding and surgically altering goats to produce living unicorns, and more recently, producing Goddess sculptures and other sacred art through the company Mythic Images. In 1990, Morning Glory coined the term "polyamory" to refer to a group marriage lifestyle and has spoken and written on this topic. Morning Glory also is a ritualist and writer of stories, chants, and poetry.

Phyllis Curott (1951–) is a Wiccan priestess, author, media spokesperson, and founder of the Circle of Ara. An attorney and Pagan civil rights activist, she helped win Wiccans the right to perform marriages in New York City and do public rituals in Chicago parks. She also has helped with many other cases and has served as a volunteer consulting attorney with the Lady Liberty League, a Pagan civil rights organization operated by Selena Fox and Circle Sanctuary. Curott is founder of the Temple of Ara and has worked with a variety of Pagan groups, including the Minoan Sisterhood and Covenant of the Goddess. Curott received her bachelor's in philosophy from Brown University and her juris doctor from New York University School of Law. Curott has traveled internationally in connection with her Wiccan writing and media work. Her books *Book of Shadows* and *Witchcrafting* have been widely read.

Marion Weinstein (1939–) is an author and one of the first witches in the United States to have a witchcraft radio show. Weinstein was born in Queens, New York, and was raised in a Jewish family. She began identifying with witchcraft as a young child and has had a lifelong affinity with the Goddess Diana. She graduated from Barnard College with a bachelor's degree in English literature. She also studied acting, dance, film, and voice. In the late 1960s she began practicing witchcraft with others, and in 1969, she began her radio show *Marion's Cauldron*, which lasted fourteen years. In 1978, Marion wrote her first book, *Positive Magic*. Also that year Weinstein began working professionally as a stand-up comic in nightclubs and using witchcraft themes as part of her routine. Over the years, Weinstein has produced a variety of books, recordings, and videotapes, as well as presented an annual Halloween performance in New York City. She is founder of the Earth Magic Dianic tradition of witchcraft.

Deborah Ann Light (1935–) is a Hedgewitch, performance artist, and Pagan elder active in interfaith work. Light was born in London to American parents and raised in Nashville, Tennessee. She received a mas-

ter's in religious studies from Norwich University, Vermont, in 1985. Her thesis explored Goddess Spirituality in the United States. In 1993, representing Earth Spirit Community, Covenant of the Goddess, and Circle Sanctuary, Light became the first Wiccan to serve on the Assembly of Religious and Spiritual Leaders associated with the Parliament of the World's Religions. She also has represented the Wiccan religion at other interfaith conferences and has supported a variety of Pagan projects and endeavors. She has traveled internationally in connection with her work.

Legacies

The Wiccan religion and other forms of Paganism continue to grow. Some report that the Wiccan religion is among the fastest-growing religions in the United States. Wiccan ritual forms, such as casting the circle and calling the sacred directions and sacred elements, have been adopted by interreligious Goddess spirituality groups and some spiritual environmental groups. Some New Age groups that previously had drawn inspiration only from Eastern religions and mystical Christianity have begun incorporating Pagan chants and Pagan sabbat customs in their practices. Some women's groups in mainline Christian denominations have adapted Wiccan croning rites to celebrate the menopause passage. Wiccan characters have begun being depicted in popular television shows, movies, and books. Wiccan and Pagan symbols and imagery increasingly are present in the art world.

The growing numbers and visibility of Paganism have been welcome by people of many religions and spiritualities, but not all. With growth also has come opposition by those unaccepting of religious diversity in general and Paganism in particular. In the United States, some attempts have been made by local, state, and federal government officials to suppress and discriminate against the Wiccan religion and other Pagan paths. Often Wiccan women have been at the forefront of religious freedom battles. For example, in 1988, Jamie Dodge (Mississippi), who had been fired from her job because she was a Wiccan, won her case in federal court. In 1999, high school honors student and Wiccan Crystal Seifferly (Michigan) successfully stood up for her right to wear her pentacle as religious jewelry in her school. In 2001, Rev. Jamyi Witch (Wisconsin) held on to her job as the first full-time Wiccan chaplain in a state correctional facility despite a campaign launched by several bigoted state lawmakers to get her fired because of her religion. In 2003, Cynthia Simpson (Virginia) filed a lawsuit against county government officials to challenge their policy that permitted only Judeo-Christian invocations to open County Board meetings. Perhaps the greatest legacy of the Wiccan religion and Paganism in the world today is heightening awareness of the importance of upholding religious freedom for all.

SOURCES: An excellent history and overview of contemporary paganism in America is found in Margot Adler, *Drawing Down the Moon*, rev. ed. (1997); and *Contemporary Paganism: Listening People, Speaking Earth* (1997), by Graham Harvey, includes some international perspectives. *Triumph of the Moon: A History of Modern Pagan Witchcraft* (1999), by Ronald Hutton, examines the development of modern Wicca in the United Kingdom, and Morganna Davies and Aradia Lynch discuss family tradition witchcraft and other paths in America in their *Keepers of the Flames: Interviews with Elders of Traditional Witchcraft in America* (2001). Several Wiccan-Pagan focused encyclopedias are *The Encyclopedia of Modern Witchcraft and Neo-Paganism*, edited by Shelley Rabinovitch and James Lewis (2002); *The Encyclopedia of Witches and Witchcraft*, rev. ed., by Rosemary Ellen Guiley (1999); *The Witch Book: The Encyclopedia of Witchcraft, Wicca, and Neo-Paganism*, by Raymond Buckland (2002); and *Witchcraft Today: An Encyclopedia of Wiccan and Neopagan Traditions*, by James Lewis (1999). Feminist women's perspectives on the Wiccan religion are included in *Book of Shadows*, by Phyllis Curott (1998); *The Grandmother of Time*, by Z Budapest (1999); and the classic *The Spiral Dance*, rev. ed., by Starhawk (1999). Pauline and Dan Campanelli's *Ancient Ways: Reclaiming Pagan Traditions* (1991) describes ancient and contemporary folkways for celebrating the seasons, and Marion Weinstein in the revised edition of *Positive Magic* (2002) discusses magical practices. *The Circle Guide to Pagan Groups*, by Selena Fox, Dennis Carpenter, and others (2003), is a directory of organizations, networks, centers, festivals, Web sites, and other contacts in the United States and other countries. *The HarperCollins Dictionary of Religion*, edited by Jonathan Z. Smith and William Scott Green (1995), with the American Academy of Religion, examines several forms of contemporary Paganism, including "Asatru," 76–77; "Goddess Religions (Contemporary)," 389–391; "Neo-Paganism," 765–766; "Wicca," 1131; and "Witchcraft: Neo-Pagan Witchcraft," 1134–1135.

Part X

Multi-denominational Movements

THE DEACONESS MOVEMENT
Cynthia A. Jurisson

THE HISTORY OF the relationship between women and institutionalized forms of Christianity is a long and complicated one. Throughout history, women's increased participation in the ministries of the church has held tremendous potential to bring about gender equality as well as social control and subjugation of women to the hierarchy of the church. Offices, honors, and positions made available for women in the church can at one and the same time increase women's participation and decrease their influence, as well as their autonomy. So it was with the introduction of the concept of the deaconess in the North American church. The development of the role held tremendous promise as a way for women to exert greater influence in both church and society. On the other hand, it held tremendous potential for increased social control and subjugation of faithful women by the church bodies that they were being called to serve. Similarly, in terms of conceptions of gender, the role of deaconess offered women an opportunity to expand the sphere of their gender, moving them legitimately into the public sphere. On the other hand, the ideology by which that was accomplished, construing deaconess work as a logical extension of women's work, also tended to reinforce traditional assumptions about gender that relegated women exclusively to the home and private life.

Connections to the Ancient World and the New Testament

The assumption is often made that the modern deaconess movement is the revival of an ancient church tradition. The term *revival* ought to be used with caution, since none of the offices of the New Testament and early church have been precisely replicated in more modern church offices, despite some similarity in terminology and notwithstanding claims to the contrary. The shape and content of church offices such as presbyter, bishop, deacon, and widow are not the same today as they were in the ancient Near East. This is no less true of the office of deaconess. Rather than a revival, it is accurate to say that there was, in parts of nineteenth-century North America, an appropriation of the term *deaconess* as the title for a newly created position for women in a number of Protestant denominations. According to Acts 6, the office of deacon was originally created by the apostles as a way to attend to the material needs of widows, and probably other impoverished or needful persons, among the early Christians. Seven men were chosen to serve as the first deacons. Their title, deacon, was taken from the Greek verb *diakonein*, to serve.

It is significant that the term *deaconess* does not appear in the Greek manuscripts of the New Testament in reference to Phoebe. Rather, she is described by Paul in Romans 16:1 as a deacon, or *minister*, as the term is frequently translated, of the church at Cenchrae. Despite the gender of the title in the original Greek, many English-language translations of the Bible have often designated Phoebe a deaconess. However, not until the third century onward and mainly in the Eastern part of the church do we find evidence attesting to the position of deaconess, using the feminine form of the title. The deaconess's primary task was to care for and assist in ministry to women, for example, at women's baptisms where a female assistant was necessary to preserve modesty.

Through the centuries there has been considerable debate about the meaning of the title deacon in reference to Phoebe. In mid-nineteenth-century North America, Romans 16:1 was often used to legitimate women's entry into professional church work as deaconesses. It may also have contributed to nineteenth-century assumptions that diaconal work was women's work, a logical extension of female maternal and domestic impulses. It is notable that there were few, if any, concerted attempts in nineteenth-century North America to organize and train groups of men for similar work.

Several impulses coalesced in the mid-nineteenth century into a movement to establish deaconess groups among a variety of North American Protestant denominations. First, the massive and rapid influx of impoverished immigrants in the mid- to late nineteenth century created a social crisis in many urban areas, taxing inadequate or nonexistent social service, educational, and health-care infrastructures. Many Americans looked with both compassion and helplessness at the misery and suffering of so many immigrants. Second, there was an enormous concern among Americans as to how the huge immigrant populace would be civilized, socialized, and transformed into virtuous citizens. Third, the primitive state of health care for all Americans and the lack of both facilities and personnel to care for the seriously ill created tremendous human suffering. Finally, during the mid-nineteenth century, the inevitable social rearrangement and dislocation brought about by industrialization and nation-building began to have an impact on conceptions of gender roles and duties. There was much agitation for, as well as anxiety about, increasing women's rights and spheres of influence and action. Deaconess work offered a professional occupation for women that, though public, was carefully circumscribed and firmly situated well within women's proper sphere of influence.

Kaiserswerth Precedent

Part of an international phenomenon in the mid- to late-nineteenth century, a large number of deaconess programs were started by North American Protestants, both intra- and interdenominationally and among both blacks and whites. Between 1870 and 1903 more than 140 deaconess homes were instituted in the United States and Canada among a diverse group of Protestant churches, Methodist, Lutheran, German Reformed, Episcopalian, Mennonite, and so forth. A bit later, beginning at the turn of the century, deaconess homes and orders began to be established in a similar fashion in Canada, particularly in the Toronto area. Though in retrospect not all those programs could be deemed a success, and many of them did not endure past the middle of the twentieth century, nevertheless they made a profound impact upon the women who staffed them, the clientele they served, and the churches under whose auspices they labored.

Almost all the first North American deaconess programs took as their inspiration the work of Pastor Theodor Fliedner (1800–1864) and his wife Friederike (1800–1842), in Kaiserswerth, Germany. Fliedner, a German Lutheran minister, had been deeply concerned about the spiritual and material conditions particularly of women and children in his congregation and the surrounding environs. On a trip to Holland he observed Mennonite congregations that frequently were served by deaconesses who looked after the women and children and assisted the sick, needy, and poor. Fliedner and his wife founded the Kaiserswerth Deaconess Institution in 1836, upon returning to Germany. Kaiserswerth initially began with a hospital and a school to train nurses and teachers, though deaconesses were also trained there for work in parishes, among indigent groups, and in foreign missions. The deaconesses were all single and lived communally. They were consecrated to their work with Fliedner's blessing, took no formal vows, and promised to remain five years. For many women the five-year promises quickly lengthened into lifelong affiliations with the community. The Fliedners' program met with great success as more women entered into deaconess work and the institution grew by leaps and bounds. In 1864 Kaiserswerth had thirty motherhouses and 1,600 deaconesses engaged in a variety of ministries. The institution would continue to grow and extend its influence worldwide in the coming years.

Fliedner's work was certainly innovative but not singular in Germany at that time. Other associations of deaconesses, and even deacons, were also founded. Pastor Johannes Wichern, for example, founded the Rauhes Haus and the Johannisstift, two organizations that trained Lutheran laymen to work with prisoners and poor families. Though Americans of many different denominations studied Fliedner's work closely, only one, Pastor William A. Passavant, sought to appropriate Wichern's work. He brought from Germany six of Wichern's brothers to oversee a Lutheran school for boys that he had started in Zelienople, Pennsylvania, but by 1864 the brothers had returned home, apparently in disagreement with the school's leadership over organizational matters. But for this one example, there were few, if any, nineteenth-century Protestants advocating for males to enter into communal living arrangements under the direction of a superior for the purpose of performing charitable ministry.

Initial Developments in North America

A Lutheran clergyman of extraordinary energy and compassion, William A. Passavant (1821–1894) was probably the first North American church person to take active notice of Fliedner's work in Germany. In 1846 while on church business to Europe, Passavant visited Kaiserswerth. He was deeply impressed with the operation there and saw it as the solution he had been seeking to help alleviate the enormous material need and social suffering he witnessed at home in Pennsylvania. He resolved to start a Lutheran deaconess community in the United States immediately upon his return to Pittsburgh and arranged with Fliedner to send four of his deaconesses to the United States in the near future. In the spring of 1848 Passavant rented a building in Allegheny to be used as a deaconess base, though as yet he had no deaconesses, no equipment, and no money. The actual beginnings of Lutheran deaconess work did not commence until January 1849, and Passavant had to aggressively seek out the first two patients, two soldiers who had just returned from the Mexican War. In July 1849 four Kaiserswerth deaconesses, accompanied by Pastor Fliedner, arrived in Pittsburgh to begin working at the hospital, which had been relocated there. At that point, the hospital was considered a branch of the Kaiserswerth Institute. In 1850 the hospital was incorporated by the General Assembly of Pennsylvania as the Pittsburgh Infirmary, under the auspices of the Institution of Protestant Deaconesses. Though similar to the Kaiserswerth model in many ways, Passavant's Pittsburgh organization had no motherhouse and offered no specific training for would-be deaconesses, other than the on-the-job training that occurred in the normal course of hospital work. This was the only training that Catherine Louisa Marthens received as the first deaconess consecrated in the United States in 1850. After only two years at the infirmary, in 1852 Marthens was tapped to run Passavant's second undertaking, an orphanage in Pittsburgh. These two tasks, orphanage and hospital work, continued to be the primary charitable activities of Lutheran deaconesses over the next seventy years.

Determined and energetic though he was, Passavant's deaconess institute and related ameliorative institutions were plagued by three chronic problems: a lack of funds, a lack of new recruits, and an inability to retain the few deaconesses that had joined his program. This did not seem to deter Passavant in any apparent way, since he went on to found three more hospitals, four orphanages, and a motherhouse for deaconesses in Milwaukee. Nonetheless, the lack of a critical mass of deaconesses was probably in itself one of the main obstacles to attracting new recruits. Between 1850 and 1891, only four women were consecrated into service with the Institution of Protestant Deaconesses. The work was extraordinarily demanding, and with a continual shortage of staff, there was never enough time for training. Passavant had precious little success attracting candidates, despite many public pleas. He continued to rely heavily on Kaiserswerth for assistance and lamented the lack of women willing to make the commitment to deaconess service. "It is strange, passing strange, that though the harvest is so great and so many stand all day idle, that so few consecrate themselves to Christ, in this service. How different in Europe with Christian females" (*The Missionary*, cited in Weiser, 31).

Though the first, Passavant was not the only nineteenth-century Lutheran cleric to be involved in organizing a deaconess society. Clergy and some lay leaders of several Lutheran church bodies sought to appropriate the concept of deaconess and interest unmarried women in making a life commitment to charitable and ameliorative work. Unique among Lutheran programs, however, was the Norwegian Lutheran Deaconess Association. Not only was it one of the more successful Lutheran programs; it also was founded, and directed for many years, by a laywoman rather than a minister. In 1883 a large community of Norwegian Lutherans in Brooklyn brought Sister Elizabeth Fedde (1850–1921) from Norway to direct charitable and relief work in their community and to train young women to serve as deaconesses. By 1889 she was already directing the opening of her second, enlarged hospital in Brooklyn. The year before that, she founded and opened a deaconess home and hospital in Minneapolis, which in turn led to the creation of the first Norwegian Lutheran deaconess home and hospital in Chicago in 1891. Among German American Lutherans, the Philadelphia Motherhouse of Deaconesses, founded in 1884, was particularly fortunate to have attracted a wealthy patron early in its existence, thus freeing it from many of the constraints that faced other programs. As with most other Lutheran institutions, its primary work was running a hospital. The Philadelphia Motherhouse also ran an orphanage, school for girls, and home for the elderly. In all, by 1914, there were ten deaconess organizations among U.S. Lutherans. The vast majority of them were closely connected to hospitals founded by their organizations, and not surprisingly, most of the deaconesses were occupied in nursing work and only secondarily in other fields such as parish work, teaching and child care, and the mission field.

Methodists were also early leaders in efforts to establish deaconess programs on both U.S. and Canadian soil. Unlike most Lutherans and other Protestants, many of their best efforts were initiated and directed by Methodist laywomen. From the start, many of these leaders, in their writings on the subject, held in dynamic tension the desperate need for social services and the opportunity to train young women for a larger role in church-related work. Theologically and ideologically, the Methodist ground was prepared by dynamic and educated nineteenth-century laywomen like Anna Wittenmeyer and Susan M. D. Fry. Wittenmeyer was a strong advocate for increased church involvement in charitable activities. During the Civil War she organized groups of women to provide nursing care to wounded soldiers. After visiting Kaiserswerth she became enthusiastic about the deaconess movement, founding a precursor to formal deaconess programs among Methodists called The Ladies' and Pastors' Christian Union and publishing a paper called *The Christian Woman* from her home in Philadelphia. Fry, another well-known Methodist laywoman and advocate for charitable causes, eventually occupied a chair at Illinois Wesleyan University. In 1872 Fry wrote a series of articles in *The Ladies Repository* making a persuasive appeal for the creation of programs to train young Methodist women to become deaconesses. The energies of both Wittenmeyer and Fry were diverted into the temperance movement starting in 1874 when Wittenmeyer was elected president of the Woman's Christian Temperance Union. It is significant that the temperance and deaconess movements alike dealt with nineteenth-century prohibitions against women's activities in the public sphere by arguing that their movements were essentially domestic in nature. Insofar as they propelled women into certain public forums, it was by rationalizing their activities as logical extensions of women's natural place and duties in the home.

In 1886 Isabella Thoburn (1840–1901), her brother Dr. J. M. Thoburn, and his wife Anna Thoburn, M.D., all of whom had spent much of their careers as missionaries in India, concluded that a deaconess program would be the best way to minister to millions of Indian women. They had in mind a sacramental function for ordained deaconesses, who would be allowed, only in India, because of cultural prohibitions against social contact between women and men, to administer baptism and communion to females.

The Thoburns were not the only American Methodists pondering how to more effectively serve the poor

Methodists were early leaders in efforts to establish deaconess programs on both United States and Canadian soil. Deaconess Ruth Lancaster of the Broadway Methodist Episcopal Church in Cleveland, Ohio, was among the thousands of laywomen who undertook social service programs such as educating recent émigrés. *Courtesy of the General Commission on Archives and History, United Methodist Church.*

and create more opportunities for service among Christian women. In October 1885 Methodist laywoman Lucy Rider Meyer founded a program in Chicago to prepare young women for missions and eleemosynary activities. In 1886 the Thoburns visited the Chicago Training School for City, Home and Foreign Missions and were deeply impressed with the program that Rider, a graduate of Oberlin College, a physician, and the wife of a Methodist pastor, had created. Meyer and the Thoburns agreed that her Chicago program was the ideal environment in which to provide practical training for deaconesses as well. In June 1887, using some empty space in the Chicago Training Home and with the support and direction of Rider, the first Methodist Deaconess Home opened for operation. Isabella Thoburn, who served as the first house mother and superintendent, was well qualified for the position. She had already distinguished herself as the first woman employed by the Methodist church in foreign missions. While in India she had established numerous ministries for women, including a school for girls. Under Thoburn and Rider Meyer's tutelage, the students spent the first summer visiting and

ministering to the poor and sick in the neighborhoods of Chicago, distributing evangelistic tracts, and bringing children to Sunday School and unchurched adults to services. In the fall they began their classwork, studying scripture, church history, Sunday School pedagogy, medicine, and singing. As the curriculum evolved, many additional subject areas were added, notable among them for a women's training program, theology, elocution, courses in social service, and even courses on the history of women's accomplishments and the history of the deaconess movement. The success of Rider Meyer's Chicago program attracted the church's attention. By May 1888, at the urging of the Chicago Preachers' Meeting, the General Conference of the Methodist church made deaconess work an official institution of the church, though it rejected the Thoburns' proposal for sacramental administration as a component of deaconess work.

The Chicago Training School and Deaconess Home continued to work cooperatively and successfully. According to ordained Methodist Episcopal Church elder Christian Golder (1849–1922), an enthusiastic, turn-of-the-century author and advocate of the female deaconate, by 1903, of the more than 2,000 young women who had received training there, 700 had gone into deaconess work, 160 into foreign mission service, and 150 into home mission work. The success of the Chicago Training School inspired the creation of many more lay education and training institutions, both in the United States and in Canada. The Methodist Deaconess Home in Toronto, Canada, was founded in 1894, the first venture of its kind in Canada. Modeled in part on the Chicago program with its emphasis on education, students attended classes taught by university professors, clergymen, and physicians. As in the United States, the emphasis on education proved attractive to young women, and the program increased from two to six residents in the first year alone. The first director, Alice Thompson, retired after two years, and in 1896 E. Jane Scott assumed the directorship. Born and raised in Baltimore, she entered the Chicago training program in 1890, arriving in Toronto with eight years of urban ministry experience. Under Scott's direction the program grew rapidly, attracting more than sixty new students within her first six years and adding a training school, midnight mission, and outreach program to impoverished children.

Many Methodist deaconess programs in the United States also owed their existence to the pioneering work of the Chicago program. The New England Deaconess Home and Training School was opened in Boston in 1889. Its curriculum was similar to that of the Chicago Training Institute, offering young women training for a variety of religious occupations. To this it also added a curriculum for those wishing to become nurses. The Scarritt Bible and Training School opened in Kansas City, Missouri, in 1892. It was founded by Belle Harris Bennett (1852–1922), a Methodist Episcopal Church, South, laywoman of extraordinary organizational talents who also presided over the Women's Home Mission Society and was responsible for the extension of laity voting rights to women in the Southern Methodist Church. When the General Conference of the Methodist Church, South, instituted an official deaconess program, Scarritt became an important training center. By 1915, Scarritt was one of sixty religious training schools for laywomen in the Methodist system.

The deaconess movement in North America sunk its deepest roots in Methodism. Of the approximately 2,000 Protestant women who served as deaconesses between 1871 and 1900 in the United States and Canada, approximately 60 percent were members of churches of the Methodist tradition. By 1903 Methodists directed 100 deaconess homes that employed some 1,400 deaconesses and probationers worldwide. Methodist deaconesses were involved in varied ministries, from foreign missions to prison missions, from running homes for the aged to directing Sunday Schools and kindergartens, from operating numerous hospitals and orphanages to doing midnight missions work in railroad stations and crime-ridden neighborhoods.

Among the many innovative programs of the Methodists was the first Deaconess Home for Colored People in Cincinnati, Ohio, founded in 1900 by African American pastor W. H. Riley. Though some young African American women had previously studied at other Methodist deaconess institutions, Riley was convinced of the value of deaconess education and the need for a training school and deaconess program designed specifically for African American women. "Ours is the only Deaconess Training-school among colored people in the United States. Only a beginning has been made in the African Methodist Episcopal Church . . . but the movement has begun, and the training schools will follow" (Golder, 412–413). Riley and his wife began by opening their own home to seven students who worked during the day and pursued their deaconess studies in the evenings. Riley was well aware of the amount of work waiting for the students but, consistent with other Methodist efforts, felt certain that proper training was essential to the success of the program. The first class of students graduated in 1902.

More than a small part of the success of the Chicago Deaconess Home and the many other deaconess programs begun by the Methodists was due to the work of women like Lucy Rider Meyer (1849–1922) and Jane Bancroft Robinson, two among many tireless workers and energetic publicists and advocates for the deaconess concept. Rider Meyer wrote numerous books and pamphlets about the deaconess movement and edited and contributed to journals promoting the female deaconate. Among the significant journals of the Methodist deaconess movement were *The Message*, the first publication of the Chicago Training School, and *The Deaconess Advocate*, the official journal of the Methodist Deaconess Society. These journals were an important public forum for Methodist women leaders, giving women like Rider Meyer and many others a "pulpit" from which to influence the public mind, comment on a variety of religious, political, and economic issues, even prod the consciences of their reading public, as with, for example, the *Advocate*'s urging of city churches not to leave their locales for the suburbs or its exhortations to teetotaling, support of Free Silver, and so on.

Jane Bancroft Robinson (1847–1932) also had a distinguished academic career. She served as a professor of French and then dean of the Women's College at Northwestern from 1877 to 1886, and later was elected a Fellow of Bryn Mawr. She also served as the secretary of the Deaconess Bureau of the Woman's Home Missionary Society of the Methodist Church. Under her supervision, at least ten Methodist deaconess houses were established. She also published several books and articles on the deaconess movement, among them *Deaconesses in Europe and Their Lessons for America* (1889).

Like other church leaders exploring ministry options for women, Episcopal clergy drew inspiration from European programs such as Kaiserswerth, as well as two English precedents, the sisterhood movement among high church Anglicans, and Mildmay, the deaconess movement started in London by William Pennefather in 1860. Sisterhoods, quite different from deaconess programs, were encouraged in those parts of Anglicanism that aspired to romanize the practices of the Church of England. Dr. Edward Pusey, member of the Oxford Movement, founded an early sisterhood in 1845. English sisterhoods of the nineteenth century had much in common with traditional Roman Catholic monastic practice. Sisters took the traditional, binding, lifelong vows of poverty, chastity, and obedience, submitting themselves to communal living under the control of a superior and a life of prayer. Education was not emphasized, and often the sisters understood their calling to be the "bride of Christ." Deaconesses in England and North America, by contrast, did not take binding vows and were free to leave the vocation at any time. According to a contemporaneous Anglican source, "The sisterhood exists primarily for the sake of forming a religious community, but the deaconesses live together for the sake of the work itself, attracted to deaconess work by the want which in most populous towns is calling loudly for assistance; with a view of being trained, therefore, for spiritual and temporal usefulness among the poor" (Robinson, 181). The first specifically deaconess enterprise in England was Pennefather's Missionary Training College for Women, later known as Mildmay House. Though Pennefather was an Anglican priest, he did not seek episcopal oversight of the enterprise. Further, he routinely welcomed women from other Protestant churches over against the objections of the Anglican hierarchy. Mildmay grew rapidly, supporting a hospital, nursing home, probationer house, night school, and so on. By 1899, the Mildmay Mission had 250 deaconesses and nurses and mission stations in Malta, Jamaica, and Hebron. At about the same time in England, the Community of St. Andrew was founded in 1861 by Elizabeth Ferard (d. 1893). This deaconess association had much closer ties to the ecclesiastical machinery of the Church of England. Ferard, who was from an old Huguenot family, had spent considerable time at Kaiserswerth, as had Pennefather. Both of them patterned their organizations on the Kaiserswerth model, including its emphasis on deaconess training. Ferard found an enthusiastic advocate for her work in Bishop Tait of London. In 1862 Tait ordained Ferard as a deaconess, and the North London Deaconess Association was born. However, deaconesses were not recognized by the Church of England until 1897 and not formally restored as an order until 1923.

Episcopal pastor William A. Muhlenberg, the great-grandson of Henry Melchior Muhlenberg (often considered one of the patriarchs of American Lutheranism), had studied both the Kaiserswerth deaconess program and the Anglican sisterhood movement with interest. He wrote several items, including a pamphlet, "The Institution of Deaconesses in the Evangelical Church," and "Two Letters on Protestant Sisterhoods" to introduce Episcopalians to these two concepts. In 1845 he founded a very small program called the Sisterhood of the Holy Communion at his church in New York City. The modest program grew slowly and by 1853 a Sister's House had been established next to the church. By 1858 a hospital, St. Luke's, had been built, which was managed by the Sisterhood.

In the beginning among Episcopalians in the United States, sisterhoods, though small in number, were yet more numerous than deaconess associations. The majority, founded by male clergy and attached to Episcopal congregations, were established in the United States in the last third of the nineteenth century. Most of them were organized to do charitable works including teaching, working with the poor, and running orphanages and hospitals, though a few were primarily devoted to spiritual retreat and contemplative living. Official recognition of the work of the sisterhoods did not come until 1869, when at its annual meeting the Protestant Episcopal Church Board of Missions passed a resolution requesting the formation of a committee to report on the organized work of churchwomen. The committee's favorable report occasioned the creation in 1870 of a board to recognize and oversee the work of sisterhoods in the church. Despite the existence of almost twenty American sisterhoods by this time, no sisters took an official role in the committee's deliberations and decisions.

The Deaconess Organization of the Diocese of Maryland was the first official Episcopal deaconess organization, established in Baltimore in 1855 under the auspices of the bishop of Maryland with two deaconesses. The deaconesses engaged in teaching and care of the poor and sick in St. Andrews Hospital. Similarly, in 1864 the Deaconess Association of the Diocese of Alabama was organized and devoted itself to teaching, nursing, and caring for orphans. Though both of these organizations supervised several charitable endeavors, they were both continually plagued with too few deaconesses to actually staff the programs they oversaw. Among young Episcopal women, the most popular deaconess-related program was a training school created in 1890 in New York City. Originally known as the Grace School for Deaconesses, the very small program later was renamed The New York Training School for Deaconesses and relocated under the direct supervision of the bishop. The two-year course of study specified classes in Bible, church history, hygiene, nursing, and liturgics, among other things. Between 1893 and 1903 the school educated fifty-four women for diaconal ministry.

The first stirrings of the deaconess movement in Canada took place in Toronto, where Presbyterians, Methodists, and Anglicans all established their first programs. Before Canada had its own deaconess programs a small number of Canadian women had attended training programs such as the Chicago Training School, the New York Training School of the Episcopal Church, and Mildmay in London. Efforts among Anglicans to establish formal women's programs in Canada were initially hampered by long-standing disagreements between evangelical and extreme Anglo-Catholic bishops on a variety of issues. As in England, Anglo-Catholic bishops favored sisterhoods, and evangelical bishops favored deaconess societies. An 1886 compromise among Canadian bishops deemed both acceptable, as long as they were established with the approval of the local bishop. By 1888 a branch of an English sisterhood called the Sisters of the Church was operating in Hamilton, Ontario. At about the same time *The Evangelical Churchman*, a publication of the low-church wing of Canadian Anglicanism, began advocating for a deaconess program. It kept readers informed of the work of the training schools and deaconesses in England and the United States. In 1890 the Alumni Association of Wycliffe College in Toronto provided the real impetus, creating a committee of Wycliff staff and local pastors to begin the work of implementing a deaconess program. The Church of England Deaconess and Missionary Training Home opened in Toronto in October 1893, though as yet it had no trainees. By the end of 1894 the institution had four trainees, and after that point, growth continued steadily, albeit very slowly. In 1895, with the arrival of Fanny Cross, the home finally found a permanent head deaconess and that same year saw its first two graduates ordained as deaconesses.

Duties and Rules for Deaconesses

Virtually all the Protestant deaconess institutions in the United States and Canada, following the Kaiserswerth precedent, drew up rules to guide their life together. The rules tended to be quite similar: Candidates were to be in good health, of a specified age, usually between eighteen and forty, and pious. Celibacy was required as a condition of service. Methodist Elder Christian Golder, one of the strongest clerical advocates for the female deaconate, was typically unequivocal on the celibacy requirement for females in organized church service. Paraphrasing Paul far too loosely in 1 Corinthi-

ans 7:34–35 (and neglecting verses 32 and 33 where Paul also urges celibacy for the male church worker), he argued,

> A married woman can have no regular calling in the exclusive service of the Church. Men are not hindered by marriage in the duties of the office but if a woman wishes to serve the Lord without restraint, in an ecclesiastical office, she must, under all circumstances, be free from the bonds of wedlock, so long as she holds the office. (Golder, cited in Ruether and Keller, *Women and Religion in America*, 1: 279)

Most deaconess associations required sisters to live communally. Many of those orders with formal motherhouses were highly structured. A clergyman director and deaconess superior functioned in loco parentis, and the deaconesses themselves occupied a subservient and obedient position somewhat analogous to children in the family home. Deaconesses and probationers had to obey the rules of the house, forsaking opportunities for entertainment, concerts, the theater, and shopping. They were expected to eschew idleness and fancy dress and live in sparse and simple accommodations, promising obedience to the superintendent and other directors. Sister Bertha Mueller (1879–1967) recalled the very strict rules that governed the Lutheran Deaconess Motherhouse in Philadelphia. "It was, as an illustration, a sin of considerable magnitude for a young sister to be late for breakfast. . . . When the kitchen work was done, all food was put under lock and key until the kitchen was opened again. No food was available between meals, nor was there, for that matter, any time available to eat it" (Weiser, 71).

The motherhouse tradition, with its highly regimented form of communal living inherited from Kaiserswerth, remained virtual dogma among Lutherans for many years, with the notable exception of the Norwegian Lutheran Deaconess Association, which did not emphasize the motherhouse lifestyle. Perhaps not coincidentally, the Norwegian Lutheran Deaconess Association was also the only Lutheran program founded and directed by a deaconess, Sister Elizabeth Fedde. In an arrangement highly unusual for Lutherans of the time, the program had no clerical rector until 1905.

Unlike the Episcopal sisterhoods, most North American deaconess organizations did not require lifelong vows. Protestant deaconess advocates in the United States carefully distinguished their programs from traditional Catholic monasticism, wanting to avoid an association that would bias people against this newly developing form of ministry for women. Though many deaconess organizations did require deaconesses and probationers to wear a uniform, they took care lest it seem too "romish." Advocates emphasized that, unlike nuns, deaconesses were volunteers with personal rights and autonomy. They could leave the organization whenever they wished, they always retained control of their personal property, and those women who remained for their whole lives would be taken care of in their old age. This was an important guarantee since deaconesses were rarely remunerated for their work, other than to receive the basic necessities of food and shelter provided by the organization.

Though the work of the first American deaconesses did vary from denomination to denomination, the majority were involved in the development of community health care, working as nurses, founding and maintaining hospitals and hospices, and providing home care for the sick. Many Episcopal sisterhoods and deaconess programs were initially founded in tandem with a hospital. The same was true for several interdenominational Protestant efforts and for most Lutherans. The Norwegian Lutheran Deaconess Association was one order that sent a particularly large number of its deaconesses into foreign missions work. The care and teaching of children and running of orphanages were also common activities among deaconesses. Canadian deaconesses found much work to do in the interior, serving missions, parishes, and schools, as well as working on reservations among Native peoples. The shortage of clergy in these areas sometimes had a salutary effect upon the status of individual deaconesses. Deaconess Winifred Stapleton distinguished herself in her work among the Sioux Indians in Manitoba, presiding at most of the services in the mission church. The Methodist, Anglican, and Presbyterian programs in Toronto also trained a number of women for foreign missions work, sending out graduates around the world in the first decades of the twentieth century, to places like China, Japan, and India.

Unlike other denominations, the earliest efforts of Methodist deaconesses were not always closely tied to a hospital or infirmary. Lucy Rider Meyer's Chicago deaconesses were in many ways pioneers in the nascent field of social services, using techniques such as the neighborhood canvas to catalog problematic living conditions in Chicago's inner-city neighborhoods. Their particular focus was the needs of women and children, providing families with domestic training and material assistance. The very real need for domestic education at this time cannot be dismissed: Before the advent of indoor plumbing, refrigeration, and antibiotics, an ignorance of hygiene, food safety, and other health issues could and often did have disastrous consequences. Meyer's deaconesses aimed to provide both spiritual and temporal assistance to the poor in order to convert them and better their social circumstances. The goals of Methodist deaconesses were consistent with the evangelistic imperative that was so central to Methodist self-understanding.

Deaconesses worked to better the circumstances of all women by training them in life skills and the Christian faith, in the hopes that, once uplifted, these rescued women could take a place on the front lines of evangelism. Strictly speaking, the work was more characteristically ameliorative than liberative both for the deaconesses and their clientele. Even so, the attempts of early Methodist deaconesses and leaders like Lucy Meyer Rider to address the systemic reasons for poverty and other social problems cannot be ignored. Their progressive and reformist spirit placed them on the leading edge of the evolving Social Gospel movement among American Protestants.

The Methodist commitment to deaconess education no doubt had a significant impact upon the status of women in that denomination. The course of study was considered essential for deaconess work, and although many women did not actually complete their studies, they all received some advanced training. This provided many young Methodist women with an opportunity to learn an occupation as well as receive an education in various theological disciplines. Though not nearly so detailed a course of study as that of male seminarians, nonetheless the theological courses functioned to elevate deaconesses' status above that of average laypersons, not so far below that of the clergy. Astute Methodist leaders such as Lucy Rider Meyer were well aware of the advantages that advanced education brought to young women.

There is evidence to suggest that the promise of training and advanced education was one of the key attractions of diaconal ministry for young women of all denominations. Between 1880 and 1915, more than sixty-two religious training schools were opened in the United States and Canada. The most numerically successful nineteenth century Episcopal venture in the United States, for example, was not an actual deaconess program but rather a training school for prospective deaconesses in New York. William Passavant's early Lutheran deaconess program floundered due to a chronic shortage of candidates. Not coincidentally, Passavant's deaconesses were offered little, if any, formal training. More than one of his imported Kaiserswerth deaconesses lamented the lack of training for their American counterparts, noting pointedly that "the probationers had too little training or pastoral care" (Weiser, 46). It would appear that Methodists were more successful than other denominations at attracting candidates for diaconal ministry precisely because their programs provided training and education for young women. Well into the twentieth century, Methodist deaconess programs continued to place a high value on education. Beginning in 1918, the Methodist Episcopal Church, South, required two years of college and two years of professional-level education for all deaconesses. Starting in 1951 all new deaconesses were required to have both a college degree and some graduate-level training.

Advocates for the deaconess lifestyle frequently used concepts like self-denial, unselfishness, and self-giving love to describe the necessary attributes of the deaconess. Often these descriptions invoked Christ's self-giving love and sometimes collapsed that concept together with sentimentalized nineteenth-century conceptions of maternal love to describe the motivation and model for deaconess work.

> The only hope and possibility of elevating and saving this class of the population in our great cities lies in the unselfish and devoted activity of such women. The sufferings, cares, and sicknesses of these most abandoned ones can only be reached by ministrations of love that will take a personal interest, nurse, encourage, counsel and assist; that will give work to the unemployed, gather the children in kindergartens and the infants in day nurseries, and be present everywhere where help is needed. These people need education . . . in the affairs of daily life, in practical economy, in the preparation of food, in sick-nursing, housekeeping and the training of children. They should also be taught the lessons of morality and practical Christianity, and this can best be done by deaconesses. (Golder, 488–489)

Isabelle Horton (1853–1933), a Chicago deaconess who served as the director of social work and education at the Halsted Street Institutional Church, put the matter most directly, "The world wants mothering. . . . The deaconess movement puts the mother into the church" (145–146).

The descriptions of the heroic task facing deaconesses provide some insights into the complicated admixture of compassion and concern that animated the charitable work of many nineteenth-century Christians as they surveyed the massive influx of immigrants: genuine compassion to alleviate the real human suffering that they witnessed, and palpable concern about the "great danger for our Nation" in bringing in "the unchristian and ignorant masses in the great cities [who were] threatening civilization" (Golder, 485). As they sought an answer to the question of how to evangelize, socialize, and civilize these poor and ignorant immigrants, the solution that frequently emerged was women: women unburdened by a family of their own who could function as mothers to the poor and sick. Indeed, for a number of church leaders, the task of the deaconess was to domesticate the new immigrants in every sense of that word. Just as a mother was called upon to train and socialize her own children to become good Christians and good citizens, so also the task of the deaconess was to domesticate her

"family," the people and neighborhoods that she was called to serve.

The maternal metaphor for the work of deaconesses proved to be very powerful, powerful enough to transcend long-standing prohibitions against women's presence and influence in both church and public life. Between 1870 and 1903, North American Protestants established over 140 deaconess homes, and over 2,000 women became deaconesses. For most denominations this was their first encounter with women as full-time, remunerated religious professionals. No doubt many were surprised by how much these women were able to accomplish in nursing, teaching, social work, immigrant resettlement, and industrial education. Deaconesses served as an early form of institutionalized charity when many churches and governments had neither the resources nor the personnel to develop adequate programs of social aid.

Despite the accomplishments of many deaconesses, the movement was never as numerically significant as leaders hoped it would be, even among the Methodists. The early twentieth century was a time of slow though continued growth for many deaconess programs and even the initiation of some new programs, such as the Lutheran Church–Missouri Synod's program, established in 1919. However, by the second and third decades of the new century it was clear that the movement was in eclipse. Most denominations had always had difficulty recruiting, but this became even more problematic after the turn of the century, even for more successful endeavors like those of the Methodists. The high point of recruitment for the Methodist Episcopal Church was between 1887 and 1910, when perhaps a thousand deaconesses had been consecrated. Recruitment statistics never reached those highs again. In this period the training schools, too, began to experience difficulty. In the late 1920s and 1930s a number of training schools closed or merged with seminaries or colleges. The Congregationalist Training School, for example, first opened its doors in 1909 but by 1926, unable to sustain itself, was forced to merge with a theological seminary. The Church of England Deaconess and Missionary Training Home in Toronto had by the 1930s restyled itself the Anglican Women's Training College. By 1969 it had merged with Covenant College in Toronto.

As the twentieth century unfolded, it become increasingly clear that the maternal metaphor, powerful as it was, had outlived its usefulness. Not only had the tidal wave of immigrants crested by the turn of the century, but also many more educational, governmental, and social services networks had developed in the interim to respond to the needs of the poor and displaced. Furthermore, many of the ameliorative tasks deaconesses pioneered in the mid-nineteenth century, nursing, teaching, social work, even foreign missions work, were by the mid-twentieth century in the hands of more highly trained and specialized professionals whose diplomas were obtained from institutes certified by their respective professional organizations. The most dramatic example of this was the nursing profession. The professionalization of medical workers, and the assumption of training responsibilities by secular colleges and universities, rendered many deaconess training schools inadequate or even irrelevant to the nursing profession. This trend was already evident by the turn of the century. The pan-Protestant Deaconess Society of Dayton, Ohio, established in 1890, had, with generous donations, built an impressive hospital in 1894. But by 1898 the Deaconess Society had been dissolved and the hospital had ceased to use deaconesses, resorting instead to the exclusive employment of professional nurses. Though a variety of factors influenced this all-too-typical course of events, ultimately the development of professional nurses rendered the already ambiguous vocation of the Dayton deaconess superfluous. A similar fate awaited those programs that pioneered social work, albeit somewhat later. The Boston Training School, for example, was eventually absorbed into the Boston University School of Social Work with little, if any, of its original mission intact.

The volunteeristic spirit of American Protestantism also contributed to the weakness and even demise of deaconess organizations. The chronic lack of deaconess candidates in various denominations may indicate that the majority of pious women felt themselves able successfully to combine church work and traditional family life. The American setting had from the beginning presented many voluntary opportunities for lay involvement by both males and females. Cent societies, women's missionary groups, Moral Reform and temperance societies, and church auxiliaries allowed many women to be deeply involved in various mission and outreach movements without forsaking children, a husband and home, and varying degrees of autonomy. The existence of institutions like Kaiserswerth in Europe reflected an overt need in that context for a formalized office of lay ministry. By contrast, in the United States, where so many denominations faced serious clerical shortages well into the late nineteenth century, laypeople had been, from the beginning, essential to the survival of the American church.

Perhaps even less attractive to the majority of North American women was the stringent and sacrificial lifestyle that excluded spouse and children. Deaconesses were subject to an extraordinary amount of social control as a condition for ministry, but their sacrifice was unaccompanied by any corresponding opportunities for greater ecclesiastical authority or influence. Throughout the history of the Christian church, visible self-sacrifice has often been a basic prerequisite of, as well as an avenue to, greater power and influence in the church, both for clerics and laity. For nineteenth- and early-twentieth-century American deaconesses, the self-sacrificing lifestyle provided no entrée to greater authority or power, either in the church or in the deaconess structure. Put simply, the majority of women wanted to be more than just metaphorical mothers.

The Early Twentieth Century

Most nineteenth-century deaconess institutions did not survive past the mid-twentieth century. Those that did had to make significant procedural and structural accommodations to changing realities, both social and ecclesiastical. Often those accommodations were not adequate and rarely were they accompanied by corresponding changes within the denominations the deaconesses served. Deaconess programs that did manage to survive did so precariously, perpetually short on recruits, financial resources, and, all too often, clear and adequate rationales to justify their continued existence. In the first half of the twentieth century, deaconess organizations and advocates typically made five common adjustments in an attempt to ensure their survival.

One common adjustment was to position deaconess programs more firmly within the ecclesiastical structures of their affiliated denominations. A statement from the *1908 Discipline of the Methodist Church* informed deaconesses, "You are to work for Jesus only" (para. 470). Within a few years however, many deaconess leaders themselves sought to make clear that deaconesses also worked for the church, hoping that this would improve their recruitment efforts and give them new funding sources as well as greater power within their denominations. Such realignments could be helpful, but they were not without their dangers and challenges. All too often they entailed the loss of both programmatic autonomy and financial control of their already limited funds, with deaconess programs becoming one of many special interest groups competing for denominational attention and resources.

A second adjustment regarded the nature of deaconess work itself in the first few decades of the twentieth century. With the professionalization of many traditional deaconess vocations such as nursing and social work, deaconess training schools increasingly focused on preparing women for parish-centered vocations, including Christian educator, pastoral assistant, music director, and church administrator. Several training schools adjusted their curriculums, adding more overtly theological coursework. However, it quickly became clear that many church leaders were more comfortable with deaconess religious work outside the walls of the church than inside, fearing that deaconesses might usurp pastoral prerogative and perhaps even overstep what were presumed to be divinely circumscribed limitations in the liturgical arena. Advocates for deaconess programs had always trod a fine line, arguing for their programs while reassuring church leaders that this office would appease women's desire for greater involvement in ministry. As one Methodist bishop put it in 1895, "Her opportunities for usefulness are now so numerous that she does not need to get into the pulpit. There must be no clashing in regard to spheres or rights" (*Deaconess Advocate*, July 1895). By 1920, however, many of those initial opportunities for usefulness in wider society had disappeared. Inside the church there was no corresponding perception of an urgent need or crisis, analogous to the mid-nineteenth-century wave of immigrants, which might necessitate and legitimate the work of professional female religious workers.

A third, frequent adjustment made by many deaconess advocates involved attempts to elevate the status and image of deaconesses. Two strategies were typically employed. The first strategy entailed imposing higher entrance standards and new educational demands upon candidates. The requirement of a bachelor's degree became common, and some programs began to require advanced professional training for all candidates. Periodic adjustments to deaconess standards became common after World War I and have continued to the present day. What appeared initially to be a small adjustment in preparation standards in fact reflected a tectonic shift in mid-twentieth-century conceptions of the vocation. In its infancy deaconess work had been understood as a definitive profession, but by the early twentieth century it came to resemble more of an ecclesiastical enhancement, an additional bit of training or certification that could complement one's real profession.

The second strategy focused on elevating deaconesses' status within their denomination. Advocates began pushing for the inclusion of the profession in denominational polities, the use of new titles and initiation ceremonies, and much later, participation in liturgical leadership, equal to the levels of participation allowed male deacons. All this, it was hoped, would lend ecclesiastical respect and weight to the profession. For some, such as various Methodist bodies, official inclusion in church polity and even ordination were achieved relatively early. But for most denominations, many years of tumultuous discussion would pass before female deaconesses would be allowed to exercise significant leadership within the walls of the congregation. The turmoil that this issue occasioned for the Anglican and Christian Reformed Churches is illustrative of other denominations. The Lambeth Conference of 1920, the decision-making body of the Anglican Church, declared that the ordination of deaconesses conferred upon them holy orders. Just ten

years later, in 1930, the same body renounced that decision. When, in 1941, the Church of England finally agreed that deaconesses were to be ordained into an official order of ministry, it narrowly circumscribed their duties to specifically exclude participation in Holy Communion services. Similarly, in 1978 the Christian Reformed Church finally decided that women could be ordained as deacons, if their work was clearly distinguished from the work of elders. The measure met with such strong protests that the next year all consistories were told to defer implementation of the decision.

Some denominations, including Methodists and Episcopalians, did eventually decide to ordain women into the office of deaconess, but even this change of initiation rite promised far more authority than it actually delivered. Some churches specified that ordained deaconesses were still laity. Those churches that deemed them an order of ministry usually carefully restricted their functions, concerned that they might usurp clerical privilege, presume clerical authority, or become the slippery slope toward women's full ordination into Word and Sacrament ministry. Well into the late twentieth century, many denominational leaders have appeared to be more comfortable dispensing ecclesiastical titles and ceremonies than allowing trained women full access to the range of ministry tasks.

Yet a fourth common adjustment made by many deaconess organizations was a relaxation of the regimentation, including an increase in the autonomy of deaconesses within their orders, and the provision of salaries. Nineteenth-century deaconesses were subject to extraordinary social control as a condition for ministry. Over time, recruitment problems, as well as evolving attitudes toward single women and married working women, resulted in greater symmetry in the lifestyle demands made upon women and men in ministry. Methodists dispensed with uniforms by 1918, and by the middle of the twentieth century most other deaconess programs had followed suit. Communal living arrangements also became less common, though some Lutheran programs, for example, the Philadelphia Motherhouse, which resettled itself in Gladwyne, Pennsylvania, maintained strict living regulations well into the 1960s. The requirement of celibacy was dropped for Methodists in 1940, simultaneous to a decision to provide all deaconesses a salary. Episcopal deaconesses were not allowed to marry until 1964. Deaconesses in the Lutheran Church in America, spiritual progeny of the Philadelphia Motherhouse, were not allowed to marry until 1969, and as late as 1964 they were still attending deaconess school, rather than an accredited college, for nursing and parish secretarial training.

A fifth common adjustment of several deaconess organizations was to create and/or participate in federative structures to promote the deaconess cause across denominational lines. In 1947, for example, the International Federation of Deaconess Associations was founded in Copenhagen. Currently, deaconesses throughout the world are represented by DIAKONIA, a worldwide, interdenominational association for the promotion and support of diaconal work. The organization holds regular international assemblies. Its publication *Diakonia News* provides ongoing information, support, and lobbying for the diaconal cause.

Beginning in the 1960s a number of denominations in North America and elsewhere undertook a reconsideration of crucial issues of theology, ministry, gender, polity, the rights and responsibilities of the laity, and the relationship of lay and clerical ministry. This resulted in, among other things, the deconstruction and preliminary reconstruction of diaconal ministry in several denominations. In 1964, Vatican Council II approved the restoration of the permanent diaconate, for men only, not as a transition to priesthood but as its own order. In 1966 the World Council of Churches sponsored ecumenical conferences on the diaconate, which culminated in two publications, *The Ministry of Deacons* (1965) and *Deaconesses* (1966). From the 1960s onward, several denominations with diaconal programs have worked to reorganize their programs and redefine their terminology, establish new rationales for diaconal work, reconsider gender and eligibility requirements, and clarify the relationship between diaconal ministers and other lay- and ordained people. This has not always been an easy or straightforward process. For example, a number of churches, including Methodists and Episcopalians, entered the 1960s with several diaconal ministries running simultaneously: deaconesses, male interim or transitional deacons who were on their way to being ordained, and male permanent deacons.

Denominational efforts to clarify terminology and job descriptions, though necessary, have also been challenging. In 1968 the United Methodist Church (UMC) created the category of lay worker. In 1976 it approved the term *diaconal ministers*, specifying that they should be consecrated to their office. Less than two decades later the UMC Commission for the Study of Ministry recommended phasing out the office of diaconal minister and replacing it with an order of lay consecrated deacons. Given the rapid changes in wider North America society, such challenges are understandable. Changing gender roles, the entrance of women into the workforce, denominational mergers, clerical shortages, and declining financial resources, to name but a few factors, have all impacted discussions of diaconal ministry. Furthermore, decisions about the identity and nature of diaconal work are inextricably connected to a host of other strategic issues facing churches in North America. One in particular is worth careful consideration. A distinctive strength of North American Christianity has

long been the high degree of leadership exerted by the laity. Many North American church leaders have quite rightly sought ways to encourage ongoing lay leadership, but it is not clear whether diaconal programs will be a help or hindrance to those efforts. Only with hindsight will we be able to ascertain the consequences of various denominational attempts to revivify the diaconate as yet another titled ministry. Ultimately, those attempts will contribute either to the democratization of the church or to its clericalization. They may help facilitate the ministries of the laity but could also further inflate church bureaucracies by adding yet another layer to the ecclesiastical hierarchy.

In retrospect it is clear that the creation and development of the office of deaconess in North America provided a good deal of impetus for the eventual decisions of many denominations to ordain women as ministers. Ironically, women's ordination into Word and Sacrament ministry probably contributed to the eventual demise of most deaconess programs. While this is lamentable, it is also a vivid reminder that throughout the history of the Christian church the shape and content of various church offices such as presbyter, bishop, deacon, and deaconess have never been static. It is not yet clear what is to be the character and content of diaconal ministry or, for that matter, clerical ministry in the twenty-first century. However, we can hope for the development of a diversity of approaches, each of which is grounded in the gospel, focused on service to those in need, and flexible enough to respond effectively in a context of rapid social change.

SOURCES: See the following: James Barnett, *The Diaconate—A Full and Equal Order* (1995); Virginia Lieson Brereton, "Preparing Women for the Lord's Work," in *Women in New Worlds*, ed. Hilah Thomas and Rosemary Skinner Keller (1981); Frederick Sheely Weiser, *Serving Love: Chapters in the Early History of the Diaconate in American Lutheranism* (1960); *Deacons in the Ministry of the Church: A Report by the House of Bishops* (1988); Mary Agnes Dougherty, "The Methodist Deaconess Movement, 1888–1918" (Ph.D. diss., University of California, Davis, 1979), and "The Social Gospel According to Phoebe," in *Women in New Worlds*, ed. Hilah Thomas and Rosemary Skinner Keller (1981); G. H. Gerberding, *Life and Letters of W. A. Passavant, D.Div.* (1906); Christian Golder, *History of the Deaconess Movement in the Christian Church* (1903); Isabelle Horton, *The Burden of the City* (1904); Rosemary Keller et al., eds., *Called to Serve, the United Methodist Diaconate* (1987); Rosemary Skinner Keller, "Lay Women in the Protestant Tradition," in *Women and Religion in America*, ed. Rosemary Radford Ruether and Rosemary Keller, vol. 1 (1981); Alison Kemper, "Deaconess as Urban Missionary and Ideal Woman: Church of England Initiatives in Toronto, 1890–1895," in *Canadian Protestant and Catholic Missions, 1820's–1960's*, ed. John S. Moir and C. T. McIntire (1988); and Mary Anne McFarlane, "A Tale of Handmaidens: History of the Deaconess Order in the United Church of Canada, 1925–1966"

(M.A. thesis, Ontario Institute for Studies in Education, 1987). For a helpful article on the role and politics of deaconesses in the early church origins, see Charlotte Methuen, "Widows, Bishops and the Struggle for Authority in Didascalia Apostolorum," *Journal of Ecclesiastical History* 46 (April 1995): 409–431; Lucy Rider Meyer, *Deaconesses, Biblical, Early Church, European, American* (1897) and *Deaconesses, Biblical, Early Church, European, American, with the Story of How the Work Began* (1892); William A. Muhlenberg, *Two Letters on Protestant Sisterhoods* (1853) and *The Institution of Deaconesses in the Evangelical Church* (1856); Jeanine E. Olson, *Deacons and Deaconesses through the Centuries: One Ministry, Many Roles* (1992); Jane Bancroft Robinson, *Deaconesses in Europe and Their Lessons for America* (1889); James Thoburn, *The Deaconess and Her Vocation* (1893); Frederick Weiser, *Love's Response: A Story of Lutheran Deaconesses in America* (1962); Abdel Ross Wentz, *Fliedner the Faithful* (1936); World Council of Churches Studies, *The Deaconess: A Service of Women in the World of Today* (1966); and Barbara Brown Zikmund, "Winning Ordination for Women in Mainstream Protestant Churches," in *Women and Religion in America*, ed. Rosemary Radford Ruether and Rosemary Keller, vol. 3 (1986).

MISSIONARY MOVEMENT

PROTESTANT WOMEN MISSIONARIES: FOREIGN AND HOME
Dana L. Robert

MISSION WORK WAS the earliest and most popular cause for which Protestant women organized themselves into gender-separate groups in the nineteenth century. In the process of spreading their religious faith across cultural barriers to non-Christians, women renegotiated the boundaries of their domestic sphere to become evangelists, teachers, physicians, and social workers—all roles seen as consistent with women's maternal nature. The distinction between home and foreign missions was geographic, with home missions designating outreach within North America. In reality, many women moved between home and foreign missions and considered them extensions of the same task. Work among Native Americans began as "foreign" missions; but with the incorporation of Indian territory into the United States, by the late nineteenth century it was organized under various "home" mission agencies.

Women missionaries outnumbered men by two to one throughout much of the twentieth century, with even greater numerical strength in the nondenominational "faith missions." Although female missionaries generally maintained the basic doctrines and pieties of middle-class Protestantism, they pushed beyond the institutional structures of the churches—founding schools, hospitals, and charitable institutions and facilitating social movements such as mass literacy and human rights campaigns. Mission work therefore provided them opportunities for independent initiative that did not exist widely in American society until the late twentieth century. Although women's involvement in missions continued into the twenty-first century, the diversification of alternative career opportunities in both church and society meant that the movement did not retain the significance it held for Protestant women a century earlier. Missionaries nevertheless remain an important channel of communication between Americans and people of other cultures, especially women and children.

Colonial Period

With missions traditionally a high-risk occupation for unmarried males, few Protestant women engaged in organized mission work before the nineteenth century. Although the English settlements in North America partly justified their existence by claiming they would evangelize the Native Americans, such work was left in the hands of a few male missionaries. The first women claiming the title of "missionary" were individuals who violated social and gender norms by preaching to the English settlers. Sustained by the doctrine of the "inner light," the first Quaker missionary women arrived in Boston in 1656, where they were examined for witchcraft and deported. But Quaker women kept entering the English colonies. After passage of a strict anti-Quaker law in 1658, Mary Dyer was hung on Boston Common for daring to evangelize the Massachusetts Puritans. During the eighteenth century, the most notable individual missionary women were Ann Lee Stanley (1736–1784), founder of the communitarian Shakers, and Quaker Jemima Wilkinson (1752–1819), the "Public Universal Friend." Inspired by millennial visions, both Mother Ann Lee and the Universal Friend undertook itinerant preaching tours and gathered converts into the denominations they founded.

The most significant organized mission work by women in the colonial period was undertaken by the Moravian pietists. Known formally as the Unitas Fratrum, the Moravians sent family groupings from Germany to live among Native Americans in Georgia in 1735. Moravians moved to Pennsylvania in 1740 and founded Bethlehem and other mission centers among Native Americans, as well as communities in New York, Ohio, and Ontario. As pacifists and egalitarians, the Moravians in Bethlehem freed women to engage in mission work by raising children in communal nurseries. Moravian women either worked in partnership with their husbands or else were organized into unmarried women's "choirs" who evangelized women, teaching them crafts and skills, and acted as nurses, teachers, and farmers. The choir system provided social support and vocational opportunities for unmarried women. Eldresses, labouresses, and deaconesses exercised spiritual leadership in the community, and fourteen women were ordained in the 1750s. The chief purpose of Moravian communities was to conduct mission work among Native Americans, African slaves, and other oppressed peoples. Living as peaceful examples of biblical communal principles, they were the most successful Protestant missionaries in the 1700s.

The Early Nineteenth Century

The mission work of women entered mainstream Protestantism during the early years of the American Republic, unleashed by the spiritual energies of the Second Great Awakening. Among followers of the "New Divinity," the theological descendants of Jonathan Edwards, cross-cultural missions became central to their millennial vision. Motives for mission included giving glory to God, rescuing the unsaved from eternal damnation, doing good as central to Christian life, and obeying Jesus' final command to evangelize the world. For many American missionaries, their goals included spreading the revolutionary ideals of democracy and human equality around the world. Women's interest in missions grew in tandem with the widening movement for women's education in the early 1800s. The earliest missionary women thus saw their primary role to be that of teachers, rather than claiming the more radical role of preachers.

By the turn of the century, women were organizing local charitable societies for outreach to poor women. Isabella Graham (1742–1814) and others founded the New York Society for the Relief of Poor Widows and Small Children in 1797. In 1800 both the Boston Female Asylum and the Female Association of Philadelphia for the Relief of Women and Children in Reduced Circumstances were founded. These early women's charitable associations were the first city mission societies. An assistant to Graham in her schools, Sarah Farquhar (1774–1839) sailed to India for her health in 1804. On shipboard, she met the first English missionary to Madras, William Loveless of the London Missionary Society. Upon marrying him, she became the first American woman to engage in overseas missions. Sarah Farquhar Loveless founded both boarding and day schools for girls in Madras, raised money for a chapel, and provided hospitality for the first American missionaries in India.

Even before Americans organized societies to send foreign missionaries, women led in raising funds. In 1800, a Baptist named Mary Webb (1779–1861) founded the Boston Female Society for Missionary Purposes, which united Baptist and Congregationalist women. Leading the society for fifty-six years, Webb raised money for diverse home and foreign missionary causes and encouraged the ecumenical cooperation of women. She eventually corresponded with over 100 women's mission groups in eighteen states. The key role of women in funding the American missionary enterprise continued after the founding of the predominantly Congregationalist American Board in 1810 as the first foreign mission–sending agency. Domestic servant Sally Thomas left $345.38 to the board as its first bequest. Among Methodists, Mary Morgan Mason (1791–1868) organized the New York Female Assistance Society in 1813 and the New York Female Missionary Society in 1819. Mason's involvement in city missions included starting Sunday Schools, mite societies (for the collection of small sums), and a maternity hospital. Besides bearing ten children and being a minister's wife, she served as head of the Missionary Society for nearly fifty years. She raised money, provided supplies, and corresponded with the society's missionary, Ann Wilkins, in Liberia.

The involvement of American women in foreign missions moved to a new phase with the founding of the American Board in 1810. Although opposition to missionary women was widespread, the insistence by newly appointed Congregationalist missionaries that they be allowed to marry provided an opening for missionary wives. Active in charitable works and highly educated for their day, several young women agreed to marry America's first missionaries and sailed with their husbands for India in 1812. They were considered "assistant missionaries" and "helpmeets" for their husbands. The youngest of the three, Harriet Atwood Newell (1793–1812), became the prototypical American martyr and icon of self-sacrificial piety when she died at age nineteen from complications caused by childbirth less than a year after her marriage and embarkation. Her diary became a devotional classic that inspired generations of missionaries. Ann Hasseltine Judson (1789–1826) and her husband became the first American Baptist missionaries when they were rebaptized by immersion upon first reaching India. Ann became a household name and heroine when as a missionary wife in Burma she taught girls, translated Bible portions, wrote the first history of an American mission, and negotiated for the release of her husband and other Europeans imprisoned by the Burmese in their rebellion against British control. She died in Burma from her hardships, but her memory continued to inspire women to missionary service in the twentieth century. The third pioneer missionary wife, Roxanna Nott (1785–1876), returned to Connecticut after two years because of her husband's ill health, but she lived a long and useful life as a minister's wife. Although controversies continued through the 1830s over the suitability of women for active mission work, the growing middle-class, home-based ideals of the era ultimately legitimated missionary wives' roles as emissaries of Christian family values in foreign cultures.

Because women were not usually allowed to preach or be ordained, they interpreted Jesus' final command to go into all the world and spread the gospel as a biblical mandate to become teachers. Teaching women and children became the major public activity of missionary women in the nineteenth century. They opened schools wherever they were stationed. In 1837, Mary Lyon (1797–1849) opened Mount Holyoke Female Seminary (the first women's college) as the preeminent training ground for women teachers who went abroad or to the American frontier. The influence of Mount Holyoke was so great that by 1887, 20 percent of missionary women in the American Board had studied there. A large number of Mount Holyoke graduates also remained unmarried for the sake of their missionary work—a feature for which the school was heavily criticized as a "Protestant nunnery." The Mount Holyoke philosophy of preparing "head, heart, and hand" emphasized high intellectual standards, disciplined piety, and practical domestic training. Its holistic approach to women's lives spread around the world through missionary schools founded by American women.

By the 1830s, women in many urban areas were starting Sunday Schools and distributing tracts among the poor. Phoebe Palmer (1807–1874) was the most important female Methodist spiritual leader of the nineteenth century, with her emphasis on "holiness" theology, or a deepened spiritual life, as a starting point for Christian activism. A class leader and evangelist who brought thousands into the spiritual experience called the "second blessing," in 1850 she founded the Five Points Mission in the Hell's Kitchen section of Manhattan. The mission introduced what became the settlement house approach and included a chapel, school rooms, apartments for the homeless, and a house of industry that provided skills and employment.

Although unmarried women readily became involved in city mission work in the early nineteenth century, the Congregationalist-dominated American Board preferred to send married women as foreign missionaries. Sarah Huntington (1802–1836) of Norwich, Connecticut, for example, found her way opened to become a foreign missionary only when in 1833 she married Eli Smith, a missionary to Syria, when she was thirty-one. But she had already spent six years as a volunteer with two different tribes of Connecticut Indians, teaching and founding Sunday Schools among them and petitioning the state legislature on their behalf. The few unmarried women who received appointments were expected to live with a missionary family. The first unmarried missionary woman was former slave Betsey Stockton (1798–1865), who went to Hawaii attached to a Presbyterian family under the American Board in 1822. She began a school for nonroyal Hawaiian children. After her return from the mission, she worked among Indian children in Canada before becoming principal of a school for black children. Despite a few notable examples like Stockton and teachers in girls' boarding schools in India and the Middle East, the American Board had made only limited progress in appointing unmarried women by midcentury. Baptists and Methodists seemed more willing to appoint unmarried women to independent ministries at that time.

The Woman's Missionary Movement

After founding numerous charitable organizations for prisoners, the elderly, and poor women, including Woman's Hospital in New York City, in 1861 Mrs. Sarah Doremus (1802–1877) founded the nondenominational Woman's Union Missionary Society (WUMS) to send unmarried women as missionary teachers. A former Presbyterian and mother of nine children, Mrs. Doremus had become Dutch Reformed upon marrying her merchant husband. Her ecumenical approach reflected both her personal experience and a strong trend among mission-minded women. The WUMS launched a new movement of nationwide women's missionary societies founded to appoint and support single women missionaries. The deaths of a generation of men during the Civil War made the idea of sending unmarried women to the mission field more acceptable to the general public. The organization of their own mission-sending agencies by Protestant women helped fuel a dramatic increase in the strength of the American missionary force. Before 1870, the United States had sent only 2,000 Protestant missionaries, roughly equally divided between men and women. But with the addition of large numbers of single women, by 1900 missionaries from the United States numbered approximately 6,000, of whom up to two-thirds were women.

Following the lead of the WUMS, women began organizing denominational women's missionary societies in response to requests from missionary wives who needed help. By 1874, women's foreign missionary societies had been founded among the Congregationalists, Methodists, Baptists, Christians, Episcopalians, African Methodists, and Presbyterians. Continuing the momentum begun by women's leadership during the Civil War, the gender-separate "woman's missionary movement" spread throughout American Protestantism. Women organizers traveled around the United States speaking and urging women in local churches to found missionary auxiliaries. Local societies prayed for missions, studied cross-cultural issues, and contributed money and goods to support missionaries. Despite opposition from many male pastors who feared women's independent initiatives, denominational networks of local societies grew and provided many women with their first taste of leadership, including speaking and praying in public, and administrative responsibilities.

In 1869, the Woman's Foreign Missionary Society of the Methodist Episcopal Church sent teacher Isabella Thoburn (1840–1901) and physician Clara Swain (1834–1910) to India as their first two missionaries. Thoburn gradually raised the level of the girls' school she started until it became the first college for women in Asia. By 1909, women's mission societies were supporting eleven women's colleges in India, China, Japan, and Korea. The first woman medical missionary, Swain opened the first woman's hospital in Asia, taught Indian women to be doctors, and provided the only Christian witness in a Muslim state. By 1909, the fiftieth anniversary of the woman's missionary movement, women's missionary societies were running over 3,200 schools, eighty hospitals, and eighty-two dispensaries, with one out of every ten female missionaries being a doctor. At a time when they could not get jobs in the United States, women physicians were actively recruited and supported by women's mission societies. Beginning with Clara Swain, missionary physicians opened the first medical schools for women in the non-Western world. Mission-

ary women also served as evangelists by visiting women in their homes or by speaking in rural areas. They were usually accompanied by indigenous "Bible women." Evangelistic partnership with indigenous women was so important that the women's societies supported nearly three times as many native Bible women as they did Western missionaries.

The ideology of the late-nineteenth-century woman's missionary movement was that of "woman's work for woman," in which Western women had the unique responsibility to reach women and children who were segregated from the larger society in countries like India, China, and Japan. Reaching segregated women with the gospel would not only bring them salvation but would educate and therefore empower them to fight against customs that oppressed women, such as foot-binding and female slavery in China, child marriage and widow-burning in India, and polygamy and low social status in Islamic countries. While it unabashedly sought social change in non-Western cultures, "woman's work for woman" was uncritical about its own middle-class, Western cultural biases. Some scholars have thus included the woman's missionary movement under "civilizing" approaches to mission—a form of "cultural imperialism" during the peak of Western colonialism before World War I.

The founding of women's missionary societies in the late nineteenth century included home missionary societies for work among poor and new immigrant populations in the United States. Under the antislavery American Missionary Association and various denominational home missionary societies, missionary teachers moved into the South to work among freed slaves starting in the 1860s. Missionaries like Joanna Moore (1832–1916) of the American Baptist Woman's Home Missionary Society spent her entire life teaching basic literacy and household skills to Southern black women, despite severe poverty and persecution from the local white society. Presbyterian women pioneered rescue work among Chinese immigrant women who were smuggled into the country and entrapped in brothels on the West Coast. Under the auspices of city mission societies in Boston, San Francisco, New York, and other urban centers, women taught English to Chinese workers in nighttime Sunday Schools, as well as other skills immigrants needed to survive in American society.

The arrival of seven British Salvation Army "lassies" in North America in 1880 put women in the spotlight as rescue mission workers among the urban poor. Although the women were arrested and reviled at first, the Salvation Army's effectiveness at converting and helping the urban poor to help themselves soon won the admiration of many in the mainline churches. Headed by the husband-wife team of Ballington and Maud Ballington Booth (1865–1948), the Salvation Army "Slum Sis-

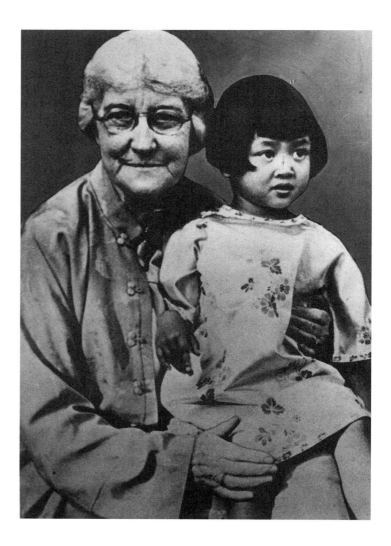

Donaldina Cameron ministered among Chinese women in San Francisco. Her urban mission helped free young women from prostitution; she worked with police to raid opium dens, brothels, and gambling houses. A Presbyterian mission in San Francisco's Chinatown, Cameron House, still bears her name. *Used by permission of Cameron House, San Francisco, California.*

ters" provided crisis care for families, founded day-care centers, and rehabilitated homeless alcoholics. Converts were integrated into the organization and became its workers. In 1896 the Booths left the Salvation Army and founded the Volunteers of America, a similar organization that also worked with prisoners and focused only on North America. In addition to the gender-integrated work of the Salvation Army, home missions by the 1880s were giving rise to deaconess and social work training in specialized women's missionary training schools. In 1881, the Woman's American Baptist Home Missionary Society founded a missionary training school in Chicago. Four years later, Methodist Lucy Rider Meyer (1849–1922), who had hoped to become a medical missionary, launched the Chicago Training School for City, Home, and Foreign Missions. The women who lived at missionary training homes studied the Bible, visited the urban poor, and soon added nurses' and social work training to the school curricula. They opened hospitals in which to care for the sick poor. Graduates of the

women's training schools served in missions around the world. Home missionaries began founding settlement houses among the urban poor in order to provide them education and social services.

In the late nineteenth century, interaction was considerable between home and foreign missionaries and their supporters. In some churches, the home and foreign missionary societies were joined. In others, they were separate organizations but had many of the same women in both. The leader of the settlement house movement, Jane Addams (1860–1935), served for a time on the board of Lucy Meyer's training school. Addams remarked how her own work paralleled the methods of foreign missionary women. Emma Rauschenbusch Clough, Ph.D. (1859–1940), a Baptist missionary in South India and sister of Social Gospel theologian Walter Rauschenbusch, argued that foreign mission work was a form of "social Christianity" and had provided a model for the Social Gospel. Isabella Thoburn helped found the deaconess training school and hospital in Cincinnati when on furlough from India in the late 1880s. Many missionary women worked among similar ethnic groups at home and abroad and moved easily between the two. For instance, former slave Fanny Jackson Coppin (1837–1913) attended Oberlin College and became principal of a teacher-training school for African Americans in Philadelphia. She later organized women's work for the African Methodist Episcopal (AME) Church in South Africa. She also served for years as president of the AME Women's Home and Foreign Missionary Society. Sometimes withdrawal from foreign missions launched a second career in home missions. Elizabeth Garland Hall (1867–1933), a mixed-race orphan adopted and raised as white, attended the Baptist Missionary Training School in Boston. In 1893 she married a black Jamaican Baptist missionary and served with him in the Congo. Upon retiring from Africa for health reasons, "Mama Hall" worked for fourteen years in Jamaica, where she ran an orphanage and founded the Jamaica Baptist Women's Federation.

In 1900, the women's foreign missionary societies launched the Central Committee on the United Study of Foreign Missions that commissioned annual mission study texts for use in local missionary circles. Leaders of the various women's mission societies had first begun meeting together in 1888 when many of them attended a missionary conference in London. The ecumenical mission study program remained in existence through 1938 and produced one of the most important bodies of missionary literature in America. The study books covered different parts of the world in sequence and also topics intrinsic to women's missions such as child welfare, pacifism, medical missions, and mission history. By 1921, total sales of the study books had reached 2 million volumes. The woman's missionary movement held annual summer schools of missions at which thousands of women studied the mission texts and enjoyed fellowship, pageants, and prayer.

Following the example of foreign mission circles, in 1903 supporters launched an interdenominational study program for home missions, supported initially by Baptist, Congregationalist, Lutheran, Methodist, and Presbyterian women. After organizing regionally, women created the national Council of Women for Home Missions in 1908 that met annually and ran committees that supported different aspects of home mission work. While foreign mission curricula focused on different parts of the world, education for home missions concentrated initially on presenting a Christian witness and citizenship training to the immigrants pouring into the United States. By the 1920s, the home mission movement had developed a strong social concern for the marginalized peoples in America, including Indians, Negroes, Mexicans, migrant workers, the blind, and "Orientals" who were discriminated against by immi-

gration policies. In addition to educating women and children about home missions, the council supported legislation upholding Asian rights and Indian land claims in the United States. As the chief providers of mission education materials, women's home mission societies helped institutionalize social justice ministries in the mainline denominations. After merging with male home mission boards in 1940, the women's home missionary movement became a founding organization of the National Council of Churches in 1950.

The ecumenical thrust of the woman's foreign missionary movement reached new heights in 1910, when the women's mission boards celebrated the fifty-year anniversary of the movement. Forty-three different women's foreign mission societies, supported by 3 million dues-paying members, demonstrated the strength of women's missions after the turn of the century. These societies had sent 2,368 missionaries by 1909. The 1910 Woman's Missionary Jubilee relied on a traveling team of inspirational speakers who visited forty-eight major cities and smaller locations where local women gathered for missionary teas and luncheons. By 1910, the unquestioned spokesperson of the woman's missionary movement was Baptist Helen Barrett Montgomery (1861–1934), author of the 1910 study text *Western Women in Eastern Lands*, which sold over 100,000 copies. Her study text for 1915 sold a record 160,000 copies. In 1914 she became president of the Woman's American Baptist Foreign Mission Society and in 1920 the president of the Northern Baptist Convention, the first woman to head a mainline denomination. A licensed preacher, she had studied Greek at Wellesley College, and in 1924 she became the first woman to translate the New Testament. Active in civic affairs in Rochester, New York, Montgomery was also the first woman elected to the school board. With the support of Susan B. Anthony, she pushed for women's rights at the University of Rochester. In 1913–1914, she and her friend Lucy Waterbury Peabody (1861–1949), a former Baptist missionary, toured the world promoting and studying women's work in missions. Their trip revealed that around the world mission-educated women were clamoring for more access to higher education. Peabody became head of a campaign by the women's mission societies that in 1921 raised $3 million for funding seven ecumenical colleges for women in India, China, and Japan in the belief that education was the key to the liberation of women everywhere. Support for the Christian colleges of Asia remained a top woman's priority for foreign missions during the mid-twentieth century.

Other ecumenical activities that grew from the 1910 missionary jubilee were the World Day of Prayer, carried throughout the world by missionary women, and a committee to sponsor Christian literature for women and children around the world. Home and Foreign Days of Prayer were combined and in 1927 became the World Day of Prayer for Missions. Divided between home and foreign missions, the funds raised on the Day of Prayer went to support cooperative enterprises like the Committee on Christian Literature for Women and Children. The ecumenical committee published magazines for different language groups, including sponsoring native writers and artists and supporting literacy training. By 1962, the committee had sponsored twenty-seven magazines around the world and had printed 500,000 children's books by 1972.

Decline of the Woman's Missionary Movement

By the 1920s, the ideology of "Woman's Work for Woman" had given way to the mission theory of "World Friendship." Repelled by the Western cultural superiority that had culminated in World War I, women's mission societies rejected maternalism in favor of partnership with non-Western women, internationalism, relief work among war refugees, and opposition to war and racism. Along with the YWCA (Young Women's Christian Association) and women in the international student Christian movement, women's missionary societies moved toward new theologies that emphasized peace and justice over "old-fashioned" conversion. By the 1930s, the voices of non-Western women had become increasingly visible in the women's mission literature, and the women's missionary societies were starting to turn over their institutions to the national churches. For example, the nationalization of foreign institutions in China in 1927 became the occasion for putting women's colleges, schools, and hospitals under Chinese leadership. But even in the midst of what seemed like the achievement of missionary goals—namely, the gradual transfer of power from Western to non-Western hands—crisis struck the movement.

The ecumenical women's missionary movement became a victim of its own success. As men in the churches eyed the millions of dollars brought in by the women, they began dismantling the women's mission organizations and forcing them to merge into church structures, all in the name of "efficiency." The first women's society forcibly restructured by male church leaders was that of the Methodist Episcopal Church, South, in 1910. Under the leadership of Belle Harris Bennett (1852–1922), southern Methodist women subsequently launched a successful crusade to gain voting rights for laywomen in the church. Bennett had founded the missionary training school for southern Methodist women in 1892, worked among the Kentucky poor, and headed the Methodist women's home mission work that founded settlement houses and opposed racism in the South. In 1923, the General Assembly of the Presbyterian Church dismantled the national women's mission organizations, both home and foreign. Women's control over mission work was dissolved and put under the administration of male-controlled denominational home and foreign missionary societies. Decades of anger and discontent among Presbyterian women followed. In one denomination after another, women found themselves helpless to stem the tide of amalgamation because they lacked laity and clergy rights in the church. In 1932, the Federation of Woman's Boards of Foreign Missions merged into the male-dominated Foreign Missions Conference of North America. By the time of World War II, the ecumenical women's missionary movement had largely ceased to exist as a gender-separate enterprise.

Another reason for the decline of the woman's missionary movement was because churches in the United States became divided in the 1920s by the fundamentalist-modernist movement, a struggle over such issues as the authority of the Bible and creationism versus evolution. Fights over doctrine pitted the ministry of women against biblical authority, and the holistic center ground occupied by the woman's missionary movement shrank. Its gender-separate agenda seemed old-fashioned to younger women who took for granted the hard-fought successes of their mothers and grandmothers. The energy of women in mainline churches moved toward ecumenical and social justice issues, such as fighting for the ordination of women and supporting the new World Council of Churches (1948) and the United Nations. The only significant ecumenical women's organization remaining in the late twentieth century that had descended from the woman's missionary movement was Church Women United, which retained the ecumenical energy and social justice commitment of the earlier woman's missionary movement but not its evangelistic zeal.

Conservative Missions

While the woman's missionary movement made the idea of the unmarried missionary woman acceptable in many quarters, it was not until the mid-1880s that women were able to move in significant numbers beyond teaching and home visitation into itinerant evangelism—an activity that involved "preaching" and so took longer to gain acceptance. Some of the strongest male supporters of the woman's missionary movement from the 1880s were pastors and mission supporters who believed that the ministry of women was a sign of the age of the Holy Spirit and preparation for the Second Coming of Jesus Christ. They defended the mobilization of women as "eleventh hour" evangelists to help bring in the harvest of souls before Jesus' return. As premillennialist, nondenominational "faith missions" were organized in the 1880s and 1890s, women eagerly joined them in hopes of being pioneer evangelists among previously unreached people. The new faith missions attracted relatively uneducated women who could not or did not obtain denominational appointments under a woman's society. Without guaranteed salaries or an emphasis on educational mission, the new wave of missions moved into mission fields among tribal peoples. Because of their lower educational requirements, and the focus on personal piety and extreme self-sacrifice, the new faith missions attracted an even higher percentage of women than had the denominational missions.

The earliest faith mission, the British-founded China Inland Mission, appointed women two by two as evangelists into the interior of China. As early as the 1870s, American women began going alone as self-supporting missionaries. Jennie Frow (1851–1900), for example, became an unmarried faith missionary in India in 1877. Later with her husband Marcus Fuller, she established a mission center in Akola. Joining the newly organized Christian and Missionary Alliance, the Fullers acted as the mentors and leaders of the first generation of Christian and Missionary Alliance missionaries in India. Jennie also wrote an important newspaper series on the social conditions of Indian women. While Jennie Fuller and other experienced missionaries joined the new missions, a few women like Lettie Cowman (1864–1960) founded their own faith missions. A participant in the late-nineteenth-century Holiness movement, Cowman and her husband were Methodists who went to Japan as independent missionaries in 1901. Launching a crusade to reach every home in Japan with the gospel, with Japanese assistance they organized the Oriental Missionary Society (OMS). Lettie Cowman served as president of the OMS from 1928 until 1949.

A striking feature of the faith mission movement was the number of women who took passage to other parts of the world as missionaries, often with no guarantee of support. As Holiness and then Pentecostal denominations were organized, independent women missionaries joined them as the "founding" missionaries of the Church of the Nazarene, the Assemblies of God, the Church of God, and so on. Interest in faith healing, Holiness, and missions coalesced among women who saw themselves as part of God's supernatural plan for the world. Many of these women entered intimate partnerships with indigenous Christians who shared their theological perspectives. An example of the complex relationships among different aspects of women's missions can be seen in the life of Minnie Abrams (1859–1912), missionary to India. Abrams attended Lucy Meyer's Methodist missionary training school and went to Bombay with the women's society of the Methodist Episcopal Church. In 1898 she left the women's society to become partner with Pandita Ramabai, a converted Brahmin woman who started a home for child widows. A Holiness believer, Abrams eagerly greeted the Pentecostal revival that began in Ramabai's mission in 1905. Her theological analysis of Pentecostalism, *The Baptism of the Holy Ghost and Fire* (1906), became the first significant statement of Pentecostal mission theology. When she sent her book to her former training school classmate, a missionary's wife in Chile, it launched Pentecostalism there. Abrams died while leading a group of unmarried women missionaries in evangelizing unreached people in India.

Despite initial openness to the leadership of women, as the faith mission movement became more conservative in the twentieth century, it began restricting women from the very evangelistic roles they had pioneered. Ironically, without the gender-separate ideology of the women's missionary movement, the faith missions had no philosophical reason to support women's ministry. By the 1920s, the fundamentalist-modernist controversy had served to push theologically conservative women into the background and disproportionately assigned them to maintenance work rather than creative evangelism. Those women who insisted on their right to be evangelists endured the marginalization of their gifts by male supervisors. Maude Cary (1878–1967) became a faith missionary in 1901 with the Gospel Missionary Union for over fifty years among Muslims in North Africa. She not only struggled in a difficult mission field, but she was repeatedly told by the mission that her work was not valued. When during World War II she remained by default the senior missionary in the field, she was finally put in charge of the work, founded a Bible institute, and trained the new missionaries. Another faith mission woman whose work was opposed in the early years was Lilian Trasher (1887–1961), who went as an independent Pentecostal missionary to Egypt in 1910. She took in abandoned babies and for over fifty years cared for thousands of orphans. In 1919, she affiliated with the Assemblies of God and became one of its most honored missionaries.

Despite great difficulties, some women in conservative evangelical missions carved out meaningful roles for themselves and became innovators in the mid-twentieth century. Eunice Pike (b. 1913) opened a whole new role for unmarried evangelical women when in 1936 she enrolled in the Summer Institute of Linguistics to become a Bible translator among the Mazatec Indians in Mexico. Despite the opposition of the founder of the Wycliffe Bible Translators, Pike moved with a female companion into a remote village, reduced the Mazatec language to writing, and began translating the New Testament. She developed a series of Mazatec primers in her focus on literacy, wrote hymns, and wrote books on phonology. Her success inspired hundreds of other evangelical women to study linguistics and become Bible translators among remote peoples. Joy Ridderhof (1903–1984) was an unmarried missionary furloughed home on sick leave when she got the idea of sending taped recordings back to the mission field. Her first batch of recordings to Honduras were so successful that she founded Gospel Recordings in 1939. She traveled to Mexico, Alaska, and the Philippines to record gospel messages and songs that would be heard by numerous peoples in their own languages. By 1997, the Global Recordings Network had distributed the gospel in nearly 5,000 languages. The careers of women like Pike and Ridderhof demonstrate that conservative evangelical women made important innovations in the context of parachurch agencies, even though they were not allowed to direct policy in evangelical churches.

While the woman's missionary movement and the faith missions easily coexisted during the late nineteenth century, with some missionaries going from one to the other, by the 1920s, a chasm was yawning between mainline and evangelical approaches to mission. Disagreements emerged over the relative merit of education versus evangelism, social service versus proclamation, and women's work versus general evangelism. In theologically conservative churches, despite the renunciation of supposedly liberal "women's work," missionary wives retained their hold on the popular imagination, especially after the martyrdom of faith missionaries John and Betty Stam (1906–1934) by Chinese communists in 1934. Wheaton College graduate Betty Stam represented a new breed of missionary educated in evangelical institutions. She and her husband went to China with the China Inland Mission in 1931. Beheaded by communists who spared their baby girl in exchange for a Chinese Christian who volunteered to die in the baby's place, the Stams came to represent the self-sacrificing ethic of evangelical missions. Betty's sister took her place on the mission field. The Stams' example propelled many young people to volunteer as missionaries.

The Late Twentieth Century

By the late 1960s, the number of missionaries from independent evangelical agencies surpassed those from mainline churches. In the 1970s, renewed emphasis on evangelizing "unreached" peoples who had never heard the gospel meant that the proportion of conservative evangelical missions kept growing through the end of the century. Traditional gender roles in most independent evangelical missions meant that distinctive women's issues did not attain the level of importance they held in the early-twentieth-century woman's missionary movement. Mainline churches, on the other hand, focused on ethnic diversity, partnership in mission, and global justice issues. The decreasing number of mainline women missionaries tended to be specialists in fields requested by partner churches, such as medicine

or education. New cultural attitudes toward personal fulfillment also meant that increasing numbers of missionaries served set terms rather than committing themselves for life. The entrance of women into the American workforce also increased women's options for satisfying careers outside the church.

The strongest gender-separate mission organization remaining in the mainline churches was the United Methodist Women (UMW; 1968), which focused on social justice, cultural and ethnic diversity, and the needs of women and children. Among conservative churches, the Woman's Missionary Union (WMU; 1888), auxiliary to the Southern Baptist Convention, was the strongest women's mission organization in the late twentieth century. Yet unlike the earlier woman's missionary movement, the UMW and the WMU were not permitted to send their own missionaries. Rather, their strength lay in local church organizations, the sponsorship of mission education literature for their denominations, and fund-raising abilities. Without the Lottie Moon Christmas offering, collected annually for foreign missions in the name of the women's pioneer China evangelist Lottie Moon (1840–1912), the Southern Baptist Convention would not have become the leading mission-sending denomination in late-twentieth-century America. Similarly, money collected by the UMW bailed out the mission commitments of the United Methodist Church on more than one occasion. Yet both groups found themselves attacked by conservatives in their churches. The WMU, in particular, underwent vicious attacks to its autonomy and leadership after the 1990 fundamentalist takeover of the Southern Baptist Convention.

By the end of the twentieth century, the distinctive contribution of Protestant missionary women lay in their partnership with Christian women across cultural boundaries. Work with marginalized populations through social services, battered women's shelters, and AIDS (acquired immunodeficiency syndrome) counseling continued occupying the "home mission" commitments of Protestant women. As the geographic center of Christianity shifted to the Southern Hemisphere in the late twentieth century, the lasting legacy of women's mission work lay in its concern for the well-being and dignity of women and children in oppressive situations around the world.

SOURCES: Gerald H. Anderson, ed., *Biographical Dictionary of Christian Missions* (1998). R. Pierce Beaver, *American Protestant Women in World Mission*, rev. ed. (1980). Gladys Gilkey Calkins, *Follow Those Women: Church Women in the Ecumenical Movement* (1961). Katherine M. Faull, trans., *Moravian Women's Memoirs: Their Related Lives, 1750–1820* (1997). Robert T. Handy, *We Witness Together: A History of Cooperative Home Missions* (1956). Dana L. Robert, *American Women in Mission: A Social History of Their Thought and Practice* (1997). Dana L. Robert, ed., *Gospel Bearers, Gender Barriers: Missionary*

Women in the Twentieth Century (2002). Jean Miller Schmidt, *Grace Sufficient: A History of Women in American Methodism, 1760–1939* (1999). Ruth A. Tucker, *Guardians of the Great Commission: The Story of Women in Modern Missions* (1988).

AMERICAN CATHOLIC WOMEN MISSIONARIES, 1870–2000
Angelyn Dries

MUCH OF THE geographic area of what became the fifty United States of America was frontier territory in the nineteenth and early twentieth centuries, and the country was considered by Vatican officials to be a "mission territory" until 1908. The predominant way for an American Catholic woman to become a missionary or an evangelist was to enter a religious order, a community of women gathered for a common purpose, shared prayer, and profession of vows of poverty, chastity, and obedience. Prior to the Civil War, a handful of these communities were started, among them the Sisters of Charity, Maryland (Elizabeth Ann Seton), the Ursulines in New Orleans, and an African American congregation, the Sisters of the Holy Family, New Orleans (Henriette Delille). After 1879 the number of communities increased dramatically, with recruits drawn from the surge of German, Irish, Italian, and eastern European immigrants. Italian-born Mother Frances Xavier Cabrini (1850–1917) had desired to be a missionary to China, but after a conversation with Pope Leo XIII, she came instead to the United States to minister to Italian immigrants. Church officials in Rome were worried that Italian immigrants would succumb to Protestant proselytizing in the new country. Foundress of the Missionary Sisters of the Sacred Heart, Cabrini took as her first mission in 1889 a parochial school on Mott Street in New York City. From there, Cabrini traveled extensively, developing schools and hospitals in Colorado, Chicago, and South America. Initially, Cabrini ran into difficulties with Church authorities because she wished to include "missionaries" as part of the sisters' incorporation title. *Missionary* had been used exclusively for clergy. Cabrini defended her use of the word: "If the mission of announcing the Lord's resurrection to his apostles had been entrusted to Mary Magdalene, it would seem a very good thing to confide to other women an evangelizing mission" (Cabrini, quoted in Sullivan, 36).

Mission acted as a place of experimentation, not surprisingly, especially when associated with the wilderness and frontier. While the public in the mid-twentieth century associated sisters mainly with teaching and nursing, their experience in the previous century provided quite diverse activities as part of their mission: housing homeless girls and women, visitation to the sick and imprisoned, teaching, homemaking, work with prostitutes, budget management, and leadership in various kinds of spiritual or devotional activities. Sisters opened or staffed some of the public schools in Colorado, New Mexico, North Dakota, and New York and built up Catholic hospital, social service, and school systems throughout the United States, serving various ethnic and racial communities.

Perhaps one of the best known frontier missionaries was Sister Blandina Segale (1850–1941), a Sister of Charity. The Italian immigrant was sent from her Motherhouse in Cincinnati to tend to the needs of the Spanish-speaking and Native Americans in Colorado and New Mexico, where she worked for eighteen years. Her journal not only recorded her activities, including her encounter in 1876 with Billy the Kid but also revealed the spirit she brought to her mission. Writing from Trinidad, Colorado, Segale sketched her plan: "Do whatever presents itself, and never omit anything because of hardship or repugnance" (Segale, 33).

Other sisters' congregations who pioneered in the western part of the United States in the nineteenth century were the Ursulines, the Sisters of St. Joseph of Carondelet, and the Sisters of Loretto from Nerinckx, Kentucky. Well-known missionaries who worked with Native Americans and Spanish-speaking groups include Sister Rose Philippine Duchesne (1769–1852), who founded the first primary school west of the Mississippi and who believed that living among Native American tribes, rather than having them come to a school in town, was a better method of evangelization; Sister Mary Amadeus Dunne (1846–1919), known by the Cheyenne as "The Great White Woman" and "Chief Lady Black Robe"; and Sister Katharine Drexel (1858–1955).

Drexel, daughter of a prominent Philadelphia banker and philanthropist, had traveled with her father to the West and South and saw firsthand the conditions of Native and African Americans. Katharine inherited the considerable Drexel fortune and used it to finance missions to these groups in the United States, British Honduras, Cuba, the Canal Zone, and several African countries. Almost single-handedly, Drexel supported the Bureau of Catholic Indian Missions. Disturbed that her contributions were so substantial and that other persons in the Church were not equally generous, the American Federation of Catholic Societies (AFCS) in 1903 cast her work as a justice issue: "Shall she alone offer her life as a vicarious reparation for the national crime, which makes the Indian an alien, an exile, a pauper? . . . Here we have a national issue—one that will reveal the faith that is in us" (AFCS, quoted in Oates, 69). In 1891 Katharine began a community of women religious, the Sisters of the Blessed Sacrament for Indians and Colored People, which continued teaching and evangelization among these populations. In the 1930s, Katharine, along

In the 1920s the call came from Rome to send missionaries to China and in the next two decades, twenty-seven women's communities responded. Mother Mary Joseph (pictured on the left) provided spiritual and practical direction for Maryknoll women. While the mission literature of the day pictured women's mission work as auxiliary to that of men, Mother Mary Joseph saw women missionaries as essential and held that a mission call urged them to "go the whole way into the wilderness." *Courtesy of the Maryknoll Mission Archives.*

with African American laity, tried unsuccessfully to convince the Catholic University of America in Washington, D.C., to admit African Americans to the school. In 1932, she founded Xavier University in New Orleans, the first college inaugurated by American Catholics for African Americans.

The first women to offer sustained mission work beyond the continental United States were the Allegany Franciscan Sisters, who sent three women in 1879 to teach in schools in Jamaica. Soon Jamaican women joined the community, and the Sisters established the first Catholic teachers' college on the island in 1897. The Sisters of the Holy Family, founded in 1842 by Henriette Delille (c. 1813–1862), a free woman of color in New Orleans, responded to the call to work among the Caribs in Stan Creek, British Honduras (Belize) in 1898.

Hawaii was considered an overseas mission not only because of its distance from the United States but because of the nature of the mission work. In 1883 Mother Marianne Cope (1838–1918) led a group of six Franciscan sisters from Syracuse, New York, along with a cousin of one of the sisters, to work with patients suffering with Hansen's disease. The women opened the first general hospital for the sick on Maui the following year. Cope's motivation was that ministry among the sick patients, especially the leprous men and women, exemplified Christ's love shown in deeds. Imitation of Christ was the women's means of evangelization.

Twentieth-Century Mission

From a handful of women's religious congregations established by 1865, the number of congregations and new provinces increased to 167 groups by 1922. The numbers of women in each of the groups grew as well. Religious life proved an attractive proposition for American Catholic women, an alternative to marriage or the single life. The work of American Catholic women missionaries overseas expanded considerably after World War I. Catholic missions throughout the world were generally under the direction of the Roman Propaganda Fide (Propagation of the Faith) Office, which assigned territories to various religious orders of men. Some mission territories were reassigned after 1919 because the French and German mission orders had suffered great losses of their priests in the war. Recognizing the increased importance of America's role in international relationships, James A. Walsh, a diocesan priest from Boston, and Thomas F. Price, an ordained North Carolinian, had lobbied for the formation of an American missionary society since the early 1900s. The Catholic Foreign Mission Society of America was authorized as a mission-sending group by the U.S. Catholic bishops in 1911. The group, known popularly as Maryknoll, sent their first four missionaries, including Price, to China in 1920.

In 1906 Mary Josephine Rogers (1882–1955), a student at Smith College in Massachusetts, had approached Walsh about obtaining mission literature for a Catholic study group at the college. Their initial association led to the formation of a group of women, "the Teresians," named for the Carmelite reformer Teresa of Avila, on whose feast day the women moved to Ossining. Preceding their decision to band together, the women gathered for prayer and retreat, after which they declared, "We were strangers to each other and differed in age, training and disposition, but we had been brought together and were henceforth to be united by the common desire of serving the cause of foreign missions" (*Teresian Diary*, January 1, 1912). The women, with Rogers as their leader, settled eventually near Ossining, New York, across the street from the Maryknoll priests and brothers. Final authorization to become a congregation of women religious was given by Church authorities in Rome in 1920. Initially the women translated letters from missionaries, answered correspondence, organized mission photographs, took care of circulation of the Maryknoll magazine *The Field Afar*, and cooked and sewed for the Maryknoll seminarians. The women's first mission assignments were to Japanese immigrants in San Francisco and Seattle in 1920. The following year the sisters went to Hong Kong. Rogers, now known as Mother Mary Joseph, worked in close association with Walsh and provided spiritual and practical direction for the Maryknoll women. She appreciated the uniqueness of the establishment of the American women's mission community and saw "American" virtues to be essential to the missionary enterprise: adaptability, initiative, and a spiritualization of the pioneer spirit in the guise of being a "living martyr." While the mission literature of the day pictured women's mission work as auxiliary to that of men, Rogers saw women missionaries as essential and held that a mission call urged them to "go the whole way into the wilderness." She maintained that while missionary priests "get the conversions" and "perform all the rites and instructions at the end . . . to teach the people how to live Christian lives, to apply the doctrines they have learned, in this the help of the sisters is incalculable" (Rogers, 59).

Other women religious were also responding to a call to mission overseas in the 1920s. By that time, many sisters' congregations, which had labored in frontier conditions, became more settled or routine in their patterns of community life and prayer. The need to manage greater numbers of sisters corresponded with the 1917 revision of Church law, which standardized the Orders' constitutions, their blueprint for life together. Just at that point of communities' homogenization, the call came to send missionaries to China in the 1920s, and in the next two decades, twenty-seven women's communities responded. An example of the pattern of pioneer foundation, settlement, and subsequent mission overseas are the Sisters of Loretto, cofounded by Mary Rhodes (1783–1853), two lay friends, and Father Charles Nerinckx (1761–1824) on the Kentucky frontier in 1812. In addition to schools in Kentucky, Missouri, and Arkansas, the Loretto Sisters established a school for Native American girls at Osage Mission, Kansas, in 1847, several schools in the New Mexico Territory in the 1850s, and an industrial school for Native American girls in 1855 in New Mexico. By the time the women went to China in 1923, the congregation had increased to over 800 members teaching throughout the South, Southwest, and Colorado. Because of their success in frontier areas and their experience of cultural adaptation, Father Edward Galvin (1882–1956) invited the Sisters of Loretto to Hanyang, Hubei Province, to serve with the priests of the Society of St. Columban, which Galvin founded in Ireland in 1918. The six women sent to China were a mixed ethnic group: three American born and the others from Ireland, Bohemia, and Canada.

Over the years they served in China, the sisters also taught in Shanghai and experienced the occupation of the country by the Japanese. Sheltering Chinese refugees from other parts of the country, finding rice to distribute to those who came to their door, and enduring the traumas of bombings in 1937 and 1938 put the women's other mission work on hold, at least temporarily, and moved them more deeply into a mission of presence and response to elemental needs of food and safety. By 1949 China had 566 American Catholic missionaries, of which 194 were women. Maryknoll Sister Joan Marie Ryan, incarcerated by Chinese communists, was one of the few American Catholic women who remained in

China after 1950 despite the triumph of communist forces and the expulsion of foreigners. That same year the total number of American Catholic women missionaries serving around the world was 1,748.

During World War II, the number of missionaries decreased overall, but almost one-fourth of the women missionaries were in Oceania, the only geographic area where women missionaries outnumbered men. After the war, the number of women entering religious congregations again increased. In 1951, the Maryknoll Sisters had 291 sisters serving abroad, including Hawaii. Five years later, they had 464 overseas missionaries and ranked first among fifty American Catholic women's groups, which collectively sent 2,212 missionaries abroad.

Medical mission work was never as popular for American Catholics as other types of mission work, but one American especially forwarded developments for medical missions. Austrian-born Anna Dengel (1892–1980), who had obtained her medical degree in 1919 at the University in Cork, worked as a laywoman with the Franciscan Missionaries of Mary at a small hospital in Rawalpindi, India. In 1925, along with the assistance of Holy Cross Father Michael Mathis, she founded the Society of Medical Mission Sisters, in spite of Church law that prohibited women religious from specific professional medical work, such as surgery and obstetrics. Scotswoman Dr. Agnes McClaren, with whom Dengel had been in correspondence over the years, made several trips to Rome, as had Dengel herself, to present the case for women religious to serve as medical mission doctors. She cited the admirable work being done by Protestant women doctors, especially in countries where custom dictated that women were not to have contact with men. Women's medical needs, therefore, received little or no response. It was not until 1936 that Vatican laws were changed to permit Catholic sisters to become medical doctors. Dengel directed professional health-care service toward women, especially in India and Africa, and put before the American public the voice of women from various religions in *The Medical Missionary*, the magazine she edited for many years. By 1957, ninety-one Medical Mission Sisters were serving overseas as doctors, midwives, nurses, and clinicians.

Throughout the twentieth century, about 1,000 American Catholic women missionaries served as nurses. Most of them lived in isolated areas and ended up performing medical procedures for which they had not been trained but which were necessary because of the condition of the patient. Much of the sisters' service was directed toward women. One researcher concluded that not only were "substantial contributions made to maternal-child health, communicable disease reduced, and the establishment and maintenance of hospitals and clinics in diverse developing countries," but the sister nurses enabled the local people to assist in the process of health-care delivery through clinical experience and through the education of local nurses and health practitioners (Kovalesky, 27–28).

Not many lay Catholic women went overseas in mission prior to the 1940s. On occasion, a young alumna of sisters' schools or a relative accompanied the sisters to their mission and worked alongside them. Laywomen evangelists were not unknown, though, especially in the Midwest. The Catholic Evidence Guild of Rosary College in Chicago sent groups of their students for several weeks in the summer to evangelize in Oklahoma, North Carolina, and other southern states. The well-trained "street preachers" interspersed music, prayer, and teaching in the 1930s and 1940s, evangelizing often from the back of a pickup truck.

In contrast to a strong corporate and business image pervading the United States, a symbol that permeated Roman Catholicism in the United States from the 1930s through Vatican Council II was that of the Mystical Body. With roots in the New Testament, the image emphasized social action and was the foundation for a surge of lay mission groups, starting with the Catholic Students Mission Crusade (1918), the Grail (1921), the Lay Mission helpers of Los Angeles (1955), the Women Volunteers for Africa (1959), and the Papal Volunteers for Latin America (PAVLA; 1960). The Grail and the volunteers for Africa were specifically women's organizations run by women. From the extant PAVLA records, it appears that more women than men were serving in Central and South American countries between 1960 and 1970, a pattern that seems to be true for other lay mission organizations of the mid-twentieth century.

One outstanding example of lay mission is the pioneer work of the Grail. International in scope and membership, the Grail moved its headquarters from the Netherlands to Loveland, Ohio, near Cincinnati, in 1940. Its mission was to develop women of all races, continents, and professions as leaders in the formation of society. In the process, the group organized a lay mission school in 1946 in the Netherlands, and a native of Chicago and pioneer of interracial work in Louisiana, Mary Louise Tully (1916–2001), went to Hong Kong the following year to work in various aspects of publication at the Catholic Center. She described her mission as "trying to live according to Christian principles—a God-centered life—in all the daily relationships, jobs, and responsibilities" (Tully, 6), whether those were in the office, dealing with printers, coolies, or living with the Chinese in their homes or hostels. In 1957, the members opened the Grail Institute for Overseas Service in two houses in Brooklyn. The women spent the year together, worked during the day, and prepared themselves for mission work in the evening and on weekends. Work, liturgical and personal prayers, study, and recreation in common were building blocks for apostolic service. By the early 1960s, thirty-five American volunteers served in Asia, Oceania, Africa, and Latin America and twenty-two more were preparing for mission assignments as catechists, nurses, doctors, agriculturalists, home economists, and teachers. Initially Grail women viewed themselves as building a Catholic culture for the modern world, but by the mid-1960s, they described themselves as more feminist in their consciousness and in the development of their educational models.

While the 1920s through the 1940s saw the largest percentage of American Catholic missionaries in China, by 1960 the numbers shifted toward Central and South America. U.S. involvement in the Alliance for Progress drew attention to economic disparity and the need for agrarian reform and improvement in health and education in Latin America. Fidel Castro's revolution (1959) and the Bay of Pigs invasion (1961) brought the threat of communism to America's very shoreline. Catholic missionaries arrived in Latin America in greater numbers in the context of the Cold War and with the endorsement of papal initiatives, which were meant to counteract communism, Protestant evangelism, and Spiritism. From 1,414 (433 women) American Catholic missionaries in 1960, the number grew to 2,863 (433 women) in 1970, the peak year numerically. Initially, many sisters carried on the same type of ministry in institutionalized settings that they did in the United States, but they quickly learned that the conditions in Peru, Bolivia, and elsewhere were quite different from the North. The experience of extreme poverty, illiteracy, and huge gaps between social and economic groups compelled the missionaries to become more vocal in speaking to the American public about the inequities faced in Latin America. Laywomen missionaries also came to Latin America through the Papal Volunteers, through over twenty other lay mission-sending groups, and through diocesan arrangements. Rosemary Smith (b. 1921), a community organizer from Cleveland, Ohio, was on the first team the diocese sent to El Salvador in 1964–1965, where she remained for fifteen years. Two members of a later team from the diocese, Ursuline Sister Dorothy Kazel and laywoman Jean Donovan, along with Maryknoll Sisters Ita Ford and Maura Clarke, were murdered by the Salvadoran National Guard in 1980, an event that galvanized Americans, highlighted the inequities in Latin America, and critiqued the role of the United States in its support of some repressive Latin American governments. The women martyrs of the twentieth century were those whose ordinary lives of teaching or work among the poor thrust them into international attention.

Black and Hispanic new consciousness of the 1960s intersected with the emerging prominence of international theologians of color. Their common agenda raised issues of justice, liberation, and structural oppression of women. Strong leadership from Dominican Sister Shawn Copeland and Mercy Sister Mary Martin de Porres Grey through the National Black Sisters' Conference, formed in 1968, reinvigorated the identity and mission of black sisters, especially in naming "black cultural, political, and economic liberation as a constitutive part of the mission of black vowed women religious" (Copeland, 124). Dominican Jamie Phelps and Diana Hayes have examined the history and theological significance of black Catholics in America. In much the same vein, Las Hermanas, a group of laywomen and sisters, was formed in 1971 in Houston, Texas, to minister to the needs of Hispanics in the United States and to affirm an appreciation of their cultures and religious history. In 1977 the group made a retreat with Peruvian liberation theologian Gustavo Gutiérrez. More recently, theologians Ana María Pineda and Ana María Díaz-Stevens have examined the role of Hispanic women as part of a theological agenda. Hispanic and black experience provided a new mission consciousness, with blurred boundaries between mission overseas and mission in the United States.

In the last two decades of the twentieth century, long-term missionaries still were being sent overseas, but a pattern of short-term missionaries, serving from six weeks to a year or longer, also became part of the picture. North American parishes and dioceses adopted parish communities in Central and South America, and the handiwork of women, such as wall hangings, banners, and embroidered items, frequently became a tangible gift exchange from one group to the other. After the China mainland opened to foreigners again in 1972, American Catholic women served as teachers, though they could not be identified as missionaries. Between 1979 and 1986, a former missionary to Taiwan, Maryknoll Sister Janet Carroll, was the delegate from the Holy See to the United Nations, concentrating on social and humanitarian issues and Asian concerns. Since 1989, Carroll has been the director of the U.S. Catholic China Bureau. The director of the U.S. Catholic Mission Association is another key national position, held by Notre Dame Sister Rosanne Rustemeyer, a former missionary to Africa. The association is an organization that unites individuals and groups committed to the cross-cultural and global mission of Jesus.

Issues and Themes

Many of the issues feminists addressed in the 1970s and 1980s revolved around economic independence for women, education, housing, health, alternative ways to exercise power, and the need for communal support of one another (Coston, 336–346). Congregations of American sisters consistently addressed these issues over the last 200 years of mission and evangelization with remarkable success. Women's mission funding groups and laywomen's mission-sending agencies were built on similar premises and were profitable for the same reasons. In this brief essay we have highlighted only a few of the hundreds of American Catholic women's groups that sent missionaries overseas. But several themes emerge from their experience, among them the importance of economic self-sufficiency, women's impact on mission theory, and women's paradigms for mission.

Economics and the Economy of Salvation

Economics and mission were invariably related because transportation, living expenses, and the work of the mission required the ability to be economically self-sustaining. Women in American parishes often banded together in groups of ten or twelve to fund missionaries and mission projects. These entrepreneurial gatherings amassed relatively good sums of money in the course of a year. Other activities, such as prayer, study about missions, and sewing handiwork, took place when the funds were counted at the monthly meetings. Control of the direction of the funds, personal contact with missionaries, an expansion of vision beyond the parish, and an opportunity for socializing drew together single and married women.

In search of funds to sustain their mission, clergy often traveled throughout Europe and America, necessitating their absence from people in their mission. But when the clergy invited sisters to serve a mission, the women were often expected to "pay their own way." For example, Father Edward Galvin invited the Sisters of Loretto to China to take charge of an embroidery factory for Chinese girls. Given a choice of the Sisters of St. Columban in Ireland and the American sisters, he chose the latter because he knew they were financially independent and able to make an enterprise economically feasible. Galvin's plan was that the factory would fill the priests' need for liturgical vestments and other clothing. He saw the marketing potential the embroidery school served for the mission. However, the sisters' idea was that the education of the young women in Christianity and the women's economic independence were more important. Further, once the level of education rose, the sisters thought that there would be no need for Americans to send money overseas to rescue abandoned children, a practice called "Pagan Baby" money. Enlightened children, grown into adulthood, would see the fallacy of abandoning babies, especially girls. Another example of women's missionary economic influence is the case of the Sisters of Mercy who accepted a teaching mission in British Honduras (Belize). While authorized to do so by the Propaganda Fide Office in Rome and

blessed by the archbishop of New Orleans, the sisters met opposition from the auxiliary bishop of New Orleans when they left the United States. He protested their departure, claiming the sisters did not have the right to take money out of the archdiocese. In reality, the money belonged to the sisters' congregation and not to the local church.

Education and cooperation to develop a sound fiscal base for women became an important aspect of mission for Maryknoll Sister Gabriella Mulherin (1900–1993). A native of Scranton, Pennsylvania, she had heard Maryknoll cofounder Thomas F. Price preach and was moved to enter the Maryknoll Sisters in 1923, after working as a legal secretary for a few years after high school. Three years later, she was missioned to northern Korea. Between then and 1941, she directed the Industry Department of a school in Yeung Yu and served in various towns, including the capital Pyongyang. After Pearl Harbor, Gabriella was repatriated, but she returned to Korea in 1952, dismayed at the devastation of the country and the plight of refugees from the North. The restoration of social agencies in the country depended on voluntary groups, and along with Maryknoll George M. Carroll, she founded the Korean Association of Voluntary Agencies. The organization shared information and resources and worked to collaborate on projects. Mulherin also organized and trained young women and war widows in arts and crafts to enable them to earn a living for themselves and their families. The work for which she became known and recognized by the Korean government was that of the Korean Credit Unions, begun in 1960, with the formation of the first union in Pusan on the Maryknoll Sisters' property. Gabriella adapted the principles she learned from the Antigonish Movement, which was under the direction of Moses Coady in Nova Scotia. This adult education program taught leadership skills as a means to promote democratic values and to develop trust and unity among groups as a first step in a Cooperative Movement. Mulherin's success with the women who worked at the hospital led to other groups forming similar cooperative movements in Korea. As a foundation for the unions, Gabriella and several women and men set up the Cooperative Education Institute in Seoul. By 1988, Korean Credit Union members numbered 1.3 million people.

Theoretical Changes in Mission

Until the early 1960s, Catholic mission literature identified women missionaries as "auxiliary," though equal to men in women's sphere of action. Women religious were needed as missionaries because their chief task was women's education, the source of women's "elevation." While acknowledging the worth of Protestant women missionaries, Catholic mission literature viewed sisters as a moral force in non-Christian countries, where men were "accustomed to see in woman a slave, an instrument, a plaything" (McGlinchey, 171). Catholicism offered an alternative view of women. While women missionaries themselves sometimes used the term *auxiliary*, they perceived themselves as essential to the missionary task.

Women's mission role was part of the larger framework of "civilization," a view that included education, health care, raised social status for women, and at least in the eyes of Americans, democratic values. By 1970, the language of *crusade* and *civilization* was no longer predominant in mission literature. Rather, *development* and *social justice* were terms that became more popular after Vatican Council II (1961–1965), due in large part to the experience of missionaries in Latin America and Africa. In many ways, women missionaries, along with indigenous groups, had raised women's issues for global consideration and response.

The Council's statement in 1965 on the relationship of the Catholic Church to other religions (*Nostra aetate*) reflected the experience and practice of women missionaries. American Catholic women missionaries practiced a kind of experiential ecumenism, because they needed to interact in a practical way on a daily basis with women from various religions. Some examples are found in Anna Dengel's story, previously mentioned in this essay, and in the good works practiced by Mother Marianne Cope in Molokai. Cope maintained, "The charity of the good knows no creed and is confined to no one place" (Cope, quoted in Hanley and Bushnell, 52). The Sisters of St. Joseph of Carondelet in Japan viewed educational excellence as evangelization in a country that placed high value on learning: "Schools operated under the auspices of the Catholic Church in Japan exercise an indirect apostolate by disposing mothers and fathers of the future favorably toward the church. The objective is to develop this favorable attitude and to give sound, moral training rather than to have a large number of baptisms" (Dougherty, 404). On a more specifically theological note, Mother Lurana Mary White (1870–1935) and the Franciscan Sisters of the Atonement had journeyed from Anglicanism to Roman Catholicism in 1909. The previous year, she, along with cofounder Father Paul Wattson, established the Chair of Unity Octave, an annual prayer week for the reunion of Christian churches, an event that impacted local Catholic and Protestant congregations throughout the United States and beyond. More recently, Maryknoll Sister Joan Delaney, who had been a missionary in Hong Kong in the 1950s, became the official Roman Catholic consultant on mission at the World Council of Churches. Over the last twenty years of the twentieth century, the ecu-menical aspects of women's mission experience coalesced with diversity issues and an emphasis in the United States on multiculturalism, a topic with which returned missionaries had much experience and shared in classrooms and other educational forums.

Women's Paradigms for Mission

Women missionaries' attention to "the body" presumed and reflected an intersection of the spiritual and the physical world. Medical healing, the reconstruction of women's social "body," through leadership training of indigenous women in small faith/bible sharing groups, as nurses, doctors, and teachers, and catechists, and the development of her economic "body," which provided self and group sufficiency, were for American Catholic women missionaries manifestations of Christ's healing and reconciliation.

By the mid-1960s, women were active participants in building missionary teams of men and women, especially in Latin America. Sisters and laywomen trained local women as leaders in health care and education, as well as in parish life. While the model for mission prior to Vatican Council II had frequently been the implantation of a Western model of church in a new context, in fact, the actual interaction women had in mission countries made them question the feasibility of that model. Women's mission life throughout the twentieth century often highlighted an authority of experience, a sense of ambiguity between religious norms of practice and the realities of mission, a lifestyle of community interaction and support, and improvisation and pragmatism, all hallmarks raised by feminists in the 1980s and 1990s.

Women's experience of mission provided a foundation for the themes of the Vatican Council II's mission document, *Missio ad gentes* (1965): inculturation, emphasis on the mission of God, rather than "church planting," the multidimensionality of mission, and the recognition that the whole church is missionary by its very nature. The witness of women's lives, their presence to the people, and experiential ecumenism intersected with the women's response to the realities of injustice, illiteracy, and poverty. The latter happened from first-hand observation of the detrimental effects of the American government or business practices abroad. Having observed the social and political consequences of their spiritual mission, American Catholic missionaries became more politically astute than when they first arrived at their mission and frequently spoke publicly on behalf of the oppressed people. Traditional women's ministry tasks of education and health care moved into the public, political spotlight. In the process, women missionaries had a direct impact on the development of women's growth, leadership development, and skill building in the countries where the missionaries served.

SOURCES: The context for women's missionary work overseas is found in Angelyn Dries, *The Missionary Movement in American Catholic History* (1998). Excellent primary resources for a study of Catholic women missionaries are located in archives of religious congregations throughout the United States. Especially noteworthy archives are the Maryknoll Sisters, Ossining, New York (*Teresian Diary;* Mary Joseph Rogers, "Reaching the Women," in *To Defend the Cross* [1923]); the Medical Mission Sisters, Philadelphia; and the Sisters of the Blessed Sacrament, Philadelphia. The standard twentieth-century perception of the role of women missionaries is found in Joseph McGlinchey, *Conversion of the Pagan World: A Treatise upon Catholic Foreign Missions* (1921). Blandina Segale's *At the End of the Santa Fe Trail* (1948), Mary Louise Sullivan's *Mother Cabrini, "Italian Immigrant of the Century"* (1992), Mary Laurence Hanley and O. A. Bushnell's *A Song of Pilgrimage and Exile: The Life and Spirit of Mother Marianne of Molokai* (1980), Camilla Kennedy's *To the Uttermost Parts of the Earth:* *The Spirit and Charism of Mother Mary Joseph Rogers* (1987), and Phyllis Zagano's *Ita Ford, Missionary Martyr* (1996) are notable biographical examples of women missionaries. Dolorita Marie Dougherty, *Sisters of St. Joseph of Carondelet* (1966), Anita Kovalesky, "American Missionary Nursing Sisters Abroad" (report to American Nurses' Foundation, January 1993), and M. Shawn Copeland, "A Cadre of Women Religious Committed to Black Liberation: The National Black Sisters Conference," *U.S. Catholic Historian* 14.1 (1996): 123–144, analyze the history and impact of particular U.S. women's groups in mission and evangelization. Mary J. Oates, *The Catholic Philanthropic Tradition in America* (1995), and Carol Coston, "A Feminist Approach to Alternative Enterprises," in *Women's Spirit Bonding*, ed. Janet Kalven and Mary I. Buckley (1984), provide more general categories of interpretation that can be applied to women's mission work. Grail missionary Mary Louise Tully, "I'm a Lay Apostle Overseas," *The Shield* (January 1950): 6–9, explains her experience of mission in China, and Janet Kalven, *Women Breaking Boundaries: A Grail Journey, 1940–1995* (1999), provides an overview of the history of the Grail movement and its changing perceptions of women's role in mission.

WOMEN'S SOCIETIES

LEADERSHIP AND COMMUNITY BUILDING IN PROTESTANT WOMEN'S ORGANIZATIONS

Rosemary Skinner Keller

SINCE THE FOUNDING of the American colonies, influential separatist women's organizations have characterized the participation of Jewish and Christian women, and women of Anglo, African, and Hispanic American descent, in sacred and secular areas of life. When not welcomed—indeed, prohibited from serving—to serve on the governing boards of established associations and institutions, women simply formed their own separatist societies to advance their religious commitments to women, churches, and social and political movements.

Prior to the Civil War, women's associations were limited to the local scene. Bible study groups, missionary societies, and prayer circles met in churches and homes. "Daughters of Liberty" organizations made supplies, medicine, and clothing for troops during the War for Independence. By the early nineteenth century, benevolence societies provided relief and employment to women in distress and started orphanages and schools to care for destitute children. Locally based activist associations worked for social justice causes such as moral reform, temperance, abolition of slavery, and women's rights.

After the Civil War, national organizations were formed to address the social, political, and religious concerns of the late nineteenth and twentieth centuries. Women provided financial and personnel resources to found hospitals, schools, orphanages, and homes for the elderly; they sent men and women into international missions to spread faith in Christ and to bring material aid to persons in underdeveloped countries; they sought laws and began unions to protect women and children from abusive working conditions.

Women's history could not be written without placing at the center the significant contribution of women's separatist associations to churches and social reform. However, when one studies women's voluntary associations through a different lens, the inner life of these organizations, another story unfolds. Separatist societies have been effective because women at the national and local levels developed an alternative style of leadership, counter to the traditional male hierarchical model.

Out of a vision of building bonds of sisterhood, community within communities, leaders of separatist societies brought thousands of women together as committed participants at the grassroots level. They provided ordinary women with larger purposes for their lives beyond the confines of their homes, networks of support for their daily needs, and education in leadership. All these fruits were crucial to the vision and power of the founders and national leaders of voluntary organizations.

This essay examines the "story within the stories," the convergence of styles of leadership and creation of community within women's communities in the American Protestant tradition. To build community within organizations, it is necessary to develop attitudes and structures of shared authority, teamwork, support, and cooperation that value the participation of all members. Creation of this environment necessitates leadership styles counter to traditional male hierarchical patterns that stress individual competitiveness and highly centralized authority. Through their leadership, feminists of the late twentieth and early twenty-first centuries profess a commitment to this alternative vision of community building.

There are historical precedents for leadership and community building growing out of this feminist vision. Focusing the lens of this essay, it concentrates on this experience of three representative women's communities that flourished during the Social Gospel period from the 1870s through the early twentieth century: the deaconess movement, women's societies of Christian service and missionary outreach, and social settlement houses. These case studies provide practical examples of the relationship between leadership and community building that reveal a side of the story of women's organizations not usually told.

Community within communities resulted from the creation of a corporate sense of members' vocations and the living out of that commitment in leadership styles, relations with each other, and daily activities. While addressing the needs of churches and social service and justice agencies, women found individual vocations, mentored each other in leadership, and developed bonds of sisterhood that previously had been inconceivable.

A Public Family and Its Mother

Leadership and community building converged in the Chicago Training School for City, Home and Foreign Missions, founded in 1885. One of the earliest and strongest deaconess institutions established within the Protestant tradition and the Methodist Episcopal Church, the school was begun after the Civil War through the partnership of Lucy Rider Meyer, who served as principal, and her husband Josiah Shelly Meyer, its longtime administrator. The Training School included a deaconess home, a residence for the young single women who joined the order of deaconesses.

Rider Meyer was known as the "mother" of the Mother House, who provided educational leadership and motherly care for the deaconesses when they ventured forth from their family of origin for the first time. Her leadership was characteristic of other female leaders in the deaconess movement of the late nineteenth and early twentieth century.

Motherly leadership was a style of soft feminism, an effort to extend the home into the public sphere. It provided protection to young women from rural environs who relocated for the first time into the inner core of cities out of their Christian conviction to serve the needy. The deaconess orders set strict limits to their female recruits' independent existence in possibly hostile environs and gently moved them into leadership and control of their own public organizations and private lives. The Chicago Training School provided less threat of the public emergence of women to traditional church leaders and laypersons than was presented by women who sought to be ordained at this time.

From 1870 until the turn of the century, over 140 training schools and deaconess homes were opened in the United States by almost all Protestant denominations and many interdenominational movements. Among the most prominent were Lutherans, Episcopalians, and Methodists. Deaconesses were pioneers who became professional female workers in Protestant churches and service institutions long before the denominations would ordain women. After being trained in Old and New Testament, theology, missions, sociology and social service, religious education, home economics, medicine, and music, as well as basic subjects of English, history, and elocution, they were sent out to establish and administer charitable institutions, including settlement houses, hospitals, schools, and churches for the poor in the United States and throughout the world. Deaconesses were equivalent to Roman Catholic nuns, though their members took no lifetime vows and were much smaller in number. They wore distinctive plain dark dresses with white collars, which they were careful to describe as "Protestant not Romish."

Deaconesses interpreted their work as a restoration of the New Testament office of a deacon, or servant. Their scriptural model was Phoebe, described in Romans 16:1–2 as a deacon of the church at Cenchreae who had a ministry of service, particularly to care for women of the churches, distinguished from other spiritual gifts or vocations such as prophecying, teaching, or working miracles. "This tradition of Phoebe's *diakonia*— her ability to see 'the world's pain' and her desire to overcome it through personal service—was just what nineteenth-century Methodist women wanted to revive" (*Women in New Worlds*, 1: 201–202).

Most of Lucy Rider Meyer's recruits were young women of strong church backgrounds, many being daughters of ministers or of churchwomen's society leaders, who responded to a call to Christian service, just as their brothers might have chosen to be ministers. While Protestant churches were fleeing to the newly created suburbs in the 1880s, 300,000 immigrants, mostly from western and eastern Europe, arrived in Chicago during that decade. In one highly populated new immigrant district of Chicago alone in the closing years of the nineteenth century, there were estimated to be two Protestant churches, 270 saloons, eighty-five wine houses, seven opium and eight gambling dens, and ninety-two houses of prostitution. To venture forth into the world of sin, squalor, and brutishness, seen as the overgrown tumor of the burgeoning inner cities of New York, Boston, Cincinnati, Chicago, and San Francisco, was a bold and courageous step for these young deaconesses to take.

Meyer was convinced of the need for the churches to reach the masses of new immigrants, both to convert them to Protestant Christianity and to provide them with spiritual and material support. She envisioned a new kind of consecrated worker essential to this cause— not amateur charity ladies but an organized force trained in ministries of care and service that grew out of woman's nature.

Meyer had an affinity with most of the young women who entered the Chicago Training School and were among the first deaconesses in Protestant churches. Born in 1849 of devoutly religious parents in the rural village of New Haven, Vermont, from early childhood she sought a religious career. She studied for two years at the Woman's Medical College in Pennsylvania, intending to join her fiancé as a medical missionary. After his premature death, Lucy Rider decided to find a vocation nearer her family. Entering the field of education, she became principal of the Troy Conference Academy in Poultney, Vermont, taught chemistry for a year at the Massachusetts Institute of Technology in Boston, and then ventured west to be a professor of chemistry at McKendree College in Lebanon, Illinois.

Drawn to the church and to direct service of humanity, she stretched her wings further to become field secretary of the Illinois State Sunday School Association in 1881. Four years later, Lucy Rider married Josiah Shelly Meyer, who was employed by the Young Men's Christian Association (YMCA) in Chicago and committed to social work within the church. She found her vocation when they initiated the Chicago Training School to prepare young women, such as herself, for the home and foreign missionary work of the churches. Sharing leadership until their retirement in 1925, the couple planned, managed, and ran the institution together, though the position of principal of the school and mother of the deaconess family was seen as primary, both inside and outside the school.

Lucy Rider Meyer had come a long way from Poult-ney, Vermont, traveling and working far from her home of origin. To bring young, innocent, and insulated young women into the day-to-day life and work in a threatening urban situation, she needed to create a community that would provide a safe homelike environment from which to venture into avowedly dangerous work situations. The community not only had to provide protection to the deaconesses but also had to assure their families and church congregations that such support was guaranteed.

To build community within the community of the Chicago Training School, Meyer employed the language and experience of the family, the community most basic and familiar to these young women. *Home, Mother House, mother,* and *family* were the words they used daily to describe who and where they were and what their purpose was to be.

"The world wants mothering," Meyer wrote, particularly the world of the immigrants new to the city and bereft of the support of family roots. The deaconess herself was to follow in the path of Lucy Rider Meyer and some day adapt the role of mother of her own institution. She described their call in these words: "Mother love has its part to do in winning the world for Christ as well as father-wisdom and guidance. The deaconess movement puts the mother into the church. It supplies the feminine element so greatly needed in the Protestant Church, and thus is rooted deep in the very heart of humanity's needs" (Horton, *Burden of the City*, 145, 146).

This image of womanhood provided the strong caring qualities essential in the young women who fanned out daily into the streets and alleys to confront the degradation of the city. The popular conception also was that a woman's nature was "so fine and delicate" that "a home dwelling in which her personal life and vocation may be grounded" was necessary for her survival. The mother image also combated the widespread fear that single women were stepping too far out of their places in moving into the public sphere. As women began to seek ordination in the churches in the late nineteenth century, some clergy and church members feared that deaconess orders might be a logical stepping stone in that direction. The "new woman," who was moving outside the home to work beside men in the business world, was a threatening specter to many substantial church people. Christian Golder, a recognized authority on the deaconess movement at the turn of the century, assured the anxious that though deaconesses were the first professional women in the churches, the Mother House "obviates all dangers of emancipation which women in public life so easily encounter" (579). To him, the family model of the deaconess movement was a highly conservative influence, keeping the young women from venturing too far on their own to become independent in the city. However, some deaconess leaders, particular among the females, hoped to make the deaconesses exemplars of "the new woman." Lucy Rider Meyer was among this avant-guarde.

Meyer's understanding of the nature of the deaconess family was complex. On the one hand, she was committed to the conservative, protective influence of the deaconess family, particularly in providing a home away from home for young women venturing from their rural environments into a sordid metropolitan world. She described the deaconesses who resided in the Mother House as her beloved family of students and deaconesses. Patterned after their families of origin, the principle of sharing all things in common was key to the family system model of the Chicago Training School and other deaconess orders. No one received an income or a salary. To do so would have degraded the spiritual value of their services. Rather, they received provisions to do the work: room, board, and basic essentials, including carfare for the day to and from their places of work. The latter was understood as an allowance, a good family term for small amounts of money doled out to children weekly to provide them the opportunity to buy a few personal items.

Before graduating their second class of fifteen students in 1887, Josiah Shelly Meyer shared this plan with them: Those who wished to stay and continue their fieldwork "could remain as a part of the family, receiving room, board, and their necessary carfare. Further than that they could promise them nothing: they 'would all work hard and share and share alike'" (Horton, *High Adventure*, 136). Recorded word that deaconesses resented maternal and paternal control exerted by the Meyers is not found. Like Roman Catholic sisters of their day, deaconesses must have so strongly felt the communal nature of their life and service that they did not consider their lack of economic control as a form of childlike dependence.

In exchange for their services over many years, the deaconesses were assured personal care in time of illness or in old age. One of their extended family members of financial supporters in the late nineteenth century, Norman Wait Harris, wealthy philanthropist and president of the Harris Banking House in Chicago, contributed $100,000 to the retirement fund of the Methodist Deaconess Association to provide suitable living conditions for elderly deaconesses who would have acquired no monetary savings to care for themselves.

Lucy Rider Meyer's leadership was not built on the manner of an employer or even a teacher. She poured her life into the work of the school, counseling, advising, praying with the girls, and sharing their burdens, wrote her biographer Isabelle Horton in *High Adventure*. She also had a charismatic quality, and her spirit was con-

tagious. Very practically, she resolved at least initially to take her part in the household tasks in which all other family members had to share. Over time, she stepped back from some jobs, including washing dishes and windows and bookkeeping, absolving herself of such responsibilities on the basis of the diversity of gifts granted to members of God's household.

Sisterhood, fostered by Lucy Rider Meyer's leadership, grew among the students and graduates. A close corps of women, such as Elizabeth Holding, stood with the Meyers at the center of a community support network within the communities of the household and school. After returning from missionary work in South Africa, "this talented woman caught the spirit of self-forgetful adventure and became an invaluable helper in laying the foundations of the new School," Horton wrote. She described Holding as "the first of a large number of women that Mrs. Meyer was able to gather around her—women of genius who found in their hearts a response to the splendor of her idealism, and who carried the influence of her dynamic leadership into every part of the homeland, and to continents beyond the sea" (*High Adventure*, 109–110).

A distinguished quartet of students at the Training School was cultivated by Lucy Rider Meyer. One of those students, Isabella Thoburn, became head of the Cincinnati Training School; Mary Jefferson took her place as head of the Chicago Home; Isabelle Reeves also remained in leadership in Chicago; and May Hilton became a missionary to South Africa. These women were the first of a large number of graduates from the Chicago Training School who, at the end of the nineteenth and early twentieth centuries, founded over forty institutions, an extended family of the Mother House, including hospitals, orphanages, schools for the homeless, and homes for the elderly.

If Lucy Rider Meyer's motherly care of the deaconess family may seem conservative and protective to readers a century later, her motivation was to liberate young women of the late nineteenth century. The "new woman of Protestantism," the single woman who could have a life and a vocation of her own, was created through the leadership and community building of Lucy Rider Meyer and the deaconess family of the Chicago Training School. Meyer sought to provide dignity and purpose for single women to gain meaningful work for themselves in the churches and in society. Isabelle Horton described the significance of Meyer's work to the women's movement of the day: "It would seem, that the time has come in the history of the work when the unmarried woman no longer needs to excuse or defend her existence, when what she had done for the betterment of humanity should silence all adverse criticism" (*Deaconess Advocate* [September 1912]: 9).

As early as 1895, Lucy Rider Meyer saw the significance of these first professional women in the churches whom she had effectively nurtured:

> A deaconess is often pictured as a goody-goody kind of woman who goes softly up dirty back stairs, reading the bible to poor sick women and patting the heads of dirty-faced children. But there is nothing a woman *can* do in the line of Christian work that a deaconess may not do. Her field is as large as the work of woman, and the need of that work. In deaconess ranks to-day may be found physicians, editors, stenographers, teachers, nurses, bookkeepers, superintendents of hospitals and orphanages, kitchen-gardeners and kindergartners. In Omaha not only the superintending nurse, but the superintendent of the Methodist Episcopal Hospital, an institution that within two years has cared for 1040 patients, are deaconesses. (*Message and Deaconess Advocate* [December 1895]: 8)

By creating a community of women within the communities of the Chicago Training School and Deaconess Home, Lucy Rider Meyer and its members inspired and trained each other. The family model and the motherly role of Meyer provided them familiar structures of support while leading them into acknowledged foreign territory. In turn, the sisterhood opened up new professions for their sisters and released them to venture into "fields of usefulness" previously barred to women of the late nineteenth century.

The Extended Family— Networks of Wider Support

The women who formed the women's societies that supported Christian service and missionary outreach contrasted dramatically with the young single women who left their homes of origin in rural areas and small towns to join deaconess orders and give themselves to full-time Christian service in urban and foreign mission stations. Women active in local churchwomen's societies were likely to be wives and mothers who had not left the towns of their birth or even traveled outside of them but who had found second homes in their congregations. However, like-minded commitments bound them to the deaconesses. The women on the home front were the mothers, grandmothers, sisters, aunts, and friends of these pioneers. They were an extended family to the women in the mission fields, women committed to the same values, who wanted to support the recruits in their newly gained freedom to work for Christ and the church.

After the Civil War, from 1861 until 1894, more women became involved in women's societies of Chris-

tian service and missionary outreach within their local churches than in all areas of social reform and women's rights movements combined. Foreign missionary societies were formed in thirty-three white and African American Protestant denominations, and national missionary societies were begun in seventeen denominations. Through these communities at the grassroots level of local congregations and the regional and national societies that brought them together, over 1,000 women, most of whom were deaconesses, were sent into foreign mission fields during this thirty-three-year period.

The most obvious meaning of the extended family lies in the connection between the female missionaries and the women in churchwomen's societies who provided them financial and moral support. Societies of Christian service and missionary outreach are grouped together in this essay. *Christian service* refers to a wide cluster of work, including national missions, aid to local congregations, and advocacy of justice issues beyond the church. Often this work was done in conjunction with foreign missionary work by one society in a congregation, while in other congregations the work might have been divided between two organizations. Most national and foreign missionaries were trained in deaconess institutions such as Lucy Rider Meyer's in Chicago. Meyer maintained close relationships with local and national women's Christian service and missionary society workers. Without the vision of vocation, its practical implementation in the training schools, and the community of support developed within the communities of women's societies of Christian service and missionary outreach, probably no corps of single female missionaries could have been sent into the national and international fields.

This essay focuses on a less obvious meaning of an extended family: leadership and bonds of vocation and sisterhood created among women in Christian service and missionary societies in local congregations. The editor of *The Heathen Woman's Friend*, the journal of the Methodist Episcopal Women's Foreign Missionary Society, stated the purpose in this way: "Apart from all considerations of duty to others, it will be *profitable to ourselves to unite together* in such associations as are contemplated by this society" (May 1869, 2; italics mine). This was the message of national and regional leaders, including Jennie Fowler Willing, and writers in women's society journals. Female members and subscribers, isolated in their homes and lacking a larger meaning for their lives, could be given new purpose, self-understandings that did not limit them to domestic duties. Now they could be laborers in the vineyard themselves. A new status of women at home being missionaries in their own right was inculcated into members of local church foreign and home missionary societies.

Willing organized the northwestern and western branches of the Women's Foreign Missionary Society of the Methodist Episcopal Church in 1870 and the Women's Home Missionary Society ten years later. She identified closely with the women at home whom she brought together into local church and national women's societies. Willing was born and grew up on a farm near Newark in downstate Illinois where she attended only a few months of formal schooling. Inspired by her mother's example of reading informational books, Fowler initiated her own program of self-education and at fifteen years old began to teach in local schools.

Four years later she married William Willing, a Methodist Episcopal pastor in northern Illinois. The couple had no children. Their marriage appears to have been one of remarkable equality in their relationship, and with her husband's support, Jennie broadened her interests outside the home. She was active in the suffrage movement at both the state and national levels and in Woman's Christian Temperance Union work, as well as in the church. With her husband's help, she gained a local preacher's license before ordination was open to women and had charge of a church in Chicago when her husband was presiding elder of the district.

At the time that the Women's Foreign Missionary Society of the denomination was being formed in 1869, the Willings were visited by missionaries from India. Mr. and Mrs. Edwin Parker, the missionaries, encouraged Jennie Fowler Willing to go into national work for the new society. She first declined, seeing herself as shy and timid, but supported by her husband, she changed her mind to become an organizer for the Women's Foreign Missionary Society and later for the Home Missionary Society. Organizing local units drew upon Willing's greatest gifts. It was said that "she went through the territory like a whirlwind" (*Notable American Women*, 3: 624). Willing traveled widely to work directly with female leaders in congregations to encourage and assist them in founding and strengthening societies throughout vast geographical regions.

Willing served for fourteen years as corresponding secretary of the Northwestern Branch of the Women's Foreign Missionary Society. She and women in similar positions in other denominations found their primary means of reaching the large number of women spread across the rural and metropolitan areas of the United States through missionary and Christian service journals, the "mass media" publications of the women's societies. By the 1890s, the three largest publications of the Presbyterian, Methodist Episcopal, and Baptist women's groups alone had over 60,000 subscribers. Women who could pay for a copy were urged to "lend it to the woman who cannot, and thereby arouse and secure

prayers" (*Lutheran Missionary Journal* [February 1890]: 261).

Writers of journal articles stated the vocation of women's society members clearly and succinctly. First, the women were commissioned to evangelize the world, to convert all men and women of the world to faith in Christ. Even more central to their vocation was their commitment to "woman's work for woman." Mrs. Lucy Williams, writing in the *Woman's Evangel*, a journal of the United Brethren Church, wrote that the Good News of new life in Christ comes to women as a "glad evangel . . . an announcement of glad tidings to some of the five hundred millions of women in the degradation and ruin of false religions and oppressive social customs of heathen nations" (*The Woman's Evangel* [January 1882]: 260). To bring the Good News meant not only to preach Christian salvation but also to work for the release of women from social and educational oppression.

Willing's leadership was demonstrated by what she wrote in *The Heathen Woman's Friend*, powerfully stating the commission of women's society members on the home front in relation to the deaconesses sent into the field:

A *few* must go forth to teach them, but the *many* must *work* at home. We now especially need the home laborers, ladies who will go to work earnestly to organize praying bands and working circles to earn and raise money to send missionaries abroad and to support native Bible women to teach heathen women.

She noted, "How many churches there are in our connection, where the women would gladly do something, if some one would but take the lead, and interest and unite them in some plan of earning or saving a little money." Willing capped her summons to commitment with these words: "Let every lady, who feels that she *would be a missionary*, go to work at home, and she may, by every dollar raised, teach her heathen sisters" (October 1869, 32). By offering these isolated women a God-given purpose for their lives, the writers inspired women to raise large sums of money through their penny mite boxes and nickel campaigns to send sister missionaries abroad.

Two kinds of community were created within the communities of women's Christian service and missionary societies. First, women's organization leaders sought sisterhood within their local churches. Their goal was that every church would have a women's society and that all women in the congregation would become members. Detailed, meticulous instructions were given in the journals for the formation of auxiliaries. Jennie Fowler Willing was especially able in developing this practical advice, putting it into print, and taking it personally to leaders and participants in congregations.

The first issue of the *Missionary Helper*, published by the Free Baptist Woman's Missionary Society in 1878, set forth the process to secure from every woman in each congregation a pledge of two cents per week or a dollar a year to carry on the work. Each woman was to write on an envelope "Woman's Work for Woman" and place two cents or more in it each week. Then she was to try to get all women in her church to do the same. When even three or four would make this weekly pledge, they were to form a Woman's Christian Service and Missionary Society auxiliary, meet once a month, and report its founding and progress to the district secretary. Finally, each woman was to ask herself if it was her privilege to become a life member. She could do so by contributing only $20.00, and that could be paid by installments over a two-year period. The hope was that through this training given in the missionary journals all grassroots members would contribute their mite for missions.

A picture printed in the January 1891 edition of *The Missionary Link* graphically portrays the purpose. A woman, clearly representing a middle-class member of a woman's missionary society, is holding the left hand of her three-year-old daughter. With her right hand the young daughter is putting a coin in a mite box, while an older daughter is pointing to a painting on the wall of a large oceangoing ship, probably carrying missionaries and supplies to those to be evangelized in China or India.

A second kind of community sought by women's society members on the home front lay in creating bonds of sisterhood with women beyond their local congregations. Raising money to support women in far-flung foreign countries was a way of bringing together women in remote reaches throughout the United States to serve a larger common purpose. The author of "Our Needs," an essay in the July 1878 edition of the *Missionary Helper*, rallied women to each contribute their small sums to support a female missionary abroad. She wrote,

The Free Baptist women of Rhode Island have pledged themselves to the support of one of these young ladies, and it is confidently expected that some part of Maine will assume the support of another. Will not the women of Ohio unite in sustaining the third? If each of the two hundred subscribers to the *Helper* in Ohio give two cents a week and influence another person to do the same, her salary will be secured. (July 1878, 74)

Beneath the duty to others to develop bonds of sisterhood and serve female missionaries in foreign countries lay a duty to self, the need for women's society members to find deeper purpose for their individual lives beyond the domestic tasks of child care and housecleaning. The writer for the *Missionary Helper* addressed her readers in these words:

In the sewing rooms of our cities, in the farhouses of the prairies, in the kitchens all through our borders, are women who have never thought of life as anything more than a "bread-winning and bread-bestowing existence." . . . in blind ignorance of their own individual capabilities, of their passing opportunities, they are wasting their substance, their lives, their all, and the golden harvests all around them are perishing for reapers. (July 1878, 74)

In reaching out to others, they gained deeper inner meaning for their own lives.

The interaction between duty to others and duty to self is also exemplified in the evolution of the Woman's Convention of the National Black Baptist Church during the Social Gospel period. The Women's Convention was the great purpose to which Nannie Helen Burroughs, founder, secretary, and president of the convention, whose leadership extended from 1900 to 1961, totally committed her life.

Born in Orange, Virginia, in 1878 to a mother determined to gain better educational opportunities for her daughter, Burroughs was educated in Washington, D.C. Unable to find suitable employment there, she moved to Louisville, Kentucky, in 1900 to become a secretary in the office of the Foreign Mission Board of the National Baptist Convention. This position and location became her launching pad to establish the Women's Convention. Evelyn Brooks Higginbotham in her book *Righteous Discontent: The Women's Movement in the Black Baptist Church, 1880–1920* shared the vision of Burroughs in her address "How the Sisters Are Hindered from Helping" at the National Baptist Convention that year. The twenty-one-year-old Burroughs summoned her black sisters to form their own female missionary and service society out of the "burning zeal" of women in her denomination to bond together, in her words, for "collective self-criticism, in order to eradicate inequalities and exclusions within the black community itself" (157).

She was elected secretary at the founding of the Women's Convention in 1900 and remained in that position until 1948. She became president that year and served until her death in 1961. From the beginning, Burroughs worked and traveled tirelessly, establishing units in congregations throughout the country, educating local leaders to run their societies, planning national meetings, and leading the Women's Convention to struggle against structural and systemic oppression and to advocate for race and gender equality in the church and society. Burroughs was credited with being the leading spirit and major strategist of the convention. Higginbotham describes her charismatic leadership as epitomizing the essence of the black Baptist women's movement, enabling the organizing women to embody the feminine presence as a spiritual, as well as a political, force within the black community.

Burroughs's purpose in initiating the call to twenty-six state representatives in 1900 was to bring them together to "rescue the world for Christ. Women arise. He calleth for thee" (Higginbotham, 157). Like most women's church organizations, which were formally or informally called missionary societies, the work of the Women's Convention of the National Baptist Church demonstrates broader kinds of Christian service within the black church and wider society to which these associations committed themselves. Resisting attempts by the male leaders to transform the women's separatist convention into a subsidiary board of the denomination, the women, under Burroughs's influence, stood firm and established their own independent governing structure.

Community, extending from the local branches to the national society, grew out of carefully nurtured structures at each level conceived in the mind and through the hard work of Nannie Helen Burroughs. Work of the branches was coordinated and regulated by handbooks that outlined organizational methods and by record books for bookkeeping and accountability, all developed to train members in how to be executive administrators. National meetings of the Women's Convention were held each year at the same time and place as the National Baptist Convention. These gatherings evoked group identity, both to be National Baptists and to be National Baptist women. They were the high point of the year for the women, resulting in shared friendships and experiences and in an agenda for fighting Jim Crow segregation laws and improving race relations. As the black churches' delegates responded to the racism that denied them accommodations in white hotels and restaurants, the women advanced community by providing housing and meals in the homes of their members.

The Women's Convention's annual meetings became "schools of methods" for local societies. They featured highly practical topics, such as "How to Increase Attendance at Each Meeting," to address their organizational growth and effectiveness. Further, they pushed their local church ministers and congregations to move from solitary focus on individual salvation to the Social Gospel emphasis on social reform.

Burroughs was the guiding light, both in educating her sisters for leadership of their convention at all levels and in broadening the outreach of their commitment to community improvement. The practical work of social salvation became her agenda and that of the Women's Convention. She advocated in her 1914 convention address that no church should remain in a community if it did not positively improve community life. Members studied issues related to social betterment: public health, crime prevention, job placement, and vocational training. Experts in their fields, including physicians, social workers, civic improvement activists, and educators, were brought to the national conventions to share their knowledge. Minutes exhibit the political philosophy and activism of the convention. They record resolutions against segregated railroad cars, stereotyping of blacks in literature, film, and other media, school textbooks that ridiculed blacks, and lynching. They advocated for black women to vote for laws to protect them from male dominance and abuse, for greater opportunities for employment of black women, and for labor laws to protect women and children.

Simultaneously, black women themselves were empowered to study and write on social conditions of their own race and not leave such work to white persons who had no firsthand knowledge of these conditions. As ideas and expertise were channeled throughout the sisterhood, the women were empowered both to be good mothers and to conceive higher and wider purposes for their individual and corporate lives.

As black sisters grew in community within their communities, they championed social reform by their national and local church bodies and were sent out individually to contribute their learning and advocacy in wider communities of social reform. The Woman's Convention was the great preparatory school of women's church societies in the name of the Social Gospel. By the second decade of the twentieth century, leaders of the convention at local and national levels branched out into secular African American reform societies, including the League for the Protection of Colored Women and the National Urban League, complementary to their continued church-related activities. The education in leadership and the networks of support they brought together in their separatist women's societies made them more valued contributors to the wider black social reform work of the new century.

A Community of Leadership

The deaconess movement and women's societies of Christian service and missionary outreach are primarily identified by their direct connection and work within the churches and secondarily by their work in relationship to the larger society. A study of settlement houses usually begins at the opposite pole. Most settlement houses were understood to be rooted in secular social philosophies and to be addressing secular needs. However, many of the founders and early leaders of settlement houses in the United States based their work, at least in part, on strong religious commitments. Many settlement houses were created out of the strong religious convictions of their founders and became primary examples of what is today described as ministry in society, social service and justice work outside of church structures.

Some settlement houses were also based on an egalitarian style of leadership, a community of leadership growing up within the membership of the residents and workers. Hull House opened on Chicago's near west side in 1889, founded both on religious beliefs and on shared community leadership. A widespread misconception relates to the kind of leadership that Jane Addams gave to it. According to popular understanding, Addams and Hull House are indistinguishable. Addams it was thought virtually *was* Hull House. Due to this traditional emphasis, the formative role she played in creating and sustaining a female network and structures of support has only recently been developed. Kathryn Kish Sklar, in her monumental work *Florence Kelley and the Nation's Work: The Rise of Women's Political Culture, 1830–1900*, returns to the evaluation made by Hull House residents and guests at the turn of the century: "Jane Addams's

personality and intelligence were the kernel around which the Hull House community took shape." Emily Balch, who visited Hull House in 1895 and the only other American woman besides Jane Addams to be awarded the Nobel Peace Prize, said that Addams "did not dominate the group. She, as it were, incorporated it and helped it to be itself" (126).

Hull House was founded on the corporate vision and community of leadership of Jane Addams and Ellen Gates Starr. Religious convictions account for much of their zeal. Within a few years, that circle of leadership expanded to include Frances Kelley, Alice Hamilton, and Julia Lathrop. Vocationally, they were all visionary social reformers of the Social Gospel and Progressive movement on the Chicago and national scenes. They differed in their religious sensibilities, however, and those differences led to changes in the understanding of Hull House's mission over the first and second decades.

Jane Addams and Ellen Gates met as students at Rockford Seminary in the early 1880s. The president, Anna Peck Sills, and teachers tried to reach both women with the message of evangelical Christianity and careers in the foreign mission field. Addams valued the evangelical zeal of the teachers and the ethos of bonding with other women at Rockford, but she personally disliked

Chicago's Hull House was founded in 1889 on the corporate vision and community leadership of Jane Addams and Ellen Gates Starr. Religious convictions account for much of their zeal. Within a few years, the circle of leadership expanded to include Frances Kelley, Alice Hamilton, and Julia Lathrop. Vocationally, they were all visionary social reformers of the social gospel and Progressive movement on the Chicago and national scenes. *Jane Addams Collection, Swarthmore College Peace Collection.*

being evangelized. Historian Anne Firor Scott described Sills's effort to lead Addams into the mission field: In Jane Addams "she encountered a vein of iron" (*Notable American Women*, 1: 16).

Addams was born in 1860 and reared in a nondoctrinaire Christian home. She inherited her religious sensibilities from her father, John Huy Addams, a Hicksite Quaker and a generic liberal Protestant who contributed to all denominations in the town of Cedarville, Illinois. He was more interested in Jesus as an earthly model than as the Son of God, a position that his daughter also would adopt. At Rockford Seminary, she affirmed a religious conviction of Jesus' teaching in the Beatitudes to care for the poor and needy. Even as a young child, Jane was morally precocious, bearing a heavy sense of responsibility to change the world. She saw the big houses and the little houses and felt a duty to bridge the gulf between poverty and wealth. Jane's understanding of Jesus' teaching and the call that it placed upon her personally were forceful in leading her to conceive Hull House.

Starr, eighteen months older than Addams, also grew up in a rural environment on a farm near Leona, Illinois. She was brought up in a mildly Unitarian family household where the Bible was not used and was given virtually no religious instruction by her parents. Her aunt Eliza Allen Starr was a devout convert to Catholicism and the strongest childhood influence on Ellen. While religion played only a minor role in her own home, much of Ellen's own life was a quest for religious truth, which led her, later in life, to also become Roman Catholic. At Rockford, she resisted being evangelized, just as did Jane. After Rockford Seminary she taught in a private girls' school in Chicago and, in 1884, joined a "low" Episcopalian Church. One year later, Addams became a member of the Presbyterian Church in Cedarville for much the same reason as Starr committed herself to an institutional church. Neither was interested or moved by the doctrine of their denominations but sought a community of believers with whom to be in fellowship.

After graduation from Rockford Seminary, Addams exchanged letters regularly with Starr. They struggled with their mutual search of how to live useful lives. Addams described these as aimless years in which she, as other women college graduates of her day, was caught in a snare of preparation: too much intellectualizing without putting her knowledge into action to address the world's needs. Both Addams and Starr rejected marriage and the mission field as rightful vocations for themselves, while the call to confront the evils in society drew them.

Addams took two trips to Europe, in 1883 and 1887, joined by Starr the second time. They were directly confronted by people displaced by unjust social systems and living in poverty. In London, Addams and Starr witnessed the strike of female match workers, women displaced by a ruthless industrial system, and visited Toynbee Hall, a settlement house begun by a group of Oxford University men in 1884. Gaining inspiration from the relief and rehabilitation work done there among the city's poor, Addams raised with Starr her idea of founding their own settlement by buying a house in a depressed area of Chicago and living there among the poor. Starr was equally enthusiastic about the plan, out of which Hull House was born two years later.

Religious motivations guided Addams and Starr's decision of what to do with their lives. They believed that the churches, with their emphasis on doctrine and dogma, had lost touch with the human needs of real people. The aim of Hull House was to enable young people "to put their beliefs into practice, to lead lives of action" (Jean Baker Elshtain, quoted in Stebner, 22). They related to many of their own generation who were disillusioned by the isolation of the churches from the realities of life and saw "involvement in the social settlement as an attempt to humanize Christianity and, at the same time, make religion less sectarian," Addams wrote in her essay "The Subjective Necessity for Social Settlements." Young people do not believe that Christianity "is a thing to be proclaimed and instituted apart from the social life of the community [but is] one manifestation of that wider humanitarian movement . . . to embody itself, not in a sect, but in society itself" (*Twenty Years at Hull House*, 18–19).

Neither Jane Addams nor Ellen Gates Starr disavowed institutional religion. Addams was a regular attendee and contributing member of the Ewing Street Congregational Church down the street from Hull House, at least through the mid-1920s. The church was an outreach congregation of the Chicago City Missionary Society and was an avowedly evangelical community. Similarly, Starr remained personally close to a Christian congregation and in 1920 joined the Roman Catholic Church, later entering a convent, "as passionate for divinity and salvation, as she ever was for beauty or for justice" (Elshtain, 132). Eleanor Stebner's words regarding Jane Addams sum up the way in which both women differentiated between their personal religious faith and the religious expression embodied in Hull House: "She desired to be authentic to her experience and participate in a religious community. She also desired to live a life of love and service based on what she perceived to be the early teachings of Jesus. But she found abhorrent the idea of dictating her perceptions to others" (82).

In founding Hull House, Addams and Starr may have intended that it be more closely related to institutional Christianity than it came to be. A notation by the pastor beside her name in the membership book of the Ewing Street Church, when she joined as a charter member in 1895, read: "First resident at Hull House. Desires to have the work of the church more closely cooperative with Hull House" (77). However, by that time, Hull House was becoming what Addams and the other women in the community of leadership also desired that it be: a spiritually grounded community based on loving God through loving one's neighbor, the model taken from Jesus' parables and the Beatitudes.

The community of leaders was highly influential in moving Hull House toward the spirituality that included all persons in fellowship and mutual responsibility and to unite them in the wider spiritual principles of service. This cadre included Julia Lathrop, Florence Kelley, and Alice Hamilton, all of whom met at Hull House and joined Addams and Starr in the 1890s.

Religious influences were present in the family backgrounds of all three women. Lathrop was born in Rockford in 1858 and enrolled in Rockford Female Seminary for one year before transferring and graduating from Vassar. She attended a Congregational Church while growing up, though probably was never active in any Protestant church. Her aunt, a missionary in India, was distressed that she never accepted a church creed. Born in Philadelphia one year later, Kelley was strongly influenced by the Quaker faith through her extended family and by her aunt's refusal to use cotton and sugar produced by slave labor. However, she did not join the Society of Friends until later in her life in 1927. Hamilton, born a decade later in Fort Wayne, Indiana, grew up in a family presided over by a widowed grandmother who was a leader in the city's charitable and religious life. While she attended the First Presbyterian Church, there is no indication that she was deeply shaped by a religious commitment.

The most formative forces in these women's lives were not agnostic but humanitarian and secular. Through the influence of her father, who was a lawyer, Julia Lathrop developed concern for women's rights, treatment of the insane, and civil service reform. Florence Kelley's early social justice concerns were evidenced in her senior thesis at Cornell University, "On Some Changes in the Legal Status of the Child since Blackstone." Traveling in Europe after college, she became caught up by the "wildfire of socialism" (*Notable American Women*, 2: 317), which deepened her understanding of the abuse of working women and children. The intellectual stimulation of Alice Hamilton's home inspired her to live an independent and useful life. She chose medicine as a profession, desiring a career in teaching and research rather than in direct care of patients, and gained scientific training comparable to that of few men or women of her day.

Kelley's socially activist work while at Hull House included leading the sweatshop investigations that resulted in passage of the Illinois Factory Acts in 1893, prohibiting child labor, limiting work hours for women, and

setting standards and procedures for inspection of tenement sweatshops. Governor John Altgeld appointed Kelley Illinois chief Factory Inspector. After leaving Hull House, she became head of the National Consumers' League, locating herself in New York City for over twenty-seven years.

Lathrop was the first Hull House resident to be employed in an Illinois State administrative position, named to the State Board of Charities by Governor Altgeld. She worked for informed personal attention in treating the insane, was pivotal in founding the first juvenile court in the United States, and was a founder and trustee of the Illinois Immigrants Protective League. Later, she became chief of the Federal Children's Bureau in Washington, D.C., as well as a member of the National Board of the League of Women Voters.

Hamilton came to Chicago as a Hull House resident when she became professor of pathology at the Women's Medical School of Northwestern University. Spending over twenty years in Chicago and at Hull House, she worked to eliminate infectious and industrial diseases and the production and distribution of cocaine. She later moved to Harvard Medical School as assistant professor of industrial medicine and outlived all other Hull House residents, dying when she was 101 years old in 1970.

Of the cadre of coworkers that formed and gave leadership to Hull House, no relationship was stronger and deeper than the one between Florence Kelley and Jane Addams. Kelley came to Hull House in late 1891, just two years after its founding. She felt immediately at home and was trusted by Addams. Within three months she wrote that she had cast her lot with Misses Addams and Starr for as long as they would let her stay there. She remained only seven years, due to her decision to lead the National Consumers' League, but she described them as the most happy, active, and influential years of her life, in providing her with powerful new means to do the nation's work. Also, as her son Nicholas pointed out, from the time of coming to Hull House until her death in 1932, Kelley counted Jane Addams as her closest friend and confidante.

Jane Addams at once experienced Florence Kelley as a deep friend and a most able surrogate. Kelley always sat beside Addams at dinner and often was in charge of events when Addams could not be present. In depth and vision, they complemented each other and formed Hull House into its distinctive self. Addams was more personally adept in relating to individual problems and persons that presented themselves, while Kelley pressed her colleague to develop a larger, more structural analysis of society's needs and programs of reform. Another close colleague, Julia Lathrop, stated that they "understood each other's powers" and joined together in a "wonderfully effective way." Addams, the philosopher, "taught

Kelley how to live and have faith in an imperfect world," and Kelley, the politician, "taught Addams how to make demands on the future" (Sklar, 183).

Kelley was highly secular in her outlook, and she moved Addams and Starr away from some practices of evangelical Christianity, such as kneeling for prayers and having evening Bible readings. Addams and Kelley both held strong commitments to social justice. Their differences in nature made for a fuller and more embracing approach, both in terms of their leadership within and beyond the Hull House community and in terms of their personal relationship. "Addams instinct for peace-making and conciliating made her see every side of social questions and feel compassion for all the actors, while Kelley's aggressive championing of the exploited usually dealt with stark contrasts behind good and evil. Kelley expressed anger against the causes of social injustice; Addams demonstrated a tragic appreciation of and sympathy with suffering" (Sklar, 185).

Addams's and Kelley's complementary dispositions provided a needed balance, both for each other and for the House. Lathrop described Addams as "serene, dauntless . . . Mrs. Kelley, alight with the resurgent flame of her zeal." Kelley's son Nicholas spoke of Addams as "firm beyond all imagining," though "I never saw Miss Addams angry and never heard of her being angry." Supreme Court Justice Felix Frankfurter, on the other hand, termed Kelley "the toughest customer in the reform riot." Another wrote, "By what rare stroke of fortune were they brought together in the days when Chicago was a great focus of our mounting industrialism?" (Sklar, 185, 183).

Discerning the corporate nature of leadership and community at Hull House, Florence Kelley interpreted Addams as the cult figure that bound together the Hull House residents. Addams's authority did not come from a heavy-handed or hierarchical leadership style, however. She provided space for companionships of mutual interests and affinities to form. These companionships were able to support more intimate communities within the larger corporate group.

The community of Lathrop, Kelley, and Hamilton within the Hull House community was one of mutual support that enabled each of them to deepen her personal vocation. Frankfurter said that of any person Kelley had "probably the largest single share in shaping the social history of the United States during the first thirty years of this [the twentieth] century" (Stebner, 128). She widened the vision and pushed Jane Addams and her other sisters into more radical social action. She was high-spirited and impatient, a fighter and a galvanizer. Lathrop, one of her best friends, was known for her pastoral presence, compassion, and patience. Some thought it was a great waste of her time and energy for such a valuable person to spend so much time with neighborhood visitors to Hull House seeking to bring them a comfort and companionship that they may not have had in years. Lathrop brought diplomacy and gentleness, never losing her temper, in relating to Florence Kelley.

They shared common traits that also brought them together, according to Frankfurter. "Both were brilliant, imaginative, humorous, and troubled by injustice. When both were at Hull House together, arguing some problem of correcting a social injustice, and disagreeing as they often did on the best method of procedure, it is doubtful if any better talk was to be heard anywhere" (Elshtain, 139f).

When Alice Hamilton came to Hull House, she felt insecure in relating to some of the residents. She especially experienced Florence Kelley as intimidating at first, while Julia Lathrop was immediately approachable. Kelley and Lathrop were both ten years older than Hamilton and must have mentored her in different ways. In time, Hamilton grew deeply fond of Kelley and found her one of the most vivid, stimulating, and challenging persons she had ever known. Lathrop must have eased the way in bringing Kelley and Hamilton closer together. Hamilton became politicized at Hull House, particularly through Kelley's influence. She found Lathrop, who became a lifelong friend, especially companionable and soon accompanied her on visits to insane asylums. The difference in what the two colleagues Kelley and Lathrop brought to Hamilton's life is beautifully complementary. Kelley challenged her to use her talents to directly confront the most serious social problems of her day, particularly as a doctor to investigate deplorable medical conditions and to become a scientific reformer. On the other hand, she wrote of Lathrop, "Julia Lathrop never roused one to a fighting pitch, but then fighting was not her method . . . [she] taught me . . . that harmony and peaceful relations with one's adversary were not in themselves of value, but only if they went with a steady pushing of what one was trying to achieve" (Stebner, 130).

When Kelley reflected on the connection between gender and class in her own life, she also challenged middle-class women to look at that relationship in their lives and to understand their own culpability as part of the problem. As she asked in her autobiography, "In the great strife of classes, in the life and death struggle that is rending society to its foundations, where do I belong?" (Sklar, 196). Kelley was reflecting vocationally on her own life, but she could have been speaking of Addams, Starr, Lathrop, and Hamilton and her other colleagues at Hull House. They belonged at Hull House and formed its community and communities, just as they were shaped by Hull House and its members.

When Jane Addams wrote *Twenty Years at Hull-House* in 1910, she reflected back on the meaning of Hull House in these words:

I remember on that exciting day when the house was first promised to us that I looked up my European notebook . . . hoping that I might find a description of what I thought a "Cathedral of Humanity" ought to be. The description was "low and wide spreading as to include all men in fellowship and mutual responsibility even as the older pinnacles and spires indicated communion with God." . . . When I read this girlish outbreak it gave me much comfort, for in those days in addition to our other perplexities Hull-House was often called irreligious. . . . [A]ll higher aims live by communion and fellowship, [and] are cultivated most easily in the fostering soil of community life. (115)

Addams symbolized Hull House as a cathedral that was an alternative structure to traditional houses of faith, one that did not separate people into communities of particular faiths, sects, or denominations. This cathedral united people around wider spiritual principles of service to each other that all people could affirm. Further, she envisioned Hull House as a way of life based on communion with God and fellowship among its members. The bonds of support and nurture cultivated by the mutual service of one to another were meant to lead its members to a deeper vision and higher ideas for their corporate life.

The three types of women's associations that are the focus of this essay, the deaconess movement, women's societies of Christian service and missionary outreach, and the settlement house movement, are very different today, both in their inner lives and in their accomplishments in society. Each has had its day in the form in which it was created and flourished near the end of the nineteenth century and in the early twentieth century. All still exist, though in radically changed forms.

Only a few deaconesses who served in national and international mission sites through the mid-twentieth century are still living, and most of those women are in retirement centers and nursing homes. Diaconal ministers, laywomen and laymen serving in a variety of professional and volunteer ministries in local churches and in other agencies, have expanded the work of deaconesses and in many cases assumed clergy functions due to the shortage of ordained ministers. Women's societies of Christian service and missionary societies in local churches are most often made up of older women. New ways to tap the volunteer resources of younger women, most of whom are employed outside their homes, are being explored. Hull House in Chicago looks very different from the many buildings that housed flourishing programs soon after it was founded. The historic site and building are still on its original location on the West Side of the city, but the social work of Hull House is now situated in multiple units throughout Chicago. As times change, so do the appropriate structures.

The inner life of these organizations is significant to women's history. Through their leadership styles, the women in this essay enabled community to be built within their communities. Lucy Rider and Josiah Shelley Meyer found ways to share partnership in administering the Chicago Training School and Deaconess Home for thirty-five years, with recognition that her position was the primary one. The genius of their leadership appears to have been in their ability to adapt a model, the family, that young women, unfamiliar and innocent to the ways of the city, could find compatible to their emerging independence. Further, they trained a host of these women to be sent out to found and lead approximately forty other service institutions for the church throughout the country. The women had to be trained practically in how to lead in order to be able to blossom on their own.

The significance of Jennie Fowler Willing's and Nannie Helen Burrough's leadership lay in their ability to empower a vast number of home-bound women to assume leadership themselves of local units in far-reaching geographical areas of the country. This took tireless energy to develop countless programs of practical training, but equally important was their ability to create extended families of support among their sisters to inspire and empower women, whose purpose and functions were narrowly constricted, to believe in their own greater personal and social self-worth.

Finally, the picture of the women of Hull House that emerges places a different face on the leadership of Jane Addams and her colleagues than has been recognized until recently. Their interrelationships demonstrate that Addams, the publicly and historically hallowed leader of Hull House, was herself vulnerable and in need of the companionship and shared authority held by her sisters. Further, the women that collectively led Hull House were persons of great strength whose identity and contribution have been overshadowed by the primary figure of Jane Addams. Their shared leadership by community, rather than by a single individual, is a distinctive gift seldom replicated.

The twentieth and early twenty-first century have increasingly integrated women into wider institutional structures of churches and the business world. There are exceptions, but integration has generally meant a continuation of traditional hierarchical styles of leadership. While individual women begin to pioneer as leaders of complex organizations, the question remains whether avant-garde feminists of the twenty-first century will notably change the nature of these institutions or continue to foster long-standing traditional patterns of leadership.

SOURCES: Anne Firor Scott, *Natural Allies: Women's Associations in American History* (1991), and Nancy Cott, *The Bonds* of *Womanhood: "Woman's Sphere" in New England, 1780–1835* (1977), establish the significance of women's separatist societies in American history and church history. Important primary sources related to Lucy Rider Meyer and the deaconess movement are Lucy Rider Meyer, *Deaconesses* (1892); Isabella Horton, *High Adventure: Life of Lucy Rider Meyer* (1928) and *The Burden of the City* (1904), and Reverend Christian Golder, *History of the Deaconess Movement in the Christian Church* (1903); also the *Deaconess Advocate* and the *Message and Deaconess Advocate*, journals of the Chicago Training School, in which Meyer's writings were published. A good modern study is Mary Agnes Dougherty, *My Calling to Fulfill: Deaconesses in the United Methodist Tradition* (1997). Recent annotated articles on Rider are included in *Women in New Worlds: Historical Perspectives on the Wesleyan Tradition,* edited by Rosemary Keller, Louise Queen, and Hilah Thomas (vol. 1, 1981; vol. 2, 1982). The authors include Virginia Brereton, Mary Agnes Dougherty, Catherine Prelinger, and Keller. Women's missionary journals of the late nineteenth century referred to in this essay include *The Heathen Woman's Friend* (Methodist Episcopal Church), the *Lutheran Missionary Journal,* and *The Woman's Evangel* (United Brethren Church). Also see Rosemary Skinner Keller, "Lay Women in the Protestant Tradition," in *Women and Religion in America*, vol. 1, *The Nineteenth Century,* ed. Rosemary Radford Ruether and Rosemary Skinner Keller (1982). For Jennie Fowler Willing, see Joanne Brown, "Shared Fire: The Flame Ignited by Jennie Fowler Willing," in *Spirituality and Social Responsibility: Vocational Vision of Women in the United Methodist Tradition,* ed. Rosemary Skinner Keller (1993). For Nannie Helen Burroughs, see Evelyn Brooks Higginbotham, *Righteous Discontent: The Women's Movement in the Black Baptist Church, 1880–1920* (1993). Jane Addams's *Twenty Years at Hull-House* (1910) is the definitive primary source document, of Addams's many writings, for this essay. Three of the recent related studies quoted here are Jean Bethke Elshtain, *Jane Addams and the Dream of American Democracy* (2002); Eleanor Stebner, *The Women of Hull House: A Study in Spirituality, Vocation, and Friendship* (1997); and Kathryn Kish Sklar, *Florence Kelley and the Nation's Work: The Rise of Women's Political Culture, 1830–1900* (1995). Biographical essays of Addams, Starr, Kelley, Lathrop, and Hamilton, as well as Meyer, Willing, and Burroughs, are found in Edward T. James, ed., *Notable American Women: A Biographical Dictionary,* 3 vols. (1971), and Barbara Sicherman and Carol Hurd, eds., *The Modern Period,* vol. 4 (1980).

"LIFTING AS WE CLIMB": NATIONAL ASSOCIATION OF COLORED WOMEN (NACW)/ NATIONAL COUNCIL OF NEGRO WOMEN (NCNW)
Marcia Y. Riggs

WHY DID AFRICAN American women organize a national club movement at the end of the nineteenth cen-

tury? There are two aspects that establish parameters for answering this question. First, the late nineteenth century through the early twentieth century was a time of such racial brutality, disenfranchisement, and legalized segregation that it has been described as the "nadir" of U.S. race relations. In fact, the plight of African Americans by the last decade of the nineteenth century has been summed up in this way: "The 1890s sounded several loud warnings of the collapse of black prospects in America. The three shrillest were Booker T. Washington's abnegation of black equality in his Atlanta Exposition speech of 1895; the U.S. Supreme Court's blessing on Jim Crow in its Plessy v. Ferguson decision of 1896; and the total eclipse by 1898 of the Populist movement with the resurgence of the solid Democratic South" (Henri, 1). In response to these circumstances, African Americans increased their self-help and racial uplift efforts within independent black churches and through social reform movements. The race-class ideologies that undergirded these responses ranged from accommodationist and integrationist to protest and nationalist; the theologies were evangelical and Social Gospel.

Second, there was a significant growth of women's organizations between 1890 and 1920 as social reform work led by women in separate groups such as the Women's Christian Temperance Unions achieved success. The growth of these women's organizations is a significant indicator of women's efforts to expand the meaning of the reigning nineteenth-century gender ideology, "the cult of domesticity." The cult of domesticity assumed that women were to be wives and mothers whose attributes were domesticity, submissiveness, piety, and purity. With social activism outside the home, women embraced a concept of "virtuous womanhood" wedded to an "ideology of educated motherhood" as they sought to transmit their morally superior values to society. Social problems were perceived to be moral problems that could be addressed by eliminating moral corruption through preventive reform programs.

Thus, the formation of a national club movement among African American women can be understood as a response to the racial situation and as part of a general trend among women to organize at the time. The interrelationship of these reasons serves as the basis for discerning the ways in which the club movement among African American women can be understood as a distinct, constructive, faith-based response to the racial, gender, and economic injustices of the era. The African American women's club movement is thus the product of the *particular* ways in which African American women interpreted and responded to the situation of African Americans and women at the close of the nineteenth century. It is the purpose of this essay to disclose the ways that social circumstances and religious motivations interacted to create and sustain the club movement. The club movement among African American women is best interpreted as a socioreligious movement aimed at reforming society through the "uplift" efforts of African American women.

The Club Movement as Socioreligious Movement

The call for a national meeting of African American women in 1895 issued by Mrs. Josephine St. Pierre Ruffin (1842–1924), an organizer of one of the first African American women's clubs, the Women's Era Club of Boston, is an important point of departure for interpreting this movement. This call and the national meeting that ensued (July 29–31, 1895) laid the groundwork for the merger of the National Federation of Afro-American Women and the League of Colored Women—the two groups that anchored the formation of the National Association of Colored Women (NACW) in 1896. Ruffin wrote:

Although the matter of a convention has been talked over for some time, the subject has been precipitated by a letter to England, written by a southern editor, and reflecting upon the moral character of all colored women; this letter is too indecent for publication, but a copy of it is sent with this call to all the women's bodies throughout the country. Read this document carefully and use discriminately and decide if it be not time for us to stand before the world and declare ourselves and our principles.

The time is short, but everything is ripe; and remember, earnest women can do anything. . . . Although we do not hope that this our first conference will in all respects meet our ideal, yet we trust that it will be the beginning of a movement for creating a community of interest among all earnest women who love purity and demand justice.

This invitation is extended to all colored women of America, members of any society or not. (*A History of the Club Movement among the Colored Women of the United States,* 3–5)

The letter by a southern editor to which Ruffin refers is one that was sent to Florence Balgarnie (a British suf-

The African American women's club movement institutionalized a distinctive religious ethical tradition. This tradition was central to what made the National Association of Colored Women and later the National Council of Negro Women impressive models of church women's activism in society. *Courtesy of the Mary MacLeod Bethune House, Washington, D.C.*

fragist and reformer) to discredit Ida B. Wells-Barnett (1862–1931) as she took her antilynching campaign abroad. In the letter, African American women were characterized as "natural thieves, liars, and prostitutes." This public assault was a harsh reminder that African American women were considered outside the norms of virtuous womanhood, and one particular aim of their club movement would be to counter this claim. The fact that a hundred women from across the country, from as far away as California, attended that meeting in Boston earmarks the significance of this initial gathering.

In an address to the 1895 meeting, Ruffin further elaborated the programmatic aims and purposes of a national club movement: vocational training, moral education, and physical development for African American boys and girls as well as "the general questions of the day," such as temperance, morality, higher education, hygienic, and domestic questions. Importantly, according to Ruffin, the movement was to challenge society's normative assumptions about African American women (particularly, their alleged immorality) as it mobilized a network of groups whose social reform work promoted justice for all African Americans—women, men, and children. Ruffin concluded her address:

Now with an army of organized women standing for purity and mental work, we in ourselves deny the charge and open the eyes of the world to a state of affairs to which they have been blind, often willfully so, and the very fact that the charges, audaciously and flippantly made, as they often are, are of so humiliating and delicate a nature, serves to protect the accuser by driving the helpless accused into mortified silence. It is to break this silence, not by noisy protestations of what we are not, but by a dignified showing of what we are and hope to become that we are impelled to take this step, to make of this gathering an object lesson to the world.

Our woman's movement is a woman's movement in that it is led and directed by women for the good of women and men, for the benefit of all humanity, which is more than any one branch or section of it. We want, we ask the active interest of our men, and, too, we are not drawing the color line; we are women, American women, as intensely interested in all that pertains to us as such as all other American women; we are not alienating or withdrawing, we are only coming to the front, willing to join any others in the same work and cordially inviting and welcoming any others to join us. (Davis, 19)

Ruffin's call and address made evident that African American women knew they were a distinct sociohis-

torical group confronted by a white racist, sexist, and classist society that placed them outside the social and moral community they sought to reform. Accordingly, their club work was to be intrinsically political, economic, and ethical. As a social movement, the African American women's clubs were the means through which African American women created a milieu wherein they could question accepted relations of power and the ideological underpinnings of those relations and develop programs, agendas, and justifications for the society they sought to reform through ideas that derived from their unique race-gender-class consciousness. It was from their experience and perspective as African American women that they generated an ethic of responsibility for themselves and society.

Likewise, the national club movement was a religious movement because of the religious influences operative within it in terms of both the motivation of its leadership and the composition of its membership. Fannie Barrier Williams (1855–1944), a club woman and journalist of the period, wrote about the leadership: "The training which first enabled colored women to organize and successfully carry on club work was originally obtained in church work. . . . The meaning of unity of effort for the common good, the development of social sympathies grew into women's consciousness through the privileges of church work" (Williams, "The Club Movement among Colored Women of America," 383). Also, as Emily H. Williams noted in her report to the ninth biennial convention of the NACW in 1914:

Many clubs are actively engaged in church work and so noticeable was the number of ministers' and bishops' wives present, that a conference of these women was held after one of the sessions. The president called attention to the importance of this phase of the work of the Association: "When you get the Negro minister's wife, you get the Negro minister; when you get the Negro minister you get the Negro people." ("Williams, The National Association of Colored Women," 481)

The religious ethical consciousness ("unity of effort for the common good") of club women that Williams described and the ability to have church groups engaged in nonsectarian social reform work are significant indicators of the socioreligious character of the movement.

In sum, when African American women formed a national club movement at the end of the nineteenth century, they created an organization through which they could address the racial, gender, and economic injustices of U.S. society. A variety of groups (e.g., literary societies, social clubs, professional clubs, prayer circles) composed the club movement. The movement was neither the department of any denomination nor an auxiliary of an organization dominated by male leadership. However, because the leadership and much of the membership were churchwomen who understood their reform work as an expression of their faith, the movement is appropriately interpreted as a socioreligious movement. Sociologist of religion Cheryl Townsend Gilkes provides an important summary:

> In addition to their organizational roles within church history, churchwomen have established an important political history. It was churchwomen who became the prominent organizers of the club movement that culminated in the formation of the National Association of Colored Women. Possibly because they could not lead from the pulpit, these women moved into the community, forming clubs and organizations that addressed the diverse social and cultural needs of the Black community of the late nineteenth and early twentieth centuries. Eschewing separatism, these women invited men to join them in a movement led by women for the benefit of women and men. In their move to uplift women, the basic Christian orientation of these women was evident in their biblical language and the dual roles they played as both community and church leaders. Their organizing was so successful that in 1935 Mary McLeod Bethune was able to form the National Council of Negro Women from the many national Black women's organizations that had been formed. (Gilkes, 969)

Finally, the basic Christian orientation of the leaders of the movement emerged as a distinctive African American women's religious ethical tradition. The club movement institutionalized this distinctive African American women's religious ethical tradition, thus making this tradition central to what made the National Association of Colored Women and later the National Council of Negro Women impressive models of churchwomen's activism in society.

A Distinct African American Women's Religious Ethical Tradition

Jualynne Dodson and Cheryl Townsend Gilkes assert: "If anything characterizes the role of black women in religion in America, it is the successful extension of their individual sense of regeneration, release, redemption, and spiritual liberation to a collective ethos of struggle for and with the entire black community" (81). This "collective ethos of struggle" is a distinctive African American women's religious ethical tradition that is operative in the public response of African American women who participated in the club movement. This tradition was at work in the lives of women during slavery as well

as in the Reconstruction and post-Reconstruction periods and into the twentieth century. African American women standing within this tradition acknowledged the call of God to challenge evils found within society, drew connections between their religious convictions and work for social justice, and offered hard-hitting analyses of racial, gender, and economic oppression. This tradition is evident in the thought and work of women from various walks of life—wealthy, educated free women; poor, minimally or uneducated bondwomen or freewomen; women reformers; preachers and/or evangelists within or outside of the organized church.

Sojourner Truth (c. 1797–1883), a former slave who became a famous antislavery lecturer and woman's rights advocate, is an exemplar of this tradition:

> The Lord has made me a sign unto this nation, an' I go round a'testifyin', an' showin' their sins agin my people. My name was Isabella; but when I left the house of bondage, I left everything behind. I wa'n't goin' to keep nothin' of Egypt on me, an' so I went to the Lord an' asked him to give me a new name. And the Lord gave me Sojourner, because I was to travel up an' down the land, showin' the people their sins, an' bein' a sign unto them. Afterward I told the Lord I wanted another name, 'cause everybody else had two names; and the Lord gave me Truth, because I was to declare the Truth to the people.
> . . . I journeys round to campmeetin's, an' wherever folks is, an' I sets up my banner, an' then I sings, an' then folks always comes up round me, an' then I preaches to 'em. I tells 'em about Jesus, an' I tells 'em about the sins of this people. (Quoted in Sterling, 151)

Sojourner Truth's words point to the interrelationship between religious belief ("The Lord has made me a sign unto this nation") and vocation or social activism ("an' I go round a'testifyin', an' showin' their sins agin my people") that is a first feature of the religious ethical tradition of African American women.

Maria W. Stewart (1803–1879), a free northeastern woman who is considered to be the first American-born woman to lecture to an audience composed of both women and men, wrote this critique in a tract titled *Religion and the Pure Principle of Morality, the Sure Foundation on Which We Must Build*:

> Oh, America, America, foul and indelible is thy stain! Dark and dismal is the cloud that hangs over thee, for thy cruel wrongs and injuries to the fallen sons of Africa. The blood of her murdered ones cries to heaven for vengeance against thee. Thou art almost become drunken with the blood of her

slain; thou has enriched thyself through her toils and labors; and now thou refuseth to make even a small return. And thou hast caused the daughters of Africa to commit whoredoms and fornications; but upon thee be their curse. (Richardson, 39)

One finds in Stewart's words a critique that recognizes the economic roots of racist injustice ("thou hast enriched thyself through her toils and labors; and now thou refuseth to make even a small return") as well as the gender oppression perpetrated against African American women ("thou hast caused the daughters of Africa to commit whoredoms and fornications"). There is in Stewart an understanding of the abuse of power in the subversion of morality and justice. Indeed, Stewart will go on to assert that America will be subject to God's wrath for the injustices that have been committed:

You may kill, tyrannize, and oppress as much as you choose, until our cry shall come up before the throne of God; for I am firmly persuaded, that he will not suffer you to quell the proud, fearless and undaunted spirits of the Africans forever; for in his own time, he is able to plead our cause against you, and to pour out upon you the ten plagues of Egypt. We will not come out against you with swords and staves, as against a thief [Matthew 26: 55]; but we will tell you that our souls are fired with the same love of liberty and independence with which your souls are fired. . . . AND WE CLAIM OUR RIGHTS. (39–40)

Within Stewart's remarks, this second feature of the African American women's religious ethical tradition comes to the fore: a belief in the justice of God. Or stated imperatively, justice for African Americans is a command of God.

Along these same lines, Anna Julia Cooper (1858–1964), born a slave in North Carolina, later attaining a Ph.D. from the Sorbonne in Paris, an educator and principal in the Washington, D.C., public schools, and club woman, poignantly described the United States' betrayal of its own religious, political, and ethical ideals to a session of the Friends General Conference in 1902. Cooper insisted that the "nation's honor and integrity are at stake" and framed the challenge to the nation in this way:

Does any one question that Jesus' vision would have pierced to the heart and marrow of our national problem, and what would be His teaching in America today as to *who is my neighbor?*

For after all the Negro question in America today is the white man's problem—nay, it is humanity's problem. The past, in which the Negro was mostly passive, the white man active, has ordained that they shall be neighbors, permanently and unavoidably. . . .

. . . God reigns and the good will prevail. It must prevail. While these are times that try men's souls, while a weak and despised people are called upon to vindicate their right to exist in the face of a race of hard, jealous, intolerant, all-subduing instincts, while the iron of their wrath and bitter prejudice cuts into the very bones and marrow of my people, I have faith to believe that God has not made us for naught and he has not ordained to wipe us out from the face of the earth. I believe, moreover, that America is the land of destiny for the descendants of the enslaved race, that here in the house of their bondage are the seeds of promise for their ultimate enfranchisement and development. (Cooper, 134–135, 141, 143)

Cooper claims that reformation of the nation on behalf of African Americans means that the nation must learn to practice love of neighbor. She also seems certain of the providential (God's providence) nature of the African Americans' destiny as equal partners in the nation. Thus, a third feature of the African American women's ethical tradition is a claim that Jesus' mandate to love our neighbor is a sociopolitical mandate for reform in the context of God's providence.

Importantly, African American women's critique was not limited to the larger society. Women speaking within this tradition criticized conditions internal to the African American community that were perceived as inhibiting progress. Julia Foote (1823–1900), a daughter of former slaves who was eventually ordained an elder in the African Methodist Episcopal (AME) Zion church, wrote in response to the patriarchialism of black clergy that "there was no justice meted out to women in those days. Even ministers of Christ did not feel that women had any rights which they were bound to respect" (*A Brand Plucked from the Fire,* in Andrews, 207). Likewise, Maria Stewart, in an address delivered in 1832 to the Afric-American Female Intelligence Society, chastised African Americans for being "so unkind and so unfeeling" toward one another that they were in one sense their "greatest oppressors." She insisted that African Americans could become a "highly distinguished and intelligent people" by marshalling their efforts, promoting and patronizing each other, and cultivating traits of character worthy of a liberated people. In fact, she admonished African Americans to walk in the ways of the Lord:

Do you ask, what can we do? Unite and build a store of your own, if you cannot procure a license. Fill one side with dry goods, and the other with groceries. Do you ask where is the money? We have spent more than enough for nonsense, to do what building we should want. We have never had an opportunity of displaying our talents; therefore the world thinks we know nothing. And we have been possessed by far too mean and cowardly a disposition, though I highly disapprove of an insolent or impertinent one. Do you ask the disposition I would have you possess? Possess the spirit of independence. ("Religion and the Pure Principles of Morality," in Richardson, 38)

But God has said, that Ethiopia shall stretch forth her hands unto him. True, but God uses means to bring about his purposes; and unless the rising generation manifest a different temper and disposition towards each other from what we have manifested, the generation following will never be an enlightened people. ("An Address Delivered before the African-American Female Intelligence Society," in Richardson, 53)

Both Foote and Stewart put the African American community on notice regarding the practices of injustice perpetrated within the community, that is, sexism and classism. Without challenging these internal practices, the community would not be an authentically liberated community. The call for communal authenticity and integrity as a manifestation of theocentric standards for African American life is the final feature of the African American women's ethical tradition.

In brief, the distinct religious ethical tradition of African American women is characterized by (1) an understanding of an interrelationship between religious belief and vocation or social activism; (2) the belief in the justice of God or justice for African Americans as a command of God; (3) a claim that Jesus' mandate to love our neighbor is a sociopolitical mandate to reform society in the context of God's providence; and (4) a call for communal authenticity and integrity in the quest for liberation.

The NACW and the NCNW: Representative Thought and Work

As stated earlier, in 1896 the National Federation of Afro-American Women and the League of Colored Women consolidated to form the National Association of Colored Women, and the NACW's first convention was held in September 1897 at Howard Chapel Congregational Church in Nashville, Tennessee. The group's constitution was adopted at that meeting; Article II declared: "The object of this Association shall be by the help of God to secure harmony of action and cooperation among all women in raising to the highest plane,

home, moral, and civil life" (*Minutes of the National Association of Colored Women*, 12).

The NACW was organized to fulfill its objective through a support network: "The structure of the organization facilitated communication: local clubs at the base, then state federations, regional federations, and at the top the national body. Information and influence flowed freely from bottom to top as well as in the reverse direction" (Neverdon-Morton, 193). The club movement's leaders were some of the most educated and economically mobile women of the late nineteenth century, and their experience had taught them that providing opportunity and the proper environment for all African American women was critical. The club women recognized the impact of systemic economic oppression upon all African Americans, and "almost every black women's club, regardless of who founded it or the ostensible reason for its establishment, focused to some extent on alleviating one or more of the many social problems afflicting an increasingly urban, impoverished, politically powerless, and segregated black population" (Hine, 238).

The motto of the NACW was "Lifting as We Climb." This motto reflected the club women's sense of the interconnectedness and interrelatedness of African Americans as a sociohistorial, sociopolitical, socioeconomic group. Historian Linda Perkins has identified this sense as one of racial obligation and duty intertwined with a notion of racial uplift and elevation.

Indeed, the club women understood: "The club movement among colored women reaches into the sub-social condition of the entire race" (Williams, "The Club Movement among Colored Women of America," 382–383). At the 1899 convention, the Reaper and Gleaner Circle of King's Daughters of the Twin Cities invoked the Holy Spirit to guide their work to open up all the trades to African American women and men. Other clubs reporting during that convention described their work in a similar vein. The Woman's Club of Atlanta, Georgia, spoke of being "women [who] were filled with the spirit of Christ . . . to save the race from immorality and vice; to put forth every effort to prevent the young from going astray" (*Mary Church Terrell Papers*, n.p.). They carried out their work through departments of prison and jail work, mother's meetings, sewing circles, history, and literature. Prison and jail work was focused upon repeal of the convict lease system. Mother's meetings were early forms of parenting classes. Sewing circles were designed to teach women a trade that would enable them to join the ranks of mill and factory workers. Departments of history and literature were aimed at empowering African Americans through knowledge of their past achievements and eradicating illiteracy. The NACW also raised funds for and established kindergartens, vocational schools, orphanages, hospitals, homes for delinquent black males convicted of misdemeanor crimes, and retirement homes, as well as opposed segregated transportation systems and supported the antilynching movement.

The initial work of the NACW expanded as the organization responded to the evolving concerns of women and the needs of all African Americans. The NACW was an early advocate of suffrage for women, participating in the suffrage movement two years before their white counterpart, the General Federation of Women's Clubs. In 1912 the organization established a national scholarship fund for college-bound African American women. During 1914, club women raised $5 million in war bonds, and many NACW women participated on the National War Council. The membership of the NACW had now reached 100,000, and it was recognized as an important agency for outreach to the African American community by the federal government. By 1916, when the association held its tenth biennial convention, it had thirty-five departments that included Legislation, Social Science, Young Women's Work, Business, Industrial and Social Conditions, Suffrage, Civics, Juvenile Court, Rural Conditions, Railroad Conditions, and Health and Hygiene.

In subsequent decades, the work of the NACW was decidedly political. In the 1930s it endorsed the Costigan-Wagner Anti-Lynching Bill and supported the defense of the Scottsboro Boys. Likewise, in the 1940s club women protested employment discrimination in the defense industries, and in the 1950s the NACW was at the forefront of discussion about the United Nations Universal Declaration of Human Rights as they applied to women. During the civil rights movement, the group was active in electoral politics, endorsed the Civil Rights Bill of 1963, and worked cooperatively with the National Association for the Advancement of Colored People, the Southern Christian Leadership Conference, and the Congress of Racial Equality.

The work of the NACW during the decades of the 1970s through the 1990s involved public health issues (operating a Health and Guidance Center out of its headquarters in Washington, D.C.), lobbying for employment equity between women and men, and programs addressing the rape and battering of women, impact of pesticides on agricultural workers, AIDS (acquired immunodeficiency syndrome), drug abuse, teenage pregnancy, and national health insurance. This work has been carried out by 300,000-plus members nationwide.

The first president of the NACW, Mary Eliza Church Terrell (1863–1954), was a freeborn southern woman, the daughter of one of the first black millionaires in the South; she was an educator, public lecturer, and social activist into her nineties when she participated in the boycotts of the 1960 civil rights movement. Terrell believed in the justice of God and justice for African Americans as a command of God as the basis for the movement's work.

Carefully and conscientiously we shall study the questions which affect the race most deeply and directly. Against the convict lease system, the Jim Crow car laws, lynchings, and all other barbarities which degrade us, we shall protest with such force of logic and intensity of soul that those who oppress us will either cease to disavow the inalienability and equality of human rights, or be ashamed to openly violate the very principles upon which this government was founded. By discharging our obligation to our children, by coming into the closest possible touch with the masses of our people, by studying the labor question as it affects the race, by establishing schools of domestic science, by setting a high moral standard and living up to it, by purifying the home, colored women will render their race a service whose value it is not in my power to estimate or express.

With courage born of success achieved in the past, with a keen sense of the responsibility which we must continue to assume we look forward to the future, large with promise and hope. Seeking no favors because of our color or patronage because of our needs, we knock at the bar of Justice and ask for an equal chance. (Terrell, 176–177)

Addie W. Hunton (1866–1943), a national organizer for the movement, placed the work of the NACW in full Christian religious ethical perspective when she wrote: "True, 'the Kingdom of God cometh not with observation,' yet its unfolding as evidenced in the awakening of our women to their needs and opportunities under the inspiration of the club spirit, must impress the most casual observer" (Hunton, 417).

With such a self-awareness of the seriousness of their work, it is thus not surprising that Mary McLeod Bethune (1875–1955), the eighth president of the NACW, went on to found the National Council of Negro Women (NCNW). The NCNW was founded on December 5, 1935. Before going on to the NCNW, Bethune during her term as NACW president encouraged the club women thus: "As we, Negro women face today our enlarged responsibilities, we should seek a fuller development of our minds and hearts, taking each day a step toward the higher ground of Christian culture, of consecrated service. With our faces toward the 'rising sun,' let us not fail to go forward, in this new day, to climb with unfaltering courage towards the 'higher ground' of wisdom, faith, of loving service, and by the Master's help, 'Lifting as we climb' " (*Mary Church Terrell Papers*, n.p.).

Bethune founded the NCNW in 1935 as the means to get African American women fully represented in national and international public affairs. It was to be an umbrella organization promoting cooperation between African American women's groups. Fourteen organizations sent delegates to the founding meeting. Today the NCNW has 4.5 million members in thirty-eight national affiliated organizations and 250 community-based sections as well as carries out its work in Egypt, Senegal, and Zimbabwe. The national headquarters was established in Washington, D.C., in 1942.

The work of the NCNW was an extraordinary enactment of the power of love as the power to transform social realities. Bethune believed that to love one's neighbor was a mandate "to create a world of fellowship and justice where no man's [sic] color or religion is held against him.... Loving your neighbor means being interracial, interreligious, and international" (Bethune, 14). This interpretation of loving one's neighbor was translated into an organizational philosophy of public education, community service, and advocacy, thus promoting, as the organization's logo reads, "commitment, unity, self reliance."

The program emphases of the NCNW from 1935 through today are employment of African Americans in federal jobs, citizenship rights and participation in electoral politics, religion and public life, and consumer education. The NCNW has established national centers for African American women: The Bethune Program Development Center (provides technical assistance and training in the areas of health, education, and community life); the Economic and Entrepreneurial Development Center (provides women technical assistance to establish and maintain businesses); the International Development Center (develops social, cultural, academic, and economic partnerships with women's organizations in Africa); the Research, Public Policy and Information Center (gathers, initiates, and disseminates information to empower African American women); and the Dorothy I. Height Leadership Institute (acts as a leadership development center for emerging and established African American women leaders in national and community organizations, on college campuses, and in other public and private sector institutions). In 1986, the NCNW's second president, Dorothy I. Height (a presidency that began in 1957 and ended in 1998), initiated the Black Family Reunion Celebration. This celebration is an outdoor, cultural event that brings families, communities, corporations, and government agencies together to focus on the historic strengths and traditional values of the black family. The event is recognized as a significant family movement that attracts more than a million attendees annually all over the country. The NCNW's health programs focus on critical health issues affecting African American women and their families, for example, the HIV/STD Prevention Initiative; the National Cancer Prevention Awareness Initiative; the National Drug Prevention Program; and the Health Protection and Reproductive Health Initiative.

In line with Bethune's concern that loving our neighbor be interracial, interreligious, and international, the NCNW was an early supporter of the United Nations and has consultative status at the United Nations today. Likewise, the group engaged in collaborative efforts with groups such as the Young Women's Christian Association, the National Association for the Advancement of Colored People, the Young Men's Christian Association, the National Council of Church Women, the National Council of Jewish Women, and the National Council of Catholic Women.

According to one interpreter of Bethune's life, as control of the school that Bethune founded, the Bethune-Cookman Institute, shifted to the Methodist Episcopal Church, the founding of the NCNW reflected Bethune's need to establish a power base outside of a male-dominated and church-controlled institution. Whether or not that was in fact her motivation, it is evident that her faith in God grounded the leadership that she provided: "My life has been a spiritual thing, a religious reality, creative and alive. Whatever 'works' I have done have 'justified' my faith.... For I have daily felt the presence of God in the tasks he has set before me in visions, and I have known his divine guidance and presence through all the years" (Bethune, 14). The National Council of Negro Women is indeed one of the works that justified Bethune's faith.

SOURCES: See the following sources: Florette Henri, *Black Migration: Movement North, 1900–1920* (1975); *A History of the Club Movement among the Colored Women of the United States* (1902, 1978); Elizabeth Davis, *Lifting as They Climb: The National Association of Colored Women* (1933); Fannie Barrier Williams, "The Club Movement among Colored Women of America" (1900), in Booker T. Washington, *A New Negro for a New Century* (1900); Addie W. Hunton, "The National Association of Colored Women: Its Real Significance," *Colored American* 14 (1908): n.p.; Emily H. Williams, "The National Association of Colored Women," *Southern Workman* 43 (December 1914): 564–566; Cheryl Townsend Gilkes, "Religion," in *Black Women in America: An Historical Encyclopedia*, ed. Darlene Clark Hine, Elsa Barkley Brown, and Rosalyn Terborg-Penn, vol. 2 (1993); Cheryl Townsend Gilkes and Jualynne E. Dodson, "Something Within: Social Change and Collective Endurance in the Sacred World of Black Christian Women," in *Women and Religion in America*, ed. Rosemary Radford Ruether and Rosemary Skinner Keller, vol. 3 (1987); Dorothy Sterling, ed., *We Are Your Sisters: Black Women in the Nineteenth Century* (1984); Marilyn Richardson, ed., *Maria W. Stewart, America's First Black Woman Political Writer* (1987); Anna J. Cooper, "The Ethics of the Negro Question," in *Can I Get a Witness? Prophetic Religious Voices of African American Women: An Anthology*, ed. Marcia Y. Riggs (1997); William L.

Andrews, ed., *Sisters of the Spirit* (1986); *Minutes of the National Association of Colored Women, Held in Howard Chapel Congregational Church, at Nashville, Tenn., September 15th, 16th, 17th, and 18th, 1897* (1901); Cynthia Neverdon-Morton, *Afro-American Women of the South and the Advancement of the Race* (1989); Darlene Clark Hine, "Lifting the Veil, Shattering the Silence: Black Women's History in Slavery and Freedom," in *The State of Afro-American History*, ed. Thomas C. Holt (1986); *Mary Church Terrell Papers* (Library of Congress); Mary Church Terrell, "What Role Is the Educated Negro Woman to Play in the Uplifting of Her Race?" in *Twentieth Century Negro Literature*, ed. D. W. Culp (1902, 1969); Mary McLeod Bethune, "What My Faith Means to Me" (1954), in *Women in New Worlds*, ed. Hilah F. Thomas and Rosemary Skinner Keller (1981); and Bettye Collier-Thomas, "National Council of Negro Women," in *Black Women in America: An Historical Encyclopedia*, vol. 2, ed. Darlene Clark Hine, Elsa Barkley Brown, and Rosalyn Terborg-Penn (1993).

RELIGIOUS EDUCATION

WOMEN AND CATECHETICS IN THE ROMAN CATHOLIC TRADITION

Mary L. Putrow

THE DEVELOPMENT OF religious education in the Roman Catholic tradition is permeated by three interrelated realities. From New Testament times to present-day practice, whether it be in the home or in a more formal situation, women are at the heart of Christian education. Also, unless women were members of religious congregations, few accounts of their work have been preserved. Finally, in most historical accounts women seldom receive due recognition for their work. Mary Charles Bryce, a historian of religious education, suggests in "Pioneer Women in Catechetics" that many times priests and bishops have been given credit for work that women have done.

Today women make up the majority of persons engaged in all aspects of religious education. While this phenomenon provides women places of influence, there is also growing concern about the feminization of religion, that is, seeing religion as the domain of women and children only.

For 2,000 years the practice of handing on the faith in the Catholic Christian tradition has had various names: catechesis, religious instruction, religious education, religious formation, faith formation, Christian formation, and occasionally, Sunday School. Today there is a movement to reclaim early Church vocabulary, using the word *catechesis* and its derivatives. *Catechesis* is described as the development of a living, active faith through instruction. Most professionals, regardless of the vocabulary used, would insist that religious education today, besides transmitting the teachings of the Church, must include formation in Catholic Christian life.

In the period of time between the early Church and the arrival of Catholics in the New World, the mode of instruction in the faith moved from purely oral teaching to the use of the written word in the form of a catechism, a summary of Jesus' teaching as interpreted and practiced by the Church. Most catechisms employed a question-and-answer form of instruction.

Initially, adults were the primary focus of religious education; with time the focus shifted to children and remained so until the present. Although today many would still equate catechesis with children, the contemporary official Church documents, particularly in the latter part of the twentieth century, strongly insist that adult catechesis should be at the center, not the periphery, of the teaching endeavors of the Church.

The Age of the Catechism

When the early European immigrants arrived on the shores of the United States, among their limited possessions one frequently found a catechism written in their native tongue. Instruction in the faith became synonymous with catechism, and the proliferation of catechisms in the nineteenth and twentieth centuries signaled a strong faith among the immigrants to the United States, even though for Christianity's first 1,400 years a common written catechism as such was basically unknown. "Throughout the Colonial Period of more than a century and a half, Catholics had only their long standing traditions of family prayer, the catechism learned and recited in the home, and, where available, the liturgy to preserve the faith of their children" (Collins, 49).

When work moved out of the home and into the shop and factory, the home became the domain of the woman. The image of children learning their prayers at their mother's knees could be said to be the symbol of catechesis during the seventeenth to the nineteenth centuries. "The prevailing concept of woman as the moral guardian was most likely as true among the middle-class Catholics as it was in the rest of middle-class America. No evidence exists to contradict this presumption" (Dolan, 244).

Religious education, and the continuation of the faith, was naturally a primary concern among Church leaders in the United States. In the statutes of Bishop John Carroll of Baltimore, Maryland, in 1784 one finds an insistence that persons "know the faith" if they are to be married in the Catholic Church. Carroll's pastoral letter assigns the primary role of catechists to parents; however, in reality "parents" meant mother.

Besides faith and moral development in the home, a traditional form of religious education was the Sunday School, more simply called "catechism." Carroll had mandated that catechism instruction for adults was to be given following Sunday evening prayer and that children should be given instruction following the Sunday Mass. This formal teaching was the prerogative of the ordained priest. In areas where there were no clergy and no churches, a sporadic "catechism" was held whenever missionaries came through. This Catholic Sunday School never did have the same enduring quality as its Protestant complement. The primary site of catechesis remained the home; the primary instructor, the mother.

When the First Council of Baltimore (1852) assembled, Church leaders were concerned to have a greater unity in the religious education provided children. Before this council numerous versions of a catechism were circulated in the United States. A single catechism to be used throughout the United States was the object of many hours of discussion and planning. During the third session of the council in 1884, a uniform instructional text was mandated for children and adults. This text came to be known as the Baltimore Catechism.

While the official Church pursued the question of one or many catechisms, Mary Anne Madden Sadlier (1820–1903) was becoming well known as one of the best Roman Catholic voices in American letters. She had emigrated from Ireland to Montreal, Canada, where she met and married James Sadlier of the Sadlier Publishing Company. Mary Anne was a great storyteller, a talent she employed in developing readers and religious materials for schoolchildren. Adults were attracted to her other writings that always conveyed a lesson in Catholicism. Sadlier published *Catechism and Examples* (1858, 1870; also known as *Catholic Anecdotes*), *A New Catechism of Sacred History* (1866), *The Great Day (on First Communion)* (1889), and *Purgatory: Doctrinal, Historical and Poetical* (1886). In 1895 Notre Dame University recognized her literary contributions by awarding her the Laetare Medal, an award given in recognition of her valuable contributions as a laywoman to the Church. As a member of a publishing family, Sadlier did not seem to confront the obstacles many other women met when they attempted to publish on theological themes under their own names. In 1930 Josephine Brownson (1880–1942), founder of the Catholic Instruction League in Detroit, encountered difficulties in publishing her religious instruction material; publishers advised her that a priest's name must appear with hers if her work was to be published (Romig, 69). Brownson herself is said to have repeated Father Aloysius Heeg's suggestion that she publish under the name of J. Van Dyke Brownson. Brownson added that if someone handed her a Doctor of Divinity degree, she would be all set. In the end, she published some of her work herself, personally assuming all costs.

The end of the nineteenth and beginning of the twentieth century saw an increased concern for the religious instruction of children, especially the children of poorer immigrants to the United States. Although the establishment of Catholic schools was a matter of great urgency to many bishops at the Second Plenary Council of Baltimore (1866), they also strongly encouraged the adoption of the Confraternity of Christian Doctrine (CCD) for those children who did not attend a Catholic school. The Confraternity is an official Catholic organization of persons devoted to religious instruction. Originated in sixteenth-century Italy, it provided a structured parish plan, outlining various roles and procedures for the religious instruction of children unable to attend a parochial school. While the Confraternity's membership was open to both men and women, in the United States women primarily constituted its membership. Catholic parish schools rose up quickly, but not until 1935 was a National Office for the Confraternity of Christian Doc-

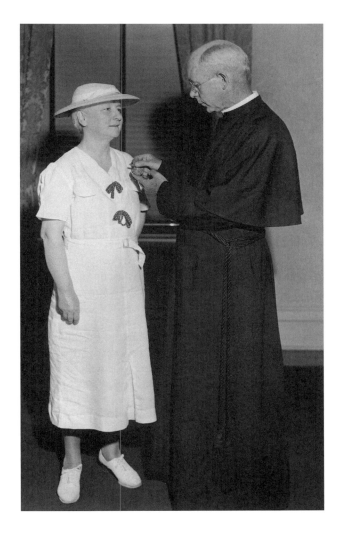

In 1930, Josephine Brownson founded the Catholic Instruction League in Detroit, Michigan, after encountering difficulties in publishing her religious instruction material. Publishers advised her that a priest's name must appear with hers if her work was to be published. *Used by permission of the Notre Dame University Archives.*

for the development and preservation of children's faith. These women religious who taught religion and other subjects during school hours often assumed responsibility for the after-school religion classes for those children not attending parochial schools.

A second group was also composed of women religious who established schools and academies independently of parishes for the education of women during a period when education was primarily the preserve of men. Like their parish counterparts, many religious came from Europe and often found numerous obstacles to their work in the United States. In some instances they lacked the support of the local bishop. Securing finances for building was always a challenge. Inadequate food and housing often marked the beginning foundations. Despite these obstacles, the women persevered; their fortitude and commitment constituted a heroic gift to the education of young women. The academies for girls had as their stated purpose the moral and religious training of their pupils as future American mothers. Religion classes were the domain of women religious with occasional appearances of a priest.

The third group was composed of new religious communities of women formed solely for the purpose of the catechesis of children who did not attend the Catholic school or academy. In many cases it was the poor and/ or recent immigrants who were not able to avail themselves of a Catholic school education. Many of these newly founded communities also provided education and formation of laity who would eventually take over this work. Countless women religious, commonly known as "the sisters," exhibited great valor and commitment amid most trying circumstances; the contributions of individual sisters to the Catholic faith, with few exceptions, are chronicled only in congregational histories.

A fourth group consisted of numerous committed and educated laywomen spurred on, no doubt, by the training and enthusiasm for the faith enkindled in them by their religious teachers. Young women with leadership skills quickly moved into positions in women's Catholic organizations. Thus as women's role within the home as the guardians of faith and morals continued, other women outside the home reinforced the faith by their teaching and example.

Laywomen whose influence was most pervasive and expansive were those who either established the Confra-

trine established by the bishops with headquarters in Washington, D.C.

Pope Pius X's (1835–1914) *Acerbo nimis* (1903) gave further impetus to religious education, as did his insistence that the Confraternity of Christian Doctrine be inaugurated all over the world; the laity were encouraged to take up the task of religious instruction. This repeated concern for religious formation and instruction sounded a trumpet call. By 1903 a small number of parishes in New York City had already established the Confraternity. The diocese of Sante Fe, New Mexico, had established the Confraternity by 1917, and Brooklyn, New York, had done the same by 1921.

The establishment of Catholic parish schools brought to the fore several groups of women committed to the task of religious instruction. One was the women religious who responded to the need for Catholic schools and staffed them. For many, the Catholic school was the vehicle for enhancing and deepening the faith developed in the home. For others the school was the only vehicle ternity of Christian Doctrine in a diocese or founded or participated in similar structures such as the Catholic Instruction League, the Settlement House, and the League of Catholic Women. By 1915 the number of Settlement Houses serving the immigrant urban population throughout the United States had grown to twenty-seven. In addition to providing social services, laywomen taught catechism to hundreds of children.

Early Pioneers

In 1872 in the city of San Francisco, Elizabeth Armer (1850–1905) became the first woman to organize a lay group for the religious instruction of children. Born in Sydney, Australia, she came to San Francisco with her parents and two brothers as a young child. Shortly thereafter, Mrs. Armer died, and Robert Armer entrusted the care of his only daughter to Richard and Mary Tobin, who raised her with their own children. Elizabeth was surrounded by the staunch religious practices of a devout Catholic family. Although baptized in the Anglican Church, Elizabeth determined at a young age that she wanted to participate in the same practices as her adoptive brothers and sisters. With the approval of her father, she was received in the Catholic Church. Lizzie, as she was commonly called, enjoyed the many advantages of music, theater, and education that the Tobins were able to offer her. As she grew into womanhood, she sensed a calling from God. With yet unclear direction, she began to gather young children around her and speak to them of God. When she presented herself to the bishop with a request to enter a cloistered community of sisters, Bishop Joseph Alemany responded that he had in mind another work for her. Thus she began an uncharted course, confident only in the Spirit of God who directed her. A young priest from Ireland, Father John Prendergast, joined with Lizzie and provided assistance and encouragement. They shared a concern for the children of Italian immigrants of North Beach. Here Lizzie began her work by forming a group of catechists who quickly caught her fire and zeal for spreading the Christian message. She converted her own home into an after-hours religion school for children. With a small group of companions she lived and worked here for eight years. On November 16, 1872, the religious community of the Sisters of the Holy Family was formed, and Lizzie was recognized as its foundress. The primary mission of this community of sisters was to become acquainted with the children of the poor, visit their homes, attract them to classes, instruct them in Christian doctrine, and prepare them for the sacraments of Holy Communion and Confirmation. In contrast to the Sunday School, these efforts became known as the Weekday Religion School. Her early interest in the cloistered life was transformed into a zeal for the poor and needy. In her direction of the sisters of her community she advised, "Hospitals shall be your monasteries; the streets of the city and the houses of the needy shall be your cloister" (Sisters of the Holy Family, 7). Sister Dolores, as Lizzie was known in religious life, died on August 2, 1905.

At the time these catechetical efforts were begun in San Francisco, Alice Vignos (1872–1940) was born in Canton, Ohio. As a young woman she volunteered to assist in the catechetical program in her local parish in Canton. Here Vignos practiced and promoted her belief that the most vital subject (religion) in a child's education need not be taught in the dullest way. Her enthusiasm for teaching the Word of God became the hallmark of her commitment to religious education. At the turn of the century, Alice arrived in southern California with her sister Blanche. The sisters committed themselves to a lifetime of catechesis among the Mexican children in the Los Angeles Diocese. With the aid of artists and educators, Alice published project books, representing the best of educational psychology, for the religious summer vacation school. At several Confraternity of Christian Doctrine National Congresses she gave presentations on the meaning and value of the project books. The books are intended to provide writing, coloring, and drawing activities related to the content of the lesson. Alice emphasized the value of such activities in creating a greater interest in the subject matter, in helping children to retain the material taught, and in stimulating the interest of parents. She was truly a pioneer and outstanding in her work with the Confraternity of Christian Doctrine. "Thousands of young men and women who are practical Catholics today owe it to her influence" (Spellmire, 501).

Verona Spellmire (1889–1975) joined in similar efforts. Born in Missouri, she grew up in Arizona and eventually moved to California with her family. Formally educated as a teacher, she worked in the schools in the poorer section of Los Angeles. She was also engaged in "Sunday School" at the Brownson Settlement House. In the summer of 1920 she and a group of teachers started weekly Confraternity of Christian Doctrine classes in a Mexican American neighborhood near Montebello. As other needs arose, she expanded her efforts throughout the diocese. In the fall of 1941 at the invitation of a longtime supporter, the now Archbishop Robert E. Lucey, Spellmire went to San Antonio and for eight years worked at establishing the CCD in that diocese. Upon her return to California, she extended her efforts in the Pasadena area. Spellmire was a cross between social worker, teacher, and evangelist. She expended incredible energy in gathering children together for religious instruction, in prodding parents to assume responsibility for strengthening the faith of the family, and in recruiting catechists to teach. No obstacle seemed insurmountable to her. It is no surprise that she was called the "Confraternity's Number One Bushwhacker" (Weber, 203). Despite all her evangelical fire, Spellmire demonstrated a sensitivity to, and a deep respect for, the culture and language of the Mexican population whom she served.

At this same time in the East other women were responding to the identical call to serve. The Mission Helpers of the Sacred Heart was formed in Baltimore in 1890 for the religious instruction of African American children; the Helpers of Holy Souls initiated weekday religious instruction in the more populous and poorer parishes of New York City in 1892. In 1914 the Religious of the Cenacle opened the doors of their New York Convent to instruct Catholic children from the public schools. The Parish Visitors of Mary Immaculate trained social workers, contacted families, and brought children to parish centers for religious education. The Missionary Servants of the Most Holy Trinity was established for settlement work and provided religious education for children not only in the North but also in Florida and Alabama.

In 1908 a devout Catholic member of St. John the Baptist Church in Pittsburgh, James Doyle, moved with his family to the small mining town of Cecil, Pennsylvania. He was alarmed by the state of Catholicity there: Many Catholics were not practicing their religion; children were not instructed in the faith; and others, baptized Catholic, were attending the services of other denominations. Doyle returned to his former parish and sought counsel from Anna Sweeney, president of the parish Confraternity of Christian Doctrine, who then sounded a call for help to attend to the Catholics in Cecil. Two young and enthusiastic volunteers, Mary Dunn and Anna Collins, took up the challenge. On their first visit to Cecil they were greeted by some forty-three children who eagerly welcomed their religion instructors. The two women traveled to Cecil regularly and conducted religious education classes under the most primitive of circumstances: in basements, boxcars, backyards, whatever was available to them. Thus began the Missionary Confraternity of Christian Doctrine. Eight years later, through the efforts of Dunn, Collins, and other catechists, sixteen sites for religious education had been established in remote areas of the diocese. Little more is known of the two pioneers other than they lived well into their nineties strongly committed to, and enthusiastic for, their Catholic faith.

In the Midwest the Missionary Catechists of Our Lady of Victory was founded in Huntington, Indiana, in 1922 to provide religious instruction for poor children in the Southwest. Because of the scattered nature of this population, Missionary Catechists would assemble a group of ten to twelve Native women, provide the instruction, and prepare them to become teachers for a given area.

Leadership for instruction in the faith was not the prerogative of women religious alone. Hundreds of committed laywomen joined in efforts to preserve and to foster the Catholic faith. Not surprisingly, a person like Josephine Van Dyke Brownson, graduate of the Academy of the Sacred Heart, distinguished herself by establishing the Catholic Instruction League in Detroit, Michigan. The majority of teachers listed in the minutes of Brownson's meetings were graduates of the same academy. This active apostolate undertaken by Detroit women focused on the recent immigrants and the poor in the city. The first formal instruction under Brownson's direction took place at the newly established Weinman Settlement House Project in 1902. Eventually as the work and number of volunteers increased, Brownson formed the Catholic Instruction League. Her own writing attends to her purpose: "Stopping the Leak." This phrase refers to concern about the loss of Catholic immigrants to other denominations. She wrote a small pamphlet of that title to rally all Catholics to remedy the situation. Brownson also identified the solution: more religious instruction of children and adults. In addition, having very strong opinions about what she as a teacher envisioned catechetical instruction to be, Brownson wrote textbooks, adapting the best of the then-known educational methodology to the enterprise. Brownson traveled extensively throughout the United States, lecturing on the Catholic Instruction League and catechetical methodology. She prepared the Missionary Catechists in the early years of their foundation for work among the poor. Her handwritten lesson plans preserved by that congregation give evidence of her own convictions and commitment in the mission of the Church to the role of religious instruction. Brownson was the recipient of the papal medal Pro Ecclesia et Pontifice in 1933 in recognition of her exceptional contributions to the faith life of the Church. That same year the University of Detroit awarded her an honorary doctoral degree. Six years later, the University of Notre Dame conferred the Laetare Medal, given to a layperson for outstanding service to the Church and society.

Contemporary with Brownson, at the encouragement of Father John M. Lyons, Elizabeth Byrne and Lillian Kubic began the work of the Catholic Instruction League in Chicago in 1912. Although Lyons was commonly associated with the league and he had personally sought approval of the league from Archbishop Quigley, it was not he but scores of women, many nameless, who brought children the Word of God and became the Church presence to their families.

The majority of the women engaged in the Catholic Instruction League and in other weekday religion schools were recruited from among the Catholic teachers in the public school system. John Archdeacon, in his 1927 study of Weekday Religious Schools, notes that in the schools he researched, sisters made up 19 percent of the catechists; female public school teachers, 67 percent; and other women, 3 percent. Priests, seminarians, and laymen made up the other 10 percent. The Catholic Instruction League expanded its work in Tampa, Tulsa, Oklahoma City, Milwaukee, Omaha, St. Louis, Albuquerque, Springfield, Illinois, and Pine Bluff, Arkansas, until it was subsumed into the Confraternity of Christian Doctrine in 1935.

These professional public school teachers began to question the adequacy of the question-and-answer catechism methodology and ushered in a new era. A parallel movement, seeking greater incorporation of the liturgy into catechetical instruction, had begun. In the United States the work of liturgist Virgil Michel was most influential. However, the Dominican Sisters of Grand Rapids, particularly Sister Jane Marie Murray (1896–1987), translated Michel's insights into practical classroom usage. Under her leadership they edited the textbook series *The Christ Life* (1934–1935), which included liturgy as an essential element of religious instruction. Joseph Collins, chronicling the phases of catechetical renewal, fails to mention the role these women played in bringing out *The Christ Life* series but credits their publication to Virgil Michel, who himself had written to the sisters, "I don't think I must be continuously in session with the sisters. You know my forte is to make others do the work" (Marx, 153). Michel had promised to guide the study of the liturgy and the intellectual preparation for the work. The writing, application, and publication were left to these Dominican women. After his death Murray continued to write and complete the high school texts, the *Christian Religion Series*, published by Bruce Publishing Company in 1952.

No list of women pioneers in religious education would be complete without the name of Miriam Marks (1896–1961), who was on the editorial staff at St. Anthony Guild, a Catholic publishing company, when the newly consecrated Bishop Edwin O'Hara visited the Guild. Because of Marks's experience in many organizations and her ability to set up and organize institutions, he invited her to assist him in establishing the Confraternity of Christian Doctrine in his diocese of Great Falls, Montana. Within a short time she was also invited by Bishop George J. Finnegan of the Helena Diocese and Bishop Charles White of the Diocese of Spokane to provide the same assistance. During her lifetime she worked with sixty dioceses in the United States and four in Canada as they began to comply with the Vatican

Directive that the Confraternity be established in every diocese.

In 1935 when the National Center of the Confraternity of Christian Doctrine was established in the United States through the efforts of Bishop O'Hara, Miriam Marks moved to Washington, D.C., where she served as secretary and field agent of the center. In this role Marks arranged many regional and national congresses of the Confraternity, where she often spoke while also managing the National Office and editing catechetical manuscripts for publication. Innumerable books have a note of gratitude to Miriam Marks in their introductions for making the work possible.

The "New Catechetics"

As the catechism came to the United States from Europe by means of families and priests intent on carrying on the traditional Catholic faith, so did the seeds of catechetical renewal find their genesis in Europe. The earlier dissatisfaction with the catechism's question-and-answer methodology found a sympathetic ear in Josef Jungmann (1889–1975), a professor of catechetics and liturgy at the University of Innsbruck, Austria. Jungmann promoted not only a different approach, called the "kerygmatic method" for religious instruction, but also a change in content from dry theological statements to the "good news of Jesus Christ." Kerygmatic methodology stressed that content be delivered in such a way that hearts would be moved and lives changed. His book *The Good News Yesterday and Today* (1962) was a watershed in catechetical studies. His influence was felt in North America principally through the work of Johannes Hofinger, a student of Jungmann who taught at various Jesuit colleges in North America.

With the publication of the Roman document *Provido sane* in 1935, the establishment of the Confraternity of Christine Doctrine in every parish was mandated once more. This instruction also called for catechists to be trained and diocesan and national offices to be erected in support of the Confraternity.

One of the women who responded fully to this mandate was Sister Rosalia Walsh (1896–1982), a Mission Helper of the Sacred Heart. Sister Rosalia, baptized Josephine Mary, was one of nine children in the prominent Walsh family of Cumberland, Maryland. At a young age, Josephine together with her father began teaching the catechism to immigrant children. Under the strong influence of this scholarly man, Josephine learned a love of her faith and the value of reading and study. She was wont to say, "I learned my religion at home and my catechism at school." As a member of a religious congregation dedicated to the religious education of the poor, Walsh easily engaged in the preparation of catechists. She was strongly convinced that instruction and formation in the Christian life needed a methodology that applied to daily life and motivated persons to act virtuously. She devised a creative methodology called the *adaptive way* that consisted of five steps: orientation to the subject matter, formal presentation by the teacher, an exercise to help children assimilate the message into their daily life, the organization of the subject matter into statements, and finally, the recitation of the content in the format of the catechism, that is, questions and answers. In 1944 she published *Teaching Confraternity Classes: The Adaptive Way,* a book that became very popular among religious educators. Her work appeared in national publications such as *The Journal of Religious Instruction, The Catholic Educator,* and *Our Parish Confraternity.* Walsh was one of three American writers who published in the first volume of *Lumen Vitae* (1947), a journal published by the International Institute of Pastoral Catechetics in Brussels. In the same year Walsh was invited by the National Confraternity of Christian Doctrine Office to incorporate the adaptive way into the Confraternity of Christian Doctrine manuals. Walsh arranged the Confraternity material according to the adaptive way. She included biblical and liturgical content and concluded each lesson with material from the catechism. Thus, while retaining the traditional form of the catechism, Walsh used it as a summary instead of the introductory piece it had been customarily. While preserving the traditional role of the catechism, Walsh clearly demonstrated a more effective use. These manuals, called *A Confraternity School Year Religion Course, the Adaptive Way,* published between 1949 and 1953, were used throughout the United States and "paved the way for later innovations" (Spellacy, "In Memoriam"). When the National Center established the Confraternity leadership courses at Catholic University, Walsh was invited to teach a methods course. Before long she was lecturing throughout the United States and Canada in institutes, at colleges and universities, as well as at National Congresses of the Confraternity of Christian Doctrine. In her retirement the passion that drove Walsh's zeal for effective religious education was transformed into a zeal for justice issues. She enthusiastically engaged in letter writing and lobbying to remind legislators of their responsibility to care for the poor and the underprivileged.

During the last decade of her life, Walsh saw another member of her congregation assume national leadership in catechetics. Sister Mariella Frye (1921–) was chosen as associate project director for the preparation of the national catechetical directory, *Sharing the Light of Faith.* Frye's vast experience in every phase of religious education from young childhood to adolescence, from catechist training to parent education, prepared her well

for this task. Her experience with the directory led her to another first, her appointment as adviser to the U.S. delegation for the international synod of bishops on catechesis in 1977. *Catholic New York* (April 7, 1988, 5) called Frye, "The Nation's Catechist" in an article reporting her reception of the prestigious C. Albert Koob Merit Award by the National Catholic Education Association. This award was granted to Frye for her professional competence and generous dedication to religious education in the United States. In 1995 Frye was awarded the Baltimore Archdiocesan Medal of Honor for her outstanding service in the Church.

A contemporary of both Walsh and Frye had begun similar work on the West Coast. María de la Cruz Aymes was born in Mexico in 1919; because the Calles government forbade the public teaching of the faith, María received her religious education at her mother's knee. In an imitative sort of way, María soon began bringing neighborhood children into the family home and instructing them in the faith. As a young woman she traveled to New York and there joined the sisters, Helpers of Holy Souls (HHS). Early in her religious life, Aymes experienced the need for better catechetical tools. When she met her first class for religious instruction in San Francisco, she realized that age, experience, and ability were overlooked in the materials and the organization of the class. This, together with what appeared to be a lackluster Office of the Confraternity of Christian Doctrine, propelled Aymes forward and tapped her creativity. She began writing lessons geared to specific abilities and specific ages. This material was soon in great demand, especially in the Bay Area of California. "There was singing, drawing, activity, prayer, games—all solidly rooted in the Catholic life of faith, prayer and action" (Reedy, 295). Although her work was highly esteemed by catechists, as many as eight publishing companies refused to publish it. Reedy suggests that it was too risky to "tackle the established way of teaching religion and a catechism once regarded as the bishops' gift to children (295). To the credit of the Sadlier Publishing Company, William Sadlier saw the value of her work, and the *On Our Way Series* was published and distributed. In 1956 the full component of grades one through eight was completed. "These catecheses are to our knowledge the first attempt (and, it may be said parenthetically, highly successful ones) to employ the kerygmatic principles of modern catechetics as early as the first years of instruction" (Hofinger, 227). Aymes became an international figure; her books were translated into at least six languages. The University of San Francisco awarded her an honorary degree. The citation read, in part, that "she has written a series of catechisms which revolutionized religious education in this country and abroad" (Reedy, 297). The question-and-answer format of the catechism, its less-than-enticing format, and dry presentation of theological principles were all giving way to a colorful, life-centered context. The material was presented in a way that motivated children to engage in the practices of Christian life. Her publications marked the beginning of a new era in religious education in the United States. In addition to writing texts, Aymes has lectured at catechetical congresses and was appointed to the International Commission on Catechetics in Rome in 1975.

Catechetics and Higher Education

Madeleva Wolff (1887–1964), a remarkable woman in many ways, was born Evaline Mary in Cumberland, Wisconsin, and raised in a family atmosphere that valued the arts and cultivated intellectual abilities. After entering the Sisters of the Holy Cross, she distinguished herself as a poet and writer. In 1919 she became one of four nuns who received a graduate degree from the University of Notre Dame and, in 1935, the first to qualify for a Ph.D. at the University of California. When it became apparent that women teaching religion had scant preparation and little access to the theological departments of the major universities that might better prepare them, Madeleva moved into action. She found that where college-university-level courses were available to women, they were the "dullest and most poorly taught in the curriculum" (Wolff, 114). As longtime president of St. Mary's College for Women in South Bend, Indiana, she took the initiative to resolve this problem. In 1942 she headed the committee of the National Catholic Education Association formed to investigate possible solutions. No midwestern graduate school was prepared to address the problem, and "Catholic University answered no to our applications to its School of Divinity" (115). In 1943, despite the many difficulties, Wolff was able to provide a graduate program in theology and scripture at St. Mary's. She thus challenged the statement of Frank Sheed, author and publisher, that there is no place in this country where anyone but a priest or seminarian can study theology.

Another contribution of higher education to the teaching of religion came in the person of Ellamay Horan (1898–1987), born into a staunch Catholic family on Chicago's South Side. With her three sisters Horan was educated in parochial schools of the city. Believing that God had called her to work in the Church, at three different times, she entered and left religious communities. It was in the academic world that Horan found her calling and made valuable contributions to the field of religious education. As a professor at DePaul University from 1929 to 1945, she was responsible for editing a catechetical journal sponsored by the university, *The Journal of Religious Instruction*. Contributors to this journal were drawn from the coterie of religion teachers

and hence provided very practical pieces to aid in instructing young children and adolescents. In 1940, about one-third of the contributors to the *Journal* were women; by 1946 almost half the articles were written by women. Besides managing the publication of the *Journal*, Horan penned many of the articles herself. She joined with others who wished to apply good educational principles to the teaching of the catechism. To this end she wrote study aids and a variety of test exercises for pupil activity and class participation to accompany the catechism, as well as numerous other materials to aid the teaching of religion. Horan's work was formally recognized by the Church in granting her the award the Ecclesia et Pontifice in 1953.

Contemporary Influences

Vatican Council II brought its own agenda of reform to the catechetical field. The informing theology suggested that the content of religious education be looked at in a contemporary way. The Council encouraged the use of the social sciences in determining better approaches to the study of religion. Experts began conversations about effective methodology and called into question the whole purpose of religious education. As important as these were, it was the reestablishment of the catechumenate, the process used by the early Church to initiate new members, that had the greatest influence on the field. In attempts to understand the process used by the early Church better, researchers began looking at the practice of the second-century Church and the original meaning and purpose of catechesis. Although the Church had never denied the need for adult religious education, the religious instruction of children has been central. *The Rite of Christian Initiation of Adults* (approved by the Vatican in provisional form in 1972 and in final form in 1988), the liturgical expression of the restoration of the catechumenate, activated greater interest and concern for the adult in the Church. Literature on adult catechesis began to appear with greater frequency.

In addition to *The Rite of Christian Initiation of Adults*, the decade of the 1970s saw the publication of the first *General Catechetical Directory*, the Roman Synod on catechesis, the very influential document *Catechesi Tradendae*, and the national catechetical directory, *Sharing the Light of Faith*. The publication of the *Catechism of the Catholic Church* in 1993 and the *General Directory for Catechesis* in 1997 prompted new work and has brought the story of catechesis full circle when it insists that *The Rite of Christian Initiation* is the norm for all catechesis. In short, religious education was to be characterized by both initiatory and instructional aspects; the community as a body was to assume a more expansive and responsible role; evangelization was to be part of the dynamic of sharing the faith, and an awareness of the many cultures served was to be fostered.

Today one can count among many contemporary leaders in religious education such women as Maria Harris, teacher, writer, lecturer, artist, and poet; Mary Charles Bryce (1916–2002), former Catholic University professor who influenced and mentored many who passed through the portals of that institution; the deceased Mary Perkins Ryan (1912–1993), author, lecturer, editor, promoter of adult catechesis and continuing education in the faith; and Janaan Maternach, author, lecturer, and one of five teachers chosen by the National Office of the Confraternity of Christian Doctrine in 1962 to do research on graded catechetical manuals of study. It was through her efforts that *Life, Love and Joy* replaced the former CCD manuals. Eva Marie Lumas, consultant and instructor in catechetics, is well known for her work with the African American community. Her sensitivity to culture and ritual in the black community has given deeper meaning to the catechetical mandate to incarnate the Word of God in every culture.

History will have no difficulty describing the catechetical achievements of such persons as Kate Dooley and Ann Marie Mongoven, both authors and professors of catechetics; Maureen Shaughnessy, of the U.S. Catholic Conference of Bishops' Education Department; and many others nationally known for their work in catechesis. However, in many ways "anonymous was a woman" still describes well the thousands of unnamed, perhaps unknown women who have tilled the soil of faith in the United States as directors of religious education, catechists, teachers, and writers.

SOURCES: Most source material of the nineteenth and first half of the twentieth centuries tends to overlook the contributions of women. While diocesan and parish archives do offer some information, the more valuable are the archives of women's religious congregations. Mary Charles Bryce offers limited information about women's contributions to religious education and encourages readers to pursue further research in "Pioneer Women in Catechetics," *Living Light* 22.4 (Summer 1986): 313–324. For general historical information about the Catholic Church in America, Jay Dolan's *The American Catholic Experience* (1985) is helpful. More precise is James Kenneally's *History of American Catholic Women* (1995). The history of religious education can be found in Joseph Collins's "Religious Education and CCD in the Early Years 1902–1935," *American Ecclesiastical Review* 169 (1975): 48–67. Johannes Hofinger's *Shaping the Christian Message* (1958) explicates the "kerygmatic approach." For information on the use of catechisms, consult Bernard Marthaler's *The Catechism Yesterday and Today* (1995). See also the brochure by Sisters of the Holy Family (Mission San Jose, California), *The Foundation Story* (n.d.); Frances J. Weber, *The Pilgrim Church in California* (1973); and Paul Marx, *Virgil Michel and the Liturgical Movement* (1957). William Reedy writes from personal experience in "Maria de la Cruz Aymes," *Living Light* 12.2 (Summer

1975): 293–297. *Living Light* is the official catechetical journal of the U.S. Catholic Conference of Bishops and is helpful for understanding the various issues of religious education. The *Proceedings of the Annual Congresses of Christian Doctrine* provide insight into the various aspects of religious education in a given year. One example is Verona Spellmire, "Helping to Safeguard Their Heritage—the Laity's Part," in *Proceedings of the 1940 Congress of the Confraternity of Christian Doctrine* (1941). Madeleva Wolff, *My First Seventy Years* (1959), describes the struggle to provide theological studies for women. An early biography is Walter Romig, *Josephine Dyke Brownson* (1955). Individuals' dissertations and theses offer valuable information and further references. Examples are Charles Carmody, "Roman Catholic Catechesis in the United States 1784–1930" (Loyola University of Chicago, 1975); and Marie Spellacy, "The Evolution of Catechetical Ministry among the Mission Helpers of the Sacred Heart" (Loyola University of Chicago, 1986). Spellacy also writes of a particular Mission Helper in "In Memoriam: Rosalia Walsh, MHSH," *Living Light* 19.2 (January 1981): 151–157.

CATHOLIC WOMEN'S COLLEGES IN THE UNITED STATES
Tracy Schier

THE DEVELOPMENT OF Catholic women's colleges at the end of the nineteenth and beginning of the twentieth centuries must be understood in light of the development and growth of the movement within America to provide educational opportunities for girls and women. To be both female and Catholic in the mid-nineteenth century in America was to be doubly handicapped as far as education was concerned. A widespread view of society's attitude toward the education of females in the Western world was enunciated by Jean-Jacques Rousseau, who wrote in *Émile* (1762) that the whole education of women ought to be relative to the needs of men.

That this attitude prevailed is evident in the pattern of development of education for girls in the United States. In the colonial period only girls from wealthy families received any education at all, and this was in such subjects as harpsichord playing, painting, and French. As girls were gradually permitted to attend elementary schools, their studies were restricted to the rudiments of reading, writing, religion, and sometimes a little arithmetic. Free education for boys, on the other hand, was a popular idea in the nineteenth century because it was understood that voters should be responsible and informed; since voting was restricted to males, there was no such argument to favor the education of girls. Many girls profited secondhand from their brothers' schooling, but the attitude that girls' and women's lives should revolve around the home prevailed. There was also fear that outside influences, especially education, might lift women above their station; even worse, there was widespread belief that the discipline required for the development of intellectual powers was physically and emotionally draining and thus detrimental to female health. Some critics of education for females went so far as to claim that because educated women were known not to marry, widespread education for women could lead to race suicide. Educational historian Thomas Woody summarized the attitude of the times: "A man would not love a learned wife. Better far to teach young ladies to be correct in their manners, respectable in their families, and agreeable in society" (157).

The growing spirit of democracy that characterized nineteenth-century America began to outweigh the fears and misunderstandings just outlined. Public elementary schools gradually admitted girls, and by the mid-nineteenth century there were female academies across the country. A notable one was Troy Female Seminary, founded in Troy, New York, in 1831 by Emma Willard. This school and others of the time made little or no attempt to achieve collegiate status or to meet the standards of schools for boys and men. These early academies had, in fact, a program of study designed to prepare young women for what society still deemed to be their proper sphere. Class content included religious and moral as well as literary, domestic, and ornamental elements such as embroidery.

The beginnings of the effort to offer women higher education can be seen in the opening of such institutions as Mount Holyoke Seminary in Massachusetts in 1837 and the chartering of Elmira Female College by the New York State legislature in 1855. These heralded the way for other institutions to begin to offer courses of collegiate status and to confer baccalaureate degrees. By the 1870s female seminaries and academies began to offer young women a better, more rounded education than heretofore had been available. As this type of education became entrenched, critics emerged who would try to improve the system. There were two prevailing attitudes at the time. The first did not favor a college education for women but demanded that seminaries emphasize substantial subjects instead of such "accomplishments" as embroidery and French conversation that could be paraded in the drawing room. The other group advocated opening institutions for women that would imitate colleges for men.

Although women were supposed to remain within the confines of their homes, there was also the widespread discovery that women were naturally suited to be teachers of youth. Accelerating this realization was the fact that women would work for one-third the pay given to men. As elementary and secondary schools proliferated throughout the United States, the result of a general movement toward compulsory education, there was great demand for teachers, and thus the need for teacher training for women became widely recognized. The Industrial Revolution, which brought large numbers of women into the labor force as full-fledged wage earners, and the suffrage movement, which mobilized women to leave their homes and make their voices heard in the public arena, also helped to crumble the taboo of women's participation in the larger social sphere. Indeed, the right to vote went hand in hand with the right to an education. Women who gained prominence in the field of teaching recognized they should have a voice in school affairs. The granting of school suffrage (voting on matters pertaining to education) in states such as Massachusetts, Kentucky, and Kansas was a precursor of complete suffrage.

Women first received baccalaureate degrees at a coeducational institution. Oberlin College, established in 1833 in Ohio, granted three young women the bachelor of arts degree in 1841 after they pursued a course of study identical to the one male candidates followed for the same degree. Antioch College, also in Ohio, opened its doors to men and women in 1853. From these initial private institutions the concept of coeducation quickly spread to those institutions established under the Land Grant College Act of 1862. Also known as the Morrill Act, this legislation stimulated the growth of technological institutions and recognized the importance of technical and scientific disciplines as important to higher education. By the 1860s the Universities of Iowa and Wisconsin were admitting women, followed closely by the Universities of Michigan and Maine, and Cornell. The motive for improving scholastic opportunity for women was not purely altruistic, however, especially in the midwestern states where leaders of the state institutions realized it made good financial sense to serve as many students as possible.

In the eastern states, during the latter half of the nineteenth century, separate women's colleges were emerging. Smith, Vassar, Wellesley, Wells, and Goucher, among others, began by offering courses of study equivalent to those offered by the men's colleges that had steadfastly resisted any attempts to become coeducational. Some institutions, as exemplified by Columbia and Harvard, made concessions for women by creating Barnard and Radcliffe as affiliated women's colleges.

Development of Catholic Education

The development of Catholic education in the United States paralleled the growth of the public school system, although, like education for women, it lagged chronologically. During the colonial days, Catholics experienced legal and social discrimination in most states. Their integration into the new nation was advanced by their demonstrated loyalty during the Revolutionary War, but their full integration, legal and attitudinal, would not take place until the twentieth century. Integration into the American mainstream was important to Catholics, but the preservation and enhancement of their faith were even more important to Church leaders. Thus, at the First Provincial Council of Baltimore (1829) the American bishops decreed the establishment of schools in which children would learn faith and morality as well as the basic secular subjects. By the Third Plenary Council of Baltimore (1884), Catholic education had advanced to the point where the bishops decreed that every parish was to have a parochial school within two years and that scholastic standards would equal those of the public schools.

As dioceses were established across the country, bishops recruited priests and congregations of religious brothers and sisters, mostly from Europe, to set up parish schools. The pattern of enlisting religious communities for the job of teaching had both religious and financial motivations: They were the obvious people to teach religion and values, and they required little financial remuneration at a time when Catholics were among the poorest Americans. It is important to recognize that studying and teaching constituted an integral part of women's monastic experience throughout the Middle Ages and the Renaissance; convents are the first Western institution that regularly provided females with formal instruction. Indeed, convents were centers for women's intellectual life, and the legacy of such women as Hildegard of Bingen (d. 1179), Herrad of Hohenburg (d. 1195), Angela Merici (d. 1540), and Teresa of Avila (d. 1582) provided a source of inspiration as well as a precedent for advanced education for women.

The first Catholic academy for girls was established in New Orleans in 1727 by ten Ursuline sisters from France. Almost a century passed before the second such school was founded in Georgetown (now Washington, D.C.) by the Poor Clares in 1801. In 1808 Elizabeth Seton, founder of the Sisters of Charity, established the third Catholic American boarding school for girls in Baltimore. By 1840 five Sisters of Providence traveled from France to Indiana to establish an academy at Saint Mary-of-the-Woods, thus evidencing the move westward of such institutions. In 1900 the Catholic Directory listed 662 academies for girls, an indication that Catholics, who were growing in numbers due to successive waves of immigration from Ireland, Germany, Italy, and the Slavic nations, were demanding that their daughters receive at least what would be known in our time as a secondary-level education. Interestingly, the Catholic academies for girls attracted a significant number of Protestant students, sometimes because these schools were the only educational option for girls in a geographical area and, in other instances, because the sisters were known to provide a genteel education that appealed to the middle and upper classes.

The development of private and Catholic higher education in the late-nineteenth-century United States presents a blurred picture: Academies offered collegiate courses, and schools calling themselves colleges offered academy-level courses. The first Catholic college, Georgetown, came into existence in 1786, 150 years after the founding of Harvard. Just as the early colleges of the colonial period were established under the influence of evangelical Protestantism, and followed closely a classical curriculum, so too did the Catholic colleges develop with religious motives and offer a similar course of study. The Third Plenary Council of 1884 defined the specific purpose of Catholic colleges: to disseminate religious truth and to train a body of cultivated young men, especially priests, who would be community leaders.

By 1900 there were 152 Catholic colleges for men, 98 of which were started by religious communities and the rest by bishops or diocesan priests. That Catholic educators gradually attempted to solve the ambiguity of what constituted a higher education can be seen in the development of Catholic University in 1887, in the evolution of graduate departments in other Catholic institutions such as the Notre Dame Law School in 1869, and by adherence to standards set by accrediting agencies and national associations.

The blurring of the distinction between academy-level and collegiate education was true in the female academies at the turn of the century as they struggled to provide advanced courses for their students. Nevertheless, the emergence of standardized exams and accrediting associations was a step toward achieving uniform quality. The fusion of the Educational Conference of Seminary Faculties (1897), the Association of Catholic Colleges (1898), and the Parish School Conference (1902) into the Catholic Educational Association (CEA) in 1904 did for Catholic education what the formation of the National Education Association in 1870 did for public schools. Through publications and conferences, the CEA (later the National Catholic Education Association) accomplished its goals of professionalization and cooperation and interpreted the need for, and the role of, Catholic education to the public at large.

The Women's Colleges Appear

At the end of the nineteenth century the American Catholic Church was struggling to emerge from its immigrant status. Both liberal and conservative Catholics worried about the inability of the American Catholic Church to offer higher education for females. Liberal Catholics were concerned that the lack of higher education for women would make the Church look as if it were against progress and the expanding vision of women's role in society; conservatives worried that Catholic women would jeopardize their faith by flocking to non-Catholic institutions.

As college attendance became more conventional across America, the religious communities that sponsored Catholic girls' academies saw the need for specifically Catholic higher education for women. A number of these academies expanded their offerings, increased and upgraded their faculties and facilities, sought state charters, and became colleges. The state of Maryland was the first to witness this evolution with the chartering of the College of Notre Dame, sponsored by the School Sisters of Notre Dame, in 1896. Other religious congregations began to add collegiate-level courses to the academy curriculum, so that by the turn of the century we see the founding of St. Mary's College (South Bend, Indiana) by the Sisters of the Holy Cross, Saint Mary-of-the-Woods College (near Terre Haute, Indiana) by the Sisters of Providence, the College of St. Elizabeth (Convent Station, New Jersey) by the Sisters of Charity, and the College of New Rochelle (New Rochelle, New York) by the Ursuline Sisters. In 1900 Trinity College, founded by the Sisters of Notre Dame de Namur in Washington, D.C., was the first to begin as a college and not evolve from an academy. The number of Catholic women's colleges increased from five in 1904 to fourteen in 1910. By 1921 there were thirty-eight, and by 1930, seventy-four. The Catholic women's colleges reached their peak in 1968 when there were over 170 four-year women's colleges as well as two-year colleges, Sister Formation colleges (founded specifically to educate nuns for the parochial schools), as well as professional schools and graduate-level programs. By the mid-twentieth century the Catholic women's colleges were educating more women than non-Catholic women's colleges.

Many of the Catholic women's colleges founded after 1920 had their origins in the needs of the religious communities themselves as they struggled to enable their members to meet state teaching certification requirements. While the earliest colleges evolved from academies, institutions such as Nazareth College in Kentucky began as a response to the need for sisters to be certified to teach at the elementary and secondary levels. Because the incomes of the religious congregations were derived from stipends earned by the sisters in parochial schools, incomes that were extremely low, there was little money for sending the sisters to the established colleges even though many of them had teacher-training programs. The competitive spirit that existed among women's religious communities had a part to play in these decisions as well. Religious congregations balked at allowing their sisters to attend a college sponsored by another sisterhood, thus prompting the founding of more than one

college in an urban area. Cleveland and Philadelphia are examples of cities where this took place.

Another reason for the development of Catholic women's colleges in the 1920s came from the bishops who were requesting that such institutions be developed for women from working- and middle-class families who could not afford the tuition nor the travel expenses demanded by the established colleges. Thus Boston's Emmanuel College and Chicago's Mundelein College opened to meet the needs of commuter students. Rivier College opened in Hudson, New Hampshire, in 1933 to educate the daughters of French-Canadian immigrants who had migrated south to work in the textile mills. Because they were small and flexible from the start, such colleges were among the first private institutions in the United States to allow students to earn baccalaureate degrees on a part-time basis. These institutions also developed curricula that differed somewhat from that of the private liberal arts colleges. Students from blue-collar families were in need of employment after graduation, and thus the schools provided, in addition to a core of liberal arts offerings, a variety of professional programs such as home economics, education, nursing, and library science. Beginning in the 1950s a number of these institutions established master's degree programs, most notably in education, that served both women and men. These programs initiated the gradual segue of male students onto the campuses, setting the stage for a high percentage of Catholic women's colleges to become coeducational after 1970. By the year 2000, only 14 of the over 110 existing colleges founded by nuns remained single sex in their full-time undergraduate programs.

As Catholic women's colleges developed, they, like men's colleges, found that the early 1900s was a time of coping with societal changes as well as a time of adopting and maintaining standards set forth by the public sector. In June 1904 the *Bulletin of the Catholic Educational Association* reported that low attendance in Catholic colleges and universities was caused by a too rigid curriculum, lack of practical courses and courses in modern languages, not enough social life, and professors out of touch with the world and thus with the needs of students. To redress this situation the CEA issued standards with which Catholic colleges had to comply in order to be recognized by the Association. In addition, the colleges sought standard accreditations. That this was done in earnest can be seen by the fact that in the early 1930s forty-five Catholic women's colleges were accredited by the National Catholic Education Association, forty-four by regional agencies, and eleven by the Association of American Universities.

It was important for the women's colleges, in their early days, to follow the curricular systems of the men's colleges in order to prove that women could endure the

Founded by the Congregation of Sisters of St. Joseph of Boston, St. Regis College was one of the small women's colleges founded in the 1920s. The development of Catholic women's colleges at this time came from the bishops, who asked that such institutions be developed for women from working- and middle-class families who could not afford the tuition or the travel expenses demanded by established colleges. *Courtesy of St. Regis College Archives.*

intellectual and physical rigors of academic life. The curriculum in the Catholic women's institutions was similar to that in other women's colleges as well, and in addition such course topics as Christian doctrine, morals, liturgy, apologetics, sacred scripture, and Church history were offered. The multiplication of courses within disciplines was obvious, exemplified by what formerly had been English becoming subdivided into the classical age, the Victorian age, romanticism, English novelists, epic poetry, and so on. Colleges also included the sciences as well as such rising new disciplines as psychology, political science, and sociology.

The daily lives of students during the early period were highly circumscribed. A composite of a day in the life of a Catholic women's college student in the early years gives an idea:

The day opens usually at six or six-thirty in the morning with the Holy Sacrifice of the Mass at which attendance, though voluntary, is generally urged. Classes begin at about eight o'clock and continue until noon. The afternoon session is usually three or four hours in length. Opportunities for recreation are provided for in the daily schedule. Quiet is required especially in the corridors of the residence halls during the day as well as at night. The bell for retiring is commonly rung at ten o'clock. (Bowler, 87)

Most Catholic colleges, men's and women's, prescribed appropriate dress. For young Catholic women, especially, modesty and simplicity were the rule of thumb, with the Virgin Mary set forth as the ideal of Catholic womanhood. These institutions also eschewed the establishment of organizations with an exclusively social aim. Sororities were seen as contrary to the spirit of a Catholic institution, but other organizations, especially those with a religious bent such as Sodalities that promoted devotion to the Blessed Virgin Mary, and Catholic Action Societies that engaged students in service activities, were encouraged. Organizations that lent support to academics—literary associations, language clubs, magazines and newspapers, and dramatic and music societies—all played an important part in the lives of the students.

The members of the religious communities that sponsored the Catholic women's colleges had multiple responsibilities—not only did they preside over the curricular and extracurricular activities of the institution, but they also were heavily involved in monitoring student dress and behavior. The doctrine of "in loco parentis" was commonplace in all American higher education in the nineteenth and early twentieth centuries, and indeed in most Catholic women's colleges, members of the religious communities resided in the dormitories and served as hall monitors and house mothers. In these colleges' early years the lives of the sisters who were the faculty and administrators were as circumscribed as the lives of the students. Religious congregations demanded of their members an unworldliness that often kept them isolated from the wider educational community. The superior general of the sponsoring religious community often held the title of college president.

Catholic higher education for women was both a religious as well as an educational experience. Religious congregations' heritage included a belief that faith was important in the development of the intellect. Thus religion permeated the curriculum as well as the daily life of the students, a fact that set these institutions apart from other women's colleges. Like the other women's colleges, however, they provided their students with role models. The sisters founded, administered, and staffed these colleges, providing young women with unprecedented opportunity to see women in powerful and influential positions.

As noted, some non-Catholic counterparts such as Radcliffe and Barnard were coordinate colleges of Harvard and Columbia. Catholic bishops did not condone the development of such coordinate institutions, yet a number of women's colleges were in close proximity to men's colleges. St. Mary's College is situated across a highway from the University of Notre Dame. Mundelein College's proximity to De Paul and Trinity College's proximity to Catholic University were not accidental.

That sisters who staffed the colleges would need an advanced education was recognized early on. Those sisters who taught in academies through the 1890s had long experience as teachers, but few had graduate or even bachelor's degrees. Independent study was a temporary solution, as was the hiring of professors from local male colleges to offer courses. A number of obstacles arose when the religious communities of women proposed to enroll their members in graduate programs in secular universities. One barrier was cost: The congregations simply could not afford to send more than a few sisters at a time for higher education. A second barrier was the vehement objection of bishops, who had authority over the congregations under canon law. Many bishops feared that educating sisters in secular universities would diminish their religious spirit and encourage an independence that would reject male direction. They also feared that sisters studying in secular universities would put an unwanted stamp of approval on these institutions by the Church. Despite these problems, however, religious congregations found ways to enroll their members in graduate programs. As the 1920s turned into the 1930s and 1940s, faculty rosters across the country more and more included sisters with doctorates from Yale, Harvard, University of Chicago, University of Minnesota, and other graduate institutions.

Governance of the early Catholic women's colleges followed closely the hierarchical governmental structure of the founding religious communities. In a typical congregation, the professed members would elect the mother superior and her councilors for specified terms. This governing group of six or seven members was responsible for the resources and activity of the community, appointing the superiors in all convents and assigning each sister to her employment. Also typically the superior served as the ex officio president of the college. A sister dean would serve as the administrator, overseeing financial and academic affairs. Faculty, in the early years composed mostly of sisters and gradually including more laywomen and -men, had little influence on governance.

The college board was usually composed of sisters who were the community councilors, with the superior serving as board chair. The invitation to laymen with legal and business expertise to serve on the boards gradually became commonplace; by the 1960s lay boards were becoming the rule and not the exception, with bylaws stipulating that members of the founding religious community would serve as a specified proportion of the membership.

Attracting laymen with business and financial contacts was especially important to Catholic women's colleges since these institutions were tuition driven with very few other means of support. Historically the women's colleges have received less support than male colleges because women's higher education was not a priority issue among the wide array of potential corporate, foundation, and independent donors. Contrary to widely held opinion, Catholic colleges founded by religious congregations, male or female, do not receive financial support from the Church. According to historian Mary Oates,

Almost single-handedly, therefore, sisterhoods financed the women's colleges from their internal resources. In a unique sense, community members, whatever their assigned employments, shared in the sacrifices required to carry out these costly projects and hence experienced a personal sense of ownership of the institutions. The financial resources of most sisterhoods came primarily from the earnings of members teaching in parochial schools, supplemented by tuitions or patient fees earned in academies and hospitals owned by communities. Whereas European communities could rely for income on large dowries required of new members, American sisterhoods, whose candidates came mainly from working class or middle class families, received only token dowries. Because the collective earnings of many communities barely supported their members, superiors often had to postpone plans for colleges. Sisters of St. Joseph in Minnesota intended to open a college in St. Paul in 1891, but financial problems delayed the enterprise for another fifteen years. (Oates, 187)

The reality that the colleges were owned by the religious congregations hampered their ability to gain financial support from foundations and corporate donors. As noted, they received no support or, in some cases, only token financial support from their dioceses. And bishops were known, on occasion, to disallow colleges' efforts to borrow funds. Such was the case at Marian College in Indianapolis. In 1939 Bishop Joseph Ritter thwarted the founding Franciscan Sisters in their efforts to fund a campus expansion by taking out loans. As a result, needed improvements to buildings, equipment, and curriculum were postponed and regional accreditation was not achieved for over a decade.

The fact that accreditation standards gradually began to mandate a minimum endowment proved to be a catalyst for the Catholic women's colleges to begin fundraising efforts in earnest. Saint Mary-of-the-Woods College in Indiana was one of the earliest of the colleges to enlist the help of laymen in such an effort. In 1923 the

Sisters of Providence formed a lay-dominated, fourteen-member Associate Board of Trustees of the Endowment Fund to conduct a four-year campaign to raise a million dollars as a beginning college endowment.

Because many bishops discouraged the women's colleges in their dioceses from holding public fund-raising campaigns, the achievement of accreditation was often delayed. Cleverly, the sisters at a number of colleges adopted the argument that accrediting agencies were narrowly defining the concept of endowment. They argued that endowment should include the equivalent financial value of the contributed services of the sisters in administrative and faculty positions. This argument was received favorably and in 1930 and 1932, respectively, the Association of American Universities and the North Central Association accepted this broadened definition of endowment. Other accrediting agencies began to follow this example so that the contributed services of the sisters remained an important underpinning of these colleges' finances until the upheavals of the 1960s.

The 1960s—that decade of ferment across all American society—precipitated other significant changes for the Catholic women's colleges. The Second Vatican Council (1962–1965), with its renewed emphasis on lay participation in the Church; the ensuing decline in membership in the founding congregations of sisters; the move toward lay boards of trustees and separate incorporation of the colleges; and the shifting landscape of American higher education all contributed to vast changes that would make the Catholic women's colleges look significantly different in the final decades of the twentieth century. As the membership in the religious communities declined, the colleges more and more relied on laypersons to fill faculty and administrative ranks; gradually they are filling the vice-presidential and presidential positions as well. As the colleges began to incorporate separately from the congregations they found that they were better positioned for government, corporate, and foundation support and for participation in federal programs. And as the board memberships included increasing numbers of laywomen and laymen, there has been an intentional effort to define what "sponsorship" means.

Boards of trustees, for the most part, retain a certain number of seats for sister-members, but this is also changing as the median age of sisters rises into the seventies. In most institutions the religious congregations retain certain "reserved powers" including such things as hiring the president, altering the mission, changing the by-laws of the college, buying/selling property, and other significant activities. The 1990s saw, on most of these campuses, a renewed interest in the history and charism of the founding sisters as the increasing numbers of laypersons tried to understand how they can carry the values and traditions of the founders into the new century. Many institutions developed special offices, often under a vice-president for mission and ministry, to study these issues and implement programming that fosters an ongoing appreciation of the founding community.

Late-twentieth-century feminism, the entry of women into professional fields in large numbers, the growth in numbers of women-headed households, and the growing numbers of first-generation women from varied ethnicities and races who were seeking advanced education all affected the colleges in several ways. Programs for non-traditional-age women proliferated across the country, often in the form of user-friendly formats such as evening and weekend programs. Chicago's Mundelein College was one of the first colleges in the nation to offer a weekend college; Saint Mary-of-the-Woods College became a pioneer in the area of distance learning with its fully accredited Women's External Degree program that allows adult women to complete bachelor's degrees through a combination of short on-campus stays followed by intensive use of technology for communication between instructor and student. The College of New Rochelle's School of New Resources for adult learners has expanded to several sites throughout the New York region. Alverno College in Michigan has achieved national recognition and significant foundation support for its program of student assessment. Barry University has forged programs that meet the specific needs of the Miami, Florida, Latino community.

The financial challenges for all higher education in the latter decades of the twentieth century are well documented. The colleges begun by Catholic women religious were not immune from such challenges. The stories are as varied as the colleges. Some colleges closed. Names like Mount St. Mary College in New Hampshire and Dunbarton College in Washington are now only in history books. Others, like Mundelein College in Chicago and Mercy College in Detroit, merged with neighboring Jesuit institutions. Still others studied the option of merger long and hard—Marygrove College in Detroit and Trinity College in Washington are two examples—and rejected it in favor of independence. Others, like St. Mary-of-the-Woods College and St. Mary's College, Notre Dame, remain single sex. The stories of all the colleges that consciously decided to adapt and be entrepreneurial are, in the estimation of historians Dorothy Brown and Carol Hurd Green, stories of "persistence and success" (Brown and Green, 235).

By the end of the 1970s it was clear to the presidents of many of these colleges that cooperation and collaboration would be important to their ongoing success. Under the leadership of Sister Jeanne Knoerle, president of Saint Mary-of-the-Woods College, fifteen presidents of colleges founded by women religious gathered in 1978 to found the Neylan Commission (so named because of original funding from the Neylan Trust). This group continues today as a subgroup of the Association of Catholic Colleges and Universities in efforts to share resources, cooperate in ventures that involve technology, seek grant funding, and identify their common legacies.

Looking around America at the beginning of the twenty-first century, over 110 colleges begun by women religious remain vigorous and intent on carrying out their educational mission in ways that are contemporary yet not forgetful of their origins. Mt. St. Mary's College in Los Angeles serves that city's increasingly diverse population with carefully designed programs, just as Trinity College serves the inner-city population of Washington, D.C.; Marywood College in Scranton is now Marywood University; seven in Philadelphia (Rosemont, Chestnut Hill, Holy Family, Immaculata, Gwynedd-Mercy, Neumann, and Cabrini) manage to coexist and collaborate. As they seek to honor the values and charisms of their founders, these colleges, in all parts of the United States, continue to adapt to changing demographics and shifting educational demands.

Dr. Rosalie Mirenda, a laywoman serving in her sixth year as president of Neumann College near Philadelphia, gives voice to the many laypersons now leading colleges founded by nuns:

> Institutions of higher education established by women religious continue to serve with excellence and integrity thousands of learners across all ages and economic strata who seek an education where character, judgment, and intuition are developed as well as intellectual competence. The greatest gift that women religious continue to give to their Colleges besides the gift of themselves and their service is distinctive identity. This distinctive identity for colleges like Neumann provides a link to the larger network of similar organizations, while allowing it to distinguish itself as possessing values and qualities that are unique. This uniqueness provides the necessary foundation for developing and nurturing loyalty, enhancing commitment, and motivating those associated with the institution to achieve organizational goals. As a lay woman to whom the mission of Neumann College in this 21st century has been entrusted, I am privileged and accountable to ensure the advancement of the legacy of the Sisters of St. Francis of Philadelphia through this higher education ministry called Neumann College. (Rosalie Mirenda to Tracy Schier, November 18, 2001)

SOURCES: The history of Catholic higher education has been documented in recent years in such works as Philip Gleason's *Contending with Modernity: Catholic Higher Education in the Twentieth Century* (1995) and David O'Brien's *From the Heart* of the American Church (1994). History and insight into the work of Catholic nuns over the centuries can be found in Jo Ann Kay McNamara's *Sisters in Arms: Catholic Nuns through Two Millennia* (1996). For the first comprehensive study of the colleges founded by nuns in the United States, turn to *Catholic Women's Colleges in America* (2002), ed. Tracy Schier and Cynthia Russett. In this work, thirteen scholars examine the colleges from a variety of historical, educational, and sociological perspectives, including Mary J. Oates, "Sisterhoods and Catholic Higher Education, 1890–1960"; and Dorothy M. Brown and Carol Hurd Green, "Making It: Stories of Persistence and Success." Older works also shed light on these institutions, including Thomas Woody's *A History of Women's Education in the United States* (1966) and Sister Mariella Bowler's Catholic University dissertation, "A History of Catholic Colleges for Women in the United States of America" (1933). Individual histories of a number of the institutions are also available.

CONSERVATIVE CHRISTIAN STRATEGIES IN EDUCATION

James C. Carper and Brian D. Ray

SINCE ITS GENESIS during the middle decades of the nineteenth century, public education often has been the subject of heated debate and controversy. In the years following the turbulent 1960s, many conservative Protestants have been critical of public education that they believe embodies a worldview—often labeled "secular humanism"—hostile to their Christian beliefs. "It's here, Jennie. Humanism in Hawkins County." So spoke Vick Frost, a leader in the Hawkins County, Tennessee, textbook protest in the early 1980s (Bates, 19). While some of these critics have attempted either to purge the schools of offending teachings and practices or to reintroduce theistic perspectives, other conservative Christians have forsaken their long-standing commitment to the public schools. They left the system to establish Christian day schools or to educate their children at home. Women have played key roles in these controversies and have been prominent in the burgeoning home school movement.

Prior to the creation of modern public schooling in the mid-1800s, the rich religious diversity that characterized overwhelmingly Protestant early America (Roman Catholics numbered about 25,000 at the time of the Revolution) was matched by an equally rich diversity of educational arrangements. With few exceptions (namely, when unable or unwilling to direct their children's instruction and upbringing) mothers and fathers fashioned an education for their offspring that embodied their religious beliefs. For most of the seventeenth and eighteenth centuries, the family was the primary unit of social organization and the most important ed-

ucational agency. As historian Steven Mintz and anthropologist Susan Kellogg point out:

> Three centuries ago the American family was the fundamental economic, educational, political, social and religious unit of society. The family, not the isolated individual, was the unit of which church and state were made. The household was not only the locus of production, it was also the institution primarily responsible for the education of children, the transfer of craft skills, and the care of the elderly and infirm. (xiv)

During the colonial period, then, mothers and fathers generally bore the primary responsibility for the education of their own children and frequently those who had been "fostered out" from other families. Although most white parents sent their offspring to school for short periods of time, much education in religion, morals, and literacy took place in the church and household.

When seventeenth- and eighteenth-century parents chose to send their children to school, their experience was quite different from that of parents today. Schooling was unsystematic, largely unregulated, discontinuous, uncontroversial, noncompulsory, and primarily the product of an individual, local community, or church efforts. The colonial education landscape was dotted with a wide variety of institutions, including town schools in New England; denominational institutions (e.g., Quaker, Presbyterian, and Lutheran in the middle colonies); old-field schools established by farm families on fallow tracts of land in the South; and academies, institutions operated by denominations, individuals, or communities that provided formal education beyond the elementary level and appeared throughout the provinces after 1750. With the exception of dame schools, in which New England women taught reading, writing, arithmetic, and Protestant Christian doctrines to young neighborhood boys and girls (most of whom received little additional formal education) in their home for a small fee, most colonial schools were conducted by men.

Although parents increasingly looked to schools to carry out what had once been primarily a family responsibility and sent more of their daughters to the growing number of quasi-public district schools funded by taxes and tuition, the colonial approach to education remained largely unchanged throughout the late 1700s and early 1800s. Educational pluralism went hand in hand with Protestant pluralism. Whether or not sponsored by a church, the vast majority of schools at that time embodied some variation of Protestant Christianity, as evidenced by an emphasis on teaching biblical principles, and parents decided whether their children would attend them.

The middle decades of the nineteenth century

marked a period of intense debate about education and reform that led to the creation of state school systems. Distressed by social and cultural tensions sparked by mid-nineteenth-century urbanization, industrialization, and immigration (which included a significant number of Roman Catholics) and energized by what historian Carl Kaestle (*Pillars of the Republic*) has called the values of republicanism, Protestantism, and capitalism, educational reformers preached the messianic power of tax-supported, state-controlled, universal, free schooling to transform American society. They believed that common schools, as early public schools were called, could mold an increasingly diverse population into a pious, disciplined, and unified people prepared to participate in a Protestant Christian society. While the most visible of the common school reformers, such as Horace Mann and Henry Barnard, were men, women also played key roles in shaping early public education. Catharine Beecher (1800–1878), the oldest child of prominent preacher Lyman Beecher and founder of Hartford (Connecticut) Female Seminary in 1823, and Emma Willard (1787–1870), founder of Troy (New York) Female Seminary in 1821 and tireless advocate for women's education, for example, crusaded for common schooling. The former urged the employment of females as teachers in the common schools, one of the lasting legacies of this period of reform, and the later wrote textbooks for common schools that embodied beliefs held in common by Protestants, example, the authority of the Bible.

With few exceptions, such as Lutheran and Reformed bodies that opted for schools designed to preserve confessional and/or cultural purity, most Protestants were supportive of common schooling. They approved of early public education because it embodied general Protestant beliefs, employed Protestant teachers, and was viewed as an integral part of the crusade to fashion a Christian—which, to the dismay of Roman Catholics, meant Protestant—America. Indeed, the pan-Protestant character of nineteenth-century public education was the primary reason that Roman Catholics embarked on the creation of their own school system.

By the dawn of the twentieth century, public education was firmly established in the United States. More than 90 percent percent of children aged five to seventeen were enrolled in public schools. And though public schooling was less Christian than it had been in the antebellum years, most Protestants still perceived it as their institution and necessary to the maintenance of a Christian society.

At this time, however, the trend toward secularization of public life was accelerating. Pointing to the disruptive effect on American Protestantism of Darwinism, higher criticism of the Bible, the fundamentalist-modernist controversy, growing cultural and religious diversity, and the failure of Prohibition, sociologist James Davison Hunter asserts that

> in the course of roughly thirty-five years (ca. 1895–1930), Protestantism had been moved from cultural domination to cognitive marginality and political impotence. The worldview of modernity [often termed secular humanism or civil humanism] had gained ascendancy in American culture. (37)

Echoing Hunter's assessment, A. James Reichley (*Religion in American Public Life*) maintains that since the 1950s this belief system—which posits a naturalistic view of the cosmos, touts science and secular reason as the keys to human progress, denies the relevance of the deity to human affairs, and claims that moral values derive from human experience—has been dominant within the intellectual community. This worldview, he asserts, has also exerted considerable influence on the entertainment industry, the news media, government, and certain parts of the educational enterprise, especially higher education.

Thus, the Supreme Court's controversial 1962 and 1963 decisions eliminating government-sponsored prayer and devotional Bible reading from state schools merely marked the culmination of more than a half-century-long process of "de-Protestantization" of public education. Many conservative Protestants interpreted the official removal of these symbols of the nineteenth-century Protestant cultural consensus as "kicking" God out of the public schools. Rather than making schools neutral on matters related to religion, they concluded that these decisions contributed to an establishment of secular humanism as the official worldview of American public education. This assessment has, in turn, led them to scrutinize public education to a greater extent than ever before. Once crusaders for the establishment of public schools, conservative Protestants are now, ironically, among its most vociferous critics.

Since the mid-1960s evangelical and fundamentalist Protestants have responded to the institution that they once considered theirs in a variety of ways. Some have acquiesced in the changes in public schooling, while others have adopted a more activist posture. Many conservative Protestants have sought to incorporate theistic symbols and perspectives in the public schools through proposals for Ten Commandments displays, discussion of intelligent design in science classes, and adoption of history texts that acknowledge the culture-shaping influence of Christianity in the United States. Others have protested curricular materials they believe advance secular humanism, which they consider as much a religion as Christianity, in the public schools. Women often have played key roles in textbook protests.

In September 1974, for example, Alice Moore, a member of the Kanawha County, West Virginia, school board and wife of a conservative pastor, led a protest against elementary language arts books that had been adopted the previous spring. She asserted, among other things, that the books taught situation ethics, contained profanity and vulgar language, emphasized the depressing aspects of life, and most significantly, denigrated Christianity. "The more I read," Moore said of the controversial books, "the more I was shocked. They were full of negative references to Christianity and God" (quoted in Fraser, 169). The protest drew national attention when violence erupted and outsiders, such as conservative textbook critics Mel and Norma Gabler, became involved in the conflict between pro- and anti-textbook forces. Only after parents were allowed to choose whether their children could use the controversial texts (better than 65 percent refused to allow their children to use the books) did the protest end.

Almost ten years later, in 1983, a Hawkins County, Tennessee, homemaker named Vicki Frost and her friend Jennie Wilson sparked a controversy over a series of readers used in their children's classes that quickly escalated into a proxy war between two national organizations deeply involved in America's "culture war"— Norman Lear's liberal People for the American Way and Beverly LaHaye's conservative Concerned Women for America, which claims to be the largest public policy women's organization in the United States. When Frost and her friends went to federal court and sought a free exercise of religion exemption for their children's exposure to the district-mandated books, which they thought promoted feminism, evolutionism, rebellion against authority, secular humanism, and anti-Christian beliefs, Concerned Women for America provided legal counsel, while People for the American Way assisted the school district's defense of the requirement that all students read the challenged texts. Though a federal district judge ordered the school district to accommodate the parents' religious objections to the reading texts by allowing their children to opt out of reading at school and learn that subject at home, a federal appellate court reversed the judge's decision on the grounds that mere exposure to objectionable material did not unconstitutionally burden the parents' religious beliefs and thus did not require an accommodation. After the U.S. Supreme Court refused to review the appellate court's ruling, Frost and several of her allies removed their children from the public schools.

Protests similar to those in Kanawha County and Hawkins County have occurred throughout the United States since the 1960s. Often they have drawn local women like Alice Moore and Vicki Frost as well as conservative national women's organizations such as Concerned Women for America and the Eagle Forum, founded in 1975 by Phyllis Schlafly, a Roman Catholic, to oppose the ratification of the Equal Rights Amendment to the federal Constitution, into the contested arena of public education. Furthermore, these clashes have contributed to the development of independent Christian schools and home schooling.

Rather than attempt to "re-Christianize" or purge the public schools of secular humanism, some conservative Protestants have forsaken their historic commitment to public education. Since the mid-1960s, evangelical Christians and their churches, few of which are affiliated with mainline Protestant denominations, have established over 10,000 Christian day schools with a current enrollment of more than 1 million students. Once thought to be mere segregation academies, the vast majority are now racially integrated and offer academic programs that embody a Christian worldview. Leadership of this movement has been predominantly male. While it is safe to assume that the majority of teachers in these schools are female, exact figures are not available.

One of the most remarkable education strategies of conservative Christians in the late 1900s and early 2000s is home schooling. Though parents' motivations for returning to an educational arrangement reminiscent of that of the 1600s and 1700s are many and varied, the vast majority have acted to a greater or lesser extent on religious convictions. In this educational milieu more than any other, women play a dominant role as teachers, support group leaders, lobbyists, and authors.

Home Schooling

I understood at an early point with my children that "The hand that rocks the cradle rules the world."
—Beverly Somogie, home school mother of four and veteran home school leader, North Andover, Massachusetts, interview, 2001

Home schooling has grown quickly to now involve about 2 million elementary and secondary students in North America during 2001, 1 million mothers, and like numbers of fathers. Home schooling in the United States has grown from 10 percent in 1990 to about 23 percent the size of private schools. Home-based education—usually called home schooling—has offered women a powerful say in their children's lives. This degree of educational influence has been virtually nonexistent during the past eighty years in North America.

In September 1974, Alice Moore, a member of the Kanawha County, West Virginia, school board and wife of a conservative pastor, led a protest against elementary language arts books that had been adopted the previous spring. She asserted that the books taught situation ethics, contained profanity and vulgar language, emphasized the depressing aspects of life, and, most significantly, denigrated Christianity. *Courtesy of the* Charleston Gazette.

Women have had an integral and often central role in the modern home-education movement. Their rationales for home schooling varied widely, but there were consistent major themes. Likewise, their roles, as far as the public is concerned, have ranged from the essentially invisible homemaker/home educator to the newspaper-quoted champion of home school–friendly legislation. Although reasons and roles may vary, most home school mothers have shared overall purposes. There are generally six categories of reasons that parents give for home schooling: (1) stronger family relationships; (2) customization of curriculum for each child; (3) strong academics; (4) guided social interactions; (5) safety in the realm of the physical, psychological, sexual, and drugs and alcohol; and (6) a set of values, beliefs, and worldview chosen by the parents rather than a school system (Ray, *Worldwide Guide to Homeschooling,* 40–43). These purposes have been especially consistent due to most home schoolers' shared Christian worldview.

During the past fifteen years, conservative Christians have represented the large majority of home school parents. Among these, women have had key roles in the modern home school movement in the United States and Canada in at least two ways. First, a significant number of the movement's current leaders and original activists have been women. Second, mothers are the key day-to-day and hour-by-hour formal educators of their school-age children, the future citizens and leaders of their local communities, churches, and nations.

Leaders: Visible and Behind the Scenes

Several women who had young children in the late 1970s and early 1980s reported that they spontaneously began having grave doubts about institutional schooling—especially government-run schooling—during these years. One woman, now in her early forties and with eight children, recalls how she was pregnant with her first child while a student-teacher in a first-grade public school classroom in Portland, Oregon. She came home one day after teaching and told her husband, "I don't know what we'll do, but I'll never put my children in a school." She had never heard of home schooling. Beverly Somogie from Massachusetts (quoted earlier), had an almost identical experience. Women like these were among the first practitioners and public promoters of home schooling.

The denominational private schools of the early to mid-1900s and the Christian day schools of the 1970s and 1980s were often founded and operated by men who used a business, organizational, and management approach to education as a service to be offered and used by customers. The bulk of home schooling activities, on the other hand, involve relationships among family members and associations with friends and small, private enterprises that do not include the payment of money. Along with this, home schooling appears to more fully blend the different and often complementary traits and traditional roles of men and women, husbands and wives. In many ways, Christian home schooling has enacted and unleashed a more relational and organic approach to education, what some biblically minded persons call *discipleship* in its most basic form. That is, these parents believe they are heeding biblical exhortations such as "[parents] teach . . . your children . . . when you sit in your house, when you walk by the way, when you lie down, and when you rise up" (Deuteronomy 6: 7) and "make disciples . . . teaching them to observe all things that I have commanded you" (Matthew 28:19–20). This educational discipleship has been encouraged and supported in many ways by key women.

The Printed Word

The printed word has often been a significant influence on the thinking of practicing and potential home school mothers. Magazines have been a mainstay of information, encouragement, pedagogical creativity, problem solving, and keeping abreast of political issues regarding home schooling. Sue Welch, a home school mother in Portland, Oregon, started *The Teaching Home* as a one-page newsletter in 1980. By 1983 it had become a national newsletter and initiated a program to work with and help statewide home school organizations that support and promote home-based education philosophy and practice. *The Teaching Home* by 2001 was a sixty-four-page, professionally produced, bimonthly magazine with a worldwide circulation of 100,000. Welch says, "Beside the benefits of academics, character, and spiritual values, I believe that homeschooling is one of the nicest things that you can do for your child. We have enjoyed learning, traveling, and living life together with our children. They have been nurtured and protected by adults that love them" (Interview, 2001). This magazine's articles on teaching practices and educational philosophy, letters to the editor, and ideas on how to lobby legislators (to protect parental rights in education) have had immeasurable effects on an untold number of adults and children.

Four of the other best-known home school magazines, *Practical Homeschooling, Home School Digest, Homeschooling Today,* and *Lifestyle of Learning,* were founded or edited by women. *Practical Homeschooling* covers almost every topic imaginable with crisp color graphics, while *Home School Digest* typically focuses on in-depth and more philosophical issues. These four magazines—each with their variegated philosophies of Christian education—have been affecting the philosophies and education of hundreds of thousands of parents and children throughout the world. Women also have produced and edited the newsletters and magazines of many state- or province-wide and local home school organizations. Most of these organizations and their publications are operated by volunteers, mostly women.

Books, too, have been a principal means of inspiring parents to home school and supporting those who do so. Christian women have been very active in this realm. Although not a part of the modern home school movement, the books of Charlotte Mason, written in the early 1900s, are now used to enlighten and motivate Christian home schoolers. Mary Pride, one of the best-known figures in the home school community, a former feminist, and a conservative Christian, first published in 1985, producing a series of books that promote her understanding of biblically prescribed social life centered around the home and family, home schooling, womanhood, and family (i.e., a husband with one wife with their biological or adopted children). She explains the ills of modern feminism in *The Way Home: Beyond Feminism, Back to Reality* (1985), *Schoolproof* (1988), and *All the Way Home* (1989). She has also reviewed numerous curricula and learning resources in her periodically updated *The Big Book of Home Learning* volumes (1986).

Ruth Beechick, among the most popular home school authors, clearly infuses biblical ideas into her work. She uses explicit Christian examples in teaching writing skills and discusses creation science. Susan Schaeffer Macaulay, daughter of the late Christian philosopher Francis Schaeffer, wrote *For the Children's Sake* in 1984. Elizabeth Wilson's main goal in *Books Children Love* is to have children read and experience the fullness and glory of God. Cathy Duffy, an expert on curriculum and the politics of education and well known in home schooling and other educational circles, authored *Government Nannies: The Cradle-to-Grave Agenda of Goals 2000 and Outcome Based Education* (1995) in which she documented and warned that government policies related to outcome-based education take from the family its historical and traditional roles regarding the education of children. Duffy writes:

Do parents have the right to pass on their beliefs to their children, or does the village [government] have the right to override parental convictions? Who determines the school agenda? Should parents have the right to reject all or part of an agenda determined by the village? I realize that these questions suggest far more than a challenge to a few programs. They cut to the heart of educational philosophy in the United States. They even question the right of government to be involved in education at all. (48)

Legislative Lobbyists

Whoever has the data controls the policy.
—Kay Coles James, former Secretary of Health and Human Resources of Virginia, African American, address to home school leaders, 1994

Women have been able to approach legislators, the media, and policymakers with their own families' testimonies and a growing base of research that documents the positive effects of home schooling. For example, students who are home schooled consistently score 15 to 30 percentile points above the national public school average on academic achievement tests (Ray, "Home Schooling: The Ameliorator," 88). Home school mothers have been principal figures in using such information to affect law and policy.

Zan Tyler of South Carolina is one of the pioneers of the modern-day home education movement. When she and her husband began home schooling in 1984, government officials threatened her with jail. In the early 1990s, Tyler spearheaded groundbreaking legislative work culminating in the establishment of the private South Carolina Association of Independent Home Schools. It is a Christian-run organization that serves persons of any faith as an approval agency for home schooling families on a par with local government school boards. Diana M. Fessler, a Christian home school mother of six children, has actively lobbied legislators on behalf of home schoolers for over a decade and is now on the Ohio State Board of Education and holds a seat in the Ohio House of Representatives, where she serves on the Education Committee and chairs the Children and Family Services subcommittee.

Organizations and Conferences

Women are also key players in organizing home school conferences and curriculum exhibits. They select speakers and therefore the messages and philosophies that are promoted among home schoolers. Women are usually the main organizers of the conferences' curriculum exhibits at which many novice and veteran home school parents evaluate and select materials for educating their children.

These women authors, lobbyists, and organizational volunteers address a wide range of subjects and hold a wide variety of particularistic Christian beliefs (e.g.,

evangelical, Reformed, dispensational, fundamental, reconstructionist, nondenominational, house churches, denominational). Their key themes, however, are rather consistent: God says that parents have the main and ultimate responsibility and authority regarding a child's education; the God of the Bible wants parents to train up and educate children so that they will for a lifetime know, love, and worship him with their whole heart, strength, soul, and mind; any parent who diligently applies his or her mind and effort can properly and successfully home educate a child (and this may include using teachers and resources from outside the home and family); putting one's child under the tutelage and indoctrination of persons who do not love the Lord Jesus Christ is a risky, if not sinful, practice.

Everyday Mothers (Educators and Philosophers)

Whether twenty-five years old with one child who is six or fifty years old with her seventh child almost ten years old, Christian home school women have learned much from being their children's main everyday teachers. The thoughts of several women flesh out the story that much scholarly research has documented.

Jon Wartes, a longtime public high school counselor, studied home school parents and gained several insights from their statements (25, 35). "I think the main benefit too is the cohesiveness of our family unit. My son said yesterday, 'Mom, I appreciate all that you do for me . . . and I love you.' The children know you are really 'for them' and that you are sacrificing for them." "Our teenage daughter wants us to be her role models and closest friends, not her peers. Our relationship with her has been strengthened in a way I never thought possible" "I've learned we are qualified to teach and guide our own children. That no one cares for your child and his future more than you." "I have learned that we do not need to turn our kids over to the 'experts' because we, as parents, are the experts. God intended for parents to participate in every aspect of their children's growing up experience."

Arné Williams, a fifty-three-year-old African American mother of four children and state leader in Tuscaloosa, Alabama, tells her story about home schooling. Her little boy was reading and doing math before they put him in public kindergarten,

then for over three years in public schools he was bored and the school taught him nothing new, academically. It was just a social situation and he became bored and became an irritant to the school people. So we put him into a Christian school where he did well academically but again there were "behavior issues." We then recognized that God was calling us to work on those problems and not the school [to fix him]. We pulled him out of school during the early part of fourth grade, and I said, "I'll teach him myself." Homeschooling wasn't a part of my vocabulary then, although we had heard of it on a radio program. (Interview, 2001)

Arné continues:

Before my son's kindergarten year, I did substitute teaching in public schools. I saw the reasons why the schools labeled children as "special needs." They would be labeled based on whether their parents were poor, how they were dressed, whether they came from a single-parent household, were raised by grandparents, and so on. There was a special code or label for each of these categories. When we began homeschooling our son, there was a public school teacher who had taught him physical education and who had begun homeschooling her children, and this teacher told me that the public schools had already begun to target our son to label him in a way that would put him on a track that would limit him. I don't like to bring this up, but there may have been a race issue.

These Christian women view home schooling as a way of acknowledging and developing their children's Creator-designed individuality. "These institutional school systems are geared toward one particular personality; just because a child's personality is different or way of learning is different doesn't mean he is not capable academically but the school cannot accommodate it or deal with it," says Williams. Somogie explains,

As a Christian, I see homeschooling as a strategy that can individualize your child's curriculum, give more time to developing special interests and skills, and provide more one-on-one time from a parent or other teacher to work on things the child is not so good at. Further, in public school, when kids go away and they are with a teacher all day, they learn to respect that teacher and get their guidance from that teacher, they see that teacher as academically stimulating and they don't see their parents that way; then what happens is a certain amount of disrespect toward parents develops in children, and I don't know whether it is intentional on the part of schools or it just happens. (Interview, 2001)

Christian women who home school their children are living what they discern to be true as followers of the Jesus of the scriptures. Somogie says,

I never thought of homeschooling in terms of being a woman. Other than when I was with my children and I would get critical stares and other women would critically ask me, "You mean you're a stay-at-home mother!?" It bothered me because my favorite thing to talk about was my vision for the family while most other women were wanting to talk about themselves. I think the women's movement has been rather self-centered rather than about a vision for others and the family.

Williams explains:

I can instill into my children what God expects of them through homeschooling. We have the time to sit down and to talk about biblical things, to do a devotional, to let them know that ultimately they are accountable to God for the decisions they make for their own lives. We could do this religious training at night and on weekends, I suppose, but from 8 AM to 3 in the afternoon my son was not getting a biblical worldview and the accountability to God was not there. There are so many teachable moments available throughout the day that we can dedicate to biblical truth in homeschooling that would be lost in the public school; in homeschooling we have these teachable moments that can pierce his spirit in a positive way.

The concept of participating in life with their children on a daily and hourly basis is key to these women and their husbands. They are concerned about both academics and the socialization of their children. Said one mother:

Schools are set up, not so much for academics, but for socialization. One of the first and most important questions our critics ask is, "What about socialization?" They don't mean just getting along with others (like being able to deal with bullies). They are really asking about a political issue. What they really mean is, "How are we going to fill your child with our liberal worldview if you homeschool him and don't put him into a public school?!"

In fact, research substantiates these mothers' claim that their children will likely be socialized in a more positive and more mature way than children and youth in institutional schools (Medlin, 119). "Getting back to the socialization issue," says Williams,

we found that our son, while in school, was being assimilated into the popular culture around him which was to gravitate to the lowest common denominator. At home his socialization was to his younger sisters and to Jesse, his father, my husband, and me so that his socialization was to be pleasing to us and not to other children who were not like us. He did not have proper leadership in his peer group.

The literature of home schoolers, especially of Christians, makes it clear that the home school movement is very much about the training of the next generation to have a heart for God and his ways of thinking and doing things. Research suggests they have both their children's and society's welfare in mind (Ray, "Home Schooling for," 289). Somogie explains it this way:

In order for the changes to take place that liberals want is for the people of the United States to not be so educated so that they [liberals] can influence people more. Homeschoolers need to know this and educate their children in a much better way. I have always felt, too, that if homeschooling is ever outlawed in the United States it will not be because of academic failure, it will be because the government does not have access to these children's socialization. The public schools are being used to socialize our children into a liberal or unbiblical and narcissistic worldview; who the leaders of public schools are in particular, I don't know. I was a very strong Unitarian (which is essentially humanism) for 23 years so becoming a Christian was a 180-degree turn and involved a complete renewing of my mind. Having been a Unitarian and completely indoctrinated in the humanistic worldview, which is what public schools do, I have an advantage in terms of understanding the other side; I look at life from a Christian perspective because it is the truth but I understand how humanists think and why they think that. Public schools were essentially humanist at least by 1985.

Conclusion

Modern home schooling women, along with their husbands, have revived the centuries-old concept of home-based and parent-led education. Whether visible home school leaders or everyday mothers and homemakers, they are practicing "rocking the cradle" so that the God of the Bible might more apparently rule individuals, families, and the world. These women know, as Warren Nord has documented (*Religion & American Education*, 159–165), that there is no educational vacuum, someone is always teaching and indoctrinating every school-age child and youth, as many scholars have documented. They are aware that many persons want to increase the number of students in state-controlled schools and reduce the number of home schooled so that more future citizens will be taught "progressive" antibiblical beliefs (e.g., abortion is good or acceptable; homosexuality is good or acceptable; the state or experts know better than parents what is good for children). These women are convinced that in order to give their children a solid academic education and to see their children, and eventually their nations, be servants of others and glorify Jesus Christ, they must do their best to educate their minds and hearts. They think home schooling is the best way to do this.

SOURCES: See A. James Reichley, *Religion in American Public Life* (1985); Stephen Bates, *Battleground: One Mother's Crusade, the Religious Right, and the Struggle for Control of Our Classrooms* (1993); Steven Mintz and Susan Kellogg, *Domestic Revolutions: A Social History of American Family Life* (1988); Carl F. Kaestle, *Pillars of the Republic: Common Schools and American Society, 1780–1860* (1983); and James Davison Hunter, *American Evangelicalism: Conservative Religion and the Quandary of Modernity* (1983). A. James Reichley, *Religion in American Public Life* (1985), comments on the fading dominance of mainline Protestant influence in American life. William Martin, *With God on Our Side: The Rise of the Religious Right in America* (1996), informs this topic by discussing so-called Religious Right organizations. See James W. Fraser, *Between Church and State: Religion and Education in a Multicultural America* (1999). Jonathan Zimmerman, *Whose America? The Culture Wars in American Education* (2002), recounts the activities of women in sex education and textbook controversies. Coauthor Brian Ray interviewed by telephone Beverly Somogie (January 17, 2001), Sue Welch (February 5, 2001), and Arné Williams (January 29, 2001). Brian D. Ray, *Worldwide Guide to Homeschooling* (2002), encapsulates twenty years of research and thinking on and by home schoolers. See Cathy Duffy, *Government Nannies: The Cradle-to-Grave Agenda of Goals 2000 and Outcome Based Education* (1995). Kay Coles James is former Secretary of Health and Human Resources of Virginia and an African American; quote is from her speech at the National Christian Home Educators Leadership Conference, Phoenix, Arizona, October 22, 1994. See Brian D. Ray's "Home Schooling: The Ameliorator of Negative Influences on Learning?" and "Home Schooling for Individuals' Gain and Society's Common Good" and Richard G. Medlin's "Home Schooling and the Question of Socialization," all published in *Peabody Journal of Education* 75.1–2 (2000). See Jon Wartes, *Effects of Homeschooling upon the Education of the Parents: Comments from the Field*, Washington Homeschool Research Project (1992); and Warren Nord, *Religion & American Education: Rethinking a National Dilemma* (1995).

WOMEN AND JEWISH EDUCATION
David E. Kaufman

BOTH AS CONSUMERS and as practitioners, women have been integral to the history of Jewish education in

America. Jewish women educators have been teachers, principals, textbook writers, curriculum developers, and leading theoreticians and advocates in the field. As students, Jewish girls formed a new constituency that helped spur a total rethinking of the goals and methods of the Jewish classroom. These innovations were all the more remarkable given that prior to the modern period Jews worldwide conformed to the traditional pattern of an all-male Jewish schooling—only men had served as classroom teachers, and only boys received a formal education. In the new world, the feminization of Jewish education would go hand in hand with the Americanization of the Jew.

The feminization of Jewish education would entail two related processes: the inclusion of women in formerly male-only domains and the expansion of educational parameters in accordance with women's sensibilities and experience. First, Jewish women in America have been newly included in formal settings of Jewish education, transcending their traditional roles as wives, mothers, and homemakers, to become teachers, communal organizers, and writers—in itself a transformation of radical proportions. Though excluded from formal education in premodern Jewish life, women did play an essential role in the cultural transmission of Jewishness. Historically, Jewish culture was disseminated via three interlocking social arenas: the public realm of community, the institutional settings of synagogue and school (often the same institution; thus *shul* is the colloquial Yiddish term for "synagogue"), and the domestic sphere of the home. Women played little role in the public and institutional realms, but their influence was great in the home. This sociological fact was later turned into conscious ideology when, during the nineteenth century, emancipated Jews assigned the religious education of the young to women. As they left the ghettos in Europe behind, modernizing Jews abandoned the schools of the Jewish community for the schools of the general society and, to replace the former educative agencies of community and school, settled upon the home as the one remaining bastion of Jewish education. Thus women, in their role as mothers, would become the chief educators of Jewish children and hence, in the 1896 words of Rebekah Kohut (1864–1951), "saviors of our people" (Hyman, 40).

In America, however, the Jewish home, like the Jewish community overall, no longer served as a principal model of Jewish life, having yielded to the disintegrating effects of assimilation. The traditional educative role of women greatly diminished; American Jewish women gravitated to the institutional realm, making it their own. Yet another key aspect of the feminization of Jewish education entailed the broadening of its scope, beyond the confines of the schoolhouse. Hence the modern term *Jewish education* construes far more than a

religious schooling in Judaism and concerns a much wider area than the pedagogic settings of synagogues and other religious centers. The term, more accurately, refers to the greater enterprise of ensuring Jewish group survival in America. In historian Jonathan Sarna's formulation: "Jewish education serves as the vehicle through which we train successive generations of Jews to negotiate their own way, as Jews, in the American arena" (10).

Two factors set Jewish education apart from other types of American religious education. First, *Jews are both a religious and an ethnic group* simultaneously and symbiotically. Jewish religious faith is couched within the idiom of Jewish peoplehood, and the historical experience of the Jewish people is an essential component of Jewish religious identity. Even when taken separately, the two sides of the identity coin recommend a special educational approach. As with American Catholics, the preservation of the Jews' ancient religious heritage may require some degree of "parochial" segregation; and, like African Americans, the harsh realities of their history—for example, anti-Semitism and the Holocaust—continue to set them apart as a people, a group identity for which they seek a more positive rationale. Hence the dual goals of Jewish education became (1) the transmission of a viable religious tradition and (2) the inculcation of a positive group identification.

A second factor is *the challenge of American assimilation*. Given their history of marginalization in European society, most immigrant Jews responded to the openness of America by quickly discarding the baggage of the old Jewish life and eagerly integrating into the new culture. Of course, such cultural assimilation is common to all ethnic groups in America, as is the preservation of some abstract remnant of group identity—that is, a symbolic ethnicity. Just such a vestigial identity characterizes most American Jews today. Jewish education is seen therefore as an imperative task facing a daunting challenge: preserving the distinct religious culture of Judaism in the midst of the most accepting society Jews have ever experienced. In the history of American Jewry, it is principally women who have risen to the task.

Nineteenth-Century Beginnings

Though in the colonial era the religious education of Jewish girls was generally neglected, some inroads were made in the decades following the American Revolution. At the turn of the nineteenth century, approximately one-third of students enrolled in the school of Shearith Israel—the original Sephardic Jewish congregation of New York City—were girls. As new congregations were founded in the first decades of the century, their full-time schools admitted girls as a matter of course. The coeducational programs offered much the same curriculum to both sexes, with the exception of special needlework classes for girls. Similarly, the 1846 institution of the confirmation ceremony (distinct from the bar mitzvah observance for boys alone) also equalized the treatment of boys and girls—both were to receive preparatory instruction "in religion in general, Jewish creed and revelations, immortality of the soul and the thirteen creeds" (Dushkin, 47).

Apart from the synagogue schools, several private institutions operated as boarding schools, necessitating separate accommodations for boys and for girls. In 1809, Hebraist and educator Jacob Mordecai opened the Female Academy in Warrenton, Virginia; his daughters Emma and Ellen were among the teachers. Two noted schools for Jewish girls in New York City were the Palache School (founded in 1840) and Mrs. Bondy's (1850s), where the general curriculum was supplemented by Hebrew reading, biblical history, and religious catechisms. As the post-Revolutionary generation of Jews further Americanized, more parents inclined to send their sons and daughters to either non-Jewish private schools or, beginning at mid-century, the growing number of American public schools. The subsequent decline of the all-day Jewish parochial school would signal the rise of supplementary schooling, a new trend in Jewish education initiated and driven by Jewish women.

The key figure in this movement was Rebecca Gratz (1781–1869), who in 1838 established the Hebrew Sunday School of Philadelphia. Gratz, a highly acculturated member of a prominent Jewish family, was active in the emerging women's culture of religious and charitable voluntarism. In 1819 she cofounded the first nonsynagogal Jewish charity in America, the Female Hebrew Benevolent Society. Jewish philanthropy turned toward educational ends when Gratz began urging its members to address "that most pressing need—the mental impoverishment of" the rising generation of American Jews. To meet this need, and to counter the apparent threat of Christian proselytization, she would model her latest initiative after the Protestant American Sunday School Union, creating a citywide educational institution for the "Hebrew" (common nineteenth-century term for "Jewish") community of Philadelphia. The Hebrew Sunday School opened with seventy students, five female teachers, and Rebecca Gratz as superintendent and head teacher. It was the first Jewish educational institution to offer a systematized religious instruction for Jewish children that would be supplementary to their studies in the public school, which remains the majority case to this day. The innovative school also represented the first attempt to shift the responsibility for Jewish education from the congregational to the communal realm. Perhaps most significantly, Gratz pioneered the training of young Jewish women to serve as teachers, albeit as un-

salaried volunteers. Truly a historic watershed, the Hebrew Sunday School is remembered as the educational setting that "allowed Jewish women to teach religion publicly for the first time in Jewish history" (Ashton, 152).

The teaching staff included the sisters Simha and Rachel Peixotto who had earlier run a women's academy in their home and would eventually write some of the textbooks for the new school. Unlike the traditional Jewish curriculum of Hebrew language (using the Bible as a primer) and rabbinic text, the Hebrew Sunday School curriculum focused on Bible study (in translation) and lessons in ethics, thus promoting an Americanized form of Judaism—a Judaism not yet reformed in practice but Protestantized and feminized in tone. According to Gratz's biographer: "The school merely continued in a systematic, public, and authoritative way the historic tradition in which stories from Scripture had been taught informally to children by knowledgeable mothers. Like Victorian culture and feminized religion, the school emphasized the importance of domestic piety, the heart's longing for and devotion to God, and God's loving kindness" (152). The biblical books of Ruth and Esther, highlighting such devoted Jewish women, were perennial favorites. The most popular modern textbook was *The Spirit of Judaism*, written by English theologian Grace Aguilar in 1842 and published in Philadelphia by Isaac Leeser, the leading American Jewish clergyman of the day and Rebecca Gratz's close colleague. By 1854, the burgeoning school had outgrown its quarters in the Peixotto home and moved into a renovated church renamed Touro Hall. In its new home, some twenty-five teachers served 250 students drawn from all sectors of the community.

The Philadelphia model was soon imitated in other cities, most notably the "Association for the Moral and Religious Instruction of Children of the Jewish Faith," formed by the women of New York's Shearith Israel congregation in October 1838. Such educational initiatives provided religious instruction to girls as well as to boys and almost exclusively employed the volunteer services of women teachers. Yet despite their early gains and the shining example of Rebecca Gratz, women continued to be relegated to the periphery in Jewish communal life for most of the period from 1840 to 1880. During this era of German Jewish immigration and adjustment to American life, new Jewish communities sprang up throughout the country. Typically, the first Jewish organization to form was a synagogue that soon took on the task of education, calling upon its immigrant rabbi to instruct the children. But not all were satisfied with this arrangement. From his initial call for the creation of a Jewish theological institute in 1841, Isaac Leeser persistently urged the training of young American men as rabbis and recommended that "young women be educated for the high calling of female instructors" (Korn, 154). Yet contrary to Leeser's pleas, no rabbinical seminary was established on a permanent basis until 1875 and no teachers training school until the end of the century. At the same time, however, a new Jewish women's movement appeared on the scene, once again linking philanthropy to pedagogy and ultimately inspiring the next phase in the feminization of Jewish education.

The social activism of late-nineteenth-century Jewish women was embedded in the general movement of settlement work and immigrant Americanization. Taking care of their own, native-born American Jews attended to the assimilation of the newly arriving Jewish immigrants from eastern Europe, establishing settlement houses and other philanthropic institutions of a particularly Jewish variety. Jewish settlements, often founded and staffed by women, tended to focus on education. Around 1880, for example, the American Jewish poet Emma Lazarus (1849–1887) urged the creation of a vocational school for immigrant children, which led to her support of the Hebrew Technical School for girls in New York City. Fanny Binswanger of Philadelphia, a latter-day Rebecca Gratz, led thirty of her friends in the Women's Auxiliary of the Hebrew Educational Society in opening a kindergarten for Jewish immigrant children in 1885. It was later reorganized as the Young Women's Union and expanded its activities to include a "Household School" for girls. In Baltimore, the young Henrietta Szold (1860–1945) established a night school for Russian Jews in 1889 in cooperation with the Hebrew Literary Society, described as being among the pioneers of its kind in America. And in the following year, Lina Hecht (1848–1921) and Golde Bamber (1862–193?) of Boston founded the Hebrew Industrial School for girls, whose motto became: "A good Israelite will make a better citizen." Every one of these individual efforts included some form of religious instruction in their program. Jewish education was thus promoted by Jewish women as an essential element of social welfare in the Jewish community.

Nationally, Jewish women's social organizations likewise devoted themselves to the "Judaization" of American Jewry. Building on the earlier example of ladies' auxiliaries and sewing circles, the first important initiative was the 1889 creation of the "Sisterhood of Personal Service" by the rabbi and women of New York's Temple Emanu-El. Such temple sisterhoods proliferated thereafter, always combining social work with education. Besides their charitable outreach and the establishment of religious schools for the community, the sisterhoods often took over the running of their congregation's school as well. At the Chicago World's Fair of 1893, Hannah Solomon (1858–1942), Sadie American (1862–1944), and others founded the National Council for Jewish Women (NCJW), "the first national organization in history to unite Jewish women to promote the Jewish religion." According to its historian, "the NCJW concentrated on combating assimilation by educating Jewish women about Judaism, hoping in the process to strengthen Jewish homes by making council members

Fanny Binswanger of Philadelphia led thirty of her friends in the Women's Auxiliary of the Hebrew Educational Society to open a kindergarten for Jewish immigrant children in 1885. The auxiliary, later reorganized as the Young Women's Union, expanded its activities to include a "Household School" for girls. *Courtesy of the Philadelphia Jewish Archives Center.*

into better Jewish mothers" (Hyman and Moore, 971). Local chapters of the NCJW were soon organized all over the country, as, for example, in the Jewish community of Denver, Colorado, whose branch established a kindergarten, night school, Americanization classes, and not least, a "mission Sunday School."

While women were active in the Young Men's Hebrew Association movement throughout the latter nineteenth century, in 1902 the first independent Young Women's Hebrew Association (YWHA) was founded in New York City under the leadership of Bella Unterberg (b. 1868). Spearheading a new movement, its stated mission was "promoting Judaism among young Jewish women and of instilling in them principles of kindness and benevolence and of improving their mental, moral, religious, social, and physical condition" (Kaufman, *Shul with a Pool*, 77). Sophia Berger, later the superintendent of the YWHA, stated in 1912 that "back of everything we do, is the thought of preserving the essential Jewishness of our people. As Jews we want to save our Judaism" (ibid., 79). Like the Sisterhood and Council before it, the YWHA embodied the American Jewish woman's penchant for social amelioration through the spiritual uplift of young Jews.

All these developments also helped to spur the widespread move of Jewish women into the teaching profession, a shift related, of course, to changes in the greater society. One historian estimates that the percentage of women teachers in the United States increased from 59 percent in 1870 to 70 percent in 1900 to 86 percent in 1920. So too did young Jewish women discover teaching as the only profession open to them—a trend most famously exemplified by Julia Richman (1855–1912), who capped a forty-year career in the New York City public school system as superintendent of the Lower East Side school district. Richman was also active in the Jewish community, teaching in the Sabbath School of her Reform temple, founding the Young Ladies Charitable Union, and attaining leadership positions in the Hebrew Free School Association, the NCJW, the YWHA, and the Educational Alliance, the leading settlement of New York's Jewish immigrant community. Another of her contributions was the establishment of Teachers' House, a settlement focusing on the problems of truancy and job placement. Ironically, however, Richman and the many other young women who embarked upon a teaching career had no corollaries within the east European Jewish community. There, women were still excluded from the Jewish classroom. The Sunday School precedent aside, the feminization of Jewish education would take place only after repeated struggle and the advent of a new American Jewish culture in the 1900s. Yet the foundations had been laid by the women's movements of the late nineteenth century.

Women and the American Profession of Jewish Education, 1900–1960

Where the earlier feminization of Jewish education was related to the subsidiary status of teaching in society, the next phase would accelerate the inclusion of women in teaching as a way to raise its status, and theirs. That is, nineteenth-century Jewish women were drawn to Sunday School teaching precisely because it was a voluntary, part-time position, whereas the twentieth century would see the professionalization of women teachers and the creation of an organized professional field. This was a decades-long process lasting from the turn-of-the-century immigrant era through the post–World War II baby boom, continuing through the present day. Moreover, it is a process that has had profound implications for Jewish women.

By 1900 the mass immigration of east European Jews to America was well under way, bringing with it hundreds of thousands of Jewish children eager to learn the ways of the "golden land." Yet the immigrants also brought with them traditional notions of Jewish education and included in their ranks many male teachers of the old type; consequently, the era of mass immigration also brought new problems in Jewish religious education. There were too many children for the available educational facilities, and those that were functioning did so poorly, staffed by ineffective teachers. Jewish leaders perceived the situation to be critical and soon began implementing various solutions, not least among them the training of Jewish teachers on the model of the American public school teacher, thus Americanizing, professionalizing, and feminizing the Jewish teaching profession.

The influence of the American public school cannot be overestimated. Specially trained in "normal schools," public school teachers soon became the standard against which parochial school teachers were measured. In 1880, for example, a Jewish assistant superintendent of schools in Milwaukee compared the public school to the religious schools of the Jewish community and harshly criticized the latter for their lack of professionalism. He contrasted the ineffectual male *melamed* (traditional teacher) of the community with the efficient female teacher of the public school and recommended that "whenever possible only experts, men and women, who have chosen to become teachers should be entrusted with the administration of the school." Since those who chose to become teachers were mainly women, he was essentially recommending that women be "entrusted with the administration" of the Jewish school (Gartner, 99–100).

The first attempts at formal teacher training were made by Rabbi Gustav Gottheil, the same rabbi who was instrumental in the creation of the temple sisterhood. From the late 1870s he had sponsored a Preparatory School for the training of teachers, and as a leader of the Hebrew Free School Association he advocated that whenever possible "gentlemen teachers were [to be] replaced by lady teachers" (Dushkin, 56). In 1882 Gottheil helped establish a normal school called the Ladies' Hebrew Seminary. Though it only existed for five years, it set a precedent soon to be followed elsewhere. Gratz College, the first permanently established Jewish teacher training school in America, opened in Philadelphia in 1898. Its first graduating class consisted of three women and one man, a ratio that would become typical. From 1902 to 1909 a series of experiments in teacher training were undertaken by the newly reorganized Jewish Theological Seminary in New York, culminating in the formation of its Teachers Institute, ultimately the most influential school of Jewish education established. Its role in the feminization of Jewish teaching was to be incalculable.

More important still was the entry of girls into the classrooms of the immigrant Jewish community. Though a group of Jewish women had launched a model school as early as 1889—the School of Biblical Instruction, in Brooklyn, New York—formal Jewish schooling was still confined to boys. Only after the turn of the century did schools catering to girls open. As Jewish educator Leo Honor explained, "[A] girls' school had a twofold advantage; it provided greater leeway for the experimenters and it concretized a new concept for the Jewish immigrants from Eastern Europe that girls as well as boys were in need of Jewish education" (10). Still, many Jewish immigrants who were unwilling to send their sons to one of the modern schools were willing to experiment with their daughters. Rebecca Aaronson Brickner recalled that her conservative mother "would allow only the girls to go to that school [the experimental Hebrew school of Samson Benderly]. The boys had to be taught by a Rebbi [sic] at home" (53).

In the early decades of the twentieth century, the fastest-growing ideology of the immigrant community was Zionism; and indeed the revolutionary spirit of early Zionism would profoundly influence the new Jewish educators. In 1905, Ephraim Kaplan opened the first "National Hebrew" [read: Zionist] School for Girls, also in Brooklyn, and another by the same name followed in 1910. The latter school was especially successful, attributed to its ambience "of joyous educational activity" and its program of "literature, drama, newspaper, singing, dancing, drawing, Zionism, and more" (Pilch, 65), a curriculum in sharp contrast to the schools of a more traditional variety. Following suit, the newly formed Bureau of Jewish Education in New York City opened a series of preparatory schools throughout the city incorporating the latest advances in educational methods and technology. Again, these model schools were for girls only. By 1912 the schools had a population of more than 1,200 girls, ranging in age from eleven to fifteen. Among other goals, one primary intent was to serve as feeder schools for the new programs in Jewish teacher training. Brickner notes the high quality of the selected students and recalls that "some of the best teachers in the entire system came from these classes" (58). Both in constituency and in scope, Jewish education had begun to open up to women.

Their entry into the profession would engender some conflict, however. Men continued to hold the leadership positions throughout this period. Rabbi Mordecai Kaplan, principal of the Teachers Institute (and later the founder of Reconstructionist Judaism), hired a staff of male teachers to instruct his largely female student body. Writing in 1928, he complained that "the proportion of male to female students was growing dangerously small"; he continued, "[A]s a matter of fact the decreasing number of boys that are taking advantage of Jewish educational courses is an evil that is flagrant already in the High School classes . . . the T.I. is apt to become a mere girls' seminary" (Kaufman, "Jewish Education," 583). Similarly, Samson Benderly, head of the Bureau of Jewish Education (and, like Kaplan, an adherent of Cultural Zionism), mentored a cadre of young graduate students to be the main proponents of the new educational approach. With a few exceptions, they were men and came to be called "the Benderly boys." Nevertheless, Benderly staunchly supported the feminization of Jewish education, writing in 1912:

If the Public Schools suffer from over-feminization, our schools, particularly the Talmud Torahs, suffer from over-masculinization. What a fund of love and devotion to Judaism lies dormant in the breast of the Jewish woman, and how little we have taken advantage of it. How much more stability would the Jewish home have, if, out of every fifty Jewish mothers, one had been a Jewish teacher, and twenty others had received a Jewish education. The penalty which our people is paying for its neglect of the Jewish education of its women is great indeed. Fortunately for Judaism, this false point of view is gradually changing. There is even now a slight demand for Jewish female teachers. The time will soon come when the Bureau will have to give attention to the training, on a large scale, of young Jewish women as Jewish teachers. (Kaufman, "Jewish Education," 583)

Though Benderly's prediction came to pass, few women attained the leading positions in the field. One significant exception among the original Benderly "boys" was a young woman named Rebecca Aaronson. As a girl in Baltimore she had been a student in Benderly's experimental school and later emulated her mentor in introducing Hebrew language study into the curriculum of Temple Emanu-El's Sunday School. Together with Libbie Suchoff (1891–1970), a new addition to the Benderly group, Aaronson organized the League of Jewish Youth and the Jewish High School Girls' Association, educational youth movements for Jewish adolescents. Since both women later married Benderly boys (Barnet Brickner and Isaac Berkson, respectively), their own stars may have been obscured by their more prominent husbands.

Nevertheless, a number of the "Benderly girls" did play a prominent part in another undertaking of historical import, the development of Jewish educational camping. Benderly acolytes Albert and Bertha Schoolman (1897–1974) first pioneered the concept with their communal Cejwin camp in 1919. Together with two other Benderly couples, Julia and Alexander Dushkin and Libbie and Isaac Berkson, the Schoolmans further refined the notion of a private summer camp as an ideal setting for intensive Jewish education. Camp Modin opened in the spring of 1922, under the supervision of the Dushkins and the Berksons. "Aunt Libbie" became especially identified with the camp, serving as director until her retirement in 1958. As the first Hebrew-speaking camp, Modin became the prototype for Jewish camps sponsored by every branch of the community, from Socialist Zionists to Orthodox Jews. The summer camp, replicating the Jewish home in its intimacy and the Jewish community in its comprehensiveness, has become one of the principal settings for contemporary Jewish education, owing in no small part to the contribution of women as camp founders, directors, and educators.

A related educational arena in which women also contributed significantly was the arts. Following John Dewey, Samson Benderly encouraged his charges to pursue the arts as an educational medium. Fanny Nimtzowitz (b. 1905) of Brooklyn, for example, graduated from the Teachers Institute and studied art thereafter; in the 1930s, she moved to Palestine, where she Hebraicized her name to Temima Gezari and later returned to teach art education and art history at the Teachers Institute from 1935. Five years later she became the director of the department of art education for the New York Board of Jewish Education (BJE). Her philosophy, which has had a profound effect on American Jewish education, is to use art to teach about Judaism and Jewish practice. Similarly, Dvora Lapson (1907–1996), also a Benderly protégée, championed the role of Israeli folk dance in Jewish education. Like Gezari, she pioneered the inclusion of her artform in the Jewish curriculum and came to direct a department of the BJE specifically geared to dance education. As Lapson wrote in 1952: "Jewish folk dance, both Israeli and European, plays an important part in any education dance program. Adolescents are particularly stimulated by the Israeli folk dances because of their vigorous and romantic character. Educators utilize this discovery for the creation of a firmer bond of confidence with the Jewish youth" (61). The premier figure in music education was Judith Kaplan Eisenstein (1909–1996; best known as the daughter of Mordecai Kaplan, who became the first bat mitzvah in history). She was the longtime instructor of music pedagogy and the history of music at the Teachers Institute. All three arts educators were also prolific authors of teaching material. Gezari illustrated educational books such as *Children of the Emek* (1937) and *Hillel's Happy Holidays* (1935) and with Deborah Pessin cowrote *The Jewish Kindergarten* (1944); Lapson produced recordings of Israeli folk dance music and developed curricula such as *Dances for Jewish Festivals* (1941) and *Jewish Dances the Year Round* (1957); and Eisenstein published *Songs of Childhood* (1935), *Gateway to Jewish Song* (1939, illustrated by Gezari), and *History of Music: The Music of the Jewish People* (1973), and many others.

Though excluded from administrative positions in Jewish education, many Jewish women exerted broad influence through the writing of educational literature, textbooks, and curricula. Women seemed to specialize in Bible primers, such as Edith Calisch's *Bible Tales for the Very Young*, Ethel Fox's *Bible Primer for Tiny Tots*, and Shulamith Ish-Kishor's *The Children's Story of the Bible: A Bible History for School and Home*, all published in 1930. Dorothy Zeligs was especially productive in writing Jewish history for the elementary grades, penning *A Child's History of the Jewish People* (1931), *A Child's History of Jewish Life in the First Sixteen Centuries of the Common Era* (1937), *A History of Jewish Life in Modern Times for Young People* (1938), *The Story of Modern Palestine for Young People* (1944), and many others. Deborah Pessin followed suit with the three-volume series *The Jewish People* (1951–1953) and *History of the Jews in America* (1957). Pessin explained her philosophy of teaching Jewish history thus:

Jewish history has been a creative history, a moving forward and development. To convey the essence of such a history, it must be taught creatively, so that the child feels himself a part of it, in harmony and in identification with his predecessors. But the feeling of identity cannot be imposed from above. It must be a development, through participation, within the child. The child must be not a recipient, but a participant. He must be a partner in the learning process. (8)

Other notable writers of children's literature in this period included Sadie Rose Weilerstein, Elma Ehrlich Levinger (1887–1958), Mamie Gamoran (1900–1984), and Lillian Freehof. Weilerstein became especially well known for her *Adventures of K'tonton* (1935), a charming story of the exploits of a diminutive Jewish boy. Levinger, wife of Reform Rabbi Lee Levinger, was exceptionally prolific, publishing titles such as *Jewish Festivals in the Religious School* (1923), *Passover Entertainments* (1924), *Great Jews since Bible Times for Young People* (1926), *Wonder Tales of Bible Days: Legends Retold for Jewish Children* (1929), *Entertaining Programs for the Assembly* (1930), *With the Jewish Child in Home and Synagogue* (1930), *Great Jewish Women* (1940), *Folk and Faith: The Confirmand's Guidebook* (1942), and *They Fought for Freedom* (1953). Gamoran was married to the leading Jewish educator in the Reform movement, (Benderly boy) Emanuel Gamoran, and herself wrote *The Voice of the Prophets* (1930), *Days and Ways—History of Jewish Holidays and Customs* (1950), and *The New Jewish History* (1953–1956). And Freehof, also married to a prominent Reform Rabbi, added *The Bible Legend Book* (1952) and *The Right Way: Ethics for Youth* (1957).

A dominant theme in this period, therefore, is the secondary status accorded women educators in relation to more prominent men. Women who would be rabbis, professors, or administrators in the post-1960s generation were then relegated to subsidiary positions and often obscurity. The phenomenon harks back to the turn of the century with leading Jewish educators such as Rebekah Kohut (1864–1951) and Henrietta Szold (1860–1945)—both of whom were daughters of rabbis (and in Kohut's case also a rabbi's widow) who became public figures themselves. Szold especially made her mark as the founder of Hadassah, the premier Jewish women's organization in America. Though they attained some prominence, Kohut and Szold were both confined to activism within the community of women, and like Rebecca Gratz and Julia Richman before them, they were unmarried throughout their public careers. Most female Jewish educators were also wives, however, and as such never attained the recognition due them. One telling example is that of Elsie Chomsky (1903–1972), whose biographer calls her "a major figure for decades in Jewish education in Philadelphia—teacher, mentor, and source of inspiration to Gratz College students and Hadassah women"; then adds that "she was overshadowed by her husband, noted Hebrew grammarian, author, and educator William Chomsky. Hence her significant contribution as a Hebraist educator, especially as a trainer of teachers, has not been adequately recog-

nized" (Feinberg, 172). Certainly, scores of other would-be leaders experienced much the same submersion of identity, and much research remains to be done before their stories can be told.

Contemporary Developments, 1960–2000

Between 1960 and the present, both the professionalization and the feminization of Jewish education have come to fruition. At the beginning of the period, enrollment in after-school religious programs still showed a marked imbalance between boys and girls. Of the estimated 261,287 total students enrolled in 1959, 71.1 percent were boys, as compared to 28.9 percent girls. The 42,651 students enrolled in all-day schools were divided 61.6 percent boys, 38.4 percent girls; yet in the more liberal Sunday Schools, the 249,662 students were divided almost evenly, with 50.5 percent boys and 49.5 percent girls. Teachers in the more traditionalist weekday and day schools were still more likely to be men, 63.6 percent and 69.2 percent, respectively, though the Sunday Schools were already dominated by women teachers at 64.2 percent. Of school administrators, fully 92.9 percent were men. These trends would soon change. Gender equality in the classroom became the norm by the 1970s. The feminist movement of that decade also helped complete the transition of the Jewish women from housewife and volunteer teacher to professional and Jewish educator. Both the earlier trends of inclusion in and expansion of the field of Jewish education proceeded apace during the following decades.

Jewish women at last attained positions of leadership throughout this period, an accomplishment often made incrementally. The career of Sylvia Ettenberg (b. 1917) is a case in point. A graduate of the Teachers Institute, Ettenberg began working at her alma mater in 1949, first as administrative secretary and then as registrar. During the ensuing years she took on many added projects such as directing extension school activities, instituting the *Prozdor* (lit., corridor) high school program, and supervising the Leadership Training Fellowship, a national organization of Jewish high school students. Yet only after 1960 was she promoted to ranks commensurate with her responsibilities, becoming dean of students in that year, associate dean in 1966, and crowning her career as dean of educational development in the 1980s. Another excellent case study could be made of the career of Sara Lee (b. 1933), who began in the 1950s as an assistant director of a college Hillel Foundation, directed religious school programs through the 1960s, began lecturing in education in the 1970s, and then, from 1980 to the present, has been director of the Rhea Hirsch School of Education at Hebrew Union College in Los Angeles, where she is also professor of education, teaching courses in curriculum, organizational development, staff development, and administration. A major influence in the field, Lee characteristically expresses her broad outlook in a focused message to students:

> Jewish educators for the 21st century are those who will create the institutions, the personnel and the programs which will continue the chain of Jewish tradition in ever-changing times for the Jewish people. The centrality of Jewish learning for building the Jewish future has never been questioned from antiquity to the present. Likewise, the role of Jewish educator in the transmission, interpretation and renewal of Jewish tradition has always been regarded as critical.
>
> We are living in a society and Jewish community where change is the one constant. In light of the centrality of Jewish learning and the changes in Jewish life, the Jewish people need creative, well-prepared, passionate and educated professional leaders for Jewish education. Many believe that the future vitality of the Jewish community is dependent on finding and educating such leaders to serve our congregations, day schools, Jewish Community Centers, camps and other programs. You can be one of those who will lead Jewish educational institutions in their critical and sacred task in the 21st century. (Rhea Hirsch School of Education, *Prospectus*, 2000)

The past generation has also seen the efflorescence of Jewish educational organization and programming on the national level. Whereas most organization in the earlier period took place on the local level of the communally sponsored Bureaus of Jewish Education, the greater American Jewish community has more recently taken up the cause of Jewish learning. One early effort was the American Association for Jewish Education, now renamed the Jewish Educational Service of North America, or JESNA, which was run throughout the 1970s and 1980s by Fradle Freidenreich, one of the better known of the new type of organizational women in the Jewish educational world. Freidenreich played a key role in several areas: in fostering innovative teaching methods and materials, in leadership development, both lay and professional, and in the area of integration—of Jewish and general subject matter in day schools, as well as the confluence of formal and nonformal Jewish education. Regarding the importance of national coordination and dialogue, she wrote: "The time has come for key people involved to discuss together the issues and problems underlying innovative efforts in Jewish education, to share materials and to evaluate, by way of media, some of the present classroom procedures" (1). Starting in the 1970s, the day school became the

fastest-growing sector in American Jewish education. By the end of the 1990s, some 184,333 Jewish children were enrolled in 676 day schools, the majority of which were Orthodox. While Orthodox day school faculties continue to be dominated by men, the flourishing movement for non-Orthodox day schools, whether Conservative, Reform, or independent, has often been driven by women. In a typical pattern, a Jewish preschool program run by women evolved into a full-time day school as the children grew older. The administrators of the preschool programs often became the principals of the new schools. Hence the non-Orthodox day school movement of the current period employs its fair share of women administrators (approximately 50 percent). Founders and principals of leading Jewish day schools have included Shulamith Elster of the Charles E. Smith Day School in Washington, D.C., Shirley Levine of the Heschel School in Los Angeles, and Metuka Benjamin of the Stephen S. Wise Temple Day School, also in Los Angeles. Across the country, the growth of the day school has provided increasing opportunities for careers in Jewish education, careers sought, more often than not, by Jewish women.

Jewish women teachers have further expanded the boundaries of Jewish education and have taken the lead in organizing on the grassroots level. In 1976, members of the Jewish Students Network convened the "Conference on Alternatives in Jewish Education." One of its organizers was a graduate student at the Harvard School of Education named Cherie Koller-Fox, who explained that "the basic conference philosophy was to offer as many of the alternative approaches to teaching in one particular area as possible, and to communicate that there was a wide range of choices available in Jewish pedagogy" (Hyman and Moore, 199). If Jewish education had earlier expanded its scope to the arts and to summer camping, the tendency toward informal education would now find public sanction and widespread appeal in the annual conferences of the Coalition for Alternatives in [later changed to Advancement of] Jewish Education, known popularly as CAJE. CAJE conferences are now major events bringing together a wide spectrum of Jewish educators who participate in workshops on every aspect of the Jewish curriculum. Not insignificantly, about 75 percent of the approximately 2,000 delegates each year are women. Without doubt, the majority of creativity and energy in the Jewish educational field today comes from the majority of Jewish teachers who are women.

As in the past, much of that energy is focused outside the formal setting of the school, and a principal setting of such "informal" education has become the Jewish museum. In American life, the museum has emerged as the primary forum for public education, and in Jewish life it has come to serve the critical ends of cultural preservation and transmission. Not surprisingly, Jewish women have played a major role in that process, as founders, directors, curators, artists, and patrons of Jewish museums throughout the United States. The Jewish Museum in New York City, for example, was established in its Fifth Avenue home through the 1944 bequest of Frieda Schiff Warburg (1876–1958) and was directed by Joy Ungerleider-Mayerson (1920–1994). Today, Joan Rosenbaum is its director, Susan Goodman its chief curator, Carole Zawatsky is director of education, and art historian Vivian Mann is scholar in residence. Across the country, in institutions such as the Skirball Museum in Los Angeles, the Magnes Museum in San Francisco, the Spertus Museum in Chicago, and the B'nai B'rith Klutznick National Jewish Museum in Washington, D.C., it is estimated that some 80 percent of Jewish museum directors and professionals are women.

In museums, cultural centers, and higher educational institutions, it is becoming ever more common to find teachers of Jewish religious studies who are women. This has been made possible by the growing number of opportunities for Jewish learning for women. Building on the model of modern, coeducational *yeshivot* (traditional schools for Jewish text study) in Israel, new programs have appeared such as the Drisha Institute in New York City, an all-women's school of Jewish studies. Drisha, as well as the numerous graduate programs in Jewish studies, enabled women to attain the same degree of Jewish religious expertise as men. In the modern Orthodox world, some of this tendency has manifested in the rising number of women's study groups and the incipient movement of Orthodox Jewish feminism. In the seminaries of the liberal religious movements of Conservative, Reform, and Reconstructionist Judaism, over half the students in rabbinical, educational, and other professional training programs today are women. Often they were inspired to enter the field by their college professors of academic Jewish studies—teachers of Jewish text such as Judith Hauptman and Aviva Zornberg, teachers of Jewish history such as Hasia Diner and Paula Hyman, and teachers of Jewish feminist thought such as Rachel Adler and Judith Plaskow.

Since women have moved into the ranks of academia, they now form a significant part of the elite cadre of theoreticians and graduate school teachers of Jewish education as well. At the Jewish Theological Seminary in New York, new professors of education following 1976 included Ruth Zielenziger, Magda Winter, Lifsa Schachter, and Carol Ingall. Currently teaching in the Seminary's Davidson School of Education, Ingall has become best known as an expert in the field of moral education. At Brandeis University, Susan Shevitz teaches education for the Hornstein Program in Jewish Communal Service, and on the West Coast, Isa Aron has attained prominence as professor of Jewish education at the Rhea

Hirsch School in Los Angeles. Shevitz and Aron—incidentally the daughter of Sylvia Ettenberg—have become leading figures in the new field of "synagogue transformation," a transdenominational movement to revitalize American Jewish life by concentrating on the synagogue. Together with colleague Sara Lee, Aron created and heads the Experiment in Congregational Education (ECE), a national program of congregational learning and renewal. Aron and Lee's ECE project thus intends to transform the synagogue through the medium of education; its "experimental" quality is the visionary application of educational theory to real-life conditions. As the academic field of Jewish education continues to grow, women are assured to be among its stalwarts.

Adult education is another area in which women have played a major part. Especially noteworthy are the "Melton Mini-Courses" in Jewish studies serving primarily women students and sponsored by the philanthropist/educator Florence Melton (b. 1911). Yet most Jewish education in this country continues to take place within the congregational community of the synagogue. Two trends in particular characterize the contemporary state of synagogue education—one inclusive, the other, expansive—a duality we have seen throughout the history of the feminization of Jewish education. The first development has been the revolutionary entry of women into the religious professions of rabbi and cantor—in the Jewish tradition, roles emphasizing the teaching function (indeed, *rabbi* is Hebrew for "my teacher"). Beginning with the 1972 ordination of Reform Rabbi Sally Priesand (b. 1946), women began to enter the rabbinate and cantorate for the first time in Jewish history. Since then, over 350 women have become Reform, Reconstructionist, and Conservative rabbis in America. Pamela Nadell, historian of this trend, notes that "as women, they offer a different model for the rabbinate . . . the female rabbis describe themselves as more approachable, prone to involve their congregants, and likely to speak sermons in a different voice" (Hyman and Moore, 1119). They are also far more likely to attend to the educational needs of their congregants. Most women rabbis and cantors tend to see themselves also as Jewish educators and often have some experience and/or professional training in the field. Thus synagogue life today, to the degree that its leadership has been feminized, is more often geared toward religious education and congregational learning.

The second significant new trend in the contemporary synagogue is family education. From the mid-1970s onward, synagogues around the country began to experiment with programs intended to educate the entire family, whether in parallel classes for adults and children, sessions in which they learn together, or in family retreats over a weekend or holiday. Often such cross-generational learning is offered in conjunction with family services, thereby further integrating the worship and study functions of the synagogue. A major initiative in family education was undertaken by Boston's Commission on Jewish Continuity when, spurred by the research of Susan Shevitz and directed by Carolyn Keller, it created Sh'arim: Gateways to Jewish Living, a communitywide program for the training and placement of family educators—thus creating a new profession in Jewish education and, almost universally, a new educational role for Jewish women. It is the quintessential example of feminization through boundary breaking. Not only have new roles been created for women in the educational sphere, but the sphere itself has been reshaped and reconceptualized based on the distinct experience and perspective of women. In the case of family education, it was a keen understanding of the centrality of family in Jewish life. In like fashion, women's energies will undoubtedly continue to drive the ongoing enterprise of Jewish education in America.

SOURCES: The most comprehensive source for the study of American Jewish women is the monumental *Jewish Women in America: An Historical Encyclopedia*, edited by Paula Hyman and Deborah Dash Moore (1997); see especially articles titled "Education of Jewish Girls in America," "Jewish Education," and "Teaching Profession." Citations of Jewish women's publications are gleaned from *A Bibliography of Jewish Education in the United States*, compiled and edited by Norman Drachler (1996). Other sources for the history of Jewish education in America include Rebecca A. Brickner, "As I Remember Dr. Benderly," *Jewish Education* 20.3 (Summer 1949): 53–58; Alexander Dushkin, *Jewish Education in New York City* (1918); Harriet Feinberg, "Elsie Chomsky—A Life in Jewish Education," in *Courtyard: A Journal of Research and Thought in Jewish Education* (1999–2000), 172–221; Fradle Freidenreich, *To Everything There Is a Time: AAJE Conference on Opening the School and Individualizing Instruction* (1975); Lloyd Gartner, ed., *Jewish Education in the United States: A Documentary History* (1969); Leo Honor, "Jewish Elementary Education in the U.S. (1901–1950)," *Publications of the American Jewish Historical Society* 42.1 (September 1952): 1–42; David Kaufman, "Jewish Education as a Civilization: A History of the Teachers Institute," in *Tradition Renewed: A History of the Jewish Theological Seminary of America*, ed. Jack Wertheimer (1997), 567–629; Deborah Press, "The Teaching of Jewish History," *Synagogue School* (September 1954); Dvora Lapson, "They Dance Together," *Jewish Education* (Fall 1952); Judah Pilch, ed., *A History of Jewish Education in America* (1969); Jonathan Sarna, "American Jewish Education in Historical Perspective," *Journal of Jewish Education* 64.1–2 (Winter–Spring 1998): 8–21; Marvin Schick, *A Census of Jewish Day Schools in the United States* (2000); and David Tyack, *The One Best System: A History of American Urban Education* (1974). Other secondary sources consulted for historical context are, for the nineteenth century, Dianne Ashton, *Rebecca Gratz: Women and Judaism in Antebellum America* (1997); Hyman Grinstein, *The Rise of the Jewish Community of New York, 1654–1860* (1945); and Bertram Korn, ed., *Eventful Years and Experiences: Studies in Nineteenth Century American Jewish History* (1954); and for the early twentieth century, Paula Hyman, *Gender and Assimilation in Modern Jewish History* (1995); and David Kaufman, *Shul with a Pool: The "Synagogue-Center" in American Jewish History* (1999). Regarding the contemporary period, the author is grateful to colleagues Isa Aron, Sara Lee, and Michael Zeldin for their generous comments and insights.

PROTESTANT SUNDAY SCHOOLS AND RELIGIOUS EDUCATION
Virginia Lieson Brereton

FROM THE BEGINNING of the Sunday School movement, Protestant women and the religious teaching of children have been intimately connected. Almost immediately—as soon as large numbers of instructors were needed—women dominated the ranks of the Sunday classrooms. This was not to say that, as in so many other fields affecting the church, women controlled the organizations, the funds, or the policymaking. Most likely a male minister and a male Sunday School superintendent oversaw their efforts—usually a prominent man in the church congregation. Furthermore, the best known Sunday School journals, which contained advice for teachers, were edited and written by men. Later on, with the rise of religious education as a profession and as an academic discipline in the early twentieth century, the most important posts in seminaries, colleges, and periodicals would be filled by men, while, as always, the teaching force remained largely female.

But the sheer numbers of women—both in the pews and in the classrooms—did make a difference. Women often had a good deal of *influence*, if not actual public authority. In fact, in scattered instances, especially early in the century, women involved in Sunday School work actually wielded power. As so often in the church, organizational independence was the key. The Female Union Society for the Promotion of Sabbath-Schools, founded in 1816 in New York City by Joanna Graham Bethune, had an autonomous existence until it had to be dissolved in 1828, thanks in part to the influence of the male Sunday School association. (Like the Female Union Society, most of the women-run Sunday School organizations would enjoy only a brief existence.) Furthermore, women often filled the vacuums that men did not want to or had not thought to fill. As Bethune had done, they organized Sunday Schools where they saw a lack. Women began to call for and create training for teachers; composed and distributed Sunday School materials for the students; and studied and publicized new pedagogical developments in Europe and the United States. The vacuums to fill—opportunities for women—have persisted throughout the past two centuries. Concepts of children have been revolutionized, as have notions of religiosity and the ways to engage the attention and assent of pupils. Women often noticed these revolutions first—indeed, sometimes they fomented them—and were the first to address them.

It is really no mystery why women became Sunday School teachers in such large numbers. While they were not supposed to speak or teach before mixed audiences of men and women, nothing forbade them from instructing children. In fact, by early in the nineteenth century women had been identified as the best teachers for the young in the public schools, or "common schools," as they were then called. After all, as mothers they taught their offspring more effectively and more regularly than fathers; for them to teach other people's children made sense as well. It did not hurt that women could be paid at one-half or one-third the rate of male teachers, nor that they had a reputation for being more amenable to suggestions from school boards and other school administrators. By the second third of the nineteenth century woman swelled the ranks of common school teaching, outnumbering men teachers. Many of the same teachers spent the week in the common schools, then taught religion on Sundays. If women were appropriate teachers of the young, surely they were even more suited to be their religious teachers. By the nineteenth century women were regarded as more "religious," more "spiritual," purer, and more virtuous than men, doubtless in part because men were increasingly leaving the home for business and industry, where their morals were assumed to be subject to corruption. A writer in the 1870s praised women for their "refined perceptions," for their "delicate intuitions," and for their "reverence" (Wyeth, 207).

The image of women had changed in the nineteenth century (from Eve or the wicked temptress Jezebel to saintly mother), and that of children as well. Once thought obdurate, sinful, and naturally inclined to wickedness—thus their wills needed to be crushed—children were increasingly seen as essentially innocent and susceptible to moral influence and good example, and thus they were not so difficult to teach after all. Women, given their gentleness, their earnestness, their beauty, and their patience, could easily win the hearts of children, even the toughest and dirtiest "street Arabs." If women were theologically unsophisticated, it did not matter, since children needed to be reached through their hearts and feelings rather than their intellects. The content and method of the early Sunday Schools were quite uncomplicated, consisting mostly of memorization of scripture verses. Women were expected to teach more by example, by *who* they were as consecrated Christian workers, than by *what* they taught. Indeed, one of their most important functions as a teacher was to visit their pupils in their homes during the week and keep in touch with them as much as possible when they grew older and left home, monitoring their spiritual and moral growth.

Men were of course highly desired as teachers for the Sunday Schools, especially if the students (or potential students) were boys. If the teachers were pastors, all the better. But by some reports men tended to be unreliable; they came late or not at all to meet their classes. They tended to be on the move from one community to another. And pastors were busy and, in any event, could teach no more than one or two classes. On the other hand, women had a reputation for arriving at teaching appointments promptly and dependably. Nor would they expect to be paid for their labor. Soon enough, it seems, a virtue was made of necessity: The Sunday School journals suggest that women were actually preferable as teachers because they spoke simply and plainly, whereas men often lectured in the class or prayed long-winded, complicated, excessively "oratorical" prayers. Already in 1855 there were signs that the Sunday School women were upstaging the pastor. A pastor J. A. James wrote, "I have heard of a case in which a pastor became jealous of his Sunday school teachers, because more were converted by their instrumentality than his own." It's clear he was speaking mostly of the women of the churches, for he had written earlier in the article, "The [Sunday school] class in our congregation has been singularly happy in the ladies who have superintended it; their ability being equal to the deep interest they take in [sic], and their intense solicitude equal to their ability. Their heads and hearts are admirably balanced in the work" (James, 62).

Another debit that men brought to the Sunday School movement besides their relatively low appeal with students is that often they did not perceive the need for educational change in a time of rapid innovation. All too often, it seemed, the very industrial and commercial leaders who endorsed the most up-to-date methods in their businesses sometimes preferred to run the Sunday Schools in the same old way as they themselves had experienced it as pupils. A fictional "Major Strong," featured in a journal of the 1870s, was described as a longtime Sunday School teacher at the largest church in "Onwardsville." Major Strong did not believe in Sunday School conventions, institutes, teachers' meetings, blackboard use, or literature. "I don't believe in Sunday-school papers," he demurred. "They recommend all sorts of innovations" (Latimer, "The Unbelieving Teacher," 129). It was a waste of valuable time, he grumbled, for him to learn anything new about teaching: "[I]t may be necessary for young men, but I have no need to study; I have been reading Scott's Commentary at family worship for twenty years, the same book my father read before me. What benefit could your talks be to a man of my age?" Major Strong is an "un-

It is really no mystery why women became Sunday School teachers in such large numbers. While not allowed to speak or teach before mixed audiences of men and women, nothing forbade women from instructing children. *Courtesy of St. Olaf College Archives.*

believer" of a troubling kind, and the author of this article concludes rather severely: "There he is in regular standing, year after year, a kind of perpetual Lot's wife, ever looking back to the days of the past, when no mention of lessons papers, teachers' meeting, no helpful hints disturbed the hour when classes repeated whole chapters without question or comment" (130). In the same decade a Mr. Slocum, a railroad director and investor in mining, is characterized as objecting to the same sorts of new-fangled notions, but on the basis of their needless expense; he wanted Sunday Schools to operate on the cheap: "The old-fashioned Bible and Catechism are good enough for me. All this money for Lesson Papers and Concert Exercises and all this stuff don't *pay*" (Latimer, "Does It Pay?" 83). Unlike the stubborn Mr. Strong, Mr. Slocum was brought around by the persuasions of "Miss Earnest," a Sunday School teacher in his church. Newly converted to reform, he ended up donating the funds for a Sunday school library.

Of course, it is not true to say that only women embraced reform and recommended investment in Sunday School education of the future. The male editors and numerous male writers of the Sunday School journals most certainly located themselves among the ranks of enlightened reformers as well, but it seems significant that those who controlled the journals were willing to credit the women with so much openness to new ways of doing things—and occasionally the persuasiveness to bring conservative businessmen along.

Indeed, Sunday School women learned a great deal about reforming pedagogical approaches from their association with the public schools, either as teachers, parents, former students, school board members, or all the above. Early in the nineteenth century public school and Sunday Schools had been intertwined, as Sunday Schools taught literacy, along with religion, in the absence of a public school. Sometimes Sunday Schools paved the way for the common school that would only arrive later in a frontier town or village. By mid-century, however, Sunday Schools and weekday schools were abundant enough in most places so that they more or less divided up the educational territory, the former handling religious knowledge and nurture, the latter dealing with the secular dimension. (Of course, *secular* had a different meaning then than it does now, and common schools diffused a sort of "nonsectarian," generic form of Protestant culture and values.)

First on the list of reforms was better preparation for teachers. Though by mid-century most common school teachers had been prepared simply by their own common school education, the ideal was coming to be an experience of two years in a normal school (as institutions for preparing teachers were called, the earliest having appeared in the 1820s). The Sunday School equivalent was the summer institute for teachers that became popular after mid-century, to which women flocked in large numbers. Another reform was the idea that a clean, well-lighted place was a necessity for a proper Sunday School—not the makeshift arrangements in the church basement, as often had been the case. Beyond that, reformers started referring to architectural schemes that would provide a special, functional place for Sunday School classes when a new church was being built—and ultimately, if the church was wealthy enough—even a separate building for the Sunday School. Yet another reform was the school library so devoutly desired by "Miss Earnest," at a time when many pupils had few books of their own and little access to a public library.

The educational reform engine was driven at a fundamental level by the ideas of the Swiss educational thinker Johann Heinrich Pestalozzi (1746–1827), who advocated a gentler, more caring pedagogy in which children's interest was appealed to, their curiosity in the world around them stimulated. Pestalozzi encouraged a turn away from strict reliance on texts, especially for very young children. Instead he recommended that children be given objects (blocks, pictures, living things) that would stimulate their senses and their emotions as well as their minds (this was called "object teaching"). Rather than being filled with information—told what they should know—children were encouraged to explore, discover things for themselves, become independent learners. Pestalozzi recommended a method of questions to students. Teachers had used questions as a pedagogical tool before, but they tended to ask questions that presupposed a "right" answer, and whose right answer might even be contained in the question. Under Pestalozzian pedagogy, the questions were supposed to become more truly open-ended, instruments of a voyage of discovery that was to be shared by pupil and teacher alike.

We see hints of Pestalozzian attitudes in Sara J. Timanus's outlines for the primary lesson, published in the *National Sunday School Teacher* of the 1870s. Timanus, a well-known Sunday School leader of the time, was addressing teachers of the younger children. Of "Lesson VI," based on Mathew 5:8, 9, she said, in part: "Jesus promised that some shall see God. See God! What a blessing! Who do you think will see God?" Then she addressed the teachers more directly: "Let the children speculate a little, then say they will see God who think only about good things; about Christ—they who do not let bad, wicked thoughts stay in their hearts. Lead the children to say, 'Such people will have pure hearts. They who keep pure hearts shall see God' " (Timanus, 58, 59). Timanus was hardly a full-blown progressive educator, for she was instructing the teachers to elicit designated answers. But she had also moved partway down the Pestalozzian route by encouraging teachers to use the language of children, to anticipate how children might conceive of a situation, and to invite children to express their thoughts along the way.

Pestalozzi's ideas entered the United States in several streams, but one of the most enthusiastic receptors was Edward Austin Sheldon, who founded the Oswego Normal School in upstate New York in 1861. The only woman mentioned on the program of the 1869 convention of the American Sunday School Association was a teacher from Oswego, Mary Howe Smith, who "taught practice lessons in her admirable way." This is all the report had to say about Smith, but we assume, from the way this statement is expressed, that Smith and Oswego—and Pestalozzian principles—were already known to the leaders of the convention (Editor, 163).

Not far behind Pestalozzi's influence in impact on American education was that of the German educator Friedrich Wilhelm August Froebel (1782–1852). Froebel's ideas gave rise to a preeminently women's reform, the American kindergarten. In the United States the first kindergartens were founded by women: Margaretta Schurz established the first one in Wisconsin in 1856, followed by Elizabeth Peabody in Boston in 1861. An early public kindergarten appeared in St. Louis in 1873, at the initiative of Susan Blow. Sunday School teachers of the youngest children quickly took Froebel's lessons to heart. A special champion of the extension of kindergarten methods to Sunday Schools was Matilda Kriege of Boston, whose articles appeared frequently in Sunday School journals, along with those of Elizabeth Harrison, a kindergarten expert from Chicago.

The Founding of the Religious Education Association

In one way, it is tempting to contradict the normal view and assert that the story of the Religious Education Association (REA) belongs at the end of the story of several decades of reform in the Sunday School, such as that urged by Sarah Timanus and Matilda Kriege and many others. The founding of the REA in 1903 represented the culmination of all these nineteenth-century reform efforts and in that sense is very much connected to them and is a monument to female educational efforts. On the other hand, the REA also was a harbinger of very different developments to come. Its organization greatly changed women's relationship to the Sunday School classroom and to the leadership of the religious education movement. In certain definite ways, the advent of the REA diminished the role of women in religious education. Historians of Protestant women have often interpreted the concern for the *profession* of religious teaching represented in the formation of the REA as a loss for women, in the sense that it seemed to privilege the education of men and to separate women more firmly than ever from the centers of power, authority, and even influence. In the case of the REA, professionalization often meant masculinization.

For instance, religious educator Sophia Fahs, one of the earliest women faculty members at Union Theological Seminary in New York City, worked in the shadow of George A. Coe on Morningside Heights, and in the early 1940s she was reduced to a one-course schedule because complaints had been received about the liberalism of her teaching and religious ideas. Women's historians sometimes see the 1890s as the heyday of women's public and political activity, followed by decline. The advent of the REA, with its considerable negative impact on women religious educators, would seem to confirm this view.

And yet the picture is more complicated than past histories have indicated. The REA brought women gains as well as losses. The organization facilitated the rise of the first women professionals in religious education—women like Fahs at Union, Edna Baxter at Hartford Theological Seminary, Adelaide Teague Case at Teachers College Columbia, and Mary and Lois LeBar at Wheaton College in Illinois. These women were professionals in the sense that they were explicitly trained for their academic careers, earned graduate degrees, drew salaries, and belonged to professional associations (like the REA), even if they seldom held top positions in those organizations. And fortunately for women, the REA did not professionalize—that is, become exclusive and dedicated to high academic standards—as fast as some of its leaders might have liked. Religious educators of whatever gender found it impossible to accrue the academic prestige of disciplines like systematic theology or biblical languages. Religious education, like education in general, remained a relatively humble profession. Thus, the "irregular" institutions, the Bible schools and the religious and missionary training schools for women—the earliest of which had begun in the 1880s—flourished well into the 1920s and were listed approvingly in the REA journal as allies to the colleges and seminaries in the struggle for pedagogical enlightenment. The first generation of women justifiably regarded themselves as professionals, even though they had not always arrived through the most orthodox channels. Edna Baxter, the first woman appointed a seminary professor (1926), had first trained as a Methodist deaconess. Sophia Fahs first raised five children and before earning her B.D. at Union Seminary at age fifty.

For several decades, an important ingredient of professionalization was familiarity with and appreciation for the thinking of educational theorists like Frank McMurry, William Heard Fitzpatrick, Edward Thorndike, and especially John Dewey. The fortunate religious educators had studied with Dewey himself at the University of Chicago or Columbia University, as well as with the lesser stars at Columbia's Teachers College. Or they had learned from Dewey disciples such as George Coe and Frank Knight Sanders. Dewey and company, as heirs of the Europeans Pestalozzi, Herbart, and Froebel, believed in the centrality of children's interests and natural abilities in determining a curriculum. They argued that children should be allowed to think for themselves. And they assumed that a "science" of education was possible.

Religious educators took the lessons of Dewey to heart. Sophia Fahs, for instance, who moved to Morningside Heights in 1902, was deeply stirred by her early months at Teachers College:

> Altogether this experience was more thrilling than any previous teaching experience I had known. When combined with the further awakening that came to my mind as a result of the dynamic courses I was taking under Dr. McMurry and others at Teachers College, and the visiting I could do in the Teachers College experimental and practice week-day school, I felt myself being born again. John Dewey's philosophy of experiential, exploratory and inwardly purposeful education interpreted by Professor McMurry came alive for me, and I became absorbed in the problem of how to adapt this educational philosophy to education in religion. (Hunter, 62)

As this passage suggests, Fahs went on to experiment with new ways of teaching Sunday School. Determining that the Bible was not a sufficient text to engage the interests and understanding of children, she tried out missionary and other kinds of biography, written at a young child's level. She thought long and hard about when might be the best age to introduce the concept of "God" (third grade, she surmised). She allowed her pupils maximum freedom and mobility in the classroom (and was criticized for her lax discipline by some who otherwise appreciated her methods). She introduced the drama, music, dance, and the fine arts; set her students on projects (e.g., a diorama, a model of the temple at Jerusalem), and took them on field trips (e.g., to a museum, a contemporary monastery, a prison—to advance a discussion of authority and punishment). She studied her own children and how they came to religious ideas. After her family had grown up, she went back to Teachers College and Union Seminary, where she acquired her B.D. and eventually her doctorate. In 1927 she joined the faculty of Union as lecturer in religious education and also became superintendent of the Union School of Religion. Until it closed in 1929 this school was the most visited and admired model Sunday School in the United States. Fahs left Union in 1944 and became a prominent Unitarian educator (she became a Unitarian in 1945).

Fahs's long life and career as a religious educator doubtless contained a number of triumphs and also some disappointments. As a teacher she was constantly elated and stimulated by new and successful ways to engage children in meaningful ideas and experiences. She was a professional in most senses of the word, and like her generation of female religious educators, she advertised her impatience with Sunday Schools staffed by untutored "amateur" teachers. She was ordained at age eighty-two on the initiative of admiring Unitarians. She left behind a large number of books, both material for use with children in classrooms and theoretical, methodological guides for teachers. But certainly her career suffered darker moments: Because of her liberal teaching her position as teacher and supervisor at Riverside Church was cut short, and she attracted the disapproval of Henry Sloane Coffin, who became Union president in 1926 and surely made her life at Union much harder. Of course, it is difficult to sort out what she suffered as a result of her religious views and what as a result of her gender. But there are hints. George Coe too ran afoul of the Union administration because of his liberality. However, Coe went on to a professorship at Teachers College when his position at Union became untenable. It seems likely that because she was a woman, Fahs's opportunities for prestigious academic and administrative appointments were more limited than Coe's.

It was not only theologically liberal women who found opportunities (and obstacles) in religious education. The LeBar sisters, Mary and Lois, studied under Rebecca Price at evangelical Wheaton College, and then as members of the Wheaton faculty they themselves taught hundreds of students in the 1940s and 1950s. Even here, the Deweyan influence was felt, albeit not as directly as at Union Seminary. The LeBars "pioneered in educational theory, arguing for a more 'child-centered' curriculum. Rather than present biblical facts from a podium, they emphasized the necessity of shaping the lession plan to the needs and interests of the individual student" (Bendroth, 87).

For a few decades the Bible Teachers Training School in New York City, founded at the turn of the century, was a bright spot for women preparing to be religious educators. (Later the name would be changed to Biblical Seminary and still later to New York Theological Seminary.) The Training School's founder, Wilbert W. White, set out with the intention of putting thorough Bible study at the center of the school's curriculum. He succeeded in making biblical scholarship respectable as well as popular, not through the teaching of the higher critical method, which it was thought led to religious skepticism, but rather through a "literary approach" to the Bible, which tended to be more appreciative and less historicist oriented than the higher criticism. Furthermore, White and his faculty welcomed laypeople, including women, into the student body. During the 1920s, also, White's institution succeeded in steering be-

tween the warring camps of fundamentalism and modernism. Thus, for a period of two or three decades, the Training School provided a well-regarded foundation in Bible study that attracted students across the theological spectrum. (Ultimately conservatives would find White's methods more useful than liberals, and a number of evangelical religious educators and biblical scholars traced their origins to the Training School/Biblical Seminary. Rebecca Price, who taught the LeBar sisters at Wheaton College, had originally studied with Wilbert White.)

The relative fluidity and flexibility of preparation and access available in the first decades of the twentieth century would not last. Ultimately it became clear to religious educational reformers that the training and Bible schools diverged from the regular academic track. Very few were graduate schools, at a time when *professional* more and more meant education beyond the B.A. or B.S. degrees. Some of these schools conferred only certificates instead of degrees. Most (except for the Bible schools, for particular theological reasons) would upgrade, or would disappear during the Great Depression—sometimes into other better-established educational institutions. The approved route for a religious education professional would turn out to be graduation from college and at least two years in a religious education department in a graduate theological seminary. The point is that the two or three decades after the founding of the REA at the turn of the century were ones of flux and fluidity, and as usual these periods offered women unusual freedom to maneuver.

The succeeding decades of the twentieth century were unexceptional ones for women and probably for Protestant religious education as well. The 1930s, taken up by economic depression, brought a shrinkage of religious educational efforts. During the 1940s world war took center stage. The 1950s, with their religious revival and booming birthrate, were bonanza years for church or Sunday Schools. In addition, the professional role of director of religious education was established in many big and wealthy churches. But even though there were signs of better things, the 1950s offered little opportunity for religious educational leadership for women. If the director of religious education position was prestigious and sufficiently remunerated, chances were that a man filled it.

In the 1970s, women started attending Protestant theological seminaries in much larger numbers. They often opted for the more prestigious ordination to the ministry over training in religious education. To make matters worse, many mainline Protestant churches have grappled with declining Sunday/church school enrollments and rising confusion about how to educate the young most effectively, given mounting competition from other societal "educators" like the media and also rising uncertainty about how much religious authority educators were entitled to invoke in classrooms. Women teachers were in a particularly vulnerable position, never having been credited with much theological sophistication or religious authority in the first place.

By a number of recent reports, religion has begun to engage larger numbers of Americans with new intensity. Contemporary religiosity is sometimes puzzling, often invoking the cliché about the superiority of being "spiritual" over being "religious" and the demurral that God is closer in the mountains or in a place of service to other people than in church. (This phenomenon is not entirely new in a nation of notoriously individualistic believers.) Furthermore, it is not really clear when religious seekers stop being Protestants in any meaningful sense of the term. Women, still marginalized from many of the centers of religious establishment, have been among the first to explore nontraditional vehicles for spirituality. It seems likely that if there is to be another reform period in religious education, one that will take seriously the new forms of religiosity and perhaps reconnect them to the more venerable roots of spirituality, then Protestant women and formerly Protestant women will once again play an important and creative role in this effort.

SOURCES: As primary sources and indications of the ideas of teachers, the journals of the Sunday school and religious education movements are invaluable, especially J. A. James, "The Pulpit and the School," *Sunday-School Journal*, April 18, 1855; The Editor, "The National Sunday School Convention," *National Sunday School Teacher* 4.6 (June 1869); Matilda H. Kriege, "Kindergarten and Sunday School," *National Sunday School Teacher* 7 (1872); Faith Latimer, "Does It Pay?" *National Sunday School Teacher* 7 (1872); Faith Latimer, "The Unbelieving Teacher," *National Sunday School Teacher* 8 (1873); Sara J. Timanus, "Outline Primary Lesson," *National Sunday School Teacher*; Mrs. Mary E. C. Wyeth, "Whom Shall We Gather In?" *National Sunday School Teacher* 8.1 (January 1873); Elizabeth Harrison, "The Child's Spiritual Nature," *Religious Education* 1.5 (December 1906); Richard Morse Hodge, "The Model Sunday School at Teachers College," *Religious Education* 1.4 (October 1906); and Ralph Bridgman and Sophie L. Fahs, "The Religious Experience of Pupils in the Experimental School of Religion," *Religious Education* (1925). For a biography of a Sunday School teacher, see Elizabeth Mason North, *Consecrated Talents: or, the Life of Mrs. Mary W. Mason* (1870; reprint). For secondary sources on the Sunday School/religious education movements, see Anne M. Boylan, *Sunday School: The Formation of an American Institution* (1988); William Bean Kennedy, *The Shaping of Protestant Education: An Interpretation of the Sunday School and the Development of Protestant Educational Strategy in the United States, 1789–1860* (1966); Robert W. Lynn and Elliott Wright, *Big Little School: Sunday Child of American Protestantism* (1971); Harris H. Parker, "The Union School of Religious Education, 1910–1929: Embers from the Fire of Progressivism," *Religious Education* 86.4 (Fall 1991); Stephen A. Schmidt, *A History of the Religion Education Association* (1983); Susan Thistlewaite, "The Feminization of American Religious Education," *Religious Education* 70.4 (July–August 1981): 391–402; and George William Webber, *Led by the Spirit: the Story of New York Theological Seminary* (1990). Helpful sources on Sophia Fahs are "Sophia Lyon Fahs," http://www.uts.columbia.edu/projects/AWTS/exhibits/fahs2.html; and Edith F. Hunter, *Sophia Lyon Fahs: A Biography* (1966). General background on women in American Protestantism is also useful, especially Margaret Lamberts Bendroth, *Fundamentalism and Gender* (1993); Margaret Lamberts Bendroth and Virginia Lieson Brereton, *Women and Twentieth Century Protestantism* (2002); and Virginia Lieson Brereton, *Training God's Army: The American Bible School, 1880–1940* (1990).

PROTESTANT WOMEN'S COLLEGES IN THE UNITED STATES
Kathleen S. Hurty

THE STORY OF Protestant women's colleges builds on the dreams and changing expectations of women yearning for higher education when little was available. Two hundred years after the founding of Harvard in 1636 by Puritan clergy for young men, the first chartered Protestant colleges for women opened their doors. The story of women's struggle for higher education in these centuries is shaped by the cultural and religious milieu—by Puritanism, by evangelical and progressive Protestantism and moral philosophy, by ideas of republican "true motherhood" for Christian women, by the Second Great Awakening with its religious revivals, by the abolitionist and the suffrage movements, and by the ever more evident threads of desire for gender equality.

The story touches on controversy—the purpose and appropriate curriculum for the education of women, women's capacity for learning, the best methods of educational reform, coordinate colleges or separate institutions, coeducation or single gender education, the question of standards and who sets them, the role of the churches in the collegiate endeavor, the essence of faith and learning.

The majority of resources chronicling the history of higher education in the United States, as well as those that focus on religious colleges, give short shrift to women's experiences and do not deal in any significant sense with Protestant women's colleges. Current feminist research is beginning to fill the gap, but much more needs to be done. The story is worth telling—women pioneers of vast skill, passion, and religious commitment forged a new day for women, providing a learning environment that not only fostered women's culture but produced impressive women leaders for church and society.

The Challenges to Women's Higher Education

Opposition to women's education was strong. The Puritans who settled the Northeast, Congregationalists and Unitarians whose beliefs grew from Puritan Protestantism, Presbyterians, and Episcopalians (rooted in the Church of England) had long felt the need for higher education for young men on American soil. So they established men's colleges in the region in order to train preachers and leaders, beginning with Harvard in 1636 and eventually including Yale, Princeton, and King's College (later Columbia University). These schools soon became nondenominational, but they had sprung from an evangelical piety that sought literate male leadership for the new colonies.

The benefactors of these schools, seeking a quality education for their sons, did not see the value of the higher education of women, whose duties were perceived to be in the home and whose bodies were perceived to be too weak to manage higher education. In 1873, Dr. Edward Clark, a retired Harvard Medical School professor, published a book titled *Sex in Education*. Fearful of the women who were demanding entrance to the university's undergraduate college, medical, and divinity schools, he argued that women who used up their "limited energy" on studying would endanger their "female apparatus," and those who embarked on education with the vigor of boys would strain their "vital organs." In a speech given in 1899 at the inauguration of the president of Wellesley College, Charles W. Eliot, the president of Harvard declared his views about colleges for women:

> Women's colleges should concentrate on an education that will not injure women's bodily powers and functions. It remains to demonstrate what are the most appropriate, pleasing, and profitable studies for women, both from the point of view of the individual and the point of view of society; and this demonstration must be entirely freed from the influence of comparisons with the intellectual capacities and tastes of men. It would be a wonder, indeed, if the intellectual capacities of women were not at least as unlike those of men as their bodily capacities are. (Horowitz, "The Great Debate")

While many argued that women were too frail to withstand the rigors of higher learning, still others argued that college education for women would reduce the number of marriages and the size of families, a challenge to a young nation.

The Roots of Protestant Women's Colleges

The roots of women's colleges can be found in the Protestant girl's academies and female seminaries (these terms are often used interchangeably—there is no distinction between them) of the early colonies, both in the South and in the North. Emma Willard (1787–1870), Catharine Beecher (1800–1878), and Mary Lyon (1797–1849) were among the pioneer women who struggled to establish schools for girls, using, among others, the arguments of "republican motherhood" to bolster their plans and to counter the men-only opportunities for quality collegiate education. In the main, they built on, rather than challenged, prevalent Protestant religious ideals—that women were to be submissive wives, be responsible for family and home, provide moral strength, and care for the religious education of their children, thus contributing to the general prosperity of the young nation. As Emma Willard noted,

> It is the duty of a government, to do all in its power to promote the present and future prosperity of the nation, over which it is placed. This prosperity will depend on the character of its future citizens, to form them such as will ensure their country's prosperity. If this is the case, then it is the duty of our present legislators to begin now, to form the characters of the next generation, by controlling that of the females who are to be their mothers, while it is yet with them a season of improvement. (Goodsell, 58)

Offering opportunity for women's participation in public life and thus stretching the mores of the day, teaching provided a natural outcome of women's interests in pursuing higher education. In a speech to the National Lyceum in 1835, Catherine Beecher, sister of Henry Ward Beecher, pleaded the cause of 2 million children in the new country without teachers and of multitudes of educated Christian women vainly seeking for schools in which to teach. She gave heart and soul to the work of securing educated women in the East willing to act as "missionary teachers" in the newly settled and "ignorant" sections of the West and South. Beecher raised money from influential Protestant women to provide teachers for the new schools. She sought cooperation in the development of these schools from religious denominations in an era when organized religion played a significant societal role.

While Willard's view was to reform the female seminaries, Beecher felt that new institutions—colleges for women—should be organized. Mary Lyon, founder of Mt. Holyoke Female Seminary, and later M. Carey Thomas (1857–1935), shaper and early president of Bryn Mawr, both strong feminists, put less stress on role dif-

These young Wellesley chemistry students seemed undeterred by Harvard President Charles W. Eliot, who had declared in 1899 that learning at women's colleges "should concentrate on an education that will not injure women's bodily powers and functions. It remains to demonstrate what are the most appropriate, pleasing, and profitable studies for women, both from the point of view of the individual and the point of view of society; and this demonstration must be entirely freed from the influence of comparisons with the intellectual capacities and tastes of men." *Courtesy of Wellesley College Archives, photo by Partridge.*

ferentiation between men and women and worked to develop rigorous educational opportunities for women. This diversity of views stimulated lively and often public debate.

Mount Holyoke (1837) as Model for Many

The dating of women's colleges is somewhat problematic, because most use the founding date of the institution, often called an academy for girls or a seminary for females. Those that evolved into full-fledged chartered colleges are the focus of this study. Current analysis suggests that some of these academies or seminaries actually provided rigorous collegiate-level education for females, often on a par with male colleges, but were devalued by historians who used the lens of male experience. This essay will use the founding dates given by the colleges themselves.

The leadership of Mary Lyons, whose path-finding creativity, passionate educational conviction, intense

evangelical enthusiasm, and tireless energy led her to found Mount Holyoke Female Seminary in Massachusetts in 1837, gives credence to this particular "first" among women's colleges. (The college uses 1837 as its founding date, although it did not call itself a college until later.) Considered as "most truly a daughter of the Puritans," Lyons was reared in a deeply religious home and adhered to a "strictly biblical" social perspective, pursuing her goal of higher education for women as a religious crusade. From the beginning Mount Holyoke's curriculum rivaled some of the best men's colleges of the time, including not only literature and philosophy but also science, mathematics, and languages. The courses were designed as an active response to the then-common belief that women were incapable of rigorous higher education. Protestant religious mores and benevolence undergirded the institution, which was founded to provide highly educated Christian women leaders for church and society. Lyons, relying on prayer and administrative skill, made Mount Holyoke into what became a successful model for many women's colleges established in the second half of the nineteenth century. These colleges, like Mount Holyoke, shaped the high quality of their educational mission around training Protestant Christian women to fulfill their duties in the home and family, to teach in the schools, and to serve as missionaries in the nation and to a broader world.

Matthew Vassar, a devout Baptist and successful brewer, was persuaded by Milo Jewett, then head of Judson Female Institute in Alabama (later Judson College, another Baptist institution) to create a school for the preparation of women teachers, following the Mount Holyoke model. He did so, endowing it generously. Sophia Smith, pious Congregational benefactor of Smith College, stated her purpose forthrightly: "It is my opinion that by the higher and more thoroughly Christian education of women, what are called their 'wrongs' will be redressed, their wages will be adjusted, their weight of influence in reforming the evils of society will be greatly increased as teachers, as writers, as mothers, as members of society, their power for good will be incalculably enlarged" (Solomon, 48).

Wellesley, too, followed the example of this early piety—the centrality of religious dedication seen as an enhancement rather than a detriment to rigorous learning. The cofounders of Wellesley, Henry Fowle Durant, a Presbyterian clergyman, and Pauline Adeline Fowle Durant, of Huguenot background, were passionate in their love of learning, radical in their belief in women's education, and strong in their commitment to evangelical Protestantism. They believed, as did Mary Lyon, that the Christian woman teacher could be an agent of national reformation. The opening announcement of the college noted, "The instruction will be Christian in its influence, discipline and course of instruction." They believed that Wellesley was "God's college, not ours." In answer to the question, What is religious truth? the response was, "What answer can there be but in the Great Protestant Faith?" (Glasscock, 17). The statutes of Wellesley provided that trustees, teachers, and officers of the college would be members of an evangelical church and that the study of holy scripture under faculty direction was to be pursued by every student each year.

Bryn Mawr was established with an endowment from Joseph Taylor, who gave generously for a conservative Quaker institution. With a purpose similar to Mount Holyoke, Vassar, Wellesley, and Smith, Bryn Mawr started with a strong commitment to moral discipline, the intention of training Quaker teachers "of a high order," and the pursuit of education so that mothers would be well prepared to train infant minds and character, making the home central. But Bryn Mawr's dean and second president, M. Carey Thomas, was of a different mind in terms of purpose. She was a strong feminist and, while not totally rejecting women's domestic

roles, focused primarily on the academic rigor she believed would make Bryn Mawr "the equal of the best men's colleges." So successful was she that Bryn Mawr "set standards of undergraduate academic competence that no male college would match for many years" (Jencks and Riesman, 302). Other women's colleges began, successfully, to choose this path.

The Seven College Coalition—"Seven Sisters"

Built, then, on foundations of excellence, committed to rigorous education for women, and organized to be nondenominational yet consistent with evangelical Protestant philosophies, these pioneer northeastern colleges—Mount Holyoke in Massachusetts (1837); Vassar in New York (1861); Wellesley in Massachusetts (1875); Smith in Massachusetts (1875); and Bryn Mawr in Pennsylvania (1888)—joined two other northeastern pioneer institutions within this Protestant mix, Radcliffe (1879) and Barnard (1889), and in 1926 formed the Seven College Coalition, also known as the "Seven Sisters" because of their parallel, to a certain degree, with the Ivy League men's colleges.

Barnard and Radcliffe differed in that they were formed as coordinate colleges—"annexes" to men's colleges. Radcliffe, with Unitarian roots, was linked to Harvard and at first offered classes taught by the all-male Harvard faculty, although later opening the faculty to women. Barnard, formed within a Protestant Episcopal milieu as a coordinate college of Columbia, became fully identified as a women's college in the early twentieth century, choosing to become a national institution and working to attract Protestant students from outside New York City.

The seven colleges had much in common with each other—a high curricular standard, a strong fiscal base, a large number of women faculty in most cases, and a sense of academic fellowship. Most, though overtly Protestant in design, were in actuality nondenominational, formed by dedicated individual Protestants, not by denominations. Their formation struggles differed, as did their religious commitment. Yet, as a group, the Seven Sisters illustrate a profound segment of the early history of Protestant women's colleges.

Early Pioneers in the South

In 1766, Moravians founded the village of Salem in North Carolina and took a lead in women's Protestant collegiate education because they believed women deserved a comparable education to that given men. Radical at the time, this idea stimulated sixteen girls and women to walk the 500 miles from Bethlehem, Pennsylvania, to Salem, North Carolina, to join the fledgling venture. A young woman—Elizabeth Oesterlein—was asked to become the founding teacher of Salem Academy. Salem College (1772) considers itself the oldest women's college by founding date. While it had a rigorous curriculum from the beginning, it was not chartered to grant college degrees until the 1890s.

Founded by another group of Protestants enthusiastic about higher education for women, Wesleyan College (1836) in Macon, Georgia, claims to be the oldest women's college by charter date. Citizen leaders of Macon developed a college with a liberal arts curriculum and an emphasis on the sciences—a progressive idea at the time. Chartered as Georgia Female College in 1836, the school granted its first degrees to women in 1840 and became affiliated with the Georgia Conference of the Methodist Episcopal Church in 1843, changing its name to Wesleyan Female College. While remaining a women's college, "Female" was eliminated from the name in 1917. Fully accredited in 1919, the school remains affiliated with the United Methodist Church.

While colleges for women had an early start in the South, development was hampered by a bias toward "southern belle" attitudes that prevailed in some, suggesting lower standards than their northeastern counterparts; by the fact that accreditation systems were based on norms established by men's colleges; by lack of money; and by their racial segregation. As Amy McCandless observes, "The earliest educational establishments in the region were the creation of various religious groups, and by the twentieth century, the major Protestant denominations had established at least one college for white men, one for white women, and one for blacks in every southern state" (8). The reality is that many southern women's colleges were quality institutions but were not heavily endowed (as men's colleges were) so could not afford the facilities and faculty salaries that were required for accreditation. In addition, they often served girls in the preparatory school levels while also offering collegiate education, but again, the ratio did not meet accreditation standards set by male colleges. In 1903, women's college presidents decided to form their own accreditation standards group and so developed the Southern Association of Women's Colleges, seeking fairness along with high standards.

The United Methodist Church has historic and ongoing relationships with four southern women's colleges: Wesleyan College (1836) and Columbia College (1854), both in Georgia, Bennett College (1873) in North Carolina, and Randolph-Macon Woman's College (1891) in Virginia. Methodists also started the Baltimore Women's College of Baltimore City (1885), the name of which was changed to Goucher College in 1910 and is now coeducational.

Randolph-Macon Woman's College was started in Lynchburg with encouragement and financial support from the Methodists because the trustees of Randolph-Macon in Ashland (a college for men) could not be persuaded to admit women. It became the first women's college in the South to be admitted to the Association of Colleges and Preparatory Schools of the Southern States. Randolph-Macon Women's College's early acceptance into the prestigious Carnegie Group of colleges speaks to the quality of the education offered from the beginning. Andrew Carnegie offered "free pensions" to certain colleges meeting specific criteria, one of which was "nonsectarian." This points to a tension over ultimate control of the college that is illustrative of many church-related colleges' struggles. In the *Encyclopedia of Southern Culture*, James Edward Scanlon tells the story:

> When the Woman's College met the exacting standards of his [Andrew Carnegie's] pension fund (the first school in the South to do so), the money came with a stipulation that meant the board would cease to be entirely Methodist. This stipulation raised the question, voiced by alumnus James Cannon, of whether the board or the Virginia Conference would own and control the [Randolph Macon] system. After a protracted, debilitating quarrel, the Virginia courts supported the trustees, but the moral victory was with the church. (Wilson and Ferris, 299)

Until 1952, all of the college's presidents were Methodist laymen from the academic arena, followed by two male clergy. The first woman president was chosen in 1987. Randolph-Macon Woman's College's Protestant roots can also be seen through the relationship between the college and the Young Women's Christian Association (YWCA), which provided a religiously based outlet for Christian young women to be involved in community service. This relationship was typical of a number of women's colleges, with YWCAs providing a spiritual dimension at a time when religious coursework and chapel services were decreasing or in some cases disappearing. Randolph-Macon Woman's College is an example of a shared historic and moral relationship with a particular denomination—in this case, the United Methodist Church—while maintaining legal separation.

Bennett College was established in 1873 as a black coeducational institution through the leadership efforts of newly emancipated slaves. The Freedmen's Aid and Southern Education Society of the Methodist Episcopal Church assumed financial responsibilities for the college. Since 1930 it has been a women's college related to and supported in part by the United Methodist Church that nurtures the development of spiritual and moral values, international awareness, and world citizenship.

Spelman College (1881) is a highly regarded college for women with a number of illustrious alumnae. Begun in Atlanta in the basement of a Baptist Church as the

Atlanta Baptist Female Seminary, the college was founded under the auspices of the Woman's American Baptist Home Mission Society. Two missionaries from Massachusetts, Sophia B. Packard and Harriet E. Giles, appalled by the lack of educational opportunity for black women, opened the school with very little money and with eleven female pupils, most ex-slaves, who wanted to learn to read the Bible and write. The two women went back to the North to secure a stronger base of fiscal support and met John D. Rockefeller at a church meeting, who gave a generous offering. The black community in Atlanta and the Negro Baptists of Georgia supported the fledgling school and helped purchase a new nine-acre site in Atlanta. On the college's third anniversary in 1884, Mr. and Mrs. John D. Rockefeller, Mrs. Rockefeller's mother Mrs. Lucy Henry Spelman, and her sister visited the school. Impressed, the Rockefellers settled the debt on the property. The college's name was changed to Spelman Seminary in honor of the Spelman family, activists in the antislavery movement. The Rockefeller support for the college continued, including money given for several major buildings on campus. Sophia Packard became Spelman's first president in 1888 when the charter was granted, and Harriet Giles became the second president. Spelman conferred its first college degrees in 1901. The first black woman to serve as Spelman's president was Dr. Johnetta B. Cole, elected in 1987 and retiring in 1997 as president emerita. Among the nationally known graduates of Spelman is Marian Wright Edelman, founder of the Children's Defense Fund and the first black woman admitted to the Mississippi bar.

The Baptists formed a number of other women's seminaries and colleges in the South. Among those still in existence are Judson College (1838) in Alabama, Blue Mountain College (1873) in Mississippi, Brenau University (1878) in Georgia—whose name means "burnished gold"—and Westhampton College (1836) in Georgia, now an accredited residential college for women within the University of Richmond. Stephens College (1833) in Missouri is also a women's college with Baptist roots, as are Hollins College (1842) in Hollins, Virginia, and Meredith College (1899) in Raleigh, North Carolina.

Mary Baldwin College (1842) in Virginia was the first for women organized by the Presbyterians. Started as a female seminary, it became a two-year college in 1916, and a four-year college in 1923, closing its preparatory department a few years later. Peace College (1857) was founded by Presbyterian elders so that there would be a school "of high grade" for women in North Carolina. Named for William Peace, a bachelor merchant who gave money and land, the college received accredited baccalaureate status in 1996. Agnes Scott College (1899) in Georgia, named for a spirited intellectually curious

Scots-Irish immigrant—Agnes Irvine Scott—is a tribute to this strong woman who valued family, faith, and learning. It was founded by a group of progressive-thinking Presbyterians in Decatur so that women could have a value-enriched intellectually stimulating education. Among the values the college believes prepare women for life and leadership in today's global society are a culture of honor, trust, diversity, and civility; the linkage of faith and learning; and religious and interfaith dialogue. These values are hallmarks of the Presbyterian heritage of the college.

The only women's college in Kentucky, Midway College (1847) was established by leaders in the Christian Church (Disciples of Christ). First known as the Kentucky Female Orphan School, the school prepared financially disadvantaged young women for teaching careers. Female orphans were seldom given even the minimal education offered other girls and women in the antebellum South and thus were destined to a lifetime of poverty. This progressive educational experiment, now an accredited college with a full liberal arts curriculum and a School for Career Development with a focus in business administration, continues its relationship with the Christian Church (Disciples of Christ).

Proliferation of Protestant Women's Colleges in the East

Heavily influenced by the commitment of educated women to high academic standards, moral discipline, and generous Christian service, yet often overshadowed by the prestige of the "Seven Sisters," other colleges for women along the Eastern Seaboard played an important early role in the higher education of women. Elmira College (1855) in New York was begun under the aegis of Presbyterians as a college on the pattern of Mount Holyoke Seminary, though with very modest resources, and was among the first northeastern colleges chartered as a separate college for women with standards of entrance and a curriculum equivalent to men's colleges. Elmira College became coeducational in the twentieth century. Wells College (1870) was established in Aurora, New York, by Henry Wells, the entrepreneur whose organizations include American Express and the Wells Fargo Bank. Wells insisted that the institution be "grounded in the Presbyterian faith." Nondenominational today, it remains committed to progressive thought, honor, and rigorous education for women.

Presbyterians also established Wilson College (1869) in Pennsylvania, through the generosity of an initial gift from Sarah Wilson, who thus became the first *living* woman in the United States to endow a college for women. Wilson College promised to educate young women in literature, science, and the arts, teaching them to think for themselves so that they could become "leaders instead of followers." Chatham College (1869) in Pennsylvania was founded by a small group of Presbyterian leaders meeting at Shadyside Presbyterian Church in Pittsburgh, seeking solid academic training for women. They named their institution Pennsylvania Female College, later called Pennsylvania College for Women, and then Chatham, beginning in 1955. While they have no formal continuing relationship with the Presbyterian Church, there is an active campus ministry at Shadyside. One of Chatham's illustrious alumnae is Rachel Carson, Nobel Prize–winning environmentalist and author of *Silent Spring*.

William Smith College for women (1908) in upstate New York was founded by the Episcopal Church as a coordinate college to Hobart College for men that began in 1822. The two colleges have the same faculty but award their own degrees, have separate deans, student government, and athletic departments, and maintain their own residential campuses. They differ in structure and philosophy from coeducational colleges, offering a particular focus on issues of female and male identity and competence in a setting that offers ways to face such issues both together and separately. A strong relationship with the Episcopal Church continues, while at the same time the college is now religiously fully inclusive.

Hood College (1893) in Maryland, with ties to the United Church of Christ, was established with the articulated desire to prepare women for lives of service both inside and outside the home—a radical idea for the time—and for the "cultivation and diffusion" of the arts, literature, and science. Five male church leaders of what is now the United Church of Christ met in Frederick, Maryland, in 1893 and successfully persuaded the Potomac Synod of the Reformed Church to establish a women's college below the Mason-Dixon Line. They appointed a young Presbyterian man to be the first president and called it The Woman's College of Frederick. The college was named Hood in 1913 after Margaret Scholl Hood, its most generous donor, who gave the land for the college. Hood continues to recognize its historic roots in the church. Cedar Crest College (1867) in Pennsylvania, like Hood College, is a women's college related historically to the United Church of Christ (UCC) and collaborates with other colleges through UCC's Council for Higher Education.

Lutherans in seven states, both North and South, took an early interest in higher education for women, participating in the humanitarian movements of the pre–Civil War years, such as women's rights, antislavery, and temperance, and opening at least fourteen female seminaries. In Pennsylvania, in 1838, the legislature passed a bill that incorporated twenty-five female seminaries, several of them Lutheran, and gave them degree-granting powers. Some Lutheran institutions for women survived the Civil War, operated collegiate departments, and later awarded baccalaureate degrees. After the war, the rapid expansion of the West opened up the need for teachers and other community service positions for women, and twenty more seminaries/colleges were opened. Irving College in Pennsylvania, founded by Methodists in 1856, came under Lutheran control in 1888, was governed for thirty years by Lutheran trustees, and served predominantly Lutheran women. Elizabeth College in North Carolina (1897) survived as a degree-granting institution until 1922, when its main building was destroyed by fire. Marion College for Women (1873)—a junior college in Virginia, the last Lutheran college for women—closed in 1967. All Lutheran colleges today are coeducational.

While a number of women's colleges began with a clearly articulated denominational perspective, others were equally clear about their *non*denominational, nonsectarian yet Protestant Christian perspective. Among these are Converse College (1889) in South Carolina and Sweet Briar College (1901) in Virginia. Douglass College (1918) in New Jersey is a women's college within Rutgers University (now a state institution), which was under the control of its organizers, the Dutch Reformed Church, up until 1920. The Young Women's Christian Association founded Hartford College for Women (1933) in Connecticut on the Mount Holyoke model, especially to educate poor young women in the depression.

Frontiers in Protestant Women's Colleges— Moving West

Educating women to be teachers became both a respected rationale for women's colleges and a national necessity as the growth in the number of academies and common schools was significant in the latter half of the 1800s. Westward expansion offered new challenges, with thousands of schools needed for the rapidly growing population. The growth and ferment within the university world itself drew women into its orbit as women sought to support themselves following the Civil War, their prospects for marriage having lessened because of the numbers of men killed in the war, along with the shifting interests of women in this time of national ferment. The post–Civil War period also drew women of an evangelical missionary mind-set into educating those released from slavery.

While arguments about the comparative values of single-gender or coeducational colleges continued into the twenty-first century, the opening of "men's" colleges to women significantly influenced women's higher education. Coeducation had an early start in the Midwest, and again, Protestants took the lead. Methodist missionary pioneers in women's education founded Oberlin Collegiate Institute in Ohio in 1833—calling it "God's college" and dedicating it to carry out God's cause on earth. Oberlin College was to become the first coeducational college in the young nation, opening its full college courses to women in 1837 and giving its first A.B. degrees to women in 1841. Oberlin remains coeducational and has also been a pioneer in matters of diversity, taking on the cause of abolition with enthusiasm and recruiting African Americans from its early days.

Rockford Female Seminary (1847) in Illinois was founded by Presbyterian and Congregational leaders to spread the intellectual and religious heritage of Puritan New England throughout the frontier. Modeled after Mount Holyoke, it became Rockford College in 1892. Building on Mary Lyon's ideas of a demanding collegiate curriculum and of preparing women for community service, Rockford spawned a number of alumnae who saw women's leadership in social service as a natural outgrowth of the moral and religious culture of the school and their academic experience. Rockford is the alma mater of Nobel Prize winner Jane Addams, pioneer of Hull House and the settlement house movement. Emmy Carlsson Evald, a well-known Lutheran leader, was also an alumna. Remaining a women's college until World War II, it became fully coeducational in 1958.

In the far West, the development of Protestant women's colleges is best represented by the story of Mills College (1852) in California. Again influenced by the Mount Holyoke model and founded by Congregationalists, the school actually began as a "Young Ladies Seminary" in Benecia started by Mary Atkins, a young Oberlin graduate. After purchase by Congregational missionaries Cyrus and Susan Mills, who had spent many years in the Pacific, the school was moved to the hills of Oakland in 1871 and named Mills College. Susan Mills, a graduate of Mount Holyoke, was a beloved dean and president of Mills for many years of its early history. Chartered in 1885, Mills College granted the first B.A. degree awarded to women west of the Mississippi River in 1889. The early curriculum matched Harvard's and that of several of the strong women's colleges. Degree requirements included Bible study all four years and in the senior year "evidences of Christianity." Mills stood for a "religious culture" but nonsectarianism. As was true of many women's colleges at the time, the aim of the founders was to establish a "Christian female institution of high order." According to Cyrus Mills, "In no way, we believe, can more be accomplished for a people and a country than in rightly educating those who are to become wives, mothers, and teachers; and hence shape the destiny of individuals and of the nation" (Keep, 60). Choosing the first trustees to honor its Christian (though nondenominational) motivation, Cyrus Mills fervently hoped that the college would not depend on any one individual but "abide a perennial blessing to the daughters of the coast."

A global perspective was present from the beginning. The experience of Cyrus and Susan Mills as missionaries in the Pacific (Ceylon, now Sri Lanka, and the Sandwich Islands, later Hawaii) stimulated strong feelings of international goodwill. The Tolman Band—a missionary society organized at the college by Susan Mills, along with a literary society and a natural history society—played a significant role for a number of years, inviting missionary speakers and contributing to varied social service enterprises in China, the Pacific, Turkey, India, South Africa, and Japan, as well as to local Bay Area causes. Later the Tolman Band merged with the YWCA on campus and after a number of years became the Mills College Association for Community Work. Divinity Church—the church built on Mills campus—had no organic connection with any sect or denominations. Members were bound into a church fellowship while on campus, holding regular Sunday services, and introduced to other churches when they left.

Issues Faced by Protestant Women's Colleges in the Twenty-first Century

THE COMPLEXITIES OF EQUAL OPPORTUNITY

In the late nineteenth century and well into the twentieth century, many small church-related colleges, originally formed to educate young men, began to allow women to enroll. While some may have deemed it just and right to educate women, the change may suggest less of a commitment to women's higher education than a need to bolster enrollment for the survival of the college and thus graft women onto the trunk of an already growing tree. The question of whether coeducation in this manner means equal opportunity for women within the educational system is still a matter for debate. Many departments are driven by male experience; many faculty members and the predominate number of board members continue to be male. While women have been pioneers and strong leaders in the development of both Protestant women's colleges and coeducational institutions, there are still many colleges who have yet to elect a woman as president. Curriculum is still, in many places, determined by and evaluated against standards set in male-dominated colleges. Ultimately questions of equal opportunity lead to the urgent need for transforming liberal education to take full account of women's dreams, aspirations, concerns, insights, and experiences. In this, women are taking the lead.

In addition, it is impossible to deny the impact of racism on women's higher education. Some religiously oriented colleges for women were not fully open to women of all races—a fact that diminishes the history of equal opportunity. Others, however, and that includes many on the list of Protestant women's colleges today, are working consciously to become fully racially inclusive.

RELATIONSHIPS TO PROTESTANT DENOMINATIONS

While many women's colleges do not call attention to their religious origins, others continue to acknowledge their historic Protestant roots. In their formation, mostly by individuals or groups of people associated with denominations, but not by the denominations themselves, the colleges made clear statements about their evangelical Protestant commitment and mission. They were usually equally clear that they were neither controlled by nor owned by the denomination of origin.

Currently, some colleges who honor their origins or the founding ethos of their institution are forming "covenants" with their denomination, recognizing a historical and ethical linkage but legal separation and academic independence. An example of the attempt to clarify current relationships is the *Education Covenant of Partnership* (2000) published by the United Church of Christ that reflects a "renewed understanding of partnership" between the church and its related institutions. The Presbyterian Church (USA) has a similar document, as does the United Methodist Church. Regional efforts to clarify relationships have also been helpful. For example, Randolph-Macon Woman's College coordinated an effort of the Methodist-related colleges in Virginia to state their relationships clearly in a document titled *In Stewardship*. Such clarity is welcomed. The spiritual health and well-being of young collegiate women has been both nurtured and respected in these relationships.

Protestant-Catholic ecumenical relations are now open and encouraged—another factor that should significantly enhance networking along a broader spectrum of church-related women's colleges. Protestant and Catholic women's colleges are likely to find more value in collaboration than was true in earlier times.

While some schools indicate relationships to the church appreciatively, others chose to hide or downplay linkages as they changed from church-related to secular institutions. But the shift away from founding purposes does not always mean total secularization, as is illustrated by a 1940 presentation by Constance Warren, then president of Sarah Lawrence College in which she discussed the global transformation under way. Noting that religious values of the older generation were under fire, while at the same time there was a yearning toward religion, she said:

> The modern college is meeting this universal need of youth in three different ways, all of them to my way of thinking preferable to a required course in Religion for all entering students. The first is by required thinking on basic human and social values in many courses and under many names. The second is by letting the questions of the students themselves decide the nature of the courses to be given in religion in any particular year. And the third is through individual guidance broad enough to include understanding of adolescent spiritual needs and problems. (Warren, 198–211)

Despite the general trend today to temper the evangelical Protestant impulses that fostered so many colleges, these very influences had an enormous impact on society in the United States. In an essay on the "Protestant College: The Integrity of Faith and Learning," Lloyd Averill (*A Strategy for the Protestant College* [1966]) suggests that the liberal arts in America are a legacy of Protestant involvement in higher education. Established on the premise that true piety and sound learning are inseparable, they equated sound learning with "liberal studies which were thought to inculcate intellectual discipline" (39). Women's colleges with a commitment to the integration of faith and learning build on and contribute to this legacy.

PLURALISM, GLOBALIZATION, AND WOMEN'S HIGHER EDUCATION

A number of Protestant women's colleges are well positioned to educate women in today's pluralistic global era. Long passionate about global missions, women's interest in global education seems a natural extension of such passion, although the move is toward partnership approaches to international learning. Educated women have become interested in networks with women around the world. Interreligious dialogue is taking root at many Protestant women's colleges as many of these colleges have opened their doors to women of all races and creeds. Clarity about the purpose of the college and the value of "particularity" in religious expression while honoring "universality" of understanding and respect is key. Protestant women's colleges can do much to stimulate interreligious understanding. Many of these colleges honor a spiritual imperative and seek ways to link faith and learning, while at the same time maintaining an authentic and respectful interreligious awareness. Inclusivity in terms of race and creed has become the norm for most women's colleges.

THE CASE FOR WOMEN'S COLLEGES

A large and persuasive body of research today supports the case for single-gender education for women. The development of leadership skills, the opportunities for full participation in all aspects of school life including student government, the palliative role of sisterhood, the values of local and global networking—all are perceived as benefits. The Women's College Coalition Web site (http://www.womenscolleges.org/) summarizes research showing that women who attend women's colleges excel in a number of ways. Their summary can be seen on a number of women's college Web sites.

An often-quoted researcher in higher education, Alexander Astin, argued in 1977, Single-sex colleges show a pattern of effects . . . that is almost uniformly positive. . . . [S]tudents become more academically involved, interact with faculty frequently, show increases in intellectual self-esteem, and are more satisfied with practically all aspects of the college experience compared with their counterparts in coeducational institutions. . . . Women's colleges increase the chances that women will obtain positions of leadership, complete the baccalaureate degree, and aspire to higher degrees. (Astin, 246)

A Carnegie Commission on Higher Education profile published in 1972 (Pace) finds that Protestant college alumni are influenced more than the average with respect to an appreciation of religion, aesthetic sensitivity, tolerance and understanding of others, broadened literary acquaintance, social development, an awareness of different philosophies and ways of life, an understanding and interest in the style and quality of civic and political life, an appreciation of individuality and independence, and the development of lasting friendships and loyalties. That is a list to surely warm the hearts of Mary Lyon, Elizabeth Oesterlein, and Susan Mills!

Graduates of Protestant Women's Colleges

North American culture has been shaped much more than is publicly acknowledged by the graduates of women's colleges and their significant role in training educational leaders. Little attention in feminist history has been paid to the contributions of the many women in the teaching profession, primarily because it has become devalued by considering it "women's sphere" work. In a challenging symposium paper celebrating Mount Holyoke's sesquicentennial in 1987, Geraldine Joncich Clifford observed that teaching has been, and remains, a mass experience of women, that it is the chief employment of educated women (as differentiated from "mere women's work"), and that teachers who are women have been, and are, strategically positioned to affect the lives of millions of young boys and girls, shaping schools for society's benefit. Women saw in teaching, she notes, an opportunity to lead a public life and put considerable energy into "organizing schools, dealing with community leaders, putting on ceremonies, collecting wages from cash-poor patrons, exercising control over nonfamily men, and providing for themselves" at a time when all of these activities were deemed inappropriate for women (165–182). Over the years, Protes-

tant women's colleges have contributed exponentially to this massive pool of talented women teachers whose lives and professional commitments have shaped the culture and the nation.

In addition to teachers, librarians, nurses, surgeons, scientists, politicians, clergy, lawyers, writers, and editors, Protestant women's colleges have produced a number of alumnae of specific distinction—at least three Nobel Prize winners; a number of senators, representatives, and federal judges; and thousands of presidents and executives of educational institutions, corporations, and nonprofit organizations.

Jane Addams, Rockford College 1881, was one of at least three graduates of Protestant women's colleges to receive the Nobel Prize—the others being Pearl S. Buck, a 1914 graduate of Randolph-Macon in Virginia, and Rachel Carson, a 1929 graduate of Chatham College. The religious imperative that shaped the graduates of these colleges focused not on narrow denominationalism but rather on the importance of living a life of service, thus building on and supporting the idealism of the young women graduates. In her commencement address at Rockford, Addams pictured "young women engaged in thought in the nursery: 'Let her not sit and dreamily watch her child, let her work her way to a sentient idea that shall sway and ennoble those around her'" (Solomon, 116). The settlement house movement, of which Jane Addams was the creative leader, offered the way for these privileged young women to become a public force for social change. Buck, author of *The Good Earth*, wrote in a letter to her alma mater, "We were very proud of our college. We still exulted when I was there in the knowledge that we were being taught what men were taught. . . . We came out ready to use our heads and accustomed to work. I have always been glad of that" (http://www.rmwc.edu/about/history.asp). In 1998 Randolph-Macon Women's College established an annual award in her name, believing that "her values are our values" (Dr. Kathleen Gill, President). Carson was an esteemed graduate of Chatham College, "who combined her love of the sciences and her gift of writing, becoming the inspiration for the modern environmental movement with her seminal work, *Silent Spring*" (Gretchen Fairley, Chatham College).

The Story of Protestant Women's Colleges Continues

The future of Protestant women's colleges is an open question. There is a distinct place for open-minded church-related colleges committed to integrate faith and learning in the rigorous academic liberal arts arena. There is an opportunity for institutions of higher education for women to continue to shape a curriculum that builds on women's experiences, fosters women's

Protestant Women's Colleges

Protestant affiliation or heritage is the common link of the women's colleges on this list. They are currently in existence as accredited four-year institutions serving women. Those on this list either acknowledge the church relationship or have historic roots in the religious perspective noted. There are no Protestant women's colleges in Canada or Mexico.

1. Agnes Scott College (1889), Georgia	Presbyterian Church USA*
2. Barnard College (1899), New York	Protestant roots—no affiliation
3. Bennett College (1873), North Carolina	United Methodist Church*
4. Blue Mountain College (1873), Mississippi	Southern Baptist roots*
5. Brenau University (1878), Georgia	Southern Baptist roots*
6. Bryn Mawr College (1885), Pennsylvania	Quaker roots—independent
7. Cedar Crest (1867), Pennsylvania	United Church of Christ*
8. Chatham College (1869), Pennsylvania	Presbyterian roots—independent
9. Columbia College (1854), South Carolina	United Methodist Church*
10. Converse College (1889), South Carolina	Protestant roots—independent
11. Douglass College (1918), New Jersey	Dutch Reformed roots—now state school
12. Hartford College for Women (1933), Connecticut	Young Women's Christian Association
13. Hollins University (1842), Virginia	Protestant roots—independent
14. Hood College (1893), Maryland	United Church of Christ*
15. Judson College (1838), Alabama	American Baptist*
16. Mary Baldwin College (1842), Virginia	Presbyterian Church USA*
17. Meredith College (1891), North Carolina	Southern Baptist*
18. Midway College (1847), Kentucky	Christian Church/Disciples of Christ*
19. Mills College (1852), California	Protestant roots—independent
20. Mount Holyoke College (1837), Massachusetts	Protestant roots—independent
21. Peace College (1857), North Carolina	Presbyterian Church USA*
22. Randolph-Macon Woman's College (1891), Virginia	United Methodist Church*
23. Salem College (1772), North Carolina	Moravian*
24. Scripps College (1926), California	Congregational roots—independent
25. Smith College (1871), Massachusetts	Protestant roots—independent
26. Spelman College (1881), Georgia	Baptist roots—independent
27. Stephens College (1833), Missouri	Baptist roots—independent
28. Sweet Briar College (1901), Virginia	Protestant roots—independent
29. Wellesley College (1870), Massachusetts	Protestant roots—independent
30. Wells College (1870), New York	Presbyterian roots—independent
31. Wesleyan College (1836), Georgia	United Methodist Church*
32. Westhampton College (1914), Virginia	Baptist roots—coordinate college
33. William Smith College (1908), New York	Episcopal Church*—coordinate college
34. Wilson College (1869), Pennsylvania	Presbyterian Church USA*

The following colleges are among those with Protestant roots but that have become coeducational and/or have closed (this listing is far from complete but is an example of major transitions).

1. Columbia College (1851), Missouri (closed)	Christian Church/Disciples of Christ
2. Elmira College (1855), New York (now coed)	Presbyterian roots—independent
3. Goucher College (1885), Maryland (now coed)	Methodist roots—independent
4. Radcliffe (1879), Massachusetts (coed, then closed)	Protestant—no affiliation
5. Rockford College (1847), Illinois (now coed)	Congregational/Presbyterian roots
6. Vassar College (1861), New York (now coed)	Baptist roots—independent

( ) = Founding dates provided by the colleges.
* = Independent but affiliated.

culture, produces women leaders, and taps the rich vein of gifts often ignored in crafting a global future for humanity. There is likely to be less stress on "Protestant" given the ecumenical strides taken in Protestant-Roman Catholic relationships. More will become "independent" colleges without religious affiliation while maintaining openness to religious studies and to an environment that values religious discernment and community. It is possible that religiously oriented Christian colleges for women will lead the way in establishing interreligious dialogue and globally focused communities of learning, while not losing their particularity as church-related institutions. Entering the public conversation in the twenty-first century, Protestant women's colleges—both those who now honor that linkage and those whose history was shaped by it—will no doubt continue to affirm the value of spiritual growth and development, the links between faith and learning, and the commitment to work toward a common humanity living together in peace.

SOURCES: Barbara Miller Solomon's *In the Company of Educated Women: A History of Women and Higher Education in America* (1985) is an essential counterpoint to earlier texts in the history of higher education and is a major resource in this essay. In addition, the following scholars pick up some of the gaps in the field: Geraldine Joncich Clifford, in John Mack Faragher and Florence Howe, eds., *Women and Higher Education in American History* (1988); Linda Eisenmann, *Historical Dictionary of Women's Education in the United States* (1998); Elene Wilson Farello, *A History of Education of Women in the United States* (1970); Jean Glasscock, ed., *Wellesley College 1875–1975: A Century of Women* (1975); Willystine Goodsell, *Pioneers of Women's Education in the United States* (1931; rept. 1970); Elizabeth Green, *Mary Lyon & Mount Holyoke: Opening the Gates* (1979); Alice Payne Hackett, *Wellesley: Part of the American Story* (1949); Helen Lefkowitz Horowitz, *Alma Mater: Design and Experience in the Women's Colleges from Their Nineteenth-Century Beginnings to the 1930s* and "The Great Debate," *Harvard Magazine* (November–December 1999), available online at http://www.harvardmag.com/issues/nd99/womanless.2.html (1984); Rosalind Amelia Keep, *Fourscore and Ten Years, a History of Mills College*, rev. ed. (1946); Amy Thompson McCandless, *The Past in the Present: Women's Higher Education in the Twentieth-Century American South* (1999); Mabel Newcomer, *A Century of Higher Education for American Women* (1956); George Herbert Palmer and Alice Freeman Palmer, *The Teacher: Essays and Addresses on Education* (1908); John Palmer Gavit, *What Are Women's Colleges Doing? A Reporter Visits Smith, Wellesley, Vassar, Bryn Mawr* (1923); Constance Warren, *A New Design for Women's Education* (1940), especially 198–211. Other sources not focused on women's colleges but offering some insight include Christopher Jencks and David Riesman's *The Academic Revolution* (1968); Alexander Astin's *What Matters Most in College? Four Critical Years* (1977, 1993); and Charles Reagan Wilson and William Ferris, eds., *Encyclopedia of Southern Culture* (1989).

Information on early church relationships of specific Protestant colleges can be found in the following books, although only limited attention is given to the discussion of women's colleges: Guy E. Snavely, *The Church and the Four-Year College: An Appraisal of Their Relation* (1955); Lloyd James Averill, *A Strategy for the Protestant College* (1966); Charles Robert Pace, *Education and Evangelism: A Profile of Protestant Colleges* (1972); and Richard W. Solberg, *Lutheran Higher Education in North America* (1985). The Women's College Coalition is a not-for-profit organization governed by a board of twelve member college presidents. Based in Washington, DC, the coalition represents the seventy women's colleges in the United States and Canada, sixty-two of which are members of the coalition. (The women's colleges in Canada are Roman Catholic institutions.) The coalition's Web address is http://www.womenscolleges.org/. The Web sites for most of the women's colleges have sections on institutional beginnings, achievements of alumne, and commentary on the values and culture of women's colleges.

WOMEN IN THEOLOGICAL EDUCATION
Jeanne P. McLean

WOMEN'S LONG HISTORY of participation in the congregational life of North American churches stands in stark contrast to the brief history of women in theological education. In recent decades, however, the number of women enrolled in theological schools has increased steadily; women now serve on the vast majority of faculties; women have achieved significant numbers among seminary administrators, and a small percentage have attained senior leadership positions. Although these positive changes for women occurred in a relatively short time, many of those who made this recent history find that women's progress in theological education has been slow in coming and hard won.

The single richest source of information on women in theological education is found in records of the Association of Theological Schools (ATS) in the United States and Canada, the accrediting agency for theological schools in North America. The Association began in 1936 with 64 schools and in the year 2000 had 235 member institutions that offered graduate theological study oriented to the practice of ministry. The seminaries, divinity schools, and schools of religion/theology of the Association are denominational, interdenominational, and nondenominational, urban and rural, and independent and university related, ranging in size from 19 students to over 3,800. The story of women's role and contributions to theological education in North America is embedded in the collective history of this broad and diverse group of theological schools.

Women's Entry into Theological Education

Women's access to graduate schools of theology was part of a long, difficult struggle for the attainment of women's basic civil rights, including the right to education, employment, and full and equal citizenship with men. During the mid-nineteenth and early twentieth centuries, women made notable but modest progress. In 1833, women had their first opportunity for higher education in the United States when Oberlin College admitted them for studies, albeit with important restrictions. As historian Rosemary Radford Ruether explains, "[E]ven then women were seen as falling under St. Paul's restrictions against public speech and thus were not allowed to speak in class. The first female valedictorian had to have her speech read for her by a male classmate" (Ruether, 270). Not surprisingly, as other colleges admitted women for theological study late into the nineteenth century, the number remained small. Historians often cite Christian teaching on the submissive role of women and limited opportunities for ordination to church ministry as significant deterrents to theological study.

At the turn of the century, women were active in many nonordained ministries within and outside the churches—they founded missionary societies and women's religious orders; they worked for moral reform through temperance movements; and they worked for social justice, ministered to the poor, and organized the women's suffrage movement. Even after 1921, when women in the United States were granted full citizenship and the right to vote, major religious denominations upheld the differentiation of men's and women's roles, denying women ordained status and full citizenship in the church. Although World War II made it necessary for women to work in the public sector, and even in churches, to fill roles vacated by men, these gains generally were not sustained in the postwar period. Not until the civil rights movement of the late 1960s and early 1970s was there a U.S. constitutional amendment that would guarantee equal rights under the law regardless of race or gender.

Although the civil rights movement had fueled the cause of women's equality and given rise to the feminist movement, educational and religious practices were slow to change. For example, although by 1900 many colleges and state universities had opened their doors to women, prestigious American universities, such as Yale, Harvard, and Princeton, did not admit women until the 1960s. Similarly, North American Protestant churches were slow to follow the postwar trend in Europe to ordain women, but by the 1960s and 1970s the practice was becoming more common in both U.S. and Canadian churches. While graduate theological education had been available to women in North America since 1889

at Hartford Theological Seminary, women did not attend theological schools in significant numbers until after 1970. Since that time, the number of women and racial/ethnic minority students enrolled in theological schools has slowly but steadily increased. These trends have occurred both in seminaries whose denominations ordain women and in Roman Catholic and conservative Protestant schools whose churches do not.

The reasons why women choose a theological education are varied and highly individual. In personal accounts women cite their love of the gospel, their conviction about the importance of education, and confidence that women have a significant contribution to make to theology and the church. Two personal stories illustrate these themes. The first woman was the daughter of a man who served as president of two small midwestern colleges before moving to the East to head a women's secondary school in Boston. She attended Wellesley College in the 1950s with a major in biblical literature and in the late 1960s received a doctorate in church history at the University of Basel, Switzerland. "I was raised with a belief in women's education and its importance.... Observing a woman president and senior administrators at Wellesley, I learned that women were quite capable of doing *anything*." Having married and returned to the States, she taught part-time at a seminary near her home, filled in one year as a sabbatical replacement, and in a highly unusual move, was invited to serve as academic dean following an unsuccessful search. This was the beginning of a lifelong career in theological school administration.

The second example is a woman who, after high school, entered a Roman Catholic religious order of women who served Catholic elementary and secondary schools, owned and staffed hospitals, and engaged in various other Church ministries. She entered religious life in the 1950s, impressed by the value placed on higher education for women and the opportunities for service that her order provided. In support of its educational ministries, her order sponsored several of its members for graduate study, both for masters and doctoral degrees. "While our particular field of study often was chosen for us based on the order's ministerial needs, we as women were able to undertake advanced study at a time when very few women outside of religious life had that chance." Women religious studied at both universities and theological schools. The high value placed on graduate education for women and the economic and moral support religious orders provided had an impact on the advancement of women not only in theological education but in other areas of higher education as well.

Women without such institutional support also began to attend seminaries in record numbers. According to the Association of Theological Schools, women comprised approximately 10 percent of all seminary students in the early 1970s, rising to 24 percent in the 1980s and to 35 percent by the year 2000. During the 1990s, there was a dramatic increase in the percentage of women students under age thirty and women students over fifty. The enrollment of women in the Master of Divinity degree, which in most denominations is required for ordination, showed a similar trend. Women accounted for only 5 percent of all Master of Divinity students in 1972, but their numbers rose steadily to 31 percent by 2000. Evangelical and Roman Catholic seminaries enrolled half of all women studying in North American theological schools. While some women who attend these schools may be members of denominations that ordain women, many are undertaking advanced theological study to prepare for a wide variety of church ministries.

By the end of the twentieth century, over 25,000 women and over 47,000 men were studying in North American theological schools, a 31 percent increase for women and a 12 percent increase for men during the last decade. Between 1990 and 2000, theological schools also experienced a dramatic increase in the enrollment of men and women of Asian, African American, Hispanic, and Native American descent. While the total number of men students was larger than that of women in all ethnic groups, the increase in the *percentage* of women outpaced that of men. Specifically, the enrollment of Asian men increased 90 percent and Asian women 169 percent; African American men increased 39 percent and African American women 126 percent; Hispanic men increased 33 percent and Hispanic women 74 percent; Native American men increased 36 percent and Native American women 179 percent.

Such changes in the overall profile of students pursuing a theological education had significant implications. The greater the gender and racial/ethnic diversity among those with advanced degrees in theology, the greater the diversity that was brought to the pool of candidates for critical leadership positions. Obtaining a graduate theological education became essential to the growing presence of women and racial/ethnic minorities in leadership roles in the seminaries, in the churches, and in society.

Women Faculty

When women entered the ranks of theological school faculty, they had opportunities to make significant and lasting contributions in several critical areas. As teachers and scholars, they prepared men and women for ordained and lay ministries, shaped their programs of study and formation, and engaged in scholarly work that contributed to theological discourse in the academy and in the church. Through these activities, women faculty played a vital role in bringing feminist perspectives to

the central issues and methods of theological scholarship and in forming future leaders for the church.

Once women had the opportunity to obtain a graduate theological education and earn doctoral degrees, they became eligible for full membership on theological school faculties. In 1971 when the Association of Theological Schools first collected gender data, only 3.2 percent of full-time faculty were women, compared to 20 percent in higher education generally. The most notable gain for women occurred between 1980 and 1990, when full-time women faculty in theological schools increased from 7.9 to 15.3 percent. By 1995, women reached 21 percent and have remained at that level through 2000. The percentage of women serving as part-time faculty, however, was nearly double the percentage serving full-time in theological education.

Despite these gains, women faculty did not keep pace with the substantial increase in women students who comprised more than one-third of students enrolled in theological education generally and as many as one-half in some seminaries. By contrast, faculties in North American theological schools have been and remain predominantly male. As a seminary president noted of her own experience, "[M]y role models along the way were all men. . . . For a time I was the only woman on the faculty. Eventually I became one of a handful of women to serve in a leadership position." Women students typically found few women on the faculty to serve as models and mentors for them during their theological education.

The story of women faculty is not fully told by numbers alone. Also important are such factors as whether they teach and do research in core theological disciplines, whether they have the same responsibilities and opportunities as their male colleagues, and whether they are promoted in rank and tenured at comparable rates. A 1991 study of theological school faculties reported that women lagged behind men on these important indicators of faculty status and influence (Wheeler, 13). The study found that women were underrepresented in proportion to their presence on the faculty in core disciplines such as Bible, theology, and ethics. Women also encountered more obstacles in their progress toward promotion and tenure, with a relatively small percentage attaining the highest academic rank. According to the Association of Theological Schools, the current pattern has been typical for women over the last three decades. In 2000, women accounted for only 14 percent in the highest rank of professor, compared to 25 percent in the associate professor rank, 28 percent in the assistant professor rank, and 33 percent in the instructor rank.

This trend, characteristic of racial/ethnic minority faculty as well, is commonly attributed to several factors. First, women and minority faculty members who serve disproportionately in the lower academic ranks tend to have heavier workloads than their male colleagues, especially in the areas of committee work and service, resulting in less time for the scholarship critical to their professional advancement. Second, women who have the primary responsibility for children and household have additional demands on their time. Third, gender and racial bias still may be prevalent in some institutions. Such factors explain, in part, why women have not advanced in rank in the same proportion and at the same rate as their male colleagues.

Even with these obstacles, the contribution of women to the intellectual, pastoral, and spiritual formation of future ministers and theologians, both men and women, was incalculable. North American women brought to the study of theology experience that differed socially, politically, economically, and religiously from that of men. This distinctive history provided a lens through which to reinterpret traditional theological study and brought women's experience into theological conversations. Feminist theology, born of the struggle for women's equality in society and in the church, also brought attention to gender inclusiveness, a redefinition of issues, and fresh interpretive methods to virtually all theological disciplines. The focus on globalization in theological education during the last decade had similar consequences for issues of race. The growing diversity among seminary students and the increasingly multicultural character of North American churches necessitated broader, more inclusive categories for theological study. While neither feminist theology nor multiculturalism were advanced solely by women and racial/ethnic minority scholars, both groups contributed significantly to broadening and deepening the theological conversation.

Women's Administrative Leadership

Women began to hold senior leadership positions in theological education in the 1970s, but the presidency eluded them until 1987 when Donna Runnalls became dean of the McGill University Faculty of Religious Studies in Toronto, a position equivalent to the chief administrator of an independent theological school. By 1990, three accredited schools had women presidents: Hartford Seminary, McGill Univesity, and Starr King School for the Ministry in Berkeley, California. A significant increase occurred between 1990, when there were three women presidents, and 1995 when fourteen women served as seminary presidents. In 2000, thirteen women comprised 6 percent of all theological school presidents.

Research in the early 1990s indicated there is no "typical" seminary president or common path to the office. However, findings showed the majority of presidents held an earned doctorate, usually a Ph.D., and nearly two-thirds had faculty experience at a seminary or church-related college. Theological school presidents tended to come either from the academy or the pastorate, and over 95 percent were ordained. In light of this research, the fact that women are underrepresented on theological faculties and in ordained ministries was an impediment to increasing the numbers of women holding presidential appointments.

Compared to the presidency, women served as academic deans somewhat earlier and in more substantial numbers. In 1980, six academic deans were women, half of whom were in Roman Catholic seminaries. By 1990, there were eighteen women deans, and in 2000, thirty-one women deans served in a broad range of seminaries. While these numbers indicate a fivefold increase in two decades, women still account for only 15 percent of all seminary deans. Since the academic dean serves as head of the faculty and the majority of deans come from the faculty, the small but growing number of women who joined seminary faculties during this period created a larger pool of women candidates for the chief academic officer position. The majority of academic deans had an earned doctorate and teaching experience, but in contrast to the presidency, ordination was rarely a requirement of the position. Consequently, the deanship was more accessible to women.

Although the percentage increase in women presidents and deans from 1970 to 2000 was noteworthy, the actual number of women in these senior leadership positions remained small. Taken together, only 44 women served as chief executive and academic officers at the close of the twentieth century, and women accounted for only 10.5 percent of seminary leaders in these two positions. Overall, women comprised about 33 percent of all administrators in North American theological schools, with the majority serving in midlevel positions and approximately half as registrars. The highest percentage of women administrators at all levels is found in mainline Protestant schools and the lowest percentage in evangelical Protestant schools. In 2000, the Association of Theological Schools indicated that women in both U.S. and Canadian schools received somewhat lower compensation than men in most administrative positions.

When women's leadership in theological education was measured by the number and percentage of women in senior administrative positions, the picture was both encouraging and disappointing. During the last twenty years, and particularly in the last decade, the *number* of women moving into senior leadership positions increased at an encouraging rate. In a relatively short time, women entered theological school administration at every level. The *percentage* of women in senior leadership positions (10 percent), however, did not keep pace with the overall percentage of women students (35 per-

Women began to hold senior leadership positions in theological education in the 1970s, but the presidency eluded them until 1987, when Donna Runnalls became dean of the McGill University Faculty of Religious Studies in Toronto, a position equivalent to the chief administrator of an independent theological school. *Courtesy of McGill University Archives, photographic collection, PR03544.*

cent) or women faculty (21 percent). Curiously, since 1995, growth in the ranks of women faculty and senior administrators in theological schools leveled off and continued to be outpaced by the steady increase in women students.

In a 1992 article on executive leadership in theological education, Barbara Brown Zikmund, then president of Hartford Seminary, asked other women presidents and deans about the character of women's leadership (Zikmund, "Walking the Narrow Path"). The respondents cited features commonly associated with women in the literature on leadership. For example, women tend to be people oriented and to have a more participatory style than men; they tend to be less hierarchical and more inclusive in decision-making processes; they are information sharers, rather than information collectors; women are less afraid to make mistakes than their male counterparts; and women who have managed a household and raised children while pursuing an academic career are experienced in balancing multiple tasks, an asset in administration.

Studies of theological school presidents and deans in the 1990s confirmed that many of the attributes and practices considered characteristic of women in fact have come to define effective leadership generally. One woman president interviewed for this essay noted that the consultative processes and participatory decision making that often characterize women leaders not only produced better and more broadly owned decisions but also served to foster inclusiveness and strengthen the sense of community. Many women who brought to their leadership positions an understanding of the long struggle for gender and racial equality also kept issues of fairness and inclusiveness on the institutional agenda.

Since the number of women serving as senior administrators reached a pleateau in the mid-1990s, many have reflected on the incentives and disincentives for women to move into leadership positions. Separate studies of seminary presidents and deans have documented the breadth and complexity of job responsibilities, the range of skills required, the rewards, burdens, and personal costs of leadership. Those who began their careers as faculty may be reluctant to give up a life centered on teaching and scholarship. Similarly, those in the practice of ministry may find theological school administration too far removed from pastoral service. Along with these sacrifices, some find themselves unwilling or unable to deal with the stresses of the job and its inevitable demands on their personal lives.

Do women and men differ in their reasons for seeking leadership positions? The answer is yes and no. A 1993 study of chief academic officers revealed that the three most important reasons both men and women deans accepted their positions were the encouragement of colleagues, their belief that they had the skills, and an interest in greater influence on academic and institutional decisions. Among the least important reasons were the higher salary and career advancement. Men and women also differed in some important respects. Being encouraged by colleagues and having the skills were more important to women than to men. Men more than women felt a sense of obligation or duty, and women more than men considered it part of their religious vocation or call. Once in their positions, presidents and deans reported many satisfactions, ranging from building a strong board and a financially stable institution to developing a faculty that could provide the educational formation needed for the next generation of church leaders.

The Leadership of the Association of Theological Schools

The Association of Theological Schools in the United States and Canada has welcomed women to the presidency of the Association and has sought gender balance on its staff and accrediting teams. Three women have served as ATS presidents since 1986: Barbara Brown Zikmund, then president at Hartford Seminary, 1986–1988; Diane Kennedy, vice president and academic dean at Aquinas Institute of Theology, 1996–1998; and Martha J. Horne, dean and president at Protestant Episcopal Theological Seminary in Virginia, 2000–2002. In recent years, ATS has added four women to its full-time professional staff, one of whom is African American.

In 1983, the Association of Theological Schools committed itself to expanding the contributions of women and minorities to theological education by establishing the Committee on Underrepresented Constituencies. The Association developed policies ensuring the participation of women and minorities in its own work and on its own committees and, in 1986, revised accreditation standards to encourage theological schools to hire members of underrepresented groups. As part of this effort, ATS sponsored workshops for women and racial/ethnic minority faculty members and administrators. In

the mid-1990s, ATS focused on the full inclusion of women and minorities in leadership, particularly in senior administrative positions.

The Association's efforts on behalf of women accelerated in 1996 when, with foundation support, it established a multifaceted program titled Women in Leadership (WIL). The program had among its goals the entry of women into administrative leadership positions within theological education. Evaluation of the program in fall 2000 indicated that its conferences, seminars, and professional development scholarships had succeeded in encouraging women to consider administrative leadership. The program built networks and created opportunities for dialogue among women aspiring to administration or serving in midlevel and senior positions. However, more work was needed to help women surmount the attitudinal and structural barriers to advancement that exist in many institutions. Even as the program has heightened the consciousness of the theological education community about the importance of women in leadership, the actual numbers of women in senior positions has remained level since 1995. With much work remaining, the Women in Leadership program won a place among a handful of priorities the Association funded through 2003.

Ongoing Challenges

When women leaders were asked to reflect on the recent history of women in theological education, they consistently noted two things. First, they cited the remarkable progress of women in recent decades, their increasing presence and vital contributions as students, faculty members, administrators, and leaders in theological education. Second, they acknowledged the long road ahead and the significant challenges that remain. As one woman dean observed,

> There have been many "firsts" and we're still dealing with "firsts" in so many places (i.e., the first woman tenured, the first woman of color, the first woman dean or president). What we don't have are many "seconds." Once a school has had a woman in senior leadership, they tend to think "We've been there, done that!" None of our organizations can say it's done.

Several challenges lie ahead. First, the representation of women and racial/ethnic minorities on the faculty and in senior administrative positions did not keep pace with the changing composition of the student body in theological education and the increasing diversity in churches and society. Since the dramatic increases in women faculty and senior administrators in the early

1990s, numbers have leveled since 1995. In 2000, women constituted only 21 percent of theological school faculties and only 10.5 percent of senior leadership positions. The thirteen seminary presidencies and thirty-one deanships held by women are few in number and relatively scarce when distributed among 243 theological schools in North America. The number of leadership positions held by African Americans, Asians, Hispanics, or other racial/ethnic minorities can be counted on one hand. Those who might consider senior administration find few role models of their own race and gender and opportunities for advancement extremely limited.

A second challenge, and perhaps the most formidable in 2000, was not only increasing the numbers of women in the ranks of students, faculty, and administrators but creating theological school cultures that are hospitable to women and racial/ethnic minorities and encouraging of their advancement. Once women and minorities entered the academy, did their work receive the attention and respect it deserves? Were they considered for faculty positions in the core theological disciplines? Did they have similar workloads and time for scholarship so they would qualify for tenure and promotion to the senior ranks? In the area of scholarship, was quality work by and about women taken seriously, engaged by those on the forefront of theological research, and published in respected journals? Was it on the fringe or at the heart of important theological discourse? Among administrators, were women limited to midlevel positions or given opportunities and encouragement to take on senior leadership roles? Some cite the progress women have made in recent decades as evidence of a gradual change from male-dominated institutions to more inclusive and accepting communities. Others believe that, despite some gains, "sexism and racism still exist covertly" in some institutional cultures.

Third, as a seminary dean observed, "The major impediment to women's progress is complacency." Another woman leader echoed this view: "Women should never say 'this is enough,' but rather, 'What can we do to move the conversation further.' Your gut tells you things are not changing very much." Several women leaders found that many young women in theological education today, for whom pioneering women have labored to pave the way, lack a sense of this historic struggle and a personal commitment to women's rights. In these relatively better times, many do not feel the urgency or need to continue the work for women's equality and opportunity. An experienced dean, whose own institution has worked deliberately over twenty years to achieve gender balance among all constituents, warned that "things will not change without strategic planning and intentionality. We can never rest even to stay at the point of the progress we've reached. If we do, we will slide back and lose our voice."

A fourth challenge is to encourage qualified women to plan and prepare for senior leadership positions in theological education. Several of the women who have become presidents and deans describe their move to administration as a combination of their own background and abilities and serendipitous circumstances. One woman considered her move to the presidency as "almost accidental." Another pointed out that "if certain people at a certain time hadn't opened doors for me and made things possible, this [move to the presidency] would never have happened." While being in the right place at the right time may have advanced the standing of individual women, it clearly does not provide a reliable path to the goal of gender and racial/ethnic balance in theological school leadership. The ATS Women in Leadership program is a deliberate effort to make women's access to leadership positions in theological education more widespread and predictable. This will take time to bear fruit. Even those who find recent changes a sign of progress wish they could hasten the process.

Another related challenge for women in theological education is overcoming barriers that still exist in religious denominations. Several denominations do not ordain women, and even among those that do, women often did not get coveted pastoral assignments and discovered a "stained glass ceiling" as they failed to advance at the same rate as their male colleagues. A woman president of a mainline Protestant seminary described with admiration the strong leadership of Roman Catholic women religious who, though unable to be ordained to the priesthood, have a long history of effective leadership within their denomination. She cited the recent example of Joan Chittister, O.S.B., whom Vatican authorities attempted to silence for her advocacy of women's rights in the Church. In June 2001, Chittister was defended successfully by the head of her Benedictine order and permitted to speak publicly at the Women's Ordination Worldwide conference in Dublin, Ireland. Whether the denomination was Roman Catholic, Protestant, or Orthodox, whether gender barriers were explicit or implicit, the question, as one woman put it, was this: "Within the confines of the denomination, how are women's issues being addressed?" The task of ensuring they are addressed effectively continues.

Whereas the progress of women in theological education has been significant, many challenges remain. In balance, however, the majority of women leaders are encouraged. Perhaps the best summation is offered by Barbara Brown Zikmund, an ordained minister in the United Church of Christ, who served theological education for twenty-five years as a faculty member, an academic dean, a seminary president, and president of the

Association of Theological Schools. Her personal witness to the changing role of women in theological education expresses gratitude and hope for the future:

[W]hen I went to seminary in the early 1960s there were very few women students or faculty. Today, although ATS members schools differ in their understanding of women's leadership in the churches, all of us applaud and benefit from the increasing numbers of women in theological education. Setting aside the ordination question, we agree that educating women for Christian service, variously defined, is worthy. We know that God is pleased and our schools are stronger and more faithful when they, and the churches, benefit from the gifts and talents of women—in governance, in administration, as part of our faculties, and (in most of our schools) as our students. I have lived through much of this change and I celebrate how far we have come. (Zikmund, "Reflections on My Twenty-Five Years in Theological Education," 24)

SOURCES: This essay was completed with the help of interviewees who participated on the condition of anonymity. Sources consulted include Rosemary Radford Ruether, "Christianity and Women in the Modern World," in *Today's Woman in World Religions*, ed. Arvind Sharma (1994); Barbara G. Wheeler, *True and False: The First in a Series of Reports from a Study of Theological School Faculty* (1966); Barbara Brown Zikmund, "Faculty as Scholars and Teachers," *Theological Education* 28.1 (Autumn 1991): 76–79; Barbara Brown Zikmund, "Walking the Narrow Path: Female Administrators in ATS Schools," *Theological Education* 29.1 (Autumn 1992): 55–65; and Barbara Brown Zikmund, "Reflections on My Twenty-Five Years in Theological Education," *Theological Education* 36.2 (Spring 2000): 23–33.

WHEN WOMEN ENTER THE CLASSROOM: THEORY, THEOLOGY, AND TEACHING
Barbara J. Blodgett

DO WOMEN WHO teach religion and theology in North America teach it differently than men? There has undoubtedly been a pedagogical shift in religious studies and theological education since women have entered academe, and many would argue that the shift is due at least in part to gender differences in teaching and learning and to feminists who have made deliberate changes in religion and theology classrooms.

Perhaps the best way to describe the pedagogical change wrought by women is to say that women's ex-perience has entered the classroom. What this means, first and foremost, is that women themselves have increasingly populated religion and theology classrooms and have thereby literally changed the face of religious studies and theological education. Seminaries, divinity schools, and religion departments have had to reckon with the presence of female students and take their distinctive needs and interests into account. For example, women students have asked for more female faculty so that they might have female mentors and role models. They have asked their professors to add texts by and about women to the syllabus. They have read and interpreted the curriculum—theology, scripture, history, and practice—from their own particular point of view. In all these ways, the experience of women has become more visible and important in religious studies and theological education.

But beyond the introduction of women themselves, female experience has changed the very way religion and theology are taught: Because female students have made a point of launching their intellectual inquiries from the standpoint of their own encounters and interests, experience itself has increasingly become both curricular content and method. For example, in addition to reading primary and secondary texts, studying historical accounts, memorizing words and actions, and honing skills, students in theology and religion classrooms are now reflecting on how texts have shaped them, examining the particular histories they have inherited, doing theology in their own words, and adapting traditional practices to fit their own contexts. All this is due in no small part to the new approaches women have brought to the practices of teaching and learning.

The pedagogical shift toward embracing women's experience finds a parallel in the development of feminist theologies and feminist approaches to the study of religion. In other words, theologians and scholars of religion have begun to think differently about the very category of "women's experience" at the same time as they have been incorporating women's experience into their teaching. In particular, scholars have wrestled with the question of how best to use concrete, everyday, lived experiences when doing theology and studying religion. How much weight should contemporary reality be given in comparison to ancient texts, long-standing and venerable traditions, timeless sacred symbols? In the earliest days of feminist theology (when one could barely speak of it as a discipline), it was enough simply to acknowledge the fact that in the history and practice of most religions women have experienced different realities than men. Then came a host of challenges to traditional religion due to its seeming inadequacy with regard to women's situation, along with creative new interpretations of religious experience from a woman's perspective. This was soon followed by questions about whether or not there was such a thing as *a* woman's perspective. Today, one might say that feminists have as many theologies as women have perspectives, and they struggle—in their scholarship and teaching—with both the benefits and challenges such proliferation brings.

Therefore, it is possible to trace the development of feminist thought on "women's experience," especially within feminist theology, and use the resulting map to follow similar developments in feminist pedagogy. One finds that just as scholars have struggled to articulate the difference women's experience makes to interpretations of scripture, God, humanity, and the church (and so forth), so too have teachers struggled with how to incorporate women's experiences into classroom discussions, writing assignments, group work, and other aspects of their teaching. And just as scholars—even those who call themselves feminist—do not all agree on how to take women's reality into account, neither do teachers all agree on how to honor students' experiences while maintaining the integrity of the educational enterprise. We shall see, therefore, that unanimity does not exist within the women's community, and there are problems.

The very first wave of feminism crashed upon the shore of theology by awakening (male) theologians to the number of women who were interested in academic study and preparation for ordained ministry. The first wave of feminism is often called *liberal feminism*—usually a secular term but one that suffices to describe early religious feminism as well. As a historical development, liberal feminism represents that phase of the women's movement that could be said to have peaked in North America during the decades of the 1960s and 1970s. Liberal feminism was (and is) characterized by a drive toward inclusion, that is, an intent to allow women into places previously dominated by men. In practical terms, liberal feminism may be credited with gaining women admission to schools of theology and religion and (in some denominations and traditions) women's ordination.

As a school of thought, liberal feminism is a response to classic liberal theory as defined by men. Liberal feminists modified the basic tenets of liberalism—the primacy of reason and the importance of the individual—to include women. They shared with classic liberals a belief in a thing called "human experience" that could be abstracted from everyone's various individual experiences across time and place. What liberal feminists did, however, was to expose the androcentrism, or male bias, behind what had long been taken to be human experience. They showed that "human" experience had all along really just meant men's experience. In other words, liberal feminists demonstrated that women had been left out of liberal theory. To correct this, they sought to incorporate women's experience into liberal-

ism. The individualistic, reasoning self, they argued, could be male or female. Women could reason just like men. They could do the same things as men. They should count as members of the human community the same way men do and share, at least in what matters most, the same experiences as men. Differences do not matter. According to liberal feminists, women's liberation would be achieved when women were made visible in the public sphere and had assumed their rightful place alongside men.

The next wave of feminists were dissatisfied with this way of thinking about gender. Called by several different names—liberationist feminism, essentialist feminism, experiential feminism (this author shall call it by the former)—the second wave was characterized by a belief in a special, separate category of human experience identified as "women's experience"—those things that all women go through in life, no matter who they are, that men do not. Feminists began to insist that experiences unique to women, such as childbearing and mothering, mattered just as much as men's experiences and equally defined what it meant to be human. They argued that acknowledging and naming female experiences, moreover, would instruct and liberate women.

In theological writing, the second wave of liberationist feminism can be detected as early as the 1960s and has continued up to today. Liberationists charge that liberal feminism is inadequate on several grounds, especially in its failure to recognize the distinctness of women as a group and their special nature. They point out that liberalism did not only leave women out but also failed to represent them accurately because it asked women to live up to basically male standards. They showed that the reasoning, individualistic "self" of classic liberal theory had been male all along, through and through. It could not suddenly become inclusively male and female. Liberationists protest that liberals are simply trying to "add women and stir." Instead, a full account of human selfhood must include a female perspective, showing that human beings are passionate *and* reasoning, social *and* individualistic. As the author of one of the first feminist theological texts put it: "It is my contention that there are significant differences between masculine and feminine experience and that feminine experience reveals in a more emphatic fashion certain aspects of the human situation which are present but less obvious in the experience of men" (Saiving, 40).

Accordingly, liberationist feminists challenge the liberal assumption that women experience the same things men do. Differences do matter, they contend. They find liberal feminist assumptions of gender parity and similarity to be false and argue instead that women share a common lot that is importantly different from that of men. When it comes to women's common experience, some liberationist feminist theologians locate its basis in biology, others in the dynamics of oppression. In other words, some argue that women share a common experience because women live in a female body, which shapes their nature. Others argue that women are bonded together by virtue of being oppressed by patriarchy—meaning, both literally and figuratively, "the rule of the fathers." Patriarchal rule, they say, is present and experienced in every woman's life, from her encounter with economics to politics to family to education. Liberation for women will arrive "after the patriarchy," that is, when all the structures of patriarchy have been removed.

In theological circles, liberationist feminism takes on special meaning due to its kinship with other liberation theologies, such as Latin American liberation theology and black theology, all of which recognize liberation as God's action of salvation for the oppressed. In liberation theology, traditional doctrines are named anew and shaped according to the particular contexts in which people experience God. Liberation theologians assume that religious experience will manifest itself in distinctly different forms, according to who is the experiencing subject. As feminist theologian Sheila Greeve Davaney argues, many of the early liberationist feminist theologians shared certain assumptions about women's religious experience without necessarily even realizing it. These assumptions include the ideas that (1) women's religious experience has a common core and (2) women's experience is a normative site against which theological claims can be tested (Davaney, in Chopp and Davaney, 198–214). Let us say more about each of these assumptions.

It was, and has remained, very important to liberationist feminists to insist on commonality among the experiences of the world's diverse women, for this shows that women form a distinct group and are *not* "just the same" as men. For one thing, naming a particular human feature as a female one serves to clear up longstanding theological misconceptions about women. For example, women's supposed passivity before evil may not be a sign that God made women inferior creatures but rather that passivity may be the particular form women's sin takes under patriarchy. Judith Plaskow began her 1980 book *Sex, Sin and Grace* by contrasting mythologies *about* women with stories *by* women in order to challenge stereotypes about female passivity and female "naturalness." "What I call 'women's situation' or 'women's experience' has two interrelated aspects: what has been said about women, mostly by men, and the ways in which women have experienced themselves" (9).

Identifying uniquely female experiences also sets women apart from men and highlights gender differences where none were previously noticed. "Women's experience" was a lever against the presumptions of male liberal theology, challenging supposedly universal truths about the nature of God and (hu)mankind. To demonstrate, for example, that women suffer at the hands not only of individual men but also of whole systems of male privilege changes the doctrine of suffering. To suggest that reforming the institution of marriage might be redeeming for many women changes the notion of redemption. Both become social, rather than purely individualistic, doctrines. Women's experience thus serves as a liberatory theological resource.

Many of the early feminist theologians also used evidence of women's commonality as a basis of truth against which the validity of ethical norms could be tested. If a doctrine did not resonate with the everyday, lived experience of women, then it needed to be changed or replaced. The logic went something like this: "If so many women experience X, that demonstrates something profound," it often became: "If so many women experience X, then any ideology that calls X wrong must itself be wrong." As *mujerista* theologian Ada María Isasi-Díaz wrote:

> Women's experiences are the locus and source of women's liberation theologies. Intrinsic to these theologies is a repudiation of universalist and transhistorical reason, hitherto elaborated and maintained as revelatory and normative by males and patriarchal structures. Instead, the daily experiences of women struggling for liberation have become the core of women's liberation theologies' critical norms. (95)

For example, feminist ethicist Susan Brooks Thistlethwaite raised questions about upholding the strict biblical laws on divorce in the face of the trauma of wife-battering in "Every Two Minutes: Battered Women and Feminist Interpretation." Lesbian theologian Anne Bathurst Gilson has challenged moral prohibitions against homoerotic love on the grounds that so many women experienced it as a good. Margaret Farley posed methodological questions about the relative authorities of text, tradition, and testimony. She argued for letting women's experience serve as a boundary around, if not judge of, interpretations of scripture and tradition that have ethical import for women's lives.

Finally, evidence of a unique and flourishing "women's experience" can be used to show the extent to which women have already been liberated, if only because they are able to name their own experiences *as women*. Naming female experience becomes the key to women's liberation, because it both justifies the need for freedom and creates solidarity among them. The lifting up and naming of experience has become a centerpiece in women's struggle for liberation and the naming activity itself salvific. Even if women's commonality lies in their oppression, by giving it a name one hints at a female experience existing beyond the layers of oppression and points eschatologically toward a time when women will rule, figuratively if not literally.

Religious hope thus lies in the identification and expression of that which is known through distinctly female experience. This idea led many theologians to claim that women possess a special way of knowing, a claim given support by researchers in psychology and education who study gender differences in learning. For example, theologian Rita Nakashima Brock has written about a special feminine form of cognition she calls "knowing by heart." She draws upon this idea to develop a feminist Christology. Brock repudiates liberal thinking because she explicitly contrasts knowing by heart with "male" reasoning—the former being subjective and passionate, while the latter is objective and detached.

Today, feminist theologians do not all necessarily share the assumptions that women's religious experience has a common core or that it has normative power. Yet another new wave of thinking is gathering force, this one characterized by doubt about the certainty of what we know and insistence that any conclusions remain provisional and multiple. Only in hindsight, of course, can liberationist assumptions be recognized as assumptions. Convictions about the uniqueness and value of women and women's experience have become so foundational that they practically constitute what it has meant to do "feminist" theology at all, and feminists who hold them have not necessarily made them explicit. Only now that these convictions are receiving direct challenge within feminist thought itself do they become more apparent—and, to many, more dubious. In any event, these are the very assumptions coming under fire within feminist theology today. Debate about them occupies, in fact, a central place within current feminist theological work.

As to the commonality of women's experience, some say that it is a short step from embracing the importance of naming and claiming women's experience to making it uniform. The temptation, and the danger, of this type of thinking is to gloss over the differences in different women's experiences in order to locate a common essence that is distinctly female. The risk is of ignoring differences of race, class, and other identities and of essentializing the category "woman," that is, falsely and prematurely identifying an authentic core to womanness. Therefore, one of the main criticisms leveled against liberationist feminists is, to put it crudely, that they merely replace *masculine* with *feminine*. Linell Elizabeth Cady writes:

This work clearly contributes to combating the fictitious neutrality in the myth of liberalism which helps to secure its hegemony. However, it does so by duplicating some of the moves by which liberalism achieves its supposed unity and universality. . . . Built into [it] is the propensity to secure unity through abstract homogeneity, a procedure that reflects the same ahistorical tendencies of the alternative it rejects. (21)

Similarly, feminists today are beginning to question whether women's experience can and should serve as a test for theological ideas. There are several concerns here. Some worry that in giving away too much authority to contemporary reality, the revelatory power of scripture and tradition is ignored. It would be as though today's concerns were given a trump card in winning theological truths. Such a shift in power bothers those who not only worry that lived experience may be fickle and flimsy (as compared to the relative stability of scripture and tradition) but who also object to theology that appears ungrounded in the historical texts and teachings of the faiths. Others question *whose* experience to use when experience is the test. Claims about God and humankind, they say, are supposed to be valid for the whole community, whereas privileging experience necessarily means privileging some women's experience over others'. Still other feminists wonder whether accounts of women's realities can simply be taken at face value. They doubt that human life interprets itself that easily. They question whether the meaning of women's experience is as readily apparent as it has been made out to be and emphasize instead its subtle complexities and nuances. They consider naive the implication that a woman's story comes vested with meaning, needing no further examination or interpretation just because she was the one to tell it.

Finally, some feminists have realized that it is disturbingly easy to win a theological argument by telling an alternative story from experience. Experience can always appear to "trump" theology. But what of those women who do not share the alternate experience? Do they have no trump cards, nothing to add to the theological enterprise? Or worse, have they simply been brainwashed by theological tradition? Feminism has begun to own up to its own rejection of traditional women's lifestyles and stories, its dismissal of them as unenlightened, unliberated people who "just don't get it." Mary McClintock Fulkerson, a theologian who has studied the experience of nonfeminist women who "fail" to see the sexism in scripture, exposes the arrogant disregard behind some feminist logic:

We would have to assume that women who do not agree with [feminist] accounts are lobotomized by distorted discourse. Even an account that explains divergence by assuming women do not know how they are oppressed cannot be satisfied with the implication that women are rendered utterly passive as readers of the tradition. (57)

As Fulkerson recognizes, the problem posed by some women's persistently nonfeminist attitudes only begs the question of what is finally "true" in women's reality. Is it accurate and fair to say that the real truth of their lives lies below a layer of ignorance and denial? She does not conclude that women's experience is a worthless category or that appeals to it can never be made. Rather, any such appeals must be modest and contextual and always open to interpretation. "My quarrel is with the notion that our knowledge of ourselves is the essentially correct reflection, a mimesis, of our real and true selves" (27).

The third wave in feminist theology, then, is a feminism that challenges other feminist assumptions about women's experience. It unmasks long-standing, even cherished, feminist beliefs and argues that they are too "felicitous" (to use Davaney's term), that is, naive and convenient. The third wave in feminist theology, not surprisingly, embraces postmodern and poststructuralist thought, that is, schools of thought that embrace ever-shifting, multiplex, socially constructed definitions of human experience. Postmodernists and poststructuralists are very suspicious of universal claims about identity and subjectivity. They would argue that the meaning of any account arises from and depends utterly on its particular context and that therefore no sweeping claims about what women experience are possible. According to this kind of thought, all accounts are limited, provisional, and complex. The meaning of experience is, so to speak, perpetually up for grabs. Among women, no single "women's perspective" can ever be held for very long because perspective is plural, and all perspectives potentially conflict.

Not all feminists embrace this wave of thought. Many feminist theologians still subscribe to and actively defend liberationist convictions about women and experience. The reason these convictions still hold sway is that many feminists recognize that to assume their utter opposite would be unwise and even dangerous for feminism. In other words, to assume that different women have nothing at all in common, that there is no normative wisdom to be gained from examining women's perspectives, and that theological doctrines are to be understood completely apart from women's stories would be to void the categories of "women" and "experience," to invite nihilism and relativism, and to risk returning to an era when women's experience was paid no heed at all. Therefore, while strong versions of these claims are increasingly rejected, weaker versions do still find acceptance. This mix of feminist approaches to the use of experience makes the current state of feminist teaching and scholarship in religion a lively one.

If feminist efforts to honor women's experience have moved beyond the attempt to "add women and stir" to the creation of whole new theologies from a female perspective, and still beyond to a recognition that women's perspectives are multiple and diverse, feminist efforts to transform the classroom have similarly matured over time. We shall now trace some of the developments in feminist teaching, primarily within theological education, to see how the more theoretical debates within feminism are played out in actual, concrete settings.

Earliest attempts to integrate women into religion and theology education concentrated on filling the most obvious gaps: recruiting women for faculty positions, adding new courses to the curriculum, supplementing course syllabi with feminist texts, and occasionally creating whole new programs in women and religion, in the form either of centers within schools and departments or independent institutions.

While feminists hailed these developments as positive, they quickly realized that they did not go far enough in terms of genuinely including women or making a real impact on theological education. Some feminists became dissatisfied and strove to create more significant change. For example, in 1980, a group of educators gathered at the Grail Center in Cornwall-on-Hudson, New York, for a consultation on the state of theological education. Working papers from the consultation were subsequently published in a book titled *Your Daughters Shall Prophesy: Feminist Alternatives in Theological Education*. The first paper in this book summarizes the impact feminism was judged to have made by 1980. Its assessment is quite critical of theological education at the time:

> As feminists, we have become increasingly aware of the ways in which women are outsiders to the process of theological education. We are not only physically outside, excluded from positions of power such as faculty appointments and top administrative positions; we are psychically outside because our history and experience are not taken seriously. . . . Questions raised by women, blacks, Hispanics, Native Americans, and the poor are seen as peripheral. . . . There are courses in "New Testament" and "Women in the New Testament," in "Church History" and "Women in Church History," but basic educational questions are not addressed. (4–5)

The Cornwall Collective, representative of many women in the field, insisted that truly feminist theological education meant more than adding a few tokens of feminism here and there. They articulated a set of feminist educational assumptions that, if fully realized, would transform theological education into what they called a "wholistic process." Their vision was (1) that disciplinary divisions become less rigid, so that learners could make interconnections between subjects; (2) that intellectual formation and skill development be integrated, so that learning would be experiential as well as purely cognitive; (3) that students become self-directed, charting their own learning; and (4) that education be recognized for the social and political enterprise that it is, capable of raising students' level of consciousness as well as knowledge. The model of theological education emerging from this set of goals would look quite different from the status quo. It would involve changes to the content, methods, and structures of teaching and learning. The Cornwall Collective authors concluded:

> If seminary curricula were interdisciplinary, experiential, self-directed, consciousness-raising, and collaborative—in other words, in the *eschaton*—what would happen to its "subjects"? Will our curriculum be radically new, or will we pour the old subjects into new wineskins? Probably that question cannot be answered, or even addressed effectively, until more changes have been made, perhaps because we, too, have been trained in the old schools. (11)

After 1980, more changes were, in fact, made, and a new generation of women began to influence educational processes. While frequently still themselves "trained in the old schools," they began to experiment with new forms of teaching, often spurred on by their students. Womanist theologian Kelly Brown Douglas, for example, described her own development as a teacher in an article for the 1992 issue of the *Journal of Feminist Studies in Religion*:

> Two years ago I anxiously prepared to teach womanist theology for the first time. My own theological training never provided me with an opportunity to do course work that involved any serious reflection on Black women's experience.... The pedagogy I initially adopted had great potential for failure. It promised to kill any enthusiasim the students might have brought to the class with them. ... Fortunately, those who entered my course were not passive learners.... Within three class sessions, "Womanist Theology" was transformed from [my original] format to one that was dialogical and interactive. In the process of this transformation I learned how to teach a course such as womanist theology. (133–134)

Douglas discovered that any course purporting to use a liberatory pedagogy must create for students three kinds of encounters. Students must encounter history ("It is through this dialogue that they can discover that their own struggle is not simply personal, but reflects a wider historical experience"). They must encounter actual women outside academe ("A womanist theology class must go beyond the four walls of the academy . . . and enter the places where Black women are actively resisting their families' and communities' oppression"). Finally, they must encounter each other ("In order to honestly confront their 'history of relationships' they have to share how that history shapes who they are and how they relate to each other"). As a result of these pedagogical discoveries, Douglas wrote that her teaching had been transformed. She changed everything from the way she seated students (now in a circle) to how she ran class (now as a seminar) to the methods she used (now taking students regularly on field trips into the local black community).

This is just one example of how a woman teaching religion put into practice the feminist assumptions that students should direct their own learning, collaborate with one another and with the teacher, widen the boundaries of learning beyond books and classrooms, and gain knowledge that is simultaneously personal and political. As women continued to gain experience (and numbers) as teachers, these assumptions and methodologies increasingly came to characterize the way they taught.

Developments in feminist teaching, it should be pointed out, coincided with a wider movement in education toward liberatory pedagogies, especially inspired by the work of Paulo Freire. Freire was a Brazilian educator who developed his methodology for teaching the illiterate poor in Brazil into a comprehensive educational philosophy. Born in 1921 into the middle class, his family fell into poverty, and he learned firsthand of the despair and passivity of the dispossessed. From then on he dedicated himself to methods of education that would contribute to their liberation from poverty. Freire's "pedagogy of the oppressed" transforms silence into critique and powerlessness into empowerment; through it people learn to name their world. Freire's ideas represented a radical departure from traditional pedagogy whereby students simply absorbed and conformed to the world as it was taught them—he dubbed this the "banking method of education" by comparing knowledge to funds deposited by the teacher and used later by the students to buy what they need. In contrast, for Freire, students took possession of knowledge themselves and participated in its use.

Feminist teaching styles also have been influenced by the psychological research on girls' and women's development that demonstrates significant gender differences in styles of learning. On the positive side, developmentalists have helped foster recognition that women may have special "ways of knowing," transcending pure cog-

Womanist theologian and teacher Kelly Brown Douglas is just one example of how a woman teaching religion put into practice the feminist assumptions that students should direct their own learning, collaborate with one another and with the teacher, widen the boundaries of learning beyond books and classrooms, and gain knowledge that is simultaneously personal and political. *Courtesy of the Office of Public Affairs, Denison University, Granville, Ohio.*

nition and including affect, emotion, intuition, and holistic (rather than linear) ways of processing information. On the negative side, however, researchers began mounting evidence during the 1980s that most North American education did a significant disservice to girls' learning. *Shortchanging Girls, Shortchanging America,* a landmark study in 1990 by the American Association of University Women (AAUW), showed that as they progress through public schools in the United States, girls lose confidence in themselves. Their self-esteem drops and so does their achievement in school. The AAUW study showed that gender biases in teaching, favoring boys, were partly to blame.

For all these and other reasons, more and more women and men in the academy began to talk in terms of a distinct "feminist pedagogy" that guided their teaching. While there is no single definition of *feminist pedagogy*, it includes at least several features. Feminist pedagogy advocates for women. It assumes that women and men students bring valuable content from life experience into the classroom and allows and even encourages them to use their experience along with the formal

course content (i.e., readings and other materials) in their work. One way of putting this is that the "subjects" of the course include the students. Course content becomes personal, and the personal becomes course content. As Ken Homan put it:

Feminist and personalist teaching begins with the recognition of personhood, of seeing and respecting self and students as subject-agents in relationship. . . . For many students it is the dawning of new insights: "I matter! What I think matters!" (253)

And because for feminists the personal is always political, to personalize teaching is to politicize it. Feminist pedagogy therefore affirms the political nature of education. Students are empowered by their learning. They gain their own voice, claim their own histories, and develop their own agency. Feminist pedagogy is political in at least two other senses as well: First, students' empowerment extends beyond the classroom once they realize that what they have learned has transformed them.

It dawns on them that what they think and say matter outside of class as well. The process of conscientization that begins in school spills over into "the real world" beyond the classroom. Sometimes teachers call this political process a circle or spiral because students' transformed experiences in the world provide, in turn, further resources for learning. In theology, it is often called a *theological spiral*. Feminist theologian Letty Russell explains:

> This style of theologizing in a continuing spiral of engagement and reflection begins with *commitment* to the task of raising up signs of God's new household with those who are struggling for justice and full humanity. It continues by *sharing experiences* of commitment and struggle in a concrete context of engagement. Third, the theological spiral leads to a *critical analysis* of the context of the experiences, seeking to understand the social and historical factors that affect the community of struggle. Out of this commitment to action in solidarity with the marginalized, and out of sharing of experiences and social analysis, arise *questions about biblical and church tradition* that help us gain new insight into the meaning of the gospel as good news for the oppressed and marginalized. This new understanding of tradition flows from and leads to *action, celebration, and further reflection* in the continuing theological spiral. (30–31)

Feminist pedagogy is also political in the second sense that power dynamics within a classroom shift as students discover their own voice. The teacher ceases to be the sole authority. As Homan says, "The teacher-as-authority shares authority with the students, and this empowers the students to author themselves as a work in progress" (255). In practical terms, this translates into strategies such as students helping to set the agenda for class, students sharing leadership of discussion, and students supporting and challenging each other. Students in a feminist classroom form bonds with one another that go beyond being merely classmates. In short, the classroom becomes a community of colearners, and the same politics arising in any community develop there.

Finally, feminist pedagogy is known for its characteristic creativity and passion. Feminist teachers have experimented with all sorts of strategies and methodologies, from field trips to interviews to dramatizations to liturgies. They feel more free to improvise within the classroom and to let both content and method remain provisional and flexible. Because of its attention to personal experience, feminist pedagogy tends to activate emotion and passion. Students in feminist classrooms cry and laugh—and become outraged—as they encounter the material and each other at levels deeper than in traditional classrooms.

One example serves to illustrate the type of creative teaching and learning made possible by feminist developments in theological education. In her book *Saving Work: Feminist Practices of Theological Education*, Rebecca Chopp recalls one particular evening in a feminist theology class:

> The class was struggling with naming the pain of patriarchy and with visualizing hope. It was obvious to the students that this naming the depth of brokenness while at the same time announcing new possibilities was a Christian enterprise. This juxtaposition of brokenness and hope, of pain and new life, was what they had heard, in a variety of ways, throughout their Christian lives and certainly throughout most of their seminary education.
>
> As we returned from break to participate in a student-led discussion section, we found the chairs placed in a circle. A wooden cross stood in the middle of the room. The women leading this part of the class session handed each of us a slip of paper as we entered and asked us to write down one specific experience of patriarchal oppression. . . . After each one read aloud the sin inscribed on the paper, she or he nailed the paper to a cross. (1–2)

As a scholar not only of theology but of theological education itself, Chopp writes that whenever she stops to ponder what is "theological education," she remembers that evening. It represents for her "a process of spiritual and ecclesial formation that is focused in and through theological wisdom" (2).

Classrooms like this are a far cry from the classrooms of old in theological education. Clearly, the inclusion within a course of a creative liturgy like this, organized by students in an effort to teach themselves a text, signals a significant change in what constitutes theology teaching and measures the depth of feminism's impact on the classroom.

Just as feminist theologians, in their speaking and writing, have ventured bold new interpretations of the Christian tradition, so too have they helped reinterpret education through their teaching. And yet just as feminist theology has invited internal criticism, so too has feminist pedagogy. Feminist teachers have noted the dangers and drawbacks of what they do, and some have begun to voice their skepticism about the assumptions regarding women students upon which feminist pedagogy rests. In conclusion, therefore, the author will identify some of the limitations of classrooms where women's experience has entered and ruled. As we shall see, these parallel the limitations of feminist theologies' use of the category "women's experience."

First, unless a teacher and her students are careful, the invitation to reflect upon experience can quickly lead to a hegemonic discourse in the classroom. That is to say, when given the opportunity to talk about actual, concrete events and perceptions, students can jump too quickly to consensus about what they mean and reinforce that consensus through their discussion. The excitement of discovering and describing their "common lot" can cause them to overlook any women who might *not* share in it. The group's tacit consensus serves, ironically, to create an "in-group" within the class, excluding the rest. A class can also reach agreement too readily on the nature and cause of women's oppression and inadvertently stifle any contributions by those who see it differently. One poignant example of this comes from an undergraduate course in feminist theological ethics where one day the topic of female genital mutilation arose. The general horror, outrage, and dismay that most students expressed upon learning of this practice served only to compound, tragically, the anguish of the one student in class who had actually undergone genital surgery. Telling her story privately to the teacher after class, she said that not only had their spontaneous reactions undermined her hard-won self-confidence as a sexual being, but it had alienated her from the rest of the group. The warning here is that unless those who adopt "liberatory" pedagogies are continually vigilant about questioning the assumed meaning of women's experience and keeping easy consensus at bay, their pedagogies may not liberate and may even further oppress. The irony of erecting yet more divisions between women is a real risk.

Second, the appeal to experience can be so compelling as to overshadow other sources of knowledge such as factual data, historical evidence, imagination, and even others' contrary experiences. Teachers who employ feminist pedagogies are all too familiar with the personal story that stops conversation. Personal narratives, particularly if they are especially vivid, seem to trump all other truth claims. Who will dare argue with her classmate's account of a real, lived experience? Who can? Imagine, for example, that the student in the example above *had* told her story to the class and had furthermore insisted that genital surgery did not "mutilate" her at all and was not an oppressive practice. Chances are that an account obtained from a secondary source (such as a text read for class) would have suddenly paled in comparison to a live, firsthand account. Chances are the secondary text would have lost some of its validity in the ethical discourse, no matter how accurate and "true"

it also was. In short, there is tremendous power in seeing a course "subject" embodied before the class's eyes, but this power cuts both ways.

The situation is further complicated when competing narratives are voiced in class. When different women have had opposite personal histories (say, of sexism in the church), and are given the opportunity to recount and defend them passionately to the group, walls of difference arise that are difficult to break down. Their differing interpretations of reality, combined with the seeming impasse, further compounds any divisiveness and threatens to harm the educational process. As Homan writes:

> In liberatory approaches there has been a focus on the shared discourse of personal narratives [that] serves both to raise consciousness and to create conditions of solidarity. Often, though, the authority of personal narrative ("In my experience . . .") creates boundaries of difference rather than interwoven narratives of solidarity. . . . When another challenges such a declarative by reference to his or her own experience, the response is frequently of the character, "That might be true for you, but it was different for me." . . . This becomes a self-referencing, self-norming process that validates the self by holding others at a distance. (259–260)

A third, and related, danger of a feminist teaching style is the tendency to postpone critical analysis in favor of extended personal discourse. If traditional pedagogies were inadequate because they made no room for students to share their experiences, feminist pedagogies can privilege experience to the detriment of intellectual content. Discussions can become sidetracked by personal stories, with students losing any critical distance on them. The extreme result is a class that simply wallows around in people's lives. As feminist theorist Jeanne Brady Giroux puts it, "A critical feminist pedagogy does not stop at entitling students to speak of their own experiences. But neither does it overly privilege voice so as to substitute critical affirmation for a vague and sloppy relativism" (9). In short, teachers are discovering the same thing as theoreticians: Experience is not inherently meaningful and does not interpret itself. Personal narrative cannot necessarily stand on its own as the "content" of a course. It requires additional sources of interpretation and the critical tools provided by history, theory, and so on.

This leads to a fourth danger, the overpersonalization of the classroom. When emotions are aroused and consciousness raised, the classroom can begin to resemble a therapy session. Students can become distraught and distracted by discoveries made about themselves and their classmates. In some cases, students cross the boundaries of proper self-disclosure, raising discomfort that is hard to dispel. Students are especially apt to disclose overly personal information when writing papers. Students have valued the opportunity to write about their lives and to treat their writing as an exercise in personal formation. Sometimes, however, they simply push too far the boundaries of what constitutes appropriate coursework and what belongs instead in a journal for therapy or spiritual direction.

One might note that the danger of over-personalization is particularly salient to the teaching of religion. In the modern college and university, departments of religion were founded on the premise that the academic study of religion properly belonged in liberal education and was not a vehicle for proselytization. Religion scholars had to justify the place of religion in the university curriculum against skeptics who could not distinguish the teaching of religion from the practice of it; some continue to face the same struggle today. They fear that their efforts will be undermined if religion classrooms give the appearance of encouraging students' personal confessional commitments. This creates a dilemma for the feminist teacher of religion. Should she encourage students to talk about their faith just as they would any other aspect of their life, according to feminist pedagogical principles? Or should she discourage confessional statements on the principle that they close the proper distance between students and course content, according to the rules of the academic study of religion? If in the study of religion the subject is not supposed to be the subject, how do the students' subjective experiences count?

As feminist theory, feminist theology, and feminist pedagogy continue to develop, no doubt they will continue to influence one another in profound ways, and women who teach theology and religion will continue to teach in different ways.

SOURCES: For feminist theology and theory, see Rebecca S. Chopp and Sheila Greeve Davaney, *Horizons in Feminist Theology: Identity, Tradition and Norms* (1997); Mary McClintock Fulkerson, *Changing the Subject: Women's Discourses and Feminist Theology* (1994); and Rosemary Tong, *Feminist Thought: A Comprehensive Introduction* (1989). For feminist pedagogy, see Margo Culley and Catherine Portuges, eds., *Gendered Subjects: The Dynamics of Feminist Teaching* (1991). For pedagogical developments within theological education, see Katie G. Cannon, Kelly Brown Douglas, Toinette M. Eugene, and Cheryl Townsend Gilkes, "Metalogues and Dialogues: Teaching the Womanist Idea," *Journal of Feminist Studies in Religion* 8 (1992): 125; The Cornwall Collective, *Your Daughters Shall Prophesy: Feminist Alternatives in Theological Education* (1980); The Mudflower Collective, *God's Fierce Whimsy: Christian Feminism and Theological Education* (1985); and Barbara Wheeler and Edward Farley, eds., *Shifting Boundaries: Contextual Approaches to the Structure of Theological Education* (1991). See also Valerie Saiving, "The Human Situation: A Feminine View," *Journal of Religion* 40.2 (April 1960): 110–112; Judith Plaskow, *Sex, Sin, and Grace* (1980); Ada María Isasi-Díaz, "Experiences," in *Dictionary of Feminist Theologies,* ed. Letty M. Russell and J. Shannon Clarkson (1996); Susan Brooks Thistlethwaite, "Every Two Minutes: Battered Women and Feminist Interpretation," in *Weaving the Visions: New Patterns in Feminist Spirituality,* ed. Judith Plaskow and Carol P. Christ (1989); Anne Bathurst Gilson, *Eros Breaking Free: Interpreting Sexual Theo-Ethics* (1995); Margaret Farley, "Feminist Consciousness and the Interpretation of Scripture," in *Feminist Interpretation of the Bible,* ed. Letty M. Russell (1985); Linell Elizabeth Cady, "Identity, Feminist Theory, and Theology," in *Horizons in Feminist Theology: Identity, Tradition, and Norms,* ed. Rebecca S. Chopp and Sheila Greeve Davaney (1997); Kelly Brown Douglas, "Teaching Womanist Theology: A Case Study," *Journal of Feminist Studies in Religion* 8 (Fall 1982): 133–138; Ken Homan, "Hazards of the Therapeutic: On the Use of Personalist and Feminist Teaching Methodologies," *Horizons* 24.2 (1997): 248–269; Letty Russell, *Church in the Round* (1993); Rebecca Chopp, *Saving Work: Feminist Practices of Theological Education* (1995); Jeanne Brady Giroux, "Feminist Theory as Pedagogical Practice," *Contemporary Education* 61.1 (Fall 1989): 6–10.

THE ORDINATION MOVEMENT

THE PROTESTANT WOMEN'S ORDINATION MOVEMENT
Barbara Brown Zikmund

DURING THE COLONIAL era the intense Puritan piety of New England, the diversity of the middle colonies, and the individualism of tidewater Anglicanism and hill country Presbyterianism created a very diverse religious landscape. Revivals regularly swept the colonies. Church and state were closely intertwined. Colonial wars, clashes with native peoples, the building of the southern slave economy, and advances in education and commerce gave women new freedoms and imposed new limits. Although women were actively engaged in Protestant church life, working out their salvation in many ways, formal questions about whether a woman could be ordained or called or appointed to serve as "clergy" did not emerge.

Colonial Women

The first glimmer of concern about Protestant women's religious leadership in North America might be dated from the Antinominan controversy of the 1630s in colonial Massachusetts. Anne Hutchinson challenged the political and theological authorities of Boston by holding meetings with women in her home to discuss the sermons of her pastor, John Cotton. The men were upset with her ideas about the relationship of grace to law, but they were also concerned that she had "stept out of" her place as a woman. In the transcript of her trial one of her prosecutors noted that she was worthy of condemnation because she had been more "like a husband than a wife, more like a preacher than a hearer, and more like the magistrate than a subject." Such behavior, he concluded, was unacceptable from a woman. She was convicted and banished to Rhode Island. After her husband's death she moved to New York, where Indians killed her and five of her children.

There were other developments in colonial America that showed woman exercising religious leadership, even though the formal question of ordination was not raised. When Quaker women shared their radical understanding of the "Inner Light," they conveyed the message that women and men were equally called to ministry. When hysteria swept the town of Salem in the late seventeenth century and a number of young women were condemned as witches, it is likely that the God-fearing people of Salem were especially apprehensive about the spiritual power of women. Most of the time, however, during the seventeenth and early eighteenth centuries the religious activities of women revolved around prayer, Bible reading, teaching children, and attending church.

Things began to change in the 1740s when the American colonies experienced a series of religious revivals known as the "Great Awakenings." Soon itinerant evangelists were moving around the countryside convincing men and women to change their ways and recommit themselves to God. Bathsheba Kingsley was a Massachusetts woman who experienced such a conversion. Kingsley stretched the boundaries of traditional religious behavior by taking on the role of a public evangelist. Although her unconventional evangelistic stance would have been condemned if she had been a man, the fact that she was a woman made her pretensions to clerical authority particularly offensive. She was repeatedly denounced and told that she could share her faith with others, but she was not to speak with the authority of an ordained minister.

Yet only a few years later certain forms of female ministry were recognized and honored, even though they were generally unauthorized. From the 1760s until her death in 1796 Sarah Osborn led many revivals near her home in Newport, Rhode Island. As a schoolteacher, mother, and religious leader she was highly respected and lauded by well-known Congregational clergyman Samuel Hopkins. Although she was never ordained, Hopkins considered her an exemplary Christian and saw to it that her memoirs were published.

Barbara Heck was part of a small group of Methodist Irish who came to New York in 1760. Out of her distress over the growing secularism of that city, she played a key role in building the first John Street Methodist Chapel. Later she moved to Canada where she started several Methodist class meetings.

Jemima Wilkinson, an African American woman raised in a Quaker family, developed a devoted following in the middle colonies around the time of the Revolutionary War. Known as the Publick Universal Friend, Wilkinson did not start a church or preach anything different than standard Quaker beliefs, but her charismatic presence led to the formation of societies of "Universal Friends." In the 1780s she moved to a "Friends settlement" west of Lake Seneca in New York where she encouraged the development of a colony where the faithful could be free of the temptations of the world.

Near the end of the eighteenth century another important utopian group emerged known as "Shakers." Shakers believed that the second appearing of Jesus Christ would be in the form of a woman. They followed a woman named Ann Lee, giving up family and property to join celibate religious communities scattered throughout the New England and the Appalachian frontier. In Shaker "families" leadership was shared equality between an eldress and an elder.

American Protestants did not ordain women, but many women functioned as religious leaders in church and society during the eighteenth and early nineteenth centuries. Women provided hospitality and/or financial support for fledgling movements. Women functioned as itinerant evangelists, moving around the countryside "witnessing" and "sharing" their faith—and even "planting" new churches. Clergy wives kept local congregations together following the untimely death of their pastor husbands. Women supported local religious life and communities in numerous ways. With the rising egalitarian ideology of the new nation, men and women grew more and more comfortable with women as religious leaders. However, as "colonial" churches severed formal ties with English and continental "mother churches," American Protestants began to impose order on earlier unregulated religious practices.

Revivalism and Congregationally Organized Denominations

After 1800 a new wave of revivalism and reform (the Second Great Awakening) swept the country. In this new religious enthusiasm women played an active role. Women organized to support mission work. Women engaged in reform movements, especially the antislavery crusade. Women took to the platform, speaking before "promiscuous assemblies" (mixed audiences) on many issues of the day.

There are stories about women like Nancy Cram and Abigail Roberts in the Hudson River Valley. In 1814, during one of the many frontier revivals that led to the formation of the small Christian denomination that later merged with the Congregationalists, Abigail Roberts was converted by a woman preacher named Nancy Cram. Nothing much is known about Nancy Cram, but records show that Abigail Roberts became an important unordained preacher, or "female laborer," for the Christian Connexion, founding many churches until her death in 1841.

The Quakers, who had long supported women leaders, became more intentional about recognizing the leadership of women. Although the Society of Friends had grave reservations about paying clergy, and never formally ordained anyone to ministry, by the early nineteenth century local Quaker meetings had developed the custom of "recording ministers." This meant that if a member spoke up regularly in a "meeting" and the members found his or her "testimony" useful, she or he might be "recorded" as a minister. Once her or his "gift for ministry" was recognized, a statement was put into the minutes of the monthly meeting and sent to the quarterly and yearly meeting. Such persons were designated as "public Friends" and expected to give up all local-meeting obligations in order to travel and share their faith with others.

One of the most famous Quaker preachers in the mid-nineteenth century was Lucretia Mott. She was almost disowned by her meeting when her radical abolitionist views led them to believe that she was compromising their pacifist principles by pressing a cause that might lead to war. Mott, however, was undaunted and firm in her faith. The great women's suffrage leader Elizabeth Cady Stanton said that it was Lucretia Mott who convinced her that she had the same right to think for herself (about religion) as Martin Luther, John Calvin, and John Knox.

The first woman who was formally ordained to the Christian ministry in an established denomination in America was Antoinette Brown (later Blackwell). Brown received her theological education at Oberlin College, although the college refused to award her a theological degree. In 1853 Brown was called to be the pastor of a small Congregational Church in South Butler, New York. She was twenty-eight years old. She was already well known as a public lecturer on reform topics like temperance and slavery.

Brown's ordination caused little controversy, because the Free Church polity of Congregationalism allows each congregation to ordain its own pastor. A progressive Wesleyan Methodist preacher, Luther Lee, preached her ordination sermon, titled "A Woman's Right to Preach the Gospel." He took his text from the prophet Joel 2: 28, as quoted by Peter on the day of Pentecost in the second chapter of Acts—"And it shall come to pass afterward, that I will pour out my Spirit upon all flesh; and your sons and your daughters shall prophesy." Her ministry in South Butler was short, however, and after a few years she resigned due to ill health and doctrinal doubts. In 1856 she married Samuel C. Blackwell, the brother of Elizabeth and Emily Blackwell, early women physicians. Antoinette Brown Blackwell raised a large family and wrote over twenty-five books on philosophy and science. After her family was grown, she returned to active ministry as a Unitarian.

The Unitarians and Universalists were strong advocates for women. The first woman ordained by the Universalists was also named Brown—Olympia Brown. She attended Antioch College, and after completing her theological studies at Canton Theological School in Canton, New York, she was ordained in June 1863. Her later ministry took her to Weymouth, Massachusetts, Bridgeport, Connecticut, and Racine, Wisconsin. Also in 1863, a second Universalist woman, Augusta Chapin, was ordained by the Universalists. Three years later, in 1866, Phebe Ann Hanaford, became the third Universalist woman pastor. The American Unitarian Association, a liberal denomination that much later joined with the Universalists (in 1961), started ordaining women in 1871, with the ordinations of Celia Burleigh and Mary Graves. By the late twentieth century the Unitarian Universalists had one of the highest percentages of women clergy among Protestantism.

After the Civil War, the movement of women into more visible leadership in many Protestant denominations continued apace. Women's missionary societies and boards sponsored female missionaries. Women served as itinerant evangelists and temporary or lay preachers. Gradually, denominations with Free Church polity, where local churches could call and ordain their own pastors without wider church authorization, moved to ordain women. In 1867, Melissa Timmons (later Terrill) was ordained at the Ebenezer Christian Church in Ohio. The local Christian Conference authorized her "standing" as a minister but commented that "we do not approve of the ordination of women to the Eldership of the church, as a general rule." In 1931 the Christians merged with the Congregationalists.

Informal records indicate that many Baptist women preached and exhorted during early revivals on the nineteenth-century American frontier. Eventually, some of these women were licensed to preach, but Baptists continued to argue about the propriety of women speaking in public. Finally, in 1894, Edith Hill became the first woman ordained among the Northern Baptists (later known as the American Baptists). When that denomination formally organized in 1907 the ordination of women was not an issue.

Women's ordination remained controversial among Southern Baptists, although from 1888 on many Southern Baptist women exercised a "ministry" through the Women's Missionary Union (WMU). Throughout the twentieth century, the conservative bent of Southern Baptist churches continued to formally resist the idea of women as preachers and pastors. Southern Baptist women became clergy wives and served as powerful lay leaders in education and music, but no Southern Baptist woman was ordained until 1964. Since that time local Southern Baptist congregations have ordained over a thousand women. Unfortunately, the careers of these ordained Southern Baptist women have been limited— with many of them only able to maintain employment as associate or assistant pastors. As a consequence, many Southern Baptist clergywomen have left the Southern Baptist Convention (SBC) to find better opportunities for ministry and a more hospitable environment for their work. After 1979, as the SBC leadership became increasingly fundamentalist and refused to approve of women serving in positions of authority, Southern Baptist women were discouraged from aspiring to ordination. Although some moderate Baptist groups, such as the Alliance of Baptists and the Cooperative Baptist Fellowship, provided alternatives, the numbers of ordained Southern Baptist women declined after a peak in the 1970s and early 1980s.

Women in most denominations with a decentralized or congregationally based form of governance, except for the Southern Baptists, were successful in gaining ordination by the beginning of the twentieth century. All that was needed was a local congregation that wanted to call a woman as its pastor. And even when objections to the ordination of a woman might arise, there was rarely any effort to undo what had been done. So it was that a Disciples of Christ congregation in Erie, Illinois, in 1888 ordained Clara Celeste Babcock. She joined a handful of women in the Quaker, Congregational, Christian, Universalist, Unitarian, Northern Baptist, and emerging Holiness denominations that ordained women to the gospel ministry and asserted that in the Christian church there should be no distinction between male nor female, because all were one in Jesus Christ.

Presbyterians

The efforts of women to be ordained in the Presbyterian tradition were not as easy. This was due in part to the fact that Presbyterians had two types of ordination. In the Presbyterian tradition, persons were "set apart" by prayer and laying of hands to ministries of "Word and sacrament" and to ministries of "governance." This practice goes back to the traditions of Calvin's Geneva and the theological idea of the "priesthood of all believers." Ordained clergy taught and preached; and ordained lay leaders served as "ruling elders" of the Session, the governing body of a congregation with responsibility for the welfare of the church.

Presbyterian attitudes toward the ordination of women were often influenced by developments on the western frontier. In 1832 the General Assembly, troubled by the unseemly involvement of women in public meetings, sent a pastoral letter to the churches. It said that "meetings of pious women by themselves, for conversation and prayer," were fine, but churches needed to be careful that the prohibitions set forth by Paul in his letters to the Corinthians and Timothy were upheld. For women "to teach and exhort, or to lead in prayer, in public and promiscuous assemblies" was forbidden. By the late nineteenth century, although American Presbyterians were divided into several denominations reflecting regional and doctrinal disputes, the pressure to change this prohibition began to increase.

First, some congregations in the small populist Cumberland Presbyterian Church elected and ordained some women as "ruling elders" in the 1880s and 1890s. When these women tried to take their seats at regional Synods and the General Assembly, however, they were denied status as commissioners. At about the same time, a woman named Louisa Woosley was able to convince the Nollin, Kentucky, Presbytery of the Cumberland Presbyterian Church that she was called to a ministry of "Word and sacrament." In November 1889 she became the first woman ordained to clergy status in any Presbyterian denomination. Later her ordination was questioned and even revoked by a Presbytery. As history unfolded, the Cumberland Presbyterian Church did not officially authorize women clergy, or teaching elders, until 1921.

Most mainstream Presbyterian bodies, however, refused to approve of the ordination of women as teaching elders until much later. In the 1920s the Presbyterian Church in the USA, the major Northern Presbyterian denomination, looked more closely at women's place in the church. Following a report titled the "Causes of Unrest among the Women of the Church," the 1930 General Assembly proposed some changes. Presbyteries were asked to consider three questions: whether they approved the full ordination of women as ruling elders and ministers of "Word and sacrament," whether they approved the ordination of women only as ruling elders, or whether they approved the licensing of women evangelists. Only the second question was approved. In 1930 Presbyterian women in the northern part of the United States could serve on local governing boards, but they could not be pastors. It took until 1955 before the Presbyterian Church in the USA approved the ordination of women to the full ministry of "Word and sacrament." In 1958 when the Presbyterian Church in the USA joined with the smaller United Presbyterian Church (UPC), North America, to create the United Presbyterian Church, USA, women from the UPC gained ordination through that merger.

The more conservative (Southern) Presbyterian Church in the United States continued to avoid the issue. Shortly after the 1955 approval of women clergy in the Northern church, an overture to grant women the right to be "ruling elders" was considered and defeated. Finally in 1964 the Presbyterian Church in the United States approved the ordination of women as deacons, ruling elders, and ministers all at once. In spite of the vote, few people thought that many women would want to or would have the qualifications to serve as pastors.

Methodists

The issue of women's ordination within Methodism was even more complex. Before the Civil War, Methodism had split into Northern and Southern bodies. It was also divided into groups that upheld episcopal forms of government and those promoting congregational polity. Furthermore, the great Holiness revivals of the mid-nineteenth century led to the formation of many small Holiness denominations committed to recovering some of the lost insights of Wesleyan theology. The first challenge to Methodism came in 1880 when two Methodist women, Anna Oliver and Anna Howard Shaw, came before the General Conference of the Methodist Episcopal Church, North, seeking ordination. They already held local preacher's licenses. Suddenly the

Methodists had to confront the question of women clergy. Unfortunately, not only was the request for ordination denied, but the conference voted to rescind the existing rule that allowed women to have a local license to preach. Soon thereafter Anna Howard Shaw left the Methodist Episcopal Church, North, and joined the more liberal Methodist Protestant denomination, where she was ordained.

The struggle for ordination and full clergy status for Methodist women took many years. In 1924 the Methodist Episcopal Church, North, voted to approve the ordination of women as local preachers but did not grant women annual conference membership. In Methodism, only ordained clergy with conference membership have full status. Being ordained did not give women a status equal to that of most male clergy in the denomination. In 1939 a church merger reunited the Methodist Episcopal Churches, North and South, and the Methodist Protestant Church to create "The Methodist Church." During the talks leading up to this merger a compromise was reached on women clergy. The southern Methodist Episcopal churches were forced to accept women as local preachers, the northern Methodist Episcopal churches retained ordination for women without conference membership, and the Methodist Protestants, who had previously ordained women and given them conference membership, were assured that women who held conference membership could keep it but full status would no longer be available to women who sought it in the future. In the end, it was not until 1956, after killing an amendment that would have limited conference membership to "unmarried women and widows," that the Methodist Church voted to give women full status in the "traveling ministry," or local conference membership.

Then again, in 1968 when the Methodist Church merged again to become the United Methodist Church (UMC) by uniting with the Evangelical and United Brethren (EUB) Church, the story of women clergy in Methodism was stretched again to embrace the unusual legacy of clergy women in the EUB Church. The EUB Church was an earlier merger of several groups of German Methodists with different histories around the issue of women's ordination. Whereas the United Brethren had ordained women as far back as 1889, the Evangelical Church and its predecessor bodies had never licensed or ordained women. In 1947, when these two churches came together to form the Evangelical and United Brethren Church, it did not allow the ordination to women. In practice, however, women who had already been ordained in the UB Church continued to serve, and UB bishops continued to ordain women. Finally, when the EUB Church united with the Methodist Church in 1968, these inconsistencies and irregularities were corrected. In the new United Methodist Church,

from 1968 on, women were ordained and guaranteed full ecclesiastical standing.

Holiness Denominations

Among the Wesleyan/Holiness denominations that broke away from Methodism in the nineteenth century, the story is quite different. Holiness denominations such as the Wesleyan Methodist Church, the Church of God (Anderson, Indiana), the Church of the Nazarene, and many other Holiness and Pentecostal denominations had no problem with the ordination of women. Phoebe Palmer, the famous nineteenth-century Holiness revivalist and writer, wrote, "Where church order is at variance with divine order, it is better to obey God than man." If the Holy Spirit gave timid women "holy boldness," removing their "man fearing spirit" and empowering them to ministry, that should be recognized. Palmer never formally endorsed women's ordination, but she was confident that women were called by God to preach and teach. The ordination of women was approved in the Wesleyan Methodist Church in 1891 and endorsed by the Church of God (Anderson, Indiana) in 1895, when it formally organized as a denomination. It was an accepted practice in the Church of the Nazarene after its founding in 1908. Unfortunately, although these denominations ordained women in great numbers around the turn of the century, after 1920 the ranks of women pastors in Holiness churches steadily declined.

The Church of God (Anderson, Indiana) is a good case in point. In 1891–1892 the Church of God magazine the *Gospel Trumpet* listed eighty-eight women active in ministry. A male church leader took pride in this situation by pointing out that the Church of God was a church "organized by the Holy Spirit." He wrote in that journal: "A man is an evangelist because he has the gift of evangelizing. It is not because he is a man, but because he has that particular gift. The gift itself is the proof of his calling. If a woman has divine gifts fitting her for a particular work in the church, that is the proof, and the only proof needed, that is her place" (F.G.S. Smith, October 14, 1920, 2). Many Holiness leaders lamented a mistranslation of Psalm 68:11 and liked to quote a better version suggested by Adam Clark, "of the female preachers there was a great host." Holiness writers consistently cited scripture passages that endorsed women's expanded role in the church and criticized interpretations of verses that prohibited women's involvement in preaching and other leadership activities.

By 1925 there were 220 women pastors in the Church of God (Anderson, Indiana), serving 32 percent of 685 congregations, but shortly thereafter the numbers of women pastors began to decline. Some people conjecture that as the focus of the Holiness movement shifted from traveling evangelistic ministers to local congregational ministry, women found fewer opportunities. Others blame the decline of women pastors on changing social attitudes toward women. Still others point out that a "fundamentalist leavening" in the Holiness movement generated a new antiwoman mentality by insisting upon a literal interpretation of the scriptures. Fundamentalists accused the Holiness churches of being unduly influenced by the secular "women's movement." Yet Holiness leaders had always rejected literal interpretations of scripture that limited women's involvement in ministry. Benjamin T. Roberts, a founder of the Free Methodist Church, declared that Christians should use Galatians 3:28 as the standard: "There is neither Jew nor Greek, . . . slave nor free, . . . male nor female, for you are all one in Christ Jesus."

The predominantly white mainline Protestant denominations sometimes like to think that the struggle for women's ordination is their story. And there is no doubt that it is important to document the advancements made by and for women within structured mainline denominations like Presbyterians, Methodists, Lutherans, and Episcopalians. However, within denominations organized around free and independent "congregational" decisions, although ordination comes earlier, it is also much more difficult to track. From the late eighteenth century on, there are local records of women "preaching" and "teaching" in revivals and in local church settings. Sometimes these women were authorized lay leaders, sometimes they were licensed to do ministry only in a specific place or only for a specific period of time, sometimes they took the place of a deceased male pastor who had been their husband, and sometimes they just started a church of their own and the people said, "Amen." Over 50 percent of all ordained women since 1853 have been in Holiness, Pentecostal, Evangelical, and paramilitary denominations. In 1870, when the Salvation Army was founded, it had no debate about ordaining women. A few years earlier, the cofounder of the Salvation Army, Catherine Booth, had published a controversial pamphlet titled *Female Ministry*. Even as recently as in a 1977 study done by the National Council of Churches of Christ in the USA, only 17 percent of women clergy were found in the top ten major Protestant denominations. Furthermore, because many of the Holiness, Pentecostal, and Evangelical denominations grew out of what were originally racially mixed grassroots movements, the issue of women's leadership and the question of women's ordination unfolded in different ways for black and Hispanic women.

African American Denominations

The black church has been, and remains, a strong force in American Protestant history. Today over 85 percent of church-affiliated black Christians in the United States belong to six major denominations: the African Methodist Episcopal Church, the African Methodist Episcopal Zion Church, the Christian Methodist Episcopal Church, the National Baptists, the Progressive Baptists, and the Church of God in Christ. The story of women's leadership and the ordination of women within these denominations is mixed.

First of all, we know that many slaves brought African religious traditions with them to North America. Because women held prominent roles in African religions, it can be assumed that slave women served American plantation blacks as healers, teachers, and preachers. And because African religious traditions were oral, and it was against the law to teach slaves to read and write, black women, as well as black men, who had gifts for storytelling and preaching were highly respected. Finally, because families were split up, and because the ministry, after Emancipation, became one of the few places where black males could exercise power in a racist society, women experienced great ambiguity when they felt a call to preach.

A small number of black women surface in the historical record: There was a former slave woman named "Elizabeth" who began preaching extensively in Maryland and Virginia in 1796. When the authorities detained her and asked if she was ordained, she answered, "Not by the commission of men's hands; if the Lord has ordained me, I need nothing better." They let her go.

A more famous black woman preacher was Jarena Lee, who was born as a free black in New Jersey. In 1809 she asked the pastor of the newly established Bethel African Methodist Episcopal (AME) Church in Philadelphia, Richard Allen, for a license to preach. He did not believe that women should preach. However, Jarena Lee was not to be stopped. She continued to preach and eventually married an AME clergyman. In 1816, shortly after the AME church organized as a denomination, she again asked Allen, who by that time was a bishop, to make her ministry legitimate. This time he was more supportive. Although church regulations did not allow female preachers, he permitted her to hold prayer meetings and to "exhort." Although she claimed to be "the first female preacher of the AME church," it was never official.

Amanda Berry Smith was another AME woman preacher. She felt her call to preach fifty years later, during the Holiness revivals of the 1860s and 1870s. She was a gifted singer, evangelist, and missionary who invited Christians to reach for "spiritual perfection" and to lead a more holy life. In 1893 she published a widely read autobiography titled *The Story of the Lord's Dealings with Mrs. Amanda Smith, the Colored Evangelist, Containing an Account of Her Life Work of Faith, Her Travels in America, England, Scotland, India, and Africa as an Independent Missionary.*

The first official female ordination in a predominantly black denomination actually took place in the AME Zion Church. In 1894 in Poughkeepsie, New York, Bishop James Walker Hood made concrete his statement that at least one Methodist Episcopal Church guaranteed women "all rights in common with men." He ordained a conference missionary, Mrs. Julia A. Foote, to deacon's orders. His action was in part a response to controversies in the white Methodist Episcopal Church, North, over seating delegates, licensing, and ordaining women like Anna Howard Shaw and Anna Oliver. The next year the Philadelphia and Baltimore Conference ordained Mrs. Mary J. Small as a deacon, and in 1898 she was ordained "elder" and given full ministerial status and conference membership. Julia Foote achieved elder's orders two years later, in 1900. It is significant to note that these ordinations were fifty years before the predominantly white Methodist Church granted full conference membership to women.

In spite of the witness of Jarena Lee in the early nineteenth century, the African Methodist Episcopal Church continued to resist ordaining women. AME women were licensed without ordination in 1884, but they were not granted full ordination until 1948. The Christian Methodist Episcopal (CME) Church was even more conservative. There were no laywomen's organizations in that denomination until after 1900, and women were not ordained as clergy until 1954.

Although one would think that black Baptists might have had an easier time, given their free-church decision-making process, female black Baptists fared no better. In fact, the important roles held by laywomen in black Baptist churches have actually made ordination for black Baptist women more difficult. This is because in many black Baptist churches there is a prevailing unexamined division of responsibilities. The formal leadership "on the pulpit" remains reserved for men, while women exercise complementary power from the pew. Within many black Baptist churches, there has never been any policy against the ordination of women, yet the climate has rarely been supportive of women preaching or pastoring churches. In recent years certain strong male pastors have "sponsored" women candidates, and the Baptist principle of local autonomy has not interfered. However, ordination for black Baptist women usually depends on her finding a powerful black male mentor.

The Church of God in Christ (COGIC), the largest black Pentecostal denomination, has formal barriers against the ordination of women. Its Official Manual argues, on scriptural grounds, that women cannot be ordained as elders, bishops, or pastors. Women may preach in churches as evangelists or missionaries, but the Bible prohibits them from serving as pastors. Yet from time to time bishops have ordained women so that they could serve as chaplains outside the church. Now and then a widow has been allowed to take over a church after her husband's death. Women's status may be changing, but at present official policy ignores such thinking.

In spite of all of these difficulties, over the years many black women have served as teachers and pastors. These women simply refused to let rules and regulations get in the way. If they felt a call to preach and the churches or male pastors did not support them, they started their own independent Holiness or Pentecostal churches. Some of them were able to build "successful" congregations and attract large numbers, but most black women pastors and preachers served small independent storefront churches. In proportion to their numbers in the population, however, there have probably been more black women preachers and pastors than white women clergy.

Lutherans

Lutheran experience in America was divided and isolated by the language and cultural legacies of European immigration. German Lutherans were different from Scandinavian Lutherans, and new immigrant Lutherans often had little in common with Lutherans who had lived in America for many generations. Until the 1940s American Lutherans were divided into ethnic and cultural enclaves generally focused on assimilation. Lutheran women related to the church in rather conventional ways, and the question of women's ordination was rarely raised.

Following World War II several progressive European Scandinavian state churches (Lutheran) endorsed the ordination of women. Although in 1938 the Church of Norway (Lutheran) formally voted to ordain women, it did not actually ordain any woman until twenty years later. And by that time, during the 1950s, Lutheran biblical scholars in Europe and the United States, who liked to think of themselves as part of a widespread ecumenical and pan-Lutheran intelligentsia, had reached the conclusion that there were no biblical or theological reasons against women's ordination.

Encouraged by this environment, in 1958 the president of Luther Seminary (in Minnesota) raised the question as to whether women should be admitted to seminaries to prepare for pastoral ministry. It was an awkward moment, because American Lutherans were in the midst of merging Norwegians, some Danish churches, and a small group of German Lutherans to create the American Lutheran Church (ALC) in 1960. Two years later, in 1962, several other American Lutheran denominations (Augustana Synod Swedes, other Danes, and several German Lutheran groups) merged to form the Lutheran Church in America (LCA). During this period of organizational consolidation, the question of women's ordination was put on hold.

In 1964, however, Luther Seminary admitted its first full-time woman student. At first, the American Lutheran Church stipulated that women seminarians could study theology, but they should not expect to be certified for ordination. Two years later, however, the ALC changed its ruling about women's ordination. And at about the same time the Synod of the Lutheran Church in America, a merger of German Lutherans, began to study the question of women's ordination. Unfortunately, the more conservative Lutheran Church–Missouri Synod (LCMS) continued to resist the idea of women's ordination.

By the late 1960s these three Lutheran bodies (the Lutheran Church in America, the American Lutheran Church, and the Lutheran Church–Missouri Synod) held an "Inter–Lutheran Consultation on the Ordination of Women." Not surprisingly, they were unable to agree. However, in 1969 the Executive Committee of the Lutheran Council of the USA (which involved these same three denominations) appointed a small subcommittee to look more closely at the question of the ordination of women. The committee concluded that (1) the biblical and theological evidence is not conclusive either for or against the ordination of women; (2) the sociological, psychological, and ecumenical considerations do not settle the question; (3) variety in practice on this question is legitimate within common Lutheran confessions; (4) the decision of individual Lutheran church bodies should be made only after consultation with other bodies and in sensitivity to the other Christian churches; and (5) the question of the ordination of women involves the broader question of ordination itself, the office of the ministry, the ministry of the whole people of God.

The report was accepted in early 1970 and sent out by all three presidents of the major Lutheran churches—placing the president of the Lutheran Church–Missouri Synod in an awkward position. In that same year several women graduated from seminary and were ready for ordination. Stimulated by their readiness, the issue of the ordination of women was promoted aggressively by several groups of Lutheran women. These women argued the case for women's ordination from sociological and feminist sources, as well as citing biblical and theological reasons. Soon thereafter, in the summer of 1970, the Lutheran Church in America approved the ordination of women. In support of that vote, the LCA Commission on the Comprehensive Doctrine of Ministry stated that "there was nothing in the exercise of the ordained ministry as a functional office that would exclude a woman because of her sex." A few months later the American Lutheran Church also approved the ordination of women. It was said that the vote reflected

"sanctified common sense," because scripture gave no clear word on the issue.

Unfortunately, the Lutheran Church–Missouri Synod was not ready to follow suit. Conflict erupted between some of its denominational leaders and a group of liberal students and faculty at the denomination's Concordia Theological Seminary. Although sparked by the women's ordination issue, the LCMS controversy revolved around the authority of scripture and basic principles of biblical interpretation. Differences eventually led a progressive group of faculty and students to leave Concordia and form a Seminary in Exile (Seminex). And a few years later, in 1977, that group became the nucleus for a new denomination, the Association of Evangelical Lutheran Churches (AELC). In 1987 the Lutheran Church in America, the American Lutheran Church, and the Association of Evangelical Lutheran Churches voted to merge to form the Evangelical Lutheran Church in America (ELCA). From its inception, the ELCA ordained both women and men. By contrast, the Lutheran Church–Missouri Synod continued to reject the legitimacy of women's ordination and reasserted its belief that the Bible limits the leadership roles of women in the church.

Episcopalians

The Episcopal Church traces its origins back to the Church of England. It was a strong force in the colonial era, and after the Revolutionary War it broke away from England to establish itself as an independent denomination—the Protestant Episcopal Church in the United States. Because of its Anglican roots and its standing in communion with worldwide Anglicanism, Episcopalians define ordination and priestly orders within the framework of "apostolic succession." This means that the authority of clergy depends on a formal unbroken progression of bishops who lay hands on priests to ordain them. Therefore, the decisions of Anglicans or Episcopalians to ordain women had implications for their relationships with Anglican churches in other parts of the world and with other branches of Christianity that affirmed "apostolic succession," such as the Roman Catholic Church.

The earliest instance of women's orders among Anglicans occurred in 1862 when the bishop of London "ordered" a deaconess by "laying on hands." In the 1880s the Protestant Episcopal Church in the United States began "setting apart" women as deaconesses. It was still unclear, however, how the status of a deaconess related to the priesthood. In 1920, the Lambeth Conference, a once a decade meeting of Anglican bishops from all over the world, discussed the issue. They concluded that the "ordination of a deaconess confers on her holy orders." Ten years later, however, the same

Lambeth Conference reversed its judgment. Deaconesses were not in holy orders. This led the Church of England to commission a study to look into the matter. Although the resulting 1935 report stated that there was no compelling theological reason for or against the ordination of women, the report insisted that an all-male priesthood was still needed for "the church of that day." During World War II an Episcopal woman was actually ordained by the bishop of Hong Kong, but his action was protested by Anglicans around the world, and after the war, she ceased functioning as a priest.

Following the war American discussions around women's ordination increased. In 1964 the General Convention of the Protestant Episcopal Church in the United States asserted that deaconesses were "ordered" rather than "appointed." Soon thereafter, in 1965 Bishop James Pike recognized Phyllis Edwards as a deacon, based upon her ordination as a deaconess. His action was controversial, and the formal decision to regularize the ordination of women as deaconesses was not voted until the General Convention in 1970. The ordination of women continued to be discussed and studied extensively, coming before several General Conventions of the Protestant Episcopal Church in the United States in various forms for vote. Finally, in 1972 the House of Bishops voted in favor of the principle of women's ordination as priests, but a year later the principle was rejected by the laity of the church voting in the General Convention. Fifty-six bishops issued a statement criticizing the convention's action; and a small group began to talk about an "irregular" ordination. Eventually, in Philadelphia on July 29, 1974, two retired bishops and one resigned bishop, in the presence of a diocesan bishop who did not actually participate, ordained eleven women deacons to the priesthood.

The Episcopal Church went into turmoil over how to deal with the renegade bishops' "violation of collegiality" and how to treat the eleven women. For two years the church debated various options, and finally, in September 1976 the General Convention approved the ordination of women to the priesthood and to the episcopate. It also agreed that the previous ordinations could be regularized, rather than repeated, by passing a new canon law authorizing the ordination of women to the priesthood in the Protestant Episcopal Church in the United States to take effect on January 1, 1977. Later that same year, recognizing that some of their colleagues still rejected the idea, the bishops adopted a "conscience clause," making a provision that any bishop who opposed the ordination of women would not to be required to ordain or oversee women priests. The General Convention, however, never approved this accommodation to those who objected.

As the years went by, many Episcopal women became priests. By 1993 over 12 percent of the priests in the Episcopal Church were women. Episcopal seminary enrollments grew, and by the mid-1980s over 50 percent of Episcopal seminarians were female. Yet although women could be priests, many people believed that the full status question for women within Anglicanism required that a woman be elected and consecrated as a bishop. Others disagreed. They felt that the consecration of a woman bishop would reflect insensitivity to Anglican diversity and to the wider Christian community. They argued for waiting. Eventually, however, the waiting ended. On September 24, 1988, the Episcopal Diocese of Massachusetts elected Barbara C. Harris, a fifty-eight-year-old black woman priest, as its suffragen bishop. Her consecration as the first female Anglican bishop in the world took place on February 11, 1989, in Boston. Five years later, in October 1993, the Diocese of Vermont elected Mary Adelia McLeod as its bishop.

Even after there were female Episcopal bishops, the issue of women priests continued to haunt the Episcopal Church. Twenty years had passed, but a handful of Episcopal bishops continued to be outspoken opponents of female priests. Their position, however, became increasingly unacceptable. Finally, in 1997 the General Convention passed Canon III.8.1, mandating the ordination of women in all 100 Episcopal dioceses in the United States. Denominational leadership continued to work with recalcitrant dioceses and "to encourage" the few remaining bishops who objected to the ordination of women to be in full compliance with church policy by

In September 1976 the Episcopal General Convention approved the ordination of women to the priesthood and to the episcopate. By 1993 over 12 percent of the priests in the Episcopal Church were women and actively carrying out their duties, such as this clergywoman administering the Eucharist on Boston Common. *Courtesy of the Archives of the Episcopal Church USA.*

2003. It was interesting that although all of the 2,000 ordained Episcopal women priests wanted full equality in every diocese, about 100 women clergy went on record against Canon III.8.1. They argued that to force women's ordination upon opponents was "to indulge in the sin of impatience" toward those who clearly differed. They suggested that it would be better to wait for the Holy Spirit than to "enshrine coercion into the canon." Their argument did not prevail, however, and Canon III.8.1 passed.

Women's Ordination and Gender Issues

Mark Chaves, in his study *Ordaining Women*, points out that until the second half of the nineteenth century arguments in favor of women's ordination among Protestants focused on the extraordinary abilities of a few women who wanted to preach or on the special religious gifts of women that were needed by church and society or on the practical demand for more workers for the gospel. The women who were actually ordained did not demand equality with men; they simply asked for freedom to do what they believed God was calling them to do.

By the 1870s, however, the rhetoric began to shift to justify the ordination of women in terms of gender equality. Writers supporting women's ordination focused on biblical texts and theological arguments that highlighted "women's rights" and emphasized the God-given equality of men and women "which the Gospel inculcates." Arguments for the ordination of women, and arguments against the ordination of women, participated in a wider social movement related to gender equality. As a consequence, denominational decisions to ordain women, or not to ordain women, were not driven by women asking to be ordained or by a desire in churches to encourage women to seek ordination or even by a need for more clergy. Decisions for or against the ordination of women increasingly depended on whether church leadership wanted to embrace, or resist, the modern ideology of gender equality and various related understandings of "modernity."

A good illustration of this shift is evident in the rationale behind the founding of several organizations to support Protestant women clergy. In 1893, Julia Ward Howe founded the nonsectarian Woman's Ministerial Conference in Boston. Its members were mostly Universalist and Unitarian women, with a few Methodists and Baptists. It inspired women clergy to think of themselves as a significant presence in modern society. Howe put together photographs of women preachers and ministers for a display at the World's Parliament of Religions during the Chicago Columbian Exposition in 1893. Female speakers at the Parliament reminded their audiences that religions subordinated women, as they set forth practical measures to raise women's status.

The International Association of Women Preachers (or International Association of Women Ministers [IAWM], as it later came to be known) was founded in 1919 by a Methodist preacher from Winfield, Kansas, named M. Madeline Southard. Membership was open to any woman who felt that she had a call to preach, whether or not she had the credentials or official authorization of her church. By 1923 the association had 189 members from sixteen denominations living in twenty-nine states and the District of Columbia, plus a handful of missionary members in Africa, China, and Japan. Although the founders of the organization were college graduates, they invited women to join whose training had "come in other ways," saying that they had no desire to appear wiser than God by denying membership to those whom "God has raised up." They also refused to limit membership only to those who were ordained. "We want to encourage those [unordained] women, not shut them out. We advise them to remain in their own churches and pioneer the way for ecclesiastical recognition." At one level the organization sought to provide fellowship among women who needed each other to survive. At the same time, from the beginning IAWM was dedicated to work toward "equal opportunity for women in the ecclesiastical world" ([Southard], 3–4).

In 1925 Southard lamented that the church seemed to be the last to yield to the growing spirit of what she called "sex-democracy." Women were serving society in many ways, but they were still not allowed to serve the ecclesiastical world. More important, women experienced great personal grief because their experiences of Christ were not valued by the church. It was a shame, she said, that young "earnest-hearted girls" were turned from preaching the gospel to social service where religion was lost. Women needed an organization to affirm the validity of their personal commitment to serve the church as preachers.

This connection between the issue of women's ordination and the modern social agenda is even more evident when examined alongside the question of biblical inerrancy and when seen in the light of assumptions about male sacramental leadership. By the mid-twentieth century the ordination of women was closely linked to gender equality, and in turn gender equality was tied to "modernity." In that context religious organizations embraced, or opposed, the ordination of women to express their self-conscious acceptance or rejection of the modern liberal agenda. Clinging to, or letting go of, biblical literalism and male sacramental leadership became the means to preserve traditional values, or to witness to the relevance of the gospel in the modern world. Furthermore, when denominational structures were decentralized, when strong independent women's organizations existed, and when the geographic center of the denomination was outside the South, social pressures for the ordination of women were enhanced.

In the late twentieth century, conflicts over the ordination of women continued. However, by that time they were driven by women, who themselves wanted to be ordained and who organized in collective advocacy for change. This often led to conflicts that were considerably more harsh and contentious than in earlier eras.

The struggle for the ordination of women in Protestant churches in the United States is not over. In recent decades the ordination issue has become much more than a question of the status of women's leadership in the churches. It involves the basic ways Christians understand gender in church and society. It is not about taking power from men and giving it to women; it is about how men and women on both sides of the controversy understand the relationship of their faith to modern culture. The conflict is between those who want their denomination to display one sort of organizational identity in the modern world and others who want their denomination to display another sort of organizational identity. Denominational rules about women's ordination give symbolic messages to the world, pointing to (or away from) the "broad liberal agenda associated with modernity and religious accommodation to the spirit of the age" (Chaves, 191–192).

In this environment, women's ordination remains ambiguous. On the one hand, Protestant theological arguments for human justice based upon baptism as a common sacrament calling all believers to Christian ministry suggest that any Christian can be "set apart" by ordination to provide leadership for the church. Yet, in practice, ordination participates in hierarchical legacies that are at odds with modernity. Roman Catholic scholar Elisabeth Schüssler Fiorenza cautions women who seek ordination. The women who succeed, she suggests, run the danger of "lording it over" other women while at the same time accepting an inferior status as a subordinate member of a male hierarchy. Women, both ordained and unordained, have mixed reactions. If they believe that they are called to ministry, they do see it as a God-given mystery; and yet they also believe that barriers to ordained ministry based on gender are unacceptable.

A study of clergy women done in the early 1990s showed that many ordained women still experience passive hostility against their ministries, and many of them still identify their problems as personal failures rather than the result of limitations created by traditionally male ecclesiastical systems. Some observers cite the dramatic increase of women clergy and argue that increasing numbers of women clergy have and will continue to force the churches to become more egalitarian. Others look at the same data and predict a backlash. Because the ordination of women is so closely aligned with the liberal modern agenda, as more conservative Christian groups grow, these observers believe that the status and support for ordained women will decline. Third, there are those who think that Protestant ministry is on its way to becoming a "pink-collar" enclave. They feel that in the future it will be easier and easier for women to become ordained clergy, but it will not make any difference. Women will simply find themselves in a "devalued vocation keeping dying denominational systems alive." Fourth, there are those who celebrate the increased numbers of ordained Protestant women but believe that real change has not occurred. There may be more and more women clergy, but they are crowded into lower and mid-level positions, and their impact is little more than token. And finally, there are those who think that a revolution is under way. They believe that clergywomen are reinventing the meaning of ordination for the whole church. Clergywomen are challenging the assumption that ordained ministry is only for ecclesiastically paid, full-time, lifelong male pastors. They are expanding the very essence of Christian ministry and guiding the whole church to rethink and renew its leadership and membership.

SOURCES: An early analysis of Protestant women's ordination is found in Inez M. Cavert, *Women in American Church Life* (1948). Documents related to the history of women in Protestant ministry appear in Barbara Brown Zikmund, "Women and Ordination," in *In Our Own Voices: Four Centuries of American Women's Religious Writing*, ed. Rosemary Radford Ruether and Rosemary Skinner Keller (1995). Focused chapters on women clergy in many Protestant denominations or movements make up *Religious Institutions and Women's Leadership: New Roles Inside the Mainstream* (1996), ed. Catherine Wessinger. A history of early women preachers is *Strangers and Pilgrims: Female Preaching in America, 1740–1845* (1998), by Catherine A. Brekus. A biography of the woman generally considered the first ordained woman in America is *Antoinette Brown: A Biography* (1983), by Elizabeth Cadzen. The most comprehensive general survey history of women clergy is Carl J. Schneider and Dorothy Schneider, *In Their Own Right: A History of American Clergywomen* (1997). Sociological studies of Protestant women clergy are Jackson W. Carroll, Barbara Hargrove, and Adair Lummis, *Women of the Cloth: A New Opportunity for the Churches* (1981); Edward H. Lehman, *Women in Ministry* (1994); Paula Nesbitt, *The Feminization of the Clergy in America* (1997); Mark Chaves, *Ordaining Women: Culture and Conflict in Religious Organizations* (1997); and Barbara Brown Zikmund, Patricia M. Chang, and Adair Lummis, *Clergy Women: An Uphill Calling* (1998). See also M. Madeline Southard, "Who Are We?" *The Woman's Pulpit* I (April 1923): 3–4; and Elisabeth Schüssler Fiorenza, "Sexism and Conversion," *Network* IX (May–June 1981): 15–22.

THE WOMEN'S ORDINATION MOVEMENT IN THE ROMAN CATHOLIC CHURCH

Maureen Fiedler and Dolly Pomerleau

DURING THE TWENTIETH century, most Protestant and Jewish denominations accepted women as ministers, priests, and rabbis—even as bishops. But the Roman Catholic Church refused to do so, and that opposition led to the growth of a movement in North America for the ordination of women as priests. As that movement has grown in the last quarter century, the Vatican has become increasingly isolated in its refusal to ordain women and, in this struggle, has lost the hearts and minds of many of its own people.

The events of the years from 1975 to 2000 provided fertile soil for the growth of the Roman Catholic movement for women's ordination. During this quarter century, the growing shortage of male, celibate priests brought the issue home to people in the parishes.

The secular women's movement in North America has constantly raised public consciousness since the 1960s on the need for gender equality in the United States and worldwide. Issues widely covered in the public media include equal pay and benefits, the "glass ceiling" for promotions, domestic violence, sexual harassment, sexual slavery, reproductive rights, women's disproportionate poverty and illiteracy, "honor killings" of women in Asia, genital mutilation in Africa, and the exposure of women's plight in countries such as Afghanistan. Meanwhile, at United Nations–sponsored Conferences on Women, held every four years, the Vatican distinguished itself by attempting to stop progress on many aspects of women's rights. Proponents of women's ordination link forms of gender oppression, noting that a failure to ordain women implies that women are not full persons and tacitly supports all other forms of societal oppression of women.

The earliest movement for women's ordination in the Roman Catholic Church dawned in the early years of the twentieth century in Great Britain as intrepid women like the Pankhursts, leaders of the suffrage movement in England, staged bold public demonstrations for women's right to vote. That energy led a group of women to found St. Joan's Alliance as a Roman Catholic organization working for suffrage in 1911.

The banner of St. Joan's Alliance moved to the United States to participate in the struggle there for the right to vote. After suffrage was won in 1920, Alliance women moved on to other issues and eventually became interested in women's ordination. Just before Vatican Council II (1962–1965), a St. Joan's member in Germany, Gertrud Heinzelmann, publicly challenged the Vatican's discriminatory policies and called for opening ordained ministries to women on an equal footing with men. But in the days before the Council met, St. Joan's Alliance's position was a fringe opinion, and it never grew beyond a small group.

The first signs of a large grassroots movement for women's ordination in the United States came in the mid-1970s. It was the natural offshoot of the secular feminist movement, struggling then for an Equal Rights Amendment to the U.S. Constitution. By then, the climate was ripe for a change. The theological ferment of Vatican Council II encouraged Church reformers. In 1962, a Dutch theologian, Haye van der Meer, published *Women Priests in the Catholic Church?* in which he argued that there is no scriptural barrier to women's ordination.

However, there were no women decision makers at the Vatican Council II, and the bishops of the world never discussed or debated the issue of women priests directly. But the Council created an aura that change in the Church was possible, even desirable. It emphasized the call of the Church to work for justice and approved a strong and unqualified statement in an official Council document: "[A]ny kind of social or cultural discrimination . . . on the grounds of sex . . . is to be curbed and eradicated as incompatible with God's design" (Pope Paul II). The next sentence offered an encouraging example: "It is deeply to be deplored that these basic personal rights are not yet being respected everywhere, as is the case with women who are denied the chance freely to choose a husband, *or a state of life*" (Pope Paul II [emphasis added]).

With the reform of the liturgy, women began to join men as readers of scripture and ministers of the Eucharist in parishes across North America. Canon law treated them as "exceptions," but in actual practice, women soon became a common sight in these roles. The visual foundations for change were laid. Women could now be seen doing things done only by priests in years past.

The 1971 Synod of Bishops in Rome urged the Church to strengthen its credibility to preach social justice by implementing justice in the life of the Church community. Justice for women in the Church was an obvious starting point.

As theologians began to raise the question of women's ordination in the early 1970s, Archbishop John Quinn of San Francisco chaired a Committee on Pastoral Research and Practices of the National Conference of Catholic Bishops (NCCB). Its report, titled "Theological Reflections on the Ordination of Women," cited the "constant teaching and practice of the Catholic Church against the ordination of women." But the report admitted that the question was complex, that it had

Since the 1960s, the secular women's movement in North America has raised public consciousness on the need for gender equality in the United States and worldwide. Proponents of women's ordination linked forms of gender oppression, noting that a failure to ordain women implies that women are not full persons and tacitly supports all other forms of societal oppression of women. *Copyright © Bettye Lane Studios.*

not yet been "thoroughly researched for Catholic theology," and that no "authoritative teaching" settled the question. Many saw the latter phrases as an invitation to deeper theological probing and advocacy.

An event in the Episcopal Church moved Catholic advocates of women's ordination to begin organizing. In Philadelphia, three retired Episcopal bishops ordained eleven women in the Episcopal Church in 1974. These were "irregular" ordinations, valid but not lawful in the eyes of Episcopal Church authorities. The national media debate intensified the issue for Catholics. By 1976 the Episcopal Church "regularized" these ordinations, admitting women to the priesthood.

The United Nations' International Women's Year in 1975 saw public signs of Catholic organizing begin to appear. In July of that year, Rev. William R. Callahan founded Priests for Equality, an organization of Roman Catholic priests and deacons who endorsed a charter

calling for the equality of women and men in church and society, including the ordination of women. In the 1990s Priests for Equality contributed powerfully to the movement for women's rights in the Church by translating and publishing the scriptures, as well as the lectionaries for Mass, in gender-inclusive language.

Mary B. Lynch, a Catholic laywoman, took the next step by asking everyone on her 1974 Christmas card list if they thought it was time to ask publicly, "Should women be priests?" Thirty-one women and one man responded with a resounding "Yes!" This small group began planning what they envisioned as a small national meeting of like-minded people. "Women in Future Priesthood Now: A Call to Action" was held in Detroit, Michigan, in 1975 on Thanksgiving weekend. "So long as women are excluded from ordination," said the sponsoring task force, "their participation in the sacramental life and ministry of the Church can only be secondary and auxiliary, reflecting a theological view of them as diminished persons."

The response of people across the United States and Canada overwhelmed the planners. Twice they were forced to move the conference to a larger site, and even then, some of the overflow crowd of 1,200 women and men had to watch the proceedings on closed circuit television from what they called their "upper room." Five hundred registrations had been returned for lack of space.

Speakers explored the issue of women in the Church thoroughly. Elizabeth Carroll expounded many meanings of the phrase "the proper place of women in the church." Rosemary Radford Ruether provided a critique of the patriarchal structures dominating women. Scripture scholars Elisabeth Schüssler Fiorenza and Carroll Stuhlmueller demonstrated that there are no scriptural barriers to women's ordination. Margaret Farley called women's ordination a "moral imperative" for the Church. Arlene Swidler offered "partnership marriage" as a model for a priesthood of equality, and speakers like Marjorie Tuite and William R. Callahan provided strategies for achieving the goal.

Other speakers at this historic assembly included George Tavard, Emily Clark Hewitt, Anne E. Carr, Rev. Richard McBrien, Marie Augusta Neal, Emily Clark Hewitt, Dorothy Donnelly, Eleanor Kahle, and Mary Daniel Turner. Mary Collins and Rosalie Muschal-Reinhardt led prayer services.

The closing ritual brought a hushed silence to the hall when all women called to priesthood were asked to stand and be blessed. Slowly, over several minutes, hundreds of women stood. The assembly was awed, and the movement was born.

The Detroit conference also produced one of the first signs of hierarchical resistance. Archbishop Joseph Bernardin of Chicago, then president of the National Conference of Catholic Bishops, issued a statement saying, "It is not correct to say that no serious theological obstacle stands in the way of ordaining women to the priesthood" (News statement, United States Conference of Catholic Bishops, October 3, 1975).

Those in the young movement, energized by the Detroit Conference and hopeful that ordinations would occur within their lifetimes, did not expect instant institutional acceptance. An organization formally called the "Women's Ordination Conference" was founded in 1976 to carry on the work begun in Detroit. The first Core Commission, the governing body of the new group, met in June 1976. Recognizing the structures of ministry in the Church as part of the problem, the organization defined its goal as the "ordination of Roman Catholic women to a *renewed* priestly ministry."

The United States Bishops convened the Call to Action Conference in Detroit that same year as a commemoration of the U.S. bicentennial. This gathering, which followed widespread hearings at the grassroots level, became a surprisingly adventurous national consultation. The delegates, of whom 93 percent were either appointees of bishops or bishops themselves, called on the American bishops to facilitate the formation of a "more fully developed position on the ordination of women to sacred orders." Delegates listed what the study must include: the rights and needs of the community, the action of the Holy Spirit, interpretive study of the human sciences, experiences of other Christian churches, contemporary biblical exegesis, as well as pontifical and episcopal statements. The study was to involve lay- and religious women, especially "women who believe themselves called to priesthood" (Call to Action: *Recommendations on Church*, II, 2).

Ironically, the Pontifical Biblical Commission already had a study under way, and its 1976 report to Pope Paul VI stated, "It does not seem that the New Testament by itself alone will permit us to settle in a clear way and once and for all the problem of the possible accession of women to the presbyterate" ("Biblical Commission Report: Can Women Be Priests?").

Arguments Advanced for Women's Ordination

Speakers at the Detroit Women's Ordination Conference advanced several arguments in favor of the ordination of women. Theologians and activists refined these arguments as the movement matured. The most prominent include these:

The Christian theology of the human person teaches that women are full human persons, made in the image of God and equal to men. Vatican Council II is cited frequently:

> All women and men are . . . created in God's image; they have the same nature and origin and, being redeemed by Christ, . . . there is here a basic equality between all . . . any kind of social or cultural discrimination in basic personal rights on the grounds of sex, race, color, social conditions, language or religion, must be curbed and eradicated as incompatible with God's design. It is deeply to be deplored that these basic personal rights are not yet being respected everywhere, as is the case with women who are denied the chance freely to choose a husband, or a *state of life*. (Pope Paul II, chapter 2, emphasis added)

Without women in the priesthood, Christ is imaged in an incomplete way. The Vatican maintains that women cannot image Jesus in the priesthood. Women's ordination activists turn that argument on its head noting that, in Catholic theology, Christ assumed, and redeemed, *humanity*, not maleness. Both women *and* men can image Christ, and the Church needs both genders to represent the fullness of humanity.

Limiting ordination to men limits God and sacralizes masculinity. Catholic theology teaches that God is beyond knowing. Language is merely a tool to image a God who cannot be expressed in images. To make God literally "male" is to confuse the essence of God with a word image. To say God cannot call women as well as men limits God's will. To make the maleness of Jesus a controlling element in imaging him is to confuse Jesus' maleness, which is *incidental*, with his humanity, which is *fundamental* to his redemptive role.

Catholic teaching on justice demands the elimination of oppressive discrimination. Women, much more than men, suffer from poverty, illiteracy, violence, and even death *because* they are women. Advocates of women priests maintain that a church that denies ordination to women participates in this sin because it sanctifies the system of sexist thought that underlies these pervasive injustices worldwide.

Jesus modeled gender equality in his dealings with women. He called both women and men to ministry, commissioning Mary of Magdala to preach, for example. He did not "ordain" anyone, men or women. The notion of priesthood evolved over time; it was not until the second or third century that it began to resemble what we know today. The twelve apostles were symbolic of the twelve tribes of Israel, Jesus' way of saying that all Jews were a part of his New Covenant. The Last Supper was a Jewish Passover Seder, a family meal, which usually included women and children.

Ordaining women reflects the finest Catholic tradition, too long buried. Scripture tells us that women were deacons, preachers, missionaries, and leaders of the early Church. New research shows that women in early centuries led house churches and presided at the table of the Eucharist, roles we now understand as priestly.

The faithful support the ordination of women, and the pastoral needs of the Church today demand it. The "canonical doctrine of reception," an ancient part of Catholic tradition, says that, for a law to be an effective guide for the believing community, it must be "received" by that community. The male-only priesthood is no longer a "received" doctrine. Polls in the United States, Canada, and Europe have shown consistently that 62 to 71 percent of all Catholics favor women priests. Moreover, there is a severe and worsening shortage of male, celibate priests. Catholics often ask, "Isn't the Eucharist more important than a male-only priesthood?"

The First Papal "No"

In January 1977 Pope Paul VI issued *Inter Insignores*, the *Vatican Declaration against the Ordination of Women*, laying the groundwork for all future official opposition by asserting that women cannot "image Christ" in the priesthood and that both scripture and the constant tradition of the Church forbid the ordination of women.

This document galvanized the fledgling movement. Public reaction was swift and stormy. While the U.S. bishops officially praised the *Declaration*, theologians like Karl Rahner and John Donohue wrote articles dissenting from virtually every section of the *Declaration*. Catholic feminists were outraged, and under the leadership of the newly formed Women's Ordination Conference, they organized demonstrations in front of cathedrals and diocesan offices nationwide. A group of theologians and leaders of the women's ordination movement held a press conference to denounce the document, calling it antiwoman and without theological credibility. The Quixote Center, a national faith-based center working on issues of justice in church and society, commissioned a Gallup Survey in February and March 1977. It measured the rapid change of Catholic opinion in the two months following the *Declaration* when public debate was the hottest. It used the question first employed by noted sociologist Andrew Greeley in a 1974 study, asking agreement or disagreement with this question: "It would be a good thing if women were allowed to be ordained as priests."

In 1974, 29 percent of Catholics agreed with this statement. By February 1977, it was 31 percent, but in only one month, it jumped 10 percentage points, to 41 percent. The Vatican was on a losing trajectory with Catholic public opinion. Professional surveys in the 1990s consistently reported that between 62 percent and 67 percent of U.S. Catholics support women's ordination.

Meanwhile, the Women's Ordination Conference launched Project Priesthood, a study of women who felt called to ordination. This 1978 survey revealed that 65 percent were nuns and 35 percent laywomen, a trend reversed twenty years later.

In response to repeated assertions that women were not psychologically suited to be priests, a sociopsychological study of a sample of these women, conducted by Fran Ferder, compared them to a sample of men studying for the priesthood. The findings, published in *Called to Break Bread* (1978), found that the women were *better* qualified than their male counterparts.

Official opposition met with righteous anger, spurring growth in movement participation, as well as Women's Ordination Conference membership. The Core Commission of the Women's Ordination Conference laid plans for a second conference on the ordination of women in Baltimore, Maryland, in 1978 with the theme of "New Woman, New Church, New Priestly Ministry." Dolly Pomerleau, a founding mother of the Women's Ordination Conference, coordinated the event.

The flyer advertising the gathering proclaimed boldly, "It's time to lay to rest the heresy that women cannot image Jesus in the priesthood."

That conference was larger than the previous one in Detroit, with more than 2,000 participants, and it began not with polite speeches but with a demonstration in the streets. Participants, carrying large silver styrofoam chains, started at Baltimore's Inner Harbor. They spilled into the streets chanting, "Burst the chains that oppress, and forge the chains that free!"

The Baltimore Conference advanced the movement by linking the evils of sexism with those of racism, classism, and social justice. Featured speakers, from Asia, Africa, Latin America, and Europe, demonstrated that the issue was not limited to North America. The conference raised publicly an issue that had been an ongoing debate in the movement from the beginning, namely: Should women accept ordination in the system as it exists or refuse ordination until Church structures underwent thorough change and renewal?

Some conference participants challenged the idea of a male-led liturgy. Although the majority of conference participants went to the official Eucharistic celebration, a small group broke off and held a women-led Eucharist.

After that conference, a group of women gathered up some of the silver styrofoam chains that had served as the conference symbol and drove to Washington, D.C., where the National Conference of Catholic Bishops was holding its annual meeting. When the women made their presence known, the Bishops' Committee on Women in the Church invited them to a meeting. Bishop Maurice Dingman of Des Moines, Iowa, stood on the floor of the Bishops' Conference and called for dialogue on the issue of women priests.

In 1979 a small group of bishops met several times to engage in a dialogue with movement representatives in what Rosemary Radford Ruether later called "a non-meeting of the minds." After one particularly frustrating session, Marjorie Tuite lamented, "They don't want us, they never wanted us, they are never going to want us ordained." At one point the women actually walked out and boycotted the meetings for a day. The talks resumed and continued for three years. Although they produced no structural or policy changes, the dialogue had a strong impact on participating bishops.

That same year, the newly elected Pope John Paul II visited the United States for the first time. In Washington, D.C., three women held an all-night vigil outside the Vatican Embassy. The next morning, Women's Ordination Conference coordinator Ruth Fitzpatrick, holding a lighted candle, greeted the pope in his motorcade by shouting the words, "Ordain Women!" Throughout his visit in Washington, D.C., protesters followed the pope with banners saying in Polish, "Sexism Is a Sin. Repent."

When the pope reached the National Shrine of the Immaculate Conception to speak to an audience of nuns, Sister of Mercy Theresa Kane, then the head of her order and the president of the Leadership Conference of Women Religious, greeted him with a gentle but firm and unmistakable message. She called for the recognition of "women as persons" in *all* the ministries of the Church. In a separately organized action, thirty nuns wearing blue armbands stood in protest during the entire ceremony at the Shrine. These events, and especially the speech of Theresa Kane, saturated the media for days. The pope rejected all pleas, but public debate on women's ordination reached a crescendo. As before, polls showed that Vatican opposition only strengthened the movement for women's ordination.

Women's Ordination Conference (WOC)

The leading organization in the movement has been the Women's Ordination Conference. In its first days, the office consisted of a card table, a chair, and a file cabinet in a back room of the Quixote Center in Mt. Rainier, Maryland. Its first national coordinator was Ruth Fitzpatrick. Within a year, she moved to a small office in the Mt. Pleasant area of Washington, D.C. Throughout the years, the office has been located in Rochester, New York, and New York City. Its national coordinators have included Ruth Fitzpatrick, Joan Sobala, Rosalie Muschal-Reinhardt, Ada María Isasi-Díaz, Fidelis McDonough, Marsie Silvestro, Dolly Pomerleau, Duffy McDermott, Maureen Fiedler, Andrea Johnson, Deborah Halter, and Genevieve Chavez.

When Ruth Fitzpatrick took the helm as national coordinator for the second time in the mid-1980s, she moved the national headquarters to Fairfax, Virginia, first to her own home, then into a second-story office over a shopping center. During her tenure, Fitzpatrick became a well-known figure in the media, responding strongly and consistently to the negative statements of the bishops and the Vatican.

Early on, the Women's Ordination Conference launched its newsletter, *New Women, New Church*. Staff traveled around the country, meeting with supporters and helping organize locally. Money was always scarce, but interest, membership, and funding surged upward every time there was a papal visit or another official document denying ordination to women once again.

The Women's Ordination Conference has sponsored public hearings on women in the Church, retreats, workshops and speeches, and a regular program of demonstrations outside churches where men are being ordained as priests. Members performed public Holy Thursday foot-washings, remembering Jesus' washing the disciples' feet at the Last Supper and his call to servant leadership. Demonstrators once wore blue armbands (the traditional color associated with Mary the mother of Jesus) but now favor the purple stole, adopted from the European movement by North Americans in the 1990s. The stole is the sign of priesthood, and the purple signifies mourning that women are barred from ordination. The Women's Ordination Conference has consistently encouraged its members to write letters to bishops and the media, to call in to talk shows, to lobby local bishops, and even to "Take a Bishop to Breakfast."

While the Women's Ordination Conference remained a focus for organizing around the women's ordination issue, a group of organizations called the "Women of the Church Coalition" met frequently to discuss a wide range of issues affecting women's status in the Church. Women's ordination was part of the agenda, but not all. Inclusive language and symbol, hierarchical structures, women's liturgies, social justice generally, reproductive rights, and gay/lesbian rights were also issues of concern. Small worshipping groups formed around the country, and women often celebrated Mass without a priest. That coalition evolved into "Women Church Convergence," and the group held its first conference in Chicago in 1983.

Both the Chicago Conference and a larger Cincinnati Women-Church Conference in 1987 addressed the question of women priests, but only as part of larger questions that included a fundamental critique of patriarchy and church governance, women-led liturgies, and all women's rights in Church and civil society.

The Women Church Convergence held its third conference in Albuquerque, New Mexico, in 1993. This time, the gathering was interfaith in scope and explored questions ranging from women in Christian ministry to Goddess worship. Few speakers touched the ordination of Roman Catholic women.

Meanwhile, in the 1980s and 1990s, many Church reform organizations added women's ordination to their agendas or were founded with that issue at the core. These included Catholics Speak Out, the Call to Action, FutureChurch, the Eighth Day Center for Justice, and CORPUS (the National Association for a Married Priesthood). In Church reform circles, women's ordination became a "settled" issue at the core of the demands for change.

Ordination Revisited, a small conference in St. Louis sponsored by the Women's Ordination Conference in 1984, brought together women who felt called to ordination. About 200 attended, and the conference led to the formation of RAPPORT, a group of "women called" who have met regularly ever since for prayer, solidarity, and strategy.

New research appeared in 1990–1991 that called into question the Vatican assertion that the Church had never "ordained" women. Giorgio Otranto, an Italian scholar, published his interpretation of icons found in the catacombs, icons that include frescos of women performing priestly functions. Mary Ann Rossi, an expert in classical studies, translated his work into English. Otranto, sponsored by the Women's Ordination Conference, lectured in the United States in October 1991, including the Catholic University of America. His findings received wide media attention.

The Vatican made a small concession in the early 1980s to the growing clamor for gender equality in the Church by permitting bishops to decide for their own dioceses whether or not women or girls might be altar servers. The vast majority of bishops in the United States approved, confirming a practice that had become commonplace. Recognizing that this was only a baby step toward its goal, the Women's Ordination Conference hailed the move nonetheless.

The U.S. bishops' Ad Hoc Committee on Women in Society and in the Church initiated a *Pastoral Letter on Women's Concerns* in the early 1990s. They began by holding public hearings held around the country. Hundreds of women testified. "Don't write about women; write about sexism," said the women of the ordination movement. "Sexism is the problem."

The first draft reflected many of the women's diverse voices, but the Vatican intervened in the process. The *Pastoral*, intended by the bishops of the United States to be an official statement of policy on women's issues, went through four drafts in two years, each becoming progressively more conservative than the last. The final and fourth draft emphatically opposed the ordination of women.

The movement organized to stop its passage. The Women's Ordination Conference, Catholics Speak Out, Priests for Equality, Call to Action, and other groups spoke out strongly against it. A national campaign was launched that included heavy grassroots lobbying of bishops, a four-page signature ad in the *National Catholic Reporter,* and multiple press releases. Just months prior to the vote, in what was believed to be a highly influential factor in the outcome, Catholics Speak Out/ Quixote Center released a Gallup poll showing that 67 percent of Catholics in the United States favored the ordination of women. In one of the first victories of the ordination movement, the bishops failed to achieve the required two-thirds vote and defeated the *Pastoral* at their November 1992 annual meeting.

Officials in Rome decided it was time to stifle the growing dissent. They began to take action against individuals and to make stronger pronouncements in an effort to quell the public support for women's ordination.

The Society of Jesus dismissed a longtime advocate of women's ordination, Rev. William R. Callahan, in 1991. Although women's ordination was not specifically mentioned in his dismissal, Jesuit officials declared that his life and preaching touched "every neuralgic issue" of the Church, and women's ordination was clearly such an issue.

Pope John Paul II issued *Ordinatio Sacerdotalis* (1994), or what became known as the "Papal No" to women's ordination. This document repeated the teachings of *Inter Insignores* but added that the teaching was "definitive" and not open to discussion. Theologians and the women's ordination movement sharply criticized the document, disputing especially the idea that so new a teaching could be "definitive."

With public discussion continuing in spite of *Ordinatio*, Cardinal Joseph Ratzinger, prefect of the Congregation for the Doctrine of the Faith, issued the Vatican's *Responsum Ad Dubium* in 1995, responding to supposed "doubts" about the teaching. *Responsum* said that the all-male priesthood is part of the infallibility of the ordinary magisterium of the Church. Leaders of the movement, alarmed by use of the word "infallibility," denounced the document. They made it clear that this teaching did not meet the standards for infallible declarations, that it was far from being "received" by the faithful, and that—in any event—Cardinal Ratzinger was not the pope.

Carmel McEnroy was fired from St. Meinrad's Seminary in Indiana in 1995 because she had signed an ad in the *National Catholic Reporter* calling for dialogue on the issue of women priests. Then the Vatican ordered the British publisher of Lavinia Byrne's book *Woman at the Altar* to destroy all remaining copies. Byrne eventually left her religious congregation. Her book was republished by New York Continuum in 1998.

With Vatican opposition intensifying, the Women's Ordination Conference was determined to tell the world that advocates of women's ordination would not be silent. A 20th Anniversary National Conference was held in Crystal City, Virginia, officially titled "Gathering '95: Discipleship of Equals, Breaking Bread/Doing Justice."

A split in the movement became evident at this public event, which drew approximately 1,000 participants. Speakers such as Elisabeth Schüssler Fiorenza argued that ordination was no longer a desirable goal because the Roman Catholic Church was hopelessly patriarchal. She urged direct work toward a "discipleship of equals" in women-church. Others, such as Maureen Fiedler, while agreeing that the "discipleship of equals" was the ultimate and desired goal, believed that women must seek ordination in order to challenge the institution and the patriarchal order and leverage other structural changes in the Church. As many conference participants

expressed doubt about the Women's Ordination Conference's commitment to its mission, the organization's board of directors reaffirmed its historic goal, the ordination of women to a renewed priestly ministry.

International Ties Are Forged

Meanwhile, fresh activities in Europe reenergized the movement in the United States. Sponsors of a *Petition of the People of God* in Austria and Germany gathered more than 2.3 million signatures for "five points" of Church reform, one of which was the ordination of Roman Catholic women as priests and deacons. This led to the founding of the International We Are Church Movement in 1997 at a meeting in Rome. Women's ordination was a prominent part of the agenda. In 1998, at an unprecedented demonstration in St. Peter's Square with more than 500 participants from seventeen countries, including the United States, a petition with the "five points"—one being women's ordination—was presented to Vatican officials, who graciously received them and promptly ignored them.

Delegates from the United States, attending the first European Women's Synod in Gmunden, Austria, joined with European and Latin American women to found Women's Ordination Worldwide (WOW) in 1996. They included Andrea Johnson, national coordinator of the Women's Ordination Conference, Jeremy Daigler, Maureen Fiedler, Suzanne Polen, and Dolly Pomerleau. WOW held the first international Women's Ordination Conference in Dublin, Ireland, in June–July 2001.

While the movement in North America and Europe was still the dream of a few in 1970, an event unknown in the West occurred in utmost secrecy in Czechoslovakia when it was under communist rule. The implications were far-reaching. On December 28, 1970, a laywoman named Ludmila Javorova lay prostrate on the floor of an upper room as Bishop Felix Davidek, a Catholic bishop in good standing, ordained her to the Roman Catholic priesthood to minister to the persecuted underground Church of that time. She carried on her ministry in secret for twenty years, serving even as vicar general of the underground diocese. In this same period, a number of married men were ordained to the priesthood to serve the persecuted Church.

The *New York Times* (December 8, 1991) revealed Ludmila's ordination, and Cardinal Miroslav Vlk of Prague admitted that Ludmila Javarova was but one of four to six unidentified women ordained for the underground Church. He characterized these ordinations as invalid. Javorova has made clear in numerous interviews and talks that she regards herself a bona fide priest. An unknown number of women were ordained to the diaconate. None of these women has made her story public.

Following the *New York Times* story, the Women's Ordination Conference organized a delegation of four women to go to the Czech Republic and search for Javorova. Dolly Pomerleau, Martha Ann Kirk, Carolyn Moynihan, and Ruth Fitzpatrick located Javorova and met with her and many others from the underground Church. Later, in her modest apartment, they heard her incredible and touching story into the early hours of the morning.

Under the sponsorship of the Women's Ordination Conference and Catholics Speak Out, Javorova came to the United States for a visit in 1997. She spoke to small groups in Cleveland, Ohio, New Jersey, and the Baltimore/Washington metropolitan area, affirming her priesthood at every gathering. She refused to grant any interviews with the media. After that trip, Javorova began collaborating with Miriam Therese Winter on a book about her life and the story of the Czech underground Church. It was published in 2001 by Crossroad of New York (*Out of the Depths, the Story of Ludmila Javorova Ordained Roman Catholic Priest*, by Miriam Therese Winter).

New Strategies in the New Millennium

New strategies began to appear in the new century. Chicago activists noted that the archdiocese of Chicago had begun a billboard campaign throughout the city to attract male candidates to the priesthood. Mirroring the archdiocesan slogan, the women created their own billboard and placed signs in the city's rapid transit system. The billboard, with a Roman collar like that used by the archdiocesan ad, read, "You're waiting for a sign from God? *This* is it! Ordain women." Media attention was instantaneous and intense. Soon the campaign spilled over into Milwaukee. Church officials were stung and responded, saying that theological debate cannot be conducted through billboards.

Many in the movement became aware that its members were graying. Most were of the Vatican II generation who remembered the excitement of change and experimentation in the 1960s and 1970s. And so the Women's Ordination Conference founded the Young Feminist Network in 1996 to attract younger people to the movement.

Under the leadership of Andrea Johnson, the Women's Ordination Conference renewed its study of women called to be priests and released its findings to the media in 1999. They showed that such women are not "radicals on the fringe of the institution. They are mature, well-educated regular churchgoers active in their faith communities. More than half are employed

by the institutional church." The study called them "benevolent subversives." In a complete reversal from the earlier study, 75 percent were laywomen and the balance nuns (Fiedler and Schwartz).

During the quarter-century since 1975, leaders and activists of the Women's Ordination Conference often discussed the question of "just doing it," that is, finding a bishop or bishops who would catapult over the regulations and actually ordain some Roman Catholic women, much as the Episcopalians had done in 1974. The issue began to gel more firmly in 1998 in Rochester, New York. Here an entire parish, then called "Corpus Christi," was expelled from the diocese over issues that included a prominent place for women at the Eucharistic table. Kevin McKenna, chancellor of the Diocese of Rochester, announced that the community had excommunicated itself, but the parish continued to consider itself Catholic.

The parish of more than 1,000 resettled itself in rented facilities and named itself Spiritus Christi. Many parishioners wanted to call two parish leaders, Mary Ramerman and Denise Donato, to serve the parish as priests, thus responding to an interior call felt by both women. As a first step, the parish sponsored a women's ordination conference in June 2000, attended by more than 200 people, to address the question. After the conference, the parish formally called the women and began to search for a bishop to perform the ordinations. They found Bishop Peter Hickman of the Old Catholic Church, a group that broke away from Rome in the nineteenth century but claims valid apostolic succession for its bishops. Bishop Hickman ordained Mary Ramerman in 2001 and Denise Donato in 2003. For Spiritus Christi, these were courageous and groundbreaking acts, firsts for a Catholic parish in the United States.

The first conference of Women's Ordination Worldwide in Dublin, Ireland, in June–July 2001, attended by 350 people from twenty-six countries and five continents, once again raised the issue to public consciousness, due largely to interventions from Rome. The Vatican forbade Myra Poole, a nun who was the conference organizer, to attend, but she came anyway. Roman officials also made unsuccessful attempts to bar Benedictine Sister Joan Chittister from presenting her keynote speech. Resolutions passed at the conference showed strong international commitment to the ordination of women.

In the summer of 2002, more "irregular" ordinations took place in Europe. Two bishops with claims to apostolic succession ordained seven women on a boat on the Danube River. There were three Germans—Ida Raming, Iris Mueller, and Gisela Forster; three Austrians—Christina Mayr-Lumetzberger, Adelinde Theresia Roitinger, and Pia Brunner. One was Austrian American—Dagmar Celeste. In 2003, Catholics Speak Out and the Women's Ordination Conference sponsored a coast-to-coast speaking tour of the United States for Ida Raming and Iris Mueller, during which they encouraged women who feel called to follow their example.

At the dawn of the third millennium, "just doing it," albeit irregularly, is gaining a foothold in the United States. At the same time, more theologians and activists on all continents are joining the movement for women's ordination. It is a movement that promises to continue until Roman Catholicism finally joins other Christian churches in accepting women fully in all its ministries.

The Women's Ordination Movement in Canada

Several different Canadian organizations have addressed the issue of women's ordination in different ways over the last thirty years. Marie-Andree Roy, Monique Dumais, and Louise Melançon founded l'Autre Parole (The Other Word) in the province of Quebec in 1976. They describe themselves as a group of Christian feminists, but they have no position on the ordination of women because of a fundamental disagreement over whether or not women should accept ordination in this patriarchal church. They publish a bulletin four times a year.

Thirty women from across Canada met in Toronto in 1981 and founded Canadian Catholics for Women's Ordination. Four theology students, Ellen Leonard, Alexina Murphy, Bernadette McMahon, and Judy Maier, were the principal initiators.

Realizing the interconnectedness of issues that women face in Church and society, the organization changed its name to Catholic Network for Women's Equality in 1988. The mission statement of the Catholic Network reflects this broad vision, and it guides the organization's strategy and program. It reads: "To enable women to name their giftedness, and from that awareness to effect structural change in the church that reflects the mutuality and co-responsibility of women and men within the church."

The organization sponsors an annual conference in a different city each year, and that gathering reflects the needs, interests, and concerns of its members. Local groups also sponsor retreat days and other events.

Femmes et Ministères (Women and Ministry) was founded in 1982 in the Province of Quebec. The organization works to improve the situation of women in the Church and educate the official Church about women's issues. It is committed to obtaining the recognition of all women's ministries in the Church and to eliminating all types of discrimination to which women are subjected.

Communication in this vast but sparsely populated country has been a challenge resolved largely through email, chat-rooms, and Web communications that enable women isolated in one part of the country to communicate with other like-minded women.

The Women's Ordination Movement in Mexico

There is no formal women's ordination "movement" in Mexico, but in the years since the Vatican Declaration against the Ordination of Women, there have been isolated voices calling for the full equality of women in the ordained ministries of the Church. In a country suffering from economic underdevelopment, the call for gender equality in ministry is usually part of a larger quest for social justice and for the equal treatment of women in economic life.

Groups such as Mujeres por el Dialogo (Women for Dialogue) and Católicas por el Derecho a Decidir (Catholics for the Right to Decide) have raised the ordination issue publicly but sporadically as part of a broader agenda of social justice and, in the case of Católicas por el Derecho a Decidir, a call for women's right to reproductive choice. The latter group is part of Movimiento Internacional Somos Iglesia (International We Are Church Movement), a worldwide coalition of Church reform groups calling for five major changes in the Church, including the ordination of women.

SOURCES: Official church documents on women's ordination are available through the U.S. Conference of Catholic Bishops or on the Web at http://www.womenpriests.org/. This Web site, created by Dutch theologian John Winjgaards, contains the largest compendium of literature on women's ordination, pro and con, on the Web. See also Pope Paul II, "Pastoral Constitution on the Church in the Modern World: *Gaudium et Spes*," http://www.vatican.va/archive/hist_councils/ii_vatican _council/index.htm; "Biblical Commission Report: Can Women Be Priests?" http://www.womanpriest.org/classic/ append2.htm; and Maureen Fiedler and Karen Schwartz, *Benevolent Subversives* (1999). Most theological work for women's ordination was done in the 1970s. Classic works include Haye van der Meer's *Women Priests in the Catholic Church?* (1973); George Tavard's *Woman in Christian Tradition* (1973); and Carroll Stuhlmueller's *Women and Priesthood: Future Directions* (1978). Compendia of important essays include Anne Marie Gardner's chronicle of the Detroit Women's Ordination Conference, *Women and Catholic Priesthood* (1976); the Proceedings of the Second Women's oOrdination Conference in Baltimore, *New Woman, New Church, New Ministry* (1978); and Leonard and Arlene Swidler's *Women Priests: A Catholic Commentary on the Vatican Declaration* (1977). By the early 1980s, most theologians believed that the issue was "settled" in favor of women's ordination, even if Rome did not recognize the fact. The scholarly conversation then shifted from "ordination" to "ministry" in a broad sense. Feminist scholars such as Rosemary Radford Ruether, Elisabeth Schüssler Fiorenza, Mary

Hunt, Elizabeth Johnson, Diana Hayes, and Ada María Isasi-Díaz led the discussion in numerous theological works. The 1990s brought fresh historical and anthropological insights to the issue. Karen Jo Torjensen's *When Women Were Priests* (1993) showed that women did indeed fill priestly roles in the early centuries of Christianity. The work of archeologist Giorgio Otranto of Italy bolstered that conclusion with iconographic evidence. See "Notes on the Female Priesthood in Antiquity," translated from Italian in *Priesthood, Precedent and Prejudice: On Recovering the Women Priests of Early Christianity* in Mary Ann Rossi, "Priesthood, Precedent and Prejudice: On Recovering the Women Priests of Early Christianity," *Journal of Feminist Studies* 7 (1991): 73–94.

JEWISH WOMEN'S ORDINATION

Pamela S. Nadell

IN 1889, ON the front page of Philadelphia's *Jewish Exponent*, the writer Mary M. Cohen (1854–1911) asked, "Could not—our *women*—be ministers?" (Nadell, 1). That question launched a century-long debate over Jewish women's right to ordination. Not until 1972 did the first American woman shatter the historic tradition of an exclusively male rabbinate, and then women became rabbis only in Reform Judaism. Thereafter, the battle over women's ordination continued—and continues today in Orthodox Judaism.

When Cohen first raised the idea of women rabbis, she did so against the backdrop of the nineteenth-century woman's rights movement. Although best known for demanding woman suffrage, the vote women won in 1920, the Seneca Falls Convention's *Declaration of Sentiments and Resolutions* in 1848 railed against men for excluding women from the learned professions—from medicine, law, and the ministry. During the nineteenth century a few women managed to break into these professions, becoming the first female doctors, lawyers, and clergy. In the 1850s Antoinette Brown Blackwell and in the 1880s Anna Howard Shaw challenged their churches and became the first women ministers in, respectively, the Congregational Church and the Methodist Episcopal Church Conference. Thus, American Jews joined their Protestant neighbors as they turned to the problem of ordaining women.

In the 1890s the question Cohen raised swirled beyond Philadelphia. In particular, it struck a chord among those in the most liberal Jewish denomination, Reform Judaism. As Reform developed in the nineteenth century, its leaders often proclaimed their intention of emancipating women in the synagogue. Thus Reform rabbis were the first to break, in 1851 in Albany, New York, with the custom of seating men and women separately during worship, and Reform Jews celebrated this as evidence of their progressive stance on women. Con-

templating women in the rabbinate, therefore, seemed consistent with Reform's championing new religious rights for women.

Not surprisingly, then, some girls and women found their way into classes at Hebrew Union College (HUC), the Reform rabbinical seminary established in Cincinnati in 1875, but none seems to have been considered a serious candidate for ordination. In the 1890s California's Ray Frank (Litman, 1861–1948) won acclaim for her lay preaching, teaching, and leading religious services. The press nicknamed her "the girl rabbi of the golden west" and asked her: "What would you do if you were a rabbi?" (39).

In 1897, in a Reform Jewish newspaper, twenty-six prominent American Jewish women weighed whether or not women should occupy the pulpit. Fifteen could imagine exemplary women, properly trained, as rabbis. Nine believed that not only did a woman's essential nature deny her this calling but that when "the crowning jewel of woman, motherhood, comes to bless her," the woman rabbi would find the struggle to balance family and career far too difficult (52). Nevertheless, Hannah Solomon (1858–1942), the founding president of the National Council of Jewish Women and a Reform Jew, boasted: "We are receiving every possible encouragement from our rabbis, and should women desire to enter the ministry, there will be no obstacles thrown in their way" (45).

Yet where were the women who wanted to be rabbis in the 1890s and early twentieth century? The Jewish women Mary M. Cohen claimed only needed a bit of encouragement to become rabbis have not left their names for the historical record. But after World War I women seeking ordination left a trail for the historian to follow, as they drove the debate about women rabbis from the realm of the abstract to the actual.

The first was Martha Neumark (Montor, 1904–1981). At fourteen, Neumark, the daughter of Hebrew Union College Professor David Neumark, became a student at the seminary. There she studied Bible and Hebrew, rabbinics, and Jewish history. In 1921, she asked the college for a high holiday pulpit. Every fall, scattered Jewish communities all over America, too small to host a permanent rabbi, called rabbinical students to lead them in prayer on the holiest days of the Jewish calendar, the New Year (Rosh Hashanah) and the Day of the Atonement (Yom Kippur). When Neumark asked for the same opportunity her male classmates had, a high holiday position, she raised the question of what would happen if she actually completed the nine-year rabbinical course. Would HUC ordain her a rabbi?

For the next two years, college faculty, alumni, and trustees debated the issue. Delving into the classical texts of Jewish tradition, scholars lined up on opposite sides, shaping the lines of the debate that would, in decades to come, echo throughout American Jewish life. Some believed Jewish law unequivocally prohibited women rabbis. Others argued that nothing in Judaism forbid this, in large measure because the great sages of old had simply never considered the question at all. In the end the HUC Board of Governors voted, six laymen to two rabbis, to exclude women from the rabbinate, even as they celebrated Reform Judaism's record of promoting the equality of women with men in the synagogue.

Martha Neumark well understood the implications of her quest. Realizing that the woman rabbi was "merely another phase of the woman question," of the struggle that "ensues each time that a woman threatens to break up man's monopoly" (71) in any field, she continued in her studies, earning for her seven and a half years in rabbinical school a certificate qualifying her to be a Sunday School principal.

Even as Neumark's hopes to become a rabbi were quashed, in New York, at the Jewish Institute of Religion (JIR), which was a nondenominational but decidedly liberal seminary, Irma Levy Lindheim (1886–1978) was raising the same challenge. By the time Lindheim joined JIR's inaugural class in the fall of 1922, she was already the mother of five and a deeply committed Zionist dedicated to transforming the ancient Jewish settlement in Palestine into a modern Jewish homeland. At first she sought an advanced Jewish education to assist her in her Zionist work. But, in the spring of 1923, she asked the faculty to change her status from that of a special student to that of a regular rabbinical student. Eventually the faculty yielded, and JIR announced that it trained men *and women* for the Jewish ministry. Nevertheless, Lindheim failed to complete the rabbinical course, traveling instead to Palestine and dedicating the remainder of her life to Zionism and the State of Israel.

But she was not the only special student at the Jewish Institute of Religion in 1922. Dr. Dora Askowith (1884–1958) was also in this class. Askowith earned a doctorate from Columbia University for her dissertation on the Jews in the ancient Roman Empire, and she taught at New York City's Hunter College. Intensely interested in Jewish life and especially in Jewish scholarship, Askowith, like Lindheim, at first simply sought higher Jewish education. As she wrote: "I took the work at the Institute because of my deep interest in Judaica and Hebraica rather than because I sought to enter the ministry though I hoped to open the road for women who might be desirous of being ordained" (79). But Askowith failed to open that road, for she left JIR without completing the rabbinical program.

Unlike Lindheim and Askowith, Helen Levinthal (Lyons, 1910–1989) stayed the course. The daughter of the prominent Brooklyn Conservative rabbi Israel Levinthal, Helen Levinthal had the intensive Jewish education typical of rabbis' children. After college and graduate school, she joined a number of Jewish women's organizations and, perhaps to occupy her time, enrolled as an auditor at JIR. But quickly she changed her status and became a regular rabbinical student. As she approached her final year, the faculty debated what to do. In the end, they concluded that, despite their decision of 1923, the time was not ripe for women's ordination. And so, in 1939, for the work she had done, as the men of her class became rabbis, Helen Levinthal received the degree Master of Hebrew Literature along with a special certificate recognizing her accomplishments.

Nevertheless, *Time* magazine proclaimed her "as near to being a rabbi as a female might be" (85). Meanwhile, she told the press, which always reported the news of women trying to break into new fields, that "it is all a process of evolution. . . . Some day there will be women rabbis" (85). Apparently, neither she nor the American press knew that already one woman had indeed become a rabbi.

In 1935 in Germany, Regina Jonas (1902–1944) became the first woman rabbi. As a student at the Hochschule für die Wissenschaft des Judentums (College of Jewish Studies) in Berlin, Jonas wanted to be a rabbi. But, when she graduated, in 1930, she received the only diploma women could earn, that of Academic Teacher of Religion. Jonas, however, remained determined and, in 1935, took an oral exam in Jewish law with Rabbi Max Dienemann, one of the leaders of German Reform Judaism, and he signed her rabbinic diploma. Although he cautioned her against using the title "rabbi" until she consulted with other authorities, from then until her death, some called her Rabbiner Doktor Regina Jonas.

What joins the 1920s and 1930s pioneers of women's ordination with those who followed them and with those who argued their cause before them is that all believed Jewish tradition permitted women rabbis. Each on her own, and largely unaware that another had already made these same arguments, used the Jewish past, especially the history of women in Judaism, to appeal to tradition, even though, as a woman who wanted to be a rabbi, she seemed destined to overturn it. So Martha Neumark, Irma Levy Lindheim, Dora Askowith, Helen Levinthal, and Regina Jonas, and those who championed their cause, all pointed to the prophetesses Miriam, Deborah, and Hulda, claiming that their religious leadership demonstrated Judaism permitted women rabbis. They brought forth—in articles and speeches, in student sermons, and for Levinthal and Jonas, in their theses—remarkable medieval and modern Jewish women, those who taught, who founded schools, and who knew Jewish law, including several "accepted by their contemporaries as 'rabbinim'" (79). In the end, they argued—as Regina Jonas did in her thesis "Can a Woman Hold Rabbinical Office?"—that "other than prejudice and unfamiliarity, almost nothing opposes a woman holding the rabbinical office *halakhically*" (87), that is, in terms of Jewish law.

Finally, what binds the pioneers of the 1920s and 1930s is that each, with the tragic exception of Jonas, who died at the hands of the Nazis in Auschwitz on December 12, 1944, would again take up the cause of women's ordination. In decades to come, these women raised the issue again, corresponding with seminary faculty and their presidents and sometimes even the press. As Martha Neumark Montor wrote in 1964:

> I have a feeling that the time is ripe for active recruitment of women students—or at least open welcome for them. . . . I remember that in that long ago I was promised the necessary blessing by a group of indignant rabbis. . . . But I guess I was just too young and too foolish then to follow through. Now I'd like to complete the circle by helping some more mature young woman to set the precedent. (104)

Later Helen Levinthal Lyons, who lived to see the first women ordained Reform and Conservative rabbis, petitioned her alma mater to grant her ordination retroactively, but it never did.

In 1947 yet another woman applied to the Jewish Institute of Religion with the intention of becoming a rabbi. This time the seminary, which once boasted it trained women for the ministry, responded that, to its regret, it was impossible to admit female students. That seemed to close the door on women rabbis. Yet during the 1950s the debate about Jewish women's ordination continued.

In fact, the decade opened with the extraordinary case of a woman succeeding her husband and becoming rabbi of their congregation. In 1924 when Temple Beth Israel in Meridian, Mississippi, called Rabbi William Ackerman to its pulpit, his wife, Paula Herskovitz Ackerman (1893–1989), was by his side. The *rebbetzin*, the affectionate Yiddish-language title for rabbi's wife, was traditionally a full partner in the rabbi's ministry, the exemplary Jewish wife, mother, and communal worker essential to her husband's success. Ackerman was no exception. She taught Sabbath school and was active in the synagogue's sisterhood and in the National Federation of Temple Sisterhoods. When her husband was ill or away, she often substituted for him in the pulpit.

In November 1950, her husband of thirty-one years died. Temple Beth Israel's president asked the widow to carry on his ministry until they could hire a new rabbi. Ackerman well understood the implications of the invitation. She wrote: "I also know how revolutionary the idea is—therefore it seems to be a challenge that I

pray I can meet . . . if perhaps it will open a way for women students to train for congregational leadership—then my life would have some meaning" (121–122). And so Ackerman became Temple Beth Israel's spiritual leader and from December 1950 until the fall of 1953 led Sabbath and holiday services; officiated at confirmations, marriages, baby namings, and funerals; and preached and sustained her congregation and its congregants.

After Temple Beth Israel hired an ordained rabbi, Paula Ackerman retired, but as she left the pulpit, she reminded her temple of its role in paving the road for women's ordination. Quoting an ancient rabbinic sage, she told her congregants: "It is not incumbent upon us to complete the work but neither are we free to desist from it altogether" (124).

Leading Reform rabbis had opposed Ackerman's religious leadership. Not only was she not ordained, not only did she not have a seminary education, but she also seemed to set a dangerous precedent. Reform leaders feared other rabbis' wives, less capable than she, might expect to follow in their husbands' footsteps.

However, that did not mean that Reform rabbis opposed women's ordination in principle. In fact, in the mid-1950s these rabbis once again examined the question, propelled not by Paula Ackerman but rather by news of women's advancement elsewhere in American religion. In 1955, the Presbyterian Church, one of the largest and most important of the mainline Protestant denominations, concluded its decades-long debate about female clergy by voting to ordain women.

Confronted by the widely publicized announcement of the Presbyterians' ruling and by Harvard Divinity School's decision to accept women on equal terms with men, the Central Conference of American Rabbis, Reform Judaism's rabbinical conclave, created a commission to study ordaining women rabbis. Its 1956 report favored women's ordination provided, of course, that women completed seminary education. Among those signing the report was Nelson Glueck, president of Hebrew Union College–Jewish Institute of Religion (HUC–JIR, the two seminaries merged in 1950). Yet the rabbis claimed they faced a purely hypothetical question—there were no female candidates for the rabbinate at that time, or so they presumed.

But they were wrong. Just as Martha Neumark and Helen Levinthal in decades past had yearned to become rabbis, now other young women dreamt the same dream. In 1957, HUC–JIR joined with its neighbor, the University of Cincinnati (UC), to offer the first year rabbinical curriculum to UC undergraduates. Several scores of students, including—probably to its creators' surprise—a dozen women, took advantage of the new program. Some of the women wanted advanced Jewish ed-

On June 3, 1972, Sally Jane Priesand was ordained rabbi, teacher, and preacher. The first American woman to become a rabbi, she would not be the last. *Courtesy of the Jewish American Archives.*

ucations in order to teach or to become Judaica scholars. But some wanted to be rabbis.

In 1964 Sally Jane Priesand (1946–   ) joined them. As a teenager in Cleveland, Ohio, Priesand found herself deeply attracted to Judaism. In her Reform synagogue, Beth Israel—The West Temple, she preached at its annual youth service and later celebrated her confirmation, graduated from Hebrew high school, and organized Sunday School services. Intensely involved in the temple's youth group, she took charge of its ritual committee, compiled prayers for its meetings, and wrote for the synagogue newsletter. Most significantly, in the summer of 1961, the temple's sisterhood gave her a scholarship to attend the Reform movement's camp institute at Zionsville, Indiana.

Jewish camping was and remains a powerful venue for molding Jewish youth. And Reform camps were no exception. These settings gave girls, as well as boys, unusual opportunities for spiritual experiences, including religious leadership. The teenagers led services, gave "sermonettes," and engaged in Torah study. Notes from friends Priesand made that summer and in subsequent

summers reveal they already knew she hoped to become Rabbi Sally Priesand, if only HUC–JIR would ordain her.

In her junior year of high school Priesand wrote to the college to find out what she needed to do to win admission. College officials responded with great caution, informing her that they had never ordained a woman and that most women preferred the field of Jewish religious education. Nevertheless, in 1964, when Priesand enrolled at the University of Cincinnati as a freshman and at HUC–JIR as a special student in its undergraduate program, the *Cleveland Plain Dealer* reported: "Girl Sets her Goal to Be 1st Woman Rabbi" (148).

By the time Priesand passed, in 1968, from the undergraduate department into the rabbinical track, the question of women in the rabbinate was inextricably tied to the new wave of American feminism. Just as in the nineteenth century the notion of a woman rabbi was set against the backdrop of the woman's rights movement, now, in the 1960s, the second wave of American feminism helped to promote the question of women rabbis. In the wake of President John F. Kennedy's Commission on the Status of Women, the publication of Betty Friedan's *The Feminine Mystique* in 1963, and Title VII of the 1964 Civil Rights Act, which prohibited discrimination in employment on the basis of race and sex, American women pushed anew simultaneously on many frontiers for women's political, social, and economic equality. In the annals of American Judaism, Priesand appeared unique. But in the annals of the new wave of feminism, her ambition to become the first woman rabbi appeared but part of the larger story of the tremendous changes under way in women's roles in American life, including religious life. As headlines blazoned "Women's 'Lib' on the March in the Churches" and reported major Protestant denominations finally ordaining women, *Time* and *Newsweek* covered "Rabbi Sally" in her student pulpits.

The publicity was crucial to Priesand's ultimate success. The attention of the press helped not only to sustain her but also to convince others to champion her cause. And it guaranteed that, in the end, if she finished rabbinical school, whatever HUC–JIR did would make national news.

The publicity led synagogues and Jewish groups to invite rabbinical student Priesand to come and speak. In these settings, she carefully distanced herself from radical women's liberation, inaccurately, but persistently, dubbed "bra-burners" by the press. Instead, she presented herself as a champion of the movement that called for the right of men—and of women—to fulfill their potential. Having spoken her piece on feminism, she turned instead to what was really important to her, to Judaism—to God, Torah, and the Jewish people. She told her audiences of the power of seeing a rabbi raise the Torah and of how she prayed to God to let her be worthy of Judaism's great heritage. "I believe that a rabbi is a scholar, a teacher, a preacher, a leader, a counselor, a comforter, a preserver of Judaism, and a human being" (155). And within a short time, she hoped to become one, desiring to serve her people and to preserve Jewish tradition, not to overthrow it.

As Priesand entered her last year of rabbinical school, one major hurdle remained—her thesis. Originally she planned a critical study of Jewish liturgy. But then she changed her mind. Instead she decided to write about women and Judaism. Unaware that all before her who championed women rabbis had done the same thing, Priesand wrote a rabbinic thesis on the historic and changing role of the Jewish woman. Here she surveyed Jewish women from the biblical era to the present. She highlighted their shifting roles in Jewish history. She described their legal position in the Bible and rabbinic literature and observed the advances Reform Judaism had made in emancipating women in the synagogue.

And she found herself turning over a few pages in the history of the women who would have been rabbis.

She located Martha Neumark's account of her experience and of the opposition she faced. She uncovered Reform rabbis' debates on the subject. She found that in 1963 the women of Reform Judaism, the members of the National Federation of Temple Sisterhoods, had resolved in favor of women's ordination. And she revealed the legacy of Regina Jonas, who, in her rabbinic thesis, had set out to prove Judaism indeed permitted women to become rabbis. That enabled her to claim that she was not violating tradition, in fact, that she "was not truly the first woman rabbi" (168), only the first to be ordained by a seminary.

On June 3, 1972, the high school junior of a decade before who had written, "Although I am a girl, I would like very much to study for a rabbinical degree" (168), was ordained rabbi, teacher, and preacher. The first American woman had become a rabbi. She would not be the last.

Yet the debate over women's ordination was never confined exclusively to Reform Judaism. Mary M. Cohen, who first raised it, was not a Reform Jew, and some of those who, in 1897, could envision a woman in the pulpit belonged to other streams of Judaism. Moreover, each time the controversy about women's ordination swelled in Reform Judaism, leaders in the more traditional center of American Judaism, Conservative Judaism, found themselves reacting to the idea, even if, as Cyrus Adler (1863–1940), president of Conservatism's Jewish Theological Seminary (JTS) of America, responded, most likely in the early 1920s: It was something his seminary would not consider even for a moment.

However, in 1972, the question, which had periodically surfaced in Conservative Judaism in the past, emerged again, and this time, with the women's movement urging it forward, would not go away. Those raising the issue knew not only of Priesand's impending ordination but also that Reconstructionist Judaism was about to ordain its first female rabbi.

Reconstructionist Judaism, for many decades the liberal wing of Conservative Judaism, had since split off. In 1968 in Philadelphia, Reconstructionist rabbis opened a new rabbinical school, the Reconstructionist Rabbinical College (RRC). Founded in the midst of the new American women's movement, RRC from its inception admitted women and men. In the fall of 1969, Sandy Eisenberg Sasso (1947–), who, although raised a Reform Jew, had become intrigued with the thought of Reconstructionism's founder, Mordecai M. Kaplan, while in college, enrolled in RRC. In 1974 she became a rabbi.

In the spring of 1972, as committed, Conservative Jewish—and passionately feminist—women vociferously demanded religious equality, they did so against the backdrop of women's ordination in Reform and Reconstructionist Judaism. Three months before Sally Priesand stood at her ordination in Cincinnati, a group of Conservative Jewish women in New York, calling themselves Ezrat Nashim (referring both to "the help of women" and also to the women's court in the ancient Jerusalem Temple), announced that they had tired of apologetics and of the parades of the great Jewish women of the past. Decrying women's second-class status in Conservative Judaism, denouncing it for treating Jewish women as "separate but equal," they demanded full religious equality, including admission to rabbinical school.

At the same time other young women began applying to the Jewish Theological Seminary. Over the course of the next decade, as more and more such women kept writing for applications, they compelled JTS leaders to keep confronting the question. Some entered other JTS graduate programs, pursuing as masters and doctoral candidates as much of the rabbinical curriculum as they could on their own, hoping that when, in the near future, their faculty changed their minds, they would be well on their way to becoming rabbis.

Meanwhile, Conservative leaders struggled with the question. For a long decade between 1972 and 1983, the issue both drained and electrified Conservative rabbis, JTS faculty, rabbinical students, the women who would be rabbis, and their supporters and opponents. Conservative leaders engaged in an intricate political dance of shifting alliances, studies undertaken, commissions formed, hearings held, motions tabled, and votes counted. For example, early in 1973, after the first women applied to rabbinical school, JTS faculty voted to refuse them admission. A few years later, Conservative leaders decided to study the question fully and appointed a national Commission for the Study of the Ordination of Women as Rabbis. The commission concluded that Jewish law indeed permitted women to become rabbis. However, the Jewish Theological Seminary actually conferred ordination, and the faculty, fearing an irrevocable split in their movement, refused then to implement the decision.

Already some young women had reluctantly abandoned Conservative Judaism and trained for the rabbinate at other seminaries. Now they tried as rabbis to join the Rabbinical Assembly, Conservative Judaism's rabbinical conclave. (The Rabbinical Assembly had long welcomed to its ranks rabbis ordained elsewhere who met its tests for admission.) As the Rabbinical Assembly went on record in favor of women rabbis and began considering whether it would admit women ordained at HUC–JIR to its ranks, JTS revisited the issue. In October 1983, the faculty voted to admit women to the rabbinical school. The following fall, Amy Eilberg, one of the women waiting in the wings for a favorable decision, biding her time by taking the curriculum necessary for ordination, entered rabbinical school. In May 1985, JTS

Chancellor Gerson Cohen, who had personally shifted his view on women's ordination over the course of the heated debate, ordained Eilberg a rabbi.

Even as those within Conservative Judaism concluded their debate on women rabbis, Orthodox Jews, the most traditional Jews in America, launched theirs. In the 1990s, some Orthodox women dared to ask the question: Would there be Orthodox women rabbis? Meanwhile, the first woman, Haviva Krasner-Davidson (now known as Haviva Ner-David), began seeking admission to the Orthodox rabbinical school, New York's Yeshiva University. Although she was denied admission, she and those raising the question in Orthodoxy have roused some of America's most traditional Jews to realize that here too the debate is under way.

Thus no sector of American Judaism has been immune from the challenge of women's ordination. As the history of Jewish women's ordination closed for Reform, Reconstructionist, and Conservative Jews, the history of women in the rabbinate opened. The reception of the first women rabbis, the questions and issues they raised for their seminaries, their congregants, and their male colleagues, and the challenges they posed in bringing women's voices and perspectives to bear on American Jewish life await the pen of a future historian.

SOURCES: Original sources for all quotations above can be found in the notes to Pamela S. Nadell's *Women Who Would Be Rabbis: A History of Women's Ordination, 1889–1985* (1988). The women who became rabbis often reflect upon their journeys. Haviva Ner-David's recounts her, to date, unsuccessful attempt to become an Orthodox rabbi in *Life on the Fringes: A Feminist Journey toward Traditional Rabbinic Ordination* (2000). Sally Priesand briefly described her path to the rabbinate in *Judaism and the New Woman* (1975). The papers of the Commission for the Study of the Ordination of Women as Rabbis were published as Simon Greenberg, ed., *The Ordination of Women as Rabbis: Studies and Responsa* (1988). Once women became rabbis, they published a great deal; a good place to begin is *Wisdom You Are My Sister: 25 Years of Women in the Rabbinate*, a special edition of *CCAR Journal* (Summer 1997). See also Gary P. Zola, ed., *Women Rabbis: Exploration and Celebration, Papers Delivered at an Academic Conference Honoring Twenty Years of Women in the Rabbinate, 1972–1992* (1996).

PROTESTANT FEMALE PREACHING IN THE UNITED STATES
Catherine A. Brekus

MOST PEOPLE TODAY assume that women did not become preachers in Protestant churches until fairly recently. Yet ever since the first British colonies were founded in North America in the seventeenth century, women have demanded the right to speak publicly in their churches. From Anne Hutchinson in the colonial era to Frances Willard in the nineteenth century to Bishop Vashti McKenzie today, Protestant women have fought to expand women's opportunities for religious leadership.

This essay traces the long history of female preaching from 1600 to the present, a history that has been characterized as much by change as by continuity. There have been significant transformations over time in how female preachers justified themselves and how they were viewed by both churches and the American public.

By an Immediate Revelation: Female Preaching in the Seventeenth and Eighteenth Centuries

Perhaps the most notorious female evangelist in early America was Anne Hutchinson (1591–1643), the "American Jezebel" who was prosecuted for sedition in 1637 in Massachusetts Bay. Like other "Puritans," the radical Protestants who wanted to reform the Church of England, Hutchinson hoped to create a more pure, godly church in America, but according to her critics, she took her beliefs to an extreme. Not only did she accuse several leading clergymen of valuing good works more than divine grace (a serious charge in a culture that prized its Calvinist heritage), but she assumed a clerical role by holding large religious meetings in her home—meetings that were condemned as "not tolerable nor comely in the sight of God nor fitting for your sex." Most radical of all, she justified herself by portraying herself as a prophet. Comparing herself to Abraham, the biblical patriarch, she claimed to have been divinely inspired "by an immediate revelation." In response, her church decided to "reduce" her: They excommunicated her and forced her to leave the colony (Hall, 312, 337).

Citing Paul's injunction to the Corinthians, "Let your women keep silence in the churches," almost all Protestant churches in early America forbade women to preach. The largest and most powerful denominations—the Congregationalists in New England, the Anglicans in the South, and the Dutch Reformed and Presbyterians in the middle colonies—claimed that women had been created subordinate to men. Just as women could not vote, hold political office, or, if they were married, own their own property, they could not sit in authority as deacons or ministers.

These churches mixed a belief in women's spiritual equality with a darker view of their sinfulness. On one hand, ministers suggested that women's "weakness" made them exemplary Christians. In contrast to men, who could be stubborn, women were supposedly more humble and submissive. Pointing to the large numbers of female converts who swelled the church pews, the Reverend Cotton Mather claimed that there were "far more godly women in the world than men" (Mather, 44–45). Yet on the other hand, ministers also claimed that women's weakness made them particularly easy to corrupt. Without the "masculine" virtues of rationality and self-control, they were easy prey for the devil. According to stereotypes, women tended to be the best of saints but also the worst of sinners. Indeed, accused witches were almost always female.

Women were excluded from the pulpit not only for religious reasons but for political ones as well. Before the First Amendment separated church and state in 1791, almost every colony had an established church that people were legally required to support. In Massachusetts, for example, people were forced to pay taxes to support the Congregational establishment, no matter what their personal beliefs. Religion and politics were closely connected, and churches, like colonial governments, forbade women to "rule." When Hutchinson refused to stop holding meetings in her home, a minister used explicitly political language to condemn her: She was accused of wanting to be a "Magistrate" rather than a "Subject" (Hall, 382–383). Similarly, other female evangelists were accused of wanting to be "Queens for Life" (Ross, 146–148).

Only the Religious Society of Friends, more popularly known as the Quakers, allowed large numbers of women to be religious leaders. Like the Puritans, they wanted to create a more perfect church, but their intense quest for purity led them in particularly radical directions. Because of their belief that every person has an inner light that allows them to communicate directly with God, they abolished an ordained ministry. All believers, whether male or female, could speak publicly as "witnesses" to the divine light within them. Between 1600 and 1800, hundreds of Quaker women traveled in both America and abroad as "Public Friends" whose mission was to spread the faith. Preachers such as Jane Fenn Hoskens (1694–1764), Sophia Hume (1702–1774), and Elizabeth Ashbridge (1713–1755) became renowned for their eloquence.

Female evangelism began to gain limited acceptance outside Quaker circles during the "Great Awakening," the religious revivals that took place in many colonies during the mid-eighteenth century. According to Ezra Stiles, a Congregationalist clergyman (and later the president of Yale), the revivals were so emotional and dramatic that it seemed as if "multitudes were seriously, soberly, and solemnly out of their wits" (Stiles, 50). Besides disturbing worship by crying out in fear or in joy, many new converts demanded the right to speak during meetings. In both the Strict Congregationalist ("Separate") and the Baptist churches, which were formed by the most radical supporters of the revivals, women as well as men were allowed to "exhort." Unlike ordained clergy, exhorters did not have any formal institutional authority: They did not have the right to deliver formal sermons explaining biblical texts, and they usually spoke from the pew rather than the pulpit. Nevertheless, some were so charismatic that they became influential religious leaders. Sarah Wright Townsend (1719–1780), a Long Island schoolteacher, exhorted in her Separate church on Sundays for more than fifteen years.

As the stories of the Quakers, Separates, and Baptists reveal, female preaching was linked to religious radicalism. The only groups that allowed women to preach were dissenters who deliberately set themselves apart from the established churches. In the South, for example, Baptists self-consciously set themselves apart from the Anglican hierarchy. Besides rejecting popular social customs such as dancing and drinking, they questioned the morality of slavery. By allowing women to exhort, they vividly symbolized their countercultural identity.

Although most female exhorters seem to have been white, there are a few clues that slave women may have spoken in religious meetings as well. Later generations of slaves passed down stories of their grandmothers and great-grandmothers testifying and witnessing during worship. It is possible that early African American Baptists may have extended their belief in gospel liberty to women as well as men.

More moderate supporters of the revivals never defended female preaching. For example, when Bathsheba Kingsley (?–1748), a Congregationalist woman from Massachusetts, began riding from town to town as an itinerant evangelist, she faced church discipline. Even though Jonathan Edwards, one of the members of the church council who met with her in 1743, defended the revivals as the work of God, he dismissed her claims to religious leadership as a delusion. In his words, Kingsley was a "brawling woman" who had "almost wholly cast off that modesty, shamefacedness, and sobriety and meekness, diligence and submission, that becomes a Christian woman in her place." Although he and the rest of the council encouraged her to read the Bible and hold private religious meetings with other women, they forbade her to speak in public. In the future, she should "keep chiefly at home" ("Advice to Mr. and Mrs. Kingsley").

In response to opposition, female evangelists claimed to have been divinely inspired. In a hierarchical culture where women were expected to be subordinate to men, they never demanded the right of ordination, and in fact, they never even dared to call themselves "preachers": Instead, they described themselves as witnesses, exhorters, or in the Quaker community, "Public Friends." Nevertheless, they claimed to speak with even greater authority than male ministers. Theologically, they tended to emphasize inspiration more than education.

They insisted that their authority had come from God himself, who had inspired them to be his prophets. Bathsheba Kingsley, like Anne Hutchinson a hundred years earlier, claimed to have received "immediate revelations from heaven."

All these women defended themselves on the grounds that they had transcended their gender. Instead of directly challenging negative stereotypes of femininity, they insisted that they were no longer ordinary women but perfect vessels of the divine. In the most extreme example of this trend, Jemima Wilkinson (1752–1819), who founded a community of more than 200 converts in western New York, claimed to have lost her gender in union with God. After an illness in 1776, she awoke and declared that "Jemima Wilkinson" had died and gone to heaven, but her body remained on earth as the "tabernacle" for a perfect, genderless spirit. She was no longer a woman but the "Public Universal Friend," a being who was neither male nor female. For the rest of her life, she refused to be addressed as "she."

Ann Lee (1736–1784), the founder of the Shakers, never denied that she was a woman, but she, too, based her religious authority on her transcendence of the female body. On the surface, she seemed to revel in her identity as a female religious leader: She encouraged her followers to call her "Mother Ann"; she portrayed herself as the "bride of Christ"; and using the language of childbirth, she described her efforts to save sinners as "bearing for souls." Yet on a deeper level, Lee valued *spiritual* more than biological motherhood. Rejecting the female body, which she denigrated as corrupt and lustful, she embraced a strict code of celibacy. In order to achieve communion with God, she believed that she had to repress her sexuality.

Although Lee and Wilkinson managed to attract hundreds of converts to their new communities, they were widely condemned as deceitful, scheming women who had duped the American public. By the end of the eighteenth century, few Protestants—with the notable exception of the Shakers, the Universal Friends, and the Quakers—still supported women's ministry. Even the Separates and the Baptists renounced their earlier tradition of female evangelism as they tried to gain greater public acceptance and respectability. Abandoning their countercultural ethic, they put strict limitations on women's public religious speech. Echoing Paul's words, they ordered women to "learn in silence with all subjection."

The consequences of this backlash against female exhorting were momentous. Because few religious leaders wanted to remember women such as Bathsheba Kingsley or Sarah Wright Townsend, their names virtually disappeared from written records. Nineteenth-century female preachers, cut off from their collective history, did not realize that other women had fought the same battles before them. As a result, the story of female preaching in America has not been one of upward progress but of disjunctions, failures, new beginnings, and reinventions.

Sisters in Christ, Mothers in Israel, Prophetic Daughters: Female Preaching in the Nineteenth Century

After the tumultuous years of the American Revolution, growing numbers of women demanded the right to preach. Besides the Quakers, who continued to encourage women as well as men to become "Public Friends," many different denominations allowed women into the pulpit, including the Methodists, the African Methodists, the Free Will Baptists, the Christian Connection, the Seventh-day Adventists, and the Holiness churches. Most radically, by the end of the century the Unitarians, Universalists, and a few local Congregational Churches allowed women to be ordained.

In contrast to their predecessors, these women identified themselves as *preachers*, not simply as exhorters, and they spoke from the pulpit, not the pew. Rather than reflecting on their own personal religious experiences or warning sinners to repent, they delivered formal sermons based on biblical texts. In another break from the past, they invented a new model of ministry that was based as much on their gender as on their transcendence of it.

Why did Protestant churches allow so many hundreds of women to become preachers? How can we explain this remarkable historical transformation? First, it is important to emphasize that female preaching continued to be linked to dissent. In general, new sects such as the Free Will Baptists, founded in 1780, and the African Methodist Episcopal Church, founded in 1816, were the most supportive of women's religious leadership. At a time of profound economic, political, and social change—the creation of the American Republic, the birth of a democratic culture, and the expansion of the market economy—they expressed profound doubts about America's future as a redeemer nation. Caught up in vast transformations that seemed beyond their control, they struggled to preserve traditional Christian virtues against the centrifugal forces of mobility and commercial expansion. By allowing women into the pulpit (an innovation that mainstream Protestants condemned as scandalous), they deliberately drew firm boundaries between their pure, covenanted communities and what they perceived as the materialism, individualism, and corruption of the secular world. Ironically, these groups tended to be theologically conservative, but because of their countercultural ethic, they were more tolerant of female preaching than religious liberals.

Second, Protestants were influenced by new ideas about women's inherent virtue. After the American Revolution, women were elevated as "republican mothers" who had a duty to raise virtuous citizens. Although older ideas about female sinfulness never entirely disappeared, ministers increasingly praised women for their qualities of piety, goodness, and compassion. By the first decades of the nineteenth century, it was common wisdom that women, not men, were the guardians of religious and political virtue.

Finally, the rise of female preaching was also connected to changing understandings of religion. After the Bill of Rights declared that "Congress shall make no law respecting an establishment of religion or prohibiting the free exercise thereof," all churches eventually lost their connection to the state. Americans no longer imagined churches as the foundation of political order but as voluntary devotional communities where people could worship with other believers. As a result, churches no longer seemed as much like public institutions that should be ruled by men alone.

Because of these transformations, women's religious leadership became less contested. In the decades after the American Revolution, women of all faiths—Protestant, Catholic, and Jewish—took an active role in the public sphere. To give just a few examples: Rebecca Gratz (1781–1869) founded the first Female Hebrew Benevolent Society in 1819; the Oblate Sisters of Providence, the first black religious order in America, taught free black children to read; and Margaret Prior (1773–1842), a devout Methodist and a member of the Moral Reform Society in New York City, visited brothels to encourage women to convert. Other women founded Sunday Schools, handed out Bibles and temperance tracts, crusaded against slavery, raised money for widows and orphans, and traveled to foreign countries as missionaries.

Of all the women who made their voices heard in the public sphere, none were more controversial than female preachers. Even though ministers applauded women for their work in charitable and reform organizations, they were still ambivalent about women's claims to the pulpit. According to the Rev. Parsons Cooke, a Congregationalist, female preachers were "shameless" women who had abandoned their "feminine delicacy," "trampling under foot the commands of God, and the decencies of [their] sex" (Cooke, 17). Only actresses, or worse, prostitutes, invited men to stare at their bodies in public.

To defend themselves against their critics, female preachers insisted that God had called them to preach. Like earlier women (for example, Bathsheba Kingsley), they portrayed themselves as prophets, or in their words, "instruments" of God. Black female preachers, who were doubly stigmatized because of their race as well as their gender, particularly emphasized their immediate encounter with the divine. According to Julia Foote (1823–1900), the first woman deacon in the African Methodist Episcopal Zion Church, she had seen an angel who held a scroll bearing the words, "Thee have I chosen to preach my Gospel without delay" (Andrews, 200). Although she was poor, black, and female, she claimed to speak with the authority of God himself, who had commanded her to preach the gospel.

Despite using the same prophetic language as earlier women evangelists, nineteenth-century female preachers did not describe themselves as "neither male nor female." Unlike Jemima Wilkinson, who had denied her gender, they compared themselves to biblical heroines. Inspired by the new language of female virtue, they described themselves as "sisters in Christ" or "mothers in Israel" who had been called to nurture converts in the faith. (The Bible describes Phoebe as a "sister," and two other women—a "wise women" who saved her city from destruction, and Deborah, the famous military leader—as Mothers in Israel.) Long before modern-day feminist theologians, female preachers combed the Bible for examples of women's religious leadership. In *The Promise of the Father* (1859), one of the most comprehensive and influential defenses of female preaching, Phoebe Palmer (1807–1874), a founder of the Holiness movement, reminded the American public that Miriam, Deborah, Huldah, Anna, and Mary had all been public evangelists.

Because many female preachers belonged to denominations that predicted the imminent end of the world, they also compared themselves to Joel's "prophetic daughters." (Describing the end of time, Joel promised, "And it shall come to pass afterward, that I will pour out my spirit upon all flesh; and your sons and your daughters shall prophesy" [Joel 2:28]). Both the Millerites, a sect that expected the apocalypse to occur in 1843, and their successors, the Seventh-day Adventists, defended female preaching as a sign of the last days, a visible reminder that the world was spinning to a close. Identifying herself as one of Joel's "prophetic daughters," Ellen Gould Harmon White (1827–1915), the visionary founder of the Seventh-day Adventists, crisscrossed the country as an itinerant evangelist. By the time of her death, she had built a powerful denomination of 125,000 members.

By describing themselves in traditionally feminine terms as mothers, sisters, and daughters, female preachers tried to assure the American public that they had no intention of usurping male authority. At the same time as Ellen White, Phoebe Palmer, and other women vigorously defended female preaching, they never suggested that women should be ordained. Because of their belief in the literal truth of the Bible, they rarely questioned the gender norms of nineteenth-century American culture, especially the belief that women had been created

subordinate to men. Conservative in their attitudes toward the family, they insisted that women's ministry was simply an extension of their domestic roles. Even Zilpha Elaw (1790–?), an African Methodist who disobeyed her husband's orders to stop preaching, claimed that women were subordinate "by nature." As she explained in her memoir *Memoirs of the Life, Religious Experience, Ministerial Travels and Labours of Mrs. Zilpha Elaw, an American Female of Color*, her own life had been exceptional because of her unfortunate marriage to an unbeliever, but as a general rule, women had a duty to submit to patriarchal authority. "These principles lie at the foundation of the family and social systems," she argued, "and their violation is a very immoral and guilty act" (Andrews, 62).

Yet after the first women's rights convention in Seneca Falls, New York, in 1848, growing numbers of women ministers identified themselves as feminists. In the Spiritualist movement, which began in 1848 when the Fox sisters claimed to be able to communicate with the dead, hundreds of female "spirit mediums" publicly defended women's rights. Although these women seemed to confirm stereotypes of female passivity by speaking only in trance, they also insisted that women should be able to vote and own their own property.

Women also began to demand more radical changes in the power structure of the churches. After Antoinette Brown (1825–1921) attended Oberlin College, which initially tried to prevent her from enrolling in their seminary program (and which never gave her a formal degree), she was ordained by a Congregational Church in South Butler, New York, in 1853. Because local Congregational churches were autonomous, with no obligations to a higher ecclesiastical authority, her church was able to ignore the protests of the Congregational General Conference. Ten years later, Olympia Brown (1835–1926) was ordained by the Universalists, the first woman to be ordained by denominational authority. Although the Methodists did not grant women the full authority of ordination until 1956, they gave local preaching licenses to several women, including Maggie Newton Van Cott (1830–1914), who was licensed to preach in New York in 1869.

Instead of defending themselves on the basis of their individual rights, these women took the language of motherhood in revolutionary directions, claiming to be uniquely qualified to preach because of their maternal qualities of compassion and understanding. For example, in Iowa during the 1880s and 1890s, Universalist and Unitarian female preachers set themselves apart from male clergy by describing the church as a home and the congregation as a family. Similarly, Frances Willard (1839–1898), a Methodist and the influential president of the Woman's Christian Temperance Union, suggested that men's preaching was too cold and formal to satisfy people's spiritual needs. "It is men who have given us the dead letter rather than the living Gospel," she argued. In contrast, women offered an emotional, experiential faith that appealed to the heart, not simply the head. In her words, "[T]he mother-heart of God will never be known to the world until translated into terms of speech by mother-hearted women" (Willard, 46–47).

Mary Baker Eddy (1821–1910), the founder of Christian Science, echoed this language by arguing that women were both religiously and morally superior to men. Inverting older stereotypes, she claimed that lustful, passionate men were responsible for the evils in the world. The key to progress was not male desire but female virtue. Like Emma Curtis Hopkins (1851–1925) and other women leaders associated with the "New Thought" movement (a broad coalition of groups that was linked by their faith in mind over matter), Eddy believed that if women were free to use their full spiritual power, they would help all of humanity triumph over sin and disease. "In this revolutionary period," she wrote, "woman goes forth to battle with Goliath" (Satter, 67).

This ideology of female virtue had both negative and positive consequences for women. On the negative side, female preachers were expected to live up to an impossible standard of selflessness and purity, a standard that required them to suppress any feelings of "masculine" ambition. In addition, since ideas about female corruption had simply been displaced onto women who did not fit the model of middle-class gentility, black and working-class women felt as if they would never be able to attain the ideal. This is why Jarena Lee (1783–?), a black female preacher, took pains to describe herself as a "lady" in the title of her memoir, *The Life and Religious Experience of Mrs. Jarena Lee, a Coloured Lady* (1836). Yet despite these drawbacks, women managed to transform the language of women's "natural" purity into a powerful justification of their right to preach.

Hoping to create an enduring tradition of female evangelism, these women published hundreds of articles and books during the nineteenth century. While many, like Jarena Lee, shared their entire life stories, others wrote biblical defenses of female preaching. In 1820, for example, Deborah Peirce, a popular preacher for the Christian Connection, a new denomination that was formed after the American Revolution, published *A Scriptural Vindication of Female Preaching*. By explaining why women's ministry was neither unfeminine nor unscriptural, she hoped to give other women the courage to become religious leaders. According to Nancy Towle (1796–1876), a nondenominational preacher who spoke to thousands of converts as she traveled in both the United States and Europe, she wrote her memoir "for the encouragement of my *own* sex, that may succeed me in the *Lord's vineyard*" (Towle, 11).

Yet despite their desire to be remembered, most nineteenth-century female preachers were forgotten by both their denominations and the American public. Few people today know the names of Harriet Livermore (1788–1868), a nondenominational preacher from a distinguished New England family, who preached in front of Congress four times, or Jarena Lee, an African Methodist who risked her freedom by traveling to preach in the slave state of Virginia. Because all of these women published their memoirs, however, they made it possible for future generations of female preachers to recover their stories.

Equal Rights: Female Preaching in the Twentieth Century

By the beginning of the twentieth century, many Protestant churches allowed women to preach. Although many people today assume that theological liberals were the most tolerant of women ministers, a large number of conservative churches also allowed women into the pulpit, including the Church of God (Anderson, Indiana) and many of the fundamentalist churches that were formed during the "Modernist Controversy." (The "Modernist Controversy" is the label historians use to describe the bitter conflicts over science and scriptural inerrancy that divided Protestant churches at the end of the nineteenth century. "Fundamentalists" claimed to uphold the fundamental truths of Christianity.) Indeed, several conservative Bible institutes, such as the Moody Bible Institute in Chicago, trained women to become evangelists. By 1910, according to the U.S. Census, 685 women listed themselves as "clergy," a number that increased to 1,787 in 1930.

Despite the wide variety of denominations that allowed women to preach, the question of women's ministry contributed to growing tensions between liberals and conservatives in the early twentieth century. Besides quarreling over biblical interpretation, most famously at the 1925 Scopes trial, fundamentalists and modernists fought over women's proper roles. The 1910s and 1920s marked a watershed in women's history: Growing numbers of "working girls" became nurses, teachers, and secretaries; outspoken female reformers founded settlement houses and other charitable organizations; and most revolutionary, in 1920 the Nineteenth Amendment gave women the right to vote.

Although liberal Protestants were often ambivalent about women's new freedoms, they slowly began to expand women's opportunities for religious leadership. Besides allowing women to serve as missionaries and religious education teachers, denominations began to give them greater power in church government. For example, in 1920 the southern Methodists began to permit women to vote on church business, and in 1929, the

Presbyterian Church in the USA allowed women to become ruling elders. (This meant that women could be lay leaders in local congregations.) Finally, in 1956, after decades of debate and controversy, the United Methodist Church and the Presbyterian Church in the USA, two of the largest Protestant denominations in the country, gave women the full rights of ordination.

Since relatively few Protestant women in the 1940s and 1950s were enrolled in seminaries, these denominations seemed to think that their support of women's ordination would cause few changes in everyday religious life. Rather than trying to change the power structures in the church, they saw their support of women's ordination as a symbolic gesture: It demonstrated their progressive attitude toward American culture. Much to their surprise, large numbers of women began entering seminaries during the feminist movement of the 1960s and 1970s, and influenced by feminist theology, these women demanded to be treated as men's equals. By 1990, 11 percent of all clergy in the United States were women.

Although conservative Protestants had been the first to welcome women into the pulpit during the nineteenth century, they were deeply ambivalent about the women's rights movement and the growing presence of women in the professions. Most important, as early-twentieth-century liberals increasingly linked the question of women's religious leadership to women's suffrage, they also began to express doubts about the wisdom of allowing women into the pulpit. For example, the Seventh-day Adventists, which had been founded by Ellen White, began to push women out of leadership positions after her death in 1915. Similarly, even though the early fundamentalists had allowed scores of women to preach, they increasingly identified women's ministry as a threat to men's authority. John Rice, a fundamentalist minister, spoke for many in the movement when he published his 1941 book decrying *Bobbed Hair, Bossy Wives, and Women Preachers*. Despite women's insistence that they had been called, the same story was repeated in several other conservative groups, including the Church of God and the Holiness churches. During the 1960s and 1970s, as growing numbers of denominations ordained women, including the American Lutheran Church in 1970, the Episcopal Church in 1976, and the Reformed Church in 1979, conservatives became even harsher in their denunciations. Quoting Corinthians 14:33–36, the Southern Baptist Convention passed a resolution in 1984 insisting that "women are not in public worship to assume a role of authority over men lest confusion reign in the local church" (Melton, 236).

By the late twentieth century, the symbolic meaning of female preaching had shifted dramatically. In a startling reversal from their earlier history, conservative Protestants no longer saw female preaching as a sign of dissent or radicalism but as an accommodation to American culture. As liberals increasingly defended women's ministry on feminist grounds, conservatives angrily condemned it as a capitulation to modern, secular values. In the nineteenth century, they had set themselves apart from American culture by allowing women into the pulpit. In contrast, in the twentieth century they symbolized their objection to modern values, especially the feminist ideal of gender equality, by excluding women from positions of religious leadership.

Hoping to disarm their critics, conservative women responded by emphasizing both their divine call to ministry and their domestic identities as church "sisters" or "mothers." For example, Aimee Semple McPherson (1890–1944), a Pentecostalist, described herself in feminine language as "Sister Aimee," and she insisted that she never would have left the domestic sphere if not for God's insistence. According to her, God had struck her down with a severe illness when she resisted her call, only saving her from death when she finally agreed to become a female preacher. Transforming herself into one of the best-known evangelists of her time, McPherson not only preached to thousands of people at revival meetings, but using modern marketing techniques, she also broadcast sermons from her own radio station. The church that she founded in Los Angeles, the International Church of the Foursquare Gospel, grew rapidly and by 2002 counted more than 3 million members worldwide.

Like McPherson, many other female preachers emphasized their "sisterly" or "motherly" nature, but as the American public grew more supportive of women's rights—first during the women's suffrage movement and then during the feminist upheavals of the 1960s and 1970s—women ministers also defended themselves on the grounds of their equality to men. Influenced by feminist theology, they argued that women should be given equal rights not only in the family and the state but also in the church. Although liberal women seemed to be especially attracted to this political language of equality, conservative women sometimes invoked it as well. In 1995, for example, when three Seventh-day Adventist women defied the church hierarchy by seeking ordination, one of them explained, "If, someday, there's going to be a world where men and women are treated equally, then we should be living that way right now" (Wilgoren, B8).

Reflecting larger divisions in the feminist movement, female preachers in contemporary America have not always agreed on how to define "equality." Echoing nineteenth-century arguments, some claim that women are essentially different from men: They have a distinctive "way of knowing" or "feminine spirituality" that makes them particularly compassionate and hence par-

Transforming herself into one of the best-known evangelists of her time, Aimee Semple McPherson not only preached to thousands of people at revival meetings, but using modern marketing techniques, she also broadcast sermons from her own radio station. The church that she founded in Los Angeles, the International Church of the Foursquare Gospel, grew rapidly, and by 2002 counted more than 3 million members worldwide. *Courtesy of the Regional History Collection, Doheny Memorial Library, University of Southern California.*

ticularly suited for ministry. They also claim to value a more inclusive, less authoritarian leadership style. In contrast, other women ministers insist that stereotypes of femininity obscure the essential similarity between male and female clergy. Despite these controversies, however, most women agree on one central issue: They should be given the same leadership opportunities as men.

At the end of the twentieth century, despite several well-publicized cases of women ministers "breaking the stained-glass ceiling," the majority of female preachers continued to face discrimination. In 1989, when Barbara Clementine Harris (1930–   ), an African American, became the first female bishop in the Episcopal Church,

many hoped that a new era had dawned for women in ministry, but older attitudes proved difficult to change. Based on almost 5,000 surveys that were done in 1993–1994, three sociologists—Barbara Brown Zikmund, Adair T. Lummis, and Patricia Mei Yin Chang—concluded that women ministers usually make less money, enjoy fewer benefits, and pastor smaller, more isolated churches than their male colleagues. Because women also have fewer opportunities to move into more prestigious positions, many have left parish work for other kinds of ministry: for example, serving as chaplains of hospitals or prisons. Ironically, even though the separation of church and state expanded women's opportunities for religious leadership at the end of the eighteenth century, it also meant that later generations of women could not sue their churches for sexual discrimination. Because churches are free from government control, they do not have to comply with the Civil Rights Act of 1964, which prohibits discrimination on the basis of sex or race.

Despite these continuing difficulties, modern female preachers cannot help but marvel at the distance they have traveled from the days of Anne Hutchinson. Because of the recovery of women's history in recent years, they have begun to understand that debates over women's religious leadership stretch deep into the American past, and they have been deeply inspired by the poignant stories of the women who went before them. In 2000, when Vashti McKenzie (1947–) was elected to be the first female bishop of the African Methodist Episcopal Church, she explained, "I don't stand here alone, but there is a cloud of witnesses who sacrificed, died and gave their best" (Goodstein, A1).

SOURCES: On the seventeenth and eighteenth centuries, see *The Antinomian Controversy, 1636–1638: A Documentary History*, ed. David D. Hall (1990); Cotton Mather, *Ornaments for the Daughters of Zion* (1692); Robert Ross, *A Plain Address to the Quakers, Moravians, Separatists . . .* (1762); Ezra Stiles, *Discourse on the Christian Union* (1761); "Advice to Mr. and Mrs. Kingsley," Jonathan Edwards Papers, Andover Newton Theological School; Catherine A. Brekus, *Strangers and Pilgrims: Female Preaching in America, 1740–1845* (1998); and Susan Juster, *Disorderly Women: Sexual Politics and Evangelicalism in Revolutionary New England* (1994). On the nineteenth century, see Parsons Cooke, *Female Preaching, Unlawful and Inexpedient. A Sermon* (1837); Frances E. Willard, *Woman in the Pulpit* (1889); Nancy Towle, *Vicissitudes Illustrated, in the Experience of Nancy Towle, in Europe and America*, 2nd ed. (1833); Beryl Satter, *Each Mind a Kingdom: American Women, Sexual Purity, and the New Thought Movement, 1875–1920* (1999); and Ann Braude, *Radical Spirits: Spiritualism and Women's Rights in Nineteenth-Century America* (1989). The memoirs of Jarena Lee, Zilpha Elaw, and Julia Foote have been published in *Sisters of the Spirit*, ed. William L. Andrews (1986). On the twentieth century, see Debbi Wilgoren, "Three Women's Acts of Devotion and Defiance," *Washington Post*, November 4, 1995, Final Edition, B8; Laurie Goodstein, "After 213 Years, A.M.E. Church Elects First Woman as Bishop," *New York Times*, July 12, 2000, Late Edition, A1; Barbara Brown Zikmund, Adair T. Lummis, and Patricia Mei Yin Chang, *Clergy Women: An Uphill Calling* (1998); Mark Chaves, *Ordaining Women: Culture and Conflict in Religious Organizations* (1997); J. Gordon Melton, *The Churches Speak On—Women's Ordination: Official Statements from Religious Bodies and Ecumenical Organizations* (1991); and Edith L. Blumhofer, *Aimee Semple McPherson: Everybody's Sister* (1993).

Music and the Arts

WOMEN HYMN WRITERS
Edith Blumhofer

WHEN THE FIRST Europeans settled in the United States, they brought with them the sacred songs that nurtured their faith. Women and children sang with men, but until the early national period, the crafting of tunes and texts remained largely a male prerogative. Musical settings often featured the melody in the tenor rather than in the soprano line. Not until the nineteenth century did women emerge as prominent composers of widely sung texts and tunes—or, for that matter, as the singers who routinely carried the melody in harmonized congregational song.

The experiences of women in the realm of English-language sacred song roughly parallel their fortunes as literary figures in Britain and the United States. At the beginning of the nineteenth century, aspiring women writers faced many obstacles, and when they wrote for public consumption, they sometimes used male pseudonyms. (British poet laureate Robert Southey's advice to Charlotte Brontë, author of *Jane Eyre*, expressed a common view: "Literature cannot be the business of a woman's life, and it ought not to be" [Gaskell, 139]. His reason: Literary pursuits inevitably interfered with woman's "proper duties.") By century's end, however, women writers on both sides of the Atlantic addressed male and female readers under their own names. Significant numbers of women contributed as well to the exploding corpus of religious song in use around the world. Translations and mounting enthusiasm for foreign missions—enhanced by an exploding mass media—rapidly gave Western women's hymn texts global reach.

When they wrote sacred song, women employed a language of devotion through which they (intentionally or unintentionally) circumvented the restricted gender roles that characterized American religious life. Although empowerment may not have been their acknowledged goal, women greatly expanded their public religious voices by offering metaphors and descriptions that popularized and sustained the nineteenth-century Christian message. Denominations barred women from addressing "mixed" audiences in the sanctuary, but they did not exclude women's hymns, and these influenced corporate understandings of faith as well as private devotions, especially when text was linked to appealing tunes. A brief historical background will introduce the nineteenth-century settings in which women's prodigious efforts expanded the course of English-language Christian song.

Background

Reformation Europe offers the immediate backdrop for American hymnody. Protestant reformers amended Christian music as well as word and sacrament. Lutherans introduced a growing body of vernacular hymns set to popular tunes and sung to musical accompaniment. The Lutheran Johann Sebastian Bach composed chorales that remain staples of classical Protestant expression, and the Lutheran Reformation unleashed a rich reservoir of untapped poetic and musical talent that made Germany an unrivaled fount of sacred song. Most of this came from the pens of men, and much of that song remained the province of German Protestants until the nineteenth century when two female English translators (Catherine Winkworth and Jane Borthwick) made it accessible in English. At the same time a German hymn writer, Dora Rappard, translated for the use of German Protestants substantial numbers of English and American hymns.

If organ-accompanied congregational song galvanized Lutherans, it dismayed Calvinists. John Calvin's followers (concentrated in Switzerland, France, Holland, and Britain), preferring to shun what the New Testament did not explicitly endorse, opted for unaccompanied psalmody. Calvin's heirs issued various psalters (collections of Psalms in meter) featuring versifications based on the familiar language of the Psalms as printed in vernacular Bibles. English psalters drew from both the Geneva Bible and the Authorized (King James) Version. Not until the early eighteenth century did Isaac Watts, an English Congregationalist, take on the challenge of "Christianizing" the psalter and, ultimately, of producing a recognized body of English hymnody. By the mid-eighteenth century, Watts's younger contemporaries, John and Charles Wesley, had launched the unprecedented evangelistic efforts that propelled them to fame. Charles offered thousands of hymn texts, some of which are among the most enduring English hymns ("Hark, the Herald Angels Sing," "Jesus, Lover of My Soul," "O for a Thousand Tongues"). John translated German hymns—especially those by his Moravian Brethren friends (for example, Nicholas von Zinzendorf's "Jesus Thy Blood and Righteousness")—and edited his brother's poetic outpouring. He also provided the burgeoning Methodist movement with "rules for singing" that helped place animated congregational song at the core of the Methodist revival and the broader North Atlantic religious awakenings of which it was part. The Methodist revival featured outdoor preaching, elicited personal response that was often emotional, and maintained that religious experiences moved people toward Christian perfection. Response among the English working class reached such proportions that historians have argued that the Methodist revival spared England an up-

heaval like the French Revolution. Participants in the revival nurtured their newly active faith with an outpouring of song, much of it provided by the Wesleys.

In the course of assembling his hymnals, Wesley introduced English-speaking Protestants to several hymns from Moravian women's pens. One Anna Dober was typical of the early female hymn writers whose words were sung in the American colonies. Born in Moravia in 1713, she lived at Herrnhut, the hub of early Moravian life on the estate of Count Nicholas von Zinzendorf in what is now eastern Germany. She poured her religious fervor into poems that expressed her longing to know Christ's love. Dober did not intend to publish her poems, nor did she write them as hymns (a circumstance also true of others who, through others' choice of their words, became hymn writers). Community leaders opted to include them in a book they called *The Moravian Brethren's Collection*, and Wesley discovered them there. By translating such Moravian women's texts, setting them to tunes, and offering them to his followers as hymns, Wesley both validated the universality of female religious aspirations and legitimated women hymn writers. Thus, women (like some men) became indirect providers of hymns when others put their poetry to an unintended use.

By the end of the eighteenth century, hymns played an established part in the worship of English Independents (as Congregationalists were known in England) and had become a feature of worship in a growing number of local Anglican parishes as well. They held a prominent place in the North Atlantic revival that was then in the throes of birthing evangelicalism. This movement embraced English Dissenters (Protestants who were not part of the Established Church) and Anglicans, German Pietists, and the Americans who reveled in the Great Awakening. Participants valued experience, testimony, and communal action and manifested a penchant for popular song. Women quickly rose to the occasion.

In the nineteenth century, evangelical stirrings animated the efforts of the first English-language female hymn writers. Middle-class Englishwomen, they tended to be wives, daughters, or sisters of Anglican clergy. A disproportionate number of these women endured long bouts with illness or took active roles in Sunday Schools. Their efforts to render Christian teaching in unambiguous language (Mrs. Cecil Francis Alexander's "Once in Royal David's City") and their appeals to the emotions—especially their sensitivity to anguish and illness (Charlotte Elliott's "Just As I Am," appeared first in a hymnal for invalids), or Sarah Adams's "Nearer, My God, to Thee"—yielded hymns that captured public imagination and quickly became standard Protestant texts. The stirring words of "Who Is on the Lord's Side?" and the plaintive prayer "Take My Life and Let It Be" came from the pen of Frances Ridley Havergal, daughter of an Anglican canon and accomplished musician. Few women hymn writers have ever attained the general influence of the mid-nineteenth-century Englishwomen Catherine Winkworth or Jane Borthwick. These translators of the substantial corpus of German Protestant hymnody (including such staples as "Praise to the Lord, the Almighty, the King of Creation" and "Now Thank We All Our God") published their collected translations in *Hymns from the Land of Luther* and *Christian Singers of Germany*. Their words became standard texts of English-language hymnody.

The work of such Englishwomen, expanded by the setting to music of a few poems not intended as hymns but written by established authors like Christina Rossetti, Elizabeth Barrett Browning, and Anne Brontë, forms a backdrop for hymn writing by American women. Americans sang British hymns. Aspiring nineteenth-century American women hymn writers felt kinship with their hymn-writing English sisters and esteemed them as collaborators in the task of expanding Christian hymnody for a nineteenth-century church on the move.

American Beginnings

English settlers brought with them to the colonies the established custom of Psalm singing. The first book to roll from the Massachusetts Bay Colony's press was the *Bay Psalter* (1640). Settlers from the continent—especially Moravians and Lutherans—transported their rich hymnic traditions to the middle colonies and North Carolina. By the end of the seventeenth century, both Psalm and hymn singing had been firmly planted in the colonies.

In the next century, amid the throes of the Great Awakening, Americans began embracing the new outpouring of hymns from Britain. Jonathan Edwards's congregation used Isaac Watts's hymnals, and by the end of the century, the growing group of American Methodists sang texts offered by the Wesleys, among them translations of some by German female authors. Meanwhile, an indigenous folk tradition of shape-note singing emerged in the colonies. Then, just after the Revolutionary War and in an energetically democratic religious setting, the Second Great Awakening unleashed a new deluge of religious song, some using a particularly American (antimonarchical) idiom. The best-known American hymn writer to date, Yale President Timothy Dwight ("I Love Thy Kingdom, Lord"), led the way in the tradition of Isaac Watts.

By enlisting women in the moral crusade to create a Christian America, the Second Awakening also helped set the stage for the emergence of an acknowledged cadre of female hymn writers. On the rapidly expanding western frontier as in East Coast cities, the Second Great Awakening fueled the astonishing growth of Methodists and Baptists and shaped the context for camp meetings and their unique musical expression, the camp meeting hymn. Camp meetings gathered the faithful for protracted meetings that featured preaching, testimony, and religious experience that often manifested intense emotion. On the frontier, camp meetings were both rare social opportunities and sacramental occasions. Among other factors, the absence of books, the crowds, and heightened emotions paved the way for simplified music and helped popularize repetitive refrains.

If one looks at the traditional hymnals of this period, one finds little evidence of women's efforts on behalf of sacred song. But a glance beyond the sanctuary into the particular settings that relied especially on women's energies suggests that women had much to contribute. In these arenas, women's additions to the hymnody that sustained and energized American religion on its march around the world can hardly be missed. As in England, the emergence of mass culture helped set the stage for women's religious verse. A growing number of women took to writing prose and poetry for public as well as private consumption, and a vastly expanded popular press proved eager for text. Some of these female authors came of well-known families and enjoyed comfortable social and economic circumstances. They often had easier access to education, money, and leisure than had their mothers. Margaret Fuller and Louisa May Alcott, like the accomplished daughters of the Reverend Lyman Beecher, for example, published essays and stories that brought them notice. At mid-century, as the movement for women's rights gained momentum, it further enhanced opportunities for female authors.

Hymn writing flowed naturally from the pens of Christian women with recognized literary competence who also felt strongly about the power of words and music combined for moral suasion. Poetry was a common form of nineteenth-century expression, attempted by millions. Of varied quality, it appeared in most newspapers, magazines, and other venues for mass consumption. Popular female poets whose lines sometimes became hymns included Alice and Phoebe Carey, sisters whose Manhattan apartment was the setting for Sunday evening literary soirees that attracted New York's prominent writers.

Repeated waves of religious revivals gave expanded visibility to women's spirituality. Revivals nurtured a piety of experience that valued a heart-felt relationship between the believer and Christ. As the nineteenth century progressed, romanticism impacted theology as well as literature, and a growing emphasis on sentiment and emotion accompanied a larger feminization of Victorian Christianity. Women wrote readily about the emotions and relationships awakened by the revivals.

The rapid expansion of the Sunday School movement

shaped a vast market for new forms of religious education. In nineteenth-century America, Sunday Schools often relied on the efforts of female teachers, and the Sunday School movement especially welcomed women's texts. In their hymns for Sunday Schools, women extended their role as mother beyond the nuclear family. They taught, cajoled, moralized, comforted, nurtured, and threatened generations of children with a vision of Christian morality, duty, and mission.

At least from the Second Great Awakening, women poured their energies into voluntary associations and moral causes dedicated to social transformation. Hymn singing rallied the faithful, beseeched the reluctant, and invited the mocker to action for the public good. Women's texts also comforted mourners and sympathized with the distressed, offering hope and uplift.

A series of new religious movements, some led by women, challenged the American status quo, modeled new options, and encouraged female hymn writers to produce texts suitable for use beyond the religious mainstream.

Literary Women as Hymn Writers

Among the women who gained literary renown in nineteenth-century America, none rivaled Harriet Beecher Stowe. Daughter of the prominent preacher, Lyman Beecher, wife of Lane Theological Seminary professor Calvin Stowe, and sister of Brooklyn's premier pulpiteer, Henry Ward Beecher, Harriet Beecher Stowe galvanized antislavery feeling in England and the United States in 1852 with the publication of *Uncle Tom's Cabin*.

Uncle Tom's Cabin made the Stowes wealthy, but success did not abate Harriet's outpouring of text. By 1853 this included several hymns. The most enduring of these, written amid the noisy commotion of Stowe's life following the release of *Uncle Tom's Cabin*, begins, "Still, still with thee when morning light is breaking" (sometimes "Still, still with thee, when purple morning breaketh"). Set to a tune from Felix Mendelssohn's collection *Lieder ohne Worte*, Stowe's hymn is an apt meditation on the wonder of quietly experiencing the presence of God amid the busyness of life. Stowe's brother, Henry Ward Beecher, included several of his sister's other hymns in *The Plymouth Collection*, the pathbreaking hymnal he published in 1855 for his Brooklyn congregation. Like "Still, Still with Thee," "When the Winds Are Raging," and "Abide in Me" manifested Stowe's longing for peace and divine presence. The most prominent single nineteenth-century hymnal, Ira Sankey's *Gospel Hymns*, included another well-known Stowe hymn, "Knocking, knocking." In this meditation on Revelation 3:20 ("Behold, I stand at the door and knock") Stowe posed a question revivalists often invested with evangelistic appeal: "Wilt thou not undo the door?"

While Stowe wrote poems that others set to music—and while she had the advantage of a brother who included her hymns in an unusually influential hymnal—Stowe's contemporary, writer and activist Julia Ward Howe, yielded to an emotional moment and gave Americans one of their best-known patriotic hymns, "Mine eyes have seen the glory of the coming of the Lord." Written in the fall of 1861 while Howe mused on the nation's future, this hymn thrived at first because it was set to the popular tune for "John Brown's body lies a-mouldering in the grave." Its millenarian language soon fired imaginations and stirred Union hearts to press on for victory in the Civil War, but its words could equally appropriately have become the Confederate anthem. Sung publicly for the first time on Lincoln's birthday (February 12) in 1862, it quickly became a national favorite, a hymn for public as well as private religious use. Written by one Unitarian at the suggestion of another—the prominent Transcendentalist author and pastor James Freeman Clarke (also a hymn writer)—it is at once a powerful declaration of public faith and a poignant expression of private devotion. Julia Ward Howe became the first—but not the last—woman to provide a hymn to sustain American public religion.

Another popular female literary figure whose hymns enjoyed acclaim was Elizabeth Payson Prentiss (1818–1878), daughter of a prominent Congregational clergyman in Portland, Maine. Prentiss had the advantage of a good education and taught school before her marriage in 1845 to the Rev. George L. Prentiss. Best remembered as the author of the bestselling *Stepping Heavenward* (1869), the novel remains in print, has sold hundreds of thousands of copies, and was immediately translated into German and French), Prentiss also wrote poetry and offered advice and consolation to a wide public through extensive correspondence. Her writings reflect her artistic eye and her spiritual sensitivity. Brimming with comfort and instruction for those who agonized in grief or languished in illness, they came from the pen of one who knew firsthand wrenching loss and the tedium of physical suffering. Prentiss filled an active role in her husband's New York City congregation despite prolonged and disabling bouts of severe anxiety. She wrote for the public all her life—assorted poems, children's books, novels, a hymn for the laying of the cornerstone of her husband's church.

Prentiss's enduring hymn "More love to Thee, O Christ" was not created for any particular occasion. Rather, it records Prentiss's consuming yearning for an intimate relationship with Christ, a desire that compelled her to pursue what she called "the consecrated life." The hymn manifests her determined resignation to the divine will, a disposition to which she often referred.

Julia Ward Howe yielded to an emotional moment and gave Americans one of their best-known patriotic hymns, "Mine eyes have seen the glory of the coming of the Lord." Howe became the first—but not the last—woman to provide a hymn to sustain American public religion. *Courtesy of the Library of Congress.*

Over her bed she hung the German motto *Stille, meine Wille* (Be still, my will). "I see now that to live for God, whether one is allowed ability to be actively useful or not, is a great thing," she wrote to a friend during a period of illness. "It is a wonderful mercy to be allowed to suffer even, if thereby one can glorify him" (Pitman, 120).

Prentiss penned "More love to Thee, O Christ" in 1856, a year filled with "sharp conflicts of soul" as well as with "great peace and joy." During that summer her journal records her preoccupation with loving God: "Saturday I had a long walk full of blissful thoughts of Him whom I do believe I love—oh, that I loved Him better!" During the same season of spiritual sensitivity she wrote the hymn "Alone with God," a text that exults in the sublime desire to be "hid with Christ in God" and so to be "At home, and by the wayside, and abroad, Alone with thee!" "Amid the busy city, thronged and gay," Prentiss wrote, "but One I see." Spiritual passion palpitates in these hymns that relish aloneness amid a crowd, a disposition later generations would disavow.

Resignation in suffering, passive submission to God, celebration of calm, and unabated longing for a more profound sense of God's presence characterized many

hymns produced by nineteenth-century American women. Elizabeth Prentiss's overwhelming desire for God in the midst of the physical ills that disrupted her otherwise happy life erupted in lines at once defiant and resigned:

Let sorrow do its work,
Send grief and pain;
Sweet are thy messengers,
Sweet their refrain,
When they can sing with me,
More love, O Christ, to thee,
More love to thee.

Reveling in intense personal piety, then, Prentiss offered texts that exalted passivity and beckoned readers to a life of reordered priorities in which the unseen appears consistently more real than the tangible. If contemporaries read these words with attention to the tumultuous public issues of the decade leading to Civil War, they found an exhortation to resignation rather than a call to action, a pronounced individualism rather than a summons to collective concerns.

The unmarried sisters Anna and Susan Warner introduced hymns through their novels. "Jesus Loves Me" appeared first in the text of a Sunday School novel that the sisters wrote when a reversal of fortune forced them to write for a livelihood. The words for Anna Warner's "We Would See Jesus" were part of the plot of her 1852 novel *Dollars and Sense*.

Stowe, Howe, and Prentiss may represent American women who are known as hymn writers as much because of their other accomplishments as because of the hymns they wrote. They brought established reputations to the writing of hymns; they did not depend on hymn writing for income; and they did not author many hymn texts. Of the three, Stowe addressed herself most directly to the ability of women to effect change. A passionate believer in the power of Christian women to feel deeply about social and religious wrongs and, by their united indignation, to be a force for change, Stowe did not find appealing the passivity that attracted Prentiss. Like Prentiss's "More Love to Thee," though, Stowe's hymn texts imply doctrine but exult in experience—in the case of "Still, Still with Thee," the nearness of God, the Christian's lover. Stowe exudes confidence in a relationship that sustains now and assures future bliss. Such sentiments of confidence as well as of passive resignation did not violate "woman's sphere." Howe's "Battle Hymn," on the other hand, offered something different, something that her female contemporaries seldom articulated with the power Howe managed: a prophetic vision and heightened sense of the religious significance of the events of the day.

Revivals and Women Hymn Writers

Nineteenth-century revivals provided another arena in which ordinary women found ample reason to express themselves in song. Women helped the revivals in many ways—visitation, follow-up, prayer, publicity, public testimony. And empowered by revivals, they often accepted the challenge to work for social change. Women labored prodigiously on behalf of the voluntary associations that roused the public to action on behalf of American civilization—the American Bible Society, the American Sunday School Union, the American Tract Society, temperance and reform movements. They enlisted support for Sabbath keeping and the Anti-Swearing League, and they wrote and sang the hymns that advanced such causes.

The best-known evangelist of the pre–Civil War era, Charles Grandison Finney, roused audiences with stern denunciations of sin, then comforted them with the promise of gracious redemption for "whosoever will." Finney's most famous predecessor, Jonathan Edwards, believed revivals were divine visitations that came and passed as God chose. By contrast, Finney taught that revivals followed predictably if people followed the right

"means." Finney fired dreams of moral renewal for the nation and then the world. In both East and West, a rash of new hymns sustained and extended the cultural hopefulness that accompanied his revivals. On the frontier, camp meeting spirituals combined simple texts and tunes, often with repetition of key phrases.

Revivals stimulated as well a bevy of new religious movements that gave women opportunities for religious leadership. One of the groups that experienced a growth spurt during the Second Great Awakening had flourished first in the wake of earlier revivals. The United Society of Believers in Christ's Second Appearing, commonly known as Shakers, were the followers of Mother Ann Lee. A radical English Quaker who insisted on celibate communal living and rethought traditional Christian teaching on the millennium, Mother Ann Lee and her successors expressed their particular tenets in an outpouring of religious song suited to the rituals that sustained their communal life. Perhaps the best-known Shaker hymn celebrates the simplicity in which the community endeavored to live:

> Tis a gift to be gentle, 'tis a gift to be fair,
> 'tis a gift to wake and breathe the morning air,
> to walk every day down the path that we choose
> 'tis a gift we pray we may never loose.
>
> When true simplicity is gained,
> to love and to learn
> we will not be ashamed,
> to turn to turn will be our delight
> and by turning, turning we'll come round right.

Shakers honored Ann Lee as divine, a female counterpart to Christ. They not only employed female imagery for the divine; they also hymned their founder:

> Let names and sects and parties
> Accost my ears no more,
> My ever blessed Mother
> Forever I'll adore:
> Appointed by kind heaven
> My Saviour to reveal,
> Her doctrine is confirmed
> With an eternal seal.
>
> She was the Lords anointed,
> To show the root of sin;
> And in its full destruction,
> Her gospel did begin:
> She strip'd a carnal nature,
> Of all its deep disguise,
> And laid it plain and naked,
> Before the sinner's eyes.

Mother Ann had endured a difficult marriage and problem pregnancies. Her gospel prohibited sex and limited to virgins the full bliss of salvation:

In Zion is a living spring,
Where virgins meet to dance and sing;
Its crystal waters flow around,
As we move in the solemn sound;
It is to virgins joy and life,
But never flows to man and wife;
But those that do our Mother's will,
May freely drink and have their fill.

More traditional were the hymns of Methodist Phoebe Palmer, a socially prominent New Yorker best known as a leading advocate of Christian perfection. She shared with Charles Finney the conviction that God often worked dramatically to purify and empower believers. Whether one called the resulting experience a "second blessing," "baptism of the Holy Ghost," or "second definite work of grace" mattered less than that one yielded one's self in a moment of consecration to purifying, perfecting grace.

Over the century, the occasional preoccupation with Christian perfection unleashed a flood of song, much of it written by women. Phoebe Palmer's most enduring text described the moment of perfecting grace:

I see the new creation rise,
I hear the speaking blood;
It speaks! Polluted nature dies!
Sinks 'neath the cleansing flood.

The cleansing stream I see, I see!
I plunge, and oh, it cleanseth me!
Oh! Praise the Lord, it cleanseth me,
It cleanseth me, yes, cleanseth me.

And the result:

I rise to walk in heav'n's own light
Above the world and sin,
With heart made pure and garments white,
And Christ enthroned within.

Such texts reinforced Palmer's teaching at weekly gatherings in her Manhattan home as well as the views she and her physician husband, Walter, expounded after 1866 in their monthly publication *The Guide to Holiness*. Known as Tuesday Meetings for the Promotion of Holiness, Palmer's weekly house meetings attracted an interdenominational mix of clergy and laity. As "social occasions" they welcomed lay participation and a new

hymnody that helped the faithful express the results of sanctifying grace.

Phoebe Palmer often collaborated with her daughter, Phoebe Palmer Knapp. The wife of a wealthy Brooklyn businessman, Joseph Fairchild Knapp, and an activist in the temperance and revival movements of her day, Phoebe Knapp composed tunes for hundreds of texts. She set many of her mother's poems to music, including several popular in their day reflecting Palmer's intense love for the Bible. A Protestant "favorite" that came from an intimate of Phoebe Palmer's circle was "All for Jesus," written by an indefatigable promoter of Holiness efforts in every form, Mary James.

With its emphases on cleansing, consecration, and empowerment, the Holiness movement latched on to graphic biblical imagery of the blood of Christ and the fire of the Spirit. Confident of "victory all the time" in their spiritual lives, they anticipated (in the words of Ohio Holiness hymn writer Leila Morris) "doing wondrous exploits with the Spirit's sword." Morris's text "Holiness Unto the Lord" aptly summarizes the movement's challenge to the church, couching it in the familiar language of the King James Version:

Called unto holiness, Church of our God,
Purchase of Jesus, redeemed by His blood;
Called from the world and its idols to flee,
Called from the bondage of sin to be free.

Called unto holiness, glorious thought!
Up from the wilderness wanderings brought,
Out from the shadows and darkness of night
Into the Canaan of perfect delight.

Women flocked to the Holiness movement, where they learned about surrender, yieldedness, and victory over personal and public evils. Using imagery of feasting, they imagined themselves at a spiritual banquet where their longings for more "heavenly manna" held them in Christ's presence. Amid life's turmoil, Palmer, Morris, Mamie Ferguson, Eliza Hewitt, Julia Johnston, and their cohorts summoned participants to live "under the precious blood" where the Holy Spirit brought "life, and health, and gladness." "Why walk in the darkness and shadows of night?" Leila Morris asked in a song she called "Live in the Sunlight," "When sunlight so full and so free is streaming around with its radiance bright to lighten the pathway for thee?" Filled with language of joy, peace, light, and power, women's Holiness hymns molded and reflected a transdenominational movement's dynamic. The palpable longing for constant awareness of Christ's presence permeated their language and made their songs appealing for use in the protracted prayer meetings at which they agonized for perfecting grace. Leila Morris expressed it clearly:

> Nearer, still nearer, close to thy heart,
> Draw me, my Saviour, so precious thou art;
> Fold me, o fold me close to thy breast,
> Shelter me safe in that "Haven of Rest."

> Nearer, still nearer, nothing I bring,
> Naught as an offering to Jesus, my king.
> Only my sinful now contrite heart;
> Grant me the cleansing thy blood doth impart.

In theory, the empowerment that accompanied the purifying moment when one received "the Holy Ghost and fire" was nothing less than direct control of one's being by the Holy Spirit rather than merely a quickening of one's own abilities. The Spirit gave gifts—prophecy, wisdom, healing, tongues—and the Spirit used those gifts through human channels, male or female, as he chose. And so the Holiness experience in which women reveled and to which their songs gave voice resulted from self-resignation or consecration through which self no longer stood in the way of the Spirit's working. In actuality, many women found their public voices while standing behind this spiritual rhetoric that effectively told them they were nothing. While attributing everything to the Spirit's inspiration, they nonetheless thrived in settings that valued their voices. In 1898 one Mrs. M. J. Harris put it this way:

> My ambitions, plans and wishes
> At my feet in ashes lay.

> Then God's fire upon the altar
> Of my heart was set aflame;
> I shall never cease to praise Him,
> Glory! Glory to His name.

In women's rationalizations of the liberating effect of the Spirit's indwelling, sequence was everything. Fire, cleansing, and power followed death to self.

Nineteenth-century women's revival songs often reminded the faithful that—despite apparent human giftedness—true success, happiness, and peace came only from total reliance on Christ through the Holy Spirit. A popular hymn by Leila Morris told them that their constant prayer was to be "wholly lost" in the "sweet will of God." Another challenged: "Will you take him now as your all in all, Let the self be slain, that the pow'r may fall?" "My all to his keeping I gladly resign," sang hymn writer Emma F. Bennett. "A vessel of clay for my Lord to design; O glory to Jesus! I'm free." This freedom was not liberation but dependence. It derived, in the words of another well-known hymn by George Matheson, from the believer's captivity: "Make me a captive, Lord; And then I shall be free."

Holiness advocates worked while they sang. The fury of effort they released had transatlantic impact, energizing publishing, missions, evangelism, and education. By the turn of the century, new denominations were spawned, all of which embraced the descriptions of holiness carried by the many hymns in which women gloried in intense experiences of submission and grace and longed for more.

Revivals associated with Finney and with the Holiness movement flowed into and out of the Revival of 1858 and the subsequent religious quickenings among the troops on both sides of the Civil War. The dominant revivalist of the postwar years was Dwight L. Moody, who enlisted the cooperation of a songster, Ira David Sankey, in an expanding cluster of endeavors. From the 1870s until Moody's death in 1899, their combined efforts took Britain and America by storm. Sankey sang solos, organized mass choirs, and combed popular Christian literature for poetry for which he composed settings. He featured a style of song known as the gospel hymn, a derivation from camp meeting spirituals and Sunday School songs. Simple and singable, gospel hymns offered words of invitation, testimony, and proclamation designed to assist evangelists in bringing souls to a point of spiritual decision. They packaged the gospel in music that featured dotted notes, simple harmonies, and familiar, often peppy, rhythms. The songs Sankey used proved so popular that he (and a changing list of coeditors) issued ever-larger hymnals that he finally combined as *Gospel Hymns 1–6*. Deemed among the most valuable musical holdings of their day, Sankey's hymnals earned millions of dollars in royalties. He and Moody dedicated the money entirely to various causes including Moody's special interests, the Northfield and Mt. Hermon Schools. (Located near Moody's birthplace along the Connecticut River in central Massachusetts, the schools provided quality education for the disadvantaged. They have become pricey preparatory schools.) The hymnals as well as Moody's campaigns popularized around the world the hymns and poems of several women who played prominent roles in crafting the genre of gospel hymns.

The best known of these was the irrepressibly cheerful blind poet Fanny J. Crosby (1820–1915). A graduate of the New York Institution for the Blind, Crosby published three volumes of poetry and wrote texts for popular music and successful cantatas before turning her attention to hymns. Thousands of hymn texts poured from her pen after 1864, many under contract to the New York publisher Bradbury and Company (later Bigelow and Main; then Hope Publishing Company). The most prolific American hymn writer, Crosby came into her own just as the demand for new religious music mounted in Protestant churches. Stimulated in part by revivals, Sunday Schools, singing schools (community opportunities for musical instruction and choral singing), and the efforts of a handful of men intent on making religious music accessible and meaningful to ordinary people, the new gospel hymns had what critics called "congregationality." They flourished first in the social meetings and extradenominational associations that convened outside the sanctuary, but they knocked relentlessly at the doors of the churches. If Sankey was their premier promoter, Crosby ranked first as their provider. Her enduring texts include Protestant favorites like "To God Be the Glory, Great Things He Hath Done," "Rescue the Perishing," "Jesus, Keep Me Near the Cross," "I Am Thine, O Lord," "Safe in the Arms of Jesus," and "Blessed Assurance." William Doane wrote the tunes for most of these, and he copyrighted tune and text together. As a result, there has not been a serious challenge in American hymnals to the marriage of Crosby's text and Doane's tune for "To God Be the Glory." (Doane also provided the tune that made Prentiss's "More love to Thee" popular.)

Phoebe Knapp collaborated with Crosby on "Blessed Assurance," a perennial Crosby favorite. One of the few women of the period who wrote tunes and edited hymnals, Knapp was unconventional in many ways. She had access to her husband's fortune (he made millions as president of the American Lithograph Company and of Metropolitan Life), which gave her ample musical and editorial resources to indulge her interests in composing. She also devoted her resources to encouraging emerging young musicians.

Revival hymnody featured several hymn tunes by women. D. L. Moody's daughter-in-law May Whittle Moody often collaborated with her father, evangelist D. W. Whittle. Her most enduring tune sets her father's text, "Moment by Moment." Carrie Rounsefell wrote the melody for "I'll Go Where You Want Me to Go" for special services in a Baptist church in Lynn, Massachusetts. This consecration hymn by Mary Brown expressed the missionary fervor of turn-of-the-century Protestant youth. The writing of tunes remained largely the province of men, but women made occasional musical contributions to the exploding corpus of gospel hymns.

Words by a high-caste Indian convert were printed in many late-nineteenth-century American and British hymnals and were used as well in the era's revival efforts. Ellen Lashmi Goreh, the daughter of Indian pastor Nehemiah Goreh, was adopted by an English family and educated in England. There in 1883 she wrote the hymn "In the Secret of His Presence." Filled with the language of consecration and devotion associated with the Keswick movement, Holiness piety, and revival aspirations,

the hymn gained wide popularity among the millions of evangelicals in the United States and abroad.

At the same time that gospel hymns and Holiness spirituality featured the hymn-writing abilities of women, the Salvation Army found its niche in American urban life. The Army offered women and men opportunities to try their hands at composing hymns of testimony. The talented women of the Army's founding family, Catherine and Evangeline Booth, Louise Booth-Tucker, and Catherine Booth-Clibborn, set an example by offering words of praise for the use of Army corps around the world. Music had a central place among the munitions in the Army's arsenal. Each early issue of the Army's *War Cry* published columns of testimony songs—words set to popular tunes—submitted by converts. The poetry may have been mediocre and the theology unsophisticated, but the vibrancy of the experiences described was undeniable. Song was a form of testimony, and catchy, irresistible melodies offered a sure way for women and men, girls and boys, to popularize the message.

A greater emphasis on individual religious experience, then, coupled with the high value placed on oral testimony and invitation, sustained this burst of religious song. Women as well as men offered testimony, envisioned a brighter future, or longed for inner peace, and so they wrote hymns. More musical instruction of whatever quality as well as more education gave women readier access than before to the tools they needed, and the simplification of religious music widened access to opportunity. One did not need to be a first-rate poet to compose a successful gospel hymn. Nor did one need to be an accomplished musician to draft an acceptable popular tune. That many gospel hymns failed to meet traditional literary standards is apparent by the biting criticism this music elicited.

In sum, by the end of the nineteenth century, the ongoing democratization of church music, revivals, education, expanding use of "social meetings," and the changing status of women in American life combined to permit women unprecedented voice in American Protestantism. Women did not celebrate this power as such, but hindsight offers abundant evidence that, by the end of the century, through their hymns, women influenced Protestant men's as well as women's vocabulary of testimony, exhortation, invitation, and praise. A religious language assuring safety, peace, comfort, love, submission, and devotion resonated with Victorian Protestant piety and seemed consonant with the notion of woman's sphere.

The Sunday School Movement

In the nineteenth century, Sunday Schools stood at the core of the Protestant vision for America, and they spawned a type of sacred song that came to be called the Sunday School hymn. Since the schools offered women an arena into which to pour their energy, it is not surprising that women gave voice to the particular concerns that drove American Sunday Schools—doctrine, manners, morals, patriotism. From small schools in the sparsely populated West to large endeavors in eastern cities, Sunday Schools filled a vital role in the religious education and direction of young Protestant Americans. Although their history reached back into the eighteenth century, their heyday arrived in the nineteenth. From 1824 the American Sunday School Union (a transdenominational association that recruited Sunday School missionaries and published children's literature) orchestrated the efforts of hundreds of local unions that spread the American patriotic and evangelistic hope for Sunday Schools and promoted the establishing of schools in prominent churches, urban missions, and western hamlets.

The first Sunday School hymnals reproduced standard hymns and tunes that seemed most appropriate for work among children. In the mid-nineteenth century, though, some promoters of music education began issuing Sunday School hymnals that included easy, lively, and rhythmic tunes. A growing national movement advocating public music education provided the rationale for these first endeavors in Sunday School music as well: "Good" music was not in itself sufficient for the education of children. Rather, successful children's music required cheerful and simple lyrics and tunes. The music that resulted gave American Protestants several enduring favorites. "Jesus Loves Me" appeared first as text in a Christian novel by Anna and Susan Warner (teachers of a Sunday School class of West Point cadets) dealing with a child's death. A tune by William Bradbury transformed the sisters' reassuring words into an American Sunday School theme song.

Soon publishers experimented with arranging sacred folk music and lyrics set to popular secular tunes for use in Sunday Schools. One of the first such attempts, *The Sabbath-School Bell*, sold nearly a million copies in its first decade. An enterprising New York music publisher named William Bradbury took the situation in hand in 1861 with the publication of a small hymnal, the *Golden Chain*. The book sold hundreds of thousands of copies, and five more immensely successful Sunday School hymnals followed in quick succession before Bradbury's death in 1868. In 1864, Bradbury enlisted Fanny Crosby to contribute weekly hymns for his company, and her name appears often above the simple songs that served as Sunday School music.

If Fanny Crosby represents the women who wrote Sunday School lyrics on demand, Phoebe Knapp illustrates those who wrote them out of the particular circumstances in the schools. Knapp took responsibility for the 200 young children enrolled in the infant class at St. John's Methodist Episcopal Church in Brooklyn, New York. With their needs in mind, she prepared over 600 Sunday School tunes and texts herself, and she enlisted as well the help of others. Knapp was one of the few women to edit a hymnal during the heyday of Sunday School song. Fanny Crosby's unusual ability to versify in any meter made her a valuable ally to Knapp as well as to Bradbury.

The financial success of Sunday School music made it inevitable that many would take up the cause. Fanny Crosby's frequent collaborator William Doane, superintendent of a Baptist Sunday School in Cincinnati, sold over a million copies of the Sunday School hymnal he edited with Robert Lowry, *Pure Gold*, which included many texts by women eager to voice faith for the benefit of children. Published by Biglow & Main, successors to Bradbury, this book and the succession that followed commanded much of the market. Traditional hymns disappeared almost entirely from such resources designed specifically for Sunday Schools, replaced by new tunes and reassuring lyrics. Eminently singable, the music was designed and arranged to fit a long list of Sunday School occasions: general worship, anniversaries, Christmas festivals, picnics, temperance rallies, social gatherings, special celebrations, deaths, revivals. A hymnal titled *Bright Jewels* offered a typical mix of Sunday School songs grouped under the following headings: Anniversaries, Atonement, Activity, Affliction, Little Children, Christ, Doxologies, Faith, Heaven, Holy Spirit, Invitation, Joy, Life and Death, Lord's Day, Missionary, Praise to God, Praise to Christ, Prayer, Repentance, Rest, Sunday School, Victory, Youth. The most songs by far fell under the category "Heaven."

Sunday School music enlisted and instructed, as in the following lyrics by Fanny Crosby:

Oh! Let us learn a simple truth,
And bear it in our mind;
That every child can praise him,
However week or small;
Let each with joy remember this,
The Lord has work for all.

Kate Cameron's lyrics offered a typical mix of pious longing and practical injunction:

Our Sabbath school, oh! May He bless,
And guard its lambs with tenderness;
And lead us gently when we die
To our Good Shepherd's fold on high.
Singing together, singing together,
Teachers and scholars gladly unite;
Singing together, singing together,
Love fills our hearts, and our faces are bright.

In an era of high child mortality when death was a regular part of the cycle of family life, Sunday Schools offered songs replete with reference to pilgrims, angel bands, and endless pleasures "beyond the river." The lyrics assured those who "tried to bear the cross in [their] youth" that they would "wear a starry crown by and by." No distinct line separated Sunday School hymns and the new gospel songs that revivalists favored: Many Sunday School songs of praise served revivals, too. Sunday School hymnals presented both since their straightforward teaching and singable tunes made them appropriate to all ages. Sunday School scholars with hymnals in hand had a blueprint for this life, assurance for eternity, and clear guidance about life's pressing public issues: Abstinence from liquor and impurity combined with careful attention to the Bible would surely result in happiness and usefulness. "Watching" as well as "praying," Lydia Baxter's lines assured, was the secret to being "more like Jesus" and to "doing good along the way." And Fanny Crosby could be counted on to express the same sentiment under many guises: "Sing always." Even the "infant class" could participate:

> Gentle Saviour, God of love,
> Hear us from thy throne above,
> While we meet to praise thee here,
> In our Infant class so dear.
> May the lessons we have heard
> From thy pure and holy word
> Make us what we ought to be,
> Lead thy little lambs to thee.

In 1881, the publishers Newhall and Company introduced *Great Joy* with a poem by Fanny Crosby that explained the hymnal's intent:

> We, for his glory send it forth,
> With this, our hearts' request,
> That through its songs, poor, hopeless ones
> May be redeemed and blest.
> We hope to see our little work
> Fast spreading, far and wide,
> And millions coming home to Him
> Who once for sinners died.

Sunday Schools offered convenient laboratories for a new brand of music geared to the young, and women's outpouring of text assured a steady supply of songs on every imaginable topic. Publishers had no problem finding new lyrics to replace any that did not gain popularity.

Social Reform and Voluntary Associations

An army of nineteenth-century Protestant women who crusaded on behalf of moral causes wrote hymns to express their vision and rally the faithful. Of all the religiously based causes, perhaps none agitated through more decades of the century than temperance. Devotees of the cause bent every effort to enlist the population in the "cold water army." Temperance hymnals offer an example of the ways women's texts addressed contemporary social issues.

Most temperance hymns assumed the errant to be males who had strayed from their mother's teaching. Often written by women—and certainly sung predominantly by women—these songs brimmed with feeling as they beseeched wanderers to come home. The image of home as sacred space over which a pious mother presided pervaded the lyrics. Temperance hymns tended to call people back rather than to summon them forward. Only infrequently did women address the problem of female intemperance.

A writer named Aunt Ann provided typical words for a tune by popular Baptist musician Robert Lowry:

> Cold water! Bright water! We thank the bounte-
>   ous giver
> Don't mix it with the poison
> That sparkles in the glass:
> It dazzles to deceive you,
> You'll find too late, alas!

The indefatigable Fanny Crosby urged those gathered around "the tempting bowl" to sign the pledge. Her language evoked the conversion experience that stood at the core of evangelical piety. Signing the pledge resembled the moment of conversion:

> I feel a quiet peace within
> I never knew before—
> The pledge is signed, my promise sealed,
> And I will drink no more.

Temperance ballads offered pathetic tales of destitute children—"poor Benny" or "the drunkard's daughter"—to implore parents to return to the right path. Appeals to the victims of drink, interspersed with hymns in praise of cold water ("Oh! Water for me, bright water for me!") and calls to arms in the battle for America's soul filled a spate of hymnals that fueled a generation of temperance advocacy. Here God became "God of the Temp'rance cause," and recruits to the cause took their places as "valiant soldiers" to "Strike for Right and Temperance" in a victorious cause. "King Alcohol reign'd all supreme a hundred years ago," wrote Mary A. Kidder, "His sword of might cut left and right, the world's most powerful foe:

> But since that day, in grand array
> Our army millions strong

Has brought him down with damaged crown
By labor, pray'r and song.

A typical text by Laura Ormiston Chant described the wrenching impact of alcoholism on the domestic circle:

O dark upon the children falls
The shadow of the strife
That robs them of the festivals
And holy days of life;
Drink is that shadow stern and grim;
Christians! Awake and pray;
Cry to your Lord for grace from Him
This curse to drive away.

In the scheme of things, temperance drove women to advocacy for children, purity, and home life, all traditionally women's concerns and all magnified in urban America. Lucy Rider Meyer, a prime mover in the deaconess movement (a movement that prepared women for religious work), provided tunes, unusual work for a woman. Frances Willard's alter ego, Anna Gordon, offered texts, as did a host of lesser known women who either crafted their own lyrics or adapted others. Traditional hymns employed the gender-specific language of the Bible to all aspects of the church. Temperance and reform hymnals often offered words directed to women, as in this adaptation of the well-known "Onward, Christian Soldiers":

Onward, sisters, onward! March with one accord:
Jesus goes before us, All victorious Lord.

Or,

Hark! 'Tis the watchman's cry, Wake, sisters, Wake!
Jesus our Lord is nigh, Wake, sisters, wake!

Hymns addressed to women enrolled in the temperance cause generally urged collective action and stressed solidarity rather than individualism. Describing the White Ribbon Army (or the Woman's Christian Temperance Union), Katherine Stevenson wrote:

Each but a unit, yet each counts for all,
What though our place and labour be small,
Our part be but to obey His great call,
We all belong, we belong.

A cry for purity pervaded many texts addressed by women to women. Though related to the concept of inner purity that animated perfectionists like Phoebe Palmer, this purity seemed more grounded in direct response to the explicit temptations of urban life. For ex-

ample, "Purer in heart, O God, Help me to be," words by a Mrs. A. L. Davidson, spoke to the goals of diligent female workers in the rescue missions that grappled with prostitution and vice.

In an effort to nip a perennial urban problem in the bud, temperance advocates prepared songs for use in infant classes in Sunday Schools:

One little life for earth and heaven,
Grant Lord, that it to Thee be given:
Guard it from snare of drink and sin;
Make it like Thine, without, within.

Women's hymns exuded confidence in their ability under God to win their cause. Motivated by a determination to be useful and dutiful, they anticipated an approaching day when "the gates of sin" would fall. In her hymn "Loyal Call," Anna Gordon voiced the call to action grounded in the absolute certainty of success:

'Tis the time for earnest doing,
Loyal hearts are needed now,
Hearts that love their homes and country,
And to evil will not bow.
Youths and maidens, little children,
You are needed one and all,
Strong in numbers, full of courage,
Soon the gates of sin will fall.

YMCA (Young Men's Christian Association) hymnals, Christian Endeavor hymnals, Chautauqua collections, and many other dedicated songbooks served the hundreds of interest groups that carried forward the hopes of nineteenth-century Protestants. All of them printed many texts by women. Most printed a mix of traditional hymns—old favorites by Watts and Wesley—interspersed a handful of patriotic texts, and offered gospel hymns dedicated to the specific interest the book reflected. Such movements also inspired hymns designed for specific occasions, and a few of these gained popularity beyond their initial audience. Two written during the 1870s for the Chautauqua Institution (a Methodist-inspired interdenominational protracted summer adult education event on the shores of upstate New York's Lake Chautauqua) illustrate movement from a particular venue to general use. They came from the pen of Mary Lathbury. "Day Is Dying in the West" became a popular evening hymn far from the spectacular lakeside sunsets that inspired its author, and "Break Thou the Bread of Life" found a place in many Protestant hymnals.

Outside the arenas nurtured by traditional Protestants, women found different opportunities to craft songs for religious communities.

Alternative Movements

While women wrote many hymn lyrics and a few tunes and edited a handful of hymnals, with few exceptions their work appeared mostly in hymnals released by nondenominational publishers and was intended primarily for use outside the sanctuary. A few nineteenth-century religious movements gave women the opportunity to attempt the preparation of hymnals intended as official denominational releases. So, for example, Emma Hale Smith, the first wife of the Mormon Prophet Joseph Smith, received by revelation in 1830 the task of selecting sacred songs for the Church of Jesus Christ of the Latter-day Saints. Her work freely adapted standard Protestant texts and featured as well some new Mormon lyrics. Nineteenth-century Spiritualists issued hymnals that reflected the importance of women's leadership in that religious movement. Mary Baker Eddy, founder of the Church of Christ, Scientist, wrote hymns, adapted traditional Protestant texts, and directed the preparation of hymnals for her followers.

Conclusion

Until the twentieth century, most mainline denominations did not seek out women to serve on hymnal editorial committees. Authorized hymnals tended to include a lower percentage of hymns by women than did the hymnals designed for general use. The most popular of women's gospel hymns slowly gained general acceptance for Sunday morning use—especially Crosby's "To God Be the Glory" and "Blessed Assurance." A few songs by Englishwomen remained popular (e.g., Frances Ridley Havergal's "Take My Life"), while translations by several women endured as standard English renderings. Denominational families also typically featured the compositions and translations of several women within their specific traditions. Baptists, Holiness denominations, and Pentecostals adopted gospel hymns as their primary hymnody, and in these traditions the contributions of nineteenth-century women to American sacred song was amply evident. In fundamentalist gospel tabernacles, the faithful also sang the gospel hymns that had helped make women prominent. Twentieth-century revivalists depended on the gospel hymn repertoire. Billy Sunday, Aimee Semple McPherson, or Billy Graham could be sure they were tapping into popular piety when they used the standard gospel hymn repertoire.

The twentieth century saw expanded roles for women in the preparation of music for Protestant use. Sunday Schools and evangelistic endeavors—including foreign missions—continued to elicit an outpouring of text. Evangelist Aimee Semple McPherson provided her sizable following with dozens of hymns and choruses that her evangelistic campaigns and radio broadcasts popu-larized. New opportunities also beckoned. Twentieth-century women were often beneficiaries of nineteenth-century movements, and they had access to better music education as well as to more education generally. Over the course of the century, mass media helped transform Christian music, opening a wide array of new opportunities for performing, arranging, accompanying, and producing texts and tunes. Especially since the 1970s, groups like The Second Chapter of Acts, with Annie Herring as its leader, and artists like Amy Grant write and perform text that both expresses and shapes the mood and tastes of contemporary Protestants. During the 1990s, the work of Carol Cymbala became increasingly influential among evangelicals. Founder and director of the (multiple) Grammy Award–winning Brooklyn Tabernacle Choir, Carol Cymbala composes texts and tunes. She also arranges well-known gospel hymns. Choirs and congregations around the world sing her music. Such artists and their cohorts influence the content and practice of the style known as contemporary worship.

Women wrote some of the century's most influential traditional hymns, too. Georgia Harkness, pioneer female seminary educator and theologian at Garrett Evangelical Theological Seminary, won a contest sponsored by the World Council of Churches (for a theme hymn for its 1954 assembly) for her hymn "Hope of the World." Evangelical Protestants appropriated texts for new hymns and adaptations of old favorites by Canadian Margaret Clarkson and Avis Christiansen. Ruth Duck, Jane Parker Huber, Mary Louise Bringle, Jann Alredge-Clanton, and Shirley Erena Murray are prominent modern hymn text writers whose work is generally characterized by fresh images and universal language about God. Sally Ann Morris composes well-received hymn tunes. Among hymn arrangers and choral conductors, few can rival the influence of Alice Parker. Active for over sixty years, Parker remains in high demand, and her choral arrangements are widely used.

The Hymn Society of the United States and Canada regularly encourages emerging text and tune writers, featuring their work at annual meetings and sponsoring occasional contests to encourage people to attempt texts and tunes. The Society provides a venue that encourages women's participation at all levels, and its activities give visibility to the large number of women who teach and study hymnology as well as write hymns. At Oberlin College, Mary Louise Van Dyke (a retired conductor) carries forward the important work of the Hymn Society in creating a vast database that chronicles the publication histories of the hymns in American hymnals. Van Dyke organizes and accesses immense amounts of data that, among other things, tracks the central roles women have played in the hymnody of American Protestantism.

Women's contributions to American sacred song have

been many and varied. While women's place at the decision-making level for standard denominational hymn repertoires is a post–World War II reality, finding women's names printed above the lyrics—and occasionally the tunes—of Protestant hymn favorites is a common occurrence. Many of those hymns were originally intended for arenas other than the sanctuary. There a handful gained such popularity that they found their way by public demand into the hymn vocabulary of American churchgoers.

SOURCES: Ian Bradley, *Abide With Me: The World of Victorian Hymns* (1997). Fanny J. Crosby, *Memories of Eighty Years* (1905). E. C. Gaskell, *The Life of Charlotte Brontë* (1901). Michael Hicks, *Mormonism and Music: A History* (1989). June Hadden Hobbs, *I Sing for I Cannot Be Silent: The Feminization of American Hymnody* (1997). John Julian, *Dictionary of Hymnology* (1892). Mrs. E. R. Pitman, *Lady Hymn Writers* (1892). Ira Sankey, *My Life and the Story of the Gospel Hymns* (1907). J. R. Watson, *The English Hymn* (1999). Paul Westermeyer, *Te Deum: The Church and Music* (1998).

AFRICAN AMERICAN HYMNODY
Cheryl A. Kirk-Duggan

HYMNODY IS THE experience of hymn singing and writing in and for a particular time, place, or church. A *hymn* is a song of adoration or praise of God, a poetic, religious proclamation appropriate for corporate expression. Hymns are sung statements of doctrinal beliefs in theological language, that is, beliefs and understandings about God's presence and work in the world. The stanzas may have an accompanying refrain/chorus that is repeated after each verse. Traditionally, hymns are those songs that express the truth claims that capture the Christian religious experience of the faithful throughout the ages. African American hymnody emerges from the African cultural, religious, and musical practices of African slaves mixed with European religious doctrines and musical styles within the United States. African traits, characteristics, myths, and hermeneutical strategies central to the development of African American music create continuity between African American hymnody and oral African cultural memories. Central to African American Christian hymnody are their experiential issues that emerge from their pain predicament—years of enslavement and ongoing oppression. Richard Allen (1760–1831), a minister and founder of the African Methodist Episcopal Church, published the first hymnal designed for African Americans, *A Collection of Hymns and Spiritual Songs from Various Authors* (two editions) in Philadelphia in 1801.

African American church hymnody categorizes music sung in a congregational style in a black church setting. This hymnody emerges from the soul as participatory, spirit-filled, holistic, celebratory, life-giving utterances and experiences, reflecting the doctrinal, theological, ethical, and sociocultural history and consciousness of diverse black churches. The songs include spirituals (folk, jubilee, arranged, protest songs); gospel music (folk, gospel-hymn, quartets, choral, contemporary); anthems (antiphonal, choral music with organ accompaniment); revival songs (music with an evangelistic fervor); hymns (standards by, e.g., Isaac Watts, Charles Wesley, Fanny Crosby, Charles A. Tindley); and praise songs (toe-tapping music of deep adoration). Central to this African American music tradition is the ring shout.

The ring shout is a cultural, expressive ritual combining the secular and sacred. The ring shout embedded the slave's musical habits into African American musical genres, where dance and holy music fuse. Such fluidity is key to all African American music. The ring shout involves feet shuffling, hand clapping, repetitive drumming, and counterclockwise movement in opposition to the sun's movement, which symbolized the bards' long, exhausting days of hard work during enslavement. The ritual embodied teaching through storytelling, trickster techniques, and other symbolic gestures and values of ancestor worship and multivalent gods; all facilitated the adaptation of the Christian doctrine of a Trinitarian God.

In addition to the ring shout, African Americans retained and embraced many African traditions and practices foundational to African American hymnody. These traditions and practices include cries, calls, and hollers; call and response; heterophony, multiple rhythms, and polyrhythms; blue notes, pendular thirds, bent notes, hums, elisions; glides, grunts, vocables; and other rhythmic-oral declamations, punctuations, and interjections. Syncopation, parallel chords and intervals, melodic and rhythmic repetitions, body movement, and distinctive timbre connected the slave bards to their African traditions and have enriched African American hymnody. African American ethnomusicologist Portia K. Maultsby tracks a three-pronged musical lineage: African American sacred traditions, African American secular traditions (nonjazz), and African American secular traditions (jazz); these traditions have multiple tentacles reflecting a continuous linkage, influence, and fluidity between the so-called sacred and secular.

The Rev. Wyatt Tee Walker notes that black singing (the joy of black worship), black preaching (the heart of black worship), and black praying (the strength of black worship) identify the sacred trilogy of African American faith. The joy of that faith comes from rootedness in God. Historically, black religious music has transmitted that faith through song.

Those enslaved brought remnants of the songs, rituals, cultures, and theologies from their home in Africa when they came to these shores. Thus, many slaves were familiar with the Christian God, as monotheism was practiced in West Africa as early as 500 C.E. Some Africans followed Islam; others followed indigenous religions. Although slaves were separated from family and those of similar language and cultural background, the slaves still managed to adapt the English language and white slave Christianity and to create and sing spirituals: the first black hymnody in the United States, the ground bass, the imprimatur for most African American music.

The Spirituals

Spirituals, songs of hope and justice, are "chants of collective exorcism" that helped an oppressed people grapple with the social evils of racism. Musically, the spirituals involved stanzas or verses and choruses built on strong, syncopated rhythmic patterns in a quadruple or duple meter. Melodically, the spirituals had three general performance formats: (1) the leader/soloist calls out and the community/congregation reacts/responds in answer; (2) the musical line consists of short syncopated rhythmic patterns; and (3) the phrases are long and sustained and the tempo is slow. This music of the preliterate antebellum church, the invisible institution, would later sustain a healing reality during the 1960s civil rights era.

These rousing, contemplative songs are living, oral testimonies that offer confession, prayer, poetry, and reflections. Slaves affirmed God, as they coped with existential angst and ontological fatigue, as well as sought healing and wholeness. The spirituals evolved during legalized slavery, between the seventeenth and nineteenth centuries, as African Americans were taken against their will—sometimes sold off by their own tribal chieftains—then legally objectified by the state and church in the United States. Having survived the Middle Passage, slaves retained their gifts of song, traditions, culture, and an unshakeable relationship with God. Believing they were created in God's image, slaves created songs in community, incubating the music until the singing helped to liberate them. Spirituals were a way to tell creative, secretive stories of survival and hope.

Black folk could cloak their identity politics in an apparently mundane song, while plotting to escape, to bolster morale and to warn others of danger through the power of song. The spiritual is one technique that links the many styles and traditions in African American music, uses figurative language to testify, call someone out, or make a rhetorical gesture; and it creates a strategy for using preexisting musical material by various treatments as a trope, for example, diverse melodic and rhythmic figures. Spirituals embody the energetic power and quintessence of African American spirituality, cre-

ativity, and sacrality. They express a collective African American folk aesthetic. This aesthetic involves the formal and folk aspects of life experiences. One sees the motivational aspects, the freedom and literacy of a politically shaped African American life, that emerges from their spirituality and embodied beauty. The spirituals signify poems, figurative language, stories, and songs as shared communal knowledge to evoke justice and often humor, naming good and evil in an imperfect world. Repetition, as a signifier, helped to empower inner strength and teach the parable to those forbidden to read and write so they could remember their culture, theology, and history, as well as orally transmit these to others.

According to John Lovell, Jr., peoples of the African diaspora created 6,000 extant spirituals that employ many traditional African musical elements, along with a distinct blending of voices to create a polyphonic sound. Slave bards composed their own tunes and appropriated tunes that they heard as they improvised songs, creating totally new communal versions. These characteristics of the spirituals declare a struggle-fulfillment scenario of the human condition from the African American perspective of anonymous composers.

During postbellum years through today, several women composers arranged the spirituals, for congregational, solo, four-part harmony, and orchestra. These composer/arrangers include Margaret Bonds (1913–1972), composer, pianist, teacher, winner of the 1932 Wanamaker prize in composition, and the first African American soloist with the Chicago Symphony at the Chicago Worlds Fair in 1933. Undine Moore (1904–1989), the "Dean of Black Women Composers," wrote vocal, piano, chamber, and choral music including sacred works and completed many arrangements of spirituals. Rachel Eubanks (1923–), the founder and director of the Eubanks Conservatory of Music, Los Angeles, composes for chorus and orchestra, for multiple instruments and solo voice, chamber works, and many songs, including arrangements of spirituals. Lena Johnson McLin (1928–) has written cantatas, masses, solo and choral arrangements of spirituals, anthems, art songs, rock operas, soul songs, works for piano and orchestra, and electronic music. During the late nineteenth and early twentieth century, the Fisk Jubilee Singers also popularized spirituals when they toured Europe.

In 1871, six years after the end of the Civil War, the nine original Fisk Jubilee singers chorus toured the United States and Europe. Fisk School, begun in 1865, in Nashville, Tennessee, was housed in the buildings of a former U.S. Army hospital in the midst of Nashville's African American community. The Jubilee Singers are the first internationally acclaimed group of African American musicians who attained recognition, fame, and financial success. This group of young ex-slaves set out on the tour to help move their financially troubled school to solvency by giving concerts. Funds raised by the Jubilee Singers during their international concerts were used to construct the school's first permanent building, Jubilee Hall. The Jubilee Singers, the first group to perform the songs of slaves publicly, introduced audiences to the power of spirituals, helping to preserve this music from extinction. On the verge of physical exhaustion and even close to death, the singers were inspiring and successful. By 1873, the group grew to eleven members and completed their second European tour. When the Fisk Jubilee Singers first performed in the late 1800s, they sang ballads and patriotic anthems. Their director, George White, suggested that they sing the songs of their ancestors, the spirituals. Though initially hesitant to share their sacred music, they agreed to add a few spirituals to their program. The music was well received, often moving audiences to tears, bringing new life to these historic, poignant songs of deep heart and faith of the African American slave. In the 1880s, the Jubilee Singers toured the American West, Asia, Australia, and New Zealand. Over a century later, the Jubilee Singers of Fisk University continue the concert tradition begun by those nine courageous bards. "Jubilee Singers: Sacrifice and Glory," part of the Public Broadcasting Service's award-winning *The American Experience* series, documents the original Fisk Jubilee Singers. For a time during Reconstruction through the early 1940s, many African Americans often did not want to sing or hear the spirituals. They wanted to forget about the songs that reminded them of the hurts and devastation of slavery. Some choral directors continued to program the spirituals, and they regained popularity during the 1960s civil rights movement.

In sum, the spirituals emerged collectively from the folk in community, from the seventeenth through the nineteenth century. Composers began arranging the spirituals, from the early twentieth century, and they continue to metamorphose. The legacy of the spirituals, black declamatory preaching style, and the movement of the Spirit gave birth to the gospel style of African American hymnody.

Gospel Music and Musicians, 1890s–1960s

Folk gospel (1890s) and the gospel hymn (1900s), like the spirituals, were connected to congregational singing. In the folk tradition, gospel songwriters are poets, composers, and performers. They disseminated their songs orally, through sheet music and recordings, attending to the song's melody and message, which draw upon personal experiences as well as scriptural verses. Gospel songs focus on the Christian church and Jesus' teaching and ministry, especially the doctrine of salvation by grace, and bear the name *gospel* because many

of the lyrics emerge from the first four books of the New Testament. This music, with its tremendous resonance among poor people, first came into its own in the northern states because there the spirituals that arose in a rural setting were not satisfactory when coping with the urban settings to which many African Americans had now migrated. William McClain argues that the sacred basis of gospel song is rooted in a theology of experience, where God creates and does not forsake, and a theology of imagination, where one's hopeful, God-focused mind's eye creates celebratory songs. Gospel songs include a theology of grace where one can be intimate with God and know liberation and a theology of survival where God assists one daily, despite monumental oppression. Melva Wilson Costen notes that African American gospel music is both a performance style and a musical genre. By improvising, a musician can "gospelize" spirituals, hymns, and anthems, to suit the musical tastes of a particular religious community.

The genres of traditional gospel (1930s) and gospel quartets (1930s) were influenced by and often grew in tandem with their more secular counterparts of rural (1880s) and vaudeville blues (1900s), boogie woogie (1900s), syncopated (1890s), and New Orleans–style jazz (1900s), as the transition into the big bands (1920s) led to swing bands (1930s). Between the 1890s and 1920s, gospel music singing received a boost from the Azusa Street Revival, in Los Angeles, that led to a nationwide expansion of Pentecostalism, 1906 to 1909. Concurrently, the ministry of sanctified singing preachers emerged along with the congregational singing in Pentecostal churches. Gospel music thus became more mainstream in African American churches nationwide, as southern, rural African Americans migrated to the West Coast and urban North during World War II. While gospel music was popularized in northern ghetto store front churches, many of the more elite African American Protestant churches did not accept this music initially, as gospel music resonated too closely with the secular blues. When the National Baptist Convention publicly sanctioned the singing of major gospel musicians, gospel music increased in popularity, beginning in Chicago in 1930. Many call Dr. Thomas A. Dorsey (1899–1993), composer of 1,000 songs, the "Father of Black Gospel music," when he shifted from vaudeville and blues to performing and writing gospel music. Dorsey credits Rev. Dr. Charles A. Tindley (1865–1933), who along with C. P. Jones created the gospel hymn of the 1900 to 1930s eras, with that honor. Dorsey and his friends advanced gospel by their strategizing and publishing businesses, as well as by establishing the National Convention of Gospel Choirs and Choruses, including friend and collaborator Mahalia Jackson.

Mahalia Jackson (1911–1972) was a world-renowned gospel singer and recording artist, entrepreneur/pro-

LEAD ME
GUIDE ME

and friend of Martin Luther King, Jr., Jackson sang a spiritual right before his famous "I Have a Dream" speech, during the 1964 March on Washington, D.C.

Several women composers/musicians transformed the congregational gospel hymn of the Transitional Period (1900–1930) into the solo, quartet, and choral gospel song of the Golden Age or Traditional Period of Gospel (1930–1969). Doris Akers (1923–1995), a native of Missouri, composed her first gospel song at age ten and organized her five-piece band. This gospel composer, singer, publisher, and choral director moved to Los Angeles in 1945 and sang with the Sallie Martin Singers. Akers and Dorothy Simmons (1948–1958) collaborated and formed the Simmons-Akers Singers, engaged in recordings, concert tours, and a publishing house. Aker's prominence grew in the 1950s and 1960s, as she helped bridge the gap between white and black gospel music. She affiliated with Manna Publishing Company and sang with a racially mixed, Los Angeles–based choir. Akers recorded with Capitol, Christian Faith, and RCA, received many awards, and sang on national television. Some of the standards for which Akers is famous appear in recent African American hymnals and include: "Lead Me, Guide Me," "God Is So Good," "You Can't Beat God Giving," and "Sweet, Sweet Spirit." Her songs proclaim the love and goodness of God, the power and gracious nature of God, faith, peace, and the power and sweetness of the Holy Spirit. In 1961 Akers was voted Female Gospel Singer of the Year and Gospel Composer of the Year. In 1992, the Smithsonian Institute honored her as the foremost black gospel songwriter in the United States. Akers died in 1995 in Minneapolis, Minnesota.

Lucie Eddie Campbell (Williams) (1885–1963), a native of Mississippi and the first woman gospel composer, helped select the music for the classic 1921 volume *The Gospel Pearls*. Essentially a self-taught musician, she later received degrees from Rust College in Holy Springs, Mississippi, and the master's degree from Tennessee Agricultural and Industrial State College. Campbell shaped the music of the National Baptist Convention (the largest body of African American Christians) through her strategizing ability and leadership, during the period 1919 to 1962. She composed songs and helped shape the singing and performance style of the pioneers of gospel

ducer, and businesswoman. Born in poverty of devout Baptists in a three-room "shot-gun" shack between railroad tracks and the Mississippi River levee in New Orleans, this New Orleans native—a niece of entertainers—sang a fusion of ragtime, blues, jazz, and gospel over against the many styles of music and performers of New Orleans in the 1920s, significantly within the Sanctified church. From the time of her baptism at age twelve, Jackson dedicated her life to God in song, whether a domestic worker doing laundry or as an international celebrity. Dorsey became her mentor and publisher and wrote over 400 gospel songs that Jackson helped popularize. "Move On Up a Little Higher" launched her career on the Apollo label, which sold over 8 million copies in the black community. With her sanctified skipping and strutting, deep breathing and irresistible swing, and her down-home southern temperament, Mahalia sang with assurance and power songs of life and death, of deep faith and comfort, of a closer relationship with God, with a penchant for singing songs about going to heaven. She recorded about thirty albums, a dozen Gold records, and had her own radio and television programs. Though her music sometimes became more commercialized as her popularity increased, Jackson's heart always returned to Dr. Watts's hymns. A loyal supporter music, notably the lined hymn style, where the song leader first recites or "calls out" the words, then the congregation responds by singing them in time and in tune. Campbell stressed the classical tradition, especially the gospel ballad. She composed original songs, used biblical narrative imagery, and arranged spirituals and jubilee songs. Jubilee songs are often used as synonyms for the earliest spirituals that evolved during slavery. Those in bondage knew a biblical sense of jubilee as their songs bolstered their morale and gave them a renewed sense of fortitude, faith in God, and hope for liberation. She created the gospel waltz, which stressed three beats in the bass with a contrasting melody in the treble, a standardized form by the 1950s. A committed educator and evangelist, Campbell's fiery temperament led to major battles with the black Baptist church administration. She was "churched," that is, excommunicated, where the right hand of fellowship was withdrawn. This experience inspired two of her most profound songs, "He'll Understand and Say Well Done" and "Just to Behold His Face." Campbell's songs express her deep Christian conviction and ethics, with words of profound sincerity. Her songs include themes of salvation, relationship with Jesus, the sufficiency of grace, humility, praise, gratitude, personal devotion, and piety. Campbell taught for over fifty years in Memphis, Tennessee. She married at age seventy-five and died in Nashville in 1963.

Sallie Martin (1895–1988) signified as orator and singer as she helped turn Dorsey's emotion-packed texts of his gospels into a highly charged hortatory or sermonic presentation. Proclaimed "The Mother of Gospel" by the National Convention of Gospel Choirs and Choruses, Martin had a deep voice and a unique speaking style of singing gospel. As a teenager, this Georgia businesswoman moved to Atlanta after her mother died and joined the Fire Baptized Holiness Church and embraced its Sanctified singing. During the 1920s, Martin, her husband, and their son relocated to Chicago. Following a 1929 divorce, she worked at a hospital and continued to pursue her interest in gospel. Martin auditioned for gospel great Thomas A. Dorsey, who was taking Chicago's music culture by storm, and he hired her. In early 1932 Martin made her debut with his group at the Ebenezer Baptist Church. Dorsey became increasingly aware of her value as a performer and entrepreneur, as she was able to help his store turn a profit within a few months. Martin traveled to Cleveland in 1933, throughout the Midwest and South to organize gospel choruses. Martin and Dorsey organized the yearly National Convention of Gospel Choirs and Choruses, and she was its vice president until her death. In 1940 Martin went solo, teaming with a young pianist named Ruth Jones (aka Dinah Washington), and began touring the country. That same year, Martin and gospel composer Kenneth Morris joined forces with financial backer Rev. Clarence H. Cobb to found Martin and Morris, Inc., a publishing company that became the biggest and the oldest continuously running national black gospel music publishing company in Chicago (1940–1980s). Martin traveled on the road with her singers, advertising the compositions they published, and Morris stayed in Chicago arranging, composing, and notating music. Martin performed with pianist and arranger Roberta Martin (no relation) for a short time, before forming the Sallie Martin Singers, the first female group in gospel history, until the mid-1950s. Among her hits were "Just a Closer Walk with Thee" and "He'll Wash You Whiter Than Snow." An astute businesswoman and tireless supporter of charitable causes, Martin's involvement in the civil rights movement led to an invitation to attend the 1960 celebration marking the independence of Nigeria. She gave support to the Nigerian Health Program, resulting in a state office building named in her honor. A pioneering gospel musician, she was widely known through the tours made by the Sallie Martin Singers.

Roberta Evelyn Martin (1907–1969), composer, singer, pianist, arranger, and group and choral organizer, introduced and developed the classical gospel choral sound that created the model for the community-based church gospel choir. Martin was the first to organize a mixed gospel choir by adding female voices into her all-male group in the mid-1940s. She founded and operated her own gospel music publishing house in Chicago. Martin combined the "moan" from her Arkansas Baptist childhood with the Dorsey bounce, a bit of semiclassical expression, and the Sanctified churches' syncopation to forge the classic gospel music sound. The Roberta Martin style fashioned a vocal sheen and collective resonance with a powerful, spiritual integrity. Martin combined African rhythm, melody, and ensemble with European form, order, and harmony through her distinct use of scales, tension, and release in each song; this marked the development of the gospel cadence formula and the use of chords to end a song. Gospel scholar Horace Boyer says that Martin's pianistic style reminded one of the subtleties of a Horowitz, the creative imagination of an Ellington, and the power of an Erroll Garner, all rooted in church piano playing. She composed about seventy songs, arranged and published 280 gospel songs, and reached and inspired thousands of listeners through performances and selling sheet music. During the 1940s and 1950s, the Roberta Martin Singers evangelized the masses. Her compositions include "He Knows Just How Much We Can Bear" and "God Is Still on the Throne." Martin earned six Gold records and sang at Gian Carlo Menotti's Spoleto Festival of Two Worlds in Spoleto, Italy, in 1963. Martin's songs offer personal testimonies of reassurance, observe the specialized power and the unfailing presence and grace of God, proclaim Jesus as comforter (one who satisfies), and honor Jesus as defender and burden bearer of the children of God. She died in Chicago in 1969. Martin moved the "Golden Gospel Age" forward with traveling choirs, ensembles (smaller in size from choirs), and sheet music. The Martin sound continues everywhere, from rock music's resiliency and symphonies to detergent commercials.

Clara Ward (1924–1973) sang in a family trio with her mother Gertrude and her sister Willarene. Settling in Philadelphia in 1920, the trio began attracting attention at the National Baptist Convention annual meetings during the 1940s. In 1947, the group expanded, was renamed the Famous Ward Singers, with the addition of Henrietta Waddy and Marion Williams, and began making recordings. During the 1950s, the Ward Singers drew crowds of up to 25,000 per event and recorded extensively, toured widely, and made controversial moves. For example, not only was the group the first to wear sequined gowns and large ornate wigs during the performance; the Ward Singers were the first gospel group to sing at the Newport Jazz Festival, the first to perform in nightclubs, the first to sing at Radio City Music Hall in New York, and among the first to appear in gospel musicals and films. They also toured regularly with the Reverend C. L. Franklin of Detroit, the father of Aretha Franklin, who also was a disciple of Clara Ward. Some describe the Ward Singers as the earliest progenitors of the pop-gospel style. Their concerts highlighted their showmanship as they honed Clara Ward's revolutionary gospel sound: They added musical elements and practices that had never been done before but are considered standard techniques and styles in gospel music. Their best-known live recordings include "Surely, God Is Able" and "How I Got Over." The Ward Singers repertoire embraced songs concerning God's power, particularly God's ability to do anything, to transform, to transcend, and the import of having a relationship with Jesus Christ. Ward formed the Clara Ward Specials in 1951 and, with her mother, started the Clara Ward House of Music publishing company in 1954. Clara had a part in Langston Hughes's play *Tambourines to Glory*. The Ward Singers appeared in the movie *It's Your Thing*. Kitty Parham, Frances Steadman, Henrietta Waddy, and Marion Williams left to form the Stars of Faith gospel group by 1958. Clara Ward's untimely death occurred in 1973.

Albertina Walker (1929–   ), the youngest of nine children, knew she wanted to be a gospel singer and began singing in Chicago at the age of four in the Children's Choir of the West Point Baptist Church; by age seventeen she was the lead singer of Robert Anderson's group. (Anderson was a renowned, influential, popular gospel male soloist, particularly in 1950s Chicago.) Wal-

ker, the "Queen of Gospel Music," organized the Caravans at age twenty-two, in 1951, and managed them for over twenty years. The original group consisted of Nellie Grace Daniels, Ora Lee Hopkins Samson, and Elyse Yancy. The Caravans launched the careers of Reverend Shirley Caesar, Inez Andrews, Delores Washington, Cassietta George, Bessie Griffin, Evangelist Dorothy Norwood, and the "King of Gospel" the Reverend James Cleveland. The Caravans achieved great acclaim with hits like "Sweeping Through The City," "Mary Don't You Weep," "Walk Around Heaven," and "Lord Keep Me Day by Day." Their singing trademarks were percussive attacks, an earthy harmony, and a precise rhythm. Walker continued to achieve success as a solo artist, with her first solo recording "Put a Little Love in Your Heart" in 1975. Her sixty albums include Gold hits "Please Be Patient with Me," "I Can Go to God in Prayer," "The Best Is Yet to Come," "Impossible Dream," and "Joy Will Come." Thematically, her songs span concerns of life and death, a close walk with God, being able to stand in difficult moments, and making testimonies of faith. Walker has five Gold records, three Stellar awards, several Gospel Music Workshop of America Excellence awards, and an induction into the 2001 Gospel Music Hall of Fame in Nashville, Tennessee. Committed to the preservation of gospel music and the enhancement of the human experience, Walker has supported many humanitarian causes and appeared on *The Oprah Winfrey Show*, *Good Morning America*, and *The Travis Smiley Show*. She is a frequent guest on the nationally syndicated BET and Word television show *Bobby Jones Gospel*, *Testify*, and *Singsation*. In addition to a street being named in her honor in her native Chicago, Walker received the honorary Doctor of Letters degree by the Chicago Theological Seminary. In addition to having sung before heads of state, Walker appeared in the motion picture *Leap of Faith* starring Steve Martin, *Going Home to Gospel* with Patti LaBelle, the off-Broadway play *The Gospel Truth*, and *The Evolution of Gospel*.

Gospel Music, 1940s–1970s

During the mid-twentieth century, gospel maintained its energetic, deeply emotional character and heightened in sophistication. The changes that emerged within the African American gospel style between 1940s and 1970s were due to changes in (1) the performers and performance practices, along with their impact on the genre itself, and (2) keyboard accompaniment style. In the 1940s, triggered by Rosetta Tharpe's performance practices in 1938 and her later debut at Harlem's Apollo Theatre in 1943, many gospel singers moved into the secular realm, forcing the question of whether gospel was for religion or entertainment. Tharpe (1915–1973), a child prodigy, combined the 1930s and 1940s spirituals, blues, and swing as she stretched gospel music, rousing both acclamation and controversy. Rivaling the status of Mahalia Jackson, Tharpe was both a singing and guitar playing sensation with strong influences from secular music, especially the blues; other than "Memphis" Minnie Douglas (1896–1973), no other woman gained fame like Rosetta Tharpe did prior to the 1930s playing the guitar as an instrument for melody-plucked lines. She performed songs about the pursuit of God by a sinner, the import of the passing of time, God's presence and power, life's challenges, the human condition, and the experience of peace. A product of the Church of God in Christ, Tharpe often ruffled the feathers of her denomination because she mixed blues and jazz with gospel. Tharpe was one of the first to sing gospel music in the nontraditional setting of nightclubs, and for the saints, this was unforgivable. In this sense, Tharpe was ahead of her times. Yet with radio gospel programs, Savoy Records gospel recordings in the 1940s, and the work of Mahalia Jackson and Theodore Fry, who organized the National Baptist Music Convention as a subsidiary to the National Baptist Convention, gospel as genre and style was legitimated.

In the 1950s, gospel music debuted at Carnegie Hall, Madison Square Garden, on television, at jazz festivals, in coffee houses, and in night clubs. Gospel ensemble accompaniment had grown to include electric organ and amplified guitars. In the 1960s the technically demanding piano style stressed the use of complex chords and harmonies, even though many gospel pianists played "by ear." By 1963 *TV Gospel Time* was broadcast every Sunday morning across the nation, as gospel musicals and gospel singing in films became popular. *TV Gospel Time* was a weekly Chicago-based television show that featured African American gospel greats during the 1950s and 1960s. In 1968 James Cleveland and friends like Helen Stephens organized the Gospel Music Workshop of America (GMWA). GMWA paralleled Dorsey's earlier organization, the National Convention of Gospel Choirs and Choruses, founded in 1933, and annually brings together thousands of songwriters and singers to be trained in the African American gospel tradition.

Dorothy Norwood, a Georgia native, began singing with Gospel Stars after moving to Chicago. Evangelist, composer, and music producer, Norwood's solo career began with Savoy Records in 1964. Known as the "World's Greatest Storyteller," Norwood recorded over forty albums, five certified Gold records, including six Grammy nominations. Having performed throughout Europe, Norwood did an American tour with Mick Jagger and The Rolling Stones in 1972. Norwood taped a special for British television along with such gospel notables as Marion Williams, the Reverend James Cleveland, the Southern California Community Choir, and special guest Natalie Cole in 1980. In 1991 Norwood signed with Malaco Records and recorded "Live with the Northern California Gospel Music Workshop of America Mass Choir"; this recording hit number one on Billboard's Top 40. Norwood has also cut "Hattie B's Daughter," "Shake the Devil Off," and "Feel Like."

In the 1970s gospel took on specific sounds and song styles and was now heard in most churches, on college campuses, in concert halls, in theaters, and all mass media. The gospel music business became a large enterprise, including the recording industry, biographies, dissertations, and ongoing workshops. Most established Protestant churches used the full corpus of African American hymnody, with the singing usually led by the senior or sanctuary choir and the gospel choir. Senior or sanctuary choirs sing the more classical music tradition of anthems, hymns, cantatas, oratorios, and spirituals. Gospel choirs may sing revised versions of spirituals, though they primarily sing gospel music and contemporary praise songs—repetitive songs usually of a few choruses to move people to ready themselves for an outpouring of the Holy Spirit and for devotion prior to worship. In smaller congregations, one choir sings everything, as worship in the African American tradition occurs through the interaction between music and the spoken word. The gospel concert might occur in sacred or secular spaces, involving singing and preaching. Many credit Willie Mae Ford Smith (1904–1994) with establishing the tradition of introducing each song with a sermonette, and an interpretation, followed by a repeat of the chorus. Smith, along with Dorsey, his partner Sallie Martin, Theodore R. Frye, and Magnolia Lewis Butts, formed the National Convention of Gospel Choirs and Choruses.

One singer-composer who emerged during the 1950s to 1970s is the Rev. Shirley Caesar (1938–   ). Caesar, a North Carolinian, is a contemporary gospel singer, evangelist, pastor, civic leader, businesswoman, and soulful spirit. When Caesar ministers, she dances, shouts, moves, preaches, and inspires, with great vitality, between pulpit, boardroom, and concert stage, as a concerned minister and citizen who focuses on the needy, giving a hand, not a handout. Caesar, one of twelve children, once knew such need because her father died when she was twelve and her mother was an invalid. Caesar began touring with the Caravans in 1958 with lead coloratura Albertina Walker, Inez Andrews, known as the High Priestess of Gospel, and Sarah McKissich, gospel ballad singer. The African American folk preacher style actualized by Mother Willie Mae Ford Smith (1904–1994) in Thomas Dorsey's Baptist gospel blues tradition in the 1920s and 1930s, and perfected by Edna Gallmon Cooke (1918–1967), the "Sweetheart of the Potomac," who did the first half of the song as a sermon and sang the second half, became Caesar's trademark:

blue notes, slurs, and achieving rhythmic effects by repeating consonants, using intense nasality, and evocative *yeah's*. (Cooke's song sermonettes usually celebrated the theme of death, in a sensual manner that enticed some and repelled others.) In addition to her sermonized singing, Caesar dramatizes her songs; for example, when singing a song about running or about not being tied, when she sings the word *running*, Caesar runs up and down the aisles. In 1966, Caesar began to sing "mother" songs and "house-rocking" songs. One of her most popular standards is "No Charge," the story of a small child who submits a bill to his mother for his chores, and the mother responds by listing all she had done for him at no charge. She performs over 150 concerts a year and pastors in Raleigh, North Carolina. Her honors include five Grammy Awards and six Dove Awards for gospel. First Lady and Queen of Gospel Shirley Caesar exudes a kind of powerful energy, soul deliverance.

Margaret Allison organized Angelic Gospel Singers in 1944 and served as lead singer, pianist, manager, and booking agent for the group. After modest local success around Philadelphia and the Carolinas, the Angelics signed with Gotham Records and recorded their first song, Lucie Campbell's "Touch Me Lord Jesus," in 1947. The Angelics teamed with the Dixie Hummingbirds to record such songs as "Dear Lord Look Down Upon Me," "Mother Left Me Standing on the Highway," and "Wondering Which Way to Go" in 1950. Through their recording, the Angelic Gospel Singers are the longest-selling female gospel group in history. In 1984, the Malaco label released an anniversary album of the Angelics commemorating over fifty years of gospel.

Contemporary Gospel, 1970s–Present

Since 1969 with the debut of Walter Hawkins's version of "Oh, Happy Day," Pentecostal artists of the Church of God in Christ have dominated the Modern Gospel Era or Contemporary Period. Many new female vocalists who have emerged within gospel since the 1960s and 1970s continue the great traditions of African American hymnody worldwide. The Anointed Pace Sisters, from a family of musicians, singers, and preachers, began singing as babies with their father at night before going to bed and later sang together in local high school talent shows and won the "Best Gospel Group" award at the Annual Church of God in Christ Music Convention in the 1970s. They became a part of the Action Revival Team led by their uncle, the Rev. Gene Martin, in the mid- to late 1970s. In 1992, these nine vivacious sisters made their debut album on Savoy Records, titled *U-Know*, which stayed on the Billboard Charts for over a year. In 1995, the Sisters released *My Purpose*. The Atlanta Choice Awards has honored them for four consecutive times as Group of the Year. The Sisters create

a distinctive balance and harmony of traditional and contemporary gospel music.

Lillian Jointer Lilly, a native of Mississippi, and her twin sister Carolyn, from a family of thirteen children, began singing duets during elementary school. During Lilly's teenage years, The Two Star Juniors expanded and became known as The Traveling Stars. From the 1970s to the 1980s, Lilly sang solos across Mississippi and Louisiana in churches on weekends and opened many gospel concerts. In 1988, Frank Williams formed Malaco's Mississippi Mass Choir and recruited Lilly, who became a principal vocalist on the albums by the Grammy-nominated choir. Her most recent album, *Gotta Have Faith*, was released in 1997. Lilly became the first solo recording artist to emerge from the Mississippi Mass Choir.

Hailing from Delaware, Linda Henry & Daughters of Faith had their break when gospel great Dorothy Norwood befriended Linda Henry. They are known for "Over and Over," "Jesus Is a Friend," and "My Rock" on their celebrated recording *If Jesus Goes With Me*, released in 1996.

La Shun Pace made her musical mark in 1988 when she recorded "In the House of the Lord" with Dr. Jonathan Greer & The Cathedral of Faith Choir. Savoy signed her to a solo recording contract, and she debuted in 1990, with *He Lives*, earning national acclaim. The album remained in the Top 20 of Billboard magazine's Gospel Albums Chart for over a year. Her second album in 1993 with Savoy *Shekinah Glory*, with The Cathedral of Faith Choir, was followed by *A Wealthy Place*, which quickly moved to Billboard's Top 15 and topped almost every gospel chart in the nation. She appeared in the movie *Leap of Faith* and has been involved with several theatrical productions and in other major venues, including the Kennedy Center, Washington, D.C.

Myrna Summer, composer and performer, delivered her first gospel message in 1970 with "God Gave Me a Song." The single gave Summer her first Grammy nomination and earned her song and album of the year awards from the GMWA. Recipient of the prestigious Mahalia Jackson Award, Summer's album titled *We Going to Make It* became a bestselling recording in 1988, receiving the Best Traditional Gospel Artist (Female) award. Summer's performances and her original compositions, classic congregational renditions, and songs of praise and worship are energetic, spiritual, and inspiring.

Ruby Terry, a native of Mississippi, coproduced her own first recording, "Heeding the Spirit," and signed with the Malaco label. In 1989 her first album, *Chapter One*, garnered a Stellar Nomination, and she recorded her second album in 1992. Her recordings include "God Can Do It" and "What a Time."

CeCe (Priscilla Marie) Winans (1964–), singer, author, philanthropist, businesswoman, actor, and television personality, sang duo with her brother BeBe for many years. CeCe and BeBe leapt into the musical mainstream in the late 1980s with smash rhythm and blues (R&B) singles, and they did well with Christian radio singles such as "Count It All Joy" and "Up Where We Belong." The two have won numerous Grammy, Stellar, and Dove Awards. In 1995 the duo decided to explore different solo possibilities. CeCe's achieved a Grammy Gold album for *Alone in His Presence*. She has recorded four albums and written a memoir, titled *On a Positive Note, Her Joyous Faith, Her Life in Music, and Her Everyday Blessings* (1999). For CeCe, music is the location for the resting of her soul. CeCe now has her own recording label, Wellspring Gospel, a subsidiary of her entertainment company. *Alabaster Box*, the label's first release in 1999, involves songs that minister to her personally and concerns spiritual brokenness, prayer, worship, and one's relationship with God. *Alabaster Box* and *CeCe Winans* are both certified Gold. Her publicist Bill Carpenter notes that new release *Throne Room* (2003) is a collaborative effort with INO Records, Puresprings, and Epic Records. Love for God and the experience of worship are central to her music. She believes that this love transcends circumstances and life; and when one understands this, then God can operate in a person's life.

The Clark Sisters, formed in the 1980s, are among the recent inductees into the Gospel Hall of Fame. Members of the group are Detroit's Twinkie Clark, Dorinda Clark-Cole, Karen Clark-Sheard, and Jackie Clark-Chisholm. Their mother, Dr. Mattie Moss Clark, was inducted posthumously. The group was influenced by the Detroit gospel style of the gospel-singing Winans family. "You Brought the Sunshine" hit the R&B charts in 1987, and the sisters later appeared in the Melba Moore video *Lift Every Voice and Sing*. Twinkie Clark considers gospel music important for reaching people who previously had no interest in religion.

Anthems and Contemporary Hymns

Along with traditional hymns and gospel music, many African American churches have senior, chancel, or sanctuary choirs, groups of young to older adults that primarily sing arranged spirituals, hymns, and anthems. With the introduction of anthems came the introduction of choral singing in African American Methodist churches. James Abbington notes the differences in function of the anthem in liturgical and nonliturgical African American churches. In liturgical churches (Episcopal, Lutheran, Catholic), the anthems are to support, complement, and reinforce the time or season of the liturgical Christian year. Some would include Methodists and Presbyterians in the liturgical group; others would not. Abbington suggests that the nonliturgical churches (Methodist, Baptist, Disciples of Christ, United

Church of Christ, Presbyterians, Seventh Day Adventists, Church of God in Christ, etc.) use anthems as they observe Christmas, Palm Sunday, Good Friday, Easter, and Pentecost, with nonliturgical days, for example, Women's Day, Men's Day, Black History Month, Children's Day, and Installation of Officers Sunday. Three factors shape the anthems sung most frequently by African American churches, particularly the nonliturgical churches. First, the texts have relevancy and meaning; are consistent; and undergird the theological, biblical, sociocultural, and justice issues essential for the African American Christian experience in its quest to be faithful, liberating, hopeful, and eschatological, in praise and worship. Second, aesthetic musical characteristics, from grandeur and power to splendor and transcendence, touch and move the hearers and please the performers and the listeners. Third, because of their longevity and use throughout the United States through the generations, these particular anthems are not in the standard repertoire or musical canon of most African American churches. Among the African American female composers are several women, who include Undine Smith Moore, Virgie Carrington DeWitty, Lena McLin, Lucie E. Campbell (See "Gospel Music and Musicians" section), and Margaret Pleasant Douroux.

Undine Smith Moore (1904–1989), a native of Virginia, received degrees from Fisk University in piano and theory and the M.A. professional diploma from Columbia University Teachers College, and had a forty-five-year teaching career at Virginia State College. She cofounded Black Music Center with Altona Trent Johns to honor and recognize what they saw as the true creative genius of everyday black people. A lecturer on the music of black composers, who traveled extensively, lecturing and conducting workshops, Moore received an honorary doctoral degree from Indiana University in 1976 and served as senior adviser to the Afro-American Arts Institute for many years. Moore composed choral works, music for solo instruments and solo voice, chamber ensembles, and orchestra; her music is heard frequently at concerts, conventions, festivals, on college campuses, and in churches. She was commissioned to do numerous works and was named Music Laureate in 1977 by the Commonwealth of Virginia. Her cantata *Scenes from the Life of a Martyr: To the Memory of Martin Luther King*, which premiered in 1982, was nominated for a Pulitzer Prize. In addition to her arranged spirituals of "Bound for Canaan's Land" and "Fare You Well," her anthems include "Let Us Make Man in Our Image," based on Milton's *Paradise Lost*, and "Lord, We Give Thanks to Thee," from Leviticus 25:9. In addition to the love and respect of generations of students, she received many awards for her contributions to education, especially in the field of choral music.

Virgie Carrington DeWitty (c. 1913–1980) was a music teacher, choir director, and composer. After her family moved from Oklahoma to Austin and joined Ebenezer Baptist Church, DeWitty began playing the piano by ear and performed her first solo at age five. DeWitty earned a degree in music and a teaching certificate in light opera (short operas with happy endings or operettas). She directed the first commercially sponsored radio program over the Texas Quality Network, 1938 to 1940. DeWitty composed or arranged more than 100 spirituals, gospels, four-part-harmony anthems, and religious music for choirs. She was a significant presence on the local, state, and national levels and was most important to the work of St. John District Association (Baptist regional entity). Her anthems include "Magnify the Lord" and "The Greatest of These Is Love." Championing her classical background, DeWitty relied heavily on the Psalms as she placed the importance of praising God front and center and the place of intercessory prayer in all of her music. Active in the National Baptist Convention of America, she died in August 1980 in Austin.

Lena McLin (1928–), the niece of gospel composer Thomas Dorsey, went to live with her uncle in Chicago after the tragic loss of his wife and child. McLin, already an accomplished musician from a deeply religious home, enjoyed living with Dorsey, who taught her gospel songs on the piano, and with her grandmother, who read to Lena from the Bible and sang the spirituals daily. Lena accompanied Dorsey to church and choir rehearsals. Eventually returning to Atlanta, McLin receive her B.M. in piano and violin from Spelman College in Atlanta and her M.M. from the American Conservatory of Music, Chicago. McLin successfully taught music in the Chicago public high schools for thirty-six years. Her composition includes masses, cantatas, solo and choral arrangements of spirituals, rock operas, anthems, works for piano and orchestra, and electronic music. The anchor of her musical style is the church and gospel. From this tradition emerges her liturgical Mass in English, *Eucharist of the Soul*, a testimony of deep faith, framed by the blues, grief-laden blues scales, warm harmonies, and improvisational-style movements that reflect and respond to her core melody. McLin is also an ordained minister. In addition to her arranged spirituals "Cert'nly Lord, Cert'nly, Lord," "Is There Anybody Here?" and "My God Is So High," her anthems include "The Earth Is the Lord's (Psalm 24)," "If They Ask You Why He Came" (text and words, composer), and "Psalm 117, Praise the Lord, All Ye Nations."

Margaret Pleasant Douroux (1941–), a Californian, is a minister of music, composer, lecturer, arranger and publisher of gospel music, hymns, anthems, spirituals, and a collection of Christmas carols. Douroux travels extensively, lecturing, teaching, and conducting workshops, particularly with the Gospel Music Workshop of America. Coming from a long family line of ministers,

Douroux is a traditionalist and engaged in Bible-based ministries and song composition. Holding degrees in music and a Ph.D. in education, Douroux has written more than 115 sacred songs, including "Give Me a Clean Heart," "He Decided to Die," and "If It Had Not Been for the Lord on My Side." Douroux's songs celebrate and proclaim the power of salvation and the importance of personal piety toward serving the Lord. The recipient of numerous awards and one who has vowed to help celebrate and preserve gospel music, she has written many booklets on music ministry, and some of Douroux's hymns appear in the *Songs of Zion*.

Theology, Themes, and Critique

The theology of African American hymnody is as diverse as the faith communities and individuals who sing them. Much of black hymnody derives from a cross section of African and European American hymnody. Some of the standard European hymns and gospel hymns embrace a Christocentric theology of grace, salvation, cross, and redemption. Some evoke a long-standing faith that daily sustains one. Many of the spirituals proclaim a "least of these theology" where God cares for everyone. Some of the spirituals and gospel hymns declare "a God who makes a way out of no way"—the God of impossible possibilities. Many of the spirituals, gospels, and other hymns ascribe a realized eschatology: One experiences a bit of heaven on earth or an intimate relationship with God so that one can persevere. One does not need to embrace a "pie in the sky" eschatology. Some gospel music declares the frailty of humanity and the power of God. The God who creates and redeems comforts, guides, and sustains. God's grace is powerful, sufficient, and ever present. Many of the spirituals and anthems have strong parallels with the Psalms. God is the one to be adored and magnified. This God is a shepherd who assures that one does not have to want. Black hymnody makes apparent the reality of being and acting in history and in the consciousness of the black church. Much of this tradition that has sustained a people through centuries of bondage and oppression is rich, empowering, and liberating. Many African American denominational hymnbooks include a varied and interesting selection of spirituals, gospels, hymns, and praise songs.

Denominational and Other Hymnals in the African American Tradition

By the nineteenth century, racism in the church pushed the further development of African American churches and thus the publishing of African American hymnody. The following African American denominations (named with their founding dates and their hymnals) have produced hymnbooks that contain music by African and European American composers. Early on, the hymnals often replicated much from their European counterpart.

Black Methodists who produced hymnbooks comprise the African Methodist Episcopal (AME, 1797), African Methodist Episcopal Zion (AMEZ, 1821), Christian Methodist Episcopal (CME, 1870), and Black Methodist Church (BMC) within the United Methodists (1939), prior to the reunion in 1970. The AME Church (begun under the tutelage of Richard Allen, cited earlier) published hymnals in 1801, 1818, 1837, 1876, 1897, 1941, and 1954 and its *AMEC Bicentennial Hymnal* in 1984. The *Bicentennial Hymnal* includes more AME denominational hymns than any other black hymnal targeting theological and cultural issues (e.g., international inclusiveness, ethnic identity, sexist language, theological relevance), deleting many of the Social Darwinist missionary hymns. AMEZ Church published hymnals in 1839, 1858, 1869, 1872, 1892, 1909, and 1957. The *AME Zion Hymnal* of 1957 boasts a variety of Wesleyan and Watts hymns, works by modern authors, hymns for young people, and songs written by AME Zion clergy, first published in the 1892 hymnbook. The CME Church published hymnbooks in 1891 and a songbook in 1904, adopted the 1939 *Methodist Hymnbook* in 1950, and published a hymnbook in 1987. In its rush to have a CME hymnbook, the CME adopted the hymnbook of the National Baptist, forsaking the gems in the 1904 *Songs of Love and Mercy* and its Methodist tradition of including a substantive number of Wesleyan hymns. Black Methodists within the United Methodist Church (UMC) coalesced when groups that came to make up the UMC voted to segregate its African American constituency in 1939, being internally segregated from 1870. *Songs of Zion*, a 1981 Supplement to the 1964 *Methodist Hymnal*, which served the denomination until 1989, includes hymns, spirituals, gospels, and special occasion music. *Songs of Zion* includes 249 songs compiled by two Black United Methodist musicians, J. Jefferson Cleveland and Verolga Nix. Seventy-one songs are by contemporary African American hymnists, including Margaret Douroux. The section of spirituals is the lengthiest, as spirituals are the largest body of black hymnody.

The black Baptists who have produced hymnbooks include the National Baptist Convention, USA (NBCUSA, 1895); National Baptist Convention of America (NBCA, 1915); and the Progressive National Baptist Convention (PNBC, 1961). The NBCUSA published its first hymnal, *The National Baptist Hymnal*, in 1903 and 1905, modeled after the *Baptist Hymnal*, 1883, and about fifteen songbooks of African American hymnody. The Sunday School Publishing Board of the NBCUSA published the *Gospel Pearls*, containing Watts and Wesley hymns, American gospel hymns, black gos-

pel hymns, and spirituals in 1921; Willa Townsend and Lucie Campbell with other distinguished African American composers served on the music committee. They subsequently published *Spirituals Triumphant, Old and New* (1927). In 1924, the Sunday School Publishing Board released *The Baptist Standard Hymnal*, a compilation of gospel hymns and classic British and American hymns, with minuscule black hymnody, edited by Willa Townsend; six women were among the sixteen music committee members. The first post–civil rights era African American church hymnal was *The New National Baptist Hymnal*, for the NBCA, 1977. Edited by Ruth Lomax Davis, with committee members and contributors including Virgie C. DeWitty and Margaret P. Douroux, *The New National* incorporates Afro-Christian social awareness and an evangelical fervor. In 1976, the PNBC published its first hymnal, *The Progressive Baptist Hymnal*, a special edition of *The Broadman Hymnal*, 1925. In 1982 the Progressive Baptists published a "special edition" of *The New National Baptist Hymnal*, named *The New Progressive Baptist Hymnal*.

Black Pentecostals and Holiness include the Church of Christ (Holiness), USA (COCUSA, 1894), the House of God Church (HGC, 1903), Mother Mary L. Tate, founder; and the Church of God in Christ (COGIC, 1907). Charles Price Jones, the organizer of COCUSA, wrote over 1,000 hymns including the various editions of *Jesus Only Nos. 1 and 2* (1899, 1901), *His Fullness* (1906), *His Fullness* combined with *Sweet Selections* (1928), culminating in the first denominational hymnal, *Jesus Only Songs and Hymns Standard Hymnal*, with nine editions between 1940 and 1966. The current *His Fullness* (1977) is the denominational hymnal now in use. These hymnals only contain European American hymnody. The hymnal's theological themes focus on sanctification and holiness, through revivalistic songs imbued with anticulturalism, separatism, antisecularism, perfectionism, and biblicism. Two women, Bishop (Mother) M. L. Tate and Bishop M. F. L. Keith, edited and compiled the HGC's first denominational hymnal, *Spiritual Songs and Hymns*. They included favorite gospel hymns, British hymns, traditional black gospel songs, and spirituals that were reinterpreted to focus on spiritual freedom from sin, not the usual references to freedom within the world. The songs, emphasizing holiness, sanctification, and faithful perseverance, included six hymns that celebrate women and women's religious freedom. With Bishop Keith's death in 1962, the new hymnal lost much of what affirmed women and made it Holiness. Pentecostal churches like the Church of God in Christ churches have relied heavily on spirituals, gospel hymns, and the hymns of Watts and the Wesleys. In earlier Pentecostalism and Charles H. Mason's COGIC churches, singing in the Spirit or Spirit baptism and singing in tongues were part of the strong sacred oral music tradition. There is, however, an early, undated collection of hymnody, *The Jackson Bible Universal Selected Gospel Songs*, by Elder H. C. Jackson, and a small collection of published hymns, *Hymnal of the F.B.H. Church* (1966) (Fire Baptized Holiness Church founded by Bishop W. E. Fuller, Sr., 1908). The first official COGIC hymnal is *Yes, Lord!: Church of God in Christ Hymnal* (1982), with Iris Stevenson as the compiler. In addition to hymns written by COGIC members Stevenson, Mattie Clark, and Betty Nelson, *Yes, Lord* includes a variety of African American hymnody and Handel's *Hallelujah Chorus*. Because most Holiness view spontaneous musical expression as more authentic, many churches do not use hymnals.

Other churches with African American hymnbooks within largely European communions include the Roman Catholic, Episcopal, Lutheran, and Methodist Churches. The impetus for African American Catholic liturgy and hymnody comes out of Vatican II and the civil rights movement. Previously, black Catholic liturgical renewal emerged in the work of Fr. Clarence Joseph Rivers, who composed *American Mass Program*, combining spirituals and Gregorian chant (1963). The work culminating in the 1987 *Lead Me, Guide Me: The African American Catholic Hymnal* began when the National Office for Black Catholics (NOBC) took black Catholic liturgy seriously. The Catholic bishops officially authorized the hymnal in 1983. Along with spirituals and contemporary hymnody by African American musicians like Evelyn D. White and Verolga Nix, there are praise songs, music of social concern, Latin and gospel masses, and Marian hymnody. Such passion for liturgy has some parallels in the Episcopalian tradition.

The roots of African American Episcopalian traditions begin with Absalom Jones, the first ordained black Episcopal priest, 1804, after he and Richard Allen withdrew from Saint George's Methodist Episcopal Church in Philadelphia when they were no longer allowed to pray at the altar in 1787. African American musical heritage was not fully integrated into Episcopal worship service until the publishing of *Lift Every Voice and Sing [LEVAS] I* (1981) to supplement the Episcopal Church's *Hymnal 1940* and *Lift Every Voice and Sing II* (1993). Like the *Gospel Pearls* and Richard Allen's *1801 hymnal*, the songs in *LEVAS* are designed to promote congregational singing. The 151 congregational songs include a variety of African American hymnody, songs from Ghana and Nigeria, civil rights songs, and mass settings, with arrangements of spirituals by Willa A. Townsend and Evelyn D. White.

In 1993, the Evangelical Lutheran Church in America (ECLA) and the Lutheran Church–Missouri Synod formed a committee to work on a hymnal to both celebrate African American cultural experiences and be faithful to Lutheran doctrine. The committee did not find all of the new hymnal, *This Far by Faith*, totally acceptable, and it was not approved doctrinally for use in the Missouri Lutheran Synod. The project was given to the ELCA and Augsburg Fortress Publishing House. The denomination strongly encourages the exclusive use of doctrinally sound worship resources but recognizes that other hymns may support a particular congregation's worship. Completed in 1999, *This Far by Faith* includes 250 hymns that represent the diversity within African American history, and African tradition rituals have also been incorporated into existing rites, with two different settings in African American styles for communion. There remains criticism of the volume by some leadership of the Missouri Synod. They challenge as to whether it upholds biblical teaching and whether certain liturgies using African kente cloth, particularly during a baptism, is appropriate. For example, the spiritual "Oh Freedom," which has the refrain, "And before I'd be a slave, I'll be buried in my grave," was deemed unacceptable. That an African American would rather die than be a slave again is read as being contrary to Luther's theology of the cross. Those who embraced the spiritual, countered, saying this spiritual actually affirms the theology of the cross, for slaves wanted true freedom, freedom only in Christ. The Missouri Synod includes a variety of cultural voices in its Hymnal Supplement 98, published in 1998, but recognizes that other hymns may support a particular congregation's worship. Though a project of both ECLA and the Missouri Synod in the United States, *This Far by Faith* was not approved as an official hymnal of the Lutheran Church–Missouri Synod, and the book was published solely by the ELCA's publishing house.

The Presbyterian Hymnal: Hymns, Psalms, and Spiritual Songs (1990) seeks to be inclusive of the many ethnic groups in its denomination, with songs of African American, Chinese, Hispanic, Japanese, Korean, or Native American origin. Similarly, the United Church of Christ (UCC), a 1957 union of the Evangelical and Reformed Church and the Congregational Christian Churches, replaced *The Hymnal of the United Church of Christ* (1974) with an ecumenical hymnbook, *The New Century Hymnal*, which significantly celebrates inclusive language, by balancing masculine and feminine images. *New Century* incorporates works inspired and composed by women and supports multiculturalism, pluralism, inclusivism, and environmentalism. All these hymnbooks provide some of the formal texts for black singing.

From the 1820s through the 1930s, several hymnbooks were published by individuals for a particular congregation. Peter Spence compiled and published *The Union African Hymnbook* in 1822 for the congregation he had just organized, the Ezion Union African Church in Wilmington, Delaware. Marshall W. Taylor compiled *A Collection of Revival Hymns and Plantation Melodies*, which he published with W. C. Echols. This volume was produced for the African American members of the predominantly white Methodist Episcopal Church, including *Revival Hymns and Plantation Melodies*. In 1908. Charles A. Tindley compiled songs as an African American gospel hymn source for his congregation, the Bainbridge Street Methodist Episcopal Church of Philadelphia, titled *Soul Echoes*. In 1934, J. Jackson compiled and published *The Colored Sacred Harp* with the Dale County Colored Musical Institute and the Alabama and Florida Union State. This work contained familiar Protestant hymn texts with new, unfamiliar melodies. Sacred Harp singing, also known as "fa-sol-la" or "shape-note" singing, is a traditional musical style that dates back to the early-nineteenth-century nationwide religious movement known as "the Great Awakening." The name *Sacred Harp singing* comes from the songbook *The Sacred Harp*, first published in 1844. The musical style has origins in eighteenth-century itinerant singing school masters who worked to devise a system for teaching their classes to sing "by-note." During the Great Awakening years, they introduced the idea of assigning different-shaped noteheads corresponding to the *fa, sol, la,* and *mi* syllables. Although shape-note songbooks had a rapid decline during the late nineteenth century, various revisions of *The Sacred Harp* remain popular in the Deep South. The Sacred Harp tradition has remained vibrant among African Americans in southeast Alabama for over a century, even though most people associate this tradition only with southern white culture.

Published by GIA, in 2001, the most recent African American hymnal, *The African American Heritage Hymnal: 575 Hymns, Spirituals, and Gospel Song*, is an ecumenical songbook edited by Delores Carpenter and Nolan E. Williams, Jr. This volume emerged from the work of more than thirty musicians and pastors, all leaders in African American worship and gospel music. This unique hymnbook includes the common repertoire of African American churches across the United States. The editors paid close attention to performance practices as they edited traditional hymns and songs to ensure that the musical notation reflects the oral tradition of African American churches in the United States. The hymnal includes litanies or responsive readings depicting an African American church year, including such special days as Mother's Day, Men's Day, Clergy Appreciation, Urban Ministry, and Martin Luther King Sunday.

Unfortunately, some of the hymns of the African American church retain racist and sexist beliefs and thought. That is, the underlying biblical analysis, hermeneutics, and doctrinal authority, symbols, and images in these songs support and often celebrate and glorify gender, class, and race oppression. For the music to help people heal and move toward wholeness, these underlying sentiments need to be exposed and explained, to help pastors and music ministers make better choices in musical selection for twenty-first-century empowering worship. In addition, another significance of consciousness raising around hymns is that many people forget the sermons, but they remember the songs. In times of trial or celebration, people tend to remember the songs of their youth and not the sermons. Thus, in singing songs that include the passage "wash me white as snow" from Psalm 51:7, one must know not to infer a washing away of one's skin color, for innocent ears hearing this could make that assumption, even though no one's skin color is whiter than snow. In matters of gender oppression, much work needs to be done regarding the "ecclesiastical apartheid," where African American women are expected to function doing the church's hard work but do not see themselves reflected back in the liturgy. This omission includes everything from ordination being withheld, and preaching biblical texts related to women, to women being ministers of music and including music written by women. Much education needs to take place with ministers of music and choral directors to help them become aware of the impact of their musical choices. Serious denominational reflection on such matters is critical. One key responsibility of musical leadership is to ensure that the underlying messages of the music are transformative, not oppressive, misleading, and harmful. Too often a beautiful melody or provocative rhythms overshadow the content and meaning of the words. Although many texts in black hymnbooks remain wedded to supremacist, hegemonic, Eurocentric, biblical Christianity, much of African American hymns of Zion illumine, empower, sustain, comfort, and signify toward hope and new life.

SOURCES: James Abbington, *Let Mt. Zion Rejoice! Music in the African American Church* (2001). James Abbington, ed., *Readings in African American Church Music and Worship* (2001). Fred R. Anderson, "Three New Voices: Singing God's Song," *Theology Today* 47 (October 1990): 260–272. Willi Apel, *Harvard Dictionary of Music* (1944, 1969). A. L. Barry, "A Statement Concerning the Hymnal, 'This Far by Faith,'" http://old.www.lcms.org/president/statements/thisfar.asp. Horace Clarence Boyer, *How Sweet the Sound: The Golden Age of Gospel* (1995). Delores Carpenter and Nolan E. Williams, Jr., *The African American Heritage Hymnal: 575 Hymns, Spirituals, and Gospel Songs* (2001). Melva W. Costen, *African American Christian Worship* (1993). Samuel A. Floyd, Jr., *The Power of Black Music: Interpreting Its History from Africa to the United States* (1995). Tony Heilbut, *The Gospel Sound: Good News and Bad Times* (1975). Darlene Hine, Elsa Brown, and Rosalyn Terborg-Penn, eds., *Black Women in America: An Historical Encyclopedia* (1993). Jamsline: The Christian Information Source, "CeCe Winans," http://www.jamsline.com/b_cece.htm. Cheryl A. Kirk-Duggan, *Exorcizing Evil: A Womanist Perspective on the Spirituals* (1997). *Lead Me, Guide Me: The African American Catholic Hymnal* (1987). *Lift Every Voice and Sing: An African American Hymnal* (1981). *Lift Every Voice and Sing* II: An African American Hymnal (1993). Austin Lovelace, The Anatomy of Hymnody (1965). John Lovell, Jr., Black Song: The Forge and Flame: The Story of How the Afro-American Spiritual Was Hammered Out (1972). David Mahsman, "Clancy Still Hopes for CPH (Concordia Publishing House) Hymnal Role. An Example of a Hymn That Failed Doctrinal Review," http://www.cuis.edu/ftp/lcmsnews/999710-AFRICAN_AMERICAN_HYMNAL_SUPPLEME.NT-980402. Margaret Allison & The Angelic Gospel Singers, http://www.malaco.com/gospel/angelics/main.html. William B. McClain, Come Sunday: The Liturgy of Zion (1990). Rachel C. Murphree, Paul G. Partington, and Dr. Udo, "Mahalia Jackson, 1911–1972" (1996), available online at http://www.lib.edu/soc/women/lawomen/jackson.htm. Skladny, "Biographies of People of the World," October 2000, http://www.philately.com/philately/biomarmaz.htm. Bernice Johnson Reagon, ed., We'll Understand It Better By and By (1992). Songs of Zion, Supplemental Worship Resources 12 (1981, 1982). Eileen Southern, Biographical Dictionary of Afro-American and African Musicians (1982). Jon Michael Spencer, "The Hymnology of Black Methodists," Theology Today 46 (January 1990): 373–385; Black Hymnody: A Hymnological History of the African-American Church (1992); and Sing A New Song: Liberating Black Hymnody (1995). Emilie Townes, Embracing the Spirit: Womanist Perspectives on Hope, Salvation & Transformation (1997). "Voices for God: The Gospel Music Hall of Fame and Museum Founders Celebrate Music and Their Faith in Life," Detroit News, October 13, 1999, http://detnews.com/1999/detroit/9910/17/10130119.htm. Wyatt Tee Walker, The Soul of Black Worship: A Trilogy—Preaching, Praying, Singing (1984). Also see Portia K. Maultsby, "The Evolution of African American Music" (1988), a poster tracking African American music from its African musical roots of the 1600s to the contemporary gospel, house music, rap, techno funk, go-go, and new jack swing of the 1990s.

WOMEN'S NOVELS AND RELIGION, 1780–1900

Diane Capitani

TO BEGIN A study of American women's novels and religion with a brief mention of a British novel, Pamela by Samuel Richardson, published in 1741, may seem out of place. This reference is important, however, because Richardson is recognized as the author of a new type of narrative writing, domestic fiction, a form that would be adopted and adapted by American women writers, eager to speak in their own voices in the New World. Richardson's novel had within it echoes of English religious works, particularly those that called for intense self-examination. His novel called attention to class struggles, to gender issues, to the rights of the individual versus society. More important, the story was of a young servant girl who resists attempts at seduction made by her master and who gains a voice through the written word: her letters to her parents. This was a sentimental novel of sorts, and it can be argued that Pamela laid the foundation for the sentimental novel of the nineteenth century in America. It is also the story of a captive, a fifteen-year-old literally held captive by "Mr. B.," the son of her late mistress. While not the type of captivity narrative that would surface in America, nonetheless it gave a grounding for works about women held against their will. Pamela speaks out vigorously, even asking in her letters, "How came I to be his Property?" How indeed? The same question was asked later in America by those kept as slaves in the South. Pamela resists seduction, Mr. B. finally marries her and all is well, but the reader has been titillated, has experienced deep swells of emotion, and has learned the moral lesson that virtue is rewarded. Pamela's voice is a sound one, and she opens the way for a genre of novel that will give later American women their best opportunity to be heard in the public sphere.

In the New World, in 1682, the first bestseller written by a woman was Mary Rowlandson's narrative of being taken prisoner during King Philip's War and held captive for four months. Later, she wrote her narrative of this experience, the first woman to do so, encouraged, she claimed, by her friends, although her husband disapproved. Like others that followed in the seventeenth and early eighteenth centuries, her narrative was a spiritual biography, written for the moral instruction of the reader. Rowlandson's story, "The Narrative of The Captivity and Restoration of Mrs. Mary Rowlandson," shaped the genre and became the paradigm for all later accounts of captivity and dreaded ordeal. Captivity was seen as God's way of instructing or punishing both the prisoner and those who heard her story. There are more than sixty-five scripture references in Rowlandson's narrative. As the wife of a minister, she certainly possessed scriptural knowledge, but what is important to note is that hers is the pattern for a genre that is followed for some time. To convince the reader of the importance of providence in the eventual release from captivity was essential.

Rowlandson's narrative is the story of a woman, voiceless, suffering in the wilderness, able to survive perhaps because she is a woman and used to being subservient. Nevertheless, Rowlandson resists captivity by reliance on God who will save her; her strong Calvinist faith never wavers. Her religious faith allows her to understand her captivity; this is God's test for her, and she relies on scripture to help her on her journey. Like most of the white colonists of the time, Rowlandson sees the Indians as instruments of the devil. She tells us that God has strengthened the Indian to be a scourge to his people, to be a scourge to the land. She quotes Hebrews 12.6: "For whom the Lord loveth he chasteneth, and scourgeth every Son whom he received." Scripture does not let her down. Suffering in God's cause is noble.

Providential guidance is there because Rowlandson realizes that she is one of God's chosen, one of the elect. The sustaining power of faith is always reinforced with biblical citations because captivity is seen as a manifestation of God's providence: "God was with me, in a wonderfull manner, carrying me along and bearing up my spirit . . . that I might see more of his Power" (in Perkins et al., 36). In the end, the captive is redeemed and reintegrated; like the Jews in Egypt, she has been led out of captivity. As a woman, Rowlandson gains a powerful voice. Articulating the experience is a strong action for her. The narrative has all the elements of the melodramatic, sentimental novel: a woman in danger, a demon "other," terrifying experiences, female physical weakness, and reliance on God's providence. In its day, it was a success.

There were many other early captivity narratives, written by both men and women. As the years went by, however, the nature of the genre changed. By the eighteenth and nineteenth centuries, there was a totally different type of writing being printed and sold. A profit motive entered the picture, and fact becomes mixed with fiction. These later narratives lose their religious focus. There seems to be a widening gap between what literature is demanding and what individuals experienced during captivity. The sense of individual redemption is gone, and the inspirational message is replaced with melodrama. "A True Narrative of the Sufferings of Mary Kinnan" (1791–1794), for example, is significant here because it demonstrates the appearance of the sentimental and the emphasis on the adventure rather than the role of Providence in human life. What Mary Kinnan wants from her readers is that their hearts "will be melted with sorrow" when they read of her terrifying suffering. While Rowlandson's style is plain, direct, and simple, Kinnan is sentimental and flowery. Note Kinnan's opening paragraph:

> Whilst the tear of sensibility so often flows at the unreal tale of woe, which glows under the pen of the poet and the novelist, shall our hearts refuse to be melted with sorrow at the unaffected and unvarnished tale of a female, who has surmounted difficulties and dangers, which on a review appear romantic, even to herself. (VanDerBeets, 320)

This is a far cry from Rowlandson's factual "On the tenth of February, 1675, came the Indians." While Rowlandson makes a moral of her story, Kinnan romanticizes. Kinnan mentions no scripture passages at all, although she does occasionally thank "the providence of God" and relies "on the beneficence of the Father of All" (326). This is a shorter piece than Rowlandson's, written for profit. Publishers know that there is a demand for this kind of writing; the public wants to know

about the demon "other." Some have argued that the early readers of these narratives in the seventeenth and early eighteenth centuries had a spiritual interest in them but that later, on into the nineteenth century, the interest, like the country, had become secular and the narratives were read for entertainment value only. Female writers had become entertainers.

Women had always had voices, of course, but society did not allow them to be public ones. What women really were and felt was not usually known to the public; any writing about them was written by men. Clergymen wrote religious tracts for female edification that concerned the duties of the female toward home, family, and church. Society had determined the role for women in America, a culturally constructed gender role organized in particular around the concept of "motherhood." Definitions of a woman's proper role changed over the centuries, from early Puritan beliefs in the inherent wickedness of women as fallen Eve to later-nineteenth-century Victorian beliefs in women as the center of the home. This became known as the "cult of true womanhood," and it determined that women could have influence over the domestic sphere where they could affect the moral development of their children and soften the harshness of the outside world on their husbands and sons. In the seventeenth and eighteenth centuries, motherhood was simply a biological necessity in the new Republic; women were seen as too irrational to be allowed to guide anyone, so the male influence in all areas of society was absolute. For this reason Mary Rowlandson's narrative is so important, because it allowed a female voice to become part of a literary canon, even though a minor one at the time. The female captive had a story to tell, but it could not be told unless it was presented as a work of God's inspiration that would morally instruct the readers. Kinnan's narrative, of course, subverted this goal because the passing centuries had brought changes in women's roles and America was becoming more and more a consumer culture. Even though women might be allowed to write, they still needed male approval to publish.

Into this climate came the slave narratives; the most famous, written by a woman, is *Incidents in the Life of a Slave Girl* by Harriet Jacobs, published in 1861. There is less of the truly spiritual in Jacobs's narrative than, for example, in the writings of Sojourner Truth. But on the whole, slave narratives followed a similar pattern to the captivity narratives: They used a journey motif, with a descent into hell, followed by personal humiliation, a bottoming out, and then redemption. The captive emerges better than she was before. Being led out of captivity in Egypt is a recurrent idea in the slave narratives; biblical imagery abounds. The importance for both types of narratives is their later influence on the fiction that dominates women's writing in the nineteenth century. There is no question, for example, that Harriet Beecher Stowe inherited the spiritual paradigm of redemption from the captivity narratives. In addition, when Stowe produces her masterpiece about the gentle slave Tom, she appropriates some of the conventions of the sentimental novel that had become popular in her day, as well as those of the slave narratives, Puritan sermons, and the idea of the captive relying only on God. In some ways, the early writings by women of their terrifying life in captivity paved the way for later tastes in popular dime novels and sentimental fiction that exploited minorities and left readers with vivid word pictures of damsels in distress. Because of gender, and because of the culturally defined role that women were forced to play, the history of female writing has in part been determined by men. The history of women and the novel is gender history, a combination of culture and biology. Out of this history women writers diverged in their emphasis and focus.

The history of female authors North and South, for example, is quite different, because northern women were able to write publicly much sooner than southern women, in part because southern culture held fast to the idea of woman as the heart of the home far longer than the North. The South was also an agrarian economy, unlike the North, which had turned from the home-based economy of earlier days to one that was market based. The publishing industry flourished in the North, but there were no major publishing houses of the same stature in the South. Thus, women had access to more reading materials and, as wealth increased, to the money to buy them. It was obvious that women could become part of the market economy, but only if they followed certain patterns in writing. Stowe, for example, was able to become a published author, in part because she was a northerner but, more important, because she wrote a novel that was sentimental, domestic, religious, and showed the influence of the captivity and slave narratives that had been so popular in America for so long. Her famous novel about Uncle Tom used all the conventions of the earlier genres and was intended to morally instruct the readers, in particular to exercise religious influence to lead to the abolishing of slavery. Stowe's white women were virtuous and demonstrated all the feminine qualities that the cult of true womanhood held to be so important. The southern women Stowe portrays, in general, are able to see the evils of slavery that their more worldly husbands do not, in part because men have become corrupted by the material outside world. The gender divisions that separated men and women into two spheres is very apparent in Stowe's work. The nonreligious character of the white men is also quite obvious; it is only the black slave Tom who is a true believer. Stowe realized, of course, that through

the years the men in America, tempted by the lure of money and material possessions, had become less and less religious. Women were the churchgoers, unlike the early days of the Republic when men controlled the pulpit and the pew. Now, men left the teaching and practice of religion to women. Stowe believed that if the women used their power to influence men by the appropriate exercise of Christian teachings, women could determine the course of government. Perhaps she was right.

Whatever the cause, there is no question that by the nineteenth century the gender division of males and females into separate spheres was well established. Males operated outside the home, where they could be corrupted by the harsh contact with business and a less homogeneous community; women stayed at home to create their own sphere and establish their own worth. By the nineteenth century, there were an increased number of women in the pews of any church. The clergy, no longer assured of a set, determined income, provided by earlier taxation laws in the colonies, began to appeal to a female constituency. Theology began to "soften"; there was less emphasis on God's wrath and more on his compassion and Christ's nurturing side. From the pulpit, clergy preached about women's gentle, sustaining role in the home, blending woman's image into that of Christ. Stowe would realize this image of Christ in the character of Tom, a man allied with Christ but not the clergy. It would be the southern woman who was allied with the clergy and through whom the southern domestic novel would be born.

Some scholars, like Anna Douglas, argue that the alliance of women and clergymen was born of necessity, since both groups' roles had shifted during the early nineteenth century. Women in the North were now consumers, not producers, of goods. Ministers were caught in clerical disestablishment; Douglas theorizes that the " 'voluntary' system in which no denomination had automatic precedence over any other and no person had any obligation to attend worship or to support religion beyond his or her desire to do so" (24) led clergymen to look for support where they could find it to survive. They would preach what the crowd wanted, and the crowd now was composed of women. Preachers, after all, had become part of the market economy. With women as the "customers" for their religious messages, ministers would cooperate by changing theology into a religion of consolation. Consequently, Christ, as well as American culture, became feminized.

Douglas's insistence that the nineteenth century was a male-dominated one is convincing. This was a century of males as power holders in an industrial society. Out of this culture, the cult of true womanhood was born, because men wanted their women home and quiet and the clergy was unimportant to them in their day-to-day lives. Powerless women and clergymen were forced to

Harriet Beecher Stowe inherited the spiritual paradigm of redemption from captivity narratives. In addition, when Stowe produces her masterpiece about the gentle slave, Tom, she appropriates conventions of the sentimental novel popular in her day, as well as those of slave narratives, Puritan sermons, and the idea of the captive relying only on God. *Courtesy of The Schlesinger Library, Radcliffe Institute, Harvard University. Portrait of Harriet Beecher Stowe after a painting by A. Chapell.*

find some area, any area, in which they could have influence. Those areas turned out to be the arts, literature, and religion. Eventually, women and clergy combined to become a powerful force, even an economic one. Both the middle-class female and the nineteenth-century clergyman had lost their productive functions. Clergy would still preach, but there was mainly one audience; women could still be mothers, but they were no longer part of the household economy, save as consumers.

The "true woman" of the nineteenth century was a fascinating creature who might have been a creation of clergymen desperate to shore up their own status, but, as Douglas points out, other men had to be willing to accept the creation. Why did they? It might be argued that when one indulges another person, one also takes away their power. The more leisure time and money a middle-class woman had, the less reason remained for her existence and usefulness, except as a producer of

children and a servant to her husband. Hence, the ideal woman became one who would exert moral pressure on society, who would defend home and hearth from the evils of the nonreligious outside world. The nineteenth century was a culture of patriarchy; women were given power of a sort, in the home, in exchange for their removal from the outside market economy, where the real power rested. Praise of motherhood would make a woman feel that her biological reproductive capacity approached the heavenly: Mary's importance, after all, was as the mother of Christ. The clergy, in both Catholic and Protestant churches, began to emphasize this role for women, more important than economic productivity. Paternal authority was lessening because men were no longer in the home all day but were out in the business world; women, therefore, needed to step into the role as moral authority for the entire family and to provide a comfortable place for a man to be revitalized before he needed to face the outside world again. With the cultivation of domestic piety, women became saints of the home and hearth and could remain chaste and pure, virtuous and moral—in fact, Christ-like.

Scholar Barbara Welter, in her 1976 book *Dimity Convictions,* has noted that the nineteenth-century man of business devoted little time to the religion of his forebears but rather spent most of his time building empires. Perhaps guilt drove him to create a new type of female, one who could be the keeper of the values he supposedly held dear but did little to exemplify. The true woman would be a constant in a man's life and would be an upholder to her family of all that the Republic stood for and represented. Welter presents a clear definition of the true woman and her attributes: They were those "by which a woman judged herself and was judged by her husband, her neighbors and society, [which] could be divided into four cardinal virtues—piety, purity, submissiveness and domesticity. . . . Without them, no matter whether there was fame, achievement or wealth, all was ashes" (21–22). Welter makes the case that "with them she was promised happiness and power. Religion or piety was the core of woman's virtue, the source of her strength. . . . Religion belonged to woman by divine right, a gift of God and nature" (22).

This divine gift would throw its beam of light over sinful man and purify him, reclaim him from sin and the material world. Religion, unlike education, would not take woman from her proper place in the home. St. Paul, after all, advised women, ideally, to be domestic. The domestic life provided security from the outside world and removed women from corruption. No group encouraged women to believe this more than the clergy, who insisted that the domestic woman remain unsullied by the outside world, submissive and Christ-like. Like Christ, woman should remain long-suffering and obedient. In this way, she could hope to bring men back to God and encourage them to support the church financially, if not physically, with their presence.

In the home, inspired by what she heard in her church pews, woman could make her worth known by bringing men back to God. Reading the scriptures by firelight, or, better yet, encouraging the man of the house to read them aloud to the family, became a woman's goal. A secondary gain for the male, of course, was that he could feel religious without actually having to attend services, while women were very happy to do so. As Mrs. Frances Trollope observed on a visit to America, "[I]t is from the clergy only that the women of America receive that sort of attention which is so dearly valued by every female heart throughout the world. . . . I never saw, or read, of any country where religion had so strong a hold upon the women, or a slighter hold upon the men" (Trollope, 75). The clergy were the one set of men who listened to women, but

they also wielded tremendous influence. When clergy preached, they spoke in a language women understood, and they used women to support their own interests, both financially and politically. (The church, or religion-based organizations and movements, also became one public arena where women would later find a voice.)

Along with encouragement from the clergy, there was another, equally strong influence on the lives of nineteenth-century women: the influence of popular literature. Women's magazines flourished in the North in the 1800s, and so did women's sentimental literature in the form of the domestic novel. Both print media encouraged domesticity, silent endurance through life's trials, piety, dignity, and faithfulness. Articles instructed women in their role as the great guardians of morality and religion. The message to greet difficulty and suffering with good cheer came through clearly in the magazines and novels of the day. And nowhere did that become more evident than in the novels and sermons of the nineteenth-century American South. Not only should women face hardship with courage and cheer, sure in the knowledge that this was their role as assigned by God, but so, too, should the plantation slave.

What had subtly changed was the older view of woman as "Eve the seductive temptress"; the voices from the pulpit had encouraged the change, and later, from the pages of sentimental, domestic fiction, it was solidified. Eve was punished because God knew she was the stronger creation and could provide the better example for men. Clergy realized early on in the nineteenth century that by presenting this enlightened view of womanhood, they would win over the women, and together both would participate in new spheres of influence, including that of the nineteenth-century sentimentalized domestic novel. Eventually this type of novel dominated the literary market and, with women of a new leisured class as consumers, sold extremely well. Husbands encouraged wives and daughters to read the sentimental novels and stories that were published because the writing was not dangerous or subversive, it encouraged domestic pursuits, and it kept the fair sex occupied at a time when low-paid domestic help created too many leisure hours to fill. Many of the novels were penned by clergymen as well as women, but all told a similar story. No matter where located, in the North or South, by the mid-nineteenth century, women writers had found a voice and a place. It was the female novelists of the North who would learn to combine the sentimental with the political, to good effect, and no one did it better than Harriet Beecher Stowe.

Into this world of the sentimentalized, domestic novel of the nineteenth century, Harriet Beecher Stowe's *Uncle Tom's Cabin* (1852) exploded, calling forth a scriptural defense of slavery from pulpit and hearth that reinforced patriarchy and its ramifications for both women and slaves. In the South, this form of fiction would be used by women novelists and clergymen to reinforce the existence of the dreadful institution of enslavement, and slaves, like women, would be urged to suffer silently and cheerfully, not because of influence it might bring them but because of future rewards in heaven. While the southern novel followed the same pattern of structural development as that of the North, it concentrated upon an enlarged definition of the cult of true womanhood and employed scripture text, often extensively, in order to defend slavery as ordained by God. A perversion, then, of biblical theology became a hallmark of the sentimental domestic novel of the South.

Stowe's novel had a dramatic impact not only because a woman had written it, and become a bestselling author as well, but because it attacked an entire way of life, the very foundations of southern culture. The southern woman of the nineteenth century was in a different economic position than her northern sister. Life on the plantation was not life in the northern, industrial cities. For one thing, southern women were extremely isolated from each other on far-flung plantations, often the only white women around until their daughters grew to adolescence. She occupied a precarious position, economically and physically. She was safe as long as she stayed within certain boundaries, physically and morally. Those boundaries forced her to do what was expected. She had fewer choices, in part because her life was so completely tied to the plantation. She ran a large household, supervised a number of house slaves, oversaw the making of their clothing, nursed and nurtured all who were ill, and provided for their spiritual comfort. In effect, she maintained the household as one might run a corporation. Her education lagged behind that of her northern sisters, and her husband often discouraged outside contacts because of the danger of corruption of her virtue and her attachment to the home. Even attendance at a Methodist Bible class meeting was challenged as dangerous by one southern husband! The cult of true womanhood not only was alive and well in the nineteenth century South but was thriving more strongly because of the nature of plantation life itself. Southern men depended on their wives by mid-century more than their northern counterparts. Husbands in turn assured their wives and daughters that their purity kept the South whole; men continued their dalliances with female slaves. And this purity, coupled with strong scriptural references used to defend the existence of the slave state, was essential to maintain the southern lifestyle. Even more than in the North, in those antebellum days, southern men insisted on the cult of true womanhood, on female purity and piety, and became almost obsessed with the ideal of the chaste woman. Men were debauched creatures, but their homes could be a domestic haven removed from the sullied evils of life. Defending

this view became the position of the southern female writer when she took to her pen and wrote to refute Mrs. Stowe's shocking exposé of the southern slave-owning lifestyle.

This image of the southern woman remained long after the close of the Civil War, and, it might be argued, still exists today in some parts of the South. Margaret Mitchell's famous 1938 novel *Gone With the Wind* brought us the southern woman we were to admire, Melanie Wilkes, not Scarlett O'Hara. The fragile, helpless heroine of southern fiction was portrayed over and over in the nineteenth-century southern domestic novel. The women they portrayed were not only helpless but self-deprecating and with an innocence that borders on the childish. Like the slaves they cared for, southern fictional heroines turned to the Bible for solace. Eventually, the southern lady became a totally dependent one, exercising, until the Civil War came and the men of the plantation went marching off to war, little power except where it caused no difficulty to the plantation master.

There is no question of Christianity's important influence on the rural plantation women of the nineteenth-century South and the equal importance it would play in the creation of the domestic, sentimental fiction that flourished in response to Mrs. Stowe's momentous work. Women had a moral duty to safeguard their loved ones and everyone around them; it became an evangelical mission. The pulpit might remain a male bastion, but the novel became women's pulpit, North and South. Southern women novelists felt compelled to combine the code of female respectability and behavior with a defense of slavery based on the tenants of Christianity. There was so little public outlet for women and their need to be more useful that it is small wonder that southern women turned to religion in droves. In consequence, the sentimental, domestic novel that sold so well, North and South, stressed the importance of the scriptures as solace to the ailing in body and spirit and as a source for help in accepting the lot in life that God had ordained.

The domestic novel became an outlet for the women who had any writing talent at all. In order for the southern domestic novelist to realize a career in writing, in a culture that would not have encouraged intellectual careers for women, her fiction had to form part of an acceptable existing genre, but more, it had to become a tool for ideological warfare: the defense of slavery through fiction, which relied heavily on the Bible itself and on the content of sermons to defend an indefensible institution. By serving the culture it represented, by defending pro-slavery male positions, the southern domestic novel would be born and thrive.

Literary historians do not question the fact that Harriet Beecher Stowe's novel made a tremendous impact on both the literary and sociocultural worlds of the mid-nineteenth century in the South as well as the North. Stowe was looking for commitment to redress the condition of slavery; it was not equality for the slaves that she sought but freedom. Indeed, much of her life Stowe seemed ambivalent about the subject of black-white equality. Nonetheless, she insisted that the conditions of slavery were horrible, and they certainly were, as she portrayed them. She forced southern novelists and preachers to defend the peculiar institution, which changed the course of southern domestic fiction. While Stowe's novel borrows from the tradition of southern domestic fiction, it does not concentrate upon the cult of true womanhood or women's domestic duties. Slavery is at the center of her novel, rather than a typical romance between a virginal and lovely southern belle and a gallant cavalier. While the settings are those of the plantation South, what happens there is significantly different than the events of the novels written in defense of the southern way of life. Stowe's substance is political; its purpose is social action and change. The southern domestic novel of the time, on the other hand, argued for a continuation of an idyllic way of life, sanctioned by scripture, ordained by God. Many of the southern novels argue for the superiority of the southern way of life, valuing the close-knit family unit of the plantation against the industrial conditions of the northern way of life. As southern novelists saw it, the North fostered greed and corruption; the South emphasized the conservative benevolence found on the plantation where God's work truly took place.

Stowe's work makes clear that religion is the answer for most of the world's problems. She was the daughter of a minister, the sister of one, and the wife of another. Because of her Calvinist upbringing, she felt a moral duty to address the nation's ills and use a Christian focus in her novels. Her New England background gave her a strong Yankee bluntness, but she remained always a lady. Indeed, it was in church where she had her vision of a bleeding, dying slave and turned the vision into words, creating a lasting political statement. After all, readers in Stowe's day were violently opinionated in regard to black people; Stowe was attempting to increase awareness of the slaves' condition.

In 1856 Stowe published another novel about the horrors of slavery: *Dred: A Tale of the Great Dismal Swamp*. While it did not enjoy the success of her story of Uncle Tom, a model of Christian virtue and forgiveness, Dred's story was of an escaped slave, an exhorter who hid in the swamps and called his people to freedom, urging them to desperate action. Stowe wrote the novel to place a moral focus on the subject of slavery. In her preface to the original edition, Stowe asks, "Is the system of slavery, as set forth in the American slave code *right*? Is it so desirable, that you will directly establish it over broad regions, where til now, you have solemnly forbid-

den it to enter?" (*Dred*, Preface to 1856 edition). Her purpose was "to do something toward revealing to the people the true character of the system. If the people are to establish such a system, let them do it with their eyes open, with all the dreadful realities before them." The Fugitive Slave Law, which declared that escaped slaves found in northern states must be returned to their owners because the slaves were property, had made a tremendous impact upon her. Both these novels were an impassioned political and religious response to it. Part of the system that she fought against, of course, was religion (specifically Christianity) used by slave owners to rationalize the enslavement of other human beings.

Stowe's novels, along with others of this genre published between 1820 and 1860, point out the intimate connections between history, literature, and religion. Her work is interesting not just as fiction but as a record of American culture and history in the 1850s. There is some question as to how Stowe attained her knowledge of slave religion, since she did not spend much time in the South. One theory is that she read clerical memoirs of missions to the slaves, but that is conjecture and needs further study and exploration. What is amazing is her grasp of the inner dimension of slave spirituality and her ability to imagine the Old Testament wrath of a slave prophet like Dred, or the long-suffering piety of Uncle Tom.

The novels are valuable not only as a record of slave religion but as a record of white attitudes toward it. Dred is a character totally different than Uncle Tom: militant, angry, willing to do battle physically for his beliefs, and to be free, willing to plan an insurrection. One might theorize that, by 1856, Stowe and other northerners had begun to fear a more apocalyptic ending to slavery, which a close reading of the southern domestic novels supports. Stowe claimed her portrayals of plantation life were accurate, and she insisted that no scripture would ever support the existence of the peculiar institution. Christianity gave slaves a voice, as it gave nineteenth-century women a voice, but these voices had to mask their political messages. Stowe is much more heavy-handed in the later novel; Dred speaks in jeremiads, those public rhetorical declamations so popular in the Great Awakening. The author uses moralizing diatribes, reminders to Methodists and Presbyterians that although their Books of Discipline condemned slavery, their southern branches had chosen to ignore them. She points out that John Wesley had denounced slavery, stating that it was inconsistent with the religion of Christ. She has a profound effect on readers because her visual pictures are so real. There is no question that Stowe caused social change with her literary strategies. She is both preacher and storyteller, and it is the preacher's voice that gave her authority that as a woman she would not have had. Stowe believed that religion is the compelling force in the world, one that gives voice to the voiceless. It certainly gave one to her.

In this way, the novel, in the midpart of the nineteenth century, entered the women's sphere as political expression, as entertainment, as voice. Stowe's battle with the tradition and justifications for slavery found in the South swept through the literary and political world like Sherman's march to the sea. This was ideological warfare at its fullest. Tailoring their work to women readers, North and South, southern female novelists not only attempted to encourage the life of devotion upon which true womanhood depended but also attempted to enter the political arena in a subtle, acceptable way, rather than to shake its foundations as Stowe had done. While southern plots emphasized home and domesticity, as did those of the North, more pages were devoted to defenses of slavery taken from pastoral descriptions of plantation scenes. Most of the southern women who wrote these novels were wives of slave owners; all had been plantation dwellers at some point in their lives. One or two were transplanted northerners won over by the southern way of life who bought into the biblical arguments for slavery's existence. Southern novelists sought not solely the integration of domestic, feminine values into contemporary culture; more important, they wished to justify their way of life as a slaveholding culture. Northern aggression was a constant threat; a way of life had to be protected. These novelists engaged fiercely in the protection of their culture.

Caroline Hentz (1800–1856) was one of the first of the southern domestic novelists to attempt to refute Mrs. Stowe's work. Like others who came after her, women authors such as Mrs. Mary H. Eastman and Maria MacIntosh, Mrs. Hentz was appalled by what she saw as a total ignorance of southern life. Mrs. Hentz, a transplanted northerner, had lived twenty years in the South and knew plantation life firsthand. Her novel *The Planter's Northern Bride* appeared in 1854 and was popular almost immediately, because not only was it a defense of slavery—it was also a romance. This established the pattern for the southern, domestic, pro-slavery novel: The opening pages present an idyllic plantation scene, usually at dusk when the slaves, finished early from their work, loll about in front of spotless, well-cared-for cabins. The owner of the plantation is always benevolent and often reads scripture in the evening to his slaves and family, creating the image of one, big, happy family. A lovely, virginal young woman, devoted to her Bible and her slaves, is always part of the family, and the slaves and the family are devoted to her as well. Propaganda rests side by side with romance; scripture references in defense of slavery abound. This would become the paradigm for the southern sentimental novel of the nineteenth century. The authors of this genre of southern fiction wrote in response to Stowe's novel, fol-

lowing her literary model, while using scripture to defend the justice and importance of slavery as a God-ordained appropriate way of life for the black race. Ironically, slaves in the southern novels use the Bible in the same way early authors of the captivity narratives did: as solace in captivity, in full belief that the Lord would lead them to freedom as He led Moses. Approving of the novels as a political weapon, the southern system seemed to miss this point that the use of the Bible encouraged a belief in slaves being free in *this* world.

In the North, the Civil War encouraged the development of a community of literary women; their work, unlike Stowe's and their southern sisters', did not necessarily have a religious focus, nor did it always employ scripture to support political viewpoints. During the war, and in the years immediately following, women writers still had to follow certain accepted conventions in their writing; they had to retain the "separate spheres" ideology so important to the male population who controlled the publishing industry. Some, like Elizabeth Stuart Phelps (1844–1911), in her novel *The Gates Ajar,* published in 1870, still retained a religious focus, but her novel is not as sentimental as Stowe's. Others, like Rebecca Harding Davis (1831–1910), began to write novels of social protest. Her story "Life in the Iron Mills" was first published in the *Atlantic Monthly* in 1861. This is not an emotional story, nor is there an emphasis on Christian faith as a support in an unfair world. Instead, the story of a tragic young factory worker was written to promote the awareness of conditions in northern mills among the middle class from which Harding Davis came. Rather than evangelizing, she encourages activism. She is one of the first American realists, who departed from the sentimental writing so popular in her time. We must remember, however, that this activism was coming from the northern women writers, many of whom were far more political than history has given them credit for.

Louisa May Alcott (1832–1888), a contemporary of Stowe and Davis, was a true feminist and abolitionist, a woman who supported women's suffrage and who, like Stowe, was able to support herself and others with her writing. Her own life, while reflected in her famous *Little Women* (1868), was not nearly the idyll the novel depicted. There are overtones of rebellion all through the work; some of Marmee's pronouncements can be read in retrospect as feminist statements, for example. Alcott was actively involved in Civil War work, nursing in a hospital in Washington, D.C. Her novel *Work: A Story of Experience* (1873) was written out of this experience. Religious references decline as she faces more ordinary life experiences, both at home and in the hospitals. The war freed many of these northern authors from previous social boundaries but also, one might argue, from religious ones as well. Southern women, we must note, were less well educated than many northern women; Alcott, for example, received an eclectic education at the hands of her philosopher father Bronson and their Transcendentalist neighbors Henry David Thoreau and Ralph Waldo Emerson. Davis was educated at Washington Female Seminary. Southern women were confined by plantation life. During the war, they were left to run the plantations as best they could (many quite successfully) but retired to their secondary position when the war was over. Northern women seemed to find a new life, both literary and political, when the war ended. There was challenge and excitement from then to the turn of the century. Many women were able to make a living at their writing in a newly literate and more affluent, northern industrial society, enjoying a freedom they had not experienced before.

Sarah Orne Jewett (1849–1909), for example, grew up in rural Berwick, Maine. Her father, a physician, took her with him on his rounds and encouraged her intellectual development. She was stirred on these visits by the situation of women who lived alone: widows, maiden ladies, some the only remaining members of once-proud New England families. Fortunately, her situation as a physician's daughter gave her a certain economic security she would not have had otherwise. She and her contemporary Kate Chopin are both remembered as excellent representatives of the "local colorist" school of writing: Their keen sense of observation, Jewett's of the coast of Maine, Chopin's of southern Louisiana, helped them create vivid word pictures of locale that, in the case of Chopin, were regarded in the North as exotic. Like Davis, Jewett did not write romances; she is a realist first and foremost: Religion is nature. Her work does not feature scripture references, and clergymen play little part in it. Like other women in the late nineteenth century, Jewett's most important friendships were with women, in her case, a devoted relationship with Annie Fields, wife, then widow of the publisher and editor James T. Fields of Ticknor and Fields, Publishing. Spending much of her time in Boston with Annie Fields, Jewett became part of the thriving literary community, male and female; she was truly born at the right time and place. Her most well known work *The Country of the Pointed Firs* (1896) is an excellent example of her work: a portrayal of universal human experience visible in the hardships and joys of the human community's relationship with nature. Jewett does not romanticize her characters; she concerns herself with studies in character and scene, not plot development. At the close of the twentieth century, Jewett's work enjoyed a renaissance, particularly in her emphasis in woman's abiding connection to nature even in the face of the booming, industrial, post–Civil War economy.

Catholic author Kate Chopin (1850–1904) was born in St. Louis, the daughter of an Irish immigrant father and a Creole mother. Educated in Catholic schools, she was fluent in French and German. She married a Creole gentleman, Oscar Chopin, and spent her married life in Natchitoches Parish, Louisiana. During her life as a wife and mother of six children, she had no time for writing. She did, however, find time to be unconventional, smoking, traveling alone, and then running the plantation after her husband's death from a fever. Some classify her as a naturalist writer, like her male contemporaries Theodore Dreiser and Stephen Crane. She was a student of the writings of Charles Darwin, which accounts in part for her refusal to include moral judgments in her writing. Adhering to the theory of survival of the fittest and that heredity and environment determine human character, virtue is not necessarily rewarded in her work, unlike the moralizing, uplifting sentiment of earlier-nineteenth-century female writers. Because she saw human will as powerless against the forces of environment, sensual reactions to surroundings are important and clearly documented. Her famous, and at the time scandalous, novella *The Awakening* (1899) makes a bridge to the twentieth century. While a local colorist like Jewett, her heroine is a much different, more sensual woman than any Jewett portrayed. Edna Pontellier is a married woman who experiences the first awakenings of desire but not for her husband. A rather reluctant mother of two, she is frustrated in marriage and wants freedom to pursue her own desires. This novel is a far cry from those sentimental, domestic novels so popular in mid-century, with their emphasis on women's place in the home as the spiritual center of her family. Edna has no interest in being the spiritual center of anyone's life, not even her own. Religion is no solace for her; she is sensual, not spiritual. Her visits to the Catholic Church leave her unsatisfied; indeed, religion itself has no answers for her. She eventually leaves her husband and children, chases a younger man, tries to become an independent artist, and eventually drowns herself, in despair over her failure to find a solution to her situation or in triumph as her final refusal to follow society's way for women. The publication of the work was greeted with scandalized shock, most particularly because Chopin offers no moral condemnation of her heroine's behavior. Edna is a woman who leaves not only her husband but also her children; some critics found this a worse sin than suicide. Surely no "natural" woman would have written such a piece. Chopin published very little after the shock that greeted this publication and died in 1904 from a cerebral hemorrhage. Classifying her only as a "local colorist," as she was for a time, is not appropriate. Only in the 1970s, with the advent of feminist studies, did she begin to be taken seriously.

As the century turned, one must marvel at the change

in women's writing from sentimental religious fiction to realist, social commentary. Perhaps, it might be argued, middle-class, more educated, and more economically secure women were finding outlets for their energies and no longer needed the church as a support. Certainly this was true for many novelists rediscovered in the latter part of the twentieth century who spoke in a different voice. Charlotte Perkins Gilman (1860–1935) was another who did not want to be a housekeeper or moral authority but chose the road of activism and writer instead. Gilman, educated at the Rhode Island School of Design, was able to support herself by teaching and writing. She married, twice, the first unhappily, and she was later divorced. After the birth of her only child, she suffered from severe postpartum depression, chronicled in her famous story "The Yellow Wallpaper." She found relief not in the church, the scripture, or charity causes but in work, with a capital "W." This is what she saw as the best state for all human beings: a life of work. She was one of the first to argue for some sort of organized day-care system so that women could work outside the home if they chose to do so, all this in 1904. She did not see church work as a release for women; she saw it as a simple continuation of women's traditional sociocultural role. In one of her works, "His Religion and Hers" (1923), she argues for what she sees as a difference in moral values between men and women, men being far more self-serving than women. Suffering with terminal cancer, she took her own life by chloroform in 1935.

The first woman to win the Pulitzer Prize for Literature, Edith Wharton established her own place in American writing in her own lifetime. She lived from the late Victorian into modern times, her life spanning the years from 1862 to 1937. Born into the privileged class of old New York money, she was well educated, traveling to Europe often as a young woman. She also married old money in the person of Edward Wharton in 1885 and became a society wife, typical of her class and time. Wharton did not share his wife's intellectual leanings, and they were divorced in 1913. Her writing, in part, took the form of novels of manners, faintly reminiscent of Jane Austen, particularly in a work such as *The Age of Innocence* (1920). What she created was a realistic picture of upper-class life in turn-of-the-century New York and what happens to those who attempt to go against the rigid system of moral behavior among the rich. The emphasis is moral, not religious. They are not the same thing in Wharton's work. Indeed, religion does not enter the works at all, but "morals" certainly do. For example, in *The Age of Innocence*, Ellen Olenska loses her place in New York society, even though she is from that set, because she has left her husband in Europe and returned to the United States, not divorced but separated. Wharton is a master of psychological portraits,

denouncing class snobbery and social presumption, as well as those gender roles society, in her lifetime, still seemed to find necessary. *The House of Mirth* (1905) and *Ethan Frome* (1911) are equally striking observations of the tragedies society inflicts upon its members. Fate seems to play a far larger role in the course of human lives for Wharton than any God ever did.

As American society moved further into the twentieth century, women as professional writers became more commonplace. Still, they often struggled with American culture's ideas of the proper subjects for female writers, and many from these years are little known today. Some, like Willa Cather (1873–1947), were regional romantic writers, but different from her predecessors in the earlier time periods, she was always a professional storyteller. Many were able to form friendships with other female writers; Cather had a lasting friendship with Sarah Orne Jewett, for example, and formed a lasting relationship with Edith Lewis, with whom she lived with in what was called a "Boston Marriage." Writers like Cather and Susan Glaspell (1882–1948) differed also from women of the nineteenth century in that their writing styles were notably sparse; flowery prose was not for them. And again, we have the turning away from organized religion so prevalent in the work of most later-nineteenth- and early-twentieth-century women authors.

It might be theorized that, beginning with those first attempts at published writing by women in early America, there was a realization that the only acceptable voice for women, in a culture that saw them as secondary, would be a religious one. The justification for writing, in the early captivity narratives and then in black women's slave narratives, had to be the moral instruction of the reader. There could be no other reason for a woman putting herself forward. By the nineteenth century, with fewer men members in the churches, women and clergy could band together for mutual support, and women could find a useful place outside the home, as long as they confined themselves to church work and did not venture into the marketplace. Eventually, there was a blurring of the lines for women when writing became an acceptable pursuit if it had a strong scriptural focus and was based on the word of God. Moral instruction was still paramount. The sentimental novel became an accepted form for such a long time, because it fit all the parameters set up by the male power hierarchy: It must be sentimental, emphasize the importance and safety of home and family, and promote religious instruction. It also continued the tradition of the dependent little woman, saint of the home. Certainly the Civil War played an enormous role, thrusting women into different roles—as nurses both in hospitals and at the front, and as workers on plantations and in mills. The industrial North saw the advantage of women, albeit lower-class women, as cheaper workers in the mills and factories; publishers saw a market for women who wrote for women in a culture that had prosperity and the time to read. The need to turn exclusively to the church as an outlet for creativity or interest was no longer there. Eventually, the writing woman was a reality, and the type of fiction she wrote emphasized reality more than romance. It was more sensible and sensual than scriptural. By the 1940s, "women's fiction" no longer fit the proscribed patterns of the past. There was no model that all must follow. Leaving the former paradigm, and its sentimental, Bible base behind, women novelists had truly become members of a profession, not scribblers with a hobby.

SOURCES: Novels include Carolyn Hentz's *The Planter's Northern Bride* (1854, repr. 1970); Maria McIntosh's *The Lofty and the Lowly* (1854); *The Gates Ajar* (1870), by Elizabeth Stuart Phelps; Samuel Richardson's *Pamela* (repr. 1971); Harriet Beecher Stowe, *Uncle Tom's Cabin* (1856, repr. 1991) and *Dred: A Tale of the Dismal Swamp* (1856); Sarah Orne Jewett's *The Country of the Pointed Firs* (repr. 1996); and Kate Chopin's *The Awakening* (1899, repr. 1981). Nonfiction sources for review include Caroline Gilman's *The Recollections of a Southern Matron* (1838); Frances Milton Trollope, *Domestic Manners of the Americans* (1832/1949); Richard VanDerBeets's *Held Captive by the Indians: Selected Narratives, 1642–1836* (repr. 1994); a sermon by Alexander McCaine from 1842 titled "Slavery defended from Scripture" and delivered to the General Conference of the Methodist Protestant Church; and an 1861 publication by Reverend Thornton Stringfellow, D.D., titled *Slavery: Its Origins, Nature and History.* See also Ann Douglas's *The Feminization of American Culture* (1977); Christie Ann Farnham's *The Education of the Southern Belle* (repr. 1994); Samuel Hill, ed., *Religion in the Southern States* (1983); Barbara Welter's *Dimity Convictions* (1976); Lyde Cullen Sizer's *The Political Work of Northern Women Writers and the Civil War, 1850–1872* (2000); and Elizabeth Moss's *Domestic Novelists in the Old South* (1992). Collections include *American Women Writers: Diverse Voices in Prose since 1845,* ed. Eileen Barrett and Mary Cullinan (1992); and *Women's Work: An Anthology of American Literature,* ed. Barbara Perkins et al. (1994).

WOMEN, RELIGION, AND AMERICAN FILM
Judith Weisenfeld

MOVIES HAVE BEEN a profoundly influential cultural force in America throughout the twentieth century, and although the nature and shape of that influence have not always been uniform, American film will certainly continue to have a powerful impact on the United States and the increasingly globalized culture in the twenty-first century. As an arena of imagination that often challenges viewers to extend themselves beyond the familiar,

the movies have helped to shape American perceptions of and attitudes toward religion in general and toward women gender, and religion more specifically. This essay considers three sets of interaction between women, religion, and film over the course of the century, focusing on women as significant agents in movements to reform the content of motion pictures, thematic patterns in representations of women and religion in American film, and women's contributions as filmmakers. Although American religious institutions have produced films (both fiction and nonfiction) for use by members in houses of worship and in religious schools, this essay instead surveys Hollywood's portrayal of women's religious experiences and expressions and women's involvement in the production and regulation of these films. The narrative codes and standards that emerged from the precursors to the Hollywood system and from Hollywood itself have dominated American film form and provided the touchstone for both imitation of and resistance to its products. Because no short essay can address every American film in which women's religious experiences are represented, this piece attempts to point to significant works and to larger themes evident in selected films.

Social Reform and Censorship

In 1917 Mary Gray Peck (1867?–1957), a leading figure in the predominantly white General Federation of Women's Clubs and the New York State Federation of Women's Clubs, announced:

Motion Pictures are going to save our civilization from the destruction which has successively overwhelmed every civilization of the past. They provide what every previous civilization has lacked—namely a means of relief, happiness, and mental inspiration to the people at the bottom. Without happiness and inspiration being accessible to those upon whom the social burden rests most heavily, there can be no stable social system. Revolutions are born of misery and despair. (*Photoplay,* 54)

In the midst of a period of progressive, often Christian-based social activism, Peck saw the movies as a force that could be put in service of the agendas of reform groups whose work focused on issues such as child labor laws, fair wages, and urban health conditions. As a representative of this influential women's organization, she emphasized the escapist nature of the movies, the possibilities of their containing the protest of the poor against their situations, and the potential of filmgoing to inspire people to uplift themselves. Other religious leaders were less optimistic about the potential of the movies to have a positive impact on American society,

In 1917, Mary Gray Peck, a leading figure in the predominantly white General Federation of Women's Clubs and the New York State Federation of Women's Clubs, announced, "Motion Pictures are going to save our civilization from the destruction which has successively overwhelmed every civilization of the past." *Courtesy The Elmira College Archives.*

leader of a gang in New York's Bowery and his subsequent turn away from crime. Owen's (played by Rockliffe Fellowes) regeneration comes through meeting Marie Deering (Anna Q. Nilsson), who herself has been transformed by an impassioned settlement house worker from a lazy, self-involved socialite to an engaged social worker. Marie takes up work at a local settlement house and, under a sign on the wall announcing that "God is Love," transforms the lives of all those with whom she comes into contact, including Owen, and eventually dies at the hands of a neighborhood gangster. Generally remembered for its detailed portrayal of New York City gangster life, *Regeneration* nevertheless places Marie at the center of the film's moral message and provides viewers with a compelling example of a Christian settlement house worker. Christian Scientist Lois Weber (1883–1939), a productive filmmaker in the silent era, directed a body of films that she called "missionary films" in which she opposed opium smuggling (*Hop, The Devil's Brew,* Bluebird Photoplays, 1916), abortion (*Where Are My Children?* Universal Film Manufacturing Co., 1916), and capital punishment (*The People vs. John Doe,* Universal Film Manufacturing Co., 1916) and lauded Margaret Sanger's campaign for birth control (*The Hand That Rocks the Cradle,* Universal Film Manufacturing Co., 1917). Despite Weber's strong religious and social reform agenda, the films did not steer clear of controversy. *The Hand That Rocks the Cradle* was banned in New York City because it advocated the use of birth control, and religious leaders attacked her 1915 allegorical film *The Hypocrites,* in which a minister uses the pulpit to rail against the hypocrisy of his congregants who show little evidence of Christian commitment in their daily lives. Perhaps the most controversial aspect of the film was Weber's inclusion of a nude female allegorical figure of "Truth," first shown in a painting within the film and who then appears to the minister in a vision to help him distinguish between the faithful and the hypocrites.

with Christians expressing considerable concern about Sunday exhibitions in violation of the Sabbath, about the saloon and nickelodeon environments in which films were shown in the early years, and about the promotion of subjects many Christians saw as sinful, particularly sex, crime, and intemperance. In the early years of film, religious leaders who were anxious about the movies were responding to the fact that a significant segment of narrative films engaged social questions of the day—including labor issues, prostitution, intemperance, crime, immigration, ethnic and race relations, divorce, birth control—in some cases seeking to shape public opinion and motivate action and in others simply using the controversial subject matter to bring in an audience. Many of the social films took up issues that were of particular importance to women in the early twentieth century and especially to women committed to religiously grounded social reform. Religious reformers remained divided on the question of whether representing social problems on film could promote social change or simply encouraged people to engage in the vices that the films represented as part of the campaign for reform.

Among the early social films, Raoul Walsh's 1915 *Regeneration* (Fox Film Corporation), an adaptation of Owen Kildare's memoir, tells the story of his life as the

More common than "social films" that proceeded from a perspective of religiously motivated reform were sensationalist films that represented women in circumstances that religious leaders found objectionable: displaying sexuality, taking drugs, drinking alcohol, and pressed into prostitution. Insistence by religious leaders that such films damaged America's children and that the movie studios reform themselves or be subjected to federal censorship grew through the 1920s into the early 1930s. Women's groups like the General Federation of Women's Clubs, the Woman's Christian Temperance Union (WCTU), the Daughters of the American Republic, the Daughters of Confederacy, as well as women in church-related groups like the Roman Catholic Legion of Decency and missionary societies were active in the campaign to regulate the movies. The WCTU engaged in a long campaign, first through its Department for the Promotion of Purity in Literature and Art and later through the Motion Picture Department, advocating federal censorship (to supersede and expand the work of existing state censor boards) in order to protect the morals of children and young women. In addition to working toward reform through public speaking and lobbying government officials and exhibitors, women's organizations promoted the formation of "Better Films Committees" to review films and make recommendations on their suitability for various audiences. In 1922, as a result of these women's work, along with that of other reformers, the major Hollywood studios established a self-regulatory mechanism in the Motion Picture Producers and Distributors Association (MPPDA) under the direction of Will H. Hays and later Joseph I. Breen, Presbyterian and Catholic laymen, respectively. Dissatisfaction with the enforcement of the MPPDA's regulations—then called the "Don'ts and Be Carefuls"—motivated additional attacks on the studios by women's groups and others concerned with the moral impact of the movies. In 1930 the MPPDA adopted the Motion Picture Production Code, which would guide industry self-regulation through the 1950s. Largely concerned with representations of sex and crime, the Production Code also insisted that representations of religion be accurate and dignified and generally insisted on consultation with clergy or other religious leaders to ensure authenticity. The Production Code also enshrined the principle of "compensating moral values" requiring that sympathy not rest with "sinning" characters and that the films provide for the punishment of these characters and denounce their actions. The Production Code, which women's religious activism played a part in formulating, had a profound impact on the content of American films, an impact that some saw as beneficial to the moral health of American society and others saw as stifling creativity and free expression.

In the early years of film, some religious Americans and filmmakers saw great potential in the medium to educate viewers by representing social problems—many particular to women's experiences—and to motivate them to support efforts at social reform. At the same time, as the industry grew and filmmakers expanded the range of films produced, some Christian reformers became concerned about the impact of the movies on the moral development of children who, they argued, would inevitably mimic what they saw on screen. This concern motivated a coalition of Christian activists, of which women were prominent members, to press for the development of censorship guidelines in an attempt to ensure that their understanding of Christian values would shape the products of the major Hollywood studios.

Representations of Women and Religion in American Film: The Bible on Film

That the Bible and female biblical characters would provide subject matter for American filmmakers should not surprise, nor should the fact that women's roles in biblical films largely follow the patterns set for women in the Bible. Filmmakers' interest in translating Bible stories to film dates back to the silent era (which began to come to a close with the 1927 release of Warner Brothers' *The Jazz Singer*) and directors confronted a number of difficult issues with regard to representing the Bible that carried over from the traditions of Passion Plays and theater. The problems of representing miracles on film, of casting people to play the parts of Jesus, who Christians believe is the son of God, and of Mary his mother, and finally of interpreting biblical stories vexed filmmakers as some religious leaders expressed discomfort with the new medium. To varying degrees throughout the century, films based on the Bible would be an important part of the fare available to filmgoers, and women would be present both on the screen and behind the scenes.

The figures of Mary and Mary Magdalene would provide staple, if limited, roles for women as filmmakers presented their versions of the life of Christ. Director Sidney Olcott's *From the Manger to the Cross* (Kalem, 1912), which he shot on location in the Middle East, was written by Gene Gauntier, the actress who would play Mary in this popular and well-received film. Cecil B. DeMille, who would prove the most important director in setting the terms for the Hollywood biblical epic, relied on Jeanie McPherson, a writer who worked with him on a number of religious films in the silent era, for the screenplay for *The King of Kings* (Paramount, 1927), his version of the life of Christ. The film starred Dorothy Cumming as Mary and Jacqueline Logan as Mary Magdalene who, the film implies, was romantically involved with Judas. Other directors had much less success than did the extremely popular DeMille in rendering the life of Christ on film and in presenting audiences with the characters of Mary and Mary Magdalene. Later in the century, George Stevens would write, produce, and direct the poorly reviewed and unpopular film *The Greatest Story Ever Told* (United Artists, 1965), which featured Dorothy McGuire as Mary and Max von Sydow as Jesus. Reviewers and audiences found this film, which was first released at four hours and twenty minutes, far less engaging than they thought the life of Christ should be despite a strong performance by McGuire. In 1988 director Martin Scorsese would encounter considerable resistance from many American Christians to his adaptation of Nikos Kazantzakis's novel *The Last Temptation of Christ* (Universal, 1988). The film emphasizes both Jesus's divinity and humanity in ways that some Christians found blasphemous. As Jesus (Willem Dafoe) waits on the cross for death, an agent of Satan tempts him by showing him the life he could have had as Mary Magdalene's (Barbara Hershey) husband. Although Scorsese presents this segment of the film as a hallucination, many American Christians objected to the implication that the prospect of a carnal life with Mary Magdalene could have tempted Jesus. Despite the attempts of protestors to prevent the distribution and exhibition of the film and the impact of public demonstrations on box-office receipts, the film was well reviewed, and Scorsese was nominated for an Academy Award for achievement in direction. More recently, actor and director Blair Underwood and writer Frank Underwood, Jr., produced a thirty-minute short film, *Second Coming* (Quiet Fury Production, 1992), in the wake of the verdict in the first Rodney King trial and the unrest that followed. The Underwoods' film presents a black Jesus and Mary and opens with Mary (Rosalind Cash) weeping at the foot of the cross and asking God to forgive those who have killed her son. The rest of the film focuses on the diagnosis of this black Jesus as insane by those he encounters in contemporary America when he returns.

More common among biblical films than ones that focus on the life of Christ have been movies of stories from the Hebrew scriptures and films focusing on fictional characters who interact with and are influenced by Jesus. Both types of films date back to the silent era but were especially popular from the late 1940s through the late 1950s and, in this period, often spoke to larger social questions like the cold war and the relationship of religious commitment to totalitarian rule. Warner Brothers' 1936 *The Green Pastures*, directed by Marc Connelly and William Keighley, was an early attempt in the sound era to present the Hebrew scriptures on film. Based on Connelly's 1931 Pulitzer Prize–winning play in which he imagines the Hebrew scriptures in a southern African American context, this was one of a number of Hollywood all-black cast films from the late 1930s through the late 1940s that set their stories in religious contexts. Women remain secondary characters in the film, with Eve (Myrtle Anderson) and "Mrs. Noah" (Ida Forsyne) having almost no dialogue. More important, women often serve as agents of destruction, as in the case of Zeba (Edna Mae Harris), who embodies the irreligion that motivates "De Lawd" (Rex Ingram) to de-

stroy humanity with a flood. Other films based on the Hebrew scriptures, like Cecil B. DeMille's *The Ten Commandments*, which he first directed in 1923 (Paramount/Famous Players-Lasky) and again in 1956 (Paramount), earning seven Academy Award nominations, including one for Best Picture, featured women in prominent roles. The 1956 version boasted an all-star cast that included Anne Baxter as Nefretiri, the Egyptian woman who loves Moses but eventually must marry Rameses, and Yvonne De Carlo as Sephora, Moses's wife. The two characters balance one another as Sephora remains supportive and committed to Moses's role as deliverer of his people and Nefretiri acts out of her own desires and becomes the agent of God's hardening his heart against Pharoah. DeMille also directed *Samson and Delilah* (Paramount, 1949), which featured Victor Mature as Samson and Hedy Lamarr, notorious for appearing nude in the 1932 Czechoslovak film *Extase*, as Delilah. 20th Century Fox released a number of biblical epics in the early 1950s including *David and Bathsheba* (1951) with Gregory Peck as David and Susan Hayward starring as Bathsheba, whose relationship with David motivates him to have her husband killed. Time and again, the female characters serve simply as temptresses who bring about or attempt to bring about the downfall of the male lead. Fox's 1960 *The Story of Ruth* (Elana Eden), while not a box-office hit, stands out as an attempt to tell a biblical story with a devout and faithful female character at the center.

Films that focused on figures influenced by Jesus include DeMille's 1932 *The Sign of the Cross*, which starred Claudette Colbert as Empress Poppaea, Charles Laughton as Nero, and Elissa Landi as Mercia, a Christian woman whom Marcus Superbus (Frederick March) attempts to seduce. *The Sign of the Cross* attracted a great deal of negative attention from religious leaders concerned about explicit images of sexuality in the movies. DeMille draws a sharp contrast between Mercia's Christian fortitude and the debauchery of the broader Roman society in a lavish and explicit orgy scene. During the 1950s era of the biblical epic, 20th Century Fox released *The Robe* (1953), the first film shot in the wide-screen format Cinemascope, which focused on the power of the robe that Jesus was wearing on his way to the crucifixion. Richard Burton is Marcellus, the Roman who takes charge of crucifying Jesus, and Victor Mature is his slave who is a follower of Jesus. Marcellus later becomes a Christian, and the film ends with Diana (Jean Simmons), his childhood sweetheart, willingly accepting death as a Christian with him. The film received a number of Academy Award nominations, including one for Best Picture.

Films that derive their stories from the Bible saw two waves of popularity in the United States, first during the 1920s and again during the 1950s when Technicolor and wide-screen formats made large-scale epics appealing to American audiences. In addition, the politics of the cold war encouraged Americans to explore some of the ways in which American political culture is grounded in Jewish and Christian traditions, and many of the Bible films from the 1950s make this connection explicit. Since the 1950s biblical epics have become less popular on the Hollywood screen, in part because of the potential for conflict over interpretations of the texts and because of the increasing recognition of religious diversity in the American experience. In both periods of popularity, however, Bible films presented limited characterizations of women, including them primarily as quiet, supportive wives or as temptresses who seek to lead devout men to ruin.

Women as Religious Leaders

A wide range of films explore women's religious experiences and expressions by focusing on women as religious leaders, especially as saints, nuns, visionaries, evangelists, and missionaries. American filmmakers have produced a number of films about Joan of Arc, including the 1895 Edison company's *Joan of Arc*, Victor Fleming's version (RKO, 1948) starring Ingrid Bergman (who received an Academy Award nomination for her work), Otto Preminger's *Saint Joan* (United Artists, 1957), based on the George Bernard Shaw play and which introduced Jean Seberg as Joan. More recently, French director Luc Besson's *The Messenger* (Gaumont/Columbia, 1999) interpreted the story of Joan of Arc (Milla Jovovich) for American audiences. And just as the story of Joan of Arc's military ventures combined with intensely spiritual motivations has captivated filmmakers, so the story of women who were believed to have seen apparitions of the Virgin Mary have made their way into American film history, indicating an ongoing interest in visionary religious experiences. 20th Century Fox's 1943 *The Song of Bernadette* won Jennifer Jones an Academy Award for her portrayal of Bernadette Soubiroux, the young woman whose vision gave rise to the belief among Catholics that Lourdes, France, is a site of healing. *The Miracle of Our Lady of Fatima* (Warner Brothers, 1952) told the story of the three peasant children who saw an apparition of the Virgin Mary in 1917 with a deeply anticommunist lesson for cold war Americans.

Roman Catholic nuns have been a large part of the American film imagination and, more often than not, have been comic characters. Nevertheless, a number of films have explored the religious experiences and commitments of nuns. Among the dramatic films, John Huston's *Heaven Knows, Mr. Allison* (20th Century Fox, 1957) featured Deborah Kerr, nominated for an Academy Award for her performance, as a nun stranded on a Pacific island during World War II and who is aided by a marine (Robert Mitchum). In *The Nun's Story* (Warner Brothers, 1959), a film based on a true story, Audrey Hepburn starred in the dramatic role of Gabrielle van der Malle, a young woman who desires to become a nun and work as a nurse in the Congo. The film provides a moving portrait of the spiritual discipline required in the novitiate and of van der Malle's struggle to achieve her goals in the context of World War II. Hepburn was also nominated for an Academy Award for her performance. *Agnes of God* (Columbia, 1985), Norman Jewison's film based on the Broadway play, stars Jane Fonda as a psychiatrist sent to determine the sanity of Agnes (Meg Tilly), a young novice who has given birth to a baby found dead in the Montreal convent. Anne Bancroft appears as the Mother Superior who provides a strong counterpoint to the agnostic psychiatrist's interpretation of events. More recently, Susan Sarandon won an Academy Award for Best Actress for her performance as Sister Helen Prejean in Tim Robbins's *Dead Man Walking* (Polygram, 1995), based on the memoir by Sister Prejean about her work with death-row inmates.

On the comic side, Ingrid Bergman received a nomination for her role of Sister Benedict opposite Bing Crosby's Father O'Malley in the popular light comedy *The Bells of St. Mary's* (RKO, 1945). Some years later, well-known actress Ida Lupino directed Hayley Mills and Rosalind Russell in *The Trouble with Angels* (Warner Brothers, 1966), set in a convent school. Warner Brothers brought out a sequel in *Where Angels Go, Trouble Follows* (1968), which follows one of the school girls (played by Stella Stevens) as she becomes a young nun. More recently, in *Sister Act* (Buena Vista, 1992) Whoopi Goldberg portrayed Delores Van Cartier, a Las Vegas lounge singer who witnesses a murder and is forced to hide under police protection in an inner-city convent and pretend to be a nun. She was joined in the cast by Kathy Najimy, as a spirited young nun, Mary Wickes, who had also appeared as a nun in *The Trouble with Angels* and its sequel, and Maggie Smith as the Mother Superior. In the sequel, *Sister Act 2: Back in the Habit* (Buena Vista, 1992), Delores works as a choir director in the convent school.

Female missionaries have appeared as characters in a wide range of films, often providing the opportunity for filmmakers to draw a contrast between American Christian cultures and other religious cultures, frequently in ways that disparage non-Christian religions. Frank Capra's *The Bitter Tea of General Yen* (Columbia, 1933) follows Megan Davis (Barbara Stanwyck) to China as she is kidnapped by a warlord and attempts to convert him to Christianity. Katharine Hepburn starred opposite Humphrey Bogart as Rose Sayer, the spinster sister of a British missionary in East Africa in John Huston's *The African Queen* (United Artists, 1951), and Anne Bancroft headed the cast of John Ford's *7 Women* (MGM, 1966), about a group of American missionaries in China attacked by bandits. Evangelists and urban missionaries have also been present in American movies and Salvation Army "lasses," of particular interest to filmmakers. In 1908 D. W. Griffith directed *The Salvation Army Lass* (Biograph), and in 1919 Paramount released *Fires of Faith*, produced with the cooperation of the army and featuring Salvation Army leader Evangeline Booth playing herself. In MGM's 1931 *Laughing Sinners* Joan Crawford starred as a nightclub performer who eventually turns her life around, through the influence of an army worker played by Clark Gable, and joins the Salvation Army. And in 1955 MGM filmed its version of the Broadway musical *Guys and Dolls* in which Jean Simmons played a Salvation Army lassie and the object of gangster Sky Masterson's (Marlon Brando) attentions. Two of the more important film investigations of the susceptibility of average people seeking spiritual fulfillment to the wiles of unscrupulous evangelists feature female evangelists modeled on Aimee Semple McPherson, the early-twentieth-century Pentecostal evangelist. Frank Capra's *The Miracle Woman* (Columbia, 1931) starred Barbara Stanwyck as Sister Florence Fallon, who begins her career as an earnest evangelist but is quickly turned by her promoters into a heavily marketed and fraudulent religious performer. Florence is redeemed in the end by her love for a sincere blind pilot and joins the Salvation Army. Richard Brooks directed an adaptation of Sinclair Lewis's 1927 novel *Elmer Gantry* (United Artists, 1960) in which evangelist Sister Sharon Falconer (Jean Simmons) falls in love with Elmer Gantry (Burt Lancaster), a con-artist preacher. Lulu Bains (Shirley Jones), a minister's daughter and one of Gantry's previous conquests, seeks revenge and ultimately brings about Falconer's death.

Exploring women's interior religious experiences, examining the various ways they act on their religious commitments, and showing them as complicated individuals who sometimes fail to live up to those commitments, this body of films in which filmmakers have presented women as religious leaders has given viewers access to a more complex range of characterizations than generally found in Hollywood biblical films. Although they often rely on romance plots that turn attention away from religion, some of these movies, ranging from comedy to melodrama to historical drama, have provided a rich portrait of women's religious lives.

Religion, Race, and Ethnicity

Films have served as an important arena in which Americans have imagined and encountered minority religious traditions as well as racial and ethnic minorities. Many early filmmakers explored the Ellis Island experience in particular and immigration more broadly in a range of films that included stories that focus on Jewish women, Irish and Italian Catholic women, and Asian women. In addition to devoting attention to religions of immigrants, the movies have also engaged African American and Native American women's religious lives. Audiences from among these groups approached the films with a great deal of ambivalence, generally excited to see films that reflected aspects of their experiences but attentive to the potential for films to present problematic images of their religious communities. MGM's 1927 *The Callahans and the Murphys*, which featured the studio's first female comedy team in Polly Moran and Marie Dressler as the matriarchs of two Irish Catholic families, generated prolonged and intense protests among Irish Americans and Roman Catholic clergy in cities across the country. Opposition to the film focused on the inclusion of stereotypes of excessive consumption of alcohol on the religious holiday of St. Patrick's Day. Many African American viewers objected to the images in King Vidor's *Hallelujah* (MGM, 1929) in which Chick (Nina Mae McKinney) cannot separate her religious emotion from sexual desire. Films featuring stories about Chinese and Japanese immigrants generally focused on crime, opium smuggling and use, and tragic deaths. Although Chinese and Japanese women appeared in many of these films, they often played only minor roles, with the possibilities of character development subordinated to the common interracial romance plot. Images of "the Orient" have been common in American film, and moviegoers took in various filmic presentations of *Cleopatra*, including J. Gordon Edwards's 1917 version (Fox Film Corporation), starring Theda Bara, Cecil B. DeMille's 1934 version (Paramount), starring Claudette Colbert, and Joseph L. Mankiewicz's 1963 production, starring Elizabeth Taylor and Richard Burton. In addition to these attempts to present historicized versions of women in ancient Egypt, American filmmakers produced a seemingly endless stream of horror films and technicolor extravaganzas that fantasize about "the Orient." Universal released a number of campy Orientalist films that starred Maria Montez, Jon Hall, and Sabu, including *Arabian Nights* (1942) and *Ali Baba and the Forty Thieves* (1944). The trio also appeared in a number of South Seas fantasies, including *White Savage* (1943) and *Cobra Woman* (1944). In all of these films, the relationship between religion, gender, and sexuality emerge as important themes.

A variety of early films take up questions of the nature and processes of Americanization, examining the role that religion plays in the production of racial and ethnic identity. Alan Crosland's 1927 *The Jazz Singer* (Warner Brothers), best known as the first feature-length sound film, follows Jakie Rabinowitz (Al Jolson) who rejects his father's (Warner Oland) plan for him to become a cantor and follow in the tradition established by the men in the family, in favor of a career as a "jazz" singer. Although the conflict between Jakie and his father sits at the story's center, his mother Sara (Eugenie Bessere) functions as an important character in shaping Jakie's new American identity. She remains loyal to her husband and to Jewish tradition but refuses to reject her son simply because he embraces American culture. More recently, filmmakers like Wayne Wang have taken up questions of conflict between traditional ways of living and secular American culture, examined through the lens of intergenerational issues between Chinese women in America in films like *Dim Sum* (Orion Pictures, 1984) and *The Joy Luck Club* (Hollywood Pictures, 1993), the latter based on Amy Tan's 1989 novel.

Despite the fact that Hollywood films frequently projected well-worn stereotypes of a range of racial and ethnic groups, the movies also proved to be a means through which moviegoers experienced the diversity of religion and race in America in ways that might not have been possible in their daily lives.

Women behind the Camera

Although there are a number of notable instances in early film and in the Hollywood studio system in which women were involved in shaping the representations of women's religious experiences, they were not present in significant numbers as film directors. In recent years there have been a number of significant productions in which female directors have engaged issues about women and religion in North America. The themes of traditional religious cultures versus secular American culture and of intergenerational conflict dominate these films in which the directors explore the implications of women moving away from family and asserting themselves as social, cultural, and religious agents. Joan Micklin Silver has directed two films that explore Jewish women's experiences in America and that take up issues of gender and secularization. *Hester Street* (Midwest Films, 1975) is based on "Yekl," an 1896 story by Abraham Cahan, and focuses on the experiences of Gitl (Carol Kane), an eastern European Jewish immigrant who joins her husband Jake (Steven Keats) in New York City at the turn of the twentieth century. Jake has embraced secular American culture—along with an American girlfriend—and Gitl desires to maintain her Orthodox beliefs and practices for herself and the couple's son. Silver took up related issues of relationships between Jewish tradition, gender roles, and American culture in the 1988 film *Crossing Delancey* (Warner Brothers) in which Isabelle "Izzy" Grossman (Amy Irving) must decide whether to submit to her grandmother's (Reizl Bozyk) desire to turn over the quest for a husband to a matchmaker (Sylvia Miles). The matchmaker's choice is

Sam Posner (Peter Riegert), the owner of Posner's Pickles. The film implies that Izzy's acceptance of Sam constitutes an embrace of Jewishness over and against the concerns and interests of secular or Christian American culture. *Yentl* (MGM, 1983), Barbra Streisand's first directorial effort, is based on an Isaac Bashevis Singer story set in eastern Europe in the early years of the twentieth century. Yentl (Barbra Streisand), an orphan, wishes to obtain a religious education reserved to men and is able to gain entrance to a yeshiva dressed as a man. The film's main concerns—women's religious experiences and access to authority—are set alongside a love story as Yentl falls in love with fellow student Avigdor (Mandy Patinkin) but finds herself pressured, because everyone takes her to be a man, to marry Hadass (Amy Irving), Avigdor's former fiancée. Yentl eventually ends the marriage, reveals the truth, and chooses an education in America over a future with Avigdor. In other cultural contexts, Mina Shum's 1995 film *Double Happiness* (Fine Line Features) brings us Jade Li (Sandra Oh), a Chinese Canadian woman, and explores her conflict with her parents over adhering to traditional family and gender roles, and Mira Nair's *Mississippi Masala* (Black River Productions, 1991) focuses on Mina's (Sarita Choudhury) attempts to shape her own future rather than conform to the life plan that her parents, South Asians in exile from Uganda, have formulated for her.

A number of female directors have emphasized questions about the transmission of religious culture across the generations and the ways in which women are sometimes central to this process. Julie Dash's 1991 film *Daughters of the Dust* (Geechee Girls) portrays an African American Gullah family in the Sea Islands on the eve of migration north in the early years of the twentieth century. The narrator of the film is the Unborn Child (Kai-Lynn Warren) of Eli (Adisa Anderson), the great-grandson of Nana (Cora Lee Day), the family's oldest member, and of Eula (Alva Rogers), who, we come to learn, has been raped by a white man. Nana has tried to convince Eli that in order for the family to stay intact in the North, he must rely on the ancestors and trust that the child that Eula bears belongs to the family. Throughout the film, we see the Unborn Child moving among the members of her family, unseen by all but felt by Nana, who called upon the ancestors for assistance in helping the younger family members to hold fast to tradition. The members of this extended family—led by the women—engage one another explicitly and heatedly on questions of African-derived religion versus Christianity, as well as about relationships between religion, gender, and sexuality. Nancy Savoca's *Household Saints* (Jones Entertainment, 1993), based on the 1981 Francine Prose novel, also engages family conflicts arising from women's different approaches to religious experience and expression. Catherine Falconetti (Tracey Ullman) finds herself caught between Carmen (Judith Maline), her mother-in-law, and her traditional approach to Italian Catholicism, on the one hand, and Teresa (Lili Taylor), her daughter whose religious life resembles her grandmother's more than that of her mother's modern, compartmentalized approach to faith. The film's humorous and eccentric approach to Catholic devotional practices provides a challenging window on broad questions about the nature of mystical religious experience.

As the United States becomes increasingly religiously diverse, viewers can expect to find more films that engage questions of religion and gender in a broad range of religions and that explore women's religious experiences in the context of immigration. The increasing presence of women behind the camera, coupled with an ongoing interest among male directors in presenting stories about women's religious experiences, assures that American film in the twenty-first century will continue to be a vibrant arena for exploring topics related to women and religion in America.

SOURCES: Mary Gray Peck's discussion of motion pictures was published in *Photoplay*, February 1917. Kevin Brownlow's *Behind the Mask of Innocence* (1990) is a useful source on early film and social reform. Matthew Bernstein, ed., *Controlling Hollywood: Censorship and Regulation in the Studio Era* (1999), and Francis G. Couvares, ed., *Movie Censorship in American Culture* (1996), contain a number of articles on the efforts of religious individuals and institutions in shaping censorship codes; Frank Walsh's *Sin and Censorship: The Catholic Church and the Motion Picture Industry* (1996) focuses on Catholic participation in this process. Lea Jacobs's *The Wages of Sin: Censorship and the Fallen Woman Film, 1928–1942* (1995) addresses discourses of gender and morality in the period in which censorship guidelines were developed. For an invaluable listing of American and foreign films that use biblical stories and themes, consult Richard H. Campbell and Michael R. Pitts, *The Bible on Film: A Checklist, 1897–1980* (1981). The articles in the special issue of *Semeia: An Experimental Journal for Biblical Criticism* 74 (1996), titled "Biblical Glamour and Hollywood Glitz" and edited by Alice Bach, provide a useful introduction to the topic, and many address issues of gender and representations of women in film.

For Reference

Not to be taken from this room